PUBLICATIONS ON ASIA OF THE
INSTITUTE FOR COMPARATIVE AND
FOREIGN AREA STUDIES

Number 25

This book is sponsored by the China Colloquium of the Institute for Comparative and Foreign Area Studies.

A Modern China
and a New World

K'ANG YU-WEI, REFORMER AND UTOPIAN, 1858-1927

KUNG-CHUAN HSIAO

UNIVERSITY OF WASHINGTON PRESS

SEATTLE AND LONDON

Library of Congress Cataloging in Publication Data

Hsiao, Kung-ch'üan, 1897–
   A modern China and a new world: K'ang Yu-wei, reformer and utopian, 1858–
1927.
   (Publications on Asia of the Institute for Comparative and Foreign Area Studies;
no. 25)
   Bibliography: p.
   Includes index.
   1. K'ang, Yu-wei, 1858–1927. 2. China—History—Reform movement, 1898. I.
Title. II. Series: Washington (State). University. Institute for Comparative and
Foreign Area Studies. Publication on Asia; no. 25.
DS763.K3H75   951'.03'0924 [B]   74-28166   ISBN 0-295-95385-3

PREFACE

While I was looking for a research subject after the completion of my work on rural China, Franz Michael, then assistant director of the Far Eastern and Russian Institute, University of Washington, turned over to me the microfilm copies of K'ang Yu-wei's writings, which the late Mary C. Wright had made from the collection of Mme. Lo Chong (K'ang T'ung-pi, the author's daughter) in the late 1940s. The four reels, I found, contained a wealth of materials, both published and in manuscript, much of which I had not seen before. With the encouragement of Professor Michael and other colleagues of the Institute I undertook to make an extended study of K'ang's thought. As it happened, Jung-pang Lo, K'ang's grandson, soon joined the Institute as visiting professor. He afforded me not only valuable suggestions but an abundance of additional source materials. I was thus placed in an unusually favorable position to carry out the project. Many years ago when I wrote the chapter on the reform movement of 1898 in my *History of Chinese Political Thought*, I had access only to a fraction of K'ang's writings. Lack of adequate knowledge of his ideas prevented me from giving anything like a perceptive account of them. I now gained an opportunity to rectify some of the misconceptions into which I had previously fallen.

My findings have been presented in a number of articles published in *Monumenta Serica, Tsing Hua Journal of Chinese Studies*, and *The Chung Chi Journal*. Complying with the wishes of my colleagues in the Modern Chinese History Project, I now republish these articles in a book.

Except for some minor changes they appear here as they were first printed. Chapters 3–6 and 8 are from *Monumenta Serica*, chapter 7 is from *Tsing Hua Journal of Chinese Studies*, and chapters 10 and 11 are from *The Chung Chi Journal*. Chapters 1, 2, and 9, however, have not been in print before. Written over a period of ten years and in a form more like separate essays than integral parts of a book, they are not free from repetitions, incongruities, and inconsistencies. Despite efforts to remove these annoying faults some inevitably remain, for which I apologize.

My aim has been a modest one: to examine in some detail the major themes of K'ang's reformist and utopian thought and, as far as I am capable, to relate them to the historical situations to which they referred and in which they developed. It is hoped that the present volume may not prove wholly useless as a supplement to *K'ang Yu-wei: A Biography and a Symposium*, edited by Professor Lo.

I wish to thank my colleagues in the Institute and the Project who gave me continued encouragement and provocative criticisms during the progress of this study. I owe a special debt of thanks to Professor Michael who in fact suggested the subject to me, and to Professor Lo for his generous help as indicated above. To the editors of the three journals, who have kindly published my articles and allowed me to reprint them here, I tender my grateful appreciation. To Margery Lang, who with admirable skill and infinite care has transformed a faulty manuscript into publishable form, I give my grateful acknowledgment. To George E. Taylor I must pay a personal tribute. Thanks to his leadership, an intellectual atmosphere that was as congenial as it was stimulating prevailed in the Institute, making scholarly pursuits a pleasant and rewarding experience for me.

KUNG-CHUAN HSIAO

Seattle, Washington
September 1973

Contents

PART ONE: THE FAMILY AND THE MAN

Chapter 1: The Family 3
Chapter 2: The Man 17

PART TWO: PHILOSOPHICAL COMMITMENTS

Chapter 3: Reinterpretation of Confucianism 41
Chapter 4: Confucianism as a Philosophy of Reform
               and a Religion 97
Chapter 5: Philosophical Synthesis 137

PART THREE: REFORM PROPOSALS

Chapter 6: Political Reform 193
Chapter 7: Administrative Reform 263
Chapter 8: Economic Reform 301
Chapter 9: Educational Reform 377

PART FOUR: UTOPIAN IDEAS

Chapter 10: Road to Utopia 409
Chapter 11: Detour to Industrial Society 515

Postscript 597
Table of Transliteration 601
Bibliography 613
Index 659

PART I
THE FAMILY AND THE MAN

Chapter 1

THE FAMILY

K'ang Yu-wei stated with obvious pride that for thirteen generations his kinsmen had been "scholars and teachers," and that none of them had ever practiced other trades.[1] This statement is somewhat misleading, as a review of his ancestry shows that no scholar of distinction appeared before the nineteenth century and some of his kinsmen engaged in professions other than that of the scholar.[2] The K'angs migrated from Nan-hsiung to Nan-hai, sometime in the Southern Sung dynasty, and settled in a village, Yin-t'ang Hsiang (also known as Su Ts'un), north of the Hsi-ch'iao hills. Little is known concerning K'ang Chien-yüan, the first settler and his early descendants. K'ang Wei-ch'ing (ninth generation down from Chien-yüan) was the first to "read books." K'ang Han-ts'ang (thirteenth generation) served as private secretary (*mu-yu*) to an official in Hunan province, probably in the early years of the Ch'ing dynasty. He was, in Yu-wei's words, "the ancestor who laid the first foundation" of the family.[3]

The status of the family rose gradually in the eighteenth century and

---

[1] K'ang Yu-wei, *Tzu-pien nien-p'u* (hereafter cited as *Nien-p'u*), p. 1a; Jung-pang Lo, *K'ang Yu-wei: A Biography and a Symposium*, p. 23. Richard C. Howard, "K'ang Yu-wei (1858–1927): His Intellectual Background and Early Thought," pp. 296–300, sketches K'ang's family background.

[2] K'ang T'ung-pi, *Nan-hai hsien-sheng tzu-pien nien-p'u pu-i* (hereafter, *Pu-i*), p. 75a; Lo, *K'ang*, p. 144, n. 2. See also K'ang "*Sung-fen chi hsü*," *K'ang Nan-hai hsien-sheng wen-ch'ao* (hereafter, *Wen-ch'ao*), 5: 33b, and *K'ang Nan-hai wen-chi* (hereafter, *Wen-chi*), *chüan* 8, p. 1a.

[3] K'ang, "*K'ang-shih chia-miao pei.*"

3

the early years of the nineteenth. K'ang Shih-yao (fifteenth generation) became "a scholar and government functionary" (*li*). It remained for K'ang Hui (Wen-yao, seventeenth generation) to achieve scholarly distinction when he passed the provincial examinations in 1804 and, later, when he became a noted teacher with whom as many as a thousand pupils studied at various times. He followed the Ch'eng-Chu school of Neo-Confucianism and was credited with having instituted the first ancestral shrine to honor Wei-ch'ing, the first scholar in the family. Thanks to Wen-yao, Yu-wei said, "our clan prospered because of the studies in filial piety, brotherly duty, rites, and propriety."[4]

K'ang Shih-p'eng (Wen-yao's third and youngest son, Yu-wei's great grandfather) carried on the family's scholarly tradition. Instead of exclusively following Ch'eng-Chu, however, he also subscribed to the doctrines of Liu Tsung-chou, a Ming-dynasty Neo-Confucian strongly influenced by the Lu–Wang school. Of Shih-p'eng's four sons no information is available regarding the third, Tzu-hsiu.[5] The others entered the lower echelons of officialdom. Hsüeh-hsiu, the eldest, was an expectant prefect; Tao-hsiu, "a devoted scholar of lofty conduct," assisted in the administration of Lei-yang hsien (Hunan province); and Tsan-hsiu (Yu-wei's grandfather), a follower of the Ch'eng-Chu tradition, became *chü-jen* in 1846 and served as subdirector of studies in Lin-shan and Lien-chou (Kwang-tung province).[6] Ta-ch'u, eldest of Tsan-hsiu's three sons and Yu-wei's father, studied with Chu Tz'u-ch'i (better known as Chu Chiu-chiang), as Yu-wei later did, and was for a time district magistrate in Kiangsi.[7]

A number of Yu-wei's ancestors pursued careers other than the scholarly. Ta-ch'ien (second of Tsan-hsiu's three sons) was rewarded with an official post (district magistracy) because of his successful military campaign against rebel bands in Lan-shan (Hunan province).[8] Ta-shou (Ta-ch'ien's younger brother) applied his talents to "industrial enterprises" and refused to seek official employment, although he was "versed in the classics and history."[9] Of Shih-p'eng's two elder brothers (Yu-wei's great granduncles) one was a merchant. In fact, according

[4] Ibid. For additional statements concerning K'ang Hui, see *"Liu-fen chi* hsü," *Wen-ch'ao*, 5: 35b, and *Wen-chi, chüan* 8, p. 3a.

[5] "K'ang-shih chia-miao pei."

[6] Ibid. For additional statements concerning K'ang's grandfather, see *"Lien-chou i-chi* hsü," *Wen-ch'ao*, 5: 36b, and *Wen-chi, chüan* 8, p. 12a.

[7] "K'ang-shih chia-miao pei."

[8] Ibid.

[9] Ibid.

to Yu-wei's own account, among Wen-yao's seventy descendants only eleven were "scholars and teachers." Fourteen of the seventy were military or civil officials who came to their positions through military service, while nine were government functionaries holding no examination degrees. It turns out, therefore, that in the five generations from Wen-yao to Yu-wei (from the seventeenth to the twenty-first) scholars and teachers constituted a minority among the kinsmen. The proportion of scholar-teachers to kinsmen in other professions was not appreciably larger in the thirteen generations (from the ninth to the twenty-first) to which Yu-wei explicitly referred.[10]

Yu-wei's estimate of the extent of scholarly commitment among his ancestors is far from accurate, but it is not without significance. In glorifying his family as one of scholars and teachers he revealed his own evaluation of that calling—and his own aspiration.

He was not unappreciative of the benefits that some of his nonscholar kinsmen afforded him. Two of them he mentioned with particular gratitude. I-hsiu (also known as Kuo-hsi), one of his great granduncles, was a commoner who organized local corps and defended his own district and three neighboring districts against the Red Turbans. He attracted the attention of Tso Tsung-t'ang because of his successful military operations. Though not a scholar himself, I-hsiu was interested in learning. He collected a large number of books that Yu-wei made use of in his childhood and youth. "Thanks to his books," Yu-wei said, "I was able to read extensively."[11] Kuo-ch'i, I-hsiu's younger brother, entered military service in the closing years of the Tao-kuang reign. When the T'ai-p'ing rebels invaded Kiangsi early in the 1850s, he raised troops to fight against them. Soon afterwards he led successful campaigns against them in Kiangsu, Chekiang, Fukien, and Kwangtung. A series of promotions made him Provincial Treasurer of Kwangsi in 1857 and Acting Governor in 1860.[12] He was the only one of Yu-wei's kinsmen to attain such official eminence. "He has brought glory and greatness to our family," Yu-wei said.[13] As I-hsiu furnished books for Yu-wei to read, Kuo-ch'i provided him elegant surroundings for study and meditation. In 1865 Kuo-ch'i, newly appointed Provincial Judge of Fukien, made a triumphant visit to his native village.[14] He ordered

[10] Ibid.

[11] Ibid.

[12] K'o Shao-min, *Ch'ing-shih kao, lieh-chuan, chüan* 220, pp. 3b–4a; *Ch'ing-shih liehchuan, chüan* 62, pp. 21b–28a; and Miao Ch'üan-sun, *Hsü pei-chuan chi, chüan* 39.

[13] "K'ang-shih chia-miao pei."

[14] Ibid., and *Nien-p'u*, p. 2b; Lo, *K'ang*, p. 25.

the construction of spacious gardens and sumptuous buildings, lending splendor to the village. The Twenty-thousand-volume Library (Erh-wan-chüan shu-lou) and the House of Calm Contentment (Tan-ju lou) soon became Yu-wei's favorite haunts. It was in the latter building where he gained his first philosophical enlightenment in 1884.[15] He was eight *sui* in 1865 and had a good time amidst all the excitement and festivities that were going on. Loved for his brightness by the elders, he was privileged to share with them much of the fun—banquets, music, games, and watching the new buildings going up in 1866.[16] For the first time in his life he experienced pomp and luxury. This did not swerve him from the scholarly path but served, in all probability, to awaken in him something like an Epicurean urge that appears to have persisted throughout his adult life, coloring his thinking and behavior.

Happy days of his childhood did not last long. He lost his father early in 1868 when he was eleven *sui*.[17] The entire burden of managing the household fell on the shoulders of his widowed mother,[18] who came from a family enjoying affluence for seven consecutive generations.[19] With his mother and a younger brother he lived in modest financial circumstances for a number of years. At one point (1880) he was so poor that he had to stay home and did not have money to buy books or pen and ink.[20]

Naturally, Yu-wei held his mother in deep affection and admiration. He dwelled at length on his indebtedness to her, in particular for her loving care during his long illness in his childhood, for her support, and for her strict discipline even long after he attained manhood. She used her dowry to meet family expenses and managed affairs in such a way as to free him of all worries, thus enabling him to devote his time and attention to study. Her guidance and encouragement in the early years of his career were especially helpful. As Yu-wei recalled after her death in 1913:

> When I pursued my studies in my youthful days, I had no desire to enter officialdom and was reluctant to compete in the examinations. My mother put pressure on me, saying, "Your grandfather expects you to achieve success in the examinations; you should not disappoint him." But when I

[15] *Nien-p'u*, pp. 5a and 6b–7a; Lo, *K'ang*, p. 39–42.
[16] *Nien-p'u*, p. 2b; Lo, *K'ang*, p.25.
[17] *Nien-p'u*, p. 3a; Lo, *K'ang*, p. 26.
[18] *Nien-p'u*, p. 3a; Lo, *K'ang*, p. 26.
[19] *K'ang*, "Hsien-pi Lao t'ai-fu-jen hsing-chuang," *Ai-lieh lu, chüan* 1, p. 3a.
[20] *Nien-p'u*, p. 5b; Lo, *K'ang*, p. 36.

earned the *chin-shih* in Kuang-hsü *i-wei* year [1895], she said, "Official life is full of pitfalls; as I wish to be with you, do not [leave me] to enter officialdom."[21]

She was no doting mother. "Even when I was fifty *sui*," Yu-wei reminisced in 1913, "I was reprimanded without leniency whenever I committed the slightest breach of propriety."[22] It may be surmised that she, together with her daughters whose character and intelligence Yu-wei also admired,[23] convinced him that women were men's equals, morally and intellectually, and led him eventually to the conclusion that the traditional conception of women must be revised. His affection for his mother was evinced in his concern for her during his exile and in his attempts to be with her whenever circumstances allowed.[24]

Yu-wei said little about his father. This relative silence may be explained by the fact that, as a government functionary in Fukien and Kiangsi, Yu-wei's father was away from home most of his short life. It was Yu-wei's grandfather and some of his paternal uncles who were largely responsible for his early education. He was particularly attached to his grandfather who, like most grandfathers in traditional China, took a keen interest in his first grandson,[25] and became Yu-wei's teacher and companion. An intensive program of study was launched in the spring of 1868, shortly after the father's death. As Yu-wei recalled, his eagerness to learn and the rate of his progress were most gratifying.

[My grandfather] instructed me day and night in the lofty principles of Confucian scholars of the past and in the rules and methodology of learning. I began to read the *Kang-chien* and thus gained knowledge of history. I then read *Ta-Ch'ing hui-tien* and *Tung-hua lu*, acquiring knowledge of political institutions. I went on to read the *Ming shih* and *San-kuo chih*. In the sixth month [of that year] I was able to write full-length essays and

---

[21] *Ai-lieh lu, chüan* 1, pp. 2b–6a.

[22] Ibid., p. 5a.

[23] Ibid., pp. 18a–22b, "Chung-tzu Lo i-jen mu-chih." Cf. *Nien-p'u*, pp. 3b and 8a; Lo, *K'ang*, p. 28. According to Chao Feng-t'ien ("K'ang Ch'ang-su hsien-sheng nien-p'u kao," p. 174), K'ang had three sisters, two of whom were older than he. The eldest was "the most intelligent" but died at three *sui*. The second, I-hung, and the third, Ch'iung-chü, were also remarkable women.

[24] *Nien-p'u*, pp. 27a, 28b, and 29a; Lo, *K'ang*, pp. 138–39. See also *Pu-i*, pp. 23b, 24a, 42b, 44b, and 50b. Cf. Lo, *K'ang*, p. 103 (no mention of Yu-wei's return to Hong Kong to see his mother), p. 195 (no mention of his mother), p. 211 ("planning to visit Australia before returning to Hong Kong to see his mother"), p. 214 ("K'ang brought his mother to Penang"), and p. 217 ("he left Singapore for Hong Kong to visit his mother").

[25] K'ang Tsan-hsiu, "Wen chang-sun Yu-wei sheng," *Wen-chi, chüan* 8.

poems. At that time my mind was open and receptive; my desire to learn was heightened. When the sun went down and the room grew dark, I leaned against a pillar under the eaves [where there was some light] and continued to read. When my grandfather found this out, he ordered me to bed. But I continued to read stealthily, with a lamp hidden behind the curtains. Frequently, I perused the *Peking Gazette* (*Ti pao*), informing myself of what transpired at the imperial court and of the achievements of Tseng Kuo-fan, Lo Ping-chang, and Tso Tsung-t'ang. I began to have long-range ambitions.[26]

A year later, when he was twelve *sui*, his grandfather initiated him into the art of writing "examination essays," which he found not difficult but distasteful.[27]

His grandfather was to him a delightful companion as well as a demanding pedagogue. The elderly subdirector of Lien-chou took the child with him on his frequent strolls in the scenic spots of the district and treated him with oral accounts of the lives and works of celebrated men of the past, including disciples and followers of Confucius, Buddhist patriarchs, famed essayists, poets, and calligraphers. Yu-wei was so inspired by these accounts that he readily identified himself with some of the luminaries of bygone ages. As Yu-wei put it:

> [I did] a certain thing and promptly regarded it as worthy of [Chang] Nan-hsüan; [I wrote] an essay and believed that it was worthy of [Su] Tung-p'o; [I had] a thought and imagined that it was worthy of the Sixth Patriarch or Ch'iu Ch'ang-ch'un. I condescended to associate with youthful students of the department, assuming an air of superiority.[28]

Yu-wei owed much to his grandfather who initiated him into Neo-Confucian philosophy, gave him his first glimpses of history, planted in him the seed of syncretic thinking, instilled in him love of learning, and above all inspired the self-confidence that was to become a permanent feature of his personality. However, he disagreed with his grandfather on one matter, namely, writing "eight-legged essays" to prepare for the examinations. When the old scholar discovered in 1870 that Yu-wei disliked writing them, he compelled the boy to turn his whole attention to the unsavory chore.[29]

Two of Yu-wei's uncles also had a hand in his early education. Im-

[26] *Nien-p'u*, p. 3a (T'ung-chih 7); Lo, *K'ang*, pp. 26–27. Translation of the passage is my own.

[27] *Nien-p'u*, p. 3a (T'ung-chih 8); Lo, *K'ang*, p. 28.

[28] *Nien-p'u*, p. 3a (T'ung-chih 8); Lo, *K'ang*, p. 28.

[29] *Nien-p'u*, p. 3b (T'ung-chih 9); cf. Lo, *K'ang*, p. 28 (1870).

pressed by his precocity they began to teach him to read, several years before his grandfather took over his education. Thanks to their efforts, he could recite from memory several hundred poems of the T'ang period, when he was only five *sui* (i.e., four years old).[30] Ta-fen (his father's first cousin) started him on writing essays and reading the *Book of History* (*Shu ching*), committing it to memory after reading the difficult passages only a few times. He was then eight *sui*.[31] Ta-chieh (son of Kuo-hsi) taught him composition, off and on during the years 1871–74.[32] Yu-wei expressed gratitude to both of them.

Yu-wei held in affection and esteem his only brother, Yu-p'u (better known as Kuang-jen). Nine years older than Yu-p'u, he served as his brother's tutor for a while in 1880. He instructed him, together with Yu-ming and Yu-p'ei (their cousins), in the classics and history, and guided them in studying other books.[33] Yu-p'u and Yu-p'ei later became active supporters of reform. The latter studied in the United States for a number of years and was a member of the Constitutional Party (Hsien-cheng tang) in the early years of the twentieth century. The former joined the reform movement in Peking, offered Yu-wei suggestions and advice, organized a school for girls, and promoted other modernizing activities, including a Society against Foot-binding in Shanghai.[34] Yu-wei mourned deeply Yu-p'u's death in 1898; two years later, when he was an exile in Singapore, he sent a friend to Peking to find Yu'p'u's remains and to bring them back home for interment.[35]

Yu-wei married Chang Miao-hua in 1876, when he was nineteen[36] and she twenty-two *sui*.[37] They did not live a full married life, as he was away from home much of the time. Between 1898 when he took refuge in foreign lands and 1909, when she joined him in Penang, the task of looking after Yu-wei's mother and managing the household devolved on her alone. In 1915 she mortgaged their house in Hong Kong

[30] *Nien-p'u*, p. 1a (T'ung-chih 1); Lo, *K'ang*, p. 24.

[31] *Nien-p'u*, p. 1b (T'ung-chih 4); Lo, *K'ang*, p. 25.

[32] *Nien-p'u*, p. 3b (T'ung-chih 10) and p. 4a (T'ung-chih 13); Lo, *K'ang*, pp. 28 (1871) and 29 (1874).

[33] *Nien-p'u*, p. 5b (Kuang-hsü 6); Lo, *K'ang*, p. 36 (1880).

[34] "K'ang-shih chia-miao pei."

[35] *Pu-i*, p. 3a; Lo, *K'ang*, p. 184.

[36] *Nien-p'u*, p. 4b; Lo, *K'ang*, p. 32. According to Chao ("K'ang Ch'ang-su . . . ," p. 180), quoting from a tomb inscription written by Yu-wei, her name was Yün-chu and Miao-hua was her *tzu*. She was betrothed when Yu-wei was eight *sui*.

[37] *Pu-i*, pp. 85a–b. Lo, *K'ang*, p. 240, mentions her death at 68 *sui*, but leaves out the passage that contains the information cited here.

to help finance the anti-Yüan Shih-k'ai movement in which he and Liang Ch'i-ch'ao played leading roles.[38] That she had won her husband's respect may be gathered from the fact that when she died in 1922, Yu-wei wrote a tomb inscription for her and conducted the funeral "fully in conformity with ancient rites."[39]

Yu-wei took a concubine in 1897[40] because he was already forty *sui* and still without a son.[41] He took another concubine ten years later, when he was in the United States. Ho Chan-li, a native of Kwangtung and a student in the United States, admired him upon seeing his picture and became his concubine on her own initiative. She accompanied him in his travels, acting as interpreter and secretary.[42] When she died seven years later (1914) at the age of twenty-four *sui*, Yu-wei expressed his grief in an elegy, "The Golden-ray Dream" ("Chin-kuang meng").[43] In taking concubines he did not live up to his principle of equality between the sexes as enunciated in the *Ta-t'ung shu* and *K'ung-tz'u kai-chih k'ao*.[44] His action, however, was in conformity to the accepted tradition. Living in an age when the social millenium was yet to come, he saw no objection to following the custom of his fellow scholar-officials.

He made frequent references to his children, especially to his two daughters, T'ung-wei and T'ung-pi, born in 1878 and 1880, respectively.[45] He showed much affection toward them and gave them a modern education. They often accompanied him in his travels, in China

---

[38] *Pu-i*, pp. 64a–b; Lo, *K'ang*, p. 229.

[39] *Pu-i*, p. 85b. Lo, *K'ang*, p. 240, makes no mention of this.

[40] *Nien-p'u*, p. 15a; Lo, *K'ang*, p. 78. According to Chao ("K'ang Ch'ang-su . . . ," p. 193), her family name was Liang and she was the mother of Yu-wei's first son.

[41] His first son, T'ung-ch'ien, was born in Penang when Yu-wei was fifty *sui*. The proud father commemorated the happy event with a poem, which was printed in the *Pu-jen tsa-chih*, 6, "wen-i" section: 54. See also Chang Po-chen, *Nan-hai K'ang hsien-sheng chuan*, pp. 51b, 74b.

[42] *Pu-i*, p. 41a; Lo, *K'ang*, p. 210.

[43] *Pu-i*, p. 62b; Lo, *K'ang*, p. 227.

[44] K'ang, *Ta-t'ung shu*, pp. 193–253; K'ang, *Ta T'ung Shu: The One-World Philosophy of K'ang Yu-wei*, trans. Laurence G. Thompson, pp. 149–67. Cf. K'ang, *K'ung-tzu kai-chih k'ao, chüan* 9, p. 15a.

[45] *Nien-p'u*, pp. 5a–b, "[Kuang-hsü 4:] Winter, twelfth month, 21st day, my eldest daughter, T'ung-wei, was born." "[Kuang-hsü 6:] Winter, twelfth month, 22nd day, my second daughter, T'ung-pi, was born" (Lo, *K'ang*, pp. 34, 36). Lo points out (p. 145, n. 8), that the date of T'ung-pi's birth as Yu-wei gave it is incorrect and that she was actually born in 1887, i.e., Kuang-hsü 13, not Kuang-hsü 6, i.e., 1880. Yu-wei's wife and concubines gave birth to a total of nine children, of whom three died prematurely. See *Pu-i*, pp. 15b, 44b, 51b; Chang, *Nan-hai K'ang . . .* ; p. 74b, and Chao, "K'ang Ch'ang-su . . . ," pp. 174–75.

and abroad.[46] T'ung-wei translated for him the Japanese books that he collected, helping him to complete in 1896 his book on Meiji Japan, the *Jih-pen pien-cheng k'ao*, an undertaking that he had begun ten years before.[47] She married Mai Chung-hua, compiler of a collection of essays on reform by over eighty authors, including Yu-wei himself.[48] Yu-wei indicated that his wife "selected the son-in-law,"[49] but in all probability he himself recommended the young man to the mother. T'ung-pi married Lo Chong, a student of Liang Ch'i-ch'ao, who had taken part in the anti-empress dowager plot in 1900. She met him in 1904 in Japan, on her way to the United States.[50]

T'ung-pi joined her father in the spring of 1901 in Penang and was with him much of the time when he traveled in India, Europe, and the United States. Late in 1902, while he was in India, he sent her to Hong Kong to visit her grandmother, and then to Europe and America "to speak on affairs of the country" (*kuo shih*).[51] Before she departed from Darjeeling, he wrote ten short poems to communicate to her his thoughts. Two of these read:

> Thousands of miles to America and Europe
>> A young girl makes the trip alone.
> Do I not have compassion on you?
>> But I cannot help having pity on all living beings. . . .
> An initial step toward women's rights—
>> A great task you now undertake.

> "People's rights" is a universal principle;
>> Constitutional government is truly an excellent plan;
> These are timely panaceas—
>> Proposals that can really save the country.
> Clearly will you enunciate my aim
>> And with zeal carry out the mission.
> The Sage Sovereign is still unharmed,
>> Such is Heaven's wish.[52]

---

[46] *Pu-i*, pp. 23a and 64a; Lo, *K'ang*, pp. 193, 227.

[47] *Nien-p'u*, p. 14b; Lo, *K'ang*, p. 76.

[48] Mai's compilation bears the title *Huang-ch'ao ching-shih wen hsin-pien*, 21 *chüan*. It was published in 1898, by Ta-t'ung shu-chü, Shanghai.

[49] *Pu-i*, p. 3a. Lo, *K'ang*, p. 183, does not mention this.

[50] "Lo Wen-chung hui Ch'ang hsien-sheng hsing-chuang," pp. 1b, 3a–b, 4b, 20b. See also *Pu-i*, p. 30a; Lo, *K'ang*, p. 196.

[51] *Pu-i*, p. 23a. Lo, *K'ang*, p. 193, says that she was sent "to the United States to study and to give speeches."

[52] *Pu-i*, pp. 23a–b. Lo, *K'ang*, does not give these poems.

The importance that Yu-wei attached to her trip and his estimation of her capacity can readily be inferred from these lines. Five years later, when he visited New York, she went to see him every day after she attended classes at Columbia University.[53]

Yu-wei's attachment to his children may also be seen from the fact that he continued to enjoy their company (and that of his grandchildren) in his late years,[54] and that he seldom failed to record the birth and death of a son or a daughter.[55] A poem he wrote in 1917 on the Chinese New Year's Eve, bearing the title "Suddenly, I Shall Be Sixty Next Year," is particularly revealing:

> Joyfully together, we drink to New Year's Eve;
>   The youngsters make noise with their drums and horns. . . .
> Wearing my ceremonial robe I pay homage to Heaven
>   And to my ancestors I offer sacrificial wine.
> Lanterns and candles shine brightly along corridors and railings.
>   Sons and daughters merrily partake food and wine. . . .[56]

Yu-wei upheld the traditional familist values in action as well as in word. This, for instance, was what he did upon hearing of the death of his grandfather in 1877:

> I lost my father when I was young. Ever since I was eight *sui* I had depended on my grandfather who personally supported me and taught me for over ten years. When I heard [of his death] I became emaciated with grief; I went without food and drink for three days; after that, I ate nothing but salted vegetables for a hundred days. When my uncles brought his remains home, . . . I lived with them in a thatched hut in front of the coffin. During the rest of the year I wore nothing but mourning clothes and ate no meat. Meanwhile, I studied the mourning rites as recorded in the three *Books of Rites*. Every movement and motion of mine was in conformity to the rites of antiquity.[57]

Likewise, he followed meticulously the rules of propriety when his

[53] *Pu-i*, pp. 40b–41a. Cf. Lo, *K'ang*, p. 205.

[54] *Pu-i*, pp. 64a and 101b. Cf. Lo, *K'ang*, pp. 227, 248.

[55] See, e.g., *Nien-p'u*, p. 6a (1883): "Fifth month. My third daughter, T'ung-chieh, died several days after she was born." This entry in the manuscript copy is missing in the mimeographed copy and not translated in Lo, *K'ang*, p. 38. *Nien-p'u* (mimeographed copy), p. 7b (1886): "My fourth daughter, T'ung-wan, died a few months after her birth." Ibid., p. 10a (1890): "In the eighth month a son was born to me, but he soon died" (Lo, *K'ang*, pp. 43, 53. See also *Pu-i*, pp. 15a, 44b, 50a).

[56] *Pu-i*, p. 73a. Lo, *K'ang*, p. 232, does not translate these lines but renders the concluding ten lines of the long poem.

[57] *Nien-p'u*, p. 4b; Lo, *K'ang*, p. 32. Translation of this passage is my own.

mother died in 1913.[58] A year later, when he returned to his native village after having been an exile in foreign lands for fifteen years, he performed sacrificial rites in the ancestral shrine and on ancestral burial grounds, in accordance with the best Confucian tradition.[59]

He upheld that tradition in many of his writings. For example, in his book on the *Ch'un-ch'iu* doctrines of Tung Chung-shu, the celebrated Kung-yang scholar of Han times, he asserted that the family and familistic morality were basic ingredients of human life. *Jen*, of course, was the central principle of the Confucian ethic, but the family was the primary arena for the development and exercise of virtue. As Mencius had said, "The course of Yao and Shun was simply that of filial piety and fraternal duty."[60] Yu-wei called attention to the fact that the Confucian school instituted the three-year mourning and produced the *Book of Filial Piety*.[61]

The Confucians were not alone in stressing the importance of the family. Mo-tzu, the prophet of "universal love" (*chien ai*), regarded love of one's own parents as man's first duty.[62] The Buddha who in his teaching treated all beings as equal effected the salvation of his own father, wife, and son, before saving all other persons.[63] The teaching of Confucius, Yu-wei added, agreed not only with those of other sages but with "heavenly reason" (*t'ien li*) as well.[64] It was therefore said that when one "serves his father filially, he serves Heaven manifestly." In fact, "the three bonds" (*san kang*) were ordained by Heaven.[65] Undoubtedly, Yu-wei's family background and his early education were responsible for this purely conventional moral outlook.

Interestingly, Yu-wei appealed to traditional morality in his attempt to discredit the empress dowager, arch enemy of his reform movement. In an undated letter to a friend, written some time after the 1898 coup d'état, he argued that the emperor had no moral or legal obligation to render her filial obedience, as she could not properly be considered his mother. In his own words:

[58] *Pu-i*, p. 62a; Lo, *K'ang*, p. 226.

[59] "Ch'u-wang huan-hsiang chi hsien-miao kao-tsu wen," pp. 16a–b, and "Ch'u-wang huan-hsiang kao hsien-mu wen," pp. 26a–27b, both in *Ai-lieh lu, chüan* 2.

[60] *Mencius*, VI.ii.4.

[61] K'ang, *Ch'un-ch'iu Tung-shih hsüeh, chüan* 6 *hsia*, pp. 1a–b and *chüan* 6 *shang*, p. 24b.

[62] Obviously, Yu-wei was referring to the words of I-chih, a follower of Mo-tzu: "To me it sounds that we are to love all without difference of degree; but the manifestation of love must begin with our parents" (*Mencius* III.i.5 [Legge]).

[63] *Ch'un-ch'iu Tung-shih hsüeh, chüan* 1, pp. 7b–6a.

[64] Ibid.

[65] Ibid., *chüan* 6 *hsia*, pp. 18a–19a.

According to the Six Classics, the *T'ung-chien kang-mu* of Chu Hsi, the *Ta-Ch'ing t'ung-li*, and the *Ta-Ch'ing lü-li*, no emperor was ever obliged to treat his father's concubine as mother. As the present emperor is heir to Wen-tsung [i.e., the Hsien-feng emperor], the Hsiao-hsien empress alone can be his mother. No other [woman] is entitled to the maternal appellation; to no other does he owe the duties of a son. The Nara empress can be regarded merely as a surviving concubine of the late emperor. Persons who do not realize that Nara is not mother and the emperor not her son, dare not expose her crime and undertake to punish her.[66]

Incidentally, in his letters to Chang Chih-tung, then governor-general of Hu-Kuang, and Liu K'un-i, then governor-general of Liang-Chiang, written after he received the news of the Boxer uprising, Yu-wei enumerated the "crimes" that the empress dowager was supposed to have committed and urged Chang and Liu to support the emperor's cause.[67]

It was said that the empress dowager called herself a "conservative" and declared her opposition to any who intended "to chop up the ancestral tablets and to burn them."[68] She was known to have "relied wholly on the influence of Confucian ethic" to maintain her authority, namely, as imperial "mother" and regent she could rightfully exact obedience from the emperor.[69] Her claim was supported, overtly or tacitly, by many a scholar-official of the time.[70] It is hardly surprising, therefore, that Yu-wei sought to invalidate her claim. Nor is it surprising that upon the collapse of the reform movement he was accused of having violated the Confucian moral code. A decree of September 29, 1898, accused him of having "gathered lawless elements and plotted to besiege I-ho yüan [the Summer Palace where the empress dowager was residing] with the intention of abducting her," thereby "endangering the moral foundations of the existing regime."[71] Obviously, Yu-wei and his opponents fought an ideological battle with the same weapon: the Confucian tradition.

A question naturally arises. What induced Yu-wei to abandon his unequivocally conservative stance in later years, when he viewed the

---

[66] K'ang, "Chih Lien-san shu," *Wan-mu-ts'ao-t'ang i-kao*, 3: 40a–b.

[67] *Pu-i*, pp. 4a–b and 9a. Lo, *K'ang*, p. 188, mentions these letters but does not give the texts.

[68] Der Ling, *Two Years in the Forbidden City*, p. 175.

[69] Li Chien-nung, *The Political History of China, 1840–1928*, p. 99. Cf. pp. 187–90.

[70] See, e.g., Yeh Te-hui, "Yü Hsü K'o-shih kuan-ch'a shu," in Su Yü, *I-chiao ts'ung-pien*, chüan 6, p. 36a.

[71] Ch'en Pao-chen, *Te-tsung shih-lu*, chüan 427, pp. 6a–b (Kuang-hsü 24/8/14).

family as a source of human miseries and predicted its disappearance in utopia?[72]

Several influences may have been at work. The Buddhist notion of *pravraj* (*ch'u chia*, "to leave the family") with which he must have been acquainted, through his study of Buddhist texts in 1879,[73] may possibly have suggested to him that the family was detrimental to happiness. The unfortunate experiences of some of his kinsfolk and friends may have confirmed or reenforced this view. For example, he was greatly distressed by the tragic lot of his sisters, I-hung and Ch'iung-chü. The former, betrothed to a sickly young man, was made to wed him when he fell critically ill in 1871. The bridegroom died nineteen days after the wedding. After witnessing the dissipation of a large family fortune by her husband's spendthrift brothers and leading the cheerless life of a widow for forty-three years, she died in 1914.[74] Ch'iung-chü became a widow shortly after marriage and "died in destitution" in 1888.[75] Yu-wei was pained by their misfortunes and expressed regret that he could lend no help to them. One of his students, K'ung Chao-yen, reported to him in a letter the "impossible family situation" he faced; he wished to pursue a scholarly career but his parents compelled him to give up his studies and to earn a living.[76] T'an Ssu-t'ung, one of his associates in the 1898 reform, lost his mother in childhood and was maltreated by his father's concubine.[77] That the emperor was maltreated by Tz'u-hsi, his "mother," had been noted by more than one writer of the time.[78] All these probably contributed to his realization that, contrary to his own personal experience and in spite of his own commitment to the Confucian ethic, the family was hardly an unmixed blessing.

[72] K'ang, *Ta-t'ung shu*, pp. 255–89; Thompson, *Ta T'ung Shu*, pp. 169–83.

[73] *Nien-p'u*, p. 5a; Lo, *K'ang*, p. 34.

[74] "Chung-tzu Lo i-jen mu-chih," *Ai-lieh lu*, *chüan* 1, pp. 18a–22b. See also *Nien-p'u*, p. 3b and *Pu-i*, p. 62b; Lo, *K'ang*, pp. 28, 227.

[75] *Nien-p'u*, pp. 9a–b; Lo, *K'ang*, p. 50.

[76] The letter is given in Su, *I-chiao ts'ung-pien*, *chüan* 4, pp. 22b–23b.

[77] Liang Ch'i-ch'ao, "T'an Ssu-t'ung chuan" (chap. 5 of *Wu-hsü cheng-pien chi*), *Yin-ping-shih chuan-chi*, no. 1, p. 106.

[78] Liang, *Wu-hsü cheng-pien chi*, p. 57; Reginald F. Johnston, *Twilight in the Forbidden City*, p. 73; and Der Ling, *Two Years in the Forbidden City*, p. 68.

Chapter 2

THE MAN

Admired by some and condemned by many, K'ang Yu-wei was one of the most controversial figures of the time. His daring and unconventional ideas brought him notoriety (which he did not seem to mind) as well as renown (which he apparently relished). His characteristic disposition and behavior did almost as much to place him in the limelight of public attention, flattering or otherwise.[1] Assuming that better

[1] Some of the most vicious attacks referred to his conduct. Yeh Te-hui, an arch-enemy of reform, e.g., said the following of K'ang: "An unprincipled man, he victimized his fellow villagers in his youthful years. After he passed the provincial examinations [in 1893], he became even more oppressive. . . . In the *i-wei* year [1895], when he organized the Society for the Study of Self-strengthening (Tzu-ch'iang hsüeh hui) in Shanghai, he was put to shame by a prostitute whose wrath he had incurred when he visited a brothel. Thereupon a cartoonist produced a "Tableau of the Sage's Tracks" ("Sheng-chi t'u") with a rhymed inscription and a couplet [in jeering reference to K'ang's supposedly indecorous behavior], and published it in a journal of humor . . . . [On another occasion] he falsely accused a fellow villager of conniving with bandits. Imitating the handwriting of his victim, he forged a letter to serve as evidence of the alleged crime. The case was not closed until a year had elapsed. Many were implicated and all the residents of the village hated him [for what he did]." "Ch'ang-hsing hsüeh-chi po-i," in Su Yü, *Ch'un-ch'iu fan-lu i-cheng*, *chüan* 4, pp. 40a–b. Cf. Hsü Ying-k'uei's memorial, in ibid., *chüan* 2, pp. 3a–5a. Yeh's allegations, obviously calumnious, were based on false or inaccurate information. Between October 29 and November 1, 1895, and again in the last days of November, K'ang indeed was in Shanghai to organize a branch of the Society for the Study of National Strengthening (Ch'iang-hsüeh hui, which Yeh misnamed Tzu-ch'iang hsüeh hui). See Kang, *Tzu-pien nien-p'u* (hereafter *Nien-p'u*), pp. 13b–14a; Jung-pang Lo, *K'ang Yu-wei: A Biography and a Symposium*, pp. 72–74. As it was not considered indecent for gentlemen to visit brothels in those days, it is probable that K'ang did

17

understanding of his way of thinking may be gained through an understanding of his personality, I propose to examine briefly some of its salient features in the following pages.

I

An intense self-confidence bordering on self-conceit was easily the most prominent trait of K'ang's personality. This was noted by some of his contemporaries and later writers.[2] He became conscious of his literary ability quite early in life. By the time when he was twelve *sui*, he was able to dash off a poem of forty lines as he watched the dragon-boat races, and was promptly proclaimed a "child prodigy" (*shen t'ung*). Accepting the compliment at its face value, he would "assume an air of superiority" over his fellow students.[3] This was not a passing phase. He was as much self-assured many years later, when he visited Peking in 1888 (thirty-one *sui*) and matched wits with the scholarly elite who happened to be there. "At that time," he reminisced, "I had already achieved the goal of learning. I stood high above the world, though I was in the company of men. Free and easy of manner, I was pleased with myself."[4] Modesty and humility, obviously, were not among his virtues.

K'ang found it difficult to admit that his views could be erroneous. If people failed to concur with him on some issues, he was inclined to think that they were simply wrong. He said to an unnamed friend, in a letter written probably after 1898:

> The Way (*Tao*) has not prevailed for a long time. It is now difficult for the lonely voice of Truth to be heard. . . . Copernicus was the first man to say that the earth goes around the sun; he went to prison. But all who

---

as many of his fellow scholars occasionally (or frequently) did. Yeh's allegation that K'ang falsely accused a fellow villager of conniving with bandits referred, obviously, to K'ang's struggle with Chang Sung-fen in 1893 over control of the Regiment and Drill Bureau of Fellow Villagers (T'ung-jen t'uan lien chü), founded by K'ang's granduncle, Kuo-ch'i, in 1854. See *Nien-p'u*, pp. 11a–12a; Lo, *K'ang*, pp. 57–61, for K'ang's own account of the incident.

[2] E.g., K'o Shao-min, *Ch'ing-shih kao, lieh-chuan, chüan* 260, p. 4b.

[3] *Nien-p'u*, pp. 1a–3a (entries for 1862–69). Lo, *K'ang*, pp. 24–27, translates K'ang's statement in part thus: "I would assume an air of superiority over the other students."

[4] *Nien-p'u*, p. 8a. Lo, *K'ang*, p. 45, "At this time, believing myself to be quite learned, I felt far superior to mundane things, and I was quite self-assured in the company of other men."

now study astronomy honor Copernicus. Ideas that are absolutely true cannot fail to gain eventual victory.[5]

Vincit omnia veritas—this was the essence of K'ang's credo. Born of self-confidence, it constituted a major source of his moral courage and intellectual firmness. "Haunted by no intellectual perplexities,"[6] he seldom paid serious attention to diverging opinions held by other men. He heartily approved of a well-known dictum of Chang Chü-cheng (1525–82), the resolute and somewhat highhanded statesman of the Ming dynasty: "In my career I have learned to take my own mind as guide; I reckon neither with the censure or praise of one time, nor with the approbation or condemnation of all times."[7] It was this unbending self-reliance that made K'ang a fearless crusader against things that he believed to be bad, a missionary preaching to the world what he thought to be good, regardless of established convention or practical consequences.

It is not surprising that he often became a victim of dogmatism. As Liang Ch'i-ch'ao, his erstwhile student, said in 1901:

> He is a man with extremely ample power of self-assurance. No one can change his views. This is true with respect to practical undertakings as well as academic pursuits. He refuses to adapt his views to fit facts but, on the contrary, he frequently recasts facts to support his views. . . . Therefore, people who decry him call him "arbitrary," "obstinate," or "overbearing."[8]

Twenty years later, Liang reiterated this appraisal and recalled his experience in assisting his teacher prepare the book on "the forged classic" (*Hsin-hsüeh wei-ching k'ao*):

> K'ang Yu-wei went so far as to say that Liu Hsin (d. 23 B.C.) interpolated dozens of items into the *Shih-chi* and the *Ch'u-tz'u*, and that Liu clandestinely cast and buried [bronze] bells, tripods, and other ritual vessels,

---

[5] "Letter to an unnamed person," microfilm, reel 1. The phrase "the lonely voice of truth" is a free translation of "ku ho . . . chih ming," literally, "the cry of a solitary crane."

[6] Loo Woon Choon (Lo Wen-chung, i.e., Lo Ch'ang), a speech delivered at the memorial service on the tenth anniversary of K'ang's death, manuscript copy in Jung-pang Lo's collection.

[7] "Letter to Shen Tzu-p'ei, of the Board of Punishment" ("Yü Shen Tzu-p'ei hsing-pu shu"). This letter was possibly written around 1889 when K'ang was about thirty-one *sui*.

[8] Liang Ch'i-ch'ao, "Nan-hai K'ang hsien-sheng chuan," *Yin-ping-shih ho-chi, wen-chi*, no. 6, pp. 87–88.

which he then later unearthed, with a view to deceiving posterity. All this is contrary to fact and reason, but K'ang stubbornly maintained his view. . . . To satisfy his desire to be catholic and original [in his scholarship], he did not hesitate to suppress or distort evidence. . . . As a man K'ang was totally subjective in myriads of things. His self-confidence was extremely strong; he held [his views] very tenaciously. As for objective facts which did not suit his purposes, he either ignored them completely or insisted on remoulding them to conform to his own view.[9]

This dogmatic frame of mind sometimes blinded him to realities. In 1898, for instance, when the emperor officially announced the reform regime (June 11), tradition-bound scholar-officials intensified their opposition to K'ang's movement. "The entire country rejoiced," K'ang observed.[10] However, voices of opposition became so loud that even he had to admit that all was not well. "When the eight-legged essay was abolished," he said, "the scholars of Chihli province wished to assassinate me."[11] To cite another instance: in 1900 he announced that he had raised substantial sums of money and rallied a sizable number of troops on behalf of his "emperor-protection" (*pao huang*) movement, which in fact he had not. Liang Ch'i-ch'ao objected strongly to such misrepresentation in a letter to K'ang: "To indulge regularly in boastful words, as Chung-shan [i.e., Sun Yat-sen] does, merely lowers people's respect for you."[12] It appears that self-assurance, though indispensable to a leader, is likely to undermine his credibility, if it turns into overconfidence, wishful thinking, or self-deception.

Self-assurance sometimes generated in K'ang an optimism unwarranted by the actual situation. Thus K'ang Kuang-jen complained to a friend shortly before the 1898 debacle: "My brother is too ambitious in his plans and overzealous in carrying out his mission. He tries to do too much and, having too few supporters, he undertakes tasks that are too big."[13] Sensing that the situation was rapidly becoming as dangerous as it had been hopeless, Kuang-jen repeatedly entreated his

[9] Liang Ch'i-ch'ao, *Ch'ing-tai hsüeh-shu kai-lun*, pp. 128–29. English translation by Immanuel C. Y. Hsü under the title *Intellectual Trends in the Ch'ing Period*, p. 93. This passage is quoted here from Hsü's translation with slight changes.

[10] *Nien-p'u*, p. 18b; Lo, *K'ang*, p. 92.

[11] *Nien-p'u*, pp. 20a–b; Lo, *K'ang*, p. 101.

[12] Ting Wen-chiang, *Liang Jen-kung hsien-sheng nien-p'u ch'ang-pien ch'u-kao*, pp. 105–6.

[13] K'ang Kuang-jen, "Chih I-i shu" (Letter to [Ho] I-i), p. 58. This passage is also quoted in Ch'en Kung-lu, "Chia-wu chan-hou keng-tzu luan-ch'ien Chung-kuo pien-fa yün-tung chih yen-chiu," p. 189.

brother to leave Peking and return home.[14] The advice fell on deaf ears. Yu-wei stayed to the bitter end; Kuang-jen did not leave and was put to death for his part in reform.

Overestimating his ability, K'ang was prone to passing snap judgments. Thanks to his "exceedingly sensitive brains," as Liang Ch'i-ch'ao put it, he could comprehend the import of a book as soon as he set his eyes on it and make instantaneous decisions when practical questions were presented to him. Unfortunately, however, "sometimes it turned out that he was not wholly right in his judgment."[15] Lu Nai-hsiang and Lu Tun-k'uei, co-authors of one of K'ang's biographies, reported that K'ang "reached an immediate decision upon being confronted with a problem and could dispose in a few words of matters that were complicated and difficult. As a result, persons who thought ill of him considered him arbitrary, strong-willed, and tyrannical."[16] In his later years K'ang himself admitted that some of his views held previously were of doubtful validity because they had been formed without mature deliberation. In a postscript (written in 1913) to his memorial petitioning the emperor to adopt Western-style raiments, he expressed regret that he had ever made such a proposal. "Men," he said, "are apt to be moved by emotions and do not think things through [before they draw conclusions]."[17]

Various historical forces combined to doom the reform movement of 1898 to dismal failure. One can hardly deny the possibility that K'ang's own disposition and attitudes had rendered success even less likely. One may, however, also pose a question. Had K'ang been more prudent and less impulsive, more diffident and less sanguine than he was, could he have launched the ill-fated movement at all?

II

Believing that he possessed unusual intellectual and moral capacity, K'ang convinced himself that it was his role to lead and to serve men. He discovered his "knack of directing the affairs of men" when he was only twelve *sui*.[18] For a while he did not concede intellectual leadership even to Confucius. He wrote in 1917:

[14] *Nien-p'u*, p. 22a; Lo, *K'ang*, p. 108.

[15] Liang, "Nan-hai K'ang hsien-sheng chuan," p. 88.

[16] Lu Nai-hsiang and Lu Tun-k'uei, *K'ang Nan-hai hsien-sheng chuan*, pp. 47b–48a.

[17] *Pu-jen tsa-chih*, 1 (1913): 15.

[18] *Nien-p'u*, p. 3a. Cf. Lo, *K'ang*, p. 27, where *chih-hui jen-shih* is translated as "to undertake more responsible work."

In my youth I had a desire to become the founder of a religion (*chiao chu*) and of surpassing Confucius. Everyday I read the books he left behind him and looked for imperfections or blemishes in them, with a view to attacking him.[19]

He bowed to the authority of the ancient sage, eventually, but he never did give up the belief that he was qualified to join the company of the sages and worthies of bygone days.[20]

He realized that to be sage or worthy he must dedicate himself to serving his fellow men. This was to him a matter of emotional demand as well as intellectual requirement. His warm-hearted concern for others—*jen* (love or benevolence) and *pu-jen* (inability to endure seeing others suffer")—was an important constituent of his mental make-up. Touched by other people's anguish or tribulation he often shed compassionate tears.[21] On more than one occasion he gave verbal expression to his humanitarian sentiments. For example, explaining his involvement in the troubled affairs of an organization in his home village in the 1890s, he said:

> As I make no distinction between what is important and what is trifling but extend my compassionate concern to all, I carry out my principle of benevolence without fear of disaster . . . and without thought of success or failure.[22]

He made a more precise statement of his principle in the *Ta-t'ung shu*. "Mankind in the ten thousand countries on earth are all my brothers. . . . I have love for them all."[23] The allegation of some his detractors notwithstanding, K'ang probably was one of the most principled men of his time.

K'ang was inclined to speak and act as his conviction dictated, irrespective of other people's feelings or established social conventions, thereby making himself a target of criticism and censure. When he

[19] "Ts'an-cheng-yüan t'i-i li-kuo chin-shen i shu-hou," *Pu-jen tsa-chih*, vols. 9 and 10 (1917), "Chiao-shuo," p. 9.

[20] *Nien-p'u*, p. 4a (statement made after failing to pass the provincial examinations in 1876) and K'ang T'ung-pi, *Nan-hai hsien-sheng tzu-pien nien p'u pu-i* (hereafter *Pu-i*), p. 75a (poem written in 1917). Lo, *K'ang*, pp. 30–31, 232 (where the concluding lines of this poem are translated).

[21] *Nien-p'u*, p. 5a (an 1878 entry); Lo, *K'ang*, pp. 33–34, "thinking of the suffering of the people in the world, I would be sad and cry."

[22] *Nien-p'u*, p. 12a; Lo, *K'ang*, p. 60 (quoted here with slight changes).

[23] *Ta-t'ung shu*, p. 4. *Ta T'ung Shu*, trans. Laurence G. Thompson, p. 65 (quoted here with changes).

was married in 1876, he firmly refused, "as a matter of principle," to acquiesce in the time-honored custom of "teasing the bride"; he was prepared to incur the displeasure of relatives and friends.[24] In 1893 he refused, again as a matter of principle, to follow the long-established usage of honoring as "teacher" the examiner who first read his essays and recommended him for the *chü-jen* degree. As expected, he brought on himself a chorus of disapprobation from the scandalized scholar-officials.[25] He even recoiled from compromising his intellectual integrity or personal dignity for the sake of his "great cause." In the autumn of 1895 he went to Nanking to solicit Chang Chih-tung's help to organize a southern branch of the Society for the Study of National Strengthening. Chang, then governor-general of Liang-Chiang, took an interest in the reform movement and received him as an honored guest, but objected to his unorthodox views as developed in his book "Confucius as Reformer" (*K'ung-tzu kai-chih k'ao*). K'ang declined to modify or abandon any of them, saying that as they stemmed from a "great principle" he did not see fit to alter them "on account of the hospitality of a governor-general of Liang-Chiang." Predictably, Chang reneged on his promise to sponsor the society.[26] In the spring of 1898, at the suggestion of Kang-i, the emperor appointed K'ang a secretary-attaché in the Tsungli yamen, after he had the historic audience with the emperor. Thinking that the assignment was calculated to insult or humiliate him, he refused to serve.[27] Regarding himself as a man of lofty aims, he could not stoop to join the rank and file of bureaucracy.

He was sometimes accused of being conceited, haughty, or power-hungry. Ku Hung-ming, an Oxford-educated conservative and Chang Chih-tung's foreign-language secretary for many years, called K'ang and his associates "extreme radicals" who were "really vain, self-seeking, ambitious, without experience, judgment, or discretion."[28] J. O. P. Bland and Sir Edmund T. Backhouse found it "difficult to acquit K'ang Yu-wei of personal and interested motives, of a desire to wield power in the state."[29] More recently, Ch'ien Mu described K'ang as a man with "an extremely strong will to lead."[30]

---

[24] *Nien-p'u*, p. 4b; Lo, *K'ang*, p. 32.

[25] *Nien-p'u*, p. 11a; Lo, *K'ang*, p. 57.

[26] *Nien-p'u*, p. 14a; Lo, *K'ang*, p. 74.

[27] *Nien-p'u*, pp. 19b–20a; Lo, *K'ang*, p. 99.

[28] Ku Hung-ming, *Papers from a Viceroy's Yamen: A Chinese Plea for the Case of Good Government and True Civilization in China*, pp. 5–6.

[29] J. O. P. Bland and Edmund Backhouse, *China under the Empress Dowager: Being the History of the Life and Times of Tz'u-hsi*, p. 189.

[30] Ch'ien Mu, *Chung-kuo chin san-pai nien hsüeh-shu shih*, p. 709.

Some of K'ang's contemporaries who had direct contact with him complained that he tended to be imperious and highhanded in dealing with people. Ch'en Shao-po, one of Sun Yat-sen's followers, reported a meeting with K'ang in 1898, in Japan:

> K'ang Yu-wei soon came out. At that moment, two other persons were in the hall, one of them was introduced by Liang Ch'i-ch'ao as Wang Chao, a man from Chihli. . . . We, seven of us, sat around a large round table. Wang Chao was on my right and said to me, "Sir, please give your judicious opinion. I live with them here. I have no freedom of speech or movement. Even my correspondence is subjected to their censorship. This is really an intolerable situation." Before he had finished talking, K'ang, sensing that something went wrong, said angrily to Liang T'ieh-chün, "Take him outside; do not leave him here to gabble." Mr. Liang rose and dragged Wang Chao away.[31]

As Wang Chao was said to be a man of strong will and hot temperament,[32] K'ang perhaps was not wholly to blame. The following excerpt from a 1902 letter from Liang Ch'i-ch'ao to K'ang, however, cannot be dismissed as sheer aspersion. Liang had published in the *Hsin-min ts'ung-pao* an article advocating anti-Manchu revolution. K'ang was furious and wrote Liang to reprimand him. In reply Liang made the following point:

> Your letter says that this journal is a Party organ and that opinions expressed therein must have the unanimous approval of all members . . . of the Party. However, as members live in widely separated parts of the world, it is absolutely impossible to obtain the signature of each and every one of them, when an article is written and ready for 'publication. Moreover, as Party members subscribe to the principle of constitutional government, they would be willing to decide matters by majority vote, [not by unanimous consent or according to the wish of any one member]. I suspect that seven or eight out of ten would endorse [my view].[33]

Admittedly, Liang deserved K'ang's censure for not following the Party line as laid down by the acknowledged leader. But in demanding conformity under the guise of unanimity, K'ang moved perilously

---

[31] Su-ch'ih [Chang Yin-lin], "K'ang Yu-wei wu-hsu cheng-pien chih hsin shih-liao," *Ta-kung pao (L'Impartial)*, "Shih-ti chou-k'an," July 24, 1936; quoted in Chien Po-tsan et al., *Wu-hsü pien-fa*, 4: 333–34.

[32] Hu Ssu-ching, *Wu-hsü li-shuang lu, chüan* 4; quoted in Chien, *Wu-hsü*, 4: 85.

[33] Ting, *Liang Jen-kung*, p. 158. See also another letter written by Liang to K'ang, rejecting the latter's charge that he was "doing things without authorization" (*chuan-shan hsing-shih*), namely, without K'ang's authorization (ibid., p. 190).

close to being dictatorial. Bertrand Russell once remarked that "the progressive" dedicated themselves to the creation of a paradise; then having been "narcissistically hypnotized by contemplation of their own wisdom and goodness, they proceeded to create a new tyranny."[34] K'ang, apparently, was not so hypnotized; he certainly had no intention of creating a tyranny. However, because of his phenomenal self-assurance, one cannot be sure that he could avoid the intellectual pitfall into which Wang An-shih (1021–86), the celebrated reformer of the Sung dynasty had fallen. "Wang was so devoted to his own unconventional ideas," as a historian recently points out, "that he became increasingly doctrinaire and intolerant of other ideas, which he often dismissed as merely conventional, worthless, and obstructive."[35]

III

K'ang derived his moral courage from another source, the belief that he was a man of destiny, to whom Heaven had entrusted a historic mission. In this he was not unlike Confucius who thought that the course of his life had been determined by Heaven for a great purpose.[36] K'ang revealed his belief in a poem written in 1917, two lines of which read:

> All my life I believe in the Decree of Heaven,
> Thus have I come into possession of fearlessness.

In the same poem he mentioned the auspicious sign that marked his birth:

> To recall the time of my birth:
> It was the Fifth Day of the Second Month,
> As crimson fire entered the house
> At midnight, I began my life.[37]

Three months after he arrived in Japan in 1898, he specified the nature of his Heaven-decreed mission. After enumerating eleven occasions on which he narrowly escaped death, he said:

---

[34] Bertrand Russell, *The Impact of Science on Society*, pp. 44–45.

[35] James T. C. Liu, *Reform in Sung China: Wang An-shih (1021–1068) and His New Policies*, p. 68.

[36] *Analects* (Legge), III.iv.4; VII.xxii.1; VIII.viii.1; IX.v.103; and XIV.xxxviii.2.

[37] *Pu-i*, pp. 73b and 75a. Lo, *K'ang*, pp. 231–32, does not translate these lines of the poem. Cf. Chao Feng-t'ien, "K'ang Ch'ang-su hsien-sheng nien-p'u kao," p. 175.

Deviously, opportunely, miraculously, my life has been spared. Perhaps my life is preserved for a purpose. Perhaps China will not be destroyed and the Great Teaching (*ta tao*) will not perish. . . . Obeying Heaven and awaiting the Decree, I shall act solely as my compassionate heart dictates, in order to save myriad people.[38]

Belief in the Decree of Heaven enabled him to overcome fear and hesitation on several occasions. In 1888, when he was about to submit the "First Memorial" to the emperor through the censorate, he was disturbed by the information that the street leading from his hostel to his destination was temporarily blocked at Ts'ai-shih-k'ou where some condemned men were being executed. This inauspicious coincidence made him pause and debate with himself.

Inwardly, I debated: "I am about to submit a memorial and coincidentally an execution takes place; the omen is not propitious. I have an aged mother; I cannot die." Then I thought: "Since I have dedicated myself to the task of saving the country, and to live or to die is ordained [by Heaven], I should not be afraid and turn back." Resolutely, I entered my carriage and went [to the censorate] through a detour.[39]

Ten years later, when his brother Kuang-jen urged him to leave Peking where the situation was becoming explosive, he replied:

To live or to die is a matter of Decree. Sometime ago, when I passed through Hua-te-li, a brick happened to drop close by my head. Had it been one inch closer, it would have hit my head and I would have died then. And, if I suffer a stroke, I might die right now. The sage Emperor is on our side. I am committed to saving China. How could I bear to think of leaving?[40]

As late as in 1924, belief in Heaven still gave him psychological strength to work for Manchu restoration, a cause that had by then become irretrievably lost. Extraordinarily auspicious omens, he said, promised success to an undertaking that transcended human power and was independent of human ability.[41]

It was a short step from belief in Heaven to commonplace superstition. When K'ang was about to leave Peking, two days before the 1898

[38] *Nien-p'u*, p. 29b; Lo, *K'ang*, p. 143. Translation of this passage is my own.

[39] *Nien-p'u*, p. 8b; Lo, *K'ang*, p. 47. Cf. Lu and Lu, *K'ang Nan-hai hsien-sheng chuan, shang-pien*, p. 14a.

[40] *Nien-p'u*, p. 22a; Lo, *K'ang*, p. 109. Cf. Ting, *Liang Jen-kung*, p. 58.

[41] "Ch'ing Chuang-shih-tun [Johnston] tai-tsou yu-shuo ching-kuo," in K'ang, *K'ang Nan-hai hsien-sheng mo-chi*, vol. 4.

coup d'état, he said that he was "inwardly alarmed" when a wall of his room fell down, taking it as a premonition of imminent disaster.[42] About a month earlier, he studied the physiognomic featues of T'an Ssu-t'ung and Lin Hsü, two of his most prominent supporters in the "One Hundred Days," and confided to Liang Ch'i-ch'ao that the features of both men were too "light" to merit the weighty positions that they would occupy as a result of successful reform. Disaster, he predicted, was impending. He cited the oracular wisdom of Kuan Lu (208–55) who accurately prognosticated the ill fortune of two contemporary officials by means of physiognomy.[43] "I am scared," K'ang said, but added that Liang's features presaged "extraordinary good luck" that might counteract the bad luck that would befall T'an and Lin.[44] In addition to augury and physiognomy K'ang also lent credence to geomancy, *feng-shui*, as two incidents clearly show. In 1877 he accepted the verdict of a geomancer and delayed the burial of his grandfather.[45] He himself practiced geomancy in 1923, when he took a sightseeing trip to Ch'ien-fu shan, a hill outside the walled city of Tsinan, Shantung. After surveying the topography of the place, with special attention to the relative positions of the city, the Yellow River, and the nearby hills, he suggested that the city be relocated because its present site violated geomantic principles.[46]

His beliefs were generally in line with Chinese tradition. Confucius' belief in Heaven is well known.[47] The *Book of Changes* was basically a book of divination. The *Doctrine of the Mean* dwells on the power of "spiritual beings" (*kuei shen*) and affirms that "when calamity or happiness is about to come, the good shall certainly be foreknown . . . and the evil also."[48] Confucius was said to have foretold his own death by analyzing a portentous dream that he had a week before.[49] Tung Chung-shu (second century B.C.) and scholars of the Kung-yang school elaborated on the ancient notions of Heaven and spirits, and attached

[42] *Nien-p'u*, p. 26b; Lo, *K'ang*, p. 126.

[43] For Kuan Lu, see Wei Shou, "Kuan Lu chuan," quoting from "Kuan Lu pieh-chuan" in *Wei shu, chüan* 29.

[44] *Nien-p'u*, p. 25a; Lo, *K'ang*, p. 121.

[45] *Nien-p'u*, p. 4b; Lo, *K'ang*, p. 32.

[46] *Pu-i*, p. 94b. Lo, *K'ang*, p. 242, mentions the visit to Tsinan but does not translate the passage referring to geomancy given in K'ang T'ung-pi's compilation. For an account of physiognomy and geomancy, see Joseph Needham, *Science and Civilization in China*, 2 : 259–64.

[47] See, e.g., Fung Yu-lan, *A History of Chinese Philosophy*, 1 : 57–58.

[48] *Chung-yung* (Legge), xvi.16 and xxiv.24.

[49] *Li-chi*, "T'an-kung shang," iii.44.

added importance to prognostication.[50] Confucius, of course, sometimes deemphasized the supernatural in order to stress man's duties to his fellow beings.[51] Hsün-tzu went one step further and rejected all beliefs in the supernatural and all forms of superstition.[52] But his arguments were all but forgotten with the rise of the Kung-yang school in Han times. It is hardly surprising that K'ang, a follower of the Kung-yang tradition in general and of Tung Chung-shu in particular, resorted freely to augury, physiognomy, and geomancy.

IV

K'ang displayed another prominent trait: a zestful outlook on life. Readers of the *Ta-t'ung shu* can hardly fail to notice his frankly hedonistic interpretation of human nature. "Under the firmament," he wrote, "all who have life only seek pleasure and shun suffering."[53] This was no fanciful, abstract philosophical construction but an expression of his own experience and conviction. A man of robust desires and stout emotions, he was inclined to regard the enjoyment of sensuous pleasures and creature comforts as a legitimate element of the good life. He developed a taste for luxury and festiveness early in his life. When he was thirteen *sui*, he went to Canton with his grandfather and was so fascinated by the gaiety of city life that he "daily roamed and played with friends, leaving no time for study." (Only two years before, he was so engrossed in learning that he used to spend an entire night to finish reading a book.)[54] He managed to live in high style even when he was an exile in foreign lands. Traveling in Italy in 1904, he hired an interpreter and a butler (who happened to be an Austrian). His attire was so "elegant and distinguished" that Roman gentlemen accompanying ladies and "riding in twin-horse carriages lifted their hats to salute" him, taking him for "a nobleman from China."[55] Apparently, he enjoyed such uninvited flattering attention. It appears that he was disposed to look upon his prolonged exile more as a pleasurable tour

[50] Fung, *A History of Chinese Philosophy*, vol. 2, chaps. 2 and 3.

[51] *Analects*, xi.11.

[52] *Hsun-tzu*, chap. 5, "Fei hsiang" (especially the opening passage) and chap. 11, "T'ien lun" (passim) (Homer H. Dubs, *The Works of Hsüntze*, Bk. 5, "Against Physiognomy" and Bk. 17, "Concerning Heaven"). Burton Watson, *Hsün Tzu: Basic Writings*, pp. 79–88, translates "T'ien lun" under the title "A Discourse of Heaven" but does not translate "Fei hsiang."

[53] *Ta-t'ung shu*, p. 9; Thompson, *Ta T'ung Shu*, p. 71.

[54] *Nien-p'u*, p. 3a; Lo, *K'ang*, p.26.

[55] K'ang, "I-ta-li yu-chi," in *Ou-chou shih-i kuo yu-chi*, pt. 1, pp. 2, 27.

that gratified his wanderlust than a bitter fruit of frustration and defeat.[56]

He was profoundly impressed by the material civilization of the West and seldom failed to show appreciation of its manifestation in luxurious and gracious living. The prosperity of Hong Kong and Shanghai aroused and intensified his interest in "Western learning," when he visited these places in 1879 and 1882.[57] Years later, in 1906–7, Monte Carlo, a playboy's paradise, enchanted him. This was what he said of his visit there:

An Englishman said to me . . . "Have you been to Monte Carlo? You must visit Monte Carlo . . . [where you will see] the best of houses, the best of *toilette*, the best of food and wine, the best of theater and entertainment, and the best of women." Previously, I heard only of the elegance of Paris; I did not know of Monte Carlo. . . . When I visited it myself, . . . [I found] its wondrous beauty coming pretty close to topping [any other place in] Europe. . . . It is indeed a supremely magnificent sight on earth.

In addition to describing in detail the things that delighted him there, he sang its praise in a poem, calling it "a country of ultimate pleasures and enjoyment untrammeled."[58]

In contrast to his ebullient enthusiasm for Monte Carlo, his keen disappointment in Athens, which was no swanky resort, is most revealing. "The hills," he lamented, "are barren and forlorn; dust obscures the sky; the hot sun burns and scorches. . . . Fortune has deserted this place for a long time. Grief stricken, I sighed and wept."[59] Similarly, he found little joy in Yellowstone Park, which he visited in September 1905. He complained of the mountains that were treeless, the rocks

[56] *Pu-i*, p. 75a, gives one of K'ang's lengthy poems, which contains these lines: "All my life I stay outside officialdom;/ I have an unquenchable desire to travel." Lo (*K'ang*, pp. 231–32), indicates the tenor of this piece and translates its concluding lines. K'ang projected his own wanderlust into his utopian world. In addition to "carriages that move of themselves" and "ships that sail of themselves," there would be "flying ships" the largest of which would be over 1,000 feet long. "Railroads would be used only to transport heavy things"; men would not travel in them because they were not fast enough. People would love to travel so much that they would live in hostels instead of fixed private houses. Indeed, there would be houses that move over land and water, dispensing with other means of travel. See *Ta-t'ung shu*, pt. 10, chap. 2, secs. 1 and 2. Thompson, *Ta T'ung Shu*, pp. 271–73, gives a very brief summary.

[57] *Nien-p'u*, pp. 5b and 6a; Lo, *K'ang*, pp. 36 and 38.

[58] "Man-ti-chia-lo [Monte Carlo] yu-chi," *Pu-jen tsa-chih*, vols. 9, 10, "Yin t'an," pp. 1–6.

[59] *Pu-i*, p. 43b. Lo, *K'ang*, p. 212, mentions K'ang's visit but does not indicate his impressions of Athens.

that were "wizened yellow in color," the heat that made the place feel like a boiler, and concluded his disparaging remarks with "my visit lasted for a total of six days; my interest sagged and petered out."[60] For him, between man-made luxury and unconverted nature, the choice was obvious.

He set forth his hedonistic philosophy in various connections. One of the most lucid statements of it was made in August, 1908, while he was in Greece.

> In a country with an agrarian economy, premium is necessarily placed on sedulity and frugality. In a country with an industrial-commercial economy, premium is inevitably placed on luxury and enjoyment. . . . Human progress has culture for its ultimate goal, and culture is measured by the degree of luxury and enjoyment. The Superior Man warned against the excessive privileges and injudicious extravagances enjoyed by a few, which surely led to the danger of destruction. However, . . . if pleasures are shared by all—if every man in the country is wealthy, happy, and equally able to appreciate beauty and attain culture—it would not be extravagance but realization of justice and reason to the highest point.[61]

This optimistic philosophy, something like "democratic hedonism," was obviously not unrelated to K'ang's philosophy of universal love, as the following statement made in 1918 suggests:

> As I am one of mankind, I love myself and my fellow men. . . . It is proper that I [together with my fellow men] enjoy all the inventions made by sages and worthies during past centuries and all the products and commodities available on the great earth.[62]

Persuaded that human desires should be gratified and not repressed, he offered a hedonistic interpretation of the history of religion. He wrote in 1904 to the effect that all religions that enforced ascetic practices failed to prosper, whereas prophets who acknowledged the legitimacy of desires achieved success. Martin Luther became the founder of Protestant Christianity because, K'ang said, he disregarded the vow of celibacy and "married a nun"; Shinran became the founder of Jōdo Shinshū because he took a wife and ate meat.[63] Indeed, K'ang

[60] *Pu-i*, p. 34b. Lo, *K'ang*, p. 199: "He enjoyed the hot springs and the mountain springs but was unimpressed by the treeless hills, the dust, and the heat."

[61] "Ya-tien [Athens] yu-chi," *Pu-jen tsa-chih*, 6 (1913), "Yin t'an": 42.

[62] "Wu-hsü lun-chou chung chüeh-pi chi wu-wu pa-hou," in Chien, *Wu-hsü*, 1: 411.

[63] "I-ta-li [Italy] yu-chi," p. 30. For a brief account of Shinran, see George Sansom, *A History of Japan to 1334*, 1: 425–26.

added, with the coming of utopia all the restraints on man's desires would be removed and even the sexual impulse would be allowed free play.

> Men are born with reproductive organs and cannot avoid having sexual intercourse. This is natural. Because it is natural, it cannot be prevented. And since it cannot be prevented, there will inevitably be actions inspired by passion. . . . Even if there were many thousands of Brahmins, Buddhas, and Christs who wished to save men by extinguishing their desires, it would certainly be impossible to extinguish men's desire for sexual union. . . . In the world of Ta-t'ung all men will give their sexual desire free play. . . . There will be men who enjoy homosexual relationships, as Socrates did. . . . There will be no reason to prohibit such relationships, if they are not results of coercion.[64]

This sounds almost like permissive America in the 1960s. However, K'ang foresaw unrestricted gratification of sexual desires only in utopia when men's thoughts and actions, free from aberrations induced by faulty institutions, would be completely beyond good and evil, no longer be amenable to rules of conventional morality. Before the arrival of the millenium, the moral and legal restraints imposed upon human desires were still to be honored.[65] Therefore, despite his refusal to practice "abstinence and frugality," he led a well-regulated life that was a far cry from libertinism.[66] His appreciation of sensual pleasures did not prevent him from conducting his life in a manner generally worthy of a respectable Confucian gentleman.[67]

V

Some of K'ang's biographers speak of what they think to be discrepancies between theory and practice in his life. This is said, for instance, in one of his biographies:

[64] *Ta-t'ung shu*, p. 420; Thompson, *Ta T'ung Shu*, p. 251. Thompson's translation is used with slight changes.

[65] *Ch'un-ch'iu Tung-shih hsüeh*, *chüan* 6 *hsia*, p. 16b, has a comment on "Yu yü" (Having Desires).

[66] Ting, *Liang Jen-kung*, p. 276, Hsü Su-fo's letter to Liang Ch'i-ch'ao.

[67] Liang, "Nan-hai K'ang hsien-sheng chuan," p. 60: "Perpetually grave, he does not speak or smile without proper reason. When he was fifteen *sui*, he already had resolved to attain the learning of the sage and the worthy. Vulgar scholars of the village laughed at him; they jeeringly called him 'Wei, the Sage' [*Sheng-jen Wei*] because he invariably had 'the sage, the sage' at the tip of his tongue whenever he spoke." Hsü Su-fo, in a letter to Liang (summer, 1908), attributed K'ang's good health to the fact that he led a well-regulated life (Ting, *Liang Jen-kung*, p. 276).

He daily commended desistance from killing [animals for meat] and yet he daily ate meat; daily he acclaimed monogamy as just and yet he took a concubine because he had no son [when he was forty *sui*]; daily he talked about equality of the sexes and yet the [female] members of his own family did not enjoy independence; daily he discoursed on equality of all men and yet he liked to employ female slaves and man servants.[68]

K'ang himself was not unaware of such discrepancies, but he had an explanation for them. Theory, he argued, served as a preview of the perfect society in the future, whereas practice must pay due regard to existing circumstances. This point was made particularly clear in connection with "killing":

> I am a man dedicated to universal love (*jen*). I preach desistance from killing. At one time I desisted from killing [animals by refraining from eating meat]. But at the end of a month, I found this impracticable under present circumstances. . . . The world of Ta-t'ung will be a world of absolute love; only in such a world would man be able to desist from killing.[69]

In short, one should not disregard the conventional rules of conduct because one has a vision of utopia. Or, as K'ang put it, "one should not consider the institutions of Ta-t'ung alone as right and those of Hsiao-k'ang as wrong; one should understand rather that they obtained in two different stages of man's social existence but did not represent two alternative ways of life for his free choice."[70] Whether or not K'ang had thus satisfactorily reconciled the discrepancies between word and deed as noted by his biographers is a question that does not concern us here. Perhaps he may have been one of those persons whom Mencius characterized as "the ambitious" (*k'uang-che*) and to whom Confucius gave qualified approbation. "Their aim led them to talk magniloquently," Mencius said. "But their actions, compared with their words, did not come up to them."[71]

One suspects that while cool reason persuaded K'ang to advocate change and innovation, emotionally he remained attached to things old. His brother, Kuang-jen, said that he was "lofty in thinking but stubborn in temperament."[72] Liang Ch'i-ch'ao put the matter more precisely in 1901.

[68] Lu and Lu, *K'ang Nan-hai . . .* , p. 48a.
[69] *Ta-t'ung shu*, p. 434. Thompson, *Ta T'ung Shu*, pp. 266–67, paraphrases but does not translate this passage.
[70] Liang, "Nan-hai . . . ," pp. 84–85, makes this clear.
[71] *Mencius*, VII.ii.37 (Legge).
[72] Ting, *Liang Jen-kung*, p. 58.

Everyone knows that he [K'ang] is a man who accepts progressivism but at the same time he is deeply ingrained with conservatism. Intensely affectionate, he is extremely fond of everything old. He loves antique bronzes and stone inscriptions, old books, ancient vessels and utensils. He is strongly attached to old friends and to his home village. Emphatically and repeatedly, he reminds Chinese intellectuals [of the importance of] preserving the nation's heritage.[73]

This bipolar or bivalent outlook may also be traced to K'ang's early training, which was thoroughly traditional, and to his later conversion to the Kung-yang school of Confucianism as well as to his eager study of "Western learning."[74]

Whatever may have been the basis of K'ang's progressive-conservative stance, which shifted in emphasis between the two as times and circumstances changed, one can safely say that Liang Ch'i-ch'ao was less than accurate (and in fact contradicted himself) when he called K'ang "a man ahead of his own time."[75] By dint of his "idealism," "zeal," and "courage," K'ang became a pioneer who blazed the trail of progress in premodern China.[76] It is of course true that K'ang had these qualities and that he was a trailblazer. But Liang overlooked the other side of K'ang's mentality, namely "conservatism," which Liang had recognized elsewhere. At any rate, as we have shown above, "the Sage of Nan-hai" was largely a conformist in personal conduct.[77]

VI

The personality traits that have been briefly noted in the preceding pages were observable during most of K'ang's life. However, for a short spell in his youth he appeared to be unsure of his place in society. He reminisced in 1918:

When I was fourteen *sui* [1871], I felt that I was feeble and fragile in body and wished to live away from the world. When I was sixteen [1873], I picked up by chance an incomplete copy of "The Dream of the Red Chamber" (*Hung-lou meng*). After reading it through in one night, I felt like having been awakened from [a dream of fleeting happiness as narrated

---

[73] Liang, "Nan-hai . . . ," p. 88.
[74] See chapter 3 of this volume: "Reinterpretation of Confucianism."
[75] Liang, "Nan-hai . . . ," p. 87.
[76] Ibid., p. 59.
[77] Lu and Lu, *K'ang Nan-hai* . . . , p. 47a.

in] "The Dream of Yellow Millet" (*Huang-liang meng*). Disconcerted, I entertained the idea of withdrawing from the world.[78]

This turned out to be a passing phase. Soon afterward, he found his goal, namely, "management of the world" and avidly read Chinese and "Western" books to prepare himself for it.[79] He emerged the confident, optimistic, and proud man that his friends and members of his family were accustomed to know.

His outlook on life changed again as time went on. His overriding self-assurance and exuberant optimism eventually mellowed into a philosophical calm reminiscent somewhat of the youthful phase of resignation. The Taoist way of looking at things, which he rejected decisively sometime after 1879, found favor with him again. He nowhere explicitly acknowledged this reversion, but the remarks he made while visiting the ruins of Pompeii in 1904 may be taken as a clue.

When Pompeii was destroyed, its destruction was regarded as an unusual and great calamity. But later, after excavation work had been done, it became a marvelous archaeological spectacle. But for the volcanic eruption, we would not now see [the ruins of] this ancient city of the Romans. [Similarly,] but for the First Emperor of Ch'in [whom historians have condemned as an evil tyrant], we would not have today the Great Walls. In our world, gains and losses complement each other, despite their polarity. Hence one who discourses on the *Tao* cannot dispense with [the notions of] negative and positive (*yin yang*). . . . Persons who see only one side, see very little; they are not qualified to discuss the *Tao*.[80]

In other words, K'ang no longer insisted, as he had earlier in his career, that truth and error, good and evil, were absolute terms, that one must suppress error and evil and support truth and good. This position curiously reminds one of the relativism of *Lao-tzu*: "Existence suggests nonexistence; easy gives rise to difficult; short is derived from long by comparison; low is distinguished from high by position.[81] So a loss sometimes benefits one, or a benefit proves to be a loss."[82]

[78] "Pa wu-hsü yü men-jen shu," *K'ang Nan-hai hsien-sheng mo-chi*, vol. 2 (no pagination). For translations of the famous novel, *Hung-lou meng*, see Martha Davidson, *A List of Published Translations from Chinese into English, French, and German*, pt. 1 (Literature), pp. 10–12.

[79] *Nien-p'u*, pp. 5b–6a; Lo, *K'ang*, pp. 37–38.

[80] "I-ta-li yu-chi," p. 11.

[81] *Tao-te ching*, chap. 2; T. K. Ch'u, *Tao Te Ching*, p. 11. Cf. R. B. Blackney, *The Way of Life*, p. 54; J. J. L. Duyvendak, *Tao Te Ching*, p. 22; and Wing-tsit Chan, *The Way of Lao Tzu*, p. 101.

[82] *Tao-te ching*, chap. 42; Blackney, *Way of Life*, p. 95. Chan, *Way of Lao Tzu*, p. 176, translates this passage thus: "Therefore it is often the case things gain by

This mellowing process reached its conclusion in the last years of K'ang's life. Instead of seeking to reform China and save mankind, he now found comfort in what he called "peregrination in the heavens" (*t'ien yu*). His *Lectures on the Heavens* (*Chu-t'ien chiang*) represented the results of his probing into the mysteries of "outer space."[83] In a 1923 postscript to a letter he wrote to Timothy Richard in 1898, he made clear how he came to make these "peregrinations."

> I, an old man who had failed to carry out [the mission entrusted to him by the emperor as specified in the secret decree transmitted to him in a] garment belt, namely, to rescue [the emperor placed under house arrest by the empress dowager]—an old man who had rendered no useful service to the empire—find no place on earth to bury my sorrow. My only recourse is to make excursions into the heavens.[84]

Thus, in his old age K'ang again "entertained the idea of withdrawing from the world" as he did in his youth, though in a different manner and for a different reason. Formerly, it was out of juvenile befuddlement; now it was because of despair born of frustration.

K'ang disclosed the philosophical implications of his new outlook. As men were born with desires that unavoidably led them to strife and to suffering, he wrote, founders of various religions invented the notions of "Paradise," "the Pure Land," and "the Wheel of Transmigration," with the purpose of directing men to happiness. These notions, unfortunately, were inadequate means to the intended ends. Accordingly, he offered his own antidote to melancholy: a trip to the starry regions where a man, leaving behind all his worldly cares, roams in untrammeled freedom. In his own words:

> I have gone through calamities unscathed and have been making daily jaunts in the heavens. My body remains in the human world of this planet; my mind roams in the boundless celestial regions. Joyously and freely [I saunter], looking down at our planet [which appears to me] tinier than a drop of water in a vast ocean, and at our human world [which seems to be] more ephemeral than the ant colony described in "The Dream of the Southern Bough" (*Nan-k'o meng*).[85]

losing and lose by gaining." Duyvendak, *Tao Te Ching*, p. 99: "For, things are sometimes increased by decrease, and decreased by increase."

[83] The contents of this book are discussed in my article, "K'ang Yu-wei's Excursion into Science: The Lectures on the Heavens," (Lo, *K'ang*, pp. 375–409).

[84] "Pa wu-hsü chih Li T'i-mo-t'ai [Timothy Richard] shu," in *K'ang Nan-hai hsien-sheng mo-chi*, vol. 3 (no pagination).

[85] *Chu-t'ien chiang, hsü*, pp. 2a–b. This book was privately printed, *circa* 1930. Author's preface was dated 1926. For a translation of Li Kung-tso's "Nan-k'o chi," see Davidson, *List of Published Translations from Chinese*, p. 110.

No longer concerned with the deliverance of man from his distressed existence through institutional reform, he now argued in effect that in the cosmic context nothing mundane really mattered. Man only had to imagine that as an "intelligent being" he in truth belonged in "the heavens." Transcendental bliss came to him who assumed the right frame of mind—by "withdrawing from the world."

K'ang's nostrum for dispelling gloom was conceivably a veiled admission of despair, an admission that the "great cause" for which he once valiantly fought lay forever beyond the reach of human endeavor.[86] These lines of an ancient poet perhaps expressed his feelings quite well:

> How can I live with men whose hearts are strangers to me?
> I am going a far journey to be away from them. . . .
> I set off at morning from the Ford of Heaven;
> At evening I came to the world's western end. . . .
> But when I had ascended the splendor of the heavens,
> I suddenly caught a glimpse of my old home. . . .
> Enough! There are no true men in the state; no one to
>   understand me.
> Why should I cleave to the city of my birth?[87]

K'ang was now in the twilight of his life. Less than a year after he wrote his *Lectures on the Heavens* he died, a disappointed but not a sullen man.

· · · · ·

Disarmingly human, K'ang was not free from foibles or fallibilities; he was no saint or sage. Fighter for a lost cause, he was no hero. For a time, he was "an object of attention in the eyes of many."[88] But cir-

---

[86] Early in 1922, when he was invited to attend a theatrical play, he wept as two actors, one impersonating the emperor and the other himself, reenacted some heart-rending scenes of 1898. He wrote a number of poems to express his feelings. Chao Ping-lin, *Pai-yen kan-chiu shih-hua, chüan* 3, pp. 8a–b, in *Chao Pai-yen chi*, gives an account of the episode and four of the poems. K'ang T'ung-pi, *Pu-i*, p. 85a, mentions it but gives no detail. Lo, *K'ang*, p. 240, makes no reference to this interesting incident.

[87] David Hawks, *Ch'u Tz'u: The Songs of the South*, pp. 33–34, lines 171, 174, 184, and 186. Cf. Yang Hsien-yi and Gladys Yang, *Li Shao and Other Poems of Chu Yuan*, pp. 13–14, give a slightly less accurate rendition.

[88] Liang, "Nan-hai . . . ," p. 88. K'ang was an impressive figure, even in the eyes of contemporaries who were neither his friends nor supporters of his cause. Tse Tsan-tai [Hsieh Tsan-t'ai], *The Chinese Republic: Secret History of the Revolution*, p. 11, describes the reformer (then forty-three years old) in these terms: "He appears to be a man of superior intelligence. He is learned and experienced, and possesses an excellent all-round knowledge. He possesses a highly retentive memory and is always busy investigating and searching for knowledge. . . . His bearing is proud and in-

cumstances soon changed. History tends to judge men in the arena of social and political action by pragmatic standards; glory seldom pertains to prophets whose visions find no confirmation in the actual course of events. It is a different matter in the realm of thought, where pragmatic judgments are not particularly pertinent. As reformist and utopian writer, K'ang had contributed significantly to China's intellectual history, because of which he is likely to remain an object of scholarly attention.

---

dependent. At a glance one can see that he is not a 'man of the common herd.' " Hu Ssu-chin, *Wu-hsü li-shuang lu, chüan* 3, reprinted in Chien, *Wu-hsü,* 1: 374, observed that with his long beard and piercing eyes K'ang was quite imposing in his appearance. When introduced to a stranger, he carefully inquired about the special products and outstanding men of the visitor's home locality, jotting down what he was told with a "Western pencil" on slips of paper which he then put into his pocket. Shen Yün-lung, *K'ang Yu-wei p'ing-chuan,* p. 69, records that when Chang Shih-chao visited K'ang in Tientsin, July 1926, the aged reformer spoke eloquently in a resonant voice. Chang said after the meeting: "Twenty years ago, men who admired Nan-hai told me that those who reviled him were people who had not met him in person. Once they came into his presence, scorn invariably turned into respect. I used to repeat these remarks as a joke. Now having met him myself, I am convinced that he indeed is no ordinary man."

PART II
PHILOSOPHICAL COMMITMENTS

Chapter 3

REINTERPRETATION OF CONFUCIANISM

Twenty years ago, an American historian called K'ang Yu-wei one of "those able and independent scholars" who, during the last period of the empire, sought to revive Confucianism by dissociating it from "the rigid state orthodoxy."[1] Ten years later, another American historian credited "the great reformer" with having offered "a remodeled Confucianism that would serve as the religion of a modernized state."[2] There is truth in both assertions. But one might add that in remodeling or reinterpreting Confucianism K'ang had in effect launched an intellectual reform that had profound significance. One suspects that he did so with a view to furnishing a philosophical basis for institutional reform; one might also surmise that the philosophical position resulting from the remodeling process convinced him that the existing institutional system stood in need of radical alteration. An examination of the contents and implications of his remodeled Confucianism, it appears, would not only throw light on the reformer's words and deeds but also help ascertain his place in the intellectual tradition of China.

A CONFUCIAN OR AN APOSTATE?

A question naturally arises (as indeed it was raised at the time): In rejecting the accepted interpretations of Confucianism, can K'ang still be considered a loyal member of the Confucian school? It is true that

[1] H. G. Creel, *Confucius and the Chinese Way* (published in 1949 as *Confucius: The Man and the Myth*), p. 279. K'ang is mentioned also in pp. 101–2, 128, 144, 308.
[2] Arthur F. Wright, *Buddhism in Chinese History*, p. 111.

K'ang professed unbounded admiration for the founding sage; but can one rule out the possibility that he paid homage to the hallowed name without in fact paying heed to the time-honored doctrine? In other words, was K'ang a faithful follower or a camouflaged apostate?

Many of K'ang's contemporaries, in particular enemies of the reform movement, unequivocally excluded him from the Confucian fold. Yeh Te-hui, one of the staunchest defenders of tradition, denounced K'ang as "a barbarian at heart," thinly disguised by the "Confucian countenance" he assumed.[3] A few recent writers are inclined to share this view.[4]

It may be recalled that in imperial China ever since Sung times one of the most convenient ways to discredit one's opponent has been to accuse him of affiliating with a "heterodox" school thus alienating himself from the "orthodox" school of thought, namely, Confucianism. For instance, Wang An-shih (1021–86), the "reformer" of Sung dynasty, was accused by the "conservatives" of subscribing to the principles of the Legalist school.[5] It is hardly surprising that centuries later K'ang Yu-wei was condemned as "un-Confucian" by some of his adversaries.

Other writers, however, answered the question differently. Liang Ch'i-ch'ao argued that K'ang's unconventional exegeses of the Confucian classics were not designed to peddle his own ideas under a false Confucian label but to reveal the real contents of the Confucian teaching.[6] A number of recent writers have echoed Liang's view and accepted K'ang as a bona fide Confucian—not one of the traditional cast but none the less a follower of Confucius.[7]

The answer to the question whether or not K'ang was a Confucian is not really difficult. Much depends on what one understands by the term "Confucianism." If one equates it with what James Legge called "imperial Confucianism," namely, the complex of ethical and philosophical precepts that were approved by the imperial government and recognized by scholar-officials as the true tradition, one can with good

---

[3] Yeh Teh-hui, "Yu Liu Hsien-tuan Huang Yu-wen liang sheng shu," in Su Yü, *I-chiao ts'ung-pien*, chüan 6, p. 17b.

[4] Ch'ien Mu, *Chung-kuo chin san-pai nien hsüeh-shu shih*, pp. 704–8.

[5] Hsiao Kung-ch'üan, *Chung-kuo cheng-chih ssu-hsiang shih*, 2: 457.

[6] Liang Ch'i-ch'ao, "Lun Chung-kuo hsüeh-shu ssu-hsiang pien-ch'ien chih ta-shih," *Yin-ping-shih ho-chi, wen-chi*, 7: 101.

[7] E.g., K. S. Latourette, *A History of Modern China*, p. 92; Li Chien-nung, *The Political History of China, 1840–1928*, p. 146; Lin Mousheng, *Men and Ideas*, p. 215; Franz Michael and George E. Taylor, *The Far East in the Modern World*, p. 197; Dai Shen-yu, "Mao Tse-tung and Confucianism," p. 4; and Wolfgang Franke, *Die staatspolitischen Reformversuche K'ang Yu-weis und seiner Schule*, p. 17.

reason describe K'ang as an apostate who forsook "Confucius" in his rejection of that tradition. If Confucianism is thought of as the totality of the doctrines actually taught by Confucius himself, so that in order to be a genuine Confucian a person must embrace these same doctrines, one can still hardly regard K'ang as a Confucian. K'ang himself claimed that in expunging what he regarded as false classics and false interpretations of the Confucian teaching, he succeeded in exhibiting the true doctrines of Confucius. Such a claim is difficult to sustain. K'ang rested his case mainly on the argument that the authentic teachings of Confucius were embodied in the *wei-yen ta-i* ("arcane doctrines and great dogmas")[8] as transmitted, largely orally, from one generation to another by the members of the New Text (in particular, the Kung-yang) school and that, therefore, all texts and exegeses at variance with these dicta and dogmas were spurious or false. K'ang's argument holds good only if it can be proved that the *wei-yen ta-i* issued actually from the mouth of the ancient sage. Unfortunately, however, there is no way of making sure that an oral tradition actually conveyed the Confucian *dogmata agrapha*.[9] Confucianism underwent many changes after the death of its founder. The Confucian school, it was said, soon split into eight separate sects.[10] We have little information concerning the doctrinal contents of these sects, but we know that Mencius and Hsün-tzu, most eminent members of the Confucian school, gave widely different versions of what Confucius taught. Other versions appeared during the next two thousand years. The doctrinal sediment in the Confucian stream had become so thick that even the most skilled diver into China's intellectual history can hardly hope to reach the rock at the bottom. Any claim to absolute knowledge of the original teachings of Confucius must therefore be discounted.

One may, however, legitimately think of Confucianism in a third sense: not as a complex of doctrines held by any particular Confucian sect or individual Confucian thinker, but a broad stream of thought that had been running its course ever since its inception in the sixth century before Christ. Understood in this sense, K'ang Yu-wei could have as much claim to being a Confucian as any of his contemporaries or predecessors. He was indeed a revisionist rather than a traditionalist;

---

[8] For a brief explanation, see P'i Hsi-jui, "Ch'un-ch'iu t'ung-lun," *Ching-hsüeh t'ung-lun*, p. 1.

[9] Hsiao, *Chung-kuo . . . ssu-hsiang shih*, pp. 67–73 and review of Wu K'ang, *Les trois théories politiques du Tch'ouen Ts'ieou, Tsing Hua hsüeh-pao*, 8, no. 1 (Dec. 1932): 1–6.

[10] "Hsien-hsüeh," in *Han-fei-tzu*, chap. 50.

so were many of the outstanding members of the school, such as Mencius, Hsün-tzu, Tung Chung-shu, Chu Hsi, Lu Chiu-yüan, and Wang Shou-jen. These men were perhaps less daring than K'ang in their interpretations of the classics; but they nevertheless gave new content and meaning to the tradition. K'ang questioned the authenticity of some of the classics; so did Mencius who doubted the reliability of the *Book of History*,[11] and remained to occupy an honored niche in the Confucian shrine. K'ang subscribed to the "unusual, strange principles" of the Kung-yang school; so did others, including scholars of the Ch'ing period whose exegeses adorn the pages of a monumental collection published in the 1880s.[12] K'ang injected alien elements (i.e., Western notions) into Confucianism; so did some of the most important Neo-Confucians of Sung times, although the alien elements they took over came from India instead of Europe.[13] K'ang was compared to Martin Luther by one of his followers (a point to which I shall return later). It seems that there is no more justification for regarding K'ang as un-Confucian because he departed from the Old Text tradition than for regarding Luther as un-Christian because he rebelled against the Roman church.

K'ang qualified for membership in the Confucian school on another count. Throughout his long career he insistently urged the government and his fellow scholars "to venerate Confucius." Despite drastic changes in the historical situation, he maintained that Confucius was still the greatest of all sages and that his teaching should serve as the infallible guide of men's social and moral life. In fact, he showed increasing admiration of Confucius during the republican years when he was more concerned with preserving what he regarded as the best of China's cultural heritage than in modernizing her social and economic structure. As early as 1895 he proposed that the imperial government give encouragement to those who "studied and disseminated Confucius' teaching" and that Confucian shrines be instituted in every corner of the empire, with a view to counteracting the trend toward "moral degeneration."[14] He made similar proposals in 1898, with added emphasis. In a memorial presented in July of that year he suggested that Confucianism be established as *kuo chiao* ("state religion"), Confucius be recognized as *chiao-chu* ("founder of religion"), the year 551 B.C. in which Confucius was born be taken as Year One of China's national

---

[11] *Mencius*, VII.ii.3 (Legge).

[12] I.e., *Huang-Ch'ing ching-chieh, hsü-pien*, 1, 430 *chüan*.

[13] Carsun Chang, *The Development of Neo-Confucian Thought*, chap. 6.

[14] Chien Po-tsan et al., *Wu-hsü pien-fa*, 2: 150.

history, and a *K'ung-chiao hui* ("Confucian Association") be organized on an empire-wide basis.[15] Between 1912 and 1927 he did much to promote the Confucian Association and renewed his efforts to establish Confucianism as state religion.[16] He was indignant upon hearing that the Ministry of Education prohibited the reading of Confucian classics in primary schools and tried to persuade the Minister to rescind the order.[17] Thus while K'ang disavowed "the spurious classics" and repudiated imperial Confucianism in the 1890s, he now cherished every bit of Confucianism and every word contained in the classics. If, as Winston Churchill reportedly said, "a fanatic is one who can't change his mind and won't change his subject," then K'ang Yu-wei was indeed a fanatic obsessed with the idea of "venerating Confucius." One can hardly accept the view that K'ang did honor to Confucius merely to camouflage his desire to westernize China.[18] Such a view is decidedly inapplicable to K'ang Yu-wei of the twentieth century and, to say the least, overshoots the mark when applied to K'ang of the reform years.

It has been suggested that K'ang's willingness to dispense with the family in his utopian world of "Universal Peace" would disqualify him for membership in the Confucian brotherhood, since the family was the keystone of the Confucian social system and moral life. This objection appears to be a grave one, but it may perhaps be met by the following considerations. In the first place, although K'ang pointed to the shortcomings of the family and envisaged its disappearance in the final stage of man's progress, he never for a moment proposed that it should be done away with prior to the time when human progress will have eliminated all the factors that made the family indispensable. Assuming that human beings as they now exist fall short of moral perfection (although they have the natural endowment to develop into perfect moral beings), the family and all the other social institutions should continue to serve useful purposes. Moreover, in men's highest social development the family will disappear not because men will lose the capacity to love but because their love will be so broadened and extended that the distinction between family and nonfamily will be unrecognizable. A man will then love all his fellow beings precisely as he

---

[15] K'ang, "Tsou-i," in *K'ang Nan-hai hsien-sheng wen-ch'ao*, 5: 10b–13a (hereafter cited as *Wen-ch'ao*).

[16] Ibid., 5: 12a–17a; 6: 63a–67b; and *K'ang Nan-hai wen-chi, chüan* 5, pp. 2a–9b (hereafter cited as *Wen-chi*).

[17] K'ang, "Yü Chiao-yü-pu tsung-chang Fan Shou-sheng ch'üan kai chin-tu-ching ling shu."

[18] Ch'ien, *Chung-kuo . . . hsüeh-shu shih*, pp. 702–9.

loves the members of his own family. Obviously, such a view of human love was based on the Confucian doctrine of *jen*, particularly as it was expressed in the well-known passage in the "Li-yün," that "men do not treat parents alone as parents, nor sons alone as sons."[19] K'ang may have stretched the meaning of *jen* beyond the traditional interpretations of it; he assuredly did not violate it.

It is significant that K'ang firmly refused to publish his *Ta-t'ung shu*, the book in which he set forth his ideal of a family-less society. After repeated requests from his students, he finally permitted a fraction of it to appear in 1913, namely, Books I and II, in which he announced his general principles and delineated his political ideals.[20] The rest of the work in which his radical social ideals are to be found was not published until 1935, eight years after he died. He explained to his students that different doctrines of social organization should be taught and practiced in different stages of human development. China in the nineteenth century could not dispense with the basic Confucian precepts of "human relationships" and social duties. His utopian ideals (which went beyond these precepts) would have dangerous repercussions if made known to the general public and must therefore be withheld. It appears, then, that while K'ang transcended Confucianism in his role as utopian philosopher, as a practical reformer he definitely remained within the Confucian fold.

Career as a Confucian Scholar

K'ang, as already said, repudiated the accepted Confucian tradition of his own age. He insisted on going back to what he claimed to have been the true teachings of Confucius, which though eclipsed during the Ch'ing dynasty,[21] could be rediscovered by a discriminating study of the classics and by doing away with the "erroneous" interpretations and "false" ascriptions that had accrued in the course of twenty centuries. Most important among these, he believed, were first, the intellectual tradition based on the doctrines of Hsün-tzu; second, "the

[19] *Li Chi, chüan* 9, sec. 1.

[20] Hellmut Wilhelm called my attention to Richard Wilhelm's catalogue of his personal collection of books, in which entry No. 497 reads "*Die grosse Gemeinschaft,* 1919." According to Professor Wilhelm, this was one of the copies printed for private distribution, which the author gave to his father. This, obviously, was a reprint of the portions that appeared in installments in *Pu-jen tsa-chih,* from February to November, 1913.

[21] Ch'ien, *Chung-kuo . . . hsüeh-shu shih,* p. 634, quoting from Ch'en Ch'ien-ch'iu, "Ch'ang-hsing hsüeh-chi pa."

spurious classics" forged by Liu Hsin (53–23 B.C.); and third, the Neo-Confucian tradition built upon the *li-hsüeh* (rationalism) of Chu Hsi (1130–1200) and dominating the minds of the majority of Confucian scholars ever since.[22] K'ang boldly and relentlessly waged war on all these. It is not surprising at all that Wen-t'i, a Manchu official and bitter enemy of reform, accused him of desiring "to sweep away the great principles and institutions of China that had been transmitted from one generation to another for thousands of years."[23]

Wen-t'i's accusation was not entirely unfounded. For what K'ang attempted to do was to discredit the tradition of imperial Confucianism—a tradition that had its roots in the Neo-Confucian philosophy of Chu Hsi and subsequently became the ideological tool of imperial rulers, with political and intellectual implications hardly foreseen by Chu Hsi. K'ang offered to replace that tradition with a Confucianism that was, in the words of Liang Ch'i-ch'ao, a "progressivism" instead of conservatism, a cult of universal love instead of personal cultivation, a doctrine of equality instead of authoritarianism.[24] K'ang made use of much of the Confucian classics, but he read them from a viewpoint that none of the traditional scholars could take.[25]

K'ang held his views firmly but not with sustained consistency. His evaluation of the various classics, as I shall venture to show, changed perceptibly at different times.[26] These changes may be partly accounted for by K'ang's phases of intellectual development. The following statement, made probably in 1901–2, indicates the major steps he took from childhood to intellectual maturity:

> I received instruction in the classics when I was a child of six. By the time I was twelve, I had read all the writings left behind by the Duke of Chou and Confucius. I then studied the commentaries on the classics and the writings of the Sung Confucians. By the time I was twenty-seven, I had acquainted myself with the views of all the scholars of the past—from Han and Wei times, through the Six Dynasties, T'ang, Sung, and Ming,

[22] Lu Nai-hsiang and Lu Tun-K'uei, *K'ang Nan-hai hsien-sheng chuan, shang-pien*, pp. 27b–29a.

[23] Wen-t'i, "Yen-ts'an K'ang Yu-wei che," in Chien, *Wu-hsü*, 2: 484; also given in Su Yü, *I-chiao ts'ung-pien, chüan* 2 and Chu Shou-p'eng, *Tung-hua hsü-lu, Kuang-hsü ch'ao, chüan* 145, pp. 14–18.

[24] Liang Ch'i-ch'ao, *Nan-hai K'ang hsien-sheng chuan*, in *Yin-ping-shih ho-chi, wen-chi*, 6: 67.

[25] Ch'en Kung-lu, "Chia-wu chan-hou keng-tzu luan-ch'ien Chung-kuo pien-fa yün-tung chih yen-chiu," p. 103.

[26] Ch'ien, *Chung-kuo . . . hsüeh-shu shih*, pp. 690–98, also points out some of the vacillating views.

and down to the present dynasty—concerning exegeses, historical research, and inquiries into moral and philosophical principles. . . .

At first, I followed the path of the Sung scholars. . . . Later, having realized that Confucius could not have been so bigoted and narrow [as they made him to appear], I followed the path of the Han scholars. . . . Then, having discovered that [the teachings of Confucius] could not have been so confused and encumbered with trifling details, . . . I departed from the classics . . . and sought [truth] in history. . . . After that I got rid of the false learning of the Old Text and sought it in the doctrines of the New Text school. . . . Thus I came upon the doctrine of the permutations of *yin* and *yang* in the *Book of Changes* and that of the Three Ages in the *Spring and Autumn Annals*. I said: "The teaching of Confucius is vast. Although I do not see all of it, I have perhaps gained a view of its outlines." . . . Accordingly, I sought truth again in the classics. When I came to the "Li-yün" [in the *Book of Rites*], I exclaimed: "Here is the true teaching of Confucius concerning the successive changes in the Three Ages and [his doctrines of] the Great Unity (*Ta-t'ung*) and the Minor Peace (*Hsiao-k'ang*)!"[27]

This may be taken as a generally faithful account. K'ang did not indicate the precise times at which he changed his views after he was twenty-seven *sui* (1884), but he gave some clues in his *Tzu-pien nien-p'u* (Autobiographical Annals). He indicated that as late as 1880, when he was twenty-three *sui*, he wrote a piece entitled "Ho-shih chiu-miu" (Ho Hsiu's Errors Exposed), with the express purpose of attacking Ho Hsiu (A.D. 129–82), author of the celebrated *Ch'un-ch'iu Kung-yang chieh-ku* (i.e., *Commentaries of the* Spring and Autumn Annals *As Interpreted by Kung-yang*), and one of the foremost scholars in the New Text tradition. K'ang said that he "realized his mistake" in so doing and promptly destroyed his manuscript.[28] Obviously he was still following "the path of the Sung scholars" (namely, scholars of the Old Text tradition) in 1880. In 1883 he engaged himself in reading various works on history, institutions, musicology, phonetics, and geography—subjects that interested those Ch'ing scholars who pursued the "Han learning."[29] This, it seems, was the time when he followed "the path of the Han scholars," although not long afterward he changed again.

[27] K'ang, "*Li-yün chu* hsü," pp. 1a–2a.

[28] K'ang, *Tzu-pien nien-p'u*, Kuang-hsü 6 (1880) (hereafter, *Nien-p'u*); Jung-pang Lo, *K'ang Yu-wei: A Biography and Symposium*, p. 36. Liang Ch'i-ch'ao, *Ch'ing-tai hsüeh-shu kai-lun*, p. 126, gives this revealing statement: "In his early years Yu-wei had a keen taste for the *Chou-li* [an Old Text classic]; he digested it and wrote "Cheng-hsüeh t'ung-i" (General Principles of Government and Education). Later, when he saw Liao P'ing's writings, he threw away all his old views."

[29] K'ang, *Nien-p'u*, Kuang-hsü 9 (1883); Lo, *K'ang*, p. 38.

About five years later (1888), K'ang "exposed the spurious nature of the Old Text classics, and demonstrated the correctness of the New Text learning."[30] He was then thirty-one *sui*, and it was three years before he began his teaching career at Ch'ang-hsing li in Canton and completed his first major work, *Hsin-hsüeh wei-ching k'ao*.[31] In 1891 he broke openly with the Neo-Confucian tradition, and soon afterward began writing his second major work, *K'ung-tzu kai-chih k'ao* (Confucius as a Reformer), which was not completed until about 1896.[32] It was in 1888 and the years immediately following, then, that K'ang, in his own words, "came upon the doctrines of the permutations of *yin* and *yang* in the *Book of Changes* and that of the Three Ages in the *Spring and Autumn Annals*."

In the statement quoted above K'ang indicated that he had discovered the doctrines of *Ta-t'ung* and *Hsiao-k'ang* in the "Li-yün" chapter of the *Book of Rites*, when he "again sought truth in the classics,"— thus implying that he had discovered these momentous doctrines sometime *after* he discovered the doctrine of the Three Ages. In other words, the concepts of *Ta-t'ung* and *Hsiao-k'ang* could not have served as guiding principles in his social philosophy prior to 1888.

K'ang hinted on more than one occasion, however, that his *Ta-t'ung* philosophy had been formulated as early as 1884–85. He dated the author's preface to his *Li-yün chu* (The "Li-yün" Annotated) "Kuang-hsü Tenth Year, *Chia-shen*, Winter Solstice Day," namely, December 21, 1884.[33] Again, in his preface to the first two books of the *Ta-t'ung shu*, published for the first time in 1919, he said that he had written that book in "Kuang-hsü *Chia-shen*" (1884), when he was twenty-seven *sui*.[34] But he wrote in his *Nien-p'u* that he "formulated the system of *Ta-t'ung*" in March 1885.[35] There is therefore a slight discrepancy in K'ang's own dating of his utopian system.

Ch'ien Mu seriously questioned K'ang's dating of these works. Ch'ien pointed out that the viewpoint taken in the author's preface to the *Li-yün chu* is at variance with K'ang's position taken when he taught at

---

[30] K'ang, *Nien-p'u*, Kuang-hsü 14 (1888); Lo, *K'ang*, p. 47.

[31] K'ang, *Nien-p'u*, Kuang-hsü 17 (1891); Lo, *K'ang*, p. 53.

[32] K'ang, *Nien-p'u*, Kuang-hsü 18, 20, and 22 (1892, 1894, and 1896); Lo, *K'ang*, pp. 54, 63, 76.

[33] K'ang, "*Li-yun chu* hsü" (*Wen-ch'ao*, 8: 19a). K'ang, *Ta T'ung Shu* trans. Laurence G. Thompson, p. 13, accepts K'ang's dating: "It was during the years 1884 and 1885 that K'ang wrote the 'Li-yun Annotated.'"

[34] Facsimile reproduction, K'ang's own handwriting, in 1935 edition of the *Ta-t'ung shu*, ed. Ch'ien Ting-an.

[35] K'ang, *Nien-p'u*, Kuang-hsü 11.

Ch'ang-hsing li in the early 1890s. K'ang made no mention of *Ta-t'ung* and *Hsiao-k'ang* in his *Ch'ang-hsing hsüeh-chi* in which he outlined the direction and scope of his instructions.[36] Ch'ien further pointed out that Liang Ch'i-ch'ao, who was then one of K'ang's favorite students, said that K'ang made him study history, Sung philosophy (namely, the philosophies of Lu Chiu-yüan and Wang Shou-jen), and "Western learning"; Liang did not mention the "Li-yün" or the doctrines of *Ta-t'ung* and *Hsiao-k'ang*.[37] It is inconceivable, Ch'ien argued, that having discovered these all-important doctrines in 1884–85 K'ang would exclude them from his curriculum. The *Li-yün chu*, Ch'ien concluded, could not have been written in the early 1890s and was probably done around 1902.[38]

Ch'ien also questioned the dating of the *Ta-t'ung shu*. He called attention to the fact that when K'ang wrote the "Jen-lei kung-li" (Universal Principles of Mankind) in 1885–87, which was probably a first draft of the *Ta-t'ung shu*, K'ang began to use the doctrine of the Three Ages as propounded by the Kung-yang school; he did not refer to *Ta-t'ung* and *Hsiao-k'ang* in that work. Later, in 1891 and 1896, when he completed the "Inquiry into the Forged Classics of the Hsin Period" and "Confucius as a Reformer," he directed his attention to the separation of the New Text learning from the Old; he was still silent on the doctrines of *Ta-t'ung* and *Hsiao-k'ang*. It is improbable, therefore, that he had completed the *Ta-t'ung shu* back in the 1880s. Liang Ch'i-ch'ao, who was in a position to know, flatly contradicted K'ang's claim that he had written the book in 1884. Liang stated that "the book was not completed at that time; he completed it in 1901–2 when he was an exile in India."[39]

Ch'ien Mu's inferences are substantially correct even though he did not know the statement (note 27, above), which shows beyond doubt that K'ang did not "discover" the doctrine of *Ta-t'ung* prior to 1888.

Further evidence supports Ch'ien's arguments. The book "Jen-lei kung-li" to which Ch'ien referred was never published, but a copy of

---

[36] K'ang's "Ch'ang-hsing hsüeh-chi" is available in microfilm, reel 1. Ch'ien, *Chung-kuo . . . hsüeh-shu shih*, pp. 634–41, summarizes the main points of this piece.

[37] Liang Ch'i-ch'ao, "San-shih tzu-shu," in *Yin-ping-shih wen-chi* 4, no. 11: pp. 16–17. Ch'ien, *Chung-kuo . . . hsüeh-shu shih*, pp. 638–39, quotes from this account, but fails to note that Liang also mentioned that in 1891 K'ang "was writing the 'Kung-li t'ung,' 'Ta-t'ung hsüeh,' and other books." See note 57 below.

[38] Ch'ien, *Chung-kuo . . . hsüeh-shu shih*, pp. 698–99.

[39] Ibid., p. 700, footnote.

the manuscript is available.[40] Another unpublished manuscript bearing the title *K'ang-tzu nei-wai p'ien* (The Esoteric and Exoteric Essays of Master K'ang), written about the same time and mentioned in his *Nien-p'u*[41] is also extant.[42] An examination of these manuscripts gives the impression that they are precursors of the *Ta-t'ung shu*. The general intellectual outlook appears to be identical although the attitude toward the characteristic Confucian values is perceptibly less radical in the manuscripts than in the published book. Some of the ideas that K'ang worked out in detail in the *Ta-t'ung shu* are found in the manuscripts in less developed form.[43] It is highly doubtful that having finally formulated his ideas in the *Ta-t'ung shu* in 1884 K'ang saw fit to express them in less finished form in 1885–87.[44]

A bit of "internal evidence" may also be cited to show that the *Ta-t'ung shu* could not have been composed in 1884. In Book VII, chapter 3, where K'ang advocated the application of "the one-world principle" to commerce, he referred to the theory of biological evolution (*t'ien-yen*).[45] As K'ang did not read English, the most likely source of his knowledge of Darwinism was Yen Fu's translation of Thomas H. Huxley's *Evolution and Ethics*, which was done in 1896 and published in 1898, under the Chinese title *T'ien-yen lun*.[46] Liang Ch'i-ch'ao had the privilege of reading Yen Fu's manuscript before publication and shared this privilege with K'ang.[47] If indeed it was from Yen's translation that K'ang came upon the concept of evolution, the *Ta-t'ung shu* could not have been completed before 1896.

While it is essentially correct to say with Ch'ien Mu that the *Li-yün chu* and the *Ta-t'ung shu* were done around 1902, it should be pointed out that the former was probably an entirely new work but the latter was the final version of earlier drafts dating back to the 1880s.

[40] A manuscript copy of the "Shih-li-kung-fa," in all probability a version of the "Jen-lei kung-li" (as I shall presently show), is available in microfilm, reel 1.

[41] K'ang, *Nien-p'u*, Kuang-hsü 11 and 12 (1885 and 1886); Lo, *K'ang*, pp. 42, 43.

[42] *K'ang-tzu nei-wai p'ien*, is available in microfilm, reel 2.

[43] These works will be analyzed in chapter 10.

[44] Ch'ien, *Chung-kuo . . . hsüeh-shu shih*, p. 699, correctly inferred that the *Ta-t'ung shu* was completed in 1901–2 but failed to take note of these earlier works which in different ways prepared the ground for K'ang's *pièce de résistance*.

[45] *Ta-t'ung shu*, p. 357. Thompson, *Ta T'ung Shu*, translates this term as "natural selection."

[46] Yen Fu, *Heh-hsü-li T'ien-yen lun* (translation of Thomas H. Huxley's *Evolution and Ethics*).

[47] Ting Wen-chiang, *Liang Jen-kung hsien-sheng nien-p'u ch'ang-pien ch'u-kao*, 1: 33, and Liang Ch'i-ch'ao, "Yu Yen Yu-ling hsien-sheng shu," in *Yin-ping-shih wen-chi*, 1: 110. This letter was written in 1896.

In a recently compiled supplement to K'ang's *Nien-p'u* the following reference is made to the *Ta-t'ung shu*. After indicating that the *Lun-yü chu* (The *Analects* Annotated) was completed in Kuang-hsü 28th year, 3rd month (April 1902), the compiler (K'ang T'ung-pi) remarked:

> At the same time he had elaborated the doctrine of *Ta-t'ung* as given in the "Li-yün." . . . He began to prepare his manuscript in *Chia-shen* year [1884] when he was twenty-seven *sui*. At first, he used [the concepts of] geometry to write the "Jen-shen kung-fa" (Universal Laws of the Human Person). Later, he changed [the title] to "Wan-shen kung-fa" (Universal Laws of All Men), and then to "Shih-li kung-fa" (Substantial Truths and Universal Laws). In a period of over a dozen years . . . he revised his manuscript several times. Finally, he brought the ten books of the *Ta-t'ung shu* to completion.[48]

She goes on to say that the *Ta-hsüeh chu* (*The Great Learning* Annotated) was completed in the 7th month of the same year. It appears, therefore, that the *Ta-t'ung shu* took its final form some time between April and August of 1902.

K'ang made, in 1919, the following remarks in a prefatory note to his *Ta-t'ung shu*:

> I was twenty-seven in Kuang-hsü *chia-shen* [1884–85]. French troops threatened the City of Rams [i.e., Canton]. For safety's sake I lived in . . . Yin-t'ang village, north of the Hsi-ch'iao hills. Aroused by the nation's calamity and commiserating with the people for their plight, I wrote the *Ta-t'ung shu*, thinking then that it would take one hundred years [to realize the ideas that I expressed therein]. Unexpectedly, the League of Nations comes into being in thirty-five years [after I wrote the book, namely, from 1884 to 1919]; I thus personally witness the realization of the doctrine of *Ta-t'ung*. This work has . . . ten books. Books I and II of which are here printed for the first time. The publication of the remainder will have to be postponed.[49]

This statement gives the erroneous impression that K'ang had *completed* the ten books of the *Ta-t'ung shu* in 1884–85, an impression reenforced by his claim, confided earlier to a friend, that his "learning had reached its final stage in the *i-yu* year [1885] and showed no further progress" after that year.[50] What he should have said is that he had written in

---

[48] K'ang T'ung-pi, *Pu K'ang Nan-hai hsien-sheng tzu-pien nien-p'u*, p. 6b; *Nan-hai K'ang hsien-sheng tzu-pien nien-p'u pu-i*, pp. 17b–18a. Cf. Lo, *K'ang*, pp. 192–93.

[49] "Nan-hai hsien-sheng i-mo chih san," *Ta-t'ung shu* (1935 ed.), pp. 8–11.

[50] K'ang, "Yü Shen Tzu-p'ei hsing-pu shu," ca. 1889, in microfilm, reel 1. Cf. Liang, *Ch'ing tai hsüeh-shu kai-lun* (written 1921), p. 149.

1884–85 an early version of the *Ta-t'ung shu,* which contained the leading ideas of his social philosophy.

Further confusion was introduced by K'ang's statements in his *Nien-p'u.* He said that after reading Buddhist texts and "Western books" he attained a sudden enlightenment, in the twelfth month of *chia-shen* year (December, 1884–January, 1885), gaining profound insight into the mysteries of the universe and human life. He thus came to the view that states, races, and religions of the world should be unified and that men and women should be treated as equals[51]—a view, as it is well known, which he developed in detail in his *Ta-t'ung shu.* Early in 1885, he said, he engaged himself in studying mathematics and "used geometry" to compose the "Jen-lei kung-li" in which he set forth "the system of *Ta-t'ung.*"[52] Then he went on to record his intellectual activities in 1886:

> This year I did the *K'ang-tzu nei-wai p'ien.* The *Nei-p'ien* deal with the principles that underlie heaven, earth, men, and things; the *Wai p'ien* deal with matters concerning government, education, the arts, and music. I also wrote the "Kung-li shu" (The Book of Universal Principles), which was done on the basis of geometry.[53]

The following statement referring to his writing done in 1887 also deserves attention:

> This year I worked on the "Jen-lei kung-li." Sending my thoughts rambling in all the heavens, I wrote them down in an endless array. I wrote the "*Nei-wai p'ien,*" in which I waded into the field of Western learning. Basing on the Confucian classics and the writings of China's ancient philosophers, I explained inferentially the matter of the great deluge . . . and the reason that China began with Yü of Hsia . . . I extended Confucius' doctrines of Disorder, Approaching Peace, and Universal Peace, and applied them to the entire globe. Being convinced that to maintain national armies and to learn different languages were detrimental to men's mind and energy, I wished to establish an institute of world languages to carry on linguistic studies, to create a world parliament to convene representatives [from all countries] to discuss the principles of uniting states [to form a world community], and to maintain a world army to get rid of states that refuse to join. All these were aimed at uniting [the states of] the globe. The thoughts that came to me each day were generally of this sort, too many to mention here.[54]

[51] K'ang, *Nien-p'u,* Kuang-hsü 11 (1885); Lo, *K'ang,* pp. 40–42.

[52] K'ang, *Nien-p'u,* Kuang-hsü 11; Lo, *K'ang,* p. 42.

[53] K'ang, *Nien-p'u,* Kuang-hsü 12 (1886); Lo, *K'ang,* p. 43.

[54] K'ang, *Nien-p'u,* Kuang-hsü 13 (1887); Lo, *K'ang,* pp. 44–45. The translation of this passage is mine.

K'ang, then, was engaged from 1884 to 1887 in writing a number of books that appear to have been early versions of the *Ta-t'ung shu*. "Jen-shen kung-fa," "Jen-lei kung-li," "Kung-li shu," and *Shih-li kung-fa*, were probably different titles that K'ang gave to these versions.[55] The *K'ang-tzu nei-wai p'ien*, however, appears to have been a separate work, representing a viewpoint different perceptibly from that of the *Shih-li kung-fa*. An examination of the two shows much more respect for traditional moral and social values in the former than in the latter[56]—too much to qualify the *Nei-wai p'ien* as a forerunner of the *Ta-t'ung shu*.

A question naturally arises: Why did K'ang write two books expressing two different points of view at about the same time? It may be conjectured that during the years 1884–87 K'ang had freshly arrived at his "universalist" point of view but not as yet freed himself of the influences of the accepted Confucian tradition. He was not completely sure of his theoretical position. Wavering between two viewpoints and not unaware of the discrepancy between them, he found it convenient to put down his thoughts in two separate works. Later, when he arrived at a more advanced stage of his intellectual progress, he abandoned the less radical position that he took in the *Nei-wai p'ien* and retained the more unconventional ideas of the *Shih-li kung-fa* to constitute his mature philosophy. Thus his claim that he had "written" the *Ta-t'ung shu* in 1884–85 was not entirely unwarranted; for he had in fact formulated the central concepts of that work and produced an early version of it in those years.

It is significant that in the *Shih-li kung-fa* and *K'ang-tzu nei-wai p'ien* K'ang made use neither of the terminology of the Kung-yang school (i.e., the "Three Ages," the "Three Systems," etc.) nor of the "Li-yün" (i.e., *Ta-t'ung* and *Hsiao-k'ang*). For it was not until after 1888 that he subscribed to the tenets of the Kung-yang school and dissolved whatever ties he previously had had with the Old Text tradition. The universalist ideas that he expressed prior to 1888, on K'ang's own showing, were largely inspired by Mahāyāna Buddhism and "Western learning." It may be recalled that he devoted himself "exclusively" to reading Taoist and Buddhist literature in 1879, after experiencing a mental crisis in the previous year. He resumed his study of Buddhism in 1884

[55] Thompson, *Ta T'ung Shu*, pp. 13–14, regards the "Jen-lei kung-li" as the first draft of the *Ta-t'ung shu* and believes that it was first written in 1884–85 and revised in 1887. This account is based on Chao Feng-t'ien, "K'ang Chang-su hsien-sheng nien-p'u kao," *Shih-hsüeh nien-pao*, 2, no. 1 (1934): 184.

[56] See especially *Shih-li kung-fa*, secs. 3–6, and *K'ang-tzu nei-wai p'ien*, chaps. entitled "Li-hsüeh p'ien" and "Hsing-hsüeh p'ien."

and meanwhile continued to read "Western books"—a task he had begun in 1879. By December, 1884, or January, 1885, he had arrived at all the basic notions that were to be expressed in the writings produced from 1884 to 1887 and eventually incorporated into his "system of *Ta-t'ung*."[57] These notions enabled K'ang to see the Confucian classics in a new light, when he studied them again in 1888. The Kung-yang doctrines with which he must have been familiar but which hitherto had made little impression on him now took on new meaning. Soon afterwards he began to initiate some of his students into his philosophy of *Ta-t'ung*. Liang Ch'i-ch'ao reminisced that in 1891, his first year as K'ang's student, he was privileged to listen to K'ang's discussions of the details of his books on *Kung-li t'ung* and *Ta-t'ung hsüeh* with another student, Ch'en Ch'ien-ch'iu.[58] Upon hearing the principle of *Ta-t'ung*, Liang was ecstatic and indicated his wish to disseminate it. K'ang restrained him but with incomplete success.[59] A few years later, perhaps around 1895, K'ang began to use the term *Ta-t'ung* for his philosophy of society.[60]

Buddhism and Western ideas helped K'ang in the early 1880s to transcend traditional Confucianism and to see the classics in a new light. But he was not persuaded to abandon Confucianism. With the help of Kung-yang doctrines he gained, in 1888, a new confidence in the teaching of Confucius. He realized that when Confucianism was purged of the "falsehoods" that had been grafted upon it, it stood as the greatest teaching of the world, embracing all the truths enunciated by the sages of India and Europe. This realization gave a new impetus to his study of the classics.

Two of the most important results of his study were the *K'ung-tzu kai-chih k'ao* and *Ch'un-ch'iu Tung-shih hsüeh* (Tung Chung-shu's Studies in the *Spring and Autumn Annals*), written respectively in 1892–96 and 1894–96.[61] K'ang made it clear that in writing the former he had relied on the Kung-yang interpretations of the *Annals*, in particular those in Tung Chung-shu's *Ch'un-ch'iu fan-lu* and on the "Wang-chih" of the

---

[57] K'ang, *Nien-p'u*, Kuang-hsü 5, 9, and 10 (1879, 1883, and 1884); Lo, *K'ang*, pp. 34, 38, 40. Onogawa Hidemi, "Kō Yū-i no hempō ron," pp. 112–13 (English summary, pp. 6–7), comes to a similar conclusion.

[58] Liang, "San-shih tzu-shu," p. 17.

[59] Liang, *Ch'ing-tai hsüeh-shu kai-lun*, p. 138.

[60] Ting, *Liang Jen-kung . . .* , p. 29, says that K'ang's group organized a publishing company in the autumn of 1897, naming it "Ta-t'ung i-shu chü." This shows that the term *Ta-t'ung* was by then widely known and accepted by K'ang's followers.

[61] K'ang, *Nien-p'u*, Kuang-hsü 18, 19, 20, and 22 (1892, 1893, 1894, and 1896); Lo, *K'ang*, pp. 54, 63, 76.

Book of Rites, the *Analects,* the *Mencius,* and the *Hsün-tzu* to reconstruct the institutional system as Confucius envisaged it.[62] He did not mention any indebtedness to the "Li-yün"—the prime source of the concept of *Ta-t'ung.* The other major work, the *Ch'un-ch'iu Tung-shih hsüeh,* published in Shanghai in 1898, still has the theory of the Three Ages and other Kung-yang doctrines as its main themes, but has also a number of specific references to *Ta-t'ung* and *Hsiao-k'ang,* and one to the famous passage in the "Li-yün," in which these concepts appeared for the first time in Confucian literature.[63] For the first time, too, K'ang linked the doctrines of the "Li-yün" with the theories of Kung-yang *Ch'un-ch'iu.*

It may be surmised that in searching for material to reconstruct the Confucian institutional system early in the 1890s K'ang went through the *Book of Rites* again and was struck with the immense significance of the "Li-yün"—passages that he had read many years before without being impressed by them—and that now in a new stage of philosophical development he was able to perceive direct connection between the "Li-yün" and the *Ch'un-ch'iu.* This was the beginning of K'ang's catholic treatment of the classics. For the time being his main emphasis remained with the *Annals.* Not too many years later, however, he set out to review all the "authentic" Confucian classics and give them that treatment. The ground was thus prepared for a number of his later writings on Confucianism: the *Chung-yung chu* (*The Doctrine of the Mean Annotated,* 1901); the *Li-yün chu* (The Evolution of Rites Annotated, 1901–2); the *Ta-hsüeh chu* (*The Great Learning* Annotated, 1902; the *Lun-yü chu* (*The Analects* Annotated, 1902); and the *Meng-tzu wei* (The Esoteric Meanings of the *Mencius,* 1902).[64] "The sage of Nan-hai" thus finally emerged as a full-fledged, independent Confucian scholar.

To sum up: K'ang's venture into Confucianism fell into three stages. The first, in which he uncritically followed tradition, commenced with his childhood and ended around 1883 when he shifted his attention from the classics to "Han learning." The second, in which he broke away from tradition, began around 1888 when he again studied the classics, discriminated against the "spurious" classics of the Old Text school in favor of the "authentic" ones of the New Text, and centered his attention on the Kung-yang doctrines of *Ch'un-ch'iu.* The third, in which he engaged himself in the catholic treatment of the classics, be-

---

[62] K'ang, *Nien-p'u,* Kuang hsü 18 (1892); Lo, *K'ang,* p. 54.
[63] K'ang, *Ch'un-ch'iu Tung-shih hsüeh, chüan* 2, p. 4a.
[64] K'ang T'ung-pi, *Pu . . . nien-p'u,* pp. 4b and 6a–7a; *Nan-hai . . . pu-i,* pp. 9b, 15b, 18a, 21b; Lo, *K'ang,* pp. 189, 192.

gan about 1892–93 and ended around 1902 when he integrated the doctrines of the Three Ages (*Ch'un-ch'iu*) and the notions of Great Unity and Minor Peace ("Li-yün") to form the guiding principles of his social philosophy.

Attitude toward Predecessors and Contemporaries

K'ang passed judgment on many Confucians of importance, commending some but criticizing or deprecating others. The only authority that he unconditionally acknowledged was that of Confucius—not Confucius as traditionally recognized but Confucius as he himself understood him. K'ang's judgments, pronounced often with a pontifical ring, were not always free from prejudice. But however unreliable they may be as measures of the intrinsic worth of the men he appraised, they nevertheless reflect his own personal conviction. A brief survey of them will throw light on his philosophical position.

Among the early followers of Confucius, Yen-tzu, Tseng-tzu, Tzu-ssu, and Mencius were traditionally regarded as the most eminent. K'ang said little about Yen-tzu, probably because "the Recurring Sage" left no writings behind him. K'ang showed a decided preference for Tzu-ssu and Mencius but held Tseng-tzu in comparatively low esteem. He accepted Ch'eng I's (1033–1107) view that Tzu-ssu was the author of the *Doctrine of the Mean* and declared that this short classic constituted the finest statement of Confucius' teaching.[65] He was even more enthusiastic about Mencius, as the following statement indicates:

> Tzu-yu received the doctrine of *Ta-t'ung* from Confucius, which he transmitted to Tzu-ssu. As Mencius received instruction from Tzu-ssu he gained a profound knowledge of Confucius' teaching concerning the *Spring and Autumn Annals*, which he elaborated and clarified. . . . O, Mencius, truly the Buddha and Paul of the Confucian school![66]

K'ang's admiration for Mencius, however, was not unlimited. On one occasion he took exception to Mencius' well-known doctrine that human nature was "good" and attached greater value to Hsün-tzu's view that it was "bad." K'ang wrote:

> Hsün-tzu contradicted Mencius' doctrine because he loathed to allow men to do as their natural inclinations lead them, thus refusing to apply themselves to learning. . . . What Hsün-tzu said is not incompatible with

[65] K'ang, author's preface to *Chung-yung chu* (Yen-K'ung ts'ung-shu ed., n.d.).

[66] K'ang, "*Meng-tzu wei* hsü" (*Wen-ch'ao*, 8: 1a–2a).

the teaching of the Sage. . . . But if we accept the doctrine of Mencius, I fear that all men would give their natural impulses unrestrained play.[67]

Tseng-tzu, to whom the *Great Learning* and the *Book of Filial Piety* have been attributed, was rated by K'ang much lower than Tzu-ssu and Mencius. Tseng-tzu, K'ang contended, devoted himself exclusively to "observing restraints" (*shou yüeh*), for he "had never heard the great teaching of Confucius," as Yeh Shih (1150–1223) correctly pointed out.[68] He was so convinced of Tseng-tzu's inferiority that he rejected Chu Hsi's attribution of the *Great Learning* to him. His arguments are simple: Being "a precious book of the Confucian school" it could not have come from a man of Tseng-tzu's caliber; moreover, Tseng-tzu is mentioned only once in the entire work and there is no evidence that he wrote any part of it.[69]

K'ang sided with Hsün-tzu against Mencius on human nature but he condemned Hsün-tzu's philosophy as a whole. The condemnation is little short of sweeping:

> Vast indeed is the Way of Confucius. In its greatness it imitates Heaven and its operations are everywhere to be seen. . . . It was, however, first corrupted by the bigoted meanness of Hsün-tzu's philosophy, later confused further by Liu Hsin's forgeries and falsehoods, and finally damaged by Chu-tzu's partiality. In this manner the Great Way of the Uncrowned King (*su wang*) was so darkened that it could not shine forth, and so stifled that it could not be manifested.[70]

K'ang continued:

> The two thousand years of our China—including the dynasties of Han, T'ang, Sung, and Ming, regardless of the prevalence of order or confusion, the rise or decline of regimes—constituted altogether the Age of Minor Peace. What Confucian scholars had said in these two thousand years— including the utterances of Hsün Ch'ing, Liu Hsin, and Chu Hsi, regardless of their truth or falsity, excellence or crudity, goodness or badness— pointed without exception to the way of the Minor Peace.[71]

In other words, Hsün-tzu, like Tseng-tzu before him, was ignorant of

---

[67] K'ang, "Ni ta Chu Yung-sheng hsien-sheng shu," microfilm, reel 1.

[68] K'ang, *Lun-yü chu*, preface (Wan-mu ts'ao-t'ang ed.).

[69] K'ang, *Ta-hsüeh chu*, preface (*Wen-ch'ao*, 5: 8b–9a, and *Wen-chi, chüan* 5, p. 21a).

[70] K'ang, *Lun-yü chu*, preface, quoted in Fung Yu-lan, *A History of Chinese Philosophy*, 2: 678 (quoted here with slight modifications).

[71] K'ang, "*Li-yün chu* hsü" (*Wen-ch'ao*, 8: 2b).

"the great teaching of Confucius" and was responsible for initiating the trend of "false" Confucian thought, which eventually led to the establishment of the Neo-Confucian tradition.[72]

Among the Confucians of Han times Tung Chung-shu alone received K'ang's unqualified approval. Tung occupied a high place in the Kung-yang school and was the author of the *Ch'un-ch'iu fan-lu* (Luxuriant Dew of the *Spring and Autumn Annals*) in which many of the characteristic doctrines of that school may be found.[73] K'ang's attitude toward Tung is clearly revealed in the following passage taken from his *Ch'un-ch'iu Tung-shih hsüeh*. He cites a number of appraisals from earlier scholars, then continues:

> He [Tung] transmitted the doctrines of his school in the most complete manner and lived not far away from pre-Ch'in times. All who wish to study Kung-yang, therefore, should turn to Tung-tzu and to no one else.
>
> Eminently worthy men like Mencius and Hsün-tzu who were the bodhisattvas of the Confucian school, did not provide the esoteric doctrines and profound principles as contained in the *Ch'un-ch'iu fan-lu*. Tung's learning [it may be asked] did not extend beyond that of Mencius and Hsün-tzu; how did he obtain these doctrines and principles? The answer is that these were the oral teachings of Confucius, which were transmitted to Tung; they were not Tung's own inventions. . . . Whatever Tung set forth, therefore, transcended Hsün-tzu and surpassed Mencius, and is not to be found in any other book of the Confucian school. But for Tung-tzu [later scholars] would find it impossible to gain an insight into the great teaching of Confucius.[74]

According to this view then, Tung Chung-shu outshone even Mencius, whom K'ang called "the Paul of the Confucian school," and the *Ch'un-ch'iu fan-lu* contained more truths than even the *Great Learning* or *Doctrine of the Mean*. It may be noted that K'ang's appraisal of Tung was made in 1897, in a period when his chief interest lay in the *Annals*, whereas his evaluation of Mencius and the Great Learning was made, in 1901–2, at a time when his interests transcended the *Annals*. This is a good example of his change of mind and his intellectual development from one stage to another.

K'ang generally spoke ill of Confucians of the Old Text tradition,

[72] Liang, *Ch'ing-tai hsüeh-shu kai-lun*, pp. 138–39.

[73] For a summary of Tung Chung-shu's philosophy see Fung, *History of Chinese Philosophy*, vol. 2, chap. 2; Lin, *Men and Ideas*, chap. 9; and Hsiao, *Chung-kuo cheng-chih ssu-hsiang shih*, 2: 293–300.

[74] K'ang, preface to *Ch'un-ch'iu Tung-shih hsüeh*, pp. 1b–2a.

especially Neo-Confucians of Sung and Ming times, but did not repudiate all of them. Sometimes he showed a degree of respect for Chu
Hsi. He admitted that men like Chu Hsi, Chang Tsai, Wang Shou-jen
and even Lao-tzu, who exerted important influences on mankind,
deserved places of honor even in the Age of Universal Peace.[75] And,
as Liang Ch'i-ch'ao pointed out, K'ang had a liking for Lu Chiu-yüan
and Wang Shou-jen.[76]

It must be emphasized that K'ang received from Sung and Ming
Confucians more formative influence on his own thinking than he admitted. An examination of his writings, in particular the *Ta-t'ung shu*,
reveals interesting resemblances between K'ang's philosophical outlook and that of Chang Tsai (1020–77). It is improbable that in his
extensive reading in Neo-Confucianism K'ang failed to be impressed
by Chang Tsai's *Hsi Ming* (The Western Inscription), which clearly
echoes the Confucian sentiment of universal brotherhood[77] and the
doctrine of *Ta-t'ung* as expressed in the "Li-yün." It is difficult to explain K'ang's failure to give credit to Chang Tsai on this score—although he did acknowledge Chang's importance in a general way.
Perhaps in his desire to dissociate his philosophy from Neo-Confucianism in general and with the Ch'eng–Chu tradition in particular, he
found it necessary not to acknowledge any indebtedness to Confucians
later than Tung Chung-shu. Chang Tsai was probably too close to the
Ch'eng–Chu school for K'ang to acknowledge safely. Liang Ch'i-ch'ao,
however, did not hesitate to make clear K'ang's intellectual relation
to the Lu–Wang school of Neo-Confucianism. According to Liang,
K'ang was initiated into the Lu-Wang philosophy by Chu Tz'u-ch'i[78]
who was K'ang's teacher in 1876–78 and he in turn initiated Liang
into it when he lectured at Ch'ang-hsing li in 1890.[79]

It is hardly surprising that K'ang was profoundly influenced by Lu
Chiu-yüan and Wang Shou-jen. Lu and Wang in their own ways rebelled against the Neo-Confucian tradition of the Ch'eng–Chu school,
the foundation upon which imperial Confucianism was built. Both men
indeed had much in common with K'ang. Lu felt mental anguish,

---

[75] K'ang, *Ta-t'ung shu*, p. 417. This passage is paraphrased in Thompson, *Ta T'ung Shu*, p. 246.

[76] Liang, *Nan-hai K'ang hsien-sheng chuan*, p. 61.

[77] Chang Tsai's "Hsi Ming" is available in translation in Fung, *History of Chinese Philosophy*, 2: 493–95 and Chang, *Development of Neo-Confucian Thought*, pp. 178–80.

[78] Liang, "Lun Chung-kuo hsüeh-shu ssu-hsiang pien-ch'ien chih ta-shih," pp. 98–99. This passage is quoted in Li, *Political History of China, 1840–1928*, p. 150.

[79] Liang, "San-shih tzu-shu," p. 16.

even in his boyhood, when he heard someone recite the utterances of Ch'eng I, founder of the Ch'eng–Chu school. "Why is it," he asked, "that the sayings of I-ch'uan [i.e., Ch'eng I] are unlike those of Confucius and Mencius?" On another occasion, while reading an ancient text, he suddenly gained the insight that "those affairs which fall within the universe are those which fall within the scope of my duty; those affairs which fall within the scope of my duty are those which are within the universe." Another philosophical insight of his was:

> The universe is my mind and my mind is the universe. If in the Eastern Sea there were to appear a sage, he would have this same mind and this same Principle (*li*). If in the Western Sea there were to appear a sage, he would have this same mind and this same Principle. . . . If a hundred or a thousand generations ago, or a hundred or a thousand generations hence, sages were to appear, they likewise would have this same mind and this same Principle.[80]

These ideas are much like K'ang's.

Lu probably appealed to K'ang in another way also. In the *Yü-lu*, Lu was recorded as declaring that he had resolved "to shatter the bondage, to clear away the brambles, and to clean up the filthy marshes" of false tradition. A kindred sentiment is expressed in the following rhymed lines:

> I raise my head and reach for the Southern Dipper;
> I turn around and stand beside the Polar Star
> I look beyond the sky's limits, holding my head high:
> I find no other man who is my like.[81]

Lu thus showed the intellectual independence and self-confidence that so strikingly characterized K'ang Yu-wei.

Foreshadowing K'ang's fearless criticisms of the Confucian classics, in a letter to Chu Hsi Lu made the following remarks:

> Sages and worthy men of old fixed their eyes on truth (*li*) and nothing else. . . . As Mencius said, "It would be better to be without the *Book of History* than to give entire credit to it. In the 'Completion of the War' I select two or three passages only, which I believe." Anything that is contrary to reason I dare not believe, even if it comes from an ancient book.[82]

[80] Huang Tsung-hsi, *Sung Yüan hsüeh-an* (Sung Yüan Ming Ch'ing ssu-ch'ao hsüeh-an ed., *chüan* 58, p. 1066.
[81] Huang, *Sung Yüan hsüeh-an*, pp. 1069–70.
[82] Ibid., p. 1073.

The similarity between the views of Wang Shou-jen and K'ang Yu-wei is equally apparent. The following passage from Wang's "Ta-hsüeh wen" would not be out of place in K'ang's *Ta-t'ung shu*:

> The great man is an all-pervading unity with Heaven, Earth, and all things. He regards all beneath Heaven as one family, and the Middle Kingdom as one man. Those who emphasize the distinction of bodily shapes, and thus make cleavage between the self and others, are the small men. The reason that the great man is able to be one with Heaven, Earth, and all things, is not that he is thus for some purpose, but because the love (*jen*) of his mind is naturally so and thus makes possible this union.[83]

It is hardly surprising, therefore, that K'ang subscribed to the philosophy of the Lu–Wang school, which "he regarded as direct, clear, sincere, lively, and useful" and consequently "adopted it as guiding principle of self-cultivation and student instruction,"[84] and I find it difficult to believe that K'ang revolted against the Neo-Confucian philosophy not only of Chu Hsi but of Wang Shou-jen as well.[85] It is conceivable that the Lu–Wang philosophy actually furnished part of the inspiration that led him to revolt against the Ch'eng–Chu tradition and thus to restore Confucianism to its "purity."[86]

But K'ang did not subscribe to the Lu–Wang philosophy in its entirety. There were elements in that school of thought which did not appeal to him. The Lu–Wang "philosophy of mind" (*hsin hsüeh*) laid too much emphasis on the study of individual morality and too little on the study of social institutions. Moreover, neither Lu nor Wang made any distinction between the "authentic" New Text and "false"

---

[83] Quoted in Fung, *History of Chinese Philosophy*, 2 : 599. Cf. Wang Shou-jen, *Wang Wen-ch'eng-kung ch'üan-shu, chüan* 2, *Ch'uan-hsi lu*, "Ta Ku Tung-chiao shu."

[84] Liang, *Nan-hai K'ang hsien-sheng chuan*, p. 61.

[85] Chan Wing-tsit, "Trends in Contemporary Philosophy," in MacNair, *China*, pp. 312–13.

[86] For a summary of controversy between Lu Chiu-yüan and Chu Hsi, see Huang Tsung-hsi, *Sung Yüan hsueh-an, chüan* 58, p. 1067 and Chang, *Development of Neo-Confucian Thought*, pp. 286–307. Before committing himself partly to the Lu–Wang philosophy, K'ang was an admirer of Chu Hsi, as two of his poems written in 1889 when he visited the Tzu-yang shu-yüan (where Chu taught) in Lu-shan, clearly show. One of these contains these lines: "When Chu and Lu contested south of the River, Hui-weng [i.e., Chu] was truly supreme." The other contains these lines: "He [Chu] truly was founder of a new Teaching [*chiao-chu*],/—a latter-day sage [*housheng*] molding an epoch." These pieces are given in *Nan-hai hsien-sheng shih-chi* (facsimile of Liang Ch'i-ch'ao's calligraphy; Shanghai, 1908), chap. 2, pp. 26a–b. Cf. another piece in ibid., pp. 26a–b. According to *Nien-p'u*, p. 9b (Lo, *K'ang*, p. 51), K'ang visited Lu-shan and other places in Kiangsi and Kiangsu in autumn and spring, 1889–90.

Old Text learning, and they showed no particular interest in the Kung-yang doctrines.

Among K'ang's contemporaries two men require mentioning here, namely, Chu Tz'u-ch'i (1807–81) and Liao P'ing (1852–1932). In his early twenties K'ang was a student under Chu for about three years (autumn 1876 to winter 1878). He eventually went farther than his teacher but remained always respectful to him and showed his gratitude in a number of ways. It appears that Chu contributed much to the early phases of K'ang's intellectual life. His influence can still be seen in K'ang's early teaching in 1890,[87] and probably helped determine the general direction of K'ang's development. Chu's eclectic approach to the diverse schools of Confucianism[88] may well have prepared K'ang for his syncretic treatment of widely different philosophical and social ideas. K'ang himself credited Chu with having set the example of going directly to Confucius for ultimate truth. In his preface to the collected works of Chu (which K'ang compiled after Chu's death) K'ang indicated what he understood to be the intellectual position of his teacher:

> He accepted the tradition of the Later Han dynasty as his criterion of moral conduct and sought rational principles in the writings of Sung scholars; later, however, he cast aside [Cheng] K'ang-ch'eng and [Chu] Tzu-yang and looked up to Confucius alone.[89]

To "cast aside K'ang-ch'eng and Tzu-yang" was K'ang's way of saying "to reject the Old Text and Ch'eng–Chu tradition." This was essentially the position that K'ang took not long after his teacher's death.

The impact of Chu's personality and scholarship upon K'ang was, according to K'ang's own testimony, decisive. In 1876 he spoke of his teacher in these glowing words:

> His learning . . . centers on practical service to mankind and the world. . . . He sweeps away the sectarian line of demarcation between Han and Sung learning, and turns to Confucius for guidance. I respectfully receive his instructions and feel like a wayfarer who has found lodging, a blind man who sees light again. I clear my mind of unscholarly thoughts and follow his guidance with a single purpose. I am convinced that sageness is assuredly attainable, that I can finish reading every book of value before I reach thirty *sui*, that I for certain shall be able to find my proper place

[87] Liang, *Nan-hai K'ang hsien-sheng chuan*, p. 61.

[88] K'o Shao-min, "Ju-lin chuan," in *Ch'ing-shih kao*, 114: 36a–37a.

[89] K'ang, "Chu Chiu-chiang hsien-sheng i-wen hsü," in *Pu-jen tsa-chih*, no. 3 (April 1913), pp. 9–12 and *Pu-jen tsa-shih hui-pien*, no. 1 (1914), *chüan* 5, pp. 14a–15a. Cf. Ch'ien, *Chung kuo . . . hsüeh-shu shih*, p. 639.

in the world, and that the world can still be saved. . . . Standing head and
shoulder above my fellow students I join the company of the worthy,
superior men of old. Truly can a great man inspire others.[90]

Chu not only imparted a high degree of self-confidence to K'ang
but also helped to foster his critical spirit. K'ang narrated a revealing
incident. Shortly before he took leave of Chu he ventured the bold
opinion that Han Yü (768–824) did not deserve the fame he had enjoyed for centuries, for what he had said concerning *tao* was extremely
superficial and much of what he had written had nothing to do with
tao at all. As Han had always been held in high esteem by scholars and
was generally acknowledged as the forerunner of Neo-Confucianism,
K'ang's remark bordered upon academic irreverence. Chu, who was
known as a stern disciplinarian, merely "smilingly chided" K'ang for
his boldness and did not chastise him as he was expected to.[91]

A mental crisis in 1878 brought to an end K'ang's association with
Chu.

> In autumn and winter, I had gained a general acquaintance with the
> contents of the important books of the [imperial] *Ssu-k'u* collection. I felt
> that in burying myself daily in heaps of waste paper I was smothering my
> intellectual faculties. I became increasingly bored and disliked doing my
> studies. . . . Suddenly, I stopped doing them and threw away my books.
> Shutting the door [of my room] and refusing to associate with my friends
> I sat in quietude to cultivate my mind. My behavior was regarded by
> my fellow students as extremely strange.
>
> [One day,] when I sat still, I perceived suddenly that I was in an all-
> pervading unity with Heaven, Earth, and all things and that light shone
> forth in great profusion. Regarding myself as a sage I smiled with happi-
> ness. But thinking of the sufferings of mankind I suddenly wept in sorrow.
>
> Winter arrived and I took leave of Master Chiu-chiang [i.e., Chu Tz'u-
> ch'i], having decided to return home and practice quiet meditation.[92]

This crisis was a turning point in K'ang's intellectual career, the
point at which he "departed from the classics" (see his statement cited
in note 27, above) and pushed his philosophical interest in several directions: Mahayāna Buddhism, institutions and practical affairs of the
state, and "Western learning."[93] He did not, however, renounce Con-

[90] K'ang, *Nien-p'u*, Kuang-hsü 2 (1876); Lo, *K'ang*, pp. 30–31. Translation of the
quoted passage is mine.

[91] K'ang, *Nien-p'u*, Kuang-hsü 4 (1878); Lo, *K'ang*, p. 33.

[92] K'ang, *Nien-p'u*, Kuang-hsü 4, autumn and winter (1878); Lo, *K'ang*, pp. 33–
34.

[93] K'ang, *Nien-p'u*, Kuang-hsü 5 (1879); Lo, *K'ang*, pp. 34–36.

fucianism, nor repudiate Chu Tz'u-ch'i. He widened his intellectual vista and was on his way to laying the foundations of his syncretic philosophy but remained essentially Confucian. He continued to refer to Chu in the most grateful manner. He wrote in 1879, for instance, "It was through my teacher, Chu Chiu-chiang, that I became acquainted with the great teachings of the Sage and the worthy."[94] Even Buddhism, it appears, came to him through Confucian channels, the philosophy of Wang Shou-jen. The phrase "an all-pervading unity with Heaven, Earth, and all things," was used by Wang on more than one occasion.

The years after K'ang left Chu Tz'u-ch'i, he returned to the classics and studied them from a new standpoint, seeing what he had previously called "heaps of waste paper" in a fresh and intriguing light. He now definitely committed himself to the Kung-yang school of Confucianism.

K'ang's relation with Liao P'ing was of a different nature. Although they were both Confucian scholars of the same school, K'ang was curiously reticent about Liao. In his extensive writings on the New Text school in general and the Kung-yang in particular, he made no mention of Liao, and consequently left himself open to accusations of plagiarism. Liao himself accused K'ang of appropriating his ideas. He said that in 1888–89 K'ang had secured a copy of his book on the classics and that K'ang had had a long conversation with him when they both happened to be in Canton. That was probably in 1889–90. In 1891 K'ang produced his *Hsin-hsüeh wei-ching k'ao*,[95] and Liao repeated his accusation with added emphasis.[96]

Liao was supported by a number of writers. Yeh Te-hui, who condemned the Kung-yang school and was strongly opposed to reform said in 1898 that "K'ang Yu-wei's learning came from Liao P'ing."[97] Liang Ch'i-ch'ao wrote in 1902 that K'ang was indebted to Liao, "the man who had brought New Text scholarship of the past decades to its highest point of development," a fact, he added pointedly, "which cannot be gainsaid."[98] Hou O who was sympathetic toward both K'ang and Liao, wrote in 1932 (the year in which Liao died) that if K'ang's books on the "forged classics" and "Confucius as a Reformer" may be

---

[94] K'ang, *Nien-p'u*, Kuang-hsü 5; Lo, *K'ang*, p. 35.

[95] Ch'ien, *Chung-kuo . . . hsüeh-shu shih*, pp. 645–46, quoting from Liao P'ing.

[96] Ch'ien, *Chung-kuo . . . hsüeh-shu shih*, pp. 645–46, quoting from Liao P'ing. Cf. Chang Hsi-t'ang, "Liao P'ing *Ku-hsüeh k'ao* hsü," preface to reprint of Liao's work in 1935.

[97] Yeh Te-hui, "Ta yu-jen shu," in Su, *I-chiao ts'ung-pien*, chüan 6, p. 31b.

[98] Liang, "Lun Chung-kuo hsüeh-shu ssu-hsiang pien-ch'ien chih ta-shih," pp. 98–99. Cf. *Ch'ing-tai hsüeh-shu kai-lun*, p. 126.

likened to a deafening thunderbolt that shook the Chinese intellectual world, then Liao P'ing's writings may be said to have furnished it with its "prodigious electrical energy."[99] Ch'ien Mu investigated the matter about the same time and came to the conclusion that K'ang indeed was guilty of plagiarism.[100]

Two facts stand out. In the first place, K'ang was in a position to appropriate Liao's ideas if he chose to do so. He published his major works on the New and Old Text school, the *Hsing-hsüeh wei-ching k'ao* (1891) and *K'ung-tzu kai-chih k'ao* (1897), years after Liao had published his on the same subjects, the *Chin ku hsüeh k'ao* (Studies in Old Text Learning, 1886), "P'i Liu p'ien" (Essay on Refuting Liu Hsin, 1888), and "Chih-sheng p'ien" (Essay on Comprehending the Sage, 1888). And while K'ang was still engaged in exposing the "errors" of Ho Hsiu, Liao had already produced his works on the "false" classics.

In the second place, there are obvious similarities between the views of the two men. In the "third phase" of Liao's study of the classics (beginning in 1888), in which Liao undertook "to exalt the New and belittle the Old," he was convinced that the Old Text school had its origin in "the elaborations of Liu Hsin and his followers" and that the New Text classics alone came from Confucius. Accordingly, Liao wrote the "Chih-sheng p'ien" "to exalt the New Text learning" and the "P'i Liu p'ien" "to refute the Old."[101] Liao also held that Confucius, in his later years, developed ideas of reform and no longer accepted the existing institutions of the Chou dynasty, thus joining the company of the "determined men" of the Spring and Autumn period, who "were anxious to reform Chou civilization."[102] It was in the New Text classics, Liao asserted, that Confucius set forth his doctrines of institutional reform. These classics, then, were *ching* ("classics") which contained the original ideas of the Sage, not *shih* ("history"), records of ancient institutions and practices.[103] These views are substantially the same as

[99] Hou O, "Liao Chi-p'ing hsien-shen p'ing-chuan."

[100] Ch'ien, *Chung-kuo . . . hsüeh-shu shih*, pp. 642–52.

[101] Fung, *History of Chinese Philosophy*, 2: 708.

[102] Ibid., pp. 706–7.

[103] Ch'ien, *Chung-kuo . . . hsüeh-shu shih*, pp. 652–53, quoting from Liao P'ing. On pp. 652–53, Ch'ien quotes the following revealing remarks made by Liao in 1913: "[In countries] beyond the seas theories of law and government are well developed, and institutions are adapted to the times. [In China] the Three Kings did not have identical systems of rites and the Five Emperors did not copy the musical system, one from another. If [these systems] were actual ancient historical facts, . . . they are already absolutely unsuitable for adoption at the present. How can they be applied ten thousand generations from now? All these must be regarded as the doctrines of

the major theses that K'ang developed in his works on the "forged classics" and "Confucius as a Reformer."

Another significant point of similarity may also be noted. In his "fourth phase" (beginning 1898) Liao broadly suggested that Confucius envisaged forms of political organization that were suitable not only for China but for mankind as a whole and that, since Confucius "extended his planning to the entire globe," the Six Classics carried doctrines of universal validity—applicable both to China and to foreign nations.[104] K'ang gave a similar universalist interpretation of Confucianism.

The similarities are striking and K'ang could easily have borrowed from Liao. In fairness to K'ang, however, the possibility of independent discovery of the same truth cannot be ruled out. K'ang presumably had read as extensively as Liao and was in a position to come to similar conclusions.[105] After all, the question of the authenticity of the Old Text classics had been definitely raised and Kung-yang studies seriously undertaken long before Liao advanced his views. K'ang could have received suggestions from such Kung-yang scholars as Kung Tzu-chen (1792–1841) and Wei Yüan (1794–1856)[106] before he came upon Liao P'ing's writings. Chu Tz'u-ch'i, K'ang's own teacher, in "casting aside K'ang-ch'eng" may have induced K'ang to take a critical attitude toward the Old Text tradition. It may even be conjectured that K'ang's acquaintance with Western ideas (beginning in 1879), fragmentary and superficial as it necessarily was, put him in a somewhat better position than Liao to arrive at the unconventional interpretations of the classics.

---

the Supreme Sage who serves as teacher and guide of ten thousand generations, not as events in the past. Only thus can the classics maintain their ground" (from Liao's lecture on "Shih-chieh che-li chin-hua t'ui-hua").

[104] Fung, *History of Chinese Philosophy*, 2: 713. Cf. Ch'ien, *Chung-kuo . . . hsüeh-shu shih*, pp. 643–62 and Ojima Sukema, "Six Stages in the Development of Liao P'ing's Theories," *Shina-gaku*, 2, no. 9 (May 1922): 70–72.

[105] K'ang, *Nien-p'u*, Kuang-hsü 2, 5, 8, 9, and 10 (1876, 1879, 1882, 1883, and 1884); Lo, *K'ang*, pp. 30–40.

[106] In the author's preface to the 1917 reprint of the *Hsin-hsüeh wei-ching k'ao*, K'ang credited Liu Feng-lu (1776–1829), Kung Tzu-chen, and Wei Yüan with having suspected Liu Hsin of forgery. K'ang, however, insisted that he had made his own discoveries. In his letter to Liao P'ing, K'ang implied denial that he was indebted to Liao. This letter, written in 1913, is available in *Nan-hai hsien-sheng nien-p'u hsü-pien*, compiled by K'ang T'ung-pi, p. 79a. For a brief account of earlier scholars who questioned the authenticity of the Old Text classics and to the Kung-yang scholars of Ch'ing times, see Liang, *Ch'ing-tai hsüeh-shu kai-lun*, pp. 23–29, 118–21; Liang Ch'i-ch'ao, *Intellectual Trends in the Ch'ing Period* trans. Immanuel C. Y. Hsü, pp. 32–36, 88–91. Hereafter, Hsü, *Intellectual Trends*.

It should be noted that there were significant differences in their views. K'ang made this point in his postscript to the 1917 reprint of his work on the "forged classics":

> There is in the present generation a scholar who is devoted to learning and engages himself in profound thinking. In his discussions of the differences between the Old and the New there may be coincidental similarities [between his views and mine]. I regret, however, that he refutes the Old on the one hand and, on the other hand, maintains a firm belief in the *Chou-li* [an Old Text classic]. . . . He thus contradicts himself and confuses the line of demarcation [between the Old and New]. One merely has to keep in mind his honoring the spurious *Chou-li* to see that his scholarship bears absolutely no relation to mine.[107]

The scholar to whom K'ang referred was Liao P'ing. K'ang was probably trying to defend himself against the charge of plagiarism, and though his argument is hardly adequate, it has some merit. Liao P'ing also pointed out their differences; but his claim is that K'ang "missed the guiding thought" when he borrowed ideas from the "Essay on Comprehending the Sage," and the "Essay on Refuting Liu Hsin."[108]

The differences between K'ang and Liao were explained more precisely by Liang Ch'i-ch'ao (K'ang's student) and Meng Wen-t'ung (Liao's student). Liang pointed out that K'ang was indebted to Liao in his Kung-yang studies but his indebtedness did not go beyond sharing with Liao the same subject matter, namely the Kung-yang doctrines based on the *Annals*. K'ang's philosophical aim differed widely from Liao's. Liao's interest remained purely academic, whereas K'ang was predominantly interested in practical reform. Herein, Liang said, lay K'ang's claim to originality.[109] Meng Wen-t'ung distinguished between two branches of the New Text school. One of these, the origins of which may be traced to the Lu school of learning in Han times, took the *Ku-liang Commentary* as its point of departure[110] and relied mainly on the *Book of Rites* to interpret the other New Text classics. Liao P'ing belonged to this branch of New Text learning. The other branch, which followed the tradition of the Ch'i school and to which K'ang belonged, took the *Kung-yang Commentary* as its point of departure and

---

[107] K'ang, *Nien-p'u*, 1: 6–7. Quoted in Ch'ien, *Chung-kuo . . . hsüeh-shu shih*, p. 648.

[108] Quoted in ibid., p. 645, from *Ching-yü chia pien, chüan* 1.

[109] Liang, "Lun Chung-kuo hsüeh-shu ssu-hsiang pien-ch'ien chih ta-shih," p. 99.

[110] Meng Wen-t'ung, "Ching-yen Liao Chi-p'ing shih yü chin-tai Chin-wen-hsüeh."

relied on the *wei-shu* ("apocrypha")[111] to interpret the classics. Thus even though K'ang may have borrowed ideas from Liao, he belonged to a different school of Confucian studies.[112]

There are two possible conclusions: First, that K'ang independently developed ideas similar to Liao's; second, that K'ang borrowed from Liao but used his ideas to serve widely different purposes. If the latter is true K'ang might be criticized for failure to give credit to Liao for whatever he borrowed from him. But, as has already been mentioned, he acknowledged indebtedness only to a few men, namely, Confucius, Tung Chung-shu, and Chu Tz'u-ch'i—men whose views he accepted with little or no reservation. He seldom if ever acknowledged others from whom he freely borrowed but with whom he was only in partial agreement, such as Chang Tsai, Wang Shou-jen, and some of the Kung-yang scholars of Ch'ing times, especially Kung Tzu-chen and Wei Yüan who, according to Liang Ch'i-ch'ao, inaugurated the modern trend of using Confucian doctrines to advance political views.[113] K'ang refused to acknowledge Liao because he did not accept Liao as his predecessor or co-discoverer of truth, although he found some of Liao's ideas acceptable. If that was plagiarism, K'ang offended not only Liao P'ing but all the scholars of the past to whom he failed to give credit.

INTERPRETATIONS OF THE CLASSICS

Changes in View

Liang Ch'i-ch'ao observed that one of K'ang's outstanding traits was his tenacity in adhering to views that he chose to hold, so much so that after reaching philosophical maturity in 1887 K'ang made no further progress and did not care to make any.[114] But Liang was merely repeating a statement that K'ang made late in the 1880s[115] and which, as I have explained earlier, cannot be accepted as accurate. K'ang, indeed, was inclined to be dogmatic and arbitrary in his views but he changed his views when circumstances changed. His general philosophical outlook and method of dealing with intellectual problems

---

[111] Fung, *History of Chinese Philosophy*, chap. 3, explains briefly the origin and nature of the *wei-shu*.

[112] See note 110, above.

[113] Liang, *Ch'ing-tai hsüeh-shu kai-lun*, p. 126.

[114] Ibid., p. 149.

[115] See note 50, above.

remained essentially unaltered throughout his long career, but the contents and direction of his thinking often showed significant variations.

This may be readily seen in his interpretations and evaluations of the classics. Despite his unvarying admiration for Confucius he entertained different views regarding the Confucian classics. Before 1888 he appeared to have accepted all of them, more or less indiscriminately, as authentic records of the Sage's teaching. In 1888 he began to segregate the Old Text classics, which he regarded as "spurious" from the New Text, which were "authentic." Thus in his *Hsin-hsüeh wei-ching k'ao*, published in 1891,[116] he undertook to demonstrate that all the Old Text classics, notably the *Chou-li*, the *Tso Commentary* on the *Annals*, and the Mao version of the *Book of Odes* were forged by Liu Hsin.[117] He reiterated this view time and again and made his position most clear in the following statement:

> Liu Hsin was the first to perpetrate forgery and confound the Sage's teaching. Cheng Hsüan [A.D. 127–200] completed the task of disseminating the spurious classics and usurping the Confucian tradition. For two thousand years . . . all scholars reverently accepted the spurious classics as [veritable records of] the teaching of the Sage. . . .
>
> All that which scholars of later times regarded as "Han learning" is nothing but the learning of Chia [K'uei A.D. 30–101], Ma [Yung A.D. 79–166], Hsü [Shen, Ma Yung's contemporary], and Cheng [Hsüan]. Even the classics that Sung scholars reverently cited were mostly spurious classics, not the classics of Confucius.[118]

With the establishment of the republic in 1912, K'ang abandoned his critical attitude and reverted to the position of his earlier years. Earnestly and insistently he argued that the Confucian classics—all of them, New or Old Text—were the most valuable repository of China's best tradition and therefore should be zealously preserved and widely read. When the Ministry of Education ordered that the practice of requiring school children to read Confucian classics be suspended, K'ang wrote a lengthy letter to the Minister, protesting strongly and urging him to rescind the order.[119]

It is not difficult to account for the changes in K'ang's attitude. As already indicated, he dropped his uncritical attitude in the 1880s

[116] K'ang, *Nien-p'u*, Kuang-hsü 17 (1891); Lo, *K'ang*, p. 53.
[117] Liang, *Ch'ing-tai hsüeh-shu kai-lun*, pp. 127–29, summarizes the main arguments of this book.
[118] K'ang, "Hsü-lu," in *Hsin-hsüeh wei-ching k'ao* (1931 reprint), pp. 2–3.
[119] See note 17, above.

partly as the result of the broadened intellectual vista gained through wide readings in Chinese literature and translations of Western books. The new point of view which led him to formulate in 1885–87 his "system of *Ta-t'ung*" fitted ill with the doctrines of the Old Text school. A reexamination of the classics became urgent and a revision of his appraisal of them was accordingly made.

The change of attitude may also have been partly the result of his acquaintance in 1888–89 with Liao P'ing's ideas. Liao's ideas may have confirmed whatever doubts about the authenticity of the Old Text classics K'ang may have already entertained. Meanwhile, the worsening conditions of the empire convinced K'ang that only extensive and timely reform could save it from dismemberment at the hands of the Western powers, and that without first demolishing the intellectual roadblock of established tradition no effective reform was possible. This, it seems, was the intellectual and political background of two of K'ang's major works on Confucianism: The *Hsin-hsüeh wei-ching k'ao* (1891) and *K'ung-tzu kai-chih k'ao* (1897).

The situation drastically changed in 1911. The imperial system with its Confucian ideology that K'ang had endeavored so laboriously to preserve by reform was replaced by a republic, a regime that K'ang for both rational and sentimental reasons found difficult to accept. Instead of working for reform he now pledged himself to the cause of restoration—restoration of the dynasty in the form of a "constitutional monarchy" and of the "Chinese tradition" in the form of unpurged Confucianism. For to him it was now no longer a problem of separating the "spurious" from the "authentic" classics but of reinstituting the authority of the classics for the moral edification of his compatriots. He thus returned to uncritical acceptance of the classics.

It may also be noted that K'ang often attached different values at different times to the individual classics that he regarded as genuine. Sometimes his estimation of a particular classic was revealed by the amount of attention he paid it. He wrote two major works on the *Spring and Autumn Annals*, for example, and annotated the *Analects* and the *Mencius* because he felt they were of the greatest importance.[120] By contrast, he did comparatively little to the *Book of History* (New Text version), the *Book of Changes*, and the *Book of Filial Piety*. He did not publish any annotation or commentary of the *Book of Rites* as a whole

[120] Namely, *Ch'un-ch'iu Tung-shih hsüeh*, written 1894–96 and published 1898; *Ch'un-ch'iu pi-hsüeh ta-i wei-yen k'ao*, and *Meng-tzu wei*, written in 1901; and *Lun-yü chu*, in 1902.

but annotated portions of it[121] and published three of his annotations as separate works.[122] He worked on the New Text version of the *Book of Odes* but did not produce anything that he regarded as worthy of publication.[123] Perhaps he paid less attention to the *Book of History* than the *Annals* because he thought the latter contained the "great teaching" of Confucius, whereas the former was merely a record of past events. He wrote little on the *Book of Changes* because it deals only indirectly with practical human affairs, which was his paramount interest. The same may be said of the *Book of Odes*. He ignored the *Book of Filial Piety* probably because it represented the philosophy of Tseng-tzu who, according to K'ang, not having heard "the great teaching," occupied a low niche in the Confucian school.

Thus it appears that of the "five classics" K'ang was seriously concerned only with the *Spring and Autumn Annals* and portions of the *Book of Rites*. He referred occasionally to or cited from the other classics in order to disparage them or, more often, to lend support to his arguments.[124] But it was these two that he chose as the media for his reconstruction of Confucianism. He did not devote equal attention to them. Between 1880 and 1902, during which he produced his major works on the classics, he at first preferred the *Annals* and turned to the *Rites* only after the stormy year of 1898. A brief survey of his interpretations of these two classics will reveal some of the significant changes in his views as a Confucian scholar and help to ascertain the extent to which he was indebted to Confucianism for his political and social philosophy.

Interpretation of Kung-yang Doctrines

Late in the 1880s and early in the 1890s K'ang was inclined to regard the Kung-yang interpretation of the *Spring and Autumn Annals* as the most complete and reliable source of Confucian truths. He said in 1894, for instance, that "although Confucius had Six Classics, he re-

---

[121] Lu and Lu, *K'ang Nan-hai hsien-sheng chuan*, pp. 51a–65b, and *K'ang Nan-hai hsien-sheng mo-chi*, vol. 4, "Fu-lu," give lists of K'ang's writings, both published and unpublished. Microfilm, reel 2, contains "Lun Yu-hsüeh"; reel 4 contains "Mao-shih li-cheng," "Hsüeh-chi ti shih-pa," "Shao-i," and "Ta-Tai li-chi pu-chu." All these are fragments of K'ang's annotations or exegeses of the *Li-chi*.

[122] Namely, *Ta-hsüeh chu* and *Li-yun chu*.

[123] Microfilm, reel 1, contains an incomplete manuscript of "*Shih-ching* Annotated," and a manuscript of forty chapters of a work designed to "expose the errors" of the Mao version of the *Book of Odes* (Old Text). The "Mao-shih li-cheng," mentioned above in note 121, also deals partly with the same classics.

[124] Ch'ien, *Chung-kuo . . . hsüeh-shu shih*, pp. 691–97, shows some of K'ang's views concerning the various classics.

posited all his great teachings in the *Spring and Autumn Annals*.[125] He expressed the same view more emphatically three years later:

> The teachings of Confucius—where do they reside? They reside in the Six Classics. The Six Classics . . . are exceedingly voluminous and divergent in their contents. Where can we find the guiding principles? They are found in the *Spring and Autumn Annals*.

K'ang then went on to quote Mencius "to prove" that what he said was true. Referring to the teaching of Confucius, he said, "Mencius mentioned no other book than the *Annals*"; Mencius attached great importance to the *Annals* because it contained the "principles" (*i*) of Confucius. Now three commentaries on the *Annals* were available. The *Tso Commentary* (Old Text school) dwelled merely on historical events; it therefore missed the significance of the *Annals* and had nothing to do with the teachings of Confucius. The *Ku-liang Commentary* (New Text school) transmitted some of Confucius' teachings but in an inadequate way. The *Kung-yang Commentary* (New Text school) alone made clear the full meaning of the *Annals*.[126]

K'ang, however, did not follow the Kung-yang tradition all the way, abiding faithfully with the established "canon of the school" (*chia-fa*). It appears that he selected from the Kung-yang doctrines those that he regarded as true (incidentally, those that served his purposes) and ignored those that failed to meet his approval or requirements. For instance, of the interpretations of the two foremost Kung-yang scholars of the Han dynasty K'ang sang high praise to those of Tung Chung-shu and relegated those of Ho Hsiu to a place of secondary importance.[127] On more than one occasion K'ang departed from Ho's views. One revealing instance suffices here. In the author's preface to his *Ch'un-ch'iu Kung-yang chuan chieh-ku* (The *Kung-yang Commentary* on the *Spring and Autumn Annals* Annotated), Ho quoted Confucius as saying, "My aim is indicated in the *Spring and Autumn Annals*, my conduct in the *Book of Filial Piety*." Ho then commented: "Both represented the attainment of the Sage."[128] K'ang glorified the *Annals* but paid scant attention to

[125] Ibid., pp. 691–92, quoting from K'ang's "Kuei-hsüeh ta-wen."

[126] K'ang, preface to *Ch'un-ch'iu Tung-shih hsüeh*, p. 1. The passages to which he referred in the *Mencius* are to be found in IV.ii.1.3; III.ii.9.8.

[127] K'ang, *Ch'un-ch'iu Tung-shih hsüeh*, *chüan* 8, p. 2b. K'ang was not always consistent; he sometimes placed Ho Hsiu and Tung Chung-shu on the same level. See, e.g., *chüan* 4, pp. 1b and 9b.

[128] Ho Hsiu, *Ch'un-ch'iu Kung-yang chieh-ku* (Shih-san ching chu-shu ed.), 1: 1a–b, quoting *Hsiao-ching kou-ming chüeh*.

the *Book of Filial Piety*; as a matter of fact, he implicitly banished the doctrine of filial piety from the utopian world of *Ta-t'ung* in which all the traditional human relationships lost their original significance.

Despite K'ang's declaration that Tung Chung-shu alone held the key to Confucian truths,[129] he did not accept every one of his ideas, but made a selective use of them, as he did with those of other Kung-yang scholars. His treatment of the Kung-yang doctrines was sometimes so cavalier that he was more than once charged with profaning the Kung-yang tradition. Chu I-hsin, a Confucian scholar in K'ang's high esteem and in frequent intellectual contact with him, observed that in K'ang's attempt to counteract Neo-Confucianism with the philosophy of Tung Chung-shu, he said things that Tung himself would not have dared say.[130] Yeh Te-hui, an archenemy of K'ang, remarked that in using the doctrines of the Kung-yang school to advance his private aims K'ang would have caused "scholars of Western Han to weep."[131] K'ang was indeed interested in the Kung-yang school not purely as a scholarly tradition but rather as a school of thought pregnant with social and political meaning. Its greatest value, he thought, lay in the "esoteric dicta and great dogmas" that had immediate bearing on the practical affairs of society and that, as he said in 1894, had the power "to dispel the smog of ignorance and deliver men from moral degeneration.[132] Liang Ch'i-ch'ao claimed that K'ang was the first to use Kung-yang doctrines to serve the cause of reform.[133] Liang may have overstated the case but he made it clear that K'ang was not at all concerned with purely academic studies of Kung-yang.

However, it should be noted that the Kung-yang tradition easily lent itself to K'ang's freehand treatment. In the first place, ever since the inception of their school, Kung-yang scholars had been inclined to interpret Confucius' teaching in the light of practical politics. Tung Chung-shu, for whom K'ang had the greatest admiration, is an outstanding example. When the dangers of autocratic rule began to show themselves, Tung undertook to interpret the Kung-yang doctrines in such a way that they might temper the authority of the emperor.[134]

[129] K'ang, *Ch'un-ch'iu Tung-shih hsüeh, chüan* 2, p. 2a.

[130] Chu I-hsin, "Ta K'ang Yu-wei ti-i shu," in Su, *I-chiao ts'ung-pien, chüan* 1, pp. 1a–b.

[131] Yeh Te-hui, "*Yu-hsüan chin-yü* p'ing," in Su, *I-chiao ts'ung-pien, chüan* 4, p. 3b.

[132] K'ang, "Chi Chu Ting-fu shih-yü wen," *Wen-ch'ao*, vol. 4, "Chi-wen:" 1a–b.

[133] Liang, *Ch'ing-tai hsüeh-shu kai-lun*, p. 130.

[134] Hsiao, *Chung-kuo . . . ssu-hsiang shih*, pp. 296–97. Ch'ien Mu dwells on the political implications of the Kung-yang tradition in his article, "K'ung-tzu yu *Ch'un-ch'iu*."

His ideas were used by later scholars also, and even for opposite purposes; in the hands of men like Ho Hsiu they strengthened rather than weakened the authority of the emperor.[135] With the revival of the Kung-yang school in Ch'ing times scholars such as K'ung Kuang-sen (1752–86) pursued for a while their studies of the *Annals* more or less with the academic detachment that characterized the "Han learning" of the eighteenth century.[136] But other members of the school, notably Chuang Ts'un-yü (1719–88), Liu Feng-lu (1776–1829), Wei Yüan, and Kung Tzu-chen, again turned their attention to political problems.[137] If, as Chu I-hsin and Yeh Te-hui implied, it was an offense to use Kung-yang doctrines to meet practical political problems, K'ang Yu-wei was not the first man to commit it, and the criticism of Chu and Yeh is valid only if the character of the Kung-yang tradition is ignored. K'ang indeed said things that Tung Chung-shu never said. But this was because he lived at a different time and was confronted with different political problems. It is conceivable that had Tung Chung-shu or Ho Hsiu lived in the nineteenth century they would have had no objection to presenting Confucius as a reformer and using the doctrine of the Three Ages to justify institutional reform.

A second characteristic of the Kung-yang school that may have inspired K'ang was the tendency to minimize the importance of historical accuracy in scholarly pursuits. It was said that in writing the *Spring and Autumn Annals* Confucius attached importance not to the recording of events (*shih*) but to the enunciation of principles (*i*).[138] K'ang cited

---

[135] Hsiao, *Chung-kuo . . . ssu-hsiang shih*, pp. 300–307.

[136] Liang, *Ch'ing-tai hsüeh-shu kai-lun*, p. 121. For K'ung Kuang-sen's views, see his *Ch'un-ch'iu Kung-yang t'ung-i*, *Huang-Ch'ing ching-chieh* edition, especially the preface. K'o Shao-min, "Ju-lin chuan 2," *Ch'ing-shih kao, chüan* 115: 25a–26a, gives a biographical sketch.

[137] Chuang Ts'un-yü, *Ch'un-ch'iu cheng-chieh, chüan* 375–87. Liang, *Ch'ing-tai hsüeh-shu kai-lun*, p. 121, regards Chuang as "the great pioneer" of New Text learning in Ch'ing times. Liu Feng-lu, *Kung-yang Ch'un-ch'iu Ho-shih shih-li*, is one of the major works of this school. K'o, *Ch'ing-shih kao, chüan* 116, "Ju-lin chuan 3," pp. 16b–18a, contains a biographical sketch. Ch'ien, *Chung-kuo . . . hsüeh-shu shih*, pp. 526–28, estimates Liu's position in the Kung-yang school. Wei Yuan, *Kung-yang ku-wei*, 10 *chüan; Ch'un-ch'iu fan-lu chu*, 12 *chüan; Shih ku-wei*, 14 *chüan*; and *Shu ku-wei*, 12 *chüan* are available in *Huang-Ch'ing ching-chieh hsü-pien*. Li Tz'u-ming, *Hsün-hsüeh-chai jih-chi, erh-chi hsia*, p. 67b, condemns Wei's views. Cf. Ch'ien, *Chung-kuo . . . hsüeh-shu shih*, pp. 529–32. Kung Tzu-chen, *Ting-an wen-chi, hsü-chi*, and *wen-chi pu* are available in *Ssu-pu ts'ung-kan*. For brief accounts of Kung's views, see Liang, *Ch'ing-tai hsüeh-shu kai-lun*, p. 122; Chu Chieh-ch'in, *Kung Ting-an yen-chiu*; and Hou Wai-lu, *Chin-tai Chung-kuo ssu-hsiang hsüeh-shou shih*, vol. 2, chap. 12.

[138] See, e.g., Liu Feng-lu, *Kung-yang Ch'un-ch'iu, chüan* 6, p. 10a, and Ch'en Li (1809–69), *Kung-yang i-shu, chüan* 1, p. 9b. However, cf. Kung Tzu-chen, *Hsü-chi, chüan* 2, pp. 54–56.

this accommodating theory repeatedly in his writings on the *Annals*,[139] obviously because he perceived that it opened wide the door to free interpretation of the Confucian teaching, regardless of known history or established tradition. The theory was rendered even more elastic by the Kung-yang doctrine that the teachings of Confucius were not all given in writing in the form of "classics" but that many of them were transmitted orally from teacher to student and that such "oral teachings" (*k'ou shuo*) constituted the most momentous utterances of the Sage. Understandably, K'ang set much store by these Kung-yang theories. He found no difficulty in maintaining that even the written word in the *Spring and Autumn Annals* and the *Kung-yang Commentary* did not convey the whole Confucian truth. Tung Chung-shu achieved eminence precisely because he went beyond the *Annals* and the *Commentary* and made clear the unwritten teachings of Confucius. Unfortunately, scholars of the past two thousand years had limited their studies to the written classics; this, K'ang said, was as foolish as "to go south by following a northward track."[140] The written word was of course not worthless. But it was no more useful than a tangible symbol whose significance could be comprehended only in the light of the oral teaching.[141] Chu Hsi, K'ang added, complained that the *Annals* was beyond his understanding. This was so simply because Chu failed to inquire into the unwritten doctrines of Confucius, in particular, the doctrine of "institutional reform" (*kai chih*). He failed to see that the Sage's dicta required no attestation, and were uttered simply as truth.[142]

In K'ang's way of thinking, then, objectivity was hardly an intellectual virtue and the study of history possessed no intrinsic value as a scholarly pursuit. The "Han learning," which he summarily dismissed as "confused and encumbered with trifling details," thus proved to be totally incompatible with his intellectual position. For K'ang, as a follower of the Kung-yang tradition, was convinced that it was altogether immaterial whether or not a particular recorded event had actually transpired and whether or not it had been accurately recorded; for "historical" records had significance only in so far as they illustrated "the principles" that Confucius had formulated. Myths and legends, in so far as they served the same purpose, possessed no less significance

---

[139] E.g., K'ang, *Ch'un-ch'iu Tung-shih hsüeh*, *chüan* 1, pp. 2a–b and *chüan* 2, pp. 3a–b.

[140] Ibid., *chüan* 4, pp. 1a–b, and "Ch'un-ch'iu pi-hsüeh ta-i wei-yen fa-fan" (*Wen-ch'ao*, 5: 5b–6b and *Wen-chi*, *chüan* 5, pp. 18a–b).

[141] K'ang, *Ch'un-ch'iu Tung-shih hsüeh*, *chüan* 2, p. 12a, comments on "kuei-ming kuei-shih." See Liang, *Ch'ing-tai hsüeh-shu kai-lun*, pp. 129–30.

[142] K'ang, *Ch'un-ch'iu Tung-shih hsüeh*, *chüan* 5, "Pien-yen," pp. 1a–b.

than authentic historical facts. Commenting on a passage in Tung Chung-shu's work in the *Annals*, in which reference was made to the "Nine Emperors," K'ang wrote that Confucius spoke not only of the "Nine Emperors" but of a great many more—in fact, of over one hundred seventy—who came before the celebrated "Five Emperors" mentioned by Chinese historians. The number of emperors really did not matter, K'ang explained, for Confucius' intention was to make clear the principle that "High Heaven helps the virtuous and Heaven's Mandate does not dwell perpetually" with any single regime, and not to give an accurate account of China's hoary past. The Sage's intellectual range was so catholic, K'ang concluded, that what he envisaged was necessarily beyond the ken of "ignorant scholars."[143]

Naturally K'ang's scholarly license drew sharp criticism from his opponents.[144] But though his speculations inspired by the Kung-yang tradition lack historical support and do not bear logical analysis,[145] they played an important role in shaping his iconoclastic social philosophy.

The Kung-yang tradition contributed to K'ang's thought in other ways also. Two of the major Kung-yang doctrines stand out prominently. One is the claim that Confucius was the originator of all the authentic classics and all the "great teachings" and that he was not the "transmitter' of a previously existing tradition. The other is the doctrine of the Three Ages (*san shih*), that the course of human history is a steady progress from the Age of Disorder (*chü-luan shih*), through the Age of Approaching Peace (*sheng-p'ing shih*) to the Age of Universal Peace (*t'ai-p'ing shih*), and that human institutions and human sentiments improve *pari passu*, so that in the final stage "all under heaven" will live together in complete unity and harmony, leaving behind the strife and discrimination of the earlier stages.[146] The doctrine of the

---

[143] Ibid., *chüan* 5, pp. 12b–13a, comment on "Chiu-huang wu-ti." K'ang did not maintain this view consistently; in a short piece, "Min-kung p'ien," probably written in his early years, he treated the legendary rulers, from P'ao-hsi down, as historic figures.

[144] In particular, Yeh Te-hui. See his "Yü Shih Tsui-liu shu," and "Yü Tuan Po-yu mou-ts'ai shu."

[145] Hsiao Kung-ch'üan, review of Woo Kang's *Les trois théories politiques du Tch'ouen Ts'ieou interprétées par Tong Tchong-chou d'après les principes de l'école de Kong-yang*, pp. 1–6.

[146] For statements of the doctrine of the Three Ages, see Ho, *Ch'un-ch'iu Kung-yang chieh-ku*, Yin-kung 1st year, 12th month, comments on "so-chien i tz'u" etc.; Tung Chung-shu, "Ch'u Chuang-wang," *Ch'un-ch'iu fan-lu, chüan* 1, passage beginning with the sentence, "Ch'un-ch'iu fen shih-erh shih i-wei san teng"; K'ung Kuang-sen,

"Three Systems" (*san t'ung*) was also of some importance. According to this doctrine, there were three institutional patterns, the "Red," "White," and "Black," each of which rested on a different principle and each of which was suitable for a given regime. A different system of institutions was adopted by a new dynasty to replace that of the defunct one, so that no single system remained in perpetual use.[147] K'ang dwelled repeatedly upon these doctrines and seldom failed to bring them into direct rapport with his ideas of reform.[148] It can hardly be doubted that he owed much to the Kung-yang interpretations of the *Annals* that he began to study in earnest late in the 1880s.

Interpretations of Other Classics

The other classics that K'ang accepted as genuine and dealt with at length, unlike the *Annals*, were not to him a source of philosophical ideas but served him in a different way. His exegeses on these were done in the years when his intellectual position had been definitely fixed and his philosophy of reform clearly delineated, and instead of deriving inspiration from them he projected his view into them and brought them into alignment with the *Annals*.

K'ang produced five works on the classics in 1901–2: *The* Li-yün *Annotated*, 1901–2; *The* Chung-yung *Annotated*, 1901; *The Esoteric Meanings of* the Mencius, 1901; *The* Ta-hsüeh *Annotated*, 1902; and *The* Lun-yü *Annotated*, 1902. Another work, *Ch'un-ch'iu pi-hsüeh ta-i wei-yen k'ao*, was rewritten from an incomplete manuscript of his pre-reform days, and as it belonged partly to the earlier period it does not particularly concern us here.

The five books written in 1901–2 were evidently the result of K'ang's endeavor to reconstruct Confucianism in the light of his studies in the classics, Buddhist literature, and Western books, and of his experiences as a practical reformer and political refugee in foreign lands. Taken together, they represent a transitional phase of his intellectual development—a stage between reinterpretation of Confucianism on the basis of Kung-yang doctrines and construction of his own philosophy without specific reference to Confucian teaching. They reflect his

Ch'un-ch'iu Kung-yang t'ung-i, chüan 11, p. 12a; Liu, "Chang san-shih li," *Kung-yang Ch'un-ch'iu, chüan* 1, pp. 1a–b, comment on the same passage; and ibid., pp. 4a–b; Kung Tzu-chen, "Wu Ching ta-i chung-shih wen-ta," *Hsü-chi, chüan* 2, pp. 61–62.

147 Tung Chung-shu, "San-tai kai-chih chih-wen," in *Ch'un-ch'iu fan-lu, chüan* 7.

148 K'ang, *Ch'un-ch'iu Tung-shih hsüeh, chüan* 2, p. 4a; *chüan* 3, 6b; *chüan* 5, pp. 3a–b, 10b–11a, 12a–b. K'ang reiterated these doctrines in 1924 in a letter, "Ta P'u chün ta-t'i-hsüeh lun K'ung-hsüeh," microfilm, reel 1.

thinking at the juncture when he was emerging rapidly from "the Martin Luther of the Confucian school" into "the Sage of Nan-hai," a full-fledged social philosopher. A brief survey of their contents will be of some interest.

The *Li-yün chu* (*The* Li-yün *Annotated*), which K'ang claimed to have written in 1884, but which was actually done in 1901–2, is perhaps the most important of his postreform writings on the classics. In this relatively short book he brought into formal rapport the doctrines of *Ta-t'ung* and *Hsiao-k'ang* (which he took from the "Li-yün") with the theory of the Three Ages (which he took from the Kung-yang *Annals*).[149] Prior to this he had made little more than occasional and casual reference to *Ta-t'ung*, but now he treated it as the cornerstone of his social thought.

An examination of this book reveals that K'ang had modified some of his earlier views on Confucians and Confucianism. One of the most significant of those modifications is his judgment of Hsün-tzu and Chu Hsi. In his earlier works he had been inclined to be generous in his appraisal of these two and to blame only Liu Hsin for falsifying the teaching of Confucius and preventing China from attaining the highest possible social development. Now he laid the blame equally on all three. The *tao* of Confucius, K'ang asserted, was "first corrupted by the bigoted meanness of Hsün-tzu's philosophy, later confused further by Liu Hsin's forgeries and falsehoods, then finally damaged by Chu Hsi's onesidedness." As a result, China was denied the benefits of that *tao* and condemned to remain in the comparatively unattractive stage of "Minor Peace."[150] He continued:

> K'ang Yu-wei . . . formally declares: In the two thousand years of our China, all the dynasties, including Han, T'ang, Sung, and Ming, irrespective of the circumstances—whether order or chaos prevailed, whether a regime was rising or declining—constituted altogether the Age of Minor Peace; in the two thousand years of China, all the utterances of Confucian scholars, including the sayings of Hsün Ch'ing, Liu Hsin, and Chu Hsi, irrespective of their quality—whether these were true or false, refined or crude, good or bad—constituted altogether the way of Minor Peace.[151]

It may be recalled that in his earlier writings on the *Annals* K'ang had given equal attention to "Approaching Peace" (the equivalent of *hsiao-k'ang*) and "Universal Peace" (the equivalent of *ta-t'ung*), and had

---

[149] K'ang, *Li-yün chu*, passim.
[150] Ibid., preface, p. 1a; "Li-yün chu hsü" (*Wen-ch'ao*, 8: 1a).
[151] Ibid., p. 2b.

not spoken disparagingly of Approaching Peace, since he treated it as a legitimate stage of social progress. But now he devoted his attention to Great Unity and regretted China's stagnation at the stage of Minor Peace. This was made particularly clear in his author's preface to a work on the *Annals*, which had been begun many years before but was completed at the same time as *The* Li-yün *Annotated*:

> In Han times every family practiced the Confucian teaching. . . . If the practice had been continued, by Sui and T'ang times China should have progressed to the Age of Approaching Peace. That was a thousand years before the present time when China should be the first on earth to achieve Universal Peace. Unfortunately, in Ch'in and Han times . . . the doctrines transmitted by Lao-tzu and Han Fei . . . which exalted the ruler and degraded the subjects, prevailed in successive dynasties, thanks to which rulers were enabled . . . to keep the people in ignorance and control them; . . . and in the time of Wang Mang's Hsin regime Liu Hsin forged spurious classics . . . to attack the Kung-yang and Ku-liang schools [of true Confucian learning]. . . . Consequently, the theory of the Three Ages no longer was recited by men and the seed of Universal Peace perished irrevocably in China. . . . In darkness for two thousand years, [the emperors] clung firmly to the institutions of the Age of Disorder to rule the empire, . . . causing China, which was the first to develop culture on earth . . . to shun progress and stagnate, and to be jeered as an uncivilized nation. Is not this a pity?[152]

Despite an obvious discrepancy in the two passages quoted above, that in one K'ang regarded the period from Han to Ch'ing as the Age of Disorder, whereas in the other he regarded it as the Age of Minor Peace, the point made was identical: that China was deprived of the opportunity of attaining Universal Peace and Great Community because the true teaching of Confucius was eclipsed by false doctrines and faulty institutions. K'ang made it clear that these doctrines and institutions were none other than those that made the autocratic imperial system what it was and that were diametrically opposed to the ideals and practices characterizing the world of *Ta-t'ung*. K'ang's change of opinion concerning Hsün-tzu and Chu Hsi then was evidently a result of his change of attitude toward the imperial system. In the 1890s, when he was actively engaged in reform, he had maintained a more or less conciliatory attitude toward the existing political order; allegations of his enemies to the contrary, he had had no intention of bringing in a new system but had sought to effect reforms, institutional and

---

[152] "Ch'un-ch'iu pi-hsüeh ta-i wei-yen k'ao fa-fan" (*Wen-ch'ao*, 5: 1a–2a, and *Wen-chi, chüan* 5, pp. 11a–12a).

otherwise, within the framework of the imperial structure. He had emphasized the necessity of making progress step by step and the folly of attempting to reach the stage of Universal Peace without going through Approaching Peace (Minor Peace). But the frustrating experiences of 1898 had persuaded him that the imperial system could not be made to serve the cause of reform. Now in 1902 as a social philosopher he spoke out against that system with all its ideological and institutional ramifications.

The social ideal that K'ang formulated in *The* Li-yün *Annotated* was the very antithesis of imperial autocracy.

> The teaching of Confucius has its roots in love (*jen*), its indwelling principle in the concept of commonwealth (*kung*), its operational principle in equality (*p'ing*), its institutional ideal in civilization (*wen*), its essence in clear definition of individual rights and duties (*ming fen*), and its application in progress with time.[153]

In more concrete terms:

> To constitute all under heaven into a commonwealth is simply to base everything on common reason [of mankind]. "Commonness" means "each and every man is treated in one and the same way." There is no distinction of noble and lowly, no racial and sex distinctions. . . . All men are supported and educated by common property and no one depends on private property.[154]

Thus K'ang denied the validity of social gradation, the family, and property, the foundation stones upon which the imperial system rested. In other words he denied the validity of the "Confucian state" that had existed in China for two thousand years and that he himself had previously recognized.

K'ang's treatment of the other four classics was similar, that is, he interpreted the texts according to what he considered the true teaching of Confucius and thus used them as a medium of expressing his own views. There was, however, a difference. The contents of these classics were difficult to align with the *Annals* and the "Li-yün," and K'ang's interpretation of them often had to be stretched. Probably he chose to reinterpret these recalcitrant texts because he felt that his arguments would be more impressive and convincing if he did not limit them to one or two items of Confucian literature. Consequently, though in

---

[153] Ibid. (*Wen-ch'ao*, 5: 1a, and *Wen-chi, chüan* 5, p. 11a).
[154] K'ang, *Li-yün chu*, p. 4b.

earlier years he had regarded the *Annals* as the chief repository of Confucian truths, now he acknowledged that the "true teaching" was to be found in the other classics as well. Thus the *Great Learning*, he now said, was a "precious book of the Confucian school," which served as vehicle of Confucius' "esoteric and great dogmas."[155] He credited the *Doctrine of the Mean* with giving "the most excellent expression to the teaching of Confucius."[156] He praised the *Analects* for containing "extremely fine and profound exposition" of the doctrine of *Ta-t'ung.*"[157] And he valued the *Mencius* because it pointed to "the shortest way to Confucius."[158]

A few instances may be cited to illustrate K'ang's approach. In *The Chung-yung Annotated* he wrote the following comment on a passage to the effect that "the superior man maintains the timely mean":

> The *tao* of Confucius comprises the doctrines of the Three Systems and the Three Ages. It changes with the times. The superior man should therefore consider making appropriate changes to accommodate the time in which he lives, so that his laws and institutions may operate usefully.... Whatever he does that fits the requirements of the time constitutes the mean for that particular time. Hence it is referred to as "the timely mean" (*shih chung*).[159]

Here, it may be noted, K'ang followed faithfully Chu Hsi's interpretation of the phrase "timely mean," obviously because it was in accord with his own thesis that Confucius was a prophet of reform.

More often, however, K'ang departed from the traditional interpretations and construed the text to suit his purposes. The *Doctrine of the Mean* contains another passage that reads: "He who attains the sovereignty of the empire has three weighty matters" (*san chung*, the character *chung* pronounced *ch'ü sheng*, 4th tone). Chu Hsi, accepting the view of another Sung scholar, identified "the three weighty matters" as "to order the ceremonies, to fix the measures, and to determine the written characters."[160] K'ang ignored this interpretation and took *chung* as "recurrence" or "rotation" (*ch'ung* pronounced *yang-p'ing sheng*

---

[155] K'ang, "*Ta-hsüeh chu* hsü" (*Wen-ch'ao*, 5: 8b–9a, and *Wen-chi, chüan* 5, p. 21a).

[156] K'ang, "*Chung-yung chu* hsü" (*Wen-ch'ao*, 5: 9a–10a, and *Wen-chi, chüan* 5, pp. 21a–22a).

[157] K'ang, "*Lun-yü chu* hsü" (*Wen-ch'ao*, 5: 10a–11b, and *Wen-chi, chüan* 5, pp. 19a–20b). In his *Ch'ang-hsing hsüeh-chi*, p. 6, K'ang expressed a somewhat different view.

[158] K'ang, "*Meng-tzu wei* hsü" (*Wen-ch'ao*, 8: 1a–2a).

[159] K'ang, *Chung-yung chu*, p. 3b.

[160] Ibid., pp. 60a–b. The passage concerned is in the "Doctrine of the Mean," chap. 19 (Legge translation).

2nd tone) thus treating the phrase *san ch'ung* as virtually synonymous with *san t'ung*, the three institutional systems as envisioned by the Kung-yang school.

Sometimes when K'ang found it difficult to stretch a passage to meet his requirements he simply denied its authenticity—an expedient to which he often resorted in dealing with the Old Text classics. *The* Lun-yü *Annotated* affords many instances of such procedure.[161] On the opening passage of Book VII of the *Analects*, for example: "The Master said, 'A transmitter and not a maker, believing in and loving the ancients, I venture to compare myself with our old P'ang (P'eng),' " K'ang commented:

> This is an interpolation, taken from the spurious Old Text. Even if it is not wholly an interpolation, it probably resulted from an alteration made by Liu Hsin on the original text in which Confucius mentioned old P'eng as "not a maker" and "loving the ancients." The character *ch'ieh* ("venture" [to]) may have originally been *pu* ([do] "not").[162]

K'ang then went on to say that according to the *Ch'un-ch'iu wei*, one of the "apocrypha" of the Kung-yang school, Confucius formulated new laws and devised new institutions for all ages to come and thus assumed the role of *hsin-wang chiao-chu* ("new king and founder of religion"). The Sage, K'ang asserted, could never have regarded himself as "a transmitter."

Thus by interpreting (or misinterpreting) suitable passages of these classics K'ang brought them into conformity with the doctrines of the Kung-yang school. One encounters here K'ang's most extensive efforts to reconstruct Confucianism and, it may be said, his final contribution to Confucian thought. In the next phase of his intellectual career he was to devote himself not to the interpretation of Confucian doctrines as such but to formulating his own philosophy. The more important ideas that he projected into the Confucian classics and that he incorporated, in modified or more elaborate forms, into his own phi-

---

[161] It may be noted that K'ang did not regard the *Analects* as a complete or necessarily truthful record of Confucius' dicta (see note 155, above).

[162] K'ang, *Lun-yü, chüan* 7, p. 1b. Ibid., *chüan* 8, p. 7b, affords another instance. Commenting on a passage in the *Analects*, VIII.9 ("The Master said, 'The people may be made to follow a path of action, but they may not be made to understand it.' "), K'ang remarked: "The *Lun-yü* and Six Classics contain many interpolations from the Old Text . . . [This passage] probably was forged and interpolated by Liu Hsin with a view to discrediting Confucius. It should be expunged and transferred to the Old Text."

losophical writings may be conveniently treated under four headings: (1) progress, (2) political institutions, (3) human relationships, and (4) economic life.

1. K'ang's idea of progress is well known. "The course of humanity," he wrote in *The* Li-yün *Annotated,* "progresses invariably in a fixed sequence: from Disorder to Approaching Peace and from Approaching Peace to Universal Peace."[163] Instead of regarding the Three Ages as simple units of time, however, as he had done previously in common with other Kung-yang scholars, he conceived of them as composite units, each of which was infinitely divisible into ever smaller units. The precise meaning of the following statement is not readily ascertainable, although it may be supposed to suggest the idea of endless progress:

> Each age (*shih*) may be divided into three ages so that the Three Ages become nine ages, nine ages multiply themselves into eighty-one, and eighty-one ages into one thousand and myriad ages—into countless ages. . . . There are, therefore, ages of Approaching Peace and Universal Peace in each Age of Disorder, and ages of Disorder and Approaching Peace in each Age of Universal Peace.[164]

2. K'ang's views concerning political institutions deserve close scrutiny. Each of the Three Ages, he argued, had its appropriate political system. Thus absolute monarchy was suitable for the Age of Disorder, constitutional monarchy for Approaching Peace, and republican government for Universal Peace. As mankind advanced from a lower stage of social development to a higher one, the form of government had to be changed accordingly. Commenting on a passage in the *Analects* in which Confucius said that "when good government prevails in the empire," the ruler holds the supreme power, the officials do not control the administration, and the people do not discuss or deliberate affairs of state.[165] K'ang contended that the character *pu* ("not"), which occurs more than once in the passage, was extraneous, "wrongly inserted" by persons who did not understand the meaning of what Confucius said, and should therefore be deleted. Having thus altered the text he said:

> A unified autocratic monarchy seldom endures one hundred generations. For when Disorder is succeeded by Approaching Peace, monarchy in all probability is replaced by the people's rule (*min-chu*). . . . "Government

---

[163] Ibid., *chüan* 2, p. 10; translated in Fung, *History of Chinese Philosophy,* 2: 680–81.
[164] K'ang, *Lun-yü chu, chüan* 2, p. 11a.
[165] Ibid., *chüan* 16, p. 2b.

in the hands of the great officials" [to which Confucius referred] is the same as constitutional monarchy. . . . [In such a system] the sovereign shoulders no administrative responsibility; the great officials conduct the administration. In the age of the Great Community (*ta-t'ung*), when all under heaven becomes a commonwealth, government affairs are decided through public discussion by the people. This is the system that obtains in the Age of Universal Peace, the acme of good government.[166]

K'ang's interpretation is obviously arbitrary, but it reveals his theory of government, which with slight modification was the essential of his political philosophy as formulated in the *Ta-t'ung shu*.

K'ang rated absolute monarchy as the lowest form of government, suitable only for a very low degree of civilization. It was justifiable only when a people remained "uncivilized." This was made clear in his comment on a passage in the *Analects*, in which Confucius said that "the barbarian tribes (*i-ti*) have their sovereigns and are not like the Chinese states, which are without them":[167]

This explains the principle of development from monarchism to republicanism. . . . What Confucius referred to as "barbarian" and "Chinese" are none other than what today we speak of as "uncivilized" and "civilized." The organization of an uncivilized people is unduly loose; it is proper to institute an absolute monarchy in order to unite the people. [This form of government] is suitable for the Age of Disorder. In a civilized age the rights of men are clearly recognized and all peoples are governed by a system of laws that are universally valid and universally applied (*kung-fa*). Government by the people through public deliberation alone exists; there is no longer any monarchical rule.[168]

To add force to his theory of government K'ang ventured into an unconventional interpretation of China's ancient history. Absolute monarchy, he asserted, did not exist in pre-Ch'in China. The government of the emperor Shun (legendary, 2255–2205 B.C.) was in essence a republic.[169] China was "civilized," then, even in antiquity. Moreover, China, which had been blessed with the teaching of Confucius since the sixth century before Christ, could not be regarded as "uncivilized." And yet the Chinese people had been ruled autocratically for two thousand years. The conclusion is obvious: the imperial system, in substance and theory an absolute monarchy, was not a form of government suitable for China.

[166] Ibid., pp. 3b–4a.
[167] *Analects*, III.5.
[168] K'ang, *Lun-yü chu, chüan* 3, p. 4a.
[169] Ibid., *chüan* 15, p. 3a.

However, K'ang did not argue that China should overthrow the monarchy immediately. Despite its theoretical excellence the republican form of government did not fit the China of the nineteenth century. "The people's rule" (*min-chu*) belonged properly to the Age of Universal Peace or the world of the Great Community—a stage of development that mankind was to attain in the future. Taking practical circumstances into consideration, constitutional monarchy (*chün-chu li-hsien*) was the only political form that China should and could adopt. Mencius, K'ang believed, delineated this form of government clearly when he said that the ruler of a state should consult the opinions of all important persons and the people.[170] What Mencius envisaged was "an excellent system suitable for the Age of Approaching Peace," which as a matter of fact had already been adopted by a number of modern states.[171] Republicanism, of course, was not a pipe dream. It was already partially realized in such countries as the United States of America and France. Commenting on Mencius' dictum, "The People are the most important element in a nation,"[172] K'ang said:

> This is Mencius' institution of the people's rule, a system for the Age of Universal Peace. . . . One who has the confidence of the people is elected the ruler of the people (*min chu*), such as the president of America or France. . . . This comes close to the world of the Great Community.[173]

Social development should be neither retarded nor unduly hastened. It was just as disastrous to try to jump from the Age of Disorder to Universal Peace as to cling to an outmoded political system when the time had come for a state to advance from Disorder to Approaching Peace. Applying this principle to China, K'ang concluded that the time had indeed come for giving the people a voice in government, for transforming the absolute monarchy that was the traditional imperial system, into a constitutional monarchy. His words deserve quoting:

> The present . . . is the Age of Approaching Peace. It is therefore necessary to disseminate the doctrines of self-rule and independence, and to strive after the actualities of parliamentary and constitutional rule. For if institutions are not reformed, great disorder will result.[174]

[170] *Mencius*, I.ii.7.3.
[171] K'ang, "Tsung-lun," *Meng-tzu wei* (*Wen-ch'ao*, 8: 10a).
[172] *Mencius*, VII.ii.14.
[173] K'ang, *Lun-yü chu*, p. 10b.
[174] K'ang, *Chung-yung chu*, p. 36; translated in Fung, *History of Chinese Philosophy*, 2: 683.

This was written in 1901, when K'ang was convinced that the autocratic imperial system had no place in the modern world, as the tragedy of the Boxer uprising had clearly demonstrated. The idea of modernizing China through the adoption of constitutional government, however, was not the outcome of temporizing; it constituted an abiding element of K'ang's political thinking.

3. Sometimes K'ang used the classics to convey his views of human values and relationships. Significantly, these views are often closer than his views on political institutions to the accepted Confucian tradition.

In line with his rejection of autocracy, K'ang revised the traditional notion of political loyalty (*chung*), the duty of subjects to remain absolutely and perpetually faithful to their sovereign, irrespective of circumstances. Commenting lengthily on a passage in the *Analects* to the effect that Wei-tzu withdrew from the court of Yin, Chi-tzu became a slave, and Pi-kan remonstrated with the tyrannical emperor Chou and died,[175] K'ang observed:

The conduct of these three men differed but they were all motivated by their sincere and compassionate desire to deliver the people from disorder . . . Confucius therefore allowed that they all possessed virtue.

Wei-tzu went to [the state of] Chou as a welcome refugee and Chi-tzu presented the "Great Plan" to King Wu [who put an end to the Yin dynasty]. From the viewpoint of later times, both were disloyal [to their former sovereign]. But Confucius praised them together with Pi-kan and did not insist that they should die for the sake of their sovereign [as Pi-kan did]. For, according to Confucius, the sole purpose of instituting rulers and ministers was to administer to the people. [As it was said in the *Tso Commentary*,] "If the ruler dies for the sake of the country, then the minister should die for his sake; and if he flees the country for the sake of the people, then they should flee with him. If, however, the ruler departs from the correct path and dies or flees, then who dare to share his responsibilities except those who are his favorites or cronies?"

Scholars of Sung times failed to comprehend this principle. It appeared to them that the people of the entire empire should perish upon the undoing of an individual ruler. That was not the teaching of Confucius.[176]

K'ang's conception of loyalty, it may be noted, agreed actually with

---

[175] *Analects*, XVIII.1.

[176] K'ang, *Lun-yü chu, chüan* 18, pp. 1a–b. The passage, "If the ruler dies," etc., was quoted by K'ang, with slight modifications, from *Tso-chuan*, Hsiang-kung 25th year, "Ch'un, Ch'i Ts'ui Chu shih ch'i chün Kuang."

the view of Confucius.[177] K'ang's conception of freedom (*tzu-yu*) betrayed the influence of Western thought, but he did not allow it to
displace the Confucian idea of social duty. This is most clearly seen in
his interpretation of the following passage: "Tzu-kung said, 'What I
do not wish men to do to me, I also wish not to do to men.' The Master
said, 'Tz'u, you have not attained to that.' "[178] These are K'ang's
words:

> Tzu-kung did not wish men to do to him [what he did not wish to do to
> men; that was to maintain his] independence and freedom. He wished to
> refrain doing [the same] to men; [that was] not to infringe upon men's
> independence and freedom.
>
> All men are born of Heaven and all belong to Heaven; each and every
> one possesses independence and freedom. . . . Each man has his sphere.
> If one infringes upon another's sphere, he suppresses the other's independ-
> ence and freedom. Such action violates the universal principle as laid
> down by Heaven and is especially condemnable.
>
> Tzu-kung, having heard the doctrine that independence and freedom
> constituted the way of Heaven, wished to see that doctrine prevail in the
> empire. Confucius, however, thought that it was premature to practice it
> in the Age of Disorder in which they lived. The doctrine was sublime but
> the world was not prepared for it. . . . It could be applied only when the
> world had advanced to the Ages of Approaching Peace and Universal
> Peace.[179]

Thus, as a Confucian scholar, K'ang was not ready to relieve man
of his obligations toward his fellow beings and to give him untrammeled
individual liberty. K'ang stated emphatically that according to the
teaching of Confucius all morality and social relationships sprang from
the very nature of man.[180] Such relationships were as unavoidable as
they were indispensable. He explained:

> As soon as a man is born, he has parents who beget other sons, and thus
> he has brothers. When he enters public service, he becomes minister to
> his sovereign. When he associates with other men, he has friends. No man
> can get away from these relations.

[177] See Hsiao, *Chung-kuo . . . ssu-hsiang shih*, p. 66, for a brief statement of Confucius'
view. K'ang's view also was similar to that of Mencius on this point (see ibid., p. 91),
and came quite close to Huang Tsung-hsi's (1610–95) position as indicated in his
Ming-i tai-fang lu, "Yüan chün," and "Yüan ch'en." Kung, *Hsü-chi, chüan* 2, "Ku-
shih kou-ch'en lun"; "Ching-shih yüeh-chi shuo"; and "Chuan ssu-teng shih-i," implicitly criticized autocratic government and thus anticipated K'ang's sentiments.
[178] *Analects*, V.11.
[179] K'ang, *Lun-yü chu, chüan* 5, pp. 4b–5a.
[180] *Chung-yung chu*, pp. 8b–9a.

The proper way to live together with one's relations, K'ang added, was to respect their feelings, rights, and interests:

> The superior man, therefore, lays responsibilities upon himself and not upon others. He performs first the duties that devolve upon him as a son, a younger brother, a friend.

At the same time, those who are fathers, sovereigns, and elder brothers should also perform those duties that properly belong to their respective positions.[181] All this was close to the traditional Confucian moral code.

The same may be said of K'ang's views concerning man's relation with Nature. Commenting on the opening passage of the first chapter of the *Doctrine of the Mean*, he wrote:

> Man [as a spiritual being] cannot be created by man but is produced by Heaven. Nature (*hsing*) is the essence of life. Man receives it as an endowment from Heaven to form his spirit soul (*shen-ming*), which is distinct from that which he inherited from his parents to constitute his body and his animal soul (*t'i-p'e*). . . . If each man follows the dictates of his own nature which he receives in common with all men, his conduct will be compatible with that of every other man.[182]

K'ang was not saying that to act in conformity with the universal principle of human nature a man had to renounce the obligations that fell upon him as a result of his specific relations with other men. On the contrary, the full realization of that principle was conditioned by the satisfactory performance of specific social and moral duties toward his family members. K'ang put the matter in the following terms:

> Heaven and Earth are the origin of human life; parents are the origin of personal existence. Speaking from the viewpoint of life's origin, Heaven is our father and Earth our mother, and fellow men our brothers. Therefore Confucius regarded universal love (*jen*) as the constituent principle of life. Speaking from the viewpoint of personal existence, parents are those who beget and raise us, and brothers are consanguineous with us. Therefore Confucius taught that they be served in accordance with the principles of filial piety and brotherly duty.
>
> The teaching of Confucius centers in the principle of universal love but, to put it into practice, one begins with the performance of filial piety and brotherly duty.[183]

[181] *Ibid.*, pp. 10b–11a.
[182] *Ibid.*, p. 1a.
[183] K'ang, *Lun-yü chu, chüan* 1, p. 3a. *Chung-yung chu*, p. 3a, contains a similar statement. Cf. Chang Tsai, "Hsi-ming" (Western Inscription), "*Ch'ien* is called the father and *k'un* the mother . . . . People are my blood brothers" (Fung, *History of Chinese Philosophy*, 2: 493, and Chang, *Development of Neo-Confucian Thought*, pp. 178–79).

Performance of social duties, however, constituted the beginning, not the end of *jen*. Taking a cue from Mencius, K'ang asserted that since love was the "constituent principle of life" man should show affection not only to his kin but also to all his fellow men and, eventually, to all living beings. The scope of man's affection was to be widened progressively as the world advanced from a lower stage of development to a higher one. Thus in the Age of Disorder priority was given to members of one's own family; "in the Age of Universal Peace all will be treated in one and the same way." Man, eventually, would extend his love to all creatures so that he would refrain from slaughtering animals for meat.[184] Racial discrimination would completely disappear; there would no longer be a line of demarcation between "Chinese" and "barbarians." K'ang's comment on a passage in the *Mencius*, in which the emperor Shun and King Wen were identified respectively as "a man of the eastern barbarian tribes" and "a man of the western tribes,"[185] merits quoting:

> Shun was a sage of the Age of Peace under the people's rule and King Wen a sage of the Age of Disorder under monarchical rule . . . . Confucius transmitted [Shun's principles] and exhibited [those of King Wen] to serve as paradigms for later ages. These sages were born among the eastern and western barbarian tribes. They did not have to be born in China [in order to attain their virtue and position].
>
> In later times, there were men such as Washington who, although they were not born in China, deserved the Sage's implicit approval, since their deeds and words were in accord with those of Shun and King Wen.[186]

The reference to Washington shows the influence of Western knowledge that K'ang began eagerly to imbibe in 1879. His cosmopolitan outlook, however, did little violence to the creed of such Confucians as Mencius, Chang Tsai, and Wang Shou-jen.

4. These four classics also served to convey some of K'ang's economic ideas. Confucius' dictum that "when equality (*chün*) prevails, there is no poverty"[187] and Mencius' ideal of land distribution[188] prompted K'ang to make the following remarks:

---

[184] K'ang, "Tsung-lun," *Meng-tzu wei* (*Wen-ch'ao*, 8: 4b–5a).
[185] *Mencius*, VII.ii.1.1–4.
[186] K'ang, "Tsung-lun," *Meng-tzu wei*, p. 7a.
[187] *Analects*, XVI.1.10. Obviously, K'ang's interpretation of this passage differs from that of Legge.
[188] *Mencius*, VII.i.22.2–3.

Equalization precludes poverty; repose produced by contentment precludes social disruption. Men of recent times have strongly advocated that the property of the rich and poor should be equalized. One hundred years from now Confucius' principle of equality will finally be put into practice. This will serve as the basis for the realization of Universal Peace.

However, in the Age of Disorder the population is relatively small and [men's economic activity] centers in agricultural production; in the Age of Approaching Peace the population is relatively large and men engage themselves also in industry and commerce. Consequently, the principle of equalization will be applied not only to agricultural wealth but also to commercial wealth.[189]

This is an excellent illustration of K'ang's way of bringing old Confucian ideas into rapport with modern conceptions. Tacitly accepting the view that China, like all modern societies, was bound to evolve from an agricultural economy into an industrial–commercial one, K'ang was led to conclude that the classical preoccupation with land distribution did not sufficiently take into account the modern economic trend. He therefore extended the concept of "equalization" beyond the agricultural sphere into the realm of industry and commerce. K'ang was here again inspired by Western ideas; he virtually equated the Confucian principle of "equalization" with socialism. These are his words:

The system that obtains in the Age of Universal Peace and Great Community does not go beyond the principle of equalization; for "when equality prevails, there is no poverty." The aim of the socialist parties (*jen-ch'ün hui-tang*) of various countries at present also does not go beyond this principle.[190]

The Western influence may be perceived in another connection also. Contrary to the view prevailing in imperial China, K'ang contended that the primary aim of economic production was to gratify human wants and desires, and that frugality as such did not constitute a virtue. Commenting on a passage in the *Analects*[191] he made this observation:

Wealth is like a spring: it is its very nature to flow and circulate. If premium is placed on thrift, wealth will stagnate and cease to flow. Utensils and implements will remain crude, intelligence and knowledge will be stifled, human life will be wretched and joyless, government buildings

[189] K'ang, "Tsung-lun," *Meng-tzu wei*, p. 9b.
[190] K'ang, *Lun-yü chu, chüan* 16, p. 2b.
[191] *Analects*, III.4.3.

will deteriorate and be out of repair, the people will be shiftless and listless, and the state will wizen and become weak.

Confucius favored refinement (*wen*), not frugality. To favor frugality was the teaching of Mo-tzu. Scholars of later times who read this chapter [of the *Analects*] improperly, mistakenly thought that Confucius disliked luxury and refinement. They therefore abhorred everything that was refined or beautiful. "The virtue of frugality" was honored in history. As a result, Chinese culture remained on the same level as that of the uncivilized.[192]

However, moral values changed with social progress. "The virtue of frugality" should be practiced by autocratic rulers of the Age of Disorder, although it should not be practiced by rulers in more advanced stages of human development. Commenting on another passage in the *Analects*, in which the ancient emperor Yü was extolled by Confucius for his austerity,[193] K'ang admitted that the autocratic ruler who employed conscript labor to serve his own needs should not be extravagant. He continued:

> If, [however,] hired labor was employed and the ruler had instituted constitutional government, then . . . the more he was able to make the palaces sumptuous and the walls elegant, the more he benefited the people and lent prestige to the state. . . . To live in a low, miserable house [as Yü did] was a practice befitting only [a ruler] of the Age of Disorder and should be abandoned in a civilized age.[194]

It may be recalled that K'ang was so impressed by the material splendor of Hong Kong when he visited it for the first time in the winter of 1879 that he began then to take a keen interest in "Western learning." The impact of this experience, reenforced by his later experience in Shanghai, must have influenced his ideas on austerity.[195]

"Refinement" did not mean the mere enjoyment of material goods. It implied the enjoyment of "the finer things of life." Music especially was indispensable to the life of a "superior man." Confucius himself showed great appreciation for music; he played musical instruments and sang whenever occasion required. Commenting on a passage in the *Analects* referring to Confucius' musical activities[196] K'ang stressed the importance of "having enjoyment in life" and condemned the Ch'eng–Chu school of Neo-Confucianism in no uncertain terms:

[192] K'ang, *Lun-yü chu, chüan* 7, pp. 16a–b.
[193] *Analects*, VIII.21.
[194] K'ang, *Lun-yü chu, chüan* 8, p. 14a.
[195] K'ang, *Nien-p'u*, Kuang-hsü 5 and 8 (1879 and 1882); Lo, *K'ang*, pp. 36, 38.
[196] *Analects*, VII.31.

Mo-tzu's repudiation of music is not in accordance with human wish. . . . Scholars of Sung times followed the rules of propriety in an extremely rigorous manner and paid excessive respect to antiquity. They taught that since ancient music had been irreparably lost, it was proper to give up singing altogether. . . . They thus caused singing to become a lost art in China—eliminating a suitable way to maintain healthy human living and thus departing from the Sage's way of having enjoyment in life (*sheng-jen lo-sheng chih tao*). They ostensibly honored Confucius but in reality followed Mo-tzu. . . . This was an error committed by Ch'eng and Chu.[197]

Classical Confucianism lent ample support to K'ang's emphasis on refinement. Confucius himself did not lead an austere life,[198] nor did Mencius shun comfort or elegance as a matter of principle.[199] Hsün-tzu made it clear that the economic policy of a well-ordered state should be to create superabundant wealth with which to gratify the desires of all, and he argued strongly against Mo-tzu's doctrine of "frugal use."[200] In all probability, K'ang was inspired by the ways and views of these early Confucians. His contact with Western civilization must have convinced him of the validity of such views and persuaded him to break away from the ascetic Ch'eng-Chu tradition.

Significance of Interpretations

The foregoing survey shows that Confucian classics served both as a source of K'ang's philosophy and as a medium for the expression of some of his own ideas. Speaking generally, the *Spring and Autumn Annals* as interpreted by the Kung-yang school, supplemented by Buddhist and Western literature, was largely instrumental in weaning K'ang from the traditional learning of his early years to the intellectual outlook that made him "a wild-fox meditator among the commentators of the classics."[201] Other Confucian texts, the *Great Learning*, the *Doctrine of the Mean*, the *Analects*, the *Mencius*, and the "Li-yün" chapter of the *Book of Rites* served mainly as vehicles for his own philosophy derived, during a period of over twenty years, from the *Annals* and from excursions into Mahāyāna Buddhism and Western learning.

The net result of K'ang's interpretation of the classics is impressive. By construing (or misconstruing) various passages in them he gave ex-

---

[197] K'ang, *Lun-yü chu, chüan* 7, pp. 15a–b.

[198] *Analects*, X.8.

[199] *Mencius*, III.ii.4.

[200] *Hsün-tzu*, no. 9, "Wang-chih," and no. 10, "Fu kuo." For a summary of Hsün-tzu's views see Hsiao, *Chung-kuo . . . ssu-hsiang shih*, p. 100.

[201] Weng T'ung-ho, *Weng Wen-kung-kung jih-chi*, 33: 43a (Kuang-hsü 20/5/2).

pression to a number of ideas among which the following are the most important: (1) that progress was the law of human society, (2) that universal love (*jen*) was the law of life, (3) that all human desires are legitimate and therefore should not be suppressed, (4) that all men should be treated as equal and given freedom, (5) that democracy (*min-chu*) was the final stage of political development and constitutional monarchy a transitional form of government between republic and autocracy, and (6) that the true teaching of Confucius lay outside the established tradition. These were the chief ingredients of K'ang's social philosophy and philosophy of reform in his *Confucius as a Reformer* and the *Ta-t'ung shu*.

K'ang ascribed all his ideas to Confucius. In some instances the classics support him; but his interpretations were often so obviously forced that Liang Ch'i-ch'ao, one of the two students whom he chose to assist him in writing his startling book on the "spurious classics," confessed that he was time and again "distressed by his teacher's arbitrariness" in dealing with the classics and by his readiness "to ignore disturbing evidence or to distort it" in drawing conclusions.[202]

K'ang's treatment of the classics admittedly was not objective.[203] But this does not make his efforts worthless. For while lack of objectivity is an unpardonable sin in a historian, it is not in a philosopher. K'ang never intended to be a historian. Following the Kung-yang tradition, he attached little value to factual knowledge and regarded the search for "principles" as the sole legitimate intellectual pursuit.[204] The criticism, therefore, that K'ang ignored or distorted evidence, merely shows that he did not give an accurate account of the Confucian teaching; it does not *ipso facto* lessen the theoretical significance of his "arbitrary" interpretations, which should be evaluated not by the criterion of objectivity but by the logic of historical circumstances.

K'ang lived in an age when drastic social and political changes dictated a thorough reexamination of the Confucian tradition and an earnest endeavor to adapt the empire intellectually and institutionally to the new conditions. His interpretations of the classics constituted the most serious attempt to date to make this adaptation. They were often forced and arbitrary because Confucianism did not anticipate the problems of modern times. In order to bridge the gap K'ang found it necessary to depart, often radically, from the accepted interpreta-

[202] Liang, *Ch'ing-tai hsüeh-shu kai-lun*, p. 437.
[203] Chang Ping-lin, *T'ai-yen wen-lu ch'u-pien*, *chüan* 1, "Hsin-shih shang," p. 36b.
[204] See notes 138–43, above.

tions of the classics, and to stretch the texts to introduce into Confucianism the novel notions of equality, freedom, republicanism, and constitutionalism. His was a well-intentioned effort to preserve China's moral heritage by modernizing it, and to save the declining dynasty by bringing its ideological foundation up to date. Had K'ang followed the rules of academic inquiry or *chia-fa*, "canon of the school," he would have become just another respectable Kung-yang commentator, something entirely different from what he actually was.

K'ang's "arbitrary" interpretations of the classics, startling as they were to the traditionalists, did little violence to the teachings of Confucius and Mencius. They often went beyond the written word, but they extended rather than negated the meanings of Confucian doctrines. Western notions made his exegeses decidedly unorthodox but not un-Confucian. Further, he was not the first to incorporate alien elements into the Confucian philosophy. Neo-Confucians of Sung and Ming times had already used Buddhist concepts to refine or extend Confucianism; these thinkers could not shut their eyes to the ideas that had been introduced into China from India. Similarly, K'ang had to take advantage of European thought. But in nineteenth-century China K'ang faced also a practical urgency for the synthesis of Chinese and foreign thought which had been unknown to his Neo-Confucian predecessors. The role that K'ang played was, therefore, not that of a closet philosopher as many a Neo-Confucian was, but a "sage" who labored "to save the world" (*chiu shih*).

That K'ang achieved revisionism without committing apostasy may be seen from another angle. K'ang's unconventional treatment of the classics was syncretic, but with a Confucian bias. In his thinking Confucian doctrines remained the frame of reference and Western ideas served to extend, modify, or replace traditional notions. His moral values remained predominantly Confucian, although his institutional ideas often betrayed Western influence.

The allegation that K'ang invoked the name of Confucius merely to silence enemies of reform obscures his sincerity. So does the suggestion that he professed Confucianism not from conviction but from necessity. A recent writer has remarked, "At a time when the old bottles of Classical Learning had not yet reached breaking point, anyone who wished to gain a hearing for his new views was still obliged to express them within the context of this Classical Learning."[205] But the "obligation"

---

[205] Fung, *History of Chinese Philosophy*, 2: 674. A roughly similar view is expressed in Richard Wilhelm, *Confucius and Confucianism*, p. 97.

to speak in Confucian terms was rooted in K'ang's own intellectual make-up and was not imposed upon him by environment. Since his childhood he had been steeped in Confucian tradition, which, despite his desire to break away from Neo-Confucianism, remained to influence him throughout his career. He was always an admirer of Confucius. He held fast to the conviction that the moral efficacy of "true" Confucianism was not irrevocably impaired by the centuries of "falsehoods" foisted upon it and could be revived to serve not only the Chinese people but also mankind as a whole; this conviction grew stronger in him as time went on. He urged his compatriots "to venerate Confucius" not merely because the bulk of Chinese scholars still swore by "the old bottles of Classical Learning" but because he had a profound admiration for Confucius. He probably was aware that some of the ideas that he expressed in Confucian terms were of non-Confucian origin. But he saw no incongruity between these ideas and the doctrines of Confucius because he believed that Confucius was a universal sage whose teaching contained all the truth. Thus he found little difficulty in weaving a synthetic philosophical fabric out of Confucian warp and Western woof. This philosophy did not produce the effects that K'ang desired. But to say that it bore no more than a Confucian veneer is to oversimplify K'ang's intellect and to do less than justice to him as a modernizer of Confucianism.

Chapter 4

CONFUCIANISM AS A PHILOSOPHY OF REFORM AND A RELIGION

CONFUCIANISM AS A PHILOSOPHY OF REFORM

K'ang's study of the classics afforded him the basis of a general social philosophy and, at the same time, an ideological justification for his reform movement. Almost immediately after he completed his book on the "false classics" in 1891 he began to write the *K'ung-tzu kai-chih k'ao*, (Confucius as a Reformer), finished it in 1896, two years before the movement was officially launched, and published it just a few months before the fateful "One Hundred Days."[1]

The central theme of this book was to demonstrate that Confucius, the supreme arbiter of intellectual and moral values, was not a transmitter of historical tradition but the creator of a "teaching" (*chiao*) that encompassed all enduring truths. Citing extensively from the classics and other ancient texts, K'ang argued that "the splendor of the institutions and principles of the Three Dynasties" was in reality Confucius' intellectual creation and that there was absolutely no way of gaining any factual knowledge of China's remote past.[2] Confucius thus

---

[1] K'ang, *K'ung-tzu kai-chih k'ao*, printed in 1897 in Shanghai, by Ta-t'ung Shu-chü; prohibited by imperial decree in 1898 and 1900; reprinted and published in 1920–22, Peking. See K'ang, *Tzu-pien nien-p'u*, Kuang-hsü 22 (hereafter, *Nien-p'u*). According to Liang Ch'i-ch'ao, K'ang's students assisted in writing this book as well as the *Hsin-hsüeh wei-ching k'ao* and *Ch'un-ch'iu Tung-shih hsüeh* ("Nan-hai hsien-sheng ch'i-shih shou-yen," in Ting Wen-chiang, *Liang Jen-kung hsien-sheng nien-p'u ch'ang-pien ch'u-kao*, 1: 17).

[2] K'ang, *K'ung-tzu kai-chih k'ao* (1920–22 ed.), *chüan* 1, p. 1a. Wolfgang Franke, "Die Lehre von den drei Dynastien in ihrer Vollkommenheit ist das von Konfuzius

had nothing to transmit to later scholars; he had to start from scratch and formulate his doctrines simply as reason directed. A "great man" like Confucius did not need any established authority or historical evidence to validate his doctrines, for he was fully qualified to found a school of thought (*ch'uang chiao*) and to formulate new systems of institutions to replace old ones that had become defective (*kai chih*).[3]

The prerogative of founding a school of thought, K'ang said, was not a monopoly of Confucius. K'ang devoted considerable space to showing that every one of the philosophers that flourished in the closing years of the Chou dynasty was the founder of a school. The following statement is particularly interesting:

> The great deluge covered the entire earth. The birth of the human race came after the deluge. Peoples of the world began to flourish in the time of Emperor Yü of Hsia dynasty [twentieth century B.C.]. With the accumulation of generations of men and their wisdom for two milleniums, all sorts of experiences and knowledge had been obtained by mankind. The most outstanding in intelligence and ability among men appeared in large numbers and distinguished themselves. . . . Each of these men took advantage of his natural endowments and life's experiences to formulate his doctrines, gathered students around himself, and proposed institutional reform, with the intention of exerting his intellectual influence upon the world.

One among these philosophers proved to be especially sagacious. Men turned to him for instruction and guidance. This was Confucius. Eventually, "a complete unification of thought" was brought about in Han dynasty, when Confucianism was accepted as the sole truth.[4] In thus "showing veneration to Confucius," K'ang added, the Han regime was unsurpassed by any of the later dynasties.[5]

After arguing at length that Confucianism owed its origin solely to Confucius, that its most potent parts were communicated orally to scholars of later times, and that Confucius was "the founder of a school of ten thousand generations" (*wan-shih chiao-chu*),[6] K'ang proceeded to

---

geschaffene Altertum," *Die staatspolitischen Reformsversuche K'ang Yu-weis und seiner Schule*, p. 15; William F. Hummel, "K'ang Yu-wei, Historical Critic and Social Philosopher, 1858–1927," pp. 347–48, and Liang Ch'i-ch'ao, *Ch'ing-tai hsüeh-shu kai-lun*, pp. 129–30, also summarize K'ang's view.

[3] K'ang, *K'ung-tzu kai-chih k'ao*, chüan 11, p. 1a.

[4] Ibid., *chüan* 2, p. 1b.

[5] Ibid., *chüan* 21, pp. 1a–b and passim.

[6] Ibid., *chüan* 7, p. 1b. Cf. ibid., *chüan* 10, p. 1a, where K'ang refutes the views of Chang Hsüeh-ch'eng.

show that the Confucian doctrines as interpreted by Kung-yang scholars constituted the Sage's philosophy of "institutional reform."[7] In formulating these doctrines, according to K'ang, Confucius virtually put himself in the position of a sovereign and exercised the royal prerogative of designing institutional systems. But as he was not an actual ruler, he lacked the authority to put his institutional ideas into practice. The fact that he was an "uncrowned king" (*su wang*) did not reduce his historical importance. By outlining his doctrines in the *Spring and Autumn Annals* and other classics he gave the substantial part of the fruit of his "kingly" undertaking, for the edification and guidance of men of later ages.[8]

Reference has already been made to what K'ang believed to be Confucius' major doctrines of institutional reform, namely, the succession of the Three Ages and the sequence of the Three Systems. Attention may now be called to other ideas that K'ang elaborated in the *Confucius as a Reformer* and which figured prominently in his other writings on reform.

K'ang contended that the systems of institutions attributed by tradition to Yao, Shun, and Wen-wang were not actually set up by those three eminent ancient rulers, and did not serve as models for Confucius to copy, but on the contrary were ideal systems that Confucius attributed to these sage-emperors. In fact, the rulers themselves were not historical figures but were created by Confucius to symbolize ideal political systems. "Wen-wang" stood for "benevolent government under monarchical rule" (*chün-chu chih jen-cheng*) while "Yao" and "Shun" stood for the governmental system obtaining in the "Age of Universal Peace under the people's rule" (*min-chu chih t'ai-p'ing*).[9]

K'ang was convinced that unity was an indispensable condition of political well-being. Disorder was an unavoidable concomitant of disunity. The history of China bore witness to the fact that peace and progress prevailed only when the empire was under a single rule. Contrary to the view of many Confucians who idealized the ancient *feng-chien* ("feudal") system and considered the unification achieved by the Ch'in dynasty a regrettable departure from the ancient "kingly way," K'ang unequivocally approved of the system established by the First Emperor, and argued that it was in full accord with "the principle of the *Spring and Autumn Annals*." "Feudalism," he declared, "was as-

[7] Ibid., *chüan* 9, passim.
[8] Ibid., *chüan* 8, pp. 4a–11b; *chüan* 11, p. 3b.
[9] Ibid., *chüan* 12, pp. 1a–b.

suredly not the Sage's idea."[10] This distaste for political fragmentation and administrative decentralization remained a permanent element of K'ang's political thought and exerted considerable influence on his ideas of reform.

K'ang did not believe that the imperial system was without serious faults. It contributed to political unity but the autocratic principle on which it rested produced many undesirable results. As circumstances changed, its defects became increasingly apparent; its shortcomings eventually outweighed its usefulness. In continuing to maintain it for two thousand years China had condemned herself to stagnation in a low stage of social development and thus denied herself the blessings of the Age of Universal Peace. China must, like all progressive states, abandon autocracy and advance steadily though unhurriedly to "benevolent" constitutional monarchy and strive to reach "the people's rule." Viewed in the context of China's political and intellectual background, K'ang's political thought as revealed in *Confucius as a Reformer* is decidedly radical.

The ideas of drastic social transformation set forth in the *Ta-t'ung shu* are absent from the *Kai-chih k'ao*. There is unmistakable respect for human relationships and traditional moral values. The basic family relationships are treated with deference. Following is his comment on Confucius' approval of the groom escorting the bride from her home to his own:

> Confucius attached the greatest importance to the relationship between father and son. But if weight was not attached to that between husband and wife, father and son would not stand to each other in the proper relationship. Hence he instituted the escorting ceremony to give importance to it.[11]

In the same vein K'ang commented on the Confucian requirement that children mourn the death of their parents for three years.[12] All this is far from the prognostication in the *Ta-t'ung shu* that the family with the multitudinous sufferings that it inflicted upon the individual would disappear in the pleasurable world of the Great Community.

This divergence of view is not inconsistent, but merely shows how K'ang at different stages of his career performed two different tasks: the formulation of a philosophy of institutional reform on Confucian

---

[10] Ibid., *chüan* 9, p. 20a.
[11] Ibid., *chüan* 9, pp. 14b–15a.
[12] Ibid., *chüan* 15, p. 8a.

principles and the construction of a general philosophy, not exclusively Confucian, of human society. In the latter he often went beyond the doctrinal scope even of New Text Confucianism, and beyond existing institutions and values; in the former he respected the accepted social and moral values and focused attention on a theoretical basis for institutional reform. The *Kai-chih k'ao* and the *Ta-t'ung shu* do not neutralize each other but represent two levels of thought.

K'ang owed much to his predecessors of the Kung-yang school but he went beyond the most daring of them in projecting into the classics the idea of political transformation.[13] Without questioning his sincerity, it may be said that he wrote the *Confucius as a Reformer* with a practical purpose: to persuade the imperial government to effect institutional changes and to convince his fellow scholars that as good Confucians they should have no objection to reform.[14] It is significant that he presented a copy of this book to the Kuang-hsü emperor, along with a memorial, in June, 1898.[15]

K'ang's efforts to convert Confucianism into a philosophy of reform, therefore, should be appraised not as a scholarly contribution to classical studies, but as a practical influence on the course of events and on the subsequent history of China. There is no doubt that K'ang achieved a measure of success in committing the youthful emperor to the cause of reform and in rallying around himself a small but dedicated group of men to serve that cause. But his success was limited. His unorthodox exegeses aroused the resentment of scholars and officials, and the reform movement of 1898 came to an abrupt end.

K'ang's bold, unconventional views prejudiced as much as helped the cause of reform. They proved to be unacceptable not only to enemies of reform but also to some supporters. Loud voices of protest were heard from the time he published his works, especially those in which he repudiated the Old Text tradition.[16] The book on the "forged classics" (published in 1891) was suppressed by imperial order in 1894, as a

[13] Liang, *Ch'ing-tai hsüeh-shu kai-lun*, p. 130. Li Chien-nung, *Political History of China*, p. 150: "K'ang Yu-wei was the first man to interpret the ideas of reform as he believed he *found them in the Spring and Autumn Annals*." Li echoes Liang's view.

[14] Ssu-yü Teng and John K. Fairbank, *China's Response to the West*, pp. 148–49.

[15] K'ang, *Nien-p'u*, Kuang-hsü 24.

[16] Weng T'ung-ho, *Weng Wen-kung-kung jih-chi*, 33: 43a. (Kuang-hsü 20); Liu K'un-i, "Fu Ou-yang Jun-sheng," in *Liu Chung-ch'eng-kung i-chi*, "Shu-tu" (also in Chien Po-tsan et al., *Wu-hsü pien-fa* 2: 633); Chu I-hsin, "Ta K'ang Yu-wei shu No. 2," in Su Yü, *I-chiao tsung-pien, chüan* 1, pp. 2a–6b; and An Wei-chün, "Ch'ing hui Hsin-hsüeh wei-ching k'ao p'ien," in Su, *I-chiao tsung-pien, chüan* 2, pp. 1b–2a. According to Su, the memorialist was Yü Chin-san.

result of such protests.[17] The view that he expressed in the *Confucius as a Reformer* further incensed traditionalists and distressed influential "progressives." Chang Chih-tung, who had previously showed lively interest in K'ang's activities, now quickly withdrew his support.[18] Chu I-hsin, a respected friend, took strong exception to K'ang's approach to Confucianism and was scandalized at the intention to capitalize on the "uncrowned king" fiction to justify the reform movement.[19] Wen-t'i, an archconservative and one of K'ang's bitter enemies, made a blistering attack on K'ang, charging him with ideological sedition, in a memorial submitted shortly after K'ang presented to the emperor a copy of his offending book.[20] It aroused so much controversy and suspicion that even Ch'en Pao-chen and Sun Chia-nai, both of whom took an active part in reform, found it necessary to indicate their disapproval of *Confucius as a Reformer*.[21] Sun proposed to the imperial court that all "perverse books," such as those that K'ang had written, be "sternly prohibited" and appropriate texts be prepared by the government for the instruction of the prospective students of the new-style schools that he was authorized to establish.[22] Violent repercussions were felt even in Hunan province where an energetic program of reform was under way.[23]

It may be asked whether it was necessary for K'ang to reinterpret Confucianism in order to advance the cause of reform.

---

[17] Ch'en Pao-chen et al., *Te-tsung Ching-huang-ti shih-lu*, chüan 344, p. 5, gives the imperial edict, dated Kuang-hsü 20/7/4 (August 4, 1894). K'ang, *Nien-p'u*, Kuang-hsü 20, refers to two memorials, one by An Wei-chün and another by Yü Chin-san.

[18] Chang Po-chen, *Nan-hai K'ang hsien-cheng chuan*, pp. 20b–21a.

[19] Chu I-hsin, "Yü K'ang Yu-wei ti-ssu shu," in Su, *I-chiao tsung-pien*, chüan 1, pp. 11a–12a.

[20] Wen-t'i, "Yen ts'an K'ang Yu-wei che" (dated Kuang-hsü 24/5/28) in Chu Shou-p'eng, *Tung-hua hsü-lu*, chüan 145, pp. 14–18; Su, *I-chiao tsung-pien*, chüan 2; and Chien, *Wu-hsü*, 2: 482–89.

[21] Ch'en Pao-chen et al., "Tsou ch'ing li-cheng hsüch-shu tsao-chiu jen-ts'ai che" (June, 1898), in Yeh Te-hui, *Chüeh-mi yao-lu*, chüan 1, p. 16; Ch'en Pao-chen and Sun Chia-nai, memorials condemning K'ang's book in Chu, *Tung-hua hsü-lu*, chüan 145, p. 29.

[22] Sun's memorial is given in Yü Pao-hsüan, *Huang-ch'ao hsü-ai wen-pien*, chüan 72, p. 5. See another memorial reporting the condition of the Imperial Peking University, in Su, *I-chiao tsung-pien*, chüan 2, pp. 15a–18b. Kung-chuan Hsiao, "Weng T'ung-ho and the Reform Movement of 1898," pp. 173–75, indicates the reactions to K'ang's book.

[23] Yeh Te-hui, "Yü Nan-hsüeh hui P'i Lu-men hsiao-lien shu," in Su, *I-chiao tsung-pien*, chüan 6, pp. 22b–23a; Tseng Lien, "Ying chao shang feng-shih," in Chien, *Wu-hsü*, 2: 491–93.

K'ang and his followers answered of course that it was. Ou Chü-chia, for example, says:

> The decadence of China must be traced to the decadence of men's mind. Men's ignorance is due to the perversion of learning, and learning is perverted because the true meanings of the Six Classics are obscured. There is no way to effect reform, if the light of the Six Classics is not made to shine again.[24]

This statement appears to be a faithful reflection of K'ang's own conviction and can be readily justified. For the traditional ideology and institutions of China were so inseparable that it was well-nigh impossible to alter the one without altering the other.[25] As a recent Western writer has put it:

> Without intellectual emancipation from the shackles of the orthodox interpretation of Confucianism, which had been so shaped as to become a chief support for a relatively static society and a decadent political regime, . . . the Chinese people would be a medieval anachronism in the modern world.[26]

Indeed, it may even be argued that K'ang's position as the intellectual leader of the reform movement rested on the "task of reforming or revolutionizing Confucianism."[27] His attempt to reconstruct the teaching of Confucius helped to dramatize his views on reform, which might be rejected or condemned but certainly could not be ignored by his fellow scholars. Men like Pao Shih-ch'en (1775–1855) and Fung Kuei-fen (1809–74) proposed reforms without questioning the validity of the orthodox Confucian tradition. Their opinions received scant attention.[28] Had they ventured to "revolutionize" Confucianism as K'ang did, they might have shocked the scholar-official world into taking notice of their proposals, even if only to reject them.

It would not be accurate to regard K'ang's attempt to equate Confucianism with reform as simply an expedient to promote institutional reform. K'ang was as much concerned with preserving China's cultural

---

[24] Ou Chü-chia, "Lun Chung-kuo pien-fa pi tzu fa-ming ching-hsüeh shih."

[25] Kenneth S. Latourette, *A History of Modern China*, pp. 221–22.

[26] Norman D. Palmer, "Makers of Modern China. I. The Reformers: K'ang Yu-wei," p. 90.

[27] Li, *Political History of China*, pp. 175–76.

[28] Pao Shih-ch'eng, *Shuo ch'u* (1801); summarized in Ch'ien Mu, *Chung-kuo chin san-pai nien hsüeh-shu shih*, pp. 537–58 and Hsiao, "Weng T'ung-ho and the Reform Movement," p. 159. Fung Kuei-fen, *Chiao-pin-lu k'ang-i* (written 1860), summarized in Hsiao, "Weng T'ung-ho and the Reform Movement," pp. 181–86.

identity (Confucianism) as with maintaining her political independence (the empire) so that neither would be engulfed by the "tide from the West." The objectives of his reform movement were clearly stated in the "Constitution" of the Pao-kuo hui (Association for Preserving the Country) which held its initial meeting in the spring of 1898. The aim of the association, as defined in Article 2, was "to preserve intact the country's territory, its people, and its tradition" (*pao-ch'üan kuo-t'u, kuo-min, kuo-chiao*), or as formulated in Article 9, "to study matters relative to the preservation of the country, the race, and the tradition" (*chiang-ch'iu pao-kuo, pao-chung, pao-chiao chih shih*).[29] Despite K'ang's interest in "Western learning," he was never convinced that China was inferior to Europe in moral values and ethical principles, even if it was inferior in science, technology, and government. Confucianism, he believed, possessed more and greater merits than any other major "teachings" of the world. This was China's tradition, the intrinsic superiority of which made its preservation mandatory; it was that tradition, in fact, that made China and the Chinese "race" worthy of preservation. Following the Kung-yang view that the distinction between "Chinese" and "barbarian" was entirely one of culture,[30] K'ang held that to lose Chinese tradition was to lose the identity of the Chinese race. The preservation of Confucianism was not less important than the preservation of the empire. To achieve the latter end China's legal, administrative, and economic institutions must be remodeled after the modern Western pattern; but to abandon Confucianism and attempt Westernization of moral life was to commit cultural suicide. The position that K'ang took in *Confucius as a Reformer* may therefore be described as "cultural nationalism," clearly different from the "cultural cosmopolitanism" of the *Ta-t'ung shu*.

K'ang was persuaded that the Confucian tradition could be preserved only if it was purged of anachronistic notions and disengaged from the outmoded institutions of the empire, and that there must be an intellectual as well as an institutional reform, although the intellectual reform must be effected within the framework of the Confucian tradition. Ingredients from foreign cultures might be borrowed, but they should enrich and supplement, not replace, the valid elements of

[29] K'ang, "Pao-kuo hui chang-ch'eng" in *Kuo-wen pao*, Kuang-hsü 24/interc.3/17; *Chih-hsin pao*, vol. 54 (Kuang-hsü 25/3/21); Yeh, "Yu Nan-hsüeh hui . . .", in Su, *I-chiao tsung-pien, chüan* 4, pp. 1a–4b; Ting, *Liang Jen-kung . . .* , 1: 50; and Chien, *Wu-hsü*, 4: 396–98.

[30] For a brief explanation of this view, see Hsiao, "Weng T'ung-ho and the Reform Movement," p. 137.

Confucianism. Accordingly, even before he undertook institutional reform, K'ang endeavored to reconstruct Confucianism with a view not only to affording a philosophical basis for institutional reform but to preserving China's best moral tradition. That K'ang was seriously concerned with the preservation of that tradition may be seen even more clearly in his attempts to promote Confucianism as a religion, as I shall discuss in the following section.

CONFUCIANISM AS A RELIGION

Liang Ch'i-ch'ao, writing in 1901, remarked that K'ang Yu-wei was a "religionist" (*tsung-chiao chia*) who rendered the greatest service to China in the field of "religion" and who, in "restoring Confucianism to its original state," was "the Martin Luther of the Confucian religion."[31] This view was echoed by a number of later writers who gave K'ang credit for transforming Confucianism from a moral philosophy into a religion.[32] It will be useful to examine briefly the manner in which K'ang tried to effect such transformation and to estimate the results of his attempt.

Liang Ch'i-ch'ao says further of K'ang's general position as a "religionist":

> Our China has not been a religious country. For thousands of years there had not been a single religionist. My teacher [K'ang Yu-wei] received Confucian learning in his youth. When he lived in seclusion in Hsi-ch'iao Hills [in his native village in 1879], he delved deeply into the Buddhist canon and attained great perspicacity and enlightenment. After his travels [in 1879 and 1882 when he visited Hong Kong and Shanghai] he also read books on Christianity. As a consequence, religious thoughts dominated [his mind]. He pledged himself resolutely to performing the tasks of continuing and transmitting [the teachings of] the Sages [i.e., the founders of Confucianism, Buddhism, and Christianity], and of bringing salvation to all men. . . . He held the doctrine that the three Sages [Confucius, Buddha, and Jesus] taught the same truths and that all religions were equal. However, [he believed that] since he was born in China, he should save

---

[31] Liang Ch'i-ch'ao, *Nan-hai K'ang hsien-sheng chuan*, p. 67.
[32] E.g., Alfred Forke, *Geschichte der neuren chinesischen Philosophie*, p. 580; Franke, *Die staatspolitischen Reformsversuche K'ang Yu-weis und seiner Schule*, pp. 52–58; and Arthur F. Wright, *Buddhism in Chinese History*, p. 111. D. Howard Smith, "The Significance of Confucius for Religion," *History of Religions*, 3, no. 2 (1963): 242–55, argues that the Confucian teaching was mainly ethical and humanistic, but it had religious significance. If one defines religion in broad terms as "Man's belief in and attitude toward superhuman and supernatural power," one can justifiably consider Confucius as "a deeply religious man." Cf. Ichiko Chūzō, "Hokyō to hempō," pp. 118–20.

the people of China first and easily lead them [to salvation] by means of China's own tradition and usages.[33]

This statement suggests first, that K'ang's interest in religion was stimulated by Buddhism and Christianity; second, that as a result of such interest he undertook to transform Confucianism into a religion; third, that all religions contained the same truths; and fourth, that the "Confucian religion" was the most suitable for the Chinese people.

Liang's observation is not entirely accurate. He correctly pointed out that K'ang owed something to Buddhism and Christianity but he failed to note that K'ang received inspiration from the Kung-yang school of Confucianism as well. It may be recalled that as early as the time of Mencius, there was already a tendency among Confucius' followers to take an interest in supernaturalism, so much so that Hsün-tzu, the most uncompromising positivist among the early Confucians, raised a strong protest against it, insisting that the pursuit of knowledge be restricted to the sphere of human affairs.[34] The tendency, however, persisted. In Han times the members of the New Text school showed a strong inclination to apotheosize Confucius, as some of the extant *wei-shu* ("apocrypha") indicate.[35] Tung Chung-shu, to whom K'ang sang high praise, did not go as far as some others in that direction, but his doctrine of "response of Heaven to man" was in line with the general development.[36] Ho Hsiu, the other leading Kung-yang scholar of the Han dynasty, definitely subscribed to the views expressed in the *wei-shu* and assigned to Confucius a sort of messianic role.[37]

An excellent instance of the apotheosis of Confucius is found in one of the *wei-shu*:

> Confucius' mother, Cheng-tsai, once while taking a walk happened upon the mound of a large tomb, where she fell asleep and dreamed that she received an invitation from a Black Emperor. She went to him and in her dream had intercourse with him. He spoke to her, saying: "Your confinement will take place within a hollow mulberry tree." When she awoke she seemed to feel [pregnant] and [later] gave birth to Confucius within a hollow mulberry. This is why he is called the Black Sage. . . .
>
> On Confucius' breast there was writing which said: "The act of insti-

---

[33] Liang, *Nan-hai K'ang . . .* , p. 67.

[34] "T'ien-lun," *Hsün-tzu.*

[35] Fung Yu-lan, *History of Chinese Philosophy*, vol. 2, chap. 3.

[36] Pan Ku, *Han-shu, chüan* 56, biography of Tung Chung-shu.

[37] Ho Hsiu, *Ch'un-ch'iu Kung-yang chieh-ku, chüan* 28, p. 10a (1872 Chiang-hsi shu-chü ed.).

tuting [a new dynasty] had been decided and the rule of the world had been transferred." . . .

After the unicorn was caught [in the fourteenth year of Duke Ai of Lu, i.e., 481 B.C.] Heaven rained blood which formed into writing on the main gate [of the capital] of Lu, and which said: "Quick, prepare laws, for the Sage Confucius will die; the Chou [ruling house] Chi will be destroyed; a comet will appear from the east. The government of the Ch'in [dynasty] will arise and will suddenly destroy the literary arts. But though the written records will then be dispersed [the teachings of] Confucius will not be interrupted."

[Confucius' disciple,] Tzu-hsia next day went to look at this, whereupon the writing of blood flew away as a red bird. This then changed itself into white writing, the composition of which is called the *Yen K'ung-t'u.* In it are delineated charts for instituting laws.

While Confucius was discussing the classics, there was a bird which [came and] transformed itself into writing. . . . A small red bird which settled on this writing became a piece of yellow jade, carved with an inscription which said: "Confucius, holding [heaven's] Mandate to act, has created these governmental institutions in accordance with the laws. . . ."[38]

A "charismatic basis"[39] was thus given to the authority of Confucius who, as "uncrowned king," was supposed to have laid down infallible laws and formulated institutions valid for all times.

K'ang accepted this conception of the "uncrowned king" and presented Confucius at once as a Heaven-ordained founder of religion and a human sage performing the task of a prescient lawgiver. The following remarks, made in 1898, indicate the trend of K'ang's thinking:

Heaven having pity for the many afflictions suffered by men who live on this great earth, [caused] the Black Emperor to send down his semen so as to create a being who would rescue the people from their troubles—a being of divine intelligence, who would be a sage-king, a teacher for his age, a bullwark for all men, and a religious leader for the whole world. Born as he was in the Age of Disorder, he proceeded, on the basis of this disorder, to establish the pattern of the Three Ages, progressing with increasing refinement until they arrive at Universal Peace. He established the institutions of these Three Ages, basing himself [initially] on those of

[38] Fung, *History of Chinese Philosophy,* 2: 129–30. The term "Black Sage" is a translation of *Yüan sheng* (translator's note, p. 129). It should be pointed out that the original term was *Hsüan sheng.* The character *hsüan* (R. H. Mathews, *Chinese-English Dictionary,* No. 2881) means "black," "dark," "profound," or "abstruse," and is the same one that appears in the concluding sentence of chap. 1, the *Tao-te-ching.* Since "hsüan" was part of the given name of the K'ang-hsi emperor (Hsüan-yeh), "yüan" became used in its stead. The translator's note misses the point when it says: "in commemoration of his [Confucius'] unusual birth."

[39] Max Weber, *The Theory of Social and Economic Organization,* p. 328.

his native state [of Lu], but stressing the idea of the one great unity that would [ultimately] bind together all parts of the great earth, far and near, large and small.[40]

K'ang's indebtedness to the *wei-shu* of the Kung-yang school hardly requires comment.

To return to the Buddhist and Christian influences on K'ang: K'ang's partial conversion to Buddhism must have occurred in 1879 (or slightly earlier) when he "studied exclusively the books of Buddhism and Taoism." He soon pledged himself to serving the world and rejected the quietist philosophy of Lao-tsu but retained some of the characteristic Buddhist ideas concerning man and the universe.[41] His interest in Buddhism was never more than eclectic; he treated it only as one of the approaches to the intellectual cultivation of a scholar. This may be clearly seen in a remark made probably early in his career:

> *Belles-lettres* are like wine which intoxicates a man, Han learning is like hash which satiates a man, Sung learning is like rice which nourishes a man, and Buddhism is like medicine which cures a man.[42]

K'ang arrived at Mahayāna Buddhism through a well-trodden Neo-Confucian bypath.[43] According to Liang Ch'i-ch'ao, he was introduced to Buddhism through his study of the philosophy of Wang Shou-jen who was profoundly influenced by Ch'an Buddhism. K'ang thus "owed the most to the Ch'an sect and abode with the Hua-yen sect."[44] That Ch'an Buddhism exerted considerable influence on K'ang, for a time at least, may be gathered from the fact that he underwent a spell of mystic "enlightenment" in 1878[45]—much as successful practitioners of

[40] K'ang, preface to *K'ung-tzu kai-chih k'ao*, in *Pu-jen*, no. 1 (1913); translated in Fung, *History of Chinese Philosophy*, 2: 675.

[41] K'ang, *Nien-p'u*, Kuang-hsü 5. For K'ang's adverse criticisms of the philosophies of Lao-tzu and Mo-tzu, see e.g. *Chung-yung chu*, p. 6b.; *Lun-yü chu, chüan* 14, p. 13b; *chüan* 9, p. 8b.

[42] K'ang, "Yü Huang Chung-t'ao pien-hsiu shu," microfilm, reel 3. Huang Chung-t'ao, namely, Huang Shao-chi (1854–1908) (Arthur W. Hummell, *Eminent Chinese of the Ch'ing Period*, pp. 343–44).

[43] Carsun Chang, *The Development of Neo-Confucian Thought*, pp. 127–35, indicates briefly the influence of Buddhism on Neo-Confucians. See also Chan Wing-tsit, "Neo-Confucianism," in MacNair, *China*, pp. 254–58. The influence was brought to bear long before Sung times. See Hellmut Wilhelm, "A Note on Sun Ch'o and His *Yü-tao-lun*," *Liebenthal Festschrift*, Sino-Indian Studies, 5, nos. 3–4 (1957): 1–11.

[44] Liang, *Nan-hai K'ang . . .* , p. 70. For brief explanations of "Ch'an" and "Hua-yen," see W. E. Soothill and L. Hodous, *Dictionary of Chinese Buddhist Terms*, pp. 269, 387, 460.

[45] K'ang, *Nien-p'u*, K'ang-hsü 4.

Ch'an experienced. But he had no taste for Hīnayāna Buddhism and did not hesitate "to accept or reject Buddhist doctrines as his whim dictated."[46]

K'ang's emphasis on human suffering and promise of "utmost joy" in a future utopia were obviously inspired by Buddhism.[47] His ability "to see universal suffering" probably owed its origin to the Buddhist doctrine of *wu k'u*, "the five forms of agony."[48] But there was a difference. Instead of tracing the source of suffering to human desires and seeking salvation in the extinction of desires as the Buddhist did, K'ang laid the blame wholly on faulty institutions and envisioned human emancipation and the complete gratification of human desires through institutional reform.[49] Therefore instead of renouncing the world, K'ang sought to reform it so that it would become a more comfortable place for men to live in. The "wholly complete" and "utmost joy" were of course to be found in the realm of *dharma* (*fa-chieh*) but after examining the Buddhist beatitudes K'ang came to the conclusion that "to abandon the world and search for the realm of *dharma*" was no way to achieve them. "He therefore devoted himself to creating the realm of *dharma* within the world."[50] He "did not long for the Pure Land (*Ching-t'u* Sukhāvatī) and was not afraid of Hell." In fact, he dwelled constantly in "hell" to work for the salvation of his fellow beings.[51] All this, K'ang believed, was the essence of the message of the Hua-yen (Avataṁsa) school of Buddhism. But he did not follow the Mahāyāna doctrines completely. He argued, for instance, that owing to wide differences in endowment, environment, and education, it was not possible for all living beings to attain Buddhahood. The task of salvation was only to provide equal environment and education to all those who assumed the human form in the process of transmigration, so that inequalities in their endowments would gradually disappear, and all of them could

---

[46] Liang, *Ch'ing-tai hsüeh-shu kai-lun*, p. 165.

[47] K'ang, "Ju shih-chieh kuan chung-k'u," *Ta-t'ung shu, Chia-pu* (*Ta T'ung Shu*, trans. Laurence G. Thompson, pp. 61–78, hereafter cited as Thompson, *Ta T'ung Shu*).

[48] These are: (1) birth, age, sickness, and death; (2) parting with the loved; (3) meeting with the hated or disliked; (4) inability to obtain the desired; (5) the five skandha sufferings, mental and physical, etc. (Soothill and Hodous, *Dictionary of Chinese Buddhist Terms*, p. 126).

[49] Thompson, *Ta T'ung Shu*, pp. 51–53.

[50] Liang, *Nan-hai K'ang* . . . , p. 83. For the meaning of the term "fa-chieh" see Soothill and Hodous, *Dictionary of Chinese Buddhist Terms*, p. 271.

[51] Liang, "Nan-hai K'ang . . . ," p. 70. Soothill and Hodous, *Dictionary of Chinese Buddhist Terms*, p. 357, give the meaning of "ching-t'u."

attain Buddhahood. It was this line of thought, Liang Ch'i-ch'ao pointed out, that led K'ang to his "system of *Ta-t'ung*."[52]

The similarity between some of K'ang's philosophical ideas and Buddhist doctrines is often striking. *Ta-t'ung*, for example, reminds one of "the Universe of One Reality" (*i-chen fa-chieh*), the highest phase of the fourfold universe envisaged by the Hua-yen school—a world brought into perfect harmony through the operation of the "Ten Profound Theories" (*Shih hsüan men*) that taught, among other things, that all things have coexistence and are united to form one entity, that all beings commune with one another without obstacle, that each identifies itself with another, thereby realizing "synthetical identification."[53] As already said, K'ang's forecast that men would abstain from eating meat in the world of *Ta-t'ung* was obviously more Buddhist than Confucian.[54]

K'ang's indebtedness to Buddhism did not prevent him from repeatedly reaffirming his affiliation with the Confucian school. For he did not give up Confucianism to become a Buddhist convert but accepted those Buddhist notions that appealed to him and projected them into Confucianism. In so doing he imparted religious overtones to Confucianism. "The teaching of Confucius," he remarked on one occasion, "was the Hua-yen sect of Buddhism," for like Hua-yen Buddhism it directed men's search for *dharma* to the world in which they lived and not to a realm lying beyond it. After all, he said, "to adorn the world is none other than to adorn the *dharma* realm."[55] Confucius, therefore, undertook to design institutions for all men and all times, so that men would be saved from interminable sufferings and given the indispensable conditions for attaining "utmost joy." He was not only a universal lawgiver; he was also a prophet who pointed the way to universal salvation.[56]

Although K'ang owed much to Buddhism, he did not possess more than a dilettante knowledge of the Buddhist religion and philosophy.

---

[52] Liang, "Nan-hai K'ang . . . ," p. 84; cf. K'ang, *Nien-p'u*, Kuang-hsü 11.

[53] Junjirō Takakusu, *The Essentials of Buddhist Philosophy*, ed. W. T. Chan and Charles A. Moore (2nd ed.; South Pasadena: Perkins, 1949), pp. 119–24.

[54] K'ang, *Ta-t'ung shu* (1935 ed.) pp. 431–39, 445–46; Thompson translation, pp. 264–69, 273. Cf. John Blofeld, *The Jewel in the Lotus* (London: Sidgwick and Jackson, 1948), p. 190.

[55] Liang, *Nan-hai K'ang . . .* , p. 84.

[56] Buddhism may be said to have thus given "cosmic significance" to K'ang's philosophy as it did to Chang Tsai's (Chang, *Development of Neo-Confucian Thought*, p. 180).

His preference for Mahayāna Buddhism was not based on a comprehensive study of Buddhist literature, nor was his rejection of Hīnayāna the outcome of critical analysis. According to Liang Ch'i-ch'ao, he did not know that his doctrines of "Universal Peace" and "Great Community" were rejected by the Buddha.[57] Whether or not Liang's opinion was correct does not concern us here. But it is interesting to note that Liang saw fit to call K'ang's attention to his inadequate acquaintance with Buddhist literature.

K'ang's understanding of Christianity was even more fragmentary. His first contact with Christian ideas must have been made in Hong Kong in 1879 when he began to collect "books on Western learning."[58] There is no evidence that he delved into the details of church history or Christian theology. His impression of the Christian religion could not have been more than superficial. The impact of Christianity on his thinking was nevertheless quite strong. His insistence on establishing Confucianism as a "state religion" was in all probability prompted by what he had heard of Western religious practices.[59] He could hardly fail to perceive the similarity between the Christian doctrine of love and the Confucian doctrine of *jen*. Ignoring (or ignorant of) the social and theological implications of the former he readily equated it with the latter. Thus Christianity, together with Buddhism, strengthened K'ang's Confucian convictions and induced him to promote Confucianism as a religion.

As K'ang's conversion to Buddhism was partial, his acceptance of Christian ideas was not without reservations. He felt that of the three religions, Confucianism, Buddhism, and Christianity, the last-named was the least satisfactory, although all of them taught essentially the same truths. His position was succinctly stated by Liang Ch'i-ch'ao in 1901:

> My teacher has his own opinion of the Christian religion. He thinks that in discussing matters relative to the spiritual realm it is less satisfactory than Buddhism; in discussing mundane affairs it falls short of Confucianism in refinement and completeness. However, it has the merit of being direct, simple, and unsophisticated; it sets forth one single principle that is at once profound, pertinent, and clear, namely, the brotherhood and equality of men. This is based entirely on truth and suitable for practical application.[60]

[57] Ting, *Liang Jen-kung* . . . , 1: 34, Liang's letter to K'ang (1896).
[58] K'ang, *Nien-p'u*, Kuang-hsü 5.
[59] As some of K'ang's contemporaries supposed. E.g., Ch'en Pao-chen's memorial (Kuang-hsü 24/5/-) in Yeh, *Chüeh-mi yao-lu, chüan* 1, p. 16.
[60] Liang, *Nan-hai K'ang* . . . , p. 70.

K'ang himself hinted at the inferiority of Christianity to Buddhism in 1904 after his extensive travels in Europe. He said in his "Record of Travel in Italy" (I-ta-li yu-chi):

> When I read books on Buddhism and Christianity twenty-five years ago I discovered that the Christian teaching came entirely from the Buddhist. Its doctrines concerning the soul, love of mankind, miracles, confessional, redemption, paradise and purgatory appeal to men's conscience. All these are no different from Buddhist [doctrines]. Its doctrines concerning creation by one god, trinity, omnipotence of God, are all found in the tenets of the non-Buddhist sects [of India]. Its doctrine of the day of Last Judgment . . . is less likely to rouse men than the [Buddhist] doctrine of the Wheel of Transmigration. Its doctrine concerning spiritual care is extremely crude and shallow, which comes only to the level of *sakradāgāmiphala* and falls short of *arhat-phala*.[61]

He said that the conceptions of soul as held by the ancient Greeks and Persians had their origin in India, since the flourishing of the ninety-six non-Buddhist sects far preceded the intellectual development of Greece, and Indian priests must have gone to Greece and Persia after Alexander's conquest and eventually introduced their religious tenets into Palestine and Judea. K'ang pointed to similarities between Christian and Buddhist rites and practices, including celibacy, renunciation of mundane life, and worship of the image of Christ as conclusive evidence that Christianity had its roots in Indian religion.[62]

K'ang regarded Christianity as inferior to Confucianism on two counts: first, because it stressed "divine authority"; and second, because it did not meet the needs of China. His argument against the adoption of the Christian religion by the Chinese is quite simple:

> The Christian religion regards God as father, causing every man to have a loving heart that considers all within the four seas as brothers. The prevalence of Christianity in Europe, America, Africa, and [some parts of] Asia has done good to men. It, however, is not to be professed in China. For all its doctrines are found in our ancient teachings. Confucianism contains detailed doctrines concerning Heaven; it also contains, in complete form, all such doctrines as concerning the soul, amending evil ways and doing good. Moreover, there is the Buddhist religion, which supplements it. [The Christian religion is therefore unnecessary.] And since the people's sentiments are against it, how can anyone force it upon them?[63]

[61] K'ang, "I-ta-li yu-chi" (1904), pp. 131–32. These Buddhist terms are explained in Soothill and Hodous, *Dictionary of Chinese Buddhist Terms*, pp. 177, 172, 374.

[62] K'ang, "I-ta-li yu-chi," pp. 133–34.

[63] Ibid., pp. 132–33.

K'ang's attitude toward Christianity seems to be far from friendly. But it differed from that of the average Chinese scholar of the time. K'ang rejected Christianity on practical grounds but recognized its theoretical merits, whereas the bulk of Confucian scholars spurned it and treated it as an uncivilized superstition.

Without expressly stating the relative merits of Confucianism and Buddhism, K'ang took it for granted that the former was the only "religion" that contained all the truths imperfectly revealed in Buddhism and Christianity, and possessed merits denied to the other two faiths. *K'ung-chiao*, "the Confucian religion,"[64] therefore was the only religion that answered the requirements of China, and K'ang undertook earnestly and tirelessly to promote it. He deplored the failure of the Chinese people "to venerate and have faith in Confucius" who was China's own "founder of religion." Europe and America, he said, had the Christian religion; even uncultured peoples were not without their religions. Would the four hundred million Chinese, he asked, be content to do without religion, "like birds and beasts"?[65]

K'ang's conception of religion then was a syncretism heavily biased in favor of Confucianism. Instead of weaving elements of Confucianism, Buddhism, and Christianity, on equal terms, into a new "unity of three religions,"[66] he drew upon the two alien religions merely to bolster up the indigenous "religion." The result was less the founding of a syncretic religion than an attempt to move Confucianism from the plane of moral philosophy to that of religious faith.

An important point may be made here. K'ang discoursed earnestly and sometimes pontifically on religion but his conception of religion was decidedly secular. He valued Buddhism and Christianity not for their spiritual or transcendental values but for their effectiveness as social or moral forces. It was precisely in this respect that he considered Confucianism superior. Some remarks made in 1904 in his "Record of Travel in Italy" show how little K'ang appreciated spiritual values and religious sentiments. Contending that it was erroneous to discount Confucius as a founder of religion because he did not talk about *shen-tao* ("divine way") he wrote:

Chiao ("teachings," "religions") are of various sorts. Some instruct men by means of the divine way, other by means of the human way, still others

[64] Liang, *Nan-hai K'ang* . . . , p. 70.

[65] K'ang, *K'ang Nan-hai Liang Jen-kung erh hsien-sheng wen-chi ho-k'e*, 2: 2a. This passage is paraphrased in Forke, *Geschichte der neuren chinesischen Philosophie*, p. 580.

[66] J. J. M. de Groot, *Religion in China*, pp. 2–3.

by means of both the divine and human way. The essential significance of any *chiao* consists in making men avoid evil and do good. . . . Anciently, men were ignorant. They believed that everything beyond their clear perception was spiritual or divine. The sages took advantage of their belief and instilled in them the fear [of the Unseen]. As a result men had something that they feared, and refrained from doing evil; and something that they longed for, and readily turned toward goodness. Hence most of the archaic religions set forth clear-cut doctrines on ghosts and spirits. The Buddhist, Christian, and Moslem religions made use of such ancient doctrines to form the conceptions of paradise and hell with which to influence men. . . .

Confucius loathed divine authority for its excessive influence [on men] and swept it away. . . . Previously, the divine way was employed to control primitive men, but the human way was employed when progress had been made. . . . As a founder of religion Confucius represented an advanced stage in cultural progress. . . . Now as men's intelligence gradually develops, divine authority gradually loses its hold on them. Confucianism therefore suits the present world best.[67]

It hardly needs pointing out that in welcoming the eclipse of "divine authority" K'ang implicitly rejected all religions based on supernatural or suprahuman sanctions. And in crediting Confucius with "sweeping away divine authority" he unwittingly brought Confucianism back from the realm of religion into the realm of moral philosophy.

K'ang's nonspiritual conception of religion, as a matter of fact, was of Confucian origin. His statement, "some instruct by means of the divine way," was based on a passage in the *Book of Changes*, i.e., "the holy man uses the divine way to give instruction and the world submits to him."[68] His atheistic attitude probably found its roots in other classics also. The *Analects*, for instance, contains this passage: "The subjects on which the Master did not talk, were—extraordinary things, feats of strength, disorder, and spiritual beings."[69] K'ang commented

---

[67] K'ang, "I-ta-li yu-chi," pp. 66–68. Obviously, part of the cogency of K'ang's argument rests on the double meaning of *chiao*, namely, "teaching" and "religion."

[68] Richard Wilhelm, *The I Ching*, 2: 125–26, "Kuan," "Commentary on the Decision."

[69] *Analects*, VII.20. K'ang may also have received suggestion from Hsün-tzu who rejected belief in the supernatural. See chapters on "T'ien-lun" and "Fei-hsiang." Hsiao, *Chung-kuo cheng-chih ssu-hsiang shih* (Taipei ed.), pp. 107–9, presents Hsün-tzu's view. Wright, *Buddhism in Chinese History*, p. 81, calls "the notion that the Chinese are rationalistic . . . and thus somehow immune to religious emotion" "a quite baseless myth that has long beclouded discussions of religion." However, he goes on to say that euphemism is a force for "Sinicization," and draws attention to the transformation of "symbols of religious ideas and aspirations" (such as "the Maitreyas, Amitābhas and other divinities" into "the potbellied patrons of one earthly concern or

on this passage in 1902 and concluded that fanatic beliefs in spiritual beings were detrimental to men and society. He cited the case of India where oxen, elephants, monkeys, and other animals were regarded as sacred, to support his contention that Confucius performed a valuable service to mankind in sweeping away "divine authority." K'ang said in his comment:

> For extraordinary things, feats of strength, disorder, and spiritual beings are to be found only in the Age of Disorder; when the Age of Universal Peace arrives, not only extraordinary things, feats of strength, and disorder disappear, but also spiritual beings which no longer exert "divine authority." Confucius did not talk on them because he wished to root out those traits of human nature, which existed in the Age of Disorder, and to prepare men beforehand for the coming of Universal Peace.[70]

In other words, religious faith, like political rulership, was useful only so long as human society fell short of perfection. With the arrival of utopia both would have served their purposes and would disappear. Prayer, which to K'ang was a confession of human weakness and imperfection, would also fall into desuetude.[71]

In the same vein K'ang discoursed on the "soul," his conception of which was also partly of Confucian origin. According to him, man had *hun* ("soul") and *p'e* ("animal spirit"), the former constituting the fine and the latter the coarse part of his nature. *Hun*, he said, inclined naturally toward "virtue," whereas *p'e* gave impetus to sensuous desires. Human behavior was determined as *hun* or *p'e* gained the upper hand. K'ang illustrated this with man's love of sensuous beauty:

> Upon receiving light and perceiving colors the eyes take delight in those colors that are agreeable to them. Electric impulses incite one another, *hun* loses its self-control and follows [the direction of *p'e*]. . . . But if the colors perceived by the eyes are changed [to those that are disagreeable to them] . . . the delight disappears immediately. All this is due to the action of *p'e*. . . . Hence one whose *hun* is pure and is master of itself, loves virtue; one who gives free rein to his impure *p'e*, loves sensuous beauty.[72]

For this reason, K'ang concluded, it was important to cultivate

---

another: pawnbroker guilds, local industry, expectant motherhood") (ibid., p. 99). One suspects that the author reaffirms, unintentionally, the "rationalistic" disposition of the Chinese.

[70] K'ang, *Lun-yü chu*, *chüan* 7, pp. 9b–10a.
[71] Ibid., p. 16a, commenting on *Analects*, VII.34.
[72] Ibid., *chüan* 9, p. 12b, commenting on *Analects*, IX.17 (cf. XI.12).

"purity of soul," so that his *hun*, like a mirror, reflected the image of everything without itself being affected by anything.[73] These conceptions of *hun* and *p'e* echoed the traditional Confucian view[74] and resembled Chu Hsi's dualistic doctrine of "Heavenly principle" and "human desires."[75]

"Soul" as K'ang conceived of it was an ethical and not a religious notion. Nor was his view concerning the relationship between "soul" and body a religious one. Unlike Buddhists and Christian theologians who renounced the carnal and stressed the spiritual, K'ang regarded both as legitimate aspects of human life. The following shows his position:

> Men are born with a *shen-hun* ("spiritual soul") and *t'i-p'e* ("animal spirits"). Those who attach importance solely to the soul regard the body as merely a temporary lodging house [of the soul] and do not love the body, such as Buddhists, Christians, and Moslems. Those who attach importance solely to animal spirits, such as Taoists following the teaching of Lao-tzu, seek physical immortality. Those who attach sole importance to the body, such as Tseng-tzu, zealously protect the body [against danger and injury]. . . . Confucius, however, . . . cultivated both the soul and body.[76]

Here K'ang revealed another reason for his preference for Confucianism to Buddhism or Christianity.

K'ang's conception of *ming*, "fate," or as Legge had it, "the ordinances of Heaven," also shows Confucian influence. Commenting on Confucius' saying, "without recognizing the ordinance of Heaven, it is impossible to be a superior man,"[77] K'ang wrote:

> *Ming* is what man receives from Heaven. In a man's life wealth, honor, poverty, humble status, longevity, premature death, frustration, and success—all these are determined by *ming* and cannot be brought about by human effort.[78]

K'ang personally believed in this doctrine of *ming*. He said in 1902:

> I lost my father [when I was a child] and did not concern myself with accumulating wealth; and yet I have never been without financial resources. Moreover, I have repeatedly met with difficulties and calamities, but I came through them all unscathed. . . .[79]

[73] Ibid., *chüan* 6, p. 2a, commenting on *Analects*, VI.2.
[74] E.g., *Li-chi cheng-i*, "T'an kung hsia," p. 59 and "Chi i," pp. 24–27.
[75] Fung, *History of Chinese Philosophy*, 2: 558–62, summarizes Chu Hsi's view.
[76] K'ang, *Lun-yü chu*, *chüan* 8, p. 2b.
[77] *Analects*, XX.3.
[78] K'ang, *Lun-yü chu*, *chüan* 2, p. 5b.
[79] Ibid., *chüan* 11, p. 8b.

But K'ang was not a fatalist. He believed that while a man should not disobey "the ordinances of Heaven," he could and should regulate his conduct in such a way as to improve his lot in a later life or to bring blessings to his offspring. He wrote in 1901:

> Wealth, honor, poverty, lowly status, distress, and calamities have their causes. The *Hsiao-ching wei* says, "Good or evil is recompense." . . . Thus in a previous life one made the causes of good or evil and receives his recompense in his present life. . . . The *Hsi-tz'u* [of the *Book of Changes*] says "A house that heaps good upon good is sure to have an abundance of blessings. A house that heaps evil upon evil is sure to have an abundance of ills." Ancestors made the causes of good or evil and the offspring receive the resultant recompense. . . . Recompense is the rational principle of Heaven; man cannot but receive it obediently. Men should therefore be careful in making the causes.[80]

The *Hsiao-ching wei*, related to the *Book of Filial Piety*, is one of the "apocrypha" of the Confucian classics. The *Hsi-tz'u* is one of the commentaries of the *Book of Changes*.[81] K'ang's doctrine of "recompense" may therefore be traced to New Text Confucianism. It may also have been inspired by the Buddhist notion of *kuo-pao*, "retribution for good or evil deeds, implying that different conditions in this (or any) life are the variant ripenings, or fruit, of seed sown in previous life or lives."[82]

K'ang's acceptance of the Buddhist theory of the "Wheel of Transmigration" may be noted in this connection. Commenting on a passage in the *Analects* concerning spirits[83] K'ang quoted from the *Book of Changes* in which it is said, "we can penetrate the *tao* of day and night,"[84] and made the following remarks:

> "To penetrate the *tao* of day and night" refers to the Wheel of Transmigration. Those who die in one place are born in another place. Men die to become spirits and spirits are reborn to be men. All this is brought about by the Wheel of Transmigration. The way of Confucius includes everything. . . . Men of later times avoided talking about anything [that the] Buddha had [also] said. They would not stop until they had drastically narrowed down the scope of Confucianism.[85]

[80] K'ang, *Chung-yung chu*, p. 12b.
[81] *Hsiao-ching wei* is one of the "apocrypha" used by Kung-yang scholars. The passage that K'ang quoted from the *I-ching* is a part of the "Wen-yen" (Commentary on the Words of the Text) of "K'un," not the "Hsi-tz'u," as K'ang indicated. See Wilhelm, *I Ching*, 2: 26–27.
[82] Soothill and Hodous, *Dictionary of Chinese Buddhist Terms*, p. 264.
[83] *Analects*, XI.11.
[84] See Wilhelm, *I Ching*, 2: 318–19.
[85] K'ang, *Lun-yü chu*, chüan 11, p. 4b.

In summary, K'ang attempted to transform Confucianism into a religion by (1) making use of whatever suitable ideas he found in Confucianism and borrowing whatever Buddhist and Christian notions that were serviceable; (2) acknowledging the "equality" of all religions but insisting on the doctrinal and practical superiority of Confucianism; and (3) contending that owing to its intrinsic superiority the "Confucian religion" was theoretically suitable for all mankind, and that it was the only "religion" suitable for China under the existing conditions.

The result fell short of K'ang's declared goal. On the one hand, in conceiving "religion" largely in moral terms and in minimizing the spiritual values or "divine authority" he did not succeed in transferring Confucianism from the sphere of ethics into that of religion. On the other hand, by grafting Buddhist and Christian notions upon Confucianism he modified or extended the scope of Confucian teaching to a certain extent, but he did not produce a true synthesis of the "three religions." It is not surprising that he achieved little more than this. For after all, he remained a Confucian in his intellectual outlook, despite his repudiation of Neo-Confucianism. Such an outlook imposed definite limitations on his syncretic endeavor and dictated the results.

Two questions may be raised here. (1) How did his attempt to promote the "Confucian religion" affect the reform movement? and (2) What was the impact of that "religion" on his contemporaries?

In answer to the first, the Confucian-religion movement affected the reform movement in much the same way as the attempt to present Confucius as a "reformer." As soon as K'ang's "religious" views became known, a chorus of violent protests rose in the scholar-official world. Tseng Lien, a tradition-bound Confucian scholar of Hunan, memorialized in the summer of 1898 that in elevating Confucius to the position of "founder of religion" K'ang "intended to treat Confucius as Moses and put himself in the role of Jesus Christ," thereby making himself the *chiao-huang* (literally, "religious emperor," i.e., pope) of China. In other words, K'ang capitalized on the name of Confucius to advance his personal ambition.[86] Ch'en Pao-chen, who was instrumental in launching the daring program of reform in Hunan province, was also greatly disturbed by K'ang's "religious" views. About two months before Tseng Lien voiced his protest, Ch'en said in a memorial to the emperor:

[86] Tseng Lien, "Ying chao shang feng-shih," in Chien, *Wu-hsü*, 2: 492.

K'ang Yu-wei living at a time when China has come into contact with the West, imagines that the cause of the strength and prosperity of foreign countries lies in the fact that European nations show reverence to the Pope. . . . Hence . . . he venerates Confucius, calling him "founder of religion," with a view to matching the strength and influence [of Confucianism] with those of Catholicism. . . . He does not know . . . that followers of Europe's Pope . . . provoked wars which lasted for decades. . . . With the rise of political and natural sciences their religion has declined.[87]

Sun Chia-nai, another high official sympathetic to reform, also took exception to K'ang's apothesis of Confucius in a memorial presented at about the same time.[88] In fact, with the exception of the small group of K'ang's most ardent supporters, all who had heard of his views objected to them. If K'ang had hoped that his Confucian-religion movement would win more support for his cause, he was foredoomed to disappointment.

Apart from its adverse effects on the reform movement K'ang's effort to develop a Confucian religion was far from successful. He was fighting against tremendous odds. The Chinese cultural background hardly favored the development of religion, Confucian or otherwise. Compared with European countries, India, and even Japan, China for centuries past had a culture that was predominantly nonreligious. "The Chinese have been primarily interested in this life," as a Western writer observed, and "their ethics emphasize man's duty to man rather than man's duty to God."[89] K'ang's claim that Confucius was a "founder of religion" must have appeared preposterous, if not sinister, to most of his fellow scholars, and anachronistic, or at least ill-advised, to intellectuals of a later generation.

K'ang was also confronted with a difficulty inherent in his own intellectual position. As the Confucian outlook was predominantly nonreligious, obviously it was impossible to create a "Confucian religion" without abandoning that outlook. Confucianism was perhaps not totally devoid of religious implications.[90] But it was essentially secular and

---

[87] Ch'en, "Tsou ch'ing li-cheng hsüeh-shu tsao-chiu jen-ts'ai che," p. 16.

[88] Sun Chia-nai, "Tsou . . . ch'ing yen-chin pei-shu shu," in Yü Pao-hsüan, *Huang-ch'ao hsü-ai wen-pien*, *chüan* 72, p. 5.

[89] Latourette, *The Development of China*, pp. 86–87. A number of Chinese writers hold a similar view, e.g., Chiang Monlin, *Tides from the West*, p. 252: "Chinese morals are derived from nature; Christian morals from divine power." See also Cheng T'ien-hsi, *China Molded by Confucius*, p. 47.

[90] E. T. Williams, "The State Religion of China," *Journal of the North-China Branch of the Royal Asiatic Society*, 44 (1913): 11; Herrlee Glessner Creel, "Was Confucius Agnostic?" *T'oung Pao*, series 2, 29 (1932): 54–99.

widely separated from such religions as Christianity and Islam, which stressed human sinfulness and the omnipotence of a personal God.[91] K'ang never gave up the Confucian outlook; in arguing that Confucianism was superior to Christianity precisely because Confucius "swept away divine authority" he reaffirmed the secular character of the Confucian teaching (and his own thinking). He may be called inconsistent, therefore, in trying to promote a "Confucian religion." Liang Ch'i-ch'ao seems to have detected this inconsistency when he rejected K'ang's religious interpretation of Confucianism and pointed out that "Confucius was an ancient sage," not a deity, and that the Confucian teaching was a "teaching in the educational, not religious sense."[92]

Conceivably, K'ang's failure to attract a large following was due partly to the manner in which he promoted the "Confucian religion." Instead of relying on persuasion, faith, and fervor, he sought the sanction of government authority, both in Ch'ing times and the early years of the republic. Thus in 1895 he proposed to the imperial court that an empire-wide effort be made to disseminate the teaching of Confucius, to convert all unauthorized temples into Confucian shrines, and to send Confucian missionaries to preach to overseas Chinese.[93] In the summer of 1898 he formally proposed that Confucianism be established as "state religion" and a Confucian "church" (*chiao-hui*) be instituted.[94] He renewed this proposal in republican times. In 1913 he proposed to the Chinese parliament that Confucianism be recognized as state religion and weekly services be performed in all Confucian shrines in the country.[95] His pleas fell on deaf ears. The Ch'ing government, which accepted Confucianism as state ideology, was not willing to treat it as state religion; it could not subscribe to K'ang's version of Confucianism, which so glaringly deviated from the state ideology. The govern-

---

[91] James W. Bashford, *China, an Interpretation*, p. 238.

[92] Liang Ch'i-ch'ao, *Yin-ping-shih wen-chi* (Kuang-chih shu-chü ed.), *chüan* 1, p. 19, quoted in Pascal M. D'Elia, S. J., "Un maître de la jeune Chine: Liang K'i-tch'ao," *T'oung Pao*, series 2, 18 (1917): 268–69.

[93] K'ang, "Shang Ch'ing-ti ti-erh shu" ("Kung-chü shang shu"), Kuang-hsü 21/4/8, in Chien, *Wu-hsü*, 2: 150.

[94] K'ang, "Ch'ing tsun K'ung-sheng wei kuo-chiao li chiao-pu chiao-hui i K'ung-tzu chi-nien che," *Wu-hsü tsou-kao*, pp. 26a–b and *K'ang Nan-hai hsien-sheng wen-ch'ao*, 5: 10b (hereafter cited as *Wen-ch'ao*).

[95] K'ang, "I K'ung-chiao wei kuo-chiao p'ei t'ien i," *Wen-ch'ao*, 4: 63a–67b and *K'ang Nan-hai wen-chi*, *chüan* 5, pp. 2a–6a (hereafter, *Wen-chi*). For brief accounts of K'ang's "Confucian religion" movement, see Reginald I. Johnston, *Confucianism and Modern China*, pp. 152–53, 157–58; P'an Shu-fan, *Chung-hua min-kuo hsien-fa shih*, pp. 42–43.

ment of the republic was too much engrossed in internal political struggles and economic exigencies to pay attention to K'ang's appeals. The
intellectuals of the time were too divided or uncertain in their opinions
to come to any agreement concerning the place of Confucianism in
modern China. Members of the Catholic, Protestant, Moslem, Buddhist,
and Taoist organizations took offense at K'ang's action and, under the
leadership of Ma Hsiang-po (Ma Liang) and Yung Chien-ch'iu (both
ardent Catholics), formed a Society for Religious Freedom to block
K'ang's state-religion movement.[96]

However, it is doubtful that K'ang could have achieved greater success if he appealed to China's intellectuals in general instead of to the
government authorities. The main opposition to his "religious" movement, after all, came from individual scholars and intellectuals, who
opposed it not because K'ang sought to invoke government authority
but because they regarded it as incompatible with the authentic Confucian tradition or unsuitable for modern China.

K'ang's personal behavior also may have contributed to his lack of
success. Throughout his entire life he deported himself not as a religious
leader but as a man of culture and learning, not inappreciative of sensuous pleasures and creature comforts.[97] Despite his repudiation of Neo-
Confucianism, he led a personal life that hardly resembled that of a
pious man of any of the major religions of the world. And despite his
willingness to dispense with the family in his utopian scheme, he was
very much a "family man" who took concubines because his wife did
not bear him any male offspring. All this was perfectly justifiable on
Confucian ethical grounds but hardly inspiring from the viewpoint of
religion. Perhaps a spiritual impetus might have been lent to his "Confucian religion," had he resorted to martyrdom in 1898. Politically
speaking, K'ang may have been perfectly prudent in saving his own
life in the coup d'état, with the intention of rendering further service

---

[96] Chang Jo-ku, *Ma Hsiang-po hsien-sheng nien-p'u* (1939), p. 222. Chang Ping-lin,
the most eminent Old Text scholar of modern times, offered strong opposition to
K'ang's movement. See his "Po chien-li K'ung-chiao i," in *T'ai-yen wen-lu, chüan* 2,
pp. 38a–41a; and Ku Chieh-kang, "Tzu-hsü," p. 24. Another (perhaps more potent)
force condemning K'ang's attempt to failure was the antireligious movement that
gathered strength early in 1920. See Tse-tung Chow, *The May Fourth Movement: Intellectual Revolution in Modern China*, pp. 320–27. Even Liang Ch'i-ch'ao opposed K'ang
in this regard. See "Pao-chiao fei shou-i tsun-K'ung lun," *Yin-ping-shih wen-chi*, 9:
50–59.

[97] K'ang gave clear expression to his hedonistic philosophy in *Ta-t'ung shu*, pp. 7,
9, 441–51 (Thompson, *Ta T'ung Shu*, pp. 68–69, 71, 271–74).

to the emperor and empire. From the viewpoint of religion, however, his Confucian cause was not served by his life of roving in foreign lands and his lack of austerity. Thus the entire Confucian-religion movement lacked emotional or spiritual appeal, whatever may have been the merits of its doctrine. Indeed one may hesitate to call it a religious movement at all.

K'ANG'S PLACE IN THE CONFUCIAN TRADITION

From the foregoing account we come to the conclusion that K'ang Yu-wei was a "patriotic" Confucian scholar who endeavored "to preserve the country, the race, and the teaching" by adapting the Confucian tradition as well as the imperial system to the new conditions that prevailed in the closing decades of the nineteenth century and the early years of the twentieth. He was not greatly different from men like Chang Chih-tung, who sought China's salvation in the formula, "Chinese learning for the fundamental principles and Western learning for practical application.[98] The difference was largely a matter of degree: while Chang wished to preserve "Chinese learning" (Confucianism) as it was maintained by tradition and to borrow from "Western learning" little more than technology, K'ang offered unconventional interpretations of Confucianism and proposed institutional reforms in addition to adoption of Western science and technology. K'ang was thus considerably more radical than Chang but no less earnest in seeking to perpetuate the authority and influence of Confucianism.[99] K'ang was as firmly convinced as Chang that "veneration of Confucius" (*tsun K'ung*) and "preservation of the teaching" (*pao chiao*) should go hand in hand with "attaining prosperity and power through reform."[100] As a defender of Confucianism K'ang may be called as "conservative" as Chang, particularly in his attitude toward China's tradition, immediately after the

---

[98] Teng and Fairbank, *China's Response to the West*, pp. 164–66, outline Chang's ideas of reform, and pp. 166–74 gives translation of portions of Chang's *Ch'üan-hsüeh p'ien*. This formula may be traced to Fung Kuei-fen, "Ts'ai hsi-hsueh": "If we let the moral principles and ethical teachings of China serve as the original foundation and let them be supplemented by the methods used by various [Western] countries for the attainment of prosperity and strength, would it not be the best for all procedures?" (Taken from Teng and Fairbank, *China's Response*, p. 52, with slight modifications).

[99] Hummel, "K'ang Yu-wei, Historical Critic and Social Philosopher, 1858–1927," p. 345.

[100] K'ang, Pao-kuo hui chang-ch'eng," in Yeh, *Chüeh-mi yao-lu, chüan* 4, p. 1a.

founding of the republic.[101] "The last stand of Chinese conservatism"[102] was not taken by the leaders of the T'ung-chih restoration in the 1860s and 1870s but by K'ang Yu-wei and a number of other Confucian scholars, working independently of one another, in the closing decades of the nineteenth century and early years of the twentieth.

It is interesting that as late as the fifth decade of the twentieth century writers of diverse intellectual backgrounds have echoed the view that Confucianism would have a bright future in the modern world. Liang Sou-ming, one of the staunchest defenders of Chinese culture, voiced the conviction that Confucianism would have an important place in "the world civilization of the future."[103] Chiang Mon-lin, a man who can hardly be regarded as a Confucian, and who is not hostile to Western civilization, says that "Confucius' teaching of proper human relations and world peace, and the democratic ideas of Mencius, will fit China to be a modern democratic state."[104] A number of Western writers have expressed similar sentiments. W. A. P. Martin asserted that "no nation, with one exception, ever received from antiquity a more precious heritage" than the teaching of the Sage.[105] Richard Wilhelm believed that Confucianism contains "certain fundamental elements which can be applied in every age and place" and that it "very definitely possesses sufficient inner elasticity to accommodate itself also to modern conditions."[106] And it may be recalled also that Confucianism commanded the attention of some of Europe's keenest minds in the eighteenth century.[107] K'ang's faith in Confucius then, was not the result of unreasoned bias.

K'ang's most important work, however, lay in his endeavor to adapt Confucianism to the needs of the time. The imperial system with its characteristic ideology and institutions was developed when the Chinese

[101] K'ang's position is most clearly revealed in his "K'ung-chiao hui hsü," in *Wen-ch'ao*, 5: 12a–13a. The following statement is particularly noteworthy: "Why was China able to achieve peace and unity, and realize good government for two thousand years? Because it was ruled by means of 'one half of the *Analects*.'" The phrase "one half of the *Analects*" was traditionally attributed to Chao P'u (A.D. 921–91).

[102] Mary Clabaugh Wright, *The Last Stand of Chinese Conservatism: The T'ung-Chih Restoration, 1862–1874*.

[103] O. Brière, *Fifty Years of Chinese Philosophy, 1898–1950*, p. 28, quoting Liang: "The world-civilization of the future will be the renovated Chinese civilization." Earlier in Brière's book (p. 27), Liang was described as "the defender of Confucianism."

[104] Chiang, *Tides from the West*, p. 271.

[105] W. A. P. Martin, *A Cycle of Cathay*, p. 59.

[106] Richard Wilhelm, *Confucius and Confucianism*, pp. 154–55.

[107] Adolf Reichwein, *China and Europe*, pp. 73–98.

empire existed largely in isolation. Confucianism, which had its inception in the last years of China's *feng-chien* ("feudal") period, had become
increasingly entangled with the imperial system ever since the Han
dynasty. It did not matter, as Chu Hsi contended, that "the way of
Confucius had not been put into practice for a single day" during the
centuries of imperial rule.[108] The fact that Confucianism was employed
as an ideological tool by the emperors was sufficient to make it virtually
synonymous with autocratic rule. There is some justification, therefore, for the view that Confucius' institutional formula "expresses in a
normative way a basic feature of Oriental despotism,"[109] or more simply, "the principles of Confucius were despotic."[110] The repeated defeats
and humiliations suffered by the empire convinced K'ang that the imperial system, both in its administrative and ideological aspects, had
outgrown its usefulness. It suited China more in the past centuries of
isolation than at a time when she had come into contact with foreign
countries. The superior strength of Western powers and Japan, a
country that had successfully copied Western ways, was compelling
evidence that China too must change her ways to meet the requirements of the modern world—not merely by adopting the technology
of the West, as the imperial government had been trying to do without
much success for the past thirty years, but by effecting appropriate institutional and ideological reforms. K'ang was probably the first man
of his time to perceive clearly and plead earnestly that such reforms
be promptly undertaken. It was to his credit also that he alone realized
that unless Confucianism was dissociated from the outmoded political
system it would be brought to ruin by the rotten weight of that system.
With rare courage he repudiated the Neo-Confucian tradition, "imperial Confucianism," in James Legge's words; he thus "challenged
the very foundation upon which traditional orthodox Chinese scholarship and political philosophy were built."[111] It is therefore hardly accurate to say with a Japanese scholar that K'ang, seeing "the eternal
element" of Confucianism, committed the error of "applying its vari-
able part to the present."[112] On the contrary, K'ang was emphatic in
rejecting any part of it that was tied to specific institutional systems of

---

[108] Chu Hsi, "Ta Ch'en T'ung-fu shu," *Chu Wen-kung wen-chi, chüan* 36, p. 579.
[109] Karl August Wittfogel, "Chinese Society: An Historical Survey," *Journal of Asian Studies*, 16 (1957): 350.
[110] Léon Wieger, *La Chine moderne*, 7: 67, quoted in Wright, *Last Stand of Chinese Conservatism*, p. 304.
[111] Ping-ti Ho, "Weng T'ung-ho and the 'One Hundred Days of Reform,'" p. 131.
[112] Kyoson Tsuchida, *Contemporary Thought of Japan and China*, p. 200.

the past. It is somewhat misleading to say simply that the ideological and institutional reforms that K'ang envisaged constituted a "change within the tradition."[113] One can hardly overemphasize the fact that the conceptual framework within which he sought to perform his tasks was not the tradition that was generally accepted by his fellow scholars (the Confucianism that determined the basic social and moral values of imperial China) but a Confucianism based on doctrines of the Kung-yang school (a school of classical commentators whose views for centuries had been regarded as unorthodox) and ideas of non-Chinese origins.

In other words, K'ang was a Confucian revisionist. In modifying and extending the contents of Confucian thought he may be said to have performed a service to Confucianism. During a period of over twenty centuries since the death of its founder, Confucianism had undergone several stages of theoretical development. The first stage was reached shortly before the First Emperor of Ch'in unified China, when Mencius and Hsün-tzu established two rival schools of thought and developed Confucius' teaching in two directions. The second stage culminated with Tung Chung-shu and other Kung-yang scholars of Han times.[114] The third was brought about by the Neo-Confucians of the Sung dynasty, when elements of Taoism and Buddhism were appropriated to give Confucianism a philosophical refinement hitherto unknown.[115] Now K'ang Yu-wei, taking clues directly from Kung-yang scholars of the nineteenth century and making use of Western as well as Buddhist ideas, gave a cosmopolitan or universalist meaning to Confucianism and thus extended the scope of its ethical and political doctrines. He may be said then to have launched a fourth stage of the development of Confucianism and so occupies a highly important position in its history.[116]

But he failed to attract supporters, because he was too much ahead of the intellectual world in the nineteenth century and too much behind it in the twentieth. In the closing decades of the nineteenth century the overwhelming majority of scholars and officials were still too profoundly

[113] John K. Fairbank, *The United States and China*, p. 148.
[114] Hsiao, "Weng T'ung-ho and the Reform Movement of 1898," chap. 2; chap. 9, sec. 1.
[115] Fung, *History of Chinese Philosophy*, vol. 2, chaps. 10–14, and Chang, *Development of Neo-Confucian Thought*, chaps. 6–12.
[116] Perhaps it is not accurate to say, as Wright does (*Buddhism in Chinese History*, p. 281), that K'ang's reinterpretation amounted to revival of an "earlier Confucianism," pure and simple.

steeped in the old tradition, too uninformed of the intellectual and political problems that faced the empire, and too blinded by their vested interests to appreciate K'ang's views. Consequently, his intellectual labors produced little more than a startling heterodoxy in the eyes of the average scholar-official. The situation after 1911 was different but hardly more propitious to K'ang's cause. Many now regarded Confucius as the sage of the imperial past, whose teaching had no bearing on republican China. To make the situation worse, K'ang, in his desire to salvage the ancient heritage, obliterated the dividing line that he had previously maintained between "false" or imperial Confucianism and "authentic" or reconstituted Confucianism, thus undoing his work of intellectual reform. Both versions of Confucianism commanded increasingly less attention in modern China. K'ang's pleas on behalf of *K'ung-chiao*, "the Confucian teaching," were not so much opposed as ridiculed or ignored by the younger generations of Chinese intellectuals. His writings on Confucius and the classics, which formerly had inspired, shocked, or incensed many a scholar-official, were now seldom read. A Western writer observed in the early 1930s that during the past eighteen hundred years the fortunes of Confucianism never fell so low as they did after the revolution of 1911.[117] It is hardly surprising that the "sage of Nan-hai" died in 1927 without winning republican China for Confucius.

Perhaps K'ang himself had unknowingly contributed to the eclipse of Confucianism in more ways than one. In the years immediately before 1898 he strove valiantly to disengage Confucianism from autocracy. However, in taking a leading role in the Pao-huang hui (Society for Protecting the Emperor) after the coup d'état, in opposing vociferously the republic in favor of "constitutional monarchy" between 1898 and 1911,[118] and in participating in the abortive attempts at Manchu restoration in 1917 and again in 1923,[119] K'ang had unmistakably identified himself with the imperial cause and was accordingly regarded by many as an enemy of the republic. And, at the same time, in assum-

[117] Johnston, *Confucianism and Modern China*, p. 125.

[118] Ting, *Liang Jen-kung . . .* , 1: 88, 99–145, indicates the activities of the Pao-huang hui. K'ang's views on monarchical and republican governments are more or less systematically presented in his pamphlet, *Kung-ho cheng-t'i lun*, written in 1911, publication date not indicated.

[119] K'ang, "Fu Ta-wei hou-chüeh shu" (Letter in reply to Marquis Ōkuma, July 1917) and "Yu Hsu t'ai-fu shu," both in *Pu-jen*, nos. 9 and 10, "Cheng-lun," pp. 1–15, and pp. 15–18. K'ang gives brief accounts of the abortive attempts in 1917 and 1923 in "Ting-ssu Mei-shen-kuan yu-chü shih-chüan," and "Ch'ing Chuang-shih-tun tai-tsou yu-shuo ching-kuo," *K'ang Nan-hai hsien-sheng mo-chi*, vol. 4.

ing a leading role in the Confucian movement he unwittingly brought Confucianism again into association with monarchism, to the detriment of that movement. Confucianism was thus thoroughly discredited in the eyes of the supporters of the republic. Understandably, it was condemned as an obstacle to political democracy and social progress.

Yüan Shih-k'ai, the first president of the republic, hardly improved matters when he declared in his inaugural address in 1912 that "the immortal tradition and precepts" of Confucianism should not be swept into oblivion, and inculcated "the duty of doing reverence to Confucius" in a presidential mandate a few months later. Meanwhile, a proposal to establish Confucianism as state religion was introduced in the ramshackle parliament. Members belonging to the Kuo-min tang vigorously opposed it, whereas those belonging to the pro-Yüan Chin-pu tang (Progressive Party) supported it. In a face-saving compromise a clause was inserted in the "draft constitution" of the republic, providing for taking "the way of Confucius as the basis of personal cultivation in national education."[120] As this document never took effect and the parliament that drafted it was soon afterwards dissolved by Yüan Shih-k'ai, the provision had no more significance than waste paper. And when Yüan betrayed the republic in 1915, Confucianism, thanks to its unfortunate association with the short-lived "Hung-hsien imperial regime," was given additional bad odor. K'ang was opposed to Yüan's move but he could not disperse the widely held view that Confucianism was firmly wedded to monarchism—a view that he had recently helped to form in another connection.

Had K'ang ceased to fight for the cause of the defunct Ch'ing dynasty and promoted modernized Confucianism as a loyal supporter of the republic, he might have had more success. In other words, had he preached after 1911 the doctrine of "Universal Peace" that implied "the people's rule" as the appropriate form of political organization, instead of clinging to the doctrine of "Minor Peace" and hearkening back to the imperial system, the cause of Confucianism might have been better served, even though the Chinese republic could not have been appreciably benefited by his efforts. He was, however, too much emotionally involved with the Ch'ing dynasty to shift his political allegiance and too deeply committed to monarchism to modify his intellectual position. His glowing description of democracy and optimistic formulations of the concepts of freedom, equality, and popular sover-

---

[120] Johnston, *Confucianism and Modern China*, pp. 152–53, 159; P'an, *Chung-hua min-kuo hsien-fa shih*, pp. 31, 42–43.

eignty remained exhilarating ingredients of his utopia, not intended for practical application. Monarchy continued for him to be the only suitable form of government, especially if the Kuang-hsü emperor or his legitimate successor was to sit on the throne. He was not aware that his loyalist commitment conflicted with his theoretical requirement to dissociate Confucianism from monarchy; he acted as if the two were inseparable. In so doing he injured the cause of Confucianism without benefiting the fallen dynasty.

K'ang may have prejudiced the Confucian cause in another way. In casting doubt on the authenticity of the Old Text classics he unintentionally opened wide the door to questioning the validity of the entire Confucian tradition. This was the verdict of Liang Ch'i-ch'ao. Writing in 1920 Liang commented on K'ang's book on the "forged classics" as follows:

> Waiving the question whether or not all his views are correct, it may be said that once his position was made known, two results were produced. First, the standpoint of the orthodox school of Ch'ing dynasty was shaken to its foundations and, second, all the ancient texts called for reexamination and reevaluation. This was in effect a gigantic cyclone blowing into the intellectual world.[121]

Liang then commented on K'ang's *Confucius as a Reformer*:

> The *Wei-ching k'ao* had already treated the major portion of the classics as sheer forgeries produced by Liu Hsin; the *Kai-chih k'ao* went further and treated all the authentic classics as Confucius' own writing that he attributed to antiquity. As a result of this, a fundamental doubt was cast upon the classics that for thousands of years had been accepted as sacred and inviolable. This produced a skeptic and critical attitude in scholars.

Liang continued:

> [K'ang] showed extreme reverence to Confucius. But since he had already asserted [in his *Kai-chih k'ao*]that Confucius' motivation, objective, and method in founding his school were no different from those of the other ancient philosophers, thus placing Confucius on the same level with them, he had in effect undone completely the notion of "distinguishing between black and white and establishing one supreme authority," and led men to the comparative study [of doctrines and schools].[122]

---

[121] Liang, *Ch'ing-tai hsüeh-shu kai-lun*, p. 128.
[122] Ibid., p. 132.

Chu I-Hsin shared Liang's opinion with added misgivings. In a letter to K'ang written before the reform days of 1898 Chu had said:

> With the circulation of the view that the Old Text classics are forgeries . . . men come to harbor the idea that all the Six Classics cannot be taken as authentic. Those who love the unusual and lack judgment resolve promptly to discard Confucianism and rely solely on the New Text. The minds of men are never satisfied. After two thousand years of the existence of the Six Classics the Old Text is suddenly pronounced unreliable. Is there any assurance that the New Text will be held reliable in another thousand or hundred years?[123]

It did not take that long to see Chu's misgivings substantiated. Only a few years after Chu wrote the letter, Liang Ch'i-ch'ao openly and directly questioned the value of K'ang's Confucian movement. In a letter (dated 1902) to K'ang, Liang bluntly stated that he did not see any sense in the attempt "to preserve the teaching," for, he explained, "to save the China of today the most urgent task is to replace old thinking with new learning," and "there is much in Confucianism that is unsuitable for the new world." He informed K'ang that he planned to write a book, jointly with a number of K'ang's followers, with the express purpose of "exposing the shortcomings of Confucianism and correcting them."[124] At about the same time, Huang Tsun-hsien, a close friend of Liang and an active reform leader, questioned the wisdom of elevating Confucius to the status of "founder of religion."[125]

Liang and Huang had ushered in a trend of challenging the authority of antiquity and discrediting Confucianism—a trend that rapidly gained momentum in the 1920s and 1930s. Ironically, K'ang's own writings on the classics constituted the chief source of inspiration for some of the later skeptics. Ch'ien Hsüan-t'ung published a new edition of K'ang's *Hsin-hsüeh wei-ching k'ao* in 1931 and said in a preface that as the major portion of the New Text classics were Confucius' own writings in which the Sage "attributed institutional reform to antiquity," scholars could only use these texts as material for "the history of Confucian thought," not for factual ancient history.[126] Ku Chieh-

---

123 Chu I-hsin, "Ta K'ang Yu-wei ti-san shu" (Su, *I-chiao ts'ung-pien, chüan* 1, p. 7).

124 Ting, *Liang Jen-kung* . . . , 1: 152–54. Liang reiterated the same sentiment in the 1920s (*Ch'ing-tai hsüeh-shu kai-lun*, pp. 143–44; translated by Immanuel C. Y. Hsü, in Liang, *Intellectual Trends in the Ch'ing Period*, pp. 103–4 [hereafter, Hsü, *Intellectual Trends in the Ch'ing Period*]).

125 Ting, *Liang Jen-kung* . . . , 1: 154–55.

126 Ch'ien Hsüan-t'ung says: "In 1911, when I went to study with Mr. Ts'ui [Shih], I borrowed from him [K'ang Yu-wei's] *Hsin-hsüeh wei-ching k'ao* and read it for the

kang, writing early in 1926, confessed that upon reading K'ang's *Confucius as a Reformer* he received the first impetus "to overthrow ancient history," as it was written and accepted by scholars of the past.[127] It was with ample justification that recent writers credited K'ang with initiating the modern "skeptic movement."[128]

It was but a short distance from questioning the authenticity of ancient history to denying the validity of Confucianism. Wu Yü and Ch'en Tu-hsiu, two of the best known leaders of the campaign "to smash the Confucian shop" (*ta-tao K'ung-chia tien*), set forth their iconoclastic views in the *Hsin-ch'ing-nien* (*La Jeunesse*) during the years 1915–21.[129] The war of extermination against Confucianism was now directed not merely against Neo-Confucianism but all schools of Confucianism, including the New Text and Kung-yang schools. Ch'en Tu-hsiu took K'ang directly to task:

> You distinguish between the Confucianism of the Confucians of Han and Sung on the one side and the "true" teachings of Confucius on the other. . . . I now wish to ask: why was it that all the Confucians since Han and T'ang times affiliated themselves with Confucius?

The answer to that question was indeed simple: "Precisely because the Confucian shop-sign had served the man-eating morality of the past two thousand years." It did not matter whether that sign was used to sell authentic or counterfeit Confucianism: "it must be taken down, smashed, and consigned to the flames."[130] Thus it was no longer a novel sentiment when the Chinese government abolished the official Confucian rites and declared in 1927:

---

first time. . . . From then on I have firmly subscribed to the view that the ancient-script Classics were forged by Liu Hsin" ("Ch'ung-yin *Hsin-hsüeh wei-ching k'ao* hsü," in the 1931 reprint of K'ang's book, 1: 16).

[127] Ku Chieh-kang, "Tzu-hsu," *Ku-shih pien*, vol. 1, p. 43.

[128] Ch'ien Mu, "K'ung-tzu yü *Ch'un-ch'iu*," *Journal of Oriental Studies*, 1: 20. Hou Wai-lu, *Chin-tai Chung-kuo ssu-hsiang hsüeh-shuo shih*, pp. 703–4, expresses a similar view.

[129] Kuo Chan-po, *Chin wu-shih nien Chung-kuo ssu-hsiang shih*, pp. 305–6; Wolfgang Franke, "Der Kampf der chinesischen Revolution gegen den Konfuzianismus," p. 6. See also Tse-tung Chow, *The May Fourth Movement*, pp. 300–313, and "The Anti-Confucian Movement in Early Republican China," in Wright, *The Confucian Persuasion*, pp. 288–375. Cf. Andrew T. Roy, "Modern Confucian Social Theory," chap. 4, "The Attack upon Confucianism from the Left: Ch'en Tu-hsiu," pp. 152–58, and chap. 5, "The Attack upon Confucianism from the Taoist and Legalist Position: Wu Yü," pp. 186–234.

[130] Hu Shih, "*Wu Yü wen-lu* hsü," dated Oct. 6, 1927, in Wu, *Wu Yü wen-lu*.

The principles of Confucius were despotic. For more than twenty centuries they served to oppress the people and enslave thought. . . . China now is a republic. These vestiges of absolutism should be effaced from the memory of citizens.[131]

A left-wing Chinese writer said in 1950 that Confucianism was the enemy of workers and peasants, the female sex, society and the state, and liberalism, and the benefactor of the wealthy, the male sex, the family and clan, and monarchial dictatorship.[132] This writer, it seems, added little to the anti-Confucian sentiment prevailing in the 1920s, beyond injecting into it a trace of "class consciousness." A few men, such as Ch'en Huan-chang and Liang Sou-ming, continued to defend Confucianism staunchly.[133] But their voices were feeble against the indifference of many and hostility of some of the intellectuals. The prospect of Confucianism appeared gloomy indeed in the years before K'ang's death.[134] In so far, therefore, as K'ang inspired skepticism of the established tradition, he may be said to have contributed to the undermining of Confucianism.[135] His attacks on the Old Text classics and Neo-Confucianism were "culturally subversive" and, by thus leading China to "cultural drift" in republican times, he may perhaps have cleared the way for the advent of Communist ideology,[136] and Communist organization.[137]

This is not saying that K'ang deliberately helped communism. He would have been horrified by the Communist regime and what it does to China—much more than by the outrageous deeds of the republican government that he lived to witness in the years 1912–27. It has sometimes been surmised that the Chinese Communists, for propaganda purposes at least, would make use of K'ang's "communistic" ideas concerning the family and property as set forth in the *Ta-t'ung shu.* But the fact

[131] Wieger, *La Chine moderne*, p. 67, quoting a Nationalist government order.

[132] Ts'ai Shang-ssu, *Chung-kuo ch'uan-t'ung ssu-hsiang tsung p'i-p'an*, pp. 70–72. Cf. Lin Yu-tang, "Some Hard Words about Confucius," *Harpers*, May 1935, p. 721, quoted by Hummel in "K'ang Yu-wei, Historical Critic and Social Philosopher, 1858–1927," p. 353.

[133] Liang Sou-ming, *Tung Hsi wen-hua chi ch'i che-hsüeh*, especially "Tzu-hsü."

[134] Johnston, *Confucianism and Modern China*, pp. 171–72.

[135] Joseph R. Levenson, " 'History' and 'Value,' " in Wright, *Studies in Chinese Thought*, p. 168.

[136] Joseph R. Levenson, *Confucian China and Its Modern Fate* (Berkeley: University of California Press), p. 163.

[137] Huang Yen-yu, "Mao's People Communes," *New York Times*, January 11, 1959. The author believes that "Mao has borrowed heavily for his ideas for communes" from K'ang's *Ta-t'ung shu.*

is that they have been in power for years and have not so far recognized K'ang as a pre-revolution prophet. This is because K'ang's philosophical standpoint was diametrically opposed to that of the Communists and his ideas of abolishing the family and private property were based on the "idealistic" notion of universal love, instead of the Marxist doctrine of class war. The Chinese Communists have even less reason to endorse K'ang Yu-wei than European or Russian Communists to acclaim Owen or Fourier.[138]

Ironically, then, K'ang praised Confucianism but ended in discrediting it. K'ang was of course not solely responsible for what happened to China's tradition. Conditions in China that prevailed for many decades made it difficult for Confucianism to survive and prosper.

The impact of the West played havoc with the native intellectual and moral values, and its total effect may be described as a cultural earthquake. Two different groups of men endeavored to save both the dynasty and the tradition. On the one side were the "conservatives" who defended the traditional political and ideological systems against any change; on the other side were the reformers who sought to adapt tradition to the altered conditions of the empire. K'ang was the leader of the latter group and undertook, in Fung Yu-lan's words, "to fill old bottles with new wine."[139] But his efforts turned out to be a "pitiable" struggle against unfavorable circumstances.[140] Others who tried "to make a revolution the heir of ancient tradition"[141] in the late 1920s were no more successful than he, and it would indeed be unfair to hold

[138] Mao acknowledged the historical significance of K'ang's reform movement, at least at one point. In his "Hsin min-chu chu-i lun" (January 1940), he regarded "the Reformist Movement of 1898" as one of the attempts made in "the preparatory period" of the Chinese revolution "to fight against imperialism and the feudal forces." See "On New Democracy," in *Selected Works*, 3: 111. But about ten years later, Mao said in his "Lun jen-min min-chu chuan-cheng" (June 1949): "Hung Hsiu-chuan, K'ang Yu-wei, Yen Fu and Sun Yat-sen were representatives of those who had looked to the West for truth before the Communist Party of China was born." Unfortunately, according to Mao, they all looked in the wrong direction. "Imperialist aggression shattered the fond dreams of the Chinese about learning from the West. . . . The Chinese learned a good deal from the West but they could not make it work and were never able to realize their ideals." Mao added: "K'ang Yu-wei wrote *Ta T'ung Shu*, or the *Book of Great Harmony*, but he did not and could not find the way to achieve Great Harmony." See "On the People's Democratic Dictatorship," *Selected Works*, 4: 412, 413, and 414. Fung Yu-lan's article, "K'ang Yu-wei ti ssu-hsiang," pp. 110–27, and Li Tse-hou's book, *K'ang Yu-wei T'an Ssu-t'ung ssu-hsiang*, pp. 1–102, represent recent views of K'ang voiced under the Communist regime.

[139] Fung, *History of Chinese Philosophy*, 2: 720.

[140] Amaury de Riencourt, *The Soul of China*, p. 203.

[141] Wright, *The Last Stand of Chinese Conservatism*, p. 300.

K'ang chiefly accountable for the general depreciation of Confucian values in modern China.

It should be emphasized that Confucianism had become preeminent in China only after the consolidation of the imperial system and primarily because of the endorsement of the imperial government.[142] With few exceptions the emperors, from Han to Ming and Ch'ing, discovered that Confucian moral precepts were a useful instrument with which to justify and strengthen their regimes. They honored Confucius even though they did not practice his doctrines or apply them in their administrations.[143] By means of these doctrines they evolved a system of social and moral values that gave the highest possible degree of political stability. Thus for two thousand years, Confucianism had been closely affiliated with the imperial system, not as an immanent principle, but as an ideological handmaid. Viewed in this light, Chu Hsi's statement that "the way of Confucius" had not been followed even for a single day during the entire imperial period appears to contain some truth.[144]

That the dominant position of Confucianism during that period was due less to its inherent strength than to the support of the government

[142] Formal actions were taken by Emperor Wu of Han when he instituted *po-shih*, "doctors," for the Five Classics in 136 B.C. and when he summoned Confucian scholars to the capital to take examinations in 134 B.C. Tung Chung-shu and Kung-sun Hung passed them with highest honors (Pan Ku, *Han-shu, chüan* 6, p. 3a). Neo-Confucianism may be said to have received official endorsement in the autumn of 1382 when Emperor T'ai-tsu reinstalled the examination system, making the exegeses of Chu Hsu and Ch'eng I the main criterion of classical interpretation (*Ming-shih, chüan* 70, p. 1b). Earlier, in 1381, the emperor ordered that the Five Classics and Four Books be distributed to the schools of the empire (ibid., *chüan* 2, p. 10a).

[143] Outstanding instances are Emperor Wu of Han and Emperor T'ai-tsung of T'ang, whose Confucianism could not have been more than skin deep (Ssu-ma Ch'ien, *Shih-chi, chüan* 120, p. 2a and Ou-yang Hsiu, *Hsin T'ang-shu*, pp. 9b–10a; cf. Liu Hsü, *Chiu T'ang-shu, chüan* 1, 9a). Emperors who did not subscribe to Confucianism included the First Emperor of Ch'in and Emperor Wen of Han (Ssu-ma, *Shih-chi, chüan* 6, pp. 18a–b, and *chüan* 23, 2b; see also *chüan* 49, p. 5b; *chüan* 107, pp. 3a–b; and *chüan* 121, p. 6a, for the Taoist influence at the imperial court in early Han times). Ou-yang, *Hsin T'ang-shu, chüan* 44, p. 3b and *chüan* 48, pp. 8b–9a, and Liu, *Chiu T'ang-shu, chüan* 24, p. 6a, indicate the presence of Taoist influence in T'ang times. Ssu-ma, *Shih-chi*, and Pan, *Han-shu*, give a number of instances in which non-Confucian scholars attained eminence in officialdom. It may also be recalled that Chu Hsi, the greatest of Neo-Confucians, was once condemned by the imperial government (in 1196) as a scholar of "false learning" (*wei hsüeh*) (*Sung shih, chüan* 37, p. 5b and *chüan* 474, pp. 3a–b). See Kung-chuan Hsiao, "Legalism and Autocracy in Traditional China," pp. 108–22, for a brief discussion of the limits of Confucian influence on emperors and the imperial government.

[144] Chu Hsi, *Chu Wen-kung wen-chi, chüan* 36, p. 579.

may be seen from the fact that, in spite of their wisdom and dedication, Confucius and his early followers had failed to make his teaching prevail in pre-imperial China. The Sage himself met frustration, ridicule, and persecution, almost at every turn.[145] The rulers of his time were preoccupied with conquest and defense, with no time for doctrine or ideology and his eloquence fell on deaf ears. But when China was united, when military affairs became less urgent and political stability became more urgent, the emperors' attention was naturally drawn to the problem of ideological control—to ways and means of insuring loyalty to the existing regime and rooting out thoughts and sentiments that might endanger it. The First Emperor of Ch'in took a negative approach to the problem. He sought to keep his vast realm in order by applying stringent laws and to keep his subjects obedient by depriving them of opportunities to form their own opinions.[146] The emperors of Han (and most of the rulers of later dynasties) took a more positive approach. Instead of trying to make men's minds intellectual vacuums they sought to fill them with notions that would make them loyal and submissive subjects. Accepting the advice of Confucian scholars they instituted Confucianism as official ideology and set up Confucius as the supreme authority of moral and political values. These scholars were able to gain the ears of their sovereigns not because they were more learned or eloquent than Confucius or Mencius—in all probability they were less so than their celebrated predecessors—but because the Confucian teaching now sounded inviting to the imperial rulers.

When the imperial system crumbled, therefore, Confucianism also failed. K'ang's efforts to salvage it were in vain because all the factors that had once made it possible to "venerate Confucius" had disappeared. He could not possibly make Confucianism prevail in post-imperial China, any more than Confucius could succeed in pre-imperial times.

This is not saying that Confucianism, as it stood in pre-Ch'in times, was predetermined by its doctrine to commit itself to the imperial cause. The autocratic system, which did not materialize until centuries after Confucius' death, was alien to his thought. He stressed the moral importance of human relationships but did not regard allegiance to the sovereign or service to the state an absolute moral duty. In the last analysis, virtue alone constituted the ultimate goal of man.[147] Men-

[145] Ssu-ma, *Shih-chi, chüan* 47, pp. 8b–22a.
[146] Ibid., *chüan* 6, pp. 17b–20b.
[147] *Analects*, XI.23. For a short exposition of this doctrine, see Hsiao Kung-ch'üan, *Chung-kuo cheng-chih ssu-hsiang shih* (Taipei ed.), 1: 58–67; (Shanghai ed.), 1: 44–52.

cius and Hsün-tzu followed the first principles laid down by Confucius but developed them in two different directions. Hsün-tzu attached importance to legal institutions and the royal authority as means to attain human purposes and thus came perilously close to the autocratic theory of government.[148] Mencius, on the contrary, championed the cause of the people. He taught that the sovereign was the least important element of the state, that "to gain the peasantry was the way to become emperor," that rulership was fiduciary in nature, and that tyrannicide was morally justifiable as well as politically necessary.[149] These doctrines could readily lead to the modern concepts of human rights and political democracy. However, this potential doctrinal development came to an end with the arrival of the imperial system. The emperors who enlisted the assistance of Confucianism to control the minds of men deliberately gave prominence to the aspect that supported autocratic rule. They, as K'ang and his followers repeatedly said, subscribed to the Hsün-tzu school of Confucian thought. K'ang's endeavor to reinterpret Confucianism constituted, in part at least, an attempt to retrace the interrupted line of its development and, with the help of imported ideas, to advance Confucian thought from the standpoint of Mencius. But K'ang could not undo that one-sided interpretation of the "Old Text scholars" that had been supported by the authority of the imperial government for many centuries. K'ang failed to convince either his fellow scholars who believed that to purge Confucianism of its imperial association was to destroy it, or the intellectuals of a later generation who felt that to honor Confucius was to acquiesce in autocracy.

Confucius was described by one of his contemporaries as a man "who knows the impractical nature of his task and yet undertakes it.[150] K'ang undertook an impractical task also. In a sense he labored under difficulties greater than those that Confucius experienced. When K'ang strove to revive Confucianism after 1911, it had already been discredited by its enemies beyond help. Few men writing in the 1920s were in a position to appraise it without prejudice and solely on the basis of its intrinsic worth. As it turned out, K'ang achieved much less than Confucius. The influence of the Sage of Tung-Lu lasted for thousands of years; that of "the sage of Nan-hai" appears to have been extremely

---

[148] Ibid. (Taipei ed.), pp. 100–107; (Shanghai ed.), pp. 77–83.

[149] *Mencius*, VII.ii.14 (on paramount importance of people); I.i.6. (on government as trustship); I.ii.7 (on public opinion); and I.i.8 (on tyrannicide).

[150] *Analects*, XIV.41.

short-lived and essentially negative. The death of "the last of the Confucians"[151] in 1927 marked the end of an epoch in China's intellectual history.

Perhaps it is too early to write the final chapter of the history of Confucianism. There may still be hope that the best in the Confucian teaching will find its place in a new cultural synthesis.[152] It is perhaps premature also to speak of "the death of Chinese civilization."[153] After all, Confucianism was originally only one of the ancient schools and never did encompass the whole of Chinese culture. Important aspects of that culture may remain, even if Confucianism can not regain its influence. One thing is certain at the moment: As long as the intellectual history of modern China is studied K'ang Yu-wei's views on Confucius and the Confucian classics will merit attention.

[151] Lin Mousheng's description of K'ang (*Men and Ideas: An Informal History of Chinese Political Thought*, p. 215).

[152] E.g., Liu Wu-chi, *A Short History of Confucian Philosophy*, pp. 190–93. Cf. Chang Ch'i-yun, *K'ung-tzu hsüeh-shuo yü hsien-tai wen-hua*, p. 2, where it is said that the present-day "new culture movement" of China under the Kuomintang is "a movement to revive Confucianism." Hung Yeh, *As It Looks to Young China* (New York, 1932), concludes the chapter on "Setting Confucius Aside" with these words: "The historic culture centering upon Confucius is disrupted. There are still some who can hear Confucius weeping in the grave. But few of them will attempt, like Tseng Kuo-fan, to set him back into the central place he once occupied in Chinese thought." Hung does not seem to rule out the possibility of a new synthesis in which some elements of Confucianism would be included.

[153] Robert Guillain, *600 Million Chinese*, pp. 257–69. Cf. de Riencourt, *Soul of China*, pp. 185–200, on "the collapse of Chinese civilization."

Chapter 5

PHILOSOPHICAL SYNTHESIS

Modern China owed her "modernity" partly to the efforts made by some of her thoughtful sons to adapt her institutional and intellectual structure to the changing conditions of the world, by introducing whatever elements of Western civilization that appeared to them to be useful for the purpose. From the 1860s to the 1910s or 1920s Western technology, natural science, principles of government, and philosophy had been the chief ingredients of a process of incomplete Westernization. There was a perceptible sequence in the adoptive process: first, technologies affecting material existence; then principles concerning state and society; and finally, ideas touching the inner core of intellectual life. The "self-strengthening" movement of the T'ung-chih period, the reform movement of 1898, and the May Fourth movement of 1919 marked the climactic points of these three stages.

K'ang Yu-wei has been generally honored as the leader of the 1898 movement and praised or blamed for promoting the idea of institutional reform, which with the support of his followers and sympathizers helped to discredit the age-long autocratic political system. But few have stressed the fact that quite apart from his role in 1898, K'ang had contributed something to China's modernization in the realm of thought, anticipating the acceptance of Western science and philosophy by many writers of the early republican years. It would be interesting to trace the pioneering efforts made by K'ang in bringing Western philosophy to bear, though only in a comparatively small way, upon Chinese thought.

137

Partly as a result of the repressive measures applied by the Ch'ing government in the seventeenth and eighteenth centuries, Chinese scholars in increasing numbers veered away from theoretical inquiries in politics and philosophy, and turned to less hazardous intellectual pursuits, such as polishing examination essays and delving into what was often known as "Han learning." Tai Chen (1723–77) was virtually the last writer of the period who could claim to having attained the stature of an independent philosophical thinker.[1] It was left to the members of the New Text school, Kung Tzu-chen (1792–1841)[2] in particular, who, traveling the tortuous paths of Han learning, rediscovered the open road to ethical and political speculation. Meanwhile, those who did not commit themselves to the Han learning generally accepted or parroted the tenets of the Ch'eng–Chu school of Sung Neo-Confucianism, which had become largely a moral code and political ideology with little contact with speculative philosophy.

This was the situation in which K'ang found himself in his childhood and youth. Up to the time when he was eighteen *sui*, his education was in line with the prevailing mode: absorbing the Confucian classics as interpreted by Sung commentators and learning the technique of composing the examination essay.[3] The first opportunity to exercise his intellect in a serious way came in 1876 when he became a pupil of Chu Tz'u-ch'i (1807–81) whom K'ang rated as comparable in learning to Ku Yen-wu (1613–82) and Wang Fu-chih (1619–92). It was Chu who inspired K'ang to advance beyond the Neo-Confucian tradition, although he did not give him anything like philosophical training.[4]

Several influences soon worked on K'ang and stimulated him into more serious inquiries into the nature of the world and the meaning of life. Shortly after he took leave of Chu (winter of 1878), he turned to Buddhist and Taoist texts for enlightenment and edification.[5] In about 1883 he became acquainted with Western thought after reading articles in missionary publications and translations from Western books issued by T'ung-wen kuan and the Kiangan Arsenal. The effect on

[1] Summaries of Tai's philosophy are given in Fung Yu-lan, *A History of Chinese Philosophy*, 2: 651–72, and in Ch'ien Mu, *Chung-kuo chin san-pai nien hsüeh-shu shih*, pp. 306–79.

[2] Ch'ien, *Chung-Kuo . . . hsüeh-shu shih*, pp. 523–68, summarizes Kung's views and those of other members of the school.

[3] K'ang, *Tzu-pien nien-p'u*, pp. 2b–4a (hereafter, *Nien-p'u*); Jung-pang Lo, *K'ang Yu-wei: A Biography and a Symposium*, pp. 26–30.

[4] K'ang, *Nien-p'u*, pp. 4a–b; Lo, *K'ang*, pp. 30–32.

[5] K'ang, *Nien-p'u*, p. 5a; Lo, *K'ang*, p. 34.

him was spectacular. "Deep reflections" brought him to what he described as "a wondrous comprehension of subtle truths." Promptly, in the summer of the next year, he formulated the *Weltansicht* that was destined to remain the foundation of his philosophical thought for almost the rest of his life.[6]

A second major influence came from the Kung-yang school of Confucianism. Partly through his own study of the classics and partly through suggestions received from reading the works of Kung-yang scholars of the nineteenth century,[7] K'ang discovered what he called the authentic teachings of Confucius.[8] Combining these with the ideas he derived from Buddhism and "Western learning" he revised and refined the "system" that he had constructed a few years before.[9]

Historical circumstances were partly responsible for preventing K'ang from developing into a full-fledged philosopher.[10] Living as he did in a period of crises during which China was threatened not only with political extinction but also cultural eclipse, K'ang must have found it difficult to concentrate on purely theoretical studies. As early as 1888 he was already profoundly disturbed by the loss of Annam.[11] He reacted to the defeat of 1894, with intensified effort "to save the country." From then on practically all his energy was directed to the reform movement that climaxed in 1898. Many years of exile followed. Returning to China in 1913 he continued his tireless campaign for constitutional monarchy against republicanism. For over a quarter of a century he had little time for calm philosophical thought. It was only in the last years of his life, especially in the 1920s, that living in leisurely retirement allowed him to concern himself with matters more transcendental than human government or public finance. It is hardly surprising that, like many Chinese thinkers before him, K'ang failed to achieve a well-articulated system of philosophy.[12]

[6] K'ang, *Nien-p'u*, pp. 6b–7a; Lo, *K'ang*, pp. 39–42.

[7] In particular, Liao P'ing. See Kung-chuan Hsiao, "K'ang Yu-wei and Confucianism," pp. 126–31, and the third section of chap. 3 in this volume.

[8] K'ang, *Hsin-hsüeh wei ching k'ao*, published in 1891, and *K'ung-tzu kai-chih k'ao*, written in 1892 and published in 1897, are his major works on the subject.

[9] K'ang called it "Ta-t'ung chih chih" ("the Great Community System") *Nien-p'u*, pp. 9b–10a (cf. pp. 6b–7a). Lo, *K'ang*, pp. 51–52; (cf. pp. 39–42).

[10] At any rate, K'ang can hardly be called a metaphysician, as Alfred Forke pointed out, in *Geschichte der neuren chinesischen Philosophie*, p. 579.

[11] K'ang, *Nien-p'u*, p. 8a; Lo, *K'ang*, pp. 45–46.

[12] Homer H. Dubs, in "The Failure of the Chinese to Produce Philosophical Systems," pp. 96–109, traces this "failure" to lack of interest in theoretical science, especially mathematics, and to the ascendance of Confucianism. It may be noted, however, interest in mathematics was not completely lacking, as Joseph Needham shows

K'ang's own tendency to be arbitrary and dogmatic, it may be noted, was far from conducive to philosophical greatness. He displayed too often an unwillingness to consider divergent views or to reckon with disturbing facts;[13] he spoke more frequently as a proselyting "holy man" than as an inquiring philosopher or scientist. This proclivity, readily discernible in his treatment of the Confucian classics,[14] hardly constituted an asset for a critical thinker. It, however, did not prevent K'ang from being the first Chinese thinker of modern (or pre-modern) China to make a serious attempt at building a philosophical system, the first to broaden and enrich Chinese philosophical thought by injecting Western elements into it. While K'ang was not a first-rate philosopher, he nevertheless made a significant contribution in revitalizing Chinese philosophical thinking. Had circumstances been favorable and had he not embroiled himself in his late years in a futile campaign for monarchical restoration, he could have become the initiator of a new philosophical synthesis comprised of Oriental and Occidental ingredients, comparable in historical importance to Neo-Confucianism, an older synthesis achieved by the infusion of Chinese and Indian thought.

K'ang's philosophical thinking fell into two distinguishable phases. In the first phase, extending roughly from the 1880s to the early 1910s or 1920s, Confucianism and Mahayāna Buddhism furnished the main sources of inspiration,[15] although Western science and history had already exerted influence on Kang's mind.[16] His *Weltansicht* as formulated in the last days of 1884[17] bears witness to this. During this period K'ang consistently took a moral view of the world and regarded meliorism as the basic law of life. Agreeing with Confucius that man's concern was with the living, not the dead, K'ang remained an agnostic (or an athe-

---

in his *Science and Civilization in China*, vol. 3. K'ang made a heroic effort to master mathematics but after a serious illness (1885) he "dared not again do mathematics" (K'ang, *Nien-p'u*, pp. 7a–b).

[13] Liang Ch'i-ch'ao, *Ch'ing-tai hsüeh-shu kai-lun*, pp. 128–29. Immanuel C. Y. Hsü, in Liang, *Intellectual Trends in the Ch'ing Period*, p. 93, translates Liang: "As a man K'ang was totally subjective in myriads of things. His self-confidence was extremely strong and he maintained it very stubbornly. As for objective facts, he either ignored them completely or insisted on remolding them to his own views. He was this way in his practical career as well as in scholarship." (Hereafter cited as Hsü, *Intellectual Trends in the Ch'ing Period*.)

[14] Hsiao, "K'ang Yu-wei and Confucianism," pp. 136–41, and the fourth section of chap. 3 in this volume.

[15] K'ang, *Nien-p'u*, p. 5a; Lo, *K'ang*, p. 34, referring to his intensive study of Buddhist and Taoist texts in 1879.

[16] K'ang, *Nien-p'u*, pp. 6a–7a; Lo, *K'ang*, pp. 38–42.

[17] K'ang, *Nien-p'u*, pp. 6b–7a; Lo, *K'ang*, pp. 39–42.

ist) for many years, one who viewed religion solely as an instrument of social betterment.[18] This phase is represented by a large number of writings, ranging from the youthful *K'ang-tzu nei-wai p'ien* (The Esoteric and Exoteric Essays of Master K'ang), done in 1886, to the celebrated *Ta-t'ung shu* (Book of the Great Community), completed in 1902.

The second phase covered the last years of K'ang's life, characterized by a higher degree of detachment in viewing man and the universe, and by a more intimate acquaintance with Western philosophical thought. He now quietly dropped his anthropocentric, melioristic approach, being convinced that man's happiness was to be attained not by remaking his world but by transcending it. He also gave up his agnosticism and insisted on the existence of God, showing a degree of intellectual humility totally absent in his earlier writings. This phase is represented by the nonscientific portions of the *Chu-t'ien chiang* (Lectures on the Heavens), especially chapters 11 and 12.

This radical change in his outlook resulted partly from lessons learned in the hard school of experience. Repeated failures in his attempts to remake China, extensive observations of Western society made during his long exile, and acquaintance with Western philosophy gained through leisurely readings of translations and articles that appeared in increasing numbers in China in the early twentieth century[19] must have been responsible for this change. His knowledge of Western philosophy was necessarily secondhand and fragmentary, but it was far more extensive than what he had in the first phase. This knowledge, together with his knowledge of Western astronomy, which he cultivated off and on over a long time, helped to widen his intellectual vista and, in fact, to alter the direction of his philosophical thinking.

It seems that K'ang's philosophical development epitomized the intellectual transition occurring in China during the closing years of the last century when innovators, including K'ang himself, directed their efforts at technological and institutional reforms with Europe as the

[18] Hsiao, "K'ang Yu-wei and Confucianism" (chap. 4, the second section, in this volume), pp. 186–89, summarizes K'ang's views on religion.

[19] E.g., *Far Eastern Miscellany* (*Tung-fang tsa-chih*), a monthly published by the Commercial Press, Shanghai; May, June, and July issues of 1916 (vol. 13), carry a long article by Liang Sou-ming, "Inquiry into the Fundamentals and Resolution of Doubts" (Chiu yüan chüeh i lun), in which Liang discusses the views of notable Western philosophers, including Kant, Schopenhauer, Spencer, and Bergson. The *Emancipation and Reconstruction* (*Chieh-fang yü kai-tsao*), a semimonthly published by the New Learning Society of Peking, 1919 (renamed *Reconstruction* in 1920) and *Philosophia* (*Che Hsüeh*), published by the Philosophical Society of Peking, 1921, also contain articles on Western philosophy.

model, and the opening decades of the present century when diverse schools of Western philosophical thought were openly (and sometimes noisily) advocated by intellectuals of the new generation. K'ang differed widely in his philosophical position from the Chinese proponents of Kant, Hegel, Dewey, Bergson, Driesch, or Bertrand Russell,[20] but even in his unsystematic and somewhat superficial way he had actually adumbrated the intellectual situation that prevailed in the 1910s and 1920s, in which many a thinking man of modern China turned to the West for philosophical enlightenment. "The tide from the West" was rising to its highest point and K'ang was one of the earliest to open the floodgate to expedite its influx.

THE FIRST PHASE: THE WORLD AS MORAL

Cosmological Ideas

K'ang arrived at his first *Weltansicht* in 1884 when he was a young man of twenty-seven *sui*. In his own words, this was its broad outline and how he came to it:

> In my early years I studied the *Doctrines of Sung, Yüan, and Ming Philosophers*[21] and the *Topical Conversations of Master Chu*.[22] While I was in the Hua-lin of Hai-ch'uang Temple,[23] I read the Four Schools.[24] Concurrently, I applied myself to mathematics and waded through books on Western learning. During autumn and winter [of that year], living alone in an upper-story room, in limpid quietude with all worldly concerns cast off, I bent to read and raised my head in thought. When the twelfth month came, my understanding had deepened day by day. Using a microscope of tremendous power of magnification[25] I saw a louse [appearing as large] as a chariot wheel and an ant [as large] as an elephant; in this way I perceived the truth that large and small are relative.[26] Knowing that a ray of light emitted by an electric machine travels several ten thou-

[20] O. Brière, *Fifty Years of Chinese Philosophy, 1898–1950*, describes briefly this situation.

[21] Namely, the *Sung Yüan hsüeh-an* and *Ming-ju hsüeh-an*, both compiled by Huang Tsung-hsi.

[22] Namely, *Chu-tzu yü-lui*, compiled by Chu Hsi's students.

[23] K'ang probably referred to his experience in early 1879 (K'ang, *Nien-p'u*, p. 5a; Lo, *K'ang*, p. 34).

[24] K'ang probably had in mind "The T'ien-t'ai Four," which included the "One-vehicle Perfect Teaching" (I ch'eng yüan chiao) represented by the *Avataṁsaka-sūtra* (*Hua-yen ching*). See Mochizuki Shinkō, *Bukkyō daijiten*, vol. 2, 1130 *shang*, 1749 *hsia*, and 1751 *shang*; W. E. Soothill and L. Hodous, *Dictionary of Chinese Buddhist Terms*, pp. 176, 397.

[25] The original has *wan shu ch'ien pei*, which obviously is hyperbole.

[26] The original has *ch'i t'ung*, literally, "equal and identical."

sand *li* in a second, I apprehended the truth that slow and fast are relative. I further understood that there are [things] larger than the largest and smaller than the smallest, that a unit is infinitely divisible, and that there is endless variety among myriad things. Taking the Primal Ether (*yüan-ch'i*) as the starting point, I extended my view to the world in the era of Universal Peace (*T'ai-p'ing*). . . . In my philosophy *yüan* is the first principle, and the *yin* and *yang* are the operative principles. As all reality has *yin* and *yang*, so air is cold or warm, forces repel or attract, substances are solid or fluid, shapes are square or round, light is bright or dark, sounds are high or low, bodies are female or male, and [man's] psyche comprises the rational and animal souls. . . . I combined the profound doctrines in the Confucian classics with those in the writings of the classical philosophers, probed into the subtle meanings of Confucianism, referred to the new truths of China and the West; thus I delved exhaustively into the hidden transformations of Heaven and man, . . . human societies, the realm of the heavens, and the generation of the stars.[27]

The cornerstone of K'ang's philosophy, then, appears to have been the concept of *yüan*, "the Prime." It has been suggested that in his thought *yüan* was just another name for the Neo-Confucian concept *T'ai-chi*, "the Supreme Ultimate," from which the *yin* and the *yang* had their origins.[28] Without denying that K'ang was indebted to Neo-Confucianism in other connections, I am inclined to think that his notion of *yüan* came directly from the *Book of Changes*[29] and from Tung Chung-shu's *Ch'un-ch'iu fan-lu*,[30] to both of which K'ang expressly referred on more than one occasion. For instance, in K'ang's own study of Tung's book[31] he said in one place, *yüan* is the root of myriad things. Man and Heaven, in having their roots in *yüan* are like waves and foams rising from the sea.[32] This followed a similar view as indicated in Tung's book:

What is called the single *yüan* is the great beginning. . . . This *yüan* is like a source. Its significance is that it permeates Heaven and Earth from beginning to end. . . . Therefore *yüan* is the root of all things, and in it lies man's origin.[33]

---

[27] K'ang, *Nien-p'u*, 6b–7a; Lo, *K'ang*, pp. 39–42.

[28] Lu Nai-hsiang and Lu Tun-k'uei, *K'ang Nan-hai hsien-sheng chuan*, p. 46a.

[29] Richard Wilhelm, *The I-ching*, 2: 2: "Great indeed is the sublimity (*Yüan*) of the Creative (*Ch'ien*), to which all beings owe their beginning and which permeates all heaven." K'ang quoted or referred to this passage many times.

[30] Tung Chung-shu (2nd cent. B.C.). *Ch'un-ch'iu fan-lu*, Pao-ching-t'ang ed. Su Yü, *Ch'un-ch'iu fan-lu i-cheng*, is useful.

[31] K'ang, *Ch'un-ch'iu Tung-shih hsüeh* (hereafter, *Tung-shih hsüeh*).

[32] K'ang, *Tung-shih hsüeh, chüan* 6 *shang*, p. 7a.

[33] Quoted in Fung, *History of Chinese Philosophy*, 2: 19–20.

K'ang came closer to Neo-Confucianism when he identified *yüan* with *ch'i,* "from which," he said, "arose the intangible and within which tangible things were separated from one another; creating Heaven and Earth it is the origin of Heaven and Earth."[34] But regrettably K'ang failed to make clear the precise meaning of the term *ch'i.* Sometimes he came close to materialism. For instance:

> Between Heaven and Earth it appears to be a void (*hsü*) but actually it is substantial (*shih*). Men move in *ch'i* as fish move in water; *ch'i* permeates water as water pervades mud. Thus everywhere is substance, [although men do not perceive it]. Men cannot see minute things. But, looking at them from the viewpoint of an extremely small creature, particles of *ch'i* (*ch'i-tien*) are very loosely connected together.[35]

Sometimes K'ang appears to have followed Neo-Confucians, such as Chou Tun-i, Chang Tsai, and Chu Hsi and perhaps also the Han philosopher Tung Chung-shu, all of whom employed the concept *ch'i,* which has been variously understood as "ether" or "force."[36] But K'ang differed sharply with Chu Hsi. According to Chu,

> There is Principle (*li*) before there can be Ether (*ch'i*). But it is only when there is the Ether that Principle has a place in which to rest. This fact applies to the coming into existence of all [things], whether as large as Heaven and Earth, or as tiny as the cricket or ant.[37]

According to K'ang, the reverse is true:

> All things have their beginnings in *ch'i;* there is already *ch'i* before there is *li* (Principle). It is *ch'i* which produces man and the things. . . . Chu Hsi believed that *li* existed prior to *ch'i;* his view is erroneous.[38]

This belief in the primacy of *ch'i* led K'ang to an interesting conclusion, that in its primitive state, nature or the physical universe, could not be said to possess moral qualities, for it was constituted of sheer, brutal force. This fact, K'ang insisted, was recognized by the Sage who designed human institutions.

[34] K'ang, *Tung-shih hsüeh, chüan* 4, p. 11b.

[35] K'ang, *Tung-shih hsüeh, chüan* 6 *shang,* p. 9a.

[36] Fung, *History of Chinese Philosophy,* 2: 20, 21 (Tung Chung-shu); p. 444 (Chou Tun-i); p. 479 (Chang Tsai); and p. 534 (Chu Hsi).

[37] Ibid., pp. 539, 544, quoting from *Chu-tzu yü-lui,* 58.11 and 1.1.

[38] Li Tse-hou, "Lun K'ang Yu-wei ti che-hsüeh ssu-hsiang," in *Che-hsüeh yen-chiu,* 1, no. 1: 75, quoting from "Wan-mu-tsao-t'ang k'ou-shuo," an unpublished MS in the collection in Peking University Library.

All institutions designed by Confucius were based on power and force (*ch'üan-shih*). He did not base institutions on shining goodness or supreme beauty because force is of Heaven and of *ch'i*. The Sage received his body (*hsing*) from *ch'i*, his reason (*li*) from Heaven. . . . Hence I say, force (*shih*) gives rise to truth (*tao*) which in turn yields reason (*li*).[39]

It is not easy to determine the meanings of "truth" and "reason"; by the former K'ang probably had in mind something like "natural order" and by the latter, man's understanding of that order. But it is clear that here again K'ang placed *ch'i* before *li*, in temporal (or perhaps logical) sequence.

A Communist writer traces the source of K'ang's "materialism" to "the *ch'i* monistic tradition of China" and to Western natural science.[40] K'ang, he said, filled the ancient Chinese "materialistic concept of *ch'i*" with modern scientific notions, such as "ether" and "electricity," and thereby gave his philosophy a scientific content.[41] Not all Communist writers, however, credit K'ang with materialism. For example, in an essay written "collectively" by six young men in the Institute of History, Chinese Academy of Science, K'ang was condemned together with T'an Ssu-t'ung for having "sunk into idealism," in their emphasis on the doctrine of "love," despite their superficial references to natural science.[42]

Both judgments suffer from oversimplification. The fact is, that as K'ang was not precise in his terminology, one cannot be sure that any of the standard philosophical labels, materialism and idealism, monism and dualism, properly describes the nature or content of his thought. If his concept of *ch'i* suggests materialism, his concept of *jen* points at the same time to idealism; if *yüan* indicates a monistic view of the universe, it is nevertheless tempered with the concepts of *yin* and *yang*, a concession to dualism. The statement following, which he made in the 1890s, is of particular interest in this connection:

Probing into the way of Heaven Confucius knew that everything contains polarity. He therefore employed [the concepts] of *yin* and *yang* to interpret the things of the world. . . . In a human body, the back is *yin* and the front is *yang*; in a tree, its branches and trunk respectively make *yin* and *yang*; with respect to light, brightness and darkness constitute *yin* and *yang*; in

[39] K'ang, *Tung-shih hsüeh, chüan* 6 *hsia*, p. 13b.
[40] Li, Tse-hou, *K'ang Yu-wei T'an Ssu-t'ung ssu-hsiang yen-chiu*, p. 77.
[41] Ibid., p. 75.
[42] Chang Ch'i-chih et al., "T'an Ssu-t'ung che-hsüeh ssu-hsiang ti chi-ko wen-t'i," in Hou Wai-lu, *Wu-hsü pien-fa liu-shih chou-nien chi-nien chi*, pp. 48, 56.

color, black and white are *yin* and *yang*. . . . There is not a single thing in
the world that lacks *yin* and *yang*. . . . Confucius who possessed an exhaustive knowledge of the nature of reality, . . . did not begin his exposition of
the *Book of Changes* with the Supreme Ultimate, but instead with *Ch'ien*
and *K'un*, which are synonymous with *yin* and *yang*. *Yüan*, the Supreme
Ultimate, and *T'ai-i*, Supreme Unity, are invisible. What is visible and
can be talked about must of necessity be the duality [of *yin* and *yang*].
Therefore he spoke of *yin* and *yang*, not of the Supreme Ultimate. Master
Chou [Tun-i] said, "The Supreme Ultimate through movement produces
the *yang*. This movement, having reached its limit, is followed by quiescence, and by this quiescence it produces the *yin*. . . ." He did not know
that when things were first produced . . . the *yin* and *yang* are manifested
at the same moment. . . . The sage of Persia's ancient religion, Zoroaster,
also believed that things have *yin* and *yang*. In all probability, he unknowingly agreed with Confucius.[43]

That K'ang took this polarity concept seriously may be seen from
the fact that he extended it to his theory of human nature and attempted thereby to resolve the age-long controversy between those
who affirmed the "goodness' of nature and those who insisted on its
"evilness," as I shall presently show.[44]

In his theory of the relationship between man and Heaven K'ang
followed the general Confucian tradition with some modifications, as
he did in his cosmological theory. Heaven and man, he believed, had
identical origins and were similarly constituted. In his own words:

The all-embracing Primal Ether created Heaven and Earth. Heaven is
[composed of] a single soul-substance (*hun-chih*). Man is likewise [com-
posed of] a single soul-substance. Although they differ in size, they are
essentially identical [in composition], for they are parts of the all-embracing Ether coming from the Ultimate Origin (*T'ai-yüan*), like drops of
water taken from the ocean. Confucius said, "The Earth began from
spirit-ether (*shen-ch'i*); the spirit-ether was thunder; thunder flowed into
form, and all things came forth to birth."[45] Spirit is electricity which has
awareness. There is nothing which the lightning-electricity cannot pro-

---

[43] K'ang, *Tung-shih hsüeh, chüan* 6 *shang*, pp. 8a–b. Fung, *History of Chinese Philosophy*, 2: 434 ff. summarizes the philosophy of Chou Tun-i (A.D. 1017–73). The quotation is taken from Chou's "Diagram of the Supreme Ultimate Explained," translated
on p. 435.

[44] Li, *K'ang Yu-wei T'an Ssu-t'ung*, remarks that in asserting the primal coexistence
of the *yin* and *yang* K'ang recognized the existence of "contradictions" but he failed
to recognize "the struggles implied in contradictions," thus greatly reducing the
"glory of dialectic method," a result of the "class character" of K'ang's thinking.

[45] *Li-chi cheng-i, chüan* 50, "K'ung-tzu hsien-chü," p. 389.

duce; there is nothing which the spirit-ether cannot affect. . . . No creatures are without electricity; no creatures are without spirit.[46]

It is difficult to make out what K'ang meant precisely in this vaguely phrased passage. In indicating that man, Heaven, and Earth were parts of the all-embracing Ether, he apparently suggested that they all came into being from the same Primal Ether, although man emerged sometime after the birth of Heaven and Earth. Man's "spirit-ether," he said, "existed before [the formation of] Heaven and Earth," although "man's nature and life (*hsing-ming*) . . . came only after countless transformations."[47] This view reminds one of Tung Chung-shu's saying that "Man's nature and emotions are from Heaven."[48] K'ang did not clarify the manner or process in which man emerged into existence. In 1890 when he instructed one of his students in the basic principles of his philosophy, he referred to the theory that "man evolved from the ape."[49] It seems, therefore, that K'ang was not at all adverse to interpreting "the way of Heaven" in terms of the evolutionary theory, thus in a small way introducing Western scientific thought into Chinese philosophy.

Ideas Concerning Human Nature

Following the footsteps of Confucian thinkers in the past K'ang speculated about man's nature (*hsing*) and undertook to resolve the conflicting views of Mencius and Hsün-tzu, leaning sometimes toward the former and at other times toward the latter. He revealed his position clearly in the *Ch'ang-hsing hsüeh-chi*, in which he outlined in 1892 the aims of his instruction and the major items of the curriculum. As the view expressed therein underlay much of his ethical and social thought, this piece merits quoting at some length.

Nature is what is received from Heaven. . . . Not only men have it, birds, animals, and plants also have it. . . . As for those [beings] called "men," their natures cannot be far different from one another. Therefore Confucius said, "By nature men are nearly alike."[50] Now to be nearly alike is to

---

[46] K'ang, *Ta-t'ung shu* (Shanghai, 1935 ed.), p. 4; (Peking, 1956, ed. and Taipei, 1958, ed.), p. 3. The translation is taken from Laurence G. Thompson's version, *Ta T'ung Shu*, pp. 64–65, with minor changes (hereafter cited as Thompson, *Ta T'ung Shu*).

[47] K'ang, *Tung-shih hsüeh, chüan* 6 *shang*, pp. 7a–b.

[48] Tung, "Wei jen che t'ien," *Ch'un-chiu fan-lu, chüan* 11, no. 41, p. 18b.

[49] K'ang, *Nien-p'u*, p. 10a.

[50] *Lun-yü*, XVII.2 (Legge trans.).

be equal. All men, then, are equal in possessing nature, previous to their
acquiring training. Being identical in sense perception, there is no distinction between what is known as mean man and the superior man. . . .
Training results from strenuous efforts made by men; it goes completely
against nature. . . . Those who act in accordance with nature remain ignorant; those who contravene nature and apply themselves to learning
become wise. . . . Therefore the reason why some men differ from their
fellow men lies in the fact that some have forced themselves to learn,
[while others have not]. . . . Now to force one's self [to learn] entails contravening the normal course. In following the normal course, man's
physical body gives rein to sensuous desires that cannot be controlled
unless [nature] is contravened, and his mind is open to the evil of selfish
and bigoted thoughts that cannot be corrected unless [nature] is contravened.[51]

This, obviously, came very close to Hsün-tzu's view that man's "goodness" was solely the result of "acquired training."[52]

K'ang, however, did not commit himself to Hsün-tzu's theory that
human nature was "evil"; instead, he set store by Kao-tzu's view that
it was ethically neutral. In a note to the passage above, he said:

Mencius' theory that man's nature is good was enunciated for special
reasons; Hsün-tzu's theory that man's nature is evil was advanced because he was aroused [by circumstances]. Kao-tzu's saying, "Life is what
is to be understood by nature,"[53] represents the true view which accords
with that of Confucius. . . . Ch'eng-tzu and Chu-tzu divided nature into
two parts, the "physical element" (*ch'i-chih*) and "rational principle"
(*i-li*). . . .[54] They gave a forced interpretation of Mencius. Actually, nature is wholly the physical element. What is called rational principle
comes out of the physical element [as the result of training]. These [two
aspects of nature] cannot be arbitrarily divided.[55]

K'ang's statement, "nature is wholly the physical element," led a
writer in Communist China to assert that K'ang showed an inclination
toward materialism.[56] Whatever may have been the metaphysical implications of K'ang's view, it is difficult to ascertain. But it is useful to

[51] K'ang, "Ch'ang-hsing hsüeh-chi," pp. 1–2; also given in Su Yü, *I-chiao ts'ung-pien*, 94:36.
[52] Homer H. Dubs, *The Works of Hsüntze*, p. 301: "The nature of man is evil; his goodness is only acquired training."
[53] *Mencius*, VI.i.3 (Legge trans.). Cf. VI.i.6: "To enjoy food and delight in sex is nature." (Legge translated this as "To enjoy food and delight in colors in nature.")
[54] Fung, *History of Chinese Philosophy*, 2: 543–45.
[55] K'ang, "Ch'ang-hsing hsüeh-chi," p. 1.
[56] Li Tse-hou, in *Che-hsüeh yen-chiu*, p. 86.

scrutinize his view in the light of the Confucian tradition. Chu I-hsin, a scholar of the traditional mold[57] and K'ang's respected friend, took him to task for following Hsün-tzu and Tung Chung-shu in his theory of human nature.[58] In reply to Chu's criticism K'ang reaffiirmed his position to the effect that the goodness in man's nature was the immediate product not of Heaven but of human effort. No man could become good, he argued, without the restraining influence of propriety (*li*). Then he went on to say:[59]

> Propriety was instituted by Confucius. Performance of the six rites in taking a wife,[60] for instance, is in accord with propriety, which is good; climbing over the wall of a neighbor's house on the east side and carrying off his virgin daughter[61] violates propriety, which is not good. If you say that the former action comes from nature, while the latter does not, I would ask, Were all men without nature before Fu-hsi[62] instituted the gift of twin [deer] hides[63] in the wedding ceremony? It is allowable to say that [moral discipline] molds man's body and mind, and brings them to [accord with] propriety. But it makes little sense to say that [discipline] restores gradually the original [nature] as Heaven has conferred [on him].[64]

Thus K'ang, in holding that "nature is wholly the physical clement" and moral goodness completely the product of postnatal discipline, went against the orthodox Neo-Confucian tradition as represented by Chang Tsai, Ch'eng I, and Chu Hsi,[65] although occasionally the difference between the views of K'ang and Chu is not readily apparent.[66]

---

[57] Chu I-hsin. Ch'ien, *Chung-kuo . . . hsüeh-shu shih*, pp. 622–32, sketches Chu's life and thought.

[58] Chu supported his view with this quotation from the *Chung-yung*, chap. 1, sec. 1: "What Heaven has conferred is called the nature; an accordance with this nature is called the path of duty; the regulation of this path is called instruction" (Legge trans.).

[59] Chu I-hsin, "Fifth Letter in Reply to K'ang" (Ta K'ang Yu-wei ti-wu shu) in Su, *I-chiao ts'ung-pien*, 1: 14a–17a.

[60] The "six rites" were: *Na-ts'ai, wen-ming, na-chi, na-cheng* or *na-pi, ch'ing-ch'i*, and *ch'in-ying. I-li chu-shu, chüan* 4, "Shih hun-li," opening passage and commentaries.

[61] *Mencius*, VI.ii.1.3.

[62] Fu-hsi was one of the three legendary emperors of antiquity.

[63] *I-li chu-shu, chüan* 4, p. 18b, col. C.

[64] K'ang, "Ta Chu Yung-sheng shu," p. 30a.

[65] See Carsun Chang, *The Development of Neo-Confucian Thought*, pp. 178, 214–17, 264–69 and Fung, *History of Chinese Philosophy*, 2: 488–91, 514–18, 551–58.

[66] K'ang probably could have assented substantially to Chu Hsi's view as expressed in this passage: "To desire food when hungry and to desire a drink when thirsty, this is the human mind (*jen hsin*). Attaining to what is correct (*cheng*) in eating and drinking constitutes the rational mind (*tao hsin*). There is [in truth] only one mind. As soon as it follows Reason (*tao*), at that moment human mind is subdued and disappears. Human mind and rational mind thus become one. . . . The rational mind has only to be pure and undivided; then all of it is manifested through the human mind." Quoted in Huang Tsung-hsi, *Sung Yüan hsüeh-an*, 1: 862.

The difficulty of interpreting K'ang springs largely from his loose use of terminology. The term "nature," for example, was used in more than one sense in various connections. Sometimes it referred to the original endowment, as in his remark, "Nature is the disposition at birth, when there is as yet without goodness or evil."[67] Sometimes he spoke of "nature" as the human mind that had been perfected through moral cultivation, as he did in 1901 when he said unequivocally that "man's nature is good."[68] And to make it even more confusing, he did not always hold firmly the idea that human nature at birth was morally neutral, as in this statement made in 1903:

> Nature is without goodness or evil but at birth it contains ether-matter (*ch'i-chih*). As it may lean too much toward the *yin* or the *yang*, it contains the defect of losing equilibrium and harmony.[69] In extreme cases men give free rein to desires and do as appetites dictate, inflicting utter injury to virtue.[70]

Substantially the same view was expressed a few years earlier, when he traced the kindly (*jen*) and avaricious (*t'an*) sides of man's nature to the *yin* and *yang* principles.[71]

K'ang sometimes hinted at a sort of Zoroastrian battle between the two sides of nature, with no assurance of victory for the better side.

> The ether (*ch'i*) of the spiritual soul (*hun*) is loving; that of the animal soul (*p'e*) is avaricious. . . . The spiritual and animal souls [of a man] struggle constantly with each other. . . . If the former wins control of the latter, then he becomes a virtuous man; if the latter imposes control over the former, then he becomes a mean man.[72]

[67] Quoted from "Wan-mu tsao-t'ang k'ou-shuo," by Li, in *K'ang Yu-wei T'an Ssu-t'ung*, p. 85. Cf. K'ang, *Lün-yü chu*, p. 1b., quoting from the *Hsiao-ching wei*: "Nature is the disposition (*chih*) at birth . . . which is received from Heaven and does not depend on discipline or instruction." Li Tse-hou condemns K'ang for holding this view (*K'ang Yu-wei T'an Ssu-t'ang*, pp. 85–86).

[68] K'ang, *Meng-tzu wei* (1901), in *Hsin-min ts'ung-pao*, no. 10 (1902) pp. 38–39; cf., no. 19, p. 58. Two editions of this work, one in the *Wan-mu-ts'ao-t'ang ts'ung-shu* with author's preface dated 1901, and the other, published by Kuang-chih shu-chü, are not available at the time of this writing. K'ang T'ung-pi, *Nan-hai K'ang hsien-sheng nien-p'u hsü-pien*, p. 31a, dates this work "Winter Solstice, Kuang-hsü 28th Year" (1902), which is probably inaccurate.

[69] Obviously, alluding to the *Chung-yung*, I. 4.

[70] *Lun-yü chu, chüan* 12, p. 1a.

[71] K'ang, *Tung-shih hsüeh, chüan* 6 *shang*, p. 28b. K'ang was probably paraphrasing Tung Chung-shu at this point. "Truly, there exists in man [both] love and covetousness, each of which lies within his body. What is thus called the body is received from Heaven. Heaven has its dual manifestations of *yin* and *yang*, and the body likewise has the dual qualities of covetousness and love." Quoted from Tung, *Ch'un-ch'iu fan-lu, chüan* 10: 7–9, in Fung, *History of Chinese Philosophy*, 2: 33.

[72] *Meng-tzu wei*, in *Hsin-min ts'ung-pao*, no. 19, p. 58.

Perhaps partly thanks to this dualistic view K'ang found it possible to speak of man's nature as good or evil, depending on which of its two sides he had in mind. Men were contentious, fighting over possession of things and struggling with one another because, K'ang said, it was their nature to do so.[73] And men were kindly and loving because they had "the mind which cannot bear to see the sufferings of others," because, in other words, they all had in themselves "ether" or "electricity."[74] K'ang, apparently, discerned no discrepancy between this and his other view that human nature was in itself morally neutral.

Somewhat curiously, despite K'ang's rejection of the Mencian theory, he eventually came to the position that the doctrines of Mencius, Kao-tzu, Hsün-tzu, and Tung Chung-shu were reconcilable. Kao-tzu's dictum, "the fashioning benevolence and righteousness out of man's nature is like the making cups and bowls from the *ch'i* willow,"[75] he said, was identical in implication with Tung Chung-shu's view that like a cocoon that requires reeling to make silk and an egg that requires incubation to produce a chick, human nature requires instruction to achieve goodness.[76] Moreover, K'ang argued, Hsün-tzu was actually in accord with Kao-tzu when he said that nature was the "original unfashioned" endowment that became refined after postnatal cultivation.[77] Finally, Mencius in saying that "from the proper feeling of it (nature), it is constituted for the practice of what is good,"[78] was in substantial agreement with Kao-tzu who remarked, "the substance of the *ch'i* willow is adapted to making cups and bowls." Therefore, K'ang concluded, little real difference existed among the views of these four men. They used divergent terminology but pointed to the same truth,[79] namely, that man could be either good or bad, depending on whether he cultivated his "nature" properly or not.[80]

This, as far as I can make out, was K'ang's basic view concerning human nature. The conviction that nature was morally tractable and indeed perfectible was a crucial one for, as it will be shown below, it served as the foundation of K'ang's ethical and social thought. But he

[73] K'ang, "I-ta-li yu-chi," p. 45.
[74] *Meng-tzu wei*, "General Discussions," in *K'ang Nan-hai hsien-sheng wen-ch'ao*, p. 3b (hereafter, *Wen-ch'ao*). Cf. ibid., in *Hsin-min ts'ung-pao*, no. 10, pp. 38–39.
[75] *Mencius*, VI.i.1.
[76] Tung, *Ch'un-ch'iu fan-lu*, chüan 35, "Shen ch'a ming-hao," p. 17b. Cf. passage quoted in Fung, *History of Chinese Philosophy*, 2: 34.
[77] Dubs, "The Nature of Man is Evil," in *The Works of Hsüntze*, Bk. 26, pp. 301–4.
[78] *Mencius*, VI.i.6 (Legge trans.).
[79] *Meng-tzu wei*, in *Hsin-min ts'ung-pao*, no. 20, pp. 1–2.
[80] Ibid., no. 19, p. 57; also in K'ang, *Wen-ch'ao, chüan* 8, p. 20a.

did not consistently hold fast to this view. Occasionally, when he was inspired by Ch'an Buddhism and in an expansive mood, he drifted back to the romantic Mencian view. He wrote in 1901:

> Man's spirituality (*ling-ming*) encompasses all existence. Mountains, streams, the Great Earth, all have manifestations in the Dharmakāya (*fa-shen*). The world, a tiny particle of dust, both have birth and death in the Ocean of Bhūtatathatā (*hsing-hai*). . . . But ordinary persons do not recognize their own nature. Incapable of having self-confidence, self-understanding, and self-attainment, they leave aside their own inexhaustible treasury and, carrying alms-bowls, beg from door to door like destitute children. If one has confidence in his own nature without the least bit of doubt, then in one moment's meditation he would attain enlightenment, dispensing with the chore of instructing himself in right conduct. . . . The Ch'an Buddhist nourishes his soul (*ling-hun*) and keeps to himself the secret of his self-attainment. Later-day Confucianists, ignorant of this, dismissed [the Ch'an doctrine] as heresy. They failed to understand that Mencius had uncovered this divinely wondrous secret and told it to scholars of the world. . . . I now again exhibit it . . . and share it with all under Heaven, who have the seed of goodness in them, so that together we shall experience the ecstasy [which it brings].[81]

Such a sally into Buddhism, however, though disturbing from a strictly philosophical point of view, did not obscure K'ang's basic tenet: Man was born with the capacity to be good, to achieve perfection through moral endeavor.

This tenet was closely connected with another of K'ang's, namely, human individuals were capable of moral progress as they advanced from infancy to maturity.

> A one-year old child does not know to be courteous and yielding. He yells when he sees food, wishing to eat it; he cries when he sees what he likes, desiring to play with it. But after he grows up, he restrains his feelings and suppresses his desires, trying to do good.[82]

Man was capable of moral development, K'ang explained, because his nature permitted it.

> Only because all men possess this nature are they alike in being capable of preferring kindness to cruelty, of preferring civilization to savagery, of

---

[81] Ibid., in *Hsin-min ts'ung-pao*, no. 17, p. 54. Dharmakāya (*fa-shen*), "embodiment of Truth and Law, the 'Spiritual' or true body; essential Buddhahood; the essence of being" (Soothill and Hodous, *Dictionary of Chinese Buddhist Terms*, p. 273). Bhūtatathatā, "the all-containing, immaterial nature of the Dharmakāya" (ibid., p. 259).

[82] *Meng-tzu wei*, in *Wen-ch'ao*, *chüan* 8, p. 18a.

preferring progress to retrogression. . . . If men were without [potential] goodness in their nature, there would only be retrogression in the world and humanity would sink into animality, devouring one another until all would be destroyed. It would have been impossible to have the civilization of today.[83]

And because individual men were capable of moral progress, human society was also capable of reaching institutional perfection. Individual development and social progress, K'ang believed, were closely intertwined. Strivings by individual men brought about social betterment, while ideal social conditions made it possible for individuals to achieve moral perfection.[84] Eventually, in the utopian world of "Universal Peace" and "Great Community" all men would be good, each completely qualified to enjoy equality and freedom under "the people's rule" (*min-chu*).[85]

In the last analysis, however, social progress hinged on the moral and intellectual progress of individual men. Therefore, it behooved thoughtful and courageous persons to break the bondage of faulty customs and to blaze the trail of progress for their fellow men. K'ang wrote in 1892:

It is men's habitual way to hold high opinions of themselves and undervalue others; thus men constantly found themselves in an environment of self-conceit. They construct theories and doctrines, performed deeds and feats. These converge into convention which dazzles the eye, blurs the vision, and overwhelms the mind. Convention is not made by one man but [results from] the accumulated doings of thousands of men—of countless men—who are confirmed partisans. Convention is not made in one day. It is composed of inveterate customs accumulated in decades, centuries—in countless ages. In order to alter it, one must go utterly contrary to it. The more one goes contrary [to convention], the greater is one's attainment in learning and the farther he stands away from the herd. Therefore, to exert oneself in practicing truth (*tao*) is a valuable thing.[86]

With such a theory of human nature K'ang must have found it easy to advocate and promote reforms, both institutional and intellectual. Even in the 1910s and 1920s when he was called by many a reactionary, he, in a way, was still trying to stand away from the herd and going contrary to convention, not the convention of the past but the convention that prevailed at the time.

[83] Ibid., p. 16a.
[84] Ibid., in *Hsin-min ts'ung-pao*, no. 19, p. 49.
[85] Ibid., in *Wen-ch'ao, chüan* 8, pp. 2b–3a.
[86] K'ang, *Ch'ang-hsing hsüeh-chi*, pp. 2–3.

Ethical Ideas

K'ang was generally inclined to take a naturalistic view of human motives and sentiments. This is especially true of his early writings, notably the two short works entitled "Substantial Truths and Universal Laws" (*Shih-li kung-fa*) and "the Esoteric and Exoteric Essays of Master K'ang" (*K'ang-tzu nei-wai p'ien*), both written in the mid 1880s.[87] This passage in the former introduces the matter.

> A man at birth has in him the disposition of love and hate. When he grows up and comes into contact with his fellow men, he benefits them as he manifests his love-disposition (*ai-chih*) and harms them as he manifests his hate-disposition (*wu-chih*).[88]

The following from the latter work makes clear what K'ang had in mind:

> I have no knowledge of the time when Heaven began to be. [I know, however, that] ether had condensed to form Heaven. After [particles of the ether] having rubbed against one another for a long time, heat and gravitational forces were generated, so were light and electricity. Matter (*wu-chih*) transformed itself and produced the sun; the sun in turn gave birth to the earth which brought forth [myriad] things. Matter possesses the life-giving property. [This property] resides in man and is called love (*jen*). The extension of this property has limits; the limits applicable to man are known as righteousness (*i*). In the way of man (*jen tao*) contention and strife make it impossible for fellow beings to live together; suspicion prevents them from getting along with one another. Consequently, trust (*hsin*) is practiced. Propriety (*li*), together with trust, completes [the complex of qualities which] constitutes humanity.[89] Men come to possess these four qualities because they have intelligence (*chih*)—because they have cerebrum and cerebellum, the nervous system that gives rise to consciousness (*ling*). . . . Knowledge increases in the aggregate of the brains of countless men; intelligence grows in the aggregate of the brain of men in countless generations. Rational principles (*li*) then appear. . . . There has been intelligence in China since [Fu]-hsi, Hsüan-[yüan], and Shen-nung;[90] there has been intelligence in Europe since Adam and Eve.[91]

In the last analysis, then, moral values and ethical principles were

---

[87] These have not been published but are available on microfilm in the collection of the Far Eastern Library, University of Washington.

[88] "Tsung lun jen-lui men," in *Shih-li kung-fa*.

[89] The text here, which has "hsing wei jen chih hou yu li yü hsin," appears to be corrupt.

[90] I.e., Fu-hsi, Hsüan-yüan (or, Huang-ti, the "Yellow Emperor"), and Shen-nung (the "Divine Farmer"), three of China's legendary rulers in remote antiquity.

[91] "Li-ch'i p'ien," in *K'ang-tzu nei-wai p'ien*, pp. 21a–b (hereafter *Nei-wai p'ien*).

crystallizations of men's psychological reactions, which in turn were manifestations of neurophysiological processes. These values and principles may be called man-made only in the sense that, in the school of experience and through the long process of intellectual development, men had learned collectively to recognize them as indispensable criteria of personal and social conduct.

In K'ang's thinking, then, "circumstance" (*shih*) was a decisive factor in man's moral evolution. K'ang put it in these emphatic words:

> I say, therefore, from circumstances are derived rational principles, from rational principles truth arises, from truth comes righteousness, and from righteousness emerges propriety. Circumstances are the forefather of human conduct; propriety is the last-generation offspring.[92]

Morality of course involved subjective emotions or sentiments. As K'ang pointed out, benevolence and righteousness were respectively expressions of "love" and "hate" or "like" and "aversion," all of which were directly "rooted in man's mind."[93] But indirectly and ultimately, subjective feelings were rooted in the cosmic process, far beyond the consciousness of any individual man.

> The *yang* makes moist warmth, the *yin* dry cold; the former gives life and growth, the latter brings death and decay, working in an endless cycle. . . . At the absolute beginning there was the moist-warm ether that steamed up to form Heaven. . . . What was close to Heaven and received the moist-warm ether produced the sun and moon. What [was far from Heaven and] received this ether produced the earth. When the earth received the steaming moist-warm ether, it produced plants, animals, and mankind. Men, having received the moist-warm ether, nourished with it their brains above and their hearts below. The moist produced benevolence and love; the warm yielded wisdom and courage. Accumulation of benevolence, love, wisdom, and courage resulted in [the making of] houses and clothes, which protected their bodies . . . and in [the institutions of] ceremonials, music, government, education, and morality, which formed their [social] order.[94]

As the moist-warm principle was not always beneficial in effect, man himself had to supplement the shortcomings of nature. For "when the moist was evil, it made greediness, deceit, and cowardice; when the warm was evil, it made oppressiveness, cruelty, and lust. . . . Strife and struggle came as a result." In order to counteract the baneful effects of

[92] "Shih-tsu p'ien" (*Nei-wai p'ien*, p. 18a).
[93] "Ai-wu p'ien" (*Nei-wai p'ien*, p. 6a).
[94] "Shih-je p'ien" (*Nei-wai p'ien*, p. 12a).

the moist-warm ether, sage men cultivated "dry-cold" virtues, such as gentleness, yielding, and frugality. Asceticism represented the acme of "dry-coldness" and was the most efficacious remedy for "moist-warm sicknesses."[95]

It is hardly surprising that K'ang's naturalistic interpretation of morality sometimes approached a materialistic interpretation of human behavior. In the last analysis, he said, everything was derived from "ether-matter" (*ch'i-chih*).[96] Man's entire mental makeup was reducible to matter, although in alone possessing intelligence he differed significantly from animals. This following discussion on "love" and "hate" reveals K'ang's view most clearly.

> Someone says to me: needles, mustard seeds, and lodestones are without intelligence, and yet they can attract [and repel] each other. These possess the love- and hate-matter (*ai wu chih chih*) but are without the intelligence-matter (*chih chih chih*). Therefore, intelligence, love, and hate, are separate entities. To which I answer: Intelligence is intangible, revealing itself through love and hate. One whose love and hate are extensive reveals [through them] that his intelligence is extensive. One whose love and hate are meager reveals [through them] that his intelligence is meager. All these [love, hate, and intelligence] are constituted of matter (*wu-chih*). What difference is there between them? [There is none.] Those who do not understand rational principles (*li*) regard benevolence and wisdom as rational principles, and physical things (*wu*) as ether-matter (*ch'i-chih*), arguing that rational principles and ether [-matter] are different.[97] These men do not know that nothing exists in the world beside ether-matter.[98]

K'ang's materialistic interpretation of human psychology was made even clearer in the following interesting statement:

> Man, born with an endowment of the *yin* and *yang* ethers, has the capacity for [sensory experience, namely,] tasting food, distinguishing sounds, and perceiving colors. Matter (*chih*) is responsible for this. He likes things [composed of] matter that is agreeable [to his senses] and dislikes things

[95] Ibid.

[96] Derk Bodde translated this term in connection with Chu Hsi's philosophy as "the physical element" (Fung, *History of Chinese Philosophy*, 2: 554). Fung Yu-lan, in a recent article explaining the meanings of some basic Taoist terms, virtually reduces everything to *ch'i*, which is "a material thing" (*Pei-ching ta-hsüeh hsüeh-pao: jen-wen k'o-hsüeh*, no. 4 [1959], pp. 22–23). Similarly, Chang Tai-nien, in an article on some of the characteristics of China's "classical philosophy," says that "Chinese classical materialism used *ch'i* as a concept to represent material phenomena," citing Lao-tzu, Wang Ch'ung, Chang Tsai, and Tai Cheng as instances (ibid., no. 3 [1957], pp. 62–63).

[97] Possibly, a veiled criticism of Chu Hsi.

[98] "Ai-wu p'ien" (*Nei-wai p'ien*, p. 7b).

[composed of] matter that is disagreeable. . . . Thus as soon as a man is born, likes and dislikes are all that he possesses [in his psyche]. Desire is the manifestation of like; delight is an expansive manifestation of like; joy is an extreme manifestation of like. Pity results when the object of extreme like is not obtained: this is what is called benevolence (*jen*).[99] All these are expressions of the *yang* ether. Anger is the manifestation of dislike. Fear is extreme dislike which one cannot [avoid]: this is what is called righteousness (*i*). All these are expressions of the *yin* ether. However, as the infant has likes and dislikes but not pity or fear, [it is clear that] at birth man has only likes and dislikes. Pity and fear come from man's intelligence [gained through postnatal experience]. With the full development of the spiritual and animal spirits (*hun p'e*), and with the complete growth of the brain, man's intelligence is increased. Knowing that knives, saws, water, and fire cause death, he carefully avoids them. . . . A sage's intelligence is even greater. He guards against harm before it comes and anticipates troubles before they arrive. . . . Therefore, the more intelligent one is, the more pity and fear he has.[100]

It was a short step from the above position for K'ang to rejecting in substance Chu Hsi's doctrine regarding "human desires" and "Heavenly reason."[101] Instead of decrying human desires and urging their eradication as a prerequisite to moral perfection, as Chu Hsi did,[102] K'ang affirmed the legitimacy of human desires, voicing a view strikingly similar to that of Tai Chen.[103] According to K'ang, "rational principles" were man-made, whereas desires inhered in man's nature. He pointed to the fact that a newborn infant did not possess moral consciousness but already had desires, without encouragement or instruction. He concluded, therefore, that "desires are natural, while rational principles are human" (*t'ien yüerh jen li*).[104] He expressed the same view in stronger terms in another connection:

All creatures that have blood and breath necessarily have desires; having desires, they invariably give them free play. To be without desires is to be

---

[99] Cf. *Chung-yung chu* (1901), p. 21a: "The character *jen* has "man" (*jen*) and "two" (*erh*) for its components, denoting "human relationship" and connoting "attraction," which is simply love-force (*ai-li*) and in reality, electrical force (*tien-li*).

[100] "Ai-wu p'ien" (*Nei-wai p'ien*, p. 6a).

[101] Fung, *History of Chinese Philosophy*, 2: 558–62, summarizes Chu's doctrine.

[102] Chu Hsi, *Chu-tzu yü-lui*, contains this passage: "Man's nature is originally clear, but it is like a pearl immersed in impure water, where its luster cannot be seen. . . . If each person could himself realize that it is human desire that causes this obscurity, this would bring enlightenment (*ming*). It is on this point alone that all one's efforts must be concentrated" (quoted in Fung, *History of Chinese Philosophy*, 2: 560).

[103] Ch'ien, *Chung-kuo . . . hsüeh-shu shih*, pp. 339–55, summarizes Tai Chen's views.

[104] "Li-ch'i p'ien" (*Nei-wai p'ien*, p. 21b).

dead. The Buddha might be said to be without [sensuous] desires; but he gave free rein to his desire for preserving his soul. The Sage might be said to be without desires [for worldly honors and riches]; but he gave free rein to his desire for benevolence and righteousness.[105]

Virtue, in other words, was not incompatible with gratification of desires. To K'ang saying otherwise was to go contrary to Confucius' teaching. "The way of Confucius," K'ang wrote in 1897, rested on "the rational principles which inhered naturally in Heaven and man." Therefore, "the Sage's way consists simply in leading the people [to act] in accordance with their own nature's dictates. . . . Hence it does not rule out gratification of sensuous desires [*sheng she*].[106]

The following statement, made in 1901, is more precise:

Confucius' teaching bases itself on human nature. It recognizes the existence [of desires relative to] sex, food, human relations, and daily needs, and [instructs men to] control and give measure to these [desires]. There are lofty, profound doctrines and extraordinary practices, such as abstention from eating meat, celibacy, mortifying the body, cultivating the soul. . . . But as these are remote from human nature, . . . they cannot be practiced by all men, and therefore cannot constitute a universally valid way [of life]. Confucius did not base his teaching [on such doctrines and practices].[107]

K'ang thus arrived at his hedonistic ethics. "The path taken by living creatures in the world," he declared, "is solely one of seeking pleasure and avoiding pain."[108] His explanation of this view is quite simple, similar in vein to his explanation of the origin of moral sentiments:

Now the awareness of living creatures [is like this]: the nerves of the brain contain the animus [*ling*]. Encountering material and immaterial [objects], there are then those which suit them, and those which do not suit them, those which please them, and those which do not please them. Those [objects] which please and suit the nerves of the brain, then cause the spiritual soul pleasure; those [objects] which do not please and suit

---

[105] "Pu-jen p'ien" (*Nei-wai p'ien*, p. 10a). One is tempted to compare this with a well-known saying of Tai Chen: "All actions involve desire. Where there is no desire, there is no action; there is action only where there is desire. When action conforms with what is perfectly proper, it is called reasonable. Where there is no desire and no action, there is no rationality" (*Meng-tzu tzu-i shu-cheng, chüan hsia*, p. 84; quoted in Ch'ien, *Chung-kuo . . . hsüeh-shu shih*, pp. 347–48).

[106] K'ang, *Tung-shih hsüeh, chüan 6 shang*, p. 31b.

[107] *Chung-yung chu*, p. 9a.

[108] K'ang, *Ta-t'ung shu, chia-pu*, p. 9; *i-pu* and *pin-pu*, p. 6; translated in Fung, *History of Chinese Philosophy*, 2: 686. Cf. Thompson, *Ta T'ung Shu*, p. 71.

the nerves of the brain, then cause the spiritual soul pain. It is especially so among humans: the nerves of the human brain being even more alert [in response] and [the human] spiritual soul being even clearer [in perception, the responses of the human body to] the stimuli of material and immaterial objects are especially complex, subtle, and swift, so that what please or do not please [the nerves] are even more clearly [experienced]. The pleasant and suitable are accepted; the unpleasant and unsuitable rejected. Therefore, in human experience there are only the suiting and not suiting. What does not suit is pain; what suits and suits again is pleasure. . . . Consequently, any planning made for humanity should seek to get rid of pain in order thereby to gain pleasure. There is no other course.[109]

It was said that here K'ang came close to Jeremy Bentham whose theory of pleasure served as the theoretical cornerstone of reform.[110] There is no evidence that K'ang had seen Bentham's writings in translation. But it is certain that K'ang's hedonistic psychology colored much of his ethical and social thought. Human progress, which was to be made possible by reforms, aimed precisely at removal of human sufferings and attainment of uttermost happiness in utopia—a veritable Epicurean paradise of boundless pleasures, sensuous as well as intellectual.[111]

Concepts that K'ang took over from the Confucian ethical theory acquired new meanings. Benevolence or love (*jen*), the most crucial of Confucian virtues, resolved itself into a matter of helping and enabling one's fellow men to gain the same pleasures that he himself sought. The realization of *jen* was not merely a matter of subjective sentiment but required the highest degree of wisdom and knowledge. For this reason, K'ang said, "Confucius often spoke of benevolence and wisdom in the same breath." For

if one is wise but not benevolent, he would refuse to lend a hand [to help others] and would, like the Taoist, take the easy way out; if one is benevolent but not wise, he would, out of compassion [for others], sacrifice himself [to assist others], like the Buddhist who treats all beings as equals.[112]

[109] K'ang, *Ta-t'ung shu, chia-pu*, pp. 7–9; *i-pu* and *pin-pu*, pp. 5–6; translated in Fung, *History of Chinese Philosophy*, 2: 686, and Thompson, *Ta T'ung Shu*, pp. 68–69.
[110] Lu and Lu, *K'ang Nan-hai hsien-sheng chuan*, p. 33a.
[111] K'ang, *Ta-t'ung shu, chia-pu*, p. 441; *i-pu* and *pin-pu*, p. 292 (Thompson, *Ta T'ung Shu*, p. 271). The entire last section (Part X) of this book deals with the various aspects of "uttermost happiness," including comfortable dwellings, luxurious clothing, and delectable food.
[112] K'ang, *Tung-shih hsüeh, chüan* 6 *hsia*, p. 8a.

Understandably, therefore, K'ang did not set store by martyrdom —inconsequential self-sacrifice that brought suffering to oneself without giving pleasure to others. This perhaps explains the fact that, upon the failure of the reform movement of 1898, K'ang chose not to die with "the six martyrs" so that he could continue to strive "to save myriad people."[113]

Aside from this important revision, K'ang followed more or less faithfully the Confucian doctrine of *jen*, in particular the doctrine that a man's moral excellence was measured by the extent of his love. K'ang echoed the classical view that the unvirtuous loved only himself, while the sage loved all.[114] The extension of love to "the barbarians," marked the crowning achievement of the virtuous man. Those who spoke of "barring and driving out the barbarians" (*jang-i*), K'ang argued, did not understand the principle of love.[115]

Also in line with Confucian thought, K'ang held that universal love did not preclude political differentiation. To implement this principle it was necessary that those who had virtue and wisdom should rule and others should obey. As K'ang put it, "those who were first informed" must instruct "those who were later in being informed."[116] Indeed, it was a moral duty for the former to serve and lead the latter. He quoted these words of Chu Tz'u-ch'i, his one-time teacher, to underscore his view.

> In endowing me with intelligence and abilities greater than what an ordinary man receives, Heaven is not partial to me but intends that I should render service to mankind. Therefore a sage shares prosperity and adversity with the common people. If I employ my intelligence and abilities for selfish ends, I would be ungrateful and repay ill Heaven's great favor.[117]

However, K'ang made it clear that inequality in service, namely, some should do more and others less proportionate to their capacities, was calculated not to perpetuate inequality but to remove it.

Though all are born of Heaven, men differ among themselves in being

[113] K'ang, *Nien-pu*, p. 29b; Lo, *K'ang*, p. 143.

[114] K'ang, *Tung-shih hsüeh, chüan* 6 *hsia*, pp. 2a–b.

[115] Ibid., p. 27b.

[116] Obviously, K'ang alluded to *Mencius*, V.i.7: "Heaven's plan in the production of mankind is this: that they who are first informed should instruct those who are later in being informed, and they who first apprehend principles should instruct those who are slower to do so" (Legge trans.).

[117] *Meng-tzu-wei*, in *Hsin-min ts'ung-pao*, no. 13, pp. 45–47.

intelligent or simple-minded, strong or weak. Not being of the same quality they naturally compete with one another. The strong win, whereas the weak lose. In this process of natural selection (*wu ching erh t'ien che*) there can be no equality. But while inequality is Heaven made, equality is the work of the sage-man. Therefore all [his] institutions and moral principles aim at eventual equality.[118]

Ideas Concerning Religion

I have treated elsewhere K'ang's attempt to transform Confucian ethics into a "Confucian religion," pointing out among other things that K'ang's conception of religion was essentially secular and that he tended to dismiss beliefs in "divine authority" as an intellectual aberration unworthy of man in his highest stage of development.[119] I shall present here only some of his ideas concerning the body and the soul, and his appraisals of the major religions of the world.

"Soul-substance" (*hun-chih*) was obviously one of K'ang's most important concepts, although it is couched in such vague terms that its exact nature is not easy to ascertain. He wrote in 1902:

The all-embracing Primal Ether created Heaven and Earth. Heaven is a single soul-substance; man likewise is a single soul-substance. Although differing in size, they both are parts of the all-embracing Ether of the Ultimate Beginning (*T'ai-yüan*). . . . Confucius said, "The Earth contains the spiritual ether (*shen ch'i*); the spiritual ether [manifests itself in] the wind and thunder. The wind and thunder flow into form; all things come forth to birth."[120] This spiritual [ether] is electricity that possesses consciousness. As electric light, it can penetrate everywhere; as spiritual ether, it can affect everything. . . . No creatures are without electricity; no creatures are without spirit (*shen*). . . . Now spirit is conscious ether (*chih-ch'i*), soul-consciousness (*hun-chih*), mental energy (*ching-shuang*), spiritual intelligence (*ling-ming*), illustrious virtue (*ming te*).[121] Though these names differ, they refer to the same activity.[122]

The "soul-substance" that K'ang mentioned appears to have been of an ambiguous character, something that was astride of the noumenal

---

[118] Ibid., p. 53. Similar ideas were more fully developed by Fang Hsiao-ju in his *Hsün-chih-chai chi, chüan* 2, "Tsung-i, no. 9, T'i-jen," and *chüan* 3 "Min-cheng p'ien."

[119] Hsiao, "K'ang Yu-wei and Confucianism," pp. 175–96; and the second section of chap. 4 in this volume.

[120] A quotation from the *Li-chi*, 29, "K'ung-tzu hsien-chü."

[121] K'ang, *Ta-t'ung shu, chia-pu*, p. 14; *i-pu*, p. 14; and *pin-pu*, p. 3. I use the translations of this passage as it appears in Fung, *History of Chinese Philosophy*, 2: 685 and Thompson, *Ta T'ung Shu*, pp. 64–65, with modifications.

[122] The phrase "illustrious virtue" occurs in the *Great Learning*, opening passage (Legge trans.)

and phenomenal realms. In fact, the nature of the universe as K'ang saw it is difficult of precise determination. K'ang's position, it appears, hovered near pantheism, animism, and materialism.

K'ang accorded a qualified recognition to the supernatural; he allowed that the occult and mystical could be inferred from the tangible. The Sage, he wrote, "exhibited the visible to make known the imperceptible and grasped the calculable to show that which was beyond calculation." As all parts of the universe were constituted of basically the same "soul-substance," each part could communicate with any other part. "This was the reason why the Sage, being prescient by virtue of his utmost sincerity, comprehended the night as well as the day, understood ghosts and spirits, and possessed comprehensive knowledge of Heaven and men."[123]

Constituted of soul-substance, man was at the same time soul and body.[124] Soul and body were equally important and, in K'ang's view, it was wrong to cultivate one aspect of man and to neglect the other.[125]

K'ang admitted, however, that from the ethical point of view, the noncorporeal part of man was "nobler" than the corporeal. The reason he gave was simple.

> The mind is intelligent; the body is without intelligence. Things are without intelligence but man has it. Therefore man is nobler than things. To realize that man is nobler than things is to know that mind is nobler than the body.[126]

It was in man's mind, K'ang added, where the ethically all-important "compassion" lay. But no insurmountable line should be drawn between soul and body. After all, the two were closely involved in the psychological process. The "compassionate mind" (*pu-jen chih hsin*) was none other than the soul's response to specific external stimuli transmitted through the sense organs.[127]

[123] K'ang, *Tung-shih hsüeh, chüan* 6 *hsia*, p. 40a. Cf. the *Chung-yung, chüan* 24: "It is characteristic of the most entire sincerity to be able to foreknow" (Legge trans.). For a modern theory of foreknowledge, see Louisa E. Rhine, *ESP in Life and Lab: Tracing Hidden Channels* (New York: Macmillan, 1967), in which Dr. Rhine states that telepathy, clairvoyance, and precognition are three different manifestations of the "psi," basing her conclusions on parapsychological researches conducted with her husband, Dr. Joseph Banks Rhine, at Parapsychological Laboratory at Duke University.

[124] *Li-yün chu* (1884?), p. 18a.

[125] *Lun-yü chu, chüan* 8, p. 2b.

[126] K'ang, *Tung-shih hsüeh, chüan* 6 *hsia*, p. 6b.

[127] K'ang, *Ta-t'ung shu, chia-pu*, p. 3; *i-pu* and *pin-pu*, p. 2; Thompson, *Ta T'ung Shu*, p. 64.

The two aspects of man became separate at death. According to K'ang, it was the animal spirits (together with the physical body) that died at the terminal of a man's life. The dismembered soul-ether (*hun-ch'i*) remained conscious and, floating above the ground, did not die at all.[128] Thus, while the body should be valued during a man's lifetime, it became completely worthless as soon as death came. As K'ang put it,

> [A corpse is destined to be] rotten flesh and dry bones. It may be preserved or it may be cremated. As it has nothing to do with soul-consciousness (*hun-chih*), it is not more valuable than fecal matter, pus, or gangrene.[129]

K'ang sometimes voiced the curious view that while all men were equally "sons of Heaven,"[130] their equality did not extend beyond death. The disembodied souls of some men existed for longer periods than those of others, depending on the personal qualities of the individual and on the circumstances under which they lived and died. The soul of a virtuous man continued to exist for a long time after death, "suffering no alteration through myriad vicissitudes."[131] That of a man who had suffered grievous injustice also persisted in postmortem existence for varying periods of time. The soul of an ordinary man, while it did not expire at the moment of death, would disperse and vanish in a month or a year.[132] Moreover, disembodied souls as a rule would sooner or later undergo reincarnation. K'ang subscribed to the Buddhist doctrine of "the wheel of transmigration" (*lun-hui*) but attributed it to Confucius.[133]

[128] *Li-yün chu*, p. 10a.

[129] K'ang, *Ta-t'ung shu, chia-pu*, p. 350; *i-pu* and *pin-pu*, p. 232 (paraphrase in Thompson, *Ta T'ung Shu*, p. 207).

[130] K'ang, *T'ung-shih hsüeh, chüan 6 shang*, p. 9b.

[131] *Meng-tzu wei*, in *Hsin-min ts'ung-pao*, no. 17, p. 55. Cf. "Li-yün," sec. 4, and "Chiao-t'e-sheng," sec. 27, in *Li-chi*.

[132] K'ang, "Chih mou chün shu," in *Wan-mu-ts'ao-t'ang i-kao, chüan* 5, p. 17a. K'ang cited in this connection Tzu-ch'an's remarks concerning the specter of Po-yu, as recorded in the *Tso-chuan*, Chao-kung 7th year. K'ang's belief in the postmortem existence of the soul led some writers in Communist China to condemn him for forsaking his "materialist inclination" and "wandering into the idealist labryinth" (Li Tse-hou, in *Che-hsüeh yen-chiu*, I, no. 1: 78–80). This condemnation rests on a misconception of K'ang's position, which was metaphysically so ambiguous that it cannot be properly identified with either materialism or idealism.

[133] *Li-yün chu, chüan* 11, p. 4b: "Men die to become spirits and spirits are reborn to be men. All this is brought about by the Wheel of Transmigration. The way of Confucius includes everything." See also "Wei wang-ying hsieh yen chih Shen I-lao shu," *Wan-mu-ts'ao-t'ang i-kao, chüan* 5, p. 16a, where, thanking a friend for sending him condolences on hearing of the death of his beloved concubine (Ho Chan-li), K'ang

K'ang also accepted the Buddhist doctrine of recompense. The following remarks made in 1901 represent the clearest expression of his view. After noting that virtuous men did not invariably receive rewards for their good deeds, he went on to say:

> Even [though men have] great virtue, the cause [*yin, hetu*] which had been created [previous to their present lives] might be divergent. Some men [do not receive rewards] because in their previous lives they had acted in a scornful way in relation to other men, or because the *karma* resulting from killing done in their previous lives has not been removed, or because though cultivating good conduct and having heard the Truth they have not extended widely their actions in saving men [from sufferings], or because though liberal in their gifts to many in need, they have not been able to free themselves of transgressions. Consequently, they receive their present recompense [in accordance with the causes established in their past lives]. Although the principle [of recompense] is far from obvious, [its operation is unerring. For] the electrical ether [*tien-ch'i*] and soul-consciousness attract and respond to each other. Even if the connections are remote, there is always a cause [for each effect]. Even though [recompense comes] after varying intervals, sometimes sooner and sometimes later, one who does good is certain to receive reward [eventually] and one who has great virtue is certain to receive the Mandate—if recompense does not come in one, two, three, or five generations, it will surely come in ten, a hundred, a thousand, or even ten thousand generations.[134]

K'ang, however, did not justify superstitious practices concerning supernatural beings. Deities and spirits, according to K'ang, should be honored, not because they had the power to dispense favors but solely because they had been in their lifetimes men of virtue as well as benefactors of their fellow men. Descendants should offer sacrifices to their departed ancestors solely to give expression to their abiding affection and respect for them. It was never ethically justifiable to ask favor of deities and spirits.[135]

As men lived and died, there would always be deities and spirits. But the number of supernatural beings was bound to decrease as man's intelligence and knowledge increased. K'ang asserted, without giving explanations or citing facts, that "spirits abounded in high antiquity,

---

said: "As I truly and profoundly believe in the doctrine of samsāra, I shall work for my own emancipation—freeing myself of worldly concerns and disciplining myself to achieve nirvāna."

[134] *Chung-yung chu*, pp. 16b–17a. For further discussion of K'ang's views concerning recompense and reincarnation, see chapter 4, this volume.

[135] See K'ang's letter cited in note 132, above.

but deities were few in middle antiquity. The wiser men became, the fewer spirits and deities.[136] For this reason, "the divine way (*shen-tao*) was useful in controlling primitive people but the human way must be used when men have made progress." K'ang was convinced that eventually, "as men's intelligence gradually develops, divine authority will lose its hold on men."[137]

It appears, therefore, that an element of "antireligious skepticism"[138] may be detected in K'ang's thinking, presumably a natural consequence of his basically rationalistic humanistic position. He was here in essential agreement with Confucius.[139] Both men refused to seek comfort in religious faith but chose to rely on man's own ability to face the facts of existence.

This rationalistic attitude revealed itself most clearly in K'ang's evaluation of the major religions of the world including Confucianism, which he regarded as one of them. K'ang at first tended to put all religions on roughly the same level. A statement he made in 1886 typifies this view.

There are many religions in the present world. There is Confucianism in China, . . . Buddhism in India, . . . Christianity in Europe, and Islam among the Moslems. In addition to these there are countless splinter religious sects. However, I say there are [in reality] only two religions. All those that [teach] the establishment of states and governments; recognize the relationships between ruler and subject, father and son, husband and wife, elder and younger brothers; authorize the occupations of the scholar, farmer, artisan, and trader; maintain the customary rituals practiced by shamans and priests in connection with [the belief in deities and spirits]; and approve of the eating of vegetables, fruits, fish, and meat, [are essentially identical with] Confucianism. . . . Those that prohibit meat-eating; require celibacy, worshipping their founders by day and by night, and refraining from carry on the four occupations; reject the four tenets;[140] follow the rules of supernatural beings; and transcend human feelings and desires, are [essentially identical with] Buddhism from which stemmed Christianity, Islam, and other [similar] religions. . . . Which of these two [basic] religions is right and which is wrong?

[136] *Chung-yung chu*, p. 14a.

[137] "I-ta-li yu-chi," pp. 66–68.

[138] See Sidney Hook, *The Quest for Being* (New York: St. Martin's Press, 1961), for an account of "pragmatic naturalism" that affords an interesting comparison with K'ang's view.

[139] *Lun-yü*, X.11 (Legge translation with modification).

[140] The original has *ssu shu*, possibly referring to "the four erroneous tenets," known also as *ssu chih*, *ssu hsieh*, or *ssu mi*—in particular, to the four tenets of the "outsiders" (non-Buddhists) (Soothill and Hodous, *Dictionary of Chinese Buddhist Terms*, p. 172).

Which will win and which will lose? My answer is, . . . Confucianism
with its [teachings concerning] the human relationships and social mores,
which are in accord with the natural reason of Heaven (*t'ien-li chih tzu-
jan*), constituted the starting point. Buddhism with its renunciation of
human relations and suppression of human desires, marks the end of man's
quest [for happiness]. . . . Without Confucianism, there would have been
nothing to prime human development at the beginning; without Buddhism, there would have been nothing to crown human achievement at
the end. . . . However, as the Buddha taught men to be kindly and meek,
they will become simple and unsophisticated again [as they had been
prior to the coming of Confucianism]. Then a sage [like Confucius] will
again rise and Confucianism will reappear. . . . Thus these two religions
[—Confucianism and Buddhism—] will succeed each other in turn . . .
and alternately guide [mankind].[141]

As time went on, K'ang showed a greater preference for Confucianism, although he continued to acknowledge the value of other religions.
Sometimes he equated Mahāyāna Buddhism with Confucianism. "The
teaching of Confucius," he said, "was the Hua-yen (Avataṁsa) of Buddhism."[142] For like Hua-yen Buddhism, Confucianism directed men's
search for *dharma* to the world in which they lived, not to a realm lying
beyond it. This was, obviously, K'ang's way of minimizing the otherworldly tendency of Buddhism. He saw relatively little value in other
Buddhist sects. As late as in the republican days he continued to com-
plain about people who talked about Buddhism (i.e., non-Hua-yen
sects) and belittled Confucianism.[143]

Christianity, in K'ang's later view was inferior to both Confucianism
and Buddhism. He contended (in a manner less than convincing) that
"the Christian teaching came entirely from the Buddhist," and was in
fact a defective copy of the latter. For "its doctrine concerning spiritual
care was extremely crude and shallow," coming up only to a lower level
of the Buddhist teaching.[144] Christianity was inferior to Confucianism
not only because it did not suit the social conditions of China but, more
importantly, because it placed emphasis on "divine authority."[145]

[141] K'ang, "Hsing-hsüeh p'ien," in *Nei-wai p'ien*. Cf. K'ang's remarks, "Sung learning [i.e., Neo-Confucianism] is like rice which nourishes a man and Buddhism is like
medicine which cures a man [of illness]," in a letter written about the same time.
"Yü Huang Chung-t'ao pien-hsiu shu," in microfilm, reel 3. This letter is not given
in K'ang T'ung-pi's compilation of her father's writings.

[142] Liang Ch'i-ch'ao, *Nan-hai K'ang hsien-sheng chuan, Yin-ping-shih ho-chi, wen-chi,* 4:
84.

[143] "Chih Chu Shih-hui shu," *Wan-mu-ts'ao-t'ang i-kao, chüan* 4, p. 35a.

[144] "I-ta-li yu-chi," pp. 131–32.

[145] Ibid., pp. 132–33.

Without denying the beneficial influences of Christianity and Islam on men, K'ang affirmed the doctrinal superiority of Confucianism precisely because it stressed the human relationships and moral duties. "Confucius loathed divine authority for its undue influence [on men] and swept it away. Therefore Confucianism suits the present world best."[146] Partly thanks to this conviction K'ang urged strongly and insistently the establishment of Confucianism as "state religion."[147]

It is clear, then, that K'ang discerned no value in religion beyond its salutary influence on men and society. It was a judgment that rested not on anything like faith or piety, but on purely utilitarian considerations. In fact, his insistence on the necessity of doing away with "divine authority" drew him perilously close to atheism, although he had nowhere expressly denied the existence of God or Providence.

K'ang's utilitarian view of religion led to an interesting conclusion. According to him, men stood in need of religion so long as they fell short of moral perfection and so long as their institutions remained defective. With the arrival of Utopia, the Age of Universal Peace and the Great Community, all religions, including Confucianism, would have served their purposes and finally become unnecessary. In his own words:

> Christianity has reverence for God (*T'ien*) and love for men as its moral teaching; it takes repentance of sin and the last judgment as [its means of making] people frightened of [doing] evil. In the Age of the Great Community [people] will naturally love one another, will naturally be without sin. Comprehending the natural workings of evolution, they therefore will not reverence God. Comprehending the impossibility of limitless numbers of souls waiting in the empty space [for last judgment], they will therefore refuse to believe in a doomsday. The religion of Jesus will then become extinct, when men attain the Great Community. Islam speaks of the bonds of the state, ruler, subject, husband, and wife. By the time we will have entered the Great Community, it will already be extinct. Although its doctrine of the soul is enunciated in God's name, it is crude and superficial, insufficient to merit credence. It was Confucius' intention [to guide men to] the Great Peace and the Great Community. Having arrived at this stage of [human development], Confucius' doctrine of the Three Ages will have been completely fulfilled [and Confucianism will also become unnecessary]. The sickness being over, there is no need to use medicine; the shore having been reached, the raft may be discarded.[148]

---

146 Ibid., pp. 66–68.
147 Chapter 4 of this volume discusses K'ang's view on religion at greater length.
148 *Ta-t'ung shu, chia-pu*, pp. 452–53; *i-pu* and *pin-pu*, p. 301; Thompson, *Ta T'ung Shu*, pp. 174–75, here quoted with modifications.

Relieved now of the onerous chores incumbent upon men in imperfect society and enjoying the fullest measure of happiness, they would have only one overriding wish. "In the state of ultimate tranquillity and joyfulness," K'ang wrote, "men will think about nothing but longevity." Two religions of an entirely different nature would come into vogue.

> Therefore in the Age of the Great Community only the studies which lead to immortality (*shen-hsien*) and Buddhahood will be widely pursued. Great Community is the ultimate law of the world. But the study of immortality, or longevity without death, is a further extension of this law. The study of Buddhahood, which transcends life and death, a setting apart from the world without going out of it, goes beyond even [the world of] the Great Community.

K'ang went on to say that there was a still higher plane of existence beyond Buddhahood, to be reached through "the study of celestial peregrination" (*t'ien-yu chih hsüeh*) and that he had written "another book" on the subject.[149] With these remarks he concluded the *Ta-t'ung shu* and, incidentally, indicated the close of the first phase of his philosophical thought and the transition to the second.

In the first phase of K'ang's thought he envisioned the world as an essentially moral system, with man as the central figure. There is often an annoying lack of clarity and consistency in his terminology—which is frequently further obscured by rhetorical furbelow. He shifted his position without notice or explanation, which adds another difficulty to grasping the precise meanings of his writings. Despite these difficulties, however, his general position is sufficiently clear. Largely in line with the Confucian tradition, he interpreted the universe and human life in ethical terms. At the same time, he took notions and precepts from outside sources, chiefly Buddhism and occasionally Christianity, and adapted them to fit into the basically Confucian frame of his thought. He thus formulated a *Weltansicht* that was thoroughly moralistic and faintly atheistic.

SECOND PHASE: BEYOND THE WORLD OF MAN

The second and final phase of K'ang's philosophical thought was given definitive expression in the *Lectures on the Heavens (Chu-t'ien chiang)*, a book dealing with astronomy and cosmology, which he completed in

[149] Ibid. The book to which K'ang referred at the end of the passage was the *Chu-t'ien chiang* (Lectures on the Heavens), the portions of which dealing with astronomy and cosmology have been discussed in my article, "K'ang Yu-wei's Excursion into Science," in Lo, *K'ang*, pp. 375–407.

the summer of 1926, about nine months before his death.[150] This, presumably, was the book to which he referred in 1902 when he mentioned "the study of celestial peregrination" as the inquiry that was to come after the study of Buddhism.

Here the mood as well as the content of K'ang's thought changed drastically. Whereas in the first phase the tone of his writings was on the whole predominantly somber, showing profound concern about the plight of his fellow humans and an earnest wish to ameliorate their conditions, one now detects a note of sublime joyfulness, gaining thereby the impression that K'ang's previous solicitude for human sufferings had given place to the conviction that happiness was readily attainable by simply maintaining the correct frame of mind. There was no need for laborious reforms, for remaking the external world. Salvation, in other words, lay not in Śākyamuni's toils in the Papaya Forest but in Kāśyapa's smile upon seeing the flower. One discerns also a hint of humility—an admission that the human intellect does not and cannot understand everything—an attitude hitherto foreign to K'ang who had been up to now a man "haunted by no intellectual perplexities."[151] Whether as leader of institutional reform or as prophet of a new Confucianism, he was characteristically self-confident almost to the point of self-conceit.[152] Closely linked with this self-confidence was his conviction that man, as Heaven's most-favored creature, possessed the power to comprehend everything worthwhile in the universe, including foreknowledge of future events; and that, while deities and spirits had their place in the world, it was man who occupied the position of central importance. Much of this anthropocentric attitude was replaced by the realization that man and his world were not more than a speck

---

[150] So the author's preface to this book indicates. This work, consisting of 14 *chüan*, was published posthumously by his students, probably after the spring of 1930, as T'ang Hsiu's colophon suggests. Thompson, *Ta T'ung Shu*, p. 67, interlinear note, appears to be inaccurate in saying that the book was "block carved in the winter of 1926, and was printed by the Chung Hwa [Book Store]." This conflicts with the date indicated in the above-mentioned colophon and with Wu Chuang's statement made in a foreword, dated 1929, to the effect that a number of K'ang's students debated on the advisability of publishing the manuscript left behind by their recently deceased teacher.

[151] Lo Woon Choon (Lo Wen-chung, husband of K'ang T'ung-pi, K'ang's second daughter), in a speech delivered at the memorial service on the tenth anniversary of K'ang's death. Manuscript copy in Jung-pang Lo's collection.

[152] See *Nien-p'u*, pp. 3a (1869, 12 *sui*), 3b (1873, 16 *sui*), and 4a (1876, 19 *sui*); Lo, *K'ang*, pp. 27, 29, 31. At the last-mentioned date he said that he "could become a sage for certain, finish reading all books before thirty, . . . and remake the entire world." Cf., the first section of chap. 1 in this volume.

in a limitless universe and that, as the extent of man's intellectual experience was narrowly circumscribed, he should not deny the existence of beings of which he had no direct knowledge.

It may be said therefore that in the last years of his life K'ang's thinking had become "otherworldly," pointing to realms far beyond the phenomenal world of man and matter. On the one hand, he transcended the narrow confines of the earth and engaged in what he called "celestial peregrination"; on the other hand, he looked beyond humanity to contemplate a Supreme Being, thus silently abandoned his earlier agnostic and atheistic sentiments.

Celestial Peregrination (T'ien-yu)

K'ang's idea of "roaming the heavens" appears to have stemmed from several sources. In the first place, it may have been suggested to him by the Lu-Wang school of Neo-Confucianism.[153] K'ang's universalistic *Weltansicht* bore a close resemblance to that of Lu Chiu-yüan; he may well have received inspiration from these oft-quoted lines of Lu:

> I raise my head and reach for the Southern Dipper;
> I turn around and stand beside the Polar Star—
> I look beyond the sky's limits, holding my head high:
> I find no other man who is my like.[154]

But the most important inspiration came from K'ang's study of astronomy, which he began in the early 1880s and carried on intermittently throughout his life.[155] The impact on him of the spectacular views revealed by the telescope appears to have been tremendous. The exhilarating experience thus gained not only quickened his interest in astronomy but also gave substance to Lu Chiu-yüan's lofty sentiments. With the help of the telescope and of whatever literature on astronomy available to him, K'ang widened greatly his intellectual vista, reaching even farther than Lu's Southern Dipper and Polar Star. A boundless realm was opened up before him, for his imagination to soar untrammeled. Incidentally, he may have received further assistance from Inoue Enryō's *Narrative of an Imaginary Journey in the Starry Regions (Hsing-chiai*

---

[153] For the influence of this school on K'ang, see chapter 2 of this volume.

[154] Quoted in Huang Tsung-hsi, *Sung-Yüan hsüeh-an, chüan* 58, pp. 1069–70.

[155] *Nien-p'u*, pp. 6b–7a (Lo, *K'ang*, p. 40), indicates that in 1884 (27 *sui*), when K'ang first marked the outlines of his *Weltansicht*, he had already come to the concept of infinite universe, and that he had used a microscope in his studies. In the author's preface to the *Chu-t'ien chiang*, however, he said that he had used a telescope when he was 28 *sui* (1885).

hsiang-yu chi), a science fiction that came to his notice sometime between 1886 and 1896.[156]

K'ang was now intellectually as well as psychologically equipped to deal with the marvelous—to roam the heavens. But it had taken many years for him to mature psychologically and finally to arrive at his new position. The events of 1894 interrupted his astronomical speculations and drew his attention to more earthly concerns. It was not until the disaster of 1898 that he again found it possible to resume this line of inquiry. The first clear indication of this resumption occurred in the opening years of the present century when he was an exile in India and was putting his book on the Great Community into final form.[157] K'ang made at least two references to "celestial peregrination" in this book. He wrote at one point:

> In my roaming through the heavens I have imagined all the worlds of uttermost happiness and all the worlds of uttermost suffering. The happy I have been happy to be together with and the suffering I have [sought to] save. Being a creature of the heavens, how could I abandon the worlds and heavens, cut [myself] off from my kind, flee from the social relationships, and be happy by myself? . . .
> [Note:] I have another book named "The Heavens" (*Chu-t'ien*).[158]

At the very end of the book he made a second reference to heaven roaming:

> After *Ta-t'ung* there will first be the study of immortality; after that, there will be the study of Buddhahood. . . . After [the studies of] immortality and Buddhahood will come the study of roaming the heavens. I have another book [on the subject.][159]

In another work written about the same time, K'ang made these remarks in which the idea of celestial peregrination was implied:

> The teaching transmitted through the Six Classics . . . deals with the nonessential matters concerning governance and legislation; it does not

[156] This book, *Seikai sōyū ki* (An Imaginary Journey in the Starry Region), a science fiction by Inoue Enryō, is listed in K'ang's bibliography of Japanese books, the *Jih-pen shu-mu chih*, *chüan* 14, "Fiction," p. 41b.

[157] K'ang T'ung-pi, *K'ang Nan-hai hsien-sheng nien-p'u hsü-pien*, p. 22b (hereafter, *Nien-p'u hsü-pien*); Lo, *K'ang*, pp. 192–93, where "ta-t'ung" is translated as "the Great Unity" instead of "the Great Community."

[158] *Ta-t'ung shu, chia-pu*, pp. 5–6; *i-pu* and *pin-pu*, p. 4; Thompson, *Ta T'ung Shu*, p. 276, here quoted with modifications.

[159] *Ta-t'ung shu, chia-pu*, p. 453; *i-pu* and *pin-pu*, p. 301; Thompson, *Ta T'ung Shu*, p. 276, here quoted with modifications.

represent Confucius' transcendental thought (*shen-ming chih i*). There is [the doctrine concerning] the limitless, numberless heavens which are absolutely intangible—a heaven-constituted world (*t'ien-tsao chih shih*) unthinkable and ineffable. There the Sage roamed, wishing to share the celestial transformation [which he thus achieved] with all the living beings. This is the ultimate doctrine of Confucius.[160]

It is important to note that in the early 1900s K'ang viewed "roaming the heavens" as an activity that should be practiced only by men who had fulfilled their obligations to society[161] and that, while he himself admittedly already practiced it, he still retained his preoccupation with "saving" his fellow men. He was, in other words, still partially earthbound.

This bifarious position, with his eyes turned toward heaven and his heart anchored in the earth, persisted for a number of years. Many of his writings done in the first and second decades of the new century testify to this. For instance, in a poem composed probably in 1904–5 on the occasion of riding in a balloon over Paris, he said in part:

> Many are lands of happiness in the heavens—
>   What prosperity on the stars, each a world in itself!
> Myriad eons have I passed in the heavens,
>   Hankering for nothing, bored by nothing, each moment at ease.
> My compassionate heart stirs and cannot be quieted;
>   Into earth-prison again I enter, to save man.
> Deliberately, vexations and worries I seek,
>   An immortal in the heavens unwilling to be.[162]

The rationale of this position was explained in his preface to the *Pu-jen* (Compassion), written in the closing days of 1912. As the earth was a very tiny globe in an infinite universe in which stars constantly came into being and passed out of existence, the "gains and losses" sustained by men were in comparison too trivial to be worthy of concern. But, he added, as a sentient being born into the world, he could not help having pity on his fellow men and wishing to free them from their miseries and pains.[163]

Repeated frustrations in his efforts to better the world eventually

[160] *Chung-yung chu*, p. 46b.

[161] *Ta-t'ung shu, chia-pu* p. 452; *i-pu* and *pin-pu*, p. 300; Thompson, *Ta T'ung Shu*, p. 275.

[162] "Pa-li teng ch'i-ch'iu ko," in *K'ang Nan-hai hsien-sheng shih-chi*, (Ts'ui Ssu-che calligraphy ed.) *chüan* 7, pp. 72–73.

[163] "Pu-jen tsa-chih hsü," in *Pu-jen*, no. 1.

brought him to despair. His part in the abortive attempt to restore the Manchu dynasty in 1917 contributed much to discourage him from taking further active interest in public affairs. This, in fact, was virtually the last manifestation of his "compassionate heart."[164] At about this time K'ang went into retirement, although he did not entirely lose contact with the outside world. He acquired a spacious estate on the shores of the scenic West Lake in Hangchow, calling it "Gardens of One Heaven" (*I-t'ien yüan*), and built a two-storied house on top of a hill, naming it "The Hall of Celestial Peregrination" (*T'ien-yu t'ang*), where he spent many a leisurely day.[165] All this constituted an eloquent testimony to the change in K'ang's attitude toward the world.

He himself clearly indicated this change. In a postscript (dated February 26, 1923) to a letter to Timothy Richard in 1898, he said, "I'm an old man . . . who has rendered no useful service to the country and found no place on earth to bury his sorrows, manage now only to make excursions into the heavens."[166] A little later, he said to his family: "I practice celestial peregrination and am not vexed by the worries and anguishes of the human world; therefore I am happy wherever I go."[167]

"Celestial peregrination," so it appears, was a sort of escapism justified by the observation that in face of the vast universe nothing in the world of man mattered at all. K'ang made this clear in 1923, in a speech delivered in Shensi.

The *Chuang-tzu* says, "Man is born with grief." In formulating institutional reforms in the *Spring and Autumn Annals* Confucius aimed solely at ridding men of sufferings. The entire body of Buddhist sūtras are calculated to serve no purpose beyond emancipation from worry and anguish. My entire life has been spent in troubles and calamities, but I manage

164 "Hsü-chuan *Pu-jen tsa-chih* hsü," in *Pu-jen*, nos. 9 and 10 (in one volume), 1917. These were the last issues ever published. I say "virtually" because K'ang made another entirely fruitless attempt at restoration, as a letter to Reginald F. Johnston, written in 1923, clearly shows ("Ch'ing Chuang-shih-tun tai tsou yu-shuo ching-kuo").

165 K'ang T'ung-pi, *Nien-p'u hsü-pien*, pp. 121a–24a, gives the text of K'ang's "I-t'ien yüan chi," written in the autumn of 1922. Lo, *K'ang*, mentions the "One Heaven Garden" (I-t'ien yüan) but does not give the text of the "I-t'ien yüan chi."

166 *K'ang Nan-hai hsien-sheng mo-chi*, vol. 3. Even at this late time, however, K'ang did not forget entirely worldly affairs. See e.g., a poem written on the occasion of the Hsüan-t'ung emperor's marriage in 1922, in *K'ang Nan-hai hsien-sheng shih-chi* (Ts'ui calligraphy ed.), *chüan* 15, pp. 32–33, and another poem (the first of a series of seven) written on the occasion of his seventieth birthday, in ibid., pp. 97–98.

167 K'ang T'ung-pi, *Nien-pu hsü-pien*, p. 146a. Lo, *K'ang*, p. 248, refers to K'ang's trips with his family but omits the remarks recorded by K'ang T'ung-pi.

to be free from both grief and fear, and to remain essentially joyous and happy. With the appearance of Copernicus, we come to the knowledge that the earth is but one of the sun's planets; the ancient doctrine of one heaven and [one] earth is shattered. . . . So numerous are the stars and so big are they that the earth-globe is [in comparison] exceedingly small. How much smaller [than the earth-globe] is one single country and family [on it]? . . . Therefore, once a person understands astronomy, all the religions lose their meaning. Infinite power and endless joy pertain to complete enlightenment gained through scientific inquiry. . . . The grief and distress of a single family or a single man are no longer worthy of mentioning.[168]

That this was not a passing mood may be gathered from another statement made a few years later, as reported by one of his students who edited the *Lectures*.

I recall that one night in that year [i.e., 1926] our teacher summoned together the students of the Academy for Celestial Peregrination, who assembled in the Western [part of the courtyard, below] the steps leading to the Hall of Celestial Peregrination where he lived. It was near midnight; . . . the bright moon was ascending from the east, pouring down its limpid rays and spilling airy shadows [of trees] on the ground. The teacher said, "Beautiful indeed is this scene; we can now proceed." Thereupon he took out the telescope, and making them look through it, one after another. . . . Then, with a smile, he said, "Born between heaven and earth men are not identical in their intelligence and worth, but [they are all alike in] being involved in lifelong toils and in being alternately visited upon by sorrows and joys that agitate their feelings within and melt away their strength without. Some [suffering these] in a small way, feel anxiety about their own lives or their families; others, in a large scale, about the affairs of the state or of the world. Men are constantly troubled because sorrow always outbalances joy. However, [a catholic view of things] will bring mental calm and composure. If we only set our minds free [from anxiety] and make them travel beyond mundane existence, we would then saunter high in the heavens and soar unshackled into infinite space—riding on vapory clouds and harnessing flying dragons; and, casting a backward glance [at the world of men] we would see that ourselves, our families, our country, or even our great earth [dwindling into insignificance before the vast grandeur of the universe], stand like gnats before Mount T'ai—absolutely unworthy of attention.[169]

[168] K'ang T'ung-pi, *Nien-pu hsü-pien*, p. 139b. Lo, *K'ang*, p. 245, indicates the "theme" of K'ang's speech but does not give the text.

[169] T'ang Hsiu's colophon to *Chu-t'ien chiang*, dated 1930. According to K'ang T'ung-pi, *Nien-pu hsü-pien*, p. 146a (Lo, *K'ang* p. 248), the Academy for Celestial Peregrination was established in Shanghai in the spring of 1926. K'ang left Shanghai for Peking in the eighth month (K'ang T'ung-pi, *Nien-pu hsü-pien*, p. 149a; Lo, *K'ang*, p. 249). The incident that T'ang recalled must have occurred sometime after the founding of the Academy and before K'ang left Shanghai.

"Riding on vapory clouds and harnessing flying dragons" was perhaps intended to be merely a figure of speech, as "celestial peregrination" itself was not meant to be taken literally. Sometimes, however, K'ang gave the impression that to rove in the heavens was actually a way of life. Subscribing to Buddhist idealism, he expressed the conviction that a man's destiny was shaped by his own thought. In a lecture to the International Moral Association in Tsingtao, delivered in 1923 (late spring or early summer), he said:

> Electricity travels three hundred thousand *li* a second. The electrical energy of man can reach up to the stars and the innumerable heavens. When one understands the principle of electrical interconnection [within the universe], one finds that the vicissitudes in the human world do not merit consideration and that the earth-globe, being tiny, is unworthy of his slightest attention. Enlightened virtue (*ming te*) . . . lies entirely in man's thought. Good comes of good thought, evil of evil thought. . . . The Sūrangama sūtra (*Leng-yen ching*) says: Pure thought [enables one] to ascend the heavens, pure passion encumbers [him and brings him] into the human world, pure desire [causes him to] fall into animality. This is a ringing truth. I take delight in thinking of celestial peregrination; often I dreamed that I fly, riding on clouds which were no more than a few feet above ground and, at the highest, only about twenty or thirty feet. This is because I have not been able to rid myself of mundane thoughts.[170]

This statement, which appears to have been made in all sincerity, reveals K'ang's new position. Having given up hope to save the world he now directed his efforts to helping individual persons to attain happiness in the same way as he himself did. In other words, having relinquished the role of social reformer he now assumed the role of a heaven-roaming prophet. An instance of his proselyting activities occurred in 1923 when he, upon hearing the sorry situation that one of his married nieces faced, wrote a lengthy letter to teach her how to emancipate herself from anguish by roaming the heavens. "My dear niece," he pleaded,

---

[170] K'ang T'ung-pi, *Nien-pu hsü-pien*, pp. 136a–39a, gives the text of K'ang's speech. The passage here quoted occurs near the end of p. 138b. Lo, *K'ang*, p. 242, mentions K'ang's visit to Tsinan and Tsingtao, but makes no mention of the speech. The International Association for Morality was formerly known as the Confucian Society (K'ung-chiao hui). I have not been able to ascertain the relationship, if any, between the K'ung-chiao hui and the "Confucian Society" (sometimes also referred to as Tsun K'ung she), founded by Richard Wilhelm and "a number of former imperial officials in the German-leased territory of Tsingtao" in 1913. For the latter, see Hellmut Wilhelm, "Lao Nai-hsüan," in Boorman, *Biographical Dictionary of Republican China*, 2: 282. Incidentally, K'ang's dreams remind one of what Sigmund Freud called "dreams of convenience" (*The Interpretation of Dreams*, trans. A. A. Brill, [New York: Modern Library, 1950] pp. 34–35).

"do try this; then you will become, together with me, a celestial human engaged in heaven-roaming."[171] K'ang did not restrict his proselyting efforts to relatives. With the establishment of the Academy for Celestial Peregrination in 1926 he undertook regularly to spread his message to a wider circle.[172]

That K'ang regarded his doctrine of celestial peregrination as a sort of religion may be seen from what he said to one of the "disciples" at the Academy:

> Jesus had [only] twelve disciples; the betrayer Judas was among them. Nevertheless, he [Jesus] was able to make his religion prevail and to propagate his teaching, which developed and spread all over the world. My students here in Shanghai number less than twenty. I do not think [the number] too small. If they really believe in my words and transmit my teaching [to others], then like what Nāgārjuna [did for Buddhism] and Paul [for Christianity], the benefits [of my doctrine] would flow down through myriad generations.[173]

The central aim of K'ang's "teaching" was to help men free themselves from the afflictions that plagued them as soon as they came into the world. This he clearly set forth in the preface to the *Lectures*.

> Born of heaven, men have desires; they cannot avoid seeking [to gratify their desires]. When what they seek is not obtained they cannot avoid contending [with one another]. Contention invariably leads to disorder.[174] A million men die grievously in a single war. In the struggle for existence the weak are the prey of the strong.[175] Therefore founders of the various religions, having pity on men and wishing to save them, feigned orders from Heaven and instructed men by means of the divine way (*shen-tao she chiao*)—frightening them with hell, enticing them with the kingdom of heaven in which utmost joy prevails, guiding them with [the doctrines

---

[171] "Yü sheng-nü T'an Ta-yin shu," in K'ang T'ung-pi, *Nien-p'u hsü-pien*, pp. 133a–34b (Lo, *K'ang*, pp. 240–41, entries for 1922 do not include this letter); and in *Wan-mu-ts'ao-t'ang i-kao, chüan* 4, pp. 126a–27a, but dated 1923, which is probably erroneous.

[172] The Academy was established in April, 1926, on Yü-yüan Road, Shanghai, with Lung Tse-hou as Dean of Studies (K'ang T'ung-pi, *Nien-pu hsü-pien*, p. 146a; Lo, *K'ang*, p. 248).

[173] K'ang T'ung-pi, *Nien-pu hsü-pien*, pp. 146b–47a (Lo, *K'ang*, pp. 248–49, entries for 1926 do not include these remarks). Nāgārjuna (Lung-shu) was the 14th of the 28 patriarchs of the Ch'an sect of Mahāyāna Buddhism.

[174] This is virtually a paraphrase of a passage in the Hsün-tzu, Book XIX, "On the Rules of Proper Conduct" (Dubs, *Works of Hsüntze*, p. 213).

[175] This is one of the few overt references to Darwinism in K'ang's writings.

of] "the six ways of sentient existence"[176] and of "the Wheel of Transmigration," or luring them with the Pure Land and the Heavenly Mansions.[177] All these were intended to soothe men's hearts and save their souls, . . . to remove their anxieties and afflictions, and to point to utmost joy as the final goal. But these do not constitute proper solutions [of the problem; to apply them] is like carrying rice to treat the starving or dispensing herbs to cure the sick [which is not as good as preventing hunger and sickness from occurring]. This is because these founders of religions did not know that our earth is a planet in the heavens and that we men are celestial beings. The remedies they prescribed therefore do not necessarily suit the disease.

K'ang's arguments betray not only his lack of understanding of the true nature of religion but also his incomplete appreciation of the meaning of human life. But this did not prevent him from confidently proferring his own "remedy."

When I was twenty-eight *sui*,[178] . . . as a result of reading the "Complete Treatise of Astronomical Calculations,"[179] I engaged myself nightly in the making of astronomical observations. Through a telescope I saw the volcanoes and arctic seas on Mars. Consequently, I inferred that humans and other living beings existed on other planets and on the stars. As there were countless heavens, there were countless humans and other living beings, governments, moral systems, customs, ceremonial and musical systems, and literatures. I therefore wrote the "Book of Heavens." It was forty-two years ago. Having gone through many calamities unscathed, I now daily engage myself in roaming the heavens. My body remains in the human world on this earth-planet, but my mind rambles in the countless heavens, freely and joyfully. Looking down at our earth-planet, it appears smaller than a drop [of water] in an ocean. Surveying the human world, it seems even more ephemeral and illusory than the Ant Kingdom on the Southern Branch.[180] . . . Now in discoursing on the heavens I desire to open the eyes and restore the hearing of my fellow men of the

---

[176] *Liu tao*, or *liu ch'ü*, i.e., the six *gati* (ways) of reincarnation: (1) *naraka-gati*, that of the hells; (2) *preta-gati*, that of hungry ghosts; (3) *tiryagyoni-gati*, that of animals; (4) *asura-gati*, that of malevolent nature spirits; (5) *manusya-gati*, that of human existence; and (6) *deva-gati*, that of divine existence (Soothill and Hodous, *Dictionary of Chinese Buddhist Terms*, p. 139).

[177] The Pure Land (*Ching t'u*), Sukhāvati, or Paradise of the West, is presided over by Amitābha. The Heavenly Mansion (*T'ien t'ang*), or the mansions of the devas, are located between the earth and the Brahmalokas (ibid., pp. 145, 256, 278, 357, 403).

[178] Namely, 1885, but according to the *Nien-p'u*, pp. 6b–7a (Lo, *K'ang*, p. 41), K'ang's astronomical insights occurred in 1884.

[179] This was the *Li-hsiang k'ao-ch'eng*, 42 *chüan*, compiled in 1713 by order of the K'ang-hsi emperor, which represented a synthesis of Chinese and Western methods. "Tzu-pu," in *Ssu-k'u ch'üan-shu tsung-mu t'i-yao*, *chüan* 106, p. 16.

[180] An allusion to the T'ang-dynasty fiction, "Nan-k'o chi," by Li Kung-tso.

heavens, so that each and everyone will realize that he is a celestial being.
. . . Then the Electrical Course (*Tien-tao*) [which leads] to uttermost joy
in the heavens, will unfold naturally before them.[181]

K'ang's preachings reached hardly beyond the handful of admiring
students who gathered around him in the Academy. But obviously he
derived much comfort and consolation from his "peregrinations," so
much so that he imparted, perhaps unintentionally, an unmistakably
buoyant and joyous mood to his magnum opus. The somberness that
characterized much of his earlier writings was gone; good cheer was
exuded at almost every turn. He sang praise to each heavenly body: the
galaxy, the sun, the planets, and their moons.[182] He "was delighted
that our earth has a moon," for if it had no moon, we would be deprived
of the pleasures that moonlit nights afforded us. "Beautiful indeed is
the moon!" he exclaimed in ecstasy.[183]

Even the prosaic earth, stage of endless human tragedies, became a
glorious planet, when it was looked at from the celestial point of view.

> Looking up at the stars in the Milky Way in the night, we see their glitter-
> ing brightness; and looking up at Jupiter, Saturn, Mars, Venus, Mercury,
> and the moon, we perceive their sparkling and limpid light. We say [that
> they are in the heavens] and admire them from below. . . . We should
> realize that inhabitants of the stars, looking up at our earth-planet, should
> see its shining beams, splendid and glorious, . . . precisely like what the
> stars appear to men on earth. . . . Therefore [it is clear that] we men who
> live on the earth-planet are at once inhabitants of a planet and denizens
> of the heavens. Thus we, 1,600,000,000 in all, are celestial beings. As soon
> as we perceive this fact, . . . we shall always be happy and utterly joyous.[184]

Moreover, despite the calamities and sufferings that befell men, the
earth-planet was a good place to live in. In addition to the natural
beauty that it afforded men, it provided also for the physical needs of
all its inhabitants, making it a much more hospitable globe than other
planets. The joy of being "men of the heavens" was thus reinforced by
"the joy of being men born-on-earth."[185]

---

[181] Author's preface to the *Chu-t'ien chiang*, written in the summer of 1929 and signed
"T'ien-yu hua-jen [A Heaven-roaming Transfigured Man], K'ang Yu-wei."
[182] *Chu-t'ien chiang*, 8: 1a–2a; 4: 4b; 5: 5a–b, 7b–8a; 3: 9b–10a.
[183] Ibid., 3: 1a.
[184] Ibid., 2: 1b–2a.
[185] Ibid., 2: 1a.

This cheerful view that suffuses the *Lectures*,[186] marks a major change in K'ang's thinking. It may be supposed that this was an outgrowth of his hedonistic presupposition, that getting pleasure and avoiding pain constituted the sole aim of human life. So just as he previously sought to bring happiness to men through social reform, he now sought to accomplish the same task by urging men to detach themselves from society and withdraw into an imaginary realm untouched by striving, strife, and disillusionment. It seems that having listened long and hard to the sorrowful tunes of the world of men, K'ang finally decided to transpose the heartrending discords into the carefree music of the spheres. This, in a sense, constituted an admission of defeat, that he was unequal to the task of elevating the rough and humble human existence to the utopian world of Universal Peace, although the admission was couched in terms that suggested victory. He claimed that in "roaming the heavens" he had transcended the human world, but he was in effect running away from it. The fact is, having traveled in it for almost seventy years he was tired of treading the same tortuous trails of mundane experience. In all probability, he had no regrets, when he actually came to the end of his earthly journey, not long after he wrote the *Lectures*.[187]

Existence of God

K'ang's prolonged interest in astronomy produced another important result: abandonment of his characteristic skeptical attitude toward religion. Astronomical studies alone, of course, did not lead to this development. His acquaintance with Western philosophy, fragmentary and superficial as it was, contributed materially. In fact, it was philosophy that convinced him of the inadequacy of the purely scientific approach to questions concerning the nonmaterial world.

K'ang took Laplace to task for his refusal to affirm the existence of God. "That there is a God in heaven," K'ang wrote, "is held in common by the religions of all countries. The term 'Heaven' used in China

---

[186] Occasionally, the somber mood recurred, e.g., ibid., 7: 4a, "Song of Meteors" (*Liu-hsing ko*):

> Forming, abiding, destruction, annihilation—a matter of course;
> Even stars fall; how can immortals endure?
> Heaven and earth will perish—the heavens are not everlasting.
> What use is there to investigate the flesh of us men?
> Night after night I gaze at the shooting stars:
> Moved and speechless, I contemplate the universe.

[187] K'ang T'ung-pi, *Nien-p'u hsü-pien*, p. 149b; Lo, *K'ang*, p. 252.

signifies 'Lord-Providence' (*chu tsai*), which is synonymous with the term 'God'. " Laplace, who (according to K'ang) developed Newton's mechanistic theory, "openly said that there is no God"[188]—an erroneous view echoed by "the materialists of modern times." Laplace was wrong because there were things in the universe that were absolutely inscrutable, whereas man, a puny creature on earth, possessed only limited knowledge. "How could we cover all the facts and reasons under heaven," K'ang asked, "by relying solely on our physical senses" as the natural scientist was inclined to do?[189] *"Ce que nous connaissons est*

---

[188] K'ang was probably less than accurate in charging Pierre Simon de Laplace (1749–1827) with gross atheism. The facts as presented by William Hastie, *Kant's Cosmology*, pp. xci–xcii, are the following: "There is a celebrated anecdote told of Laplace to the effect that when he presented the first edition of his *Exposition du Système du Monde* to General Napoleon Bonaparte, then the First Consul, Napoleon, himself a considerable mathematician—said to him: 'Newton has spoken of God in his book. I have already gone through yours, and I have not found that name in it a single time.' To which it is stated that Laplace replied: 'First Citizen Consul, I have not had need of that hypothesis.' This has been generally taken to mean that Laplace regarded the existence of God as a hypothesis. M. Blanchet gives the story in his Preface to his translation of Lucretius, and represents Laplace as proclaiming himself to be an Atheist. M. Barthèlemy Saint-Hilaire, in the Preface to his translation of Aristotle's *Treatise on the Heavens*, takes the same view. . . . But M. Faye gives the saying a different interpretation, and exonerates Laplace entirely from the charge of Atheism. He holds that it meant only that Laplace did not accept Newton's hypothesis of the *intervention* of God, from time to time, to modify the movements of the world, especially in its perturbations, 'and that he (Laplace) had not the need of such a supposition.' It was not God that he treated as an hypothesis, but his direct intervention at a determinate point. . . . M. Faye maintains that Laplace 'did not profess Atheism,' and . . . that shortly before his death he begged that the anecdote be suppressed. Nor were his last pathetic words, 'ce que nous connaissons est peu et ce que nous ignorons est immense,' those of a dogmatic Atheist." Cf. Clement C. Webb, *Kant's Philosophy of Religion*, p. 14. Peter Doig, *A Concise History of Astronomy*, p. 91, summarizes Laplace's views on the matter. Isaac Newton's view on God is given in "General Scholium," in *Fundamental Principles of Natural Philosophy* (Motte trans.), reprinted in *Theories of the Universe from Babylonian Myth to Modern Science*, Milton K. Munitz, ed. (Glencoe, Ill: The Free Press, 1957), p. 208: "This most beautiful system of the sun, planets, and comets could only proceed from the counsel and dominion of an intelligent and powerful Being. And if the fixed stars are the centers of other like systems, these, being formed by the like wise counsel, must be all subject to the dominion of One. . . ." Ibid., p. 209: "The Supreme God is a Being eternal, infinite, absolutely perfect, but a being, however perfect, without dominion, cannot be said to be 'Lord God'; . . . It is the dominion of a spiritual being which constitutes a God. . . . And from this true dominion it follows that the true God is a living, intelligent, and powerful Being. . . . He is not eternity and infinity, but eternal and infinite; he is not duration or space, but he endures and is present. . . ."

[189] *Chu-t'ien chiang*, 11: 3a–b. Ibid., *chüan* 11, entitled "On God" (*Shang-ti p'ien*), is devoted entirely to this topic.

peu et ce que nous ignorons est immense."[190] K'ang would have readily approved of these last words of Laplace. Two other Western thinkers attracted K'ang's attention here. He mentioned without comment Aristotle's view that the Prime Mover of the universe was God;[191] and, after presenting Ptolemy's system of epicycles[192] (in a less than intelligible manner), he commented that "looking at this theory today it appears mostly laughable."[193]

What then was the correct view? K'ang mentioned five different "proofs" of the existence of God, the ontological, the psychological, the cosmological, the physico-theological, and the ethical, and considered them all inadequate. After summarily dismissing atheism as "untenable," he went on to state briefly each of these proofs. "Those who advanced the ontological argument," he said, "proved God's existence from God's perfection." Those who advanced the psychological argument, such as Descartes, maintained that "the idea of God in a man's mind is caused by God's very existence." The cosmologist held that "there must be a cause for the existence of the universe, and God is this cause." The physico-theologian held that "the universe is a work of art and that its possession of such good order presupposes a maker who, if not its Creator, must be its architect." Finally, the moral philosopher believed that "it is God, the unseen power that makes man sacrifice the individual for the good of the group."[194] None of these arguments "proved definitely the existence of God." "As Kant had said, the existence of God is an existence judgment that is *a posteriori*. From our experience we can neither assert that there is no [God] nor that there is one."[195]

Unable to read books in Western languages and without technical

---

[190] Quoted in Hastie, *Kant's Cosmology*, p. xcii.

[191] *Chu-t'ien chiang*, 11: 1a–b. For Aristotle's theory of the spheres and the Prime Mover, see W. K. C. Guthrie, *On the Heavens* (London: Heinemann, 1939), lines 268b 11 to 269a 32, 270a 15 to 270b 25, 271b 1–10, 271b 28 to 272a 20, 276a 16 to 276b 22, 278b 5 to 279a 18, 286b 10 to 287a 22, and 296a 24 to 298b 20. Cf. Aristotle, *Metaphysics*, trans. John Warrington (London: Dent, Everyman's Library, 1956), Book A, chap. 8. For a summary, see J. L. E. Dreyer, *A History of Astronomy, from Thales to Kepler*, 2nd ed. (New York: Dover Publications, 1953), pp. 108–22.

[192] For Ptolemy's system, see Doig, *Concise History of Astronomy*, pp. 37–39; Rudolf Thiel, *And There Was Light*, trans. Richard and Clara Winston (New York: Knopf, 1927), pp. 49–51; and Dreyer, *A History of Astronomy*, pp. 191–206.

[193] *Chu-t'ien chiang*, 11: 1a–b.

[194] For summaries of these arguments, see T. W. Crafer's article on "Apologetics" in James Hastings, *Encyclopaedia of Religion and Ethics*, 1: 611–22, and V. Ferm, *Encyclopedia of Religion*, pp. 301–2. The latter is a briefer but less satisfactory account.

[195] *Chu-t'ien chiang*, 11: 1b–2a.

training in philosophy, K'ang could hardly be expected to present the well-known proofs in a sufficiently accurate way.[196] His understanding of Kant's philosophy of religion seems to have been less than perfect. The view that he cited was probably based, indirectly, on Kant's *Critique of Pure Reason* (1781) in which, in dealing with "the ideal of Pure Reason" Kant gave an account of the illusory reasonings that owed their origin to an attempt to employ the categories of the under-standing beyond the realm of possible experience, by means of the senses to which they alone were applicable.[197] K'ang apparently was not aware that in Kant's precritical view of religion[198] he was not above employing categories of the understanding beyond the realm of sense experience,[199] nor was he aware that in Kant's critical philosophy God's existence was affirmed precisely on moral grounds ("the ethical proof"). As Kant made it emphatically clear, while "all attempts to employ reason in theology in any speculative manner are altogether fruitless and by their very nature null and void," it was still possible to have a "theology of reason" which was "based upon moral laws" or sought "guidance from them."[200] Thus, as it was said, by means of the magic wand of practical reason Kant undertook to bring to life again "the deism which the theoretical reason had slain."[201]

[196] See Hastings, *Encyclopaedia of Religion and Ethics*, 1: 558 ff. and W. T. Jones, *A History of Western Philosophy*, pp. 433–34, for more precise statements of St. Anselm's "ontological proof." For other proofs, see Aquinas, *Summa Theologica*, Pt. 1, Quest. 2, art. 3 (fourth and fifth proofs) in *Basic Writings; The Philosophical Works of Descartes*, 1: 162–67; Hastings, *Encyclopaedia of Religion and Ethics*, 4: 646; Elwes, *The Ethics of Spinoza*, Pt. I, Prop. xi, "Another Proof."

[197] Webb, *Kant's Philosophy*, p. 46. For Kant's own statement and criticisms of "the arguments of speculative reason," including the ontological, cosmological, and physico-theological proofs, see *The Critique of Pure Reason*, Bk. 2, chap. 3, secs. 3–7.

[198] Webb, *Kant's Philosophy*, pp. 37–38.

[199] E.g., Kant, *Universal Natural History and Theory of the Heavens* (1755), "there is a God, just because nature even in chaos cannot proceed otherwise than regularly and according to order" (Hastie, *Kant's Cosmology*, "Translations," p. 26. Cf. Webb, *Kant's Philosophy*, pp. 25–26).

[200] "Now I maintain that all attempts to employ reason in theology in any merely speculative manner are altogether fruitless and by their very nature null and void, and that the principles of its employment in the study of nature do not lead to any theology whatsoever. Consequently, the only theology of reason which is possible is that which is based upon moral laws or seeks guidance from them" (*Critique of Pure Reason*, p. 528). This passage occurs in *Werke*, ed. Wilhelm Weischedel (Weisbaden: Insel-Verlag, 1956–64, 6 vols.), 2: 559. Cf. *The Critique of Practical Reason*, vol. 2: chap. 2, sec. 5, "The Existence of God as a Postulate of Pure Practical Reason." Webb, in *Kant's Philosophy*, gives a brief exposition of this view.

[201] Heinrich Heine's remarks on Kant, in *Zur Geschichte und Philosophie in Deutsch-land*; quoted in Webb, *Kant's Philosophy*, pp. 48–49. See F. E. England, *Kant's Concep-tion of God*, for a critical exposition of Kant's religious thought in its various stages of development.

If K'ang's understanding of Kant's view appears somewhat hazy, his presentation of the views of other European philosophers is no more accurate or precise. After blaming dualism for making it difficult to assert positively the existence of God,[202] he stated that there were two views concerning the matter, *monotheism,* which envisaged God as "the highest entelechy," and *pantheism,* which held that God's essence resided in the universal flux, the infinite and continuous process of cosmic renovation. He elaborated on pantheism in these words:

> The pantheism as we understand it differs slightly from that conceived of by men like Spinoza and Goethe. In their view God is everywhere, hence the name pantheism. In our view, importance is attached to God's being a continuous process of change, not a fixed entity. This is what Bergson says. Bergson equates freedom with absolute nondetermination, because he thinks God himself is in the process of change.[203]

K'ang's own conception of monotheism was as indicated in the following passage:

> Monotheism divides itself into two schools of thought, the doctrine of emanation (*liu-fa shuo*) and the doctrine of creation (*ch'uang-tsao shuo*). Followers of the former doctrine held that God and the universe through which he manifests himself are the reality with the same power for future development. Neo-Platonism, Indian philosophy, and [the philosophies of] Spinoza, Schelling, and Hegel, all belong to this school. Followers of the latter doctrine held that there is a Creator who existed outside and

---

[202] *Chu-t'ien chiang,* 11: 2a. K'ang mentioned three dualistic doctrines: (1) that both perfection and imperfection came from God; (2) that God was perfection, matter which represented imperfection did not come from God; and (3) that there were God [Ahura Mazda] and devil [Angra Mainyu], the former representing light, the latter darkness. See Ferm, *Encyclopedia of Religion,* pp. 573, 842–43, and Hastings, *Encyclopaedia of Religion and Ethics,* 5: 109.

[203] *Chu-t'ien chiang,* 11: 2b. For Goethe, see Hastings, *Encyclopaedia of Religion and Ethics,* 6: 307 and Ferm, *Encyclopedia of Religion,* p. 306. For Spinoza, see *Ethics* in A. Boyle, *Chief Works of Benedict de Spinoza* (London: Dent, Everyman's Library, 1951), Proposition XVIII, "God is the indwelling and not the transient cause of all things." Proposition XXV, "God is not only the effecting cause of the existence of things, but also of their essence." "Corollary. Particular things are nothing else than modifications of attributes of God, or modes by which attributes of God are expressed in a certain and determined manner." A. E. Garvie's introductory essay to the article on Pantheism, in Hastings, *Encyclopaedia of Religion and Ethics,* 9: 609, is useful as a general statement. For Bergson, see *Creative Evolution,* (Mitchell trans.), especially pp. 43–45, 54–58, 99, 215; and *The Two Sources of Morality and Religion,* (Audra and Brereton trans.), especially pp. 22–24, 48–50, 255–57. Bergson's philosophy is summarized in Jones, *A History of Western Philosophy,* pp. 929–58, and Ferm, *Encyclopedia of Religion,* pp. 66–67.

beyond the world and who, having created the world, exists together with
it. Judaism, Christianity, and Islam subscribe to this doctrine.[204]

K'ang raised three questions concerning monotheism:

> First, if it is said, the world has come as the result of God's creation, then
> when did the creation begin? Second, if mankind is regarded as free, then
> God's attributes of omniscience and omnipotence are affected; for the two
> [God's attributes and man's freedom] are incompatible. Third, if the doc-
> trine of emanation is accepted, then the day of man's emancipation (*chieh-
> t'o*) should be also the day of God's emancipation; if the doctrine of
> creation is accepted, according to which God stands outside the world,
> then even if all mankind achieves redemption (*shu tsui*), it would be no
> more than the redemption of his creatures. What would then be the posi-
> tion of God?[205]

With these questions that were intended to be unanswerable, K'ang
concluded the section on "European Philosophers' Utterances Concerning God." Few, if any, philosophers would take these objections,
which stemmed from imperfect understanding of the issues involved,
as damaging criticisms of monotheism. K'ang did not expressly say
that he favored pantheism, but was clearly partial to the sort of pantheism that he attributed to Bergson. K'ang thus shared with a number of
Chinese thinkers of the republican period their predilection for Bergson,[206] although his grasp of the Bergsonian philosophy was less firm
than that of men like Chang Tung-sun.[207]

Keeping in mind K'ang's inveterate commitment to the idea of progress, it is not difficult to see the reason for his taste for the Bergsonian
philosophy. However, there was an important change in his amelioristic
attitude, from the "radical finalism" (Bergson's phrase)[208] which was

---

[204] *Chu-t'ien chiang*, 11: 2b. For Neo-Platonism, see Ferm, *Encyclopedia of Religion*,
p. 525, and W. R. Inge's "Neoplatonism," in Hastings, *Encyclopaedia of Religion and
Ethics*, 9: 307–19. For Spinoza, see *Ethics* (Boyle trans.), Pt. 1, "Concerning God,"
especially "Definitions"; England, *Kant's Conception of God*, p. 25 ("God is *causa sui*
in the sense that he is a self-complete being whose essence involves existence"); and
Ferm, *Encyclopedia of Religion*, p. 731. For Shelling, see ibid., p. 692; for Hegel, see
ibid., pp. 327–29.

[205] *Chu-t'ien chiang*, 11: 2b–3a.

[206] Brière, *Fifty Years of Chinese Philosophy*, pp. 22, 48, 67, 105.

[207] Chang Tung-sun, translator of Bergson's *Creative Evolution* into Chinese (*Ch'uang-
hua lun*) and *Matter and Memory* (*Wu-chih yü chi-i*).

[208] Bergson, *Creative Evolution*, p. 45: "But radical finalism is quite as unacceptable
[as radical mechanism], and for the same reason. The doctrine of teleology . . . implies that *things and beings merely realize a program previously arranged* [emphasis supplied].
. . . As in the mechanistic hypothesis, here again it is supposed that *all is given* [em-

very much in evidence especially in the reform days, to a willingness to leave matters to man's "free act" and to the God that was eternal change.[209]

Conceivably, K'ang shared Bergson's objection to a static conception of God, "an ineffectual God who simply sums up in himself all the given."[210] Conceivably also, K'ang was willing, in Bergsonian terms, to establish a contact "with the creative effort which life itself manifests," an effort which "is of God, if it is not God himself," and thus to transcend "the limitations imposed on the species by its material nature," in order to continue and extend "the divine action"[211]—i.e., roaming the heavens. And, finally, K'ang may have endorsed Bergson's distinction between "open society," a community of all mankind, and "closed society," a particular group of men,[212] and regarded the former as the ultimate basis of morality. Regrettably, K'ang was silent on these interesting points in his all-too-short discussion on Western philosophers. But this much is clear. K'ang in 1926 had ceased to be the dogmatic reformer who sought to fashion the Chinese state according to a definite, preconceived model, and had, in other words, given up Confucian rationalism in favor of Bergsonian mysticism.[213]

It is as unjustifiable to suppose that K'ang accepted every aspect of

---

phasis original]." Ibid., p. 50: "The error of radical finalism, as also that of radical mechanism, is to extend too far the application of certain concepts that are natural to our intellect. Originally, we think only in order to act. . . . Now, in order to act, we begin by proposing an end; we make a plan, then we go on to the detail of the mechanism which will bring it to pass. This latter operation is possible only if we know what we can reckon on. We must therefore have managed to extract resemblances from nature, which enables us to anticipate the future. Thus we must, consciously or unconsciously, have made use of the law of causality." Ibid., p. 58: "It would be futile to try assigning to life an end, in the human sense of the word. To speak of an end is to think of a pre-existing model which has only to be realized. It is to suppose, therefore, that all is given, and the future can be read in the present."

[209] Ibid., p. 54: "A conduct that is truly our own . . . is that of a will which does not try to counterfeit intellect, and which, remaining itself—that is to say, evolving—ripens gradually into acts which the intellect will be able to resolve indefinitely into intelligible elements without ever reaching its goal. The free act is incommensurable with the idea, and its 'rationality' must be defined by this very incommensurability, which admits the discovery of as much intelligibility within it as we will. Such is the character of our own evolution; and such also, without doubt, that of the evolution of life."

[210] Ibid., p. 215.

[211] Ibid., p. 209.

[212] Bergson, *Two Sources of Morality and Religion*, pp. 22–24, 48–50, 255–57. Summary in Jones, *History of Western Philosophy*, pp. 945–48.

[213] Bergson's definition of mysticism, in *Creative Evolution*, p. 209.

Bergson's philosophy as to allow that he accurately apprehended it. For K'ang sometimes said things that would have proved unacceptable to Bergson. A particularly revealing instance appears in the short section on "God Must Exist" in the *Lectures*. After asserting that there must be a God, he went on to expound the theory of predestination.

> As for predestination of human fate: Both Aristotle and Leibniz[214] thought that God predetermines [human fate], in agreement with the doctrines of predestination and predetermined fate known in our country. In our country, physiognomy, fortune-telling, and divination are often marvellously accurate. As the *Doctrine of the Mean* says, "It is characteristic of the most entirely sincere to be able to foreknow."[215]

K'ang obviously was not aware that this went contrary not only to Bergsonianism but to his own statements made earlier in the same book where he condemned in strong language the superstitions in connection with astronomy.[216]

It is interesting to note that K'ang offered no rational proof for the existence of God. He merely stated that all religions affirmed God's existence and that ever since ancient times the Chinese also had the same belief. But scientists like Newton, Laplace, and Darwin, who subscribed to the mechanistic view, denied or doubted the existence of a supernatural being because they did not find evidence of such existence in their study of the visible world. K'ang felt they were all mistaken. For some of

> the things under heaven are extremely inscrutable and men's knowledge is extremely limited. How can we cover all the facts and reasons under heaven by merely relying on our senses? . . . Newton, Laplace, and Darwin were able to comprehend tangible, material things. They could not apprehend beings and events that are intangible. The *Chuang-tzu* says, "A man's life has limits but knowledge is limitless." Newton, Laplace, and Darwin, whose knowledge was extremely limited, could hardly understand everything under heaven. How could they say for sure that there is no God? They only showed that they did not know [the limits of] their own [intellectual] capacity [in denying the existence of a being beyond the visible world].[217]

[214] K'ang probably had in mind Leibniz's doctrine of "pre-established harmony," *The Monadology* (Latta trans.), pp. 262–63, sec. 78, and Latta's introduction, pp. 41–42.

[215] *Chu-t'ien chiang, chüan* 11: 3b. The quotation is from the *Chung-yung*, 23 (Legge trans.).

[216] *Chu-t'ien chiang, chüan* 1, pp. 6b–7b.

[217] Ibid., *chüan* 11, pp. 3b–4a. These are the concluding words of the chapter on God. The last sentence of this passage is a quotation from the *Lun-yü*, XIX.24 (Legge trans.). (The original is in third person singular and present tense.)

It is implied, then, that K'ang joined Bergson in denouncing "radical mechanism," which was related to "radical finalism" and equally untenable. It is interesting to note that Bergson also took Laplace to task for believing in the inclusiveness and adequacy of scientific knowledge.[218] K'ang, however, did not quite follow Bergson in his confidence in the power of philosophy, even the Bergsonian philosophy. Approaching the problems of religion and philosophy through astronomy instead of biology, K'ang shared with some of the Western thinkers who traversed the same road their sense of humility in front of the overwhelming grandeur of an infinite universe. K'ang showed clearly this sense in the *Lectures*, in the concluding paragraph of chapter 12.

The Heavens of the Prime-Prime (*Yüan-Yüan t'ien*)[219] are [like] a speck of dust in the innumerable heavens; the Heavens of Whirling Clouds (*Wo-yün t'ien*)[220] are [like] a speck of dust in [the extragalactic] heavens. The earth is [like] a speck of dust in the solar system. The various founders of religions, born on this tiny earth-globe and enjoying eminence on it, possessed no more than a slightly higher degree of intelligence than the dull-brained masses. Now as these founders of religions were living creatures, their knowledge was necessarily limited—however intelligent they were. The founders of religions in the heavens who dominate their respective globes, are countless. . . . Their intelligence is infinitely higher than that of those of our earth-globe. Even their knowledge is not without limits. . . . Therefore Confucius said, "Am I indeed possessed of knowledge? I am not knowing."[221] Thus was [Confucius] a sage.[222]

About fifty years before K'ang made this statement, when he was a young man of nineteen *sui*, he felt sure that he could acquire enormous knowledge and "read all the books" before he was thirty.[223] Now this rather impudent youthful self-confidence gave way to mellow humility, the reward of a more mature assessment of man and the universe.

K'ang was not alone in attaining humility through star gazing. Long before him Kant had already done so, though in a different way.[224]

---

[218] Bergson, *Creative Evolution*, pp. 43–45.

[219] This, according to K'ang, was the highest of "the Heavens of the Prime" (*Yüan t'ien*) and therefore the highest of all the heavens to which he was able to assign names. Countless other heavens existed above the *Yüan t'ien* (*Chu-t'ien chiang, chüan* 10, p. 10b).

[220] This was the heaven immediately above the *Yin-ho t'ien* ("Heaven of the Silvery Stream," i.e., the galaxy) (ibid., *chüan* 10, p. 1a and *chüan* 11, p. 1a).

[221] *Lun-yü*, IX.7 (Legge trans.).

[222] *Chu-t'ien chiang, chüan* 12, pp. 11a–b.

[223] *Nien-p'u*, p. 4a; Lo, *K'ang*, p. 31.

[224] Kant, *Critique of Practical Reason*, p. 260: "Two things fill the mind with ever new and increasing admiration and awe, the oftener and the more steadily we reflect on them: the starry heaven above and the moral law within." Hastie, *Kant's Cosmology*, introduction, p. xcvii, gives a slightly different translation of this celebrated passage.

Harlow Shapley, a modern astronomer, counseled that in view of the vastness of the cosmos man should not take himself too seriously.[225] People in other walks of life had comparable experiences and came to a similar insight in contemplating the heavens.[226] Whatever may have been K'ang's intellectual shortcomings, he was in good company in this one aspect at least.

In desisting from offering a rational proof of the existence of God K'ang seems to have followed Kant's view that belief of God was not a matter of speculative reason but of moral (or psychological) necessity. Thus without subscribing to any formalized creed or being converted to any specific religion, K'ang made peace with the unseen power that transcended the physical world. Now to him all the efforts in search of human perfection through social reform, all the attempts at achieving personal happiness through heaven-roaming, had become really super-fluous.

I have noted previously that K'ang's understanding of Western philosophy was imperfect. This is not intended to be a damaging criticism. Liang Ch'i-ch'ao, who disagreed with his teacher on many issues, had come to a reasonable appraisal of K'ang as a philosopher.

> My teacher is a born philosopher. Without a knowledge of Western languages, with no instruction in Western thought, without reading [original] Western books, he reaches beyond the heavens and into his own independ-

[225] Harlow Shapley, *Of Stars and Men*, pp. 142–43: "Don't take man too seriously . . . certainly not when comparing him with possibilities elsewhere in the richly endowed Metagalaxy." Ibid., p. 149: "The new discoveries and developments contribute to the unfolding of a magnificent universe; to be a participant is in itself a glory. With our confreres on distant planets; with our fellow animals and plants of land, air, and sea; with the rocks and waters of all planetary crusts, and the photons and atoms that make up the stars—with all these we are associated in an existence and an evolution that inspire respect and deep reverence. We cannot escape humility."

[226] E.g., Theodore Roosevelt and Harry Golden. Harold E. Kohn, *Thoughts Afield* (Grand Rapids, Mich., 1959) p. 98, reports William Beebe's visits to Roosevelt at Sagamore Hill. They often walked over the lawn and looked up into the night sky, vying with each other to see who could first identify the pale bit of light-mist near Pegasus. The host or the visitor would say, "This is the Spiral Galaxy of Andromeda. It is as large as our Milky Way. It is one of a hundred million galaxies. . . . It consists of one hundred billion suns, each larger than our own sun." Then Roosevelt would smile and say, "Now I think we are small enough. Let's go to bed." Harry Golden had this to say: "I have a rule against registering complaints in a restaurant; because I know that there are at least four million suns in the Milky Way—which is only one galaxy. How many galaxies are there? Billions. . . . When you think of all these, it is silly to worry whether the waitress brought you string beans instead of limas" (*Only in America*, pp. 1–2).

ent thought which often accords with the views of Western thinkers. An outstanding figure indeed in the intellectual world![227]

It would be a mistake, of course, to think that Liang regarded K'ang as a great philosopher. What Liang had actually indicated in this statement is simply that despite K'ang's lack of training he had, thanks to his native ability, gained insights into things worthy of true thinkers.

Liang offered an assessment of K'ang's philosophical attainments in another connection. According to Liang, K'ang was the first modern Chinese thinker to make a serious attempt at a new philosophical synthesis that would be "neither Chinese nor Western but in fact both Chinese and Western."[228] The attempt was not entirely successful. But the fact that such an attempt was made at all is of considerable historical significance.

---

[227] K'ang died March 31, 1927, less than a year after he wrote the preface to the *Lectures* (K'ang T'ung-pi, *Nien-p'u hsü-pien*, p. 149b; Lo, *K'ang*, p. 252).

[228] Liang, *Ch'ing-tai hsüeh-shu kai-lun*, p. 161; Hsü, *Intellectual Trends in the Ch'ing Period*, p. 113.

PART III
REFORM PROPOSALS

Chapter 6

POLITICAL REFORM

INTRODUCTION

K'ang Yu-wei earned a place in history partly (and perhaps chiefly) because of his leading role in the 1898 reform movement. His outspoken opposition to the 1911 revolution and the 1912 republic, as much as his earnest pleas for "preserving the national essence," had led many of the younger intellectuals of the 1910s and 1920s to regard him, often scornfully, as a hopeless reactionary. However, a careful scrutiny of his views as expressed during the republican years should reveal that even then he had remained basically a reformer,[1] although the historical context had changed drastically since 1898. In the 1880s and 1890s he endeavored to reshape the imperial system together with its outmoded social and intellectual ramifications; he now tried to correct what he believed to be foolish errors that were being committed in the fumbling republic. Adverse circumstances eventually persuaded him, in the last years of his life, to refrain from taking direct or overt action in the affairs of the country.[2] Nevertheless, his deep concern for the future of

---

[1] *Webster's New International Dictionary*, 3rd ed. (Springfield, Mass: G. C. Merriam, 1961): "reformer 1: . . . one that works for or urges reform . . . ; "reform *n* 1a: amendment of what is defective, vicious, corrupt, or depraved . . . b: a removal or correction of an abuse, a wrong, or errors."

[2] Yang Fu-li "K'ang Liang nien-p'u kao-pen," 3: 46a: "From now on [1918] Mr. K'ang lived regularly in Shanghai and occasionally visited Hangchow, roaming on streams and lakes and paying no attention to affairs of the world." This, even on Yang's own showing, is not entirely true. E.g., ibid., p. 72a, indicates that in 1923 K'ang made another attempt at monarchical restoration.

China continued to prompt him to pour forth an almost endless succession of biting criticisms of the ways of his contemporaries and of impassioned appeals for intellectual reorientation as well as political amendment, until about 1926, a year before his death.

For four decades the central aim of K'ang's reform efforts stood practically unchanged. In the simplest terms, it was the political, economic, and intellectual transformation of China, with the modern West as his prime model. His formula for achieving this aim remained also unaltered, which was to transform, in measured steps, China's antiquated tradition into the general institutional and value patterns obtaining in the modern West—patterns, in his view, suitable for all nations at comparable stages of development.

China's autocracy must go; but considering the stage of her political development she must first pass through the intermediate stage of constitutional monarchy before she could reach full-fledged democracy. Her primitive agricultural economy must give way to industrial economy; but private capitalism and not socialization must serve as the driving force. New social and intellectual values must be introduced to prepare the coming of a modern way of life; but valid elements of the native culture should not be swept away.[3]

The emphasis, then, was on gradualism. However, it may be noted that the aim of K'ang's reform efforts went far beyond the modernization of China. To put the country on an equal footing with the Western powers and Meiji Japan constituted merely the first step toward the realization of a world society in which men's concern would no longer be "wealth and power" for the sake of national survival but universal peace through freedom and equality for all. Thus, in K'ang's grand design of reform, to modernize China was not merely to bring into being yet another great power in the "family of nations" but rather to prepare a "backward" nation for participation in the forward march on the road to world harmony and human happiness. Here, again, the gradualist principle was to be maintained. The "Great Community" (*Ta-t'ung*) was to be realized not by summarily destroying the imperfect but by striving constructively toward perfection, not by snatching at the distant goal but by making the best of what was on hand. One must, in short, be constantly in touch both with the present and the future. K'ang, we recall, had delineated the salient features of his utopia and the precise steps men should take to reach it.[4] In the same

[3] See chapter 11 of this volume.

[4] *Ta-t'ung shu*, parts 2–10; K'ang, *Ta T'ung Shu*, trans. Laurence G. Thompson, pp. 61–276 (hereafter cited as Thompson, *Ta T'ung Shu*).

spirit he confided his aspirations to some of his favorite students in
1891:

> Our mind shall we nurture;
> Our people from ignorance shall we deliver.
> To its utter limits our insight shall we enlarge
> A universe infinite and boundless to behold:
> How can the earth, a small thing,
> Into West and East divide?
> But to begin: love our own kind;
> Our fatherland shall we not neglect.[5]

In K'ang's thinking, then, just as constitutional monarchy should
serve as a transition from autocracy to democracy, so should patriotism
or nationalism constitute the prelude to cosmopolitanism. That being
the case, the task of reform within China would not stop with the realization of constitutional monarchy nor would the road to human perfection terminate with China's modernization. Further and continuing
reforms must be carried on before republicanism in one country and
unity of mankind could become a reality.[6] This ultimate commitment
separated K'ang not only from the leaders of the "self-strengthening
movement" of the 1860s and 1870s but also from the collaborators in
the 1898 reform movement. For despite divergencies in their views concerning modernization, both groups agreed on one point: they were
"nationalists" whose sole objective was to help China to acquire "the
Faustian character of Western civilization."[7]

Precisely because K'ang was at once an imaginative idealist who
dared to be audacious in thought and an incurable gradualist who refused to be rash in action, he became a despicable villain alike to conservatives (who opposed change) and to radicals and revolutionaries

---

[5] A poem sent to Liang Ch'i-ch'ao and two others, given in K'ang, *Nan-hai hsien-
sheng shih-chi*, (Liang calligraphy ed.), *chüan* 3, p. 3b. "A universe infinite and boundless" is translation for *chu t'ien wu ch'iung*, literally, "heavens countless."

[6] K'ang's note to the first two books of the *Ta-t'ung shu*, reprinted in 1919, available
in the first complete edition of the book, Shanghai, 1935.

[7] Benjamin Schwartz, *In Search of Wealth and Power: Yen Fu and the West*, pp. 238–
39 et passim. It may be noted in this connection that K'ang differed also from other
modernizers of the 1890s (whose writings K'ang probably had seen and some of
whose ideas he conceivably had adopted without acknowledging his indebtedness)
in one crucial point: while these men saw in democratization China's only way to
survival, he went beyond them and entertained the ideal of a world society. See,
especially, T'ang Chen, "I-yüan," in *Wei yen, chüan* 1 (1890); Ch'en Chih, "I-yüan,"
Yung shu, Wai-p'ien, chüan hsia (c. 1896); Cheng Kuan-ying, "I-yüan," *Sheng-shih wei
yen, chüan* 1; and Ho Ch'i and Hu Li-yüan, "Hsin-cheng lun-i," *Hsin-cheng chen-ch'üan*.

(who wanted to change in a hurry). He assessed in 1925 the price he had paid for being such a reformer:

> Ever since 1898 those of the old school have been attacking me for being too modern, whereas the moderns have been assailing me for being overly tradition-bound. Meanwhile, the revolutionists have been falling upon me for "protecting the emperor."[8]

Much of this hostility can be traced to misapprehension of K'ang's theoretical position, which was neither that of an impatient radical nor that of a short-sighted conservative, but that of an insistent reformer believing in the possibility of perfection through progress.

In the pages following I propose to show (1) that despite K'ang's opposition to the 1911 revolution, he was dedicated to the task of politically modernizing China through progressive democratization of her institutions; (2) that his ideas of reform were, in the light of the historical context, as understandable as alternative proposals for China's "salvation"; and (3) that although his reform efforts did not produce the results he expected them to have, they nevertheless had significant bearing on modern Chinese history. As I have dealt partially with his ideas of economic and intellectual reform elsewhere,[9] I shall restrict myself here to political reform. The story of the 1898 reform has been told by more than one scholar.[10] I shall therefore refer to events transpiring in and

---

[8] "Kao kuo-jen shu," in K'ang, *Wan-mu-tsao-t'ang i-kao* (hereafter cited as *I-kao*) *chüan* 4, "Shu-tu, part 2, p. 130b. Liang Ch'i-ch'ao commented in 1901: "My teacher is progressive. . . . Superficially, he appears to be a radical (*chi-chin p'ai*, 'one who wishes to advance in a hurry'), but in his heart he is really a gradualist. I know that from now on, young intellectuals will increasingly laugh at him for his conservatism. But if this be the case, it would be good for China." One may well doubt that Liang would have written the last sentence in the above passage, if it had been the 1910s or 1920s.

[9] See chapters 3, 4, 5, 10 and 11, this volume.

[10] Accounts in Western languages include Maribeth E. Cameron, *The Reform Movement in China, 1898–1912*, pp. 23–55; Te-chih Ma, "Le mouvement réformiste et les événements de la cour de Pékin en 1898"; Wolfgang Franke, *Die staatspolitischen Reformversuche K'ang Yu-weis und seiner Schule*; and S. L. Tikhvinsky, *Dvizhenie za reformy v Kitae v kontse XIX veka i Kan Iu-wei*, especially chaps. 7–12. Chinese sources are K'ang, *Tzu-pien nien-p'u*, pp. 15a–29b (hereafter cited as *Nien-p'u*); Liang Ch'i-ch'ao, *Wu-hsü cheng-pien chi*; K'ang T'ung-chia, *K'ang Yu-wei yü wu-hsü pien-fa*; Yang, "K'ang Liang nien-p'u," part 1, pp. 79a–101a; and T'ang Chih-chün, *Wu-hsü pien-fa chien-shih*. The last-mentioned book contains a convenient chronology of major events in K'ang's life and of the 1898 reform movement (beginning with 1884 and ending with the execution of the "Six Martyrs" on September 28, 1898) and a useful index to over 100 articles (in Chinese) on various aspects of the movement, published Oct. 1949–Dec. 1959. Yano Jin'ichi, "Bojutsu no hempō oyobi seihen," pp. 54–67, 30–44, 81–100, gives an account of the main events. T'ang Chih-chün, "K'ang Yu-wei ti

after that fateful year only where they seem to be pertinent to the discussion.

THEORETICAL POSITION

Remodeling of China's antiquated political system loomed large in K'ang's reform thought, as even a cursory reading of his writings readily shows. He was convinced that the surest way to "wealth and power" (for China as for other countries) was a government that operated on the principle of popular sovereignty (*min-ch'üan*) and an efficient administration that met the requirements of modern life. He kept on reiterating this theme, especially in the 1880s and 1890s. He said, for instance, in a memorial submitted to the emperor in 1888, that to make "suitable changes" in the centuries-old "decayed governmental system" would result in a wealthy and powerful country "within ten years."[11] Much of what he wrote in the late 1880s was devoted to giving details of such changes.

Miyazaki Torazō, in a conversation with two of K'ang's students in 1899, commented that while K'ang and Sun Yat-sen differed in upbringing and temperament, they were alike in cherishing the principles of republicanism and democracy (*kung-ho min-ch'üan*).[12] This observation, especially noteworthy as it came from a man not particularly sympathetic with K'ang's gradualist approach to reform, identifies correctly one of his fundamental tenets.

That K'ang was committed to democracy in the general sense of the

---

hsin-cheng chien-i ho Kuang-hsü-ti ti hsin-cheng shang-yü," pp. 154–221, and Onogawa Hidemi, "Kō Yū-i no hempō ron," pp. 101–99, summarize K'ang's views and proposals. Jérôme Tobar, *Koang-siu et Ts'e-hi, Empéreur de Chine et Impératrice douairière Décrets impériaux 1898*, gives a total of 178 decrees issued between June 10, 1898, and Feb. 23, 1899.

[11] "First Memorial to the Emperor," in Chien, *Wu-hsü*, 2: 129. Mai Chung-hua, *Wu-hsü tsou-kao* is a smaller compilation printed in 1911. According to Tikhvinsky, *Dvizhenie za reformy*, p. 203, K'ang wrote over fifty memorials between June 16 and September 20, 1898, a few of which were submitted under other people's names. It may be noted that a few others of the period also saw the need of political or administrative reform, but their demand for change was far less bold than K'ang's. See, e.g., Tseng Kuo-fan, *Ch'iu-ch'üeh-chai jih-chi*, "Chih-tao" in *Tseng Wen-cheng-kung ch'üan-chi*; T'ao Mu, "Fu-ch'en tzu-ch'iang ta-chi shu" in Yü Pao-hsüan, *Huang-ch'ao hsü-ai wen-pien*, chüan 3, pp. 4a–b; and Ho Ch'i and Hu Li-yüan, "*Ch'uan-hsüeh p'ien shu-hou*," chüan 7, pp. 29a–b. Interestingly, when General U. S. Grant visited China in 1879, he suggested that China should reorganize her government, pointing to Japan as a successful example. Tseng Yu-hao, *Modern Chinese Legal and Political Philosophy*, p. 41 and n. 3, citing Grant's letter to Prince Kung, from *John Russell Young Papers*, vol. 33, "Ulysses S. Grant World Tour."

[12] Miyazaki Torazō, *Sanjūsan-nen no yume*, p. 126.

term can be readily seen in many of his writings. He became acquainted with the ideas and institutions of modern democracy when he read what he called "Western books" in the late 1870s and early 1880s,[13] and undertook to bring these ideas into rapport with the "true teachings" of Confucius.[14] Confucius, K'ang asserted, "paid special attention to [the ideal of] universal peace and equality," when he characterized the governments of the emperors Yao and Shun as practical expressions of that ideal operating under "the people's rule" (*min-chu*).[15] *Min-chu*, by which K'ang meant republican government, was the highest and most perfect form of democracy. Constitutional monarchy, which he variously referred to as "benevolent government under monarchial rule" (*chün-chu chih jen-cheng*) or "joint rule of monarch and people" (*chün-min kung-chu*),[16] was a less perfect form suitable for a country at a lower stage of political development. Autocracy (*chuan-chih*) was the lowest and worst possible form of government which only prevailed in a politically backward country. At its best, autocratic government could not offer anything better than "Minor Peace."[17] An autocrat, interested only in keeping his subjects under control, gave no thought to their welfare. At its worst, therefore, autocracy degenerated into tyranny to the detriment of the people, a fact to which Chinese history bore uncontested witness. Moreover, autocracy spelled social and intellectual stagnation. As K'ang put it,

> In the darkness of two thousand years [of autocratic rule the emperors] clung tenaciously to the institutions of the Age of Disorder, to maintain

[13] K'ang began to read such materials in 1879 (*Nien-p'u*, p. 5b), which included *Hsi-kuo chin-shih hui-pien* (Periodical Digest of World News, published by the Kiangnan arsenal translation bureau); *Wan-kuo kung-pao* (*Wan Kwoh Kung Pao*) (*International News Bulletin*; Timothy Richard referred to it as "Review of the Times"), edited at different times by Young J. Allen and others; and Timothy Richard's translation of Robert Mackenzie's *The Nineteenth Century, a History*, 4th ed., Chicago, 1882, the Chinese title of which is *T'ai-hsi hsin-shih lan-yao*. This last work sounded a distinctively optimistic note regarding political progress in the direction of liberty and corresponding decrease of tyranny in nineteenth-century Europe. Wang Shu-huai, *Wai-jen yü wu-hsü pien-fa* chap. 1, outlines the ideas introduced into China by Richard and other Westerners.

[14] See chapter 3 of this volume.

[15] *K'ung-tzu kai-chih k'ao*, *chüan* 12, pp. 1a–b. Significantly, K'ang presented a copy of this book to the emperor, early in the summer of 1898.

[16] Ibid., p. 2b, where K'ang attributed this form of government to King Wen of the Chou dynasty.

[17] "*Li-yün chu* hsü," in *K'ang Nan-hai hsien-sheng wen-ch'ao*, *chüan* 8, p. 1a (hereafter, *Wen-ch'ao*). The preface was dated 1884 but the book was possibly completed in 1901–2.

control of the empire . . . thus causing China, the first nation to evolve culture on earth, . . . to shun progress, to stagnate, and to be jeered at [by Westerners] as an uncivilized nation. . . . Is not this a pity?[18]

K'ang accepted, virtually without reservation, the basic democratic values of "liberty" and "equality." He formulated in 1901–2 his political ideal in these terms:

> To constitute all under heaven into a commonwealth is simply to entrust everything to the common sense [of mankind]. "Commonness" (*kung*) means "each and every man is treated in one and the same way."[19]

That being the case, a monarch who ruled according to the "true Confucian" (i.e., democratic) principles would never imagine that he was intrinsically superior to the people. He regarded himself as one of them and occupied the throne not in order to exalt himself but only in order to serve them.[20] For, K'ang explained, "As all men are born of Heaven and belong to Heaven, each and every man is independent and free."[21] And as each had in him the "common nature" of humanity, he had the ability to act in accordance with reason. His conduct would be "compatible with that of every other man,"[22] without the benefit of arbitrary external control. Theoretically, therefore, there was no room for autocracy, a political system that denied free and independent men the right to rule themselves. The state, in truth, was the people's "common possession" (*kung ch'an*; *kuo wei kungyu*). The only rightful and dependable political authority was the authority of the people (*min-ch'üan*).[23]

---

[18] "*Ch'un-ch'iu pi-hsüeh ta-i wei-yen k'ao* fa-fan," *chüan* 5, p. 1a. This book was completed in 1901 when K'ang was in Penang; it was published in 1913. Cf. "Ts'ai hsing-sheng i," *chüan* 4, p. 31a, where he blamed autocracy for making China remain "uncivilized like an aboriginal tribe" and sang high praise to Western material civilization which, he said, was of an order higher than that of imperial China during the heyday of Han and T'ang dynasties.

[19] *Li-yün chu*, p. 4b.

[20] *Ch'un-ch'iu Tung-shih hsüeh*, *chüan* 6, part 2, pp. 24a–b. Repeatedly, K'ang pointed to the detrimental effects of the isolation of the emperors as a result of excessive reverence. See, e.g. "Seventh Memorial to the Emperor," in Chien, *Wu-hsü*, 2: 203–4.

[21] *Lun-yü chu*, *chüan* 5, pp. 4b–5a. K'ang went on: "This doctrine is sublime, but the world [of Confucius' time] was not ready for it. . . . It could be applied only when the world has advanced [through] the Age of Approaching Peace to the Age of Universal Peace."

[22] *Chung-yung chu* p. 1a.

[23] *Wen-ch'ao*, *chüan* 12, p. 20a. K'ang formulated his theoretical position in a poem written shortly after the inception of the Pao-kuo hui (April 12, 1898) which reads in part as follows:

Autocracy, in K'ang's view, was responsible for the sorry situation that had faced China ever since she came into contact with Western powers. Her salvation, therefore, hinged on the transformation of the imperial system into a democratic form of government.[24] However, it would not be prudent to move precipitantly from autocracy to democracy. China had suffered more than enough from the former but she was not ready for the latter. Progress, political and otherwise, had to be an orderly evolutionary process. It was as perilous to rush into a higher form of government before conditions were ripe as it was to maintain institutions that had outlived their usefulness.[25] Existing forces and circumstances had to be taken into account; inveterate malpractices could not be cleared away in one sweep. The final outcome of political reform would be radical, but the process of change had to be gradual and "peaceful."[26] In short, before implementing republicanism (full democracy) China must go through a transitional phase—constitutional monarchy (prelusive democracy).

Proposals for Constitutional Monarchy (1898)

Among the various changes proposed by K'ang in 1898 none was quite as important as his suggestion that the imperial system be con-

---

The Empire is sorrowfully being dismembered.
Good people, perturbed, hasten to save the nation.
Realizing that the Empire is a common possession (*kung ch'an*),
    It is fitting to do so by dint of popular sovereignty (*min-ch'üan*).
Brief accounts of the Pao-kuo hui are in K'ang, *Nien-p'u*, pp. 17b–18a and Ting Wen-chiang, *Liang Jen-kung hsien-sheng nien-p'u ch'ang-pien ch'u-kao*, pp. 50–53. Tikhvinsky, *Dvizhenie za reformy*, pp. 185–89, is useful.

[24] K'ang's position was so manifest that even writers in Communist China (who in other connections do not hesitate to misinterpret or denigrate the reform movement) admit that it in fact represented "a political demand for the reform of the institutions of feudalistic absolute monarchy" (Li Tse-hou, *K'ang Yu-wei T'an Ssu-t'ung ssu-hsiang yen-chiu*, p. 30).

[25] For summaries of K'ang's theory of social progress and his interpretation of the Kung-yang doctrine of the "Three Ages" see chapters 3 and 4 of this volume; Hsiao Kung-ch'üan, *Chung-kuo cheng-chih ssu-hsiang shih*, 6: 699–700; and Fung Yu-lan, *A History of Chinese Philosophy*, 2: 180–81.

[26] Woodbridge Bingham, Hilary Conroy, and Frank W. Iklé, *A History of Asia*, 2: 337. Franklin W. Houn [Hou Fu-wu], *Central Government of China, 1912–1928: An Institutional Study*, p. 6: "This [reform] movement was sanctioned by the open-minded Emperor Kuang-hsü, and the so-called 'Hundred Days' of reform marked the attempt to patch up the government structure without fundamentally altering it." The concluding remark rests upon a misconception.

verted into a constitutional monarchy.[27] With apparent pride (and not without justification) he claimed that the notion of the body politic as a commonwealth (*kuo wei kungyu*), the suggestion that constitutional government be instituted in China, originated with him in 1898.[28]

K'ang advanced two lines of argument for constitutional monarchy as China's initial form of democratic government. On the one hand, he appealed to "Confucian teaching." Commenting on Confucius' dictum, "The rude tribes of the east and north have their princes, and are not like the States of our great land which are without them" (*The Analects*, III. 5; Legge tr.), K'ang wrote that while backward peoples had to maintain the autocratic rule of princes, civilized people who upheld human rights (*jen-ch'üan*) did well under the rule of law, dispensing with the authority of an absolute monarch.[29] On the other hand, K'ang pointed to modern Western countries where democratic and constitutional governments had attained success as shining examples of human progress. In implementing the doctrine of "three powers"—in evolving a political system in which "deliberative officials" (i.e., members of parliament) and "judicial officials" shared authority with "executive officials"—Western nations had given reality to democratic government, which previously existed in China only in theory.[30] China lagged behind the West in democratic practice not because the teaching of Confucius was defective but merely because many of his followers had misconstrued it.[31]

The parliamentary institution, K'ang believed, was vital in a constitutional system. For it was parliament that served to bring ruler and

[27] Scholars generally agree. E.g., Cheng-fu Lung, "The Evolution of Chinese Social Thought," p. 314, identifies K'ang as a political reformer "advocating constitutional monarchy for China"; Tikhvinsky, *Dvizhenie za reformy*, p. 193, suggests that the adoption of a constitution was "the principal political demand" of K'ang and his associates; and T'ang Chih-chün, *Wu-hsü pien-fa jen-wu chuan kao*, 1: 15, describes the reform movement as "a bourgeois-class movement demanding *min-ch'üan*."

[28] K'ang T'ung-pi, *Nan-hai K'ang hsien-sheng nien-p'u hsü-pien* (hereafter, *Nien-p'u hsü-pien*), p. 106b. Liang Ch'i-ch'ao, for one, supported this claim (*Nan-hai hsien-sheng chuan*, in *Yin-ping-shih ho-chi, wen-chi* 6: 85). As indicated in note 7, above, this notion was shared, broadly, by a number of other writers of the period. K'ang could claim credit for being the first to dwell on it and to attempt to implement it.

[29] *Lun-yü chu, chüan* 3, p. 3. Similar arguments for constitutional government and democracy are found in the same work in his comments on another passage in the *Analects*, XV. 4, and in his *Meng-tzu wei*, pp. 12, 15–16, in his comments on two passages in the *Book of Mencius*, I.ii.7 and IV.i.9.

[30] "Sixth Memorial to the Emperor," Jan. 29, 1898, given in Chien, *Wu-hsü*, 2: 199.

[31] "*Lun-yü chu hsü*," *Wen-ch'ao, chüan* 8, p. 2b. A fuller treatment of the theme is found in his *Hsin-hsüeh wei-ching k'ao*.

people into direct communication and thus to bind them into a healthy body politic. In addition to facilitating the levying of taxes (apparently referring to British experiences), parliament made it possible for the people, through their representatives, to voice their views and grievances, and to play their part in achieving national consensus regarding public policy.[32] K'ang identified the central features and chief advantages of parliament in a memorial (written for a Manchu official committed to his cause) early in the summer of 1898:

> The secret of the strength of Japan and Western countries lies solely in their adoption of constitutional government and convening of parliament (*kuo-hui*, literally, "national assembly"). Parliament is a body through which the sovereign and the people deliberate together the laws and policies of the country. Since the appearance of the doctrine of three powers [there has come into being a political system in which] laws are made in parliament and enforced by the judiciary, and administrative matters are conducted by the government, while the ruler stands above them all. A constitution is enacted, which binds the ruler and all others alike. The ruler's person is inviolable; he can do no wrong, as administrative responsibilities are shouldered by the government. In this way the sovereign and the people are welded together into one body politic. How can the nation not be strong?[33]

K'ang then went on to specify the basic disadvantages of autocratic government.

> In our country autocratic government (*chuan-chih cheng-t'i*) prevails. One ruler and a few high ministers govern the country. How can the country not be weak? For it is the nature of things that the many are better than the few.

To add cogency to his argument K'ang warned that unless political reform was effected in time, China would suffer the calamity of revolution, as France and Poland in fact did. The lesson of France was particularly instructive. The French people, K'ang wrote in 1898, inspired by the American revolution and encouraged by the fall of Charles I and James II of England, resolved to overturn the long-continued oppressive rule of the Bourbon monarchy and readily succeeded. The explanation was not far to seek.

When the people's passion was aroused, their mood changed drastically.

[32] "Fourth Memorial to the Emperor, June 30, 1895, in Chien, *Wu-hsü*, 2: 176.
[33] "Ch'ing ting li hsien-fa k'ai kuo-hui che," p. 236.

The dignity and prestige [of the sovereign] no longer sufficed to keep them in place. Instead, these served only to excite them. [His] authority and power no longer could suppress them. On the contrary, these worked merely to enrage them.[34]

The authoritarian regime of France thus came to an abrupt end. Had Louis XVI understood the dangerous situation confronting him and decided, of his own accord and with dispatch, to promulgate a constitution, defining appropriately the respective rights of the people and the ruler, he would have saved not only his own life but the monarchy itself. Unfortunately, he failed to comprehend a universal truth:

That the few cannot match the strength of the many nor can the private interests [of the ruler] override the common interests [of the people].

The tragedy of Poland taught the same lesson, though the historical situation was different. K'ang pointedly mentioned that the king of Poland, rendered powerless by conservative high ministers and hamstrung by a domineering queen-mother, was unable to make his own decisions. How much better would it have been for him "to have given power to the people" before the situation became completely hopeless?[35]

The French revolution, K'ang continued, quickened the pace of the trend toward democracy. In fairly rapid succession one modern state after another replaced autocracy with constitutional government—discarding *chuan-chih* and inaugurating *min-ch'üan*.

This is the trend of history which has greatly changed the mood of the people. Surging waves and rolling waters [of revolution] are engulfing the great earth—a profoundly awesome trend![36]

The conclusion was obvious. As it would be futile to breast the tide, China must move with it: prepare for the coming of constitutional government while circumstances remained still favorable. Accordingly,

[34] "Chin-ch'eng *Fa-kuo ko-ming-chi hsü* (Chien, *Wu-hsü*, 3: 7–9; available also in *Wen-ch'ao, chüan* 5, pp. 20b–21a).

[35] "Chin-ch'eng *Po-lan fen-mieh-chi* hsü" (Chien, *Wu-hsü*, 3: 10 and *Wen-ch'ao, chüan* 5, p. 24a). In a postscript written late in 1912 or early in 1913 K'ang said that upon reading this book, the emperor broke into tears. He took decisive actions soon afterward, including granting common people the privilege of submitting memorials to him and dismissing the entire panel of the ranking officials of the Board of Rites who were archenemies of reform. The latter action was taken on September 4, less than twenty days before the coup d'état that ended the reform episode.

[36] Chien, *Wu-hsü*, 3: 9 and *Wen-ch'ao, chüan* 5, p. 21b.

K'ang made the following proposal to the emperor, about five months before the "Hundred Days":

> I humbly beg Your Majesty . . . to summon talented men for consultation with a view to broadening Your Majesty's understanding, to encourage men of the empire to voice their sentiments so that they may be brought to [Your Majesty's] attention, and to announce formally a policy of reform, thereby inaugurating a new era for the empire. From now on all affairs of the state are to be turned over to parliament for deliberation and decision.[37]

The convening of parliament, which was to mark the beginning of constitutional government, was to be preceded by several preliminary steps. On several occasions between 1888 and 1895 the emperor was advised to select and appoint consultative personnel, variously described by K'ang as "advisory-deliberative officials" (*hsün-i kuan*)[38] or simply "counsellors" (*i-lang*).[39] Then, in the summer of 1898, during the frantic days of bitter struggle between reformers and conservatives, K'ang urged the emperor to call into session a sort of prelusive parliament, to be composed of a number of officials without administrative duties selected and appointed by the emperor.[40] A little later, K'ang made a double proposal to him:

> Both Europe and Japan owe their strength to the convocation of parliament and the adoption of constitutional government. Now Your Majesty has approved the splendid plan [of convening parliament as submitted by K'uo-p'u-wu-t'ung] and is ready to proceed with resolve and determination. This is the good fortune of the country and the people. I beg Your Majesty to announce in an official decree to the empire that constitutional government is to be adopted and that a date for convening parliament has been set. . . . I [further] beg Your Majesty, as of now, before the convening of parliament, first, to assemble talented persons of the realm and to discuss with them the details of the [projected] political system; and, second, to listen to the opinions of the people of the empire and to permit them to submit in writing their views [concerning national affairs].[41]

[37] "Fifth Memorial to the Emperor" (submitted between December 25, 1897 and January 21, 1898) (Chien, *Wu-hsü*, 2: 194).

[38] "First Memorial to the Emperor" (1888) (Chien, *Wu-hsü*, 2: 129).

[39] "Second Memorial to the Emperor" (1895) (Chien, *Wu-hsü*, 2: 152–53).

[40] *Nien-p'u*, p. 24b, gives K'ang's view that it was unthinkable to have a government that had only executive and administrative officials and was without "deliberative officials" and that he had accordingly written a memorial recommending the appointment of such officials and had Hsü Chih-ching, a vice president of the board, submit it in midsummer, 1898.

[41] "A Memorial . . . Begging [the Emperor] to Set a Date for Convening Parlia-

These proposals, taking preliminary steps before actually launching constitutional government, are of particular interest. K'ang made them not only because they were in line with his gradualist approach to reform but because the situation prevailing at the time called for circumspection. "The court," he said, "was filled to overflowing with conservatives." To push for immediate convocation of parliament would arouse undue opposition and endanger the entire program.[42] The emperor, he suggested, should not for the moment go beyond holding discussion sessions with a group of selected advisers who would constitute a working prelude to parliament.[43]

It may be interesting to note that K'ang's 1898 recommendations foreshadowed the moves actually made by the Ch'ing court in 1906–8: announcing the intention to adopt a constitution and setting a date for convening parliament.[44] The resemblance, however, was no more than superficial. While K'ang intended the preliminary measures he suggested to lead to a basic transformation of China's political system,[45]

---

ment, to Select Qualified Persons to Deliberate Affairs of Government, and to Permit the People to Present Their Views" (midsummer, 1898) (Chien, *Wu-hsü*, 2: 241). K'ang went on to say that before the institution of constitutional government the emperor of Japan invited "talented people" of the country to discuss affairs of government. As a result, Ōkubo Toshimichi (1831–78), Kido Takayoshi (1833–77), and others appeared on the scene. Hugh Borton, *Japan's Modern Century*, pt. 2, passim, refers briefly to the roles of Ōkubo and Kido in the Meiji reform.

[42] *Nien-p'u*, p. 24b. Cf. ibid., p. 25a, where it is said that late in the 7th month K'ang dissuaded T'an Ssu-t'ung and Lin Hsü, two of his most ardent followers and of the "Six Martyrs" of 1898, from again proposing parliament.

[43] Ibid; p. 22b, indicates that the request was actually made by Li Tuan-fen in a memorial written for him by Liang Ch'i-ch'ao. According to Chao Feng-t'ien, "K'ang Ch'ang-su hsien-sheng nien-p'u kao," p. 206, K'ang himself wrote a memorial, which he asked Sung Po-lu to submit, in which he made the same request and recommended Huang Tsun-hsien and Liang Ch'i-ch'ao to serve as kind of co-chairmen of the would-be consultative body. The side hall mentioned by K'ang was identified as the Mou-ch'in tien by Chin-liang (*Kuang Hsüan hsiao-chi*, pp. 52–53).

[44] See Cameron, *Reform Movement in China*, pp. 103–4 (decree of Sept. 1, 1906, pp. 114–15, and Appendix A, pp. 205–6 (nine-year program of constitutional government). The basic philosophy of all this was stated by the high ministers who went abroad to study governmental forms in a memorial submitted in the first month of Kuang-hsü 32nd year (1906) requesting the court to make known its intention to adopt a constitution. The same view was stated by Tsai-tse in the seventh month of the same year in another memorial. Texts of these documents are in Shen T'ung-sheng, *Kuang-hsü cheng-yao*, *chüan* 32, pp. 1a–2b and 28a–30a; see pp. 30a–b for a decree of the same date concerning preparations for constitutional government.

[45] Pierre Renouvin, *La question d'Extrême-Orient, 1840–1940*, p. 189: "Dans tout ce vaste programme de réformes administratives et techniques, aucune allusion n'était faite à une modification du régime politique de l'Empire." This, obviously, is inaccurate.

the Ch'ing court's constitutional gestures amounted to little more than dilatory tactics calculated to prolong autocracy and forestall democratization. In the words of a French journalist of the time, "her [the empress dowager's] expressed intention to create a constitutional monarchy was her method of fooling the people."[46]

In K'ang's way of thinking, to carry out reform step by step did not mean to be satisfied with half measures. He demanded, repeatedly, the institution of a "planning bureau" (*chih-tu chü*) to draft new laws, to design new institutions, to formulate new policies, and in short to deal with the entire range of political reform.[47] He explained the rationale of such a bureau in these terms:

> At present, after having repeatedly suffered foreign aggression, the people of the empire are aware that the old institutions have outlasted their usefulness and consider reform the only way to survive. However, if we . . . carry out [reform] piecemeal, pursuing unimportant or nonessential matters, . . . we would end in failure. . . . Your servant is of the opinion . . . that if we resolve to change the institutions, we must necessarily aim at their complete transformation.[48]

And, with a view to symbolizing the emperor's determination to break away from the old imperial tradition, K'ang suggested that a new reign name be adopted, the capital be moved to south China, a modern style of official garbs be designed, and the queue be done away with.[49]

---

[46] Quoted in Li Chien-nung, *The Political History of China, 1840–1928*, p. 209. Li did not give the journalist's name but corroborated his view with: "As for the empress dowager's policy, her intention was procrastination" (p. 208). Tsai-tse admitted that one of the advantages of announcing the government's intention to adopt a constitution was to deprive the revolutionists of their "pretext" that China was still under a "semi-civilized autocratic rule." See memorial cited in note 44, above.

[47] This proposal was made at least three times, namely, in the "Sixth Memorial" (Jan. 29, 1898), in "Ching hsieh t'ien-en ping [ch'ing] t'ung-ch'ou ch'üan-chü che" (June 21) and in "Ch'ing k'ai chih-tu-chü i hsing hsin-cheng che" (submitted between August 17 and September 15). These documents are given in Chien, *Wu-hsü*, 2: 197–202, 214–17, 251–53.

[48] "Ching hsieh t'ien-en ping [ch'ing] t'ung-ch'ou ch'üan-chü che" (Chien, *Wu-hsü*, p. 215).

[49] "Ch'ing she hsin ching che," and "Ch'ing tuan-fa i-fu kai-yüan che" (both submitted early in September, 1898), in Chien, *Wu-hsü*, 2: 263–65, 259–62. K'ang may have been indebted to an article in the *Wan-kuo kung-pao*, 90: 3, which deals with the same matters and was written by Chiang Shu-tzu. This article is reprinted in *Wu-hsü*, 3: 200–201. Years later, K'ang expressed regret for having made the proposal to discard the native-style clothing. This, together with the other two requests, he said, were made for a psychological reason: to dramatize the emperor's resolve to implement thoroughgoing reform. In so doing, however, he had committed a tactical

It is hardly surprising that these suggestions were loudly condemned by his foes as a call for Westernization and abandonment of China's heritage.[50] They served to show, nevertheless, that while K'ang was a gradualist in method, he was really a radical in aim. To him reform was fruitful only when it was thorough.

AGENTS OF POLITICAL TRANSFORMATION

As it is well known, K'ang relied heavily on the Kuang-hsü emperor to implement his program of reform. He sought to initiate, in other words, a process of democratization in China by enlisting the service of the most decisive factor in an autocratic system. Liang Ch'i-ch'ao gave in 1901 this explanation of K'ang's position:

> My teacher is the first to advocate popular sovereignty (*min-ch'üan*) in China. (Many perhaps are acquainted with the notion but he is the first to champion it.) In dealing with practical policies [of reform], however, he attaches importance to the authority of the monarch (*chün-ch'üan*). He thinks that given the habits accumulated during several thousand years [of autocratic rule] and a people who have no knowledge [of democracy], to turn over to them the rights and powers [of government] would inevitably entail difficulties. Moreover, as the authority of the emperor has gained so much force and strength [in the past], it can become a most efficacious instrument [of reform] in the hands of an enlightened ruler. . . . My teacher has said, therefore, that we should make use of the monarch to implement the principle of democracy.[51]

The idea of making use of the monarchy to effect political modernization was suggested to K'ang not only by Chinese history but possibly also by the history of England, Russia, and Japan. Recent events in China undoubtedly gave him encouragement. The emperor had come of age and had formally assumed imperial authority in 1889.[52] The

error because he thereby made the conservatives even more determined to oppose reform. See his postscript to the second of the memorials cited above, in Mai, *Wu-hsü tsou-kao* (see note 11), pp. 73a–b.

[50] Wen-t'i, "Yen ts'an K'ang Yu-wei che" (Chien, *Wu-hsü* 2: 485).

[51] *Nan-hai K'ang hsien-sheng chuan, Yin-ping-shih ho-chi, wen-chi,* 4: 85; also in Chien, *Wu-hsü,* 4: 34.

[52] The history of China (and of England) may have also suggested to K'ang the rationale of political reform by means of the monarchical authority. Commenting on Wang An-shih's reform in eleventh-century China, James T. C. Liu said, "To introduce his sweeping reforms and to overcome strong opposition within the bureaucracy, Wang had to rely mainly upon the support of the Emperor" (*Reform in Sung China,* p. 21). Simon de Montfort's "Great Parliament" of 1265, summoned after his victory over Henry III, pointed also to the possibility of initiating constitutional government by monarchical fiat, even if only unwittingly.

empress dowager still wielded power and influence, as K'ang himself was aware. But the emperor was a young man who might be receptive to new ideas and even be willing to try them. Thus, in 1895, shortly after the crushing defeat by Japan, K'ang for the first time openly proposed that the emperor exercise his authority to rid China of her outmoded ways and to remodel her anachronistic institutions.[53] It is important to note that K'ang did not act on a belief in the supremacy or permanence of the monarchy;[54] actually, he was proposing that it take the first steps to liquidate itself.

K'ang's major argument for using monarchial authority to implement political change may be briefly recalled here. In one of the important memorials to the emperor, submitted on June 21, 1898, K'ang said:

> The ruler of men possesses overwhelming authority; nothing can withstand its awesome force. [I beg Your Majesty] to use the authority you have to carry out tasks that should now be undertaken and to perform those that are essential. It will then be possible to change immediately the habits of the empire and to arouse the minds of the people.[55]

Apparently to give confidence and encouragement to the youthful ruler, K'ang cited Russia's Peter the Great and Japan's Meiji as living examples of successful reform by dint of monarchical authority, worthy of imitation. Peter and Meiji achieved phenomenal success precisely because they had the courage "to break away from the thousand-years-long habit of self-conceit and self-delusion" and "to effectuate sweeping institutional changes, including the adoption of a constitution."[56] The best course for the Chinese emperor to follow.was therefore simply, in K'ang's words,

> To adopt the mental attitude of Russia's Peter the Great as the dictate of the mind and to take the governmental system of Japan's Meiji as the archetype of [proficient] government.[57]

[53] "Tien-shih ts'e," in an appendix to *Nan-hai hsien-sheng ssu shang-shu chi*, p. 49b.

[54] Ch'ien Tuan-sheng, *The Government and Politics of China*, p. 51, asserts that "K'ang Yu-wei was a Confucianist and believed in the supremacy of the monarchy. In this he was not different from Tseng Kuo-fan and Li Hung-chang." Professor Ch'ien, obviously, failed to grasp the true significance of K'ang's position.

[55] "Ching hsieh t'ien-en ping [ch'ing] t'ung-ch'ou ch'üan-chü che" (Chien, *Wu-hsü*, 2: 215).

[56] "Chin-ch'eng *O-lo-ssu Ta-pi-te pien-cheng-chi* hsü" (Chien, *Wu-hsü*, 3: 2; "Chin-ch'eng *Jih-pen Ming-chih pien-cheng-k'ao* hsü" (Chien, *Wu-hsü* 3: 3); and the "Sixth Memorial" (Chien, *Wu-hsü*, 2: 189). All three were written early in 1898.

[57] "Fifth Memorial to the Emperor" (submitted between December 24, 1897 and January 21, 1898, Chien, *Wu-hsü*, 2: 195).

In the early phase of China's political transformation, K'ang explained, the experiences of Russia and Japan were more pertinent as guideboards than the ideas and institutions of the advanced democracies of Europe and America. Russia's experience was particularly germane to the Chinese situation. As K'ang put it in February 1898:

> Of all the countries on earth, none is as prosperous and contented as the United States of America, but her republican political system is different from China's [autocratic] system; none is as powerful and wealthy as England or Germany, but the governments of these, being mixed monarchies (*chün-min kung-chu*) differ also from that of China. Only in Russia where the monarchical authority is supreme, the political system resembles that of China. Previously, Russia was weakened by Sweden [*sic*] and scorned by the West. In this she is also like China. But by making use of the monarchical authority to reform her institutions she has emerged from weakness to strength and has turned degeneracy into progress, with unmatched speed. . . . Therefore, in reshaping our own institutions China would do well to follow the example of Russia; in implementing reform it would be best [for the emperor] to adopt the ways of Peter.[58]

The emperor was convinced. In the famous decree of June 11,[59] he officially committed himself to reform and thus implied his willingness "to adopt the ways of Peter." From now on K'ang shifted his emphasis and began to dwell on the importance of following the example of Meiji of Japan, namely, the wisdom of making the transition from autocracy to constitutional monarchy.[60]

According to K'ang, the emperor was also agreeable to the idea of constitutional monarchy. In a postscript to the memorial proposing parliament for the empire (referred to in note 41), K'ang said that the emperor had indeed decided to implement the idea and was stopped from taking action by the empress dowager's firm opposition. When Sun Chia-nai remonstrated that if parliament was convened, the people would deprive the ruler of his authority, the emperor was quoted as saying, "We wish only to save China. If the people are thereby [also] saved, it matters not that We have no authority." K'ang then commented that only a sovereign "who sincerely intends to make the

---

[58] "Seventh Memorial to the Emperor" (submitted February, 1898) (Chien, *Wu-hsü*, 2: 203). K'ang added that the secret of Peter's success lay in his willingness to "condescend," "to waive rank and dignity" in order to learn the modern ways of the West.

[59] This decree is given in *Te-tsung shih-lu, chüan* 418, p. 115 and in Chien, *Wu-hsü*, 2: 17.

[60] See, e.g., the memorial cited in note 33, above.

empire a commonwealth (*kung t'ien-hsia*) could have uttered these words."[61] K'ang must have thought at the time that with the unreserved commitment of the emperor, China's political modernization was within reach.[62]

But there was a fatal flaw in K'ang's plan. The emperor had the best intentions in the world but was without real power to translate those intentions into action. Miyazaki observed in 1899 that to wish to sweep away "China's accumulated malpractices" by means of imperial decrees (which were no better than scraps of paper) was sheer folly, and that K'ang failed to effect reform precisely because he "relied solely on monarchical authority."[63] K'ang himself, of course, was not unaware that the emperor was less than a free agent. "What can I do," the latter said to K'ang on one occasion, "with so much hindrance?" Nevertheless, K'ang felt that it was still possible for the emperor to do something. His advice was,

> Exercise whatever authority Your Majesty possesses to bring about whatever changes that may be effected. By working on the most important things, China can be saved, even though the change may not be complete.[64]

Occasionally, K'ang spoke as if he believed in something like the mystique of the monarchical hero. For example, while he was traveling in Italy in 1904, he sang high praise to Julius Caesar who (he said)

---

[61] Mai, *Wu-hsü tsou-kao*, p. 34b; also in *Pu-jen*, no. 5 (June 1913), p. 2, and in *Wench'ao*, p. 10a.

[62] K'ang continued to affirm the emperor's willingness. See, e.g., "Chi Te-tsung huang-ti wen," quoted in Chao, "K'ang Ch'ang-su hsien-sheng nien-p'u kao," p. 271; and "An Open Letter to My Countrymen," *I-kao, Shu-tu*, pt. 1, pp. 130a–b. Historians do not doubt the reliability of K'ang's report. See, e.g., T'ang Chih-chün, *Wu-hsü pien-fa jen-wu chuan kao*, 1: 12, and Chang Po-chen, *Nan-hai K'ang hsien-sheng chuan*, pp. 36a–b.

[63] Miyazaki, *Sanjūsan-nen no yume*, p. 144. Miyazaki, who was partial to Sun and his cause, suggested alternative courses of action that were, under the circumstances, hardly more practicable. If, he said, the Chinese Emperor was truly as enlightened as K'ang thought him to be, he could put Charles I and Louis XVI to shame by abdicating his throne and becoming a commoner, thus giving the people the right and opportunity to choose their own ruler and transforming China into a republic. Or, K'ang could organize a revolutionary army among the people, waiting for the emperor to join him. To hope "to wipe out corrupt practices in one stroke without bloodshed" was an absolute impossibility (ibid., p. 145).

[64] *Nien-p'u*, p. 19a, a conversation between K'ang and the emperor in the June 16, 1898, audience. Earlier, in 1895, Weng T'ung-ho had already told K'ang that the emperor was powerless (ibid., p. 13a). Cf. the translation of this conversation in Ssu-yü Teng and John K. Fairbank, *China's Response to the West*, pp. 177–79.

surpassed even Alexander and Napoleon in talent and achievement. Only Emperor T'ai-tsung of T'ang China compared favorably to him. All the other kings and emperors in history were "mostly clumsy geniuses" (*ts'u ts'ai*).[65] K'ang did not compare Caesar and Kuang-hsü. However, the fact that K'ang consistently showed the greatest admiration to the latter, even years after 1898,[66] tempts one to surmise that K'ang probably would not hesitate to rate him as potentially worthy of a place alongside Caesar and T'ai-tsung. Unfortunately, Kuang-hsü proved in 1898 to have been far less than what K'ang had wished him to be. It is indeed doubtful that he had the personal qualifications to carry out the difficult program of political reform, even if he had real power.[67]

It must be noted, however, that K'ang did not rely solely on the emperor. He did in fact seek to activate other possible agents of reform —members of the scholar-officialdom, the lettered elite, and even the common people. Understandably, he paid a great deal of attention to earn the support of the first group. Political reform, he said in 1895, must necessarily begin in the imperial capital and with high officialdom.[68] He endeavored earnestly in 1888 to gain the attention of such high court officials as Weng T'ung-ho, P'an Tsu-yin, and (of all people) Hsü T'ung, an archconservative.[69] It happened that he was only able to convince Weng of the importance of reform, and only after the humiliating conclusion of the Sino-Japanese War.[70]

K'ang did not restrict his campaign to high officialdom. He tried strenuously to win the support of the lettered elite in general and middle and lower officials in particular. He conducted a sort of educational and propaganda campaign among them, familiarizing them with world affairs and China's problems, and urging them to make concerted efforts "to save the country" through reform. Together with his fellow

---

[65] "I-ta-li yu-chi," in *Ou-chou shih-i kuo yu-chi*, pp. 40–41.

[66] E.g., he sometimes referred to the emperor as "sage" (*sheng*). Chao, "K'ang Ch'ang-su hsien-sheng nien-p'u kao," p. 271.

[67] For a brief analysis of the emperor's personality and the situation confronting him, see K. C. Hsiao, "Weng T'ung-ho and the Reform Movement of 1898," pp. 136–49. Li Hung-chang's assessment of the emperor was not entirely groundless. He told Timothy Richard in 1895 "that the Emperor had no mind of his own, but depended on every last adviser" (Timothy Richard, *Forty-five years in China*, p. 207).

[68] *Nien-p'u*, p. 13a.

[69] Ibid. This was in 1888 when K'ang began his reform activities, having been aroused by the situation created by the Sino-French conflict of 1884–85.

[70] Ibid. For Kang's relationship to Weng, see Hsiao, "Weng T'ung-ho," pp. 149–79.

reformers he published newsletters and newspapers, and formed "study associations" (*hsüeh-hui*) in and out of the capital.[71] To bring like-minded people into *hsüeh-hui*, he believed, would not only facilitate the introduction and dissemination of new ideas and the formation of modern intellectual attitudes, but also enhance the strength and influence of these people.[72] The activities of *hsüeh-hui* were to be large in number and many-sided, including collecting books translated from Western languages, translating selected Western-language books, circulating these books among the members; translating newspapers published in foreign lands and distributing them in the provinces; promoting scientific studies by providing laboratory facilities and establishing museums; encouraging "useful knowledge" by requiring each member to pursue a specific field of study; and sending "accomplished members" to travel in China and abroad, with a view to giving them opportunities to acquire further knowledge and to contribute to it. Contacts were to be made with prominent officials, with sympathetic overseas Chinese, with Western scholars residing in China, and with learned societies in other countries.[73]

The idea of *hsüeh-hui* took its initial and somewhat dramatic shape in the Ch'iang-hsüeh hui (Society for the Study of [Self-]strengthening, known in some Western circles as "The Reform Club") which held its inaugural meeting in Peking on August 22, 1895.[74] A number of officials in the capital joined or took an active part. Timothy Richard lent it his support.[75] Charles Denby, the American minister to China, and Sir Nicholas O'Connor, the British minister, offered help in procuring Western books and scientific-technological equipment. High officials in the provinces, civil and military, including Liu K'un-i, Chang Chih-

---

[71] As T'ang Chih-chün correctly pointed out, memorializing the emperor, organizing *hsüeh-hui*, and publishing periodicals were the major undertakings of the reformers ("Wu-hsü pien-fa shih ti hsüeh-hui ho pao-k'an," *Wu-hsü pien-fa shih lun-ts'ung*, p. 222).

[72] *Nien-p'u*, p. 13b. K'ang made these remarks in August, 1895.

[73] Liang Ch'i-ch'ao, "Lun hsüeh-hui," which forms the fifth section of his *Pien-fa t'ung-i, Yin-ping-shih ho-chi, wen-chi*, pp. 33–34. This piece is also available in Chien, *Wu-hsü*, 4: 376.

[74] *Nien-p'u*, pp. 13b–14a, gives K'ang's own account of the association. K'ang's statement of its aims, "Ch'iang-hsüeh-hui hsü," is in *K'ang Nan-hai wen-chi, chüan* 8, p. 20, and in Chien, *Wu-hsü*, 4: 384–85. A translation of the text is given in Teng and Fairbank, *China's Response to the West*, pp. 152–53.

[75] Richard, *Forty-five Years in China*, pp. 254–55. William E. Soothill, *Timothy Richard of China*, p. 235, describes Richard's role thus: "The influence of the latter's [Richard's] writings and his personality had been very great on many of the reformers, so he was naturally a keenly interested spectator of the doings of 1898."

tung, Wang Wen-shao, Sung Ch'ing, and Nieh Shih-ch'eng, contributed sums of money.[76] The beginning appeared auspicious.

Conservative opposition soon persuaded the government to suppress the society. But the idea of organizing like-minded people to pursue a common objective (as advocated by K'ang and his collaborators) persisted and spread. Small groups were formed in the capital and more ambitious ones appeared in the provinces. The most well-known of the latter included the Hsiang-hsüeh hui and Nan-hsüeh hui in Hunan, the Chih-hsüeh hui in Hupeh, the Sheng-hsüeh hui in Kwangsi, and the Su-hsüeh hui in Kiangsu. In addition to these were a few groups organized to pursue specific objectives, such as the I-shu kung hui (Book Translation Society) of Shanghai and the Fa-lü hsüeh hui (Society for the Study of Law) of Hunan.[77] The Ch'iang-hsüeh hui of Shanghai was founded in autumn 1895, thanks partly to K'ang's own efforts.[78] In the imperial capital itself the work of the defunct Ch'iang-hsüeh hui was carried on briefly by the Pao-kuo hui (Society for National Preservation), formed in the spring of 1898, on the eve of the fateful "One Hundred Days," which like its predecessors became in turn the forerunner of a number of societies organized for the avowed purpose of "preserving" the provinces concerned.[79] None of these existed for long. Their practical influence is difficult to estimate; their impact on the contemporary scene seems to have been limited and ephemeral. However, their very appearance showed that K'ang saw the possibility of enlisting agents of reform other than the emperor.

In addition to seeking the cooperation of governmental officials K'ang and his colleagues perceived the advantage of spreading the gospel of reform among younger men, of exposing them to modern knowledge through Western-style education, "Western books," newspapers, and other facilities. They launched in fact a program of intellectual reform,

[76] *Nien-p'u*, 13b–14a. According to K'ang, Li Hung-chang "voluntarily offered to contribute 2,000 [taels?] and to join the Society." Many members, however, were against accepting the offer and precipitated much debate and generated ill-feeling. "Decline and failure," K'ang observed, "sprouted as soon as the Society attained to prosperity."

[77] Wang Ch'i-chü, "Hsüeh-hui teng tsu-chih," in Chien, *Wu-hsü*, 4: 373–478, gives accounts of these and other *hui*.

[78] *Nien-p'u*, pp. 14a–b. Wang, *Hsüeh-hui teng tsu-chih*," pp. 385–86 and 389–94, includes Chang Chih-tung's statement for the Society and the Society's constitution which, incidentally, echoed some of Liang Ch'i-ch'ao's ideas as set forth in his essay on *hsüeh-hui*, cited in note 73, above.

[79] *Nien-p'u*, pp. 17b–18a. Chien, *Wu-hsü*, 4: 399–417, gives the Society's constitution, roster of names of people who allegedly joined it, text of K'ang's speech, summary of Liang's speech, and Liang's account of the impact of the Society.

alongside of political reform, each of which was calculated to reinforce and facilitate the other. As I propose to deal with intellectual reform· in another connection, it suffices to note here that K'ang was inclined in 1898 to pay greater attention to political reform and to place more trust in the monarchical authority as an instrument of change than some of his followers.[80] The fact remains, nevertheless, that on the whole and over the years he devoted about as much of his energies to intellectual as to political reform.

As the ultimate aim of K'ang's reform movement was the transformation of China into a "commonwealth," it is hardly surprising that even in 1898 he had already sought to prepare the common people, psychologically at least, for the momentous change. Thus he requested the emperor to distribute copies of his portrait, to issue a decree expressing his "affection for the people," and to send copies of the reform decrees to every nook and corner of the empire, including "remote hamlets and out-of-the-way spots," so that the common people would become acquainted with their sovereign and his program.[81]

Even more important was K'ang's insistence that the people must be made to prepare themselves for the coming of democracy. He maintained, emphatically, that local self-government was the very foundation of democratic government. He must have come to the realization by 1898 that while the emperor and the elite together could furnish the initial motive force of political modernization, the people themselves alone could give substantive reality to democracy. Before the arrival of constitutional government, therefore, be it monarchical or republican

---

[80] E.g., when the situation in the capital became perilously explosive shortly after the abolition of the "eight-legged essay" on June 23, 1898, K'ang Kuang-jen, his brother "martyred" in the September *coup*, advised him repeatedly to suspend the campaign for political reform and to turn his attention to education instead. On one occasion, this advice was offered him: "As the emperor has no power he surely cannot implement the reform measures. It is better to return home where you can select scholars versed in Chinese and Western learning and indoctrinate them with your principles. In three years you should certainly accomplish something. Then it will be the time to advocate political reform" (*Nien-p'u*, p. 22a). K'ang, however, chose to continue to push political reform until the disastrous days of September. He then directed his efforts to "protecting the emperor," especially among overseas Chinese (K'ang T'ung-pi, *Nien-p'u hsü-pien*, p. 4b, and Ting, *Liang Jen-kung hsien-sheng nien-p'u ch'ang-pien ch'u-kao*, p. 88). According to Wu Hsien-tzu [Wu Chuang], *Chung-kuo min-chu hsien-cheng-tang tang-shih*, p. 25, the official English name of the emperor protection society was "Chinese Reform Association."

[81] *Nien-p'u*, p. 23b. The proposal was made in the summer of 1898. The emperor, K'ang said, agreed to broadcast the reform decrees. It is doubtful that the measure was actually carried out.

in form, the people must be ready for active participation in the political process; and the best way to learn to govern themselves was to begin at the local level.

"All local government," K'ang said early in 1898, "should stem from the people." The people were of course not as yet prepared for self-rule. But precisely because they were not it was important that steps be taken promptly so that they would become acquainted with its principle, structure, and functions. The services of the local elite, the gentry, should be enlisted as a first step. Assisted by an official appointed by the government in a "Bureau of People's Affairs" (*min-cheng chü*), they were to be responsible for initiating matters that properly pertained to local government. When satisfactory progress had been made in local self-rule, the people then would be ready for constitutional government on an empire-wide basis.[82]

K'ang reiterated his demand for local self-rule, with added emphasis, when in 1905 the Ch'ing court made known its ostensible willingness to consider constitutional government. He now argued that although circumstances still precluded the convening of a national assembly, the time had indeed come for the institution of village, district, prefectural, and provincial assemblies. That, he said, was the only practical way to give expression to popular sovereignty and to prepare the people for full-fledged constitutional government that was to come.[83] He described in some detail the local governments of Germany, England, the United States, and other countries, and suggested that China adopt a system that would combine the best features of all these.[84] People in culturally backward countries (*yeh-se chih kuo*), he pointed out, lived in scattered villages, whereas those in civilized countries (*wen-ming chih kuo*) concentrated in cities. In the modern West a concentration of population was called a "town" (*i*); when it developed a high degree of industrial and commercial activities, it became known as "city" (*shih*). In order to attain to the status of a civilized country China must develop industry and commerce; she must, in other words, join Western countries in the march toward urbanization. Cities then would become units of local self-government, alongside villages and metropolises (*tu-hui*). When local self-government became a reality in

[82] Chien, *Wu-hsü*, 2: 202.

[83] "Lun sheng fu hsien hsiang i-yüan i chi-k'ai wei pai shih chih pen," *Wen-ch'ao*, *chüan* 4, p. 67a.

[84] "Lun tzu-chih," *I-kao*, *chüan* 1, pp. 40a–43b. K'ang also described the self-government systems of Berlin, New York, Birmingham, Marseilles, Milan, and other cities.

all parts of the empire, China would then have acquired the solid foundations of constitutional government. Nothing, therefore, was "as essential as local self-rule."[85] In reply to the inquiry of a modernizing provincial official, K'ang suggested that the inhabitants of the villages of each district be instructed to elect their own representatives to form an assembly and to select their own leaders so that matters such as census, roads, public health, schools, irrigation, etc., could be appropriately dealt with.[86]

Liang Ch'i-ch'ao, again, correctly identified K'ang's position in saying that his erstwhile teacher "attached the greatest importance to local self-government" operating through a system of local assemblies because, in K'ang's view, these bodies would afford the people opportunities to gain experience in government and thus lay the foundations of democracy.[87] The people themselves would have become in this way agents of political transformation.

THE CASE FOR CONSTITUTIONAL MONARCHY

1911 saw K'ang's hope for constitutional monarchy irretrievably dashed. In pragmatic terms, all his work for China's political transformation came to naught. A lost cause, however, is not necessarily devoid of historical meaning. K'ang's cause, at any rate, merits scrutiny by standards other than the strictly pragmatic.

Given the facts of political life as it existed at the time, the course that K'ang plotted for China was not an unreasonable one. That the autocratic system was egregiously outmoded was allowed by all except the die-hard conservatives or the completely uninformed. It was natural

---

[85] Ibid., pp. 44b, 47a–b, and 48a.

[86] "Fu Liu kuan-ch'a Shih-chi shu," *I-kao, chüan* 4, p. 47b. Liu was then Intendant for Economic and Industrial Affairs of Kweichow, and was put in charge of the Bureau of Local Self-government by Governor Chang Ming-ch'i in 1908.

[87] *Nan-hai K'ang hsien-sheng chuan*, p. 86. Lu Nai-hsiang and Lu Teng-k'uei, *K'ang Nan-hai hsien-sheng chuan, shang-pien*, pp. 19b–20a, put the matter somewhat differently: "Our teacher thought that although constitutional government had not been established for the country, it was inevitable that the people's right [to govern themselves] should be recognized. . . . Therefore, he vigorously advocated a system of local self-government [for China] and was the first to do so, being convinced that self-government of citizens formed the basis of democratic government." Occasionally, K'ang was inclined to regard the self-help organizations that existed in many parts of rural China as counterparts of modern Western self-government. In his account of an organization formed in 1854 in his home village, under his granduncle's leadership, he described it as "a system of local self-government" (*Nien-p'u*, pp. 11a–b). This was an overestimation. See K. C. Hsiao, *Rural China: Imperial Control in the Nineteenth Century*, pp. 261–322.

for men like K'ang, after applying themselves to discovering the secrets of the West's success, to come to the conclusion that democracy, a form of government under which in K'ang's phraseology, "the state is the people's common possession," was the only alternative. It was reasonable also for K'ang to conclude that, as the Chinese people having lived for centuries under autocratic rule had neither the capacity nor the desire to take possession of the state, it would be sheer folly to hand political authority to them before they were qualified to exercise it, and that, therefore, the safest way of democratizing the country was to make use of existing facilities to prepare them for the radical change. This, in short, was the case for constitutional monarchy.

One can hardly exaggerate the political unpreparedness of the Chinese people. Mai Meng-hua, one of K'ang's loyal followers, observed in the summer of 1898, when some talk about *min-ch'üan* was heard in and out of Peking:

> As the people of China are unable to manage their own [political] affairs, they cannot have [political] authority. To give them such authority would result in the possession of authority not by men that are decent but by those who are objectionable.[88]

The immediate reaction of "the people" to an imperial decree of August 2, 1898, calling for presentation of their views and suggestions[89] (a move recommended by the protagonist of reform as a way to encourage popular concern for public affairs)[90] gave some substance to Mai's misgivings. An avalanche of memorials descended upon the court, coming from people of diverse stations. Dozens of these went to the emperor each day; he hardly found time to read them through.[91] Many of the documents turned out to be simply nonsensical or downright bizarre, in content or form, although a few of them showed bona fide attempts to

[88] Mai, "Lun Chung-kuo i tsun chün-ch'üan i min-ch'üan," Chien, *Wu-hsü*, 3: 113. This article was published originally in the *Ch'ang-yen pao*, a journal published by Wang K'ang-nien in Shanghai, Aug. 17 to Nov. 19, 1898, a total of ten issues. See T'ang Chih-chün, "Wu-hsü pien-fa shih ti hsüeh-hui ho pao-k'an," p. 255.

[89] This decree is given in *Te-tsung shih-lu, chüan* 421, pp. 15b–16a.

[90] In the concluding portion of the memorial "Ching hsieh t'ien-en [ch'ing] t'ung-ch'ou ch'üan-chü che," K'ang requested (summer of 1898) the emperor "to permit the people of the empire" to present their views in writing (Chien, *Wu-hsü*, 2: 242).

[91] See a report reprinted from the *Kuo-wen pao*, Sept. 22, 1898, under the title "Kuang-kuai lu-li" (Chien, *Wu-hsü*, 3: 412). Liang Ch'i-ch'ao made a similar assessment of these documents. See his "Wu-hsü cheng-pien chi," pp. 44–45, and Chang, *Nan-hai K'ang hsien-sheng chuan*, p. 35a. The contents of the less bizarre of these memorials, submitted by a *chü-jen* of Yunnan province, were revealed by the emperor (*Te-tsung shih-lu, chüan* 423, p. 2b).

tender pertinent advice.[92] Some of the most ridiculous pieces, presumably, came from the foes of reform who wished thus to discredit the idea of paying heed to "popular opinion." But the very fact that this happened and that little useful result came of this experiment in prelusive democracy constitutes good evidence that the Chinese people were far from prepared to exercise *min-ch'üan* in 1898. K'ang and his associates were not unduly pessimistic when they thought that an enlightened monarch was the most suitable agent to initiate the arduous process of democratic transformation in China.[93]

At the risk of overlaboring an obvious point, I wish to cite the observations of a number of men not involved in the reform movement. An official criticizing the editor of *The Times* (*Shih-wu pao*, June 11, 1898) for suggesting that convening parliament was the first step of political reform, pointed out that the parliamentary institution fared well in Western countries only where there was, in addition to an educated elite, a class of "the wealthy and talented" who understood what was good for the nation. Such an elite and class did not exist in China.

> The gentry (*shen*) of China came to their status through the examinations, purchase, or inheritance. Its members are inclined to be boastful and to indulge in useless babble. Those that are poor are mercenary and avaricious; even wealthy gentry are not free from greed, being less concerned about the interests of the country than about their own private gains. . . . From this it can be seen that proposing parliament [for China] is a great mistake.[94]

Such an appraisal of the quality of China's traditional elite may perhaps be a little overly pessimistic.[95] But the assertion that China did not have a "wealthy and talented" middle class, which contributed to the successful operation of Western democracies, is essentially well-founded. The absence of such a class remained, in fact, a limiting factor in China's

---

[92] Chien, *Wu-hsü*, 2: 362–74, gives the text of three of the four pieces that have been preserved.

[93] Franke, *Die staatspolitischen Reformsversuche K'ang Yu-weis und seiner Schule*, p. 39, interprets K'ang's position thus: "Die Beteiligung des Volkes an der Regierung wird nach den Reformatoren am besten durch die Einrichtung eines Parlamentes gewährleistet. Jedoch ist vorläufig nicht der richtige Zeitpunkt hierfür gekommen, da das Volk noch zu ungebildet ist und zu wenig Verständnis und Interesse für die Regierungsangelegenheiten hat."

[94] Yüan Ch'ang, "I-fu chi-yü shih-chien t'iao-ch'en," (dated September 8, 1898; in Chien, *Wu-hsü*, 2: 452). Yüan went on to suggest that "outstanding local gentry" be chosen by local officials to constitute a sort of advisory body. That, he said, would be the best way to enjoy some of the benefits of the lower house of Western parliaments.

[95] See Chang Chung-li, *The Chinese Gentry* and *The Income of the Chinese Gentry*.

struggle to develop a viable democratic system of government, even after the 1911 revolution, as more than one writer has noted.[96]

The remarks of a district magistrate who had personal experience with district and municipal assemblies in localities near Peking in 1914, merits quoting:

> . . . each district had its own Local Assembly . . . and Local Municipal Committee. . . . According to the fixed regulations the members of these organs should be upright members of the gentry. In reality, however, these Yi-yüan (deliberative members) usually gained their position by means of bribes and threats. They are "local" but not "representative." If the magistrate is honest, . . . these members attack him with all their might and hamper his every move. If the magistrate should prove as corrupt as they, they at once form a league with him and begin a systematic process of oppression and squeeze.[97]

Nor did the general populace make much headway toward democracy. Liang Sou-ming, leader of the Rural Reconstruction movement and a reformer in his own right,[98] said in the early 1930s that "given the right to vote but without previous training, people in North China would certainly vote against the prohibition of foot-binding."[99] Tsiang T'ing-fu, then professor of history at Tsing Hua University, said in 1935: "If the people do not want a share in government, no constitution can present them with any political power."[100] C. K. Yang, an American-trained sociologist, found in the late 1940s that much of the Chinese peasantry, including those dwelling in villages near Nanking (then the nation's capital) remained generally indifferent to and ignorant of political affairs.[101] The basic fact that the Chinese people, gentry

[96] Houn, *Central Government of China*, p. 175: "The most significant social problems in China during recent centuries have been those which resulted from economic and technical backwardness. As a result, a powerful and enlightened middle class, which has been the backbone of constitutional democracy in the Western world, was still not yet in existence in China."

[97] *Letters from a Chinese Magistrate*, reprinted from the *Peking and Tientsin Times* (Tientsin, 1920), p. 51.

[98] For a detailed account, see Harry J. Lamley, "Liang Shu-ming: The Thought and Action of a Reformer."

[99] Quoted by Chu Ching-nung, in "Chieh-shu hsün-cheng ti shih-chien wen-t'i," p. 18.

[100] "Kuo-min-tang yü Kuo-min-tang-yüan," *Tu-li p'ing-lun*, no. 176 (November, 1935), p. 14.

[101] C. K. Yang, *A Chinese Village in Early Communist Transition* (Cambridge, Mass.: Technology Press, MIT; dist. Harvard University Press, 1959), passim. Cf. Hsiao Kung-ch'üan, "Ti-tiao t'an hsüan-chü: Ti-fang min-i chi-kou ti ch'u-pu chien-t'ao," pp. 104–9 and 110–33. The latter reference is to a paper based on a field survey conducted by the writer in the early 1940s in western Szechwan province.

and peasant alike, were not ready for democracy lent cogency to K'ang's argument for evolving constitutional government by utilizing the existing monarchical authority as an initial motive force and by simultaneously enlisting the support of the lettered elite.

K'ang's commitment to gradualism made him a determined opponent of the revolutionist and republicans. A few of his arguments against sudden, violent political change may be briefly indicated here. He rested his arguments sometimes on theoretical grounds, that is, political change must be compatible with the historical circumstances prevailing at a given period of time. He appealed often to the Kung-yang doctrine of the "Three Ages" each of which called for a particular form of government.[102] As China had still to make the transition from "the Age of Disorder" to "the Age of Approaching Peace," she should at the moment strive to replace autocracy with constitutional monarchy. Republicanism (*min-chu*) was suitable only for "the Age of Universal Peace." It was intrinsically desirable but lay beyond China's immediate reach. As he said in 1900,

> Popular sovereignty (*min-ch'üan*), equality, and liberty are values that coincide with universal truth and accord with human wish. . . . It is absolutely certain that they will [eventually] prevail in the whole world. . . . However, appropriateness in time and place must be taken into consideration; it is premature to try to realize them in China. Therefore, . . . to engage ourselves in revolution [with a view to attaining these values now] . . . would do much harm.[103]

K'ang refused to budge from his gradualist position even when in 1902 some of his followers, despairing of the Ch'ing court's behavior and impressed by the revolutionists' contention that under the existing circumstances nothing could be accomplished without bloodshed,[104] suggested to him that "to follow the example of George Washington" was the only way to save China.[105] And, in fact, when it become obvious that the revolutionary tide was reaching its crest, K'ang redoubled his

---

[102] Hsiao, *Chung-kuo cheng-chih ssu-hsiang shih*, pp. 687–91 and 702–3, summarizes K'ang's interpretation of this doctrine.

[103] "Kao t'ung-pao Yin [-tu] shih shu-hou," *I-kao, chüan* 2, pp. 28a–b.

[104] See Sun Wen, "Po Pao-huang pao," written in 1904, in *Kuo-fu ch'üan-chi*, 6: 226–32. Cf. Jen Cho-hsüan, "Kuo-fu ti ko-ming ssu-hsiang," *Ko-ming ssu-hsiang*, 1, no. 1 (July 25, 1955): 7, a brief summary of arguments in favor of effecting "national," "political," and "social" revolution simultaneously and the argument that no change could be brought about without destroying the existing order.

[105] *Nien-p'u hsü-pien*, p. 20a. K'ang was traveling in India when a letter from Chinese businessmen in North and South American countries reached him.

efforts to check it and poured forth a torrent of antirevolution writings. Among these were the "Essays on Rescuing [China] from Destruction" (*Chiu wang lun*) written shortly after the outbreak of the 1911 revolution.[106] In these essays K'ang pointed to the dire perils that would befall China if the revolutionary course was followed to its bitter end (essays 1 and 2); he repeated his contention that republicanism ill suited Chinese conditions (essay 3); he argued, less than convincingly, that the Chinese and Manchus were descended from the same ancestors and that therefore "nationalism" (*min-tsu chu-i*) constituted no valid ground for revolution (essay 10); he asserted, above all, that what really mattered was the fundamental democratic principle, namely, that "the state is a commonwealth," and that it was folly to wreck the country in fighting over nonessential issues such as governmental forms and racial differences (essays 3, 4, and 5); and, finally, asserting that constitutional monarchy was "an ingenious and marvellous system of hidden republicanism" (essay 8), he set forth his theory of "a republic under a titular monarch" (*hsü-chün kung-ho*, essay 9). To placate those who insisted on ridding China of the Manchu rule he proposed that the linear male descendant of Confucius be elected China's titular king who would enjoy no more power than that exercised by "an earthen idol in a deserted shrine." The rationale of such an arrangement, K'ang explained, was that it was useful to have a symbol of political unity and stability, and thus to spare the nation the contention and strife that too often attended the elections of chiefs of state in some modern republics.[107]

K'ang's willingness to abandon the Ch'ing house as indicated in the above-mentioned proposal, is significant, for it reveals his fundamental position. During the reform days of 1898 he was suspected of desiring only to save China but not the Manchu dynasty.[108] This suspicion was

---

[106] Ibid., pp. 73–74a, and Yang, "K'ang Liang nien-p'u kao-pen," pt. 2, pp. 62b–63a. These essays, "Chiu wang lun," ten in number, were first published in *Pu-jen*, no. 7 (August, 1913), pp. 1–55 and reprinted in *Pu-jen tsa-chih hui-pien*, 1st series (Shanghai, 1914), 1: 22b–39a. The possibility of China's partition as a result of revolution was not a sheer figment of K'ang's imagination. According to Masaru Ikei, "Japan's Response to the Chinese Revolution of 1911," pp. 215–16, there actually had been proposals "to use the existing situation to forward Japan's continental policy" and some military men called for the division of China.

[107] "Chiu wang lun," pp. 36b–37a.

[108] *Nien-p'u*, p. 20b, gives K'ang's own account of Wen-t'i's impeachment. Wen-t'i's memorial is given in Chu Shou-p'eng, *Tung-hua hsü-lu*, *chüan* 145, pp. 14a–18a and in Chien, *Wu-hsü*, 2: 482–89. Wen-t'i charged that K'ang intended "merely to preserve the 400 million people of China" and had "no concern for our great Ch'ing."

not unfounded. As our survey of his writings has shown, his primary concern was to preserve China through reform. He would like to preserve the Ch'ing dynasty as an instrument of change; he was not adverse to the idea that by preserving China the dynasty would also preserve itself. But if to preserve the dynasty meant to block the road to modernization—to make it impossible to effect peaceful and orderly transition from autocracy to constitutional government—he was willing to let the dynasty go. Furthermore, it should be borne in mind that in K'ang's grand scheme of political transformation even constitutional monarchy itself would ultimately make way for "people's rule." K'ang was, in other words, no loyalist or even monarchist, pure and simple, as he was sometimes taken to be.

K'ang had made another and more hopeful attempt at forestalling revolution a few years before 1911. The imperial court sent five high ministers abroad to investigate constitutional government in 1905 (the same year in which the revolutionary organization, T'ung-meng hui, was formed in Tokyo), and officially announced in the following year its intention to adopt a constitution. K'ang wrote a petition for overseas members of the newly named China Constitution Society,[109] in which he urged the Ch'ing court to implement constitutional government without delay. Contradicting his own argument advanced shortly before, that the Chinese people were unprepared for participation in government, he now asserted that they in fact were ready for it. Constitutional government, he wrote,

> has already been unequivocally promised in an imperial decree. That it is slow in coming is due to the fact that some are not sure that the people are sufficiently enlightened and fully qualified [for parliamentary government]. China is a vast country with an immense population of 400 million people; her schools have developed and new knowledge has been pursued in earnest. There must now be countless persons well versed in affairs of the world. To say that we cannot find a few hundred individuals qualified to be members of parliament is unduly to belittle China and her people. . . . Most of the officials now serving in the government have never traveled abroad or even in all the provinces. They have no understanding of matters relating to agriculture, industry, commerce, mining, or to the customs and usages of the people. . . . It is exceedingly strange indeed . . . to entrust

[109] On February 13, 1907, the Pao-huang hui was renamed Chung-hua hsien-cheng hui (China Constitution Society), while K'ang was on his way to the United States from Europe (*Nien-p'u hsü-pien*, p. 59b). Wu Hsien-tzu, *Chung-kuo min-chu hsien-cheng-tang tang-shih*, pp. 47–48, gives "Kuo-min hsien-cheng hui" (National People's Constitution Society) and "Kuo-min hsien-cheng tang" (National People's Constitution Party) as the group's name.

China, an enormous country facing a very dangerous situation, to a few uninformed men. . . . Why should we disparage the ability of the people of the empire, alleging that none among them are qualified to discuss affairs of the country? . . . We, overseas merchants, therefore are of the view that constitutional government must be established before we can save our country, that parliament must be convened before we can have constitutional government, and that to determine what type of constitution we need it is better to ask the people of the whole country to elect several hundred outstanding men to perform the task than to send a handful of high officials who do not even know any foreign language, to go abroad and to study [constitutional government].[110]

It is of course inconceivable that the Chinese people who were unfit for parliamentary government in 1898 suddenly became fit in 1907. This abrupt reversal of K'ang's judgment, however, can be explained. He was now trying hard to ward off revolution by persuading the Ch'ing court to embark promptly China's political future in constitutionalism. It appears that a man who normally spoke only from conviction, was not above indulging in propaganda in his very zeal to advance his cherished cause. At any rate, his argument that China should no longer entrust her political future to a few uninformed officials is not without cogency.

The sorry situation that emerged after the inauguration of the republic confirmed many of K'ang's misgivings regarding premature political change. He soon reverted to his original view and restated it with added emphasis. He said in 1913,[111] for instance, that the republic had not bestowed liberty and equality on the people, simply because they themselves did not deserve these blessings of democracy, which could be enjoyed only when each citizen conducted himself as befitted a perfect gentleman (*shih-chün-tzu*). On the other hand, when a people unworthy of democracy degenerated into a mob, then

what is called popular sovereignty would merely serve as instrumentality of oppression in the hands of mobocrats, . . . what is called equality would spell the utter disruption of social and moral order, and what is called liberty would give rise to profligacy and shamelessness.

This sounds more like an angry denunciation of the republic than a calm analysis of its problems. Nevertheless, it reflected K'ang's basic

---

[110] "Hai-wai Ya Mei Ou Fei Ao wu chou erh-pai pu Chung-hua hsien-cheng hui ch'iao-min kung-shang ch'ing-yüan shu," *Pu-jen*, no. 4 (May 1913), *i-lin*, pp. 3–4.
[111] "Wen wu ssu-wan-wan kuo-min te min-ch'üan p'ing-teng tzu-yu hu," p. 3.

conviction, that forced, premature change must necessarily result in disaster.[112]

To resume our account of K'ang's antirevolution campaign: K'ang sought to strengthen his case for constitutional monarchy by arguing that it was a mistake to overthrow the Manchu role, thereby depriving China of the opportunity to make a smooth transition from autocracy to preliminary democracy. In addition to the arguments set forth in 1911 in essay 10 of his *Chiu wang lun* (cited in note 106), he now contended also that the only valid distinction between "Chinese" and "barbarian" was on cultural and not on racial grounds. The Manchus in having honored and maintained China's tradition, had not "undone" China and therefore should not be spurned as aliens. Fratricidal struggle between Chinese and Manchus, as the revolutionists advocated, would surely invite conquest by Westerners who could hardly be expected to respect China's cultural heritage. China would then be really lost.[113]

In the last years of the dynasty K'ang also undertook to convince the Manchus that it was in their own interest to dissolve the line of segregation between the Chinese and themselves. The emperor, he said, should take a Chinese name, following the example of Toba Hung, Emperor Hsiao-wen-ti of the North Wei dynasty, who, among other measures of frank Sinification, adopted a Chinese surname in A.D. 495.[114] K'ang also suggested that the emperor change the official appellation of China from "Ch'ing-kuo" to "Chung-hua" in diplomatic communications. The Manchus as well as the Chinese would benefit, if they forgot their "racial" differences and cooperated in ridding the

---

[112] Commenting on the 1917 Russian Revolution, K'ang wrote: "Lenin and his followers in the party have put into practice the Socialist doctrine of equality of property (*she-hui chün-ch'an i*). . . . This is the lofty ideal of the Great Community (*Ta-t'ung*) which cannot be realized today." *Kung-lo p'ing-i, chüan* 3, *Pu-jen*, nos. 9 and 10 (1917), p. 5. T. Pokora, in his review of S. L. Tikhvinsky's book on the 1898 reform, p. 144, wrongly translated the last sentence of the passage quoted here as "This is the mighty ideal of the Great Unity which is realizable today in this way."

[113] "Chün yü kuo pu-hsiang-kan . . . lun," pp. 30–33. K'ang's arguments are summarized in Hsiao, *Chung-kuo cheng-chih ssu-hsiang shih*, pp. 701–2. According to Masaru Ikei, "Japan's Response to the Chinese Revolution," pp. 217–24, foreign governments, including those of Japan, England, Russia, and the United States, viewed the Chinese situation differently from the standpoints of their diverse national interests, but they tended to agree on one point, that constitutional monarchy was more suitable to China at the time than republicanism. They all refrained from intervention.

[114] Wei Shou, *Wei shu, chüan* 7, pt. 2, p. 11a.

country of the unbearable burden of autocracy.[115] Under constitutional monarchy (the first fruit of political modernization) there should be no reason on the part of the Chinese to oust or destroy the Manchus, as they far outnumbered the latter.[116] There was, in short, no need for "nationalist revolution."

This somewhat diffusive presentation of K'ang's case for constitutional monarchy, I hope, serves to make clear the real objective of the political aspect of the 1898 reform movement. His gradualist approach to the problem of modernization, his rejection of instant democracy through revolution, should not obscure the fact that his insistence on constitutional monarchy was meant to be only an initial step toward radical democratization. Constitutional monarchy, in other words, was not to be an alternative to democracy; it was to be merely China's first installment of democracy. As K'ang himself remarked in 1911, "To propose the adoption of a constitution is to propose a great revolution, a revolution which will put an end to a system in which the ruler possesses the state."[117] This, I take it, constituted the most important political implication of the 1898 reform movement.

K'ANG YU-WEI AND SUN YAT-SEN: POINTS OF CONTACT

It may be said, then, that the constitutionalist and the revolutionists shared an essentially identical goal, namely, the democratic transformation of China, although they chose different ways to achieve it, the former preferring peaceful, orderly progression to the latter's violent, cataclysmic change.[118] Conceivably, it was this identity of goal that

[115] "Ch'ing chün min ho chih Man Han pu fen che," in Chien, *Wu-hsü*, 2: 239–40. Tikhvinsky, *Dvizhenie za reformy*, p. 200, surmises that K'ang being "a capitalist thinker of China" was interested in struggling against the Chinese peasantry and therefore could not be hostile to the Manchu court as it, too, had the same interests, i.e., those of the landowner. This is one of the instances of Tikhvinsky's facile application of the Marxist formulas to interpret Chinese history. In this case, it makes little sense.

[116] Liang, *Nan-hai hsien-sheng chuan*, p. 85.

[117] "Hsin shih-chieh cheng kuo wei kung-yu . . . shuo," p. 29. Joe Chou Huang, "The Political Theories of K'ang Liang School and Their Application to the Reform Movement in China, 1895–1911," gives Liang credit for advancing the movement to its "second stage," while K'ang persisted in promoting "the cause of political and institutional reforms." Apparently, the author does not recognize the true significance of K'ang's "political reform."

[118] K'ang warned against the threat of revolution in 1898. "Chin-ch'eng *Fa-kuo ko-ming-chi* hsü," in Chien, *Wu-hsü*, 3: 7–10. Cf. Tikhvinsky, *Dvizhenie za reformy*, pp. 6–7: "The practical measures envisaged by K'ang Yu-wei and his followers included restriction of the Manchu rule, which was to be achieved by peaceful means, with a view to preventing a revolutionary outburst."

led some well-meaning people to try to persuade K'ang and his associates to cooperate with Sun Yat-sen and his group; and it was the difference in approach between them (among other factors) that rendered
collaboration impossible.[119]

A closer look reveals that similarities existed even in their approaches.
As already mentioned, K'ang attached great importance to local self-
rule as an indispensable premilinary step in the evolvement of democratic government. It is well known that Sun, too, held the view that
local self-government was the foundation of democracy.[120] On a number
of occasions in 1916, for instance, Sun repeated, unknowingly, some of
K'ang's ideas which he advanced nearly a decade earlier, that "the
root of political order lies in local self-government," that "local self-
government is the foundation stone of the state," and that census,
roads, schools, etc., were the proper concerns of local self-government.[121] He also echoed K'ang's thought with little variation, when in
1920 he specified the steps required in developing local government in
China.[122] When in the spring of 1924 Sun outlined the "General Principles" which were to guide China's political upbuilding, he again indicated that local self-government, with the *hsien* as the basic unit, was
to serve to effect the transition from "military" to "constitutional government."[123] And, faintly reminding one of K'ang's 1898 proposals,[124]
was Sun's directive that

> during the period of political tutelage (*hsün cheng*) the government shall
> send personnel that have been trained and found qualified after examina-
> tion, to the various districts (*hsien*) to assist the people to make preparations
> for self-rule.[125]

[119] Miyazaki, *Sanjūsan-nen no yume*, p. 146. Inukai Tsuyoshi also made unsuccessful
attempts. See Washio Yoshinao, *Inukai Mokudō den*, 2: 626–27. Chang P'eng-yüan,
Liang Ch'i-ch'ao yü Ch'ing-chi ko-ming, p. 131, explains that K'ang and Sun could not
cooperate because they despised each other, the former considering the latter un-
couth, while the latter regarded the former as pedantic. On pp. 207–21, he summarizes the main arguments between the *Min pao* (organ of revolutionists) and the *Hsin-
min ts'ung-pao* (organ of the constitutionalists). Li Shou-k'ung, "Kuang-hsü wu-hsü
ch'ien-hou ko-ming pao-huang liang p'ai chih kuan-hsi," pp. 10–15, 52–56, is useful.
[120] Chang Ch'i-yün, *San-min chu-i kai-lun* (Taipei, 1950), pp. 46–47.
[121] *Kuo-fu ch'üan-chi*, 3: 40–41, 140, 144, 149–50.
[122] "Ti-fang tzu-chih k'ai-shih shih-hsing fa," 6: 160–65.
[123] "Kuo-min cheng-fu chien-kuo ta-kang," 2: 366–69.
[124] Chien, *Wu-hsü*, 2: 202.
[125] Article 8 of the document referred to in note 123, pp. 366–67. Some Western
thinkers also pointed to the "educative" function of local self-government. E.g.,
Alexis de Tocqueville, *Democracy in America*, trans. Henry Reeve (London: Oxford
University Press, 1952), p. 57: "Town meetings are to liberty what primary schools

Another and more significant similarity may be noted. Both recognized the fact that the Chinese people stood in need of guidance or leadership in getting themselves ready for democratic government, although occasionally they spoke as if they thought otherwise. K'ang's overestimation of the political capacity of the Chinese has already been mentioned. For tactical reasons Sun, too, chose to be overgenerous in his assessment. Thus in the fall of 1898 in a conversation with Miyazaki and another Japanese friend, Sun claimed that the Chinese were indeed ready for democracy. As he told them,

> Some people say that republicanism does not suit China. This view stems from lack of understanding of the true situation. Democratic spirit underlay the government of our country's golden age and is the legacy of our ancient sages. . . . The government of the Three Dynasties operated on democratic principles. . . . Even now people in remote hamlets and inaccessible places, who have not been deeply contaminated by the vices of the Manchus . . . are all capable of self-rule.[126]

Later, however, when Sun was not concerned so much with justifying revolution (or arousing revolutionary zeal) as with planning revolutionary action, he was far less sanguine and, somewhat like K'ang, predicated a transitional stage between the end of autocracy and the emergence of democracy, during which stage the people were to be taught the theory and practice of democratic government.

One of Sun's earliest formulations of the concept of political transition under elite leadership appeared in 1905. In an article in *Min pao*, Wang Ching-wei quoted Sun at length:

> The aim of revolution is to institute popular sovereignty. But during the progress of the revolution military power must have precedence. . . . In my view, the key to the transition from military [power] to popular sovereignty lies in defining, at the very beginning of revolution, the precise relationship between the two, . . . so that they do not infringe upon but

---

are to science; they teach men how to use and how to enjoy it. A nation may establish a free government, but without the spirit of municipal institutions it cannot have the spirit of liberty." James Bryce, *Modern Democracies*, 1: 131: "The best school of democracy, and the best guarantee for its success, is the practice of local self government." Harold J. Laski, *A Grammar of Politics* (New Haven: Yale University Press, 1931), p. 413: "Local government . . . is educative in perhaps a higher degree, at least contingently, than any other part of government."

[126] "Chung-kuo pi hsien ko-ming erh-hou neng ta kung-ho chu-i," 4: 451–52. Sun arrived at Yokohama from Canada on Aug. 2, 1897, when Miyazaki Torazō and Hirayama Shū met him. In October the two men introduced Liang Ch'i-ch'ao to Sun, in an unsuccessful effort to make them cooperate.

rather support each other. . . . When the revolution draws to a successful close, military power will dissolve itself, giving place to popular sovereignty. The instrument that defines that relationship is a provisional constitution (*yüeh fa*).[127]

Obviously, the "military power" that was to put an end to autocracy was the counterpart of the authority of the "constitutional monarch" with which K'ang hoped to bring about the same result. The difference between the two schemes lies chiefly in the mode of effecting the change: the revolutionary as opposed to the gradualist, the violent as opposed to the peaceful. Wang then continued on with Sun's views:

At the start of the revolution a military government is to be set up, which exercises both military and political power. As soon as a *hsien* comes under its control, it defines all the basic rights and obligations of itself and of the people. It institutes a local government by order and appoints an official to conduct that government. The people institutes a local assembly (*ti-fang i-hui*) which is not a full-fledged parliament as it obtains in a democratic country, but which has the sole important function of chaperoning the military government.

When the above procedure was completed in each and every *hsien* of the eighteen provinces, a "provisional constitution" for the entire country would be in force and serve to insure smooth transition to full democracy. Sun explained:

As the people of the country have applied themselves to local self-government since the beginning of the revolution and have thus trained their minds and habits for a long time, they by now have the qualifications that pertain to the citizens of a democratic state. Then, [finally,] when a constitution is enacted on the basis of the provisional constitution, constitutional government under popular sovereignty will have an absolutely secure foundation.

It hardly requires pointing out that Sun's projected government under a provisional constitution was the rough equivalent of K'ang's constitutional monarchy, serving essentially the same prelusive function.

The notion of elite leadership, vaguely implied here, was made explicit later by Sun. One of the clearest statements of it came out on July 17, 1916, in a speech before members of the Chinese parliament:

In order to realize [democratic government in China] men of foresight

[127] Wang Ching-wei, "Min-tsu ti kuo-min," pp. 20–22.

and prevision (*hsien-chih hsien-chüeh*) must assume their responsibility. . . . Previously, I had said that we should serve as the people's preceptors, instructing them in the value of popular sovereignty. Now I invite you gentlemen all to be their regents and guardians so that popular sovereignty will have a firm foundation. . . . If our conscience is clear, then even if we deal [with the people] with a somewhat heavy hand (*yen-li shou-tuan*), we would be only performing our duty as their regents and guardians.[128]

This of course is Sun's celebrated concept of "political tutelage." He elaborated on this notion two years later in one of his major works. Precisely because the Chinese people lacked knowledge and experience of democratic government, he wrote, they should be taught, even as children were taught by their teachers in school. He continued:

> The people of China have today just entered into the democratic political order. It is proper that there is a revolutionary government with foresight and prevision to tutor them. This is why the period of political tutelage constitutes an indispensable transition between autocracy and democracy.[129]

The reason for Sun's insistence on elite leadership is not far to seek. Like K'ang and the constitutionalists, he and his followers were aware of the fact that the Chinese people being politically apathetic knew nothing about democracy and lent no support to any movement of political change, be it reform or revolution, and had to depend on a small segment of the elite for "enlightenment."[130]

Understandably, Sun continued to insist on elite leadership in the last years of his life. He said in 1924, for instance, that many blamed the Provisional Constitution[131] for the failure of republicanism in China. The 1911 revolution, they rightly pointed out, had made China "a republic in name" only and had brought upon her ever deepening

---

[128] "Ti-fang tzu-chih wei chien-kuo chih ch'u-shih," 4: 143–44. "Preceptor" is translation for "Shu-sun T'ung" in the original, "regents and guardians" for "I Yin Chou-kung" and "performing our duty as their regents and guardians" for "I Yin chih fang T'ai-chia" (banishment of T'ai-chia, youthful ruler of the Shang dynasty, by I Yin, the regent). For Shu-sun T'ung, who taught Emperor Kao-tsu of the Han dynasty some of the techniques of government, see his biography in Ssu-ma Ch'ien, *Shih-chi, chüan* 33; and for I Yin, who put T'ai-chia on the throne and disciplined him for misrule, ibid., *chüan* 3.

[129] "Sun Wen hsüeh-shuo," 2: 59–60.

[130] See, e.g., Ssu Huang [Ch'en T'ien-hua], "Lun Chung-kuo i kai-ch'uang kung-ho cheng-t'i," p. 49.

[131] P'an Shu-fan, *Chung-hua min-kuo hsien-fa shih*, pp. 11–29, gives an account of this document.

crises. They were mistaken, however, in thinking that the remedy lay in making a new constitution. They did not see that the root of the trouble lay in the fact that "we had skipped the stages of military government and political tutelage and had gone on directly into the constitutional stage." Sun then offered the "General Principles of Political Reconstruction" ("Chien-kuo ta-kang") to guide his party, in which he restated his theory of the three stages (Article 5) and specified his plan for democratic upbuilding by means of local self-rule (Articles 8–18).[132]

To Westerners accustomed to the democratic way of looking at things, the thought that democracy (whether in the form of constitutional monarchy or constitutional republic) could be reached through the intermediary of "enlightened autocracy"[133] or "political tutelage" may sound strange. They sometimes tend to forget that the modern Western democratic tradition is a product of slow and sometimes troubled evolution, and to overlook the fact that stagnating for centuries under autocratic rule, China, a politically "underdeveloped country," had to build democratic habits and institutions from scratch.[134] The handful of men in China who knew something about Western political history and saw the urgent need for political modernization in their own country (such as K'ang and Sun), could not afford to wait for or count on the leisurely process of evolution. Unavoidably, they faced a dilemma: to institute "people's rule" among a people who had neither the desire nor the capacity to rule themselves. They found only one solution to this "Chinese puzzle"—training the people for democracy by a resolute elite. Their seemingly strange proposal is therefore historically understandable.

Indeed, their solution seems to have relevance even in mid-twentieth-century situations in the "developing" nations of Asia and Africa. A

---

[132] "Chih-ting Chien-kuo ta-kang hsüan-yen," *Chien-kuo fang-lüeh*, p. 363.

[133] "Enlightened autocracy" was Liang Ch'i-ch'ao's phrase. See his "Kai-ming chuan-chih lun," *Hsin-min ts'ung-pao*, no. 74 (February 1906), p. 11; reprinted in *Yin-ping-shih ho-chi, wen-chi* 17, p. 39. This article was Liang's response to Ssu Huang [Ch'en T'ien-hua], cited in note 130, above. See *Hsin-min ts'ung-pao*, no. 73, p. 1 (*Yin-ping-shih ho-chi, wen-chi* 17, p. 13). Chang, *Liang Ch'i-ch'ao yü Ch'ing-chi ko-ming*, pp. 232–41, notes similarities between Liang's notion of "enlightened autocracy" and Sun's ideas of "provisional constitution" and "political tutelage."

[134] Houn, *Central Government of China*, pp. 161–63, reiterates the obvious truth that revolution and a democratic constitution alone did not guarantee democratic government. "What really prevented China from building up a democratic government was the fact that the Chinese people never had any actual experience in controlling government, nor had they even tried to study the method of achieving that result."

British writer has recently suggested that one of the main tasks of these countries is "to produce a new elite of reformers and innovators, ready and willing to assume the hardships and risks of modernization," and that, as such a group "will find it impossible to carry out all these tasks [of reform] in a liberal democracy," they will "organize an authoritarian (if not totalitarian) state," and be prepared "to jolt the people out of their ruts."[135] They will, in other words, resort to the equivalents of "enlightened autocracy" or "political tutelage" to achieve modernization. An American political scientist in his analysis of what he calls the "predemocratic" modernizing societies of Asia, Africa, and Latin America, points in the same general direction. He underscores "the need for an examination of the role of predemocratic forms of government" in which uses are made of "predemocratic and nondemocratic institutions."[136] Conditions in China that confronted K'ang and Sun differed widely of course from those prevailing in contemporary modernizing countries. One may still justifiably regard the proposals of these two men as intelligible formulas for political modernization by means of predemocratic institutions.

Even the notion of "enlightened autocracy" by which K'ang and his group set store, makes sense in the contemporary scene. It has been noted that working instances of "modernizing autocracy" are found in Thailand, Morocco, and Ethiopia, where "authority remains at the top, although in fact, it may be shared through a variety of instrumentalities such as councils, parliaments, party groups, and so on." There is an advantage to such an arrangement: "well-institutionalized modernizing autocracies can experiment with goals without paying the penalty of immediate instability."[137] K'ang would have agreed heartily.

Unfortunately, a sensible formula in itself carries no warranty of success. Feasibility of political modernization by means of predemocratic institutions is conditioned by the availability of a modernizing elite.[138] K'ang had counted on the Ch'ing emperor and discerning scholar-officials to administer his prescription for curing China's political malady. But he was destined to be disappointed. Those whom he had won over to his cause were in no position to apply his ideas, whereas those in power refused to accept them. In a sense the Manchus (including the empress dowager) were not entirely to blame. For K'ang's pro-

---

[135] I. R. Sinai, *The Challenge of Modernization*, pp. 217–19.
[136] David E. Apter, *The Politics of Modernization*, p. 3.
[137] Ibid., pp. 37, 360, 397, and 402–5.
[138] Ibid., pp. 138–44.

posals amounted to nothing short of eventually ending Manchu domina-
tion in China.[139] To implement them was tantamount to committing
political suicide; to ask the Manchus to give up autocracy was like, as
a Chinese proverb goes, "to negotiate with a tiger for his hide."

The unwillingness of China's ruling elite, the Manchus in particular,
to modernize by peaceful measures became so patent that arguments
for revolution gained force. Even Liang Ch'i-ch'ao became disillusioned
and impatient. In a letter to K'ang written late in 1902 he joined opponents of constitutionalism in predicating the impossibility of political
innovation without revolution. Many of the overseas members of
K'ang's "party" had begun openly to revile the Manchus.[140]

Revolution in fact came. But it put an end to autocracy without making China fit for democracy. It appears that K'ang failed to give constitutional monarchy to China partly because the monarch that was to
effectuate it proved to be willing but unable, and that Sun did not give
democracy to China because he did not command enough "men of
foresight and prevision" to complete the task of political tutelage. Circumstances were far from favorable. For years his party had to battle
hostile forces; it faced a generally discouraging international situation.
After the establishment of the National Government in Nanking it had
to devote more attention to consolidating its control over the country
than to coaching the people in *min-ch'üan*. From 1898 to 1948 one unhappy fact of Chinese political life stood unchanged: the bulk of the
people were still not ready for democracy. Ch'en Tu-hsiu in his rebuttal
of K'ang's criticisms of the republic, acknowledged this fact and cast
doubt on the feasibility of achieving democracy by way either of republicanism or constitutionalism. He wrote in 1918:

> If the qualifications of the people fall short of those required for national
> survival, it is as mistaken to wish to accomplish preservation by means of
> [constitutional monarchy] as by means of republic. Considering the quali-

---

[139] Tikhvinsky, *Dvizhenie za reformy*, p. 5: "It would be extremely naïve to expect
that having read the emperor's [reform] decrees, the Manchus will readily renounce
their privileges and titles." Cf. Mu Fu-sheng, *The Wilting of the Hundred Flowers*, p.
111, where it is said that "nationalism" and nearsightedness on the part of the Manchus stood in the way of reform.

[140] Ting, *Liang Jen-kung hsien-sheng nien-p'u ch'ang-pien ch'u-kao*, p. 157. Liang continued to favor revolution as may be gathered from his letter to Hsü Ch'in (ibid., pp.
181–82). But Liang soon reverted to constitutionalism. See his letter to Chiang Kuan-
yün [Chiang Chih-yu], July, 1903, in ibid., p. 186. See also Liang, *Ch'ing-tai hsüeh-shu
kai-lun*, p. 142, and Liang, *Intellectual Trends in the Ch'ing Period*, trans. Immanuel C. Y.
Hsü, p. 102, in which the foregoing is translated (cited hereafter as Hsü, *Intellectual
Trends in the Ch'ing Period*).

fication of [the people of] our country, it is indeed doubtful that a democratic republic can be attained. But can one be sure that their qualifications are really sufficient for the implementation of a republic under a titular king or a constitutional monarchy?[141]

Ch'en soon lost faith in "Mr. Democracy" and "Mr. Science" (the two main pillars of modern Western civilization in his way of thinking) and sought "truth" in Marxism. The stage, in fact, was set for the Communist victory. Disunity, warlordism, economic difficulties, and foreign invasion,[142] in addition to the people's political backwardness, provided ample opportunity for Mao Tse-tung. Despair and anxiety consequent upon the fruitless West-inspired endeavors at modernization suggested to some young intellectuals the likelihood that communism was a workable alternative (if not exactly "the only solution"), worth trying.[143] As Mao had said, after having "looked to the West for truth" in vain, the time had come to look to Soviet Russia for enlightenment.[144]

It is not our task here to identify the factors and circumstances that led to Mao's phenomenal rise. But it may perhaps be pertinent to suggest that the Chinese people, in their very political inertness, had contributed to it. It might be said, indeed, that Mao had shrewdly made use of that characteristic to his advantage. Instead of trying to work a radical change in the people as a preparation for political transformation, as K'ang and Sun each in his own way had done, Mao simply used them as "the material force of history"—as a "natural source of energy"—to attain his immediate objective,[145] namely, the establishment of "New Democracy," euphemism for totalitarian dictatorship. Dictatorship, like autocracy, thrives on that popular indifference and submissiveness that constitute a stumbling block to democratization.

A Soviet writer in his book on the 1898 reform labeled as "idealistic" the view that the masses were incapable of conscious, organized activities and had to leave the work of history-making to the elite.[146] Compared with Mao, K'ang was indeed "unrealistic" in believing the possibility of leading, step by step, a people long habituated to autocratic

---

[141] Ch'en Tu-hsiu, "Po K'ang Yu-wei *Kung-ho p'ing-i*," p. 192.

[142] Cf. Chalmers A. Johnson, *Peasant Nationalism and Communist Power* (Stanford: Stanford University Press, 1962), passim.

[143] Mu, *Wilting of the Hundred Flowers*, p. 113.

[144] "On the People's Democratic Dictatorship," *Selected Works*, 4 (Peking, 1961): 412–13.

[145] Cf. Suzanne Pepper, "Rural Government in Communist China: The Party-State Relationship at the Local Level," pp. 33–34.

[146] Tikhvinsky, *Dvizhenie za reformy*, p. 219.

rule onto the path of democracy. However, K'ang was hardly a pedantic fool. He was, in all probability, the first of his generation to see that political backwardness was China's crucial problem and that no modernization could be effected without radical political change. He was among the very few, if not actually the first, of the time to realize that democratic government in the broad sense was the basis of the modern West's strength. Accordingly, the most important of his 1898 proposals of political reform aimed not merely at reshaping the administrative apparatus but also at conditioning the people for their eventual participation in the political process. He hoped, in short, to evolve democratic institutions both from the top down and from the bottom up. He rejected revolution as a reliable method of change, but the objective he envisaged was in truth nothing short of revolutionary—the liquidation of the age-old autocracy. Liang Ch'i-ch'ao had a glimpse of the political import of the 1898 reform movement when he wrote in 1901:

> Focusing its attention on the common interests of the people, it sought to transform China's political system by cultivating talented men of the country and by adopting Western ideas to solve her problems.[147]

"Emperor Protection" and Constitutional Monarchy, 1899–1910

K'ang's opposition to the 1911 revolution and the 1912 republic, and his involvement in the 1917 restoration have been widely condemned as activities that were reactionary, if not also treasonable. However, a careful examination of what he said and did in the decade following 1898 suggests a different verdict. In continuing to espouse the cause of constitutional monarchy, in conducting a sustained compaign against a form of government that in his view was ill suited to the needs of China at the time, and in contriving ways and means to ameliorate the disheartening situation that prevailed since 1912, he was as much a reformer as he had been in 1898, although the object of his reform had changed from the faltering autocracy to the floundering republic.

It appears that between 1899 and 1925, with changes in the historical situation, K'ang shifted his position several times, though he held steadfast to his central objective, namely, the political modernization of China by progressive democratization of her institutions. First, between 1899 and 1905, his major concern was the restoration of the Kuang-hsü emperor to power, in whom he still lodged his hope of realizing a constitutional monarchy in China. Then, between 1906 and

---

[147] *Nan-hai K'ang hsien-sheng chuan*, p. 64.

1910, he centered his efforts on translating into reality the Ch'ing court's professed willingness to adopt a constitution and, at the same time, to forestall revolution. When the revolution and the republic became *faits accomplis* in 1911–12, he set about to expose the shortcomings of the new regime and to propose ways to render it more viable. Finally, realizing that all his endeavor had been in vain, he joined others in a counterrevolutionary movement that culminated in the fiasco of the 1917 monarchical restoration, and continued his bootless attempt underground into the 1920s.

K'ang's initial resolve to restore the emperor to power led to the formation of the Pao-huang hui (Emperor Protection Society). After a brief stay in Japan and Canada and a short visit to England, K'ang returned to Canada in the spring of 1899. More successful for the moment than Sun Yat-sen in enlisting the support of overseas Chinese,[148] he persuaded a number of what he called "righteous persons" to form the Pao-shang hui (Merchant Protection Society) early in July, in Victoria, B. C. Arguing that "protecting the emperor" from the empress dowager's "plot to endanger him" was more urgent and crucial than protecting the merchants, he had the name of the group readily changed to Pao-huang hui. By the spring of 1903 branch societies were said to exist in many major cities in Canada, the United States (including Seattle), and Japan, with most of the members of the Chinese communities joining.[149] The Japan branch in Yokohama under Liang Ch'i-ch'ao's immediate leadership conducted an intensive campaign of indoctrination and propaganda, against first the conservatives in China and then the revolutionists abroad, through school education and periodical journalism.[150]

It is difficult to see how K'ang and his overseas friends could bring about any practical results beyond keeping their cause alive and getting ready for action when opportunity came. They did not have to wait

[148] Li Chien-nung, *Political History of China*, p. 179.

[149] K'ang T'ung-pi, *Nan-hai K'ang hsien-sheng tzu-pien nien-p'u pu-i*, p. 2b (hereafter, *Nien-p'u pu-i*); K'ang Tung-pi, *Nien-p'u hsü-pien*, p. 4b; Wu, *Chung-kuo min-chu hsien-cheng-tang tang-shih*, pp. 24–27; Yang, "K'ang Liang nien-p'u kao-pen", 2: 2a–b; and Ting, *Liang Jen-kung hsien-sheng nien-p'u ch'ang-pien ch'u-kao*, p. 88.

[150] Wu, *Chung-kuo min-chu hsien-cheng-tang tang-shih*, pp. 29–30. The Society claimed to have founded three schools in Japan: the Ta-t'ung hsüeh-hsiao (Yokohama), T'ung-wen hsüeh-hsiao (Kobe), and Kao-teng ta-t'ung hsüeh-hsiao (Tokyo), all in 1899. Members of the Society carried on a sustained campaign against both conservatism and revolutionism, mainly through the *Ch'ing-i pao* (1898–1901) and the *Hsin-min ts'ung-pao* (1902–5).

long. The "Boxer catastrophe" of 1900[151] persuaded both the emperor protectors and the revolutionists that the time had arrived for direct action.[152] From K'ang's viewpoint, to overthrow the empress dowager by taking advantage of the turbulent situation was not only strategically desirable but morally necessary. Early in the previous year, at the recommendation of Hsü T'ung and other arch enemies of reform, the empress dowager decided to depose the emperor and stopped short of so doing because of strong remonstration from various quarters.[153]

[151] The uprising broke out in Peking in the spring of 1900; by June the Boxers had overrun all Chihli province. The Ch'ing court fled the capital in July. Chester C. Tan, [T'an Ch'un-lin], *The Boxer Catastrophe* (New York: Columbia University Press, 1955), remains the most extensive study. Li, *Political History of China*, pp. 173–83, gives a brief account. Teng and Fairbank, *China's Response to the West*, chap. 19, give a few important documents. Huang Ta-shou, *Chung-kuo chin-tai shih*, vol. 3, chaps. 15–16, furnishes some useful details.

[152] Sun Yat-sen wrote to Sir Henry Arthur Blake, Governor of Hong Kong, to solicit support for revolution (*Kuo-fu ch'üan-chi*, 5: 17–19). Rivalry and friction inevitably developed between the revolutionists and constitutionalists. Ting, *Liang Jen-kung hsien-sheng* . . . , p. 103, indicates: "Chung-shan [i.e., Sun] is daily making preparations [for action]; if we do not plan quickly and if Kwangtung falls into his hands, where then shall we make our start?" Tse Tsan Tai [Hsieh Tsan-t'ai], *The Chinese Republic: Secret History of the Revolution*, pp. 16, 20, 25, records: "4th November, 1899—I wrote to Kang Yu-wei, severely denouncing his 'Protect the Emperor' (Po Wang Whui) Society." "26th August, 1900—Kang Yu-wei and his followers successfully planned a revolutionary [sic] movement at Ta Tung, in Anhui province, and Hankow, in Hupeh province. Dr. Yung Wing, Ph. D., and his nephew, Yung Sing-kiu, were connected with this movement, and narrowly escaped with their lives." Fung Tzu-yu, *Chung-hua min-kuo k'ai-kuo ch'ien ko-ming shih*, 1: 57, states that T'ang Ts'ai-ch'ang, leader of the Hankow uprising against the empress dowager, began his career as a collaborator (with Liang Ch'i-ch'ao and others) in the modernization program in Hunan province. Upon the collapse of the 1898 reform movement he resolved to overthrow the Manchu regime by force and went to Japan to plan with K'ang and Liang. Pi Yung-nien, his friend and Sun Yat-sen's follower, introduced him to Sun who invited him to help consolidate the revolutionary forces in the provinces south of the Yangtze river. Attracted by the prospect of using the funds of the Pao-huang hui to finance his projected revolt, T'ang thought it "inconvenient to cooperate actively with the Hsing-chung hui." Nevertheless, through the mediation of Pi and Hirayama Shū, an agreement was reached that each group would pursue "a different course of action leading to the same end." Li, *Political History of China*, p. 182, puts the situation thus: "T'ang Ts'ai-ch'ang, in particular, found himself in a difficult situation. Pi Yung-nien tried to enlist him under Sun Yat-sen's banner, while K'ang and Liang were pulling him firmly to their side."

[153] The decree of Feb. 11, 1899, announcing the institution of T'ung-chih emperor's heir apparent, is given in Chu, *Tung-hau hsü-lu*, *chüan* 157, p. 13. Wang Chao, *Fang-chia-yüan tsa-yung chi-shih*, pp. 8–9, suggests that Hsü T'ung and other high officials advised the empress dowager to depose the Kuang-hsü emperor. But as Jung-lu strongly opposed the move, she compromised by instituting an heir apparent for the T'ung-chih emperor. Chang Chien, *Se-weng tzu-ting nien-p'u*, *chüan hsia*, p. 10, credited Liu K'un-i with dissuading the empress dowager from going through with the plan to depose the emperor.

Convinced that the emperor was in danger, K'ang decided to take drastic measures.

Despite extensive preparations that involved practically all the leaders of the society stationed in Singapore (K'ang), Honolulu (Liang), Yokohama, and other places, the 1900 uprising was poorly coordinated.[154] The uprising in Hankow had to be postponed again and again pending the arrival of funds which never came; the plot was uncovered (August 21) by Chang Chih-tung. T'ang Ts'ai-ch'ang and a number of others were summarily executed the next day,[155] marking the tragic end of the undertaking. Meanwhile, Sun Yat-sen's uprising at Hui-chou was also quickly quelled.[156]

It was reported that agreement existed between T'ang Ts'ai-ch'ang and the revolutionists to the effect that the two groups were to move along different paths toward the same goal.[157] But, as a matter of fact, K'ang and Sun envisioned widely different objectives. Whereas the latter aimed at the complete elimination of the Manchu rule, the former intended only to remove the empress dowager and her supporters from positions of power so that the emperor could regain his authority. K'ang made this clear in a number of writings done during the 1900 uprising and immediately after the Hankow debacle. Unless the "immoral empress dowager" was removed by force, he wrote, nothing useful could ever be accomplished. In personally leading the uprising T'ang Ts'ai-ch'ang was rendering service to the emperor; he was not a "bandit" as some newspapers had falsely identified him.[158] In an earlier piece K'ang argued that the net result of the Boxer uprising and the consequent ravaging of Peking by foreign troops might be in a way beneficial to China:

> All the conservatives would be destroyed; the sage emperor would be safe. This could be Heaven's way of laying the foundation of China's modernization and of preparing the ground for the sage emperor's restoration.[159]

[154] Ting, *Liang Jen-kung hsien-sheng* . . . , pp. 101–3, gives details of the preparation and mentions some of the problems encountered.

[155] Fung, *Chung-hua min-kuo k'ai-kuo ch'ien ko-ming shih*, 1: 58–80, relates the story of the uprising from its beginning to end. Ting, *Liang Jen-kung hsien-sheng* . . . , pp. 143–45, gives Liang's letter to K'ang, dated April 17, 1901, indicating the difficulties encountered in raising funds.

[156] Sun Wen, "Tzu-chuan," *Kuo-fu ch'üan-chi*, 1: 36–38. Li, *Political History of China*, pp. 182–83, mentions briefly this incident.

[157] Fung, *Chung-hua min-kuo k'ai-kuo ch'ien ko-ming shih*, p. 57.

[158] Ch'in-wang luan-fei pien", *I-kao, chüan* 1, pp. 19a–21a.

[159] "Ch'üan-fei chih luan wei fu Sheng-chu erh ts'un Chung-kuo shuo." Cf. another piece, "Yü tang-jen lun O pai . . . ", in microfilm, reel 3.

After the fall of Peking in mid-August K'ang felt that it was advisable to make known his views to the foreign powers concerned. In one of the essays written for that purpose he made a sharp distinction between "the pro-emperor party" (*Ti tang*) and "the pro-empress dowager party" (*Hou tang*), a vital distinction that should be recognized by the powers in dealing with post-Boxer China.

> The pro-emperor party is none other than the party of the reformers, whereas the pro-empress dowager party is simply a coterie of wicked men (*tsei tang*). [Members of] the pro-emperor party are well versed in diplomatic matters, loyal to the emperor, friendly to foreign countries, and have a liking for Western civilization. . . . [Members of] the pro-empress dowager party are imperious, stupid, perverse, and violent; ignorant of international law and profoundly resentful of foreigners, they entertain constantly the desire to kill and to expel them all.

The foreign countries, K'ang went on, had now learned the "ugliness" of the pro-empress dowager party. But, if in effecting a post-bellum settlement with China they did not know well enough to support the pro-emperor party, all their efforts would be futile.[160]

K'ang's advice went unheeded. The Ch'ing court returned to Peking in 1902, with the empress dowager in full control. K'ang, however, had not given up the idea of getting rid of her.[161] He now initiated a plot of assassination, with her as the principal target. Large sums of money were spent between 1900 and 1906 by his group to enlist would-be "knights-errant" (*hsieh-shih*). Liang T'ieh-chün, K'ang's trusted friend, was sent to Peking to direct the operation. Nothing ever happened, except that Liang was apprehended and put to death.[162] That

---

[160] "Hsin-tang tsei-tang pien," *I-kao, chüan* 1, pp. 21a–22a. "Ch'a Chung-kuo shih tang pien tang-p'ai shuo," *I-kao, chüan* 1, pp. 17a–18a, in which K'ang expressly identified Prince Ch'ing, Jung-lu, and Li Hung-chang as members of the pro-empress dowager "party," and Chang Chih-tung and Liu K'un-i as men wavering between the two "parties." Another piece on the same theme, written two months after the fall of Peking, is "Ko-kuo chin-jih chih mu-ti", in microfilm, reel 2.

[161] According to K'ang, the empress dowager was sure to bring about China's dismemberment ("Lun Chung-kuo pi fen-ko," in microfilm, reel 1).

[162] Ting, *Liang Jen-kung hsien sheng* . . . , p. 198. Early in the autumn of 1903 Liang Ch'i-ch'ao said in a letter to K'ang that leaders of the "nihilists" (*hsü-wu tang*) carried out assassination missions themselves, and that to rely on hirelings, as K'ang did, would be unwise. Now "Lin, the knight errant" (on whom K'ang depended to execute his assassination plans) spent the money received from K'ang in pursuit of pleasure and made no mention of the mission for which he was hired (ibid., p. 190). Marius B. Jansen, *The Japanese and Sun Yat-sen*, p. 77, paraphrases a passage in Miyazaki (*Sanjūsan-nen no yume*, p. 164) describing K'ang's encounter with Miyazaki in

ended another tragic episode of K'ang's perennial campaign for emperor protection. As one of his followers remarked years later, the 1900 venture was an extremely dangerous one with very little hope of success.[163]

K'ang himself, in all probability, was not unaware of the risk involved. He nevertheless decided to commit his entire organization and all its resources to try to reinstate the emperor, for the simple reason that he saw no possibility of political change unless "the sage ruler" regained his authority. It was a risk worth running. Understandably, therefore, the disaster of 1900 did not dampen K'ang's resolve to "protect the emperor" in order to promote constitutional monarchy. He still regarded the Boxer calamity as a blessing in disguise. In an unpublished and little-known piece written probably late in 1900 or early in 1901, he again sounded a cheering note of optimism, to the effect that with many of the archenemies of reform put to death or dismissed from office and with the government's ancient records destroyed, the backbone of conservatism was broken and the way to reform was finally clear. The empress dowager and some of her servants were still around; but by a strange twist of fate they had, by their very perversity, unwittingly paved the way to reform. K'ang concluded by calling upon fellow reformers to rejoice and to rededicate themselves.[164]

His optimism was not justified by subsequent events. Early in 1901, while still in Sian, the empress dowager issued a decree in the emperor's name paying lip service to reform but at the same time denouncing K'ang's "treasonable" activities.[165] Early next year she was again firmly entrenched in power in Peking, with the emperor serving as her involuntary rubber stamp. Worried by the situation but still hopeful,

---

Hong Kong in 1898, shortly after the *coup*: "He [K'ang] told Miyazaki that the empress dowager was the only obstacle to reform in China, and expressed a desire to eliminate her by hiring some Japanese *sōshi*. Miyazaki regarded this as a reflection on the character of K'ang's followers. One determined patriot was all that was needed; was there not one such among the reformers? Evidently, K'ang took this to heart, for the next day a very nervous young man came to Miyazaki to take a tearful farewell." Miyazaki was perhaps not entirely fair to K'ang's followers. Did not Liang T'ieh-chün go to Peking and lose his life in the attempt to carry out his mission? It should be admitted, however, that physical courage, apparently, was not one of K'ang's virtues.

[163] Wu, *Chung-kuo min-chu hsien-cheng-tang tang-shih*, p. 37.

[164] "Chung-kuo pu-hsin ch'u-chiu lun," *I-kao, chüan* 1, pp. 23a–25a.

[165] Chu, *Tung-hua hsü-lu, chüan* 164, pp. 2b–3b and Shen, *Kuang-hsü cheng-yao, chüan* 26, pp. 28b–29a, give the decree of January 29, 1901 (Kuang-hsü 26th year, 12th month, 10th day). Cameron, *Reform Movement in China*, chaps. 3–8 and Li, *Political History of China*, pp. 194–98, give accounts of the post-Boxer reforms.

K'ang wrote a lengthy memorial in 1903, petitioning the empress dowager, among other things (1) to return the reins of government to the emperor, (2) to condemn Jung-lu and Li Lien-ying to death, and (3) to adopt a constitution and to recognize the people's political rights.[166] It requires no profound analysis to see that the last request represented K'ang's basic aim. These words of his are significant:

> Recently, everyone in the country talks about reform. In one decree after another issued in 1900 and 1901, adoption of Western ways has been consistently urged. As our weakness has been recognized all of us, in high and low stations, have become alarmed. Thus, even people who were previously conservative and strongly opposed reform, now are also compelled to change their minds. But China's basic infirmity cannot be remedied by simply concerning ourselves with such nonessential undertakings as . . . schools, railroads, and mining.

The really crucial task, K'ang said, was the political transformation of China from an autocracy into a constitutional monarchy resting upon the foundation of popular sovereignty (*min-ch'üan*).[167]

Repeating essentially what he had said in the 1890s, K'ang pointed to democratic government (*i min-ch'üan wei kuo*, government by popular sovereignty) as the secret of the amazing strength of modern Western countries. Democracy, he explained, implied the adoption of a constitution, the convening of a popularly elected parliament, and the institution of local self-government. Such an arrangement was far superior to a system in which a few ignorant and selfish individuals controlled the destiny of millions.[168]

K'ang warned the empress dowager that to persist in her old ways was to invite disaster, not only to the empire but to herself also. As the history of China and other countries testified, long-continued misrule brought despots to inevitable ruin. "Popular sovereignty" had become by now an irresistible historic force that no ruler could withstand.[169] The Chinese people were already dissatisfied with her misrule. They had not as yet taken any action simply because they had heard that she had the intention of turning back the reins of government to the emperor "who had risked his own life to save the people and had demonstrated his ability to strengthen the country through reform." The people had waited for an entire year; but she still remained in power.

[166] This document is available in *Wan-mu ts'ao-t'ang i-kao, chüan* 3, pp. 9a–20a.
[167] Ibid., p. 16b.
[168] Ibid., p. 17a.
[169] Ibid., pp. 10a–11a and 17b–18a.

Would they be willing to allow their country to be ruined eventually by Jung-lu and Li Lien-ying, in deference to her wishes?[170]

K'ang's memorial sounded more like an ultimatum than a petition. We have no evidence that it actually reached the empress dowager. Even if it did, it is highly improbable that she would be in a mood to heed K'ang's counsels. It appears that having failed to remove "the immoral empress dowager" by force, he now tried to do so by persuasion!

K'ang soon found it increasingly imperative to campaign against revolutionary republicanism, which was rapidly gaining ground under the leadership of Sun Yat-sen and other young intellectuals. In the summer of the same year in which the Ch'ing court sent five high officials abroad to study political institutions, the revolutionary organization T'ung-meng hui was formed in Tokyo, the avowed aims of which were, among other things, "to expel the Manchus" and "to establish a republic."[171] With the appearance of *Min pao*, the organ of Sun's group, the constitutionalists intensified their propaganda. Liang Ch'i-ch'ao bore the main burden and proved to be the most effective in the war of words between the two camps.[172] K'ang must have also written in defense of his cause, but for reasons yet to be ascertained we find little in his writings done at the time that bear directly on the matter.[173] However, on one occasion at least he voiced his opposition to premature republicanism. People, he wrote in 1905, who had come into contact with the social and political ideas of Europe and America, were dazzled by them and thought mistakenly that these ideas constituted a ready panacea for all of China's ills. "This is why," he complained, "from 1901 onward the tide of revolutionary thought has been threatening to engulf all. 'Liberty' and 'revolution' have become clichés on youngsters' lips."[174]

[170] Ibid., p. 11a.

[171] From the oath administered to the seventy-odd persons, including Sun, Huang Hsing, and Ch'en T'ien-hua, who were present at the founding ceremonies of the organization. Shelley H. Cheng, "The T'ung-meng-hui: Its Organization, Leadership, and Finances, 1905–1912," p. 102.

[172] Yang, "K'ang Liang nien-p'u kao-pen," pt. 2, pp. 36a–b, 42a; Ting, *Liang Jen-kung hsien-sheng . . .* , p. 221.

[173] One possible explanation: during these years he was engaged in writing or rewriting works on Confucianism, on utopia (*Ta-t'ung shu*), and on reforming the bureaucracy (*Kuan-chih i*); in addition he wrote accounts of his travels in Europe (*Ou-chou shih-i kuo yu-chi*) (K'ang T'ung-pi, *Nien-p'u hsü-pien*, pp. 12b–50b and *Nien-p'u pu'i*, pp. 9b–33b).

[174] Author's preface to *Wu-chih chiu-kuo lun*. This essay is now also available in *Shih-chieh p'ing-lun* (The World Review), 10th year, nos. 18 and 19 (Feb. 16 and Mar. 10, 1963), pp. 6–15, with an introduction by Hsü Kao-yüan.

K'ang interpreted the death of Jung-lu (April 11, 1903) as the end of the necessity to "protect" the emperor. He promptly left India for southeast Asian countries to engage himself in active campaigns for the constitutional movement.[175] The Ch'ing court issued a decree (August 31, 1906) saying in part that as various countries achieved power and wealth because of constitutional government, China should now follow their example. But as the people did not as yet possess "wisdom and knowledge," measures must be taken "to acquaint the gentry and common people with affairs of the state, thus to lay the foundation of constitutional government."[176] K'ang took this decree as a signal for action. After deliberating with his associates he announced (October 10, 1906) that the Pao-huang hui was to be known as Kuo-min hsien-cheng hui (National Constitutional Society) as of the first day of the *ting-wei* year (February 13, 1907),[177] thus formally inaugurating a new phase of his constitutional movement.

K'ang's basic tenets were reaffirmed in the constitution of the society (known also as The Constitutional Party). "The Party," so reads the first article, "has for its resolute aim the transformation of China into a constitutional state."[178] K'ang's aspirations were further revealed in a four-quatrain anthem of the society, written at the request of its members residing in the United States, which may be rendered in part as follows:

With talents and rights Heaven endows the people he creates,
To enable them to support and defend themselves so that their tribe
    survives.

[175] K'ang T'ung-pi, *Nien-p'u hsü-pien*, p. 33b and *Nien-p'u pu-i*, p. 24a. K'ang T'ung-pi is obviously mistaken in suggesting that K'ang had at that time changed the name of the Pao-huang hui to "Hsien-cheng hui"; the change, as we shall see, came a little later.

[176] The text is given in Chu, *Tung-hua hsü-lu*, *chüan* 202, pp. 2b–3a.

[177] Wu, *Chung-kuo min-chu hsien-cheng-tang tang-shih*, pp. 46–48. According to Wu, K'ang wrote the announcement. Cf. Ting, *Liang Jen-kung hsien-sheng . . .* , pp. 215–18 and Wu, *Chung-kuo min-chu . . .* , p. 48, for the different names proposed.

[178] "Hsien-cheng-tang chang-ch'eng," a short document of six chapters (eighteen articles) is available in microfilm, reel 3. K'ang formulated (Art. 2) a twelve-point platform that included "allocation of political powers," "promotion of local self-government" and "emphasis on political education." Liang Ch'i-ch'ao, arguing that K'ang was too much of a *persona non grata* to lead the constitutional movement, organized a party of his own, the Cheng-wen she (Political Information Club), which held its inaugural meeting in Tokyo, Oct. 17, 1907. Its constitution, written by Liang, echoed the basic ideas espoused by K'ang. A decree of Aug. 13, 1908, interdicted Liang's organization (Ting, *Liang Jen-kuang hsien-sheng . . .* , pp. 215–20, 284–88; Wu, *Chuang-kuo min-chu . . .* , pp. 50–55; and Li, *Political History of China*, pp. 216–18.

To honor the many's opinion is the way of social union,
And when private interests yield to public good, constitutional govern-
    ment thrives.
Sages, seeking to help the people, rid them of sufferings and to them
    happiness give:
But the sovereign's love for the people is poor substitute for their self-rule,
And the loving sagacity of the one matches not the insights of the many
    combined.
To follow their own dictates is unerring justice to achieve.[179]

With a view to quickening the process of political transformation,
K'ang and his associates sought by various means to mobilize public
opinion, both in China and among overseas Chinese, and to put pressure on the Ch'ing court.[180] K'ang himself wrote in 1907 a long petition
for overseas members of the society, in which he demanded among
other things that parliament be immediately convened to give reality
to constitutional government, that the "distinction" between Manchu
and Chinese be abolished, and that China be known as "Chung-hua
kuo" instead of "Ch'ing kuo."[181]

He began by pointing to the perilous situation that still confronted
China about which overseas Chinese were deeply concerned. The
measures of reform announced or being implemented since 1901 hardly
met the requirements of the situation. As he bluntly observed,

Recently, the Court has effected some modest reforms which of course
represent an important departure from the conservatism of the past. And
yet people grow increasingly anxious and perplexed. This is because a
great undertaking [such as reform] can be accomplished only on the basis
of honest intention, not of empty promise. . . . It has now been repeatedly
said that affairs of the state will be amenable to public opinion. . . . But
the government has been applying measures that are more repressive than

---

[179] "Chung-hua ti-kuo hsien-cheng-hui ko," *Nan-hai hsien-sheng shih-chi*, Liang calligraphy ed., *chüan* 1, pp. 9a–b.

[180] The activities were carried on mostly by members of Liang's Political Information Club, some of whom went back to China to agitate for constitutional government
and to make plans for a training school and a newspaper in central China. The Club's
headquarters were moved from Tokyo to Shanghai to facilitate coordination of these
activities. (Ting, *Liang Jen-kung hsien-sheng* . . . , pp. 258–84).

[181] Available accounts do not completely agree as to the demands. See Wu, *Chung-
kuo min-chu* . . . , pp. 55–56; Ting, *Liang Jen-kung hsien-sheng* . . . , p. 287; and K'ang
T'ung-pi, *Nien-p'u hsü-pien*, p. 59b; *Nien-p'u pu-i*, p. 41a. The text of the petition is
given in *Pu-jen*, no. 4 (May, 1913), "Wen-i," pp. 1–26, and no. 6 (July, 1913), "Wen-
i," pp. 27–33, as well as in *Wen-ch'ao*, "Tsou-i," pp. 13a–25b. The demand that the
empress dowager return the reins of government to the emperor is not included in
the *Pu-jen* and *Wen-ch'ao* texts.

before. . . . Does this not go directly contrary to the principle of constitutional government? This is why people have no faith in the Court.[182]

The first demand mentioned a moment ago, that parliament be promptly convened, was obviously the most important. K'ang restated his old argument that experiences of mankind as well as "true Confucian teaching" predicated constitutional government as a political system suitable for the modern age. The lack of the parliamentary institution in China during the past centuries had reduced the "Confucian" notion of constitutional government to a "pious word" without substance. "Because of this the government [of China] has remained inferior to those of modern Western nations that have adopted constitutions, and the country itself has become enfeebled and faces danger." Parliament, therefore, was the key to China's political problem. K'ang concluded his argument in these terms:

> Now a constitution is just a piece of paper, if no parliament exists to sustain and guard it. Therefore, . . . before we can really save the country, we must first adopt a constitution; and before we can have constitutional government, we must first convene parliament. And, wishing to determine the type of constitutional government that would suit [China], it is far better to make the determination by [relying on] the wisdom of the hundreds of outstanding men in parliament than on the investigation of a few high officials traveling abroad without even command of a foreign language.[183]

As one expects, the Ch'ing court was outraged and took further repressive measures against the constitutionalists. K'ang's language was unnecessarily offensive; some of the demands were utterly unacceptable to the empress dowager and to the bulk of the Manchu ruling class. His suggestion, in particular, that China be known as "Chung-hua kuo" was tantamount, in the eyes of the Manchus, to obliterating the dynasty, symbolically if nothing else. The request that the line of demarcation between Manchu and Chinese be eliminated may well have sounded in Manchu ears as a device to liquidate their status as the ruling class. K'ang's argument, that to merge with the Chinese was the best way to insure the safety of the Manchus themselves and to void Sun Yat-sen's justification for nationalistic revolution, reasonable as it was in itself, could hardly allay the deep-seated suspicion of the Man-

[182] "Hai-wai . . . Chung-hua hsien-cheng-hui ch'iao-min kung-shang ch'ing-yüan-shu," p. 2.
[183] Ibid., p. 4.

chus.[184] Some of them, in all probability, did not forget the accusation leveled against K'ang in 1898 that he was committed only "to saving China but not the Great Ch'ing."[185] Even the demand for an immediate convening of parliament could easily be construed by some of the Manchus as a ruse to deprive them of power. Being a tiny minority among the colossal Chinese population it must have been obvious to them that they would be the losers in a system in which matters were to be decided by counting heads.

Undiscouraged, K'ang continued to agitate for parliament. As late as 1909 he wrote a memorial proposing that parliament be convened in the autumn of the next year because, he argued, the situation had become so critical that it would be folly to postpone the implementation of constitutional government to later years, as the Ch'ing court decided to do.[186] Meanwhile, K'ang went on to campaign against revolution, against the clamor for "liberty" and "equality." Freedom without discipline, he said, was no political blessing. He praised Germany for her "matchless" administrative and military system, her literature, science, and technology, and traced the source of her superiority to her constitution in which popular rights and monarchical authority were articulated into an efficient order. Neither the United States nor France could compare to her because "there was too much freedom" in these two countries, a shortcoming from which even England, pioneer in constitutional government, was not entirely free. China should learn from these lessons and avoid the pitfalls into which some Western countries had fallen.[187] K'ang was not arguing against democratic government. He was arguing rather for a proper balance between *min-ch'üan* and *chün-ch'üan*—for a "mixed monarchy" in which neither the king nor the people enjoyed overwhelming authority. The principle of check and balance, K'ang believed, was applicable also to the parlia-

[184] Ibid., pp. 6–9. Cf. "Ch'ing chün min ho chih Man Han pu fen che" (summer, 1898), cited in note 115, above.

[185] *Nien-p'u*, p. 20b.

[186] "Tsou-ch'ing k'ai kuo-hui che." The Ch'ing court proclaimed (Sept. 22, 1908) an outline of the projected constitution and laws governing the election and organization of parliament (as drafted by the Bureau for Compilation of Constitution), and set a time limit of nine years for actualizing constitutional government (Li, *Political History of China*, pp. 218–20).

[187] "Pu Te-kuo yu-chi hsü," *Wen-ch'ao*, 2: 43b–44a. According to K'ang, Presidents William McKinley and Theodore Roosevelt of the United States had set a new trend in constitutional government in exercising ever stronger executive powers. Cf. "*T'u-chüeh yu-chi* hsü, *Wen-ch'ao*, 11: 1a (*Wen-chi, chüan* 6, p. 1a), where K'ang said that in demanding "equality and freedom" Turkey would face ruin.

mentary institution; the bicameral system therefore was preferable to the unicameral.[188]

It may be said, then, that in the decade immediately following 1898 K'ang worked consistently to help China achieve political modernization by means of a peaceful transition from autocracy to constitutional monarchy. This explains his seemingly contradictory position: "aiming at popular rights" and at the same time "laboring to protect the emperor."[189]

CAMPAIGN AGAINST PREMATURE REPUBLICANISM, 1911–1925

"Republic with a Titular Monarch"

A drastically new situation emerged with the outbreak of the revolution in 1911 and with the inauguration of the republic in 1912. K'ang kept on fighting for disciplined democratization but now found it necessary to adapt his strategy to the altered circumstances.

He made his last attempt to stave off republicanism late in 1911. In a letter to Li Yüan-hung and other commanders of the revolutionary forces he asked them to transmit his views to leaders of the provinces.[190] He began by acknowledging the rapid success of the revolution and the demise of the Manchu dynasty, calling them events that had "the sanction of Heaven and the support of men." He then went on to warn them of the dangers of adopting the presidential form of republican government, a political system that had never been tried in China. He pointed to the chaotic conditions that resulted from experimenting with such government in Latin American countries. He argued that it had fared well in the United States only because of uniquely favorable circumstances. The colonists carried with them to the New World the deep-rooted democratic tradition of England; moreover, at the time of the American revolution the population was small. China, a country without the benefit of a democratic tradition and encumbered with a huge population, could not be expected to operate successfully the intricate machinery of republican government.

He himself, too, subscribed to the principle of "government by the people." But as the actual conditions in China did not permit the immediate application of that principle, it would be a grave mistake to apply it prematurely. The important thing was to give China a govern-

---

[188] "Ou-tung A-lien wu-kuo yu-chi," *Pu-jen*, no. 5, "Ying-t'an," p. 20.
[189] Lu and Lu, *K'ang Nan-hai hsien-sheng chuan*, p. 19b.
[190] "Chih Li Yüan-hung teng shu," *I-kao, chüan* 4, pt. 1, pp. 61a–69b.

ment that was democratic in essence. Now a "presidential republic" (*tsung-t'ung kung-ho*) as exemplified by France or the United States differed from a "monarchical republic" (*chün-chu kung-ho*) as exemplified by England only in form; they both were "replacements of absolute monarchy." For a country like China, which was accustomed to autocratic rule and lacked democratic experience, "monarchical republic" offered advantages not found in the "presidential republic." In the former, a constitutional (or titular) monarch, standing above political rivalries and competitions, would serve as a working symbol of national unity and stability. And as he was to reign but not to rule, he did not have to possess outstanding personal talent. That being the case, the abdicated Ch'ing emperor or even "the Holy Duke" (Yen-sheng kung, the lineal descendant of Confucius) could easily qualify for such a position.

K'ang elaborated on his notion of "titular-monarch republicanism" (*hsü-chün kung-ho*) in two essays written about the same time, one "On Rescuing China from Destruction" and the other "On the Forms of Republican Government."[191] After a theoretical and somewhat pedantic discussion of the forms of "republican government" (among which he included the aristocracy of Athens and the Triumvirate of Rome), he drew the conclusion that each of the historical and existing forms had its particular defects and that the English form, a "monarchical republic," was comparatively free of them. As "presidential republic" was a relatively inferior form of democratic government, to risk political strife and confusion in trying to realize it in China would be too high a price to pay.[192]

In the years immediately following, K'ang reiterated the same view in a number of writings, notably, "Proposals for China's Rehabilitation" (1916),[193] "Letter to Hsü [Shih-ch'ang], the Grand Tutor"

[191] I.e., "Chiu-wang lun" (autumn, 1911), *Pu-jen*, no. 7, "Cheng-lun," pp. 1–55 and "Kung-ho cheng-t'i lun," microfilm, reel 2.

[192] K'ang now argued against electing the "Holy Duke" to be the titular monarch, on the ground that he might not enjoy the moral support of the non-Chinese minorities of the republic. It would be better, he said, to have the "old sovereign" occupy the throne (ibid., pp. 14–15). This suggests the possibility that the piece was written a little before his letter to Li Yüan-hung and others. Cf. Liang Ch'i-ch'ao, "Hsin Chung-kuo chien-she wen-t'i," pp. 27–47, in which Liang expressed roughly the same view regarding the relative merits of the various forms of democratic government but refrained from recommending constitutional monarchy (which he granted was the best of all the existing forms) because he doubted that the Manchus were qualified to implement it.

[193] "Chung-kuo shan-hou i," *I-kao, chüan* 1, pp. 97a–100b. This was written after the collapse of Yüan's monarchical movement. Early in 1916, K'ang sent a letter to

(1917),[194] and "An Open Letter to My Countrymen" (1925).[195] He stoutly maintained that "titular-monarch republicanism" was the only solution to China's baffling political problems.

It should be noted that while K'ang consistently opposed premature republicanism, he modified his views regarding the form of democratic government suitable for China as time went on. As he himself remarked in 1917, "Since 1898 I had advocated constitutional monarchy; since 1911 I have been advocating republicanism under a titular monarch."[196] The main difference between the two forms was that in the former the monarch was to have actual authority, even though it was to be limited by a constitution, whereas in the latter he was to have no power at all. His thinking was thus described as "progressive" by some writers.[197]

Attempts to Reform the Republic

K'ang's extremely pessimistic view of the 1912 republic[198] did not deter him from making recommendations to help make it work, espe-

---

Yüan, "the Hung-hsien emperor," advising him to abdicate. "Republicanism, constitutionalism, and monarchism," K'ang wrote, "are like physicians' prescriptions. As prescriptions are not good or bad by themselves and a good prescription is one which cures the sickness, so are forms of government not intrinsically good or bad and [one that] makes a country strong is a desirable system" ("Chih Yüan Shih-k'ai shu," *Nien-p'u hsü-pien*, p. 94a; *Nien-p'u pu-i*, p. 65a).

[194] "Yü Hsü t'ai-fu shu," written after the collapse of the 1917 restoration, *Pu-jen*, nos. 9–10, pp. 1–5. K'ang pointedly recalled that in some Western countries foreigners were "invited" to serve as constitutional monarchs: in England, Henry II from France, 1154; William from the Netherlands, 1650; and George I from Hanover, 1660.

[195] "Kao kuo-jen shu," *I-kao, chüan* 4, "Shu-tu," pt. 1, pp. 128a–31a.

[196] In a telegram to Feng Kuo-chang, then Provisional President of China, sent after the collapse of the restoration when Feng ordered his arrest (K'ang T'ung-pi, *Nien-p'u hsü-pien*, p. 107a; *Nien-p'u pu-i*, p. 77b). In these sources the date of the telegram is given as July 4, 1917, which is probably incorrect. The restoration was announced July 1; Tuan Ch'i-jui assumed command of the "punitive forces" at Ma-ch'ang on July 5; a week later, Chang Hsün fled and found asylum in the Dutch Legation, two days before Tuan led his troops into Peking. See Li, *Political History of China*, pp. 370–71. K'ang could not have sent the telegram on July 4.

[197] Chao Feng-t'ien, "Ch'ing-mo wei-hsin jen-wu chih-i, K'ang Yu-wei," *Ta-kung pao*, quoted in Yang, "Kang Liang nien-p'u kao-pen," pt. 2, p. 76b.

[198] In addition to what has already been referred to, it may be interesting to cite an unpublished essay on "The Chinese Should be Concerned about Foreign Aggression and Avoid Internal Strife" ("Han-tsu i yu wai-fen wu nei-cheng lun"), written after Sun Yat-sen set up his Military Government at Canton, Sept. 3, 1912. The simultaneous existence of two governments, one in Peking headed by Yüan Shih-k'ai and the other in Canton headed by Sun, highlighted the struggle among the Chinese and portended political chaos. See Li, *Political History of China*, p. 377.

cially in the first two years of its existence. In an open letter to overseas members of the Constitutional Party (written early in 1912) he in fact indicated his acceptance of the new political order. He began by recalling the history of his party:

> I have just heard that the old dynasty has come to an end with the [emperor's] abdication. . . . The functioning of popular sovereignty presupposes the existence of political parties. . . . Fourteen years have passed since our Party has come into being. . . . At first, our hope was placed in the Emperor who sacrificed himself for the sake of the people. Hence in the seven years between 1899 and 1905 our group labeled itself "the Emperor Protection Party" to show our opposition to the tyrannical clique under the empress dowager. In the next phase of our Party, having resolved in 1906 to promote constitutional government, we changed its name, from "Emperor Protection" to "National Constitutional Party." . . . Between 1906 and 1911, a period of six years, we, through the media of numerous letters and telegrams, had endeavored to organize our countrymen in a common crusade for constitutional government. . . . If, since the institution of the Regency [in 1909], those who held the reins of government had not resorted to sham constitutionalism, the objective of our Party would have been attained. . . . For, following the English model, the ruler would have relinquished his powers and the people would have taken part in deliberating affairs of the state. . . . The tragic bloodshed and the constant fear of disintegration [brought about by the 1911 revolution] which we are witnessing today, would have been rendered unnecessary.

He then went on to urge his comrades to dedicate themselves anew and to work for the republic:

> Now as time and circumstances have changed, the new has replaced the old. Five Nations are united into one body politic; the imperial title [of the Manchu ruler] is allowed to stand while republican government prevails. . . . Even though our Party had no part in the destructive revolution, we cannot shirk our responsibility in the task of reconstruction that is to come. . . . I therefore earnestly beseech you, my comrades, to redouble your efforts [in serving our country]. However, as our form of government is not a constitutional monarchy [I suggest] that . . . we change the name of our Party to "National People's Party" (Kuo-min tang). . . . Much remains to be done of the great undertaking of making China strong and powerful; we shall exert ourselves and shall advance together toward new achievements.[199]

An incident attested to K'ang's decision to commit his group to the

[199] "Jen-tzu chih ko-pu shu," *I-kao, chüan* 4, pt. 1, pp. 70a–b. A curious coincidence: the new name of K'ang's party is exactly the same as that of Sun's.

cause of the 1912 republic. Late in that year Hsü Ch'in, his most trusted disciple and one of the active leaders of the constitutionalists, was "elected" by overseas members of his party to represent them in the Chinese parliament. Hsü, however, had some misgivings about returning to China. K'ang gave him assurance and encouragement, vouching that with Hsü's dedication and talent, he should be effective even in difficult situations.[200]

For a while, then, K'ang was willing to serve the republic. He remained critical of the failings of premature republicanism but his criticisms were often constructive, aiming not at destroying the new order but rather at reforming it, at making it viable.

The guiding principle of republican reform can be simply stated. In his view, China's new political system should be a happy combination of the best features of modern democratic governments and valid elements of the native tradition.[201] In a number of writings done in 1912–13 he suggested solutions to many of the perplexing problems of the time. In one of these, the "Essay on China's Salvation," written in the summer of 1912, he proposed among other things that China would do well to adopt the cabinet form of government and the two-party system. He rejected the idea of a federation of autonomous provinces and argued for a strong central government.[202] Early the following year he completed a "Draft Constitution of the Chinese Republic," when preliminary steps were being taken by the government at Peking to make a new constitution to replace the provisional one.[203] A little earlier (April 1912) he prepared a draft law governing parliamentary election and another governing senatorial election.[204] In these and other writ-

[200] K'ang T'ung-p'i, *Nien-p'u hsü-pien*, pp. 77b–78b. A much briefer account in *Nien-p'u pu-i*, p. 53b.

[201] "*Kung-ho chien-she t'ao-lun-hui tsa-chih* fa-k'an-tz'u," microfilm, reel 1.

[202] "Chung-hua chiu-kuo lun."

[203] *Ni Chung-hua min-kuo hsien-fa ts'ao-an, Pu-jen*, no. 3 (April, 1913), pp. 1–54; *Pu-jen tsa-chih hui-pien*, 1st ser., *chüan* 2, pp. 1 ff.; and *Wen-ch'ao*, 6: 1a–58b. K'ang said in the preface that the essay was actually done in 1908–9 and the system envisaged was patterned after the British constitution. At the suggestion of his students he revised it; taking into consideration the fact that China had now become a republic, he took the French constitution as his model. K'ang appears to have made a serious study of the matter, e.g., he cited James Bryce's views as expressed in *The American Commonwealth* (1888) when he discussed federal government. P'an, *Chung-hua min-kuo hsien-fa shih*, pp. 30–39, gives a short account of the so-called "Temple of Heaven Constitution."

[204] "Chung-hua min-kuo kuo-hui tai-i-yüan hsüan-chü fa-an," and "Chung-hua min-kuo yüan-lao-yüan hsüan-chü fa-an," microfilm, reel 3. In the former document K'ang proposed imposition of property, professional, and educational restrictions on the suffrage. In the latter document he made the senate represent "special interests," "special classes," and "localities."

ings of the time K'ang tended to attach importance to personal qualification in the exercise of the franchise and to place political unity above
individual rights. Mere counting of heads, he said, would easily lead to
the tyranny of majority and turn democracy into mobocracy.[205] The
doctrine of *min-ch'üan* (people's rights) which had dominated European
and American political thinking many years ago, was now being replaced by the concept of *kuo-ch'üan* (rights of the state) to which many
Western leaders, including Theodore Roosevelt, subscribed. In the
competitive world of modern times a state that allowed itself to be
weakened by unrestricted popular rights was to court ruination.[206]
Incidentally, this sentiment of K'ang's was echoed, in different words,
by Sun Yat-sen ten years later.[207]

K'ang made what appears to have been his last attempt to salvage
the battered republic in 1916, shortly after Yüan Shih-k'ai discarded
his imperial pretensions (March 23). K'ang proposed three alternative
methods to deal with the unsettled situation. One was to recognize Li
Yüan-hung as the legally instituted president of the republic, with no
real power like the French counterpart, and to permit his descendants
to inherit the office, thereby eliminating presidential elections, which
had been a source of intrigues and strifes. A second method was to
institute a "senate of elders" (*yüan-lao yüan*) the members of which were
to be elected by residents of the twenty-two provinces, and of Mongolia,
Chinghai, and Tibet, and were to elect among themselves a ten-man
council much like the Swiss system. If neither of the above was considered acceptable, then, as a last resort, a "republic under a titular
monarch" must replace the existing republic.[208] Not unexpectedly, his
suggestions found no response. He now decided to join others to work
for monarchical restoration.

[205] "Chung-kuo i ho fang chiu wang lun," pp. 16–18.
[206] Ibid., p. 19.
[207] Sun Yat-sen, *San Min Chu I*, pp. 212–13: "Now how shall the term 'liberty' be
applied? If we apply it to a person, we shall become a sheet of loose sand; on no
account must we give more liberty to the individual; let us secure liberty instead for
the nation." This is from the second lecture on "Principle of Democracy," delivered
March 16, 1924. It may be noted that as late as 1916 K'ang had not completely given
up hope for the 1912 republic. In a letter to Fung Kuo-chang and seven other *tu-chün*
(military governors) he appealed passionately to these war lords, beseeching them to
stop civil wars and to restore peace, so that they would be able to devote themselves
to constructive undertakings such as drafting a constitution and convening a parliament (*I-kao, chüan* 4, pt. 1, pp. 80a–b).
[208] "Chung-kuo shan-hou san ts'e," *Nien-p'u hsü-pien*, pp. 70a–71b.

It is not my purpose here to assess the merits of K'ang's proposals for reforming the republic. Under the well-nigh impossible circumstances in which the infant republic found itself, K'ang's recommendations probably had no more chance of effective application than a host of other views that came from different quarters. In making these suggestions, however, K'ang had unintentionally but conclusively refuted the allegation that from beginning to end he was an enemy of the republic, working always to undermine it.

Attempts at Restoration: Last Crusade for Constitutional Monarchy

The abortive attempt to revive the fallen Manchu dynasty in 1917 marked the culmination of a restoration movement that, in fact, had begun almost as soon as the last emperor's abdication was proclaimed,[209] although K'ang did not join it until the spring of 1913, as he himself confessed.[210] In 1917 he was among those who actively plotted with General Chang Hsün to mount a military coup.[211]

Yüan Shih-k'ai's monarchical scheme gave a new impetus to the restoration movement.[212] K'ang took Yüan's action as clear evidence

---

[209] Aisin-gioro Pu Yi, *From Emperor to Citizen*, 1: 77–78: "One would be safe in saying that they [restoration efforts] did not cease for a day from the abdication proclamation in 1912 to the establishment of the 'Empire of Manchukuo' in 1934." The same statement occurs in the Chinese edition, *Wo-ti ch'ien-pan sheng*, 1: 81–82. In an interview with G. E. Morrison, *London Times* correspondent, when negotiations between the north and the south were going on, Yüan Shih-k'ai was quoted as saying: "I firmly believe that seventy percent of the Chinese people are conservative. . . . If we overthrow the Manchu family now, the conservatives must, before long, try to restore the monarchical system" (Li, *Political History of China*, pp. 304–5. For details of the interview, see *Far Eastern Review*, 12 [1915]: 105).

[210] "Fu Ta-wei hou-chüeh shu," p. 17: "General Chang [Hsün] was deeply loyal to the imperial house. Previously, in the 3rd month of the *kuei-ch'ou* year [i.e., 1913], I had secretly planned with him, intending to restore the Dynasty. Unfortunately, our plan was uncovered and it had to be dropped."

[211] Shen Yün-lung, *K'ang Yu-wei p'ing-chuan*, pp. 59–65, gives a brief account of the abortive 1917 restoration. See also Aisin-gioro Pu Yi, *Wo-ti ch'ien-pan sheng*, pp. 156–67, 331. These and other accounts give the impression that K'ang operated quite independently of the loyalist officials. In fact, some of them thought so ill of K'ang that they were even opposed to granting him a posthumous title by the dethroned emperor. Incidentally, the well-known scholar Lao Nai-hsüan (1843–1921) paralleled K'ang's condemnation of the republic. See Lao, "Jen-sou tzu-pien nien-p'u," in *T'ung-hsiang Lao hsien-sheng i-kao, chüan shou*, p. 20a, under *chia-yin* year, where it is said that he wrote an essay in 1911 bearing the title "Kung-ho cheng-chieh" and that he now (1914) wrote two additional pieces, "Hsü kung-ho cheng-chieh," and "Chün-chu min-chu p'ing-i."

[212] Li, *Political History of China*, p. 305, dated the inception of Yüan's monarchical movement from the time of the constitution revision, late 1913 and early 1914. (The

that republicanism in China was mortally ill, although at the same time he regarded the medicine that Yüan proffered as worse than the disease. With Liang Ch'i-ch'ao and others he worked for Yüan's downfall.[213] An important difference in objective, however, separated K'ang and Liang. Whereas K'ang wished to undo the "Hung-hsien" regime in order to make room for Manchu restoration and "titular monarchism," Liang aimed simply at the restoration of the republic and was unequivocally opposed to K'ang's aim.[214]

There is no need here to relate the events connected with the 1917 restoration.[215] Suffice it to say that K'ang played an active, though not necessarily crucial, part in bringing it to pass. Several times before June he had written letters to Chang Hsün, urging the latter to take Peking by force as an indispensable step.[216] Together with three others he arrived at Peking on June 27, four days before the restoration was announced. The republican government ordered his arrest on July 17, five days after the collapse of the restoration and nine days after he was granted asylum in the American Legation.[217]

---

articles of organization of the Constitutional Conference were proclaimed January 26, 1914; the first meeting of the Conference fell on February 18.) The movement was formally launched with the forming of the Peace Planning Society (Ch'ou-an hui) by Yang Tu and five others in August, 1915. Yüan's "Hung-hsien" regime was abolished March 23, 1916. Kao Lao, "Ti-chih yün-tung shih-mo chi," *Tung-fang tsa-chih*, 13, no. 8 (Aug., 1916): 6–28; no. 9 (Sept., 1916): 9–32; and no. 10 (Oct., 1916): 9–22, is useful.

[213] See K'ang's letter to Ts'ai O in *I-kao, chüan* 4, pt. 1, pp. 76a–b. Liang left Peking for south China on Dec. 12, 1915, to take a personal part in organizing the military operations against Yüan (Ting, *Liang Jen-kung hsien-sheng* . . . , pp. 444, 460–61).

[214] On the same day on which the restoration was announced (July 1, 1917), Liang issued a circular telegram that was printed in *Ta-kung pao* (Tientsin, July 3). This is given in Ting, *Liang Jen-kung hsien-sheng* . . . , pp. 519–20. Earlier, Liang wrote an essay to refute arguments for restoration, "P'i fu-p'i lun," pp. 117–19. Yang Fu-li recorded that after being informed of Liang's position, K'ang "gravely and in a loud voice" restated his own views concerning restoration and added that, if Liang and others failed to support him, he would regard them as his enemies. Cf. Wu Hsiang-hsiang, "K'ang Liang yü fu-p'i yün-tung," pp. 59–67. For Liang's anti-Yüan writings, see especially "Tun-pi chi," sec. 4, in *Yin-ping-shih ho-chi, chuan-chi* 33, pp. 85–117.

[215] Brief accounts in Li, *Political History of China*, pp. 370–71. The following are also useful: Aisin-gioro Pu Yi, *From Emperor to Citizen*, pp. 85–95 (Chinese ed., 1: 90–101); Ting, *Liang Jen-kung hsien-sheng* . . . , pp. 519–20; and Hsü Shu-cheng, *Hsü Shu-cheng hsien-sheng wen-chi nien-p'u ho-k'an, Nien-p'u*, pp. 197–99.

[216] One of these letters is available in microfilm, reel 1.

[217] K'ang T'ung-pi, *Pu K'ang Nan-hai hsien-sheng tzu-pien nien-p'u*, p. 26a. The then American minister to China, Paul S. Reinsch, provided a convoy for K'ang when he left Peking for Shanghai, Nov. 25, 1917. K'ang revealed some of his thoughts and

The editor of *The China Press* reporting K'ang's death in 1927 asserted that K'ang's "monarchist leanings" were never "definitely proved."[218] If by "monarchist leanings" was meant leanings toward autocratic monarchy, the charge that had been direct against him could not indeed be sustained. But if the phrase was taken to mean "titular monarchism," then there is absolute proof that K'ang had in truth seriously attempted to undo the 1912 republic. On more than one occasion K'ang himself had confessed as much. For instance, he said explicitly in his "Suggestions for China's Reconstruction" (written in 1916) that "republic under a titular monarch" to be brought about by Manchu restoration was China's only way out of the political muddle.[219] As late as 1925 he was still harping on the same theme with slight variations. He now argued that as the installation of the abdicated Manchu ruler as titular monarch would give him neither authority nor prerogatives, the action could not even be properly called "restoration."[220] Above all, one cannot overlook the fact that he was actively and deeply involved in the 1917 coup.

Precisely because K'ang harbored no true loyalist sentiments and worked for titular instead of absolute monarchism his recommendations were ignored by Chang Hsün and other leaders of the restoration. K'ang drafted a number of "decrees" for the would-be imperial court, but none of these was used.[221] K'ang commented after the debacle that had his view prevailed, the restoration could have succeeded. It was those "ignorant bigots," including Chang Hsün, devoid of knowledge of Western constitutional government and lacking understanding of the affairs of the world, that insisted on restoring the Ch'ing as an absolute monarchy and thus invited disaster.[222] One cannot help recalling that it was K'ang himself who gave encouragement to Chang and negotiated with the other "ignorant bigots," imagining that he

---

sentiments while a political refugee in the American Legation in a number of poems. These are given in "Ting-ssu Mei-shen-kuan yu-chü shih-chüan."

[218] *The China Press*, April 2, 1927, "The Passing of K'ang Yu Wei."

[219] See note 193, above.

[220] "Kao kuo-jen shu," *I-kao, chüan* 4, "Shu-tu," pt. 1, p. 129b.

[221] "Letter to Hsü Shih-ch'ang," *Pu-jen*, nos. 9–10, "Cheng-lun," pp. 13–14; K'ang T'ung-chia, *K'ang Yu-wei yü wu-hsü pien-fa*, pp. 11–12; Chang, *Nan-hai K'ang hsien-sheng chuan*, p. 69b; Hu Ying-han, *Wu Hsien-tzu hsien-sheng chuan-chi*, p. 67. Aisin-gioro Pu Yi, *From Emperor to Citizen*, pp. 85–95 (Chinese ed., 1: 90–101), makes no mention of K'ang in his account of the 1917 episode, though K'ang's name is included in the list of "officials."

[222] "Kao kuo-jen shu," p. 13b.

could make use of "the northern army" and depend on "the matchless loyalty and courage of General Chang" to carry out his objective.[223] As it turned out, Chang and all the others were of little use to K'ang; and they had little use for him.[224] Moreover, given the existing circumstances, the restoration of the abdicated emperor as titular monarch could hardly be achieved, even with the full-hearted support of the "bigots."

K'ang was correct in saying that Chang Hsün and the other Ch'ing loyalists knew too little of the world outside of China. His knowledge of Western history, it seems, was quite considerable. On more than one occasion in 1917 he mentioned that although England had become a republic with the execution of Charles I in 1649, she became a constitutional monarchy when his son was restored to the throne as Charles II in 1660. Therefore, K'ang said, "The Europeans still describe England as a democracy (*kung-ho kuo*)."[225] The history of Western countries, he argued, gave no reason why any country that had become a republic could not revert to constitutional monarchy.[226] Such reversion was not political regress as some thought but represented, in some instances at least, a decisive step in the direction of progress. The restoration of Charles II afforded one such instance.[227]

---

[223] "Letter in Reply to Marquis Ōkura" ("Fu Ta-wei hou-chüeh shu"), *Pu-jen*, nos. 9–10: 17. It may be noted that as the Peiyang military clique was so badly troubled by internal dissension "the northern army" would prove useless for K'ang's purpose, even if Chang Hsün and others involved in the restoration accepted his point of view.

[224] K'ang himself realized the futility of the attempt soon enough. K'ang T'ung-pi, *Nien-p'u hsü-pien*, p. 106b, records that three days after he arrived at Peking, he sensed that something was wrong and considered the advisability of quietly slipping away. He decided against it because, as he enjoyed so much prestige, to withdraw his support would further endanger the movement. Hu Ying-han, *Wu Hsien-tzu hsien-sheng chuan-chi*, p. 68, tells a slightly different story, to the effect that Wu Hsien-tzu, a prominent member of K'ang's group, advised K'ang to leave promptly, as all his suggestions had been rejected by Chang Hsün and his associates. K'ang was quoted to have said: "I know for sure it [the restoration] is going to fail; I shall be taken, inescapably, as the chief culprit . . . ; no matter what I do I cannot clear myself [of the accusation]."

[225] Text of a telegram to Feng Kuo-chang, given in K'ang T'ung-pi, *Nien-p'u hsü-pien*, p. 105b and *Nien-p'u pu-i*, p. 76b.

[226] "Letter in Reply to Marquis Ōkuma," *Pu-jen*, nos. 9–10, "Cheng-lun," p. 18. Porfirio Diaz (1830–1915), president dictator of Mexico, was overthrown by a revolution in 1911.

[227] Incidentally, the restoration was engineered by General George Monck (1608–70) who at first was loyal to Cromwell but later decided that order could be main-

K'ang traced the source of the opposition to constitutional monarchy to ignorance and prejudice which he proposed to dispel.

> Before the 1911 revolution no one in the country knew that there was such a thing as republican government; after the revolution no one in the country permitted anybody to speak of the shortcomings of republicanism. . . . I do pity those [who are ignorant and prejudiced] and have written a book titled "Impartial Words on Republicanism" to treat extensively of the subject. Humbly I hope that some day our people will gain a clear understanding of the nature of government. We can then look forward to good order in our country when the necessary changes in our government will have been made.[228]

K'ang's knowledge, however formidable, did not serve him well in pragmatic terms. The 1917 restoration attempt was in fact doomed to failure even before it was made. The warlords on whom K'ang relied to carry out his plan had no understanding of nor sympathy for titular monarchism. The history of seventeenth-century England to which K'ang hopefully appealed could not repeat itself in early twentieth-century China. For one thing, Chang Hsün was no George Monck. And even though England repudiated the political consequences of the Puritan Revolution and preferred monarchy to republic,[229] she already had a centuries-long parliamentary tradition (to mention just one important factor) to serve as an effectual instrumentality to push the country's political institutions toward that form of democracy that K'ang admired and would have liked China also to attain. None of these democratic potentials obtaining in seventeenth-century England was available in China.

---

tained only by restoring the Stuarts to the throne. Godfrey Davies, *The Early Stuarts, 1603–1660*, pp. 256–58, refers briefly to Monck's part in the restoration.

[228] "Letter in Reply to Marquis Ōkuma," p. 18.

[229] Interestingly, Sun Yat-sen came close to K'ang's view of the 1660 English restoration. Sun said in 1924: "The first instance of actual democracy in modern times was in England. A revolution of the people took place about the same time as the close of the Ming dynasty and the beginning of the Manchu dynasty in China, under a leader named Cromwell, which resulted in the execution of King Charles I. . . . Europeans thought that the English people would defend the rights of the people and thus give a great impetus to democracy. But, to the surprise of all, the English preferred monarchy to democracy; although Charles I was dead, they continued to long for a king. Within less than ten years the restoration of the monarchy had taken place and Charles II was welcomed back as king" (*San Min Chu I*, trans. Frank Price, pp. 171–72, quoted here with slight modifications. Price rendered *chün ch'üan* in the original as "autocracy," which is hardly accurate). The passage in the original is in

In K'ang's statement quoted above he expressed the hope that he could enlighten his countrymen and prepare them for the momentous political transformation he envisioned. Political enlightenment, in short, should precede political reform. That being the case, one might justifiably raise the question, was not the 1917 venture a rash and in essence revolutionary move that transgressed against his own gradualist canon of political change? In helping to engineer the restoration had he not adopted a wrong strategy, even though his basic aim was perhaps commendable? And, in failing to see that the last opportunity for the Ch'ing regime to adopt constitutionalism had irretrievably slipped away by 1910, was he not guilty of being blind to the realities of the historical situation?

In fairness to K'ang it should be noted that he soon realized his mistake and decided to resume the efforts of peaceful reform, which he had been making in 1912–13, without slackening his biting criticism of premature and misbehaving republicanism. The essay, "Impartial Words on Republicanism," written while a political refugee in the American Legation quarters in Peking, was the most important piece of writing in this connection.[230] Much of what he now said was essentially an elaboration of earlier arguments, though new ones were occasionally introduced in view of recent developments. For example, he asserted that the Russian revolution was bound to spell disaster for the country and that communism, though a noble ideal in itself, should not be tried before the advent of utopia.[231] And to reassure his readers that he was not at all opposed to democracy as such, he reproduced parts of the *Ta-t'ung shu* where man's eventual progress toward world-wide democracy was delineated.[232]

One way to render the republic workable, he believed, was to convene a national assembly to discuss constitutional government. This was the gist of his answer to questions put to him by Ts'ao K'un who became president of the republic after the war of 1922 between the Chihli and Fengtien cliques. "Whatever may be the form of govern-

---

Sun's *Kuo-fu ch'üan-chi*, 1: 82.

[230] This work, *Kung-ho p'ing-i*, in three *chüan*, appeared first in *Pu-jen*, nos. 9–10, "Cheng-lun," pp. 1–48, 1–80, and 1–73. It was issued in book form in Shanghai, 1918. That it was taken seriously by supporters of the republic may be seen from the fact that Ch'en Tu-hsiu wrote a point-by-point rebuttal in the *Hsin ch'ing-nien*, 4, no. 3 (Mar. 15, 1918): 190–211.

[231] *Kung-ho p'ing-i*, *chüan* 3, in *Pu-jen*, nos. 9–10, pp. 3–5.

[232] Ibid., pp. 13–42.

ment," K'ang wrote, "be it monarchical or republican, a constitution is indispensable." A national assembly was the only way to give the republic a new start; "to retrace the ruinous track" which had been followed since 1912, would be a painful mistake.[233] He proposed, in other words, to invoke *min-ch'üan* in order to save the republic.

Again he was destined to be disappointed. The situation remained as hopeless as before. Once again he tried to put an end to the republic and began to plot another restoration coup in 1923.[234] In a letter to Reginald F. Johnston[235] asking him to inform the abdicated emperor of the results of his maneuvers, K'ang stated (with unwarranted optimism) that after a year's negotiations with provincial military leaders the situation was ripe for another restoration attempt. Shensi, Hupeh, Hunan, Kiangsu, Kiangsi, Anhwei, and Kweichow, he claimed, had all consented to act.[236] Obviously, he mistook noncommittal response for firm pledge; at any rate, nothing materialized.[237] That K'ang took the matter seriously may be seen from the fact that he undertook to

[233] Yang, "K'ang Liang nien-p'u kao-pen," pt. 2, pp. 61b–62a, quoting from K'ang's telegram to Ts'ao. K'ang made seemingly identical proposals in 1917, in an open letter to provincial high officials and newspapers, but with an entirely different objective and under different conditions. He implied support of Li Yüan-hung's dissolution of the old parliament because, he explained, unless a new parliament was elected and the Provisional Constitution was replaced, "China could not be saved." He seems to have believed that such a course of action might open the way to a constitutional monarchy through lawful procedures, or perhaps might give a semblance of legality to the restoration that was soon to be attempted ("Ch'ing k'ai kuo-min-ta-hui kung-i li-hsien shu," pt. 1, pp. 92a–b).

[234] Ting, *Liang Jen-kung hsien-sheng* . . . , p. 654, "January [1924]—Nan-hai *hsien-sheng* undertook to foment restoration a second time without success." Actually, as K'ang's own account shows, the attempt was made in the previous year.

[235] For Johnston's relationship to the "Ch'ing court," see Aisin-gioro Pu Yi, *From Emperor to Citizen*, pp. 188–216 (Chinese ed., pp. 118–25).

[236] "Ch'ing Chuang-shih-tun tai-tsou yu-shuo ching-kuo," *K'ang Nan-hai hsien sheng mo-chi*, vol. 4 (pages are not numbered). The letter was dated "chia-tzu, 1st month, 18th day," i.e., Feb. 16, 1924.

[237] There is evidence that K'ang took part in yet another restoration plot. "Chia-tzu Ch'ing-shih mi-mou fu-p'i wen-cheng," *Ku-kung ts'ung-k'an*, Palace Museum, Peiping, 1929. This is a collection of facsimile reprints of "memorials" and letters dated 1923–24. One of the letters was from K'ang. Hsü Shu-cheng in a letter to Tuan Ch'i-jui, then the Chief Executive, written in 1925, advised Tuan not to probe into the restoration movement, naming Chin-liang as one of the two persons involved, and arguing that "restoration" (like "the presidency" or "provincial federalism") was just one of the political issues arising from the unsettled conditions of the country, and that these men were "powerless bookish scholars" incapable of effective action ("Shang Tuan chih-cheng shu," *Shih-hsi-hsüan i-kao*, "Wen 1," pp. 47–48, in Hsü, *Hsü Shu-cheng hsien-sheng wen-chi nien-p'u ho-k'an*).

indoctrinate P'u-i, the abdicated emperor, in the theory and practice of constitutional monarchism.[238]

The year 1923 saw K'ang's last endeavor to turn the republic into a "republic under a titular monarch." After that and until his death in 1927 he devoted his time mostly to nonpolitical activities, including travels in various parts of China, discoursing on "authentic Confucianism," and lecturing on his philosophy of "celestial peregrination."[239] Not that he had repudiated his long-held view that restoration of the Manchu ruler as a titular monarch was China's only way out of the republican quagmire. As late as in 1925 he still maintained that it was "the absolutely best plan."[240] But it had become, so far as he was concerned, a purely theoretical issue. The ouster of P'u-i from the Forbidden City in the previous year presumably convinced him that restoration had in fact become for him another lost cause.

The foregoing discussion points to the conclusion that K'ang Yu-wei was an inveterate reformist who believed that democracy, China's political destiny, could be reached only through a process of guided evolution. Therefore, while his opposition to revolution as a method of change was intransigent, his objection to republicanism was conditional. Republicanism was undesirable only when it was invoked without due preparation.

A Chinese historian wrote recently that in continuing to promote constitutional monarchy after the 1911 revolution K'ang was guilty of cleaving to an "old delusion" and of closing his eyes to progress.[241] This appears to be an oversimplified judgment stemming from inadequate understanding of K'ang's position. In so far as K'ang failed to effect China's political modernization through progressive modernization— in so far as he mistook what he believed to be politically desirable for what was historically feasible—he had indeed worked under delusion. To that extent our historian is right. But it is hardly accurate to say that in preferring the method of gradual reform to sudden revolution K'ang had thereby resigned himself to unmitigated conservatism. Moreover, one should not overlook the fact that in spite of his misgivings about premature republicanism, he had made honest efforts to help make the 1912 republic work—under the delusion that it could really be helped!

[238] "Tsou-hsieh yü-tz'u fu-shou-tzu che," microfilm, reel 3.

[239] K'ang T'ung-pi, *Nien-p'u hsü-pien*, pp. 134b–49b. See my article "K'ang Yu-wei's Excursion into Science," in Lo, *K'ang*, pp. 375–409.

[240] Yang, "K'ang Liang nien-p'u kao-pen," pt. 2, p. 76a.

[241] Wu Hsiang-hsiang, *Min-kuo cheng-chih jen-wu*, p. 67.

K'ang was not alone in having tried vainly to render help. Even the wholehearted commitment of Liang Ch'i-ch'ao and Sun Yat-sen to the republican cause brought no tangible results. As soon as the republic was proclaimed Liang pledged his services without reservation. He played an active role in forming political parties and served conscientiously as Minister of Justice (1913). He risked his life to defend the republic when Yüan Shih-k'ai launched his monarchical movement in 1915. He opposed resolutely the 1917 restoration and for a second time he accepted a cabinet post as Minister of Finance after Yüan's fall. However, eventually disillusioned and thoroughly disgusted, he withdrew from the political arena and engaged himself in educational and scholarly work.[242] His dedication to the republic produced no more positive results than K'ang's devotion to the "old delusion."

Sun, too, found his initial enthusiasm for republicanism belied by later events. In 1917 he launched the "Constitution Protection Movement" against the northern war lords. In 1924 he mounted the "northern expedition" that terminated in the victory of the Nationalist Revolutionary Army,[243] thus in effect giving the *coup de grâce* to the ailing republic that he had called into existence twelve years before. China's second republic, so to speak, came into being in 1928 with Nanking as its capital. The National Government reaffirmed his doctrine of political tutelage as a means to preparing the people for democracy.[244] Republican constitutionalism was promised anew in 1932,[245] but a host of adverse conditions, including the Communist threat and Japanese invasion, long delayed its fulfillment. At last the National Assembly met in Nanking (November 15, 1946) and the "Constitution of the Republic of China" was formally promulgated (January 1, 1947).[246] Time, however, was running short. Mao Tse-tung was soon to try his "New Democracy" on China and Taiwan to become the bastion of the democratic republic founded on Sun's "Three Principles of the People."[247]

[242] Ting, *Liang Jen-kung hsien-sheng* . . . , pp. 379–569, passim.

[243] Brief account in Li, *Political History of China*, pp. 376–77, 462–505. The victory was not complete. War lords continued to defy the authority of the National Government; some of them broke out in open revolt in 1930. The next year Japan attacked Mukden, thus initiating the series of her military aggressions against China, which led to the second Sino-Japanese war.

[244] Ch'u Yü-k'un, *Chung-kuo hsien-fa ta-kang*, p. 72, gives the text of "The Principles of Political Tutelage" (*Hsün-cheng kang-ling*), issued Feb. 3, 1928.

[245] Ch'u, *Chung-kuo hsien-fa ta-kang*, pp. 264–65.

[246] Ibid., pp. 138–65. Text of the Constitution is given on pp. 261–70.

[247] "The Constitution of the Republic of China" (Dec. 25, 1946), Article 1, Ch'u, *Chung-kuo hsien-fa ta-kang*, p. 261. A translation of this is available in Ch'ien Tuan-

Will the 1947 Constitution, so far as the Chinese people on the main-land are concerned, remain another tantalizing hope?

At the moment few, if any, can give a sure answer. However, one conclusion suggests itself, that democracy cannot be made on short order, not even on the order of the most resolute of reformers or revo-lutionists. If history affords any clue, it appears that one way to build a democratic country in a hurry is to have, in addition to a combination of fortunate circumstances and enlightened, dedicated leadership, a lot of farmers like Captain Preston who fought in 1775 in colonial America to secure the right of self-rule, although they had never heard of "the eternal principles of liberty" so confidently enunciated by James Harrington, Algernon Sidney, and John Locke.[248]

---

sheng, *Government and Politics of China*, p. 447.

[248] Samuel E. Morison, *The Oxford History of the American People*, pp. 202–3, relates this illuminating incident. To the question "What made the farmers fight in 1775?" —put by Judge Mellen Chamberlain in 1842—Captain Preston, a ninety-one-year-old veteran of Concord, answered: "We had governed ourselves, and we always meant to. They did not mean we should." It was neither the feeling of oppression, he made it clear, nor "reading Harrington or Sidney and Locke about the eternal prin-ciples of liberty" that made them go for the redcoats. Chang Peng-yuan, *Li-hsien-p'ai yü hsin-hai ko-ming*, draws the conclusion that the constitutional movement was bound to fail because "the West's human rights movement" (*jen-ch'üan yün-tung*) at-tained its goal only after many long years had passed and only in gradual stages. It was therefore impossible for China to adopt Western democratic institutions in a few years (p. 239). He does not assess the results of the 1911 revolution beyond saying that it put an end to the Manchu monarchy, nor does he take up the obvious question whether it would be possible for the revolutionists to transplant Western democracy on Chinese soil simply by doing away with autocracy.

Chapter 7

ADMINISTRATIVE REFORM

REORGANIZATION FOR EFFICIENCY AND DEMOCRACY, 1888–1898

The long-range aim of K'ang Yu-wei's political reform was the radical but gradual transformation of China's autocratic system into a constitutional democracy. Pending the realization of that aim (which would take years to attain) it was necessary, in K'ang's view, to effect without delay extensive changes in the existing administrative structure, which, owing to faulty structural design and functional deterioration, had become a hopeless anachronism. All efforts at reform would be in vain unless the political apparatus was appropriately renovated.

K'ang voiced his dissatisfaction with the existing system in his "First Memorial" to the emperor, submitted in the autumn of 1888. "The institutions of the empire" he wrote, "have degenerated to the extreme." The shortcomings were many and grave.

> Myriad government affairs devolve on the Six Boards. Not one of the presidents and vice-presidents has definite responsibility. There are numerous secretaries, but these too have no specific assignments. They all make their presence each day in the offices, merely to countersign the documents. . . . Moreover, the presidents and vice-presidents do not devote their whole attention [to the affairs of the respective Boards] as most of them hold concurrent posts in other parts of the government. . . . As a result, even men of ability and knowledge fold their arms [and do nothing].[1]

[1] "Shang Ch'ing-ti ti-i shu" (Kuang-hsü 14th year, 9th month), (Chien Po-tsan et al., *Wu-hsü pien-fa*, 2: 128).

263

Local administration on the *chou* and *hsien* level was in no better shape.

> Affairs pertaining to the military, law enforcement, revenue, education, and economic welfare are all responsibilities of one man [namely, the district magistrate]. He is liable to punishment, if a single bandit escapes, a single lawsuit is improperly handled, or a single coin is misappropriated.

Local officials became, inevitably, more concerned with saving their own necks than with serving the people or the government. The situation was made even worse by the fact that local administrative posts could be purchased with money. Corruption thus became virtually a regular feature of the system.[2]

K'ang of course was not alone in calling attention to administrative defects and deterioration. Some of his contemporaries that shared his misgivings were at least as outspoken as he in their criticism of the demoralized bureaucracy.[3] Nor was K'ang the first man to raise the question of administrative reform. Robert Hart for one had already broached it in 1865. He pointed out, among other things, in his "Spectator's Memorandum" that although the system was carefully designed, it had become ineffectual with the passage of time. Few officials serving outside Peking fulfilled their duties, while many of them engaged in corrupt practices. Officials in the capital were so overburdened with multiple assignments that none of them could attend to their proper duties, even if they wished to do so. Scholars who aspired to officialdom had no knowledge of practical affairs, even though some of them indeed had considerable literary skill. Unless these and other faults were corrected in due course, the imperial administration would remain unprepared for meeting the challenge of the new situation.[4]

---

[2] The pace of administrative decay quickened appreciably under the empress dowager, Tz'u-hsi. Chao Erh-hsün et al., *Ch'ing-shih kao*, Mukden ed., 1927, 107: 5a; Hong Kong reprint 1960, 2: 1377. The trend began much earlier. See, e.g., H. B. Morse, *Trade and Administration of China*, 2: 439–40.

[3] See, e.g., Chin-liang, *Kuang Hsüan hsiao-chi*, pp. 55–56; Chang Jo-ku, *Ma Hsiang-po hsien-sheng nien-p'u*, pp. 119–20; Huang Chün, *Hua-shui-jen-sheng-an chih-i*, pp. 55–56. Instances of factionalism, corruption, incompetence, and irresponsibility are authentically described in these works. Even the Censorate, supposedly the watchdog of the imperial administration, did not escape the process of deterioration. For additional information, see Li Tz'u-ming, *T'ao-hua sheng-chieh-an jih-chi*, and *Hsün-hsüeh-chai jih-chi*, both in *Yüeh-man-t'ang jih-chi*, *ts'e* nos. 28–51, passim. See also Weng T'ung-ho, *Weng Wen-kung-kung jih-chi*, 35: 44b, entry of Kuang-hsü 22nd year (1896), 5th month, 17th day.

[4] This piece bears the title, "Chü-wai p'ang-kuan lun," and is given in Wen-ch'ing et al., *Ch'ou-pan i-wu shih-mo*, T'ung-chih period (Peiping, 1929–30), *chüan* 40, pp.

However, K'ang went beyond his contemporaries in one important way. He probably was the only man at the time who traced the root of the difficulties to the nature of autocratic rule. As he said in his "Fourth Memorial" (June 30, 1895):[5]

Since ancient times China has been under unified rule. Surrounded by small barbarian tribes [the emperors had] no desire to contend for supremacy against outsiders but wished only to forestall trouble from below. With the Ming dynasty the methods of control became even more thoroughgoing than before. Officials were recruited through "the eight-legged essay"; promotion was on the basis of seniority; . . . several persons shared a single administrative function, while one man concurrently held several government posts, thereby dividing the authority and hamstringing the functionaries, none of which had opportunity to exercise their abilities to the full.

This device of "dividing authority and hamstringing functionaries" had served well its intended objective. During Ming times no important official was known to have created any "untoward incident." In the age of isolation, administrative impotency was not too high a price to pay for political security. The situation, however, had drastically changed. China, with her outmoded administrative system, had proved unable to cope with the problems arising from confrontation of the Western Powers. On the other hand, thanks to the practice of "honoring merit" and "attaching importance to efficiency" as well as to political institutions that served primarily the interests of the people, these countries had developed great strength.[6] China would do well to learn this lesson of the West and revise her philosophy of government accordingly. The cardinal principle of administration should no longer be dynastic safety at the expense of effective operation; it must be proficiency in service of the nation.

14a–15b. It was sent to the Tsungli yamen, Oct. 27, 1865, which together with another memorandum (ghost-written by Thomas Wade) submitted by the British minister, Sir John Rutherford Alcock, was transmitted to high provincial officials, including Kuan-wen, Tseng Kuo-fan, Tso Tsung-t'ang, Li Hung-chang, and a few others for comment.

[5] "Shang Ch'ing-ti ti-ssu shu" (Chien, *Wu-hsü*, 2: 177). Modern scholars tend to corroborate K'ang's view. E.g., Pao Chao Hsieh, *The Government of China, 1644–1911*, pp. 390–97, points to some of "the undesirable results"; and T'ung-tsu Ch'ü, *Local Government in China under the Ch'ing*, observes that stagnation was the price of stability and inefficiency of conformity. Cf. Kung-chuan Hsiao, *Rural China: Imperial Control in the Nineteenth Century*, pp. 3–5.

[6] K'ang, "Shang Ch'ing-ti ti-ssu shu" (Chien, *Wu-hsü*, 2: 175).

Efficiency, K'ang believed, could be attained through rationalization. Some of his suggestions in this direction were made in his "Second Memorial" (May 2, 1895). He called for a number of changes in the bureaucratic structure so that each functionary would have specific duties and adequate authority to perform them. Supernumerary offices and personnel, therefore, should be abolished. The practice of assigning "important" officials to concurrent posts should stop. As the district magistracy formed the core of local administration, its incumbent should be an official who had "loving concern for the people"; he should be paid a decent salary, given an appropriately high rank, and freed from the cumbersome and unnecessary "supervision" of intendants and prefects. The province was altogether too large a division to allow effective administration and therefore should be reduced to the size of a circuit (*tao*).[7] K'ang restated these suggestions in his "Fourth Memorial" (June 30, 1895) and denounced in emphatic terms "the practice of hamper and obstruction" that inhered in the existing system.[8]

These and other related suggestions that K'ang made in the early 1890s were calculated primarily to enhance the efficiency of the administrative apparatus by ridding it of the debilitating devices resulting from the autocratic concern for security. He proposed, in other words, a revision of the operational principle of the bureaucracy without altering its general structure. In 1898, however, he went much further. Early in that year he urged that the administration be thoroughly reorganized and brought in line eventually with the modern constitutional systems of the West. He was now concerned not merely with operational efficiency but radical political transformation.

"In recent times," he wrote in his "Sixth Memorial," "Westerners who discoursed on government referred invariably to the 'three powers.' There were in China rough counterparts of the executive and judicial branches of government as it existed in Western countries, but there was lacking an organ which exercised 'the deliberative power.' As a sesult, the Chinese government was not properly equipped to undertake ruch a crucial task as the formulation of a reform program." To bridge this important gap, K'ang urged that a "planning bureau" (*chih-tu chü*) be instituted at once.[9] This was not to be a legislature or parlia-

---

[7] "Shang Ch'ing-ti ti-erh shu" (sometimes referred to as "Kung-chü shang-shu") (Chien, *Wu-hsü*, 2: 150–51).

[8] "Shang Ch'ing-ti ti-ssu shu" (Chien, *Wu-hsü*, 2: 182).

[9] "Shang Ch'ing-ti ti-liu shu" (original title, "Ying-chao t'ung-ch'ou ch'üan-chü che") (Chien, *Wu-hsü*, 2: 199–200).

ment in the true sense of the word, but a new government body by means of which K'ang hoped to bypass the existing administrative structure and to carry out his reform program. It would have twelve departments dealing severally with matters pertaining to law, finances, education, agriculture, industry, commerce, railroad, post, mining, association and travel, and navy.[10] It thus assumed the form of an embryonic cabinet with twelve ministries that together would perform the "deliberative," executive, and administrative functions of a modern government. K'ang, conceivably, saw in the *chih-tu chü* a useful device to initiate the transition from the traditional administrative structure to the modern cabinet.

K'ang revealed even more clearly his desire to change the existing system in the direction of democracy as well as administrative efficiency in his 1898 proposals regarding local government. He still attached great importance to the district magistracy, but he now emphasized the view that "local rule should come from the people themselves." Accordingly, he suggested the institution of a system of "bureaus of people's affairs" (*min-cheng chü*) as an initial form of local self-rule.[11] At this point, he was not asking for constitutional or democratic government as such. What he sought was a modification of the autocratic structure at its lowest level, thereby laying the first foundation stone of "government by the people."

As time went on, K'ang made more sweeping demands. By mid-spring of that year he had come to the conviction that a thorough overhaul of the administration was in order. Half measures would be self-defeating. As he memorialized on May 22:

> After repeated onslaught of foreign aggression, people in the empire have now come to the realization that the old institutions are decayed and are thinking of preservation through reform. But, to change A and leave out B, to do one thing and leave out other things, proceeding piecemeal . . . and missing what is fundamental, would surely spell failure. . . . In your servant's view, therefore, . . . we must change our institutions completely, if the decision is to change them.[12]

[10] Ibid., pp. 200–201.

[11] Ibid., pp. 201–2. *Contemporary Review*, 76 (July–September, 1899): 191–95, summarizes the contents of this memorial. *Min-cheng chu* is referred to as "People's Council."

[12] "Chin-hsieh t'ien-en ping t'ung-ch'ou ch'üan-chü che," in Chien, *Wu-hsü*, 2: 215. K'ang restated his position after the September *coup* in these terms: "a government is a very complex machine; the elements of government are very various. . . . Thus we find that unless we change the whole [system] with all our might, we shall never succeed in our efforts but only aggravate the evils" (*Contemporary Review*, 76: 187–88).

This insistence on all or nothing in administrative reform also separated K'ang from most of his contemporaries who favored limited innovation.

It might be of some interest to examine briefly K'ang's concrete suggestions regarding administrative regeneration—changing methods of personnel recruitment and adopting measures to eliminate bureaucratic deadwood.

He made two major suggestions regarding recruitment. Convinced, like many others of the time, that skill in composing the "eight-legged essay" constituted no index to a man's administrative ability, he repeatedly requested the emperor to modify the examination system in such a way that it would serve to gauge the true qualifications of aspirants to officialdom. For example, he told the emperor, in the nearly three-hour-long audience on June 16, 1898, that ignorance was the root of the current difficulties and that the eight-legged essay must be blamed for this ignorance.[13] The examination system was condemned in even stronger terms in a memorial submitted about a month earlier:

> Because of government requirements [scholars] pay attention only to Chu Hsi. . . . Ignoring all the other Classics they read only the *Four Books*; foregoing true learning they concern themselves only with the eight-legged essay. The records of knowledge accumulated in two thousand years have thus ceased to have value [for them] and are allowed to gather dust on inaccessible shelves. Among men of "pure talents" in the Hanlin College are some who do not even know the time in which Ssu-ma Ch'ien or Fan Chung-yen lived, or of what dynasties were emperors Kao-tsu of Han and T'ai-tsung of T'ang. If questions concerning the geography of Asia or Africa, or political and educational institutions of Europe and America, are put to them, they would not know what to say—agape with astonishment.[14]

The remedy was obvious. Candidates must demonstrate their knowledge of the Confucian Classics, and such knowledge was to be conveyed through free-form discourse instead of the eight-legged essay. In addition, they must demonstrate their acquaintance with practical affairs, both domestic and foreign. Authors who set forth new truths that were capable of practical application should be admitted into the Hanlin College, even though they had not taken the examinations.[15]

[13] *Tzu-pien nien-p'u*, p. 19b (hereafter, *Nien-p'u*). Cf. Shen T'ung-sheng, *Kuang-hsü cheng-yao, chüan* 34, pp. 17a–b, for a fuller account of K'ang's proposals.

[14] "Ch'ing fei pa-ku shih-t'ieh k'ai-fa shih shih kai yung ts'e-lun che" (Chien, *Wu-hsü*, 2: 209–10).

[15] "Shang Ch'ing-ti ti-erh shu" (Chien, *Wu-hsü*, 2: 149). K'ang's emphasis on practical knowledge was shared by some of his contemporaries. Yen Hsiu, in particu-

A second way to revitalize the administration was to infuse it with new blood—by drawing into service men of special talents who were relatively young in age and low in official position. K'ang was highly critical of the recruitment and promotion practices that had been in use for centuries, namely, promotion on the basis of seniority[16] and assignments by lot.[17] Neither method, he observed, conformed to the principle of "honoring the worthy and employing the capable" or to "the Confucian way."[18] Both should be promptly abandoned to make room for procedures based on the principle of merit. He elaborated on this idea in his "Third Memorial" (June 3, 1895) in which he urged the emperor "to seek men of talent and promote them without regard to established routine," and to replace the high officials who had become unduly cautious and decidedly senile—useless in a time of crises.[19] The same theme was reiterated later in another memorial[20] and in his audience with the emperor.[21]

Incidentally, this was one of K'ang's proposals that took immediate effect. In a decree of January 17, 1898, issued to the Grand Secretariat, the emperor ordered provincial authorities to recommend "talented

---

lar, proposed the establishment of "special courses in practical affairs" in a memorial, "Tsou-ch'ing she ching-chi chuan-k'o che" (Jan. 27, 1898), given in Chien, *Wu-hsü*, 2: 329–32 and Chu Shou-p'eng, *Tung-hua hsü-lu, Kuang-hsü chao, chüan* 142, pp. 6b–7b. The decree which set up the "courses" is in Chu, pp. 7b–8b. According to Liang Ch'i-ch'ao, *Wu-hsü cheng-pien chi*, pt. 4, p. 148, the emperor's action turned out to be an opening wedge in the 1898 reform. The "courses" were suspended (Oct. 9) shortly after the collapse of the movement.

[16] Ts'ui Liang's device, known as "t'ing-nien-ko chih," Chinese equivalent of "seniority rule," was instituted in A.D. 519 when he was President of the Board of Civil Office and found it difficult to evaluate the personal qualifications of the great number of office seekers. The results were said to be less than encouraging; "mediocre and inferior men" often received consideration before men of talent who happened to be newcomers to officialdom. See biography in Wei Shou, *Wei shu, chüan* 66 (Chung-hua ed.), p. 9a.

[17] The *ch'e-ch'ien fa*, i.e., "lot-drawing method," initiated in 1594 by Sun P'i-yang, President of the Board of Civil Office, was calculated to forestall influence peddling by the all-powerful eunuchs of the Ming dynasty. See biography in Chang T'ing-yü, *Ming-shih, chüan* 44 (Chung-hua ed.), pp. 8b–9a.

[18] K'ang, *Ch'un-ch'iu Tung-shih hsüeh, chüan* 6, pt. 2, p. 31a.

[19] "Shang Ch'ing-ti ti-san shu" (June 3, 1895), in Chien, *Wu-hsü*, 2: 171–73.

[20] "Shang Ch'ing-ti ti-ssu shu" (Chien, *Wu-hsü*, 2: 186).

[21] *Nien-p'u*, p. 19a. The passage quoted here is modified from the partial translation of this conversation in Ssu-yu Teng and John K. Fairbank, *China's Response to the West*, p. 178, from the original given in Chang Po-chen, *Nan-hai hsien-sheng chuan*, pp. 26b–28a.

men" for office.[22] A number of such people, including K'ang himself, Liang Ch'i-ch'ao, and others active in the reform movement, were actually nominated for imperial consideration.[23]

To insure a constant source of new administrative talents K'ang deemed it important to develop a modern Western-style school system.[24] In a memorial petitioning the establishment of schools (submitted in the summer of 1898, after the emperor issued the decree abolishing the eight-legged essay), K'ang called attention to the fact that Western countries launched modern school systems as early as the eighteenth century. It was Prussia's Frederick the Great who initiated a system of universal primary education that marked the beginning of modern education in Europe. With the development of higher education appeared large numbers of "men of talent" to serve their respective countries. Therein lay the strength of the modern West. The same was true of Japan.

> Recently, Japan defeated us in war. It is not that her ministers, commanders, or soldiers are better than ours. It is because she, having established schools all over the country, is in possession of a sufficient number of men of ability and skill better than what we have.

It was high time, therefore, for China to follow the example set by

[22] This decree is given in *Te-tsung shih-lu, chüan* 413, pp. 16b–17b and reproduced in Chien, *Wu-hsü*, 2: 7–8. In another decree, issued June 11, 1898, the emperor ordered that persons qualified for diplomatic service be recommended for his consideration (*Te-tsung shih-lu, chüan* 418, pp. 15b–16a).

[23] Notably, recommendations of "men of ability" were made by Hsü Chih-ching in memorial of June 9, 1898 (in behalf of K'ang Yu-wei, Huang Tsun-hsien, T'an Ssu-t'ung, Chang Yüan-chi, and Liang Ch'i-ch'ao), given in *Chih-hsin pao*, no. 63, pp. 8a–9b and reproduced in Chien, *Wu-hsü*, 2: 7–8 and by Wang Hsi-fan, in memorial of August 29, 1898 (in behalf of Lin Hsü, Yen Fu, and two others), given in Chien, *Wu-hsü*, 2: 374–75, and Yeh Te-hui, *Chüeh-mi yao-lu, chüan* 1, pp. 18a–b. Hu Ssu-ching, *Wu-hsü li-shuang lu, chüan* 4, shows in a table the names of over 200 persons recommended by Chang Chih-tung (Liang Ch'i-ch'ao, Yang Jui, T'ang Shou-ch'ien, and others), Ch'en Pao-chen (Liu Kuang-ti, Yang Jui, and 13 others). On the question of who recommended K'ang Yu-wei to the emperor, see Kung-chuan Hsiao, "Weng T'ung-ho and the Reform Movement of 1898," pp. 166–79. Huang Chün, *Hua-sui-jen-sheng-an chih-i*, accepts the view that it was Chang Yin-huan's "secret memorial" that brought K'ang and the emperor together. Ho Ping-ti, "Chang Yin-huan shih-chi," in Pao Tsun-p'eng et al., *Chung-kuo chin-tai-shih lun-ts'ung*, 7: 108–9, states categorically that Chang indeed was responsible. Perhaps the last word on the question remains to be said.

[24] See "Second Memorial," May 2, 1895; "Third Memorial," June 3, 1898; "Fourth Memorial," June 30, 1898; and "Ch'ing k'ai hsüeh-hsiao che" (submitted between June 19 and July 18, 1898), all in Chien, *Wu-hsü*, 2: 147–48, 170–71, 180–81, 217–19.

Japan and the West. Primary and secondary schools should be established in every village and district, and institutions of higher learning in the prefectures and provinces wherever conditions permitted. The proposal to set up an imperial university in the capital had been made years ago; it was time now to make it a reality.[25] To reduce the need of building new school houses, which would entail heavy expenditures at the outset, he suggested that the facilities of the traditional academies (*shu-yüan*) and "unauthorized" shrines (*yin tz'u*) be made use of.[26] To help provide suitable instructional material, he proposed a translation bureau that would make available to Chinese scholars selected books in Japanese language on modern government, literature, and military science.

Promising young students should be sent to Japan and Germany to acquire knowledge in science and technology, subjects that could not be adequately studied by reading books nor properly taught in domestic schools.[27] Eventually, China would also have an ample supply of well-trained men from whom administrative functionaries could be recruited.

These then were the measures by which K'ang hoped to rejuvenate the bureaucracy—to change the character if not also the structure of the existing administrative system. It should be noted, however, that in 1898 K'ang did not advocate the replacement of the old high-echelon personnel, though he would like to see changes effected at the lower levels.[28] He made it particularly clear during his audience with the emperor:

> Old offices should not be abolished but new ones should be created, the incumbent high officials should not be dismissed but minor officials should

[25] "Ch'ing k'ai hsüeh-hsiao che" (Chien, *Wu-hsü*, 2: 217–19). K'ang mentioned that Frederick the Great invited Voltaire to Sans Souci; one is thereby tempted to suppose that K'ang had an inkling of the Enlightenment. His call for establishment of schools was echoed by Li Tuan-fen, a high official who supported reform, in a memorial of June 20, 1898, in ibid., pp. 297–300.

[26] "Ch'ing ch'ih ko-sheng kai shu-yüan yin-tz'u wei hsüeh-t'ang che" (late June or early July, 1898) (Chien, *Wu-hsü*, 2: 219–22). Hu P'ing-chih and Ch'ien Chün-hsiang, "Ch'ing pien-t'ung shu-yüan chang-ch'eng che," submitted sometime between July 19 and August 16, 1898, sought to preserve the *shu-yüan* by introducing "useful learning" such as mathematics, astronomy, geography, etc., into their curricula, without abandoning the study of Confucian classics and Chinese history (Chien, *Wu-hsü*, 2: 297–300).

[27] "Ch'ing kuang-i Jih-pen-shu ta-p'ai yu-hsüeh che" (late June or early July, 1898) (Chien, *Wu-hsü*, 2: 222–25).

[28] See notes 7 and 8, above.

be gradually promoted. . . . The high officials, thus spared the burden of attending to government affairs and relieved of the fear of losing their positions, would not become resentful and would cease to oppose [reform].[29]

As we recall, K'ang took the position in 1895 that sinecures and superfluous offices should be abolished. This change of heart, presumably, stemmed from his desire to abate the opposition of the high officials.

However, the matter soon went out of control, despite his circumspection. Overzealous partisans of reform talked volubly about abolishing this or that office, or dismissing this or that official early in the summer of 1898.[30] A flurry of memorials proposing the abolition of various offices descended on the emperor's desk.[31] Against K'ang's advice and the opposition of some high ministers the emperor decreed (August 30, 1898) the abolition of the Imperial Supervisorate of Instruction (Chan-shih fu), the Office of Transmission (T'ung-cheng ssu), the Banqueting Court (Kuang-lu ssu), the Imperial Stud (T'ai-p'u ssu), and other courts, governors serving in the same cities with governors-general, Director-general of the Yellow River (Tung-ho tsung-tu), and a number of other posts considered supernumerary.[32] This action presumably put a stop to wild rumors mongered by various people.[33] It, however, did not pacify the "conservatives"; on the contrary, it added fuel to their angry opposition and made new enemies of reform. Thousands of people were estimated to have lost their jobs as a result of the liquidation of half

[29] Chu, *Tung-hua hsü-lu, Kuang-hsü chao, chüan* 144, pp. 18b–19a. Cf. *Nien-p'u*, p. 19a, "as for the incumbent personnel, they should be left alone."

[30] Cited in note 12 above.

[31] Among these were memorials from Chang Yüan-chi (abolition of the Hanlin College and the Censorate), Ts'en Ch'un-hsüan (doing away with the Courts), Yang Shen-hsiu (dismissal of "incompetent" and "decrepit" officials), Yüan Ch'ang (abolition of supernumerary functionaries and offices, including the Imperial Supervisory of Instruction, Directorate-general of the Grain Transport, Governors and Governors-General having offices in the same cities, i.e., those in Hupeh, Kwangtung, and Yunnan, and all Circuit-intendents), and Ts'ai Chen-fan (wide-ranging reorganization of the bureaucracy) (see *Nien-p'u*, pp. 22b—24b). For Yang Shen-hsiu, see Chao Erh-hsün et al., *Ch'ing-shih kao, chüan* 251, pp. 3b–4a. Memorials of Ts'ai and Yüan are given in Chien, *Wu-hsü*, 2: 381–92 and 449–54.

[32] The decree announcing the dismissals is given in *Te-tsung shih-lu, chüan* 424, pp. 6b–8a. Hsieh, *The Government of China, 1644–1911*, p. 345, mentions the "superfluous offices" abolished by the decree. H. B. Morse, *The International Relations of the Chinese Empire*, 3: 141, notes that "the former incumbents were generally left undisturbed in their posts."

[33] E.g., the rumor that "the Six Boards and Nine Courts will be abolished and foreign-devil offices (*kui-tzu ya-men*) will be established." See Su Chi-tsu, *Ch'ing-t'ing wu-hsü ch'ao-pien chi*, reprinted in part in Chien, *Wu-hsü*, 1: 337.

a dozen of government offices in the capital alone.[34] Spiteful personnel sacked the building of one of the offices affected by the abolition decree.[35] An American scholar blamed the "strenous campaign against sinecure posts" for the sudden change of attitude on the part of "many an official who at first viewed the Emperor's reform effects with equanimity."[36] K'ang himself admitted after the September 21 coup d'état that "the present crisis" was precipitated by the emperor's premature action in administrative reform, even though such reform was an indispensable step in modernization.[37] Perhaps the emperor was not solely responsible. K'ang himself had previously (1895) suggested such a measure,[38] even though he later (1898) counseled caution.

[34] *North China Herald*, 61, no. 1634 (Sept. 19, 1898): 521. Ch'en K'uei-lung, *Meng-chiao-t'ing tsa-chi* (Chien, *Wu-hsü*, 1: 485), indicates that over a dozen offices were abolished, causing, directly or indirectly, some ten thousand people to lose their positions or assignments.

[35] Ch'en, *Meng-chiao-t'ing tsa-chi*, quoting an eyewitness report.

[36] Meribeth E. Cameron, *The Reform Movement in China, 1898–1912*, pp. 44–45.

[37] K'ang's statement as reported in the *China Post* (*Chung-kuo yu-pao*, Hong Kong) under the title "China's Crisis" ("Chung-kuo ti wei-chi"), Oct. 7, 1898, available in Chien, *Wu-hsü*, 3: 503. K'ang seems to have faced the same problem confronting Wang An-shih who, in implementing a reform program eight centuries before, had to warn Emperor Shen-tsung against premature action, but to no avail. See Hsiao Kung-ch'üan, *Chung-kuo cheng-chih ssu-hsiang shih*, 4: 459–60.

[38] In addition to advocating reshaping the administrative structure, K'ang also saw the advisability of simplifying and expediting administrative procedures by ridding the system of multifarious and cumbersome regulations or precedents that had accumulated over the centuries. See his "Shang Ch'ing-ti ti-ssu shu" (Chien, *Wu-hsü*, 2: 182). The emperor issued a decree (July 29, 1898) ordering various government offices to undertake a thoroughgoing review of rules and precedents and to make appropriate changes (*Te-tsung shih-lu, chüan* 421, pp. 11b–12a). According to Su, *Ch'ing-t'ing wu-hsü ch'ao-pien chi*, p. 338, the emperor's order was generally ignored. However, the Board of Civil Office and the Board of Revenue reported that actions had been duly taken, in separate memorials submitted Sept. 1, 1898 (Chu, *Tung-hua hsün-lu, chüan* 127, pp. 10b–11a). K'ang also proposed revision of the legal code. In a memorial, "Ch'ing k'ai chih-tu-chü i hsing hsin-cheng che," submitted sometime after August 17, he said in part: "As for the laws of our country, they differ from those of all other countries. Therefore, it has been impossible to do away with the extraterritorial jurisdiction [enjoyed by foreign Powers]. Moreover, in our existing legal system there is no distinction between civil and criminal law, and commercial as well as maritime law is lacking. This renders it even more difficult to deal with other countries." Accordingly, he recommended that a special bureau, *fa-lü chü*, be set up and attached to the planning bureau (Chien, *Wu-hsü*, 2: 252–53). *Wu-hsü tsou-kao*, compiled by Mai Meng-hua and published 1911, lists K'ang's undated memorial "Ch'ing ting fa-lü che" among other 1898 memorials but indicates in a note that the text was "at the time unavailable." It should be pointed out that K'ang was not in favor of indiscriminate Westernization of China's legal system, as his remarks made in 1917 apparently show. See "Ts'an-cheng-yüan t'i-i li-kuo ching-shen i shu-hou," *Pu-jen*, nos. 9–10 (Dec., 1917), "Chiao-shuo," pp. 1–2.

POST-BOXER ADMINISTRATIVE REFORM, 1901–1910

With the collapse of the 1898 reform movement all the alterations in the governmental structure decreed by the emperor were promptly annulled. K'ang's efforts at administrative reform thus came to naught in the empress-dowager's "counterreform."[39] The disaster of the Boxer uprising, however, convinced her that some modifications of the old ways had to be accepted, even if only half-heartedly or in less than good faith. Accordingly, she launched a reform of her own, in which among other measures a number of seemingly significant changes in the administrative system was introduced between 1901 and 1910.[40] A student of Chinese government aptly summarized the changes made in 1906 in these words: "the age-long traditional administrative sextet was turned into a body of ten ministries corresponding to the cabinets of European countries."[41] This process of reorganization was completed in 1910 with the addition of a ministry of navy.[42]

The decree announcing the post-Boxer reform, issued in the emperor's name on January 29, 1901, is of some interest. It began by declaring that while principles of morality were immutable, there were no unalterable methods of government. In view of the changed conditions a revision of the existing political system was necessary. However, it would not be a repetition of 1898; for "the disaster wrought by K'ang the traitor was worse than what the Red Turbans had perpetrated." The decree then went on:

> The root of China's weakness lies in the harmful habits that have become too firmly entrenched and in the rules and regulations that have been too minutely drawn; in the overabundance of inept and mediocre officials and in the paucity of outstanding, talented ones; and . . . in the ubiquitous paper work which reduces all matters to fiction and in the strait jacket of the seniority rule which condemns men of ability to languish in oblivion.

Such a state of affairs must not be allowed to continue. Accordingly, high officials both in and outside the capital were ordered to make sug-

---

[39] The phrase is H. B. Morse's (*International Relations*, 3: 149). The decree announcing the "counter-reform" issued on September 26, 1898, is given in *Te-tsung shih-lu, chüan* 427, pp. 1a–2b.

[40] Brief accounts in Cameron, *Reform Movement in China*, pp. 105–11, and Hsieh, *Government of China*, chap. 13.

[41] Hsieh, *Government of China*, p. 348.

[42] Ch'ien Shih-fu, *Ch'ing-chi Chung-kuo chung-yao chih-kuan piao*, p. 114. Chang Ch'i-yün et al., *Ch'ing shih* (Taipei, 1961), 4: 2833–36, give names of the incumbents.

gestions concerning "ways and means of full-range reform: (*ch'üan-mien wei-hsin*) within two months' time."[43]

The response, apparently, was less than enthusiastic. The two-month deadline had passed but only a few had submitted the required proposals. About three months later (April 21) the court issued another decree urging the delinquent officials to send in their views and setting up a committee to evaluate them and to draw up an integrated program on the basis of the acceptable suggestions. Known as the Board of State Affairs (Tu-pan cheng-wu ch'u) it was composed of six top-echelon officials: Prince Ch'ing, I-k'uang; Grand Secretaries Li Hung-chang, Jung-lu, K'un-kang, and Wang Wen-shao; and President of the Board of Revenue, Lu Ch'uan-lin. In addition, Liu K'un-i, governor-general of Liang-chiang, and Chang Chih-tung, governor-general of Hu-kuang, were "to participate from a distance" in the deliberation.[44]

Yüan Shih-k'ai, then governor of Shantung and a little later governor-general of Chihli, was active in the post-Boxer reform,[45] but Chang Chih-tung appears to have played a more decisive role. The three memorials that he submitted jointly with Liu K'un-i in the spring of 1901 attracted wide attention and were said to have served as basis of a new reform program. At first, Chang proposed that all the provinces submit a collective memorial. Liu concurred and prevailed upon him to prepare a draft. Thereupon Chang invited Chang Chien, Shen Tseng-chih, and T'ang Chen,[46] all of whom had advocated reform in the 1890s, to send in their suggestions to him. Assisted by staff members of the governor-general's office, Chang then proceeded to write the three memorials that took him more than a month to complete. Informed by Yüan Shih-k'ai that the throne wished the provinces to submit separate proposals, Liu decided nevertheless that he and Chang

---

[43] Chu, *Tung-hua hsü-lu, chüan* 164, pp. 2b–3b and Shen T'ung-sheng et al., *Kuang Hsü cheng-yao, chüan* 26, pp. 28b–29a, give the text of the decree issued Kuang-hsü 26th year, 12th month, 10th day. Cameron, *Reform Movement*, pp. 57–58, uses the translation of this document by J. O. P. Bland and E. Backhouse, in their *China under the Empress Dowager* (1st ed.), pp. 419–24. The date is wrongly given as January 8 and the translation is inaccurate.

[44] The decree of Kuang-hsü 27th year, 3rd month, 3rd day, is given in Chu, *Tung-hua hsü-lu, chüan* 166, p. 11b.

[45] Cameron, *Reform Movement*, pp. 61–64, identifies Yüan's part in reform but omits to mention Chang in this connection.

[46] Both Shen and Chang had taken an active part in the Ch'iang-hsüeh hui of 1895. T'ang Chen was the author of *Wei Yen*, in which he advocated wide-ranging reforms. T'ang Chih-chün, *Wu-hsü pien-fa jen-wu chuan kao*, 1: 156–57, contains biographies of Shen and Chang; cf. *Nien-p'u*, p. 13b.

do so jointly.[47] According to Jung-lu, the empress dowager was favorably impressed by their suggestions.[48]

Chang Chih-tung, author of these three memorials, was in all probability the chief architect of the initial post-Boxer reform program.[49] Some of the guiding principles and many of the important measures adopted by the Ch'ing court paralleled fairly closely his recommendations. Each of these documents dealt with a separate topic: the first, with education, the second, with administration, and the third, with economic and military affairs.[50] Only the second concerns us here.

According to the memorialists, it would be fruitless to attempt modernization in the economic and military spheres without first effecting administrative reform. As they put it,

> Three things are essential to a state: the first is government, the second, wealth, and the third, power. If a state has good government, it can strive to achieve prosperity and strength; otherwise, a hitherto prosperous and strong nation can become poor and weak. The way to attain good government is to reform the native institutions; the way to pursue wealth and power is to adopt Western methods.

They then went on to make twelve concrete proposals that, when carried out, would yield "good government." Most of these, significantly, pertained to administrative reform and were calculated to enhance (in a limited way) the efficiency of the administrative apparatus. Among the more important were: making appointments without regard to the accustomed rules and practices, suspending the selling of official posts, training government functionaries and paying them adequate salaries, and simplifying rules and regulations to give them opportunities to assume responsibilities proper to their respective offices. These, it might be noted, remind one of some of K'ang Yu-wei's ideas set forth in the 1890s.

[47] Hsü T'ung-hsin, *Chang Wen-hsiang-kung nien-p'u* (1939 ed.), *chüan* 7, p. 20, author's note.

[48] Ibid. Jung-lu was quoted as saying that "the proposals are good but only no body is there to carry them out."

[49] The empress dowager gave her approval in a decree (Oct. 2, 1901) to the effect that the proposals of Liu K'un-i and Chang Chih-tung concerning "revitalizing the Chinese system in order to apply Western methods" should be implemented in so far as they are practicable (Chu, *Tung-hua hsü-lu*, *chüan* 169, pp. 41–42). For Chang's other proposals and the projects he launched in the areas under his jurisdiction between 1901 and 1908, see Hsü, *Chang Wen-hsiang-kung nien-p'u*, *chüan* 7 to 10, passim.

[50] The aim, as Chang put it, was "the adoption of Western methods as a means to achieving wealth and strength." Texts of these memorials are available in Chu, *Tung-hua hsü-lu*, *chüan* 169, pp. 7a–41a.

They gave their reason for recommending a new approach to the matter of official appointment and promotion. Their view again was not greatly different from K'ang's.

> While in times of peace people are mostly employed on the basis of their seniority [in office] . . . in times of crises men of outstanding qualifications must be preferred. For those who advance through the regular channels are mostly fence-sitters (*ch'i ch'iang*); being old and tired they dread change; and occupying lofty ranks they regard it shameful to seek advice from people in lower positions.

The established practice, therefore, should be discarded and recommendation (made solely on the basis of personal merit and ability) be relied upon as a regular method of recruitment. The old device of giving assignments by lot should also be abandoned.[51]

The rationale for giving special training to provincial officials was explained in these terms:

> At present when so many unsettling things occur each day, the duties that devolve on the various provincial officials cannot be properly performed by men who are versed only in writing the examination essay or skilled only in locating administrative precedents. For to be able to serve the needs of the time a functionary must have [special] knowledge.

Academies and institutes for training officials should, therefore, be set up in each province, in which instruction in international law, educational systems, military organization, as well as mathematics, astronomy, geography, and technological subjects such as agriculture, industry, and mining was to be provided for the students. All expectants must successfully complete a course of study before they received assignments. At the same time, the salary scale must be adjusted upward so that bribery and embezzlement would no longer remain an economic necessity on the part of government functionaries.[52]

These and some other proposals submitted by Chang and Liu remind one of 1898, although K'ang Yu-wei's suggestions were comparatively more far-reaching. Indeed, one might even discern a measure of continuity between 1898 and 1901. As it had been pointed out, the plan for modifying the examination system jointly submitted by Chang and Liu was "based on the general principles" underlying the program as

[51] Text in ibid., pp. 15a–27b; see especially pp. 16b–17a and 22b–23b. Cf. K'ang's views as referred to in notes 16–20, above.
[52] Chu, *Tung-hua hsü-lu, chüan* 169, p. 40a.

authorized by the emperor in 1898.[53] Presumably, to make their views acceptable to the empress dowager, who harbored ill will toward K'ang and his movement (and possibly on account of significant differences between their position and K'ang's), they found it appropriate to denounce "K'ang Yu-wei's heresies and errors" and to claim that what they now recommended was "totally different!"[54] One is tempted to suspect that they had knowingly or unknowingly taken over some of K'ang's ideas but rejected him as the prophet of reform. This is not saying that K'ang had a monopoly on reform ideas. The problems that confronted China of the time were so obvious and the solutions so manifest that they could hardly escape any who addressed their attention to them.[55]

Though pointing still in the same direction, the post-Boxer administrative reform eventually went beyond the suggestions of Chang and Liu. On September 1, 1906, the Ch'ing court issued a decree that called for extensive administrative reform as the first step toward constitutional government.[56] This, too, reminds one of the sentiments of 1898 and deserves quoting at length.

> The institutions and ordinances of our country have successively come into being and have undergone no change for a long time. Now as we are constantly in danger and in fact faced with impending disaster, we are no longer in a position to carry out the wishes of our founding ancestors and to fulfill our subjects' desire for peace and order. We have accordingly sent high ministers to various countries to study their governmental institutions.
>
> Tsai-tse and the other ministers have now returned and made their report. They feel that our weakness is due really to the lack of communication between ruler and subject, between the capital and the country at large, and to the fact that officials do not know the correct way to serve the people and that the people are ignorant of their obligation to defend the state. [They are persuaded also] that thanks to constitutional government under which public opinion makes decisions, foreign countries have achieved prosperity and strength. . . . Therefore, living in the present

[53] Hsü, *Chang Wen-hsiang-kung nien-p'u*, p. 21a.

[54] Chu, *Tung-hua hsü-lu, chüan* 169, p. 40a.

[55] Gilbert Chinard, *The Correspondence of Jefferson and Du Pont de Nemours*, p. xi, "We shall have to admit that there are times when ideas are 'in the air,' when they seem common property, and when the attribution to any one man of the paternity of any particular idea is well nigh impossible. The eighteenth century was undoubtedly such a period." To a lesser degree, the 1890s and 1900s in Chinese history was such a period, so far as idea of "reform" was concerned.

[56] Chu, *Tung-hua hsü-lu, chüan* 202, pp. 2b–3a.

age we cannot but, after careful consideration, follow these examples and adopt constitutional government. . . .

However, as [appropriate] laws and institutions still have to be developed and as the people are not properly informed, to adopt hasty measures would do service merely to empty formality. . . . We must begin with [renovating] the administrative system—with clearing away the inveterate malpractices and defining precisely duties and responsibilities. . . . We must, in addition, revise our laws and regulations, develop education, put our financial house in order, revitalize the military services, and institute an empire-wide police system, so that gentry and people will gain a clear understanding of public affairs, thereby laying the foundation of constitutional government.

It hardly needs pointing out that this was a restatement in different terms of K'ang's general idea that administrative reorganization constituted a preliminary phase of constitutional government. Perhaps this was no mere coincidence. Among those who helped Chang Chih-tung in the preparation of the memorials were men who had been active in the 1898 reform movement and had even collaborated with K'ang Yu-wei.[57]

On September 2, 1906, the imperial government appointed fourteen top court officials (eight Manchus and six Chinese) to draw up a plan for administrative reorganization and ordered Chang Chih-tung and other governors-general to work with them. I-k'uang (Prince Ch'ing), Sun Chia-nai, and Ch'ü Hung-chi were given the task of scrutinizing the proposals and making recommendations to the throne.[58] The three reported their findings two months later:[59]

We humbly think that as the present administrative reorganization is intended to serve as a basis for constitutional government, it is important so to effect the changes that the resulting system will approximate the spirit of constitutionalism. Now in the governmental structures of those countries that have adopted constitutionalism, the three powers, legislative, executive, and judicial, stand side by side, each having its exclusive sphere of action and each operating to supplement the others. The underlying principle is excellent and the institutional form is good.

[57] See note 46, above.

[58] The decree is in Chu, *Tung-hua hsü-lu, chüan* 202, p. 3b. The eight Manchus were Tsai-tse, Shih-hsü, Na-t'ung, Jung-ch'ing, Tsai-chen, K'uei-chün, T'ieh-liang, and Shou-ch'i; the six Chinese were Chang Pai-hsi, Tai Hung-tz'u, Ko Pao-hua, Hsü Shih-ch'ang, Lu Jun-hsiang, and Yüan Shih-k'ai.

[59] Text of this memorial (Nov. 1, 1906) is in Chu, *Tung-hua hsü-lu, chüan* 202, pp. 11b–13b.

They then went on to analyze the shortcomings of the Chinese system. All the administrative difficulties, they said, were traceable to three main defects: that authority was not clearly demarcated among various government organs, that responsibility was not definitely fixed on any functionary, and that in the performance of administrative functions "reality" did not correspond to "name." They illustrated their contention with concrete examples. Administrative officials also exercised law-making power; regulations were often laid down that were neither just nor had the people's support. Where several officials presided over one single office, some of them must obviously be supernumerary. When one man held posts in various boards, it was clear that he could not be an expert in any field. And when one functionary was given several assignments at the same time, he could hardly find time to do justice to any one of them. To make the situation worse, more than one important administrative organ was not in a position to do what it was supposed to do: the Board of Civil Appointments had no authority to select appointees beyond making assignments by lot, the Board of Revenue was in fact no more than a cashier's office, and the Board of War neither controlled nor commanded troops.[60]

They accordingly outlined a new administrative system that would work toward "correcting the inveterate abuses, defining responsibilities, and realizing gradually constitutional government." Separation of powers was to be the central feature of the proposed reorganization.[61] Pending the convening of parliament, legislative power was to be lodged (in part) in an Advisory Council (Tsu-cheng yüan), while powers of impeachment and auditing would devolve respectively on the Censorate and an Auditing Department (Shen-chi yüan). Judicial power was to be exercised by a Supreme Court of Justice (Ta-li yüan), with a Ministry of Justice (Fa pu), replacing the old Board of Punishments as a supervisory organ. Executive power was to be lodged completely in a cabinet, composed of a premier and the ministers of various ministries. Each ministry was to have one minister (*shang-shu*), two vice ministers (*shih-lang*), and a number of lower functionaries. Each ministry was to be individually responsible for its appropriate duties; collectively, they would form "the Government" (Cheng-fu). "Centralization of power" (*chung-yang chi-ch'üan*) would thus be achieved. Concurrent posts and assignments were expressly ruled out; it was

[60] Ibid., pp. 11b–12a.
[61] Hsieh, *Government of China*, p. 361.

implied that the established practice of balancing Manchu and Chinese appointments was to be abandoned.[62]

There was more than one point of contact between this plan and K'ang Yu-wei's 1898 program of administrative reform: that governmental reorganization should serve to prepare for eventual adoption of constitutionalism, that separation of powers should be an essential feature of the new administrative system, and that administrative efficiency should be attained through structural and functional rationalization. In fact, K'ang could hardly have been able to improve upon what was proposed here (which involved the replacement of the traditional "administrative sextet" by a Western-type cabinet).[63]

However, the co-sponsors of the plan did not achieve very much more success than K'ang in translating their ideas into practice. As records show, the Ch'ing court adopted only a part of the 1906 plan, being not willing to make more than a half-hearted move toward the avowed goal. In the decree of November 1,[64] no mention was made of separation of powers, although an Advisory Council (Tzu-cheng yüan) was promised and later instituted. Dual presidency in the boards was to be discontinued, but holding of concurrent posts was allowed. The distinction between Manchu and Chinese in appointing high officials was to be discarded but, ironically, among the high-echelon appointees to the newly organized imperial government, Manchus outnumbered Chinese.[65]

Let us now take a quick look at the changes in the provincial administration as proposed in 1906–7. In response to a decree issued November 1, 1906,[66] Tsai-tse and his group proceeded to draft a plan of reorganization and to consult appropriate provincial officials. I-k'uang, Sun Chia-nai, and Ch'ü Hung-chi then reviewed the plan and made their own recommendations to the throne, July 7, 1907. They began by quoting from the decree, to the effect that as the people were not qualified for local self-government (*ti-fang tzu-chih*), it was important to reorganize the *chou* and *hsien* administrations as a preparatory measure.

[62] Chu, *Tung-hua hsü-lu, chüan* 202, pp. 12b–13a. I have used the Brunnert and Hagelstrom translation of these names (*Present Day Political Organization of China*).

[63] See, e.g., "Shang Ch'ing-ti ti-liu shu" and "Ch'ing ting-li hsien-fa k'ai kuo-hui che" (submitted under K'uo-p'u-wu-t'ung's signature), in Chien, *Wu-hsü*, 2: 199–200, 236–37.

[64] Chu, *Tung-hua hsü-lu*, pp. 13b–14a.

[65] Hsieh, *Government of China*, pp. 351–52 and Cameron, *Reform Movement*, p. 107. Chang, *Ch'ing shih*, 4: 2833–36, lists the names of the eleven ministries as reorganized in 1906.

[66] Chu, *Tung-hua hsü-lu, chüan* 202, pp. 14a–b.

The changes they went on to suggest were quite limited in scope. The structure of the provincial government, especially the levels above the *ssu-tao*, was left virtually untouched. The most important changes that they envisaged in the lower levels were calculated to attain two objectives, initiating "judicial independence" and laying groundwork for "self-government."

To accomplish the former, they suggested that local courts be set up, which would take over the judicial powers of the magistracy. The magistrates, relieved of the heavy burden of hearing litigations, would have more time to look after the local inhabitants' needs such as education, agriculture, industry, and police. They also proposed that the number of subordinate functionaries be increased and their quality be improved. With more adequate supporting personnel, the magistrates should be in a better position to take the first steps of "self-government"—in particular, to organize local deliberative assemblies (*i-shih tung-shih*). It was further recommended that the changes be first made in the Three Eastern Provinces (Fengtien, Kirin, and Heilungkiang) because of their importance and that reorganization also be promptly effected in Chihli and Kiangsu because means of communication were most highly developed and the inhabitants better informed than those of any other province.[67]

The Ch'ing court approved of the plan and set a time limit of fifteen years for all the provinces to complete the authorized reorganization. This, it was expressly said, would constitute "preparation for constitutional government."[68] It might be noted that the idea of "self-government" figured prominently in the 1907 blueprint for local administrative reform. Was not this also a prominent feature in K'ang Yu-wei's program?[69]

[67] Ibid., *chüan* 206, pp. 17a–19a. Cameron, *Reform Movement*, pp. 107–10, summarizes the contents of this document.

[68] Chu, *Tung-hua hsü-lu, chüan* 206, p. 19a, gives the text of the decree issued Kuang-hsü 33rd year, 5th month, 27th day (July 7, 1907).

[69] The Ministry of Interior (Min-cheng pu, literally, "ministry of people's affairs"), submitted a memorial on March 26, 1907, which contains this interesting observation: "No [country] has achieved wealth and strength without devoting attention to people's rule (*min chih*). . . . Although at present the knowledge and intelligence of the people in the provinces remain undeveloped . . . thus making it impractical to institute local self- government immediately, . . . it would be proper to begin with a study of the actual functioning of the village association (*hsiang she*)." The Minister was then Hsü Shih-ch'ang, who later (April 20) was appointed governor-general of the reorganized Three Eastern Provinces. Chu, *Tung-hua hsü-lu, chüan* 205, pp. 1b–2b, gives the text of the memorial just cited.

"ESSAYS ON THE OFFICIAL SYSTEM"

K'ang could scarcely find comfort in the fact that his ideas of administrative reform did not all die at the end of the Hundred Days. The changes advocated and actually made after 1901 had left untouched the major defects of the old structure. Worse still, the innovations adopted were more in the nature of political window dressing than honest efforts at constitutional government. K'ang made his feeling known in a memorial to the empress dowager in 1903. "The nonessential undertakings" authorized in 1900–1901, he wrote, could not save the country because they did not go to the root of the matter, namely, reorganization as a step toward constitutionalism.[70]

Insistent reformer that he was, K'ang refused to be discouraged. He continued to apply his thoughts to the problem. By early 1903, while he was in India, he had completed a book, *Essays on the Official System (Kuan-chih i)*[71] in which he developed his ideas on the subject in a systematic way.[72] The fact that he used "Ming-i" as his pseudonym when he published these essays for the first time suggests that he had not given up the hope of eventually bringing his views to bear on the actual situation.[73]

This book was probably the most systematic treatise on government that appeared in China at the time. After setting forth what he con-

[70] "Tsou wei kuo-shih wei-chi . . . ho ch'ing . . . kuei cheng huang-shang li-ting hsien-fa . . . che," *Wan-mu-ts'ao-t'ang i-kao, chüan* 3, p. 16b. K'ang went on to reiterate the necessity of convening a popularly elected parliament. It is doubtful that this memorial actually reached the empress dowager.

[71] It was published in book form in Shanghai, 1904, and reprinted (at least three times) in 1905, 1906, and 1907. Author's preface was dated Feb. 4, 1902. The preface and eight of the fourteen essays appeared first in Liang Ch'i-ch'ao's *Hsin-min ts'ung-pao*, nos. 35–52, under the pseudonym Ming-i. That K'ang attached much importance to this book may be gathered from the fact that he had it reprinted several times. The *Pu-jen*, nos. 9–10 (2 nos. in 1 vol., Shanghai, 1918), carried an advertisement, showing that it was still available at that late date.

[72] In a telegram to Chao Heng-t'i (military governor of Hunan), summer of 1922, K'ang mentioned this book as "Kuan-chih k'ao." K'ang T'ung-pi, *Nan-hai K'ang hsien-sheng nien-p'u hsü-pien*, p. 88b, gives the text of this telegram. Lu Nai-hsiang and Lu Tun-k'uei, *K'ang Nan-hai hsien-sheng chuan*, pp. 20a–25b, summarize the contents of this book.

[73] *Ming-i* is an allusion to the thirty-sixth hexagram of the *Book of Changes*, in particular, to these lines:

> Darkening the Light. In adversity
> It furthers one to be persevering.

(Richard Wilhelm, *The I Ching*, 1: 150, and 2: 210). Cf. James Legge, *The I Ching*, p. 134: "*Ming-i* indicates that (in the circumstances which it denotes) it will be advantageous to realize (the difficulty of the position) and maintain firm correctness."

sidered the fundamental principles of government (essay 1), K'ang
went on to evaluate, on the basis of these principles, modern Western
political institutions and those obtaining in China from ancient to Sung
times (essays 2–4). He then subjected the existing Chinese system to a
searching criticism (essay 5). In the remainder of the book (essays
6–14) he offered suggestions for improvement and reform. Much of
what he set down had been said previously in less elaborate ways. It
suffices here to mention only a few salient points.

Governments, K'ang believed, should be judged by their ability to
serve the interests of the people. For "as the people constitute the basis
of the state, the affairs of the people are the primary concern of government." Livelihood, education, protection of "life, property, and rights"
(*sheng-ming ts'ai-ch'an ch'üan-li*), and many other matters that pertained
to the people's material and mental welfare were within the scope of
the government's service. Functionaries who rendered such services
were therefore properly called "the people's officials" (*min-kuan*).[74]

There were, however, other functions that, though they did not bear
directly or completely on the people's welfare, were nevertheless necessary or useful. The state must keep its financial house in order; it must
defend itself against external aggression; it must conduct its peaceful
relations with other states. Those who performed these functions were
"the state's officials" (*kuo-kuan*), in contradistinction to "the people's
officials." A third type of function, such as the maintenance of posts,
railways, telegraph, and banks, served the interests both of the people
and the state. There must be, accordingly, another group of officials
(K'ang omitted to label them) to carry out these useful if not also necessary tasks. In monarchical states, past and present, were a fourth group
of officials who looked after the needs of the ruler and his household.
They were "the ministering officials" (*kung-fung chih kuan*) who found
no place in republican states and whose functions therefore could not
be regarded as universally indispensable.[75]

No government was complete without "deliberative officials," as execution presupposed deliberation. In K'ang's words, "It is the nature
of things that administration follows legislation."[76] Local officials, too,
were of paramount importance to a state. For "while administering
(*cheng*) proceeds from the state, governing (*chih*) stems from the peo-

---

[74] "Kuan-chih yüan-li," in *Hsin-min ts'ung-pao* (hereafter, *HM*), no. 35, pp. 21–23.
[75] Ibid., p. 25.
[76] Ibid., p. 24.

ple." The establishment of local governments was a practice followed by all states.[77]

Serving the people's interests, then, constituted the essential duty of government. Evidently, the greater capacity a government had for discharging that duty, the better it would be. Administrative efficiency, in other words, was vitally desirable. One way to achieve efficiency, according to K'ang, was to divide functions precisely and to define responsibilities clearly. Anciently, when life was simple, there was no need to institute a plurality of governmental offices. But in the modern "civilized world" in which governing and administering had become a complicated matter, it was unavoidable that administrative functions multiplied and the number of functionaries, each with specific duties, correspondingly increased. A well-articulated system of functional division thus insured proficient government.[78]

A second way to attain this end was to maintain effective central control over the administrative structure. Local governments should of course have adequate authority to perform their appropriate tasks. However, it would be determinental to administrative efficiency in general if the authority of the central government was countervailed by regional authorities. Formerly, when political unity was still a thing of the future and when means of communications were rudimentary, such as in ancient China, "division of authority among feudal lords" had to be allowed. But modern conditions made administrative centralization not only feasible but desirable. A government (such as the imperial government of late nineteenth-century China) that did not have real and complete control of the economic and military affairs of the country would be a poor instrument to meet the challenges of a Darwinian political world.[79]

The scope of the government's authority should not be unduly restricted. It should be sufficiently wide to permit effective action in serving the people. In the past, when China remained in blissful isolation, with no concern about aggression or competition from without, her government had wisely avoided interfering with the ways and lives of the people. Absence of governmental control gave them a sort of freedom (*tzu-yu*). But noninterference did not suit modern times when states competed and struggled constantly with one another, and when the fate of a nation hinged on the degree of cohesion achieved by its

[77] Ibid., p. 26.
[78] "Kuang-chih i hsü," in *HM*, no. 35, p. 33a.
[79] Ibid., p. 33b.

members as a result of political discipline. To bring a people such as the Chinese under the traditional rule to confront a well-ordered modern nation would be like "driving riffraff to face an organized army." One could hardly expect victory.[80] The people's best interests, in fact, were served not by giving them unlimited freedom but by guiding them with a competent administration. In a constitutional state, whether monarchical or republican in form, in which the people's interests stood paramount and protected by law, there was little danger of the government becoming arbitrary or oppressive, even though it exercised substantial authority over the people. Political democracy, in other words, did not preclude administrative efficacy; the former required the latter for successful operation.

With the basic principle of government thus established, K'ang proceeded to use it as a criterion to evaluate Chinese and Western governments as he knew them. Some of the highlights of his lengthy discussion will suffice to indicate the drift of his thinking.

K'ang had high opinion of what he regarded as the government of the legendary emperor Yao. Each office was designed to serve the people; functions were minutely divided; each office had only one incumbent at a time; all local officials were under central control. Of the eight principal offices not a single one was *kuo-kuan*, and preponderant emphasis was on nonmilitary affairs. "That, indeed, was a system truly befitting an age of perfect peace and unity." "Even the present European and American systems" had nothing to add to its excellence.[81]

K'ang traced the source of imperfections that he discerned in the administrative structures of imperial China to the *Chou-li*.[82] The most glaring of the departures from the perfect system of antiquity was the conversion of most, if not all, of the government officials into servants of the autocratic ruler. Thus, most functionaries of Han times were "in truth no better than slaves who had nothing to do with the people's affairs."[83] This was true generally of all subsequent dynasties.

Another pernicious influence exerted by the *Chou-li* was the adminis-

[80] Ibid., p. 34b.

[81] "Chung-kuo ku kuan-chih p'ien," *HM*, no. 37, pp. 27–30. K'ang traced the changes occurring in Hsia and Shang times, described the resulting systems, and compared them with what he knew of Western systems (ibid., pp. 31–33).

[82] Ibid., nos. 38–39 (2 nos. in 1 vol.), pp. 73–76. The *Chou-li*, according to K'ang, was a forgery from the pen of Liu Hsin and a product of Ch'in and Han times when autocracy began to prevail (ibid., p. 76). However, he conceded that some ideas in the work were not without merit (ibid., nos. 40–41 [2 nos. in 1 vol.] pp. 31–39).

[83] Ibid., p. 78.

trative sextet, the division of the central government into six "Boards," which persisted down to 1907. As a result of such an arrangement, functions could not be precisely and logically separated, nor could responsibilities be clearly defined.[84]

K'ang admitted that there were a few saving features in the generally faulty structures of China's imperial government. The Han system, for instance, deserved praise because it avoided the pitfall of the seniority rule (which was destined to sap the strength of the Ch'ing system) by making it possible to recruit officials on the basis of personal qualifications through an institutionalized recommendation procedure.[85] The Sung dynasty system, too, had a number of merits. It achieved effective centralization of administrative, financial, and military powers in the imperial government; at the same time it succeeded in reducing the size of the main administrative division, the *chou*, to no larger than one quarter of that existing in Han times. Regrettably, however, this "most excellent" arrangement was later replaced by the unwieldy provincial division (the *hsing-sheng*) of the Yüan dynasty.[86]

Assuming that China could learn much from the West, K'ang devoted a chapter of his book to analyzing the political institutions of over a dozen European and American countries, both large and small. He found that in general these countries attached most weight to four main functions, namely, those relative to economic, military, domestic, and foreign affairs. Facts of modern political life had dictated a broad principle, that "while the people are paramount, the state must nevertheless be given priority" in fashioning the governmental structure.[87] This, K'ang believed, was one lesson for China to learn.

Another desirable feature should be noted. European governments usually were manned by "officials with specific duties" (*chuan-wu chih kuan*), each of whom performing only a single function. In this respect, the English system was a worthy counterpart of the Sung structure, in that it was also characterized by the practice of instituting governmental offices as needs arose from time to time and by the existence of a large number of ministries and other administrative bodies. Such arrange-

---

[84] Ibid., pp. 42–43.

[85] "Chung-kuo Han-hou kuan-chih p'ien," *HM*, nos. 42–43 (2 nos. in 1 vol.), p. 37.

[86] "Sung Kuan-chih tsui-shan p'ien," *HM*, nos. 46–48 (3 nos. in 1 vol.), pp. 89–98. K'ang noted several other "merits" (ibid., pp. 98–103).

[87] "Ko-kuo kuan-chih p'ien," *HM*, no. 50, pp. 17–18.

ments were conducive to efficiency. "For when functions are properly divided and defined, they are easily performed."[88]

K'ang then turned his attention to the existing Chinese system. He found that almost everything was wrong with it, both with respect to fundamental aim and to mode of operation.[89] As his criticisms (made in other connections) have already been mentioned, we shall here refer briefly only to what he considered the directions in which changes should be effected.

K'ang ruled out at once the possibility of facile Westernization or "returning to antiquity." Because of wide differences in physical and historical conditions, no Western system, however excellent in itself, could serve as China's model. And because the country was in a process of far-reaching political transformation, China's past experience could not afford any reliable guide.[90] Her present administrative malady— lack of concern for the people and of efficiency—which inhered in faulty organization, irrational procedures, and undue centrifugal forces, called for special corrective treatment.[91]

The nature of administrative functions, K'ang believed, should dictate the form of administrative organization. There were (we recall) three main types of government functions, those serving the people, those serving the state, and those serving both the people and the state. Under the present circumstances, the best way to evolve a genuinely efficacious people-serving system would be the institution of "citizens' self-rule" (*Kung-min tzu-chih*); the best way to improve the quality of the dual-service officialdom would be to reduce the size of local divisions and simultaneously to increase the number of local functionaries; and the best way to enhance the efficiency of the state-serving apparatus would be to realize administrative centralization. "Self-rule" and centralization were the most crucial of these three.[92] To condition the people for "self-rule," it would be useful to launch a program of study and discussion of political affairs to be carried on by locally organized "study associations" (*hsüeh hui*). To facilitate central control, railway, telegraph, and postal systems should be developed.[93]

It is unnecessary to go into K'ang's concrete proposals beyond noting a few major points. First, regarding the central structure. As adminis-

[88] Ibid., pp. 18–23.
[89] "Chung-kuo chin-jih kuan-chih ta-pi i-kai lun," *HM*, no. 51, pp. 59–67.
[90] Ibid., p. 61.
[91] Ibid., pp. 61–65.
[92] Ibid., pp. 60–61.
[93] Ibid., pp. 60–61, 67.

trative reform was to be but a preliminary step leading to eventual constitutional government, K'ang did not wish to have the existing system completely swept away. Some offices, such as the Six Boards, should be retained and reformed pending the institution of new organs to take over their functions.[94] Others, including the Censorate, the Hanlin College, and the Grand Court of Revision, should also remain but with their functions modified to suit modern needs. The Censorate, in a sense, was "China's deliberative body"; it should be allowed to stand, even after a parliament had been convened, and to function as a sort of administrative court. The Hanlin College, to be renamed "Hsüeh-shih yüan" (Academy of Scholars), would after reorganization become an advisory body. The Grand Court should be "elevated to become the Ministry of Justice." Still other offices, namely, the various courts and all sinecures should be converted into brevet ranks and thus cease to be integral parts of the administration.[95] Finally, those officials that served the emperor and his household should be drastically reduced in number. Eunuchs, in particular, should all be dismissed and their duties taken over by members of the lettered elite (*shih-jen*).[96]

The reorganized administrative structure as K'ang envisaged it was a somewhat elaborate one. It was to be comprised of thirty-three ministries (*pu*), falling into six groups according to function. These together with a "law ministry," an "exterior (i.e., foreign affairs) ministry," and a ministry serving the imperial household were to constitute "the government." An administrative court (formerly the Censorate) and an audit department (*shen-chi yüan*) completed the central system.[97] Such

[94] "Ts'un chiu-kuan lun," *HM*, no. 52, pp. 44–47.

[95] Ibid., pp. 47–48.

[96] "Kung-fung sheng-chih lun," *HM*, no. 55, pp. 33–37. Cf. "Hai-wai . . . Chung-hua hsien-cheng-hui . . . ch'ing-yüan shu" (1907), *K'ang Nan-hai hsien-sheng wen-ch'ao*, 5, *tsou-i*: 15a–b.

[97] "Fen-tseng hsing-cheng pu," summarized in Lu and Lu, *K'ang Nan-hui hsien-sheng chuan*, pp. 20–22. The ministries envisioned by K'ang were: Group I, dealing with Interior Affairs: (1) Northern Ministry (for Chihli, Shangtung, Shansi, and Shensi); (2) Eastern Ministry (for Kiangsu, Chekiang, Kiangsi, and Anhwei); (3) Central Ministry (for Honan, Hupeh, and Hunan); (4) Southern Ministry (for Kwangtung, Fukien, and Kwangsi); (5) Western Ministry (for Kansu, Yunnan, Kweichow, and Szechwan); (6) Liao Ministry (for the Three Eastern Provinces); (7) Meng (i.e., Mongol) Ministry (for Inner and Outer Mongolia); (8) Hui (i.e., Moslem) Ministry (for Singkiang); (9) Tsang Ministry (for Tibet). Group II, dealing with financial matters: (1) Finance; (2) Currency; (3) Banking; (4) Maritime Customs; (5) Salt Administration; (6) National Debts. Group III, dealing with "people's affairs": (1) Agriculture; (2) Industry; (3) Commerce; (4) Forestry; (5) Mining; (6) Husbandry; (7) Silk and Tea; (8) Reclamation. Group IV, dealing with communication and transportation: (1) Posts; (2) Telegraph; (3) Railway; (4) Sea Ports.

an arrangement, K'ang thought, would do some justice to the principles of precise separation of functions and clear definition of responsibilities.

In the sixth and seventh essays of the book,[98] K'ang called for drastic changes in the local government, seeking to introduce an element of constitutional government at local levels and to eliminate the province, which he considered an obstacle to centralization. He reiterated much of what he had said in connection with his campaign for constitutional monarchy,[99] that it was better to rule oneselves than to be ruled by others, that "government by the people" had brought wealth and power to Western countries, that the absence of self-rule was a cause of China's stagnation, and that, therefore, "local self-rule" was an essential part of administrative reform.[100] Adapting Western ideas to Chinese conditions, he suggested a three-level structure of local government: rural, *hsien*, and metropolitan. At each level was to be a "bureau" (*chü*), with a sort of mayor, a judge, a police chief, a tax collector, and a postmaster, all to be elected by qualified voters. There was also to be a council ("deliberative assembly," *i-shih hui*) each member of which would represent an electorate of 300 or 400 citizens. Members of the local elite, known as "gentry councilmen" (*shen i-yüan*), were to take part in the council's deliberations concerning matters of local interest, such as census, roads, schools, hygiene, taxation, and police.[101] This would then be the initial setup for "local self-rule."

The province, an area "extending over a thousand *li*," and containing millions of people, was too large an administrative division to permit effective government. It should be broken into units no larger than the

---

Group V, dealing with cultural affairs: (1) Literature; (2) Education; (3) Fine Arts. Group VI, dealing with military affairs: (1) General Staff; (2) Army; (3) Navy. In addition to these thirty-three, there were to be a Ministry of Justice, a Ministry of Foreign Affairs, and a Ministry of Supply and Service (*kung-feng pu*), making a total of thirty-six.

[98] "Kung-min tzu-chih," in *Hsin-min ts'ung-pao hui-pien*, 2 (1902): 103–15 and "Hsi chiang tseng li," in ibid., pp. 138–55.

[99] See the first three sections of chapter 6, this volume.

[100] "Kung-min tzu-chih," pp. 103–7.

[101] Ibid., pp. 108–15. K'ang believed that possession of considerable property should be a qualification for citizenship and that persons otherwise not qualified to vote might be franchised by contributing suitable sums of money. This latter idea probably was inspired by the traditional practice of purchasing official ranks and posts, which he elsewhere condemned (ibid., pp. 106–7). Liang Ch'i-ch'ao objected strongly to this idea, as he indicated in an editor's note (ibid., pp. 103–4). K'ang continued to advocate self-rule in the years following. See, e.g., "Lun sheng fu hsien hsiang i-yüan i chi-k'ai wei pai shih chih pen" (1905), *Wen-ch'ao, chüan* 4, p. 67a, and "Lun tzu-chih" (circa 1908), pp. 40a–43b.

existing circuit (*tao*) and would thus cease to be an administrative division. The intervening divisions between the existing province and the district (*hsien*), namely, the circuit and the prefecture, served no useful administrative purpose and merely impeded the free flow of communication between higher and lower levels of government. They too should be abolished as administrative divisions, leaving the equivalents of the circuit, the district, and the village (*hsiang*) to form a three-tiered structure. The district, which should be a vital link in local administration, had hitherto been rendered ineffectual because the magistrate was given too little power, treated too shabbily in point of rank and salary, and permitted too few subordinate functionaries to help him carry out his duties. All this must change.[102]

As a transitional measure, K'ang would let the province and the prefecture stand as a "supervising" but not administrative organ; a "governor-general" would preside over both. A "superintendent of people's affairs" (*tu-pan min-cheng ta-ch'en*) would head each circuit in the reorganized system, with authority comparable to that enjoyed by the existing governor. Citizens of each circuit would send representatives to form a "people's assembly" (*min i-hui*) with the superintendent as presiding officer.[103]

The rank and salary of the "district administrator" (*hsien ling-shih*) should be appreciably higher than those of the existing magistrate; the number of his subordinate functionaries should be greatly enlarged. To enhance efficiency, the district administration should have under it four offices (*ts'ao*), each with subdivisions, to take charge separately of matters relating to agriculture, trade, police, education, and others. The judicial powers hitherto exercised by the magistrate should be transferred to a court, which, with an appropriate number of judges, was to be independent of the district administration. Voters of each village would send representatives each year to a district "people's assembly," which, with the district administrator as presiding officers, would operate in accordance with the principle of majority rule. This deliberative body would lay down policies; the administrator would then carry them out. The old regulation that prohibited local officials to serve in their native provinces was most detrimental to administra-

---

[102] "Hsi-chiang tseng-li p'ien," *Hsin-min ts'ung-pao hui-pien*, 2: 138–44. Incidentally, the circuit intendant exercised jurisdiction over two or more of the prefectures in a province. The number of prefectures in each province varied. Kiangsi had 13 while Shensi only 7, the average being around 10.

[103] Ibid., pp. 144–49.

tive efficiency; for it resulted in handing over local administration to men who knew nothing of the needs and conditions—not even the dialect—of the place to which they were assigned. This regulation, if not rescinded outright, should be relaxed.[104]

CENTRALIZATION VERSUS "FEDERALISM"

In the *Kuang-chih i* of 1903, as we have just seen, K'ang laid clear emphasis on administrative centralization and local self-rule, the former to insure governmental efficiency and the latter to prepare for the eventual adoption of constitutionalism. This latter emphasis separated K'ang's proposals from the reorganization measures recommended and executed in the post-Boxer years. Despite lip service to constitutional government, the changes that were effected in the administrative structure in 1906–7 amounted to little more than what might be called political paramorphism—alteration in form without modification of the essential character of the existing system. On the other hand, the institution of "people's assemblies" and "deliberative assemblies" on local levels as demanded by K'ang was intended to be a decisive step toward radical transformation of the imperial structure.

K'ang insisted emphatically on administrative centralization. Between 1902 and 1922 he had written on this theme probably as much as he did on "self-rule." Greatly alarmed by increasing velocity of the play of centrifugal forces in China during the last decades of the nineteenth century and the first years of the twentieth,[105] he stoutly and consistently maintained that political unity must be preserved and that only a strong centralized government could cope with the difficult situation. Centralization, he believed, was not incompatible with self-government, as democracy did not preclude political unity. The two, in fact, complemented each other. With the people taking part in government from the village up to the national level, tyranny no longer constituted a threat; and standing in a competitive world, only a centralized administration, unhampered by the divisive pressures of power-

---

[104] Ibid., pp. 149–55. K'ang attached so much importance to the adverse effects of this practice that he devoted an entire essay to urge its abandonment, namely, "Hsüan chin-ti-jen wei kuan," the fourteenth piece of the book.

[105] See, e.g., Lu and Lu, *K'ang Nan-hai hsien-sheng chuan*, p. 20b and K'ang T'ung-pi, *Nan-hai K'ang hsien-sheng tzu-pien nien-p'u pu-i*, p. 24a. Mary C. Wright, *The Last Stand of Chinese Conservatism*, pp. 57–59, refers briefly to "the breach between central and provincial authority" which widened toward the end of the nineteenth century.

ful regional governments, could deal competently with the many critical problems that confronted the nation.[106]

Enhancing the authority of the central government involved, in practical terms, the liquidation of the province as a virtually autonomous political entity. K'ang did not, however, arrive at this conclusion until sometime after 1898. As late as 1897 and 1898 he was willing to entrust the provinces with the task of reform. "For the time being," he remarked, "it does no harm to permit divergencies; we can expect general consensus (regarding reform) in three years."[107] In fact, as we recall, he had tried two years earlier to enlist the support of provincial officials, notably Liu K'un-i and Chang Chih-tung, for his "Reform Club" (Ch'iang-hsüeh hui).[108] He must have been gratified that a number of provinces, with or without his direct encouragement, launched reform programs of their own.[109] At the same time, however, he must also have been piqued by provincial officials who refused or neglected to carry out the reform measures as decreed by the emperor.[110] These officials conceivably aided K'ang to come to the realization that the province was a stumbling block to good government.

K'ang's opposition to provincial autonomy sometimes took the form

[106] The author's aim, as just indicated, was to prepare the people for constitutional government. See Lu and Lu, *K'ang Nan-hai hsien-sheng chuan*, pp. 20a–b; K'ang T'ung-pi, *Nan-hai K'ang hsien-sheng tzu-pien nien-p'u pu-i*, p. 24a; and Liang Ch'i-ch'ao, *Nan-hai K'ang hsien-sheng chuan*, p. 85. The last item is available also in Chien, *Wu-hsü*, 4: 34–35.

[107] "Shang Ch'ing-ti ti-wu shu" (Kwang-hsü 23rd year, 12th month), in Chien, *Wu-hsü*, 2: 196, where K'ang referred to what he called the "third alternative policy," namely, "permitting provincial officials to launch institutional reforms of their own."

[108] *Nien-p'u*, pp. 13b–14a.

[109] The most important of these was the program implemented in Hunan under Governor Ch'en Pao-chen's leadership and with Liang Ch'i-ch'ao's active participation. Charles M. Lewis, "The Reform Movement in Hunan, 1896–1898," pp. 62–90, is a useful account. See also Cheng T'an-chou, "Shih-chiu shih-chi-mo Hunan ti wei-hsin yün-tung," and Ch'en Hsiung, "Wu-hsü cheng-pien ch'ien-hou Hu-nan wei-hsin yün-tung ti she-hui chi-ch'u ho ssu-ch'ao ti yen-pien." Less ambitious programs were adopted in a few other provinces. Tikhvinsky, *Dvizhenie za reformy v Kitae v kontse XIX i Kan Iu-wei*, chap. 6, describes the situations in various provinces in the years 1895–98.

[110] Prompted by K'ang, Yang Shen-hsiu requested the emperor to commend Ch'en Pao-chen, leader of the reform movement in Hunan; Sung Po-lu, also inspired by K'ang, memorialized the emperor that T'an Chung-lin be punished for his failure to implement reform measures in Kwangtung (*Nien-p'u*, pp. 23a–b; Chang Po-chen, *Nan-hai K'ang hsien-sheng chuan*, p. 33a; and Chao Feng-t'ien, "Kang Chang-su hsien-sheng nien-p'u kao," p. 204). Chu, *Tung-hua hsü-lu, chüan* 147, pp. 25a–b, gives the text of an imperial decree severely reprimanding T'an. The text is available also in *Te-tsung shih-lu, chüan* 423, pp. 14b–15b.

of opposition to "federalism." Liang Ch'i-ch'ao appears to have been the first to raise this controversial issue, in the autumn of 1900 while K'ang was an exile in Penang. Apparently impressed by the American experience, Liang suggested that China would do well to adopt a federal system by converting her eighteen provinces into independent states and then effecting a union among them. To this K'ang objected vehemently and firmly.[111] A few years later, while he traveled in Italy, he explained at some length his adamant opposition to "federalism." It was the nature of men, he said, to compete and to struggle, especially when they formed themselves into states. War could be avoided among smaller units only when they integrated themselves into a larger body politic, a truth to which European history as well as the history of China bore witness. Therefore, to break up a unified empire, such as China, into fragments was political retrogression—reversion to the conditions prevailing two thousand years before.[112] "Federalism" would be a step decidedly in the wrong direction.

Most of the time, however, he argued for the abolition of the province as an administrative division. In a petition submitted in 1907 in the name of the overseas members of the China Constitutional Association (Chung-hua hsien-cheng hui) he in effect started an open campaign against the province.[113] In the years immediately following he wrote a number of pieces to advance his cause, the most noteworthy of which being "Essay on Abolishing the Province" ("Ts'ai hsing-sheng i").[114] He pointed again and again to the many serious administrative problems created by the undue size of the province and the excessive powers of the governor-general and governor. He was convinced that these problems would surely continue to plague the country, if the province was allowed to exist when China became a constitutional state. For it would be impossible for China to have a workable administrative system if the province continued to exercise power over such vital matters as finance, army, and justice. It was indeed inconceivable that without a

[111] As K'ang recalled in the summer of 1922, in his telegram to Chao Heng-t'i, governor of Hunan (K'ang T'ung-pi, *Nan-hai K'ang hsien-sheng tzu-pien nien-p'u pu-i*, p. 88a). Liang perhaps had received inspiration from Rousseau. See his "Lu-so hsüeh-an" (1901), *Yin-ping-shih ho-chi, wen-chi* 6, p. 110, final paragraph.

[112] "I-ta-li yu-chi," *Ou-chou shih-i kuo yu-chi*, pp. 45–46. This piece is available also in K'ang T'ung-pi, *Nan-hai K'ang hsien-sheng nien-p'u hsü-pien*, pp. 36b–38b, bearing the title, "Lun Lo-ma li-kuo te-shih."

[113] "Hai-wai . . . Chung-hua hsien-cheng-hui . . . ch'ing-yüan shu" (1907), *K'ang Nan-hai hsien-sheng wen-ch'ao*, 5, *tsou-i*: 17b–19b (hereafter cited as *Wen-ch'ao*).

[114] This essay, published in 1910, is available in *Wen-ch'ao*, 4: 28b–46b. K'ang set forth similar ideas in another piece, "Wai-kuan-chih i" (*Wen-ch'ao*, 4: 46b–59b).

strong central administration China could attain prosperity and strength, prerequisites for a modern "civilized" state.[115]

K'ang's misgivings were soon to be confirmed by the situation that the "war lords" brought about in republican China—by men who in effect inherited the powers of the governors and governors-general and materially extended them. K'ang renewed with added vigor his campaign against administrative fragmentation about the time when the 1911 revolution broke out, with the completion of the "Essay on Abolishing the Province"; in the summer of the next year he came out with an "Essay on China's Salvation" in which he reiterated his opposition to "federalism."[116] Given the widely different conditions in China and the United States, he said, it would be folly for the former to adopt the American form of government, which showed "nine harmful features" without possessing a "single advantage."[117] Moreover, the damage that was being done by the military governors (*tu-chün*), was already worse than anything their predecessors (the *tu fu* of late Ch'ing times) had done. The root of the evil lay in the province, an unruly administrative division on account of its size. The remedy, K'ang said, was simple: abolish the province but retain the prefecture as the largest unit of local government.[118]

In the 1910s and early 1920s persons with diverse motivations promoted what they called the "self-government of federated provinces" movement (*lien-shen tzu-chih*). It appears to have reached its height in 1922 when Hunan promulgated a "provincial constitution" and several

[115] "Ts'ai hsing-sheng i," *Wen-ch'ao*, 4: 32b–35a.

[116] "Fei sheng lun" is in *Wen-ch'ao*, 2: 32a–58a; *K'ang Nan-hai wen-chi* (hereafter *Wen-chi*), *chüan* 2, pp. 21b–45b; and *Pu-jen*, no. 1, pp. 5–11. According to K'ang T'ung-pi, *Nan-hai K'ang hsien-sheng tzu-pien nien-p'u pu-i*, pp. 21b–22a, "the declaration of independence" from the Ch'ing government by one province after another in the autumn of 1911 prompted K'ang to write this essay, hoping that it would serve to convince the revolutionary government and the military governors of the vital importance to preserve China's political unity. For brief accounts of the situation, see Li Chien-nung, *Political History of China*, pp. 248–49. The "Chung-hua chiu-kuo lun" is available in *Wen-ch'ao*, 1: 1–22; *Wen-chi*, *chüan* 1, pp. 1a–21a; *Pu-jen*, no. 1 (Feb., 1913), pp. 1–58; and *Pu-jen tsa-chih hui-pien*, 1st ser., *chüan* 1, pp. 1a–18a. At about the same time, K'ang wrote another piece, "Lun kung-ho li-hsien" in which he maintained that "even a republican state should be unitary, with centralized authority lodging in the national government," and that China should not follow the United States and adopt a federal system (*Wan-mu-ts'ao-t'ang i-kao, chüan* 1, pp. 69a–71b).

[117] "Fei sheng lun," *Pu-jen*, no. 1, pp. 5–11. Cf. "Chung-hua chiu-kuo lun," *Pu-jen*, no. 1, pp. 28–30.

[118] "Fei sheng i" (pt. 2 of "Fei sheng lun"), *Pu-jen*, no. 2, pp. 21–29, and "Ts'un fu i" (pt. 3 of "Fei sheng lun"), *Pu-jen*, no. 2, pp. 43–47.

other provinces attempted to do the same.[119] In K'ang's view all this reflected nothing more than the desire of the war lords to perpetuate their own personal power by thus institutionalizing it. He did not hesitate to make known his views to these men. When Chao Heng-t'i, governor of Hunan, sounded him out on the matter, he raised strong objections to federalism, repeating some of his old arguments, that the historical experiences of both China and European countries pointed to the desirability of political unity and the danger of division, that Western countries adopted federalism because of special historical circumstances, and that federalism constituted no remedy for the unsettled conditions of republican China. Unless and until the country could get rid of the war lords, loose talk about "self-government" could only serve as a pretext for political fragmentation. He restated his position in equally uncompromising terms on several other occasions.[120] Indeed, he was so convinced of the necessity of achieving political unity that he urged Wu P'ei-fu, one of the most powerful war lords of the time, to "unify China" by military force.[121]

K'ang's opposition to federalism was as much a logical consequence of his view on government as a reaction to the conditions of the period. It was his basic tenet, we recall, that strong centralized government must go hand in hand with local self-rule to give practical meaning to constitutional government. The following remarks, made in 1912, serve to make emphatically clear his position, although it involves questionable political theory as well as dubious history in denying the fact and desirability of "separation of powers" between central and local governments in certain systems.

[119] Li, *Political History*, pp. 401–5, gives a brief account. The actual beginnings of the movement might be traced to the declaration of independency by Shantung province in 1911 in which, among other things, it was said that the constitution of the republic should provide for federalism. The Hunan provincial constitution of Jan. 1, 1922, remained in force until 1926. It marked the episode following the downfall of the "self-government" declared by Chao Heng-t'i in 1920.

[120] Text of K'ang's telegram to Chao (summer, 1922) is in K'ang T'ung-pi, *Nan-hai K'ang hsien-sheng tzu-pien nien-p'u pu-i*, pp. 85b–91b. Yang-Fu-li, "K'ang-Liang nien-p'u kao-pen," pt. 2, pp. 61a–b, summarizes the contents of this document. In a letter in reply to Wu P'ei-fu (who was appointed Inspecting Commissioner of Hunan and Hupeh by the Peking government, Aug. 9, 1921) and Hsiao Yao-nan (Tuchün of Hupeh), written sometime in 1921, K'ang restated his opposition to federalism and his preference for self-rule at the prefectural and lower levels. *Wan-mu-tsao-t'ang i-kao*, *chüan* 4, pp. 104a–110a. A telegram on the same theme sent to Wu in the same year is available on microfilm, reel 2.

[121] K'ang T'ung-pi, *Pu K'ang Nan-hai hsien-sheng tzu-pien nien-p'u*, manuscript copy in the collection of Jung-pang Lo, p. 28b, mentions K'ang's telegram (March 5 and 6) to that effect.

To implement . . . great policies one cannot but pin one's hope on a strong government. . . . Therefore, whatever may be the form of government, be it monarchical or republican, no state can dispense with a centralized administration. [A constitutional government] differs from an autocracy in the division of powers [between its executive branch and] the legislative assembly. Under no circumstance should powers be divided between [the central and] local governments.[122]

The last sentence justifies the conjecture that K'ang saw no distinction between constitutional delegation of authority to local governments and arrogation of powers by local governments resulting from the play of centrifugal forces. He was inclined to confuse the notions of "political unity," "unitary government," and "administrative centralization," not being aware that a unified country could adopt a system of administrative devolution or that federalism necessarily precluded national unity. As a practical reformer speaking with reference to the situation in China, however, he had made his position unequivocally manifest, that political fragmentation must be stopped and a strong central administration must be evolved. It should be noted, however, that despite his stout objection to "federalism" he had no intention to advocate anything like "authoritarian rule" or "modernizing autocracy," favored by those wishing quickly to lift their countries out of stagnation.[123]

Somewhat curiously, in insisting upon the necessity of having a strong central government, K'ang adumbrated a view that Sun Yat-sen took years later. K'ang believed, we recall, that with the people's will articulated in representative assemblies, a powerful administration should serve to carry out its dictates in an efficient manner. This assumption appears to have underlain Sun's well-known theory of the relationship between "sovereignty" (or, "the political power of the people") and "ability" (or, "the administrative power of the government"). With the people exercising the former, there should be no danger that the government possessed too much of the latter. For the government, power was none other than that authority "which centralizes the great forces managing the affairs of the people."[124] Indeed, the more capable the government was, the better it would perform its

---

[122] *Chung-hua chiu-kuo lun, Pu-jen,* no. 1, pp. 37–40.

[123] David E. Apter, *The Politics of Modernization,* pp. 396–97 and passim; Maurice F. Neufeld, *Poor Countries and Authoritarian Rule,* pp. 144–60.

[124] Sun Yat-sen, "The Principle of Democracy," Lect. 6 (delivered April 26, 1924), *San min chu i,* in *Kuo-fu ch'üan-chi,* 2d ed., 1: 165; *San Min Chu I,* trans. Frank Price (Chungking, 1943), p. 342. Price's translation is here used with slight modifications.

services to the people. "An all-powerful, all-competent government in the employ of the people," therefore, would be "the finest thing" in political life.[125] Furthermore, like K'ang he believed in the desirability of unitary government and at the same time considered local self-government the foundation of democracy. And, like K'ang also, he did not hesitate to advocate the use of military force as a means to achieving political unity.

Here, however, the parallel ended. While both set store by unitary government, they did not agree as to its operational form. Sun, especially in the last years of his life, favored party dicatorship as a means to a political end—a democratic China as he envisioned it. His inspiration came largely from the Russian revolution. "The fruits of the (Russian) revolution," he declared late in 1924, "are greater and more perfect than what had been gained by the American or the French Revolution." In demanding the individual's absolute obedience to the party, Lenin was a "revolutionary sage" (*ko-ming sheng-jen*).[126] Such sentiments, it appears, were reminiscent of his pronouncements regarding "the military phase" of revolution heard around 1905.[127] To him, now as it was then, personal freedom might be a final product of revolution, but it could not be its immediate aim nor its watchword. K'ang, on the other hand, did not go so far as to recommend dictatorship, whether by one man or by one party, as a suitable means to bring about political unity and administrative centralization. His conception of the preconstitutional structure, as we have seen, came nearer to something like a pseudo cabinet government than the legacy of the Russian "revolutionary sage."

Whatever the similarities and differences between the views of K'ang and Sun concerning administrative centralization, one conclusion might be safely drawn, that while Sun achieved success in what he set out to accomplish, all K'ang's efforts amounted to exercises in futility. Sun's "northern expedition," launched in 1924, culminated in the establishment of the National Government in Nanking in 1928. The unity thus

[125] "The Principle of Democracy," Lect. 5 (delivered April 20, 1924) (*Kuo-fu chüan-chi*, p. 141); Price trans., p. 293, here quoted with modifications. Sun elaborated on this theory in *Kuo-fu ch'üan-chi*, pp. 144–54 and in Lect. 6, pp. 165–75 (Price trans., pp. 294–319 and 341–60), where he developed his elitist conception of government as a corollary to this theory.

[126] "Ko-ming ch'eng-kung ko-jen pu-neng yu tzu-yu . . ." (farewell speech to the cadets of the Huangpo Military Academy, Nov. 3, 1924), *Kuo-fu ch'üan-chi*, 3: 475.

[127] For an early formulation, see Wang Ching-wei, "Min-tsu-ti kuo-min," *Min pao*, no. 2 (Nov., 1905), pp. 20–22.

attained was far from complete or enduring. A number of war lords that survived the campaigns continued to defy the central authority, covertly or openly. The newly inaugurated government had to fight to preserve this hard-earned partial unity in the 1930s and 1940s against Japanese aggression and the Communist threat—in fact, to fight for its own very existence. In 1937 Nanking and most of China were lost to the Japanese occupation armies; 1949 saw the loss of the entire mainland to the Communists. Nevertheless, so long as it lasted the result was better than what K'ang had hoped to produce. Without power, political or military, and a *persona non grata* to the Ch'ing court and republican leaders, he exerted no influence on the actual course of events, despite his arguments for unity and efficiency—despite his conviction that China could not attain political modernity while remaining a divided house with an enfeebled, inept management.

This conviction, however, was not without indirect or implied support from his contemporaries. The endeavors of Sun and his followers constituted, in a sense, an unintentional endorsement of it. The Ch'ing government itself subscribed in effect to K'ang's idea of administrative centralization, when it adopted in 1906 the policy of reducing the governor-general's authority,[128] although it was calculated merely to perpetuate the Manchu regime and fell short of effective implementation. Chinese intellectuals, especially those writing at the beginning of the twentieth century and wishing to see "the strengthening of China within the shortest period," tended also to emphasize "group solidarity" and to rely on the state as an indispensable instrument of national regeneration.[129] Finally, support came from an unexpected quarter. A Japanese journalist editorialized in 1906 that as the crux of China's organizational problem lay in "the governor-general system," centralization of administrative power would be impossible as long as that system continued to exist.[130]

[128] Li, *Political History of China*, pp. 209–12.
[129] Y. C. Wang, *Chinese Intellectuals and the West*, pp. 358–60.
[130] *Shun-t'ien shih-pao*, Nov. 12, 1906, quoted in Li, *Political History of China*, p. 211.

Chapter 8

ECONOMIC REFORM

K'ang Yu-wei shared with many of his contemporaries the conviction that China stood in need of economic reform—that China would be doomed to remain poor and helpless, if she failed to transform her stagnant agrarian economy into an industrial-commercial one—and, together with them, he suggested ways and means to effect such a transformation. In the following pages I propose to examine these suggestions (made mainly between the 1890s and 1910s), with a view to showing their relationship with the trends of economic thinking current at the time, to ascertaining their theoretical relevance to the existing historical situation, and to explaining the lack of pragmatic success in his efforts to implement them.[1]

PROPOSALS FOR ECONOMIC MODERNIZATION AND THEIR IMPLICATIONS

K'ang made known his views concerning the empire's economic affairs in 1888 while he visited Peking. He had been "studying China's domestic problems and foreign relations," he said; the 1884 defeat by the French convinced him that unless China arouse herself and reform her institutions, she would not be able to survive.[2] It was not until the

---

[1] Chao Feng-t'ien, *Wan-Ch'ing wu-shih-nien ching-chi ssu-hsiang shih*, pp. 301–5, sketches K'ang's "economic ideal" as presented in the *Ta-t'ung shu*, but does not deal with his ideas of economic reform. K'ang took up the problem of economic modernization again in 1905 and wrote the *Wu-chih chiu-kuo lun* which, for sake of convenience, will be discussed in a later chapter.

[2] Jung-pang Lo, *K'ang Yu-wei: A Biography and a Symposium*, pp. 45–47.

autumn of 1888, however, that he succeeded in gaining a hearing by the imperial government, indirectly through T'u Jen-shou, a censor who was also deeply concerned about the fate of the country. K'ang drafted several memorials for him requesting, among other things, the minting of silver coins as a modest measure of currency reform. Meanwhile, he supported Chang Chih-tung's proposal to build a railroad between Lukouch'iao and Hankow and suggested to T'u "the idea of utilizing the grain transport system, along a route in which eighteen stations are already in existence," thereby reducing the cost of construction.[3]

The humiliating Sino-Japanese War of 1894 and the subsequent peace negotiations prompted K'ang to urge reform in more comprehensive terms. In a memorial, signed by K'ang and a large number of provincial graduates then in Peking to take the metropolitan examinations, the imperial government was asked to launch wide-ranging reforms, military, administrative, educational, and economic.[4] Instead of limiting himself to one or two specific problems, as he did in 1888, K'ang now presented a broad plan of economic development. To insure the country's economic prosperity he outlined a six-point program: a sound system of paper currency, minting of silver coins, machinery, mining, railroads and steamships, and a modern postal service. To improve the economic lot of the people he recommended four policies: attention to agriculture (adoption of new techniques), promotion of industry (development of science and technology), encouragement of commercial enterprise (government assistance and protection), and relief for the needy (appropriate measures to aid the unskilled, unemployed, and disabled).[5]

An important assumption underlay these proposals, namely, that the objective of economic reform was not only to enrich the state but to give an affluent life to the people. K'ang, in other words, did not think of "wealth" primarily as a means to attain "power," as modernizers of the 1860s tended to do,[6] but rather as an end desirable in itself, especially on the part of the Chinese people. K'ang departed from the position taken by the leaders of the "self-strengthening movement" in an-

[3] Ibid., pp. 47–49. K'ang also discussed the problem of financing the projected navy.

[4] This document, sometimes referred to as the "Kung-chü shang-shu" or "the Second Memorial to the Ch'ing Emperor," was drafted by K'ang and submitted May 2, 1895. The text is available in Chien Po-tsan et al., *Wu-hsü pien-fa*, 2: 131–54.

[5] Ibid., pp. 140–47. Lo, *K'ang*, p. 150, n. 26, summarizes these points.

[6] See, e.g., Ssu-yü Teng and John K. Fairbank, *China's Response to the West*, chaps. 5–9; cf. Chao, *Wan-Ch'ing . . . ssu-hsiang shih*, pp. 41–181.

other way. In his view the modernizing process must be left basically to the genius of private enterprise, although because of the general ignorance and apathy of the populace, the government must take appropriate actions to expedite or to initiate the trend of economic growth. He would like to see at the very beginning private capital and enterprise work hand in hand with government undertakings. Thus, in his 1895 memorial he suggested that private funds invested in the existing native banks (*yin-hao*) should form a part of the reserve in a paper currency system authorized by a government-controlled banking system; that private entrepreneurs, licensed by the government, were to build railroads in the eighteen provinces, in accordance with a general plan formulated by the government and in conformity with regulations laid down by the government; that licensed private investors should make all types of machinery and engage in every form of industry, including armament manufacturing; and that, finally, for the benefit of private entrepreneurs, the government should disseminate modern mining know-how and remove all the existing restrictions on mining.

The role of government in economic development was to be chiefly educational. The government should foster the spirit of business venture and cultivate the capacity for innovation, partly by helping private entrepreneurs to acquire modern managerial and technical skills, in agriculture as well as in industry and commerce. It should, for example, make it possible for inhabitants of every locality to form "agriculture societies" (*nung hui*) to facilitate transmission and exchange of new methods of farming, fishing, and forestry. Armed with such knowledge they would greatly increase their production and thus rise from bare subsistence to economic affluence. In order to develop industry, the government should take steps to introduce modern industrial know-how by preparing textbooks and establishing schools in all parts of the empire. It should, in addition, institute patent rights to protect inventions and give recognition to inventors of new industrial designs or processes. But, K'ang made it clear, while the government must exert vigorous leadership to set in motion the process of economic expansion, it was nevertheless ill-suited to engage in economic undertakings. Experience showed that government enterprises had too often been inefficient and unproductive. This was true not only in China but in Western countries as well. "Krupp cannons and Mauser rifles, valued by every nation as indispensable," he said, "are all products of private industry."

Government leadership, in short, was needed to stimulate private initiative, but it could not be a substitute for it. The same assumption underlay K'ang's recommendations concerning "encouragement of commercial enterprise." The government's role was essentially to enlighten, to encourage, to assist, and to protect private business, in particular, large-scale joint-stock companies with ample capital and a wide scope of operation and thus in a position to compete in the arena of foreign trade.

Other things the government should and could do. To relieve the pressure of population growth and to lighten the burden on the economy, the government should adopt measures to provide occupation to the unemployed, to teach a trade to the unemployable, and to implement programs of land reclamation and colonization. In addition to helping the economy such moves should also contribute to social order and gratify humanitarian feelings. Charity work, care of the destitute and disabled, would be most effectively undertaken by the government in conjunction with private organization. In K'ang's view, it was a mistake to think solely or primarily of "the public interest" and to relegate the people's welfare to a place of secondary importance. In economic life at any rate, the interests of the state and those of the people were inseparable; the best way to promote both was to give priority to the latter. "When the people are destitute," he remarked, "there is no means whereby the country can prosper."[7]

K'ang's 1895 position, as just indicated, reminds one of the Confucian sentiment, "If the people have plenty, their prince will not be left to want alone."[8] K'ang's words were possibly a reflection of that sentiment. It is quite likely, also, that he had derived inspiration from a more recent source, i.e., modern British experience as he knew of it.[9] It is equally conceivable that he had learned from Meiji Japan, where energetic government leadership of the late 1860s prepared the way for the phenomenal development of a capitalist economy since the early 1880s.[10] More directly, K'ang must have been in varying degrees indebted to his predecessors and contemporaries (although he seldom acknowledged indebtedness to other writers), such as Hsüeh Fu-ch'eng, Ma Chien-chung, Cheng Kuan-ying, and others.[11] Whether he had

[7] "Second Memorial," in Chien, *Wu-hsü*, 2: 143.

[8] The Confucian *Analects*, XII. 9, part of Yu Jo's reply to Duke Ai's question regarding government finances (Legge trans.).

[9] As Lo has suggested in *K'ang*, p. 150, n. 27, K'ang's view regarding the need to encourage commerce "appears to be derived from the nineteenth-century British interest in commerce."

[10] Richard C. Howard, "Japan's Role in the Reform Program of K'ang Yu-wei," in Lo, *K'ang*, pp. 280–312, discusses K'ang's indebtedness to Japan.

[11] Chao Ching, "K'ang Yu-wei ti ching-chi ssu-hsiang," p. 35.

gone beyond the ideas of these men, whether he had formulated in final form the demands and proposals of the reformists who preceded him,[12] will become clear when we examine in more detail his specific ideas.

Agriculture

K'ang rejected the traditional view, which minimized the importance of industry and commerce in economic life. But, unlike some of the leaders of developing countries of the twentieth century, he did not place an undue emphasis on nonagricultural enterprises. Explicitly, he favored a balanced growth of all sectors of the economy.

China's survival in the modern world, he argued, hinged on the abandonment of the outmoded traditional attitude.

> When China stood in isolation, it was necessary to regard agriculture as the [economic] foundation of the state, so that the people's minds could be set at rest. But when she stands among contending nations [as she now does], it is inevitable that commerce should be considered the foundation of the state, so that the profits [that have been lost] to her competitors could be recovered. . . . In the past, nations have been destroyed by wars; everyone knows that. Now a nation can be ruined by commerce, but nobody pays attention to it.[13]

Essentially the same argument was restated in another connection. The old policy of "building the base [i.e., agriculture] at the expense of the extremities [i.e., industry and commerce]" was economically unsound. Instead of developing the country's resources (which K'ang thought to be ample), the government knew only to exploit the agrarian populace of the provinces. It was high time indeed to give up that policy and to endeavor to meet the threat of economic imperialism on its own ground.[14] K'ang did not imply that agriculture should be downgraded. Agricultural growth and industrial development were both prerequisites to commercial expansion. As roads and ships facilitated the flow of trade, so agriculture, industry, and mining furnished goods and commodities for the market.[15] Nor did K'ang suggest that industrialization should be achieved at the expense of agriculture, as it has been alleged.[16]

Agricultural pursuits, in K'ang's view, were not merely "livelihoods"

[12] Ibid., p. 34.

[13] Chien, *Wu-hsü*, 2: 145; the translation is adapted from Lo, *K'ang*, p. 150, n. 27.

[14] *Jih-pen shu-mu chih*, preface to section on agriculture and commerce, *chüan* 7, p. 1b; cf. Lo, *K'ang*, pp. 150–51.

[15] "T'iao-ch'en shang-wu che" (Chien, *Wu-hsü*, 2: 246).

[16] By So Kwan-Wai in his "Western Influence and the Chinese Reform Movement of 1898," pp. 183–85.

that enabled those who engaged in them to subsist, but in reality productive enterprises yielding surplus commodities to sell in the market
for a profit. His conception of agriculture thus came close to that prevailing in industrialized societies, according to which the pattern of agricultural production was determined largely by the requirements of the
customer rather than by the wants of the producer.

K'ang did not formulate a detailed program of agricultural development. In his writings during the 1890s he merely indicated the general
areas to which the government should direct its attention. Thus, to
reverse the disastrous unfavorable balance of trade with foreign countries, he suggested that the government adopt measures to help pro-
ducers improve the quality and increase the quantity of native products, such as tea and silk, that had a place in foreign trade; that it should
undertake to introduce modern farming methods to the farmers, acquainting them with Western knowledge of soil analysis, fertilizer, plant
and animal breeding, and mechanization; and that it should encourage
the formation of "agriculture societies" throughout the empire, with a
view to facilitating the dissemination of such knowledge. Similar measures, K'ang indicated, should be adopted with regard to forestry and
fishery as well as other related industries.[17] Later, in 1898, he proposed
that schools of agriculture be established in each *chou* and *hsien* of the
provinces, that books on agriculture in foreign languages be translated
into Chinese, and that chemists (presumably from foreign countries) be
invited to China to make a study of the soil of various regions of the
country. A "bureau of agriculture and commerce" (*nung shang chü*), he
added, should be instituted in the capital, with branch offices in the
provinces, to direct the modernization program.[18]

Industry

K'ang attached equal importance to the introduction of Western
knowledge in mining, industry, and commerce. He took his contemporaries to task for rushing into mining projects without first acquiring
the necessary know-how. This was why, despite the institution of an
Imperial Commissioner for Mining Affairs in Yunnan and a government mining bureau in Jehol, the undertakings achieved no success.[19]

[17] "Second Memorial" (Chien, *Wu-hsü*, 2: 143–44).
[18] "Ch'ing k'ai nung-hsüeh-t'ang ti-chih-chü che" (Chien, *Wu-hsü*, 2: 250–51).
Another memorial, "Ch'ing ch'üan nung che," submitted in the same year, is listed
in Mai Chung-hua, *Wu-hsü tsou-kao*, but its text is unavailable.
[19] "Second Memorial," "Third Memorial" (Chien, *Wu-hsü*, 2: 142; 2: 168).

Such an approach, he said, might be likened to treating patients without having first studied medicine. He went on to say:

> If we wish to open mines under the ground, we should first open the mines that are in our minds and before our eyes. How to open the mines that are in our minds and before our eyes? Simply by establishing mining schools and translating books on mining.[20]

As the Belgians were at the time most advanced in mining technology, the government should invite Belgian experts to teach in mining schools and to survey the country's underground resources. It should import machines to replace human labor and construct railroads to speed up transportation.[21]

Without underestimating the importance of agriculture, K'ang devoted much of his time to advocating industrialization. For about two decades following 1895, he wrote repeatedly, often at length, on the matter. He noted that the many inventions made in Europe and America since the beginning of the nineteenth century, including the steamship, railroad, telegraph, balloon, electric lamp, and farm machinery, had worked to enhance the power of the state and promote the welfare of the people. It was true that, following the pioneering moves of Tseng Kuo-fan, efforts at introducing machine manufacture had been made in some provinces. But because no attempt had been made to educate the people in modern industrial knowledge, these enterprises did not achieve notable success.[22] In K'ang's view, in other words, technological education must precede industrialization.

K'ang did not stop at a call for bringing modern technology to bear on native industry; he in effect urged a change of attitude toward economic life itself. He traced the cause of China's lack of economic progress to the fact that standing in isolation for centuries the rulers and their subjects were satisfied with the status quo in which "having few desires" constituted a virtue for the former and "freedom from hunger" a blessing for the latter. Such an attitude, he argued, was as ill-suited to the conditions of the modern world as it was incompatible with the true demands of human nature. It was man's efforts to gratify his desires that led to progress. "As human desires know no bounds, so the advance of civilization has no end." For many years people of the West, who

---

[20] *Jih-pen shu-mu chih*, preface to section on mining books, *chüan* 2, p. 11a.

[21] "Second Memorial" (Chien, *Wu-hsü*, 2: 142).

[22] Ibid., pp. 144–45. K'ang wrongly identified Robert Fulton, builder of the *Clermont* (1807) as an Englishman.

refused to curtail desires, had been achieving spectacular technological progress. Rapid multiplication of inventions led to industrialization, which, in addition to enabling people to satisfy their expanding appetite for commodious living and their countries to gain unprecedented power and prosperity, had in effect "transformed an old world of unnumbered centuries into a completely new one."[23]

The transformation was not merely economic. In the process of passing from agrarian to industrial-commercial society, "conservatism and ignorance" were replaced by "progressivism and enlightenment." In creating "an industrial world," K'ang observed, Western countries had at the same time fashioned "a world in which progressivism and enlightenment became dominant values." It would be sheer folly for China to try to survive in such a world by persisting to maintain the attitudes and ways of "conservative and ignorant people in an agrarian society." To make China worthy of this new world, it was necessary to transform her into an "industrial country" (*kung kuo*) and, at the same time, "to change the minds of the people," persuading them "to forsake conservatism and ignorance and to prize progressivism and enlightenment."[24]

Significantly, K'ang realized that modern technology had its roots in physical science, as the following statement shows.

Industrial technology is the adaptation and application of the [knowledge gained from the study of] the natural processes of material things.[25]

The specific measures by means of which K'ang hoped to bring about the desired changes need not detain us here. Briefly, they were similar to those that he suggested to the Kuang-hsü emperor in connection with agricultural development: establishment of "special schools to nurture talents" and encouragement of discoveries of new scientific principles as well as inventions of new industrial devices.[26] And, as he had made it clear in an earlier connection,[27] private enterprise should have a free hand to contribute to industrial development; the government did not have to do more than licensing and offering general guidance.

[23] "Ch'ing li kung-i chiang ch'uang-hsin che" (June 25 or 26, Chien, *Wu-hsü*, 2: 225–27).
[24] Ibid., p. 227. Cf. Chao, *Wan-Ch'ing . . . ssu-hsiang shih*, pp. 74–75 and So, "Western Influence and Chinese Reform Movement," pp. 184–85.
[25] Chien, *Wu-hsü*, 2: 226.
[26] Ibid.
[27] See pp. 303–4, this chapter.

The above account shows that K'ang's proposals made in the 1890s touched upon three major issues. First, he called for parallel growth of industry and agriculture, and was frankly critical of the old notion of subsistence farming. Secondly, he was skeptical of the government's ability to manage or promote economic enterprise (a view undoubtedly based on his observations of the performance of government-run projects in various parts of the empire), while at the same time he acknowledged the fact that the people at large were unprepared to embark on modern entrepreneurship. He therefore wanted the government to furnish leadership in inaugurating the process of economic modernization but to leave the actual sustainment of the process to private entrepreneurs. Thirdly, believing that the traditional attitude toward economic life was a stumbling block to progress—the "Confucian" or, more accurately, Neo-Confucian, view that gratification of human desires was not conducive to moral virtue or political stability[28]—he demanded a change in people's minds and vouched the legitimacy of these desires in which he located the fountainhead of modern Western industrial civilization. He was convinced that there could not be an economic breakthrough without a psychological breakthrough.

In the years immediately following 1898 K'ang turned his attention mainly to China's political problems and wrote little on economic re-

---

[28] It appears that by 1886 K'ang had come to a hedonistic view of human nature. In his *K'ang-tzu nei-wai p'ien*, we find this passage in the "Essay on Compassion" (Pu-jen p'ien): "All creatures that have blood and breath necessarily have desires; having desires they inevitably give them free play. To be without desires is to be dead." For a brief discussion, see chapter 5, this volume. This hedonistic view was reiterated and elaborated in the *Ta-t'ung shu*. It is not easy to trace its origin. One might conjecture that it stemmed in part from his own mental makeup. A man of robust desires, he abhorred asceticism and frankly enjoyed sensual pleasures, considering them legitimate ingredients of the good life (See this volume, chapter 3). Despite his rejection of Hsün-tzu's teaching, he may have received suggestion from a passage in the eleventh essay of the *Hsün-tzu* ("Wang pa p'ien") in which it is said: "It is human to desire utmost gratification of the eyes with color, of the ears with sound, of the mouth with tasty food, of the nose with fragrance, and of the mind with joyful ease. . . . A state of ten thousand chariots may be called extensive, commodious, prosperous, and affluent; it has in addition [a government which] commands the way of good order, strength, and security. Thus there will be satisfaction and contentment. . . . All happiness, therefore, obtains in a well-ordered state." (Homer H. Dubs does not translate this passage in *The Works of Hsüntze*; Burton Watson in his *Hsün Tzu: Basic Writings*, leaves out the entire essay.) Confucius gave a hint of asceticism, on one occasion at least. "The Master said, 'He who aims to be a man of perfect virtue, in his food does not seek to gratify his appetite, nor in his dwelling-place does he seek the appliances of ease' " (*Analects*, I. 14; Legge trans.). It was Chu Hsi who in his teaching on "Heavenly Principles" and "human desires," gave Confucianism a puritanic cast. See Fung Yu-lan, *A History of Chinese Philosophy*, 2: 500–501, for a brief account.

form. It was not until 1905 that he again concerned himself with industrialization. His essay on "National Salvation through Material Upbuilding" has been dealt with in another connection.[29] It will suffice
here to indicate the general drift of his thinking.

Changed circumstances persuaded K'ang to shift emphasis and to
introduce new issues in this essay, but he retained many of his old ideas.
Alarmed by the rising tide of revolutionary sentiments among overseas
Chinese intellectuals, who rallied around Sun Yat-sen and his colleagues, K'ang now maintained that any attempt to disrupt the existing political order or to undermine the traditional culture would not
only be fruitless but decidedly dangerous. "Liberty," "rights," "constitution," and other notions borrowed from the West and circulated
among youngsters enrolled in what he called "schools of empty words,"
were no more pertinent to problems of China's salvation than the
"eight-legged essay" of old. There was only one thing that could save
China: speedy and full-fledged industrialization. There was only one
thing she should and could learn from the West: scientific and technological knowledge.[30]

K'ang was now even more firmly convinced that the way to industrialization was through private enterprise. The government of China
was unsuited for the task because, in addition to the fact that it did not
command sufficient financial and other resources, public management
of industry could not foster the spirit of competition or encourage the
desire to excel, both indispensable to economic progress. He pointed to
Krupp and Armstrong, as he did before, as shining examples of successful private entrepreneurship, worthy of emulation. He did not oppose
socialization in principle but warned sharply against its premature in-
vocation. Unlike Sun Yat-sen, who would like to see "social revolution"
and "political revolution" carried out at the same time,[31] he saw in

[29] Chao, *Wan-Ch'ing . . . ssu-hsiang shih*, pp. 77–88, summarizes the contents of this
essay. For a discussion of the historical significance and theoretical implications, see
chapter 10, this volume. Lo, *K'ang*, p. 198, refers to K'ang's essay as "Economic Reconstruction to Save China."

[30] In K'ang's own terminology, *wu-chih chih hsüeh*, "knowledge of material things."
Visiting the United States from Canada, K'ang arrived at Los Angeles on March
16, 1905, where he remained for two months. The industrial development there
deeply impressed him, as did the factories of other large American cities, which inspired his essay mentioned in the previous note (Lo, *K'ang*, p. 198; cf. K'ang T'ung-
pi, *Nan-hai K'ang hsien-sheng tzu-pien nien-pu-i*, p. 34a, and *Nan-hai K'ang hsien-sheng
nien-p'u hsü-pien*, pp. 51a–53a).

[31] See, e.g., an address delivered on Oct. 17, 1906, in Tokyo, "San min chu-i yü
Chung-kuo min-tsu chih ch'ien-t'u" (*Kuo-fu ch'üan-chi*, 3: 11), where he indicated in

private capitalism a logical intervening phase of economic development, lying between stagnant agrarian economy and socialistic utopia.

Another point might be noted. Although he strongly opposed overthrowing the existing regime by force, he recognized the need of radical political reform. He said near the end of the essay:

> Industrialization depends upon [sound] financial management, and financial management presupposes [efficient] administration which in turn rests upon the foundation of the self-government of citizens. . . . Therefore, before the institution of provincial, prefectural, district, and village assemblies, all that I have set forth here is of no [practical] significance.

Obviously, K'ang had come to the realization that it was futile to rely on the demoralized and bungling Ch'ing government to implement measures of economic modernization.

Commerce

K'ang's basic tenet regarding commerce has already been mentioned. As with agriculture and industry, he considered government leadership indispensable and private enterprise the sinew and muscle of commercial development. Like many of his contemporaries, he focused his attention on foreign trade.

Long continued unfavorable balance of trade, he pointed out, was draining China's financial resources and forcing her onto the path of economic ruin. To fight "the commercial war" waged by foreign countries against China with their own weapons he urged the government to encourage, enlighten, and protect private businessmen who worked to counter the torrents of foreign import by exporting native products and selling them in international markets. His arguments often remind one of mercantilism, though his economic theory in general seems to have been inspired chiefly by the Industrial Revolution.

Government action should be relevant and effective in several areas. Drawing lessons from the modern West and Meiji Japan, he called for the establishment of business schools (*shang hsüeh*), publication of business journals (*shang pao*), and promotion of trade fairs (*shang-hsüeh pi-chiao ch'ang*), all of which were calculated to spread modern commercial knowledge and to foster the spirit of innovation and competition. A ministry of commerce (*shang pu*) should be instituted in the capital to

---

effect the desirability of solving "the social problem" arising from industrialization while it was still in its infancy. More on Sun's views in "An Alternate Approach," later in this chapter.

take over-all charge of the nation's commercial affairs. Chambers of commerce (*shang hui* or *shang-hsüh hui*) should be organized in all parts of the empire with a view to lending strength to entrepreneurs. Taxes and imposts on business should be lightened, a code of commercial law enacted, insurance made available to businessmen, consulates set up in foreign countries, and naval vessels charged with the duty of protecting native commercial interests commissioned. All these, he thought, would give entrepreneurs convenience and security. In this way "government and business would work in smooth cooperation" resulting, eventually, in "a prosperous people in an affluent state." The unhappy situation in which officials looked down upon merchants and merchants distrusted officials would thus be brought to an end.[32]

To facilitate cooperation between government and business, K'ang suggested that bureaus of commercial affairs (*shang-wu chü*) be formed in all provinces, each of which was to be placed in charge of "persons of ample means and tested ability," selected by their fellow merchants, and each was to have the responsibility of setting up commercial schools, publishing business journals, and organizing chambers of commerce. If, for the time being, the government did not see fit to institute a ministry of commerce, the Tsungli Yamen should be authorized to supervise and control these bureaus. K'ang referred to the policies of Meiji Japan;[33] one readily sees a broad resemblance of his proposals to these policies. He would have found it easy to declare with the members of Japan's Liberal Party (Jiyutō) who formed in 1887 the Asian Commercial Institute (Ajiya Bōeki Shōkai), "Let us become known as Yankees of the East."[34]

Probably taking a hint also from Japan's post-Restoration economic development (as well as from the industrial West), K'ang maintained that small enterprises owned and operated by single individuals could not have sufficient strength to play an effective part in modern foreign trade. China must have large companies (*ta kung-ssu*) which, sustained by stockholders and assisted by the government, would command enough financial power to trade effectively in distant lands.[35] Such commercial giants would be a far cry from the family-owned small firms of old. By implication, K'ang rejected the idea of government enter-

[32] "T'iao-ch'en shang-wu che" (Aug. 2, 1898) (Chien, *Wu-hsü*, 2: 244–46).

[33] Ibid., pp. 248–49.

[34] Marius Jansen, *The Japanese and Sun Yat-sen*, p. 239, note 59, citing Itagaki Taisuke, *Jiyūtō shi* (Tokyo, 1910), 2: 289–406.

[35] "Second Memorial" (Chien, *Wu-hsü* 2: 146).

prise and the formula "official supervision and merchant management."[36]

Transportation and Communication

K'ang was not particularly concerned with what economists sometimes call the infrastructure of a nation's economy, but he did reveal his thinking on railroads, steamships, and postal service. He echoed the view of his contemporaries that railroads played a decisive part in Western economic development and that, therefore, China should promptly initiate a program of systematic railroad building. The benefits were more than economic. Besides facilitating the flow of large quantities of industrial goods and agricultural products, railroads afforded means of rapidly moving men and matériel in times of war and, in times of peace, helped to dissolve the barriers arising from differences in dialect and custom, by making it easy for inhabitants of one locality to travel to another. Railroad construction required large expenditure; lack of capital had so far been the stumbling block. He suggested, accordingly, that the government should encourage and help private entrepreneurs who invested in railroad building by offering them viable plans, equitable regulations, and dependable protection. With an optimism not justified by the existing situation, he wrote, "Our own people should raise their own capital; they have the ability to do it and to prevent foreign countries from reaping the profits that are ours."[37]

Foreign capital, then, should not be used to build Chinese railroads. Differing with some of his contemporaries, K'ang ruled out the possibility of financing railroad projects by contracting foreign loans or inviting foreign investments. In fact, he would like to lessen the commercial importance of Shanghai and Tientsin, the two largest treaty ports, by constructing a railroad system that would bypass them. This was one of his major arguments for building a line between Peking and Ch'ing-chiang-p'u and against one connecting Tientsin and T'ungchou.[38] K'ang was here a "nationalist," overestimating China's financial capabilities and unaware of the role that industrially advanced

---

[36] At any rate, K'ang made no mention of it in the writings of this time.

[37] Ibid., p. 141.

[38] In 1888–98 the Ch'ing government was considering Li Hung-chang's proposal for extending the Tientsin-Tangku line to T'ungchou and Chang Chih-tung's plan for building a line between Lukouch'iao and Hankow. Sometime in 1888 K'ang wrote "Ch'ing k'ai Ch'ing-chiang-p'u t'ieh-lu che," the text of which is available on microfilm, reel 3. K'ang supported in effect Ch'ang's position. See Li Kuo-ch'i, *Chung-kuo chao ch'i ti t'ieh-lu ching-ying*, pp. 74–85, for an account of this episode.

regions could play in initial capital formation in underdeveloped economies.

K'ang suggested in a memorial (midsummer 1898) that the ailing
grain transport system be done away with and that the funds allocated
for its operation be used for railroad building. The system, he pointed
out, was never an economic success; it had now become an anachronism, "a laughing stock to foreign nations." Modern railroads could
move grain quickly and efficiently from one place to another. Actually,
it was unnecessary for the government to involve itself in food transportation. With modern facilities for the exchange of commodities
made available, "merchants and traders would apply themselves, of
their own accord, to meeting the people's demand for food." The government did not have to intervene.[39] Here K'ang appears to have come
close to the notion of free enterprise.

The question of modern shipping was dealt with in the same vein.
"Steamships," he said, "offer advantages equal to those afforded by
railroads. The common people, merchants, and the government would
be benefited by both; the people should be free to build them both."[40]

The government, however, should establish and maintain the postal
service. Pointing to British experience K'ang argued that a modern
post-office system operated by the government would help to augment
imperial revenues and, at the same time, provide a much needed convenience to the people. It would supplement the railroad system and
enhance its usefulness.[41]

Finance

Between the mid 1890s and mid 1910s, K'ang at times addressed
himself to the question of capital formation as a prerequisite to the development of modern enterprise. He seems to have gained some insight
into the problems involved, although he was inclined to offer solutions
that were somewhat simplistic if not also naïve.

"Financial management" (*li ts'ai*), according to him, held the key to
rapid capital formation. A suitable currency system and a nationwide
banking system were the most efficacious means to achieving solvency
in the impoverished empire.

[39] "Ch'ing fei ts'ao-yün kai i ts'ao-k'uan chu t'ieh-lu che" (Chien, *Wu-hsü*, 2: 253).
Harold C. Hinton, "The Grain Tribute System of the Ch'ing Dynasty," pp. 339–54,
and "The Grain Tribute System of China, 1845–1911" (doctoral dissertation, Harvard University, 1951), chapter 3, are useful.
[40] "Second Memorial" (Chien, *Wu-hsü*, 2: 141–42).
[41] Ibid., p. 143.

This was essentially the position he took in 1898, when he spoke briefly on the banking and currency systems of Meiji Japan, in reply to the emperor's question concerning the method of fund raising.[42] A few years earlier, he proposed a banking system that was faintly reminiscent of the American national bank as authorized by an act of 1864. In K'ang's view, private banks should deposit their capital (silver) with the Board of Revenue or provincial treasuries, which would in effect become the reserve for the paper currency notes to be issued by the Board. As the total value of these notes was to be one and one-half of the value of silver deposited with the government, the money thus put in circulation would, according to Kang's estimate, amount to some 100,000,000 units (taels?) in the eighteen provinces. Meanwhile, to stem the tide of foreign silver coins that were steadily pouring into China, the government should authorize a silver coinage of its own. Every country of the Far West, he said, had its own hard currency; "Russia, for example, has the ruble, Germany the mark, Austria the florin, and England the shilling." No Western country permitted circulation of foreign coins within its boundaries. It behooved China to follow this Western practice.[43]

K'ang continued to discuss financial problems long after 1898. He consistently applied his basic formula: greasing the fiscal wheels with paper money backed with appropriate reserves and circulated through banks. This, he remarked, was "to make something out of nothing" (*i wu wei yu*).[44] He was, however, aware of the necessity of maintaining the value of the paper currency and insisted on an adequate silver reserve.[45] Alarmed by the fiscal chaos in the first months of the republic, he wrote an essay on "Saving the Country through Financial Management" in which, in addition to restating his old proposals for a banking system and issuance of paper money, he emphasized the wisdom of building up a silver and gold reserve.[46]

[42] The exchange took place on June 16, during an audience with the emperor. K'ang also mentioned "the land tax in India" (Lo, *K'ang*, p. 98).

[43] "Second Memorial" (Chien, *Wu-hsü*, 2: 140–43).

[44] In a letter in reply to an intendant serving in Kwangsi, "Fu Liu kuan-ch'a Shih-chi shu," written in 1908; text available in *Wan-mu ts'ao-t'ang i-kao* (hereafter, *I-kao*), *chüan* 4, p. 50a, where K'ang said, "the bank makes something out of nothing; bank notes are tokens that stand for real [money]."

[45] *Chin chu-pi chiu-kuo i*, pp. 26b–28a. After commenting on the extreme usefulness of paper currency, he warned that "in issuing paper money the quantity must be limited and backed by a gold reserve." The idea of a reserve remained unchanged, although now he preferred gold to silver.

[46] "Li-ts'ai chiu-kuo lun" (*Pu-jen*, no. 2: p. 8a). Part ii of this essay, which was to deal with taxation, is unavailable to this writer. Perhaps it was never written.

It would be erroneous to suppose that K'ang relied solely on money and banking to recruit capital. He saw the usefulness of government bonds and corporate stocks as means to raising capital for agricultural, industrial, and commercial enterprises.[47] In addition to issuing paper money, the banking system, comprising a central bank, local banks, and banks serving special enterprises (*ch'üan-yeh yin-hang*), would assume the responsibility of buying and selling all stocks and bonds.[48]

K'ang saw in the rise of land value both a contributing factor and a consequence of general economic growth. He wrote in 1908:

> With the development of diverse enterprises, [agricultural, industrial, and commercial,] land value will rise. More bonds then can be issued, more profitable local businesses can be inaugurated, and more banks can be opened. Each of these contribute to [the growth of] the others and is in turn stimulated by the others.[49]

He did not, therefore, share Sun Yat-sen's view that unearned increment of land value as a result of economic development should be taken away from private owners.[50]

K'ang was convinced of the vital importance of maintaining currency stability against undue fluctuation, especially in relation to foreign currencies. Accordingly, he advocated the adoption of a gold standard, which, he believed, was the only way to avert financial disaster. In a series of essays written between 1904 and 1908 dealing with the subject,[51] he showed considerable acquaintance with it, both in its historical and practical aspects. He theorized that money came into use as an inevitable consequence of the expansion of trade. Since earliest times gold had been found to be the most suitable medium of exchange. Gold coins first appeared in ancient Egypt. Later, silver also occupied an honored place in monetary systems. Recently, however, since Eng-

---

[47] "Letter in reply to Liu Shih-chi" (*I-kao, chüan* 4, p. 50b).

[48] "Li-ts'ai chiu-kuo lun," pp. 8b ff.

[49] "Letter in reply to Liu Shih-chi" (*I-kao, chüan* 4a, pp. 48b–51b). To K'ang, "land and real estate values" constituted the major element of a nation's wealth.

[50] The final formulation of this view is in Sun's "Second Lecture on the Principle of People's Livelihood," *San Min Chu I* (Price trans.) pp. 418–23; *Kuo-fu ch'üan-chi*, 1: 203–5, 209–12.

[51] *Chin chu-pi chiu-kuo i*, manuscript copy available in Hoover Library, with a preface by Wang Chüeh-jen dated Hsüan-t'ung 2nd year, 1st month (early 1910). This collection of twenty-three essays with an appendix of five essays on paper money was possibly a draft version of the work cited in note 45, above. K'ang T'ung-pi, *Nan-hai K'ang hsien-sheng nien-p'u hsü-pien*, pp. 64a–65b, indicates that K'ang wrote these essays in 1908 while living in Penang. See also Lo, *K'ang*, p. 214, where mention is made of this work.

land adopted the gold standard by virtue of the acts of 1798 and 1816, the tendency had been away from bimetallism. There was then a world-wide tendency toward the depreciation of the value of silver relative to gold. This tendency, he thought, had been noticeable in China for a long time, from a gold to silver ratio of 1:5 in Ch'in and Han times to about 1:30 in the early years of the twentieth century. To persist in maintaining the silver standard, as China then did, was tantamount to eventual financial suicide.

He believed that China should promptly adopt a gold standard, fixing the rate between gold and silver at about 1:20 and minting gold coins in various denominations, in addition to subsidiary coins of silver and brass. But as China was not in possession of sufficient quantities of the yellow metal to make a large number of coins, she might resort to a transitional measure, adopting "a legally established gold currency" (*fa-ting chin chu-pi*), roughly as it obtained in India, where the government held a gold reserve and fixed the exchange rate between gold and the currency in circulation.[52]

K'ang's attitude toward foreign loans and investment was not a consistent one. On some occasions, as already noted, he was inclined to share the misgivings of many of his contemporaries regarding the influx of foreign capital. As late as 1916, he still saw "no necessity of inviting foreigners" to take part in the economic development of Szechwan and Yunnan, although he had no objection to purchasing weapons from foreign countries.[53] In midsummer, 1912, he raised strong protest against a foreign loan that the republican government under Yüan Shih-k'ai was negotiating. Such a loan, K'ang said, amounted to "giving China away as a free gift to foreigners."[54]

On other occasions, however, K'ang approved of importing foreign capital, provided it was to be invested in undertakings that contributed to the nation's economic growth. Thus, although he roundly denounced the Yüan government for contemplating the loan, he allowed that to contract a foreign loan for the purpose of modernizing the banking and currency systems would be acceptable, if it was proved to be necessary. Years before, in the summer of 1898, he suggested to the emperor that Jung Hung (Yung Wing) be sent to the United States to negotiate a "huge loan" of the equivalent of 600,000,000 taels, which, when deposited in the central bank to form a 60-percent reserve for paper cur-

[52] *Chin chu-pi chiu-kuo i*, essay 11 et seq.
[53] "Chih Ts'ai Sung-p'o shu" (*I-kao, chüan* 4, pp. 6a–b).
[54] "Ta chieh-tsai po-i" (*K'ang Nan-hai wen-chi, chüan* 3, pp. 36a–39b).

rency, would yield a working capital of one billion taels. This, he said, should adequately finance his modernizing programs and stimulate private enterprise. He explained that the foreign loans made in the past failed to produce positive results because none of them had anything to do with economic development. Such nonproductive loans further drained the economy instead of contributing to its expansion.[55] He made a similar proposal to Yüan in 1912, calling for a foreign loan of over a billion dollars.[56]

Our brief account of K'ang's ideas of economic reform, which he set forth mostly between the 1890s and 1910s, yields the impression that he placed his hope for China's future in the development of something like a market economy resting largely on private enterprise. There seems to be a touch of mercantilism and economic nationalism in his thinking;[57] he might even be accused of being a spokesman of "the capitalist and landlord class."[58] At any rate, it is clear that as a practicing reformer he had no use for the utopian socialistic scheme that he outlined in his *Ta-t'ung shu*, nor did he have faith in state control and state management as a fruitful approach to economic development. He wanted the government to set the process in motion, but he doubted that it had the capacity to carry the process into advanced stages of agricultural, industrial, and commercial growth, which in his view should be left largely to private enterprise. He aimed not merely at preserving the existing regime; he wished in fact to change it in the direction of constitutional government, which would be able to usher in the dawn of China's bright economic future.[59] He was concerned not merely with making the state prosperous and strong; he was primarily interested in giving his countrymen a commodious and affluent life—a life that Westerners were already enjoying.

[55] "Ch'ing chi ch'üan-chü ch'ou chü-k'uan i hsing hsin-cheng chu t'ieh-lu ch'i hai-lu-chün che" (Chien, *Wu-hsü*, 2: 255–58).

[56] "Chih Yüan tsung-t'ung shu" (*I-kao, chüan* 4, p. 72a).

[57] Hou Wai-lu, *Chin-tai Chung-kuo ssu-hsiang hsüeh-shuo shih*, 2: 650–55, where the author makes the point that the economic thought of K'ang (and his followers Liang Ch'i-ch'ao and T'an Ssu-t'ung) echoed Western mercantilism.

[58] S. L. Tikhvinsky, *Dvizhenie za reformy v Kitae v kontse XIX veka i Kan Iu-vei*, p. 193, credits K'ang with having given the most clear and exhaustive exposition of the views of capitalist and landlord class reformers. Cf. Chao Ching, "K'ang Yu-wei ti ching-chi ssu-hsiang," p. 34, where it is said that prior to 1902 K'ang's thinking reflected "the demands of the new capitalist class for the development of national industry and commerce."

[59] Chao, "Kang Yu-wei . . . ," p. 47, condemns K'ang for "attempting to confound the true issues and to save the moribund dynasty." This is hardly an accurate assessment.

VIEWS OF CONTEMPORARIES

Reserving the question of the theoretical validity or pragmatic relevancy of K'ang's ideas of economic reform for a later occasion, it might be useful at this point to view them in the context of the trend of economic thought prevailing in China between the 1870s and 1890s. As the following survey will show, K'ang shared many convictions of the writers of the period. A sampling of the more representative should suffice.

Chu Ts'ai, a protégé of Li Hung-chang and Chang Chih-tung, appears to have been the first to stress the importance of technological education. He wrote in 1873 that unless members of the scholar-officialdom apply themselves to the study of engineering and mathematics (*ch'i shu chih hsüeh*), China would not be able to build steamships of her own. The government should set the trend by rewarding inventors of new machines and discoverers of new scientific principles with honor and emolument, so that talented and ambitious men would no longer belittle technological knowledge and skill.[60] In the next year, he proposed that technological schools be established in the capital as well as in all the coastal provinces, in which shipbuilding, engineering, mathematics, geography, and other related subjects would be taught. Students would be given stipends while they were attending these schools, and later appointed to government positions upon successful completion of a course of study.[61]

Li Fan, a supervisory censor, advanced the idea of meeting Western economic imperialism on its own ground, by "fighting commerce with commerce" (*i shang ti shang*). In a May 20, 1878, memorial he traced China's woes to one source, trading with foreign countries. In the West, he said, government and merchant joined effort in commercial ventures; in this way merchants gained great strength and in turn helped their country to become prosperous and powerful. Unlike aggressors of the past who sustained economic losses in wars of conquest, modern Western nations achieved territorial expansion through economic expansion. The situation in China was entirely different. The government did not support the merchant. "The country becomes poorer and weaker day by day."

---

[60] Chu Ts'ai, *Ch'ing-fen-ko chi, chüan* 2, p. 20a; reprinted in Chung-kuo shih-hsüeh hui, *Yang-wu yün-tung*, 1: 331–32. Chu, a man from Chekiang, was prefect of Fenchou, Shansi, and later intendant of the Ch'iung-Lei Circuit, Kwangtung.

[61] Chu Ts'ai, "Hai-fang i," p. 349.

Li suggested that the government take measures to encourage "patriotic inhabitants of the coastal provinces" to follow the example of merchants of foreign countries: organizing joint-stock companies and engaging in overseas trade. It should help these people to find the necessary capital and to form the appropriate organizations; it should give them "unobstrusive consideration" so that they, knowing that they could depend on the government, would feel free to dedicate themselves to waging "the commercial war." In twenty years, Li estimated, China should be in a position "to thwart the military might of foreign countries, without actually resorting to armed conflict."[62]

Without industry there could be no commercial expansion. Foreign trade, Li said, was a two-way traffic, importing goods that China needed and exporting commodities to meet the demand of foreign markets. Chinese merchants should import foreign goods; Chinese industrialists should manufacture commodities with which Chinese exporters would then supply the foreign consumer. The government must help private entrepreneurs to acquire new techniques and to buy the indispensable machines with which to modernize the textile and other industries.[63]

A year after Li memorialized the throne, Lo Ying-liu, an expectant circuit intendant, made similar recommendations regarding commerce and industry. "Westerners," Lo wrote, "rest their government policy on commerce," whereas China, clinging to "moral persuasion," became a victim of Western commercial exploitation. To reverse the situation China must pursue "wealth and power" through a program of commercial-industrial development. In other words,

> We should develop our own resources which Westerners covet; . . . we should ourselves manufacture what we have been depending on foreign lands for and export ourselves what foreign lands have been depending on us for.

More specifically, China should open mines, develop modern industry, build railroads and steamships, and expand foreign trade. In order to foster entrepreneurship the government should encourage and protect private industrial and commercial interests. This could be accomplished by rewarding notable success in business ventures with official honors, by adopting a protectionist tariff that would impose heavier duties on imports than on exports, especially on Western-style goods manufactured in China; and by establishing consulates in all foreign

[62] Ibid., pp. 165–67. Li was a supervisory censor for the Hu-Kuang Circuit.
[63] Ibid., pp. 167–68.

lands, e.g., Singapore, Penang, San Francisco, and other localities where large numbers of overseas Chinese resided. The guiding principle, obviously, was government leadership in priming the development of private enterprise.[64]

Kuo Sung-t'ao, who gained knowledge of Western countries during his missions abroad in the late 1870s, joined Li and Lo in advocating the same formula of economic development: government encouragement—private entrepreneurship. In a letter to Li Hung-chang, written probably about 1878, Kuo made the observation that "the West owes its prosperity and power to private entrepreneurs (*min-shang*)." It was these men who built the economic foundation of a country, while the government did its part by affording them protection and security. The people and their government thus joined hands to develop the economic resources. In China there was too little community of interest between the government and the people. This, Kuo concluded, explained the lack of success in the modernizing projects that had been going on in the previous decades.[65]

Kuo raised another interesting point in a letter to an unnamed friend, written about the same time. Prosperity and strength, he said, must rest on the foundation of social and political stability. It was inconceivable that a country could acquire wealth and power while the people remained in economic poverty. He continued:

Nowadays men who talk about wealth and power invariably regard these as weighty affairs of the state—matters that have nothing to do with the people. They do not realize that in Western countries wealth resides in the people, not in the state.[66]

Hsüeh Fu-ch'eng, another well-known official and diplomat of the period, came even closer to an endorsement of something like private

[64] Lo was an expectant intendant in Kweichow. His memorial, submitted July 23, 1879, is given in *Yang-wu yün-tung*, 1: 170–81; see especially pp. 177–80. In addition to economic modernization, Lo urged the government to reform the educational system and to revitalize the military structure. His piece received considerable official attention. Li Hung-chang, then governor-general of Chihli, approved of his economic proposals (ibid., 1: 205). Shen Pao-chen, then governor-general of Liang-Chiang, however, doubted that China's businessmen were at the time ready to respond to government leadership (ibid., 1: 183–84).

[65] "Chih Li fu-hsiang shu," in *Yang-chih shu-wu i-chi*, chüan 13, p. 17a; reprinted in *Yang-wu yün-tung*, 1: 315–16.

[66] "Yü yu-jen lun fang-hsing hsi-fa shu," written probably in late 1870s (*Yang-chih shu-wu i-chi*, chüan 13, p. 36b; *Yang-wu yün-tung*, 1: 322).

capitalism. In a memorial submitted in 1895 while he was on diplomatic missions in Europe, he pointed out that

> Western countries vie with one another in contriving means to store wealth with the people (*ts'ang fu yü min*) and then find it easy to achieve political order and military power.

Commercial development was the main road to economic affluence. To attain it the government should make it possible for the people to invest in railroad building (which did not have to involve public financing) and to adopt modern methods in textile and other industries (which could be done by private companies with suitable government assistance).[67]

In an 1891 essay Hsüeh explained the method of "guiding the people to economic productivity (*tao min sheng ts'ai*)." Western countries were more densely populated than China and yet they enjoyed prosperity while China remained poor. This was because they were able "to open up the sources of wealth" through agricultural, industrial, and commercial development. If China continued to default—to fail to learn the lesson of the West—she would soon be in an even worse economic plight as population pressure increased.[68]

He identified the basic aim of Western economic policies in another essay written the next year. Western governments imposed much heavier taxes on their people than the Chinese government, but few felt that the burden was intolerable simply because "what is taken from the people is spent for the people." Even military expenditures were calculated basically to benefit the people. Moreover, when armaments were manufactured, iron-clad ships were built, and railroads were constructed, many workers, skilled or unskilled, found their livelihood. And, what was even more important, Western governments made sure that their economic undertakings would result in "lodging wealth in private enterprise" (*ts'ang fu yü shang*).[69] In fact, Hsüeh was so committed to the idea of private enterprise that he would like to have railroad building taken over by businessmen, after the government had

---

[67] "Ch'iang-lin huan-ssu chin ch'en yü-chi shu," *Yung-an nei-wai p'ien* n. p., 1898; *Hai-wai wen-pien, chüan* 2, p. 6a (reprinted in *Yang-wu yün-tung*, 1: 260–61).

[68] "Hsi-yang chu-kuo tao-min sheng-ts'ai shuo" (*Hai-wai wen-pien, chüan* 3, pp. 5b–6a).

[69] "Hsi-yang chu-kuo wei min li-ts'ai shuo," ibid; pp. 7a–b.

made a start. After all, he argued, railroads "from the very beginning should have the people's convenience as its basic aim."[70]

Even more interesting is Hsüeh's recognition of something like the profit motive as a dynamic force in economic life. In an essay on "Commercial Affairs" he argued that in order to end China's chronic unfavorable balance of trade, it was necessary to modernize her domestic industry, chiefly tea, silk, and textile manufacture, and to develop a system of modern transportation. All these, he insisted, should be left to private entrepreneurs; government supervision (such as in the case of the China Merchants Steam Ship Navigation Company) should be dispensed with.[71] He justified his view in these terms:

> It is natural that men are engrossed in their private interests. Merchants do sometimes sustain losses in the market, but they still carry their money and go there. The reason? They all wish to gain profits for themselves. And precisely because all wish to do so the state is, in the long run, benefited greatly without expending public funds.[72]

Commenting on Hsüeh's view, a Chinese writer says that "the 'commercial affairs' which he [Hsüeh] talked about was none other than capitalist development," even though he did not have a complete understanding of capitalism.[73] This, so it appears, is a fair judgment.

Hsüeh was aware of the close relationship between industry and commerce and the importance of industrialization. In an essay on the need to develop industry he criticized the traditional view, which looked down upon the craftsman. He noted that the sudden rise of Western countries must be accounted for by the fact that industry (which formed the backbone of commerce) was honored together with the latter as pillars of the state. Scientists (*shih*) formulated the principles and engineers (*kung*) applied these principles to achieve technological success. In this way "the scholar" and "the craftsman" worked in intimate cooperation. The government, too, played a part. It gave distinction to scientists and technicians who had made outstanding discoveries and inventions in the recent decades. China, evidently,

---

[70] "Ch'uang-k'ai Chung-kuo t'ieh-lu i, *Yung-an wen-pien, chüan* pp. 12b–13b (*Yung-an ch'üan-chi* ed.). In an earlier piece, "Tai Li po-hsiang i-ch'ing shih-pan t'ieh-lu shu," *Yung-an wen hsü-pien* (*Yung-an ch'üan-chi* ed.), *chüan* 1, pp. 6b–7b, Hsüeh said that it was feasible to invite "merchant capital" (*shang ku*) or to make foreign loans with which to finance railroads.

[71] "Shang cheng," *Ch'ou yang ch'u-i*, written about 1880, *chüan* 1, pp. 10b–12a, available in *Yung-an ch'üan-chi*.

[72] Ibid., p. 11a.

[73] Huang Tzu-t'ung, "Hsüeh Fu-ch'eng ti ssu-hsiang," pp. 51–56.

must dissolve the age-old prejudice against the craftsman—a prejudice sustained and reenforced by the examination system—before she could inaugurate the process of technological modernization.[74] Unless, he warned, China moved forward, from handicrafts to machine manufacturing, she could never trade with foreign nations on equal terms. To the objection that modern factories would deprive the people engaged in handicraft manufacture of their livelihood, he countered that those who wished to see the impoverished people cling to handicraft were actually wishing to keep them poor and helpless.[75]

Like many of his contemporaries Hsüeh blamed the failure to explore China's natural resources for her poverty; accordingly, he urged the government to initiate a positive program of mining development. Both government and private enterprise, he believed, should play active roles in this area.[76] And, like many others, he urged the abolition of the likin.[77]

Ma Chien-chung, who was sent by Li Hung-chang to study in France, reported his findings in an 1877 letter. A year's study, he wrote, had convinced him that in European countries "the pursuit of wealth has for its basis the protection of commercial interests [by government] and the search for power must begin with winning the support of the people."[78] In an essay on "Enriching the People," written in the spring of 1890, he advanced the proposition that "wishing to make China prosperous, we can do no better than increasing exports and reducing imports." The way to bring this about was to modernize agricultural and industrial methods so that Chinese goods could command

---

[74] "Chen pai-kung shuo" (*Hai-wai wen-pien, chüan* 3, pp. 16b–17b). Hsüeh had already stressed the importance of introducing modern technology in an 1875 memorial, "Ying chao ch'en yen shu" (*Yung-an wen-pien, chüan* 1, p. 12a; reprinted in *Yang-wu yün-tung*, 1: 157). A similar view was expressed in a May 19, 1890, entry in his diary (*Ch'u-shih Ying Fa I Pi ssu-kuo jih-chi*, 2: 11b–12a, available in *Yung-an ch'üan-chi*). The text has been translated in Teng and Fairbank, *China's Response to the West*, p. 144.

[75] "Yung chi-ch'i chih ts'ai yang min shuo" (*Hai-wai wen-pien, chüan* 3, pp. 8b–9a).

[76] "K'uang cheng" (*Ch'ou yang ch'u-i, chüan* 1, pp. 13b–15a).

[77] He saw the advisability of abolishing the *likin* as early as 1865, when the campaign against the Taipings was still going on. In a letter to Tseng Kuo-fan ("Shang Tseng hou-hsiang shu, *Yung-an wen wai-pien, chüan* 3, pp. 11b–13a), he said that while the *likin* was useful, it was not "something which benefits the people's livelihood." The rate should be progressively lowered and the levy itself should finally be abrogated. He reiterated the same view ten years later ("Ying chao ch'en yen shu," *Yung-an wen-pien, chüan* 1, pp. 6a–b).

[78] "Shang Li Po-hsiang yen ch'u-yang kung-k'o shu," *Shih-k'o chai chi-yen, chüan* 2, p. 6b; partial translation in Teng and Fairbank, *China's Response*, p. 96. The edition here used is the one included in Liang Ch'i-ch'ao, *Hsi-cheng ts'ung-shu.*

foreign markets, and to develop coal, iron, silver, and gold mining so that full use could be made of "the resources that are already there."[79] He, too, was in favor of building a railroad system. To raise capital for the undertaking, he suggested that loans be negotiated with government and private banks of France and England.[80]

Ma's discussion of China's economic problems was little more than cursory. Cheng Kuan-ying, a comprador in Dent and Co. and Butterfield and Swire for about thirty years, had a great deal more to say on the subject. Speaking from personal experience and knowledge gained through reading, he presented a broadly conceived plan for China's economic development in his *Sheng-shih wei-yen* (Words of Warning in a Seemingly Properous Age).[81]

A viable political system, he argued in effect, was indispensable to achieving prosperity and strength. Implicitly critical of China's age-old autocratic government, he recommended the establishment of a parliament through which ruler and people would reach mutual understanding and work together for the good of the country. "In a monarchy the ruler holds too much authority; in a republic the people hold too much authority. Where ruler and people share control [i.e., as in a constitutional or "mixed" monarchy], there is a happy balance of authority." With the appropriate political framework thus defined, he went on to lay down the guiding principles of economic modernization. Following the example of advanced Western countries China should endeavor to achieve three things: "that human talents are fully developed and employed, that natural resources are thoroughly explored and

[79] "Fu min shuo," *Shih-k'o chai chi-yen, chüan* 1, pp. 3a–6b. Ma thought, mistakenly, that the sudden growth of Western industry was due to the discovery of gold in America, referring obviously to the gold rush in California (ibid., p. 4b).

[80] "T'ieh-tao lun," and "Chieh-chai i k'ai t'ieh-tao shuo," both in *Shih-k'o-chai chi-yen, chüan* 1, pp. 6b–9b; 9b–12b.

[81] Teng and Fairbank, *China's Response*, p. 113, give a brief sketch of Cheng's career. He joined Li Hung-chang's enterprises in 1882, serving in directorial capacities in the China Telegraph Company, the China Merchants Steam Ship Navigation Company, Li's cotton mill, and briefly as manager of the newly founded Hanyang Iron Foundry. In the 1890s he was a patron and enthusiastic reader of the *Wan Kwok Kung Pao*; he liked Robert Mackenzie's *Nineteenth Century* (in Chinese translation) so much that he distributed one hundred copies of it to his friends. His essays on diverse aspects of modernization were collected in the *Sheng-shih wei-yen*, which was first published in 1893 and underwent several successive editions. The 1893 version was actually a revision of an earlier collection, which was in turn a revision of "Chiu-shih chieh-yao," with a preface dated 1884. A sequel to the *Sheng-shih wei-yen, Sheng-shih wei-yen hou-pien*, 15 *chüan*, contains accounts of his experiences in the various enterprises: textile, railroad, steamship, ironworks, mining, and telegraph.

utilized, and that the flow of commodities is free and unimpeded."[82]

A substantial portion of the book deals with virtually the entire range of economic matters, agriculture, industry, commerce, finance, and transportation.[83] Cheng's treatment of China's economic problems was more systematic and thoroughgoing than any of his contemporaries, but his viewpoint and specific suggestions often paralleled theirs. A few points will serve to make his position clear.

Cheng recognized the importance of agriculture and proposed its modernization. Taking the West as his model he envisioned a ministry of agriculture to formulate general policies, permanent agricultural expositions in all the provinces to stimulate technological improvements, and schools of agriculture to advance and disseminate new knowledge.[84] To effect industrialization, he suggested that special schools be established to teach science and technology. These words of his merit quoting:

> The prosperity and strength of Western countries rest on the foundation of industry. But . . . without knowledge of mathematics and science, it would be difficult to penetrate the mysteries of industrial technology. . . . It is proper that our country should promptly set up schools of science and technology to educate talented young men so that they will be able to apply science to industry, thereby achieving continued industrial progress.[85]

Understandably, Cheng had much to say concerning commerce. In his essay on "Commercial Affairs" and "Commercial Warfare," he advanced the familiar argument that China must counter the economic encroachment of Western powers on their own ground. He called for a ministry of commerce to give guidance and protection to commercial enterprises; he urged that machine manufacturing be developed in

[82] *Sheng-shih wei-yen*, preface, dated 1892 (Shanghai, 1905 ed.). Interestingly, Fung Kuei-fen offered somewhat similar formulations years before Sun Yat-sen. Teng and Fairbank, *China's Response*, p. 53: "in making use of the ability of our manpower, with no one neglected, . . . in securing the benefits of the soil, with nothing wasted, . . . in maintaining a close relationship between the ruler and the people, with no barrier between them, we are inferior to the barbarians." Sun's formulation was: "The basis of Europe's wealth and power . . . lies in the fact that men are able to make full use of their talents, the land is able to yield the fullest measure of its productivity, resources are completely utilized, and commodities enjoy unimpeded circulation."

[83] Namely, essays nos. 23 through 46 (24 out of a total of 55); in addition, 6 of the 10 essays comprising the appendix deal with machine manufacturing, textile industry, steamships, railroads, electricity, and telegraph service.

[84] *Sheng-shih wei-yen*, *chüan* 4, especially essay 28, "Nung kung," pp. 39b–40b.

[85] Ibid., *chüan* 3, essay 26, "Chi-i."

order to give the necessary backbone to commercial expansion; and, while he wished the government to provide the framework of economic development, he insisted that commercial enterprises should be privately owned and privately managed. His own experience persuaded him that government interference was detrimental to economic growth. He described various ways in which officials extorted money from businessmen or meddled with business management. He was particularly critical of the practice of recommending people who had no training or experience in commercial undertakings "to serve" in business firms. Such personnel were not only inept but were inclined to indulge in malpractices and embezzlement. As a result of such interference "there have been few shareholders who have made a profit and many who have lost their capital in the last several decades." One way to remedy the situation was to enact a commercial code, as modern Western countries had done, which would protect private enterprise against official encroachment.[86] To insure further commercial growth, means of communication and transportation must be developed[87] and a modern banking and currency system instituted.[88]

Ch'en Ch'iu, whose work on "General Suggestions for Good Government" was listed in Liang Ch'i-ch'ao's *Bibliography of Books on Western Learning*, devoted considerable attention to economic matters,[89] touching upon a wide range of subjects pertaining to agricultural modernization, industrialization, commercial expansion, opening of ports of China's own to compete with the existing treaty ports dominated by foreign interests, and banking and paper money. Agreeing with many a writer of his time, Ch'en recognized the legitimacy of "private profit" (*ssu li*). Industrialists manufactured goods and merchants sold them in the market; each did so to make money for himself. But at the same time they both contributed to the economy of the country. Government therefore should give encouragement to private entrepreneurs, by conferring official ranks and titles on the most successful ones. It should, more importantly, allow ample room for them to exercise their talents in such areas as railroads, postal service, mining, textile, and other industrial ventures that were beyond the capacity of the government to promote or manage.[90]

---

[86] Essays 24 and 25, "Shang-wu" and "Shang-chan."

[87] Ibid., *chüan* 4, essays 33, "T'ieh-lu"; 34, "Tien-pao"; and 35–36, "Yu-cheng."

[88] Ibid., essays 37–38, "Yin-hang," and 40, "Chu yin."

[89] *Chih-p'ing t'ung-i*, Shanghai (?), 1893; author's preface dated 1892.

[90] See, especially, *Ching-shih po-i*, 4 *chüan*, and *Chiu-shih yao-i*, 1 *chüan*, both included in the work cited in the preceding note.

The views of one more representative writer might be mentioned before we bring this short survey to a close. Ch'en Chih, a secretary in the Board of Revenue and an active participant in K'ang's 1898 reform movement,[91] gained much of his knowledge of "current affairs" through reading and travel.[92] Ch'en underscored the importance of agricultural modernization as much as the necessity of industrial development. He saw the value of an agricultural surplus in economic growth. He pointed out that in Western countries development of industry did not involve neglect of agriculture. In fact, as a result of the application of new farming techniques (thanks to scientific and technological progress) production had increased tenfold, thus relieving the continued pressure of population on land. It behooved China to set up a special government office whose duty would be to bring about the country's agricultural modernization through proper measures.[93]

Ch'en explained the impact of modern industry on Western societies in these words:

> Since the advent of machines, the work of one man can adequately support ten people. The wealthy furnish the capital to establish factories which give work to thousands of poor people. The profit reaped by the wealthy amounts to no more than 10 or 20 percent; but the wages earned by the poor have increased many times and are still increasing. Thus the rise of machine manufacturing has primarily benefited the poor.[94]

Industrialization, therefore, would not deprive Chinese people of their livelihood; on the contrary, it would relieve the chronic population pressure that too often condemned men to die of starvation or to rise in futile rebellions.

Modern scientific knowledge, in his view, was the first foundation of industry. He sang praise to Western science which had been developing in the recent three hundred years. "Probing into final causes and first principles," he wrote, Western scientists "discovered what is unknown from what is already known." And, applying their knowledge to develop new technology and machinery, they benefited both the coun-

---

[91] K'ang, *Nien-p'u*, pp. 13a–b; Lo, *K'ang*, pp. 63–73.

[92] I.e., *Yung shu* (the title incorrectly rendered by So, "Western Influence and the Chinese Reform Movement of 1898," as "Trite Writings") and *Hsü fu-kuo ts'e* (*Fu-kuo ts'e* being William A. P. Martin's work on economic matters).

[93] *Yung-shu, chüan* 2, "Nung cheng" and *Hsü fu-kuo ts'e, chüan* 1, "Chiang-ch'iu nung-hsüeh shuo," pp. 13a–14a. See also *Yung shu, chüan* 1, "Shui-li," and *chüan* 2, "Ts'an sang."

[94] *Yung-shu, chüan* 8, "Yang min."

try and the people. As a result, "a brand new world has emerged."[95]
By adopting Western science and technology, Ch'en concluded, China
could not only assure herself of national survival but also earn a rightful
place in this new world which, eventually, would be a "great community of cultures" (*sheng-chiao ta-t'ung*).[96]

Ch'en was confident that such a splendid goal could be attained.
Meiji Japan afforded a clue.

> Japan is but a small nation in the eastern sea. During the three decades
> in which the country has been opened to commerce, it has learned all
> that the Westerners can do and all that the Chinese are now incapable
> of doing.[97]

As Japan was on her way to become a member of the "great community
of cultures," China should follow her footsteps without delay.[98] Scientific and technological education was crucial. The industrial growth of
Western countries had its foundation in epoch-making inventions, such
as the steam engine and the telegraph, which in turn had their roots in
the various branches of natural science.[99] Mathematics, he pointed out,
was the key to science. The Chinese attached little importance to it, not
knowing that all sorts of new scientific principles and technological inventions had, in the last analysis, come from the study of mathematics.[100] Science itself, of course, should be seriously taught in the schools.
Chemistry (including biochemistry), mechanics, optics, electricity, and
geology—all of which bore directly on agriculture, industry, and commerce—should be included in the curricula.[101] Technological training
should also be provided.[102]

[95] Ibid., *chüan* 7, "Tien hsüeh," p. 8a. Anticipating the objection of conservatives
who would repudiate science because it was "foreign," Ch'en argued that Western
science had its origin in ancient China and that to adopt modern science was tantamount to retrieving what China has lost (ibid., *chüan* 7, "Ke-chih," p. 9a).

[96] Ibid., *chüan* 5, "K'ao kung," p. 6a.

[97] Ibid., *chüan* 8, "Tzu li," p. 4b.

[98] Ibid., pp. 4b–5a and *Hsü fu-kuo ts'e, chüan* 3, "Ch'üan kung ch'iang kuo shuo," in
which Ch'en traced China's weakness, economic and military, to the inveterate
tendency to look down upon craft and craftsman, and explained the West's scientific
and industrial achievements by the effects of government promotion. Like K'ang, he
was greatly impressed by the Krupp works of Germany.

[99] *Hsü fu-kuo ts'e, chüan* 3, "I ch'eng yü hsüeh shuo," pp. 3a–b.

[100] Ibid., essay 3; "Suan-hsüeh t'ien-hsüeh shuo," pp. 3b–4b. Accordingly, he
proposed that all candidates taking the civil examinations be required to show knowledge of mathematics.

[101] Ibid., essay 4, "Hua-hsüeh chung-hsüeh shuo," pp. 4b–5a, and essay 5, "Kuang-
hsüeh tien-hsüeh shuo," pp. 5a–6b.

To counter the widely prevailing sentiment that machine manufacturing would destroy handicraft industry and deprive many people of their livelihood, Ch'en wrote an essay on "Industry Supports the People."[103] He condemned those who clung to this view as "great criminals bent on impoverishing and weakening China."He cited the experience of England where handicraftsmen found work in the newly evolving factory system and earned their living. Without industrialization, he argued, China would not be able to compete with Western countries in trade and would, by that very failure, doom the native handicraft economy—and countless people—to poverty. He went on to glorify the machine, which, being endowed with "superhuman skill and intelligence," was truly a great blessing to mankind. Only when man came into possession of machines was he worthy of "standing together with heaven and earth to form a trinity."[104] Such a nearly worshipful attitude toward technology reminds one of Ch'en Tu-hsiu's exaltation of "Mr. Science"; at any rate, it clearly adumbrated the position K'ang took in his 1905 essay on industrialization.

Our survey of the views of eight writers points to one conclusion, namely, while they differed in details and emphasis, they concurred generally on a number of major issues: that improvement in agricultural production was vital to economic growth; that industrialization was necessary and urgent; that, in order to achieve agricultural and industrial modernization, scientific technological knowledge must be introduced from the West, disseminated in the country, and pursued by native scholars; that railroads, steamships, telegraph, and postal services were indispensable to a modern economy; that to facilitate capital formation and flow, a modern banking and monetary system must be instituted; and that, finally, government action was necessary to encourage and assist private entrepreneurship in various sectors of the economy, especially in the initial phases of modernization, but the government should avoid meddling in the actual process of economic development. None of these writers favored state control or management of economic enterprises. Unlike the modernizers of the 1860s, they focused their attention more on the economic welfare of the people

---

[102] Ibid., essays 6–13, on metallurgy, minerology, textile and food manufacturing, and manufacturing of utensils, glassware, watches and clocks, etc., as well as weapon-making, machine-making, and road-building, pp. 6b–14a.

[103] I.e., ibid., *chüan* 3, "Kung-i yang min shuo," pp. 14b–15b.

[104] Ibid., p. 15a. Like others of his time, he regarded the *likin* as an obstacle to economic growth and urged its abolition (*Yung shu, chüan* 2, "Li-chin," pp. 3a–b).

than on wealth as a means to state power.[105] K'ang, as already indicated, shared these convictions; his position was in fact a reflection of the dominant trend of economic thinking of the time.

"Western Learning" and Economic Reform

That men of such diverse backgrounds and careers should hold so much in common can be readily explained by the fact that they had derived knowledge and inspiration from roughly the same sources, namely, "Western learning" transmitted largely through the writings of missionaries,[106] translations of Western books (and their Japanese versions) by government and other institutions,[107] and personal ob-

[105] Chao, *Wan-Ch'ing . . . ssu-hsiang shih*, p. 315: "In the Hsien-feng and T'ung-chih periods the emphasis was on the search of power; in the Kuang-hsü and Hsüan-t'ung periods the emphasis was on achieving wealth." This work mentions several other writers of the time (see pp. 19–301). I have not included Chang Chien in my account because he was notable chiefly as China's "pioneering industrialist" rather than as a writer on economic reform. See, however, his essays "Nung-hui i" and "Shang-hui i" both written in 1896, in which he recommended the formation of empire-wide networks of commercial and agricultural associations to stimulate growth in these sectors. He also supported the view that economic enterprises should be privately owned and operated, while government should encourage and protect them (*Chang Chi-tzu chiu lu, Shih-yeh lu, chüan* 1). Samuel C. Chu, *Reformer in Modern China: Chang Chien, 1853–1926*, chap. 3, gives an account of Chang's industrial enterprises. Chang Chih-tung, however, relied more on government action than private enterprise. See, e.g., "Cha t'ung-chü she chü chiang-ch'iu yang-wu," written 1884 while serving as governor of Shansi, and "Cha ssu-tao chiang-ch'iu yang-wu," written in 1886 while he was governor-general of Hu-Kuang, both in *Chang wen-hsiang-kung ch'üan-chi, chüan* 89, p. 22, and *chüan* 93, p. 22. Essay 9 of *Chüan-hsüeh p'ien*, "Nung kung shang hsüeh," contains his views on the importance of agriculture, industry, and commerce, on their relationship to one another, and on the ways and means to modernize them.

[106] See Teng and Fairbank, *China's Response*, pp. 134–35, for a brief reference to missionary influence on reform thought. Kikuchi Takaharu, "Kōgakkai to hempō undō—Kōgakkai no setsuritsu ni tsuite," pp. 305–17, is useful. People active in the Society (established in 1888) were among the most important in exerting influence on the reformers. A contributor to the *Wan Kwok Kung Pao*, no. 88 (ca. 1896), who used the pseudonym "Ku-wu k'un-hsüeh chü-shih," praised the Society's work in "supplementing China's old learning with the new knowledge of Western countries" through the publication of over one hundred books. This article, "Kuang-hsüeh-hui ta yu-tsao yü Chung-kuo shuo," is reprinted in Chien, *Wu-hsü*, 3: 214–17. That K'ang owed much to the Society's publications was testified by Timothy Richard, *Forty-five Years in China*, p. 253; "He [K'ang] . . . drew up a Memorial . . . praying that the Emperor should immediately take steps for reform. The lines . . . advocated were similar to those laid down by the publications of the S. D. K." Richard also pointed out that the official paper of the Ch'iang-hsüeh hui not only bore the title "Wan kuo kung pao" but at first "consisted mainly of reprints from our magazine" (p. 254).

[107] E. R. Hughes, *The Invasion of China by the Western World*, pp. 108–9, points out that by the beginning of the 1870s there were three translation bureaus at work, one in Peking, another in Shanghai, and the third in Canton. For a survey of works

servations made by men who went abroad to study or on diplomatic missions and by those who visited or worked in China's treaty ports.[108]

The Society for the Diffusion of Christian and General Knowledge among the Chinese (Kuang-hsüeh hui) exerted wide influence through its publications, the sales of which increased almost a hundredfold between 1893 and 1907.[109] Men like Young J. Allen, Joseph Edkins, John Fryer, William Muirhead, Alexander Williams, and Timothy Richard, active members of the society, introduced Western science, technology, economics, through the pages of the *Wan Kwok Kung Pao* (International News Bulletin), especially in the years after 1874, and through a number

---

translated, see Tsuen-hsuin Tsien, "Western Impact on China through Translation," pp. 305–27. So, "Western Influence and Chinese Reform," gives a general but not particularly perceptive survey.

[108] Among persons mentioned above, Ma Chien-chung, Cheng Kuan-ying, and Hsüeh Fu-ch'eng were the most outstanding instances. K'ang had first-hand contact with Western civilization when he visited Hong Kong (1879) and Shanghai (1882), which prompted him "to study Western books on a large scale" (*Nien-p'u*, pp. 5b and 6a; Lo, *K'ang*, pp. 36, 38). Japan became an indirect source of Western ideas for K'ang and Liang. See Philip C. Huang, "A Confucian Liberal: Liang Ch'i-ch'ao in Action and Thought," chap. 4.

[109] I.e., from 817 *yüan* to 21, 146 *yüan*, according to a report published in the *Chih-hsin pao* (*China Reformer*), an organ of K'ang's reform movement, published in Macao; no. 103 (Sept. 15, 1899), p. 9a.

[110] Chao, *Wan-Ch'ing . . . ssu-hsiang shih*, pp. 305–11, identifies some of the publications dealing with agriculture, industry, and commerce. Henri Bernard, "Notes on the Introduction of the Natural Sciences into the Chinese Empire," pp. 220–41, is a comprehensive survey. Adrian Arthur Bennett, *John Fryer: The Introduction of Western Science and Technology into Nineteenth-century China*, pp. 89–96, lists Fryer's translations of works on manufacturing, engineering, agriculture, and other technological subjects.

[111] *Nien-p'u*, p. 6a; Lo, *K'ang*, p. 38. Lo cites this journal as the "Review of the Times." K'ang indicated that he had turned his attention to "acoustics, optics, chemistry, electricity, and mathematics," besides history and other subjects. The following articles in the *Wan Kwok Kung Pao*, e.g., presumably influenced K'ang's economic ideas: Alexander Williams, "Chih kuo yao wu," chap. 3, in no. 4 (May 1889), pp. 16a ff., discussing the facts and prospects of coal mining; Joseph Edkins, "T'ieh-lu i k'uo-ch'ung lun," in nos. 5–11 (June–Dec. 1889), suggesting that the existing railroad system be expanded; Chü-wai p'ang-kuan jen (i.e., Robert Hart), "Lun t'ung-shang ta-chü," n.s., no. 10 (Nov. 1889), pp. 3b–5b, arguing that foreign trade should benefit China and that railroads, electric power, mining, steamship navigation, and banks should be developed; Ernst Faber, "Shen li kuo-ts'ai," no. 14 (March 1890), pp. 190a–91b, recommending machine manufacturing, development of a transportation system, abolition of *likin*, and issuance of government bonds; Ernst Faber, "Tzu hsi tsu tung," no. 15 (April 1890), pp. 189b–291a, 307a–9a, and 316a–17a, vouching the importance of modern agricultural techniques, machine manufacturing, and protection of industrial inventions with patent laws. A number of articles on science also appeared in the journal. Tseng Hsieh-kang (Tseng Chi-tse)'s preface to Williamson's

of other publications.[110] K'ang became a reader of the International News Bulletin in 1883;[111] he acquainted himself also with books and pamphlets on economic affairs written by various authors.[112]

Timothy Richard, "perhaps the most influential missionary who advocated reform" in China,[113] must have made a profound impression on K'ang. At any rate, many of K'ang's ideas appear to have borrowed from Richard, as a survey of the latter's writings readily suggests.[114] The "Hsin cheng-ts'e" (New Policies) is especially interesting in this connection.[115] After pointing out in a short introduction that the only way to meet the challenge of population pressure on land was to develop commerce and that it was a serious mistake to attempt to close the country to commercial intercourse with foreign nations by means of military force, Richard defined four main areas in which reform must be effected: "first, measures to enlighten the people; second, measures to nourish the people; third, measures to give peace to the people; and

articles on Western science, "Hsi hsüeh lüeh shu," no. 6 (July 1889), pp. 1a–2a, is an endorsement of science as enthusiastic as Ch'en Chih's.

[112] As his *Jih-pen shu-mu chih* shows. *Chüan* 7, 8, and 9 of this bibliography of Japanese books list works on various aspects of agriculture, industry and commerce. In his *Hsi-cheng ts'ung-shu*, Liang Ch'i-ch'ao included, among other works, the texts of John Fryer's *Kung-ch'eng chih fu lun* (Essay on Achieving Wealth Through Engineering, translation of a work by an English engineer), 12 *chüan; K'ao-kung chi-yao* (Essentials of Engineering, a sequel to the above), 17 *chüan*; Joseph Edkins' *Fu-kuo yang-min ts'e* (A Treatise on Enriching the State and Nourishing the People), 16 chapters; and Fryer's *Pao fu shu yao* (Essentials of Protecting Wealth, translation of an English author's work on money and banking), 17 chapters.

[113] Teng and Fairbank, *China's Response*, p. 134. Richard, *Forty-five Years in China*, chap. 6, "Working among Officials and Scholars, 1881–84," and chap. 12, "The Reform Movement in China, 1895–1898," narrated his own experiences in promoting reform.

[114] Richard, *Forty-five Years in China*, p. 261, said that when the "Reform Society" published a new collection of *Tracts for the Times* early in 1898 in Shanghai, it included thirty-one of his articles touching on government, economics, education, religion, and military matters. Richard probably helped K'ang see new significance in the ancient Chinese notion *ta-t'ung*. Thus Richard wrote, on p. 254: "On October 17, 1895, occurred my first meeting with Kang Yu-wei. . . . He had brought a copy of his work to present to me, before leaving for the south next day. He told me he believed in the Fatherhood of God and in the brotherhood of nations as we taught in our publications, and he hoped to cooperate with us in the work of regenerating China." A bibliography of Richard's writings published by the Society, appended to Ts'ai Erh-k'ang, *Chung Tung chan chi*, includes this item: "Ta-t'ung hsüeh, 30 cents." It appears that Richard was correct in saying that K'ang believed in "the brotherhood of nations," but it is doubtful that K'ang believed in "the Fatherhood of God"—at any rate, not in the religious sense.

[115] Written in the autumn of 1895, this piece first appeared in the *Wan Kwok Kung Pao*, no. 87 (April 1896) and was reprinted in Ts'ai, *Chung Tung chan chi, chüan* 8. It is now available in Chien, *Wu-hsü*, 3: 232–41.

fourth, measures to renovate the people" (*chiao min chih fa, yang min chih fa, an min chih fa, hsin min chih fa*).[116] The phrase *yang min chih fa*, significantly, was exactly the same one that K'ang used in his memorials submitted to the emperor in May and June 1895.[117] Similarities in contents between these documents and the *New Policies* are striking. Of the ten points made by Richard, transportation, postal service, mining, land reclamation, industry, mechanization, banking and paper currency, silver coinage, commerce, and newspapers, only the tenth was not covered by the proposals in K'ang's memorials.[118] A comparison of Richard's other relevant works with K'ang's writings on economic affairs yields the same conclusion, that K'ang accepted virtually all of Richard's ideas of economic reform. Richard's 1894 "Tracts for the Times" (*Shih-wu hsin lun*),[119] e.g., dealt in part with "Nourishing the People," "Sources of Wealth," "Science," "Foreign Affairs," and "Road Building." These, too, were K'ang's favorite themes. In an essay written probably in the early 1890s, "Beseeching Scholars to Save the People" ("Ch'iu ju chiu min shuo"), Richard urged "the book-reading men of the eighteen provinces of China to study Chinese and Western methods of nourishing the people," to seek the emperor's approval of their findings, and to put them to use. The "excellent methods" that he recommended were incorporated by K'ang in his 1898 reform program: land reclamation, mining, road building, currency reform, postal service, and industrialization.[120] Both men held similar views regarding agricultural modernization[121] and emigration as a measure to relieve poverty and overpopulation.[122] Both agreed that improvement of the economic welfare of the people should be the primary aim of reform.

It is unnecessary to pursue further the parallels of thinking between

[116] "*Hsin cheng-ts'e* tzu hsü," reprinted in Chien, *Wu-hsü*, 3: 231–32. This formulation was repeated in the opening paragraph of the essay (p. 233).

[117] Namely, in the "Second" and "Third Memorials," May 2 and June 3, 1895 (Chien, *Wu-hsü*, 2: 143, 168). Some of the measures that Richard proposed came under another topic, "Methods to Enrich the State" (*Fu-kuo chih fa*). Richard's work in question was published after K'ang wrote these memorials, but conceivably the former had earlier communicated his views to K'ang.

[118] Chien, *Wu-hsü*, 4: 234–36; 2: 140–47, 168. Instead of newspapers, K'ang had "caring of the destitute and disabled."

[119] *Shih-wu hsin lun* (sometimes cited as *Shih-shih hsin lun*, e.g., by So, in *Western Influence and Chinese Reform*, p. 56), 12 *chüan*, Shanghai, 1894. This was a collection of articles previously printed in the *Tientsin Times*.

[120] This was reprinted in Yü Pao-hsien, *Huang-ch'ao hsü-ai wen-pien*, chüan 2, pp. 17b–19b.

[121] Liang Ch'i-ch'ao included this pamphlet in his *Hsi-cheng ts'ung-shu*.

[122] Richard, *Forty-five Years in China*, pp. 137, 142.

K'ang and Richard—and between other advocates of economic reform and other Westerners connected with the society. An interesting fact, however, should be noted. As a recent study has shown, of the thirty-nine men who in 1889 formed the moving spirit of the society, most had come from Great Britain. The next large group hailed from the United States. Very few Germans and no Frenchmen or Russians took part in its activities. And of the thirty-nine, sixteen were businessmen, nine missionaries, eight functionaries in the maritime customs, one a lawyer, one a doctor, one a newspaperman, and the remaining three in diplomatic service.[123] It was natural that China's economic problems were a major focus of their attention and that the Anglo-American outlook pervaded their views concerning economic development and China's proper course of action. As K'ang and his fellow reformers (and other modernizers who were not directly involved in his movement) were greatly influenced by these men, they naturally tended to reflect the sentiments prevailing in late nineteenth-century Great Britain and the United States, in particular, a predilection for private enterprise, a mercantilist notion of foreign trade, and a reliance on the banking and monetary system as a means to help capital formation. They did not, however, borrow exclusively from Westerners. The spectacularly successful modernization of Japan persuaded K'ang and others that China could learn much from her island neighbor.

Meiji Japan as a Model of Economic Modernization

A few months before the official inauguration of the 1898 reform, K'ang Yu-wei advised the emperor that China would do well to take Meiji Japan as a particularly suitable model of modernization.[124] That K'ang had some knowledge of the economic and political developments in post-Restoration Japan may be gathered from the fact that he had not only compiled a bibliography of "Japanese books" but actually written a book on Meiji reform.[125]

[123] Wang Shu-huai, *Wai-jen yü wu-hsü pien-fa*, pp. 33–34.

[124] "Fifth Memorial" (Chien, *Wu-hsü*, 2: 195). This undated document was submitted to the emperor sometime late in 1897 or early in 1898.

[125] In K'ang's *Jih-pen Ming-chih pien-cheng k'ao*, which he began in 1886 and completed late in 1896, he gave an account of the changes effected in Meiji Japan from 1868 to 1890 (microfilm). As already noted, his *Jih-pen shu-mu chih*, printed in the winter of 1897, lists books on various aspects of agriculture, industry, and commerce (*chüan* 7, 8, and 9). K'ang of course was not alone in taking a keen interest in Meiji Japan. An anonymous article, "Cheng-ling i-hsin shuo," *Wan Kwok Kung Pao*, n.s., no. 5 (June 1889), pp. 11a–12a, outlines the reform measures implemented in post-Restoration Japan and concludes that China too could achieve equality with Western

A brief review of Japan's experience shows that there were obvious reasons for K'ang's choice. The achievements of the island nation were truly dazzling. In the early nineteenth century the economy was hardly more advanced than that of Western Europe in the Middle Ages. The overwhelming majority of the people were unfree, poverty-stricken peasants who supported a ruling hierarchy of shōgun, daimio, and samurai. Some 40 percent of their produce was annually appropriated by the daimio and shogun. On such a seemingly unpromising foundation a prosperous and powerful state was rapidly constructed.[126] Only a little over a year after the Restoration, the young samurai reformers began to do away with the feudal system under which they had grown up. In 1871 the fiefs were abolished and the land was divided into prefectures (ken). The old daimio gradually left the political scene; some of them became members of the emerging capitalist class. Those samurai that refused to accept the new order of things mounted a series of revolts; the abortive Satsuma rebellion of 1877 marked the end of the feudal society. Something like a middle class appeared. Businessmen and financiers, some of whom were former samurai or daimio, contributed their talents to the nation's economic development. Later on, many of their sons became government officials, army officers, or businessmen; from the last group came leaders of the business empires, the *zaibatsu*.[127] "The young reformers," as it has been said recently, "who started in 1868 to make Japan a modern nation able to hold its own on terms of equality with the Western powers, saw their ambitions realized within their lifetimes."[128] It is hardly surprising that they became a source of inspiration to K'ang and his collaborators in reform.

The Chinese reformers drew lessons from Meiji Japan to formulate their programs. As students of Japanese economic history have pointed out, agricultural expansion played a notable part in the country's

---

powers by following Japan's example. Joseph Edkins, "Jih-pen ko-ku ting-hsin chih ku," *Wan Kwok Kung Pao*, no. 12 (Jan. 1890), p. 298a, explains and summarizes the Meiji reforms. Huang Tsun-hsien, *Jih-pen-kuo chih*, an extensive work of 40 *chüan* completed in 1890 (published probably in Shanghai), deals with various aspects of the Meiji Reform, beginning with 1868 and ending at about 1880. The final *chüan*, entitled "Kung-i chih," describes the industrial development.

[126] William W. Lockwood, "Foundations of Japanese Industrialism," in *The Economic Development of Japan: Growth and Structural Change, 1868–1938*, pp. 3–34; reprinted in Barry E. Supple, *The Experience of Economic Growth: Case Studies in Economic History*, pp. 372–93.

[127] Edwin O. Reischauer, *Japan, Past and Present*, especially pp. 119–56, gives a concise account of this development.

[128] Ibid., p. 134.

growth. Thanks to the adoption of new techniques in farming—extended use of commercial fertilizers; selective breeding, propagation, and distribution of rice strains; improved methods of water and pest control, etc.—all of which came from knowledge made available by government-sponsored agricultural schools, research and extension services, and experimental stations; thanks to experts imported from foreign lands and to native students who studied in European universities, an accelerated growth in the agricultural sector took place in the closing decades of the nineteenth century and continued into the early years of the twentieth.[129] And thanks to the rising productivity of the land and the cultivator, and to the fact that savings were not squandered in increased consumption but were siphoned off to economic development, Japan was able to accumulate capital to finance her industrial and other aspects of expansion.[130] It is entirely conceivable that K'ang knew something of this development; his suggestion that the government should undertake to introduce modern knowledge and techniques of farming may well have stemmed from what he knew

[129] Bruce F. Johnson, "Agricultural Production and Economic Development in Japan," pp. 499 ff. The author estimates that in the thirty years following 1881, Japan increased the per capita food supply by over 20 percent and the output per farm worker by 106 percent. A summary of Johnston's findings is given in William H. Nicholls, "The Place of Agriculture in Economic Development," in Kenneth Berrill, *Economic Development with Special Reference to East Asia*, pp. 352–53. James I. Nakamura, "Growth of Japanese Agriculture, 1875–1920," in William W. Lockwood, *The State and Economic Enterprise in Japan: Essays in the Political Economy of Growth*, pp. 249–324, revises downward the agricultural growth rate as estimated by Johnston, but admits that increased agricultural productivity "was an important source" of savings contributive to development in the early stage. Shūjirō Sawada, "Innovation in Japanese Agriculture, 1880–1935," in Lockwood, *State and Economic Enterprise*, pp. 325–51, points out that a "steady growth in output" was achieved "by a long, slow process of technical innovation," both land-saving and labor-saving. But the persistence of the "traditional structure of the Japanese village and small-scale farming" made it increasingly difficult to achieve further advances in later decades.

[130] Gustav Ranis, "The Financing of Japanese Economic Development," pp. 440–54; reprinted with omissions in Supple, *Experience of Economic Growth*, pp. 399–412. Cf. William McCord, *The Springtime of Freedom: The Evolution of Developing Societies*, p. 61. Capital formation was facilitated by what Ranis calls "a severely regressive tax structure," and by the stable sociopolitical conditions that favored the propensity to save among the upper income group. Kazushi Ohkawa, "Agricultural Policy: The Role of Agriculture in Early Economic Development, A Study of the Japanese Case," in Berrill, *Economic Development*, pp. 322–35, brings together the views of English-speaking scholars, including Johnston, Lockwood, Ranis, and H. Rosovsky, and adds his own analysis based on quantitative data. Johannes Hirschmeier, *The Origin of Entrepreneurship in Meiji Japan*, pp. 690–710, discusses the economic and social institutions that contributed to Japan's agricultural growth.

of Japan's experience, in addition to what he learned from reading "Western books."

Japan's story of agricultural success was matched in the industrial and commercial fields. The government played an important role in the early phases of modernization and continued to be a factor in the economic life of the nation. "The start of industrialization in Japan," it has been observed, "was principally a political event. Even after some while when industrialization had become established in many fields the government remained its leader."[131] Vigorous leadership in economic reform furnished "the stimulant to growth." The Meiji government built the nation's first railroads and steamships; it established the first telegraph lines; it financed and operated various Western-type factories, which employed foreign technicians and new methods; it created special banks and adopted the gold standard; it introduced technical education at the college and secondary-school levels, covering a broad range of scientific and practical instruction in agricultural, commercial, and industrial technology; in addition, it aided new enterprises and industries in a variety of ways.[132] In fact, "from the time of the Restoration, the stimulation of economic development became a leading objective of national policy,"[133] although a perceptible emphasis was placed on undertakings that were considered to be essential to achieving military power.[134] The government's investment and involvement in economic enterprise were not necessarily extensive in absolute terms.[135] Nevertheless, its limited commitment was sufficient to set in

[131] Ichiro Nakayama, *Industrialization of Japan*, Introduction, p. 1.

[132] See, e.g., Lockwood, in Supple, *Experience of Economic Growth*, pp. 381–82; Hirschmeier, *The Origin of Entrepreneurship*, pp. 127, 136–41; Nakayama, *Industrialization of Japan*, p. 35; G. C. Allen and Audrey G. Donnithorne, *Western Enterprise in Far Eastern Economic Development*, pp. 191–92; and McCord, *Springtime of Freedom*, pp. 60 ff. According to Henry Rosovsky, *Capital Formation in Japan, 1868–1940*, p. 23, even after the initial phase of economic endeavor the government was "the largest and most important investor in the economy during the period 1887–1940."

[133] Allen and Donnithorne, *Western Enterprise*, p. 242. Hirschmeier remarks that "Modern shipping in Japan was . . . from the beginning strongly stimulated by military considerations" (*Origin of Entrepreneurship*, p. 142).

[134] Reischauer, *Japan, Past and Present*, p. 130. Cf. William W. Lockwood, "The Political Consequences of Economic Development in Japan," a paper presented at the Japanese Studies Seminar, 1962, cited in Nakayama, *Industrialization of Japan*, p. 4. Seymour Broadbridge, *Industrial Dualism in Japan*, p. 10, makes this point: "In Japan the clarion call of the Meiji period was *fukoku kyōhei*, 'a rich country, a strong army.'"

[135] Hirschmeier, *Origin of Entrepreneurship*, p. 150. See also Thomas C. Smith, *Political Change and Industrial Development in Japan: Government Enterprise, 1868–1880*.

motion the process that was soon to make Japan a prosperous and strong modern state.

The young emperor of Japan was of crucial importance as the symbol of national unity and purpose in the early Meiji years, even though control of the empire was actually in the hands of the Restoration leaders.[136] Despite the conservative ring of their watchword, *Sonnō jōi* (revere the emperor, expel the barbarians), their movement turned out in fact to mean the restoration of the emperor to his ancient position of authority in order to serve as the rallying point of their modernizing (and, to some extent, Westernizing) endeavors. The symbolic value of the emperor can hardly be overrated. "At times the very name of the emperor would break down resistance to the industrialization and modernizing efforts."[137]

As the traditional merchant and manufacturing groups lacked knowledge as well as capital to initiate modern enterprises, the government took an active and direct part in the first stages of economic transformation;[138] shortly afterwards, it decided to rely more and more on private entrepreneurship for further development.[139] When the government faced financial crises—when inflationary pressures developed as a result partly of the heavy investments in industry, partly of the costly liquidation of the feudal system, and partly of the military expenditures incurred in the 1873 (Formosa) and 1877 (Korea) expeditions—it was forced to make an important shift in economic policy. In 1881 the new minister of finance, Matsukata Masayoshi, curtailed government outlays drastically and initiated the sale of government enterprises (often at bargain prices). The latter move plugged one of the main drains on the treasury, even though the government continued to grant subsidies, direct or indirect, and monopoly rights to industrial-

[136] Reischauer, *Japan, Past and Present*, p. 113, notes that as the Meiji emperor was a boy of fifteen when he ascended the throne, he was too young and inexperienced to be a dominant figure in the early years of his reign, although eventually he became one of the great men of Japan. The celebrated "Charter Oath" which he proclaimed in April 1868 as an official expression of the nation's resolve to break with the past, was the result of discussion on the part of the Meiji leaders.

[137] Hirschmeier, *Origin of Entrepreneurship*, pp. 118–19.

[138] Hirschmeier points this out and remarks that "The greater the backwardness that has to be overcome, the greater will be the guidance and help required from the state" (ibid., p. 8).

[139] Ibid., pp. 33–37. The author observes that long before the decisive shift of policy in 1881, the government already undertook to draft merchant capital but with little success. Under the auspices of the Ministry of Transportation and Trade (*Tsūshōshi*) a trading operation was started in 1869 in a number of key cities, even though the response from the merchants was generally less than enthusiastic.

ists. This was in effect a decisive step in the direction of private capitalism.[140]

The Meiji leaders did not turn the nation's economy entirely to free enterprise. In the later years of the Meiji era, the chief entrepreneurial function was exercised "by the State and the Zaibatsu together."[141] Moreover, Meiji Japan's private enterprise was not "private" in the full sense of the term as it is understood in the English-speaking world. The great entrepreneurs, the leaders of big business houses, commonly described as the *zaibatsu*, were not the common variety of businessmen. They were, so to speak, "political merchants" (*sei shō*). Government sale of plants, government contracts, and government subsidies helped to bring about a concentration of heavy industry and transportation in the hands of a small group of families that had financial and political ties with factions in government. In some instances the *zaibatsu* were in intimate connection with the *hanbatsu*, at any rate in the early Meiji years. These people contributed greatly, particularly in the 1890–1910 period, to the development of Japan's modern capitalism.[142] Since the

[140] Ibid., pp. 148–50, 152–56. Sung-jae Koh, *Stages of Industrial Development in Asia*, pp. 29–30, takes a less optimistic view of the role of the Meiji government in economic development. The government, he says, "in its hasty effort, made idealistic plans and fell short of developing realistic policies. . . . After several years of reflection, the government began to realize the futility of idealistic planning, and started to encourage the new industrialists. . . . In 1881 the new Minister of Finance, Count Matsukata, pointed out the inefficiency of the government policies toward the model or sponsored mills" (ibid., p. 33). William W. Lockwood, "Adam Smith of Asia," *Journal of Asian Studies*, 23, no. 3 (May 1964): 352, takes an almost opposite view. "Initially," he writes, "the Meiji state intervened in passive fashion. . . . Yet policy was directed from the beginning to building up the private sectors and widening their capacities rather than stifling them."

[141] Allen and Donnithorne, *Western Enterprise*, p. 194.

[142] Broadbridge, *Industrial Dualism in Japan*, pp. 11–12, citing from Tsuchiya Takao, *Nihon no seishō* (The Political Merchants of Japan), Tokyo, 1956, and Smith, *Political Change and Industrial Development*, pp. 85–100. Broadbridge agrees with Lockwood that one should not overemphasize the role of the state but, at the same time, one should not overlook it. He argues that without the "political merchants" the growth would not have been so fast or so extensive. Godai Tomoatsu, 1834–85, afforded an interesting example of a political merchant. Second son of Naozaemon, a Confucian scholar of the Satsuma *han*, Kagoshima Prefecture, he went in 1857 to Nagasaki to study the Dutch language at the order of his lord. He was subsequently appointed secretary of the Marine Commissioner of the *han* and was sent to England in 1865 with an elderly member of the *han* to arrange for the training of young *han* members in that country. Returning the following year, he was appointed a Councilor by the Restoration authorities and ably assisted Itō, Inoue, Ōkuma, and other leaders in the difficult early Meiji years. Retiring from government, he engaged himself in such enterprises as shipbuilding, spinning, mining, and others, and helped to establish the Osaka Stock Exchange, Osaka Chamber of Commerce and Industry, and other modern-

1890s, with the assimilation of machine technology, the accumulation of banking and industrial capital, and the expansive influences of world prosperity and rising prices, the Japanese industrial-commercial system showed a rapid growth in output and profit. Two victorious wars gave added impetus to the development of transport, banking, and strategic industries under the dual leadership of government and *zaibatsu*. Although in the early 1910s Japan's industrial capitalism was still weak compared with advanced countries of the West, it had definitely emerged from its formative stage.[143]

It has been said of England that "the industrial revolution was also a revolution of ideas" and that, more specifically, "the growth of industry was connected historically with the rise of groups which dissented from the Church by law established in England."[144] Under different circumstances and in a different way, Meiji Japan's "industrial revolution" was also accompanied by a revolution of ideas. Government leaders who felt that economic development depended as much on cultural and ideological as on material premises, adopted a number of measures to foster a new outlook on life. Travel and study in Western lands were encouraged; a system of general compulsory education was instituted in 1870; based largely on the teaching experiences of the modernizer, Fukuzawa Yukichi,[145] Western-style textbooks were compiled by the Ministry of Education. The over-all aim was to spread *bummei kaika*. To symbolize this movement Western-style buildings were constructed and Western-style haircut and dress were popularized.[146]

---

type institutions (Hirschmeier, *Origin of Entrepreneurship*, pp. 38–39, 122, 171–72, 251, 279; Godai Ryūsaku, *Godai Tomoatsu den*).

[143] Lockwood, *Economic Development of Japan*, pp. 3–34; reprinted in part in Supple, *Experience of Economic Growth*, pp. 372–97. The disastrous World War II only temporarily checked the momentum of Japan's growth. In 1966 she was ahead of Great Britain and behind the United States, West Germany, and France in gross national product (*Japan Report*, vol. 13, no. 16 [Aug. 31, 1967], issued by the Japan Information Service, New York).

[144] T. S. Ashton, *The Industrial Revolution, 1760–1830*, pp. 1–22; reprinted with omissions in Supple, *Experience of Economic Growth*, pp. 146–58, where the author shows how intellectual dissent led to scientific and technological inventions and to entrepreneurial adventures.

[145] For the life and thought of Fukuzawa (1835–1901), see Carmen Blacker, *The Japanese Enlightenment: A Study of the Writings of Fukuzawa Yukichi*.

[146] Hirschmeier, *Origin of Entrepreneurship*, pp. 120–25. K'ang obviously received inspiration from Japan, when in the summer of 1898 he proposed in a memorial that Western-style haircut and dress be adopted, and that (following the Meiji emperor's example) the Kuang-hsü emperor officially pledge himself to reform and designate the 24th year of Kuang-hsü as *Wei-hsin yüan-nien* (Year One of Reform) ("Ch'ing tuan-fa i-fu, kai-yüan che," Chien, *Wu-hsü*, 2: 263–64).

The *bummei kaika* campaign was a success.[147] The emergence of "a mentality of progress" was of the greatest importance in the course of Japan's economic development.[148] Unlike England, where such mentality was an indigenous product, Japan's new way of thinking was transplanted. It took root, thanks to a native receptiveness and a combination of propitious historical circumstances.[149] A newborn faith in modern technology and industry permeated first an entrepreneurial elite and then virtually the entire population. The samurai's traditional disdain of pecuniary matters began to disappear;[150] entrepreneurs came to call themselves *jitsugyōka* (industrialists, businessmen) with pride.[151] This new outlook, a key factor in economic growth,[152] must have contributed materially to Japan's industrial and commercial expansion.

Understandably, Meiji afforded an attractive model to K'ang Yu-wei and others who knew something about her recent economic history. There was more than one point of contact in K'ang's plan and Japan's development: that government should furnish leadership, that the emperor should be a key figure, that private enterprise should be the basic dynamic force, and that educational and economic modernization must

---

[147] G. B. Sansom, *The Western World and Japan*, gives an account of the transition from "hate the barbarians" to learning from the West. The Meirokusha (Sixth Year of Meiji Association), founded by a group of intellectuals in 1873, helped to spread Western ideas of education, government, business methods, and other subjects. Many of the prominent members of the association were government officials. Fukuzawa played a key role as its most active member. This organization may have suggested to K'ang and his associates the usefulness of *hui*. See also Hirschmeier, *Origin of Entrepreneurship*, p. 120.

[148] Hirschmeier, *Origin of Entrepreneurship*, pp. 111–13.

[149] Ronald Philip Dore, *Education in Tokugawa Japan* (Berkeley: University of California Press, 1965), argues that much of the mentality of progress that characterized post-Restoration Japan was indigenous. One might note that without denying their creative genius, the Japanese seem also to possess a remarkable aptitude of adopting and adapting elements of foreign culture to form an integral part of their tradition. Confucianism and Buddhism were outstanding instances. Naturalized Confucianism, in fact, may have contributed to "the mentality of progress" that Dore considers to be indigenous. Yasuzō Horie, "Modern Entrepreneurship in Meiji Japan," in Lockwood, *The State and Economic Enterprise in Japan*, p. 169, traces the willingness to Westernize to Confucian tradition: "Its rationalism bred habits of mind which facilitated the introduction of Western technology."

[150] Hirschmeier, *Origin of Entrepreneurship*, p. 50, cites from Kiyooka Eiichi, trans., *The Biography of Fukuzawa Yukichi* (Tokyo, 1948), p. 11, that Fukuzawa refused to follow the samurai convention of wrapping their faces with hand-towels and going out in the darkness of night to handle money transactions.

[151] Hirschmeier, *Origin of Entrepreneurship*, p. 173; cf. p. 3.

[152] Joseph A. Schumpeter, *The Theory of Economic Development*, pp. 128 ff.

go hand in hand. K'ang must have believed that as Japan succeeded, so could China build her own economic future—with Japanese experience as a guide.

K'ang, however, failed to see that while the situations in mid-nineteenth-century China and Japan were in some ways broadly comparable, the latter was blessed with a number of factors that were absent (or that operated differently) in the former.

The main contributing factors to Japan's success can readily be identified. In the first place, Tokugawa Japan contained features that facilitated the historic transformation. The nation, in fact, was not wholly unprepared for the reception of Western ideas. Through the medium of the Dutch language, knowledge of Western technology became widely diffused during the first half of the century, especially among the samurai of the western han. Several of the daimio, notably those of Satsuma and Chōshū, launched a number of modernizing projects.[153] Before Commodore Perry's arrival in 1853, Japan had already gone through the preliminary phases of transition from an agrarian to a mercantile economy; even manufacturing industry was being developed in some lines, including textile, mining, and shipbuilding.[154] All this eased the task of the Meiji reformers.[155] The emergence of a money economy prompted by the rapid growth of cities and the development of transportation, the formation of *kabunakama*, a sort of company resembling the European guild, the fact that landlords began to leave their traditional professions to engage in trade and manufacturing led a recent writer on Asian economic history to remark that in Japan "the transition from a feudal to a modern industrial society" was essentially "the outcome of industrial and commercial progress in the Tokugawa era." The pressure exerted from the West "was not the cause of, but merely the occasion for" the momentous changes that transpired in Meiji times.[156]

Another factor was perhaps even more important. Meiji Japan appears to have had the knack of turning constituent elements of the old

---

[153] Allen and Donnithorne, *Western Enterprise*, pp. 188–90.

[154] Sansom, *Western World and Japan*, p. 527.

[155] McCord, *Springtime of Freedom*, p. 59.

[156] Sung-jae Koh, *Stages of Industrial Development in Asia*, pp. 28–29. See also E. Sydney Crawcour, "The Tokugawa Heritage," in Lockwood, *The State and Economic Enterprise in Japan*, pp. 17–44, where it is said that although the Japanese economy of the 1860s was not "outstandingly productive for a traditional economy," it was more "responsive than most traditional economies to economic stimuli," thanks, among other factors, to "a high potential for saving," "a well-developed system of national markets," a population "comparatively well educated and economically motivated."

society into contributive ingredients of economic growth in the new order. Propelled by vigorous leadership and aided by happy fortuities of history, different classes of the people, knowingly or unknowingly, directly or indirectly, worked to realize a common goal. Landlords and peasants, merchants in towns or villages, adapted themselves to the new situation. Many of the displaced samurai rose in unsuccessful armed revolts, but at the same time some members of the lower warrior class engaged themselves in intellectual reform, in the Restoration movement, and in shaping the Meiji new order. Even the daimyo had a part in economic modernization.[157] The feudal code of ethics, instead of working to impede change, lent moral strength to Meiji society and, in fact, served "as a basis for large-scale administration by the government and business." As a student of Japanese economic history puts it, "the respect for hierarchy, group discipline and teamwork—the virtues characteristic to the system of feudalism did not work against the introduction of industrialization. . . . On the contrary they played a vital role in promoting the whole process of modernization."[158] Confucianism, naturalized to fit the Japanese requirements, became "a way of life and thought widely disseminated through every stratum of society." Instead of acting to stymie progress, it helped to produce Meiji leadership from commoners as well as from samurai.[159] Moreover, its influence furnished "a strong ideological basis for a concern with the economic life of the people which was characteristic of the Tokugawa Period."[160]

[157] Horie, "Modern Entrepreneurship in Meiji Japan," pp. 194–95, points out that the social origins of the Meiji industrial pioneers were diverse and that the role of the samurai families was crucial. The ambitious minority among them, especially those of lower rank, accomplished the Restoration; thereafter, "concious of their elite status and responsibilities, they appeared in every field of new activity including business entrepreneurship." Robert N. Bellah, *Tokugawa Religion: The Values of Pre-industrial Japan*, pp. 117–31, shows how peasants and merchants contributed to the process of modernization by turning traditional values to good account.

[158] Nakayama, *Industrialization of Japan*, p. 37. Nakayama draws attention also to the persistence of "feudalistic heritage with its hierarchy, the sense of responsibility, and the ability to work in a team together with the family system" (ibid., p. 47).

[159] Horie, "Modern Entrepreneurship in Meiji Japan," p. 196, commenting on the "Confucian education" of both samurai and commoner, points to the fact that Confucianism, instead of being merely a "learned specialty," "was a way of life and thought widely disseminated through every stratum of society," and that it differed importantly from the Chinese original.

[160] Ibid., pp. 108–17, the influence of "Confucianism" on the Japanese economy is discussed. According to the author, that influence furnished "a strong ideological basis for a concern with the economic life of the people," by evolving a "Japanese" view of political economy, which placed an emphasis on "one-way dynamism in the attainment of goals and the selfless subordination of all collectivity members to the

The social characteristics of the Japanese villages, too, were helpful, particularly in the initial stages of economic development. The absence of divided inheritance in Japan meant that as soon as there were opportunities for younger sons to move out of agriculture, these opportunities were promptly utilized. Migration into towns and cities was steady and rapid. As the younger sons manned the new industries, their elder brothers who inherited the family property were able to supplement the workers' low wages, at least in emergencies. This was helpful in accumulation of industrial capital.[161] Furthermore, prosperous merchants and big landlords, instead of spending their resources to buy luxuries, invested their savings to modernize the spinning section of the cotton industry, just as wealthy farmers used theirs to modernize the weaving section. In this way the existence of the wealthy classes constituted "one of Japan's initial conditions for industrial development."[162]

Political stability and efficient central administration, two achievements of the Restoration, contributed importantly to economic progress. But these political assets were to some extent legacies of the feudal past. As it has been noted, the new regime "inherited the strong and reasonably efficient Tokugawa government intact."[163] A political, social, and institutional framework was thus available at the very beginning of the Restoration. This helped the effective and powerful leadership of the early Meiji government to keep at a minimum whatever dissension or conflict there existed between people who favored change and those who opposed it.[164] The inauguration of the imperial order indeed put an end to the shogunate, but it involved largely a redistribution of political power within the governing class rather than a destruction of the political fabric. It was in essence an "aristocratic revolution," which ushered in no democratic tradition but made it possible for the country to move from an agrarian to an industrial society without entailing serious internal strife. There was "no class or party war in which the skirmish line was drawn between new and old, revolutionaries and

---

goal effort." (One might add that K'ang Yu-wei made a valiant effort to develop a new brand of Confucianism which also stressed "one-way dynamism" but the endeavor of one man was poor substitute for the ethos of many.) Bellah also notes that even Zen monks played a very important part in the trade of the Ashikaga period (1338–1573) (*Tokugawa Religion*, p. 107). Japan, it appears, has demonstrated that traditional values as such do not necessarily preclude economic innovation.

[161] Tadashi Fukutake, *Asian Rural Society: China, India, Japan*, p. 5.
[162] Sung-jae Koh, *Stages of Industrial Development in Asia*, pp. 52–53.
[163] Reischauer, *Japan, Past and Present*, p. 117.
[164] Nakayama, *Industrialization of Japan*, pp. 26, 34.

conservatives"; regardless of status or profession, all were "more or less reformist, more or less traditional, and more or less modern."[165] Thanks to continuity and stability Japan underwent immense economic changes without losing social cohesion.[166] "Forced industrialization" may have given a "dualistic" character to Japanese economy in which "huge combines co-exist with thousands of small businesses."[167] But this phenomenon—a linkage with the economic past—hardly detracts from the modernity of the economy.

It might be suggested that post-Restoration Japan herself was a dualism—a dualism of old and new, the result of a creative synthesis of tradition and innovation. In the words of a recent writer, "the modern sector has succeeded because it climbed onto the shoulder of the traditional sector."[168] Or, as another writer puts it, "Japan exchanged the sword for guns and steam engines in order to preserve . . . the Chrysanthemum, that is, her national identity and self-respect."[169] In plain language this simply means that she has achieved economic modernity without wholesale cultural Westernization.[170]

The Chinese Situation: A Case of Retarded Development

To have the correct approach or to choose the right model was in itself no guarantee for fruitful economic modernization. As records

---

[165] Thomas Smith, "Japan's Aristocratic Revolution," pp. 381–83.

[166] Allen and Donnithorne, *Western Enterprise*, p. 188. Kamishima Jirō suggests that the traditional notion of "family" (*Ie*) had become "the driving force to construct the Meiji new society." See his "Modernization of Japan and the Problem of 'Ie' Consciousness," pp. 1–54.

[167] Broadbridge, *Industrial Dualism in Japan*, Preface, p. xi.

[168] Ibid., p. 53.

[169] Hirschmeier, *Origin of Entrepreneurship*, p. 114.

[170] This seems to be the view of more than one student of Japanese history. See, e.g., McCord, *Springtime of Freedom*, pp. 62–64; James C. Abbeglan, *The Japanese Factory: Aspects of Its Organization*, p. 2: "Japan . . . for all its industry remains clearly and consistently Asian"; Broadbridge, *Industrial Dualism in Japan*, especially pp. 23–24, discussing Japan's "dual industrial structure" and its relationship to her social and cultural dualism; and Nakayama, *Industrialism of Japan*, p. 32, note, criticizing W. W. Rostow for seemingly excluding "the possibility of different industrial systems" in his book *The Stages of Economic Growth: A Non-Communist Manifesto*. Simon Kuznets recently observed that as economic growth implies a variety of rapid accommodations and changes in economic and social structure, "a major challenge to a society that wants to take advantage of modern economic growth is to be able to make these revolutionary changes without breaking down, without allowing the conflicts usually generated by these changes to impair the unity of the society" ("Methodological Problems in the Study of Economic Growth," *Economic Papers, Special English Series*, no. 1, The Institute of Economics, Academia Sinica [Taipei, Taiwan, March 1969], p. 2). Japan successfully met that challenge.

show, K'ang's proposals received scant attention from the Ch'ing government. His dream of an industrial-commercial China rising from her stagnant agrarian economy was thus doomed to remain a forlorn hope. Indeed, one is tempted to surmise that, given the historical conditions prevailing in the closing decades of the past century, even if the Ch'ing rulers saw fit to adopt his economic program *in toto*, it is highly doubtful that it could have been carried out with a degree of success comparable to the Japanese precedent. The explanation is obvious: the crucial factors and forces that made modern Japan did not obtain in China.

The most important difference between the two situations was that, while the Restoration infused a new outlook and a new vigor into a system that had been on the whole administratively and morally sound, the 1898 reform movement appeared when the Chinese dynastic system under the Manchus was dying from inner decay.[171] Whatever were the faults of the Tokugawa government, it was able to give the country general peace, order, and a fairly effective administration, all of which became valuable legacy to the Meiji regime. The Ch'ing government's performance was far less satisfactory. The inherent weaknesses of the autocratic system, abeyant in the heyday of the dynasty, developed into a host of chronic administrative ailments.[172] Dissension and suspicion between Chinese and Manchu officials and, in the crucial 1890s and 1900s, between the emperor and the empress dowager; ineptitude, apathy, ignorance, and corruption in central and local officialdom; outmoded administrative precedents and regulations—these and other symptoms of political degeneration that prompted K'ang and others to demand institutional reform[173]— could hardly have yielded favorable conditions for economic improvement. Had Western expansion coincided not with China's political decadence, and had modernizing efforts been made in K'ang-hsi or Yung-cheng times, the outcome could conceivably have been different.

The scholar-official elite, China's civilian equivalent of the samurai, showed signs of intellectual and moral malaise. As early as in the 1810s

[171] Reischauer, *Japan, Past and Present*, pp. 117–18. The author goes on to say that the fall of the Manchu regime did not help matters. Instead of the political unity and efficient administration which the Meiji leaders inherited from Tokugawa Japan, republican China inherited "the political disunity and disrupted central government" from the Manchu dynasty.

[172] For a brief reference, see Kung-chuan Hsiao, *Rural China: Imperial Control in the Nineteenth Century*, pp. 503–10.

[173] See chapter 7, this volume, "Administrative Reform," especially the first three sections.

a famous writer had already noted with alarm the atrophy of intellectual capacities among all classes of people, so much so that even thieves lacked talent or ingenuity.[174] It has often been observed that traditional attitudes in general and Confucian values in particular, which tended to oppose innovation and to belittle or despise gainful enterprise, acted as an obstructive influence on economic development.[175] It is, however, possible to overstress this influence. Meiji Japan, too, had to reckon with traditional forces and her own brand of Confucianism, and yet she succeeded in effecting far-reaching changes in her economy, by harnessing old forces to serve new aims.[176] Something else, it seems, spelled the difference between the Chinese and Japanese experience.

Conceivably, power of regeneration belonged to a living tradition, however old, but not to a tradition that had lost much of its vitality. The value system of feudal Japan was capable of serving as a moral or psychological prop in the Meiji reform because it had been, down to the last Tokugawa days, a code of conduct actually honored by the bulk of the populace. The "Confucian tradition" of China did not fare so well. The political intrigues, factional rivalries, official corruption, and bureaucratic irresponsibility,[177] which violated both the letter and spirit of Confucian teaching might be taken as an index of the degree of elite demoralization reached in the declining years of the dynasty. Lip service was still rendered to Confucianism, but too often it was more *pro forma* than a matter of inner conviction or personal commitment. Few among the Chinese elite showed anything that could be

---

[174] Kung Tzu-chen, "I-ping chih-chi chu-i," no. 9, in *Kung Ting-an ch'üan-chi lei-pien* (Taipei, 1960), pp. 68–69. The same essay bearing a different title ("I-ping chih-chi shu-i," no. 2) is in the same volume, *chüan* 6, pp. 116–17.

[175] Albert Feuerwerker, *China's Early Industrialization*, p. 8, blames "the institutional and ideological obstacles to change" for China's inability to accomplish the transition to an industrial society. Fang Hsien-t'ing, "Chung-kuo kung-yeh-hua yü hsiang-ts'un kung-yeh," in *Chung-kuo ching-chi yen-chiu*, 2: 616–32, regards traditional attitudes and institutions as the chief cause of economic stagnation.

[176] Hirschmeier, *Origin of Entrepreneurship*, p. 174, cites Shibusawa Eiichi (1840–1931), a samurai, an activist in the *sonnō jōi* movement, and a distinguished business-man-industrialist of the Meiji and Taishō eras, as a revealing instance of the fruitful fusion of traditional and new attitudes. Shibusawa channeled the Confucian outlook, which had been an instrument to preserve the status quo, to help the country attain economic modernity—"to manage business enterprise using the *Analects* of Confucius." Hirschmeier bases his account on Tsuchiya Takao, *Nihon no keieisha seishin*, p. 76. Cf. references cited in notes 158–160, above.

[177] Some of the diaries written by men of the period contain much firsthand information. Particularly useful are Chao Lieh-wen, *Neng-ching-chü jih-chi*; Li Tz'u-ming, *Yüeh-man-t'ang jih-chi*; and Weng T'ung-ho, *Weng-kung-kung jih-chi*.

considered the counterpart of "the spirit of the samurai."[178] Explicit avowals notwithstanding, they can hardly be credited with having conserved the traditional values; in their failure to practice them they might be charged with undermining them. Reformers would have found it difficult to recruit sufficient personnel to carry out their programs with the necessary dedication, even if the Kuang-hsü emperor had the power to authorize them. "Rotten wood cannot be carved; a wall of dirty earth will not receive the trowel."[179] A decaying tradition, so it seems, could not stand remaking. This, however, does not justify the conclusion that tradition necessarily precluded innovation. The case of Meiji Japan should be kept in mind in discussing the question of the relationship between tradition and change.

The quality of leadership, admittedly, was vital in successful modernization.[180] The competence of China's reform leaders has been pertinently called into question.[181] But it should be granted that, while China did not have exact equivalents of Japan's samurai, some of the reformers did show a degree of perceptiveness and dedication. K'ang and his collaborators may not have fully understood the structure of China's traditional economy or the problems of economic development. Viewed in the historical context, however, their suggestions for reform were not without plausibility. The "Six Martyrs" of 1898 (T'an Ssu-t'ung, at any rate) compared not unfavorably with Yoshida Shōin in willingness to die for a worthy cause. One suspects that, for one thing, the enormous difference in size between the two countries (China proper's 2,279,234 square miles to Japan's 142,726 square miles) and

---

[178] Hirschmeier, *Origin of Entrepreneurship*, p. 44, describes "the spirit of samurai," which not only determined official policies but became something of a public attitude, as "a happy mixture of militant patriotism and economically rationalized Confucian ethics."

[179] *Analects*, V. 9 (Legge trans.).

[180] Allen and Donnithorne, *Western Enterprise*, p. 190.

[181] Feuerwerker, *China's Early Industrialization*, pp. 39–40, suggests that the reform leaders lacked understanding of "the structure of the traditional economy and the influence of the traditional values as they affected the inadequate supply of capital for the new ventures they proposed," recognition of "the necessity for forced saving in agriculture as a basis for the initial growth of industry," and realization of "the progressive decay of the Ch'ing government structure" in assigning "a major role to the state in the execution of their program." This assessment, though well grounded, does not seem to be entirely fair, especially with reference to K'ang who wished to make private enterprise the backbone of China's new economy and was very much concerned with administrative and political reform. As for assigning a major role to the state in the initial phases of modernization, one might raise the question: What could have been the alternative?

corresponding difference in population worked to the disadvantage of China. The influence of the small number of men who committed themselves to change was easily lost in a population of hundreds of millions; whereas the impact of the Meiji leaders (who perhaps outnumbered K'ang's group) was decisive in the island nation. The process of economic development at its early stages, it has been said recently, involves "the building of organs of public administration and the provision of an educated minority," who will then undertake "the task of popular enlightenment."[182] In China the task of enlightenment—of cultivating "the spirit of innovation"[183]—must have been much more difficult than in Japan. One should not of course overlook the fact that illiteracy was considerably higher in imperial China than in Tokugawa Japan. The quality of the people at large, it appears, rather than merely the quality of leadership, could have adversely affected the Chinese situation. Immense size might also disadvantage a country in the process of economic development itself. In a compact country like Japan a little innovation went far to change the economic structure. Japan's achievements in the first Meiji years would have been not much more than drops in a bucket if they were transferred to China and, conversely, what China attained, especially between 1912 and 1949,[184] could possibly have also worked wonders in early Meiji Japan.

It might be useful to take a brief look at the economic situation in the China of the time. There is no gainsaying that China presented a case of retarded and interrupted development. Nevertheless, from the 1860s onward, efforts at industrialization had been made, though only on a limited scale.[185] By the turn of the century a wide variety of industrial projects had been started, either by native promoters or by foreign in-

[182] John Kenneth Galbraith, *Economic Development* (1964) p. 46. This book is a revised and expanded edition of *Economic Development in Perspective*, 1962.

[183] Robert J. Alexander, *A Primer of Economic Development*, p. 142, suggests that the problem of getting the process of economic change started is to develop a group within the economy whose role is to innovate and to spread the spirit of innovation throughout the community.

[184] John K. Chang, "Industrial Development of Mainland China, 1912–1949," especially pp. 65–81. One might cite the Chee Hsin Cement Co. to illustrate this point. Albert Feuerwerker, "Industrial Enterprise in Twentieth-century China: The Chee Hsin Cement Co.," p. 341, observes that "the substantial forward linkage" of the company (cement to China's railroads and to factories and other buildings in the treaty ports) amounted to "a mere drop in an oceanic society which boiled and stormed." One might add that compact size must have been helpful in attaining economic successes in Taiwan, an island of 13,886 square miles, where social and political stability prevailed.

[185] Feuerwerker, *China's Early Industrialization*, pp. 1–2.

terests in the treaty ports. These did not bring about any structural change in the economy, but "signs of growth" had been detected in the mid 1890s.[186] The growth of the cotton industry was particularly noticeable. Beginning with 11 mills (65,000 spindles) in 1891, the industry boasted 120 mills (3,850,000 spindles) in 1928.[187] With the exception of the agricultural sector, which had been plagued by repeated natural disasters and "political disorganization,"[188] there was perceptible though restricted growth in other sectors, in the infrastructure, and in commerce.[189] "Comprador capital" and private enterprise showed some expansion, mostly in the treaty ports and coastal provinces.[190] All this was not substantial enough to match Japan's achieve-

[186] R. S. Gundry, *China Present and Past*, pp. 85–116. The author, correspondent for the *London Times*, made a survey of "industries and resources," pp. 116–40.

[187] Franklin L. Ho and H. D. Fong, "Extent and Effects of Industrialization in China," p. 8.

[188] Walter H. Mallory, *China, Land of Famine*, pp. 1–4, 189, explains China's agricultural stagnation by referring to the fact that there were 1,828 famines between 108 B.C. and A.D. 1911 and that political disorganization tended to aggravate the economic situation.

[189] For the armament industry, see Wang Erh-min, *Ch'ing-chi ping-kung-yeh ti hsing-ch'i*. For iron and steel industry, Fang Hsien-t'ing and Ku Yüan-t'ien, "Wo-kuo kang-t'ieh kung-yeh chih niao-k'an" in *Chung-kuo ching-chi yen-chiu*, 2: 633–51; Hou Hou-p'ei, *Chung-kuo chin-tai ching-chi fa-chan shih*, pp. 120–32; and Sun Yü-t'ang, *Chung-kuo ching-chi-shih tzu-liao*, 1: 743–892. For cement industry, Hou, *Chung-kuo chin-tai ching-chi fa-chan shih*, pp. 132–39 and Feuerwerker, "The Chee Hsin Cement Co.," pp. 304–41. For chemical industry, Hou, *Chung-kuo chin-tai ching-chi fa-chan shih*, pp. 139–47. For mining industry, Sun Yü-t'ang, *Chung-kuo ching-chi-shih tzu-liao*, 2: 567–669 (coal) and pp. 670–743 (metal), and Li En-han, *Wan-Ch'ing shou-hui k'aung-ch'üan yün-tung*. For textile industry, Han-sheng Ch'üan, "The Cotton Industry in Kiangsu before the Opium War" (in Chinese with English summary), *Tsing Hua Journal of Chinese Studies*, n.s., 1, no. 3 (Sept. 1958): 25–51; Allen and Donnithorne, *Western Enterprise*, pp. 166–67, 174–79; Sun Yü-t'ang, *Chung-kuo ching-chi-shih tzu-liao*, pp. 893–956 (wool) and pp. 905–37 (cotton and silk); and Hou, *Chung-kuo chin-tai . . . ching-chi*, pp. 89–108 (cotton) and 103–12 (wool). For flour milling industry, Hou, *Chung-kuo chin-tai . . . ching-chi*, pp. 112–20 and Allen and Donnithorne, *Western Enterprise*, p. 174. For railroad, Li Kuo-ch'i, *Chung-kuo chao-ch'i ti t'ieh-lu ching-ying*; P. H. Kent, *Railway Enterprise in China*; Hou, *Chung-kuo chin-tai . . . ching-chi*, pp. 291–305; and Chang Kia-ngau, *China's Struggle for Railroad Development*. For shipping, Lü Shih-ch'iang *Chung-kuo tsao-ch'i ti lun-ch'uan ching-ying*, (Taipei, 1962); and Sun Yü-t'ang, *Chung-kuo ching-chi-shih tzu-liao*, pp. 375–443. For money and banking, Hou, *Chung-kuo chin-tai ching-chi . . .*, pp. 155–91 (currency) and 191–203 (banking). Wang Ching-yü, *Chung-kuo chin-tai kung-yeh-shih tzu-liao* (a sequel to Sun Yü-t'ang's compilation cited above), contains much relevant material.

[190] Feuerwerker, *China's Early Industrialization*, pp. 16–21. Y. C. Wang, *Chinese Intellectuals and the West*, pp. 471–96, surveys the activities of businessmen, bankers, and industrialists, and points to them as "instances of successful private enterprise." Sun Yü-t'ang, *Chung-kuo ching-chi-shih tzu-liao*, 2: 957–1173 and Wang Ching-yü, *Chung-kuo chin-tai kung-yeh-shih tzu-liao*, passim, give additional material showing growth and limitations of private enterprise.

ment.[191] Nevertheless, China was beginning to move in the general direction in which K'ang and many of his contemporaries wished to see the economy move.

The movement, however, was slow and hesitant. Instead of following a smooth, upward trend, it slithered along by fits and starts, in broad response to shifting circumstances. A student of modern Chinese economic history discerned "three industrial surges" in 1914–20, 1926–36, and 1938–42. There was no long-term stagnation, nor was there a consistent pattern of growth. The pace was on the whole not brisk. In 1933 China's industrial output in national income (about 11 percent) was comparable to Japan in 1880 (9 percent) and lagged far behind her in 1900 (22 percent).[192] The efforts at industrialization made between 1862 and 1911 by the government and by private entrepreneurs, both native and foreign, were not fruitless, but they did not bring about alterations in the essential character of the economy.[193]

Two questions suggest themselves. What made it possible for China to escape complete economic stagnation? Why did the modernizing efforts fail to produce sustained progress and to induce structural changes in the economy?

In answer to the first question, it might be said that some of the factors contributive to economic development were not totally absent in China. Such factors as a capacity to innovate, a spirit of business adventure, and a technological aptitude were not entirely suppressed by ignorance and bigotry. "Conservative attitudes," it appears, did not necessarily rule out innovation. England afforded a revealing instance: when a railroad system was proposed in the early 1830s, a loud cry against it was raised by people in diverse walks of life, including lawyers and medical men. Dire consequences would ensue, they predicted, if "the fiery monsters" were sent forth to overrun the country. Their opposition did not silence the innovators, nor did it prevent England from building the railroads that contributed much to her economic growth.[194]

---

[191] Reischauer's phrase. See his "Time Is on Our Side in Asia," pp. 55–60.

[192] Chang, "Industrial Development of Mainland China," pp. 73–74, 78. Albert Feuerwerker, *The Chinese Economy, 1912–1949*, does not recognize these "surges."

[193] Kung Chün, *Chung-kuo hsin kung-yeh fa-chan-shih ta-kang*, pp. 13–14, 49–50, 65–69. Ku Yüan-t'ien, "Chung-kuo hsin kung-yeh chih hui-ku yü ch'ien-chan" in Fang Hsien-t'ing, *Chung-kuo ching-chi yen-chiu*, 2: 581–602, takes the years 1914–22 as the "golden age" of Chinese- and Japanese-owned enterprises and considers 1923–35 a period of decline for Chinese-owned industrial undertakings.

[194] Harold E. Gorst, *China*, pp. 106–7, commented on the situation in China in the 1890s when many a scholar-official opposed the introduction of Western technology.

Chinese history, too, seems to support this conjecture. In Sung times some of the "Confucian" officials were known to have engaged in clandestine commercial enterprises.[195] Legal proscription and moral scruple did not deter some nineteenth-century gentry from trying their hands in mercantilist undertakings, the more successful of whom became "gentry-merchants,"[196] and who might be considered as harbingers of the "bureaucratic capitalists" of later years. The accomplishments of Chang Chien, a Confucian scholar-official who turned reformer and pioneer industrialist in the late nineteenth century, demonstrated that traditionalism and entrepreneurship were not of necessity incompatible. He was one of the Chinese people of the time who, feeling the need of change, were ready to give up the old methods of manufacture and make use of machinery.[197]

That the Chinese (tradition-bound or otherwise) were not devoid of entrepreneurial talent or the spirit of enterprise was evidenced by the economic successes of immigrants in Southeast Asian countries,[198] by the emergence of a modern business class in China proper, and by the rise of the comprador-entrepreneur in Shanghai.

The development of China's modern business class was occasioned by the First World War. Foreign firms had hitherto dominated the

[195] Ch'üan Han-sheng, "Sung-tai kuan-li chih ssu-ying shang-yeh," pp. 199–253.

[196] Chung-li Chang, *The Income of the Chinese Gentry*, chap. 6.

[197] *The North China Herald* (*Pei Hua chieh-pao*), Sept. 18, 1886, published a report of the British consul-general at Ningpo in which he made the observation that although there had been little industrial development, the establishment of a modern cotton gin made it clear that "the Chinese people," etc. Chu, *Reformer in Modern China: Chang Chien, 1853–1926*, and Chang Hsiao-jo, *Nan-t'ung Chang Chi-chih hsien-sheng chuan-chi*, are useful.

[198] One might recall that in much earlier times Chinese merchants had been carrying on trade with distant foreign lands. For a particularly notable instance, see Friedrich Hirth and W. W. Rockhill, *Chau Ju-kua: His Work on the Chinese and Arab Trade in the Twelfth and Thirteenth Centuries, Entitled* Chu-fan-chi. Kuwabara Jitsuzō, *Hojukō no jiseki*, pp. 84–96, gives a brief account of trade between China and such places as Arabia, Persia, and India. It is said that in the late ninth and the early tenth century Arabian merchants going to the east mostly used Chinese ships. By the middle of the fourteenth century, most ships that sailed between China and India belonged to the Chinese, the largest of these vessels carrying about a thousand passengers. The interdictions imposed by the Ming and Ch'ing governments put an end to this situation. Although many of the seafaring merchants were domiciled Arabs and other West Asians, and P'u Shou-keng (Ho Ju-kō) was a Sinicized Persian, their entrepreneurial spirit and skill could not have been lost on the native Chinese. After the decline of the Western Asian trade in the last quarter of the thirteenth century, the Chinese themselves developed the "Nan-yang" trade. See Wang Gungwu, "The Nanhai Trade: A Study of the Early History of Chinese Trade in the South China Sea," 31: 2.

commercial and industrial centers in the coastal provinces. The war
changed the situation. Native enterprisers, many of whom had received
a Western education or gained experience in modern factories or business houses, filled the vacancy left standing by their foreign predecessors.
Bringing modern industrial techniques and managerial methods to
bear, they achieved gratifying results in their endeavors.[199] The comprador, "never allowed to forget his inferior position in regard to his
Western employer," shrewdly learned from the latter modern business
or industrial know-how. He was likely to be talented enough to apply it
effectively to ventures of his own or to government-sponsored enterprises that he was invited to manage or supervise.[200]

Among the most notable comprador-entrepreneurs who figured
prominently in the second half of the past century were T'ang T'ing-
shu, Hsü Jun, and Cheng Kuan-ying.[201] T'ang T'ing-shu (Ching-hsing;
known to foreigners as Tong King-sing) was not wholly free of the
traditional outlook, but his ten-year experience as the Shanghai comprador of the British firm of Jardine, Matheson and Co. equipped him
with enough knowledge and skill to take a leading part in China's incipient shipping enterprise, in particular, the China Merchants Steam
Ship Navigation Company (as manager) and the China Coast Steam
Navigation Company (as director). His understanding of modern
methods was so thorough and his managerial ability so outstanding
that a Western businessman was led to remark that his thinking was
really that of a foreigner instead of a Chinese.[202] Hsü Jun (Yü-chai)

[199] Shih Kuo-heng, "The Early Development of the Modern Chinese Business
Class," in Marion J. Levy and Shih Kuo-heng, *The Rise of the Modern Chinese Business
Class*, pp. 54–55. Shih mentions, among successful businessmen and industrialists, Jen
Tsung-ching (Jung Tsung-ching), Moh Ou-ch'u (Mu Ou-ch'u), Fan Hsiu Tung (Fan
Hsü-tung), Lu Tso-fu, and Chang Kia-ngau. See also P'eng Chang, "The Profes-
sional Merchants in China, 1842–1911" chap. 4, sec. 2.

[200] Y. C. Wang, "Tu Yüeh-sheng (1888–1951): A Tentative Political Biography,"
Journal of Asian Studies, 26, no. 3 (May 1967): 434–35.

[201] Yen-p'ing Hao, "Cantonese Comprador-Merchants: A Study of Their Functions and Influences—1842–1884," deals with their immediate predecessors. The
story of their early counterparts, the *hang* merchants of Kwangtung who flourished
from about the 1760s to the 1840s, is told in some detail in Liang Chia-pin, *Kuang-tung
shih-san hang k'ao*.

[202] Liu Kwang-ching, "T'ang T'ing-shu chih mai-pan shih-tai," pp. 143–80;
English abstract, pp. 181–83. T'ang, a native of Hsiang-shan, Kwangtung, was born
in 1832. He received his early education at the Morrison Educational Society School.
After some noncommercial work in Hong Kong he joined the British firm and became its Shanghai comprador in 1863. He was appointed general manager of the
China Merchants Steam Ship Navigation Company in 1873 and was awarded a
brevet second rank and expectant circuit intendant for Fukien province. He died in

began as an apprentice in Dent and Co. in Shanghai when he was about fourteen years old. In less than ten years he rose to a responsible position in the firm. Convinced of the usefulness of government contacts he purchased an official title (*Kuang-lu-ssu ch'ing*, Superintendent of the Banquet Court) in 1862 and another (*Yüan-wai lang*, Second-class Secretary of a Board) in the year following. Meanwhile, he launched business ventures of his own. Soon he was called upon by the government to assist in the organization of the China Merchants Steam Ship Navigation Company and to serve as co-director of the K'ai-p'ing Coal Mines.[203] Cheng Kuan-ying, author of the *Warnings to a Seemingly Prosperous Age*, whose views have been mentioned in a previous connection, learned his trade also in Dent and Co. and was engaged, like some of the other compradors, in tea, silk and shipping enterprises. In 1877, when he was thirty-six, he was appointed manager of the Shanghai office of the Tientsin-Shanghai Telegraph Line and was soon authorized to extend service to other localities. In addition, he was given the task of establishing modern cotton-weaving and paper-making factories and a shipyard in Shanghai.[204]

Nor was China devoid of people with modern technological knowledge or skill. While lagging behind the West in science and technology in modern times, she had made some notable contributions in these fields in earlier periods.[205] The efforts made in the late nineteenth and early twentieth centuries were not without results. Hua Heng-fang and Hsü Shou, for instance, succeeded in constructing a steamship engine for Tseng Kuo-fan in 1862.[206] Chan T'ien-yu (educated in the United

---

1892. The remark referred to is given in *Yang-wu yün-tung*, Shanghai, 1961, 8: 401, a translation from H. H. Shore, *The Flight of the Lapwing: A Naval Officer's Jottings in China, Formosa, and Japan* (London, 1881).

[203] Hsü Jun, *Hsü Yü-chai tzu-hsü nien-p'u*, in *Yang-wu yün-tung*, 8: 88–227.

[204] From Cheng's own *curriculum vitae* included in a letter to an official, "Fu k'ao-ch'a shang-wu ta-ch'en Chang Pi-shih shih-lang," *Sheng-shih wei-yen hou-pien, chüan 8*; reprinted in *Yang-wu yün-tung*, 8: 83–84.

[205] Joseph Needham, *Science and Civilization in China*, especially vol. 4, sections on mechanical and civil engineering, textile technology, and chemical industry. He assesses China's attainments in these terms: "There was a Chinese contribution to man's understanding of nature, and his control over it, and it was a great one" (ibid., 1: 9).

[206] Tseng Kuo-fan, *Tseng wen-cheng-kung jih-chi*, entry of T'ung-chih 1st year, 7th month, 4th day (July 30, 1862). Arthur W. Hummel, *Eminent Chinese of the Ch'ing Period*, 1: 540, contains brief biographical notes on Hua (1833–1902), Hsü (1818–84), and Hsü's son, Hsü Chien-yin (1845–1901), who visited European factories in 1879–84 and at different times, directed the arsenals and Tientsin, Tsinan, Nanking, and Hanyang.

States) became the chief engineer of the Peking-Kalgan and other railroads; he also founded the Chinese Association of Engineers in 1911.[207] In fact, by the 1930s Chinese technicians were able to replace foreigners who in the past had normally supervised the operation of railroads in China; some of this native personnel became fully competent to direct large-scale civil engineering works.[208] A Western observer felt that Chinese workmen were ready as well as willing to learn the delicate and complicated machine operations, even in the days when industry had gained no more than a foothold in the country.[209]

With entrepreneurial and technological talents available, even only in a very modest measure, the situation was hardly hopeless. Why, then, did China fail to achieve a degree of economic growth sufficient to lead her to modern industrial-commercialism?

RELEVANCE OF THE POLITICAL FACTOR

Economic growth does not occur in a social vacuum. A number of conditions must be present before it takes place in a given society. A country is fortunate indeed if it has the ability to construct "a social framework which will provide incentive and opportunity for human enterprise in new forms," at a time when no such framework exists.[210] A sound government, it might be surmised, constitutes a basic element of the framework.[211]

Japan succeeded in economic modernization in a short period of time; she was blessed with a number of propitious factors, some of which existed already in Tokugawa days. Without minimizing the importance of other factors it can be safely suggested that the Meiji government, with its intelligent and vigorous leadership, was historically decisive. The new political order alone, in all probability, would not have been sufficient to transform an agrarian society into a modern nation, but it can be argued that without that order Japan could not have evolved

---

[207] Chan studied civil engineering at Yale University, 1878–81. Construction of the Peking-Kalgan line, a difficult piece of engineering work, was his crowning achievement. Kuan Lü-yin, "Chan T'ien-yu yü Chung-kuo t'ieh-lu," pp. 4–5, 35.

[208] Allen and Donnithorne, *Western Enterprise*, pp. 141–42.

[209] Gorst, *China*, pp. 108–9.

[210] Lockwood, *Economic Development of Japan*, p. 499.

[211] Galbraith, *Economic Development*, p. 42, referring to the new African states and parts of Latin America, points to the importance of administrative efficiency in economic development. "It is idle to imagine," he writes, "that good development plans can be created or carried on without a reasonably good government to do it. And neither technical assistance nor trained technicians do well, or are even much needed, where administration is indifferent or bad."

into a full-fledged industrial-commercial economy. It is true of course
that the Meiji leaders did no more than "pioneering industry" in the
post-Restoration years and that they were forced by economic necessity
to replace state entrepreneurship with private enterprise in the early
1880s.[212] Nevertheless, if there had not been such a leadership, it is
doubtful that Japan could have produced a brand of industrial revolution that was distinctively her own.

China demonstrated the relevance of effective government to successful economic transformation in a negative way. She was not without
certain elements that could have contributed to sustained, if slow, economic growth. She had no samurai, but the modernizers among the
scholar-official elite might have accomplished something more or less
comparable to the achievements of "the Meiji bureaucrats"—if, like
the latter, they had occupied positions of power and commanded the
services of a proficient administrative apparatus. She had no daimio to
lay the first industrial and commercial foundations of the country, but
those few provincial leaders who launched programs of modernization
did make a somewhat promising start. She did not develop *zaibatsu*,
but there were enterprising and talented people whose skill in applying
"Western methods" in manufacturing and business often impressed
European observers. However, because of crucial differences in the
political situations prevailing in the two countries, China was condemned to halting and interrupted industrial development, while Japan
attained speedily the status of a modern power.[213] A much larger country than the island neighbor, China of necessity would have required
much more time than the latter to make the transition from an agrarian
to an industrial-commercial economy. It would take more than a few
decades (the time which it took Japan to accomplish the Meiji "mira-
cle") for the constructive impact of "the thin line of European civilization on the coast"[214] to penetrate the vast hinterland and to induce

[212] Lockwood, *Economic Development of Japan*, pp. 506–8. Cf. Eijiro Honjo, *The Social
and Economic History of Japan*, chap. 12, sec. 1, "Financial Distress of the Meiji Government."

[213] Kenneth Berrill, "Historical Experience: The Problem of Economic Takeoff,"
in Berrill, *Economic Development with Special Reference to East Asia*, pp. 243–45: "Indians,
Greeks, Chinese, Levantines, all showed their power of entrepreneurship when
translated to other lands. They failed to achieve much result in their own country
because the other conditions were not ripe." Again, "it is easy to exaggerate the
importance of inventions triggering the 'take-off' of an economy. The mechanical
innovations of the English cotton industry were trivial compared with the skill and
ingenuity of the Chinese centuries earlier. . . ."

[214] Lord Charles William de la Poer Beresford's phrase. See his book, *The Break-up
of China*, p. 443.

empire-wide economic change. Nevertheless, it remains doubtful that, without decisive improvement in the political situation, there could be successful economic transformation.[215]

One can hardly overstress the fact that when China was forced by Westerners to modernize, she was in the process of "rapidly advancing disintegration" leading to eventual "internal collapse of authority."[216] It was China's misfortune that the European industrial revolution and the expansionist phase that accompanied it coincided with an era of her political decadence, when the emperors fell far below their predecessors in administrative ability.[217] The enfeebled regime with its largely demoralized bureaucracy was in no position to furnish leadership in economic or other reforms. It was, in fact, incapable of providing even elementary conditions of order and stability.

Students of economic development generally attach importance to government leadership. Late comers to industrialization, they point out, cannot afford the luxury of leisurely evolution available to "pioneer countries" favored with special circumstances. It is better therefore for the late comers to rely on government planning and direction—on "government-sponsored imposition"—to effect speedy and orderly development.[218] Well-conceived plans of industrialization and other types of economic endeavor, irrespective of the government's ideological commitments, can be a way of giving impetus to growth.[219] Public planning does not have to encompass every aspect of the economy, leaving no room for private initiative. The government, however, should define the goals of national effort, mobilize and allocate main sources of capital and manpower, inaugurate enterprises in the public sector of the economy, and guide or assist private entrepreneurship.[220]

[215] Chu, *Reformer in Modern China: Chang Chien*, p. 179, commenting on K'ang Yu-wei and Sun Yat-sen: "It was their contention that without fundamental political change there was no hope of effecting basic social or economic changes in China."

[216] Beresford, *Break-up of China*, p. 448. He suggested that England help China to bring about military, currency, and fiscal reforms and to construct railroads, waterways, and telegraph lines (ibid., pp. 449–50).

[217] Allen and Donnithorne, *Western Enterprise*, p. 13.

[218] Alan B. Mountjoy, *Industrialization and Underdeveloped Countries*, p. 81. Government planning is relevant also to countries other than those in which "the economic well-being of their population was secondary to increasing the power of the state" (ibid., p. 97).

[219] Alexander, *A Primer of Economic Development*, p. 68. The author cites the Germany of the kaisers and Meiji Japan as instances in which the government played a dominant role as the innovating force (ibid., pp. 142–45). Cf. Galbraith, *Economic Development*, pp. 64–68.

[220] Gerhard Colm and Theodore Geiger, "Public Planning and Private Decision-

The government should at least provide certain political conditions that are conducive to economic growth. It must maintain law and order, laying down institutional rules according to which private economic decisions can be made and carried out, and giving protection to economic assets against expropriation or encroachment. Without law and order there can be no untroubled development of industry and commerce.[221] The government would do well also to invest actively in the field of essential public works and services, in "the overhead capital structure," ranging from roads, railroads, waterways, and telegraph and telephone lines to power plants and even schools and hospitals. The absence of these facilities would tend to hamper expansion; "the yield of any injection of private capital may turn out disappointingly small."[222] Unwise or excessive government intervention can of course be economically obstructive,[223] but a delinquent government that fails to act where action is needed can be equally detrimental. Rare indeed is the case in which appropriate government leadership is not helpful.[224]

A student of Chinese economic history calls attention to the need of nationwide direction in economic development. Without denying the value of the modernizing efforts made by provincial officials, he argues that the type of "regional power" such as held by Li Hung-chang "could not take the place of a vigorous national directing authority comparable, for example, to the Meiji oligarchy which governed

making in Economic and Social Development," in Richard J. Ward, *The Challenge of Development: Theory and Practice*, pp. 5–7.

[221] Bert F. Hoselitz, "The Entrepreneurial Element in Economic Development," in Ward, *Challenge of Development*, p. 126. Cf. Edward P. Holland, "Principles of Simulation," in Ward, *Challenge of Development*, pp. 19–20, where the writer enumerates a number of other objectives to which government policies can contribute.

[222] Ragnar Nurkse, *Problems of Capital Formation in Underdeveloped Countries and Patterns of Trade and Development*, p. 152.

[223] Cranley Onslow, *Asian Economic Development*, p. 225, draws this conclusion from surveys of six Asian countries, Burma, Ceylon, India, Malaya, Pakistan, and Thailand, made by various authors. Malaya is "an honorable exception," as is Thailand.

[224] Berrill, "Historical Experience: The Problem of Economic Takeoff," p. 238, concludes from surveys of England (1780), the United States (1840), Germany (1870), Japan (1880), Russia (1890), and Australia (1900): "History teaches us that in every case of 'take-off' the Government has played a major role." He further comments (pp. 238–39) that it is not the intentions of the governments that mattered but rather their sense of urgency, their "continued thrust" and their "efficiency." "As far as intentions went, there was not all that to choose between . . . the Japanese Government and the Chinese Government of the 100 days." The author, it might be suggested, probably overestimated "the intentions" of the Ch'ing government; at any rate, it was easy to choose between the Meiji leaders and the empress dowager with the conservative high officials around her.

Japan." Had the outcome of the 1898 reform been happier, the economic situation could have changed for the better.[225] Another writer who shares this view remarks that "in most cases of economic change centralized national government played an important role."[226] (K'ang Yu-wei, by the way, would have heartily supported this view. He was so convinced of the importance of centralized direction that he recommended the abolition of the provincial system.[227])

Favorable political conditions, in short, are indispensable to economic development. A central administration sufficiently sound to insure political unity and social stability, a bureaucracy basically honest and scrupulous to win the confidence of industrialists and businessmen, and a political elite adequately intelligent and knowledgeable to afford constructive leadership—these together should constitute a wholesome environment for economic expansion. These, unfortunately, were not present in late nineteenth-century China. The decaying imperial regime was in no shape to pursue a meaningful economic policy or to carry out any realistic project to successful conclusion,[228] if indeed it could see the wisdom of having such a policy or launching such a project at all. In those instances in which industrial undertakings had been started by provincial officials or private entrepreneurs, the government was unable to exercise intelligent direction or supervision; on the contrary, it allowed them to suffer from faulty planning, mismanagement, economic waste, official encroachment, or unfair foreign competition.[229]

[225] Feuerwerker, *China's Early Industrialization*, pp. 246, et passim.

[226] Galbraith, *Economic Development in Perspective*, p. 13. In his view, economic growth has usually begun only in nations with a history of political unity, as economic development in its earliest stages requires the building of public administration and the provision of an educated minority. In many of the currently developing countries the state does not exhibit the same unity as in Meiji Japan. This lack of unity complicates the problem of economic growth.

[227] See, in particular, K'ang's essay 'Ts'ai hsing-sheng i," *K'ang Nan-hai hsien-sheng wen-ch'ao*, 4: 28b–46b.

[228] Allen and Donnithorne, *Western Enterprise*, pp. 165–66. The silk-weaving industry of China afforded a concrete instance. Shih Min-hsiung, *Ch'ing-tai ssu-chih kung-yeh ti fa-chan*, pp. 132–33, shows that "because of the lack of political support, the [once commanding] position of the silk-weaving industry was seized by the Japanese."

[229] Gorst, *China*, pp. 264–65, quoting the United States consul at Hankow, concerning the Hanyang iron and steel mills: "If ever finished, it will be one of the most complete rolling mills in the world, as expense seems to have been a secondary consideration in the erection of this immense establishment." Gorst commented: "The practical results of Chang Chih-tung's enormous and wasteful expenditure appear to be thoroughly unsatisfactory. Lord Beresford, during his tour of inspection in the Yangtze valley, visited the iron works in November, 1898, and found them in a de-

The Ch'ing government did not even provide the minimal conditions under which entrepreneurial efforts could succeed. Uprisings, large- and small-scale, had beset various parts of the empire in the previous century. Humiliating wars with foreign powers from 1840 on seriously drained its strength in addition to damaging its prestige. The Taiping rebellion threatened the very existence of the dynasty.

The 1911 revolution delivered the *coup de grâce* to the moribund regime, but the new republican government did no better (possibly worse) than its predecessor in providing a congenial environment for economic development. Decades of civil wars precluded even a semblance of political order or social stability. For years the central government, while not indifferent to the economic problems that confronted the nation, was quite incapable of affording leadership even in areas where national security was involved.[230] Less fortunate than Meiji Japan, republican China inherited no legacy of competent administration. A defaulting government had the effect of discouraging long-term investment and of persuading people to apply whatever capital they had to traditional ways of "making money." To avoid "exposing one's wealth to society" and thus inviting possible trouble,[231] even the most venturesome would think twice before risking financial resources in

---

plorable state of inefficiency owing to the chaotic administration of the native officials." Similarly, Beresford (*Break-up of China*, p. 303): "My visits to the arsenals showed me that enormous sums of money are being expanded on war material that in most cases is absolutely useless." Allen and Donnithorne, *Western Enterprise*, p. 68, point out the problems that beset the silk industry: (1) no central authority capable of or interested in establishing a licensing system for egg production; (2) no security in the interior; and (3) no central supervision and government intervention at key points to assist the industry. "China lacked a government competent to exercise the supervision and it was largely because of this that she lost so much of the silk trade [to Japan]." Inefficient administration and incompetent officials also hampered undertakings operating according to the *kuan-tu shang-pan* formula. James Morrell, "Two Early Chinese Cotton Mills," pp. 43–98, identifies the basic weaknesses of the system, one of which was inept official direction. Armament enterprises established and supported by provincial officials had some beneficial effects, especially in helping to introduce modern technological and managerial practices into China and in furnishing personnel to some of the newly started nonmilitary industrial undertakings. But the impact was small. See Wang Erh-min, "Ch'ing-chi ping-kung-yeh lüeh-lun," pp. 15–19.

230 Allen and Donnithorne, *Western Enterprise*, pp. 179, 243; also pp. 149–64 and 247–48.

231 Shih Kuo-heng, "Early Development of Modern Chinese Business Class" in Levy and Shih, *Rise of Modern Chinese Business Class*, pp. 38–39: "Under an uncertain situation, they [merchants] felt that there was no economic security. The better way for self-protection was not to expose one's wealth to society."

industrial projects that were intrinsically profitable and significant.[232] "The spirit of enterprise" would be very slow to emerge in the circumstances. Almost inevitably, the field was left to foreign interests, especially in the treaty ports.[233]

Officials and the government itself (at least in Ch'ing times) too often stood as stumbling blocks to business or industrial enterprise. Entrepreneurs faced exactions by central or local authorities.[234] One particularly damaging practice was to permit nepotism or favoritism to interfere with the management of business firms. Unqualified personnel not only impeded operations but tended to lower the morale of rank and file, who were thus led to feel that it was more advantageous to curry favor of influential people than to do honest work.[235] Keeping inept personnel on the payroll was, at any rate, not a sound business practice.[236] Even the mere presence of official influence could exert a restraining effect on entrepreneurship. Chang Chien, China's noted industrialist, once complained that "with officials standing in your way and with merchants as by-standers, any hopeful task might be defeated at any time."[237] "Enterprising" merchants might find a measure of security by ingratiating themselves with officials, thereby becoming in

[232] Feuerwerker, *China's Early Industrialization*, p. 187, points out that because of unstable political, social, and economic conditions, the China Merchants Steam Ship Navigation Company diverted its earnings to large, short-term profits for its managers and used its reserves for the purchase of real estate, instead of investing them for further expansion of the enterprise itself.

[233] Allen and Donnithorne, *Western Enterprise*, p. 19: "The contrast between the security that could be found under foreign jurisdiction and the insecurity that prevailed elsewhere produced a chain of consequences that left the foreigners in an ever stronger political position vis-à-vis the Chinese government."

[234] Ibid., p. 15.

[235] Shih, "Early Development of Modern Chinese Business Class," pp. 45–47. Government-controlled enterprises often suffered from the hands of official inspectors who might write adverse reports, if they were not properly "entertained" or bribed outright (ibid., p. 48).

[236] Gorst, *China*, pp. 104–5, quoting from a report of the Blackburn mission concerning situations in cotton mills in various parts of the Yangtze region: ". . . onc is surprised to see in every department numbers of richly-dressed, indolent gentlemen, lolling about, or deeply engrossed in the study of Chinese classics. Inquiry from the English manager elicits the information that these are the friends of the controlling officials, and that, although they know absolutely nothing of the work, . . . they are all on the pay list, as superintendents, overseers, and as upper hands, with similar euphonious titles." The report went on to say that in native-owned mills which were under the supervision of a European, no harm was done by "these parasites" other than entailing useless expenditure; but in cases where everything was left to Chinese management, the machinery was neglected, the operatives were not properly treated, and the accounts were badly kept.

[237] Quoted by Shih, in "Early Development . . . Business Class," p. 38.

effect the latter's protégés.[238] But such maneuvers contributed little to the spirit of enterprise as such. There was the additional drawback that those who practiced the political art in business tended to pick up "the officials' way of life." As a result,

> Instead of setting up their own behavior pattern, Chinese businessmen tried to imitate official behavior and introduce bureaucratic tactics and traditions into their business area. Gradually, all the bad habits and practices, such as inefficiency, red tape, and smuggling, which originated in the political circles, were found in business.[239]

There were many exceptions. But the fact remains that China's "political merchants," unlike their Japanese counterparts, the *seisha*, of Meiji times, did not develop into the *zaibatsu* that did much for the island empire's economic growth.[240] Moreover, one should not overlook the fact that those merchants who did not consort with officials and had no confidence in them often remained unwilling (or unable) to risk investment in any sizable venture.[241]

That political factors were relevant to economic development was further illustrated by the fact that in some areas of China and during certain periods, where and when the government was able to provide a degree of leadership and a measure of stability, the economy tended to move forward. It has been noted that in the early 1930s when the administration was "more stable than that of any Chinese government for decades," the economic prospects became decidedly encouraging. There emerged something like a confidence in the future of the country —a confidence "based on the remarkable growth of stability achieved in recent years and the improved political, financial, and economic conduct of affairs, government and private." This hopeful situation did not last long. With the outbreak of the Sino-Japanese War in 1937, the bright promise of economic growth disappeared with "the newfound stability of the State."[242]

[238] This was an old game in imperial China. For a late Ming observation, see Chu Ch'ien-chih, *Li Chih: Shih-liu shih-chi Chung-kuo fan-feng-chien ssu-hsiang ti hsien-ch'ü-che*, p. 21, quoting Li Chih to the effect that merchants who risked their lives and capital, must try to be on friendly terms with high officials in order to reap profits and ward off disaster.

[239] Shih, "Early Development . . . Business Class," pp. 48–50, identifies three types of harmful political influence on private enterprise.

[240] See note 142, above.

[241] *Chinese Maritime Customs Decennial Report, 1892–1901* (Chungking): 135 (quoted in Sun Yü-t'ang, *Chung-kuo chin-tai kung-i-shih tzu-liao*, 1: 982), cited a revealing instance of an unsuccessful attempt to start a cotton mill with initial capitalization at 400,000 taels.

[242] Allen and Donnithorne, *Western Enterprise*, pp. 28–29.

The Nanking government did more than achieve stability. Actually, it "played an active and positive role in the economy and brought about institutional changes which had far-reaching effects on China's industrialization and modernization." During the brief period of 1930 to 1936, a number of major economic measures were adopted, including the restoration of tariff autonomy (1930), abolition of the likin (1931), currency reform (1935), and decision to draft a four-year industrial expansion plan (1931). The plan was never implemented, but it gave evidence of the government's intention to involve itself in industrialization. The rate of growth was accelerated in these few years, even though the country remained still far behind Japan in development.[243]

The relevancy of the political factor was also illustrated by the situations in Hong Kong,[244] Manchuria,[245] and Taiwan in recent years.[246]

[243] Chang, "Industrial Development of Mainland China," pp. 73–81. According to Chang's calculation, the rate of growth was from 4.7 in 1925–30 to 9.3 in 1931–36 (pp. 73–74). He attributes "a large percent of the remarkable increase in output that has been achieved in China since the Communists took over" to "the substitution for chaos of something resembling public order" and concludes that "China's economic progress could have been achieved by any government capable of maintaining internal peace." One does not of course have to subscribe to this somewhat simplistic view in order to emphasize the importance of the political factor.

[244] In an interview with reporters, Sir David Trench, governor of the colony, printed in the *U. S. News and World Report,* May 29, 1967, explains Hong Kong's prosperity by referring to "the character of the Hong Kong Chinese people—in their industrious way of life, and in their ability, given a reasonably free economic climate, to win through against all odds" and to "the stability of Hong Kong—both political and economic." "Stability," he adds, "naturally makes for a favorable investment climate."

[245] Allen and Donnithorne, *Western Enterprise,* p. 181: "These achievements [in industrial growth in Manchuria] were possible largely because Manchuria had passed under the control of a Government capable of maintaining order and intent upon fostering industrial growth." Without justifying "imperialist aggression," the authors observe that "the experience of Manchuria . . . demonstrates how largely the slow rate of progress in China's economy as a whole, and especially her extreme backwardness in modern manufacturing enterprises, were attributable to the absence of ordered government and of competent economic administration at the center."

[246] Melvin Gurtov, "Recent Developments on Taiwan," pp. 59–95, describes the situation, pointing out that the four-year plans have been so successfully carried out that "The growth rate in 1966 [second year of the fourth Four-year Plan] was 8.1 per cent, surpassing the 7 per cent goal," and that the rate is the second highest in Asia, below Japan's (p. 74). Charles Hsi-chung Kao, "An Analysis of Agricultural Output Increase on Taiwan, 1953–1964," pp. 611–26, has this to say: "A favorable government agricultural policy can accelerate the rate of agricultural development. . . . In addition, there have been three Four-year Development Plans since 1953. The overriding goal of these plans has been to insure a simultaneous growth of both agriculture

One should not of course overrate the importance of the political factor. Given an efficient government, there might not necessarily be economic growth, as other contributing factors might be lacking. But it is reasonable to suppose that without political stability and appropriate government guidance, even though other favorable conditions were present, there could be no sustained, untroubled economic expansion.[247] K'ang was perhaps aware of this when he pleaded for renovation of China's political and administrative structure, especially in the 1890s and 1900s.[248] He believed that fruitful industrialization depended on sound "financial management," which in turn presupposed efficient administration. He went even so far as to declare that unless a viable political order could be established, all that he wrote concerning reform would be devoid of practical significance.[249] Such an order never did emerge. His vision of an industrial China remained a mirage in the quagmire of dynastic decay and social disruption.

AN ALTERNATE APPROACH

K'ang's plan for economic modernization derived its inspiration partly from nineteenth-century Europe and America and partly from Meiji Japan. It presupposed a regenerated imperial government that would, like the Meiji government, set the process of economic growth in motion and eventually bring into being an industrial-commercial economy resting on the foundation of private enterprise. By itself the plan did look reasonable and attractive, but the circumstances that created modern Japan did not prevail in late-Ch'ing China. The Kuang-hsü emperor, for one thing, was no Meiji; whatever may have been his personal abilities, he occupied a far less enviable position than his Japanese counterpart. He died not long after 1898 and the dynasty itself fell soon after.

Sun Yat-sen, "father of the republic," took an alternate approach to the problem of economic modernization. The central difference between Sun and K'ang can be simply stated: whereas the latter banked his hope on private enterprise, the former leaned toward socialization.

---

and industry." Again: "The agricultural output increased at an average annual rate of 4.6 per cent during the period 1953–64. Such a record is highly impressive in comparison with both developed and developing nations" (p. 626).

[247] One might recall a passage in the *Mo-tzu* as quoted in Fung Yu-lan, *A History of Chinese Philosophy*, p. 258: "A minor cause is one with which something may not necessarily be so, but without which it will never be so."

[248] In particular, his *Kuan-chih i* of 1903 and *Wu-chih chiu-kuo lun* of 1905.

[249] *Wu-chih chiu-kuo lun*, p. 89.

Sun's early views regarding economic development were outlined in his 1894 letter to Li Hung-chang.[250] His position then was hardly a radical departure from that of the reformers. "The roots of Europe's wealth and power," he wrote, did not lie wholly in "solid ships, efficient guns, strong forts, and crack troops," but also in the full development and employment of human talents as well as natural resources. A situation must be created, in China, therefore, in which "men are able to make full use of their talents, the land is able to yield the fullest measure of its productivity, resources are completely utilized, and commodities enjoy unimpeded circulation." He called, in particular, for the establishment of a department of agriculture to render service to farmers, the introduction of modern farm machinery, and the institution of schools of agriculture to develop scientific knowledge and techniques. Science and technology, he said, formed the foundation of industry; full utilization of natural resources presupposed industrialization; commercial growth would lead to unimpeded flow of goods and commodities. The government must play a dual role: giving assistance and protection to private enterprises and developing shipping and railroad transportation.[251]

Soon afterward Sun's outlook changed. Seeing that the existing regime was unwilling and unable to reform, he committed himself to revolution and brought the republic into being. Circumstances persuaded him to resign from the provisional presidency (April 1, 1912) of the newly founded republic. At Yüan Shih-k'ai's invitation he went to Peking (August 24) to discuss with the new president problems of railroad construction and industrial development and in the ensuing months he set forth his view on these matters in a number of speeches and articles. At this point he had not ruled out the possibility or desirability of assigning a place to private enterprise in industrialization, although he had already begun to make clear the socialistic implications of his plans. Thus, in an article published in the *China Press* (October 10) he stated that to carry out his project of a nationwide

---

[250] Available in *Kuo-fu ch'üan-chi*, 5: 1–12. Excerpts of this lengthy document are translated in Teng and Fairbank, *China's Response to the West*, pp. 224–25.

[251] Letter to Li Hung-chang, *Kuo-fu ch'üan-chi*, 5: 1–9. Sun went on to say that in view of China's population pressure, agricultural development was even more important than other modernizing tasks and that, accordingly, he had made promising experiments in Hawaii and asked Li to help him carry out a world-wide tour to investigate agricultural science and technology (ibid., pp. 11–12; hereafter, all references to Sun's work included in *Kuo-fu ch'üan-chi* will be by volume and page number only).

network of railroads, it was necessary to make use of foreign capital, namely, to invite individual persons or private firms to invest in the enterprises that, having nothing to do with government, would be of a "purely commercial nature" (*ch'un shang-yeh hsing*).[252] He made this point, however, later in the same article:

> Industrialization is what China needs. Civilization and progress necessarily depend on it, which cannot be forestalled by any human effort. . . . [But] in the natural evolution of modern capitalism workers have been given unfair treatment. We should strenuously avoid it. Pondering deeply I have found a solution to this problem. What is the solution? It is simply the principle of people's livelihood.[253]

"The principle of people's livelihood" was the label he chose for his own brand of socialism. He did not envisage "the redistribution of all property," which, according to him, was "extremely absurd." He was interested rather in an economic system in which benefits were so distributed that "those who work would receive all the fruits of their labor." Thus, railroads, public utilities, canals, and forests should be nationalized and all income from land and mines should be the state's revenue to meet administrative costs and finance social welfare programs.[254]

The same thought appeared in other connections. Earlier in 1912, Sun acknowledged that as industry had made foreign powers prosperous and strong, industrialization should be China's urgent concern. However, "failure to understand the socialist teaching [on the part of these powers] has resulted in economic inequity, thus making it difficult for them to achieve further industrial development. This is regrettable." It behooved the industrialists of China, therefore, to learn this lesson and "to study socialism."[255] When a newspaper editor criticized him for advocating nationalization of railroads, he retorted that the objection was based on the economic theory of "capitalist monopoly," whereas he subscribed to the principle of people's livelihood.[256] He pursued much the same line of thinking in subsequent years.[257]

[252] This article was first written in English; its Chinese version, which is here used, bears the title "Chung-kuo chih t'ieh-lu chi-hua yü min-sheng chu-i" (6: 8).

[253] Ibid., pp. 10–11.

[254] Ibid., pp. 11–12.

[255] "Hsing-fa shih-yeh wei chiu p'in chih yao-chi," a speech at the Industrial Association of Shanghai, April 17, 1912, (3: 29–30). Cf. another piece written just after he resigned from the Provisional Presidency (April 1), "Chung-kuo chih ti-erh pu" (6: 256–58).

[256] "Hsiu-chu t'ieh-lu nai Chung-hua min-kuo ts'un-wang chih ta wen-t'i" (2: 77).

[257] See, e.g., *San Min Chu I*, 1919, in which he condemned the West's capitalist

"The principle of people's livelihood," then, separated Sun from K'ang and other reformers. Nevertheless, Sun's plans for economic modernization contained items that were similar to or even identical with those found in K'ang's programs. The economic portion of the Kuomintang platform that he drew up in 1913 suffices to illustrate. He demanded that efforts be directed toward the modernization of agricultural, industrial, commercial, and financial sectors of the economy; more specifically he wanted the government to include in its program land reclamation, institution of national forestry, flood control, promotion of mining and manufacturing industries, encouragement of export trade, and development of transportation and communication systems; he urged, in addition, an overhaul of the fiscal system, to be effected, among other measures, by the establishment of a central bank with the exclusive authority to issue paper currency and by the adoption of a gold exchange standard.[258]

Sun did not explicitly rule out private enterprise, but he gave the impression that he was wholeheartedly in favor of socialism or, in his terminology, "state capitalism" (*kuo-chia ch'an-yeh chu-i*).[259] It appears that while he often talked the language of the Communists, he had in mind not totalitarian communism but a mixed system, "combining in uncertain proportions elements of controlled democracy and state socialism," a position hardly acceptable to "a Western devotee of political and economic liberalism"[260]—or to K'ang Yu-wei who had greater confidence in private enterprise than he.

---

economy because it entailed economic inequality and exploitation, and "Chung-kuo shih-yeh tang ju-ho fa-chan," 1920, in which he warned against monopoly and "capitalist tyranny" (*tzu-pen chih chuan-chih* (6: 272–83, 301). Cf. "Chung-kuo kuo-min-tang hsüan-yen," Jan. 1, 1923, in 4: 92–95, in which socialistic ideas were incorporated into the Party's platform, especially where it was said that all large-scale industrial and commercial enterprises should be undertaken by the state.

[258] "Kuo-min-tang cheng-chien hsüan-yen," 1913 (4: 77–80). Cf. "Ch'ien-pi ko-ming," a circular telegram of 1912 (6: 1–5); "Cheng-chien chih piao-shih," a speech at a Shanghai press conference, Oct. 1912, in 3: 93; and "Chien-she i hsiu-chih tao-lu wei ti-i yao-cho," Aug. 16, 1916 (3: 48) contain more of his views on fiscal and monetary reform.

[259] E.g., he wrote on Jan. 20, 1923: "In Europe and America the phenomenon of economic inequality appeared with the invention of machines. . . . Consequently, after comparing the views of various schools and ascertaining their relative merits and demerits, I have come to feel that state capitalism (*kuo-chia ch'an-yeh chu-i*) is the safest and most practical" ("Chung-hua ko-ming shih," 6: 150).

[260] Shao Chuan Leng and Norman D. Palmer, *Sun Yat-sen and Communism*, pp. 179–80. For an example of Sun's talking the language of the Communists, see his "Chi Lieh-ning wen" (6: 316–17).

Sun made his position particularly clear in his "Plan of Industrialization" (Shih-yeh chi-hua), written at the end of the First World War.[261] "China's industrial development," he said, "should proceed in two ways: first, private enterprise (*ko-jen chi-yeh*) and, secondly, state enterprise (*kuo-chia ching-ying*). He then went on to define the scopes of these two sectors. State enterprise should include undertakings that, being monopolistic in nature, could not be entrusted to private entrepreneurs. All others belonged in the private sector. The government, however, was not to stand aloof. It must encourage and protect private enterprises, abolish all taxes that were economically depressive, rectify the chaotic monetary situation, and remove all other obstacles to growth. To further the development of private enterpreneurship, the government should place at its service an efficient system of transportation and communication.[262] But he placed an unmistakable emphasis on state enterprise and, in the closing section of this lengthy work, he again sounded warnings of the dangers that inhered in free enterprise. Economic expansion, he feared, would inevitably give rise to huge corporations that would in turn result in economic inequity—a development contrary to the principle of people's livelihood. Eventually, therefore, all large corporations resulting from economic expansion should be nationalized; only small business, presumably, would remain in the private sector. The ultimate aim of his industrialization plan, he pointed out, was "to make use of the capitalism of foreign countries (*wai-kuo chih tzu-pen chu-i*) to construct China's socialism (*Chung-kuo chih she-hui chu-i*)."[263] It turns out, then, that in Sun's thinking, private enterprise and state enterprise, which were to begin as two parallel ways of economic development, should end as two successive phases of the process, with "socialism" as the crowning achievement.

It is unnecessary to go into the details of Sun's extensive plans, which included the construction of a nationwide system of railroads, highways, canals, telegraph, telephone, and wireless services; the establishment of steel and cement works; and the development of metallic and non-metallic mines—in short, practically every aspect of heavy industry found in advanced Western countries. Light industry also received his attention. He observed that industries that produced consumer goods

[261] "Shih-yeh chi-hua," a lengthy document comprising an introduction, six individual plans covering major aspects of industrialization, a conclusion, and six appendices, is available (2: 101–278). Originally in English, it was translated into Chinese by four of his followers.

[262] Ibid., p. 106.

[263] Ibid., pp. 263–65.

and services constituted "industry proper" (*kung-yeh pen-pu*), as they furnished "what a family needs and what gives comfort to life."[264] (Here, it might be noted, he agreed essentially with K'ang regarding the ultimate aim of industrialization, namely, to improve the economic lot of the people and not to aggrandize the state's "wealth and power.")

To finance his ambitious programs Sun would rely heavily on foreign loans.[265] He estimated on one occasion that if China could raise ten million yuan each year, it would take her sixty years to complete the projected two hundred thousand li of railroads. It would be wise, therefore, "to open the door" to foreign capital, "to absorb" foreign investments in railroad (and mining) projects.[266] "Thanks to foreign capital and foreign techniques," he remarked, "Japan became a powerful country in a few decades."[267] The situation prevailing after the First World War convinced him that it was both feasible and desirable to invite international cooperation to develop China's industry.[268]

Positive action of the government, Sun believed, was necessary to set in motion the process of industrialization. At any rate, the government must initiate such basic industries as mining and machine making.[269] It must continue to play a prominent part in the nation's economy even after China had achieved modernization, in particular, as owner and operator of those industries that were nationalized.[270] Obviously, in order to carry on its function as "state entrepreneur" the

[264] Ibid., p. 242. "Industry proper" included (1) food industries, (2) clothing industries, (3) housing industries, (4) travel industries (automobile making, highway building, fuel-oil production), and (5) printing industries, etc. Sun devoted 141 pages to heavy industry and only 14 pages to light industry because he considered the former "key and basic" and believed that the latter would readily and quickly emerge as the former attained full development (ibid., p. 241).

[265] Ibid., pp. 261–65. He did not rule out the possibility of raising funds through domestic loans, especially at the provincial level (p. 182). He took this position ten years before (1912) when he accepted Yüan Shih-k'ai's invitation to formulate a nationwide railroad plan. See, e.g., "Su hsiu t'ieh-lu i li fu-ch'iang chih chi," a speech made on Sept. 2, 1912 (3: 65).

[266] "Cheng-chien chih piao-shih" (3: 89–91). He expressed substantially the same view in "Shih-hsien t'ieh-lu cheng-ts'e hsü ch'ü k'ai-fang men-hu chu-i," a speech made in Nanking, Oct. 22, 1912 (3: 99–100).

[267] "Tsai-fu Li Ts'un-nung lun wai-chai shu," 1917 (5: 275–76). Sun added that "foreign loans need not mean money, exclusively. . . . The capital which China lacks today is not gold or silver but production machinery."

[268] "Kuo-chi kung-t'ung fa-chan Chung-kuo shih-yeh chi-hua," 1920 (6: 293–98). This plan, which received high praise from Paul S. Reinsch, then United States minister to China, forms the introduction to the "Shih-yeh chi-hua" (2: 101–5).

[269] Ibid., p. 255.

[270] Ibid., p. 102; "When machine-manufacturing industry replaces handicraft," it should be "centralized and nationalized."

government must command technical and managerial skill, in addition to possessing a high degree of general administrative efficiency.

Somewhat curiously, Sun argued, on one occasion at least, that China could not solve her political problems before she had successfully coped with the unsatisfactory economic situation. Thus he wrote in August 1912:

> The general situation in which the Republic finds itself being such, any person holding the reins of government cannot now implement any constructive measures. . . . Political remedies will unavoidably cause more confusion and further deterioration [of the situation]. We should begin with what is fundamental: development of our material resources. When the people's livelihood has become affluent and the state has thereby attained stability, then and only then will there be political viability.[271]

One wonders how, in the absence of a sound political order, the process of industrialization could be started.

This is not saying that Sun's plans were not well conceived. For instance, his emphasis on the development of harbors, waterways, railroads, lines of communication— all important components of the infrastructure of a modern economy—was in line with modern economic thought.[272] Lenin's theory of colonialism and leftist opposition to foreign firms notwithstanding, there is a place for foreign loans, investments, and technical aid in the economic planning of underdeveloped countries, as many writers agree.[273] But, however sound the plans, they could not be carried out in the absence of political stability. The unsettled condition of republican China well-nigh precluded the formation of the necessary infrastructure; it hardly gave encouragement

[271] "Lun ch'ou-chu t'ieh-lu shih chih Sung Chiao-jen han" (5: 155). Perhaps Sun implied justification of his acceptance of Yüan Shih-k'ai's invitation to discuss railroad planning.

[272] See e.g., Richard J. Ward, *The Challenge of Development*, part 5, "The Challenge in Developing Infrastructure."

[273] See e.g., McCord, *Springtime of Freedom*, pp. 148–68. Cf. Galbraith, *Economic Development*, pp. 28–29, and Alexander, *A Primer of Economic Development*, pp. 105–11, 119–36. Allen and Donnithorne, *Western Enterprise*, pp. 134–42, discuss the role of foreign investment in Chinese railroads under less than satisfactory conditions prevailing from the 1860s to the 1930s. Ivory Coast, a small country in West Africa, illustrates the possibility of economic growth with the help of foreign investment. Felix Houphouët-Boigny, elected president eight years after the country won independence from France (Aug. 1960), leads it in a massive development drive. While other African leaders preach a hazy socialism, he accomplished his country's transformation by openly luring overseas capital and know-how. See e.g., a report in *Time*, March 8, 1968.

to foreign investment or international cooperation. When the political situation improved during the late 1920s and early 1930s, the economy began to move forward. But the protracted Sino-Japanese War intervened. China had to fight for survival as a nation and to forget for the time about economic development. The postwar years were spent largely in rehabilitation and in contesting, unsuccessfully, with the Communists for the control of an impoverished and weakened country.

It appears then that Sun's alternate approach to China's problem of economic modernization (which had more than one point of contact with K'ang's) did not produce much greater results than the latter's. This was due not so much to any inherent shortcomings of their approaches as to the unfavorable political climate. K'ang had hoped to bring about modernization by innovating the decaying imperial government; Sun realized that modernization could come only with the establishment of a new political order. Failure of the 1898 reform and of the constitutional monarchy movement rendered revolution inevitable. Republican China, did not provide a milieu conducive to sustained industrial and commercial growth. It merely confirmed, negatively, the relevancy of the political factor to economic development.

PROSPECT OF THE AUTHORITARIAN APPROACH

Neither Sun nor K'ang favored the authoritarian or totalitarian approach to economic modernization, an approach often preferred by leaders of developing nations of today, especially by those who commit themselves to Marxism. The question arises: Would the authoritarian approach have been more fruitful than the approaches chosen by Sun and K'ang?

Leaders of the developing nations are, understandably, anticolonial; they are often suspicious of the ways of the former colonial powers, such as England and France, which happen to be democracies. Being consciously or unintentionally nationalists and in a hurry to achieve industrialization, these leaders are not inclined to follow the model of England or the United States, each of which accomplished economic development basically through private enterprise. Disillusioned with and unprepared for Western parliamentary government and influenced by the Marxist analysis of capitalism, they tend to share the Communists' faith in the efficacy of authoritarianism as a means of modernization.[274]

---

[274] Sukarno's words might serve as an example: "I have said over and over again

A few students of economic development have recently undertaken to explain, if not to justify, the trend toward regimentation. One, for instance, gives an historical reason for this. The conditions of the nineteenth century that facilitated industrial growth through "free enterprise" prevail no longer in the twentieth century, certainly not in the developing nations of our time. With changes in the historical circumstances came changes in men's attitudes and ideas. The Industrial Revolution was essentially an evolutionary process; it was not planned. But the industrial economy that came upon its heel is now seen by the leaders of these countries as a desirable goal to be reached by a forced economic march. Accordingly, they prefer "regimentation and planned growth" to "spontaneous generation." Moreover, unacquainted with the old assumptions that the individual is the best judge of what is in his own interest and that individual wishes are congruous with social welfare, they do not have to reckon with the "liberal tradition" and unhesitatingly adopt the authoritarian approach to economic problems.[275] Another writer has arrived at essentially the same conclusion. He is convinced that "the explicit premise that democratic capitalism, as a model for economic and political organization, is unlikely to exert its influence beyond the borders of the West, at least within our lifetimes." In order to make the "Great Ascent" to economic modernity, it might be necessary for "the backward nations" even to sacrifice human liberties and perhaps human life.[276]

This line of argument is not without cogency. For one thing, peoples of underdeveloped countries do not know much about modern eco-

---

our political atmosphere is an unhealthy one, a liberal political atmosphere, an atmosphere of 'free-fight liberalism.' . . . We must abandon this free-fight liberalism completely, if we want to develop and build up in the right way." From a lecture to the students of Hasanuddin University, Oct. 31, 1958, reprinted in Paul Sigmund, Jr., *Ideologies of Developing Nations*, p. 60. Editor's introduction on pp. 11–28 is helpful. McCord got the following response to his question about the desirability of the repressive measures being applied in Ghana by Nkrumah's government: "We must govern an uneducated, superstitious, violent people, a nation divided by tribal, religious and economic conflicts. . . . Above all, we wish to modernize our society and end poverty. . . . How could we possibly do this if every bush farmer were given the power to decide whether to build the Volta Dam or accept an increase in taxes, or agree to a reduction in consumer imports?" (*Springtime of Freedom*, p. 5).

[275] Karl de Schweinitz, Jr., *Industrialization and Democracy: Economic Necessity and Political Possibility*, pp. 272–79. Maurice F. Neufeld, *Poor Countries and Authoritarian Rule*, offers a more detailed analysis.

[276] Robert L. Heilbroner, *The Great Ascent: The Struggle for Economic Development*, pp. 148–49.

nomic life nor do they care for democratic values. Mass ignorance and apathy seem to make leadership imposed from above a logical choice. That Sun and K'ang failed to achieve their objectives might also lend plausibility to arguments in favor of the authoritarian approach to modernization.

Other students of economic development, however, do not take this position. It has been pointed out, for instance, that those leaders of "poor countries" who, seeking to achieve political stability and economic progress by resorting to various forms of authoritarian rule, have not realized their dreams. The explanation is not far to seek. Such rule "did not advance industrial progress against the backward pull of historical forces any more swiftly than the looser and less involved devices of liberal parliamentary systems."[277]

There is also the view that modernization does not require political tyranny and economic collectivism, that authoritarian rule is likely to hinder instead of expediting growth, and that economic progress is possible under democratic rule. Admittedly, authoritarianism is not without apparent advantages. It often can facilitate capital formation by forcing the transfer of an economic surplus from consumer to the planning elite.[278] It can prosecute its projects with a ruthlessness eschewed by or impossible in democratic societies.[279] The fact that the forces and circumstances that made the Industrial Revolution possible in the eighteenth and nineteenth centuries in Western Europe do not obtain in the developing nations today constitutes an obviously valid argument that Soviet Russia instead of Hanover England should be the model for economic development.[280] But authoritarian rule also has certain drawbacks. As actual experience shows, totalitarianism or dictatorship does not afford the best or true solution to economic problems. Waiving the question of human liberty, it in itself contains no guarantee of economic success. Unleashed political authority can make economically foolish decisions. Power need not corrupt, but in the hands of people not well versed in economic matters, it can do damage to the economy, in their very effort to improve it. There is no assurance that reliable intelligence on the state of the economy is available to men holding unlimited power. Rigorous control and rigid pro-

---

[277] Neufeld, *Poor Countries and Authoritarian Rule*, p. 144. Chap. 11 of this book deals especially with the question of authoritarian rule.

[278] McCord, *Springtime of Freedom*, pp. 68–69.

[279] Ibid., p. 13.

[280] Ibid., pp. 52–53.

gramming can hardly foster enterpreneurial incentive or the spirit of inventiveness so necessary to economic expansion. Soviet Russia has indeed achieved considerable success in industrialization. But it can be argued that "greater freedom would in all probability have avoided the sad effects on agriculture of Stalin's attempt to force higher production" and that "more flexibility would have forestalled the immensely wasteful impact" of centralized economic decisions and controls.[281] It might be suggested that, in forcing industrialization down the throat of the Chinese people, Mao Tse-tung has yet to demonstrate that he has solved China's problem of modernization.[282]

Studies of the situations in six Asian countries have persuaded a contemporary writer that inept or unwise action of a government (authoritarian or otherwise) can prove detrimental to economic growth. Policies that stemmed from inflexible and uncritical attitudes in planning—concentration of efforts and resources on uneconomic projects, undue restrictions on private industry and commerce, erection of barriers against foreign private enterprise, and neglect of the basic needs of agriculture—tend to impede progress.[283] Exclusive reliance on the public sector can be self-defeating.

Theoretically at least, one should not rule out the possibility of a "pluralistic solution" of the problem of development, a solution that aims at "collaboration between the state and private groups," diffusing

---

[281] Ibid., pp. 69–70, 242–43.

[282] Except for the first decades of the Chinese Communist rule, when it achieved a degree of apparent success, thanks in part to the newly gained political unity and administrative efficiency, the economic situation has not been consistently gratifying. Unwise economic policies and bungling in implementing otherwise helpful measures aside, there is the possibility that "rising political power inputs might lead to declining economic outputs, particularly after a certain point" (Alexander Eckstein, "Economic Planning, Organization and Control in Communist China," *Current Scene: Development in Mainland China*, 4, no. 21 [Nov. 25, 1966]: 11). See also W. K. [Werner Klatt], "Communist China's Agricultural Calamities" (covering 1949–1961), pp. 64–75. Li Ming-hua, "The Industrialization Problem on the Chinese Mainland," *Issues and Studies*, 6, no. 5 (Feb., 1970): 34–36, suggests that "Mao has wavered all along in his handling of the relationship between industry and agriculture, and between light industry and heavy industry, because of the contradiction between Mao's subjective requirement— preparedness against war—and the basic need of human life. Mao's policies and measures are neither consistent nor indisputably correct." At any rate, "To use industrialization as a means to mobilize for war is itself a mistake, because it contradicts the objective principles of economics." One might add that Mao's position reminds one somewhat of that of the leaders of the self-strengthening movement, to whom "wealth and power" of the state was the direct objective of economic modernization.

[283] Onslow, *Asian Economic Development*, pp. 225–26.

both economic and political power as widely as possible throughout the society."[284] "The democratic method," as it has been noted, can be compatible even with a socialistic economy; it does not have to become obsolete even if "capitalism is being killed by its achievement" in advanced industrial countries. "General election, parties, parliaments, cabinets and prime ministers may still prove to be most convenient instruments for dealing with the agenda that the socialist order may reserve for political decision."[285]

That the political factor is relevant to economic construction is no justification for the authoritarian approach. One could as readily err in predicating the all-sufficiency of government control as in clinging to economic laissez faire. Government action and individual effort should be combined and should not be regarded as mutually exclusive; they are complementary factors rather than alternatives.[287] The experience of Meiji Japan points to the possibility (and desirability) that while the government usefully took the lead in modernization, it judiciously invited private enterprise to carry on the process.[278] As authoritarian rulers are prone to claim infallibility,[288] they can hardly be expected to exercise restraint or to countenance private initiative.

It is beyond the scope of this paper to judge the merits of the two approaches, democratic and authoritarian, relative to economic development. Experts in the field do not agree. One thing, however, might be said. The failure of K'ang Yu-wei and Sun Yat-sen to start China on her way to industrialization constitutes no proof that the democratic approach lacks intrinsic value, whereas the experiences of Soviet Russia, Communist China, and certain African and Southeast Asian countries seem to suggest that the authoritarian approach is no foolproof panacea for economic backwardness.

---

[284] McCord, *Springtime of Freedom*, pp. 6, 76; cf. pp. 69–70.

[285] Schumpeter, *Capitalism, Socialism and Democracy*, pp. 269, 300–301, 415.

[286] Nurkse, *Problems of Capital Formation in Underdeveloped Countries and Patterns of Trade and Development*, pp. 154 56. The late Professor Nurkse held the view that "capital formation can be permanently successful only in a capital-conscious community" and that "nothing matters so much as the quality of the people." Personal habits and traits associated with the use of capital, such as "initiative, prudence, ingenuity and foresightedness—give a deeper and surer base to a nation's economic advance than the blueprints of a planning commission." Referring to Meiji Japan, he favored government action at the start and its withdrawal from areas where success had been achieved.

[287] Robert T. Holt and John E. Turner, *The Political Basis of Economic Development: An Exploration in Comparative Political Analysis*, pp. 100, 105–11, 237, 246.

[288] Harry R. Davis, "Toward Justifying Democracy," *The Key Reporter*, 32, no. 2 (Winter 1967–68): 3.

Chapter 9

EDUCATIONAL REFORM

PROPOSALS

K'ang Yu-wei's reform movement aimed at changing "the sternly conservative mentality and behavior of the nation" as much as at modifying the outmoded and decaying political structure.[1] Educational reform, therefore, constituted an integral part of his 1898 program.

Convinced that the traditional examination system was chiefly responsible for much of the ignorance and bigotry of the average literatus, one of his first proposals made to the emperor was the abolition of the "eight-legged essay." He presented his case against it in strong and incisive terms.

> Those who learn to write the eight-legged essay do not read any book written after Ch'in and Han times. They do not study the affairs of the the countries of the world. . . . Today there is an abundance of officials [recruited through the examination system]; none of them have the knowledge or skill to deal with any emergency or crisis. All this is due to the eight-legged essay. It is the eight-legged essay . . . that is responsible for the loss of Taiwan and Liaotung, . . . of Kiaochow, Lüshun, Talien, Weihaiwei, and Kwangchowwan.[2]

[1] Ma Te-chih, *Le mouvement réformiste et les événements de la cour de Pékin en 1898*, p. 9.
[2] K'ang, *Tzu-pien nien-p'u*, p. 19b; Jung-pang Lo, *K'ang Yu-wei: A Biography and a Symposium*, p. 97. Some of K'ang's contemporaries shared this view. Yen Fu, e.g., said that of all necessary reforms abolition of the "eight-legged essay" was the most urgent ("Chiu wang chüeh lun," reprinted in Chien Po-tsan et al., *Wu-hsü pien-fa*, 3: 60–71). Liang Ch'i-ch'ao, in a letter to K'ang, considered changing the examination

The emperor took action after several others urged him to change the examination system.[3] On June 23, 1898, he issued a decree abolishing the eight-legged essay and requiring aspiring scholars to give evidence of their acquaintance with "practical affairs" as well as their knowledge of the Confucian classics and Chinese history in free-style written discourses.[4] K'ang attached great importance to this action. He said to a Japanese friend after he reached Tokyo late in October 1898, that although the reform movement collapsed, the abolition of the eight-legged essay would unshackle the minds of China's literati and, as a consequence, intellectual enlightenment would become a reality.[5]

To give encouragement to persons who cultivated knowledge of current affairs, K'ang suggested that they be admitted outright into the Hanlin College or given regular official appointments.[6] He prompted Yen Hsiu to petition the emperor to institute special examinations for scholars accomplished in various fields of "practical learning," i.e., government administration, public finance, diplomacy, military affairs, science, and technology.[7] This he did on January 6, 1898, and as a result,

---

system "the foremost task" of reform ("Yü K'ang Yu-wei shu," given in Yeh Te-hui, *Chüeh mi yao-lu*, chüan 4, pp. 21b–22a). Cf. the first section in chapter 7 of this volume, passim, where K'ang's suggestions for administrative reform through renovating the educational system are discussed.

[3] E.g., Chang Chih-tung and Ch'en Pao-chen said in a joint memorial (June 4, 1898): "to deliver the country from the present predicament, the first thing to do is to foster human talent; before we can foster human talent, we must change the examination system." They went on to detail the unsalutary effects of the "eight-legged essay" (*Chang Wen-hsiang-kung ch'üan-chi*, chüan 48, *tsou-i*, pp. 2b–9a). Hsü Chih-ching's memorial, "Ch'ing fei pa-ku shu," petitioning the emperor to do away with the "eight-legged essay," was drafted by K'ang. Chien, *Wu-hsü*, 2: 339, gives excerpts from this document. Years before 1898, attention had already been drawn to the shortcomings of the examination system, notably, by Hsüeh Fu-ch'eng, "Hsüan-chü lun" (1864), *Yung-an wen nei-wai-pien*, wai-pien (Shanghai, 1901), chüan 1, pp. 1a–6b, and by Li Tzu-ming, *T'ao-hua-sheng-chieh-an jih-chi, jen-chi*, pp. 14b–15a, an entry of Feb. 18, 1874, in *Yüeh-man-t'ang jih-chi*.

[4] *Ta-Ch'ing li-ch'ao shih-lu, Kuang-hsü*, chüan 419, pp. 5–6.

[5] K'ang's undated letter to Okada Masaki, "Chih Kang-t'ien Cheng-shu shu," *Wan-mu-ts'ao-t'ang i-kao*, 4: 32a–b.

[6] K'ang first made the suggestion in 1896, in his "Tien-shih ts'e," *Nan-hai hsien-sheng ssu shang-shu chi*, pp. 47a–b. In 1898 he drafted a memorial for Sung Po-lu, requesting annual examination of scholars possessing "practical knowledge" (Sung Po-lu, "Tsou-ch'ing ching-chi sui-chü . . . che" [July 1, 1898], in Chu Shou-p'eng, *Tung-hua hsü-lu, Kuang-hsü*, chüan 145, pp. 6b–7a; Chien, *Wu-hsü*, 2: 347–48).

[7] Yen Hsiu, "Tsou-ch'ing she ching-chi chuan-k'o che" (Chien, *Wuhsü*, 2: 329–32). Reportedly, Yen submitted the memorial at K'ang's prompting. Years before 1898, Hsüeh Fu-ch'eng made a similar proposal. See his "Ying chao ch'en yen shu" (1875), *Yung-an wen-pien*, chüan 1, pp. 1a–12a, in *Yung-an ch'üan-chi*.

Ching-chi t'e-k'o soon came into being, following the two decrees issued on January 27, 1898, and July 13, 1898.[8]

Agreeing with some of his contemporaries, K'ang regarded the development of a new school system as an essential and urgent task. To have an examination system without a school system, he argued, was merely to recruit talent without making an attempt to foster it. Inevitably, there would be a dearth of talent. He told the emperor of what he knew of the situations in foreign countries—Germany, France, England, Japan, and others. He was particularly impressed by the German educational system. Frederick the Great, he said, inaugurated a system of modern schools in which subjects ranging from history to science were taught. Elementary schools prepared children for citizenship; high schools trained youths for various professions; universities, by affording instruction in higher learning, produced leaders and teachers who formed the nation's elite (*shih ta-fu*). It was a superior educational system rather than a superior army that, in the last analysis, decided the outcome of the Franco-Prussian war. And yet, K'ang added, "we still compel an entire nation to engage in writing the eight-legged essay, . . . thus stunting and smothering human talent." Despite a population of four hundred million, China did not have enough men of knowledge and understanding to enable her to stand as a truly independent country. The conclusion was obvious. China must follow the example of Prussia and establish a full-fledged modern school system.[9]

A number of Western-style schools existed in China before 1898,[10] but in the eyes of K'ang and his friends, they were far from adequate. Their curricula were usually limited to foreign-language courses; subjects imparting knowledge concerning "wealth and power" were seldom included. Students were not given opportunities to gain knowledge through experimentation in laboratories or travel in foreign lands. There was only a small number of schools in the eighteen provinces, far

---

Sheng Hsüan-huai suggested in a memorial that a new category be instituted in the examination system for scholars of "new learning" ("T'iao-ch'en tzu-ch'iang ta-chi che," in Chien, *Wu-hsü*, 2: 442; cf. note 16, chapter 7, this volume).

[8] See *Te-tsung shih-lu, chüan* 414, pp. 4b–5a, and *chüan* 420, pp. 12a–b. Paul Pelliot, "La réforme des examens littéraires en Chine," is useful.

[9] K'ang, "Ch'ing kuang k'ai hsüeh-hsiao i yang jen-ts'ai che" (late June, 1898) (*K'ang Nan-hai hsien-sheng wen-ch'ao*, 5, *tsou-i*: 6b–8a, hereafter, *Wen-ch'ao*; Chien, *Wu-hsü*, 2: 217–19).

[10] Knight Biggerstaff, *The Earliest Modern Government Schools in China*, surveys the steps taken between 1861 and 1894, and gives details concerning the T'ung-wen kuan, the Kiangnan Arsenal foreign language school, and the Foochow Naval Yard school. Cf. Meribeth E. Cameron, *The Reform Movement in China, 1898–1912*, chap. 4.

too small to answer the needs of the situation.[11] Many more should be established; curricula and teaching methods must be improved.

The reformers placed special emphasis on the founding of a university in the imperial capital, which would serve as a spearhead in the development of a school system. In the "memorial requesting the establishment of schools,"[12] K'ang advised the emperor to speed up the founding of the university. He referred to Li Tuan-fen's memorial submitted in the summer of 1896 and to the fact that after deliberation by court officials, Li's proposal for a *Ching-shih ta-hsüeh-t'ang* was approved in principle.[13] K'ang must have been gratified that two years later, under the direction of Sun Chia-nai, the university finally took shape.[14]

To expedite the development of a school system in the provinces, K'ang suggested that the traditional academies (*shu-yüan*) be converted into "middle schools" and the buildings of "unauthorized shrines" (*yin tz'u*) be used to house elementary schools, which all children six years old should be required to attend. Middle schools should have "Western subjects" in their curricula. K'ang cited the example of Meiji Japan to support his argument. Thanks to modern education, which gave her leaders knowledge in Western government, literature, and technology, the island country was strong enough to defeat China in war.[15] In a

---

[11] Li Tuan-fen, "Ch'ing t'ui-kuang hsüeh-hsiao che" (June 20, 1898) (Chien, *Wu-hsü*, 2: 292–93). Li went on to propose that a network of modern schools be established in the empire. His suggestions differed from K'ang's in details but reflected the same general point of view. Li was related by marriage to Liang Ch'i-ch'ao and was one of the very few high officials who supported reform. The manuscript copy of K'ang's *Tzu-pien nien-p'u* (microfilm, reel 3) carries an interesting marginal note: "Winter of *i-wei* [late 1895 or early 1896]—drafted a memorial for Li Pi-yüan [i.e., Li Tuan-fen], requesting the establishment of a university." Li's memorial proposing the university was submitted in the summer of 1896 (see note 13, below). Conceivably, this 1898 memorial of Li's was inspired by K'ang or Liang, if not drafted by either of them. A little earlier, on April 9, 1898, Li Sheng-t'o, a censor, petitioned the emperor to order all provincial authorities to establish schools within six months (*Te-tsung shih-lu, chüan* 416, pp. 13a–b).

[12] See note 9, above.

[13] As indicated in an imperial decree issued on June 11, 1898: "the imperial university, which will set an example for the provinces, shall be the first to be founded" (*Te-tsung shih-lu, chüan* 418, p. 15a; Chien, *Wu-hsü*, 2: 17).

[14] In an 1896 memorial, "I-fu k'ai-pan Ching-shih ta-hsüeh-t'ang che," Sun Chia-nai made several concrete suggestions concerning organization, curriculum, and recruitment of faculty and students of the projected university (Shen T'ung-sheng, *Kuang-hsü cheng-yao, chüan* 22, pp. 21b–24a; Chien, *Wu-hsü*, 2: 425–29). On Aug. 9, 1898, Sun made a progress report in a memorial, "Tsou ch'ou-pan Ching-shih ta-hsüeh-t'ang ta-kai ch'ing-hsing che" (Chu, *Tung-hua hsü-lu, chüan* 146, pp. 14a–15a; Chien, *Wu-hsü*, 2: 435–37).

[15] K'ang, "Ch'ing ch'ih ko-sheng kai shu-yüan yin-tz'u wei hsüeh-t'ang che"

decree issued on July 10, the emperor adopted his suggestions without reservation.[16]

To furnish the new schools with suitable teaching and reference texts, and to provide reading materials for the general public, K'ang urged that the translation work that had been going on in Shanghai, Foochow, and Canton[17] be greatly expanded.[18] Previous endeavor had been un-

---

(Chien, *Wu-hsü*, 2: 219–22). About two years earlier, Ch'en Chih had proposed conversion of *shu-yüan* into schools, in his *Yung shu, chüan* 2, p. 59. Hu P'ing-chih and Ch'ien Chün-hsiang jointly petitioned the emperor (late spring or early summer, 1896) to order inclusion of "useful subjects," such as mathematics, astronomy, agriculture, etc., in the curriculum of the *shu-yüan* ("Ch'ing pien-t'ung shu-yüan chang-ch'eng che," Chien, *Wu-hsü*, 2: 297–300). Cf. chapter 7 of this volume, at note 27. Chang Chih-tung, in a telegram to the Tsungli yamen (Sept. 3, 1898), reported that he had converted all the *shu-yüan* in Hupeh province into schools in which foreign languages, mathematics, astronomy, geography, natural sciences, and technology were taught, together with Chinese history and the Confucian classics (*Chang Wen-hsiang-kung ch'üan-chi, chüan* 80, pp. 4b–6a). Hsieh Kuo-chen, "Chin-tai shu-yüan hsüeh-hsiao chih-tu pien-ch'ien k'ao" (Hu Shih, *Chang Chü-sheng hsien-sheng ch'i-shih sheng-jih chi-yen wen-chi*, pp. 281–322), tells the story of the transition from *shu-yüan* to schools.

[16] *Te-tsung shih-lu, chüan* 420, p. 9a. As expected, the action aroused much opposition. Tseng Lien, an avowed "conservative," condemned the conversion of *shu-yüan* into schools, alleging that "Western learning will play havoc with the Sage's Way" ("Ying chao shang feng-shih" [written sometime after Aug. 2, 1898], Chien, *Wu-hsü*, 2: 493–94). Wu Ching-heng (Wu Chih-hui) recalled that "public opinion" was against the use of shrines as school houses. "A peddler of vegetables," shouted angrily: "temples and shrines have been here since antiquity; how can we do away with them?" (quoted in Ch'en Kung-lu, "Chia-wu chan-hou keng-tzu luan-ch'ien Chung-kuo pien-fa yün-tung chih yen chiu," *Wen-che chi-k'an*, 3, no. 1 [1933]: 104). Renville C. Lund, "The Imperial University of Peking," deals with the founding of the University.

[17] Obviously, K'ang had in mind the translation bureaus in Shanghai (founded in 1863 and later attached to the Kiangnan Arsenal), Canton (founded in 1864), and Foochow (founded in 1866 and attached to the Foochow Shipyard). Curiously, he did not mention the T'ung-wen kuan in Peking, which was established in 1862 as a result of Prince Kung's suggestion in 1861. Perhaps K'ang was unaware that the T'ung-wen kuan translations included Fawcett's *Political Economy*, Wheaton's *International Law*, De Marten's *Guide diplomatique*, Tytler's *Universal History*, books which K'ang would have deemed "essential" or at least useful. W. A. P. Martin, who took charge of T'ung-wen kuan in 1869, said: "The works translated comprised . . . such subjects as international law, political economy, chemistry, natural philosophy, physical geography, history, French and English codes of law, . . . diplomatic and consular guides, etc. . . . Such works are a lever which, with such a fulcrum, must move something" (*Cycle of Cathy*, pp. 319–20). See Biggerstaff, *Earliest Modern Government Schools*, chapter 2, and "The T'ung Wen Kuan," pp. 307–40.

[18] K'ang was not alone or the first to stress the importance of translating books on Western government, law, education, and related subjects. See, e.g., Ma Chien-chung, "Ni she fan-i shu-yüan i" (winter, 1894), *Shih-k'o-chai chi-yen*, in Liang Ch'i-ch'ao's *Hsi-cheng ts'ung-shu, chüan* 4, pp. 6b–9b. Adopting Censor Hu Fu-ch'en's sug-

satisfactory for two reasons: the scope was too narrow and the speed was too slow. Most of the books rendered into Chinese were mostly out-of-date works dealing with what he considered "nonvital" subjects such as agriculture and technology; few, if any, could serve "to develop the intelligence and understanding of men." This mistake must be corrected. Moreover, the books selected for translation have so far been written originally in Western languages. The task was unavoidably laborious and snail-paced. Japan, in a period of thirty years, had translated virtually all the "good books" on government, literature, and military affairs published in Europe and America. It would be wise, therefore, to render these books into Chinese. As the Japanese and Chinese languages were quite similar, the task would be easier and more quickly accomplished. To further expedite the work, translation bureaus should be set up in Peking and all the provinces.[19]

China must send students abroad to acquire firsthand knowledge of the modern West, as Japan did. Science and technology (*wu-chih chih hsüeh*) were most highly developed in Europe and America; for this reason Western countries were preferable to Japan. Unlike government, history, and philosophy, these subjects could not be properly studied by reading translated books or taught in Chinese schools. At the start, each district of the eighteen provinces should be required to finance from one to three promising young men to study in foreign countries; later on the number of students should be increased. However, not every Western country was suitable. Germany, for instance was preferable to France because the former not only was most advanced in learning but also had, like China, a monarchical form of government. Meanwhile, young men should be encouraged to go to Japan to study on their own. As the expenses incurred would not be very great, there was no need for government support.[20] It may be noted in pass-

---

gestion, the government established a publication bureau, the Kuan-shu chü, early in 1896 (*Te-tsung shih-lu, chüan* 382, p. 7). This bureau, which was under Sun Chia-nai's direction, carried on several functions: maintaining a library, translating and printing books on jurisprudence, international law, commerce, agriculture, industry, etc.; establishing a museum to display scientific apparatus and specimens; and conducting a school for the younger members of Peking officialdom. See Sun's memorial, "Kuan-shu chü chang-ch'eng shu" (Chien, *Wu-hsü*, 2: 422–24).

[19] K'ang, "Ch'ing kuang-i Jih-pen shu ta-p'ai yu-hsüeh che" (*Wu-hsü tsou-kao*, pp. 15b–18a; *Wen-ch'ao*, 5, *tsou-i*: 8a–9b; Chien, *Wu-hsü*, 2: 222–25). K'ang did not specify what books would serve the stated purpose, but taking a clue from the curriculum of his private academy in Canton, one may surmise that they would be in the fields of social science and humanities. See note 35, below.

[20] Ibid. (*Wu-hsü tsou-kao*, pp. 17a–b; *Wen-ch'ao*, pp. 9a–b; Chien, *Wu-hsü*, p. 224).

ing that K'ang was not the first to see the necessity of sending students abroad; the government in fact was already doing so, though on a small scale.[21]

ASSUMPTIONS

Three assumptions appear to have underlain K'ang's proposals: (1) that education must be universal and compulsory, at any rate at the elementary level; (2) that education should not only impart useful knowledge but also foster a new intellectual outlook, a new frame of mind, unshackled by antiquated conventions; and (3) that the pursuit of Western learning should not entail the abandonment of China's cultural legacy.

As noted above, K'ang borrowed his idea of universal education from what he knew of Prussia. Frederick the Great, he said, had elementary schools built in the villages and ordered all children six years old to attend them. . . . Parents of those who failed to attend were punished."[22] China should also have "all children of the common people" enrolled in schools.[23] One is tempted to speculate that had the reform movement achieved unqualified success, China conceivably could have drastically reduced illiteracy in a matter of decades.

That K'ang saw in educational reform a means to bring about an important change in China's intellectual climate, from the accustomed conservative temper to a new progressive outlook, may be gathered from what he said in his "Fourth Memorial to the Emperor."

In Sung and Ming times [countries of] the Far West were kept in ignorance by the popes. [Thus enfeebled,] they were repeatedly invaded by Moslem nations. Pei-ken [Bacon?], an Englishman, living in Yung-lo times, set forth new principles. He believed that the more challenge human intelligence faces, the more it develops and that as civilization moves forward, ever greater glory is added to each new phase. He held

---

Somewhat curiously, K'ang made no mention of the United States. One may safely assume that he would have thought it unsuitable on account of its form of government.

[21] Largely as a result of the joint petition of Tseng Kuo-fan and Li Hung-chang (Dec. 23, 1871), the first batch of 120 students arrived in the United States in 1872. The Educational Mission was in operation until 1881. See Ssu-yü Teng and John K. Fairbank, *China's Response to the West*, pp. 91–94; for students sent to Europe, see pp. 95–97. Cf. Shu Hsin-ch'eng, *Chin-tai Chung-kuo liu-hsüeh shih*. Li Tuan-fen was one of the high officials who supported the idea (*Te-tsung shih-lu, chüan* 390, p. 1b).

[22] K'ang, "Ch'ing k'ai hsüeh-hsiao che" (1898) (*Wu-hsü tsou-kao*, p. 12b; Chien, *Wu-hsü*, 2: 217).

[23] K'ang, "Shang Ch'ing-ti ti-erh shu" (May 2, 1895) (Chien, *Wu-hsü*, 2: 149).

that man should explore the new and not abide with the old, adapt himself to the present and not cling to the past. . . . Decades later [sic] Columbus discovered the vast land of America and Copernicus demonstrated that the earth moves around the sun. . . . In the present century, new knowledge has increased even more.[24]

Accordingly, K'ang advised the emperor to encourage the growth of new knowledge by conferring honors on authors who expounded new truths and inventors who devised new instruments. Subjects that tended to broaden the student's perspective, such as history and geography, should be included even in the curricula of elementary schools.[25] K'ang wished, so it seems, to put an end to the baneful influence of China's "popes" and to welcome a Chinese Bacon who would usher in an era of enlightenment. Presumably, he would not object to playing such a role himself.

K'ang admired the Western spirit of progress and recognized the crucial importance of science and technology, but he did not commit himself to worshipping "science" as "omniscient, omnipotent, and the bearer of man's salvation,"[26] as some leaders of the New Culture movement did in the 1910s and 1920s.[27] He never wanted to forsake China's moral values. Complete Westernization or "smashing the Confucian shop" was to him as pernicious as hidebound conservatism. In this sense, he was a moderate or, in Liang Ch'i-ch'ao's words," "a progressive and a conservative at the same time."[28] As a "conservative," K'ang attached great value to "the national essence" (*kuo ts'ui*) with "authentic" Confucianism as its highest expression. He affirmed this position on more than one occasion. In 1895, for example, he memorialized the emperor to establish Confucianism as a special and honored field of study, and to encourage "men of superior talent and great learning"

[24] K'ang, "Shang Ch'ing-ti ti-ssu shu" (June 30, 1898) (Chien, *Wu-hsü*, 2: 175–76). K'ang was not as careful as he should have been about dates in European history. The Englishman he mentioned was more likely Francis Bacon (1561–1626) than Roger Bacon (ca. 1214–94). Both men were innovators in their own ways, but neither lived in Yung-lo times (1403–24). Columbus discovered America in 1492–93, two centuries after Roger died but only about seven decades before Francis was born. The immortal work of Copernicus was completed probably by 1530 and was published in 1543, nearly two and a half centuries after Roger died and about three decades before Francis was born.

[25] Ibid., p. 180.

[26] R. G. Owen, *Scientism, Man and Religion*, p. 20.

[27] See the fourth section of chapter 11 in this volume for more detailed discussion of the intellectual issues involved in modernization.

[28] Liang Ch'i-ch'ao, *Nan-hai K'ang hsien-sheng chuan, Yin-ping-shih ho-chi, wen-chi*, 6, p. 88a.

to disseminate the Confucian teaching in foreign lands.[29] He proposed in 1898 that Confucianism be elevated to the status of "state religion" (*kuo chiao*).[30] In the early years of the republic, he continued to extol Confucianism and strove to extend its influence.[31] The Confucianism he promoted, however, was not identical with the traditional variety.[32] He was in reality a Confucian revisionist and thus cannot be accurately described by the simple label "Confucianist."[33]

K'ang himself put into practice the conviction that sound education should combine Chinese studies and Western learning. In his own private academy in Canton, where he taught in 1891–93,[34] he lectured on "Western philosophy, sociology, principles of politics, and histories of China and foreign countries" in addition to Confucianism, Neo-Confucianism of Sung and Ming times, Buddhism, and the philosophies of the late Chou thinkers.[35] He endeavored in this way to introduce "Western learning" to his students and, at the same time, to make them pay due attention to China's own intellectual heritage.

In thinking that Chinese culture was not without value and therefore deserved preservation, K'ang was in fairly good company. For instance, this was said of W. A. P. Martin's estimation of it.

> Martin had not recoiled from the Heathen's absorbing philosophy and his delightful literature, as many of his missionary colleagues who took "the narrow way" of Christian sectarianism. In fact the intellectuals among the missionaries, from the famed Jesuit scientists of the seventeenth and eighteenth centuries onward, were profoundly moved (though for policy's sake they sometimes sought to conceal it) by the breadth and depth of that Chinese culture which had made China the mentor of the Far East.[36]

[29] K'ang, "Shang Ch'ing-ti ti-erh shu" (1895) (Chien, *Wu-hsü*, 2: 150).

[30] K'ang, "Ch'ing tsun K'ung-sheng wei kuo-chiao li chiao-pu chiao-hui i K'ung-tzu chi-nien erh fei yin-ssu che" (1898) (Chien, *Wu-hsü*, 2: 233).

[31] K'ang, "Chung-hua chiu-kuo lun" (1912) (*Pu-jen tsa-chih hui-pien*, 1st ser. [Shanghai, 1914], *chüan* 1, pp. 15b–17b).

[32] See chapter 4 of this volume, "Confucianism as a Philosophy of Reform and as a Religion."

[33] Benjamin Schwartz, "The Intellectual History of China: Preliminary Reflections," in *Chinese Thought and Institutions*, ed. John K. Fairbank (Chicago: University of Chicago Press, 1957), p. 19.

[34] K'ang, *Tzu-pien nien-p'u*, p. 10a; Lo, *K'ang*, p. 53.

[35] K'ang T'ung-chia, *K'ang Yu-wei yü wu-hsü pien-fa*, pp. 26–27. The author adds that music and gymnastics were also included in the curriculum. Liang, *Nan-hai K'ang hsien-sheng chuan*, pp. 64–70, explains K'ang's educational ideal and the guiding principles of the curriculum of his academy at Ch'ang-hsing li, Canton.

[36] Esson M. Gale, *Salt for the Dragon: A Personal History of China, 1908–1945*, p. 23.

An American diplomat who served in China made these remarks some sixty years ago:

> China cannot, indeed, make herself over into an efficient nation unless she is willing to learn from other peoples the ways in which they excel and to consider the moral elements of their success; but she must also be true to the best in her own civilization. . . . Turning her back upon abuses current in the past, she will make herself strong by becoming different without ceasing to be essentially herself.[37]

Interestingly, even Hu Shih, prophet of the New Culture, sometimes showed appreciation of China's "old civilization." These words are especially noteworthy:

> . . . it would surely be a great loss to mankind at large if the acceptance of this great new civilization [of the West] should take the form of abrupt displacement instead of organic assimilation. The real problem, therefore, may be restated thus: How can we best assimilate modern civilization in such a manner as to make it congenial and congruous and continuous with the civilization of our own making?
> . . . The solution of this great problem . . . will depend solely on the foresight and the sense of historical continuity of the intellectual leaders of China, and on the tact and skill with which they can successfully connect the best in modern civilization with the best in our own civilization.[38]

K'ang, too, was concerned with solving this great problem and offered a solution that he thought would assimilate the new without displacing the old. His judgment regarding what was the best in Chinese and Western civilizations may not have been necessarily correct; in applying his solution he may not have been sufficiently tactful and skillful, but his approach to the problem can hardly be called unreasonable.

Gale met Martin in 1908 when the latter was eighty-four years old. In the past, China was not withoit impact on European thought. See, e.g., Geoffrey Hudson, *Europe and China: A Survey of Their Relations from the Earliest Times to 1800*; Lewis A. Maverick, *China, A Model for Europe*; D. F. Lach, *Contributions of China to German Civilization, 1648–1740*; and A. Reichwein, *China and Europe: Intellectual and Artistic Contact in the Eighteenth Century*. A few studies by Chinese scholars may also be cited: Ho Ping-sung, "Chung-kuo wen-hua hsi-ch'uan k'ao," Pao Tsung-p'eng et al., eds., *Chung-kuo chin-tai-shih lun-ts'ung*, 1st ser. (Taipei, 1956), 2: 33–62; Fang Hao, *Chung-hsi chiao-t'ung shih*, vols. 4 and 5; and Chu Ch'ien-chih, *Chung-kuo ssu-hsiang tui-yü Ou-chou wen-hua chih ying-hsiang*.

[37] Paul S. Reinsch, *Intellectual and Political Currents in the Far East*, p. 186.

[38] Hu Shih, *The Development of the Logical Method in Ancient China* (written in 1917; published in Shanghai, 1922), Introduction, pp. 6–7. Hu came back to this position in his later years. See this volume, chapter 11, at notes 220 and 221.

De-Sinification, K'ang feared, would spell "abrupt displacement" and damage the cohesive force that sound tradition could supply. In that event, China would simply become different without making herself strong. Students of twentieth-century "emerging nations" have come to the conclusion that between preserving the old culture at any cost, a choice favored by the "traditionalists," and destroying the entire fabric of traditional society, the choice of the "modernizers," there is a third choice—"modification of the institutions, practices, and structure of a traditional society in the direction of modernization while retaining some of its traditional cohesive features."[39] Broadly speaking, this was the course that the reformers of Tokugawa Japan followed and that K'ang wished to take.

It has been pointed out that Hu Shih, in exploiting experimentalism as a rationale for cultural revolution, departed from the intent of William James and John Dewey. According to James,

> New truth is always a go-between, a smoother-over of transition. It marries old opinion to new fact so as ever to show a minimum of jolt, a maximum of continuity. . . . The point I now urge you to observe particularly is the part played by the older truths. . . . Loyalty to them is the first principle.

In Dewey's view, "the office of intelligence in every problem that either a person or a community meets is to effect a working connection between old habits, customs, institutions, beliefs, and new conditions."[40] As we have mentioned, Hu at one point believed in the importance of having "the sense of historical continuity" and of effecting an "organic assimilation" of modern Western civilization within traditional Chinese culture. He was then, presumably, abiding by the principles laid down

[39] Max Millikan and Donald Blacker, *The Emerging Nations* (Boston: Little, Brown, 1961), quoted in William McCord, *The Springtime of Freedom: The Evolution of Developing Societies*, p. 147. McCord, on p. 144, says, "man and institutions in developing nations must change, but in the process of transforming man, no government has a duty to dismember an entire tradition." Cf. Bert F. Hoselitz, "Tradition and Economic Growth," in *Tradition, Values, and Socio-Economic Development*, ed. R. Braibanti and J. Spengler, excerpted in McCord, *Springtime of Freedom*, pp. 146–47; and I. R. Sinai, *The Challenge of Modernization*, p. 215. These writers deal with problems of economic modernization, but their conclusions are not irrelevant to educational reform.

[40] William James, *Pragmatism and Four Essays from the Meaning of Truth* (New York: Meridian Books, 1955), p. 51; John Dewey, *Intelligence in the Modern World: John Dewey's Philosophy*, ed. Joseph Ratner (New York: Modern Library, 1939), p. 452. Both passages are quoted in Jerome B. Grieder, *Hu Shih and the Chinese Renaissance: Liberalism in the Chinese Revolution, 1917–1937*, p. 118.

by James and Dewey. But the disheartening conditions that prevailed in republican China may have convinced him that the old culture was beyond salvage, and he was thus persuaded to revise his experimentalist position. "Clearly," he wrote in 1918, "ours is a government of corrupt officials and vile bureaucrats—but we perversely sing of merit and chant hymns to virtue."[41] Now, instead of insisting on the importance of historical continuity, he urged a break with the past. The family, the cornerstone of traditional society, was condemned because it fostered dependence. Changed conditions had rendered "nonsense" the "unalterable principles" of old.[42] He conceded that it was not "virtue" that was responsible for China's plight but rather the failure to practice it. Nowhere did he say that "benevolence," "righteousness," "reciprocity," and other cardinal Confucian values are in themselves morally or socially irrelevant in modern Western lands.

K'ang Yu-wei, too, was critical of Confucianism—of a moral tradition that was honored not by deed but mostly by word. He made a distinction between a Chinese tradition that had decayed and was outmoded, and another tradition that deserved preservation and should be "married" to the new situation, thereby minimizing "jolt" and maintaining "a maximum of continuity" in the process of modernization. One may surmise that in this respect K'ang, unwittingly, was a more consistent experimentalist than Hu.

AFTERMATH

K'ang's efforts at renovating the educational system were not entirely abortive, even though they did not reach his ultimate goal, namely, intellectual enlightenment through transfusion of new blood without entailing cultural hemophilia. Some of his ideas of education did not die with the 1898 debacle, but were embodied in substance in the post-Boxer reform, particularly as planned by Chang Chih-tung and Liu K'un-i. In the first of the three memorials they jointly submitted to the throne in the spring of 1901, it was said:

[41] Hu Shih, "I-pu-sheng chu-i," *Hu Shih wen-ts'un*, 4: 904; quoted in Grieder, *Hu Shih and the Chinese Renaissance*, p. 94.

[42] Hu, "Shi h-yen chu-i," *Hu Shih wen-ts'un*, 2: 435–36; quoted in Grieder, *Hu Shih*, pp. 114–15. Grieder adds this comment: "In Hu Shih's hands experimentalism was thus a weapon turned against the tradition" (p. 115). Again: "The Chinese were little interested in an attempt to 'marry old opinion to new fact.' Their aim, rather, was to use new fact to discredit old opinion, and an appeal to 'experience' was necessarily an appeal to a past largely repudiated. Even Hu Shih's demand for a 'transvaluation of all values' was designed not 'to effect a working connection' with the past, but to serve as the justification for a new beginning" (p. 120).

We humbly believe that China is poor not in economic resources but in human talent, and that she is weak not in military power but in mental vigor. Intellectual isolation and useless learning have resulted in a dearth of men of ability. Contented to live in a fool's paradise, people have no far-sighted plans to meet impending disaster; nor do they have energetic resolve to acquire true knowledge. They are consequently feckless.[43]

In the schools of the Far West, the memorialists continued, students were taught useful knowledge together with "moral principles," gaining understanding of the affairs of both foreign lands and their own countries. China would do well to follow their example and revamp her educational system.[44]

"Western methods" must be adopted. They presented their arguments for selective Westernization in the third of the memorials.

At present, constant progress is being made in various countries of the world. The larger ones have attained both strength and prosperity; even the smaller ones do not suffer from weakness or poverty. The forms of their government and the contents of their scholarship are the fruit of centuries of study and represent the cumulative accomplishments of many men. . . . One country emulated another; America followed the footsteps of Europe and Japan took her pattern from the West.[45]

Among other measures they recommended were the following which they thought were easy to implement: sending a large number of promising persons to study abroad; extensive translation of books published in Japan and Western countries; and establishing institutes of technology and schools of agriculture—[46] Some of the measures were curiously similar to those K'ang suggested a few years before. Chang and Liu were probably not unaware of the similarity. They pointedly stated that their suggestions were "patently different" from the "evil and perverse words" of K'ang Yu-wei.[47]

Ten years after the 1898 coup d'état, Chang Chih-tung and Sun Chia-nai formulated a course of study for the child emperor P'u-i,

---

[43] Chu, *Tung-hua hsü-lu, Kuang-hsü, chüan* 169, p. 7a. Teng and Fairbank, *China's Response to the West*, chap. 20, "The Conservative Reform Movement," give a brief account and selected documents.

[44] Chu, *Tung-hua hsü-lu, Kuang-hsü, chüan* 169, p. 8a. The memorialists went on to sketch a three-tier school structure and to propose that elementary schools be established in districts, middle schools in prefectures, and advanced schools in provincial capitals. The Confucian classics, Chinese history, "Western learning" (law, science, technology, etc.), they said, should be included in the curricula (ibid., pp. 8a–10b).

[45] Ibid., pp. 27b–28a.

[46] Ibid., pp. 28a–41a.

[47] Ibid., p. 40a.

which included lectures by various tutors on the Confucian Four Books, Chinese history, general history of the West, history of Japan's Meiji reform, and principles of constitutional government.[48] K'ang Yu-wei could hardly have any objection to such a curriculum. In the republican years, the Imperial University was reorganized as Peking University and became the center of radical thought, home of the New Culture movement, and cradle of Chinese Communism. Translation of Western and Japanese books continued with increased speed in the twentieth century. The "enthusiasm for natural and applied sciences of the past century shifted to the social sciences and humanities,"[49] a trend that K'ang had wished to set in the 1890s. Other measures of educational reform advocated by him, particularly, establishment of schools, publication of newspapers, and formation of "study societies," carried on since 1901, exerted an "enlightening influence" on China's intellectuals.[50]

However, K'ang's central objective was far from realized. Instead of a blending of East and West, which might serve as an intellectual foundation for social, political, and economic reform, the new education brought about a depreciation of Chinese values without reaping constructive benefits from Western ideas.[51] Many of the intellectuals soon wallowed in a veritable whirlpool of cultural confusion. Thanks to superficial Westernization and erosion of native values, the country was on the verge of losing her identity. A British observer recorded his impression in 1909 in these terms, perhaps with unintentional hyperbole:

> China has fundamentally altered. She used to be absolutely the most conservative land in the world. Now she is a land which is seeing so many radical changes, that a missionary said, when I asked him a question about China, "You must not rely on me, for I left China three months ago, so that what I say may be out of date."[52]

He went on to predict the fall of Confucianism.

Western thought is very powerful. The way it has dominated the forces

---

[48] Hsü T'ung-hsin, *Chang Wen-hsiang-kung nien-p'u, chüan* 10, p. 10b and compiler's note.

[49] Tsuen-hsuin Tsien, "Western Impact on China Through Translation," pp. 318–19. The author shows that in 1902–4, of the 533 works translated, those in the humanities amounted to 60.8 percent, whereas those on sciences only to 31.5 percent.

[50] For *hsüeh-hui*, see chapter 6, this volume, at notes 71–79.

[51] Shen Yün-lung, *Hsien-tai cheng-chih jen-wu shu-p'ing*, pp. 1–10, and T'ang Chih-chün, *Wu-hsü pien-fa chien-shih*, p. 50.

[52] Gascoyne Cecil, *Changing China*, p. 4.

of nature gives it a great prestige. . . . Confucianism must fall before Western materialism. . . . China will be left stripped of religion, robbed of her old ideas, and not clothed with new ones, wandering into all the misery and humiliation that vice and sin can bring upon mankind.[53]

Sounding like a prophet of doom, he spoke with an obvious missionary bias. He would like to have China reject Western science and technology but embrace the Christian religion. Very few Chinese intellectuals of the time would go along with him. (K'ang, for one, would see no sense in spurning "Western materialism" and replacing "the Confucian religion" with Christianity.) However, as later developments showed, his grim prediction was correct to a suprising extent.

One suspects that given the existing circumstances, K'ang's hope of achieving a constructive synthesis of Chinese and Western values through educational reform was impossible of fulfillment. The most crucial fact was the advance necrosis of China's own cultural tissue. For a long time the teachings of the ancient Sage had been in general honored more by word than by deed. Scholars aspiring to higher status must of course read Confucian texts and compose essays on themes taken from them. Officials must pay lip service to the Sage or suffer the consequences of not so doing. But, by and large, Confucianism was not a pervading, living creed, guiding the everyday thoughts and actions of the lettered elite. In a China that was at most only partially Confucian,[54] "the national soul" (*kuo hun*, to use K'ang's terminology) faced the prospect of disembodiment.

This was true at least in late Ch'ing times when K'ang lived and worked. The empress dowager, like many emperors in the past, understood the usefulness of "imperial Confucianism" as an ideological tool and did not hesitate to employ it.

As Li Chien-nung said, "Although she herself did not pay much attention to Confucian moral principles, she always used the majestic power of the Confucian moral code when she dealt with others."[55] Li could have added that although few among the men with whom she dealt practiced Confucian principles and that although they presumably knew that the Confucian moral code was a mere tool in her hands, none dared openly question its power. The whole thing, so it appears, amounted to a sham. Outward conformity with the traditional rules of

[53] Ibid., pp. 40–43.

[54] Kung-chuan Hsiao, "Legalism and Autocracy in Traditional China," pp. 108–21.

[55] Li Chien-nung, *The Political History of China, 1840–1928*, p. 99.

conduct and verbal commitment to the "Five Constants" constituted no proof that these were expressions of inner conviction. Tradition was not completely dead. A few scholar-officials were known to be bona fide practicers of Confucianism. But these exceptions did not alter the general situation and by republican times even these few probably had disappeared. Hsü Chih-mo, the well-known poet, called attention to the "mutilated corpses of benevolence, righteousness, propriety, wisdom, and trustworthiness" floating in the "filthy stream of humanity."[56] Carsun Chang hardly exaggerated matters in describing the last hundred years as "the period of spiritual vacuum because in the Chinese mind there remained no conviction by which scholars and masses could live and for which they could fight."[57]

Chang blamed K'ang Yu-wei, Hu Shih, and Ch'en Tu-hsiu for having created the vacuum. "To speak frankly," he wrote, "Confucianism or Neo-Confucianism almost became moribund after having been the target of attack since the middle [sic] of the last century." K'ang was, he added, "the first creator of China's spiritual vacuum."[58]

One is not sure, however, that Chang's verdict was really fair to K'ang, or even to Hu and Ch'en. The "vacuum" was in the making (thanks to a combination of historical forces) long before K'ang arrived on the scene. His Confucian revisionism was calculated precisely to remedy the disease of sham Confucianism.[59] He strove to breathe new life into a waning tradition, not to destroy it. To hold him responsible for the atrophy of Confucian values was not unlike blaming a physician who did not succeed in reviving a patient for having caused the death. "The small band of Chinese intellectuals" indeed wanted to bury Confucianism. They were (perhaps with the exception of Hu Shih) uncompromising Westernizers, advocating in effect cultural decalcomania, wholesale transfer of patterns of modern Western civilization onto Chinese society. One might justifiably criticize them for their simplistic approach to the problem of modernization, or for their

---

[56] Hsü Chih-mo, "Tu-yao" (Poison), *Chih-mo ti shih*, p. 140.

[57] Carsun Chang, *The Development of Neo-Confucian Thought*, 2: 410.

[58] Ibid., pp. 410, 415. Chang allowed that K'ang acted "unconsciously," Hu and Ch'en, deliberately. In an earlier place Chang said that "the conscious effort on the part of a small band of Chinese intellectuals to destroy the Confucian tradition" was particularly damaging. Two among them stood prominently. "One is Mr. Ch'en Tu-hsiu who inspired the Communist Party and the other is Dr. Hu Shih, avowedly a disciple of John Dewey. . . . Dr. Hu coined a slogan, 'Down with the house of Confucius' and attained a certain measure of success" (ibid., p. 6).

[59] Cf. this volume, chapter 3, secs. 1 and 2, and chapter 4, sec. 3.

étrangisme—a belief in the absolute superioriy of all things foreign.[60] One might even condemn them for having given added impetus to the process of cultural decline. (K'ang Yu-wei was open to the same charge.) But to credit them with the annihilation of China's moral tradition was to attribute to them a power they did not possess. Shaped by a complex of historical forces operating over a long period of time, a functioning value system was not the product of a day, nor could it be demolished by a small band of intellectuals, however iconoclastic their views or eloquent their arguments. Moreover, once its vitality had sagged, it could not be revived quickly by the efforts of a few well-meaning men.

Contributors to and products of the new education, China's new intellectuals were involved, unintentionally or knowingly, in the process of cultural erosion. The process quickened its pace as time went on, and their attitude toward the old values became increasingly hostile; their hostility in turn worked further to weaken the fading tradition.[61]

Several generations of these intellectuals can be identified. First, there was "the transitional generation of the late nineteenth and early twentieth century," men whose intellectual roots lay in the old culture but whose concern about the future of their country persuaded them to acknowledge the necessity of adopting new ideas. K'ang Yu-wei, Liang Ch'i-ch'ao, and Yen Fu were outstanding members of that generation. Then came "the student generation of the beginning of the twentieth century, many of whose members must be considered as the first truly 'alienated' intellectuals of modern China." These men, the first fruits of the new educational system that K'ang among others helped to bring into being, were no longer generally committed to the traditional moral and intellectual values, even though they were in varying degrees acquainted with them. Hu Shih and Ch'en Tu-hsiu were among them, although the two men's thinking did not entirely coincide. They were followed by young intellectuals who knew very little of Chinese tradition and were not necessarily well informed of Western civilization— "the student generation of the May Fourth period"—"the young men, who had found modern schools and colleges waiting for them, containing a whole world of modern-minded people ready to give sympathy and encouragement in the inevitable fight against the family."[62]

[60] Henri Baudet, *Paradise on Earth: Some Thoughts on European Images of Non-European Man*, p. 50.

[61] Cf. Benjamin Schwartz, "The Intelligentsia in Communist China: A Tentative Comparison,' in *The Russian Intelligentsia*, ed. Richard Pipes, p. 172.

[62] Bertrand Russell, *The Problem of China*, pp. 76–77. Martin Malia, "What Is the

Two major factors seem to have molded the attitudes of this generation. The fall of the dynasty not only brought discredit to "imperial Confucianism" but ushered in a period of unrest and uncertainty. It was quite easy for many of the intellectuals of republican China to trace all the political, social, and moral maladies to "Confucianism." By equating "Confucianism" with Chinese culture, they called, not without apparent plausibility, for a radical transvaluation of all old values.

Another factor that directly shaped the attitudes of the young intellectuals was the new education itself, which worked out to be far more "Westernized" than its original proponents had intended. Soon after the inauguration of the republican government, the Confucian classics were no longer required reading in the schools; the time and attention of the students were devoted to pursuing non-Chinese subjects. By the early 1920s, not only the majority of the texts used in the colleges and schools were in foreign languages but examples cited by teachers to illustrate a principle were to a surprising extent of Western origin.[63] The younger generation was denied opportunities to gain adequate understanding of the native culture.[64] Uncritical acceptance of "democracy" and "science" proved to be a poor antidote against the chronic sicknesses of Chinese society.[65] Western-inspired "liberalism" domi-

---

Intelligentsia?", in *The Russian Intelligentsia*, p. 12, identifies two generations of Russian intelligentsia, "the fathers" of the 1840s drawn mostly from the gentry, and "the sons," or the *raznochintsy* (people of no estate in particular) of the 1860s. The fathers introduced into Russia the great ideals of humanity, reason, liberty, and democracy; the sons tried to translate these ideals into reality. But a "generation gap" developed: "the sons were more bitter and irascible than their better-bred fathers." The Russian and Chinese situations were different, but the change of attitudes among earlier and later intellectuals in both countries presented a striking similarity. Tsi C. Wang, *The Youth Movement in China*, surveys the changing attitudes and ideals of the leaders of "the youth movement," 1911–25.

[63] Y. C. Wang, *Chinese Intellectuals and the West*, p. 372, quoting from *The Reorganization of Education in China* (Paris, International Institute of Intellectual Co-operation, 1932), p. 165. This Paris publication was the result of a 1931 mission of experts sent by the League of Nations to China. The following remarks are also interesting: "A visitor who examines the plan of work in History, Political Science, or Economics in some universities in China may be pardoned if he feels uncertain whether it is for Western students who are studying in China or for Chinese students who are studying in the West" (ibid.). To the present writer's knowledge, "Westernization" was far less in evidence in inland provinces.

[64] Cf. Wang, *Chinese Intellectuals and the West*, pp. 378–421, where it is argued that modern education rendered Chinese intellectuals "politically weak."

[65] Chiang Meng-lin [Chiang Monlin], "T'an Chung-kuo hsin wen-i yün-tung," *Chung-kuo wen-i-fu-hsing yün-tung* (Taipei, 1960), reprinted in *Chuan-chi wen-hsüeh*, 11, no. 3 (Sept. 1967): 105.

nated the academic scene for a time and went out of fashion, partly because the liberals could not "manufacture the opportunity they needed."[66] Hu Shih, for his unavailing attempt to transplant a Western brain in the Chinese social body, was denounced as "one of the viruses that have made China sick."[67]

Deprived of accepted standard or criterion of thought and action, many members of the new generation became "psychologically and socially displaced persons."[68] The chaotic political situation intensified their plight. They were often as intellectually befuddled as they were emotionally frustrated. "I don't know what to do that can be considered correct," wrote Mao-tun. "This world is changing too fast, becoming too complex, too contradictory. I really am lost in it!"[69]

Moral insensibility tended to accompany intellectual bewilderment. Mao-tun characterized the aimless, hypocritical intellectual thus: "Each man has concern only for the moment. . . . Each man seeks his own personal advantage. . . . There is no reason, no purpose, no principle. And yet what each says sounds equally good."[70] One wonders how much had improved from the old days when each man's lip service to Confucius sounded equally good.

Mao-tun perhaps was a bit too sweeping in his judgment. One cannot deny that there were many among the twentieth-century intellectuals who honestly and seriously worried about the future of their country, just as many of their predecessors did in the 1890s. Time, however, had changed and their approaches to the problem of national salvation widely differed. "Nationalists choosing to sacrifice traditional culture in order to attain modernization now superseded culturalists who had hoped to modernize without giving up 'the national essence.' "[71] K'ang

---

[66] Grieder, *Hu Shih*, p. 343.

[67] Ibid., p. 359.

[68] John Israel, *Student Nationalism in China, 1927–1937*, p. 1. The author tends to overrate the influence of Chinese intellectuals on history. "In a country of illiterates, where political environment was traditional, the educated, sensitive, and mobile school population was the *vox populi*. . . . More than once, student demonstrations influenced the decisions of powerful generals and statesmen" (p. 9). It can be argued also that more than once their voice was not heard or heeded by those who wielded power, and that, in Grieder's words, they were unable to "manufacture the opportunity they needed" to put their ideas into practice.

[69] Mao-tun (Shen Yen-ping), *Mao-tun wen-chi*, *chüan* 1, "Tung-yao," p. 163. Mao-tun put these words in the mouth of "Mrs. Fang."

[70] Mao-tun, *Tsui-ch'iu*, pp. 5–6.

[71] The terminology is borrowed from Stuart R. Schram, *The Political Thought of Mao Tse-tung* (New York: Frederick A. Praeger, 1963), p. 6, which the author uses in somewhat different contexts.

Yu-wei's attempt to stem the ebbing tide of "Confucianism" was doomed by the circumstances to come to naught. But those who were ready to deal the *coup de grâce* to waning tradition also failed to achieve their aim. Rejecting everything old, the "liberals" championed Western values that the bulk of China's young intellectuals did not fully understand and for which they were not really ready. The old mental habits and behavior patterns that had undermined the native tradition could furnish no fertile soil for "democracy," "science," or "liberalism." Given peace and sufficient time, these might conceivably take root and slowly grow. But there was neither peace nor time. Civil wars came to a partial and temporary halt in the late 1920s, but the threat of foreign aggression became increasingly evident. By the late 1930s even the physical existence of the country was in grave doubt. All values, Chinese and Western, appeared to be woefully irrelevant to the critical situation. The younger intellectuals, baffled, confused, and desperate, grabbed at any "ism" that came their way, like a drowning man grabbing at any slippery plank that floated by him. "Marxism," which afforded the dubious comfort of a new faith (thanks to its dogmatic certainty) and which gave the promise of a new order, appealed particularly to them. It was preferable to "reformism," which hearkened to a past of which they knew little, and to "liberalism," which seemed to require them to be critical of everything and to assure them of nothing. The way was paved for "Maoism," a cult dedicated to sweeping away every last vestige of "feudal" (i.e., traditional) culture and every little trace of "capitalist" (i.e., Western) thought that new education had erratically disseminated in the schools.[72]

[72] Richard L. Walker, *China under Communism: The First Five Years*, p. 193, points out that of the publications put out by the Commercial Press and the Chung Hua Book Company since the turn of the century, more than 86 percent were destroyed. From January to December, 1951, in the Shanghai office alone, a total of 237 tons of books were destroyed or sold as waste paper. In Hsiang-t'an, the Hunan provincial government burned 17,000 cases of books belonging to a priceless collection; in Swatow more than 300,000 volumes were collected and burned in a bonfire that lasted over three weeks in May, 1955. Book burning was just one of the measures that the Communist rulers employed to achieve de-Sinification. One need not accept the view that "The Marxist revolution in China is a mass adoption and complete imitation of international Communism," or that the rise of Maoism means "the Russification of China," as propounded by Robert Guillan, *600 Million Chinese*, p. 27 and chapter 17. It seems clear, however, that Communism as a doctrine and as a way of life is alien to the Chinese. It is difficult to accept the view that "Red China is a more up-to-date, more ruthless, more efficient version of what the Celestial Empire had been for thousands of years" (Amaury de Riencourt, *The Soul of China*, p. 264). H. A. van Oort comes closer to the truth when he says, ". . . taking into account the mate-

It has been recently said that a society such as China's finds it difficult to modernize because of the strength of its tradition. "China is probably destined to profit from foreign models less than countries with less deeply rooted traditions."[73] This widely held view is not without general truth. However, there may be significant exceptions. Nineteenth-century Japan, for example, was a tradition-bound society, and yet its efforts at modernization achieved phenomenal success. Transformation of the Tokugawa into the Meiji order was accomplished largely by linking time-honored traditional values with constructive innovations. The samurai code and, in fact, the native version of Confucianism formed a basis for launching *bummei kaika*, a movement of intellectual reform.[74]

Perhaps a distinction could be made between a live and a moribund tradition. A live tradition evolves in a long period of time as generations of men commit themselves to its component values and vindicate them through their deeds. Thus, a society's ability to sustain an old tradition is an index to its own vitality, an indication of the fact that its members, by and large, are concerned with things that go beyond the sphere of their immediate interests. In such a society conservatives (to whom the tradition is the essence of their moral existence) can assume the role of innovators when circumstances make it clear that reorientation of their purposeful energies is necessary in order to preserve that essence. In an old society, on the other hand, in which tradition has lost its hold on the bulk of its members, opposition to change is likely to flow not from a genuine desire to uphold the waning tradition but rather from a reluctance to alter habitual modes of behavior, or from a fear of damaging vested interests. "Tradition" assumes the character of a cultural hangover; it hardly constitutes a motivating force. "Conservatism" does not entail personal commitment but is often used as a pretext. In such a society nothing constructive can really be accomplished—evolving a new social order or merely preserving the existing social fabric.

This appears to have been the situation prevailing in the last years of imperial China and the early days of republican China. All efforts at reform were bound to be utterly frustrating. Hu Shih, normally a buoyant optimist believing in the viability of a democratic way of life and

---

rial level [i.e., norms and values] of Maoism and Chinese civilization, it soon becomes clear that Maoism is a flat contradiction of the essence of the Chinese cultural heritage" ("Chinese Culture-Values, Past and Present," p. 34).

[73] Michael Gasster, *Chinese Intellectuals and the Revolution of 1911*, pp. 246–47.

[74] See the fourth section of chapter 8 in this volume.

the "New Culture," made a gloomy assessment of his efforts at modernization in the summer of 1926.

> In the last analysis, what have I done in the nine years since I returned to China? Where are the achievements? I see with my own eyes the politics of the nation going from bad to worse. . . . We may, of course, shift the responsibility by saying that this is the evil results of [the actions of] our predecessors and has nothing to do with us. But where, then, are the consequences of our own actions? Periodicals dealing with the "new art and literature" are everywhere. Everywhere one finds shallow and foolish discussions of art and literature and politics. Are these [the consequences of] our fresh endeavor?[75]

Hu said later in the same year that every institution that worked properly in Western countries functioned strangely when it was adopted in China.

> Parliament serves only to sustain shameless politicians; presidential government lends support only to [unscrupulous men like] Fung Kuo-chang and Ts'ao K'un; schools produce only good-for-nothings; political parties merely give opportunities to vend one's soul. You see, everything becomes distorted in our hands.[76]

Failure of Hu Shih and his fellow liberals to show positive results persuaded impatient intellectuals to look for salvation in other directions. Some of them cast their lot with the "radicalism of impotence."[77] It is hardly surprising that when "slaves of Confucius and Chu Hsi" became virtually extinct, "a breed of slaves of Marx and Kropotkin" readily sprang up.[78] K'ang's reformism and Hu's liberalism both failed

[75] Hu Shih, "Ou-yu tao-chung chih shu" (No. 4, to Hsü Chih-mo; Paris, Aug. 27, 1926), *Hu Shih wen-ts'un*, 3, no. 1: 77–78; translated in Grieder, *Hu Shih*, p. 218; quoted here with slight changes. Incidentally, these writers on "new poetry" remind one somewhat of the "Younger Set" among the Houyhnhnms who "knew little about the traditional Epicks" and who "scorned the painful Craft of Verse-making, preferring the Spontaneous Over-flow of their Feelings, even when they were but giving Vent, like the Aeolists, to Wind" (Matthew Hodgart, *A New Voyage to the Country of the Houyhnhnms* [London: Duckworth, 1969], pp. 59–60).

[76] Hu, "Ou-yu tao-chung chih shu" (No. 5, to Hsü Chih-mo; Nov. 14, 1926), *Hu Shih wen-ts'un*, 3, no. 1: 85.

[77] Gasster, *Chinese Intellectuals*, p. 243. Joseph A. Schumpeter uses these words in a different context. Referring to the Russian situation in 1905, he wrote, "it was precisely because of the fundamental stability of the social structure that the intellectuals, who could not hope to prevail by anything like normal methods, were drawn into a desperate radicalism and into courses of criminal violence. Theirs was the kind of radicalism whose intensity is in inverse proportion to its practical possibilities, the radicalism of impotence" (*Capitalism, Socialism, and Democracy*, p. 328).

[78] Hu, "Wo-ti ch'i-lu" (1922), *Hu Shih wen-ts'un*, 2, no. 3: 102; quoted in Grieder, *Hu Shih*, p. 189.

to achieve their respective goals. One may, however, give K'ang credit for having diagnosed China's malady more correctly than Hu. K'ang recognized the symptoms of cultural degeneration and tried to alleviate them; Hu did not see that "the Confucian shop" no longer had customers and that to smash it made no better sense than "beating a dead tiger."

K'ANG YU-WEI AS REFORMER

The chief architect of the reform program of 1898, K'ang was naturally held responsible for its failure. For over a half century various criticisms of him have been advanced by writers of diverse persuasions. The censorious words of the enemies of reform are so obviously biased that no useful purpose can be served in analyzing them.[79] However, a brief examination of some of the views of other critics may help us to arrive at a fair appraisal of K'ang's role as reformer.

Promotion of ill-considered measures by K'ang Yu-wei has often been cited as the main cause of the failure of the reform movement. A recent writer points to a lack of "real understanding of the relation of ideas and social forces" as K'ang's fatal weakness.[80] Another writer says that K'ang made proposals that were actually impossible to implement because he had grossly understimated the difficulty of the task.[81] Moreover, lacking practical experience in government and carried away by naïve idealism, K'ang and his associates demanded too much and moved too boldly for the situation, thereby generating powerful opposition and resentment.[82]

Some of K'ang's contemporaries thought that tactical and strategical errors prejudiced his cause. Sir Claude M. Macdonald, British Minister to China at the time, commented after the 1898 debacle that China's "legitimate reform efforts" were ruined by the "unwise actions" of

[79] Su Yü, *I-chiao ts'ung-pien*, collected some of the anti-reform writings of the time. Naturally, writers committed to revolution had little good to say of K'ang and his friends. Chang Ping-lin, e.g., accused K'ang of harboring unworthy motives and the "partisans of 1898" of being "immoral," although he allowed that T'an Ssu-t'ung and Yang Shen-hsiu were brave men ("Po K'ang Yu-wei lun ko-ming shu," *T'ai-yen wen-lu*, *chüan* 2, pp. 29b–30a, and "Chen hsin-tang lun," *T'ai-yen wen pieh-lu*, *chüan* 1, p. 24a).

As Shen Yün-lung points out, Chang's judgment was patently partisan (*K'ang Yu-wei p'ing-chuan*, pp. 127–28).

[80] Andrew T. Roy, "Modern Confucian Social Theory: Social Change and Its Concept of Change," p. 126.

[81] Ch'en Kung-lu, "Chia-wu chan-hou keng-tzu luan-ch'ien Chung-kuo pien-fa yün-tung chih yen-chiu," *Wen-che chi-k'an*, 3 (1933): 110–11.

[82] Ch'en Kung-lu, *Chung-kuo chin-tai shih*, *chüan hsia*, p. 486.

K'ang Yu-wei and his friends.[83] Timothy Richard, sympathetic to
K'ang and his movement, had "steadily warned the reformers against
undue haste"[84] and voiced regret after the September *coup* that they
had worked, unwisely, to do away with the existing institutions without
mature thought and careful planning.[85] Robert Hart communicated
his feelings to H. B. Morse in these terms:

> The emperor's head is set in the right direction, but his advisers, Kang
> Yu-wei and others, had had no experience of work, and they simply killed
> progress with kindness—they stuffed it, against its power of assimilation
> and digestion, with food enough in three months for three times as many
> years.[86]

Charles Beresford, after interviewing K'ang in late September in 1898,
remarked that although K'ang was a patriot, he failed because his efforts were misdirected and made too much haste.[87] Joseph K. Goodrich
wrote in 1911:

> Unfortunately for the Emperor, for all of China, Kang Yu-wei was not
> the statesman that he was reformer; had there been coupled with his
> enthusiasm a commensurate discretion, he might, thirteen years ago,
> have inaugurated the reform which shall ere long bring about "the
> coming China"; . . . But enthusiasm carried away both would-be adviser
> and his Imperial pupil.[88]

Several years later, H. B. Morse reported that "foreign opinion . . . has
generally approved the project of Kang Yu-wei, but condemned his
precipitancy."[89] Some of K'ang's Chinese contemporaries, it may be
noted, held similar views.[90]

One of the severest criticisms came from Yen Fu, who in his earlier

[83] *London Times*, Nov. 23, 1898, quoting Sir Claude McDonald.

[84] W. E. Soothill, *Timothy Richard of China*, p. 242.

[85] *Wan Kwok Kung Pao*, 12, no. 135: 2, reporting Timothy Richard's remarks at the
twelfth annual meeting of the Kuang-hsüeh hui.

[86] H. B. Morse, *The International Relations of the Chinese Empire*, 3: 155. The letter
was dated Oct. 24, 1898. F. L. Hawks Pott, *A Short History of Shanghai*, p. 145, also
quotes this letter "to a friend."

[87] Charles Beresford, *The Break-up of China*, pp. 194–95.

[88] Joseph K. Goodrich, *The Coming China*, pp. 92–93.

[89] Morse, *International Relations*, p. 154. Chap. 6 of this volume deals with "The
Hundred Days of Reform."

[90] See, e.g., Liu K'un-i, "Fu Feng Hsin-i" (Nov. 3, 1898), *Liu Chung-ch'eng-kung
i-chi, shu-tu, chüan* 13; Chien, *Wu-hsü*, 3: 634; Fei Hsing-chien, *Tz'u-hsi ch'uan-hsin lu*
(Chien, *Wu-hsü*, 1: 476); Anonymous, "K'ang Yu-wei lun," *Hsin-wen pao* (Shanghai,
Oct. 12, 1898) and *Kuo-feng pao* (Nov. 5, 1898) (Chien, *Wu-hsü*, 3: 368–71).

days was as strongly in favor of reform as K'ang. Writing in 1922, however, Yen alleged that in forcing reform in an extremely rash and im-
prudent manner, K'ang Yu-wei and Liang Ch'i-ch'ao had in effect
brought about the downfall of the Ch'ing dynasty. Had they showed a
little more patience, waiting for the time when the empress dowager
was dead and the emperor held undivided authority, then gradually
made the desired changes, the outcome would have been totally different.[91] Even K'ang Kuang-jen, who took an active part in the 1898
venture, thought his brother too ambitious and too zealous in pushing
reform and implored him to leave Peking as the situation became clearly
dangerous.[92] At about the same time, Liang Ch'i-ch'ao, too, urged
K'ang to suspend his efforts at reform and to turn his attention to education for the time being.[93]

The criticism that K'ang tried to do too much at too fast a pace
was not groundless. He indeed called for extensive and prompt changes.
Unrealistically optimistic, he expected "a complete change of the institutional system" (*kang-chi i pien*) in a matter of months and a permanent transformation within two decades.[94] He told the emperor that
"not to change would invite disaster, a complete change would bring
strength, but insignificant changes would still end in ruin."[95] Piecemeal
reform, doing the unimportant and leaving out the essential, was merely
an exercise in futility.[96] Accordingly, he and some of his colleagues
advocated various measures that were wide-ranging in scope and far-
reaching in effect. These, they believed, were necessary and not unreasonable.[97] They were not alone in taking this view. Wen Ching, who
had no part in the movement, commented sometime after 1898 that as
all previous half-hearted efforts at reform had come to naught, "a new
school of reformers" adopted "bold and comprehensive measures of

[91] Yen Fu, "Yü Hsiung Shun-ju shu," *Hsüeh-heng* (The Critical Review), no. 8
(Aug. 1922); reprinted with deletions in Chien, *Wu-hsü*, 2: 600.

[92] K'ang Kuang-jen, "Chih I-i shu," quoted in Ting Wen-chiang, *Liang Jen-kung
hsien-sheng nien-p'u ch'ang-pien ch'u-kao*, p. 58. Cf. K'ang, *Tzu-pien nien-p'u*, p. 22a; Lo,
K'ang, p. 108.

[93] Liang Ch'i-ch'ao, "Yü K'ang Yu-wei shu" (Chien, *Wu-hsü*, 1: 544).

[94] K'ang, "Shang Ch'ing-ti ti-i shu" (autumn, 1888) (Chien, *Wu-hsü*, 2: 129).

[95] K'ang, "Shang Ch'ing-ti ti-liu shu" (Jan. 29, 1898) (Chien, *Wu-hsü*, 2: 197).

[96] K'ang, "Ching-hsieh t'ien-en ping t'ung-ch'ou ch'üan-chü che" (Jan. 19, 1898)
(Chien, *Wu-hsü*, 2: 215).

[97] As it was argued in an unsigned article, "Lun Chung-kuo pien-cheng ping-wu
kuo-chi" (That the institutional reforms in China are not excessively radical), *Chih-
hsin pao*, nos. 74, 75, 76 (Dec. 13, 23, and Jan. 2, 1899), reprinted in Chien, *Wu-hsü*,
3: 290–304. The *Chih-hsin pao* (The Reformer China), published in Macao from early
1897 to late 1900, was an organ of the reform movement.

national reform, aiming not at the addition of this or that new [government] department but laying the axe at the root of the tree."[98] E. T. Williams gave a qualified approval of K'ang's endeavor. "Every one of the proposed changes in 1898," he wrote, "was practicable and looked toward the modernization of the state," although in trying to effectuate them "the pace was too swift and the method lacked tact."[99]

K'ang was in a hurry because he feared that China might soon be "sliced like a melon" by the Western powers and Japan. His fear was not entirely unfounded. Kenneth Scott Latourette, commenting on the Treaty of Shimonoseki in 1905, notes that "soon the powers began carving out for themselves leaseholds and spheres of influence," a situation not unlike Africa in the 1880s and 1890s when much of the continent was "partitioned among the earth-hungry European governments." "The prospect for China's continued independence and territorial integrity," he concludes, "was grim."[100] Victor Purcell calls attention to "the battle of concessions" fought among Japan and European powers in 1895–1900. "It seems likely," he writes, "that China was about to disintegrate, and Germany, Russia, France, Japan, and even the new 'Power,' Italy, hovered like vultures over the anticipated corpse of the 'Middle Kingdom.' " "In the middle of this scramble (the prelude to partition, it seemed), there occurred the last desperate attempt at reform under Manchu Rule."[101]

Subscribing to the Kung-yang doctrine of "the Three Ages," K'ang was basically a gradualist in his philosophical thinking. Shortly before 1898 he stated that "institutional reform should be carried out in a gentle and smooth manner; it should not be forced or done precipitately."[102] In fact, it took him some twenty years to come to the realization that only radical reform could save China.[103] All previous attempts at limited reform having proved inadequate and ineffectual,[104] he saw

[98] Wen Ching, *The Chinese Crisis from Within*, pp. 29–30.

[99] E. T. Williams, *China Yesterday and Today*, p. 415.

[100] Kenneth Scott Latourette, *A History of Modern China*, p. 88.

[101] Victor Purcell, *The Rise of Modern China*, pp. 15–16. It may be recalled that John Hay sought to forestall China's dismemberment by enunciating the "Open Door" doctrine (July 3, 1900), declaring the intention of the United States to preserve the "territorial and administrative entity" of China in the years ahead.

[102] K'ang, *Ch'un-ch'iu Tung-shih hsüeh, chüan* 6 *hsia*, p. 32b. "Gentle and smooth" is translation for *hsün shun*.

[103] He began studying "Western books" in 1879; in 1882 he "abandoned completely" his "old views" and decided to work for China's transformation (*Tzu-pien nien-p'u*, pp. 5b, 6a; Lo, *K'ang*, pp. 36, 38).

[104] Immanuel C. Y. Hsü, *The Rise of Modern China*, p. 423: "ever since China's de-

no alternative to making a "last desperate attempt" at extensive reform, and to making it as speedily as it was possible.

A British observer opined that remodeling China's political system was an "impossible reform," but, given "the present moral conditions," changing laws, the currency, etc., were "possible reforms."[105] As subsequent events show, no reform, comprehensive or piecemeal, hurried or leisurely, yielded any material benefit to the country. By the late 1890s the imperial system had deteriorated beyond repair; it was to be toppled by a revolutionary movement that was soon to materialize.[106] Any reform was impossible. Critics who faulted K'ang for being too ambitious or too hasty did not quite hit the mark.

K'ang realized that reform was not to be easy, but he did not think it impossible. Knowing that the emperor did not enjoy full authority, he advised him to carry out reform with whatever power his majesty then possessed.[107] K'ang was ridiculed by a Japanese writer for relying on imperial decrees to sweep away "the dirt which had been accumulating for thirty centuries."[108] He was criticized, by implication, of pinning his hope on an emperor who was not only powerless but personally ineffectual—"a neophyte,"[109] "an inexperienced weakling,"[110] "a sickly, worried young man"[111] stupid enough to challenge the empress dowa-

feat in the French war in 1885 the inadequacy of limited modernization had been obvious, and her defeat in the Japanese war in 1895 was irrefutable proof that the Self-strengthening Movement had failed." Wen Ching noted seventy years ago that efforts at self-strengthening had "come to naught." See note 98, above. The following conversation between Ito Hirobumi and Li Hung-chang in 1895 is revealing. Ito: "Ten years ago when I was at Tientsin, I talked about reform with the Grand Secretary. Why is it that up to now not a single thing has been reformed?" Li: "At that time when I heard you, sir, I was overcome with admiration, and furthermore I deeply admired, sir, your having vigorously changed your customs in Japan so as to reach the present stage. Affairs in my country have been so confined by tradition that I could not accomplish what I desired" (translated in Teng and Fairbank, *China's Response to the West*, p. 126). Li should have blamed bigotry and ignorance instead of tradition (in the proper sense of the word) for his lack of accomplishment.

[105] F. S. A. Bourne, "Possible and Impossible Reforms," p. 4.

[106] Kung-chuan Hsiao, "Weng T'ung-ho and the Reform Movement of 1898," pp. 197–98.

[107] K'ang, *Tzu-pien nien-p'u*, p. 19a; Lo, *K'ang*, p. 96.

[108] Miyazaki Torazō [Miyazaki Tōten], *Sanjusan-nen no yume*, p. 144. The criticism was not really fair, as K'ang sought to activate other agents of reform. See the third section in chapter 6 in this volume.

[109] P. Leroy-Beaulieu, *Awakening of the East*, p. 278.

[110] Morse, *International Relations*, 3: 153.

[111] S. L. Tikhvinsky, *Dvizhenie za reformy v Kitae v kontse XIX veka Kan Iu-wei*, p. 231, quoting the Russian Minister Cassini's report to the foreign office, dated Nov. 12, 1894. For another view of the young emperor's personal traits, see Hsiao, "Weng T'ung-ho and the Reform Movement," pp. 141–42.

ger's immense power[112] which she wielded for over three decades. One could hardly rely on such a person to carry out an extensive reform program.[113]

K'ang held a different opinion of the emperor, repeatedly referring to him as "the sage sovereign."[114] Der Ling, a Western-educated Manchu lady who had ample opportunities to watch the emperor at close range, found him "a most intelligent man with a wonderful memory."[115] That he had an accurate understanding of the political situation may be seen from what he said to Der Ling in 1903:

> I have plenty of ideas regarding the development of this country, but . . . I am not able to carry them out as I am not my own master. I don't think the Empress Dowager herself has sufficient power to alter the state of things existing in China at present. . . . I am afraid it will be a long time before anything can be done toward reform.[116]

It appears that while Kuang-shü was hardly "sage" (as K'ang said), he most probably was not stupid.

Whatever may have been the emperor's personal qualities, K'ang really had no choice but to depend on him to implement the empire-wide reform program. He was legally the supreme ruler of the realm and he heartily endorsed K'ang's ideas. The empress dowager held *de facto* power, but she did not favor K'ang's brand of reform, even though the limited reforms she authorized had fallen far short of expectations. It may be noted that K'ang did not rely exclusively on imperial decrees; he sought other means to facilitate reform, one of which was to promote "study societies" (*hsüeh hui*). The most important instance of these was the Society for the Study of National Strengthening (Ch'iang-hsüeh hui) formed in 1895 in Peking.[117] Such societies, he hoped, could galvanize scholar-officials into action, generating additional support for the movement. But the activities of Ch'iang-hsüeh hui and similar

[112] Tikhvinsky, *Dvizhenie za reformy*, p. 282, quoting *London Times*, Nov. 23, 1898.

[113] Ch'ien Mu, *Kuo-shih ta-kang* (6th printing, Taipei, 1958), p. 649.

[114] See, e.g., K'ang's letter to Liu K'un-i (autumn, 1900) (K'ang T'ung-pi, *Nan-hai K'ang hsien-sheng nien-p'u hsü-pien*, pp. 11a–12a).

[115] Der Ling, *Two Years in the Forbidden City*, p. 374. It may be recalled that Weng T'ung-ho was impressed by his imperial pupil's intelligence (see his *Weng Wen-kung-kung jih-chi*, 15/32b, 15/76a, 16/2b, 18/52b, 19/98a, and 23/101a).

[116] Der Ling, *Two Years in the Forbidden City*, pp. 190–91.

[117] Kwan-wai So [Su Chün-wei], "Western Influence and the Chinese Reform Movement of 1898," pp. 251–52. So mentions other factors that doomed the movement. For K'ang's own statement concerning the Ch'iang-hsüeh hui, see *Tzu-pien nien-p'u*, pp. 13b–14a; Lo, *K'ang*, p. 72.

organizations were no substitute for decisive moves of the government.

Some historians believe, as K'ang did, that had the emperor "actually had undisputed control" of the destiny of the country, the outcome of 1898 would have been different. Of course, it would have brought happier results, but one cannot be sure that they could be exactly what K'ang had wished to see. Many formidable obstacles stood in the way of successful modernization. Just to mention one of them: as the reform program envisioned important changes in the political, economic, and educational institutions of the empire, there must be a sizable personnel composed of men who were not only talented and knowledgeable but at the same time dedicated and courageous to carry out each of these changes. Where could the emperor (or K'ang) find a sufficient number of such men? K'ang advised the emperor to disregard established procedure of appointment and to entrust minor officials with the task of reform.[118] The question still remains: given the generally demoralized officialdom, what assurance was there that he could recruit enough worthy men among the junior functionaries to serve him? Wang An-shih, the celebrated reformer of eleventh-century China, enjoyed the full confidence of the Jen-tsung emperor, but found recruitment of reliable personnel a baffling problem.[119] In the spring of 1901, Chang Chih-tung and Liu K'un-i jointly submitted to the imperial court their plans of post-Boxer reform. After seeing the documents, Jung-lu commented, "The proposals are good, but there is nobody to carry them out."[120] It is difficult to ascertain what he had in mind when he uttered these words. Taken at their face value, they clearly point to a serious predicament.

An even more serious obstacle to reform was, of course, the hopelessly dilapidated political structure itself. As I have said in another connection,

> The imperial system, beset with personal and factional strifes, cursed with an inept and decaying administration, and perplexed by recurrent internal and international crises, was in an advanced stage of disintegration. It could not furnish the conditions for accomplishing anything of positive benefit to itself; the elixir of reform could not be administered

---

[118] K'ang, *Tzu-pien nien-p'u*, p. 19a; Lo, *K'ang*, pp. 96–97.

[119] James T. C. Liu, *Reform in Sung China: Wang An-shih (1021–1086) and His New Policies*, chap. 4, discusses the problem of "bureaucratic practices below the Confucian standards."

[120] Hsü T'ung-hsin, *Chang Wen-hsiang-kung nien-p'u*, *chüan* 7, p. 20, compiler's note.

to a dying regime. . . . A worthy cause was thus doomed to be a lost cause.[121]

Chang Yüan-chi, who took an active but subordinate part in 1898, reminisced fifty years later: "At that time we wished to change the destiny of our country by reform. Only later did we realize that it was all a dream."[122] K'ang Yu-wei, in his later years, must have had similar feelings when in his "heaven roaming"—a sort of transcendental day-dream—he viewed the human world about which he once had been deeply concerned, as "more ephemeral than the ant colony in 'Nan-k'o meng.' "[123] Perhaps he could have found consolation in the thought that there is no comparison between that which is lost by not succeeding and that which is lost by not trying.

[121] Hsiao, "Weng T'ung-ho and the Reform Movement," p. 196. Historians have mentioned various factors that prevented the reform movement from attaining success. See, e.g., Hsü, *The Rise of Modern China*, pp. 530–36; Huang Ta-shou, *Chung-kuo chin-tai shih*, 2: 591–98; and Tikhvinsky, *Dvizhenie za reformy*, p. 343.

[122] Chang Yüan-chi, "Wu-hsü cheng-pien chih hui-i," transcription of an oral statement published in *Hsin chien-she*, vol. 1, no. 3 (Oct. 6, 1949) and reprinted in Chien, *Wu-hsü*, 4: 329.

[123] See chapter 2 in this volume, at note 85.

PART IV
UTOPIAN IDEAS

Chapter 10

THE ROAD TO UTOPIA

LEVELS AND PHASES OF THOUGHT

K'ang Yu-wei's social thinking moved on two levels. On one level, he directed his attention to the practical affairs of China in the last decades of the nineteenth century when he endeavored to salvage the sinking empire through reform and, later, in the first decades of the twentieth when he engaged himself in scathing criticisms of the tottering republic. On another level, he disengaged himself from concerns with immediate situations and sallied forth into theorizations and speculations which had little direct contact with reality. Often he moved simultaneously on both these levels; sometimes he shifted back and forth from one level to the other. In this way he assumed a double role: as a practical reformer and as a utopian thinker.

He was reported to have said that his intellectual position had become permanently fixed by the time he reached thirty *sui*.[1] This claim was refuted by the fact that he modified his views perceptibly on more occasions than one during his long career.[2] However, so far as his social thought is concerned, this claim is not entirely groundless. A survey of his writings shows that some of the basic ideas concerning man and

---

[1] Liang Ch'i-ch'ao, *Ch'ing-tai hsüeh-shu kai-lun*, p. 149. *Intellectual Trends in the Ch'ing Period*, translation of the above by Immanuel C. Y. Hsü, p. 109 (hereafter cited as Hsü, *Intellectual Trends in the Ch'ing Period*).

[2] Ch'ien Mu, *Chung-kuo chin san-pai nien hsüeh-shu shih*, pp. 634–62 and 689–709; Hsiao Kung-ch'üan, *Chung-kuo cheng-chih ssu-hsiang shih*, 5: 704–10; Kung-chuan Hsiao, "K'ang Yu-wei and Confucianism," pp. 132–62; the fourth section of chapter 3 of this volume.

society that came to him in the 1880s remained with him essentially unaltered for many years.[3] When later experience proved some of his earlier views to be untenable, he met the requirements of the situation largely by giving prominence to some of his ideas that appeared to be relevant and letting others drop into the background or, momentarily at least, entirely out of sight. Thus he moved from one level of thought to another, giving rise to different phases of thought. But, as one phase followed upon another, little that was really new appeared. These phases, therefore, did not constitute true developmental stages but were rather successive alternations of levels of thought.

Several such phases can be distinguished. Having prepared himself for independent thinking through studying texts of Confucianism and Buddhism, Chinese institutional history, and "Western books" in 1878–84,[4] he began to lay the first foundations of his social thought. He outlined his ideas in two unpublished works, "Substantial Truths and Universal Principles" (*Shih-li kung-fa*; hereafter cited as *Truths*) and "Esoteric and Exoteric Essays of Master K'ang" (*K'ang-tzu nei-wai p'ien*; hereafter, *Essays*).[5] In these youthful works he devoted much attention to such matters as moral values and social relationships. He was not, at this time, concerned with practical affairs of any particular time or individual country, but with "truths" and "principles" that he believed to be universally and eternally valid. He was not as yet ready for the construction of a utopia; but here he had in fact laid the earliest foundations of his utopian thought.

He suspended his theoretical inquiries in 1888 when he made his first attempt at calling the government's attention to the need of reform.[6] From then on until the autumn of 1898 he became increasingly involved in the reform movement that culminated in the historic "one hundred days." During these years part of his time was taken up by other intellectual activities—lecturing to a small group of students and

[3] This tenacity may have been due partly to his unusual self-confidence (see the first section of chapter 2 in this volume).

[4] K'ang, *Tzu-pien nien-p'u*, pp. 4b–6a (hereafter, *Nien-p'u*); Jung-pang Lo, *K'ang Yu-wei: A Biography and a Symposium*, pp. 32–45.

[5] K'ang referred to the first of the two works as *Jen-lei kung-li* in *Nien-p'u*, pp. 7a, 8a. A microfilm copy made from manuscript copies of these works is available in the Far Eastern Library, University of Washington. The *Wan-shen kung-fa, Jen-lei kung-li*, and *Shih-li kung-fa*, all of which K'ang mentioned in his *Nien-p'u*, were probably early drafts of his *Ta-t'ung shu* (1902). See Hsiao, "K'ang Yu-wei and Confucianism," pp. 106–15 and chapter 3, second section, of this volume.

[6] A long memorial submitted to the emperor, known sometimes as "the first memorial," in late 1888; available in Chien Po-tsan et al., *Wu-hsü pien-fa*, 2: 123–31.

setting forth his interpretations of Confucianism.[7] For the time being
he postponed his search for "universal principles."

Living as an exile in foreign lands in the years immediately following
the collapse of the reform movement he found opportunities to resume
the line of thought interrupted in 1888. In 1902 he put into final form
his utopian work, *The Book of the Great Community* (*Ta-t'ung shu*; hereafter, *Community*).[8] Fully aware of the far-reaching implications of some
of his ideas expressed in that book, he withheld its publication until
1913 when he printed the first two books (the less startling portions) in
the periodical *Compassion* (*Pu-jen*).[9] That he continued to regard his
utopian ideal as valid and valuable may be seen from the fact that he
reprinted in 1919 the same portions that had appeared in *Compassion*
and wrote a short preface together with three didactic poems to introduce them.[10]

Meanwhile, he turned his attention to another direction. The *Proposal
Concerning the Official System* (*Kuan-chih i*) of 1903 marked the beginning
of the second period of his interest in practical affairs.[11] A succession of
essays and treatises on China's current problems appeared between 1903
and 1922, among which the most important for our purpose are *An Essay on National Salvation through Material Upbuilding* (*Wu-chih chiu-kuo lun*;
hereafter, *Salvation*), 1905; "Discourse on China's Perilous Situation
Caused by the Error of Completely Following Europe and America,
and Abandoning *in toto* the National Heritage" (Chung-kuo tien-wei
wu tsai ch'üan-fa Ou-Mei erh chin-ch'i kuo-ts'ui shuo; hereafter, *Dis-*

[7] Namely, in his *Hsin-hsüeh wei-ching k'ao*, begun in 1892 and completed in 1896;
and a number of commentaries on various Confucian classics done around 1901–2.
See *Nien-p'u*, pp. 10a–b, 11a, 14b, and K'ang T'ung-pi, *Nan-hai hsien-sheng nien-p'u
hsü-pien* (a sequel to the *Nien-p'u* mimeographed for private distribution, 1958; hereafter, *Nien-p'u hsü-pien*), pp. 12b–33a; Lo, *K'ang*, pp. 53–57, 76, 189, and 192–93.

[8] *Nien-p'u hsü-pien*, p. 22b; Lo, *K'ang*, pp. 192–93.

[9] The complete work was not published until 1935, about eight years after K'ang's
death.

[10] The concluding lines of the second poem read somewhat as follows:
  "To the Great Community I point the way,
  To which I wish men to lead."
He said in the preface: "I was twenty-seven *sui* . . . when I wrote the *Ta-t'ung shu*,
thinking then that I had to wait a century before I would see its fulfillment. Unexpectedly, within thirty-five years the League of Nations was formed and I personally witness the realization of *Ta-t'ung*." The poems and the preface, given in the
1935 edition, are unfortunately omitted both in the 1956 Peking edition and the
1958 Taipei edition.

[11] *Nien-p'u hsü-pien*, p. 34a; Lo, *K'ang*, p. 192. This work of K'ang was completed
in 1901 and published in 1905, by Kuang-chih shu-chü, Shanghai. Portions of it appeared in various issues of the *Hsin-min ts'ung-pao*, edited by Liang Ch'i-ch'ao, 1902–3.

course), 1913; and "Essay on China's Spiritual Revival" (Chung-kuo huan-hun lun; hereafter, *Revival*), 1913.[12] K'ang now descended from the lofty utopian level and reverted to a position somewhat similar to that taken in the last decades of the previous century by men like Fung Kuei-fen, Wang Hsien-ch'ien, and Chang Chih-tung,[13] that China's future lay in Western-style industrialization and, at the same time, in the preservation of her own nonmaterial culture.

Deeply disturbed by the political changes occurring since 1898 and repeatedly frustrated in his well-intentioned attempts "to save the country," he finally became discouraged. Slowly but surely he turned his eyes away from the perplexed world of men and toward a transcendental region above and beyond even the "Great Community." He now ceased virtually to be either a social or utopian thinker and assume the role of a prophet of "outopia"[14]—a "Never-never-land" in which human beings, blissfully unencumbered with moral values or social relationships, would be completely emancipated from worldly care. If the vision that K'ang unveiled in his final major work, the *Lectures on the Heavens* (*Chu-t'ien chiang*; hereafter, *Lectures*) written in 1926,[15] can in any sense be called utopian, then in Lewis Mumford's terminology, it pointed not to a "utopia of reconstruction" but a "utopia of escape."[16]

UNIVERSALIZATION AND WESTERNIZATION

Intellectuals of the late nineteenth century reacted generally in three

[12] The first-mentioned piece was written in 1905, while K'ang was in Los Angeles. It was printed in his "Records of Travels in Eleven European Countries" (*Ou-chou shih-i kuo yu-chi*), as an appendix, and published in book form in 1919, by Ch'ang-hsing shu-chü, Shanghai. The second work appeared in the *Pu-jen*, nos. 6 and 7 (July and August, 1913). The third work appeared in the same journal, no. 8 (November, 1913), pp. 1–8.

[13] Fung Kuei-fen, *Chiao-pin-lu k'ang-i*, 1860. Wang Hsien-ch'ien, "Fu Pi Yung-nien shu," reproduced in Su Yü, *I-chiao ts'ung-pien* (1898), *chüan* 6. Chang Chih-tung, *Ch'üan hsüeh p'ien* (Hu-pei kuan-shu chü ed., 1898), passim. This book was partially translated by Samuel I. Woodbridge as *China's Only Hope* (Edinburgh and London: Oliphant, Anderson and Ferrier, 1901).

[14] Lewis Mumford, *The Story of Utopias*, preface: "utopia might refer either to the Greek 'eutopia,' which means the good place, or to 'outopia,' which means no place."

[15] This was privately printed in 1930. I wish to thank Dr. Jung-pang Lo for giving me a copy of this fascinating book together with the *Nien-p'u* and *Nien-p'u hsü-pien*. For a partial account of it, see my article, "K'ang Yu-wei's Excursion into Science," in the symposium edited by Dr. Lo cited in note 4, above.

[16] Mumford, *Story of Utopias*, p. 15, indicates that the latter "leaves the external world the way it is," whereas the former "seeks to change it so that one may have intercourse with it on one's own terms." The *Ta-t'ung shu* is a utopia of reconstruction in this sense.

ways to the impact of Western civilization. At one extreme were the "conservatives" who found nothing wrong with the Chinese tradition and everything distasteful in "learning from the barbarians."[17] At the other extreme were those who saw nothing good in that tradition and every reason for unconditional Westernization.[18] Between these extremes stood two groups: a large number of men who, in varying degrees, acknowledged deficiencies in "Chinese learning" and recommended in effect partial Westernization;[19] and a smaller number who believed that, as differences between East and West were more nominal than basic, to reform China's outmoded political, economic, and educational systems was not Westernization but in reality universalization—bringing Chinese culture up to that stage of civilization to which all mankind should do well to attain.[20] There is good reason for supposing that those who took this position were persuaded, somewhat like a Chinese philosopher of Sung times, that as "the truth permeates all under Heaven," the same "principle" holds good for all;[21] or perhaps like an international statesman of today, that "civilized men everywhere have common ideals."[22] Whatever may have been the motivation or basic philosophy of these Chinese universalizers, there is little doubt that their efforts possessed considerable significance in modern Chinese intellectual history. For they in effect were consciously or unknowingly working at an intellectual synthesis. Crude and unconvincing as their efforts must be, since their knowledge and understanding of

[17] Wo-jen was the most outstanding representative of this view. See Document 19, "Wo-jen's Objection to Western Learning, 1867," in Ssu-yü Teng and John K. Fairbank, *China's Response to the West*, pp. 76–77.

[18] Ho Ch'i and Hu Li-yüan came close to this position. See their *Hsin-cheng chen-ch'üan*, especially the "Ch'ien tsung hsü" and "Tseng lun shu-hou."

[19] See Teng and Fairbank, *China's Response*, passim, for brief excerpts from writings of those who recommended partial Westernization.

[20] E.g., T'ang Chen, who came close to this position. According to T'ang, "the Westerners' political and educational systems were based mostly on [principles indicated in] the *Chou-li* and their technology, mostly on [the writings of] the philosophers [of the pre-Ch'in period]" (*Wei yen, chüan* 1, p. 11b).

[21] Lu Chiu-yüan (Lu Hsiang-shan, 1140–1225). Quoted in Fung Yu-lan, *A History of Chinese Philosophy*, 2: 573, 574.

[22] Remarks made by U Thant, Acting Secretary General of the United Nations, reported in *NEA Journal* (National Education Association, Washington, D.C.), July 1962: "It seems to be assumed that there is one civilization in the East and quite a different one in the West, and that this inevitably results in tension or conflict between people of different geographical regions. I consider this concept a fallacy. A civilized Burman will not differ essentially from a civilized American, but both will differ widely from their relatively uncivilized compatriots. Civilized men everywhere have common ideals, and these ideals have a force that unites."

Western civilization were, under the circumstances, bound to be superficial and fragmentary, nevertheless, they must be recognized as men
with better qualifications for places of honor in the history of social
thought than the pure traditionalist or the simple Westernizer.

K'ang Yu-wei, on one level of his social thought and during certain
periods of his career, belonged unquestionably to this last group and
was in fact its leading figure, even though on another level he must be
counted among the half-way Westernizers. Obviously, it is in the former
capacity that he could lay claim to historical eminence.

The impact of the West on K'ang tells an interesting story. It yields
clues not only to the process through which his own social thought took
shape but also to the way in which a person thoroughly steeped in the
native tradition undertook to resolve the challenging problem of assessing the value of that tradition in the light of "Western learning."
K'ang's soul-searching efforts inaugurated in effect a historic trend;
the net outcome marked the first major item of a series of intellectual
transformations that came about in the first half of the twentieth century.

He came into contact with Western civilization when he was about
twenty. Prior to 1879 his intellectual horizon did not extend beyond
books on Confucianism, Taoism, and Buddhism. But in that year he
began to read "Western books."[23] The political, social, and material
conditions of New York, Washington D.C., London, and Paris described glowingly in one of these books must have aroused his curiosity,
if not genuine interest. He soon paid a visit to Hong Kong, which impressed him greatly and confirmed what he read about Europe and
America. He now collected and studied in earnest "books on Western

---

[23] These included "A Compendium of Recent Events in Western Countries" (*Hsi-
kuo chin-shih hui-pien*), by John Young Allen and others, which carried translations of
news items from foreign newspapers; and Li Kuei's "New Notes on Travels Around
the Globe" (*Huan-yu ti-ch'iu hsin-lu*), published in 1878, with a preface by Li Hung-
chang, then Governor-general of Chih-li. This four-*chüan* work consists of three main
parts: (1) "Brief Notes on the American Exposition" (*Mei-hui chi-lüeh*), relating his
observations made in the centennial international exposition held in Philadelphia,
May 10 to November 10, 1876; (2) "Sight-seeing Jottings" (*Yu-lan sui-pi*), reporting
on his trip through Philadelphia, Washington, D.C., Hartford, Conn., New York
City, London, and Paris; conditions of the Chinese students in Hartford and Chinese
immigrants in San Francisco; history of Suez Canal; discussion with a Western friend
concerning businessmen living in foreign lands; life generally in Western countries,
etc.; (3) "Diary of An Eastern Trip" (*Tung-hsing jih-chi*), describing his journey to
the United States by way of Japan, with a map of the world showing his itinerary.
This book is reprinted in Wang Hsi-ch'i, comp., *Hsiao-fang-hu-chai yü-ti ts'ung-ch'ao*
(Shanghai, 1877–97), 12th *chih*, pp. 78a–90a and 91a–125a, with minor changes.

learning."[24] A visit to Shanghai in 1882 prompted him to make "extensive purchases" of such books and "to change completely" his old views. One result of this intellectual metastasis was K'ang's decision to give up his studies for the examinations so that he could devote himself exclusively to "new knowledge and deep thinking."[25] One is tempted to surmise that K'ang's desertion from the Old Text school and conversion to the New Text was also in part a consequence of his newly developed enthusiasm for Western learning. It may be recalled that as late as 1880 he was still committed to the Old Text and wrote a treatise with the avowed purpose of "exposing the errors" of one of the most renowned of the masters of the rival school. But he soon realized his own "mistake" and relented. Publication of the *Study of the Classics Forged in the Hsin Period (Hsin-hsüeh wei-ching k'ao)* in 1891[26] marked the consummation of the change referred to above. Meanwhile, he started to formulate a social theory of his own. With the writing of the two unpublished works in 1885–87, of which mention has already been made, he ceased virtually to be "the last of the Confucians"[27]—Confucians who carried on the hallowed old tradition—even though he continued to profess and defend "Confucianism" as he understood it.

In this phase of his thought covering the years from the early 1880s to the 1900s, K'ang's attitude toward Western civilization appears to have changed several times. At first, apparently fascinated by its contents and awed by its successes, in both its technological and institutional aspects, K'ang was inclined to endorse it with little reservation. He did not advocate the abandonment of Chinese tradition but worked in effect to transform it. This was done partly in his reinterpretation of the Confucian classics, rejecting the Old Text and honoring the New in which he saw essential agreement with Western learning, and partly in the unconventional ideas which he sketched in the *Truths* and, to a lesser extent, in the *Essays*.

Ch'ien Mu was of the opinion that in reinterpreting Confucianism K'ang was actually "using the barbarian to convert the Chinese."[28] There is some truth in this observation. However, it must be stressed that K'ang's implicit endorsement of Western ideas did not amount to

---

[24] *Nien-p'u*, p. 5b; Lo, *K'ang*, p. 36.

[25] *Nien-p'u*, p. 6a; Lo, *K'ang*, p. 38. The next year (1883), he bought issues of the *Wan Kwok Kung Pao* (A Review of the Times) and studied in earnest mathematics, natural sciences, histories of Western countries, and records of travels in foreign lands.

[26] *Nien-p'u*, pp. 5b and 10a; Lo, *K'ang*, pp. 36, 53.

[27] Lin Mousheng, *Men and Ideas*, p. 215.

[28] Ch'ien Mu, *Chung-kuo chin san-pai nien hsüeh-shu shih*, p. 660.

a deliberate attempt at Westernization. It stemmed rather from the conviction that at their best East and West were identical in essence. Confucianism itself may have afforded a basis for such a conviction. The concept of "all under Heaven" was universalist in implication. The notion that "to the true king nothing was external or foreign" and the ideal that "the world was common to all"[29] added concrete meaning to that concept. It was but a short step from this classical outlook to the Neo-Confucian sentiment that truths are universal, to which reference has been made a while ago. It is entirely conceivable that K'ang, who was fully acquainted with the Confucian classics and with Sung Confucianism, readily came to the position that so far as truths were concerned "nothing was foreign" and that therefore for a social thinker what really mattered was whether or not a given institution or value possessed intrinsic (i.e., universal) validity, instead of whether it was of native or foreign origin. From such a position he found it easy to reject specific Chinese institutions and values that he considered unacceptable and, at the same time, to fit Western ideas into his universalist scheme.

It is interesting to see that K'ang, a man steeped in the Confucian tradition, came to such an intellectual position as a result of his reaction to the early waves of the "tide from the West." Some of his views anteceded ideas that came into vogue in the 1920s and 1930s—in particular, socialist ideas and ideas concerning "democracy and science." There was, however, a significant difference. While the latter-day radical thinkers who had little or no real training in Chinese tradition and therefore did not hesitate to "smash the Confucian shop,"[30] worked for Westernization pure and simple, K'ang tried in effect to accomplish a synthesis by means of his universalizing formula, which itself had some of its roots in Confucian tradition.

K'ang was not alone in discovering the universalizing formula. It appears that other thoughtful men of his generation who were versed in Chinese tradition and brought into contact with Western culture often tended either to view the latter in the light of the former, or conversely, to scrutinize the former in the light of the latter, and eventually to discover basic similarities between the two.[31] A younger con-

---

[29] Chiang Monlin, *Tides from the West*, p. 75.

[30] See Tse-tsung Chow, "The Anti-Confucian Movement in Early Republican China," in Arthur F. Wright, *The Confucian Persuasion*, pp. 288–312; Andrew T. Roy, "Modern Confucian Social Theory," chap. 4; and Hsiao, "K'ang Yu-wei and Confucianism," p. 206 (cf. chapter 4 in this volume).

[31] Chiang, *Tides from the West*, pp. 43–44. Years before, Wang T'ao had already seen the essential identity of human minds and cultures. See "Yüan jen" (On Benevolence)

temporary of K'ang reported his intellectual experience, as a student in the United States, in the years immediately following the Russo-Japanese war, in these terms:[32]

> I began to see the oneness of the East and West and appreciate the dictum of Lu Hsiang-shan . . . that "the sages born of the Eastern Sea will have the same mind and therefore the same reason as the sages of the Western Sea. . . . " So I followed the teachings of Mencius and Lu Hsiang-shan that in learning we must grasp the essential [i.e., basic similarities] and neglect the trifles [i.e., non-essential differences] and make our reasoning power the sole arbiter. Thus I began to establish myself on the solid rock of reasoning instead of traditional beliefs.

Apparently, K'ang went through a comparable experience after he studied "Western books," although the "reasoning power" that he thus developed led him to more daring and more extensive experiments in social thought than his younger contemporary. At any rate, both these men should be called universalizers rather than Westernizers.[33]

In the case of K'ang this universalizing phase eventually gave place to another in which he became critical not only of Chinese tradition but of Western civilization as well. This change became discernible in a number of writings produced after 1898, when he lived for many years as an exile in foreign countries. Direct observation of social institutions and usages in the West afforded him a more intimate acquaintance with, though not necessarily a more accurate knowledge of, Western civilization. Close-range scrutiny dispelled his adulatory view of Western social and political institutions but, somewhat paradoxically, intensified his admiration for Western material civilization. Two works completed in the first decade of the new century reflected most clearly this important change. In the *Community* (1902) he condemned by implication the basic institutions of China and the West as they existed—the state, the family, and private property—but pointed to further advancement of science and technology as a basis of man's hope for attaining unmixed blessings in utopia.[34] In the lengthy *Salvation*

---

and "Yüan tao" (On the Way), in *T'ao-yüan wen-lu wai-pien*, *chüan* 1, pp. 4b–5b, and p. 2b.

[32] Chiang, *Tides from the West*, p. 62.

[33] Their position thus differed from that of post-Tokugawa Japan's "first-generation intellectuals" who were said to have "plunged blindly" into the "progressive and aggressive civilization" of the West and "learned blindly from it." Makato Oda, "Third-Generation Intellectuals," pp. 101–6. Oda is a student at Tokyo University.

[34] K'ang's veiled but ruthless criticisms of existing social institutions are found in most of the first nine books of the *Ta-t'ung shu*, and his "naïve confidence" in science and technology is clearly implied in the final book. The phrase in quotes is Derk Bodde's. See translator's note, Fung, *History of Chinese Philosophy*, 2: 690.

(1905) he stated emphatically that as the strength of the West lay entirely in its material civilization and China's weakness was due exclusively to the lack of modern science and technology, the only way for China to survive and achieve greatness was to adopt Western technology and retain her own nonmaterial culture.[35] Accordingly, in the first years of the Republic he pushed with increased vigor his campaign to establish Confucianism as "state religion"[36] and implored his countrymen not to commit themselves to "complete Westernization," thus forsaking the "national heritage"—China's traditional political, social, and moral values.

Thus having traversed, both physically and intellectually, the Eastern and Western world, K'ang offered a drastically different guidebook to his compatriots, pointing the way not to utopia of the future but to a viable fatherland realizable at the present. But instead of advocating institutional and intellectual reform as he did in 1898, he recommended simple industrial upbuilding. In so doing he came superficially close to the position taken by Chang Chih-tung in his *Exhortation to Learning* (*Ch'üan-hsüeh p'ien*) written, ironically, with the purpose of refuting K'ang's "radical" ideas of reform.[37]

PATH FINDING IN TWO WORLDS

"The Esoteric and Exoteric Essays of Master K'ang" and the "Substantial Truths and Universal Principles," which he wrote in 1885–87,[38] represented the first constructive results of his reaction to Western civi-

---

[35] This essay was written while he was in Los Angeles, California, and was printed as an appendix to his "Record of Travels in Eleven European Countries," published in Shanghai, 1906. The author's preface to this essay, written in 1904, shows clearly that K'ang was deeply impressed by the results of Western industrial development. The essay was reissued separately later, the sixth printing of which was issued in 1919, by Ch'ang-hsing shu-chü, Shanghai.

[36] Hsiao, "K'ang Yu-wei and Confucianism," pp. 175–96, discusses K'ang's "Confucian religion" movement; see also chapter 4 in this volume.

[37] More on this point later in this chapter. Chang's book, as already indicated, was partially and somewhat unsatisfactorily translated by Samuel I. Woodbridge.

[38] In the *Nien-p'u*, pp. 7a–8a, passim, K'ang gave the impression that he started to write the "Universal Truths of Mankind" (*Jen-lui kung-li*), which presumably was the same essay known otherwise as "Substantial Truths," in 1885 and to do the *Essays* the next year, and that he continued to work on both of them simultaneously until 1887. It is possible, however, as internal evidence shows, that the *Essays* was actually completed a little earlier, as it represented a slightly earlier stage of his thinking. One revealing clue is found in the *Truths*, in the section on "Husband and Wife" (*Fu-fu men*), where he referred to 1891 as "the present year," the year in which he began to teach in Ch'ang-hsing li, in the city of Canton, after he returned from Peking late in 1889 and cited from what he called the "Paris census" of 1891.

lization. According to his own statements, the influence of Western science on him was at least as decisive as Western social ideas. From the periodical *A Review of the Times* (*Wan Kwok Kung Pao*)[39] and other sources he gained some knowledge of mathematics, astronomy, geography, physics, chemistry, and Western history.[40] Geometry proved to be, for a while, particularly intriguing to him and suggested to him a novel methodology for studying man and society.[41] The microscope and telescope opened up for him an entirely new intellectual perspective.[42] These and other elements of Western knowledge produced a number of crucial changes in him. They enabled him to break out of the confines of the traditional outlook and prepared him for the universalizing tendency that was to dominate his social thought for many years to come. They gave him a sort of scientific (or pseudoscientific) approach to philosophical enquiry and brought him occasionally close to a materialistic interpretation of human life. All this was given expression, though in a somewhat confused and limited way, in his first ambitious work, the *Essays*.[43]

The fifteen essays comprising this book do not present anything approaching a systematic philosophy, but they serve to indicate the general tenor of K'ang's thinking at this stage. Like many a social thinker he began with certain assumptions about human nature. Man's intelligence, he said, was the product of cosmic and biological evolution. Moral sentiments, together with consciousness itself, were functions of "the cerebrum and cerebellum" (*ta-nao, hsiao-nao*) and "the nervous system" (*nao-ch'i-chin*).[44] This was K'ang's way of saying that human

---

[39] K'ang probably had consulted at this time at least vols. 14 and 15 (1881–82 and 1882–83). Publication of this periodical was suspended with vol. 15.

[40] *Nien-p'u*, p. 6a; Lo, *K'ang*, p. 38.

[41] *Nien-p'u*, pp. 7a–b; Lo, *K'ang*, p. 42. K'ang mentioned in the *Essays*, in *Ch'ao-yü p'ien*, the *Chi-ho yüan-pen*, translation made in 1852–55 by Alexander Wylie and Li Shan-lan of Euclid's *Elements*, which presumably was the main source of his mathematical knowledge. John F. W. Herschel's *Outlines of Astronomy* (1851 ed.) translated by Wylie and Li as *T'an t'ien* (Discoursing on the Heavens), published sometime after 1855, may have furnished some of K'ang's knowledge of Western astronomy.

[42] *Nien-p'u*, pp. 6b–7a; Lo, *K'ang*, pp. 40–42. In the *Essays*, in the section on "Perception and Understanding" (*Chüeh-shih p'ien*), K'ang mentioned both the microscope and the telescope; in the section on "Creation of the World" (*Ch'ao-yü p'ien*) he showed some knowledge of astronomy.

[43] This collection of fifteen pieces was given the title *K'ang-tzu nei-wai p'ien*, literally, "inner and outer essays." K'ang explained that the "inner" or esoteric essays deal with the principles governing Heaven, earth, man, and things, while the "outer" or exoteric essays cover matters relative to government, education, arts, and music (*Nien-p'u*, p. 7b).

[44] *Essays*, "Li-ch'i p'ien."

behavior and human values were conditioned, in the last analysis, by neurophysiological processes.

Man was capable of sensory and emotional experiences—psychological responses to external stimuli—because, according to K'ang, he was born of the yin and yang ethers (*ch'i*), which were material or substantial (*chih*). He had a liking for things composed of matters which "agreed" with his senses; he disliked those composed of matters which "disagreed" with them. Basically, "likes and dislikes" were all that man possessed in his psyche; these, in fact, constituted the primary psychological states from which all others evolved. In K'ang's words:

> Desire is the manifestation of like; delight is an expansive manifestation of like; joy is an extreme manifestation of like. Pity results when the object of extreme liking is not obtained. This is what is called love (*jen*). . . . All these are expressions of the yang ether. Anger is the manifestation of dislike; fear is extreme dislike which one cannot avoid. This is what is called righteousness (*i*). All these are expressions of the yin ether.[45]

Human nature being essentially identical, the possession of the capacity for experiencing "likes" and "dislikes" was common to all races of men, Chinese or European. Even nonsentient things, such as the lodestone, were capable of attracting and repelling. Difference between man and things was solely a matter of degree: the latter experienced smaller quantities of "likes" and "dislikes" than the former.[46]

K'ang attached importance to "desires," which existed in all sentient beings. "All creatures," he wrote, "that have blood and breath, necessarily have desires. Having desires they invariably give them free play. To be without desires is to be dead."[47] This readily led to K'ang's hedonistic view that even the sage could not do without the enjoyment of pleasurable things, such as elegant clothing and sumptuous dwellings, although he judiciously placed limitations on such enjoyment by means of appropriate institutions.[48] For this reason, social and political institutions existed universally, in China and all other countries, European as well as Asian; they were "a natural consequence" of imposing restrictions upon man's desires.[49]

[45] *Essays*, "Ai-wu p'ien."
[46] Ibid. Cf. the passage in "Shih-je p'ien," where he linked virtues and vices respectively to the "wet-warm ethers" and "dry-cold ethers" that emanated from the *yin* and *yang* ethers.
[47] *Essays*, "Pu-jen p'ien," 2nd. par.
[48] *Essays*, "Jen-wo p'ien," 1st par.
[49] *Essays*, "Hsing-hsüeh p'ien."

The universal existence of institutions, however, constituted no guarantee that the institutional system of a particular country would reach perfection or be free from degeneration. As a matter of fact, K'ang pointed out, China was at the time suffering from defective institutions that sanctioned and perpetuated human inequalities. As K'ang put it:

To exalt the sovereign and to look down upon the subject, to attach importance to men and to slight women, to show consideration to "honorable" people and to repress "dishonorable" ones—these constitute China's custom and right conduct. [In the past] the positions of the subject and wife had been depressed to the lowest possible level. Coming down to the present, ministers of state, kneeling in abject submissiveness [before the sovereign] are so awed by his majestic presence that they dare not speak out. Wives, downtrodden and repressed, remain untutored and unenlightened. . . . I am afraid all these are merely results of convention; they do not accord with the highest principles of justice and reason. Now according to the nature of things, whatever is put under excessive pressure will inevitably break away [from that pressure]. I say, at the end of one hundred years all these will change. The sovereign will no longer be exalted nor the subject looked down upon, men and women will be regarded as of equal importance, and there will be parity between the honorable and dishonorable.[50]

K'ang equated this view with what he called "the Buddha's doctrine of equality." In all probability, he received inspiration also from what he read about Western social and political ideas. However, it would be incorrect to conclude from this that K'ang had at that time committed himself to renouncing Chinese traditional values *in toto*. The fact is, when he wrote the *Essays* he was not as yet quite sure of his basic standpoint and vacillated between two almost opposite positions. On the one hand, he adopted the universalizing approach that was destined to characterize much of his social thought; on the other hand, he clung, implicitly and perhaps unintentionally, to certain aspects of the Chinese tradition. He identified himself with all mankind declaring that "the Heavens" were his home;[51] at the same time, he justified conformity with Chinese institutions and values, on the ground that what was absolutely right and reasonable could not be known for sure. The following words of his are particularly revealing.

[50] *Essays*, "Jen-wo p'ien," 3rd par. The "honorable" and "dishonorable" people referred to the commoners and the "mean" people. See Ch'ü T'ung-tsu, *Law and Society in Traditional China*, pp. 128–35.
[51] *Essays*, "Chüeh-shih p'ien," 1st par.

Former kings had instituted the relationships between sovereign and subject, father and son, husband and wife, elder and younger brothers, and between friends. As I was born into these relationships I should comply with the established tradition: I should recognize as sovereign who is sovereign, as subject who is subject, as father who is father, as son who is son, and so forth. And as I was born in a particular period of time, I should accept whatever style of dress and dwelling, whatever calendar system, whatever form of writing and speaking, whatever sort of moral principles that are accepted by society at that time.[52]

Sometimes K'ang went even so far as to glorify the traditional autocratic government. He spoke approvingly of the tremendous authority of the Chinese emperor and of the absolute control that he exercised over the empire. He could exercise such control, K'ang explained,

not because China has an extensive territory, a vast population, or an abundance of natural resources, but simply because his authority is absolute. His authority does not rest on physical coercion or depend upon material inducement. It is rather the cumulative result of the benevolence (*jen*) of the Two Emperors and Three Kings, of the righteousness (*i*) of the [rulers of] the Han, T'ang, Sung, and Ming dynasties, and the teaching and encouragement of countless sages and worthy men of the past.[53]

Naturally, K'ang showed little confidence in the wisdom of the common people.

The people may not be made to understand it [i.e., a path of action]. Therefore in conducting government the sage always carries in his heavy heart secrets that he cannot divulge to the world. In carrying out his policies he is prepared at the start to go against the moral judgments accumulated through many generations and to thwart the wishes of all the people. . . . His manipulations are known neither to his contemporaries nor to men of later times.[54]

Here, presumably, K'ang followed the teaching of Confucius, as the opening sentence, a quotation from the *Analects*,[55] clearly shows. But

---

[52] *Essays*, "Li-hsüeh p'ien."

[53] *Essays*, "Ho-p'i p'ien," 2nd par. K'ang went on to say that with such authority it would be easy to make China strong, despite all difficulties. This view partly explains K'ang's reliance on the Kuang-hsü emperor's authority to effect far-reaching reforms in 1898, for which K'ang was criticized by Miyazaki Torazō. See anonymous Chinese translation of his *Thirty-three Years' Dream* (*Sanjūsan-nen no yume*), p. 40.

[54] *Essays*, "Ho-p'i p'ien," 4th par.

[55] An allusion to a passage in the *Analects* (Legge trans.), viii. 9: The Master said, "The people may be made to follow a path of action, but they may not be made to understand it." Cf. W. K. Liao, *The Complete Works of Han Fei Tzu*, 2: 309. "The in-

this teaching, we recall, was stressed and developed not by Mencius but by Hsün-tzu, whom K'ang identified elsewhere as the first to "corrupt" the true doctrines of the Sage and therefore the founder of that intellectual transition that K'ang, as an independent thinker, rejected unequivocally and undertook resolutely to transcend.[56]

Curiously, K'ang came, on one occasion at least, perilously close to the Legalist position. He defended the actions of Kuan Chung and Shang Yang and vouched for the efficacy of "the art of expedients" (*ch'üan shu*). The end, K'ang argued in effect, always justified the means.[57] So long as the ruler of men had the interests of his subjects in mind he should be allowed to achieve his aim by whatever means he deemed appropriate. For instance, it was entirely justifiable, and indeed necessary, to channel the people's actions and thoughts into the desired direction by means of rewards and punishments.

Interestingly, K'ang set store by ideological control as a legitimate and effective political instrument.

> What is that which possesses the greatest power of moving men? Nothing surely has greater power than words and ideas. It is natural that the child loves his parents; and yet the Buddha could override this love and institute the master-disciple relationship. Nothing is stronger than the instinct of self-preservation; and yet the Sage could neutralize it and persuade men to die for their parents and sovereigns. If by pronouncing a doctrine or setting up a principle one could nullify the love of oneself and of one's parents, then there is nothing else in the world that cannot be set aside by the same means.[58]

K'ang, however, did not really believe that words and ideas in themselves had such power. Ideological control could be effectively implemented only by applying the technique of "opening and debarring" (*k'ai se*, namely encouraging by rewards and deterring by punishments).[59] K'ang supported this view by citing a number of historical

---

telligence of the people . . . cannot be depended upon just like the mind of the baby"; and p. 310: "the intelligence of the people is not adequate for use as directive."

[56] See Hsiao, "K'ang Yu-wei and Confucianism," p. 118.

[57] *Essays*, "Ho-p'i p'ien," 3rd par.

[58] Ibid., 1st par. In another essay, "Chih-yen p'ien," he suggested that in writing, prolixity rose from the kindly intention of making the reader understand, whereas laconism was dictated by "the desire to control and restrain." K'ang appears to have understood the psychological effects of slogans and shibboleths.

[59] Interestingly, the phrase as well as the thought was taken from Shang Yang, one of the great Legalist thinkers of antiquity. See *The Book of Lord Shang*, trans. by J. J. L. Duyvendak, pp. 225–33.

instances in which such technique was successfully employed in the past, including the measures applied by the early rulers of the Ch'ing dynasty.[60] K'ang was also persuaded that in order to cope with special situations, such as those that existed in his own day, it was necessary to adopt unusually harsh and repressive measures—wholesale executions, to begin with those who stood close to the sovereign and occupied high, official positions.[61]

Here in the *Essays* K'ang took a rather dim view of men. Persons with intelligence and talent, he believed, were invariably ambitious whereas those who had little desire for worldly honor and wealth were not anxious to do the ruler's bidding. Therefore it behooved the ruler to adopt the "stick and carrot" technique, to tantalize the ambitious with guerdon and to terrorize the lazy or unruly by chastisement. This was the only way in which a ruler could get things done as he wished.[62] It is also interesting to note in this connection that K'ang virtually upheld the principle that might makes right:

> Strength and weakness constitute the decisive principle in human affairs. Strength lies sometimes in [superior] force and sometimes in [superior] intelligence. . . . Power is the first postulate of human action, while propriety is its last corollary.[63]

Obviously, K'ang's sanguine view of autocratic rule harmonized ill with his utterances concerning justice and equality as recorded in different portions of the same work. It is possible that K'ang unknowingly contradicted himself. But this lack of agreement permits another explanation. Without the benefit of training in strict logical reasoning K'ang felt no difficulty in proceeding simultaneously on two levels of thought. On one level he concerned himself with the problem of how to make the best of the existing situation; on another level he looked forward to a future that was to be radically different from and decidedly

[60] "Ho-p'i p'ien," 6th par. K'ang pointed to the institution of the *Po-hsüeh hung-tz'u* by the K'ang-hsi emperor in 1678 as one of the means whereby the government "netted all the eminent scholars of the late Ming dynasty and thus captured the hearts of the people of the empire." In the following paragraph (7th par.), K'ang alleged that the Meiji emperor of Japan, whom he referred to as "the Japanese Prince Mutsuhito," employed the same technique of "opening and debarring" to effectuate his reforms. For the *Po-hsüeh hung-tz'u*, see Chang Ch'i-yün et al., eds., *Ch'ing shih* (Taipei, 1961), 1: 75.

[61] *Essays*, "Ho-p'i p'ien," 9th par.

[62] Ibid., 10th par. This also reminds one of legalism. See, e.g. Liao, *Han Fei Tzu*, 1: 46–47.

[63] *Essays*, "Shih-tsu p'ien."

better than the present. It appears, therefore, that he already adumbrated vaguely in the 1880s the idea of stages of social progress, which he later developed into the theory of the "Three Ages."[64]

There was a touch of pessimism in this early writing of K'ang. Theorizing on the fact that the *Book of Changes* ends with the hexagram "Before Completion" (*Wei chi*)[65] K'ang said in part:

> Heaven cannot make all men sages or worthies. Even if all men were sages and worthies, they cannot be free from sicknesses, poverty, or premature death. Human desires are limitless; consequently, men's hopes for good order remain forever unfulfilled. They can only voice their regrets, to no avail. To make the matter worse, Heaven produces more evil men than good ones. [Under the adverse influences of a capricious natural environment:] fitful storms, erratic climates, skittish topography, frivolous material surroundings, . . . men are unable to cope with the struggles among their burning desires and the battles between the heart and blood that go on within themselves. Fidgety persons who fail to understand this go on hastily to seek accomplishment in a day. But Heaven has his hand in human achievement. Even when Heaven lends a helping hand, what men achieve amounts really to very little.[66]

Such pessimism, however, did not lead K'ang to despair. Following more or less the Confucian tenet that a virtuous man should love and serve his fellow beings, whatever might be the outcome of his efforts, K'ang voiced this conviction:

> Heaven and earth, standing in an infinite universe, are extremely puny entities. Man, living between Heaven and earth, is an even more insignificant creature. Whatever talent or ability he might possess, he is frequently plagued by illness and hamstrung by unfavorable circumstances. Deducting the time consumed in childish play and old-age infirmity, opportunities for him to accomplish worthwhile things are rather scant. . . . The maximum extent of his achievement cannot possibly extend over more than a few thousand *li* and his fame cannot last beyond three thousand years. What then is man's purpose for occupying a place in the infinite universe? . . . So far as I am concerned, it is to extend to the utmost the feeling of compassion that is in my heart and to do what my own nature insistently dictates. I covet nothing that lies outside myself. . . . I shall study the institutions of past centuries, discovering their merits

[64] For one of K'ang's own statements of this theory, see K'ang Yu-wei, *Ta T'ung Shu*, translated by Laurence G. Thompson, p. 72 (hereafter cited as Thompson, *Ta T'ung Shu*).

[65] For significance of the hexagram, see Richard Wilhelm, *The I Ching*, 1: 265–69 and 2: 367–71. K'ang's interpretation of this hexagram differed from the above.

[66] *Essays*, "Wei-chi p'ien."

and shortcomings, successes and failures; I shall envision the institutions of future centuries, anticipating their strengths and weaknesses, efficacies or lack of them. I shall do all these not because I entertain any ulterior motive but simply because I like to do them and have an aptitude for doing them. However, if I discover that I possess no such aptitude, I would detach myself from human affairs and from the world itself, and withdraw myself into inaccessible mountains [to become an anchorite].[67]

This statement is extremely interesting, for it foreshadowed some of K'ang's roles that he assumed successively in later years—as practical reformer, utopian thinker, and "roamer of the Heavens."

Much of the hesitant and ambiguous posture that K'ang assumed when he wrote the *Essays*, disappeared in the second major work of this early period, namely, the "Substantial Truths and Universal Principles"[68] (*Shih-li kung-fa*; hereafter, *Truths*). As the title itself suggests, K'ang was now definitely committed to the universalizing point of view.[69] He relinquished the basic traditional social and political values of China, and accepted implicitly the Western-inspired notions of love, liberty, equality, and democracy, which were to constitute chief ingredients of his ideal of a universal society as delineated in detail in the book on the "Great Community."

After giving a number of prefatory remarks and preliminary definitions, K'ang went on to deal with the basic human relationships and social institutions.[70] His universalizing predisposition is in evidence almost at every turn. Here he took a somewhat more benevolent view of man and human nature. The following propositions were assumed to

[67] *Essays*, "Pu-jen p'ien."

[68] The relation of this work to the *Essays* and the *Community* is briefly discussed in Hsiao, "K'ang Yu-wei and Confucianism," pp. 112–13. K'ang wrote in *Nien-p'u*, p. 7a (Lo, *K'ang*, p. 42) that he "had worked out" his "Universal Principles of Mankind." The extant manuscript bearing the title "Substantial Truths and Universal Principles" (*Shih-li Kung-fa*) probably represents the final version of the work.

[69] K'ang intended the *Truths* to be the first of a series of books to which he gave the general title, "Books on the Universal Principles of Myriad Persons" (i.e., all men; *Wan shen kung fa shu-chi*). The *Truths*, he said, pointed to the "root and source" of mankind's universal principles. The second item of the series was to be "Guide to Universal Principles" (*Kung-fa hui-t'ung*), of which only small fragments exist. The other items included: "The Complete Book of the True Principles of Good and Ill Fortune" (*Huo-fu shih-li ch'üan-shu*), "The Authentic History of the World" (*Ti-ch'iu cheng-shih*), "The Philosophies of the World" (*Ti-ch'iu hsüeh-an*), "International Law" (*Wan-kuo kung-fa*), and "The Laws of Various Countries" (*Ko-kuo lü-li*).

[70] This book has a total of sixteen sections, of which six deal with human relationships, four with rites and ceremonies, law and punishment, education and government. There is a chapter on social and moral judgments. In the final chapter is K'ang's recommendation for compiling "World Books."

be axiomatic (or, in his terminology, "substantial truths"): that "men" born of Heaven and earth, are originally equal"; that each man received a part of the substance of Heaven and earth to constitute his being; that each had a soul, which made him an intelligent being; that each possessed at birth the capacity to love and to hate; and that at birth man was incapable of deceit, which he learned only through postnatal experience.[71] From these postulated "truths" K'ang derived several corollaries ("universal principles"): that "each man has the right of self-determination," that "man-made laws shall be applied in the spirit of equality," that "legislation shall aim at promoting love and suppressing hate," and that "importance shall be attached to laws that reward honesty and penalize deceit."[72]

K'ang then proceeded to lay down the "universal principles" that he believed should govern the various human relationships. Among the most unconventional of his views were those concerning marriage. He began with this "substantial truth":

Medical science has now demonstrated that no material difference exists in [marriages in which] a husband and a wife are permanently mated, one husband is wedded successively to several wives, and one wife is married successively to several husbands; and that it is most difficult for two souls to be joined together permanently, as love deteriorates when [two persons] live together for a long time.[73]

The "universal principle" that followed from the above was formulated by K'ang as follows:

Freedom shall be granted to a man and a woman who are in love. But they shall take no action which sets up a binding contractual relationship between them. They shall not be required to live together, if there is the least bit of dislike or repugnance between them.[74]

K'ang, in other words, advocated free love, an idea which he retained with little modification in his utopian work, the *Ta-t'ung shu*.[75] Natur-

[71] *Truths*, "P'eng-yu men," "shih-li," 1st par.
[72] *Truths*, "Kung-fa," 1st–4th pars.
[73] *Truths*, "Fu-fu men," 1st par.
[74] *Truths*, "Fu-fu men," "Kung-fa."
[75] Books 5, chap. 9; Thompson, *Ta Tung Shu*, pp. 163–67. However, cf. *Truths*, "Fu-mu men," "Pi-li," 1st par., where K'ang indicated that men and women in love should be permitted to bind themselves with a three-month contract, renewable only after the elapse of three months following upon the termination of the previous contract.

ally, he condemned the traditional monogamous marriage precisely because such an institution involved a permanent conjugal tie that could not be dissolved without a divorce on "justifiable grounds." Such a relationship, K'ang asserted, was "incompatible with substantial truth and without benefit to humanity." Moreover, monogamous marriages were often reduced to a sham by couples who failed to find happiness in their unions. K'ang cited from what he took to be the Paris census for 1891 to the effect that in a single year there was reported 5,572 cases of divorce in France, and that in the same year 73,936 of the 866,377 children there were born out of wedlock. These figures, he argued, showed that a large number of men and women joined in monogamous marriages "resented and hated each other." Furthermore, the 73,936 illegitimate children bore eloquent witness to the fact that in France at least, 147,872 men and women actually practiced free love, obeying clandestinely the "universal principle" governing the sexual relationship.[76]

To K'ang monogamous marriage was bad enough, but even worse were marriages dictated by parents, with the concomitant practices of inequality between the sexes and the institution of concubinage. And the only thing that was worse than any of these was celibacy.[77]

K'ang's views concerning the parent-child relationship were no less a radical departure from Chinese tradition. By minimizing the importance of parenthood he sought to free the child from the performance of filial duties as prescribed by the Confucian code. According to him, that the child owed little to his parents and therefore should not be subordinated to them, might be seen from the following "substantial truth." In the first place,

> Matter (*yüan-chih*) pertains to Heaven and earth; it is not created by parents. Parents can only use the matter pertaining to Heaven and earth to beget children. That is all. . . . Moreover, as in most cases, the characters of the children's souls differ from those of the parents' souls. As a result of the incompatibility of their souls, affection between parents and children degenerates, when they live together for a long time.[78]

Secondly, as souls of human individuals went through reincarnation in diverse ways after their deaths, "the souls of deceased parents might become reincarnated [in the bodies of] the descendants of their own

[76] *Truths*, "Fu-mu men," 3rd par. and note.
[77] *Truths*, "Fu-mu men," 5th par.
[78] *Truths*, "Fu-mu tzu-nü men," 1st par.

children." And, thirdly, as there was a continuous exchange of matter between human beings of the world, through the physiological processes of breathing, eating, and excretion, and through the chemical process of "material transformations" (*ch'i hua*), "there was also an interchange of matter between parents and their children." Thus, parents and children being ultimately identical in substance, the former were not in any real way superior to the latter.

If there was nothing sacrosanct about parents and parenthood, then it would be wrong for society to require subjection of children to their parents. The first "universal principle" applicable here was, accordingly:

> Parents shall not demand performance of filial duties by their children and children shall not demand affection and care from their parents. Each person shall enjoy the right of self determination.[79]

Society, according to K'ang, was to undertake the task of supporting and rearing of children. Public nurseries were to be established and, to compensate the parents for their labor in begetting children, they were paid suitable remuneration—thus absolving all the indebtedness that their children owed them.[80]

On roughly the same grounds K'ang demolished the traditional precepts governing the relationship between the elder and the young. He denied, by implication, that it was proper to require the latter to show unqualified respect to the former, thus doing violence to the "truth" that both were basically equal as human beings. As K'ang put it:

> The elderly and the youthful are simply people who happen to be born in the world [at different times], the former preceding the latter. . . . Seniors and juniors in age are like old and new utensils or articles; [there is no reason for attaching greater importance to the former]. And, according to the veritable doctrine of transmigration of souls [and the law of succession of generations], the elderly will in time become the youthful, and vice versa.[81]

The "universal principle" that followed from the above was obvious: "Equality shall exist between the old and the young."[82]

[79] Ibid., 2nd and 3rd pars.
[80] Ibid., "Kung-fa."
[81] *Truths*, "Chang-yu men," 1st and 2nd pars.
[82] Ibid., "Kung-fa."

One is tempted to ask, how did K'ang, at this stage of his career, arrive at such an iconoclastic view, amounting to a negation of the traditional conceptions of the family? No definite answer can be found. It may be surmised that his interest in Western social institutions and customs,[83] his disrelish of the less attractive aspects of the Chinese family system,[84] and his fertile imagination[85] contributed, in all probability, to this unconventional view.

K'ang treated of the sovereign-subject relationship in a similar vein. Contrary to tradition (and to his own view as expressed in the *Essays*), he denied not only that the ruler of a state should possess absolute or exclusive authority, but also that there should be a single supreme ruler for all. Persons who conducted the government, according to him, were arbitrators or administrators elected by the people "for their own protection." The only true form of government was one in which a "parliament" took charge of all public affairs and all government functionaries were elected by the people. Thus, even a republic was not an ideal government because there was still a chief executive. A constitutional monarchy in which "the sovereign and the people shared the authority" was not to be recommended; an absolute monarchy was of course the worst of all.[86] All this, obviously, was K'ang's way of showing his preference for something like democracy—a form of political organization which was so "democratic" that all persons who served in the government, including those on the lowest echelons, might be referred to as "rulers."

K'ang added the notion of progress to that of equality in his views concerning intellectual life. Truths, he declared, inhered in nature and were discovered by the application of human intelligence. As discoveries were successively made, man's knowledge of the universe increased as time went on. K'ang stated this optimistic view thus:

Knowledge of men of a later age surpasses inevitably that of men of a previous age. Those who came later reap the harvests realized by those who preceded them. The late comers not only take possession of the knowl-

---

[83] In 1892, K'ang's eldest daughter, T'ung-wei, compiled "Studies in the Customs and Institutions of Various Countries" (*Ko-kuo feng-su chih-tu k'ao*) with a view to showing "the principle of the evolutionary progress of mankind" (*jen-ch'ün chin-hua chih li*)—undoubtedly, under his supervision (*Nien-p'u*, p. 11a; cf. Lo, *K'ang*, p. 56).

[84] See the concluding paragraph of chapter 2, this volume.

[85] There is no way of finding out how K'ang came to the idea of free love.

[86] *Truths*, "Chün-ch'en men" and "Chih-shih men."

edge based on the discoveries made by their predecessors but also are able to add discoveries of their own. . . . To that extent at least, their knowledge goes beyond that of their predecessors.[87]

This, K'ang believed, was the case for intellectual freedom. As discovery of truth was not the exclusive prerogative of any individual or group of individuals, "each man should enjoy the right of self-determination." It was wrong, therefore, as it was done in traditional China to deny intellectual independence to students, requiring them to submit themselves unconditionally to the authority of their teachers.[88] The truth was that even a sage, the greatest of all teachers, should not lay claim to absolute authority. For, in the last analysis, truth itself alone could serve as infallible criterion of human opinions. K'ang put the matter in these words:

> The sage holds no authority which pertains to all men. Ancient and modern doctrines shall be judged in the light of Truth; they shall not be measured by [the words of] sages or worthies. All dicta shall be evaluated on the basis of their intrinsic validity, without considering the persons who uttered them.[89]

K'ang certainly was no skeptic. As just indicated, he believed in the existence of objective truth, which was discoverable by man and ascertained by general consensus. He suggested that a number of "sacred scriptures" that contained incontestably valid precepts and principles be selected every five years by popular vote, for the edification of young people not yet ready to exercise independently their own intellectual faculties.[90]

This implied that intellectual freedom was to be enjoyed only after an individual had attained intellectual maturity. According to K'ang, the aim of education and religion was precisely to help him to attain to such maturity. Making no distinction between the two, which he denotes with the same character, *chiao*, he defined their aims thus:

> The substantial truths of *chiao* are two: first, to develop men's intelligence, talent, and ability, and to enhance their love and integrity; second, to transmit to them the true doctrines and beneficial institutions which have been developed by fellow men of the five continents, so that all may

[87] *Truths*, "Shih-ti men," 4th par.
[88] *Truths*, "Kung-fa," 2nd par.
[89] *Truths*, "Kung-fa," 1st par.
[90] *Truths*, "Cheng-ch'i ti-ch'iu shu-ch: mu-lu kung-lun," 2nd par.

enjoy the benefits [of these developments]. . . . In this way their intelligence, talent, and ability would not be wrongfully employed.[91]

In line with his objection to concentration of authority and probably taking a hint from Western experience, K'ang laid it down as a "universal principle" that the spheres of religious and political authority should be clearly demarcated so that one would not encroach upon the other. He condemned strongly the infringement upon political authority by the priest as much as usurpation by the political ruler "the authority that properly belongs to the priest."[92]

Much of what K'ang wrote in the *Truths* stemmed in part from his acquaintance with European ideas gleaned through reading the "Western books," which he began to collect in 1879. The impact of the West, it appears, produced in him no xenophobia, as it did in many of the enemies of the 1898 reform. However, it may be noted that K'ang did not regard the imported ideas that he freely borrowed as something alien but rather as elements belonging in a system of universally valid principles. One can therefore hardly charge him with consciously trying "to smuggle western values into Chinese tradition."[93] For here K'ang was not concerned with preserving or renovating Chinese tradition but rather with constructing a system of social thought that would transcend geographical or national boundaries. Instead of injecting Western values into Chinese tradition, he actually threw some of the most hallowed of Chinese values out of his universalized scheme. There is no ground for doubting that he honestly was convinced that valid principles were universal in their application. To him universalization was not a methodological device but a matter of intellectual conviction—a conviction

---

[91] *Truths,* "Chiao-shih men," 1st par.

[92] *Truths,* "Kung-fa" and "Pi-li," 1st par. That K'ang had no conception of religion in the strict sense may be gathered from his discussion of "God's appellations." He mentioned a number of designations for "Lord on High" (*Shang-ti*), including "the Ether-flux" (*ch'i-hua*), "Prime Substance" (*yüan-chih*), "the Great Lord" (*Ta chu-tsai*), "the Lord Creator" (*Tsao-wu chu*), Deus (*Ti-wu-ssu*), and Jehova (*Yeh-ho-hua*), and commented that only the first three names were suitable and proper, the rest being not in accordance with "substantial truths" (*Truths,* "Li-i men," section on "Shang-ti ch'eng-ming").

For a discussion of K'ang's views on religion, see the second section of chapter 4 in this volume. It may be noted in this connection that K'ang did not believe in the continued existence of the soul after death, and insisted that there could not be communication between the living and the dead. Funeral and sacrificial rites, therefore, were meaningful only from the point of view of the living (*Truths,* "Chih-shih men," sections on "Burial" and "Sacrifice").

[93] Joseph R. Levenson, *Liang Ch'i-ch'ao and the Mind of Modern China* (Cambridge, Mass.: Harvard University Press, 1953), p. 48.

that was to become, in the well-known *Ta-t'ung shu* of 1902, the central theme and guiding spirit of his social thought.

In a small way universalization had already become K'ang's preoccupation in the *Truths* of 1885–87. There he proposed that all men live together in harmonious unity, speaking a common language and served by a common government. To help break down particularisms born of the divisive effects of different political and religious systems, he condemned all calendar systems that reckoned the years on the basis of the births of individual sages or by the reigns of individual rulers, and recommended the adoption of a common calendar to be used by all peoples of the world.[94]

Such, briefly, are some of the leading ideas that K'ang set forth in the *Essays* and the *Truths*. One can hardly fail to note that a significant change of outlook had occurred during the time when he wrote these two books—from a way of looking at social institutions and moral values, which still showed unmistakable influences of tradition, to a theoretical approach that was little short of tradition shattering. It appears that between 1879 when he first came into contact with Western learning, and 1887 when he completed the second of the two works, he had indeed arrived at the position that, as he himself said with apparent pride, was to remain with him for many years to come.

This position was gained not without laborious soul searching and path finding. Tired of wading in the stagnant waters of traditional learning, K'ang went through in 1878 a tremendous mental crisis that shook his faith in amost everything he had previously learned with diligence.[95] Then, after a spell of Taoist and Buddhist studies he turned to books on Western learning in 1879, thus inaugurating a new phase of his intellectual life.[96] In the years 1880–87 he experienced within himself a period of intense intellectual ferment. Freed, partially at least, from the bondage of classical learning and greatly fascinated by

[94] *Truths*, "Li-i men," section on "Chi-yüan chi-nien yung-li." This universalist proposal affords an interesting contrast to his later view on such matters. He proposed, especially in the 1900s and after, that the year of Confucius' birth be taken as "Year One" and actually adopted this method of reckoning in some of his writings done in these years: e.g., "Commentaries on the Evolutions of Rites" (*Li-yün chu*), completed probably in 1901–2, was dated "the 2435th Year of Confucius, i.e., Kuang-hsü 10th Year"; "Commentaries on the *Analects*" (*Lun-yü chu*), completed in 1903, was dated "The 2453rd Year after Confucius' Birth, i.e., Kuang-hsü 28th Year"; and the first issue of the "Compassion" (February 1913), was dated "The 2464th Year of Confucius, First Month."

[95] *Nien-p'u*, pp. 4b–5a; Lo, *K'ang*, pp. 33–34.

[96] *Nien-p'u*, pp. 5a–b; Lo, *K'ang*, pp. 34–36.

Western ideas, he found himself engaged in prolonged inquiries into an almost bewildering variety of matters.[97] For a time he must have been groping excitedly in the confusion brought about by the sudden confrontation of heterogeneous notions that came to him through his diversified readings. Thanks to an active intellect and a lively imagination, he managed to bring some order to the chaos resulting from the collision of two worlds in one mind. However, uncertain at first about what he saw, he wavered between two positions, one rooted in the East, the other biased toward the West. Such a double orientation could not but be intellectually perplexing. It is probable, therefore, that much of the "deep thinking" that K'ang did at this time[98] was devoted to finding a way out of his quandary. He soon came to the realization that after all there was no insuperable gulf between East and West, and therefore, no double orientation. With this universalizing approach that he discovered when he set about to write the *Truths*, he had found his way to social theory and, at the same time, laid the foundation for his "one-world" utopian ideal. He had, in fact, found an alternative to Westernization.

It was to K'ang's credit as a thinker that he did not take the simple way out. Assuming that intellectual and social reforms were due in China and that in its pragmatic successes Western civilization had proved its merit, it was easy indeed for patriotic and open-minded persons to prescribe Westernization in technology or in nonmaterial culture, or in both. It required more insight to see the possibility of an East-West synthesis by whatever method that might be deemed appropriate. Such a view, however, had little appeal to those who preferred the simple way out. Even Liang Ch'i-ch'ao, K'ang's erstwhile favored student, doubted seriously the value of synthesis through universalization. He charged K'ang and men who supported his cause with loving Confucius at the expense of truth. "They follow the new learning and new principles," Liang wrote in 1902, "not precisely because those latter are palatable to their minds but because these things secretly coincided with 'their' Confucius. Thus, what they love is still Confucius and not truth."[99] In view of the fact that K'ang in large part had drastic-

[97] *Nien-p'u*, pp. 5b–7a; Lo, *K'ang*, pp. 36–42.

[98] *Nien-p'u*, 6a, Lo, *K'ang*, p. 38, where the original "hsin-shih shen-ssu" is freely rendered "as I learned about new things I began to perceive the principles behind them."

[99] Liang, *Ch'ing-tai hsüeh-shu kai-lun*, pp. 144–45; Hsü, *Intellectual Trends of the Ch'ing Period*, pp. 103–4. This passage was quoted by Liang from the *Hsin-min ts'ung-pao*, 1902.

ally revised the Confucian value and institutional system, Liang's charge can hardly be accepted as well founded. It resulted obviously from his failure to appreciate the significance of K'ang's position and that failure in turn may have flowed from Liang's inability or unwilling-ness to recognize the possibility of intellectual synthesis. In effect, therefore, Liang was, at this point, a Westernizer. He made his position clear in 1915, by way of a metaphor:

> I will never pick the tempting and luscious peach and plum blossoms of my next-door neighbor to set off the old trunk of fir and pine around my house, thereby becoming elated and self-satisfied. If indeed I love peaches and plums, I should think of ways and means of transplanting them.[100]

But to return to K'ang's *Truths*. It should be noted that while it fore-shadowed the *Community*, an important difference stood between the two books. In the former K'ang adopted a consistently individualistic viewpoint, stigmatizing every institution contrary to the desires of in-dividual man as incompatible with "substantial truth" or "universal principle," but in the latter he set store by ideas and ideals that might be described as socialistic or communistic. This vital difference, how-ever, did not lessen the merits of the earlier work—his first credentials as an independent social thinker.

ROAD TO UTOPIA

Liang Ch'i-ch'ao aptly likened the overpowering impact of K'ang

[100] Liang, *Ch'ing-tai* . . ., p. 146; Hsü, *Intellectual Trends of the Ch'ing Period*, pp. 103–4. This passage was quoted by Liang from the *Kuo-feng pao*, 1915. Evidently, Liang still held this view in 1902, for he quoted the above statements in his *Intellectual Trends*, which was completed late that year. Prior to 1902, in particular between 1873 and 1898, Liang largely followed K'ang in his efforts at syncretism. See Levenson, *Liang Ch'i-chao*, pp. 34–41. I cannot, however, go along with Professor Levenson in his basic approach and in many of his conclusions. For instance his concepts of "analogy of patterns of culture-growth" and "analogy of cultural values" (ibid., p. 41) ,offered to explain the intellectual process which led Liang to the idea of reform, show that he is "alien" to Liang Ch'i-ch'ao's mind as well as "to the spirit of civilization." (Arthur W. Hummel's review of Levenson's book, *Far Eastern Quarterly*, 14, no. 1 [November 1954]: 111.) As Hummel correctly points out, Liang was engaged in differentiating the transient from the permanent elements in Chinese culture and in interpreting the new knowledge from the West. "It was a soul-searching experience for Liang—not an exercise in dialectic" (ibid., p. 110). This holds true with K'ang, though he came to that experience before Liang and in fact initiated Liang into it. See Liang's own account of his first encounter with K'ang, "San-shih tzu-shu" (written 1902) in *Yin-ping-shih ho-chi, Wen-chi*, 11, pp. 16–17; quoted in part in Ting Wen-chiang, *Liang Jen-kung hsien-sheng nien-p'u ch'ang-pien ch'u-kao, chüan* 3, p. 15.

Yu-wei's *Ta-t'ung shu* (The Book of the Great Community) to "a mighty volcanic eruption and huge earthquake."[101] Not unaware of the far-reaching implications of his book, K'ang firmly refused to publish it, averring that premature disclosure of its contents, at a time when the world was not ready for them, would be "to consign mankind to a vast deluge or ravening beasts."[102] Rightly indeed K'ang considered his ideas dangerous, for they contravened almost at every turn the very traditions and values that for many centuries had shaped Chinese society and held it together. The phrase "Great Community" was taken, to be sure, from one of the Confucian texts.[103] But K'ang gave it such startlingly new meanings and connotations that it cannot be identified with any of the recognized doctrines of the Confucian school.[104] One may well raise the question whether K'ang, as the author of the *Ta-t'ung shu*, can be properly regarded as a true follower of the ancient Sage.[105]

Whatever may have been his relationship with Confucianism, there can be no doubt that he was in "a utopian state of mind" when he wrote the *Ta-t'ung shu*.[106] While utopian thought was born of dissatisfaction,[107] it attained to maturity only when the thinker, thanks to a broadened intellectual vista, had reached a certain degree of philosophical detachment from the immediate situation. Dissatisfaction with

---

[101] Liang, *Ch'ing-tai* . . ., p. 129; Hsü, *Intellectual Trends* . . ., p. 94.

[102] Liang, *Ch'ing-tai* . . ., p. 136; Hsü, *Intellectual Trends* . . ., pp. 97–98. According to Liang, "Among his students only Ch'en Ch'ien-ch'iu and Liang Ch'i-ch'ao were permitted to read this book at first."

[103] I.e., the *Li-yün*, ninth section of the *Book of Rites*. Thompson, *Ta T'ung Shu*, pp. 27–29, gives various translations of the relevant passage.

[104] Liang, *Ch'ing-tai* . . ., p. 133; Hsü, *Intellectual Trends* . . ., p. 96. Liang suggested that K'ang "developed" the ideas contained in the *Li-yün* into "democracy" and "socialism."

[105] Richard C. Howard, "K'ang Yu-wei (1858–1927): His Intellectual Background and Early Thought," p. 295, says, "in revising Confucianism, K'ang not only transformed but transcended it: in his *Ta-t'ung shu* Confucianism . . . was no longer the doctrine dominating the intellectual and spiritual life of the only true civilization, but merely a basis for man's progress to a higher level of existence in the world of the 'grand unity.'" Cf. Hsiao, "K'ang Yu-wei and Confucianism," pp. 97–103 and the first section of chapter 3 in this volume.

[106] Karl Mannheim, *Ideology and Utopia: An Introduction to the Sociology of Knowledge*, p. 192: "A state of mind is utopian when it is incongruous with the state of society within which it occurs."

[107] K'ang, *Nien-p'u*, p. 6b, indicates that in the early summer of 1884 he returned to his native village from Canton because martial law was declared in the city as French troops had overrun Annam and were about to invade Taiwan and Fukien. This was K'ang's first personal experience of the threat of foreign aggression.

the present might evoke an urge to reform; only a transcendental look into the distant future could lead to utopian construction. In the case of K'ang, the transition from the former to the latter occurred in the few years immediately following 1898. Travels in Europe and America gave him opportunities to take a closer view of Western civilization. The abortive attempt in 1900 to unseat the empress dowager ended for the time being his hope for practical reform. Penang and Darjeeling afforded him almost three years of quiet and leisure to ponder more deeply than ever before problems of human life and society.[108] He thus became psychologically conditioned to tread the road to utopia. Turning his back to "crystallized and perverted institutions and social practices," he undertook to "imagine society under revised and perfect institutions and ideals" and delineated his vision of "the Great Community."[109] He might be called justifiably China's first utopian writer who, by virtue of the boldness of his conceptions, was a worthy colleague of the great utopians of other lands.[110]

As the title of the book suggests,[111] K'ang was here concerned not with defending Chinese values or with transplanting Western ideas, but with defining for all mankind a way of life that would be psychologically satisfying and morally justifiable. It was here, in fact, that he gave the fullest expression to the universalizing phase of his social thought.

Theoretical Standpoint

K'ang began his utopian construct by offering a universalistic interpretation of morality. His theory of the nature and origin of "love"

[108] K'ang T'ung-pi, *Nien-p'u hsü-pien*, pp. 10b–33b, passim. Lo, *K'ang*, pp. 188–93.

[109] Joyce O. Hertzler, *History of Utopian Thought*, pp. 259, 260.

[110] See in addition to Hertzler, *History of Utopian Thought*; Marie Louise Berneri, *Journey Through Utopia*; Mumford, *The Story of Utopias*; and Raymond Ruyer, *L'utopie et les utopies*. A word will be said on K'ang's place in the utopian tradition later in this study.

[111] It is difficult to give a fully satisfactory translation of *"Ta-t'ung"* for which Thompson (*Ta T'ung Shu*, pp. 29–30), gives (among others) the following translations: "the Great Unity" (Fung Yu-lan), "Grand Union" (Elbert D. Thomas), "Cosmopolitan Society" (Teng and Fairbank), "The Great Commonwealth" (Lin Mousheng), "the Great Communion" (Richard Wilhelm and John H. Reece), and "Grand Harmony" (Tseng Yu-hao). The present writer apologizes for introducing yet another translation, "the Great Community." There is some merit in the word "community": it covers a variety of meanings thus making it come closer to the term *t'ung* as K'ang used it. *Webster's New International Dictionary of the English Language*, 2nd ed. (Springfield: G. C. Merriam, 1951) gives seven different definitions; of these only No. 4 does not fit the connotations of *t'ung*.

(*jen*) or "compassion" (*pu-jen*) carries a curiously materialistic ring. He put it in these terms:

> Vast is the primal energy (*yüan ch'i*), the creator of heaven and earth. Heaven is a single spiritual substance (*hun chih*; literally, "soul substance"), and man, too, is a single spiritual substance. Though different in size, they both share the vast energy derived from the Great Origin (*t'ai yüan*), . . . Confucius had said: "Earth contains the spiritual energy (*shen ch'i*), which [produces] the wind and thunder-clap. By the wind and thunder-clap the [seeds of] forms are carried along, and the multitude of creatures show the appearance of life."[112] This spiritual thing is electricity, possessed of consciousness. As electric light, it can be transmitted everywhere; as spiritual energy, it can activate everything. . . . There are no creatures who are devoid of this electricity, this spirit. It is a conscious energy (*chih ch'i*). . . . To whoever possesses consciousness it gives the power of attraction, like that of the lodestone, but how much more so in the case of man! The inability to endure [seeing the sufferings of others] is a manifestation of this power of attraction. This is why both love and wisdom are stored [within the mind], where wisdom holds precedence; it is why both love and wisdom are exercised [in external conduct], where love is more noble.[113]

These notions, purely speculative and rather fanciful, can hardly stand the test of experimental science or technical philosophy; nevertheless, they formed the metaphysical foundation of K'ang's ethical and social thinking.

From the assumption that love was inherent in all creatures, K'ang came to the view that love of one's fellow beings was the basic law of life and that love must be universal in scope or it was no love at all. This was particularly true of man.

> Being that I was born on earth, then mankind in the ten thousand countries of the earth are all my brothers of different bodily types. Being that I have knowledge of them, then I have love for them.

This love, he continued, was rooted in and intensified by a basic community of life-experience, irrespective of geographical or racial differences.

> All that is finest and best of the ancient wisdom of India, Greece, Persia,

---

[112] Quoted from the *Book of Rites*, sect. 30, "K'ung-tzu hsien-chü."

[113] *Ta-t'ung shu* (hereafter, *Community*), Shanghai ed., 1935 (hereafter, 1), p. 4: Peking ed., 1956 (hereafter, 2), p. 3; and Taipei ed., 1958 (hereafter, 3), p. 3. This passage is translated by Derk Bodde, in Fung, *A History of Chinese Philosophy*, 2: 685; quoted with modifications. Cf. Thompson's translation (*Ta T'ung Shu*, pp. 64–65).

Rome, and of present-day England, France, Germany, and America, I have lapped up and drunk, rested on, pillowed on; and my soul in dreams has fathomed it. With the most ancient and noted savants, famous scholars, and great men, I have likewise often joined hands, to sit on mats side by side, sleeves touching, sharing our soup; and I have come to love them. The wonders and beauties of the dwellings, clothing, food, boats, vehicles, utensils, government, education, arts, and music of the ten thousand countries of the world I have daily received and enjoyed. Thereby the mind's eye and my spiritual energy have been stimulated. Do they [men of other countries] progress?—then I progress with them; do they retrogress?—then I retrogress with them; are they happy?—then I am happy with them; do they suffer?—then I suffer with them.[114]

Men in different parts of the world shared common experiences in life because, K'ang explained, they were basically identical in their physical and psychological make-up. This identity accounted also for basic similarities of their attitude and behavior.

In his *Essays*, K'ang made it clear that moral sentiments, together with consciousness itself, were functions of the brain and nervous system, and that emotional as well as sensory experiences ("likes" and "dislikes") were simply nerve responses to external stimuli that might be either "agreeable" or "disagreeable." Now in the *Community* he elaborated this view into a clear-cut hedonistic theory of psychology and ethics.

The awareness of living creatures [is like this]: the nerves of the brain possess sensitivity. Encountering material and nonmaterial [objects], there are those which suit it, and those which do not suit it, those which please it, and those which do not please it. Those [objects] which please and suit the nerves of the brain then cause the spiritual soul (*shen hun*) pleasure; those [objects] which do not please and suit the nerves of the brain then cause the spiritual soul pain. It is especially so among humans; the nerves of the human brain being even more sensitive and [the human] spiritual soul being even more pure and clear, the stimuli of the material and immaterial [objects] which enter into the [human] body ['s awareness] are even more complex, subtle, and swift [in their effects]; and [those objects] which please or do not please it are even more clearly [perceived]. What pleases and suits it, it receives; what does not please it or suit it, it rejects.

[114] *Community*, 1, pp. 4–5; 2 and 3, pp. 3–4; Thompson, pp. 65–66. Obviously, this way of thinking was in line with the sentiments of Wang Shou-jen (Wang Yang-ming) as he expressed them in his "Questions on the Great Learning," translated in part in Fung, *A History of Chinese Philosophy*, 2: 599–601. Concrete meaning was given to the notions of all-embracing love and unity of all living beings, probably as a result of K'ang's personal experiences gained in contacts with peoples of the various countries he visited during his self-imposed exile.

Therefore, in human life there is only suiting and not suiting. What does not suit is pain. What suits and suits again is pleasure. Thus the way of man depends upon [the nature of] man; the way which depends upon [the nature of] man is simply pain and pleasure. What is schemed for by man is simply to abolish pain so as to find pleasure. There is no other way.[115]

K'ang assumed that what was pleasurable was what was good and that what man desired was what was desirable. This assumption served for him as the sole criterion by which to judge all social institutions and moral doctrines.

The establishment of laws and the creation of teachings which cause men to have pleasure and to be without suffering: [this] is the best of the Good. [The establishment of laws and the creation of teachings] which cause men to have much happiness and little suffering: [this] is good, but not the perfect good. [The establishment of laws and creation of teachings] which cause men to have much suffering and little happiness: [this] is the not-good.[116]

Judged by this standard, according to K'ang, the teachings of Mo-tzu fell short of perfection. For it was "good" to teach men to practice the doctrines of "agreement with the superior" and "universal love"; but it was "not-good" to require men to lead a life of oppressive austerity.[117] "Indian religion," which required mortification of the body in order to cultivate the soul, and Christianity, which sought the blessings of the Kingdom of Heaven and denounced the carnal, were not suitable for all men. Thus it is clear that by "pleasure" or "happiness" K'ang meant, chiefly if not exclusively, sensuous enjoyment of things that afforded creature comfort or delighted the senses.[118]

Human institutions were to be judged by the same criterion. K'ang set forth a theory of the origin and development of social institutions that was at variance with the accepted Confucian view. He wrote:

Laws of society were made by the strong, which invariably benefited [the lawgivers] themselves and worked to oppress the weak. Laws of the state evolved from military rules. When rules which were [originally] calculated to insure obedience to officers' commands and to keep soldiers in awe were applied [by the sovereign of a state], a situation arose in which

[115] *Community*, 1, p. 7; 2 and 3, p. 5; Thompson, pp. 68–69.
[116] *Community*, 1, p. 9; 2 and 3, p. 7; Thompson, p. 71.
[117] K'ang obviously referred to the *Mo-tzu*, sections 11–16, 20, 21, 25, 32.
[118] *Community*, 1, pp. 9–10, 441–51; 2 and 3, pp. 7, 293–300.

the sovereign was venerated, officials were held in low esteem, and the common people were reduced to servitude. Laws of the family grew out of the clan organization. When rules designed to honor clan leaders and to keep clan members under control were applied in the family, they resulted in elevating [the position of] men, lowering that of women, and treating its junior members as inferiors. Even when the sages undertook to make [new] laws, they could not but formulate them with due regard to the existing circumstances and old customs. With the general trend thus established and oppression continued for a long time, [laws which were socially inequitable] became accepted as morally right. Thus what at the beginning had been rules useful in affording mutual assistance and protection, ended by causing sufferings through oppressiveness and inequity—directly contrary to the fundamental principle of seeking happiness and avoiding pain. This is the case with India; and China has not escaped it. Europe and America are nearer to [the Age of] Ascending Peace (*sheng p'ing*); but as their women are still men's private possessions, they are far from [according with] universal principles (*kung li*); and as to the way of finding happiness, they have likewise not attained it.[119]

Utopians are critics of their age[120] and K'ang for one was indeed critical, as the passage above clearly shows. He was critical not only of traditional Chinese institutions but also of Western institutions as he knew them. As Confucian precepts had contributed importantly to shaping Chinese institutions of imperial times, K'ang's criticism of these institutions amounted in effect to a criticism of these precepts themselves. It is true that after damning Chinese institutions K'ang went on to sing praise to Confucius:

The sage-king Confucius, who was of god-like perception, in early times took thought [of the problem]. Therefore he set up the law of the Three Systems (*san t'ung*): following [the Age of] Disorder (*chü luan*), [the world] will change to [the Age, first of] Ascending Peace [and finally of] Universal Peace (*t'ai p'ing*); following [the Age of] Minor Peace (*hsiao k'ang*), [the world] will advance to [the Age of] the Great Community (*ta t'ung*).[121]

---

[119] Ibid., 1, pp. 10–11; 2 and 3, pp. 6–7; Thompson, pp. 71–72. K'ang's theory of the origin of inequality as stated here reminds one of Pao Ching-yen's statement given in Ko Hung, *Pao-p'u tzu, chüan* 48.

[120] Hertzler, *History of Utopian Thought*, p. 260.

[121] *Community*, 1, p. 11; 2 and 3, p. 7; Thompson, p. 72. For meanings of the terms "Three Systems" and "Three Ages," see Hsiao, "K'ang Yu-wei and Confucianism," pp. 136–62 and chapter 4 in this volume. There is something to be said for Thompson's rendering of *p'ing* as "Peace-and-Equality." But even this translation does not give the full sense of the original term. For the sake of simplicity I have rendered it simply "Peace."

But, obviously, the Confucius whom K'ang thus apotheosized was not the Confucius of Chinese tradition. It was, as K'ang made clear in the *Community* and other writings, a Confucius universalized in such a way that he was no longer the supreme Sage of China but became in effect prophet of an ideal commonwealth for all mankind. Thus the net result of K'ang's deification of Confucius appears to have been de-Sinification of Confucius. For, as the author of the *Community*, K'ang was as a matter of fact concerned not so much with glorifying Confucius as with pointing the way to human happiness through perfection in human institutions. That K'ang did not write as a sectarian Confucian-ist is most clearly evinced in the concluding portion of the book where he forecast the eventual eclipse of Confucianism along with all other religions identified with particular civilizations.

Several leading ideas served K'ang as conceptual bases upon which to evaluate existing institutions and to construct his utopian system. As already noted, happiness, enjoyment of pleasure unmixed with pain, constituted the supreme and sole aim of human existence.[122] This hedonistic premise was conjoined with the principle of "love" (*jen*), a principle that undoubtedly was suggested to K'ang by the Confucian tradition and for which probably he found confirmation in the Christian religion. K'ang also assumed that as all men were equal no one should be deprived the opportunity to gain happiness or to lose his freedom. Thus *hedonism*, *humanitarianism*, and *egalitarianism* appear to have con-stituted the main props of K'ang's social thought, from which arose other ideas that might be described roughly as "democracy," "social-ism," and "science"—the first stemming largely from egalitarianism, the second from humanitarianism, and the third from hedonism. All the above might be called constitutive ideas of his thought. In addition to these, the idea of progress also figured prominently in his thinking, serving as an all-important operative principle under which man's so-cial life was conceived of as a dynamic process moving step by step, through deliberative efforts, from imperfection to perfection.

Criticism of Traditional Institutions

Judging from what K'ang said in the book about social and political institutions, in particular those of imperial China, he was indeed a severe critic of his age. He "surveyed the multitudinous sufferings of

[122] In the *Community*, 1, pp. 11–77; 2 and 3, 8–51, K'ang grouped "sufferings" under six major headings and elaborated on them, thus offering the most complete array of human miseries in all Chinese literature.

men and traced them all to faulty institutions" ("boundaries," in his terminology).[123]

He began with the state.[124] As a result of natural development and chiefly for the purpose of protection, he believed, men had since earliest times lived in groups of various sizes—families, clans, tribes, and states. These institutions, while useful and unavoidable, were not unmixed blessings. One of the misfortunes they brought upon men was organized conflicts, and the most baneful of these were the wars of conquest, which appeared with the establishment of the state, the largest so far of human organizations. War was inherent in the nature of political organization; for states and empires had their origin in the process of forcible annexation of smaller entities by means of military might. Thus as long as states existed, wars would always be fought, not only on earth but conceivably in "star clusters and nebulae" and other parts of the universe.[125] Civilization did not stop war but simply helped to make it more fierce and destructive.

> Anciently, wars were fought with knives, in which men were killed singly; now wars are fought with fire and poison. Several hundred thousand men could be slaughtered in one evening, as at Sedan. Alas, how grievous and lamentable are [the aftereffects of] the establishment of the state![126]

K'ang then went on to condemn social stratification. As political organization interfered with men's right to live, social distinctions infringed upon their right to be equal. Equality, K'ang maintained, was a natural right upheld by "universal principle."

> The coming to birth of all men proceeds from Heaven. All are brothers and all are truly equal. How can [men] wrongfully be divided into higher

---

[123] K'ang mentioned nine such "boundaries": (1) state, (2) class, (3) race, (4) sex, (5) family, (6) property, (7) "disorder," namely, "the existence of unequal, unreasonable, dissimilar, and unjust laws," (8) "kind," i.e., "the separation between men, and the birds, beasts, and fish," and (9) "suffering-boundaries," i.e., sufferings giving rise to further sufferings without end. K'ang's classification is hardly logical. Not all the "boundaries" are established institutions; the last item does not even refer to "boundary."

[124] K'ang devoted an entire chapter (Part 2, chap. 1) to "the evils of having states."

[125] *Community*, 1, p. 82; 2 and 3, p. 54; Thompson, p. 80. K'ang stated in the same passage that as a result of territorial wars waged by "the people of Mars" countless human lives were lost. This curious statement stemmed obviously from K'ang's misunderstanding of Roman mythology.

[126] *Community*, 1, p. 102; 2 and 3, p. 68; Thompson did not translate this passage.

and lower classes and some be treated as important while others as insignificant?[127]

Inequality, unlike warfare, did not involve destruction of human life. But its effects were nevertheless baneful. "Of the sufferings due to inequality," K'ang declared, "none compare to [those which stem from] unjustifiable class distinctions."[128]

Unfortunately, institutions that upheld and perpetuated inequality prevailed in practically every age and every place of the world. They existed in various forms in ancient Egypt, Babylonia, Greece, medieval Europe, feudal Japan, and India, which with its caste system enjoyed the dubious distinction of having the worst type of them all. China, together with the United States, led the nations of the world in moving toward social equality. K'ang said approvingly of the latter:

> The people of America enjoy the highest degree of equality. There is no monarch but there is a president. Since Washington established the constitution, hereditary nobility has been regarded as perverse. Although there are high priests, they cannot hold [government] office or interfere in public affairs. [When] Lincoln freed the negro slaves, a war was fought over it, strongly contested with much bloodshed. As a result [of the emancipation], all of America's people are common citizens, all have attained equality. Even though negroes are [still] not treated equally, [America] is nevertheless the harbinger of the Age of Ascending Peace. Therefore, [that country] is most tranquil, strong, prosperous, and happy.[129]

The highest praise, somewhat surprisingly, was reserved for China, or, more accurately, for Confucius, the Confucius as K'ang made him to be. According to K'ang, social and political inequalities prevailed before and during Confucius' lifetime, creating a situation comparable to that existing in feudal Japan or medieval Europe, though appreciably better than that obtaining in India. But by dint of his teaching, Confucius "abolished" all these inequalities.

> Confucius originated the idea of equality. [He] made clear the unityl [of the empire] so as to do away with feudalism and derided the [institution of] hereditary nobility so as to do away with hereditary office. [He trans-

[127] *Community*, 1, p. 170; 2 and 3, p. 110; Thompson, pp. 135–36. Similar sentiments are seen in K'ang's earlier works, "Substantial Truths and Universal Principles." Part 3 of the *Community*, which deals with "class boundaries," is one of the shortest sections of the book and bears marks of hasty writing (and perfunctory editing). This, together with Parts 4–10, remained in MS when K'ang died in 1927.

[128] *Community*, 1, p. 167; 2 and 3, p. 108; Thompson, p. 134.

[129] *Community*, 1, p. 169; 2 and 3, p. 109; Thompson, p. 134.

mitted the idea of the ancient] assigned-field system so as to do away with slavery and wrote the constitution of the *Ch'un-ch'iu* so as to put a limit to the monarch's power. [He] did not exalt his followers and thus precluded [the appearance of] high priests. Caste was thereby completely eliminated in Chinese institutions . . . and the evils of caste did not exist. Verily this was an extraordinary accomplishment of Confucius, and he did it two thousand years before [a comparable achievement] in Europe. It is entirely due to this that China has been stronger and more flourishing than India.[130]

China, however, did not completely follow Confucius' teaching. Slavery remained, together with the inferior status of such people as "boatmen" and "entertainers." The Chinese, really, were not to blame. The chief culprits were the Mongols of the Yüan dynasty, who enslaved vanquished peoples, and the Manchus who carried on the Mongol tradition, in the institution of "bondservants" thus reverting to the pre-Confucian tradition, in violation of the "universal principle" as embodied in the Confucian teaching.[131]

Racial discrimination, according to K'ang, constituted a third source of human "sufferings." Somewhat inconsistently with the "universal principle" that he enunciated in connection with his condemnation of institutions of social inequality, namely, that all men were brothers and "truly equal," he refused to regard the "races" of the world as equal in mental capacity or physical excellence. In no uncertain terms he described the "white" and "yellow races" as superior to the "brown" and "black."

> The silver-colored race is spread out over the globe, while the gold-colored race is more numerous [though concentrated on one continent]. These two kinds—the yellow and the white—possess the whole world. The strength of the white race is assuredly superior, while the yellow race is more numerous and also wiser.[132]

In equally clear terms K'ang characterized the brown and black races as inferior, mentally as well as physically. Members of the brown race had lackluster eyes and dark-colored complexion; "tired in spirit, hot in temper, lazy in disposition, and dull in mind," they stood just one "notch" above the blacks, the "most inferior" of human races.[133] K'ang painted an insulting picture of negroes.

[130] *Community*, 1, pp. 169–70; 2 and 3, pp. 109–10; Thompson, p. 135.

[131] *Community*, 1, pp. 172–73; 2 and 3, pp. 111–12; Thompson, p. 137.

[132] *Community*, 1, p. 178; 2 and 3, p. 114; Thompson, p. 141. Some notable textual variations exist between 1 on the one hand and 2 and 3 on the other. Thompson used edition 1 in making his translation.

[133] *Community*, 1, p. 186; 2 and 3, p. 115; Thompson, pp. 147–48.

With their iron faces, silver teeth, slanting jaws like a pig, front view like an ox, full breasts covered with long hair, their hands and feet deep black, stupid like sheep or swine, they bring fear to [one who] beholds them.[134]

It was understandable, K'ang continued, that despite Lincoln's "noble intention in liberating the black slaves" and the bloodshed entailed in bringing about their emancipation, people of America persisted in refusing to treat negroes as their equals.

Americans talk about equality, but refuse to elect negroes to office, to permit negroes to enter their hotels, to ride in first class trains. . . . because their skin color is different.[135]

Instead of condemning racial discrimination, K'ang offered an explanation of it, an explanation which amounted virtually to justification.

That all men should be equal, that mankind should be completely unified in the Age of the Great Community and Universal Peace, is of course a universal principle. But the inequality of creatures is a fact. Whenever we speak of equality, it is necessary that creatures have the capacity to be equal in abilities, knowledge, appearance, and bodily characteristics, before equality can be effected. If not, then even though it is enforced by state laws, constrained by a ruler's power, and led by universal principles, it still cannot be effected.[136]

K'ang, of course, did not really approve racial inequality. But he wished to eliminate it, as we shall see, by methods other than simple legislative action.

K'ang's criticisms of "sex boundaries" and "family boundaries," two other major sources of sufferings, were far more severe than the above. His views in these connections were, at the time when he expressed them, by far the most novel and provocative. He condemned the subjection of women in extremely strong terms. In an impassioned passage he said:

In the world, when there are cases of injustice and inequality in which

---

[134] *Community*, 1, p. 180; 2 and 3, p. 118; Thompson, p. 144. Cf. *Community*, 1, p. 187; 2 and 3, p. 115; and Thompson, p. 148, where K'ang depicted their "extreme stupidity and ugliness" in similar terms.

[135] *Community*, 1, p. 187; 2 and 3, pp. 115–16; Thompson did not translate this passage.

[136] *Community*, 1, pp. 179–80; 2 and 3, p. 118; Thompson, p. 143.

there are only one or two persons being unduly repressed, and one or two persons being unduly favored, many will go to law for them and help them. . . . Now for ten and some thousand years and in all the countries of the globe, incalculable, inconceivable numbers of beings who have all alike had human form, have all alike had human intelligence, who have all been in intimate relation with and loved by men, have been callously and unscrupulously repressed, restrained, kept in ignorance, shut up, imprisoned, and shackled by [these same men]—prevented by men from attaining independence, from taking part in public affairs, from becoming officials, from being citizens, from participating in public assemblies; still worse, from doing scholarly work, from voicing their opinions, from having their names heard by others, from free social intercourse, . . . from [even] leaving the house; and still worse, [forced by men] to bind and constrict their waists, to veil their faces, to deform their feet, to tattoo their bodies—the guiltless being thus universally oppressed and the innocent punished. These are worse than the worst immoralities. And yet throughout the world, past and present, for thousands of years, those whom we call charitable and righteous men, having been accustomed to the sight [of such things], have sat and looked and considered them to be matters of course; no one has demanded justice for these [oppressed ones] or helped them. This is the most appalling, unjust, inequitable thing . . . under heaven.[137]

K'ang paid special attention to women's lack of freedom in choosing their mates. He criticized severely marriages arranged "by parents' command" and lifelong widowhood, institutions sanctioned in China by the Confucian moral code and upheld by established tradition. He dwelled on the evils resulting from lack of "matrimonial freedom" (*hun-yin tzu-yu*), a phrase used for the first time in imperial China and destined to become current in republican and communistic China.[138] Denial of freedom to choose one's mate often led to ill-matched marriages, and women suffered more than men on this account because of the former's position in family and society. Sometimes girls were betrothed to their future husbands even before they were born; young women were promised in marriage to young men simply because the fathers of the families were wealthy or eminent. In many instances the young men turned out to be woefully unworthy—defective in body or despicable in character—or utterly incompatible in temperament with

[137] *Community*, 1, p. 193; 2 and 3, p. 126; Thompson, pp. 149–50. K'ang was apparently not aware of the woman suffrage movements that developed in the second half of the nineteenth century in the West, nor acquainted with J. S. Mill's views as expressed in his *Subjection of Women* (1869).

[138] See C. K. Yang, *The Chinese Family in the Communist Revolution* (Cambridge: Harvard University Press, 1959), chap. 2, "Freedom of Marriage," for a summary of changes from traditional marriage to marriage under the Marriage Law of 1950.

their wives. K'ang cited instances of which he had personal knowledge
to underscore the disastrous results of the popularly honored precept,
"Married to a rooster, follow the rooster; married to a dog, follow the
dog."[139]

All this was contrary to reason and justice. K'ang declared:

> As all humans have bodies given by Heaven, they all have the right to
> freedom given by Heaven. . . . To withhold [freedom] from any person is
> to usurp human right and to violate heavenly reason.[140]

The argument that there were differences between the sexes constituted no justification for subjection of the "weaker sex." K'ang
pointed out that one could not be sure that such differences as actually
existed worked necessarily in favor of the male. So far as mental capacity
was concerned, there had been on record dull males and intelligent
females. No woman, it was true, had been counted among the few outstanding men distinguished in learning such as Yang Hsiung, Chang
Heng, Copernicus, and Newton. But it could hardly be denied that
given equal opportunity women could make comparable contributions.[141] In fact, K'ang argued, women's contribution to civilization
was as important as men's, though in different direction. Under primitive conditions survival of mankind owed much to men's superior physical strength, which was indispensable to hunting and war, but the invention of arts and crafts, essential ingredients of civilization, must have
been largely the work of women who stayed home and applied themselves to such work.[142] To deny equality to women, therefore, involved
a double injustice: violation of the basic principle of human equality
and failure to show appreciation for the crucial role of women in the
history of civilization.

K'ang traced the origin of inequality to the time when men's physical
might made right. Later, with the development of social institutions
and values, repression of women hardened into inveterate tradition.
They lost their rights as independent human beings; nominally men's
"peers," they became virtually their slaves and chattels. Eventually,
the husband was recognized as the counterpart of the sovereign. The

[139] *Community*, 1, pp. 206–10; 2 and 3, pp. 136–39; Thompson, p. 153.

[140] *Community*, 1, p. 206; 2 and 3, p. 136; Thompson, pp. 152–53. The Chinese
character *t'ien* in the original, which is here translated as "Heaven," can also be
rendered as "Nature." Conceivably, K'ang was restating the Western idea of *natural
rights* as he understood it.

[141] *Community*, 1, pp. 229–30; 2 and 3, pp. 150–52; Thompson, pp. 155–56.

[142] *Community*, 1, pp. 224–26; 2 and 3, pp. 147–48; Thompson, p. 155.

overpowering doctrine of "the three bonds" (*san kang*) with all its implications soon became established.[143]

K'ang held the Neo-Confucians of Sung times responsible for the one-sided moral code imposed upon Chinese women. Whatever pleasure it might have given to men, this code, especially in imposing the duty of chastity on women, caused untold sufferings on the part of the latter. In K'ang's words:

> The Sung Confucians loved lofty principles. They sought to surpass the Sage and succeeded in causing countless widows to grieve in wretched alleys, harassed by hunger and cold—their hidden heartaches filling the firmament—but [these Confucians] thought it a beautiful custom![144]

Interestingly, K'ang's views concerning the position of women adumbrated those of a number of writers in the 1920s, who loudly decried traditional moral values in general and feminine chastity in particular.[145] In fact, it would not be unreasonable to suggest that K'ang had actually initiated a trend that continued in the republican period and culminated in Communist China.[146]

K'ang's most startling views, however, were reserved for Part VI, the longest section of the book, where he dealt with the evils of the family as a social institution. He began with an inquiry into the origin and basis of the family. In the earliest time of human existence, he believed, there had been no family because men and women lived in sexual promiscuity, in "a manner not different from dogs and foxes." Children recognized their mothers but not their fathers, and they had no inkling of the paternal family of later times. Eventually, some males who had particularly strong affections for their mates managed to make their unions permanent, by means of sheer force, thereby giving rise to the institution of marriage. With the relationship of husband and wife thus established, it became possible to define the father-child relationship, which in turn gave rise to the institutions of the family and the clan.[147]

[143] *Community*, 1, pp. 231–36; 2 and 3, pp. 152–56; Thompson, pp. 156–57.

[144] *Community*, 1, p. 241; 2 and 3, p. 159; Thompson, p. 157.

[145] Notably, Hu Shih, "Chen-ch'ao wen-t'i," *Hsin ch'ing-nien*, 5, no. 1 (July 1918): 5–14 (Japanese reprint, pp. 9–18); and T'ang Ssu (Lu Hsün), "Wo-chih chieh-lieh kuan," *Hsin ch'ing-nien*, 5, no. 2 (Aug. 1918): 92–101 (Japanese reprint, pp. 103–12).

[146] See Yang, *Chinese Family in Communist Revolution*, pp. 45–54, for a sketch of the history of remarriage of widows under the traditional system, in republican times, and under Communist rule.

[147] *Community*, 1, pp. 255–58; 2 and 3, pp. 168–70; Thompson, pp. 169–70. As

The family and the clan served useful purposes in the Age of Disorder. China owed much to her well-developed family system and well-defined family ethic. Filial piety, K'ang admitted, deserved to be stressed as the most appropriate way to requite the affection and care that children received from their parents, as long as the family was allowed to exist. K'ang deprecated Europeans and Americans for their "ingratitude towards parents," and regarded Christianity as "inferior" to Confucianism because the former taught men "to honor God but belittle parents." "I follow Confucius," K'ang declared.[148]

Unfortunately, however, filial duty was honored in China more by words than deeds. Selfish desires and economic necessity prevented most from recompensing their parents. Psychologically, it was far easier to love children than to cherish parents. Few could resist the charm of little children; many found it impossible to tolerate "divergence of views" between their parents and themselves. Thus this cardinal Confucian virtue remained an "empty word."[149] The family was thus marred by a serious flaw in the parent-child relationship; the flaw was somewhat less obvious in China than the West, but no family was free from it.

If children found it difficult to show affection to their own parents, it was even more difficult for other members of the family, less intimately related by blood, to love one another. Constrained by tradition to live together, relatives were too often driven by prejudices, dislikes, frailties, or cross-purposes into personal conflicts that might end in litigations, fights, murders, or sucides. Chinese family life presented to K'ang an extremely gloomy picture.

> There are times of peace in a country but there are no days of tranquility in a family. . . . [People] calling one another brothers or sisters actually hate one another worse than enemies; [people] calling one another daughters-in-law, mothers-in-law, or sisters-in-law become in fact perfect strangers because of disaffection. . . . The wealthier and higher in social position a family finds itself, the less affectionate and filial are its members; the stricter the rules of propriety are applied, the deeper become the troubles

---

K'ang cited only instances from China's prehistory, there is no ground for supposing that he had known the views of Western writers on the subject, e.g., Lewis Henry Morgan.

[148] *Community*, 1, p. 271; 2 and 3, p. 179; Thompson, p. 176. Cf. however, K'ang's statement in his early work, the *Truths*, "Fu-mu tzu-nü men," "kung-fa": "Parents shall not demand performance of filial duties by their children." See Path Finding in Two Worlds, an earlier section in this chapter.

[149] *Community*, 1, pp. 271–76; 2 and 3, pp. 179–82; Thompson, pp. 176–79.

and sufferings [experienced by its members]; the more numerous are its offspring and womenfolk, the more extensive the suspicion and resentment among them.[150]

In most cases the family did not readily break up as a result of dissension and conflict. They often maintained, for a while, an appearance of harmony. But no family could show such a false front forever. In the almost thirty years in which he lived in his home village, K'ang said, loud altercations between daughters-in-law and mothers-in-law, angry words among sisters-in-law were all that he heard, and open fights among brothers were all that he witnessed. "Axioms of past sages were just empty words" to these people.[151] The family, he concluded, which conferred advantages on its members by requiring them to live permanently together, brought endless "sufferings" upon them by this very requirement.

There was an even more serious objection to the family as a social institution: its continued existence was detrimental to the common good of society and to human progress in general, because it was the breeding ground of selfishness, the root of many evils, and because it encouraged dependence and perpetuated inequality. It therefore had no place in the Age of Universal Peace.[152] The family thus stood condemned in K'ang's thinking.

This, obviously, is a matter of major significance. In condemning the family, he in effect demolished, theoretically, the cornerstone of the social structure of traditional China and the keystone of the Confucian moral system, despite K'ang's overt statement that he "followed Confucius." K'ang himself certainly was aware of the iconoclastic implications of his position; he firmly refused to publish the portions of the book that contained these and other "shocking" suggestions.

As already mentioned, K'ang came to a highly unconventional view concerning the parent-child and husband-wife relationships in the 1880s.[153] But he did not hold this view consistently. In a major work on New Text Confucianism, done in the 1890s, he unequivocally upheld the traditional Confucian values, in particular filial piety and fraternal duty, contending that the Confucian teaching was in accord with "heavenly reason." "The three bonds," he asserted, "may be

---

[150] *Community*, 1, pp. 218–19; 2 and 3, pp. 183–84; Thompson, p. 179.

[151] *Community*, 1, p. 279; 2 and 3, pp. 184–85; Thompson did not translate this passage.

[152] *Community*, 1, pp. 286–88; 2 and 3, pp. 186–91; Thompson, pp. 180–82.

[153] See Path Finding in Two Worlds, in this chapter.

traced to Heaven itself."[154] Interestingly, during much of his lifetime, K'ang maintained the traditional familial values in actual conduct, showing impeccable filial piety toward his grandfather and parents, and unallayed affection for his brother and children.[155] All this was a far cry from what he wrote in the *Community*.

What made K'ang change his attitude toward the family and persuaded him to become the harshest critic of China's time-honored moral tradition? A combination of factors, as I have suggested elsewhere, appear to have contributed to this change.[156] In addition, his observations of European and American societies made during his extensive trips, must have convinced him that no social institutions, not even those of the countries he then admired, were free from serious defects and that, therefore, human happiness must be found in a social order entirely different from what was known in China or the West. Thus K'ang became the first uncompromising critic of China's traditional value system.[157]

Private property was to K'ang another faulty institution that stood in the way of happiness. Together with the family, private property engendered competition and conflict. It is interesting to note that while K'ang's criticisms of the family were based largely on his observation of the Chinese situation, his objections to private property stemmed mostly from what he knew of the conditions in Western industrial society.

K'ang obviously was concerned with a moral problem arising from modern technological and industrial developments to which they offered no solution. As he put it:

> Things which satisfy human needs are grown by farmers, manufactured by workers, and supplied by merchants. . . . With the arrival of modern times, . . . there come schools of agriculture, industry, and commerce; machines and chemical fertilizers are used in farming; the marvels of industry [have made it possible] to ascend the skies in balloons, to "shrink the earth" by railways, and to communicate across oceans by wireless telegraphy. Compared with the medieval, ours appears to be a brand-

---

[154] K'ang, *Ch'un-ch'iu Tung-shih hsüeh, chüan* 6 *hsia*, pp. 1a–b; *chüan* 6 *shang*, p. 24b; *chüan* 1, pp. 7b–8a.

[155] See chapter 1, this volume.

[156] Ibid., concluding paragraph.

[157] In pre-republican years, K'ang's vehemence against traditional social values was matched only by T'an Ssu-t'ung, who regarded himself as one of K'ang's students and became one of the "six martyrs" of the reform movement. T'an echoed K'ang's denunciation of the "three bonds" in his *Jen-hsüeh*, especially pp. 1a–4a and 7b–10a.

new world. In addition, commerce has grown to such an extent that ships sail busily to bring merchandise to all parts of the five continents. . . . Advancing day by day, [modern] civilization is certainly better than anything of the past. But the new technologies, although marvellous, represent only a superficial aspect of the world. They cannot contribute anything to rectify the unsatisfactory situation existing in the livelihood of the people— destitution and sufferings of the individual, and deficiencies in our regard for public welfare.[158]

After thus sounding the keynote of the discussion, K'ang went on to exhibit the shortcomings of private enterprise in agriculture, industry, and commerce. He did not write in the most logical manner, but he made the drift of his thinking very clear. He traced all the inequities and difficulties in agriculture to the fact that "people could buy and sell land." With the exception of "newly opened" America where arable land was ample, all countries of the world were plagued by the same problems. The situation was bad in China and worse in other "old countries of Asia." Various solutions had been proposed. In China, Confucius "devised the well-field system" as a means to implement his principle, "with equality, without poverty."[159] But this "checkerboard" arrangement of land distribution could hardly be carried out in countries other than those that were just being developed. Wang Mang applied the principle of equality in a reckless way and brought on disaster.[160] In the West, "the Englishmen [sic], Mr. Fourier," suggested, in this theory of livelihood, a system of huge "well-fields." This was another good but impracticable idea.[161] All these methods of reform proved to no avail because they missed the root of the evil.

> If we permit people to buy and sell private property [in agricultural land], that is, if people have such property, then there would not be a leveling of wealth and there would never be any way [to bring about] equality.[162]

[158] *Community*, 1, p. 353; 2 and 3, p. 234; Thompson, p. 210.

[159] *Lun-yü*, XVI.i.10.

[160] Wang Mang usurped the throne in A.D. 9–22 and instituted sweeping social and economic reforms. See Pan Ku, *Han shu, chüan* 99. Wang prohibited buying and selling of land in A.D. 9, thus virtually abolishing private landownership. Thompson (p. 211) misunderstood K'ang in translating the passage as "Wang Mang did not follow this path, but recklessly abandoned it."

[161] *Community*, 1, p. 353; 2 and 3, pp. 234–35; Thompson, p. 211. Fourier (1772– 1837), whom K'ang referred to as "Mr. Fu, " was French, not English. See Thompson, p. 228, n. 5. For a brief statement and evaluation of Fourier's utopian socialism, see W. A. Dunning, *Political Theories from Rousseau to Spencer*, pp. 352–54.

[162] *Community*, 1, p. 354; 2 and 3, p. 245; Thompson, p. 211.

The reference to Fourier constitutes definite proof that K'ang had come into contact with socialistic ideas, probably for the first time during his short sojourn in Japan.[163] His knowledge of socialism must have been, under the circumstances, quite hazy and fragmentary. It would be unwarranted to suppose that he had understood or accepted the central tenets of Marxism.[164] But however defective was his grasp of socialistic (or communistic) ideas, K'ang was one of the first Chinese writers to recognize their significance and to give them notice in writing, antedating by a number of years the flow of "early socialist currents" among the Chinese revolutionary writers.[165]

K'ang's leaning toward socialistic ideas became quite pronounced in his diagnosis of the ills of the capitalist industrial system. He wrote:

> With regard to the struggle between labor and capital: in recent years they have become more intense, because of machines being used to make things and completely replacing the artisan. . . . But men who have the ability to set up the machines of large factories must necessarily be big capitalists. Hence nowadays the large factory, the large railway or ship-building shop, the large emporium, and the large farm—all are run by big capitalists. A thousand or ten thousand laborers depend upon one factory or shop for their living, while the capitalist can fix wages as he sees fit, controlling and exploiting the laborers. Whereby the rich become richer and the poor become poorer.[166]

But this was not the worst. In a few more decades, K'ang predicted,

---

[163] Namely, October 26, 1898, to March 22, 1899 (*Nien-p'u*, p. 29b and *Nien-p'u hsü-pien*, p. 4a; Lo, *K'ang*, pp. 144, 179).

[164] On a few occasions K'ang employed the terms *kung-ch'an* ("community of property") and *chün-ch'an* ("equalization of property") in the *Community*; e.g., 1, pp. 105, 354, 356; 2 and 3, pp. 70, 235, 236. Apparently, he used these terms as equivalents of "communism." K'ang's relation to communism will be taken up later in the present study.

[165] See Robert A. Scalapino and Harold Schiffrin, "Early Socialist Currents in the Chinese Revolutionary Movement: Sun Yat-sen versus Liang Ch'i-ch'ao," pp. 321–42. The authors point out that "Liang wrote what was probably the first article on socialism in Chinese in the Ch'ing-i pao in 1899" (p. 335). Presumably, K'ang shared Liang's interest in socialism and may even have been introduced to socialism by Liang.

[166] *Community*, 1, p. 355; 2 and 3, p. 235; Thompson, p. 212. The word "wages" is a free translation of *k'ou-shih* (literally, "mouth food"). Thompson rendered *ts'ao-tsung* (literally, "grasp and let go") *ch'ing-chung* (literally, "light and heavy") in the original as "be strict and lenient, easy and hard." R. H. Mathews, *A Chinese-English Dictionary* (Shanghai, 1931), No. 6732, translates *ts'ao-tsung* as "to control the market and raise and lower the prices according to one's desires," which roughly covers the meaning also of *ch'ing-chung* as K'ang used it here. I have freely rendered both phrases as "fix" for the sake of simplicity.

with further expansion of capitalist industry, disparity in wealth would become extreme and mankind would face incalculable calamities. Even at the moment danger signs were clearly discernible.

> In recent years there has been a sudden rise of struggles by labor unions to coerce the capitalist, in Europe and America. This is only the beginning. The formation of labor unions will certainly increase in the future. One fears that this will lead to the calamity of bloody conflicts. . . . A hundred years hence it will certainly draw the attention of the entire world. Therefore nowadays socialist and communist doctrines are gaining increasing popularity, which will constitute the most important subject of discussion.[167]

This was almost prophetic, though the timing was incorrect. He did not know, at the time when he wrote the above, that the first waves of Marxism were to reach the Chinese intellectual world about two decades later and to engulf the entire country in less than fifty years.

K'ang shifted his standpoint when he discussed commerce. Here he was not primarily concerned with economic inequality but with the detrimental effects of free competition. The profit motive inevitably led merchants to unethical practices: shameless swindling of the public by charging high prices for inferior goods, or ruthless subverting or crushing of competitors. All this could not but prove morally degrading. K'ang attributed the spread of the competitive spirit to Darwinism and condemned it in these terms:

> Nowadays the theory of natural selection is being proclaimed, and the idea of competition is being regarded as most rational. Hence state and state, they marshal their troops and confront each other, considering annexation and conquest as a matter of course; man and man, they cunningly deceive and entrap each other, considering cheating and abuse to be the proper measure. . . . It is thought that talent and knowledge advance through competition, that tools and techniques are refined through competition, and that survival of the fittest is a law of nature. Competition is more seriously honored in commerce as the greatest principle [of life] than in any other occupation. [This principle] not only corrupts a man's mind but also brings ruin to his life.[168]

---

[167] *Community*, 1, p. 356; 2 and 3, p. 236; Thompson, p. 213. The term "socialist" is translation for *jen-ch'ün* (literally, "human group" or "society"); the term "communist" is translation for *chün ch'an* (literally, "equalization of property" or "equal possession").

[168] *Community*, 1, p. 357; 2 and 3, pp. 236–37; Thompson, pp. 214–15. K'ang repeated his opposition to Darwinism in *Meng-tzu wei*, in *Hsin-min ts'ung-pao*, no. 13 (1902), p. 53.

The effects of competition on society, K'ang continued, were as bad in commerce as in industry; in either case competition, which was the basic *modus operandi* in free enterprise, led directly to inequality.[169]

K'ang raised other objections, largely economic in nature, to free or private enterprise. The private farmer, unable to predict the market for his produce, was at a loss as to how much land to cultivate or what crops to raise. He was often confronted with short supply or overproduction. The private manufacturers were troubled by a number of problems: fluctuations of consumer demand, of labor supply, of costs, of quality of products. He was powerless to solve any of these problems and had to allow resources and manpower to go to waste. The private merchant was plagued by similar difficulties, to the injury not only of his own interests but also of the consumer.[170] It appears that K'ang had a fair knowledge of the "capitalist" economic system, even though his "socialism" reminds one of the armchair variety.

This concludes K'ang's criticism of specific social institutions. Keeping in mind the time at which he wrote, the beginning of the present century, one can hardly deny the revolutionary nature of his ideas. Liang Ch'i-ch'ao therefore quite justifiably compared these to "a mighty volcanic eruption and huge earthquake."[171] It is noteworthy that K'ang's criticisms were directed to institutions that were typical both of China and Western countries. If his objections to the autocratic state and male-centered family (conceptualized in the Confucian moral code as the "three bonds") were more pertinent to traditional China, his denunciation of racial discrimination and capitalist inequities was more applicable to the modern West. It seems that the universalizing tendency of K'ang's thinking was working here also. But instead of pointing to universal truths, he now pointed to the universal incidence of institutional imperfections. These objectionable components of Chinese and Western civilizations must be done away with. He called for, in other words, a thoroughgoing remaking of human institutions by de-Westernization as well as de-Sinification. Only thus could the ground be cleared for the construction of his utopian society—the ultimate fruit of universalization.

Institutions of "The Great Community"

The main features of K'ang's utopia can be briefly described. It

---

[169] *Community*, 1, p. 357; 2 and 3, p. 237; Thompson, p. 215.
[170] *Community*, 1, pp. 358–62; 2 and 3, pp. 237–40; Thompson, pp. 216–18.
[171] See note 1, above.

would be at once a world state under a democratic government, a society embracing all mankind without kinship, racial, or class distinctions, and an economic system maximizing the benefits of technological developments without the drawbacks of capitalism. It would be, in short, a form of existence in which complete happiness would materialize through the unity and equality of all men. The road to such a paradise on earth was to be paved on the foundation of a fourfold transformation of man and society: political, social, economic, and racial.

K'ang's plan for the political transformation of the world, namely, abolition of all individual states and autocratic systems and establishment of a democratic world political organization, was in some ways the least startling of his utopian ideals. It reminds one of such ancient Chinese conceptions as "all-under-heaven for all alike" (*t'ien-hsia wei kung*)[172] and "all-under-heaven as one family" (*t'ien-hsia yu i-chia*),[173] conceptions familiar to K'ang. It also reminds one somewhat of Immanuel Kant's "Project for a Perpetual Peace,"[174] although K'ang's theoretical standpoint was widely different from that of the German philosopher. Proceeding from the assumption that the existence of "state boundaries" invariably involved armed conflicts between states, K'ang drew the obvious conclusion that only by doing away with these boundaries could men live in lasting peace. It was impossible, K'ang argued, to curb the will of a sovereign state, "the highest form of human organization."

> Outside of Deity in Heaven there is no superior law to govern it. Each state plants for its own benefit. No public law can restrain it, no high principle can affect it.[175]

Individual states, then, must go. This was to be accomplished not through sudden revolution but as a result of gradual development. K'ang was optimistic in this connection. "Speaking in terms of universal principles and viewing the matter from the tenor of men's minds," he said, the tendency was assuredly and unmistakably toward world unity and peace.[176] Two political developments testified to this. On the one

---

[172] From the *Li-yün*; translation in William de Bary, Wing-tsit Chan, and Burton Watson, *Sources of Chinese Tradition*, p. 502.

[173] Wang Shou-jen, "*Ta-hsüeh* wen" in *Wang Wen-ch'eng-kung ch'üan-shu (Ssu-pu ts'ung-k'an), chüan* 26, p. 736; or in *Yang-ming ch'üan-chi (Ssu-pu pei-yao), chüan* 26, p. 1b. Translation in de Bary et al., *Sources of Chinese Tradition*, p. 571.

[174] Immanuel Kant, *Project for a Perpetual Peace*.

[175] *Community*, 1, p. 102; 2 and 3, p. 69; Thompson, p. 84.

[176] *Community*, 1, p. 104; 2 and 3, p. 69; Thompson, p. 84. In this passage, K'ang

hand, states were being combined to form ever larger political entities. Asian as well as Western history bore witness to this integrating process. For instance, the Chinese empire created in the third century B.C. was the product of the successive amalgamation of many states of antiquity; Aśoka united India at about the same time; similar processes took place in ancient Rome, modern Germany, and Italy. Despite the sufferings entailed in the wars of conquest the outcomes were desirable. K'ang continued:

> As the tendency toward fusion is a matter of natural selection, the swallowing up by the strong and large and the extermination of the weak and small may be considered as a prelude to the Great Community. Germany and the United States of America, both being federal states, point to an even better method of political integration. . . . Some day the latter will combine [all the states of] the American continents and the former, [all the states of] Europe. Such [developments] will hasten the world along the road to the Great Community.[177]

Another trend, the shifting of political authority to the people, moved also toward world unity and peace. The American revolution initiated the democratic movement that spread to other countries as revolutions occurred successively. With the establishment of political democracy came socialist movements with their "doctrine of communism" (*chünch'an chih shuo*), further quickened the march toward *Ta-t'ung*. For, K'ang explained, as democracy dispelled political selfishness, which characterized autocratic rule, communism would banish economic selfishness, which inhered in private property.[178] To do away with human selfishness was to facilitate the realization of universal harmony.

While K'ang admitted that political integration by military conquest had contributed to unity in the past, he preferred using peaceful methods to achieve the desired end. He envisaged three preliminary stages in man's progress toward utopia.

> Now if we wish to bring about the Great Community, first we will initiate it by disarmament conferences, next we will bind states together into alliances, and then we will lead to it by means of a world parliament.

---

mentioned "Darwin's utopia" among others. Thompson (p. 130, n. 16), was puzzled by the inclusion of Darwin. Apparently, K'ang had in mind here Darwin's theory of natural selection that, K'ang believed, would eventually lead to "one-world" as a result of its operation. See below.

[177] *Community*, 1, pp. 104–5; 2 and 3, p. 70; Thompson, p. 85.
[178] *Community*, 1, p. 105; 2 and 3, p. 70; Thompson, p. 86.

Proceeding in [this] order, it is certain that one day we shall arrive at the Great Community.[179]

Optimistically, K'ang estimated that the time required for completing this three-stage progress was between two and three centuries. He said in a note that in view of the invention of "flying ships" (aircraft)[180] he felt that the Great Community might come even within a century's time.[181]

K'ang regarded the establishment of a world parliament (*kung-i cheng-fu*, literally, "public deliberation government") as the first concrete step in the development of the Great Community itself. This parliament was to be composed of representatives elected annually, on the basis of equal or proportional representation, from all states. There was to be no president (chief executive) to challenge the sovereignty of the individual states, but a speaker was to be elected by majority vote from among the representatives. All matters were to be decided by majority vote. This arrangement, K'ang pointed out, resembled the Swiss but differed completely from the American system. This world-wide deliberative-legislative body was to have the authority to deal with matters specifically designated as falling within its competence; authority to deal with all other matters was to remain with the individual states.[182]

The world parliament would exercise control over such matters as the "universalization of international intercourse," which included formulation of international law, adjudication of international disputes, equalization of tariff rates, standardization of weights and measures, and development of a universal language to replace the existing languages; it would have authority to control all peoples, lands, and seas not under the jurisdiction of individual states; it would enforce, by military power if necessary, its rules and regulations over all states; and

---

[179] *Community*, 1, p. 105; 2 and 3, p. 70; Thompson, p. 86. K'ang pointed to the Hague Peace Conference of 1899, called by Czar Nicholas II of Russia and attended by delegates of twenty-six states (four of which were Asiatics) as a sure sign that the world was moving toward *Ta-t'ung*. K'ang failed to note that because some of the delegates, notably those from Germany, blocked every attempt at reducing the armed forces, the conference did not quite achieve its aim (*Community*, 1, p. 112; 2 and 3, p. 75; Thompson, pp. 90–91).

[180] To recall: Otto Lilienthal constructed his first glider in 1891; Samuel P. Langley commenced experiments with his model craft in 1892; Wilbur and Orville Wright produced the first power-driven machine in 1903. Thus, K'ang's reference to "flying ships" constitutes internal evidence that the book could not have been completed in 1884, as he claimed.

[181] *Community*, 1, p. 113; 2 and 3, pp. 75–76; Thompson, p. 91.

[182] *Community*, 1, pp. 113–14; 2 and 3, p. 76; Thompson, p. 91.

it would require all states to report to it the extent of their armaments and set limits to military equipment and armies. To insure that its will would prevail, it could call armies of individual states into its service or raise its own troops.[183] Thus the world parliament that K'ang designed would possess powers far more extensive and substantial than the United Nations of today. The idea that a universal language would eventually replace all existing languages is particularly interesting; it hints at K'ang's wish to eliminate national cultures and national feelings and reveals the extremely cosmopolitan nature of his utopia.[184]

The second (or "middle" in K'ang's terminology) stage of development would be reached when the situation favorable to the establishment of a "common government" for all men (*kung cheng-fu*) gradually appeared, in a number of decades after the institution of the world parliament. By then, K'ang believed, the power of the individual states would have greatly diminished, the desire to attain selfish ends at the expense of other nations would have decreased, and "democratic organization" would have multiplied and become firmly established; the world would be ready for a form of government similar to the American federal system.

The major functions of the world government, as outlined by K'ang,

[183] *Community*, 1, pp. 114–18; 2 and 3, pp. 76–79; Thompson, pp. 92–96.

[184] K'ang did not hold this view consistently, at least with regard to language. According to the editor of the *Community*, K'ang inserted a statement at the end of the passage dealing with language, when the first two parts of the book were published in 1919: "The Chinese language is expressive and elegant; it would be difficult to eliminate it" (*Community*, 1, p. 116; 2 and 3, p. 77; Thompson, p. 94). K'ang's interest in language reform began early in his career. He said in 1887 (*Nien-p'u*, p. 8a) that he "considered maintaining armies and learning languages to be greatly detrimental to man's mind and wasteful of his time" and that he "wished to formulate a plan for an Institute for Universal Language" (*Ti-ch'iu wan-yin yüan*, literally, "Institute for Myriad Languages of the Globe"). He appears to have made an effort to learn foreign languages. The late Professor Erwin Reifler showed me two books on the Egyptian language in his personal library, both of which bear K'ang's handwritten inscriptions. One is *First Steps in Egyptian: A Book for Beginners* (London: Kegan Paul, Trench, Trübner and Co., 1895), and the other is *An Egyptian Reading Book for Beginners*, issued by the same publisher in 1896. On the front flyleaf of each K'ang wrote: "Ancient Egyptian literature. Confucius 2460, *chi-hai*, Second Month. Bought in Cairo. Keng-sheng." "Keng-sheng" was the pen name that Kang often used after the collapse of the reform movement. This dating is confused. K'ang was in Japan in 1899 (*chi-hai* year); in the second month (March) of that year he left for America and Europe, sailing from Ottawa for Europe on May 21 and arriving at London May 31. It was in 1908 (*wu-sheng* year, or Confucius 2460) on his second European trip, when he went from Constantinople to Egypt (Second Month, or March). See K'ang T'ung-pi, *Nien-p'u hsü-pien*, pp. 4a and 60a. Despite K'ang's faulty dating, these volumes bear witness to his interest in foreign languages.

were calculated to quicken further the march toward world unity. The first among these was annual reduction of troops of each state until no standing armies of any size would remain. Another task was to liquidate the states themselves, to expunge even the term "state."[185] The earth then would be divided into "provinces" and "areas," each with its own local self-government. And to expedite further the process of integration the world government would adopt a new calendar to replace the existing ones,[186] to adopt the decimal system and with it a uniform system of weights and measures to replace the diverse systems in current use, and finally to adopt a single language for the entire world.[187] It appears that K'ang regarded this world government as the chief instrument of utopian construction.[188]

Interestingly, in a "Chart of the Three Ages in which Nations Unite into the Great Community," K'ang equated the three stages of development from the existing world to perfect society with the three stages of progress conceived of by the Kung-yang school of Confucianism: "the Age of Disorder," "the Age of Ascending Peace," and "the Age of Universal Peace."[189] This is one of the few places in the book where K'ang, unintentionally perhaps, showed his intellectual ties with Confucianism.

With the world integrated into one universal state, all men would become "world citizens" (*shih-chieh kung-min*) whose authority would be exercised through "public deliberation" (*kung-i wei ch'üan*),[190] in electing representatives to the world parliament and in conducting local self-government. The governmental structure as K'ang described it was a simple one. It was to consist of a bicameral parliament. Members of the upper house were to be elected by inhabitants of the various geographical divisions, those of the lower house by the people at large.

[185] Thompson, p. 99, misread this passage as meaning abolition of national languages.

[186] *Nien-p'u*, p. 7b (Lo, *K'ang*, pp. 43–44), indicates that K'ang had already worked out a new calendar system in 1886 when he was twenty-nine *sui*. He proposed that dating of events be according to the *Ta-t'ung* era, taking 1900 as Year One, and that all "private systems of dating" by births of monarchs or religious leaders be abolished. By this, he implicitly rejected his own practice of dating by Confucius' birth.

[187] K'ang made a similar proposal in 1887 (*Nien-p'u*, p. 8a). Cf. note 84, above.

[188] K'ang developed these ideas in *Community*, 1, pp. 118–36; 2 and 3, pp. 79–90; Thompson, pp. 96–104.

[189] *Community*, 1, pp. 136–65; 2 and 3, pp. 90–107; Thompson, pp. 105–27. For an account of K'ang's indebtedness to the Kung-yang school, see this volume, chapter 3, the concluding paragraph of the fourth section.

[190] Thompson's translation of this phrase as "under the authority of the public parliament" (p. 106) is doubtful.

There would be no speakers and all decisions were to be made by majority vote. In addition to legislative powers, the upper chamber would have authority to hear impeachments submitted by the people against administrative officials and to punish those who were thus found to be guilty. The executive branch of the world government was to have a number of "executive officials" (*hsing-cheng kuan*) and a "chief executive" (*hsing-cheng chang-kuan*), to be elected by the two houses of parliament. Each division of the earth would enjoy self-government, with the authority to make laws and to conduct administration within its area of competence.[191]

K'ang had no use for political parties. He argued that even though competition was conducive to progress, it "depraved" human nature and thus was too high a price to pay for progress. The existence of parties necessarily involved politics, and politics spelled competition. K'ang took an extremely dim view of electioneering.

> Nowadays under constitutional governments executive officials are all elected through nationwide competition of political parties. . . . [When the candidates stand for election, they] go clamoring about the roads, calling for partisan followers; secretly, [they] plot against one another, sometimes going as far as to use weapons to assassinate [their opponents]. Before the election, when multitudes of people mill about aimlessly, [they] spread out large quantities of food and wine [before the crowds] to curry favor [and thus to win votes]. Those whom the voters select are not necessarily deserving; even if the choice is justly made, it nevertheless involves competition, which depraves man's moral nature.[192]

No such behavior, according to K'ang, would be seen in utopia. There would of course be elections in the Great Community, but they would be conducted with justice and dignity, namely, without competitive electioneering. Compared with these elections the partisan competitions of the present would appear "barbarous" and indeed ridiculous. Incidentally, K'ang was dissatisfied with the operation of parlimentary institutions of his own time. His dissatisfaction was revealed in the observation that in the Great Community members of all the deliberative and legislative bodies would conduct themselves with unimpeachable

[191] *Community*, part 8, chap. 4: 1, pp. 388–91; 2 and 3, pp. 258–60; Thompson, pp. 233–34. It was to be composed of twenty ministries or boards; including, among others, ministries of welfare, agriculture, industry, finance, transportation and communication, moral and religious instruction, and entertainment and amusement. There was no ministry of war or foreign affairs, for in a world of absolute peace without individual states, there would be no place for either war or diplomacy.

[192] *Community*, 1, pp. 391–92; 2 and 3, p. 260; Thompson, pp. 234–35.

decorum, quite unlike "present-day partisan members of parliament" (*cheng-tang i-yüan*) who "fiercely attack one another, laugh noisily, and speak loudly." Such "extremely uncivilized" behavior would surely incur parliamentary censure or public scorn in the Age of Universal Peace.[193]

In addition to the central world government, there were to be local governments and local self-governments. K'ang proposed that the earth be divided into one hundred "degrees" and that each of the degrees would have its own government patterned after the central government with one important difference: the local government would have no authority to deal with matters concerning communication and transportation. Each degree was to be subdivided into smaller units, each of which would enjoy self-government.

K'ang's ideas of local self-government are quite novel. He forecast that as people of the world would live either in public buildings devoted to various enterprises (agriculture, industry, transportation, development) or in public institutions (schools, hospitals, homes for the young or aged), there would be "practically no private houses" nor "people living scattered in villages." As population concentrations would be basically agricultural (i.e., rural) or industrial (i.e., urban), centering respectively around extensive farms or large factories, the divisions for local self-government would be made not on a territorial but on a functional basis. Each farm or factory would constitute a unit of local self-government, the director of the farm or factory would be the head of local government, and all inhabitants working in the unit would take part in making decisions. Each farm or factory would have its own educational and welfare institutions: schools, public nurseries, hospitals, homes for the aged, and institutions for the destitute, in addition to bureaus of public works and economic affairs. Each local self-governing unit was to be a self-sufficing integral community, operating on thoroughly democratic principles.[194]

Thus, according to K'ang, there would be three levels of government in the Great Community: world government, "degree" government, and farm or factory self-government, all of which were "indispensable to man." In this governmental system the principle of equality was to be fully realized and the authoritarian principle to be reduced to a minimum. Indeed, all men were to become members of a community

---

[193] *Community*, 1, pp. 392–93; 2 and 3, p. 261; Thompson, pp. 235–36.

[194] *Community*, part 8, chap. 8: 1, pp. 401–5; 2 and 3, pp. 266–69; Thompson, pp. 238–39.

organized and operating in accordance with the principle of division of
labor among equals for the good of all. K'ang wrote:

> In the era of the Great Community there will be no subjects,[195] for all
> men of the world will perform in common the tasks of the world, like
> members of a family; there will be no rulers,[196] for although functionaries
> will be high or low, they will be so only in so far as concerning their func-
> tions. Outside the performance of specific functions all men of the world
> will be equal. There will be no distinctions in rank or position, no differ-
> ence in attire, no special privilege to use insignia or enjoy retinue which
> mark off some men from others.[197]

Political organization represented just one aspect of K'ang's utopian
construct. Basic social transformation had to be accomplished before
the development toward the Great Community was complete. In his
criticisms of existing social institutions (see above), K'ang clearly implied a classless communistic world-society that would materialize
through gradual orderly evolution, not as a result of sudden, violent revolution. He now sketched the main directions in which such transformation would take place.

The first was abolition of social classes. K'ang believed that in China
as well as in Western countries considerable progress had already been
made in this direction, although China lagged somewhat behind in still
allowing slavery to persist, despite Confucius' teaching. Emancipation
of slaves was absolutely proper and necessary; and the reason for so
doing was self-evident to K'ang. "All men," he declared, "are born of
Heaven and all citizens belong to the state. No one can be private possession of any person or any family."[198] However, a hasty order by government to manumit slaves would arouse bitterness and resentment
on the part of slaveowners. It would be much better to sweep slavery
away step by step.[199] First, slaves who had served their masters many
years should gain their freedom by paying the latter nominal sums of
money; second, newly bought slaves should be given the status of hired
hands and reimburse whatever purchase prices their would-be masters

---

[195] The original text has *min*, "people."

[196] The original text has *kuan*, "officials."

[197] *Community*, 1, p. 393; 2 and 3, p. 261; Thompson, p. 236.

[198] *Community*, 1, pp. 173–74; 2 and 3, p. 112; Thompson's translation, p. 137, is
unsatisfactory.

[199] *Community*, 1, p. 173; 2 and 3, p. 112; Thompson did not translate this passage.
K'ang mentioned in this connection that his grandfather, K'ang Tsan-hsiu, who once
served as subdirector of studies in Lien-chou, Kwangtung, set free a slave he just
purchased, and praised the old gentleman for his *jen* ("humaneness").

had paid by working without wages for a proper number of years; and third, a date would be set after which no purchase of slaves would be allowed.[200]

An even more basic task was transformation of the traditional familial institutions that perpetuated inequalities among persons related by blood or by marriage. K'ang was especially concerned with ending inequality between the sexes. He indicated a two-phase development. In the first phase, a "system of increasing equality and independence for women"[201] would be worked out. All women would receive education exactly as men, exercise political rights on a par with men, enjoy complete freedom of social intercourse and of choosing their mates; they would be spared of such "degrading" and painful practices as foot-binding, face-veiling, ear-piercing, waist-compressing. Married women would no longer be required to "obey the husband" or to use their husbands' surnames. And as a visible badge of their independence and equality, all women would wear the same style of clothing as members of the opposite sex.[202]

In the second phase of transformation women (and men) would attain further freedom, when marriage as an institution would be abolished. Instead of marriage there would be mating by free choice. The man and woman thus mated were to enter into a "contract of intimate relationship" (*chiao-hao chih yüeh*). In such an alliance, the parties were not to be known as "husband and wife" and each party was to stand on an entirely equal and independent footing; for, K'ang explained, the contract that bound them together was "like a treaty of alliance between two states," not affecting the sovereignty of the contracting parties. K'ang made it emphatically clear that the slightest distinction of superior and inferior between men and women joined in such alliances would constitute "a flouting of the nature-conferred human rights of equality and independence"[203] and would eventually lead to the subjection of women as hitherto prevailing in all societies.

To guard against reversion to the traditional form of marriage, K'ang suggested that a time limit be placed on all contracts of intimate rela-

---

[200] *Community*, 1, p. 174; 2 and 3, pp. 112–13; Thompson skipped this passage.

[201] This is the title of chap. 8 (part 5), missing in *Community*, 1, but given in 2 and 3, p. 162.

[202] *Community*, 1, pp. 246–48; 2 and 3, pp. 162–64; Thompson, pp. 160–63.

[203] *Community*, 1, p. 248; 2 and 3, p. 164. The original text has *tien-fu jen-ch'üan p'ing-teng tu-li chih i*. K'ang probably had in mind the Western concept of natural rights. Thompson's translation of *t'ien-fu* as "heaven-conferred" (p. 163) is not necessarily accurate.

tionship, so that any agreement to mate for life would be null and void.[204] Temporary mating, K'ang pointed out, would have the further advantage of not forcing people who were no longer in love to continue to live together. For, explained K'ang, "all whom we call humans necessarily have natures which are unlike." Even two persons "extremely in love" could not be completely compatible in their feelings, desires, and inclinations. To bind them in a lifelong union would end in disaster. Moreover, humans were fickle. Bored by one's mate in a long alliance, one would naturally wish to come into a new relationship with a person of the opposite sex] who appeared to be "more talented or learned, more beautiful or handsome, more congenial, or more wealthy" than the present mate. To perpetuate the existing alliance would spell unhappiness for both parties involved. In Asia where men were permitted by tradition to take concubines but women were condemned to remain faithful to their husbands, lifelong marriages meant for the wives adding inequity to injury.

Above all, the institution of marriage would find no place in the Great Community. Marriage once had its place in the history of man's social development. In the Age of Disorder, the patrilineal family served as the cornerstone of social structure. Without permanent unions between men and women the relationship between father and son would have been impossible to maintain. But in the Great Community the patrilineal family must be scrapped to make room for universal equality and freedom. With the patrilineal family gone, patrilocal marriage would lose its raison d'être.

Kang's proposal is simple.

(1) The length of the mating period may not exceed one year, nor be less than one full month. Those couples remaining in love may renew their [mating] agreements. (2) "Marriage agents' offices" shall be instituted [in different parts of the world]. When a man and a woman wish to be joined in union, they shall go to the marriage agent of the locality where they live, receive an official certificate, and write their agreement in the document. They shall vow to love each other for the duration of the contact.[205]

---

[204] K'ang expressed substantially the same view in his *Truths*, "*Fu-fu men*," "Pi-li," paragraph 1, which he wrote in the 1880s. In this early work K'ang proposed that the length of the mating contract be limited to three months, after which the parties would be free to mate with other persons, although they would also be free to renew the contract, *after a three-month interval*.

[205] *Community*, 1, p. 252; 2 and 3, p. 167; Thompson, p. 116. K'ang imposed restrictions on the freedom of "marriage" on women who had not gone to school and completed their education and who could not be "independent," financially or otherwise (1, p. 253; 2 and 3, p. 167; Thompson, p. 166).

K'ang was not disturbed by the fact that his proposal went contrary to the Confucian concept of marriage as clearly formulated in the *Book of Rites*:

Marriage is to make a bond of affection between two surnames, the object of which is to serve the ancestors in the temple and to perpetuate the coming generations.[206] Once married [a woman] does not change [spouse] for the rest of [her] life. Therefore [she] does not remarry after the husband's death.[207]

Ignoring such principles as these K'ang came out simply with what he believed to be the true basis of "marriage" in the Great Community.

The relation between men and women rests solely on the fulfillment of personal love, and not on the assurance of the continuation of the line from father to son.[208]

The time-honored and, especially since Sung times, the all-important womanly "virtue" of chastity, therefore, had no significance in K'ang's thinking. To him it was far better, in compliance with the principle of happiness, to allow people to follow the dictate of their hearts. Divorce would thus be rendered unnecessary and fornication, as a legal crime or moral sin, would no longer exist. K'ang's position was radical to the extreme, especially when one bears in mind that he wrote at the beginning of the present century, years before Ch'en Tu-hsiu, Hu Shih and others came out with their views on the emancipation of women and feminine chastity, and who by comparison were somewhat less thoroughgoing than K'ang.[209]

K'ang, however, did not close his eyes to the dangerous implications of his proposal. Accordingly, he concluded his chapter on marriage with this warning:

What has been said above is intended only to serve as a plan of future progress. If at present, when the education of women is incomplete and their personal character is not fully developed, we recklessly apply the rule of independence to women who would turn their backs on their husbands and give free rein to lustful passions, we would then open the road

[206] *Li-chi cheng-i* (Ch'i-ming shu-chü reprint, Taipei, 1959), 61, "Hun-li," p. 452.

[207] Ibid., 25, "Chiao t'e-sheng," p. 225, where it is said in effect that a married woman never changes her spouse to the end of her life. See T'ung-tsu Ch'ü, *Law and Society in Traditional China*, chap. 2, for legal aspects of traditional marriage.

[208] *Community*, 1, p. 250; 2 and 3, p. 165; Thompson, p. 165.

[209] See the section on the "Great Community" in Historical Perspective, later in this chapter.

to chaos. "Linens for summer; furs for winter": to everything its appointed time. Until we have arrived at that time, we must not prematurely apply this rule. The author does not want to corrupt the moral customs; he does not wish to be guilty of that.[210]

With the institution of marriage done away with, the traditional patrilineal family, "the most serious impediment" to the realization of the Great Community, would cease to exist. For the basic familial relationships, husband-wife, father-son and brother-brother, could no longer be recognized when mating of men and women became temporary. K'ang proposed the establishment of "public" institutions to take over the functions that previously were largely if not exclusively performed by the family. These institutions would serve the needs of every person, from cradle to grave, to an extent greater than anything known in the most advanced "welfare state" of modern times. It is unnecessary to go into details of K'ang's plan,[211] but it is useful to note some of its salient features.

K'ang began by stating its theoretical basis. As he put it:

Man is not [a being] that can be produced by man. All men are [beings] to whom heaven has given birth, and are therefore directly subject to heaven.[212] The free government [of the Great Community] is instituted publicly by men. Such a publicly established government should publicly nurture, educate, and succor men.[213]

Accordingly, there would be three types of public institutions to render three types of services: "public nurture," "public education," and "public succor." Institutions of public nurture included those that would care for pregnant women, infants, and young children; institutions of public education ranged from nursery schools to colleges; and institutions of public relief included those that would look after the aged, the destitute, the sick and disabled, and "public crematories." Thus every phase of a man's life, "from begetting to burying," would be completely managed by government through these institutions. As a consequence,

---

[210] *Community*, 1, p. 253; 2 and 3, p. 167; Thompson, pp. 166–67.

[211] K'ang gave considerable space (roughly, one-seventh of the book) to delineate this plan (*Community*, 1, pp. 290–352; 2 and 3, pp. 192–233).

[212] This is substantially reiteration of a view advanced earlier in the *Truths*, "Fu-tzu men," par. 1.

[213] *Community*, 1, p. 290; 2 and 3, p. 192; Thompson, p. 184.

parents will not have the toil of nurturing and caring for children, nor the expense of educating them. Moreover, the children thus cut off from the parents . . . will not recognize them. Men do not have to "leave the family";[214] they will automatically be without families.[215]

We cannot go into the rules and principles that K'ang formulated for the operation of these institutions. Some of the rules are quite interesting, but the most significant were those he laid down for guiding the educational institutions. His conception of education was obviously influenced by his knowledge of modern Western industrial societies. He stressed strongly the importance of specialization in learning, especially at the college level.

> When the Great Community becomes a reality, every profession will be specialized, and every man will have specialized training. Indeed, the higher the civilization advances, the more specialization in profession will ensue. . . . As time goes on, countless fields of specialization will appear.[216]

This emphasis on specialization constituted in effect a negation of the traditional Chinese ideal of scholarship: catholic knowledge of "all affairs under heaven." Significantly also, K'ang attached great importance to knowledge gained through practice and experimentation, as against speculative or "book knowledge." Thus, to study agriculture, one should work on a farm; to study medicine, one should gain experience in a hospital; to study law, one should practice in a court. Education, K'ang said, was not a matter of "empty writings or lofty discourses."[217] This, again, was a far cry from the traditional ideal: "discussion of the principles sitting down." Perhaps unknowingly, K'ang sponsored the technological-scientific, as against the "liberal" humanistic education of the modern West. Incidentally, it may be

---

[214] "To leave the family" (*ch'u chia, pravraj*) is a Buddhist term. K'ang rejected this Buddhist practice because it would logically lead to the extinction of mankind.

[215] *Community*, 1, p. 291; 2 and 3, p. 193; Thompson, p. 186.

[216] *Community*, 1, p. 328; 2 and 3, p. 217; Thompson, p. 198.

[217] *Community*, 1, p. 330; 2 and 3, p. 218; Thompson, p. 199. In another connection (1, p. 418; 2 and 3, p. 278; Thompson, pp. 246–47), K'ang outlined the curricula of these schools: "aside from moral, intellectual, and physical education, practical education will be most important. . . . Ancient history serves merely to inform scholars of the past; its usefulness is very slight. . . . As for the subtleties of logic and transcendental [speculation] on the soul, scholars will be allowed to pursue on their own. . . . As these will not be the concern of the public schools, they will not be taught in them." Foreign languages, K'ang added, would also be excluded. With the time thus saved "educational progress will be countless times faster than at the present." Thompson's translation misses the point entirely. Interestingly, time-saving was one of the chief arguments advanced by supporters of the "literary revolution" of republican times.

mentioned that this line of thought was to come out in even stronger terms about three years later in the *Essay on National Salvation through Material Upbuilding*.

The Great Community presupposed economic as well as social transformation. K'ang's economic ideal was in substance communistic both with respect to production and distribution. Every aspect of economic life was to be "nationalized" or "communized"; agriculture, industry, and commerce were to be "public" or "common" (*kung*). The institution of private property, land or otherwise, would be banished from utopia.[218] The government would set up appropriate offices to manage the economic affairs of the world.

There would be a central ministry of agriculture and a number of local boards and offices of agriculture, with authority to plan, regulate, and manage all phases of farming, husbandry, forestry, fishing, and mining. Government control would be so complete that not the least room would be left to individual choice or discretion. All the "agricultural" workers, recruited from men who had successfully completed the prescribed courses of public education, would be regimented "almost as under military command."

> In cultivating the soil, harvesting the crops, raising and breeding animals, or fishing, they will be mustered and organized; specific tasks will be assigned to them; and the working hours of each day will be fixed. . . . [The regulations governing] their movements will be virtually like military commands.[219]

Each farm would be an integral unit of self-government, in addition to being a unit of production. The director of the farm would be the head of the "local" government and the directors of the establishments subsidiary to the farm (including institutions for "public nurture," "public education," and "public succor") would be his assistants. "Local affairs would be openly discussed and voted upon by all members of the farm. Public dormitories, restaurants, and other facilities would render private housing unnecessary.[220] The structural similarities between K'ang's plan and the rural commune of Communist China are too obvious to require comment.

"Public industry" and "public commerce" would be similarly patterned. Each factory would constitute a unit of self-government as well

[218] *Community*, 1, p. 362; 2 and 3, p. 240; Thompson, p. 218.
[219] *Community*, 1, p. 368; 2 and 3, p. 244; Thompson, p. 219.
[220] *Community*, 1, p. 401; 2 and 3, p. 267; Thompson, pp. 238–39.

as a unit of production; the factory director would be the head of the "local" government and all the workers took part in deciding "local" affairs.[221] Premium would be placed upon technological progress and honor attached to industrial workers. New inventions and expanding mechanization would progressively reduce working hours—eventually to no more than an hour or two a day for each worker. Completely relieved of family burdens and financial worries (as both family and private property had been abolished) and freely enjoying the ample advantages afforded by the communal cultural and recreational facilities, the workers would be supremely happy, "like immortals in heaven." As supply and demand would be precisely controlled by the world government, overproduction or unemployment resulting from oversupply of manpower would be unknown.[222]

Commercial enterprises, like agriculture and industry, would be owned and operated "publicly." The central ministry of commerce would direct factories located in various parts of the world to manufacture exact quantities of goods to meet the demands of the total population of a given year, and would distribute these commodities to "retail stores." All prices would be fixed by the government; the most speedy and convenient means made possible by automation would be used to deliver goods ordered by consumers. All employees in the stores would be public functionaries. As the "profit motive" would be ruled out, middlemen's profit eliminated, and taxes done away with, the cost of commodities would be very low indeed.[223]

K'ang dismissed the possibility of bureaucratic corruption. With the liquidation of the family, and a complete change of social institutions and human psychology, he argued, not only the objective conditions that made fraud and embezzlement possible would disappear but the desire to steal would not arise. Therefore, K'ang concluded, abolition of the family was crucial to the economic and social transformation of society.[224]

From the above it can be gathered that what K'ang had in mind was something like complete socialization of human relationships and economic life. However, man could not attain utopia without achieving one more transformation: the elimination of racial inequality. In his enumeration of the "races," he expressed the view that the white and

[221] *Community*, 1, p. 402; 2 and 3, p. 267; Thompson, p. 329.
[222] *Community*, 1, pp. 371–75; 2 and 3, pp. 246–49; Thompson, pp. 221–22.
[223] *Community*, 1, pp. 375–79; 2 and 3, pp. 249–51; Thompson, pp. 223–25.
[224] *Community*, 1, p. 380; 2 and 3, p. 252; Thompson, p. 226.

yellow were superior to the brown and black. He recognized two ways to bring about racial equality: allowing the process of "natural evolution" (*t'ien-yen*)²²⁵ to run its course and thus eventually eliminate the "inferior" races, or merging the divergent races into one single breed by systematically applying measures of amalgamation. While the operation of the "principle of survival of the fittest" (*yu-sheng lieh-pai chih li*) would bring about the elimination of the black people of Africa "after a thousand and several hundred years,"²²⁶ it was far better and more humane to achieve racial equality through racial unity.

K'ang's suggestions betray his lack of acquaintance with the basic facts of biological life. Racial differences, he said, could be dissolved by the application of four methods: "the method of migration," "the method of intermarriage," "the method of dietary change," and "the method of elimination."

As a first step toward the goal, the world government should order all peoples dwelling in localities on or near the equator to move to cooler regions, such as Canada, lands by the Baltic, North, and Black seas, and areas lying between the thirtieth and fortieth parallels in South America. The next step was "to encourage mixed marriages." Any yellow or white person who mated with brown or black would be awarded the "race-reformer" decoration and accorded special consideration. Ruling out the possibility of racial degeneration as a result of intermarriage, as Houston Stewart Chamberlain and his fellow racists believed, K'ang was certain that the offspring of parents of different races would inherit the characteristics of the parent with the lighter skin color. Meanwhile, the process of amalgamation would be expedited by altering the diet of the "inferior" races, so that even their offensive bodily odors would disappear completely in a number of generations. And, finally, to guard against degeneration, black and brown individuals whose disposition was "unduly evil" or who had bad diseases, would be prevented from having offspring.²²⁷

K'ang expected fantastic results from these methods. He was convinced that intermarriage would set in motion a process of progressive bleaching so that

²²⁵ K'ang probably owed this term to Yen Fu's translation (1896) of Thomas Henry Huxley's *Evolution and Ethics* (1893), which bears the Chinese title *T'ien-yen lun.*

²²⁶ *Community*, 1, pp. 178–79; 2 and 3, pp. 117–18; Thompson, pp. 141–42.

²²⁷ *Community*, 1, pp. 184–89; 2 and 3, pp. 121–22. Minor differences are found in the texts, between 1 on the one hand and 2 and 3 on the other; Thompson's translation, pp. 146–48, is based on 1.

in from seven hundred to a thousand years, . . . all the negroes will be transformed into white persons. Thus, with the arrival of the Great Community, thanks to the transformative processes of a thousand years, the people of the entire world will be of the same color, the same appearance, the same size, and the same degree of intelligence. All human races will then constitute one great unity.[228]

K'ang, in other words, sought to bring about racial equality not by taking the races as they were and treating them as equal, but by tranforming the "inferior" races and making them indistinguishable from the "superior." This reminds one of a recent American writer who suggested that the best way to end segregation is "to make every negro a first-class citizen" by helping him to cease to behave like a negro.[229] Similarly, K'ang would like to make every negro a first-class member of mankind, by helping him to cease to be a negro.

Utopia of Universal Peace and Consummate Happiness

The process of social transformation having been completed, human attitudes and behavior would meanwhile have undergone significant changes. With nothing to warp or stultify men's heaven-endowed nature, they would leave behind them all the sins and crimes that perplexed pre-utopian society. The Great Community would indeed be crimeless. For as the perfect society would make perfect men, so perfect men would make the perfect society.

In K'ang's view, men committed crimes because of frustrations: inhibitions of their natural desires as the result of restrictions imposed upon them by social institutions, in particular, the state, family, and private property, with their obstructive and repressive effects. Removing such restrictions would amount to removing the compulsive conditions that led to adultery, rape, theft, robbery, assault, rebellion, and war. "Public" education, which would bring the principles of freedom, equality, and fraternity to bear on each and every individual, would constitute a further insurance against misconduct.

In the Great Community, therefore, laws and courts would be unnecessary. The only useful regulations would be those governing performance of administrative and productive functions.[230] Even a fixed

[228] *Community*, 1, p. 188; 2 and 3, p. 116; Thompson, p. 148.

[229] John Fischer, "What the Negro Needs Most: A First-Class Citizen's Council," *Harper's*, July 1962.

[230] *Community*, 1, pp. 419–26; 2 and 3, pp. 279–83; Thompson, pp. 247–54. K'ang would permit the common people to bring suits to the public parliaments against officials, and specified that judicial officials be instituted in the world government (1,

moral code would be inappropriate for, according to K'ang, it was difficult to establish a standard of good and evil.

> According to the universal principle (*kung li*) nothing is inherently good
> or evil. Right and wrong are all according to what various sages have
> established. . . . Thus . . . good and evil are difficult to determine, and
> right and wrong shift with the times. Indeed, as good, evil, right, and
> wrong are all man made, universal principles themselves are determined
> by the [circumstances of] a given time.[231]

But relativity of moral values should not prevent men from having a
universally valid pragmatic rule to guide their action. K'ang invoked
a precept that he set forth in earlier portions of the book: "As I figure
it," he said, "whatever is injurious to man is wrong; whatever is not
injurious to man is right."

K'ang formulated four rules ("four prohibitions" in his terminology)
that would insure the continuity of the Great Community: prohibitions
against laziness, idolizing an individual, competition, and abortion.

Childbirth being painful and rearing of offspring troublesome, K'ang
assumed that women in utopia would eagerly seek abortion. Unless
stringent regulations were enforced against it, mankind would eventually disappear from the world.[232] Laziness should be prohibited for
the obvious reason that when people were too much given over to
pleasure, as they surely would in utopia, they would refuse to work and
thus bring the world back to the Age of Disorder.[233] Equally apparent
was the reason for prohibition against idolizing an individual. Equality
was a basic principle of the Great Community and one of the indispensable conditions for human happiness. If undue importance was attached to a single individual, the door to inequality—and to "disorder"
—would be opened.[234] Competition was not allowable because it would
lead directly to conflict and confusion. Somewhat inconsistently with
his suggestion that man's psychology would drastically change in utopia, K'ang persisted in taking a rather dim view of "human nature."[235]

---

pp. 158–59; 2 and 3, p. 103; Thompson, p. 112). K'ang's optimistic idea that laws
and courts could be eventually dispensed with was obviously inspired by an old Confucian ideal. See the *Shih-chi, chüan* 4, "Chou pen-chi," p. 13b (Chung-hua shu-chü
ed.), to the effect that during the reigns of King Ch'eng and King K'ang the empire
was in such good order that penal laws were not applied for over forty years.

[231] *Community*, 1, p. 424; 2 and 3, p. 282; Thompson, pp. 251–52.
[232] *Community*, 1, pp. 306–12; 2 and 3, pp. 203–6; Thompson, p. 190.
[233] *Community*, 1, pp. 426–27; 2 and 3, p. 284; Thompson, pp. 254–55.
[234] *Community*, 1, pp. 427–28; 2 and 3, pp. 284–85; Thompson, pp. 255–57.
[235] See *Essays*, "Ho-p'i p'ien," par. 10.

From the very beginning, he said, man had been motivated by selfishness. And because of selfishness there was competition and struggle between individuals, families, states, and races. "The strong oppressed the weak; the majority harried the minority." Thereupon K'ang launched a scathing attack on Darwinism.

> People who had a little knowledge and held mistaken views, such as Darwin, invented the theory of evolution, making out that it was natural [for men to compete]; he taught men that competition was a great principle. As a result, competition, which proves to be an extremely evil thing for the whole world, past and present, is being carried on openly and accepted even by honorable men without shame. Thus the earth becomes a jungle in which all is "iron and blood."[236]

All this was contrary to the principle of universal harmony and mutual help—a principle beautifully expressed in the *Li-yün*, from which K'ang quoted these well-known words:

> They hated to see goods lying about in waste, yet they did not hoard them for themselves; they disliked the thought that their energies were not fully used, yet they used them not for private ends.[237]

[236] *Community*, 1, p. 429; 2 and 3, p. 285; Thompson's translation, p. 258, is unsatisfactory. "Iron and blood," as Thompson pointed out, alludes to the "blood and iron" policy of Bismarck. Liang Ch'i-ch'ao, K'ang's one-time student and collaborator in reform, took a different position, at about the same time that K'ang completed his *Community*. Liang, in an interesting biographical sketch of Darwin ("T'ien-yen hsüeh ch'u-tsu Ta-erh-wen chih hsüeh-shuo chi ch'i lüeh-chuan," in *Yin-ping-shih ho-chi, wen-chi*, 5, no. 13: 12–18), rated "the principle of natural selection and survival of the fittest" as universally valid, and suggested that the ideas of "competition and progress" would completely dominate the twentieth century. In another piece, the fourth section of his "Hsin-min shuo" (1902), Liang attributed the supremacy of Anglo-Saxon England and America as well as the ascendance of white men in general to the operation of "the principle of survival of the fittest," and suggested that China should follow the Anglo-Saxons ("Hsin-min shuo," *Chuan-chi*, 3, no. 4: 7–11). About twenty years later, however, Liang came around to K'ang's position. World War I convinced Liang that something was wrong with Western civilization and he laid the blame partly on Darwinism. He wrote: "This great European War nearly wiped out human civilization; although its causes were very many, it must be said that the Darwinian theory had a great influence" ("Lao-tzu che-hsüeh," in *Yin-pin-shih wen-chi, chüan* 63, pp. 14a–b, quoted by Levenson, *Liang Ch'i-ch'ao and the Mind of Modern China* (Cambridge, Mass.: Harvard University Press, 1953), p. 203.

[237] *Community*, 1, p. 430; 2 and 3, p. 286; Thompson, p. 259. In part 9 (1, pp. 431–39; 2 and 3, pp. 287–92; Thompson, pp. 264–69), K'ang argued that men should not compete even with other living creatures. Man, after all, was but one species among many, and he had no justification for struggling against another species. He, therefore, should refrain from killing birds and beasts and stop eating meat. Science would come up with meat substitutes which would be so delicious that man would shun meat, even if it was available. "Brahmanical Buddhism," K'ang said, attained the highest degree of humaneness in its insistence upon vegetarianism.

Not all competition, however, would be ruled out. For to suppress all striving would make progress impossible. Stagnation would surely spell social decay. The world government, therefore, should undertake to encourage men's strivings for excellence, knowledge, and virtue. Constant progress would then bring about a state of human existence so perfect that it would go far beyond the purview of men living in a previous age.[238]

The Great Community, as K'ang described it, appears to be a veritable paradise in which every human need would be amply met and every human desire fully gratified, without hard toil or anxiety. Life would be an unbroken succession of pleasurable experiences. Food, clothing, housing, and travel facilities would not only afford the highest degree of creature comfort but also give the fullest aesthetic satisfaction. Music would be heard everywhere; chairs, tables, beds, and all other pieces of furniture would send out exquisite strains of soothing sounds. Sanitation and health would engage the government's constant attention. Everything would be mechanized and automation would reign supreme. Unlike men of pre-utopian times, people would love to travel and dislike living in one place. There would be "mobile houses" and "flying ships" to carry them to whatever place they would wish to go.[239]

All this presupposed a high degree of industrialization, made possible through scientific and technological advances. K'ang's social ideal thus appears to have been at once an idealization and a criticism of modern Western industrial society.[240] The prosperity and splendor of Hong Kong, Shanghai, and other modern metropolises seldom failed to arouse his interest and admiration.[241] At the same time, he was not unaware of the social and moral problems that confronted the industrial West. His Great Community, which clearly implied the socialization of human as well as economic relationships, can with good reason be regarded as an attempt to forestall these problems. In this way he unknowingly joined the company of many a modern Western utopian

[238] *Community*, 1, pp. 407–18; 2 and 3, pp. 271–78; Thompson, pp. 241–46.

[239] *Community*, 1, pp. 442–51; 2 and 3, pp. 294–300; Thompson, pp. 271–74. In a way, K'ang had a preview of twentieth-century America "a nation on wheels" and in house boats.

[240] See Lin K'e-kuang, "Lun *Ta-tung shu*" (written in November, 1956) in *Chung-kuo chin-tai ssu-hsiang-chia yen-chiu lun-wen hsüan*, p. 19: "This society [the Great Community] is built on the foundation of a highly advanced material civilization."

[241] *Nien-p'u*, pp. 5b and 6a; K'ang T'ung-p'i, *Nien-p'u hsu-pien*, passim; and K'ang, *Ou-chou shih-i kuo yu-chi*, passim. K'ang's visit in Los Angeles, California, March 1905, convinced him even more of the vital importance of "the material civilization of the [Western] countries." This conviction prompted him to write *Wu-chih chiu-kuo lun*.

who, despite different backgrounds and differences in the details of proposals, moved in the same general stream of utopian thought.[242]

K'ang's utopian ideal, then, rested on two major principles: industrialization and socialization. It should be recalled also that K'ang relied heavily on a third principle in constructing his utopia, a principle of political organization that may be broadly characterized as democratic. It has been observed that "far too large a number of classic utopias were based upon conceptions of authoritarian discipline," thus exhibiting "dictatorial tendencies" and "creating an order too inflexible and a system of government too centralized and absolute, to permit any change."[243] K'ang was not entirely free from the authoritarian bias of some of his Western counterparts, especially in his conception of economic organization. In the socialized farm, for instance, agricultural workers would be regimented "almost as under military command."[244] Nevertheless, at the risk of contradicting himself, K'ang repeatedly stressed the value of personal freedom and equality. In fact, the political system that he envisioned for the Great Community was a republican government based upon the principle of popular consent. He did not call for anything like a stage of political tutelage to prepare men for full exercise of their rights. The individual man would not become an instrument of society. On the contrary, his happiness would always constitute the ultimate and immediate aim of all social organization. Economic regimentation was calculated, after all, only to insure the production in the fullest measure of goods that would make his life pleasurable, and to do nothing else. When his obligations to his fellow men were fulfilled, he would be free to leave society, to place himself in effect outside the sphere of social control, and to seek transcendental forms of individualized existence—to become a Taoist "immortal" or a buddha that would leave even the Great Community behind.[245] One can hardly detect social authoritarianism here.

Moreover, the Great Community itself was not intended to be a

---

[242] See Glenn Negley and Max J. Patrick, *The Quest for Utopia*.

[243] Mumford, *Story of Utopias*, p. 4.

[244] In his earlier writing, the *Essays*, "Ho-p'i p'ien," paragraphs 2 and 4, K'ang appears to have been positively sanguine about the efficacy of the monarchical authority and skeptical of the common people's ability. But apparently he had come gradually to a different view after 1898, when he began to appeal to as many people as he could reach for support of his cause. Forced by circumstances, he thus became one of the first among Chinese leaders to attempt to generate something like a popular political movement (K'ang T'ung-pi, *Nien-p'u hsü-pien*, passim).

[245] *Community*, 1, pp. 451–53; 2 and 3, pp. 300–301; Thompson, pp. 274–76.

"closed society for the prevention of human growth."[246] It was in fact permeated by the idea of progress. K'ang insisted upon both the necessity and possibility of the continuous improvement of social institutions and life conditions. "To be able to increase men's happiness and reduce their sufferings," K'ang wrote, "is progress."[247] To achieve this end it was necessary, according to him, not only to perfect social organization but also to make unlimited technological and scientific progress. What is more, men would not be bound even to dwell forever in social perfection. The Great Community would leave its exit doors always open —for qualified individuals to move on to "immortality" and "buddhahood," and finally "to roam in the heavens" in a blissful state of absolute transcendental freedom.[248] If authoritarianism indeed characterizes the majority of Western-conceived utopias, K'ang's Great Community constitutes a notable exception.[249]

"The Great Community" in Historical Perspective

I suggested earlier in this chapter that K'ang took his ideal of the Great Community seriously, intending it to be a practical plan of social transformation, which was to be carried out by appropriate means and at the proper time. Others, however, including one of his own students, tended to view the matter differently. Liang Ch'i-ch'ao confessed that he was at a loss as to why his teacher formulated a brilliant ideal but "did not desire its realization and even fought with all his might to suppress it."[250] Ch'ien Mu, the well-known historian, argued that as China did not provide objective conditions for the materialization of *Ta-t'ung*, K'ang "came close to indulging in inane speculation for self-amusement" in depicting it.[251] Communist writers saw no greater value in it than utopian socialism. Mao Tse-tung remarked in 1949 that K'ang wrote the *Ta-t'ung shu* but he did not and could not find the way

---

[246] Mumford, *Story of Utopias*, p. 4.

[247] *Community*, 1, p. 442; 2 and 3, p. 293; Thompson, p. 271, has not included this passage in his translation.

[248] *Community*, 1, 453; 2 and 3, p. 301; Thompson, p. 276. K'ang, therefore, differed in this respect with most Western utopian writers who "could conceive of no progress beyond their projected states" (Hertzler, *History of Utopian Thought*, p. 307).

[249] Interestingly, K'ang did not refer in his book to anarchism, which had considerable influence on Chinese intellectuals of the time. In suggesting the possibility of these forms of transcendental existence beyond utopia, however, he gave a faint hint of anarchistic sentiments.

[250] Liang, *Ch'ing-tai hsüeh-shu kai-lun*, p. 136; Hsü, *Inlellectual Trends . . .* , p. 98.

[251] Ch'ien Mu, *Chung-kuo chin san-pai nien hsüeh-shu shih*, p. 664.

to "Great Harmony."[252] Writers in Communist China generally echoed this view. One dismissed K'ang's ideal as "dismembered thought" without basis in social reality; another identified it as "a sort of fanciful agrarian socialism"; a third disparaged it for "bogging down in pure fancy," even though it pointed to the "progressive notions" of democracy and freedom; and a fourth charged K'ang with using it "to deceive and dope the masses with a view to staving off the high tide of people's revolution."[253]

None of these appears to have taken note of K'ang's subjective intent or made an effort to understand the historical significance of his ideas. There is absolutely no doubt that he regarded *Ta-t'ung* as a practical ideal which would guide man's future social development. In 1919 when he published the first two portions of his book, apparently believing that time had arrived for implementing the political aspect of his utopia, he introduced them with three poems and a prefatory note. He said in one of the poems:

> To the Great Community I point the way,
> To which I wish men to lead.[254]

K'ang was in fact persuaded, as he clearly hinted on at least two occasions, that the political aspect of the Great Community was already taking shape in his own day. The First Hague Conference for international peace of 1899 was to him "a great event" that fittingly marked the beginning of world unity.[255] Upon learning of the founding of the League of Nations in 1919 he remarked with joy that he lived to "witness the realization of *Ta-t'ung*."[256] He still felt, however, that the other aspects of utopia lay in the distant future.[257]

---

[252] Mao Tse-tung, *Lun Jen-min min-chu chuan-cheng* (Hong Kong, 1949), p. 6; "On the People's Democratic Dictatorship" (June 30, 1949), in *Selected Works*, 4: 414. Mao's statement reminds one somewhat of Friedrich Engel's assessment of the effectiveness of utopian socialism. See *Socialism Utopian and Scientific*, trans. by Edward Aveling, pp. 74–75. S. L. Tikhvinsky, *Dvizenie za reformy v Kitae v kontse XIX veka i Kan Iu-vei*, chap. 14, deals with the *Ta-t'ung shu* and echoes the view of Mao whose words are quoted (p. 341). A Chinese translation of Tikhvinsky's book by Chang Shih-yü, Liang Chao-hsi, Lu Shih-lun, and Chiang Chen-yin appeared in Peking in 1962.

[253] Li Jui, "Mao Tse-tung t'ung-chih ti ch'u-ch'i ko-ming huo-tung," *Chung-kuo ch'ing-nien* (1953), no. 13, p. 9. Lin K'e-kuang, "Lun *Ta-t'ung shu*," p. 26. Hsi Wen-fu, "Yu-li-liao-ti hsüeh-shuo," *Hsin shih-hsüeh t'ung-hsün* (June, 1953), p. 6. Mao Chien-yü, "Wen-t'i chieh-ta," *Hsin shih-hsüeh tung-hsün* (May, 1953), p. 19.

[254] *Community*, 1, pp. 5–6.

[255] Ibid., 1, p. 135; 2 and 3, p. 90; Thompson, p. 104.

[256] *Community*, 1, pp. 8–10. See this chapter, Path Finding in Two Worlds, note 10.

[257] See note 250, above.

The *Ta-t'ung shu*, it seems, was in effect "a direction for action."[258] In addition to giving detailed explanation to the formal structures and operative principles of social institutions, it outlines the successive stages through which man would march, surely but gradually, to utopia. The process of transformation was to be something like "piecemeal utopian engineering."[259] The author showed no interest in remaking society at one stroke or attaining *Hua-hsü* in daydream.[260]

The allegation that K'ang's social ideal had no contact with reality is open to challenge. His trenchant criticism of existing institutions touched the core of some problems that confronted men of the late nineteenth century, both in China and the West. His suggestions for meeting these problems pointed to the general direction in which the historical process actually moved. Some of his radical ideas were clearly ahead of the time and consequently found little response. But his other notions, which he put into their final form in 1902, were later championed by a sizable number of intellectuals or subsequently became social realities. In the 1910s and 1920s "liberty" and "equality" were household words in intellectual circles; "democracy" and "science" enjoyed passionate and often vociferous sponsorship. The Chinese family did not disappear as K'ang had recommended, but it underwent in the republican period changes so far reaching they were virtually "revolutionary."[261] A Woman's Rights League was organized in 1922 in Peking;[262] a year later, a group of college students in the south advocated "family democracy" and "full freedom" in marriage.[263] Equal-

[258] Mannheim, *Ideology and Utopia*, p. 40.

[259] Karl Popper, *The Open Society and Its Enemies* (Princeton: Princeton University Press, 1950), vol. 1, chap. 9.

[260] "Hua-hsü" was a Taoist utopia which could be reached only by a journey of the spirit, described in the *Lieh-tzu*. See A. C. Graham, *The Book of Lieh-tzu*, p. 34, and Lionel Giles, *The Book of Lieh-tzu*, p. 35.

[261] See, e.g., Olga Lang, *Chinese Family and Society* (New Haven: Yale University Press, 1946); Marion J. Levy, *The Family Revolution in Modern China*; Yang, *Chinese Family in the Cultural Revolution*, especially pp. 10–17; and Chow Tse-tung, *The May Fourth Movement: Intellectual Revolution in Modern China*, chap. 10.

[262] Zung Wei Tsung, "The Woman Movement in China," *The Y.W.C.A. Magazine* (Shanghai, June 1923), pp. 2–3, quoted in Tsi C. Wang, *The Youth Movement in China*, p. 236. Cf. Chow Chung-cheng, *The Lotus Pool*, trans. from the original German by Joyce Emerson (New York: Appleton-Century-Crofts, 1961), an autobiography of a Chinese woman who defied tradition.

[263] See resolutions adopted by Zingnan [Lingnan?] College Students' Summer Conference, July 2–8, 1923, given in *The Chinese Recorder*, Aug. 1923, p. 435; quoted in Wang, *Youth Movement in China*, pp. 237–38. See also Chow, *The May Fourth Movement*, pp. 257–59, "The Emancipation of Woman," Kao Chung Ju, *Le mouvement intellectuel*

ity of the sexes and freedom in choosing one's mate found expression in government legislation.[264]

These developments did not come as a result of K'ang's influence. Intellectuals of the period knew only of K'ang's dogged opposition to the republic, his attempts at dynastic restoration, his futile efforts to establish "the Confucian religion," his somewhat paradoxical protests against "Westernization" in the turbulent 1910s and 1920s; they did not see his book on the Great Community, which was not published until the mid-1930s. No wonder, therefore, that these people regarded him with disdain or disgust, as a reactionary fighting against the rising tide of the "new culture." He remained a prophet unrecognized by the very same people who moved in the direction to which he firmly pointed years before. The fact is, both K'ang and his unwitting followers reflected the same trend of historic changes that for better or worse, freed China from the shaky grips of traditionalism and brought her to the unfamiliar portals of modernity in a matter of decades. To K'ang, however, belonged the credit of being the first to seize the currents already present in society and to chart a precise course of social transformation. Lack of recognition by his contemporaries and successors does not really detract from his historical importance.

K'ang's Great Community, then, was "an effective utopia" and not a fanciful dream divorced from the social process or the intellectual development of modern China.[265] The succession of cataclysmic events that occurred during his lifetime so badly shook the institutional and intellectual foundations of China that he was convinced not only of the desirability but also the possibility of radical transformation. His knowledge of the Chinese tradition and his acquaintance with modern Western civilization placed him in a position to see with an amazing degree of perspicacity what was wrong with China and how to change the situation. In the reform movement of 1898 he attempted reconstruction on a less ambitious scale. It represented, so to speak, his minimum program. In the book on the Great Community he laid down a plan of reform that was far greater in scope and far more profound in theoretical implications than anything that appeared in his generation. It

en Chine et son role dans la révolution chinoise, pp. 49–52, "L'emancipation féminine dans le domaine intellectuel (1860–1919)."

[264] See *The Civil Code*, Part IV, "Family Relations," promulgated May 5, 1931, especially chap. 2 on marriage.

[265] Mannheim, *Ideology and Utopia*, p. 207; and "Utopia," an article in the *Encyclopedia of the Social Sciences*," ed. Edwin R. A. Seligman and Alvin Johnson (New York: Macmillan Co., 1930–35), 15: 200–203.

was a uniquely imaginative and provocative utopian construct that should qualify its author for a niche in the hall of the world's greatest utopists.[266] One may well question the wisdom of some of his proposals, such as those concerning the family and property. But one cannot ignore the historical meaning of his social thought as a whole.[267]

The "Great Community" and "New Culture"

A brief examination of some of the ideas propounded by the leaders of the "New Culture" movement that crested in the later 1910s and early 1920s might be of some use here. Ch'en Tu-hsiu and Hu Shih were unquestionably among the most important of these leaders. Ch'en acknowledged that he was indebted to K'ang for initially broadening his intellectual horizon beyond China's old tradition, thanks to K'ang's writings produced during and prior to 1898, but took K'ang to task for his opposition to republicanism and his efforts to establish the "Confucian religion."[268] As Ch'en did not see the *Ta-t'ung shu*, at least not in its totality, he did not realize that K'ang's ideas of social transformation as set forth in 1901–2 not only anticipated some of his own but in some ways went even beyond them.

In an article published in 1915, Ch'en urged China's youth to embrace six principles that would be appropriate for the modern age. The first of these was "To be independent and not to be slavish." He explained:

> Men call the history of modern Europe "a history of emancipations." To achieve political emancipation monarchism was destroyed; to attain religious emancipation the authority of the church was denied; to bring about economic emancipation doctrines of socialism were developed; to emancipate women from men's domination suffragist movements were promoted. Emancipation means breaking off the shackle of slavery and preserving free and independent human personality.[269]

---

[266] More on this point later. For the term "utopist," see Negley and Patrick, *The Quest for Utopia*, introduction.

[267] Some of the writers in Communist China appear to admit this. E.g., Mao Chien-yü, "Tsai wei-hsin pien-fa yün-tung kuo-ch'eng-chung K'ang Yu-wei wei-shih-mo chu *Hsin-hsüeh wei-ching k'ao, K'ung-tzu kai-chih k'ao*, ho *Ta-t'ung shu*," *Shih-hsüeh t'ung-hsün* (May 1953), pp. 1–6; Lin K'e-kuang, "Lun *Ta-t'ung shu*," pp. 1–2; and "Yu-li-liao ti hsüeh-shuo" ("Disembodied Doctrines"), *Shih-hsüeh t'ung-hsün* (June 1953), pp. 3, 6.

[268] Ch'en Tu-hsiu, "Po K'ang Yu-wei chih tsung-t'ung tsung-li shu," *Hsin ch'ing-nien*, 2, no. 2 (Oct. 1916): 127–30; and "K'ung-tzu chih tao yü hsien-tai sheng-huo," *Hsin ch'ing-nien*, 2, no. 4 (Dec. 1916): 295–301.

[269] Ch'en Tu-hsiu, "Ching-kao ch'ing nien," *Hsin ch'ing-nien*, 1, no. 1 (Sept. 1915): 1–6. Cf. *Hsin ch'ing-nien*, 2, no. 4: 3.

Ch'en's other principles were equally interesting, in that they also clearly and closely approximated some of K'ang's ideas. It was necessary, Ch'en said, "to be progressive and not conservative," because all people who clung to old ways sooner or later came to grief, whereas those who strived forward were rewarded with endless prosperity; "to advance and not to retreat," for it was better to be a Columbus than to be a Tolstoi or a Tagore; "to be cosmopolitan and not to be isolationist," for all countries, however divergent they were in their ways, moved inexorably though gradually toward uniformity in spirit; "to rely on science and not on imagination," for it was science that accounted for the superiority of modern Europe; and finally, "to seek the practically beneficial and not to deal in empty words," for only practical knowledge possesses real value.[270]

It was such sentiments as these that underlay Ch'en's vehement campaign against China's old tradition and his earnest plea for honoring "Mr. Democracy" and "Mr. Science."[271] However, Ch'en did not really advocate wholesale abandonment of past achievements. In the belatedly issued "Manifesto" of the *Hsin ch'ing-nien* (December 1, 1919), which set forth the collective position of its editors and contributors at the time, it was clearly indicated that while "old conceptions" were being discarded,

> new conceptions concerning politics, morality, and economics are to be created by synthesizing ideas of worthies and sages of the past and present, and of our own, with a view to defining the spirit of a new age, compatible with the conditions of a new society.

This new society would be characterized by progressiveness, freedom, equality, peace, mutual aid, and happiness. In this new society men would transcend their instinctive aggressiveness and possessiveness; they would "show sentiments of friendly affection and mutual help to all races of the world." In this society also true democracy would materialize by "distributing political power to all people, including women."[272] None of these ideas, obviously, would be out of place in K'ang's utopia.

[270] *Community*, 1, p. 333; 2 and 3, p. 218; see above, note 217.

[271] Ch'en Tu-hsiu, "Pen-chih tsui-an chih ta-pien-shu," *Hsin ch'ing-nien*, 6, no. 1 (Jan. 1919): 10.

[272] Ch'en Tu-hsiu, "Pen-chih hsüan-yen," *Hsin ch'ing-nien*, 7, no. 1, (Dec. 1919): 1–4. This "Manifesto" contains a total of twelve points. Others, in addition to those mentioned here, are: repudiation of "the principles of military state and money power"; recognition of "the dignity of labor," regarding it not merely as a means to

Shortly after returning to China upon completing his schooling in the United States, Hu Shih began to express his views concerning social and intellectual reconstruction. Some of these views bore a curious resemblance to K'ang's, even though Hu objected to K'ang's way of thinking because it was "too old."[273] In the same issue of the *Hsin ch'ing-nien* that carried Ch'en's manifesto, Hu undertook to specify the contents of the "New Intellectual Tide." "A transvaluation of all values," he said, was due to be effected through critical study of concrete problems. Confucianism and indeed the entire system of traditional values must be subjected to searching scrutiny, so that anything that was outmoded would be discarded. The real objective of the new current was "cultural reconstruction," which was to be achieved by introducing modern Western knowledge on the one hand and by systematizing and reinterpreting the native tradition on the other.[274]

Pragmatism, as it turned out, was the most important single element of Western knowledge that Hu introduced into China.[275] Another item that he set about to introduce was what he called "Ibsenism." In one of the articles on the subject written in 1918 he called attention to a "clearly discernible doctrine" implicit in Ibsen's dramatic writings, namely, that society tended to smother the spirit of independence in the individual, to the detriment of individual liberty and social progress alike. Hu also gave special notice to Ibsen's cosmopolitan outlook, quoting from a letter written in 1888, to the effect that intelligent men invariably felt dissatisfied with the "old conception of the state" and that such conception would surely be replaced by the "conception of humanity."[276]

---

make a living but as "a sacred thing"; social reconstruction through mass movements; recognition of social progress and material needs as the central goal of all efforts; rejection of all literature and morality that no longer meet the requirements of a new society; recognition of the natural sciences as necessary elements of progress; and repudiation of "absolute skepticism." The influence of socialist thought is apparent.

The same issue carried Ch'en Tu-hsiu's article, "Shih-hsing min-chih ti chi-ch'u," pp. 13–21, in which Ch'en, citing John Dewey's views, concludes that the people themselves must unite to develop self-government that would take two forms: village self-governing organizations and trade self-organizations. This affords an interesting comparison to K'ang's idea of local self-government, namely, farm and factory as the basic units.

[273] Hu Shih, "Kuei-kuo tsa-kan" (written Jan. 1918), *Hu Shih wen-ts'un, ch'u-chi, chüan* 4, pp. 10–11.

[274] Hu Shih, "Hsin ssu-ch'ao ti i-i," *Hsin ch'ing-nien,* 7, no. 1 (Dec. 1919): 5–12.

[275] Hu Shih, "Shih-yen chu-i," *Hsin ch'ing-nien,* 6, no. 4 (April 1919): 342–58.

[276] Hu Shih, "I-pu-sheng chu-i" (first draft, May 1918; final version, April 1921), *Hu Shih wen-ts'un, ch'u-chi, chüan* 4, pp. 24, 29–31.

A revealing instance of Hu's way of reassessing the value of Chinese tradition is found in his preface to Wu Yü's *Collected Essays*, written in 1921. He spoke approvingly of the furious onslaughts on Confucianism made by Wu and Ch'en Tu-hsiu. In addition to praising their efforts to clear away the "intellectual smog" born of "Confucian dregs," Hu alleged that Wu had in fact applied the "pragmatic criterion" in evaluating Confucianism, by implication, when he asked these pertinent questions:

> What sort of institutions has it produced? Have these institutions increased or diminished human happiness? What sort of national character have they formed? Have they helped or impeded progress?[277]

The answers to these questions were self-evident to Hu—and to his friends. Confucianism had indeed produced institutions that worked to impede progress and to bring miseries to countless generations of Chinese. It hardly requires pointing out that the "Confucianism" that Hu and his group condemned was the same system of social and moral values condemned by K'ang as "false Confucianism" (or "imperial Confucianism" in James Legge's phraseology), and K'ang condemned it for substantially identical reasons: its adverse effects on human happiness and social progress. The *Hsin ch'ing-nien* writers, in a small way, went a step further than K'ang. While the latter honored the "authentic teachings" of Confucius (i.e., Confucianism outside the established tradition), the former argued that as "Confucius" had become the "shop sign" of those who traded in "the man-eating institutions of two thousand years," "it should be taken down, demolished, and consigned to flames."[278]

Similarities between the positions taken by K'ang and the *Hsin ch'ing-nien* group toward human relationships are quite striking. Just as K'ang repudiated the traditional value and institutional systems, Ch'en, Hu, and others of the group likewise urged their rejection. According to Ch'en, one of the fundamental differences in attitude between peoples of the East and West was that in the West importance was attached

---

[277] Hu Shih, "*Wu Yü wen-lu* hsü," in *Wu Yü wen-lu* and *Hu Shih wen-ts'un, ch'u-chi, chüan* 4, p. 258.

[278] Hu, "*Wu Yü wen-lu* hsü," p. 259. Hu, however, approved of Confucius for the following reasons: that Confucius was one "who knows the impracticable nature of the times and yet will be doing them" (*Lun-yü*, 14: 41, Legge trans.) and "who does not perceive that old age is coming on" (ibid., 7: 18, Legge trans.). Hu continues: "Knowing this true Confucius, one can do without [all the rest of] the *Analects*." "Pai-hua shih," *Hsin ch'ing-nien*, 2, no. 6 (Feb. 1917): 6.

to the individual, whereas in the East the family was regarded as the basic social unit.[279] Writing in 1916, Ch'en asserted that as the result of her contact with European civilization China experienced a series of social and political crises. Each crisis galvanized the Chinese into intellectual awakening, highlighted in particular by Hsü Kuang-ch'i's (1562–1633) acceptance of Western science and religion in mid-Ming times, K'ang Yu-wei's reform movement after the Sino-Japanese war, and the controversy between the republicans and constitutionalists in the years immediately preceding and following the 1911 revolution. A "final awakening" was due, when the constitution of the republic was to be put into force. But while it was important to achieve "political awakening," it was even more crucial to attain a "moral awakening" which called for unconditional renunciation of traditional values, such as the precept of *san kang* ("the three moral obligations"). For without personal liberty, equality, and independence there could be no political democracy.[280]

Believing that the traditional family was inseparably bound together with autocratic government,[281] Ch'en and his group made determined assaults on it. Hu Shih's views are particularly interesting in this connection. In a piece entitled "My Son" he implicitly but deliberately undermined the old conception of filial duty. "As a tree does not purposely bear its fruits," he wrote, "so have I conferred no favor upon you. . . . I wish you to be a dignified human being; I do not want you to be my filial and obedient son."[282] This reminds us readily of one of K'ang's "universal principles" laid down in the last decade of the previous century:

> Parents shall not demand performance of filial duties by their children and children shall not demand affection or care of their parents. Each person shall enjoy the right of self-determination.[283]

Hu, together with others of the group, advocated the emancipation of

[279] Ch'en Tu-hsiu, "Tung hsi min-tsu ken-pen ssu-hsiang chih ch'a-i," *Hsin ch'ing-nien*, 1, no. 4 (Dec. 1915): 1–4.

[280] Ch'en Tu-hsiu, "Wu-jen tsui-hou chih chüeh-wu, *Hsin ch'ing-nien*, 1, no. 6 (Feb. 1916): 1–4.

[281] Wu Yü's views are representative. See his "Chia-tsu chih-tu wei chuan-chih chu-i chih ken-chü lun," *Hsin ch'ing-nien*, 2, no. 6 (Feb. 1917): 1–4, and "Tui-yü ssu-K'ung wen-t'i chih wo-chien," *Wu yü wen hsü-lu*," pp. 13–28.

[282] Hu Shih, "Wo-ti erh-tzu," quoted by Wang Ch'ang-lu in his letter to Hu, in *Hu Shih wen-ts'un, ch'u-chi, chüan* 4, pp. 96–97.

[283] K'ang, *Truths*, "Fu-mu tzu-nü men." See Path Finding in Two Worlds, earlier in this chapter.

women. He urged Chinese women to follow the example of American women who, he said, showed a "spirit of independence," committed themselves to a *Lebensanschauung* that transcended the ideal of "good wife and worthy mother," and took their "life careers" so seriously that they sometimes by-passed marriage.[284] He strongly opposed what he called "the unilateral chastity" imposed upon Chinese women,[285] and made clear that one should be free to choose one's own mate, even if it involved contravening parental wishes.[286] Morally speaking, "free love" was not wrong; even if it led to unstable mating, the only legitimate question to raise was whether or not the separation was "reasonable." However, Hu did not go all the way with K'ang. He stopped short of advocating the abolition of the institution of marriage or the family.[287]

This was left to another contributor to the *Hsin ch'ing-nien*. In an article appearing in 1919, entitled "Public Rearing of Children: Method of Radical Solution of the Woman Problem, Key to Disposition of all Problems of the New World," Shen Chien-shih declared, "The greatest stumbling block to solving the woman problem is the family institution,"—an "evil heritage" of mankind inseparably connected with the equally odious institution of private property. Because of the family every factor of social progress had been slowed down. Its poisonous influence was felt everywhere, although it was worse in Asia than in Europe. With the end of the World War "democracy" would become the sole principle of social reconstruction. But unless man seized the opportune moment to destroy the family, women would remain in bondage and the democracy that emerged could only be a halfway house. Accordingly, Shen proposed a four-point program. First, women would receive an education absolutely equal to and exactly identical with that given to men; second, women would be financially independent and in a position to render all services to society; third, "family in its existing form" would be abolished; and fourth, all children would be "publicly

---

[284] Hu Shih, "Mei-kuo ti fu-jen" (a speech at the Normal School for Women, Peking, Sept. 1918), *Hu Shih wen-ts'un, ch'u-chi, chüan* 4, pp. 39–61.

[285] Hu Shih, "Chen-ts'ao wen-t'i," *Hu Shih wen-tsun, chüan* 4, pp. 63–77. Cf. T'ang Ssu [Lu Hsün], "Wo-chih chieh-lieh kuan," *Hsin ch'ing-nien*, 5, no. 2 (Aug. 1918): 92–101. Lu Hsün concluded with a vow "to make all mankind enjoy proper happiness."

[286] Hu Shih, "Chung-shen ta-shih" ("The Great Affair of a Lifetime," i.e., marriage; a farce with a happy ending, in which a girl eloped with her love leaving a note for her parents: "This is the great affair of my life-time; the decision should be mine"), *Hsin ch'ing-nien*, 6, no. 3 (March 1919): 311–19.

[287] Hu Shih, "Hu Shih ta Lan Chih-hsien shu," *Hsin ch'ing-nien*, 6, no. 4 (April 1919): 422.

reared" in a variety of institutions which together replaced the family
—institutions such as pediatric clinics, nurseries, kindergartens, primary schools, and children's hospitals. Thus freed entirely from the
burdens of the family, women would attain complete freedom and
true equality. Shen concluded:

> By means of these measures, the family institution, the autocratic state,
> and economic classes will be demolished, permanently and irrevocably.
> Then and only then can there be a radical solution of the labor problem
> and the problem of economic equality.[288]

One almost suspects that Shen had seen K'ang's *Ta-t'ung shu* and was
paraphrasing freely what K'ang wrote in 1902.[289] Shen, of course, cannot be charged with plagiarism because he had no access to the pertinent portions of that book, which K'ang refused to publish.

Other parallels between K'ang's views and those of his critics may
be added, but it is hardly necessary to do so. I have cited the writings
of Ch'en Tu-shiu and other contributors to the *Hsin ch'ing-nien*, easily
the most progressive and influential periodical of the time, with the
purpose of lending more cogency to the thesis that K'ang's ideas of
radical social transformation were not devoid of historical significance.
As he and the other men concerned themselves with the same general
problem (i.e., modernizing China through social and intellectual reconstruction), reflected the same general historical trend (i.e., transition
from a traditional to a modern China), and derived their inspiration
largely from the same source (i.e., modern Western civilization), it was
inevitable that they arrived at broadly similar positions, despite the
wide gulf that separated them in intellectual background, methodological approach, and personal temperament. The existence of this gulf,
obviously, explains the many differences in detail and emphasis between K'ang's "Great Community" and the "new society" as envisioned by the *Hsin ch'ing-nien* group. But there were sufficient similarities
between the two to warrant the suggestion that even though K'ang's
message was not heard by the intellectuals of the time, it was, in substance, not really *vox clamantis in deserto*.

---

[288] Shen Chien-shih, "Erh-t'ung kung-yü: ch'e-ti-ti fu-jen wen-t'i chieh-chüeh fa
ch'u-fen hsin shih-chieh i-ch'ieh wen-t'i chih so-yüeh," *Hsin ch'ing-nien*, 6, no. 6
(Nov. 1919): 563–67.

[289] Namely, *Community*, parts 4–7, where K'ang dealt with equality of the sexes, the
family, and private property.

The "Great Community" and Socialism

Utopian thought, it has been said, marked the inception of modern socialism.[290] K'ang Yu-wei wrote years after the appearance of socialism in the West so it is hardly surprising that socialistic sentiments colored the utopian thought of a man who, from 1879, had made efforts to acquaint himself with "Western learning."[291]

Recently, writers in Communist China have paid considerable attention to K'ang's *Ta-t'ung shu*, although they not all agree as to its significance. Some are inclined to dismiss it as reactionary. Thus, Fan Wen-lan, a historian, asserts that K'ang's objective in writing the book was "to point the way out for China's capitalist class." By concealing the "reality of class struggle" with the concept of "the Great Community" K'ang sought to help perpetuate that class.[292] Fung Yu-lan, the noted philosopher, charges K'ang also with denying the importance of class struggle. All the "seemingly leftist theories" that K'ang advanced served merely "to camouflage the reactionary contents" of his book. "The Great Community" was, in the last analysis, simply a "capitalist society idealized."[293] T'ang Chih-chün, a member of the Chinese Communist Party, summarily condemns the book as in substance counterrevolutionary.[294]

[290] Hertzler, *History of Utopian Thought*, p. 298, quoted from Karl J. Kautsky, *Die Vorlaufer der neuren Sozializmus*, p. 466.

[291] Thompson, *Ta Tung Shu*, p. 52, points out that K'ang's notion of communism is very vague: "he thinks of it as a form of economic democracy. . . . He does understand that it is a movement which has arisen because of the struggling of the 'unequal' labouring and poor groups against the capitalist rich group. (We will not fail to note, in passing, his prescience as to the importance of this struggle in the coming years.)" Some writers in Communist China agree in part with Thompson, e.g., Hu Pin, *Wu-hsü pien-fa*, pp. 22–39.

[292] Fan Wen-lan, *Chung-kuo chin-tai shih*, p. 322.

[293] Fung Yu-lan, "K'ang Yu-wei ti ssu-hsiang," *Chung-kuo chin-tai ssu-hsiang-shih lun-wen chi*, pp. 123–24.

[294] T'ang Chih-chün, "Kuan-yü K'ang Yu-wei ti *Ta-t'ung shu*," *Wen-shih-che*, 1957, no. 1, p. 43. Other writers criticized K'ang in the same vein. E.g., Ch'en Chou-yeh, "Shih-lun K'ang Yu-wei k'ung-hsiang li-lun (*Ta-t'ung shu*) ti chieh-chi chi-ch'u," *Chung-hsüeh li-shih chiao-hsüen*, 1957, no. 11, p. 4, describes K'ang's utopian thought as "a product of the thinking of China's immature capitalist class, a companion of the production-relationship of immature capitalism." Chu Ch'ien-chih, "*Ta-t'ung shu* shih chüan," *Tu-shu yüeh-pao*, 1957, no. 1, pp. 22–23, characterizes K'ang's "ideal state" as representing an attempt to effect a gradual transformation of feudal system into capitalist system. Li Tse-hou, "Lun Chung-kuo shih-chiu shih-chi kai-liang-pa'i pien-fa wei-hsin ssu-hsiang ti fa-chan," *Hsin chien-she*, 1956, no. 5, pp. 58–59, and "Lun K'ang Yu-wei 'Ta-t'ung' li-hsiang," in *K'ang Yu-wei T'an Ssu-t'ung ssu-hsiang yen-chiu*, p. 102, identifies K'ang's ideal as a "capitalist, liberal, reformist utopia."

Perhaps because of their commitment (honest or feigned) to the ideological line laid down by the Communist regime, these writers have to close their eyes to the socialistic sentiments that K'ang so clearly exhibited in his book. Other writers in Communist China, however, for reasons to be ascertained, are willing to accept K'ang as a socialist even though his thinking fell definitely short of "scientific socialism." One, for instance, credits K'ang with "reformist socialism," which, unfortunately, propagandized not class struggle but class cooperation. According to this writer, K'ang not only attacked China's "feudal institutions" but also exposed the faults of the capitalist system of Europe and America.[295] Another writer equates K'ang's "Three Ages" of historical progress with the Marxist three stages of social development. The ages of "Disorder," "Ascending Peace," and "Universal Peace" were K'ang's way of referring to feudalism, capitalism, and communism.[296] A third writer perceives a shift in K'ang's view regarding the economic aspect of utopia. Whereas in the "earlier drafts" of his book K'ang criticized feudal institutions but looked up to capitalism, he criticized capitalist institutions in his "final draft" and looked forward to institutions of Communist society—[297] even though in so doing K'ang involved himself in "obvious inconsistency."[298] Broadly speaking, the assessment of K'ang by these writers has come nearer to the truth. They would not be mistaken at all if they credit K'ang with contributing to the early currents of Chinese socialist thought and thus consider him an outstanding forerunner of the socialist movement in modern China.

It is well known that around the turn of the century the influence of socialist thought became clearly discernible among Chinese intellectuals in Japan, in particular the revolutionaries rallying around Sun Yat-sen. With the publication of the *Min pao* in 1905,[299] socialism became a

[295] Lin K'e-kuang, "Lun *Ta-t'ung shu*," pp. 7–19 and 30–31.

[296] Li Chu, "Lun she-hui chu-i tsai Chung-kuo ti ch'uan-po," *Li-shih yen-chiu*, 1954, no. 3, p. 2.

[297] Chang Yü-t'ien, "Kuan-yü *Ta-t'ung shu* ti hsieh-tso kuo-ch'eng chi ch'i nei-yung fa-chan pien-hua ti t'an-t'ao," *Wen-shih-che*, 1957, no. 9, pp. 55–60. Chang, however, agrees with Fan Wen-lan on several other points.

[298] Chang Ch'i-chih and others, "Kuan-yü K'ang Yu-wei *Ta-t'ung* ssu-hsiang shih-chih ti shang-chüeh," in Hou, *Wu-hsü pien-fa liu-shih chou-nien chi-nien chi*, p. 78. The divergent views concerning K'ang's thought perhaps do not constitute a sign of ideological split among these writers, but point rather to different efforts to determine K'ang's significance in the historical process as viewed from the general Marxist-Leninist standpoints—efforts which parallel those made by other writers to ascertain the historical significance of Confucius. See Joseph R. Levenson, "The Place of Confucius in Communist China," *The China Quarterly*, no. 12 (Oct.–Dec. 1962), pp. 1–18.

[299] *Min pao* ("People's Report," English title given in no. 3, April 1906), appeared

major plank in their platform. A survey of the early issues of this periodical would suffice to make our point. In the very first number (October 1905), in a "Notice of Publication" under the signature of Sun Wen
(Sun Yat-sen), the well-known "three principles," nationalism, democracy, and socialism were formally announced.[300] The first two
principles, it was said, had already been largely realized, in Europe and
America, while fulfillment of the third remained the most outstanding
task of the twentieth century. China should work immediately for the
realization of nationalism and democracy, and *at the same time* implement the principle of socialism, before "the economic problems" that
were plaguing the West had time to develop. Sun continued:

> Recently, thoughtful men have talked themselves hoarse in urging
> China to achieve strength on a par with European and American na-
> tions. But [they fail to see that] while these countries are strong, their
> peoples are really in distress. General strikes [break out], anarchist and
> socialist parties multiply and gain strength each passing day. In view of
> this [one surmises that] social revolution probably will soon come. . . . In
> our country [where economic problems have not as yet become serious],
> it would really be possible to accomplish both political and social revolu-
> tion at one stroke.[301]

This theme was echoed, with variations, by other writers in Sun's
group, notably, Hu Han-min, Fung Tzu-yu, and Chu Chih-hsin. Hu
wrote an article to elucidate the "six principles" (i.e., the six objectives)
of the journal.[302] He identified "state ownership of land" (the third
principle) as a "part of state socialism" and set forth his arguments
against private property, which immediately remind one of K'ang's.
Land, Hu wrote, was an "essential element" of economic production
and therefore should not be privately owned. The landlord system led
to glaring disparity in wealth and to oppression of labor by capital.
China should learn the lesson of the West. If she failed to abolish private
property in land after completion of her political revolution, "eco-

---

from 1905 to 1910, a total of 26 issues. Photographic reproduction in four volumes,
Peking, 1957.

[300] *Min pao*, no. 1 (Oct. 1905), pp. 1–3. In the terminology of the revolutionary
writers, "socialism" (*she-hui chu-i*) was synonymous with "the principle of the people's
livelihood" (*min-sheng chu-i*), as made clear by Chu Chih-hsin in a note to the title
of his article "Ts'ung she-hui chu-i lun t'ieh-tao kuo-yu chi Chung-kuo t'ieh-tao chih
kuan-pan ssu-pan," *Min pao*, no. 4 (May 1906), p. 45.

[301] Ibid., no. 1, p. 2.

[302] The "six principles" are found in ibid., no. 1, an announcement at the end of
the issue.

nomic classes" would replace "political classes"—thus repeating the
sad experience of the West.[303] Fung Tzu-yu recommended "state socialism" for China, namely, "equalization of land ownership" as advocated
by Henry George.[304] Chu Chih-hsin traced the cause of "social revolution" to "imperfect social and economic organization" which meant
"free competition and absolute property right." He did not suggest
"pure communism" for "immediate application" but, in a somewhat
confused manner, argued that one should have no "absolute objection"
to "scientific socialism" and no objection at all to "state socialism."[305]

K'ang's socialistic ideas, to recall, were quite a bit more radical than
those subscribed to by Sun and his supporters. Although K'ang contributed nothing really original, his anti-capitalist formulations preceded the *Min pao* articles by at least three years and were done in a
more coherent form. His socialism remained practically unnoticed for
years; Sun's socialism (officially called "the principle of people's livelihood") was widely publicized and insistently proclaimed, though his
followers did little to implement it.

Socialist currents of thought flowed in another channel. In the late
1910s and early 1920s, the *Hsin ch'ing-nien* became in part an important
vehicle of socialist sentiments.[306] As early as 1915, Ch'en Tu-hsiu considered socialism, together with the doctrine of human rights and the
theory of biological evolution, as the "distinguishing mark" of modern
civilization. The socialism he had in mind at that time was not that of
Marx but of Babeuf, Saint-Simon, and Fourier.[307] As time went on

[303] Hu Han-min, "*Min pao chih liu ta chu-i*," *Min pao*, no. 3 (April 1906), pp. 1–22.

[304] Fung Tzu-yu, "Lu *Chung-kuo jih-pao* 'Min-sheng chu-i yü Chung-kuo cheng-chih
ko-ming chih ch'ien-t'u,' " *Min pao*, no. 4 (May 1906), pp. 97–122.

[305] Hsüan-chieh [Chu Chih-hsin], "Lun she-hui ko-ming tang yü cheng-chih ko-
ming ping-hsing," *Min pao*, no. 5 (June 1906), pp. 43–66. Under the pseudonym
Chih-shen, Chu published another article, "Te-i-chih she-hui ko-ming-chia lieh-
chuan," *Min pao*, no. 2 (March 1906), pp. 1–17 (Marx) and no. 3 (April 1906), pp.
1 19 (Lassalle). He criticized Marx for regarding *all* capital as robbery and rated
Lassalle below Marx. *Min pao*, no. 5 (June 1906), pp. 79–105, carried an article on
the "Brief History of the Communist International" (Wan-kuo she-hui-tang ta-hui
shih-lüeh) by Ch'iang-chai (pseudonym). This was a translation of a Japanese article,
with comments and modifications. For a survey of the socialist ideas of the revolutionary writers, see Scalapino and Schiffrin, "Early Socialist Currents in the Chinese
Revolutionary Movement," pp. 321–42.

[306] For brief accounts of Chinese exponents of diverse brands of socialism, see Li
Chien-nung, *The Political History of China: 1840–1928*, pp. 439–40 and Chow, *The
May Fourth Movement*, passim (see Index under "Socialism," "Chiang K'ang-hu,"
"Chang Tung-sun," etc.).

[307] Ch'en Tu-hsiu, "Fa-lan-hsi-jen yü chin-shih wen-ming," *Hsin ch'ing-nien*, 1,
no. 1: 1–4.

contributors to the *Hsin ch'ing-nien* showed increasing interest in other schools of socialist thought, culminating in unreserved commitment to Marxism.[308]

Ch'en Tu-hsiu wrote in 1920 that industrialization, an indispensable step in China's modernization, could be accomplished only on socialist principles. Capitalism had developed industry and education in Western countries and Japan, but "at the same time it had rendered Europeans, Americans, and Japanese avaricious, mean, deceitful, ruthless, and unconscionable." China should not miss the opportunity to industrialize herself before capitalism took hold of her.[309] Li Ta-chao, one of the first to introduce socialism into China and a founder of the Chinese Communist movement, condemned (in 1920) the Chinese family system on the basis of Marxist ideas. Every social and intellectual movement, he argued, pointed to the destruction of the traditional Confucian moral code, with its precepts of monarchical loyalty, filial duty, wifely obedience, and feminine inferiority. China's incipient "labor movement," in particular, constituted "a movement to destroy the Confucian doctrine of classes, which persistently placed the working class in the position of the ruled for the exploitation of the ruling class.[310] It is a matter of record that with the forming of the Chinese Communist party in July 1921, Marxism had become the social gospel with the vanguard intellectuals of the *Hsin ch'ing-nien* group. "The communism of Marx," it was said, "can certainly be practiced in China."[311] Ac-

---

[308] Some of the articles in *Hsin ch'ing-nien* dealing with Marxism included: Ch'i-ming, "O-kuo ko-ming chih che-hsüeh-ti chi-ch'u," vol. 4, no. 4 (April 1919); and no. 5 (May 1919); Ku Chao-hsiung, "Ma-k'e-ssu hsüeh-shuo," vol. 6, no. 5; Ling-shuang, "Ma-k'e-ssu hsüeh-shuo p'i-p'ing," vol. 6, no. 5; Liu Ping-lin, "Ma-k'e-ssu chuan-lüeh," vol. 6, no. 5; Li Ta-chao, "Wo-ti Ma-k'e-ssu chu-i kuan," vol. 6, no. 5, and no. 6 (May, Nov. 1919); Li Ta-chao, "Yu ching-chi-shang chieh-shih Chung-kuo ssu-hsiang pien-tung ti yüan-yin," vol. 7, no. 2 (Jan. 1920); and "Wei-wu shih-kuan tsai hsien-tai shih-hsüeh-shang-ti chia-chih," vol. 8, no. 4 (Dec. 1920); Li Chi, "She-hui chu-i yü Chung-kuo," vol. 8, no. 6 (April 1921); Li Ta, "Ma-k'e-ssu p'ai she-hui chu-i," vol. 9, no. 2 (June 1921) (Lenin's *State and Revolution* was one of the references cited); Ch'en Tu-hsiu, "Ma-k'e-ssu hsüeh-shuo," vol. 9, no. 6 (July 1922). Interestingly, vol. 7, no. 6 (May 1, 1920), was a special Labor Day commemorative issue.

[309] Ch'en Tu-hsiu, "Kuan-yü she-hui chu-i ti t'ao-lun," *Hsin ch'ing-nien*, 8, no. 4 (Dec. 1920): 8. In a letter to Chang Tung-sun, Ch'en said, "I profoundly believe that foreign capitalism constitutes the sole cause of China's economic want. Therefore it is necessary to topple foreign capitalism" (p. 18).

[310] Li Ta-chao, "Yu ching-chi-shang chieh-shih Chung-kuo chin-tai ssu-hsiang pien-tung ti yüan-yin," *Hsin ch'ing-nien*, 7, no. 2: 47–53.

[311] Ts'un-t'ung, "Ma-k'e-ssu ti kung-ch'an chu-i," *Hsin ch'ing-nien*, 9, no. 4 (Aug. 1921): 10.

cordingly, in a July 1922 article, Ch'en Tu-hsiu undertook to propound
the basic tenets of Marxism: surplus value, historical materialism, class
struggle, and "workers' dictatorship."[312]

Even Hu Shih, whose philosophical outlook precluded subscription
to Marxism, showed "admiration" for "the large-scale political experiment" conducted in Soviet Russia. It was, Hu said, an unprecedented
"gigantic 'utopian' plan" matched only by the "experiments in state
socialism" launched in China in A.D. first century by Wang Mang and
a millenium later by Wang An-shih. But Hu disapproved the method
adopted by the Soviets to achieve socialism. He explained:

> Modern history points to two different methods: One is the Soviet
> Russian method which, operating through the dictatorship of the prole-
> tariat, does not permit the existence of the propertied classes. The other
> method is one which avoids "class struggle" and, following the trend
> toward socialization . . . seeks to realize gradually a society in which
> liberty and happiness will be enjoyed. This method I like to describe as
> "New Liberalism" or "Liberal Socialism."[313]

Thus, in the first two decades of the present century diverse currents
of socialist thought, ranging from utopian socialism to Marxism, from
capitalism tempered with socialization to unmitigated communism,
found expression in the writings of Chinese intellectuals. K'ang's Great
Community stood as perhaps the most systematic and imaginative socialist construct of all. More radical than Hu Shih's "liberal socialism,"
it might be characterized as "democratic communism" and as such
was much more akin in spirit to utopian socialism than to revolutionary
Marxism. It appears that the flow of socialist currents in China, from
K'ang Yu-wei to Ch'en Tu-hsiu, paralleled the development in Europe
from eighteenth-century utopian socialism to nineteenth-century scientific socialism.

This observation should suffice to warn against giving more credit
to K'ang than he deserved, as some recent writers seem to be doing,
One of them has suggested that K'ang's ideal of the Great Community
is indistinguishable from "Western communism";[314] another claims

[312] Ch'en Tu-hsiu, "Ma-k'e-ssu hsüeh-shuo," *Hsin ch'ing-nien*, 9, no. 6 (July 1922):
1–9.

[313] Hu Shih, "Ou-yu tao-chung chi-shu," *Hu Shih wen-ts'un, san chi, chüan* 1, pp. 75–
76, 84. These letters were written in 1926.

[314] Kyoson Tsuchida, *Contemporary Thought of Japan and China*, p. 196, asserts that
K'ang's *Ta-t'ung* was "the same social ideal as in Western communism or anarchism."
This is untrue because K'ang's ideal was not identical with either of these isms. De-

that Mao Tse-tung "has borrowed heavily for his ideas for commune" from K'ang Yu-wei.[315] There are of course striking points of contact between the Great Community and Communist society, beyond obvious structural similarities. Both are universalistic ideals based on the assumption that human development is rigidly unilinear. But such similarities do not obscure the fundamental differences between the two. As Laurence G. Thompson has correctly pointed out, K'ang's assumptions about human nature, method to attain the ideal, and the guiding spirit of utopia are widely different from those of the Marxist.[316] In fact, the essentially humanistic outlook of K'ang was diametrically opposite to the Communists' brutally cynical view of man and society. K'ang therefore was inherently unacceptable to Mao Tse-tung as Mao would certainly have been unacceptable to K'ang Yu-wei.

That K'ang Yu-wei, Hu Shih, Ch'en Tu-hsiu, and other men of modern China whose temperaments and persuasions were as divergent as they could be, proposed to modernize China through the highways and byways of socialism was perhaps no more than historical coinci-

---

spite some similarities between the "Great Community" and the anarchist ideal, especially as it was espoused by the Chinese anarchists, there is a crucial difference between the two: the latter called for abolition of government, whereas the former envisaged a comprehensive world government. Some of the similarities, however, are interesting. With the anarchists as with K'ang universal love was the first principle of life. The anarchists also spoke of "ta-t'ung" as the ultimate goal, condemned competition and struggle, opposed traditional values and institutions, advocated "promiscuous sexual intercourse" (i.e., abolition of marriage and the family) in the interest of individual freedom, equality, and happiness. For surveys of Chinese anarchist thought, see Robert A. Scalapino and George T. Yu, *The Chinese Anarchist Movement*, and Michael Gasster, *Chinese Intellectuals and the Revolution of 1911*, chap. 5.

[315] Huang Yen Yu, "Mao's People's Communes," *New York Times*, Jan. 11, 1959.

[316] Laurence G. Thompson, "*Ta T'ung Shu* and the Communist Manifesto," in Lo, *K'ang*, p. 351: "They [K'ang and Marx] differ completely as to the method of establishing this polity [i.e., communistic utopia]: Marx advocates a revolutionary seizure of power by the proletariat which will result in centralization of the means of production and eventually in a 'vast association of the whole nation'; K'ang believes that the basis for the establishment of One World is replacement of the family system by the system of public institutions, and feels confident that the ideal polity will come about in the natural course of evolution." K'ang probably would disagree with Liang Ch'i-ch'ao, who, writing in the early 1920s, argued that China should first allow a capitalist class to develop, to serve as the motive force of industrialization and later implement the principle of socialization. Liang believed that the evils of capitalism could be attenuated by "rectifying" and "supervising" its operation through "social legislation" and concurrent development of state enterprises together with a cooperative movement. "Fu Chang Tung-sun shu lun she-hui chu-i yün-tung," in *Yin-pin-shih ho-chi, wen-chi* 36 (vol. 13), pp. 1–12. See also Liang's "Wu-ch'an chieh-chi yü wu-yeh chieh-chi" (written in 1925), and "Wu-yeh yu-min yü yu-yeh p'ing-ming," *Ho-chi, Wen-chi*, 42, pp. 1–3, and 43, pp. 19–20.

dence. A recent writer has remarked that in the "developing nations" of today, where there is a strong desire as well as an urgent need to industrialize, leaders are inclined to favor "socialist methods" of diverse sorts to bring about rapid economic growth. "The socialism of the developing countries," he continues, "is said to be directed at the establishment of a society based on justice rather than profit, national planning rather than the blind operation of the market."[317] The conditions in late nineteenth-century and early twentieth-century China were of course not identical with those prevailing in contemporary developing nations. But one is tempted to think that as K'ang and other men of the period were not unaware of the problems that the industrial revolution created in the advanced countries, they too became concerned more with justice than profit and saw greater promise in "rational planning" than "the blind operation of the market."

It is interesting to retrace briefly the history of China's attempts at modernization since the 1860s: first there was the "self-strengthening movement" aiming at achieving the West's "wealth and power," then the 1898 reform movement with its variety of economic measures, and finally the program of industrialization as envisioned by the revolutionaries. Leaders of these movements, Mao said in 1949, "had looked to the West for truth," seeking to find the key to social progress in "the new knowledge from the West."[318] These leaders indeed had looked to the West, but they did not all see the same "truth." K'ang Yu-wei, as we have suggested, was inclined, as many of his contemporaries were, to endorse the capitalist methods of postindustrial revolution Europe.[319] However, at the beginning of the present century K'ang, as author of the *Ta-t'ung shu*, sounded a clear note of socialism, soon to be echoed and reechoed with strident modulations. The historical situation required a radical reorientation of thought. Socialism, so to speak, was in the air and K'ang was among the first to inhale a robust whiff of it. Thus he, like many others of the time, banked hope on socialist methods. Disenchanted with capitalism, he proposed a new road to utopia. One cannot be sure that it was a viable road; but one can safely say that in proposing it K'ang had a part in writing the brief history of modern Chinese socialist thought.

[317] Paul E. Sigmund, *The Ideologies of the Developing Nations*, editor's introduction, pp. 11–12.

[318] Mao Tse-tung, *Selected Works*, 4 (Peking, 1961): 412.

[319] For a brief survey, see *Chao Feng-t'ien, Wan-Ch'ing wu-shih nien ching-chi ssu-hsiang shih, Yen-ching hsüeh-pao, chuan-hao*, no. 18.

The Ta-t'ung Shu and the Utopian Tradition

S. L. Tikvinsky, in his book on the 1898 reform movement, devotes no less than an entire chapter to describing and evaluating the *Ta-t'ung shu*. He suggests that Buddhism, Taoism, and the communistic ideas of the T'ai-p'ing rebellion, in addition to Confucianism, contributed importantly to K'ang Yu-wei's utopian thought. However, because of K'ang's "purely abstract approach," his utopian ideal was foredoomed to failure, even though it reflected "the Chinese peasant's wish" to do away with the "feudal state" and to attain economic equality.[320]

Overburdened with Marxist-Leninist biases, Tikhvinsky's analysis falls short of objectivity or accuracy. It does point to the fact, however, that K'ang was indebted to diverse elements of Chinese tradition, some of which suggested "utopias of construction" (or "speculative utopias")—perfect societies realizable in the future—and others "utopias of escape" (or "satiric utopias")—imaginary golden ages in the past as substitutes for the actual world of "hard facts" too complicated to carry through and too tough to face.[321] The idyllic communities pictured by Taoist writers are instances of the latter, while the humanistic ideals set forth by Confucianists come close to the former.[322]

K'ang owed relatively little to Taoism. The "small state with few people" portrayed in the eighth chapter of the *Lao-tzu*,[323] "the Age of Supreme Virtue" and "the State of Established Virtue" in the *Chuang-tzu*,[324] and the countries of *Chung-pei* and *Hua-hsü* in the *Lieh-tzu*[325] are

[320] Tikhvinsky, *Divizenie za reformy*, pp. 331–32.

[321] See Negley and Patrick, *The Quest for Utopia*, p. 5 and Mumford, *The Story of Utopias*, p. 15.

[322] Communist China's Academy of Science, Institute of Philosophy, Section on the History of Chinese Philosophy, has compiled a "Source Book in Chinese Utopian Thought" (*Chung-kuo ta-t'ung ssu-hsiang tzu-liao*, Peking, 1959), which conveniently gives selections from various texts, from the *Li-yün* to Sun Yat-sen's writings. Unfortunately, the selections are not always made with sound judgment.

[323] Many translations are available. Among the more satisfactory are: J. J. L. Duyvendak, *Tao Te Ching*, p. 162; Lionel Giles, *Tao Te Ching* (London, reprint of 4th ed., 1948), p. 93; Arthur Waley, *The Way and Its Power* (1934. New York: Grove Press, 1958), p. 241; and Paul K. T. Sih, *Tao Teh King* (New York, 1961), p. 113.

[324] The *Chuang-tzu*, chap. 2, "Mountain Trees" (*Shan mu*), trans. Herbert A. Giles (Shanghai: Kelly and Walsh, 1926), pp. 107–8, 248, and James Legge, *The Texts of Taoism* (1891. New York: Dover Publications, 1959), pp. 325–26, 470.

[325] The *Lieh-tzu*, chap. 2, "The Yellow Emperor" (*Huang-ti*) and chap. 5, "T'ang's Questions" (*T'ang wen*), trans. A. C. Graham, in *The Book of Lieh-tzu*, pp. 34, 102–3 and Lionel Giles, in *Taoist Teachings* (London, 1959 reprint), pp. 35–36. Giles omitted translating the passage from chap. 2.

all frankly fictitious communities in which men, completely unspoiled by artificialities of civilization, were supposed to have lived in absolute contentment. Accessible only in dreams or the imagination, they fit perfectly the original meaning of the word "utopia"—nowhere; attributed to the remote past, they are most appropriately described as utopias of escape. This Taoist tradition persisted in later time. Two of the most interesting restatements of its utopian ideal were made by the famous poet-hermit T'ao Ch'ien (365–427)[326] and a less well-known writer K'ang Yü-chih (12th century),[327] although the philosophical background of the latter is uncertain.

K'ang Yu-wei, undoubtedly, was acquainted with this Taoist tradition.[328] He in fact made mention of Chang-tzu's "State of Established Virtue" and Lieh-tzu's "Country of the Utter North" (*Chung-pei*).[329] Even though K'ang eventually became disenchanted with Taoism, it is conceivable that some Taoist ideas remained with him and contributed something to his utopian thought. Thus in the State of Established Virtue, it was said, people "labor but do not lay up their gains" and "give but do not seek for return." Similarly, in the Country of the Utter North men "do not know how to prefer themselves to others." These sentiments run closely parallel to the altruistic ideas set forth in the *Li-yün*, a major source of K'ang's inspiration, to the effect that men did not hoard goods for their own enjoyment, nor use their energies for private ends.

There is no evidence that K'ang had seen K'ang Yü-chih's writings, though being a widely read man he possibly had. At any rate, he might have readily approved of the communistic arrangement obtaining in the utopia as depicted in the "Record of Yesteryear's Dreams":

> Nothing is privately hoarded but everything is shared equally by all; which makes living together feasible. Land is assigned [to each family] according to size; each person supports himself by farming or agriculture, as it is improper to appropriate other people's food or clothing.

K'ang owed more to Confucianism than to Taoism. As already noted,

[326] T'ao Ch'ien [T'ao Yüan-ming], "T'ao-hua-yüan chi" (A Note on the Peach-blossom Spring), in *Ching-chieh hsien-sheng chi, chüan* 6, pp. 1a–2a.

[327] The "great cave" which was supposed to be located near Lo-yang, is described in his *Tso-meng lu* (A Record of Yesteryear's Dreams), in T'ao Tsung-i, comp., *Shuo-fu* (Shanghai, 1927), *chüan* 21, pp. 28a–29a.

[328] K'ang studied Taoism and Buddhism, and wrote a commentary on the *Lao-tzu* when he was about twenty (K'ang, *Nien-p'u*, pp. 4b, 5a; Lo, *K'ang* pp. 33–34).

[329] *Li-yün chu*, p. 3a.

he derived much inspiration from the *Li-yün* for which he wrote exegeses to explicate what he believed to be its true teaching. The following passage from his *Li-yün chu* shows the extent of his indebtedness:

> Now to have states, families, and selves is to allow each individual maintain a sphere of selfishness. This infracts utterly the Universal Principle (*kung-li*) and impedes progress. . . . Therefore, not only states should be abolished, so that there would be no more struggle between the strong and the weak; families should also be done away with, so that there would no longer be inequality of love and affection [among men]; and, finally, selfishness itself should be banished, so that goods and services would not be used for private ends. . . . The only [true way] is sharing the world in common by all (*t'ien-hsia wei kung*). . . . To share in common is to treat each and every one alike. There should be no distinction between high and low, no discrepancy between rich and poor, no segregation of human races, no inequality between sexes. . . . All should be educated and supported with the common property; none should depend on private possession. . . . This is the way of the Great Community which prevailed in the Age of Universal Peace.[330]

The *Li-yün*, important as it is, was not the sole source of K'ang's utopian thought. He owed to the Kung-yang school the doctrine of "the Three Ages," which helped him to envision *Ta-t'ung* as utopia of the future, not a golden age of the past. In addition, Western notions such as progress, democracy, and socialism contributed materially to shaping his way of thinking. Thus the Great Community was not a simple product resulting from rehashing the Confucian tradition; it was rather a composite picture with intervolving motifs taken from divergent sources. It appears that in carrying out his universalizing procedure (see the Universalization and Westernization section in the first part of this chapter), K'ang translated modern Western notions into Chinese terms and, conversely, traditional Confucian and Taoist notions into Western terms.[331] Understandably, therefore, the tenor and tempera-

---

[330] Ibid., pp. 2b–4a. K'ang dated his preface to this book "Confucius 2435, Kuang-hsü 10th year, *chia-shen*, Winter Solstice Day," which places the time of composition in 1884–85. Ch'ien Mu, *Chung-kuo chin san-pai nien hsüeh-shu shih*, pp. 698–99, suggests that K'ang probably did not finish writing this book before 1901–2, at about the same time he completed the *Ta-t'ung shu*, but for some reason chose to antedate it. Thompson, in the introduction to his translation of the *Ta-t'ung shu*, pp. 27 and 34–35, rejects Ch'ien's view because "the conception of *ta-t'ung* does come from the famous passage in the "Li Yün." Thompson, obviously, misses the point at issue. Significantly, in K'ang's *Nien-p'u* (pp. 6b–8a) where he sets forth his "system of *Ta-t'ung*" and lists the books he wrote at the time (1884–87), no mention is made of the *Li-yün chu*. See chapter 2 in this volume.

[331] See Liang, *Ch'ing-tai hsüeh-shu kai-lun*, p. 133; Hsü, *Intellectual Trends* . . . , p. 96.

ment of the Great Community are both akin to the modern West and Confucian China. The outcome was hardly unhappy—the most imaginative utopian construct in Chinese intellectual history.

Tikhvinsky made another observation. The "Land System of the Heavenly Dynasty"[332] drafted by leaders of the T'ai-p'ing rebellion, he said, exerted considerable influence on K'ang's utopian thought. According to Tikhvinsky, the communistic and equalitarian ideas as set forth in this document had "circulated widely among the peasants of Nanhai" (K'ang's native district); as a result they became "completely sympathetic to the side of the rebel armies." In K'ang's *Ta-t'ung shu* one can still see "the lingering waves of these ideas."[333]

This claim is not borne out by fact. K'ang's personal experience as well as his philosophical outlook would have made it difficult for him to be receptive to T'ai-p'ing ideology. Several of his relatives served actively in the government campaigns against the rebels; one of these, K'ang Kuo-ch'i (Yu-wei's granduncle)[334] so distinguished himself in the operations in Kiangsu, Chekiang, Fukien, and Kwangtung that he was rewarded with high provincial posts. "He," said Yu-wei, "has made our family glorious and great."[335] Indeed, loyalty to the existing dynasty appears to have become a family tradition that contributed to shaping Yu-wei's own political attitude. He, too, remained loyal to the dynasty, even after its downfall, although his loyalty was more a matter of theoretical conviction than personal sentiment. There is no mention of T'ai-p'ing ideology in his writings; quite likely, he did not see any of the rebel documents, which were strictly interdicted by the government.

Some similarities do exist between T'ai-p'ing ideology and K'ang's utopian thought. But this does not constitute grounds for asserting that K'ang was indebted to the T'ai-p'ing leaders. It is more plausible to explain these similarities by tracing them to a common source, the *Li-yün*. In one of the early T'ai-p'ing documents in which the doctrine of "one world" is expounded, it is said that as Huang-shang-ti (God) is "the common father of all men under heaven," no one should treat another as stranger or enemy. Then the very same passage of this

---

[332] This document, "T'ien-ch'ao t'ien-mou chih-tu," is available in Hsiao I-shan, *T'ai-p'ing t'ien-kuo ts'ung-shu*; Ch'eng Yen-sheng, *T'ai-p'ing t'ien-kuo shih-liao*, and Chung-kuo shih-hsüeh hui, *T'ai-p'ing t'ien-kuo* (*Chung-kuo chin-tai-shih tzu-liao ts'ung-k'an*, no. 2; Shanghai, 1952.).

[333] Tikhvinsky, *Dvizhenie za reformy*, p. 332.

[334] See chapter 1, notes 12 and 13, in this volume.

[335] K'ang, "K'ang-shih chia-miao chih pei," manuscript copy in Lo's collection.

Confucian text from which K'ang derived the notion of *Ta-t'ung* is quoted in full.[336] The fact appears to be that *Ta-t'ung* was a sufficiently appealing concept to attract persons of widely divergent persuasions— and with sufficient ambiguity and flexibility to allow diverse interpretations. Hence it had been used with equal facility in the T'ai-p'ing rebellion, the Chinese anarchist movement, the revolution led by Sun Yat-sen,[337] and in K'ang's utopian thought, to convey vastly different social ideals. It is unwarranted to suppose that any one of these was inspired by any other.

Assuming that K'ang had knowledge of Western utopian thought, Tikhvinsky compares K'ang's ideas with those of European utopists, from Thomas More to Charles Fourier.[338] He suggests that varying degrees of similarity exist between K'ang and his European counterparts, though on the whole differences outbalance resemblances. However, either owing to his Marxist bias or insufficient understanding of K'ang's position, Tikhvinsky says things that border on the superficial or tend to be misleading.

He believes, for instance, that K'ang had little in common with Etienne Cabet[339] but stood quite close to Robert Owen[340] and Charles Fourier.[341] Even a cursory examination should reveal that the reverse

---

[336] "Yüan-tao hsing-shih hsün," available in Ch'eng Yen-sheng, *T'ai-p'ing t'ien-kuo shih-liao*, 2: 5b; Lo Yung, *T'ai-p'ing t'ien-kuo shih-wen ch'ao* (Shanghai, 1934), 1: 13b; and Chung-kuo shih-hsüeh hui, *T'ai-p'ing t'ien-kuo*, 1: 91–92. The text given in Hsiao, *T'ai-p'ing t'ien-kuo ts'ung-shu*, 1: 5b–7a, bears the title "Yüan-tao hsing-shih chao," apparently a later and revised edition, and does not contain the crucial quotation.

[337] The concept of *Ta-t'ung* was widely known among Chinese intellectuals and used by many of them, e.g., the anarchists (see note 314, above) and Sun Yat-sen (see his "Autobiography" written early in 1923, where he said that nationalism, *min-tsu chu-i*, was a preliminary step to "Ta-t'ung"; his lecture on "Min-sheng chu-i" delivered Aug. 3, 1924, where he equated his "principle of people's livelihood" with "socialism," "communism," and "the principle of Ta-t'ung"; and an undated letter to the Japanese statesman, Inukai Tsuyoshi, in which he said: "Sovietism is exactly what Confucius called 'Ta-t'ung,' " and then quoted the celebrated *Li-yün* passage). Sun's "Autobiography" and lectures are available in *Sun Chung-shang ch'üan-shu*, vol. 2; the letter is given in *Chung-kuo ta-t'ung ssu-hsiang tzu-liao*, pp. 94–95.

[338] Tikhvinsky, *Dvizhenie za reformy*, pp. 335–38. The others mentioned are Campanella, Morelly, Cabet, and Owen.

[339] Etienne Cabet (1788–1856), *A Voyage to Icaria* (Paris, 1840); abridged translation from the 1845 reprint by Negley and Patrick, *Quest for Utopia*, pp. 543–74.

[340] Robert Owen (1771–1858), *Book of the New Moral World*, (London, 1842), and many other writings. See G. D. H. Cole, *Life of Owen*, 2nd ed. (London: The Macmillan Co., 1930).

[341] Charles Fourier, see above, note 161. For succinct accounts of Fourier's ideas, see Harry Ross, *Utopias Old and New*, pp. 125–28, and Mumford, *Story of Utopias*, pp. 117–23.

is true: that more similarities exist between K'ang and Cabet than between him and either of the other two men. Owen's small community of families with a total of from 500 to 3000 persons living on a tract of land, or Fourier's "phalanx," a group of 500 families living in a single building and enjoying modified and controlled private ownership of property, is a far cry from K'ang's world community in which the institutions of family and property would be completely eliminated. On the other hand, Cabet's Icaria contains a number of features that remind one of K'ang's Great Community. To mention a few: the assumptions that love and altruism are natural instincts and that inequality is a breach of the law of nature; the proposals that in utopian society men should be absolutely equal in every respect, that all should work and all occupations are of equal importance, that private property should be done away with and the state should control the processes of production and distribution, that government should be completely democratic, that every detail and every moment of life should be organized to serve a common purpose, that education should be public and equally available to all, and that as the "once-useful" Christian Bible would be out of date, its sway would be replaced by that of a "real religion," the "religion of communalism and happiness";—all these, obviously, are akin in spirit with certain features of K'ang's Great Community. The ultimate aim of Icaria, in fact, appears almost identical with that of the Great Community. In Cabet's words:

> Remember also that the purpose of all our laws is to render the people as happy as possible, beginning with the necessary, then adding the useful, and finishing with the agreeable without setting any limit.[342]

This is not saying that the two agree in all important details. For instance, Cabet allowed both the family and the state to exist in Icaria, thus leaving K'ang the more radical thinker of the two.[343]

There is, really, little meaning in pointing to the similarities or differences between K'ang and Western utopists, beyond showing that K'ang, a writer without knowledge of foreign languages and with only indirect and restricted access to Western literature, succeeded in constructing a utopia that compares favorably with any of the modern

[342] Negley and Patrick, *Quest for Utopia*, p. 558.

[343] This account is based largely on the translation by Negley and Patrick. See also Sylvester A. Pietrowski, *Étienne Cabet and the Voyage en Ecarie*; Hertzler, *History of Utopian Thought*, pp. 204–8; M. Kaufmann, *Utopias*, pp. 123–42; and Ross, *Utopias Old and New*, pp. 128–39.

Western utopias in boldness of conception and fullness in structural detail. There is little doubt that he borrowed both from Chinese traditional and Western sources; nevertheless he deserves credit for having combined commonplace elements to form a unique whole. He had, as he put it, imbibed "all that is finest and best of the wisdom of India, Greece, Persia, Rome, and of present-day England, France, Germany, and America."[334] But he did not remain a mere imitator. In borrowing freely and widely from others, he attained a utopian wisdom (or extravagance) that is characteristically his own.

Comparison might serve another purpose: to show that the seemingly fantastic ideas that K'ang set forth in the *Ta-t'ung shu* were shared by other utopists, though advanced in different connections and various forms, and with divergent implications.

In stressing the necessity of radical social transformation K'ang unknowingly shared the views of many Western utopists, in particular those who were convinced that men could not realize ideal values unless the social environment provided satisfactory conditions of existence and that such conditions could not materialize without the socialization of all economic activities.[345] K'ang thus joined the company of such men as Thomas More in whose Utopia "all things being held in common, every man has abundance of everything";[346] Tommaso Campanella who recognized no family institution or individual property;[347] James Reynolds in whose Lithconia "no such words as mine and thine are ever heard";[348] Edward Bellamy who, certain of the breakdown of the capitalist system, envisaged a society in which everyone would labor according to his aptitude and choice, and share alike in the economic products;[349] and, as already mentioned, Etienne Cabet.

[344] See Note 114, above.

[345] Negley and Patrick, *Quest for Utopia*, p. 7.

[346] Sir Thomas More, *Utopia* (Leyden, 1516; English trans. by Ralph Robinson, London, 1551; by Gilbert Burnet, London, 1684; definitive edition in St. Thomas More, *The Complete Works* (New Haven: Yale University Press, 1961); excerpts in Negley and Patrick, *Quest for Utopia*, pp. 258–83. According to George H. Sabine, *A History of Political Theory*, 3rd ed. (New York: Holt, 1961), pp. 436–37, however, More "was really motivated by a longing for the past," when he expressed his dislikes of the acquisitive society of his time.

[347] Tommaso Campanella, *Civitas solis seu ides reipublicae philosophicae* (written, 1602; published, 1623); Eng. trans. as *The City of the Sun*, in *Ideal Empires and Republics* (New York, 1901) and Negley and Patrick, *Quest for Utopia*, pp. 311–42.

[348] Excerpts from *Equality or a History of Lithconia*, attributed to James Reynolds (first published in 1802; Philadelphia, 1947), in Negley and Patrick, *Quest for Utopia*, p. 506.

[349] Edward Bellamy, *Looking Backward: 2000–1887* (written in 1888; published in

Agreeing with many Western utopists, K'ang took equality as one of the basic principles of perfect social organization; and concurring with almost every utopian writer from Plato onward,[350] he advocated strongly equality of the sexes, which to him as to many of his Western counterparts, implied woman's freedom to choose her own mate. Bellamy made this point particularly clear and went even so far as to suggest that in utopia it would be "the custom for the young women to propose marriage to the man."[351] Significant differences of course exist. H. G. Wells, K'ang's younger contemporary, afforded an interesting example. Although Wells believed that as a result of "the complete absence of any economic inequality between the sexes," every match in Utopia would be a "love match," he would nevertheless impose unilateral chastity upon women.[352] This would certainly be unacceptable to K'ang.

One of K'ang's most "shocking" proposals, abolition of marriage and the family, was made by some Western utopists, notably Campanella, Fourier, and Reynolds. In Campanella's City of the Sun, however, mating would not be a matter of personal love and free choice, but would be regulated by government. "Large and beautiful women are mated only with large and aggressive men, fat ones with lean men, and lean ones with fat men, so as to moderate all excesses."[353] Fourier excluded individual households from the phalanx and gave the right of free choice to women even though it would spell the doom of monogamic marriage.[354] In Reynold's Lithconia marriage "fell gradually into disuse," children became "property of the state," and no one took the trouble to find out who was the father of a given child. "Marriages" could be easily dissolved, by simply announcing the intention to erase the opposite party's name from the "matrimonial register."[355]

Chicago, New York, and Boston, in various editions, 1888–1929); excerpts in Ross, *Utopias Old and New*, pp. 143–46.

[350] Hertzler, *History of Utopian Thought*, p. 287, commenting on ideas held in common by European utopists.

[351] Ross, *Utopias Old and New*, p. 152.

[352] H. G. Wells, *A Modern Utopia*, chap. 6. For a summary, see Ross, *Utopias Old and New*, pp. 129–80.

[353] Campanella, *Civitas solis seu ides reipublicae philosophicae*, trans. by William J. Gilstrap, in Negley and Patrick, *Quest for Utopia*, p. 324.

[354] Mumford, *Story of Utopias*, pp. 121–22.

[355] Quoted in Negley and Patrick, *Quest for Utopias*, pp. 508–512. The English anarchist, William Godwin, in his *Enquiry Concerning Political Justice and Its Influence on Morals and Happiness*, advocated free love in addition to abolition of government. Wu Ching-heng [Wu Chih-hui], one of the leaders of the Chinese Anarchist movement,

In delineating the political aspect of the Great Community K'ang showed at least as much preference for democracy as many of the well-known Western utopists who, as already noted, were often inclined to be authoritarian. To mention just two: Thomas More subscribed to the elective principle just as K'ang did, but his Utopia is in its essence a benevolent despotism.[356] H. G. Wells' "Samurai"—a "voluntary leadership" furnished by men "dominated by a desire to serve and a determination to rule"—is distinctly elitist in conception.[357] Cabet's Icaria is one of the relatively few Western utopias that match K'ang's Great Community in democratic commitments. "The Icarians," according to Cabet, "constitute a society founded on a basis of perfect equality." The people being sovereign, rule through a popular assembly and an elected executive "subordinated to the popular assembly." The political organization of Icaria is thus "an almost pure democracy,"[358] as K'ang's Great Community appears also to be.

K'ang's "one-world" idea is found in the writings of a number of Western utopists.[359] One of the most notable instances was afforded by the celebrated French "utopian socialist," Saint-Simon, who advocated "the religion of humanity." The aim of this religion, in his words, was

> to realize and maintain the association of all the men on the surface of the globe, in which each shall be placed according to the capacity that he shall have received from God, and rewarded according to his works.[360]

H. G. Wells's Modern Utopia, like K'ang's Great Community, embodied the idea of world organization and unity of mankind, to be reached through such means as universal education, interracial marriage, and a single language for all. Thus

> The Chinaman will speak the same language as his wife—whatever her

argued that as love was universal in scope and should not be monopolized by anyone, the marriage institution had no raison d'être and that men and women should "intercourse promiscuously." That would be the first step toward human progress ("P'ing Chü-p'u chün 'Nan-nü tsa-chiao shuo,'" *Wu Chih-hui hsien-sheng wen-ts'ui*, 3: 274–80). Both these are more radical than K'ang's proposals.

[356] Ross, *Utopias Old and New*, pp. 57–58.

[357] Wells, *A Modern Utopia*, p. 181. The entire ninth chapter deals with this topic.

[358] Negley and Patrick, *Quest for Utopia*, pp. 547–50.

[359] Ibid., pp. 13–14, where the authors point out that utopists writing before the industrial revolution were as a rule attracted by the ideal of a secluded, small, self-sufficient community. During the nineteenth century, however, when nationalistic sentiments were still strong, utopists had come to realize that not even national entities could stand as self-sufficient units of social organization.

[360] Saint-Simon, quoted in Ross, *Utopias Old and New*, p. 124.

race may be—he will wear costume of the common civilized fashion as his European rival, read the same literature, bow to the same tradition.[361]

K'ang's hedonistic principle is not without parallel in the West. Cabet's words to the effect that the purpose of legislation is to render happiness to the people have already been mentioned above. Nearly a half-century earlier, Reynolds asserted that he who was able to show the manner of multiplying human enjoyments would deserve well of the human race. Happiness, Reynolds explained, was what men always sought after; it eluded them because of "the folly of human institutions."[362] In More's Utopia, men would enjoy pleasures of both body and mind, including the "delights let in" through the eyes, ears, and nostrils. Music, in particular, would be constantly heard. The Utopians, More observed, were convinced that "all our actions, and even all our virtues, terminate in pleasure."[363] The pleasure of travel to which K'ang attached great importance, was also stressed by Wells. "In the modern Utopia," he wrote, "travel must be in the common texture of life."[364]

This should suffice to demonstrate that K'ang's leading ideas fall well within the recognized territory of utopian speculation, Western as well as Chinese. Many of these he had knowingly or unwittingly borrowed from his predecessors. However, the borrowings were so thoroughly assimilated and combined with so much imaginativeness they had in fact become his very own. With them he had created "a new ideal"[365] and thus qualified himself as China's foremost utopist and a worthy peer of the outstanding utopists of the West.[366]

---

[361] Wells, *A Modern Utopia*, p. 342.

[362] Excerpts in Negley and Patrick, *Quest for Utopia*, pp. 603–4.

[363] More, *Utopia*, Eng. trans. in *Ideal Empires and Republics*, pp. 188–94; cf. Negley and Patrick, *Quest for Utopia*, p. 170.

[364] *A Modern Utopia*, p. 43.

[365] Liang Ch'i-ch'ao's phrase (*Ch'ing-tai hsüeh-shu kai-lun*; p. 136; Hsü, *Intellectual Trends* . . . , p. 98).

[366] Francis L. K. Hsü, "Cultural Differences between East and West and Their Significance for the World Today," p. 224, contrasts the wealth of utopias in the West to the paucity of utopian writing in China, citing T'ao Ch'ien's "T'ao-hua-yüan chi" as the sole instance of Chinese utopian construction. Hsü of course is not correct in saying that this delightful piece was the only example of it. There were a few others, including the "Ta-t'ung" in the *Li-yün*, the "small country" in the *Lao-tzu*, and the two or three others mentioned above. Somewhat curiously, Hsü ignores K'ang's *Ta-t'ung shu*. One wonders how he would rate it.

APPENDIX: THE *Ta-t'ung shu* AND THE "HOMELY WORDS TO AID GOV-
ERNMENT"

S. L. Tikhvinsky suggests that among the books issued by the translation bureau of the Kiangnan Arsenal, which K'ang presumably had
read, John Fryer's *Tso-chih chu-yen* ("Homely Words to Aid Government," published in 1885) exerted the greatest influence upon him.
Tikhvinsky believes that K'ang made use of portions of this book, when
he wrote the *Ta-t'ung shu.*[367]

Tikhvinsky's conjecture appears to be partly correct. K'ang himself
confessed that he was very much impressed by Fryer's works, as this
entry in his autobiographic annals (for Kuang-hsü 12th year, or 1886)
shows:

> At the time, Chang Chih-tung was governor-general of Kwangtung. In
> the spring I sent Chang Yen-ch'iu, Hanlin Compiler, to inform him:
> "China has all too few [translations of] Western books. Those translated
> by Fryer deal mostly with nonurgent subjects such as military science and
> medicine; but those that deal with government are exceedingly impor-
> tant. Western books [on government] contain many novel principles
> which are not found in China. A bureau should be established to trans-
> late these. This is a most pressing task.[368]

The treatise "Homely Words to Aid Government" may well have
been one of the "Western books" in which K'ang discovered "novel
principles."[369] It is altogether possible that along with other books it
contributed to determining the general drift of K'ang's social thought
which, between the 1880s and the early 1900s, was given diverse expressions in his reform writings, in such early pieces as "The Esoteric
and Exoteric Essays" and "Substantial Truths and Universal Principles," and finally, as well shall see later, in the "Essay on National
Salvation through Material Upbuilding" of 1905. This is not saying
that in writing the *Ta-t'ung shu* he actually adopted the basic premises
of Fryer's book. An examination of the "Homely Words" compels the
conclusion that there is a fundamental difference in outlook between
the two works. The "Homely Words" vouches for "an idealized capitalist society," whereas the *Ta-t'ung shu* represents a version of utopian

---

[367] Tikhvinsky, *Dvizhenie za reformy*, p. 397, note 65.

[368] K'ang, *Nien-pu*, p. 7b. Lo, *K'ang*, p. 43.

[369] I have used the reprint included in Liang's *Hsi-cheng ts'ung-shu*, vol. 4. The
"Homely Words" was "orally translated" (*k'ou i*) by John Fryer and put in writing
by Yin Tsu-hsi. The original author and title of this work have not been identified.

socialism. To a certain extent, K'ang used Fryer's book as a target of criticism rather than as a model of construction.

There are, of course, obvious similarities between the two books, similarities that lend ground to Tikhvinsky's assertion that K'ang was indebted to Fryer.[370] The chapter on "General Principles" of the "Homely Words" begins with the statement that it is the wish of the Creator

> to enable all men on the face of the earth to have sufficient food and comfortable clothing, to enjoy peace and happiness together, to be without want or disappointment during their entire life—from childhood to old age.[371]

Later in the book it is said:

> In a society or state are unavoidably some people who due either to sickness . . . or want of skill . . . cannot support themselves by their own labor and have to depend on others for charitable help. Therefore all who are able-bodied and in possession of technical expertness must devise ways and means to assist them.[372]

Sentiments such as these run closely parallel to notions set forth in the *Li-yün* and in the *Ta-t'ung shu*.

The obligation to look after unfortunate fellow men does not controvert the obligation to work. One sees another point of agreement between the two books. It is Heaven's wish that "each person diligently pursue his proper occupation" and that society punish laziness as a crime.[373] This reminds one immediately of the first of the four rules, "prohibition against laziness," formulated in the *Ta-t'ung shu*.[374]

The concepts of independence and equality, to which K'ang attached great importance, are clearly stated in the "Homely Words":

> Having endowed men with life, Heaven must also give them capacity and power to protect their life. . . . Thus irrespective of nationality, race, or color, each man being his own master (*tzu-chu*) cannot [yield his right of independence] to another even in the slightest degree. If a man has committed no crime nor violated any law, then even the government or its officials cannot take away his basic right of independence.[375]

---

[370] Tikhvinsky, *Dvizhenie za reformy*, p. 397.
[371] *Tso-chih chu-yen* (hereafter, *Chu-yen*), "Tsung lun," sec. 1, p. 1a.
[372] Ibid., chap. 2, sec. 12, p. 2b.
[373] Ibid., "Tsung lun," sec. 2, p. 1a and chap. 2, sec. 14, p. 3a.
[374] Community, 1, pp. 426–27; 2 and 3, p. 284; Thompson, pp. 254–55.
[375] *Chu-yen*, chap. 2, sec. 9, p. 2a.

Equality should prevail among citizens of a state and members of the human race as a whole. "Irrespective of social position, the people of a state should be regarded as equal." As inequality exists among "uncivilized" peoples, it is the duty of those that are civilized to work for human equality.

> The peoples on the globe resemble one another in some respects and differ among themselves in other respects. . . . Greater inequalities in rank or class prevail among uncivilized peoples. Consequently, the strong over-power the weak, resulting in even greater calamities. Civilized states should bring equality to all races of men; then there would no longer be the phenomenon of oppression and aggression.[376]

Slavery, which constitutes a direct violation of the principles of inde-pendence and equality, and which exists in "uncivilized" societies, should be done away with.

> With the rise of civilization the state is governed with impartial and equitable laws. Moreover, people are moved by the religious sentiment of mercy, which makes them love others as they love themselves. The old evil practice of buying and selling slaves is now completely abolished.[377]

All this may have helped to convince K'ang that the concept of *t'ien-hsia wei kung* as expounded in the *Li-yün* embodied the true Confucian teaching and was a "universal principle."

K'ang probably derived information concerning forms of Western government from the "Homely Words." Chapter 10 contains this statement:

> All governments on earth fall in general into three sorts: the monarchi-cal system, the aristocratic system (*hsien-chu shan wei*, literally, "succession of worthy rulers to the throne."), and the republican system. In some in-stances, one of the three systems is adopted; in others, two of the three are combined; in still others, all three are combined, as in England today.

The republican form of government is described in these terms:

> In a republican state (*min-chu chih kuo*) the basic aim is to have the people elect, publicly and at intervals, a number of men to represent them in legislation and select a man of ability and integrity to be their chief of state. In the American state this system has been in operation for several generations. The people regard it as convenient.[378]

[376] Ibid., chap. 4, sec. 22, p. 4b and chap. 9, sec. 64, p. 11a.
[377] Ibid., chap. 11, sec. 86, p. 15a.
[378] Ibid., chap. 10, sec. 73, 74.

The idea of parliament, which figured prominently in K'ang's utopian scheme as well as in his reform thought, is also dealt with in Fryer's book. The parliamentary system (*kung-i-yüan chih fa*) is rated as a most important legacy of the past and "the best system" of all existing political institutions.[379] The evolution of the British parliament is sketched and its composition and powers are briefly explained.[380] Interestingly, K'ang used the same term *kung-i-yüan* to designate the parliamentary body that would obtain in the Great Community, in all the stages of its development.[381]

Chapters 7 and 8 of the "Homely Words" deal with international relations and with war and peace. Some of the ideas and information presented here may also have been useful to K'ang. The process of integration, from tribal groups to nations and from small to large states, as Europe witnessed through the centuries, is briefly described and the advantages resulting from it are pointed out.[382] The development and working of international law (*kung-fa*, a term K'ang used often and in various senses), it is said, tend to render the task of maintaining peace among nations appreciably easier. Moreover, international trade helps to draw many nations of the world into friendly relations with one another. War, in fact, is not a concomitant of civilization. The more civilized the nations become, the greater will be their capacity for mutual friendship. Continual advancement of civilization will eventually bring universal peace (*t'ai-p'ing*) to the entire world.[383] It is but a short step from this optimistic forecast to K'ang's vision of the Great Community.

K'ang probably received suggestion (or confirmation) from Fryer's book regarding social progress in measured stages as against sudden change through violent revolution. The following passage from the "Homely Words" is particularly interesting:

> The excellence of the English system has not been achieved at a stroke or as a result of internal upheaval. It is rather the product of prudent conservatism (*hsiao-hsin chin-shou*)—the promotion of everything useful and the elimination of anything harmful—which has made it possible to pro-

[379] Ibid., chap. 11, sec. 98, p. 17a.

[380] Ibid., chap. 11, sec. 105, pp. 17b–18a. Cf. ibid., chap. 2, sec. 15, p. 3b.

[381] *Community*, 1, pp. 136–65; 2 and 3, pp. 91–107; Thompson, pp. 105–27. K'ang also used the term *kung i-hui* interchangeably with *kung i-yüan*.

[382] *Chu-yen*, chap. 7, especially secs. 47–53, p. 7b–9a.

[383] Ibid., chap. 8, sec. 63, p. 11a. Cf. sec. 60, p. 10b: "In the last analysis, war is not a mark of advanced civilization"; and sec. 61, p. 10b: "As civilization advances the disaster of war can be gradually eliminated."

gress in an orderly manner toward perfection. . . . The political system of England today differs widely from that existing three centuries ago. Upon scrutiny [one realizes that] all this [progress] has come from gradually reforming the three-centuries-old system. By following this practice the political system of any country can attain excellence—by degrees and in an orderly way. If, however, because the political system of a country falls short of excellence, one wishes to eliminate evil practices through rebellion or revolution, it is feared that what follows the upheaval and chaos will not be satisfaction or excellence.[384]

One can hardly see any material difference between this and K'ang's approach to social change.

These and other significant similarities, however, should not obscure the crucial difference in basic standpoint: K'ang was concerned with depicting a socialistic utopia, while Fryer endorsed, in Tikhvinsky's terminology, an idealized "capitalist class society" (or, more specifically, idealized Victorian English society). This being the case, the former could not help rejecting some of the latter's central tenets.

The idea of "free enterprise" stands as the cornerstone of the social structure in the "Homely Words."[385] The proper functions of the state, it is declared, are maintenance of peace, enforcement of law, and conduct of foreign affairs. Most other matters should be left to the people themselves. This is the explanation:

> If matters which are properly done by the people themselves, are managed by the state, the latter would find itself unequal to the task and would inevitably work to the disadvantage of the former.[386]

Again, more specifically:

> Many matters fall outside the sphere of government. To impose [government] control over them would not only injure the people but also prove detrimental to the state itself. . . . In the first place, as the state cannot support all the people, it cannot control the people's economic enterprises; second, workers' wages, working hours, and the amount of work done each day cannot be fixed by the state; third, the quantity of commodities (food, clothing, and other articles of daily use) that should be produced each month or year, the method of marketing them, and commodity prices are not for the state to determine.[387]

This, it hardly needs pointing out, goes directly contrary to the eco-

[384] Ibid., sec. 105, pp. 17b–18a.
[385] Chiefly, in chaps. 14–24.
[386] Ibid., chap. 12, sec. 107, p. 18a.
[387] Ibid., chap. 12, sec. 118, p. 19a.

nomic theory underlying K'ang's Great Community which would be an out-and-out socialized system.

The "Homely Words" summarily rejects socialistic ideas:

> Formerly, a noted French engineer said that a man who creates property by accumulating wealth is doing something no different from robbing the wealth of others and appropriating it. Another man in France proposed that the wealth of a country be evenly divided among all the people, each sharing it equally [with all others]; for this was the only fair and just way. . . . As soon as such views became known, ignorant and unreasonable persons of that country refused to work, hoping to appropriate other people's property for their own use. . . . No Englishman has ever lightly subscribed to these views.[388]

The author of the *Ta-t'ung shu*, as we have already seen, preferred the views of the "French" to that of the "Englishman."

Another crucial difference stands between K'ang and the author of the "Homely Words": the former saw no use for the family as a social institution, whereas the latter regarded it as indispensable:

> The state has its roots in the family. For in giving life to man, Heaven of necessity makes man and woman mate themselves as husband and wife and thus form a family. Later, when children are born to them, they, as parents, following the dicates of their Heaven-endowed nature, rear them, nurture them, until they grow into adulthood, before they are allowed to leave home and set up families of their own. . . . All social mores and [political] regulations are subsequent developments.[389]

This is certainly a far cry from K'ang's suggestion that the institutions of marriage and the family itself would disappear in utopia.

Again, in accepting class distinctions as both natural and reasonable, the author of the "Homely Words" takes a position diametrically opposite to K'ang's. Men should be equal before the law, it is said; but as individual abilities and accomplishments must differ, distinctions between "the worthy and unworthy, honored and lowly, have existed

---

[388] Ibid., chap. 18, sec. 196, p. 30b. Arguments against socialism are continued in secs. 197–208, pp. 31a–32a. Chaps. 23 and 24, dealing respectively with wages and capital, reveal the author's position clearly. In the passage quoted here Fryer perhaps had in mind something like the sentiment, "Property is robbery," elaborated by Pierre Joseph Proudhon in his *What is Property?* (1840; Eng. trans. by the American anarchist, Benjamin R. Tucker in 1876). Dunning, *Political Theory from Rousseau to Spencer*, pp. 365–71, gives a brief account of Proudhon's ideas.

[389] *Chu-yen*, chap. 1, sec. 4, p. 1b. Cf. sec. 6, p. 2a: "The husband-wife relationship is in truth the source of all civilization."

ever since antiquity." It is proper for the government to award official positions and nobiliary ranks to outstanding persons; equally proper is it for descendants of the recipients of such awards to inherit them.[390] By the same token, property, which is the reward of personal industry, should also be inheritable.

> A person who has accumulated wealth during his lifetime cannot take any of it with him when he dies. Therefore, he must hand it down to his offspring, to be preserved generation after generation without fail. This is a principle of nature.[391]

Private property, we recall, finds no place in the *Ta-t'ung shu*.

In view of such vital differences in standpoint between the "Homely Words" and the *Ta-t'ung shu*, it is difficult to accept Tikhvinsky's suggestion without important reservations.

---

[390] Ibid., chap. 4, sec. 22–25, pp. 4b–5a.
[391] Ibid., sec. 26, p. 5a.

Chapter 11

DETOUR TO
INDUSTRIAL SOCIETY

CHANGE OF CIRCUMSTANCES AND SHIFT OF EMPHASIS

The *Ta-t'ung shu* was completed under somewhat special circumstances. Between January 1902 and April 1903, K'ang lived in northern India (Darjeeling) where he enjoyed peace and quiet under the protection of British colonial authorities. His attempts to overthrow the empress dowager in 1900 during the Boxer uprising ended in tragic failure. Isolated for the time being from the troubled world, he detached himself from practical concerns of the present and directed his attention to matters relative to the remote past or distant future. It was in such circumstances that he resumed his work of reinterpreting Confucianism and gave the finishing touches to his utopian construction.

Circumstances soon changed. Jung-lu, his arch enemy, died in April 1903; he deemed it now safe to leave his asylum and to lead a more active existence. After short trips in Southeast Asian countries and a brief revisit to Hong Kong to see his mother, he set out (March 22, 1904) for Europe and America, chiefly to promote the cause of constitutional monarchy and to acquaint himself with the situations in the Western countries. A significant shift of emphasis in his social thinking came about as a result. Instead of fixing his gaze on social perfection and human happiness, he now concerned himself with saving China from being overwhelmed by the powerful nations of the twentieth-century world. Thus three years after he finished the *Ta-t'ung shu* he wrote the *Wu-chih chiu-kuo lun* (Essay on National Salvation Through Material Up-

515

building),[1] putting forth his impassioned plea for China's industrialization.

Apparently, K'ang's travels in Western countries in the early years of the present century intensified his admiration for modern industrial civilization[2] (an admiration to which he gave expression for the first time in 1879), and deepened his fear that China might be destroyed by the great powers which that same civilization had helped to create (a fear that motivated his reform efforts in 1898). He came to the inescapable conclusion that China could avert impending destruction only by bringing herself to the same level of industrialization attained by the West.

Meanwhile, another disturbing fact claimed his attention. In the last years of the preceding century, revolutionary sentiments had begun to loom large among Chinese intellectuals in Japan and other parts of the world; an organized revolutionary movement actually took shape with the formation of the T'ung-meng hui in Japan in July 1905.[3] Later in the same year, the *Min pao*, organ of the revolutionary movement, made its appearance, against which Liang Ch'i-ch'ao and other members of K'ang's group carried on a sustained ideological and propaganda battle. K'ang joined in the struggle, defending the cause himself of constitutional monarchy against revolutionary republicanism, in many of his writings, notably his "Essay on Averting Destruction" and "Essay on the Republican Form of Government," both written just before the fall of the dynasty.[4] The 1905 essay on material upbuilding was written partly with the purpose of stemming the revolutionary tide by diverting attention to what he believed to be a more constructive and less hazardous approach to the problem of China's modernization.

K'ang himself made this clear in his preface to the essay. After indicating with regret the failure of Tseng Kuo-fan, Li Hung-chang, and

---

[1] *Wu-chih chiu-kuo lun* (hereafter cited as *Essay*). (This piece, with introductory remarks and notes by Hsü Kao-juan, is available in *Shih-chiai p'ing-lun*, 10th year, nos. 18 and 19 [February 16 and March 10, 1963], pp. 6–15).

[2] *Essay*, pp. 54–57, describes in glowing terms the prosperity and beauty of modern industrial cities, including Los Angeles, California, and Vancouver, B.C.

[3] See Shelley H. Cheng, "The T'ung-meng-hui: Its Organization, Leadership, and Finances, 1905–1912," especially chaps. 1–3.

[4] K'ang T'ung-pi, *K'ang Nan-hai hsien-sheng nien-p'u hsü-pien*, pp. 73b–74 (hereafter, *Nien-p'u hsü-pien*). Jung-pang Lo, *K'ang Yu-wei: A Biography and A Symposium*, p. 218. These pieces are cited by Lo as "On Saving China from [the Danger of] Collapse" and "The Political Structure of a Republic."

other leaders of the "self-strengthening movement" to recognize the
true basis of Europeans' strength, he goes on to say,

> After the defeat of 1894 by Japan and as people's understanding grad-
> ually improved, they came to the view that the basis of Europe and
> America's strength lay in an educated citizenry and that education de-
> pended upon the development of a school system. Consequently, in the
> past ten years, the entire country has focused its efforts on establishing
> schools. Ever since 1898 more and more people have read Japanese books.
> All of a sudden, they came into contact with the social and political ideas
> of Europe and America, ideas which hitherto had been unknown in
> China. Dazzled by these ideas . . . they imagined that the foundation of
> wealth and strength in Western countries lies in the subtlety and profun-
> dity of Western philosophy, in that liberty which came with revolution.
> Without locating the root of China's trouble, they discarded the teaching
> and learning that has been accumulated in thousands of years, and em-
> brace those [of the West]. Hence, from 1901 onward, the tide of revolu-
> tionary thought has been threatening to engulf all. "Liberty" and "revo-
> lution" have become clichés on young people's lips.[5]

This shift of emphasis, which involved important modifications of
K'ang's social thought, did not imply a radical change in his general
outlook. There is no evidence that he now renounced his utopian ideal
—his hope that social perfection could be attained eventually through
radical intellectual, institutional, and material transformation. One
unmistakable clue to this is that he continued to expound *Ta-t'ung* to
overseas Chinese, including those residing in the United States.[6] It is
conceivable that having finished sketching the Great Community he
felt that it was time to show the ways and means of realizing it, taking
existing circumstances into consideration. As already noted, the affluence and splendor of the Great Community could not be achieved
without a very high degree of scientific and technological advancement.[7] In the *Ta-t'ung shu* K'ang chose to center his attention on the
nonmaterial aspect of utopian construction; the millenium was to
come after radical intellectual, social, and political transformation.
But now persuaded that China must address herself to the urgent prob-

---

[5] *Essay*, preface.

[6] K'ang T'ung-pi, *Nien-p'u hsü-pien*, p. 51a (Lo, *K'ang*, p. 198), indicates that K'ang
"frequently expounded the ideal of *Ta-t'ung*" to members of the Los Angeles branch
of the Constitutional Association, March, 1905.

[7] As Derke Bodde has pointed out, in his translation of Fung Yu-lan's *History of
Chinese Philosophy*, 2: 690, translator's note, the *Ta-t'ung shu* shows "a curiously naïve
confidence in technological progress as the key to human happiness," thus "makes it
quite un-Chinese."

lem of national survival before she could march toward universal peace, K'ang took up the question of industrialization in earnest.

Development of material civilization would serve a twofold purpose: to preserve China by making her a worthy member of the family of modern nations and to lay the material foundations for the eventual realization of utopian society. To K'ang it was unthinkable that the Chinese, a "superior" race of men, should or could be eliminated in the process of progress. No world community would be complete without China as an integral component. His pleas for China's preservation stemmed from something like patriotism and carried overtones of nationalism. But he was not a nationalist, pure and simple;[8] he committed himself too firmly and deeply to cosmopolitanism to be that.[9] Maintaining national identity was but a necessary step to "Universal Peace." Industrialization constituted, so to speak, a byway, a detour that would lead China into the utopia of all nations.

It should be emphasized that while industrialization was K'ang's preoccupation in 1905, China's political problems did not cease to interest him. In fact, he continued to dream of a China rendered strong through political reconstruction. He revealed the outlines of this dream on more than one occasion. For example, when he was in Italy (June 1904), he sang praise to Cavour for his role in the unification of Italy and claimed spiritual kinship with this Italian statesman, "the truly greatest" among leaders of Europe.[10] A little later, while visiting Berlin, he eulogized the "blood-and-iron" chancellor who in addition to making Germany great by developing industry and commerce, "saved the country by means of monarchical authority,"[11] a feat that K'ang him-

---

[8] I.e., as defined in *Webster's Third International Dictionary* (Springfield, Ill.: G. C. Merriam Co., 1963), "Nationalist. 1. an advocate of believer in nationalism (a true nationalist places his country above everything)," "Nationalism: loyalty and devotion to a nation; esp.: an attitude, feeling, or belief characterized by a sense of national consciousness, an exaltation of one nation above all others, and an emphasis on loyalty to and the promotion of the culture and interests (as political independence) of one nation as opposed to subordinate areas or other nations and supernational groups."

[9] The *Ta-t'ung shu* shows this most clearly. However, K'ang occasionally came close to being an "imperialist." E.g., in the *Essay*, pp. 33–34, he argued for a strong navy and suggested that China should implement a colonial policy, for "only through expansion could preservation be assured."

[10] K'ang T'ung-pi, *Nien-p'u hsü-pien*, pp. 35b–36a. Lo, *K'ang*, p. 196, mentions the poem in which K'ang voiced his admiration for Cavour but does not give the text.

[11] K'ang T'ung-pi, *Nien-p'u hsü-pien*, pp. 45b–46a. Lo, *K'ang*, p. 196, says K'ang "went via Milan to Paris" on June 26 without visiting Berlin.

self had hoped to accomplish in 1898 and still hoped to do as late as in 1917.

For years K'ang held fast the conviction that in the Kuang-hsü emperor lay the key to China's modernization. One of the major objectives of the 1898 reform movement was with Kuang-hsü's consent and cooperation to transform the autocratic regime of China into a constitutional monarchy. The collapse of the movement did not put an end to K'ang's conviction. He kept on fighting for the cause and adjusted his strategy to the changing situations. As long as the captive emperor lived, he sought to restore him to power by every available means. Under his leadership the Society for Protecting the Emperor (Pao-huang hui) was organized on July 20, 1899, in Vancouver, B.C., Canada, marking the formal beginning of a political movement that persisted in years to come.[12] He made speeches in behalf of constitutional government and, on several occasions, lectured on "the idea of *Ta-t'ung*," for the benefit of members of the Los Angeles branch of his organization—at about the same time that he composed the essay on material upbuilding.[13] The importance of institutional reform, too, was not forgotten. For instance, while he was in Hong Kong in October 1903, he completed an essay on administrative reorganization, on the assumption that China could not achieve modernization without modernizing her administration.[14] All this shows that K'ang's plea for industrialization represented a shift of emphasis, a modification of procedure, in his plan of social reconstruction, but did not imply any radical revision of his social thought in general.

Perhaps it was no mere chance that K'ang wrote his essay on material

[12] K'ang T'ung-pi, *Nien-p'u hsü-pien*, p. 4b; Lo, *K'ang*, p. 181. According to Wu Hsien-tzu, *Chung-kuo min-chu hsien-cheng-tang tang-shih*, passim, the English name of this organization was "Chinese Reform Association" (Wei-hsin hui). Branches were soon established in other cities, including Portland, San Francisco, New York, New Orleans, and a few other cities in Central and South America. Between 1906 and 1911 it was known as the Chinese Constitutional Party (Chung-kuo hsien-cheng tang), in response to the situation created by the Ch'ing court's declared intent to adopt constitutional government. K'ang T'ung-pi, *Nien-p'u hsü-pien*, p. 33b, however, says that the name Pao-huang hui was changed to Hsien-cheng hui in 1902.

[13] Namely, March 1905. K'ang T'ung-pi, *Nien-p'u hsü-pien*, p. 51a; Lo, *K'ang*, p. 198. Earlier, in December 1902, when he was in India, he decided to send K'ang T'ung-pi to Europe and America to lecture on "affairs of the country" (K'ang T'ung-pi, *Nien-p'u hsü-pien*, p. 33a; Lo, *K'ang*, p. 193).

[14] K'ang T'ung-pi, *Nien-p'u hsü-pien*, pp. 34a–b; Lo, *K'ang*, p. 143. This book was published in 1903 in Shanghai, with author's preface dated 1903; 3rd printing, 1904; reprinted in 1905, 1906, and 1907. It also appeared in installments in Liang Ch'i-ch'ao's journal, *Hsin-min ts'ung-pao*, no. 35, and following issues.

upbuilding in the United States. In 1905 Theodore Roosevelt had just begun his second term; under his vigorous leadership the country was rapidly coming of age, both industrially and as a world power. K'ang's lack of both modern training and command of Western languages did not prevent him from seeing with his own eyes the tremendous progress that had been made in the rapidly growing industrial centers of the country, confirming his long-held belief that in industrialization lay power and prosperity. This, in his own words, was how he felt when he toured the United States.

Having traveled in all the countries of Asia and eleven countries of Europe I have now come to America. Between 1898 and the present, I have been journeying outside [of China] for eight years. Intimate acquaintance with the social and political systems of Europe and America [has enabled me] to compare Europe and Asia, assessing their respective advantages and shortcomings, finding out their similarities and differences, tracing the factors which have made the modern world, and analyzing carefully the trend of the great changes [that have taken place]. The causes and antecedents are so immensely complex that they cannot be mentioned in one word. But viewing the matter with reference to the condition of our country . . . [I am convinced that] the root of China's weakness lies solely in not knowing well enough to develop science and technology (*wu-chih hsüeh*, literally, "study of the material"). The Chinese civilization, which is thousands of years old, is actually the foremost on earth. But it has placed undue emphasis upon ethics and philosophy, and is extremely deficient in science and technology. . . . I pity my countrymen who have lost their way in a quagmire of futile discourses on lofty themes; for their enlightenment I offer my Essay on National Salvation Through Material Upbuilding.[15]

This was not a transient sentiment. As late as in 1919 when K'ang reprinted this essay, he reaffirmed the overriding importance of industrialization with an added note of warning against premature application of "novel" political principles.

Stimulated by the effects of the present great European war, scientific discoveries and technological inventions have multiplied at an even faster pace. Fifty-six centimeter guns have a range of 200 *li*; aircrafts span the Atlantic Ocean in sixteen hours. Industrialization has made Germany

[15] Preface to *Essay*. Cf. K'ang T'ung-pi, *Nien-p'u hsü-pien*, p. 51a: "Seeing with his own eyes the development of material civilization in various countries and being persuaded that China, which still clung to her old ways without change, would be unable to compete with them in the world, he wrote the *Wu-chih chiu-kuo lun*." Lo, *K'ang*, p. 198, makes no mention of this observation.

powerful and prompted her to harbor the ambition of swallowing up all Europe; industrialization has enabled England and France to resist [German aggression] for four years; industrialization has made the United States the most wealthy country in the world. All this progress has been made on the foundation of science and technology. . . . Nevertheless, when formerly I wished to publish this book, Liang Ch'i-ch'ao, my student, strongly opposed it, thinking that liberty, revolution, and constitutional government would be sufficient to effect our country's reconstruction. . . . Recently, many people in our country do talk about industrialization, but they do not know the proper approach. . . . Some of them have advocated the principle of absolute social equality. What they hold is not unreasonable. But if we apply it prematurely, ahead of the proper time, we would merely open the way to chaos.[16]

Keeping in mind the fact that in 1919 the *Hsin ch'ing-nien* had already been in circulation for four years and diverse brands of socialism were being promoted by ardent but not necessarily well-informed exponents, one should find it easy to see the significance of the concluding sentences in this passage.

These statements show clearly that K'ang had revised his attitude not only toward "Western learning" but also toward Chinese learning. He condemned "futile discourses on lofty themes"; this was tantamount to condemnation of the traditional mode of learning, of book knowledge culled from the classics. He cautioned against subscribing to "the principle of absolute social equality"; this was opposition to accepting "novel principles" imported from the West. And in laying preponderant emphasis on material upbuilding, he virtually reversed his view concerning Western civilization. In 1886 he had dismissed "Western books" on science and technology as "nonurgent" and attached paramount importance to those dealing with government.[17] This was the line of thought that underlay his reform program of 1898.[18] But now in 1905 (and 1919), he argued that the only thing that China should and could learn from the West at the time was its science and technology.

The "Essay on National Salvation Through Material Upbuilding," therefore, represented a modification of K'ang's thinking concerning

[16] Colophon to 1919 reprint of the *Essay*. The original for "principle of absolute social equality" is *she-hui chih-p'ing chih i*. K'ang referred obviously to socialism and possibly to the socialistic ideas appearing in the earlier issues of the *Hsin ch'ing-nien*.

[17] K'ang, *Tzu-pien nien-p'u*, p. 7b (hereafter cited as *Nien-p'u*); Lo, *K'ang*, p. 43.

[18] Liang Ch'i-ch'ao's preface to his compilation of translations of "Western Books on Public Affairs" (*Hsi-cheng ts'ung-shu*), indicates this line of thought most clearly and concisely.

the problem of China's modernization. Here he de-emphasized (but did not abandon) his assumption that basic human values knew no national boundaries, but stressed the necessity for China to match the modern West in material civilization. In other words, he found it necessary in 1905 to descend from one level of his social thought to another:[19] instead of occupying himself with spreading the idea of cultural cosmopolitanism, he advocated here something like selective Westernization. In so doing he set himself apart both from Chang Chih-tung and other partial Westernizers who had no use for Western values, and from the exponents of the "new culture" who had no use for Chinese values.

ARGUMENTS FOR INDUSTRIALIZATION: THEORETICAL IMPLICATIONS

K'ang's main argument is quite simple. In a word, as Western countries had become powerful through phenomenal advancement in science and technology, China must attain the same advancement in order to survive and prosper.

K'ang was aware that Western industrialization presupposed something more than technological inventions—the proliferation of new machinery and expansion of factory production. In a highly interesting passage in the 1905 essay he pointed definitely to science as the foundation of modern material civilization.

> Nowadays, military might and national wealth all depend upon science. . . . The physical sciences and mathematics furnish its general principles; mechanical and civil engineering are its application. . . . All these constitute science. With it [men live in] the New World; without it [men find themselves in] an old world and will gradually perish.[20]

Nineteenth-century modernizers of China failed to attain their goal,

---

[19] See chapter 9 of this volume, the sections on Levels and Phases of Thought and Universalization and Westernization. Cf. Joseph R. Levenson, " 'History' and 'Value': The History of Intellectual Choice in Modern China," in *Studies in Chinese Thought*, ed. Arthur F. Wright, pp. 161–66, and *Liang Ch'i-ch'ao, The Mind of Modern China* (Cambridge, Mass.: Harvard University Press, 1953), pp. 6–8. Meribeth E. Cameron, *The Reform Movement in China, 1898–1912*, p. 42, suggests that K'ang Yu-wei and Chang Chih-tung "differed chiefly in tempo." This hardly touches the essential point.

[20] *Essay*, pp. 41–42. "The natural sciences" is translation for *po-wu hsüeh* in the original text. This term was used in K'ang's time in two senses. In a narrower sense, it covered roughly the biological sciences, but in a broader sense, it denoted the general study of natural phenomena. See *Tz'u-yuan*, 18th printing (Taipei, 1949), "po-wu hsüeh." *Tz'u-hai*, 3rd printing (Taipei, 1958), p. 483, gives only the narrow sense. K'ang apparently used the term in its broader sense.

K'ang said, precisely because they did not understand that science was the basis of material civilization. As he put it,

> I have read all the documents kept in the Tsungli yamen, which were prepared prior to 1894 by high officials serving both in and outside the imperial court. Without exception [these officials] realized that it was necessary to build a modern army and navy, or to manufacture guns and construct warships. But unfortunately, they did not recognize science, the foundation of all technology and engineering. Their efforts in developing a modern army and navy, in manufacturing guns and constructing warships inescapably failed to bring them the desired results.[21]

K'ang's recognition of "science" as a basis of industrialization, even though his conception of science was of necessity rather hazy, represents perhaps one of the most significant points made in the essay. This recognition marks a turning point in the thinking of the period. It set K'ang apart from the leaders of the self-strengthening movement of the late nineteenth century and qualified him as a forerunner of the advocates of "scientism" in the twentieth century.[22]

In stressing the overriding importance of science and technology K'ang minimized the value of "ethics" and "philosophy." A year before he wrote the essay, when he was in the Netherlands, he visited the place where Peter the Great of Russia worked in a shipyard to learn modern industrial techniques, K'ang wrote a long poem that contains these lines:

> The foundation of Europe's power:
> Science and technology.
> Inventions achieved in a century—
> Marvellous, imposing, matchless!
> Thanks to them the whole globe
> Under Europe's sway has come.

He went on to say that because of false pride in China's moral tradition, nineteenth-century leaders refused to "condescend" themselves to learn from Europe.[23] Exactly the same sentiment was expressed, in plainer language, in the essay of 1905:

> That which enabled the Europeans to occupy a position of power on earth is not their philosophy, nor their [doctrines of] popular sovereignty

---

[21] *Essay*, pp. 19–20.

[22] The views of Ch'en Tu-hsiu will be briefly stated in a subsequent section.

[23] K'ang T'ung-pi, *Nien-p'u hsü-pien*, pp. 48b–49a. Lo, *K'ang*, p. 197, mentions K'ang's visit to the historic shipyard but omits the poem.

and liberty; it is the power of science and technology [which has lent them power]. . . . Wei Mo-shen had suggested, "learn the superior techniques of the barbarians in order to curb the barbarians". . . . Wei Mo-shen's view remains absolutely correct even now.[24]

Accordingly, K'ang opened his essay with a section on "Peter Studies Shipbuilding." Russia, he argued, was at first "uncivilized," without either government or law worthy of the name. But Peter modernized the country by simply adopting the material civilization of the West. China, which had a civilization of several thousand years, should easily become stronger and more prosperous than Russia—if her leaders would only follow Peter's example.[25]

The experiences of the other leading countries of the West—England, Germany, and the United States—were equally instructive. England, "the strongest of European powers," could claim no superiority over France and Germany in nonmaterial culture. Kant, Hegel, Montesquieu, Rousseau, Condorcet, and others were great thinkers; the doctrines of equality and liberty ridded France of the *ancien régime*. But it was England that defeated France and took India, Canada, and Australia—thanks to her matchless navy and commerce—all "because England made the greatest effort in developing science."[26] Germany and the United States told a similar story. Formerly, when Germany devoted her energies to philosophy, she remained weak for a long time. But after defeating the French, she focused her attention on material development. In less than twenty years she became stronger even than mighty England. The United States "had not produced a single philosopher" but had made spectacular progress in science and technology. Her national strength became most impressive. On the other hand, Western nations that neglected science remained weak. Witness Italy and Spain, two countries dominated by religion and engrossed in theological and philosophical speculations.[27] Indeed, K'ang continued, even the greatest of prophets who did nothing about material upbuilding were of no avail in face of national calamities.

Jesus became the religious leader of Europe but did not save Judah

[24] *Essay*, pp. 21–22. K'ang referred to Wei Yüan's preface (pp. 1a–b), to his *Hai-kuo t'u chih*, dated 1842: "For what purpose is this book written? I reply: 'It is written for the purpose of [demonstrating the advantages of] learning the superior techniques of the barbarians with which to curb them.'"

[25] *Essay*, pp. 1–2, 49.

[26] Ibid., pp. 23–24.

[27] Ibid., p. 44.

from destruction; the Buddha became the religious leader of East Asia but did not save India from destruction.[28]

Similarly, Confucius, China's "religious leader," was unable to give China strength and prosperity but had, in fact, allowed the country to remain agricultural for thousands of years, comparing most unfavorably with the "affluent and happy" industrial countries of the modern West. Not that the Confucian teaching was without intrinsic value; the trouble lay in China's failure to develop science and technology to supplement that teaching.

K'ang confessed frankly that his own learning, which was not "material," could not be serviceable to China.

> Among the four hundred million people I am not without some knowledge. I have not only read all Chinese books but also studied and gained understanding of ideas, events, and customs of Europe and America. . . . But if China eventually fails to attain industrialization, then even everyone of the four hundred million is as [well informed as] I, there would be no way to escape ruin. For although I have a measure of earnestness and possess some knowledge, I am most useless concerning the work of national salvation—because I know nothing about the practical enterprise: industry.[29]

By the same token, all persons who did not concern themselves with "material learning" were equally useless to the country. Even if each and every one of the four hundred million attained the wisdom or knowledge of "Rousseau, Voltaire, Montesquieu; or perhaps of Kant, Bacon, Descartes; or even of Plato, Aristotle, Christ, the Buddha," none of them could escape the fate of slaves.[30]

Efforts to modernize China had of course been made. But all these were in the wrong direction: hope had been mistakenly placed in "the schools of empty words."[31] (In K'ang's view, anything that did not contribute to "actual living" was empty words.) Such words, "even if they were legacies bequeathed by forefathers or doctrines handed down from sages or worthies," were "valueless."[32]

[28] Ibid., p. 10.
[29] Ibid., p. 49.
[30] Ibid., p. 10.
[31] Ibid., p. 11.
[32] Ibid., p. 46. Unwittingly, K'ang echoed in effect the sentiment of Wang Hsien-ch'ien (a staunch opponent of K'ang's institutional reform) expressed in 1898: "Japan's modernization began with industry: China's reform began with chatter" ("Letter in Reply to Pi Yung-nien," in Su Yü, *I-chiao ts'ung-pien, chüan* 6, p. 7b). One is also reminded somewhat of the concluding words of Chang Chih-tung's essay on the

There were different sorts of empty words, some of which were useless without being dangerous and others were pernicious in addition to being unavailing. The curriculum of the Western-style schools was as useless as the "eight-legged essay" of old, but it gave currency to a harmful sort of empty words. Neither yielded scientific and technological knowledge, but the former taught scholars to desert Chinese tradition and thus block their way to moral betterment. China must industrialize, but modernity was not to be achieved by denying her people the opportunity to be virtuous. The Confucian classics were "empty words" only is so far as they contributed nothing to material life; but as valid guides to the good life they should have a place in modern China. Therefore, traditional values should not be traded for imported newfangled empty words that had nothing to do with science and technology, and were unsuitable for domestic application at the present stage of development.

This, obviously, was the line of thought that underlay the following important statement.

> In the past, though the eight-legged essay cultivated by scholars was remote from timely practical use, it at any rate drew them to the classics and the exegeses, thereby enabling them to develop their character and lessen their faults. In this way it contributed to good mores. But now [due to the influence of the schools of empty words] people summarily discarded China's great teachings—the precepts as contained in the classics and their exegeses. Youthful students readily pick up clichés such as "liberty," "constitution," "rights," and "struggle," . . . but they are not in possession of practical knowledge. . . . What, really, is the purpose of converting the old-fashioned academies into Western-style schools, [a change] earnestly and loudly demanded by well-intentioned men of the country?[33]

It may be noted that the "clichés," which K'ang said were parroted by students in the 1900s and regretted their doing so, were in truth none other than the "novel principles" which he spoke of with enthusiasm in the 1880s.[34] Time and circumstances had changed, and so did his view on education. Twenty years before, he was concerned with over-

---

importance of agriculture, industry, and commerce in his "Exhortation to Learning," written in the same year. A scholar, Chang said, who studied the classics for the examinations but knew nothing about these practical subjects was a wholly useless individual, not an "effective scholar" (*Ch'üan-hsüeh p'ien*, "wai-p'ien," no. 9, "Nung kung shang hsüeh," p. 33a). Samuel I. Woodbridge did not translate this piece in *China's Only Hope* (Edinburgh: Oliphant, Anderson, & Ferrier, 1901).

[33] *Essay*, pp. 46–47.

[34] *Nien-p'u*, p. 7b (Lo, *K'ang*, p. 43). K'ang quoted his friend and obviously agreed with him.

coming the prevailing "conservatism" of the bulk of the scholars and officials; now he had become deeply disturbed by the rising tide of "radicalism" that arrived with a new generation of intellectuals. But, to repeat, he had not altered his fundamental conviction that China must modernize in a judicious manner and at a measured pace. This meant that she should not commit herself to republicanism before she had matured as a constitutional monarchy, nor should she cast aside the national ethos before the advent of cosmopolitan utopia.

K'ang's arguments for industrialization, as explained above, are not without cogency. Unfortunately, however, these arguments were not stated as carefully or clearly as they should have been. Sometimes he actually involved himself in inconsistencies. A particularly significant instance may be noted. With a view apparently to giving the strongest possible emphasis to his thesis that industrialization was of paramount importance, he argued that "fine customs and good morals" were, so to speak, a by-product of material civilization. He cited what he believed to be the situation in the United States to sustain his point. Personal character and social mores, he said, were "in former times extremely rotten" in that country, but with industrialization came moral improvement. Now not only wealthy people like Rockefeller, Stanford, and Carnegie unselfishly contributed their riches for their follow men's benefit, but even common "laborers behaved as befitted gentlemen."[35] Unfortunately, China had failed to industrialize. Therefore, despite the presence of great sages with their superb teachings, the morals of the Chinese were actually no better than the worst of Westerners. Without the material basis, what the Americans had achieved in the realm of morality was absolutely impossible in China, "even if Yao and Shun [the noblest of sage-emperors] came back to life, and I-yin and Chou-kung [the ablest of worthy ministers] held the reins of government."[36]

[35] *Essay*, p. 50. Cf. a letter written sometime after 1912, in which K'ang repeated the same view with slight changes. Fifty years ago, he said, Europeans and Americans were not only ignorant but also immoral. But thanks to the rapid advancement of material civilization, they "not only have become increasingly wealthy and strong day by day but have gradually improved their character and customs . . . which is a truly surprising thing." He then went on to say that he had written two books: (1) Essay on National Salvation Through Material Upbuilding, (2) Essay on National Salvation Through Financial Management (*Li-ts'ai chiu-kuo lun*, 1912), dealing with the two most urgent tasks which must be done to save China. However, China's superb moral tradition must be preserved ("Fu Liu Kuan-ch'a Shih-chi shu," *Wan-mu-ts'ao-t'ang i-kao, chüan* 4, pp. 47b–48a, hereafter, *I-kao*).

[36] *Essay*, p. 54.

Apparently, K'ang was not aware that this clashed with an observation made earlier in the essay:

> Europeans and Americans, compared with the Chinese, . . . are surely superior to the Chinese, if one refers to material civilization. But if one speaks of them with reference to morality, then one can say that the Chinese, who have been receiving instruction from the Sage's classics and following the way defined by the Sung learning—who value benevolence, yielding, filial piety, brotherly love, loyalty, and reverence—are superior to the Europeans and Americans.[37]

One wonders how China, which even Yao and Shun could not help, managed to attain such a lofty state of goodness.

This obvious inconsistency, it may be surmised, stemmed from the fact that K'ang held two divergent assumptions concerning the relationship between the material and nonmaterial aspects of civilization. On the one hand, he assumed that science was the key to moral advancement as well as material progress. Had he pursued this line of thought to its logical end, he would have to argue, with the exponents of scientism, that in adopting the industrialization of the West, China was bound to evolve a value system essentially identical with the modern Western value system; that, in other words, there was no need to preserve China's indigenous tradition and that modernization was in effect equivalent to total Westernization. On the other hand, K'ang assumed that science and morals were two independent, separable aspects of civilization. Any one country, therefore, might make strides in one but lag behind in the other. Thus it was possible for China to be superior to the European countries in moral development and yet inferior in industrialization; and conversely, for Europeans to be superior in science but to remain backward in moral life. K'ang sometimes stressed the first or monistic assumption but at other times he emphasized the second or dualistic assumption, apparently unaware of their incompatibility.

K'ang's inconsistency may be annoying, but it is not without historical meaning. In assuming that science was the basis of human values, he anticipated in effect the position of Ch'en Tu-hsiu and his fellow admirers of "Mr. Science," although in opposing republicanism K'ang, as the author of the essay of 1905, had no use for "Mr. Democracy." (See the section, The Great Community and the 'New Culture' in chapter 10.) And in assuming that a nation could develop a wondrous

[37] Ibid., p. 8.

value system and yet remain woefully deficient in material civilization, he prefigured some of the arguments against total Westernization set forth by such writers as Liang Ch'i-ch'ao and Liang Sou-ming. (See following section, Problem of Modernization: Evaluation of the Chinese and Western Civilizations.) K'ang, in fact, grappled in a preliminary and somewhat confused manner with the same issues that later became sharply drawn in the lengthy debates on "science and view of life" and "Eastern and Western Civilizations." His two assumptions foreshadowed the credos of intellectuals in opposite camps and his essay of 1905 afforded a preview of the controversies of the late 1910s and 1920s.

PLAN OF INDUSTRIALIZATION

K'ang's plan for industrialization as outlined in the essay requires only a brief examination. In some respects, this plan is reminiscent of his reform program of 1898.[38] With a view to laying a solid foundation for industrial development, he suggested as a first step the training of personnel. Students should be sent abroad to study science and technology, and "famed technicians" of foreign countries should be invited to give instruction in Chinese schools. He designated Germany, Scotland (for mechanical engineering) and the United States (specifically, Cornell University, the University of Chicago, and "Berkeley") as the best countries to send the students.[39] At the same time, technological institutes and industrial schools should be established in China, and courses teaching the use of machinery and skill in wood working introduced in elementary schools. Modern factories, of course, should be built as time went on.[40]

Private enterprise, he believed, was the proper way to implement his plan. He therefore rejected both "government management" (*kuan pan*) and socialization. He rested his objections to the former on practical grounds:

> All the new machine enterprises launched in the decades of the T'ung-chih and Kuang-hsü reigns were under government management. Now to rely on the government to raise additional capital [for industrial expansion] would not only be infeasible because [the government] does not have sufficient economic resources to do so but also undesirable, even if

[38] See K'ang's memorials submitted to the imperial court in 1898, concerning schools, given in Chien Po-tsan et al., *Wu-hsü pien-fa*, 2: 217–19, 222–25, 250–51.

[39] *Essay*, pp. 66–81.

[40] Ibid., pp. 81–88.

it had sufficient resources, because it is doubtful that [government management] can foster the spirit of competition for excellence.

K'ang pointed to Krupp of Germany and Armstrong of England as shining models of successful private enterprise, worthy of emulation.[41]

His objection to socialization was somewhat qualified. He wrote in the colophon:

> Recently, many people in our country . . . talk about industrialization, but they do not have the correct approach. . . . Some of them have expounded the doctrine of absolute social equality. What they hold is not unreasonable. But if we apply it prematurely, before the proper time arrives, we would merely open the door to chaos.[42]

It should be noted, however, that K'ang was not opposed to socialism in principle, nor did he favor private enterprise as a permanent economic system. Private enterprise in his thinking was but a transitional arrangement that would prove useful in speeding up China's industrial development.[43] "Material upbuilding," which would turn

[41] Ibid., p. 20.

[42] Ibid., colophon. It is interesting to note that according to Chao Ping-lin (*Pai-yen kan-chiu shih-hua*, in *Chao Pai-yen chi*, *chüan* 3, p. 8b), when K'ang heard in the early 1920s that Yen Hsi-shan, *tu-chün* (military governor) of Shansi, honored the Confucian tradition and planned for the province's industrial development, he sent two of his students to Shansi and suggested to Yen that industrialization should begin with attracting capital from overseas Chinese. Chao commented: "At that time, Shansi was entertaining the idea of applying the ancient 'well-field' principle of public ownership of land to mining enterprises, namely, all mines were to be public property but operated as private enterprises, in order to forestall monopoly of capitalists. When [K'ang] Nan-hai heard of it, he gave his approval." For Yen's undertakings, see his *Chih Chin cheng-wu ch'üan-shu*, vols. 10 and 11 (on mining). For Yen's views on Confucianism, see "K'ung-tzu shih ko shih-mo chia?" (What Was Confucius?, Taipei, 1950). Yen also subscribed to the idea of *Ta-t'ung*, which in some respects, approximated K'ang's "Great Community." See Yen, *Shih chieh ta-t'ung*.

It may also be noted that Chang Chien, "who advocated a substantial program of modernization for China, but one which was to be based on the traditional culture," succeeded to a remarkable extent in transforming Nan-t'ung, his native district and one of the most backward areas of Kiangsu province, into what was regarded by many as a "model district" resting on the foundation of private enterprise (see Samuel C. Chu, *Reformer in Modern China, Chang Chien, 1853–1926*). K'ang made no mention of Chang but it is certain that he would have approved of what he thought and did. (For China's early efforts to industrialize, see Ch'üan Han-sheng, "Chia-wu chan-cheng i-ch'ien Chung-kuo kung-yeh-hua yün-tung," pp. 59–80 and Albert Feuerwerker, *China's Early Industrialization: Sheng Hsüan-Huai (1844–1916) and Mandarin Enterprise*).

[43] In insisting upon private enterprise, K'ang differed from leaders of the preindustrial countries of today, who generally favor "socialistic" methods. See Paul E.

China from an agricultural into a modern industrial society, was not to sidetrack her from the Great Community, but would serve as a byway leading eventually to it. In other words, K'ang did not abandon the socialistic ideal which he had delineated a few years ago in the *Ta-t'ung shu*, but warned only against its premature application, in violation of his principle of social progress in orderly stages.

K'ang recognized capitalization as a crucial problem in industrialization but he did not overlook the importance of stable political conditions, which could be realized only through modernization of the political system. China's age-old autocratic rule must be replaced by constitutional government (which, in his view, had its ultimate foundation in local self-government) before industrial development could take place. He wrote near the end of the essay:

> Industrialization depends upon [sound] financial management, financial management presupposes [efficient governmental] administration which in turn rests upon the foundation of the self-government of citizens. . . . Therefore, before the establishment of provincial, prefectual, district, and village assemblies, all that I have set forth here is of no [practical] significance.[44]

This, of course, is not an unreasonable view. However, haunted by the specter of revolution, K'ang made statements that sounded like arguments against constitutionalism and self-government. The following serves to illustrate:

> Any political system could be adopted as soon as we wish to have it.

Sigmund, *The Ideologies of the Developing Nations*, especially pp. 11–22. However, in stressing the importance of industrialization, K'ang was in essential agreement with them. Nehru of India, e.g., was convinced that "cottage industry" must give way to an economy based on "the big machine and industrialization," that "a child's education should be intimately associated with some craft or manual activity," and that "set phrases and old formulas" were worthless and therefore should be discarded (see excerpts from *The Discovery of India* in Sigmund, pp. 93–95). Hsü Kao-yüan, in his introduction to an annotated reprint of the *Essay*, suggests that K'ang's plan for industrialization "came fairly close" to Sun Yat-sen's program as outlined in the "Chien-kuo fang-lueh," showing "the same degree of zeal" toward development of science and technology (see *Shih-chieh p'ing-lun*, no. 18, p. 6). Obviously, Hsü refers to Sun's "Shih-yeh chi-hua." There is indeed some resemblance in aim, namely, modernization through industrialization, but the two plans differ widely in more than one respect. E.g., while K'ang insisted on private enterprise, Sun argued that "social revolution" must be implemented together with "industrial revolution," that, in other words, certain modern industries were to be nationalized ("Shih-yeh chi-hua," *Sun Chung-shan ch'üan-shu*, 2: 5).

[44] *Essay*, p. 89.

But industrialization cannot be achieved in short order, whenever we wish. From this it can be argued that if the government exerts itself, with resolve and dispatch, and effects [political reforms] throughout the country—making [a reality] parliament, constitution, popular sovereignty, public opinion—it still would not be able to fend off the aggression threatened by our powerful neighbors.[45]

This not only obscures his real position, i.e., that political reform and economic development were both necessary but also belied his sustained efforts to promote constitutional government, which were being made at the very moment when he wrote the essay. His frustrating experience could hardly lend ground to the optimistic view that "any political system could be adopted as soon as we wish to have it."

PROBLEM OF MODERNIZATION: EVALUATION OF CHINESE AND WESTERN CIVILIZATIONS

It may be said that the problem of China's modernization, as it was posed in the last decades of the nineteenth century and the first of the twentieth, resolved itself in part into an evaluation of Chinese and Western civilizations. Each advocate of modernization undertook, overtly or implicitly, systematically or in a random manner, to make his own appraisal. In general, the older writers who were steeped in the native tradition and possessed relatively little intimate knowledge of the West tended to take a more favorable view of Chinese civilization, while writers of the younger generation who had no close ties with China's past, both intellectually and as a matter of sentiment, were much more ready to accept Western culture without reservation. Living in historical situations decades apart, these two groups of writers acquired widely different outlooks and did not even speak the same intellectual language. Neither could really understand the position of the other. Consequently, just as the older writers viewed with alarm their younger contemporaries' "uncritical acceptance" of the modern West, so the new intellectuals frowned upon their predecessors for their "blind worship" of China's past. Incompatible as they were, the two groups represented in fact two successive phases of one and the same intellectual development. The earlier writers set the trend and the later ones pushed it to its logical extreme.

K'ang Yu-wei stood as the most important spokesman for the first phase of this development, although some of his views foreshadowed those of the new intellectuals. In a large number of writings done mostly

[45] Ibid., p. 48.

between the 1890s and 1910s, he pointed to merits and shortcomings of both civilizations. Each, he contended, had within itself ingredients of universal value, worthy of adoption or preservation; each was marred by features that were detrimental to human happiness and therefore fit to be discarded and shunned. Instead of drawing an insuperable line between East and West, he often dwelled on the essential identity of the "twins" who must eventually meet on a common cultural ground. He was inclined to relate ideas and institutions to historical conditions —to what he believed to be regular stages of human development— and to appraise them according to their suitability to the requirements of changing situations. A society ready to enter a given stage of development should adopt the ideas and institutions appropriate for that stage, irrespective of their geographical or ethnic origins; it should, on the other hand, reject those that had outlived their usefulness and refrain from applying others that suited a later time. Anachronism in either direction would spell disaster.

A nation must therefore make cultural adjustments from time to time. And, living among nations which have come into close contact, it must also make proper adjustments with reference to the cultural developments of its neighbors. Thus, as it happened that China was behind the West in material civilization, she must, for her own sake, bring herself up to the level of the scientific and technological progress attained by Europe and America.[46] And, as it also happened that the West could claim no superiority over China in moral development, it would be wise for China to retain her superior tradition, the "Confucianism,"[47] which was valid not only for the Chinese but for all other civilized people as well.

Modernization was, therefore, a continual process of cultural adjustment aiming at progress. The march of civilization was, in the last analysis, toward the common good of all mankind; it was not the exclusive responsibility or privilege of any particular nation. Each made its contribution from which others might derive benefit, but no nation should relinquish its individual achievement in order to copy the ways of another. Just as "Confucianism" was not exclusively Chinese, evolved only for the benefit of the Chinese, so was not *wu-chih* an ex-

[46] This was the central theme of K'ang's 1905 essay.

[47] For K'ang's conception of "Confucianism," see Liang Ch'i-ch'ao, *Ch'ing-tai hsüeh-shu kai-lun*, pp. 126–28; Liang, *Intellectual Trends in the Ch'ing Period*, translated by Immanuel C. Y. Hsü, pp. 91–92 (hereafter, Hsü, *Intellectual Trends . . .*). Cf. Kung-chuan Hsiao, "K'ang Yu-wei and Confucianism," pp. 136–66, and the section on Universalization and Westernization in a previous chapter.

clusive Western phenomenon, good only for Europeans and Americans. And it would be equally foolish for the West to give up science and technology in exchange for China's moral tradition and for China to repudiate her own value system in order to make room for industrialization.

This, in short, was K'ang's general position regarding Chinese and Western civilizations. As already hinted before, this position implied three related propositions: (1) that the valid elements of any civilization obtaining at a given stage of development were appropriate for any country moving into or reaching that stage; (2) that while China lagged behind the West in material achievement, she was equal or superior to the West in moral advancement; and (3) that China should bring her material culture up to the modern Western level, and, at the same time, preserve the best of her moral tradition. One may of course question the correctness of K'ang's assessment of the Chinese and Western civilizations, the practicability of his plan of modernization, or the soundness of his theoretical assumptions. But one can hardly deny that his general position is a highly interesting one worthy of consideration.

There is no evidence that K'ang had abandoned this position at any time between the 1890s and 1910s, except, perhaps, when he was engaged in utopian construction. However, as the historical circumstances and his intellectual objectives changed, he did not hesitate to shift the emphasis from one to another of the above-mentioned propositions. In general, he tended to stress the first in the earlier years and the other two in later times.

Partly with a view to counteracting the bigotry and ignorance of the hidebound traditionalists, K'ang often reiterated the argument that what had made Western countries strong and prosperous were basically the same principles that China's sages had laid down thousands of years ago. For instance, he said in 1897:

> There is no better science of government than [what is found in] our Six Classics. According to my investigation, what has made the West strong are [principles which] conform completely to those contained in the Classics. The foundation of Western strength lies in educating, nourishing, and protecting the people, in assuring all the people liberty and happiness, [the same things that are held essential in China's political tradition]. . . . The cause of China's weakness lies in [doing things] contrary to the principles contained in the Classics.[48]

[48] K'ang, *Jih-pen shu-mu chih*, "Kuo-chia cheng-chih-hsüeh shu t'i-yao."

This, as it has been pointed out, was tantamount to saying that the existing political system of China was "thoroughly un-Confucian."[49]

In a letter to one of his friends, written probably also in the 1890s, K'ang stated his belief in the universality of social values in somewhat more general terms. The true principles of China, he said, "are followed by all mankind. How can there be any difference between the Chinese and other peoples," including those portions of humanity erroneously referred to as "the Western barbarians?"[50] As late as 1903 he restated this view without change. The Confucian moral principles, he wrote, "prevailed widely in Europe and America but [ironically] had been lost in the country of their origin."[51]

K'ang made it clear, however, that essential identity of moral principles did not preclude divergencies in the cultural patterns of different countries. As a matter of fact, dissimilar geographical or historical factors often induced diversities in social customs and caused different countries to attain varying degrees of advancement in different aspects of civilization.[52] Thus the Chinese had their distinctive ethos that set them apart from the Westerners, and were advanced in one aspect of culture (morals) but were far behind the latter in another (industry). It would be folly, K'ang argued, for his countrymen to neglect science and technology and thus to forfeit the opportunity of modernization, but it would be equally unwise for them to give up the Chinese ethos and thus "to become Westerners" (*hua wei hsi-jen*).[53]

[49] Otto Franke, "Der Ursprung der Reformbewegung in China," p. 22.

[50] K'ang, "Yü Ting-fu," manuscript copy on microfilm in the collection of the Far Eastern Library, University of Washington. This letter is not included in *I-kao*. Cf. another letter written 1891, "Yü Hung Shih-ch'en chi-chien lun Chung-Hsi i-t'ung shu," given in K'ang, *I-kao, chüan 4 shang*, pp. 9a–10a and in microfilm, reel 1. In the 1891 letter K'ang explained the differences between China and the West by divergencies in historical circumstances (*shih*) and customs (*su*). For centuries China had been a unified empire, whereas Europe since the fall of the Roman Empire had been a collection of independent states. Consequently, autocracy prevailed in China and Chinese laws and institutions were permeated by conservatism. On the other hand, competition and struggle among European states put a premium on change and progress, while active citizenries tended to curtail absolutism. Because of such wide difference in circumstances there arose differences in customs. In China the "Three Bonds" became the ruling principle of social life; in the West equality became the cardinal principle. K'ang denied that the West had achieved social perfection, but he pointed out what he believed to be the serious shortcomings of the traditional Chinese social and political system.

[51] K'ang, *Lun-yü chu, chüan 8*, p. 6b and *chüan 15*, p. 3a. Similar sentiments were expressed in other works of this period.

[52] "Yu Hung Shih-ch'en chi-chien lun Chung-Hsi i-t'ung shu," (see note 50).

[53] "Yu Ting-fu" (see note 50).

It appears clear, then, that while K'ang envisaged the eventual emergence of a universal civilization encompassing all peoples of the world, he did not propose to arrive at that goal by erasing the cultural identity of a nation. On the contrary, pending the coming of utopia, it was advisable for a civilized nation such as China to strive toward universality without surrendering its cultural individuality. Ethnic suicide was no way to progress. Viewed in this light, K'ang's opposition to indiscriminate copying of Western ways did not constitute conservatism, in the sense of opposition to cultural change as such.

K'ang, in fact, recognized the value and necessity of cultural change resulting from interaction of different ethnic groups. No civilization could prosper (and, indeed, exist for long) in stagnant isolation. He made this observation in 1902, while he was in India:

> The mingling of diverse elements constitutes what is called culture (*wen-wu*); the more mingling, the more developed is the culture. When a culture reaches full development [with concomitant advancement of] knowledge to full complexity, it is known as civilization (*wen-ming*). . . . Just as in marriage only when the wife is selected from [a family bearing] a surname differing from [that of the groom's family] will there be an abundance of progeny,[54] so in society only when it has contact with other societies will its culture attain complete development.[55]

This appears to be K'ang's theoretical justification for his attempts at cultural synthesis, which was to be realized by a happy combination of the most advanced elements of Chinese and Western civilizations, or, in Liang Ch'i-ch'ao's words, at "founding a new school of learning which would be 'neither Chinese nor Western but in fact both Chinese and Western.' "[56]

Such a broad-minded approach to the problem of culture was made possible by K'ang's appreciative attitude toward both the Chinese and Western civilizations. As a Western writer put it,

K'ang had not only read the story of other nations and realized that

[54] An allusion to the ancient Chinese principle of exogamy. See the *Tso-chuan*, Hsi-kung 23 (Ch'i-ming shu-chü ed., *chüan* 15, p. 113); Séraphin Couvreur, trans., *La chronique de la Principauté de Lou* (Paris, 1951), 1: 345: "quand l'homme et la femme portent le même mon de famille, leur postérité n'est ni florissante ni nombreuse." Cf. James Legge, *Chinese Classics*, V.i.187 and V.ii.580. A similar statement of this principle in the *Kuo-yü* (1876 Tsun-ching shu-yüan ed.), *chüan* 10, p. 6a. This principle is briefly explained in T'ung-tsu Ch'ü *Law and Society in Traditional China*, pp. 91–92.

[55] K'ang, "Yin-tu yu-chi hsü," in K'ang T'ung-pi, *Nien-p'u hsü-pien*, pp. 18a–b.

[56] Liang, *Ch'ing-tai hsüeh-shu kai-lun*, p. 161; Hsü, *Intellectual Trends . . .*, p. 113. Cf. the introductory section of chapter 3 in this volume.

China was "only an eighty-oneth part of the world": he had also made this story part of his own experience as a Chinese. He was neither crushed nor dazzled by what he read. On the contrary, his mind was stimulated and invigorated, and the measure of this is found in the easy, natural way in which he turns from Chinese history to Western and vice versa. There is no discounting of foreign history in favor of Chinese, just as there is no sign of indiscriminating admiration of the West.[57]

This is not to claim that K'ang's approach was unique. Far from it. K'ang's belief in the universality of basic human values and the necessity of cultural adjustment was in fact shared, with variations in detail, by a number of writers of the period, writers who were more or less steeped in the Chinese intellectual tradition and who wished to see China transformed into a modern country. Among these the views of T'ang Chen came particularly close to those of K'ang.[58] Liao P'ing, a Confucian scholar of the Kung-yang school, argued that as there was no hard and fast line between cultures, it was advantageous for both China and the West "to learn from each other."[59] T'an Ssu-t'ung and Liang Ch'i-ch'ao, as one would expect, echoed their teacher's convictions.[60] Even Ts'ai Yüan-p'ei and Chiang Meng-lin, men who had no intellectual kinship whatever with K'ang, came to the conclusion that "truth has no national boundaries"[61] and that "Chinese and West-

[57] E. R. Hughes, *The Invasion of China by the Western World*, p. 114; cf. p. 115: "In K'ang Yu-wei we can see an instance, not of a struggle between East and West, but of the way in which the Chinese mind when presented with a whole new world of political experience could retain its initiative and derive inspiration."

Joseph R. Levenson, who perhaps commands less insight into the "Chinese mind," had also suggested, implicitly, that K'ang recommended not simple Westernization but universalization. "The reformers," Levenson wrote, "disparaged neither the Western spirit nor the Chinese spirit but prized them both and tried to believe them identical" "('History' and 'Value': Tensions of Intellectual Choice in Modern China," in *Studies in Chinese Thought*, ed. Arthur F. Wright, p. 162).

[58] T'ang Chen, "Chung hsüeh," *Wei Yen, chüan* 1, pp. 10a–12b.

[59] Liao P'ing, "Kai wen ts'ung chih shuo," in Yü Pao-hsüan, *Huang-ch'ao hsü-ai wen-pien, chüan* 6, pp. 14b–17a. Liao recognized two patterns of culture, "the refined" (*wen*) and "the practical" (*chih*, or "the unadorned"), which followed each other in an endless cycle, so that in any given period one of the two characterized the culture of a given country. Thus, at a time when the Chinese civilization was "refined" (i.e., predominantly moral), the Western civilization was "practical" (i.e., materialistic). Obviously, Liao saw no intrinsic difference between Chinese and Western civilizations, which were to him two phases of the same cultural cycle.

[60] T'an Ssu-t'ung, *Jen hsüeh, chüan shang*, "Chieh-shuo" nos. 1–4, in *T'an Liu-yang ch'üan-chi*, 4: 1a. Liang Ch'i-ch'ao, "Hsi-cheng ts'ung-shu hsü," in *Yin-ping-shih ho-chi, wen-chi*, 2, no. 2: 62–63.

[61] Quoted by Levenson, in Wright, *Studies in Chinese Thought*, p. 174. See Robert K. Sakai, "Ts'ai Yüan-p'ei as a Synthesizer of Western and Chinese Thought," for a useful but somewhat inadequate account. Ts'ai's dates were 1867–1940.

ern ideas concerning certain matters are similar or identical."[62] Bertrand Russell apparently failed to reckon with the views of these men (and of K'ang himself), when he remarked that the Chinese intellectuals "have not grasped that men's morals in the mass are the same everywhere."[63]

K'ang's position, then, was not eccentric or unintelligible but, regrettably, it was seldom understood by his contemporaries. At any rate, it was unappreciated by those who assumed that as East and West could never meet on common or equal terms, China's choice was either to cling stubbornly to the indigenous old or to accept everything new from abroad. K'ang complained that "scholars of the new learning cast away completely China's ancient [tradition], whereas tradition-bound scholars, like pedants of tiny thorps, are too far behind times."[64] His complaint was not unfounded. On the one side, he was often accused by the latter of "desiring to destroy completely China's institutions and customs," and "to turn, silently and unseen, all the people of China into Westerners,"[65]—the very thing that K'ang firmly opposed. On the other side, he was dismissed by the former as a reformer turned reactionary, fighting futilely against the growing demand for modernization[66]—a thing which K'ang had never intended to do. Historians who failed to perceive K'ang's true position took him for a worshipper of the West thinly disguised as a disciple of Confucius.[67]

[62] Chiang Monlin, *Tides from the West*, p. 61. Incidentally, Chiang went to the United States to study in 1908.

[63] Bertrand Russell, *The Problem of China*, p. 81. Russell obviously had in mind the views of such radical Westernizers as Ch'en Tu-hsiu and other contributors to the *Hsin ch'ing-nien*. K'ang, however, could have readily accepted Russell's assessment of Western morals: "In so far as there is a difference of morals between us and the Chinese, we differ for the worse, because we are more energetic, and can therefore commit more crimes *per diem*" (p. 80). K'ang would have had little objection to this observation: "What we have to teach the Chinese is not morals or ethical maxims about government, but science and technical skill" (p. 177).

[64] K'ang, "Chih Chang I-shan shu." This undated letter must have been written sometime before 1919, as this statement, "till now the *Ta-t'ung shu* has not been published," suggests.

[65] E.g., Wen-t'i, "Yen ts'an K'ang Yu-wei che" (Chien, *Wu-hsü*, 2: 484–85).

[66] This was the judgment of such writers as Hu Shih and Ch'en Tu-hsiu. Hu Shih said in 1934 that K'ang's "intellectual leadership" in the 1898 reform was "truly spectacular" but his "downright reactionism" in subsequent years helped to convince the nation of the impossibility of "peaceful reformation" (*The Chinese Renaissance*, pp. 34–36). See Ch'en Tu-hsiu, "Po K'ang Yu-wei chih tsung-t'ung tsung-li shu," *Hsin ch'ing-nien*, 2, no. 2 (Oct. 1, 1916): 127–30.

[67] E.g., Ch'ien Mu, *Chung-kuo chin san-pai nien hsüeh-shu shih*, chap. 14, passim, Charles Beresford, *The Break-up of China*, pp. 191–92, credited K'ang with endeavor-

K'ang had himself partly to blame for being called a reactionary. For one thing, he often unwittingly invited misunderstanding. The confused political, social, and intellectual situation prevailing in the early republican years alarmed him. Instead of regarding the drastic changes as "for the better," as some writers of the time rightly or wrongly did,[68] he took them as confirmation of his theory that premature cultural changes were always disastrous and had brought calamities to China. Accordingly, he fought savagely against the new political system and the "new culture" movement. Too often he overstated his case or contradicted his statements previously made. For the sake of argument he was willing even to depart for the moment his reformist, universalist position and assume the stance of staunch defender of native tradition. Instead of cultural cosmopolitanism, he now stressed cultural nationalism; instead of prizing both the "Western spirit" and the "Chinese spirit," he now came close to envisaging "struggle between East and West." China was superior to the West in morals, he concluded; the West could teach her nothing besides "science and technical skill."

Contrary to his earlier convictions, K'ang now held that Westerners, despite their advanced industrial civilization, were not as "civilized" as their Chinese admirers imagined. He censured, in 1916, his compatriots who were dazzled by the splendor of the major cities of Western industrial countries.

> They who passed through Paris were amazed by its dominating influence and buoyant gaiety; they who passed through New York, Chicago, and San Francisco were overwhelmed by the dizzy height of the skyscrapers and astonished by the marvellous, great achievements of industry; thereupon they mistakenly inferred that the political life [of Western countries] was also good. . . . These people have no knowledge of the evil ways of America [and Europe].[69]

---

ing "to introduce Western ideas" into China and trying to make China see "the necessity of adapting herself to Western ideas," in other words, simple Westernization. This does less than full justice to K'ang. This writer, too, fell into the error of presenting K'ang as a reformer turned reactionary, when he wrote the *Chung-kuo cheng-chih ssu-hsiang shih.* This error may be explained by the fact that at the time he did not have access to K'ang's unpublished works, paid insufficient attention to the *Ta-t'ung shu,* and uncritically accepted the view referred to in note 66, above.

[68] Hu Shih, *The Chinese Renaissance,* pp. 100–110, where he pointed to three "important changes in the social life of the Chinese people," and hailed them as "the greatest gains which Chinese civilization has received from its contact with the life and institutions of the West."

[69] K'ang, "Chung-kuo shan-hou i." This undated piece is available in microfilm,

Even in 1904, a year before he wrote the essay on industrialization, he already showed disenchantment with the nonmaterial culture of Europe. Italy confirmed his disappointment:

> People who have not visited Europe imagine that it is a dreamland and that all its inhabitants are endowed with superhuman talents and goodness. How would they know that it is so filthy and disorderly, infested everywhere with swindlers and thieves? Thus it may be said that "to take one look is better than listening to hearsay a hundred times." Previously, when I visited England, I already felt that what I saw fell short of the image formed of it from what I read in books. I was disappointed. Now coming to Italy, I was even more so as soon as I stepped on her shores.

Italy, he went on to say, compared unfavorably with China, even in architecture.[70] This assessment pointed not only to an important revision of his attitude toward Western civilization which he maintained after his visit to Hong Kong in 1897[71] but also to a departure from some of his statements made in the 1905 essay.

A question may be raised here. What happened to K'ang's view that Chinese and Western values were basically the same? Or, in revising his appraisal of Western civilization did he modify, implicitly at least, this view also?

A close examination of K'ang's writings shows that he had not altered his universalist position but merely changed his assessment of the moral situations as they existed in different times. He appears to have maintained, implicitly, a distinction between the ideal value system and the morals as actually exhibited by men—between the "authentic teachings of Confucius" and the institutions and usages prevailing in China throughout the ages, or between the teachings of Western "sages" and the actual conduct of Europeans and Americans. As all men were still far from perfection, their performance necessarily fell short of the ideal, in various degrees and at different times. China, for instance, did well in the Eastern Han period (see below, note 75); Westerners in more recent times had acted in substantial conformity with "Confucian" principles (as well as the best teachings of Western sages). Thus the development of international law in the West reminded K'ang of the conditions in China during the Ch'un-ch'iu period.[72] But on the whole

---

reel 2. Cf. "Yü Teng chi-chien T'ien-hsiang shu," microfilm, reel 1. This must have been written before 1898, and K'ang still used his old given name, Tsu-i.

[70] K'ang, "I-ta-li yu-chi," pp. 3, 49–53, 100–104, and 142–48.

[71] K'ang, *Nien-p'u*, p. 5b.

[72] "I-ta-li yu-chi," pp. 68–69.

the behavior of both the Chinese and their Western neighbors had been disappointing: neither had advanced beyond the "age of disorder."[73]

So far as morals were concerned, then, both at their best and at their worst, Western civilization was in general no better or no worse than the Chinese. But taking the latter at its best and the former at its worst, one could not but reject the one in favor of the other. The conclusion was inevitable: the only thing that China could learn with advantage from the Westerners was their scientific knowledge and technical skill, or, in K'ang's terminology, "the material sciences dealing with the tangible" (*hsing-erh-hsia chih wu-chih hsüeh*) and having nothing to do with "morality which is beyond the tangible" (*hsing-erh-shang chih tao-te*.)[74]

In order to give emphasis to his defense of moral tradition, K'ang dropped temporarily his distinction between "ancient-script" and "modern-script learning," together with his preference for the latter brand of Confucianism. One of the clearest instances of such change was his unreserved praise for the "Eastern Han,"[75] a period which witnessed the ascendance of the moral values to which scholars of the ancient-script school subscribed and, concurrently, the decline of the influence of the rival school. This change of view, however, did not imply that K'ang was ready to abandon his fundamental position regarding Confucianism. It should be recalled that while he extolled the perfection of the modern-script teaching, he did not dismiss the ancient script as worthless. On the contrary, he made it clear that the latter was appropriate for men in the "age of minor tranquility" (or, "age of ascending peace"). In more concrete terms, he held that although the moral values that constituted what James Legge called "imperial Confucianism" fell short of the ideal, they nevertheless represented the "second best" and must serve to effect man's emergence from the "age of disorder" and to guide his conduct in the next and higher stage of development. The modern-script value system (which in his view coincided in substance with the Western ideals of democracy and socialism) could be realized only in man's final stage of development and was

---

[73] Ibid., p. 65.

[74] K'ang, "Ts'an-cheng-yüan t'i-i 'li-kuo chih ching-shen i' shu-hou." This undated piece was published in *Pu-jen*, no. 9 (1917), "Chiao-shou," p. 8.

[75] Ibid., p. 9. In Eastern Han times, K'ang said, "every person understood the principles (*kang*) which guided the relationships between ruler and subject, between father and son, and each family knew the path that led to what was right and away from what was wrong. . . . The calamities visiting late-Ch'ing [China] were due not to any defect in the Confucian way but to failure to honor and follow that way."

therefore too advanced for the existing situation. It would be foolish to discard tradition before it had exhausted its usefulness.

This, so it seems, was how K'ang arrived at the seemingly contradictory position: that in order to modernize, China must industrialize in earnest and at the same time preserve her old moral tradition, that in other words, she must not trade China's "national essence" (*kuo ts'ui*) for the Western way of life, as a condition for industrialization.[76]

Contrary to the view of his critics, K'ang was not arguing for maintaining the status quo or for returning to the ancestral ways, to the social and intellectual conditions existing in pre-republican days. He was not guilty of advocating cultural atavism. Despite the many shifts of emphasis, he never did forsake his consistently reformist position nor his lifelong objective, namely, revitalizing China through appropriate measures of modernization. He opposed the republican regime, not because he wished to perpetuate the autocratic dynastic system but because he believed that China was not prepared for republicanism[77] and that the new regime, in addition to being administratively inept and ineffectual,[78] was responsible for the social and intellectual chaos brought about by indiscriminate Westernization. Rightly or wrongly he simply could not concede that republicanism could come before

[76] K'ang reiterated this view in a number of writings done in the 1910s and 1920s; one of the most noteworthy of these is "Chung-kuo tien-wei wu tsai ch'üan fa Ou-Mei erh chin ch'i kuo-ts'ui shuo" (hereafter cited as "China's Peril"), *Pu-jen*, nos. 6 and 7 (July and August 1913), "cheng-lun," pp. 1–42; also available in *Pu-jen tsa-chih hui-pien*, 2nd collection, *chüan* 1, pp. 1a–13b.

[77] K'ang said in "China's Peril," *Pu-jen*, no. 7, p. 39 (*Pu-jen tsa-chih hui-pien*, pp. 12a–b): "Previously, I had written three books, namely, Treatise on the Administrative System [*Kuan-chih i*, also known as *Kuan-chih k'ao*, 1902–3], Essay on National Salvation through Material Upbuilding [1905], and Essay on National Salvation through Financial Reconstruction [*Li-ts'ai chiu-kuo lun*, 1913]. I thought that when these three matters [which were dealt with in these books] had been taken care of, parliament then could be convened. Therefore I dared not expound such doctrines as liberty and equality [in these books or elsewhere]. In my youth [sic] I wrote the Book of the Great Community, in which I touched upon every matter relative to the future world; but I dared not allow the doctrines of revolution, republicanism, and socialism [which were expounded in this book] to circulate openly. It was not that I did not believe that these [doctrines] would [eventually] prevail in later times. [I withheld them because, I was convinced,] they should not be applied before the arrival of the appropriate time."

[78] K'ang opposed the republic on practical as well as theoretical grounds. Theoretically, republicanism was unacceptable because China was not ready for it; pragmatically, because it failed to work satisfactorily. To help it function more properly K'ang offered, in 1913, a "Proposed Draft Constitution of the Republic of China" (*Ni Chung-hua min-kuo hsien-fa ts'ao-an*), which he published in installments in the *Pu-jen*, nos. 3 and 6 (April and July 1913), pp. 1–90.

constitutional monarchy and that in order to achieve modernity China must cease to be Chinese.

In insisting strongly upon the necessity of preserving China's "national essence," K'ang came close to what I have ventured to call cultural nationalism. It has been suggested that nascent nationalism tended to look for its justification in the heritage of the past, to talk about "the national soul."[79] K'ang perhaps was not a nationalist in the ordinary or full sense of the word. Whatever nationalism he embraced was alloyed with the cosmopolitan elements that figured prominently in his thinking. Nevertheless, he did talk earnestly about *kuo hun*, "the national soul," at least in the early decades of the present century. The following should serve to make clear what he meant.

> Each country must have something whereby it exists as an independent entity. This something, which [manifesting itself in various ways,] from political, intellectual, and moral life, to social customs and usages, enters deeply into the hearts and minds of the people, permeates their flesh and marrow, molds their feelings and thoughts, and shapes their folkways; which consolidates itself ever more firmly with the passage of time and with which [the people] become so accustomed that its presence is not consciously felt—this something is called the National Soul. No country, large or small, long existing or newly established, can stand on its own feet without it. . . . This is a universal law of politics, which admits no exceptions.[80]

The culture of a country, of course, could not stand still; it must progress with time and through judicious adaptation to circumstance. But this constituted no justification for its wholesale condemnation. To throw away the "national essence" was, in K'ang's view, tantamount to reducing the nation to cultural slavery—the greatest of all follies. Unfortunately, that was exactly what the Chinese had been doing since the inauguration of the republican regime. He put it in strong terms:

> In recent years the entire country has gone crazy: people discard every bit of China's political, moral, and social tradition without finding out

[79] Hans Kohn, *Nationalism: Its Meaning and History* (Princeton: Van Nostrand, Anvil Books, 1955), p. 30. Cf. Ernest Renan, "a nation is a soul" "Qu'est-ce qu'une Nation?" (a lecture delivered at the Sorbonne, March 11, 1882, after the end of the Franco-Prussian war), p. 308.

[80] "China's Peril," *Pu-jen*, no. 6, (July 1913), p. 1a; also in *K'ang Nan-hai hsien-sheng wen-ch'ao*, 3: 32 (hereafter, *Wen-ch'ao*) and *K'ang Nan-hai wen-chi, chüan* 2, p. 1a (hereafter, *Wen-chi*).

what is right or wrong, what is advantageous or harmful; they copy all the political, moral, social, and religious practices of Europe and America, without knowing which is right or wrong, which is advantageous or harmful.[81]

In this mad rush toward cultural suicide, "the more Western ways were copied, the greater injury was done to the country."

K'ang's opposition to borrowing Western social and moral values appears to have further stiffened after the first World War. Sometimes he became outspoken in his criticism of Western civilization itself, although unlike Liang Ch'i-ch'ao, he made no disparaging remarks about "science." The war, K'ang argued, was a natural product of modern Western civilization of which "utilitarianism and Darwinism" were potent ingredients. It was high time for Westerners as well as the Chinese to recognize the value of "Confucianism."[82]

Accordingly, K'ang assumed in effect the role of a latter-day Confucian prophet preaching cultural nationalism. "The Confucian teaching," he declared, "was the National Soul."[83] To revive and honor that teaching was to save China from cultural death. This was the rationale of his persistent but fruitless efforts to establish Confucianism as "state religion."[84] He now felt that even the defunct examination

[81] "China's Peril," *Pu-jen*, no. 6, pp. 1b–2a. Cf. "Chung-kuo huan-hun lun," *Pu-jen*, no. 8 (Nov. 1913), p. 5. K'ang also protested strongly against attempts to temper with Chinese customs in "I-yüan cheng-fu wu kan-yü min-su shuo," *Pu-jen*, no. 2 (March 1913), pp. 1–14. The "folkways" which K'ang would allow to persist included taking concubines, gambling, using the old calendar, and offering sacrifices in Taoist and Buddhist shrines. He regretted that he had petitioned the Ch'ing government in 1898 to abolish the queue and the old-style attire (cf. "Chung-kuo huan-hun lun," pp. 1–8).

[82] "Chih Li Chung-hao teng shu," *I-kao, chüan* 5, p. 46a.

[83] "*Chung-kuo hsüeh-hui pao t'i-tz'u*," *Wen-ch'ao*, 5: 28a.

[84] "Chung-kuo huan-hun lun," pp. 3–4. See also *Kung-ho p'ing-i* (written in 1917, shortly before the abortive Manchu restoration). Ch'en Tu-hsiu wrote a rebuttal to this piece, "Po K'ang Yu-wei *Kung-ho p'ing-i*," *Hsin ch'ing-nien*, 4, no. 3 (March 15, 1918): 190–211. In a number of other writings of this period, K'ang carried on his "Confucian religion" campaign, among which were "K'ung-chiao hui hsü," *Wen-ch'ao*, 5: 13a–17a; "I K'ung-chiao wei kuo-chiao p'ei t'ien i," *Pu-jen*, nos. 3, 6, 7, and 8 (April, July, Aug., and Nov. 1913); "Fu Chiao-yü-pu shu" *Pu-jen*, no. 4 (May 1913); and letters to President Li Yüan-hung, Minister of Education Fan Yüan-lien, and members of the National Parliament (written in 1916), *I-kao, chüan* 4 *shang*, pp. 82a, 83a–84b, and 85a–90a. (For a brief account of K'ang's attempt to establish Confucianism as a religion, see chapter 4, this volume).

The only tangible results of the efforts made by K'ang and his associates were (1) the organization of the Confucian Society (K'ung-chiao hui, 1912), which published the *Confucian Magazine* [*K'ung-chiao tsa-chih*], a monthly, in February, 1913, and the appearance of societies with a similar aim in some provinces (Chihli, Shantung,

system (which in the 1890s he had helped to discredit) had at least one virtue, namely, that in compelling scholars to read the Confucian classics, it gave them opportunity to attain goodness—an opportunity denied to students of republican China.[85]

K'ang was resolved to save China's "soul" at any cost, even to giving up some of his cherished views and seeking an alliance with Yüan Shih-k'ai, a man whom he took to be an enemy of everything he held dear. Despite his firm opposition to Yüan's "monarchical movement,"[86] he tried to enlist the latter's support to his "Confucian movement." It was not entirely without reason, therefore, that the Confucian Society was widely condemned as being "in league with the reactionary and monarchist movement." His involvement in the short-lived restoration of the Manchu emperor in 1917 brought further disrepute to Confucianism in general and his position in particular.[87] Thus, partly as a result of his desperate but unwise measures, his soul-saving cause, a very unpopular one in the first place, became a lost cause, forever beyond redemption.

To do K'ang justice, however, it should be said again that he was not really a reactionary, nor did he intend to be one. As I have contended in the previous section that in arguing that China's requirement for modernization consisted in adopting the material civilization of the

Honon, Hunan); (2) inclusion of Article 19 in the "Draft Constitution of the Chinese Republic" (the so-called "Temple-of-Heaven Constitution" of 1913), which reads in part: "The way of Confucius shall constitute the great foundation for the cultivation of moral character in national education," and of Article 12 in the "Constitution of the Chinese Republic" (known sometimes as the "Ts'ao K'un Constitution," 1923,) which reads: "The people of the Chinese Republic shall have the freedom of honoring Confucius and embracing any religious faith, which [freedom] shall not be unlawfully abridged." The texts of these documents are given in P'an Shu-fan, *Chung-hua min-kuo hsien-fa shih*, pp. 346–61; and (3) Yüan Shih-k'ai issued a presidential decree on November 26, 1913, in which it was declared: "The whole people hold the doctrines of Confucius most sacred," and in 1915, when he became the "Hung-hsien emperor," he officially honored Confucius (see Paul S. Reinsch, *An American Diplomat in China*, pp. 23, 26–27).

[85] "Chung-kuo huan-hun lun," pp. 3–4.

[86] K'ang supported Liang Ch'i-ch'ao's active role in organizing the military campaigns that contributed directly to Yüan's quick downfall. K'ang even attempted to persuade Yüan to call off the monarchical movement in the eleventh hour. See "Chih Yüan Shih-k'ai shu," written early 1916, in *I-kao, chüan* 4 *shang*, pp. 77a–79a.

[87] Hu, *The Chinese Renaissance*, pp. 89–90, referring to Yüan's monarchical movement and the Manchu restoration, pronounced this verdict: "These political intrigues greatly discredited the new Confucianist movement, which as the radical thinkers had predicted, was proved to be in league with the reactionary and monarchist movement" (see Chow Tse-tsung, *The May Fourth Movement*, pp. 291–93, for a concise account of the Confucian Society, 1912–16).

West, K'ang did not become a renegade from utopia but was pointing to a byway to it. He was convinced that the disruptive cultural avalanche precipitated by the revolution did not expedite modernization but constituted a roadblock to orderly progress. As the maximum program of social and cultural transformation (which he sketched in the *Ta-t'ung shu*) now had to be further postponed, he offered a minimum program of social and cultural reconstruction: Modernization through industrialization (which was the burden of the 1905 essay). The unsteady republican regime, he hoped, would be replaced by a constitutional monarchy with a Manchu emperor or a lineal descendant of Confucius on the throne and indiscriminate Westernization would give way to selective cultural adjustment. In entertaining such hope he was woefully unrealistic; at any rate, it proved to be a forlorn hope. The trend was against him: too many were his opponents. And yet, in daring to stand against the rising tide of iconoclasm, he must be credited with that courage which was born of conviction. In fact, as a professed follower of Confucius, he did what his predecessor had done centuries before him: who "knowing it's no use, but kept on doing it."[88] In one sense, K'ang was a reactionary, one who reacted against the determined efforts to discredit Chinese tradition and against the loud pleas for total Westernization, which by the 1920s had become a sort of convention among the "new youth" of China. K'ang had said in 1892 that going contrary to convention meant standing "away from the herd."[89] In fighting against the iconoclasts of the time K'ang had indeed chosen to stand away from the herd, a move that neither helped his reformist cause nor exerted any restraining influence upon the drift toward cultural disintegration. The real tragedy lay perhaps not so much in K'ang's failure to convince his compatriots of the advantages of his program of modernization, industrialization without de-Sinification, as in the failure of his opponents to bring about constructive Westernization as an alternate method of modernization. Eventually, China came under the sway not of "Mr. Science" and "Mr. Democracy," but of "comrades" Marx, Lenin, and Mao Tse-tung.

"Science" versus "Metaphysics"

K'ang Yu-wei's evaluation of Chinese and Western civilizations, as

---

[88] *Analects.* XIX.41 (Waley trans.), with slight changes.

[89] *Ch'ang-hsing hsüeh-chi*, quoted in Kung-chuan Hsiao, "The Philosophical Thought of K'ang Yu-wei," p. 150: "The more one goes contrary [to convention], the greater is one's attainment in learning and the farther he stands away from the herd."

briefly explained in the foregoing sections, anticipated the major issues raised in the spirited controversies among a large number of intellectuals, which reached a dramatic climax in the polemic on "science" and "metaphysics" (or "view of life") in 1923, and in the controversy over Chinese and Western civilizations in general, began shortly after the end of the first World War and continued with reduced intensity into the 1930s.[90] It may not be out of place to relate K'ang's ideas to those of the later writers, with a view to showing his position in the intellectual history of modern China. By way of anticipation, it may be said that except for a few extreme instances, the difference between K'ang's basic position and those of the "new intellectuals" was not as wide as it appears.

We may conveniently begin with the "science" and "metaphysics" controversy. It may be recalled that in the essay of 1905 and in some other writings of the period, K'ang recognized two equally important and indispensable ingredients of civilization: "the material sciences dealing with the tangible" (in which the West excelled) and "morality which is beyond the tangible" (highly developed in China). Significantly, while K'ang believed in the superiority of Chinese "morality," he did not hold the view that "correct ethical sentiments are more important than detailed scientific knowledge," nor did he subscribe to the opposite view that "technical efficiency is everything and moral purpose nothing."[91] His dualistic position, which was a concomitant to

[90] Carsun Chang, "Reflections on the Philosophical Controversy in 1923," pp. 19–22, recalls the circumstances leading to the controversy and its outcome. Briefly, (1) the Tsing Hua Students Association invited Chang to talk on "Life-view" (which was his translation of Eucken's term *Lebensanschauung*). He stressed "very much the factor of free will in human affairs"; (2) after publication of the speech Hu Shih told him that he and V. K. Ting would start a debate; (3) more than thirty scholars joined "the science versus metaphysics debate," with the majority on Hu's side and a minority declaring "neutrality"; (4) even though it appeared that Chang was "defeated" at the end of the debate, he restated and refuted Hu's arguments for the all-sufficiency of scientific knowledge. Chow, *The May Fourth Movement*, pp. 327–32, "The Controversy over Eastern and Western Civilization," and pp. 333–37, "The Polemic on Science and Metaphysics," and Kao Chung Ju, *Le mouvement intellectuel en Chine et son rôle dans la révolution chinoise*, pp. 123–51, summarize these debates. W. T. de Bary, Wing-tsit Chan, and Burton Watson, *Sources of Chinese Tradition*, pp. 834–43 and 846–57, give abridged translations of some of the important writings. The writings produced during the time of the latter controversy have been collected in *K'o-hsüeh yü hsüan-hsüeh* (Science and Metaphysics), by editors of the publisher, Ta-tung t'u-shu kuan, 2 vols. (Shanghai, 1923) and in *Jen-sheng-kuan chih lun-chan* (Polemic on Views of Human Life), edited by Kuo Meng-liang, 3 vols. (Shanghai, 1923); 3rd printing, 1928. According to Hu Shih, "when a part of the controversial literature was collected, it amounted to over 250,000 words" (*Chinese Renaissance*, p. 91).

[91] Russell, *The Problem of China*, pp. 78–79.

his syncretic approach to the problem of civilization, separated him on the one side from the ethnocentric apologists of the spirituality of the East who would defend China against "Western materialism" and, on the other side, from the exponents of scientism who perceived little or no value in "Chinese morality." As a matter of fact, he adumbrated to some extent the tenets of both groups.

As already said, K'ang recognized "science" (*wu-chih chih hsüeh*, "study of the material") which derived its "general principles from the physical sciences and mathematics, constituted the basis of technology and the secret of Western strength."[92] He began to appreciate the value of Western science in the late 1880s. Avidly he read books on various aspects of physics and mathematics when he was a young man of 25.[93] Soon he began to study astronomy in earnest, an adventure that contributed importantly to shaping his *Welt-* and *Lebensanschauung*.[94] When he was seriously ill in 1885, he placed confidence in Western medicine,[95] one of the first Chinese intellectuals to make what was in those days a bold (and risky) experiment. His interest in astronomy persisted for many years, He was still making nightly observations with a telescope just a year before he died.[96]

K'ang, therefore, had a more than casual acquaintance with modern science. Apparently he derived much inspiration from it, so much so that he showed, in some of his early writings, a perceptible tendency toward materialistic interpretation of morality and human nature.[97] In later writings he sometimes even suggested that man's moral and intellectual advancement was conditioned by his scientific and technological progress. Thus he wrote in 1905 that as a result of material development a "totally new morality and society" came into existence in modern Western countries.[98] "From machines," he remarked, "has come full-fledged civilization."[99]

[92] K'ang, "China's Peril," pp. 40–41.

[93] *Nien-p'u*, p. 6a; Lo, *K'ang*, p. 38.

[94] *Nien-p'u*, pp. 6b–7a; Lo, *K'ang*, pp. 40–42.

[95] *Nien-p'u*, p. 7a; Lo, *K'ang*, p. 42.

[96] See my article, "K'ang Yu-wei's Excursion into Science," in Lo, *K'ang*, pp. 375–407.

[97] See chapter 5, this volume.

[98] *Essay*, p. 24.

[99] From a long poem composed in late November, 1905, when he visited the Rocky Mountains. The original is *kai ts'ung chi-ch'i pei wen-ming* (K'ang T'ung-pi, *Nien-p'u hsu-pien*, pp. 53b–54b). Lo, *K'ang*, p. 199, mentions the "long poem on the scenic beauties there" but does not give the text of the piece. About seven years before, K'ang, in a memorial requesting the emperor to give encouragement of technological

Modern technology and industry, K'ang pointed out, had their roots in science and the scientific method. It was the "English school of thought which stressed science" that ushered in the modern era. In his own words:

> Bacon, founder of the school of empiricism (*shih-yen hsüeh-p'ai*), was the forerunner of European science. He dispelled the darkness of a thousand years and [opened] the unlimited vista of enlightenment. Later thinkers of England, from Locke, Hobbes, Milton [sic] to Spencer, had ,all placed special emphasis upon the material (*wu-chih*). This accounts for the great achievement [of modern Europe].[100]

K'ang's knowledge of the history of Western science was necessarily limited. However, he knew enough of it to take note of some of the thinkers who had contributed to the development of science or of the scientific method. Thomas Hobbes, in particular, exerted influence on English thought in the direction of mechanistic interpretation of human psychology.

Years before Ch'en Tu-hsiu, then, K'ang had made the acquaintance and recognized the importance of "Mr. Science." In fact, K'ang did more than that. After making a serious effort to study science he sought to incorporate his findings (modest and of doubtful validity as they had to be) in his social and philosophical thought. His mechanistic, if not exactly materialistic, interpretations of human psychology and morality, and his cosmological views were based in part at least on his knowledge of Western astronomy,[101] on his understanding of Copernicus, Galileo, and Newton.[102] Indeed, his entire philosophical outlook showed the impact of what he knew about Western science and appeared so alien to some of his contemporaries that they accused him of "losing every bit of the Confucian spirit."[103]

It was not a very long step from K'ang's admiration for Bacon and Hobbes to Ch'en Tu-hsiu's adulation of "Mr. Science." However, K'ang did not believe that science alone could answer all the problems

---

inventions, said that industrialization gave the West not only economic prosperity but a new outlook and mentality, progressiveness and enlightenment replacing conservatism and ignorance (Chien, *Wu-hsü*, 2: 225–27).

[100] *Essay*, p. 24. Hsü Kao-juan, "*Shih-chieh p'ing lun*," p. 15, note 10, points out that it was probably James Mill, not Milton, whom K'ang had in mind. It may well have been J. S. Mill.

[101] See notes 96 and 97, above.

[102] K'ang, *Chu-t'ien chiang, chüan* 1, pp. 5a–b and *chüan* 2, pp. 2a–b.

[103] Liang Sou-ming, *Tung-Hsi wen-hua chi ch'i che-hsüeh*, p. 135.

of life. In the essay of 1905 and in many other writings of the 1900s and 1910s he laid unmistakable emphasis on "Confucianism," as strongly as he did on science. Significantly, in his last major writing, the *Lectures on the Heavens*, he criticized Laplace for his failure to affirm the existence of God and insisted on the indispensability of supernatural religion.[104] Science, K'ang said, told men nothing about the transmaterial world. In this way K'ang approximated the position of Chang Chün-mai and Liang Ch'i-ch'ao in the science-metaphysics polemic. As the *Lectures* were written in the mid-1920s, K'ang presumably was informed of the polemic, but for some unknown reason he made no mention of it in the book or elsewhere. It may be conjectured, however, that his criticism of Laplace and others who refused to admit the relevancy of "metaphysics" constituted an indirect reply to the worshippers of "Mr. Science." If this was the case, then K'ang had in effect joined the controversy without involving himself in the hue and cry of the participants.

Chang Chün-mai and Ting Wen-chiang precipitated the "polemic battle over science and metaphysics" as the result of the former's speech on "View of Life" (February 14, 1923) and the latter's article on "Metaphysics and Science" written about two months later. Actually, however, the main issues of the polemic had been raised years before by supporters of "science" and defenders of "metaphysics," although these earlier writers did not engage themselves in direct controversy as the later disputants did. Thus as K'ang set forth his pro-science arguments in the 1905 essay, Ku Hung-ming fought against "the destructive forces of the materialistic civilization of Europe" (*die zerstoerenden Kraefte der materialistischen Zivilisation Europas*) in order to preserve "the true culture" (*die wahren Kultur*) of China.[105] However, neither K'ang's essay nor Ku's book was read by many; it was in the polemic of 1923 that the problem of "science" and "metaphysics" first attracted wide attention.

Ch'en Tu-hsiu and some of his associates may be credited with having set the stage for the polemic. In his "Call to Youth" (September 15, 1915), Ch'en urged the young people of China to "Be scientific, not imaginative." "Religion, art, and literature," Ch'en declared, "were

---

[104] *Chu-t'ien chiang, chüan* 11, pp. 3b–4a and passim. See summary of his views in chapter 5, this volume.

[105] Ku Hung-ming, *Chinas Verteidigung gegen europäische Ideen*, p. 230. The same view was expressed in his *Story of a Chinese Oxford Movement*, p. 99. Ku was also highly critical of the parliamentary systems of the West. See his "Hsi-yang i-hui k'ao-lüeh," *Chang wen-hsiang-kung mu-fu chi-wen, chüan hsia*, pp. 2a–3a.

the products of the era of imagination" and as such flourished only "in the unenlightened days of old."[106] In two other articles written in 1919 he denounced "the old culture and sang praise to 'Mr. Science' and 'Mr. Democracy.'"[107] Social progress, he argued, was absolutely impossible without the instrumentality of the natural sciences and pragmatic philosophy.[108]

Ting Wen-chiang, a British-trained geologist, became the chief exponent of scientism in 1923. Despite the claim of one of his admirers, who described him as "a high-powered machine using scientific knowledge for fuel" in his argumentation,[109] Ting's approach to the problem of "metaphysics" can hardly be accepted as strictly objective or scientific. "Metaphysics," he said, was a "bewildered specter" which had haunted Europe for twenty centuries and which was now out "to lure and fool the Chinese people," with Chang Chün-mai as its medium.[110] In fact, metaphysics had already done much damage to China. The Lu–Wang school of Neo-Confucianism, in particular, must be held responsible for China's loss of "national independence" and for her helpless intellectual stagnation. The first World War, he added, was not the work of science but of unscientific politicians; Western peoples had made good use of science in developing industry but Western societies and governments were "absolutely devoid of the scientific spirit."[111] In other words, even the West stood in need of science, more of it.

"Mr. Science" found an even more devout worshipper in Wu Chih-hui, referred to by some as "a comet in the intellectual world" of modern China and (with much less justification) as "the representative thinker of modern China."[112] In an article "Essay on the Promotion of

---

[106] "Ching kao ch'ing-nien," *Hsin ch'ing-nien*, vol. 1, no. 1 (Sept. 15, 1915), trans. in Teng and Fairbank, *China's Response to the West*, pp. 244–45.

[107] "Pen-chih tsui-an chih ta-pien-shu," *Hsin ch'ing-nien*, 4, no. 1 (Jan. 15, 1919): 10–11.

[108] "Pen-chih hsüan-yen," *Hsin ch'ing-nien*, 7, no. 1 (Dec., 1919): 4.

[109] Fu Ssu-nien, "Wo shuo-jen-shih-ti Ting Wen-chiang hsien-sheng," quoted by Hu Shih, "Ting Wen-chiang chuan-chi," *Annals of Academia Sinica*, no. 3 (Taipei, 1945), p. 1.

[110] Ting Wen-chiang, "Hsüan-hsüeh yü k'o-hsüeh," *K'o-hsüeh yü jen-sheng-kuan*, 1: 1–19; originally published in *Lu-li*, nos. 48, 49 (April 15 and 22, 1923). Excerpts trans. in de Bary et al., *Sources of Chinese Tradition*, pp. 838–40.

[111] Ting, as summarized by Hu, "Ting Wen-chiang chuan-chi," pp. 48, 54. Some of the arguments advanced by Ting, Ch'en, and others of the group are summarized in Chow, *May Fourth Movement*, pp. 333–35, and Hughes, *Invasion of China by the Western World*, pp. 196–228.

[112] Chiang Meng-lin (Chiang Monlin), "Chin-shih wo-kuo hsüeh-shu-chieh-ti i ko

the Great Community by Machines" written in 1918, Wu envisaged a
utopia to be brought about through the advancement of material
civilization in a socialistic world society which curiously reminds one
of K'ang's ideal as sketched in the *Ta-t'ung shu*. All forms of manual
labor would be replaced by machinery and no person would work for
more than two hours a day. The leisure thus obtained would be used
for rest, amusement, study, and scientific invention. Goodness and
beauty would be everywhere.

> Everyone would have an exalted, pure, and excellent character. All
> buildings would be beautiful and elegant, and all the roads would be
> wide with nine lanes. . . . The whole world would not have one place
> that is neglected, dirty, or blighted; it would be virtually like a huge
> park. . . . Machines would be available [for carrying passengers] to dis-
> tant places, into space, or underground. . . . This is not an [impossible]
> utopian ideal. There is already evidence of its realization in countries
> that have superior machines.[113]

In Wu's thinking, "material civilization" was to form the basis of
"spiritual civilization." The two moved forward *pari passu*: the more
advanced the former, the more developed the latter became. "Therefore," he concluded in 1916, "a huge element of material civilization
must be included in [human] welfare."[114] A few years later (1924), he
reaffirmed his confidence in the power of science and technology in
these words:

---

hui-hsing," *Chung-yang jih-pao*, March 25–26, 1963. See also Alfred Forke, *Geschichte
der neuren chinesischen Philosophie*, p. 646. D. Wynn-ye Kwok, "Wu Chih-hui and Scientism," pp. 160–85, gives a good account of Wu's views. Michael Gasster, *Chinese
Intellectuals and the Revolution of 1911: The Birth of Chinese Radicalism*, pp. 177–82, deals
with "Wu Chih-hui and Anarchism." See also Gasster's unpublished Ph.D. dissertation, "Currents of Thought in the T'ung-meng-hui" (University of Washington,
1962), pp. 191–96. For Wu's own account of anarchism, see his "T'an wu-cheng-fu
chu-i hsien t'ien," *Wu Chih-hui hsien-sheng wen-ts'ui*, 2: 282–87. Wu's views on "science" are treated by Gasster in his book, pp. 179, 180–81, 189.
   [113] "Chi-ch'i ch'u-chin ta-t'ung shuo," *Wu Chih-hiu hsien-sheng wen-ts'ui*, 2: 236.
This piece appeared in the *Hsin ch'ing-nien*, 5, no. 2 (April 15, 1918): 158–60. This
affords an interesting comparison with K'ang's *Ta-t'ung shu* (Shanghai, 1935), pp.
241–44; (Peking, 1956, and Taipei, 1958), pp. 271–73. One important theoretical
difference between the two lies in the fact that Wu's ideal of universal anarchistic
society was partly inspired by the philosophy of Lao-tzu and Chuang-tzu, whereas
K'ang rejected Taoism. See Chiang Meng-lin, "Chin-shih wo-kuo hsüeh-shu-chieh-
ti i ko hui-hsing," *Chung-yang jih-pao*, March 25 and 26, 1963.
   [114] "Ch'ing-nieu yü kung-chü," (June 11, 1916) *Wu Chih-hui hsien-sheng wen-ts'ui*,
2: 239.

Iron is the most important raw material from which machines are made. . . . China's inferiority to foreigners lies in the [lack of] the iron-forging-devil (*ta-t'ieh kuei*, i.e., scientist-engineer). Iron-forging-devils of foreign countries possess substantial knowledge; clever men of China look down upon iron-forging as something below their dignity.

Was it really wise and prudent, he asked, for the Chinese to devote all their attention to the "study of spiritual civilization?"[115] K'ang Yu-wei could hardly have put the matter in stronger terms.

To give a philosophical basis to his views, Wu wrote a 70,000-word piece in 1923 on "A New Conception of the Universe and Life, Based on a New Belief,"[116] which was his contribution to the science-metaphysics polemic. Assuming that "spirit" did not exist apart from "matter," he sketched a mechanistic and materialistic *Welt-* and *Lebensanschauung*. "Everything in the universe," he said, "can be explained by science." Indeed science in which modern material civilization had its roots held the key to all human problems. For

the more advanced material civilization becomes, the more plentiful material goods will be, the human race will tend more and more toward unity, and complicated problems [of life] will be more and more easily solved.

Refuting the pessimistic view (which he attributed to Liang Ch'i-ch'ao) that Western material civilization was already "bankrupt," Wu predicted that thanks to the advancement of scientific knowledge it would develop incessantly for countless years to come.[117]

Wu did not exclude "morality" as a legitimate ingredient of civilization; on the contrary he regarded it as "the crystallization of civilization." Morality was necessary in self-discipline of the individual man as science and democracy were indispensable to the proper management of society.[118] Morality, however, also had its basis in science. Somewhat like K'ang, Wu gave a mechanistic interpretation of psychology. Real-

---

[115] "*K'o-hsüeh chou-pao* pien-chi-hua" (Science Weekly Editorial Notes, dated August 18, 1924), *Wu Chih-hui hsien-sheng wen-ts'ui*, 2: 210–11.

[116] "I ko hsin-hsin-yang-ti yü-chou-kuan chi jen-sheng-kuan," available in *K'o-hsüeh yü jen-sheng-kuan*, 2: 24–137; *Wu Chih-hui hsien-sheng wen-ts'ui*, 2: 1–112; and as a separate pamphlet in the "Huang-p'u hsiao-ts'ung-shu" series, issued by the Political Department, Central Military And Political Academy, Nanking, 1927.

[117] Ibid., in *Wu Chih-hui hsien-sheng wen-ts'ui*, 2: 78–79, 81–82, 93. Summarized by Hu, *Chinese Renaissance*, pp. 91–92; de Bary et al., *Sources of Chinese Tradition*, pp. 840–41; and Chow, *May Fourth Movement*, pp. 236–37.

[118] Ibid., pp. 88–93.

ity, he said, was "alive" for it had "energy" as well as "substance." In this sense, then "the universe is a greater life," its energy (or power) gave rise to its "will" which in turn, at a particular moment of its incessant activity, gave rise to man. Man, a miniature copy of the macrocosm from which he had come, derived from the latter his "mechanistic form of life" (*chi-hsieh-shih chih sheng-ming*). As man's will was a manifestation of matter and energy, its responses were mechanistically determined.

> When the will comes into contact with the external world, sensations ensue, and when these sensations are welcomed or resisted, feelings arise. To make sure that the feelings are correctly [channeled], thoughts arise which constitute the intellect. . . . Each of these functions takes place in the nervous system.[119]

It was therefore entirely unnecessary, Wu concludes, to invoke the concept of soul, which offered no help at all in explaining human psychology.[120]

Wu's "new conception of the universe and life" bore remarkable resemblance to K'ang's view. As early as the mid-1880s, K'ang had come to the belief that man possessed intelligence because he had "cerebrum and cerebellum, the nervous system which gives rise to consciousness." Sensations, emotions, and intelligence itself, according to K'ang, "are constituted of matter (*wu-chih*) which accounted for varied reactions to stimuli: "Man likes things that are agreeable to his senses and dislikes those that are disagreeable."[121] K'ang, too, regarded "matter" not as something static or inert, but intrinsically dynamic, as his concept of "spirit-ether" indicates.[122]

The one most important difference between K'ang and Wu appears to be this: the latter did not build a hedonistic ethic on the basis of his mechanistic-materialistic philosophy, as K'ang did.

Another similarity may be noted. K'ang, we recall, condemned in strong terms in his 1905 essay what he called "empty words" and took

[119] Ibid., pp. 16–20; partial translation in de Bary et al., *Sources of Chinese Tradition*, p. 841.

[120] Ibid., p. 21.

[121] *K'ang-tzu nei-wai p'ien*, "Li-ch'i p'ien," and "Ai-wu p'ien." K'ang set forth essentially the same view in the Ta-t'ung shu (Shanghai, 1935), pp. 7–8; (Peking, 1956, and Taipei, 1958), pp. 5–6. Translations in Laurence G. Thompson's, *Ta T'ung Shu*, pp. 68–69, and Fung, *History of Chinese Philosophy*, 2: 686. See chapter 5 in this volume for a study of K'ang's philosophical thought.

[122] *Ta-t'ung shu* (Shanghai, 1935), p. 4; (Peking, 1956, and Taipei, 1958), p. 3; Thompson, *Ta T'ung Shu*, pp. 64–65.

a dim view of "philosophy." Likewise, Wu saw little value in anything other than the physical sciences. "Metaphysicians and artists," he wrote in 1924, "are people whose minds are defective and slothful," because "they do not seek to conquer nature."[123] Literary men," he said two years later, "are lunatics; they do nothing but talk nonsense." He was more lenient with philosophers who, standing midway between scientists and literary men, discoursed on things that "generally transcend the common sense of men." It was impossible to do away with any of the three. But as "China cannot be saved without science," it would be wise for her intellectuals "to study science in addition to literature and philosophy."[124] Understandably, therefore, despite Hu Shih's efforts to popularize "the scientific method," he was disparagingly referred to by Wu as "the founder of the imported eight-legged essay," obviously because Hu devoted too much time to the "literary revolution" and the "new culture" movement and too little to the study of natural science. China, Wu said, could not afford to have too many men like Hu Shih.[125]

One important difference existed between Wu and K'ang. While K'ang subscribed to a mechanistic-materialistic view of reality and life, he nevertheless recognized the relevancy of philosophy and religion;[126] and while he admired Western science and technology, he attached great value to Chinese tradition. Wu, on the other hand, had little use for metaphysics, religion, and Chinese tradition. He spoke of Chinese tradition in these terms:

> The national heritage, this ill-smelling thing, has been thriving inseparably together with concubinage and opium-smoking; concubinage and opium-smoking in turn have coexisted inseparably with office-seeking and money-making. Thus each time traditional learning flourished, government was corrupt: witness the emergence of Confucius, Mencius, Lao-tzu, and Mo-tzu, all products of the chaotic Spring-Autumn and Warring-States periods. It [traditional learning] should be dumped into the cesspool and left there for thirty years. At present we should promote an austere, unsavory material civilization. Then, when others shoot at us with machine guns, we shall fight back with machine guns. After China

---

[123] "*K'o-hsüeh chou-pao* pien-chi hua" (May 18, 1924), *Wu Chih-hui hsien-sheng wen-ts'ui*, 2: 150, also available in *Wu Chih-hui wen-chi*, p. 343.

[124] "K'o-hsüeh yü jen-sheng" (Science and Human Life, dated Aug. 1926), *Wu Chih-hui hsien-sheng wen-ts'ui*, 2: 114–15, 118; *Wen-chi*, pp. 131–37.

[125] "Chen Yang-pa-ku-hau chih li-hsüeh," *Wu Chih-hui hsien-sheng wen-ts'ui*, 3: 322.

[126] See the sections on Ideas Concerning Religion and Existence of God in chapter 5, this volume.

can stand on her legs, then it will not be too late to study the national heritage.[127]

Wu's emphasis on industrialization stemmed from the same conviction that prompted K'ang to write the 1905 essay. Both men agreed that first things must come first, although K'ang did not take a contemptuous view of the "national heritage." Even here the difference between them was not really as wide as it appears. For Wu allowed that after China had been modernized through industrialization, it would be relevant to take a second look at Chinese civilization. There is no ground to suppose that Wu had seen K'ang's essay. Interestingly, however, Wu praised K'ang in 1924 in these words:

> Twenty years ago, men like Chang Chih-tung, Wang Hsien-ch'ien, and Li Wen-t'ien rekindled the sorcerous flames of Ku [Yen-wu], Wang [Nien-sun], Tai [Chen], and Tuan [Yü-ts'ai] . . . thus unwittingly brought about the premature death of the spirit that underlay Tseng Kuo-fan's [Kiangnan] Arsenal and produced the face-saving Westernized "national heritage." . . . Fortunately, there was K'ang Tsu-i [i.e., Yu-wei] who resolved to go beyond the Uncrowned King [i.e., Confucius] and thus sent forth a spark of the revolutionary spirit.[128]

Another difference between the two men should not be overlooked. Generally speaking, K'ang paid greater attention to the results of science, while Wu and other supporters of "Mr. Science" were more inclined to stress the importance of the "scientific spirit" or "scientific method." For instance, Wu wrote in 1924:

> It is easy for men to think loosely, in fuzzy generalities. A person who has received scientific training observes and studies everything in his environment in a systematic, orderly manner; he gains a clearer understanding of the universe and is thus enabled to build a proper view of life.[129]

[127] "Chen yang-pa-ku-hua chih li-hsüeh," *Wu Chih-hui hsien-sheng wen-ts'ui*, 3: 319. This passage has been translated by Kwok, "Wu Chih-hui and Scientism," p. 175, with minor inaccuracies. In another piece dated May 4, 1924, Wu suggested that at least in so far as students were concerned, all the old Chinese books should be thrown into the latrine, so that they might be able to turn their undivided attention to science (*Wu Chih-hui hsien-sheng wen-ts'ui*, 2: 145).

[128] *Wu Chih-hui hsien-sheng wen-ts'ui*, 2: 319. For Wang Hsien-ch'ien and Li Wen-t'ien, see sketches in Arthur W. Hummel, *Eminent Chinese of the Ch'ing Period*, pp. 140, 349, 401, 483, 494–95; for Ku, Wang, Tai, and Tuan, see Liang, *Ch'ing-tai hsüeh-shu kai-lun*, pp. 6–80 (translated in Hsü, *Intellectual Trends . . .* , pp. 21–68).

[129] "K'o-hsüeh chou-pao fa-k'an yü," *Wu Chih-hui hsien-sheng wen-ts'ui*, 2: 127; *Wen-chi*, pp. 313–14.

This sentiment was echoed, among others, by Chiang Meng-lin, who credited the "method of the natural sciences" with having contributed to all the great movements in modern European history and with furnishing, in part at least, the starting point of China's "intellectual emancipation" as reflected in the May Fourth movement.[130]

Hu Shih was possibly the stoutest exponent of the scientific method. He accepted all the results produced by modern science and constructed on the basis of these results his ten-point "credo" (facetiously referred to by some Christian missionaries as "Hu Shih's Decalogue").[131] But far more well-known and influential was his formulation of the "evidential method of research": "Respect and attach importance to fact and evidence," "make hypothesis boldly but seek evidence carefully." K'ang Yu-wei's mode of thinking was a far cry from this. As already said, his conception of "science" itself was vague and "scientific method" was hardly the focal point of his intellectual purview. For many years steeped in the Kung-yang tradition of classical studies, in which normative principles loomed more prominently than objective truths, he held little respect for historical facts. The "Han learning," which was extolled by Hu Shih as an outstanding instance of the application of the scientific method in humanistic research, was to him "confused and encumbered with trifling details."[132] Even this crucial difference, however, should not obscure the fact that K'ang and Hu were in substantial agreement concerning the proper subject matter for scientific research. In the 1905 essay K'ang recognized the overriding necessity for studying "material things." In the *Lectures on the Heavens*, written twenty years later, he dismissed China's traditional astronomy, which was not based on actual observations by means of "refined" instruments, as a body of sheer errors.[133] Hu Shih voiced the same view. According to him, it was not enough to have knowledge of the scientific method; one must apply it to the study of material objects in order to realize its full benefit. Ku Yen-wu and other masters of the Han learning employed the scientific method; but as they applied it only to "paper data," their achievement was regrettably limited. Their European contemporaries—Galileo, Kepler, Harvey, Boyle, and Newton —applying a similar method to the study of concrete, material objects,

---

[130] "Kai-pien jen-sheng-ti t'ai-tu," *Hsin chiao-yü*, vol. 1, no. 5 (1918), quoted in Liang Sou-ming, *Tung-Hsi wen-hua chi ch'i che-hsüeh*, pp. 58–59.

[131] Hu Shih, "What I Believe," *Living Philosophies*, pp. 260–62.

[132] See chapter 3, this volume, and *Monumenta Serica*, n.s., 18 (1959): 138–41.

[133] *Chu-t'ien chiang*, *chüan* 1, pp. 1a–7b.

"created a new science and a new world."[134] This difference in choosing subject matter, Hu concluded, made all the difference between Chinese and Western civilizations.[135] K'ang should have no quarrel with this conclusion.

A remarkable approximation to K'ang's position came from a most unexpected quarter. Lu Hsün, prophet of Westernization in the Chinese literary world, wrote a little-noticed essay in 1907[136] (then a young man of twenty-six), in which he discussed the problem of civilization and came to the conclusion that "to accept the modern but to revive the old" was the soundest course for China to follow. This was a far cry from his views as expressed in the "Madman's Dairy" of 1918 or in the conversation with a friend in 1922.[137]

Lu Hsün's reasoning of 1907 paralleled rather closely K'ang's thinking in 1905. China, Lu Hsün wrote, had been known all over the world for her self-conceit and had been ridiculed for her obstinacy—as a country doomed to destruction because of her refusal to reform. But now, after having heard "a little about the new learning" men of China suddenly decided to change.

> They refused to mention any idea that is not from the West and to do anything that is not in the style of the West. They attack everything old, with all their might and main, saying, we are only trying to correct our previous mistakes and to work for [China's] prosperity and strength.[138]

Lu Hsün then went on to give what he believed to have been the reasons for China's self-conceit and stagnation. Surrounded by less advanced peoples and being creator of a splendid civilization, it was only natural for the Chinese to be proud; and it was almost inevitable

[134] Hu, *Chinese Renaissance*, pp. 70–71. The same sentiments were expressed in an earlier piece, "Chih-hsüeh-ti fang-fa yü ts'ai-liao," *Hu Shih wen-ts'un*, 3rd ser., *chüan* 2, pp. 187–205.

[135] "*K'o-hsüeh yü jen-sheng-kuan* hsü," *Hu Shih wen-ts'un*, 2nd ser., *chüan* 2, p. 2. Hu praised Wu Chih-hui for his frankly materialistic view of life. Hu did not subscribe to materialism and, significantly, acknowledges his indebtedness to Yen Fu and Liang Ch'i-ch'ao ("What I Believe," pp. 247–48).

[136] "Wen-hua p'ien-chih lun," *Lu Hsün ch'üan-chi*, *chüan* 1, "Fen," pp. 38–54.

[137] "K'uang-jen jih-chi," *Hsin ch'ing-nien*, vol. 4, no. 5 (May 15, 1918). The conversation with Chin Hsin-i was recorded in 1922 in "*Na-han* tzu-hsü," *Lu Hsün chüan-chi*, *chüan* 1, pp. 274–75. Signs of Lu Hsün's change of view were discernible in a piece on literature, written in 1907, in which he extolled Gogol and commented that a newly emerged country, despite its undeveloped culture, gave greater hope for the future than an old country with resplendent culture in the past but "out of touch with the present" ("Mo lo shih-li shuo," *Lu Hsün ch'üan-chi*, *chüan* 1, p. 57).

[138] "Wen-hua p'ien-chih lun," p. 38.

for a proud people to persist in their honored tradition and eventually to become victims of Western aggression. Unfortunately, many a well-meaning man, "without knowing the true situation of China and without looking carefully into the conditions in Europe and America," plunged headlong into a campaign of Westernization, glibly parroting such doctrines as "materialism" (i.e., "science") and "majority rule" (i.e., "democracy"). They did not see that these were no longer potent elements of Western civilization nor did these meet the current needs of China. For Western civilization had not progressed in a straight line but swung in a pendulumlike movement, veering first in one and then in the opposite direction. In fact, "in their evolution, all civilizations have their roots in the past: polarity is produced when reactions against a preceding situation take place." The "materialism" and "majority rule" that characterized nineteenth-century Western cvilization represented reactions against the religiosity and political absolutism of the previous age. Before the century came to an end reactions against materialism and majority rule were already under way: witness the writings of such men as Kierkegaard, Ibsen, Nietzsche, and Stirner, in which various types of "individualism" were propounded.[139]

Somewhat like K'ang Yu-wei, Lu Hsün was inclined to think that civilization could not be appraised by any fixed, absolute criterion but must be judged by its ability to serve specific purposes in specific periods of time. He did not however, subscribe to K'ang's optimistic theory of progress. He believed rather that each stage of cultural development contained elements that eventually brought about their opposites. In the present zigzag of civilization, majority rule had come upon the heel of autocratic rule. However, the rule of the many soon revealed its own shortcomings; the multitude seldom was able to distinguish between right and wrong. "Only when the Superman arrived would the world see peace." This was the case for "individualism."[140] Similarly, materialism called forth a direct reaction against itself. When in the late nineteenth century "spirituality became eclipsed day by day and human thoughts turned toward shallowness and mediocrity," "idealistic thinkers" began to attach importance to the "mind" or the "will," seeking to stem the tide of immorality that came as an aftermath of materialism. The twentieth century would see further increase of the "light of spiritual life."[141] To him, therefore, China's course was clear:

[139] Ibid., pp. 41, 44, 47, and 52.
[140] Ibid., pp. 48–49.
[141] Ibid., pp. 49–52.

After studying the past and surveying the future, we should strike down materialism and enhance the spiritual, rely on the individual instead of the multitude. When each individual is vigorous and active, the country as a result will prosper. Of what use is it to demand only industry, parliament, and constitution—to clutch the branches and pick up the leaves [without touching the more vital parts of a tree]?[142]

Lu Hsün did not counsel against change. He was opposed only to a change that involved the abandonment of the native tradition. He put his views in these striking terms:

To those who are known as well-intentioned men I venture to pose these questions: Do you think that wealth creates civilization? Then how have the descendants of Judah fared, who are born financial wizards? Do you think that railroad and mining constitute civilization? Then what is the civilization of the natives of Australia and Africa where for the past fifty years efforts have been directed to these enterprises? Do you think that majority rule makes civilization? Then what is the condition of Spain and Portugal, countries which for a long time have had constitutions?[143]

"Materialism" and "majority rule" benefited these countries little, because one crucial element was lacking—spiritual values, which gave character to a civilization and to the individuals sustaining it. This should serve as an object lesson for China. She should modernize herself in order to survive in a competitive world, but it was essential that the changes thus entailed would

neither lag behind the intellectual currents of the world nor do violence to the lifeblood of native tradition: it was essential, in other words, to accept the modern and to revive the old, and thus to create a new civilization. The meaning of life will be deepened. People will attain self-realization and individuality will be developed. Consequently, the country, which is now like a pile of sand, will become a nation . . . standing in the world with proud uniqueness.[144]

This, I suggest, came quite close to K'ang's arguments for preserving the "national soul" and for insuring personal independence. Perhaps this unintentional *rapprochement* of views may be partially accounted

---

[142] Ibid., p. 41. The word "industry" is translation for *chin-t'ieh* (literally, "gold-iron"), chosen by Lu Hsün probably to symbolize "materialism."

[143] Ibid., pp. 53–54.

[144] Ibid., p. 53.

for by the fact that there was a rough parallel in the two men's intellectual experiences. Both in their early years were steeped in the old scholarly tradition and both received a broadening influence from the study of science.[145] We must not, of course, push the parallel too far. For reasons which do not concern us here, Lu Hsün was to renounce Chinese tradition altogether a few years after he wrote the essay mentioned above, whereas K'ang continued to plead for the preservation of the national essence with unabated fervor. It appears that each man followed his own basic assumption. Lu Hsün let his own intellectual pendulum swing away from "the old" and toward "the modern," while K'ang held fast to his premise that before the coming of utopia the values and institutions appropriate for the present age must be retained as China strove to become an industrial society. It is difficult to say which Lu Hsün, author of the 1907 essay or author of the 1915 diary, made the correct judgment. But one may speculate that had he lived long enough and had the circumstances in China been other than what they were since the 1920s, he might have let his pendulum swing once more toward "the old."

Indirect confirmation of K'ang's views came from a less unexpected direction. Liang Ch'i-ch'ao who, according to K'ang, opposed publication of the 1905 essay on industrialization because it minimized the importance of democratic ideas and institutions, came around in the 1920s to a position that approximated that of his one-time teacher. The first World War convinced Liang that something was wrong with the modern Western civilization. His visit to Europe at the end of 1918 (made with Chang Chün-mai and others) brought him into contact with such philosophers as Eucken and Bergson who, each in his own way, represented a reaction against materialistic thought. They confirmed Liang's disillusionment with the West. In the following year Liang put his thoughts in his widely noted "Impressions of a European Journey."[146] The phenomenal success of Western science, Liang wrote, led to a "purely materialistic and purely mechanistic philosophy of life" (using Hu Shih's phrase), at the expense of the "idealistic tradition." People sang praise to the "omnipotence of science"; they chased after the

---

[145] Ts'ai Yüan-p'ei, "*Lu Hsün hsien-sheng ch'üan-chi* hsü," *Lu Hsün ch'üan-chi, chüan* 1, p. 1. According to Ts'ai, Lu Hsün was "originally steeped in the scholarly tradition of the Ch'ing period, but he also delved deeply into science." Medicine was the science Lu Hsün studied in Japan. K'ang, on the other hand, took a keen interest in mathematics and astronomy but received no formal training in either.

[146] Liang Ch'i-ch'ao, "Ou-yu hsin-ying lu," abridged in *Yin-ping-shih ho-chi, chuan-chi,* no. 23.

mirage that was "Mr. Science" (using Ch'en Tu-hsiu's phrase). But they found out that science had brought to them not happiness but catastrophe. Rudely awakened from their "vast dream of the omnipotence of science," Europeans were now decrying its bankruptcy.[147]

In thus opposing the extreme scientism of the *Hsin ch'ing-nien* group, Liang did not deny the relevancy of science in the modern world. "I absolutely refuse to admit," he wrote, "that science is bankrupt, though at the same time I refuse to allow that science is omnipotent."[148] Like his former teacher, Liang was concerned at the time with making best use of the modern scientific civilization, preserving the best nonmaterial tradition of China, and fusing the two strands into a new cultural synthesis. For like K'ang he saw abiding value in Chinese civilization, a realization that Boutreu, Bergson's teacher, had helped to strengthen. Agreeing in part with Lu Hsün,[149] Liang believed that Western civilization tended to be "one-sided." Idealism prevailed at one moment, but at another moment materialism gained the upper hand; now religionists laid exclusive emphasis on the life to come and idealistic philosophers devoted themselves to metaphysical subtleties, then came "scientists" who would in effect persuade men to throw away their cherished "noble ideals." In view of this vacillating movement of Western civilization, Liang argued, it would be a grave mistake for the thinking men of China "to become intoxicated with Western influence" and to call everything Chinese worthless. A civilization formed by "harmonizing and extending" China's best moral tradition and the West's modern science should prove beneficial not only to China but to the entire human race as well.[150]

---

[147] Ibid., pp. 10–12. Excerpts translated in de Bary et al., *Sources of Chinese Tradition*, pp. 847–49.

[148] Ibid., p. 12, author's note.

[149] Liang's characterization of European civilization reminds one somewhat of Lu Hsün's theory of shifting polarity in civilization.

[150] Ibid., *hsia-p'ien*, sec. 13, pp. 35–36. With slight shifts of emphasis but expressing basically the same view are the following: "K'o-hsüeh ching-shen yü Tung-Hsi wen-hua" (dated 1922), *Yin-ping-shih ho-chi, wen-chi*, no. 39, pp. 1–9; "Shen-mo shih wen-hua," *Ho-chi, Wen-chi*, no. 39, pp. 97–104; "Yen-chiu wen-hua-shih ti chi-ko chung-yao wen-t'i (dated 1923), *Ho-chi, Wen-chi*, no. 40, pp. 177; "Tung-nan ta-hsüeh k'o-pi kao-pieh-tz'u," (Aug. 20, 1922) *Ho-chi, Wen-chi*, no. 40, pp. 7–15; and his contribution to the science-metaphysics polemic, "Kuan-yü hsüan-hsüeh k'o-hsüeh lun-chan chih 'chan-shih kuo-chi kung-fa'—tsan-shih chü-wai chung-li-jen Liang Ch'i-ch'ao hsüan-yen" (May 5, 1923), *Ho-chi, Wen-chi*, no. 40, pp. 27–28, and "Jen-sheng-kuan yü k'o-hsüeh: tui-yü Chang-Ting lun-chan ti p'i-p'ing" (dated 1923), *Ho-chi, Wen-chi*, no. 40, pp. 21–27. I have not discussed Chang Chün-mai's views for two reasons: first, because they are too well known to require presentation here and secondly, because

Admittedly, the views of the men just mentioned were not entirely free from difficulties. But one should not overlook the weakness that inhered in the position of the advocates of stark scientism. Worshippers of "Mr. Science" took an overly simple view of a complex problem. By recognizing only the importance of the material (in particular, Wu Chih-hui) and by equating "science" with the quintessence of Western civilization (in particular, Ting Wen-chiang), they readily came to the conclusion that China's future lay in ceasing to be Chinese in order to become "scientific." Their iconoclastic ideas appealed strongly to all who were despaired of the unsatisfactory conditions of the period and found in the "old tradition" a convenient scapegoat. The acquaintance gained by many of them with the "unscientific" native civilization was no more than casual, making it difficult for them to perceive any merit that may have lain beneath the values and institutions outmoded with the passing of the dynastic system. And, with the exception of a few, their knowledge of Western science (and civilization) was no better than superficial or half-baked, making it difficult for them to see through the glamorous haze of novelty the imperfections of that "scientific civilization." Their ideas, often couched in rousing language, found ready acceptance among young people whose knowledge of China and the West was even flimsier than theirs and whose ruling passion was to shake off whatever restraining influence of tradition that still remained to annoy them.[151] The "new culture," the "scientific view of life," with its twin slogan of "science" and "democracy" afforded them a most welcome justification for their revolt against the accepted moral code. Hence the wide prevalence of the demand to banish Confucianism and "metaphysics." It appears that the shock that resulted from the impact of Western industrial civilization upon their minds and the traumatic

---

they are rather close to Liang's. The following statement from Chang's "View of Life," as quoted by Hu Shih, "Ting Wen-chiang hsien-sheng ti chuan-chi," *Annals of Academia Sinica*, no. 3, p. 42, suffices to indicate the tenor of his thinking. "From Confucius and Mencius to the Neo-Confucians of Sung, Yüan, and Ming times [all Chinese thinkers] had stressed the cultivation of the inner life of the mind; the result is a spiritual civilization. For the past three centuries, Europe has been stressing man's conquest of nature; the result is therefore a materialistic civilization. . . . Is it a proper and correct view of life, or a proper and correct civilization, for a country to place an exclusive emphasis on industry and commerce? This has now become a great question in the minds of Europeans." In alleging that European civilization was materialistic, pure and simple, Chang made himself an easy target of Hu Shih's criticism.

[151] It appears that the new generation of Russian intelligentsia also showed a predilection for something like scientism. See Martin Malia, "What Is the Intelligentsia?," in Richard Pipes, *The Russian Intelligentsia*, p. 12.

experiences they suffered in the chaotic republican days had brought to them something like cultural amnesia with respect to China's past.

The situation was not helped by the fact that many of the exponents of scientism did not possess adequate knowledge of science or understanding of the implications of industrialization. Ch'en Tu-hsiu, for one, was not unjustifiably criticized for failure to grasp the significance of the term "science."[152] The outpourings of his associates and friends were longer in denunciation of "metaphysics" and "tradition" than in contribution to scientific research or methodology.[153] It is hardly surprising, as a writer commented in 1926, that the New Culture movement "has not yet helped many to acquire the habit of scientific thinking" and that "much of the writing today is not very much more than thinking aloud."[154] In contributing to hastening the "cultural drift" without achieving tangible success in propagating the "scientific spirit" imported from the West, the worshippers of "Mr. Science" may have effectively prepared the way for the acceptance of "scientific socialism" which neither in spirit nor content was scientific at all. Ch'en Tu-hsiu himself exemplified in fact that transition from pseudo-conversion to the "scientific philosophy of life,"[155] to quasi discipleship in Marxism.

This is not to condemn scientism or its ardent sponsors. Historians would agree that it was a natural, and the most obvious response to the intellectual situation of the time. However, it must be admitted that the most obvious was likely to be the most naïve. Writers who were better informed or more sophisticated than others of the period were able to take a less hysterical view of the problem. They pointed to the truth (which was virtually a truism) that the natural sciences served many vital purposes of life but did not cover its entire range. That was why the "metaphysical ghost" continued to haunt Europe and was able to obtain a willing "medium" through which to lure the Chinese people, as Ting Wen-chiang said. This, in the broadest terms, was the position taken by such men as Chang Chün-mai, Liang Ch'i-ch'ao,

[152] Hu Shih's statement, as reported by Vincent Y. C. Shih, "A Talk with Hu Shih" in the spring of 1959.

[153] An inventory shows that from vol. 1, no. 3, to vol. 9, no. 3, inclusive, the *Hsin ch'ing-nien* carries a total of 21 articles relative to scientific subjects. Of these 6 are on science in general (its nature and methodology) and 15 on biology and geology—a very small fraction of the total number of articles printed and a very limited coverage of science.

[154] Timothy Tingfang Lew, "The New Culture Movement and Christian Education in China," pp. 60–61.

[155] Hu Shih's phrase (*Hu Shih wen-ts'un*, 2nd ser., *chüan* 1, p. 139; trans. in de Bary et al., *Sources of Chinese Tradition*, p. 843.

and Lu Hsün (in 1907). This was also essentially K'ang's position. K'ang, who had arrived at a philosophy of life of his own in the 1880s after acquainting himself with aspects of Western science—a philosophy that underlay much of his social thought—made it emphatically clear that "national salvation" (and utopia) could not be achieved without science and that in the brave new world to emerge, which would have science and industry for its material foundation, there would be a place of honor for "metaphysics" of which China's best heritage was to form a part. That this plan of cultural construction was a feasible one was illustrated by Chang Chien's success in Nan-t'ung where he made both Western "science" and Chinese tradition serve his program of local modernization. Significantly, Chang had a healthy regard for science and technology in his theory of education. At the same time, however, he insisted upon the importance of "Chinese": "A school," he said, "which does not emphasize the study of Chinese has no hope of achieving a balanced curriculum, even if its science courses are adequate."[156]

The fact that views such as these were overshadowed, temporarily, by narrow-visioned scientism does not necessarily constitute a true index to their intrinsic worth. It is just possible that something like Gresham's law operated in the intellectual world of twentieth-century China: bad intellectual coins drove out good. Very soon, however, an entirely different currency, imported also from the West, began to flood the country, threatening to drive out both.

East and West

The polemic on "science" and "metaphysics" was part of a broader controversy over the merits of the Chinese and Western civilizations. It should be noted that these were no mere "academic discussions," no idle pastime. Those who took part were in fact attempting, knowingly and otherwise, to find answers to two critical problems that confronted China: How to preserve China as an independent nation in face of social, economic, and political crises precipitated partly by actions of foreign powers? and, What to do with the native tradition which was eroding away, thanks partly to the impact of Western civilization? Answers to the first question appeared mostly as proposals of reform; answers to the second mainly took the form of polemics on civilization.

As in the science-metaphysics polemic, the fiercest and longest battles were fought not between the ultra "conservatives" who insisted on un-

---

[156] *Chang Chi-tzu chiu-lu*, iii, chap. 1: 4a–b, 14b–16b, 17b–18a; chap. 2: 16b–27a. See also P'eng Tse-i, "Chang Chien ti ssu-hsiang chi ch'i shih-yeh," *Tung-fang tsa-chih*, 40 (July, 1944): 54–60. Cf. note 42, above.

conditional preservation of Chinese tradition, and the ultra "radicals" who advocated total Westernization, but between the latter and a third group of people who saw China's future in a cultural synthesis in which East and West would meet. Many an accusing finger had pointed at K'ang Yu-wei for his allegedly reactionary social thought. The accusation, as indicated earlier in this study, stemmed largely from misunderstanding or insufficient knowledge of K'ang's views and was therefore not well founded. K'ang was not at all opposed to innovation. Clearly and decidedly, he was in favor of modifying China's existing value and institutional systems in the light of the experience of the most advanced modern Western countries, without forfeiting her cultural identity. He did not write much concerning the problem of civilization as such, but he had written enough to justify the conclusion that he not only belonged definitely to the third group but anticipated in more ways than one the position of some of the "radicals" who in moments of maturer reflection departed unmistakably from the position of unconditional or wholesale Westernization.

In order to show more clearly the position occupied by K'ang Yu-wei, I propose first to outline the typically "conservative" and "radical" views and then to analyze the views of writers who in effect approximated more or less those of K'ang, even though they might continue to disparage him.

Ultra conservatives were not particularly active in the polemic partly because very few of them were still around at the time and those who lived to witness the debate probably thought it beneath their dignity to have anything to do with "the native snobs who sought western culture."[157] Ku Hung-ming's European education and firsthand acquaintance with Western civilization qualified him as the most remarkable defender of China's Confucian past.[158] He saw everything distasteful

---

[157] Mu Fu-sheng, *The Wilting of the Hundred Flowers*, p. 76; "The Chinese resented the superiority of western arms, but they abhorred more the native snobs who sought western culture." This observation applies more appropriately to the "conservatives" of the old school than to any other group.

[158] See Andrew Tod Roy, "Modern Confucian Social Theory," pp. 75 ff. For brief sketches of Ku's life and thought, see Hummel, *Eminent Chinese of the Ch'ing Period*, p. 28; Hu Shih, "Chi Ku Hung-ming," *Ta-kung Pao*, Literary Supplement, no. 164 (Aug. 1935); and a number of articles by Lin Yu-t'ang and others in *Jen-chien shih*, no. 12 (Sept. 1934), no. 18 (Dec. 1934), no. 28 (May 1935), and no. 34 (Aug. 1935). Ku's major writings in order of publication are: *The Discourses and Sayings of Confucius* (translation of the *Lun-yü*) (1898); *Papers from a Viceroy's Yamen: A Chinese Plea for the Cause of Good Government and True Civilization in China* (1901); *The Conduct of Life, or, The Universal Order of Confucius* (translation of the *Chung-yung*) (1906); *Chang Wen-hsiang-*

in modern Western civilization and nothing wrong with China's cultural heritage. If there was a "last Confucian," Ku had as good a claim as any other man of the period.[159]

Ku's opposition to "Europeanization" or Westernization, the imposition upon China of "democracy" and "science," was absolute and unwavering.[160] The "true civilization" that he staunchly defended was that brand of Confucianism that James Legge had aptly called "imperial." Every one of the traditional values honored in the dynastic system was to him inviolable.[161] He took Chang Chih-tung to task for his part in the reform movement, but praised him for the support he once lent to the Ch'ing-liu tang, which he chose to call "the Chinese Oxford Movement."[162] "The Chinese Oxford Movement," he wrote, "was also directed against Liberalism, against the modern European ideas of progress and learning."[163] Naturally, Ku condemned K'ang Yu-wei for his unconventional ideas:

> Matthew Arnold says: "Violent indignation with the past, abstract system of renovation applied wholesale, a new doctrine drawn up in black and white for elaborating down to the very smallest details, a rational society for the future: these are the ways of Jacobinism." These are also the ways of K'ang Yu-wei which the Rev. Timothy Richard and foreigners who called themselves friends of China so much admired.[164]

This grossly inaccurate assessment of K'ang indicates most clearly Ku's extreme Sinocentric position.

---

kung mu-fu chi-wen (ca. 1910); *The Story of a Chinese Oxford Movement* (1910); *Chinas Verteidigung gegen europäische Ideen* (1911); *The Spirit of the Chinese People* (1915); *Le catéchisme de Confucius: Contribution à l'étude de la sociologie chinoise* (1927). Some of his shorter writings have been collected by Ku Neng-i and Ku Wen-ching in *Tu-I-t'ang wen-chi*.

[159] Lin Mousheng, *Men and Ideas: An Informal History of Chinese Political Thought*, pp. 215 ff., rates K'ang as "the last of the Confucians." Incidentally, Ku died a year after K'ang, in 1928.

[160] George Young, "Europeanization," 5: 623.

[161] Ku defended the Manchu dynasty and the empress-dowager, in his *Papers from a Viceroy's Yamen*.

[162] Yen-p'ing Hao, "A Study of the Ch'ing-liu Tang: The 'Disinterested Scholar-Official Group' (1875–1884)," Harvard University, *Papers on China*, 16 (Cambridge, 1962): 40–65. Ku referred to this group as "die Partie der nationalen Reinigung" in *Chinas Verteidigung gegen europäische Ideen*, p. 32, and as "the Party of National Purification" in *The Story of a Chinese Oxford Movement*, p. 5. Ku's translation comes closer to the literal and connoted meaning of the term *ch'ing-liu*.

[163] *The Story of a Chinese Oxford Movement*, introduction, p. 3. Anti-Westernization forms the burden of this book.

[164] Ibid., pp. 25–26; cf. *Chinas Verteidigung*, pp. 56–57.

It was Ku's assumption that the correct way to measure a civilization was by the type of man it produced. A civilization was superior not because it yielded superior science and technology that gave rise to ample supplies of material goods, but because it nurtured a race of superior men through a superior way of life. Thus he wrote in 1915, the year in which the *Hsin ch'ing-nien* had its debut:

> Now in order to estimate the value of a civilization . . . the question we must finally ask is not what great cities, what manufacturing houses, what fine roads it has built . . . : the question we must ask . . . is, what type of humanity, what kind of men and women it has been able to produce.[165]

The civilization of China was superior to that of Europe precisely because, thanks to Confucianism, which "without being a religion can take the place of religion," it had produced the Chinese people, a superior race of men whom Westerners found it difficult to understand.[166] The Chinese had "made little or no progress not only in the physical but also in the pure abstract sciences such as mathematics, logic and metaphysics"; but that was nothing to be ashamed of, for in minimizing the intellectual or scientific they were able "to live a life of the heart" and to heed the Confucian teaching: "Love Mankind *with good taste.*"[167]

Liberty and equality, which K'ang accepted as true "Confucian values," were summarily dismissed by Ku as worthless. "Subordination," Ku said, "is in itself a better thing than independence."[168] "The Chinese feminine ideal" as summed up in the "Three Obediences" and "Four Virtues" and China's "Magna Charta of Loyalty," which enabled the Chinese people "to behave themselves as good citizens," had so far eluded Europeans.[169] Unfortunately, however, the revolution of 1911 (thanks to the "Magna Charta of liberty and constitution") changed all this. Having lost their sense of loyalty which gave them "moral liberty," "the modern queueless, up-to-date Chinamen, the returned students," now learned "from the people of Europe and America. . . how to misbehave themselves."[170] Men should realize that not liberty or constitution, but "right and tact" made "good citizens and healthy states." Ku quoted Goethe with approval: "*Es gibt zwei friend-*

[165] *The Spirit of the Chinese People*, preface, p. 1.
[166] Ibid., p. 20.
[167] Ibid., pp. 10–11, 17. Original emphasis.
[168] Ibid., p. 167.
[169] Ibid., pp. 78–79.
[170] Ibid., pp. 7–8, 168.

liche Gewalten auf der Welt: Das Recht und die Schicklichkeit," and added this comment:

> Now this Right and Tact, *das Recht und die Schicklichkeit,* is the essence of good citizenship which Confucius gave to the Chinese here in China; this Tact, this *Schicklichkeit,* especially, is the essence of the Chinese civilization.[171]

Ku was not pessimistic about the future of the Chinese civilization. In common with all staunch conservatives he was convinced that because it was "moral" its validity was necessarily universal and abiding. As he wrote in 1920:

> Most people now believe that the old order of things in China is passing away, and they hail the coming era of the new learning and of the civilization of progress into this country. I for one do not believe that the old order of things in China can pass away. The reason is because I feel that the old order of things—the Chinese civilization and Chinese social order —is a moral civilization and a true social order, and cannot therefore, in the nature of things, pass away.

Chinese civilization was "moral" because it was "Confucian." Confucianism, he said, embodied "the sense of responsibility in human conduct that makes not only civilization but human society possible."[172]

Ku's claim that Chinese civilization could not possibly pass away must have sounded preposterous, especially to what he called the "up-to-date Chinamen, the returned students." However, there were some who would have no objection to this claim, not only among Chinese writers but also among Western scholars. An eminent Sinologue of

---

[171] Ibid., p. 16. Ku praised almost everything Chinese, including the sharp distinction between the spoken and written language. The former, he said, was the language of the uneducated and the latter, the educated. "In this way half-educated people do not exist in this country." In Europe and America, since the disuse of Latin, there arose a class of half-educated people "who talk of civilization, liberty, neutrality, militarism, and panslavism without in the least understanding what these words really mean."

[172] *The Conduct of Life,* introduction, p. 9. Cf. this interesting narration of a conversation between him and Marquis Ito of Japan, who visited him in Wu-ch'ang: "Marquis Ito said to me, 'I have heard that you are well versed in Western learning; don't you know yet that Confucius' teaching which could prevail thousands of years ago, cannot be applied in the twentieth century of today?' I replied, 'Confucius' precepts for the edification of men are like the methods employed by mathematicians. Thousands of years ago, three multiplied by three gave nine; now in the twentieth century three multiplied by three still gives nine. You cannot change nine to eight' " (*Chang-wen-hsiang-kung mu-fu chi-wen,* preface, p. 12a).

modern times, for instance, admired the "Chinese ethos" so much that instead of seeking to superimpose Occidental ideas on the Chinese, he upheld "the right of the Chinese to intellectual, political, aesthetic, and social self-determination."[173] This appreciative attitude, it may be recalled, was shared by some thinkers of the European Enlightenment.[174] Leibniz, in particular, was of the opinion that while the Chinese compared unfavorably with Europeans in speculative science and the art of war, they excelled the latter in "practical philosophy."[175] Later, in the years immediately following the first World War, a few European thinkers repeated in effect the old sentiment that *"La sagesse est l' Orient."*[176] In fact, it was these thinkers who confirmed the view that science could not solve all the problems of life and indirectly gave rise to the polemic mentioned above.

I have stated Ku's Sinocentric ideas at some length, not because they are necessarily valid but because they represent, in the most clear-cut manner, a position that differed significantly from that of K'ang Yu-wei who, while honoring "Confucius" and valuing China's "national essence," did not fail to recognize the cultural contributions of the West. It was men like Ku, and not K'ang, who stood diametrically opposed to the "extreme radical"—the anti-Confucians and total Westernizers of the 1910s and 1920s.

Damning the Chinese civilization, like glorifying it, resulted partly from reactions to the frustrating situations that prevailed in China after the 1911 revolution. As defenders of tradition blamed the floundering republican regime for the troubles, those who lodged their hope in the new order traced all social and political ills to the old tradition. In the simplest terms, this was the case for complete Westernization (or absolute de-Sinification) vehemently demanded by the leaders and supporters of the "new culture" movement.[177]

---

[173] George H. and Annina Periam Danton, preface to their translation of Wilhelm's *Confucius and Confucianism*, p. iii.

[174] For brief accounts of the influence of Chinese texts on European thought and government see Fang Hao, *Chung-Hsi chiao-t'ung shih*, 5: 183–204; Gorai Kinzō, *Ju-chiao tui-yü Te-kuo cheng-chih ssu-hsiang ti ying-hsiang*; Lewis A. Maverick, *China, A Model for Europe*; and Adolf Reichwein, *China and Europe*, trans. J. C. Powell.

[175] Fang, *Chung-Hsi chiao-t'ung shih*, 5: 199. Goethe, whom Ku quoted, had some knowledge of Chinese books in translation (ibid., p. 203). H. C. Creel, *Confucius, the Man and the Myth*, pp. 254–78, discusses the influence of Confucian thought on Western thinkers, including Voltaire, Leibniz, Quesnay, and others.

[176] Chow, *May Fourth Movement*, p. 328.

[177] Cf. Mu, *Wilting of the Hundred Flowers*, pp. 91–92. It might be noted that such a demand had been made in the closing years of the previous century by Ho Ch'i and

The views of these men are well known and need not detain us long.[178] In general, they condemned Chinese civilization by equating it with "Confucianism" and linking the latter to autocratic government or to Yüan Shih-k'ai.[179] With "guilt by association" thus established, it was an easy matter to discredit everything that was characteristically Chinese or non-Western. It did not occur to them, apparently, that a case might be made for the view that Chinese civilization contained other ingredients than what they called Confucianism and Confucianism in turn was broader than autocracy or Yüan Shih-k'ai.[180] Lu Hsün (since 1918), Ch'en Tu-hsiu (especially 1915–20), and Ch'en Hsü-ching (1932–36), each in his own way, stood as the most representative of the wholesale Westernizers. Hu Shih started as an ardent supporter of the cause of Westernization but later showed definite signs of modifying his early position. He thus afforded a clue to a significant intellectual trend away from Westernization and toward cultural synthesis, as we shall see in the pages following.

Lu Hsün, who in 1907 suggested the formula "to accept the modern and to revive the old," changed his views about ten years later and joined the *Hsin ch'ing-nien* group to condemn "the old" in the harshest of terms. "Humaneness" (*jen*), "righteousness" (*i*), and "morality" (*tao-te*), which filled the pages of Chinese history, he wrote in 1918, were in fact merely euphemisms for "men-eating." "Perhaps," he continued, "there are still some children who have not yet devoured human beings? Save these children!"[181]

According to him, therefore, "to preserve the national essence" was to invite self-destruction,[182] and to remain Chinese with their characteristic cultural traits was to forfeit the opportunity to find a place in the modern world. This was his argument:

Hu Li-yüan in their *Hsin-cheng chen-ch'üan*, "Ch'ien tsung-hsü," pp. 7–8, 12, where it is said that Chinese classical learning no longer suited the modern world and that K'ang was wrong in saying that the best of Confucian teaching coincided with Western principles of government.

[178] Summaries of their views and excerpts from their writings are in Chow, *May Fourth Movement*, pp. 300–313, and de Bary et al., *Sources of Chinese Tradition*, chap. 28, passim.

[179] As Ch'en Tu-hsiu said in effect in his article "Yüan Shih-k'ai fu huo," *Hsin ch'ing-nien*, 2, no. 4 (Dec. 1, 1916): 1–4 (1962 reprint, pp. 311–13).

[180] Chow, *May Fourth Movement*, p. 311, rightly points out that "Varying emphases or distortions will certainly paint a different Confucius."

[181] "K'uang-jen jih-chi," *Hsin ch'ing-nien*, vol. 4, no. 5 (May 15, 1918); reprinted in *Lu Hsün ch'üan-chi*, 1, 281, 291.

[182] T'ang Ssu [Lu Hsün], "Sui-kan lu," no. 35, *Hsin ch'ing-nien*, vol. 5, no. 3 (Oct., 1918); 1962 reprint, pp. 513–14.

In order to grow together [with other peoples] in the present world and to earn a place in it, it is necessary [for the Chinese] to gain an appropriate measure of progressive knowledge, morality, character, and thought. . . . A people that possess too much national essence . . . possess also too much idiosyncrasy; too much idiosyncrasy makes it difficult for them to grow together with other peoples and to obtain a place among them.[183]

It was a simple task to rid China of "idiosyncrasy"; she had only to adopt the ways of Western peoples, without any reservation. For Western ways were always superior to Chinese ways, even in the matter of "idolatry." Idolatry, of course, was never as good as "self-reliance." But if one had to practice idolatry, worshipping Western idols was preferable to worshipping native ones. As Lu Hsün himself put it:

Rather than worship Confucius and Kuan-kung ["god of war"], one should worship Darwin and Ibsen; rather than sacrifice to the god of pestilence and the five spirits (*wu-tao shen*), one should sacrifice to Apollo.[184]

It is hardly surprising that he joined Wu Chih-hui in a campaign against Chinese books. Lu Hsün counseled Chinese youth to spend their time in reading Western books, instead of wasting their time on Chinese books. Chinese books, he said, tended to isolate their readers from the active world of men and thus to render them ineffectual and useless.

Even though some Chinese books contain words that urge men to go into the world, they represent mostly the optimism of lifeless corpses. Some foreign books may carry dejection and despair, but at least they voice the dejection and despair of live men.[185]

He himself confessed regretfully in 1926 that as the result of having read a lot of Chinese books, he was unable to shake off "the suffocating burden"—"the ancient ghosts"—that he carried on his back.[186]

Ch'en Tu-hsiu shared Lu Hsün's worshipful attitude toward Western civilization, with equal if not more intensity. Like many of the anti-Confucians of the time, Ch'en traced what he regarded as the worst elements of Chinese civilization to "Confucianism." To make his attack

[183] Ibid. (1962), p. 514.

[184] Ibid., no. 46 in *Hsin ch'ing-nien*, 6, no. 2 (Feb. 15, 1919): 213.

[185] "Ch'ing-nien pi-tu shu" (Feb. 10, 1925), *Lu Hsün ch'üan-chi*, 3 ("Hua-kai chi"): 18.

[186] "Hsieh-tsai *Fen* hou-mien" (Nov. 11, 1926); *Lu Hsun ch'üan-chi*, 1: 263–64. Lu Hsün added that the "poison" of Chuang Chou and Han Fei was still with him in his thinking, though Confucius and Mencius no longer bothered him.

more effective, he identified "Confucianism" with the complex of traditional moral values as upheld by the imperial system and denied that the doctrines of the "Three Bonds" and "Five Constants" "originated in the apocryphal texts (*wei-shu*)" and were promoted only by Sung Neo-Confucians, and that these doctrines were therefore not authentic elements of the Confucian teaching (as K'ang Yu-wei contended years ago). Thus, to him, pristine Confucianism and Neo-Confucianism amounted to the same thing: both taught doctrines of "one-sided duty, morality of inequality, and social stratification."[187]

"Confucianism," Ch'en concluded, was absolutely incompatible with "modern life,"[188] namely, the democratic way of life as obtaining in the West which had been recently introduced into China. The alternatives therefore were quite clear: either Confucianism or democracy and modern life:

> If we think . . . the Confucian way will serve us to set up our political organization, order our society, and thus to make us fit for survival in the competitive world of today, then not only the republican constitution can be done away with, even all the reforms of the last decade, the bloodshed and revolution, the convening of parliament, the revision of the legal code, and all other measures of political and educational innovation would have been wasted efforts and, indeed, egregious mistakes. . . . On the other hand, if we are not satisfied with remaining in stagnation and if we have the courage to wish to establish a Western-type modern state, to organize a Western-style modern society, in order to qualify ourselves for survival in the present world, then the basic step would certainly have to be to import [into China] the ultimate foundations of Western state and society, namely, faith in human equality and human rights. We must achieve a complete awakening and muster a resolute determination regarding the Confucian teaching which is incompatible with this faith. The one will not prevail unless the other is blocked.[189]

This, then, was the case for complete Westernization (or complete de-Sinification). Implicitly equating democracy and science with modern Western civilization, Ch'en summed up his view in a well-known statement made in 1919:

[187] Ch'en, "Hsien-fa yü K'ung-chiao," *Hsin ch'ing-nien*, vol. 2, no. 3 (Nov. 1, 1916); reprint, pp. 201–2.

[188] Ch'en further suggested that Confucianism reflected the life of "feudal times" and was therefore unsuitable for modern men. "K'ung-tzu chih-tao yü hsien-tai sheng-huo," *Hsin ch'ing-nien*, 2, no. 4 (Dec. 1, 1916): 295–301.

[189] "Hsien-fa yü K'ung-chiao," *Hsin ch'ing-nien*, 2, no. 3 (Nov. 1, 1916): 203. This passage has been translated with minor inaccuracies by Y. C. Wang in "Intellectuals and Society in China, 1860–1949," p. 403.

In order to lend support to Mr. Democracy, we cannot but oppose Confucianism, feminine chastity, old morality, and old politics; in order to lend support to Mr. Science, we cannot but oppose the old arts and old religions. In order to lend support to both Mr. Democracy and Mr. Science, we cannot but oppose our national heritage and our traditional literature.[190]

Ch'en worshipped Mr. Science, but somewhat curiously, he insisted on the relevancy of supernatural religion in modern life. After Mr. Science had disposed of the "old religions" Christianity should be accepted as a legitimate item in the program of Westernization. "Faith" and "love," he believed, constituted the essence of the Christian religion. He urged his countrymen to "cultivate in our blood" the "lofty character" and "fervent affection of Jesus," thereby "to save us from the cold, cruel, dark, filthy pit into which we have fallen."[191]

Apparently unaware of the inconsistency involved, Ch'en hailed the "spiritual impulse," which according to him was the common source of both Chinese and Western civilizations. These were unlikely words from one who wished "to smash the Confucian shop":

The highest cultural [element] dominating the minds of the Chinese is the moral principle [which has existed] since the time of the T'ang, Yü, and the Three Dynasties [of antiquity]. The highest cultural [elements] dominating the minds of the Westerners are the Greek sentiment and the Christian sentiments of faith and love. These two civilizations [Chinese and Western] are similar in their sources, both of which flowed from supramaterial spiritual impulses.

However, Ch'en continued, as morality (the essence of Chinese civilization) "pertains to the intellect and is rationalistic," "there is lacking in the source of Chinese civilization the purely aesthetic and religious sentiments" which existed in Western civilization.[192] From a man who

---

[190] "Pen-chih tsui-an chih ta-pien-shu," *Hsin ch'ing-nien*, 6, no. 1 (Jan. 15, 1919): 15.

[191] "Chi-tu-chiao yü Chung-kuo-jen," *Hsin ch'ing-nien*, 7, no. 3 (Feb. 1920): 16–17. Not many of China's young intellectuals followed Ch'en in this respect. In fact, not long after he published the article, another group of intellectuals launched an anti-Christian movement, which soon became The Anti-Religion Movement, in the spring of 1922, in which Li Shih-tseng played an active part. See Tsi C. Wang, *The Youth Movement in China*, pp. 187–88 and 201–3. According to Wang, some of the Christians answered the challenge, mainly in the Baptist journal, *The True Light Review* published in Canton (ibid., pp. 201–12).

[192] Ch'en, "Chi-tu-chiao yü Chung-kuo-jen," pp. 17–18.

committed himself to "science" (and to "socialism"),[193] these are surprising words indeed. One suspects that Ch'en's evaluation of the civilizations of China and the West—and his preference for the "aesthetic and religious" to the "rationalistic" (namely, moral) reflected his subjective predilection and were hardly the result of mature thought.

The views of Lu Hsün and Ch'en Tu-hsiu, as summarized above, pointed to an obvious conclusion, that the entire complex of Chinese civilization should be discarded in order to make room for complete (in Hu Shih's phraseology, "wholesale" or "wholehearted") Westernization. This conclusion was explicitly drawn by Ch'en Hsü-ching in 1932, in a book on *The Future of Chinese Civilization*.[194]

The most important point made by Ch'en Hsü-ching was that the Chinese and Western civilizations differed in the degree of advancement, not in kind. The former was not exclusively "spiritual" as the latter was not "materialistic." On the one hand, China had contributed to material civilization: witness silk for clothing, delicacies for the table, the Great Wall and Grand Canal. These contributions had aroused the admiration of Europeans who read Marco Polo's accounts of his visit to Cathay. On the other hand, Europeans were not without spirituality. Besides the steamship and aircraft they also had literature, philosophy, and religion; among their eminent men were Rousseau and Hegel as well as Thomas Edison and Henry Ford.[195] Actually, the spiritual and the material were two inseparable aspects of civilization, so that it was impossible for any country to advance in one aspect while lagging behind in the other. Those who claimed that China was superior to the West in spirituality were mistaken. In fact, she was behind the West not only in material civilization but in "spiritual civilization" as well. Ch'en Hsü-ching explained:

---

[193] In 1915 Ch'en took socialism, the doctrine of human rights, and the theory of biological evolution to be "the distinguishing marks of modern Western civilization" (*Hsin ch'ing-nien*, 1, no. 1 (1915): 1–4).

[194] *Chung-kuo wen-hua ti ch'u-lu*, author's preface, dated January 28, 1932. Ch'en remarked later, in 1936, that "a decade ago" he together with Lu Kuan-wei and Ch'en Shou-i "had already felt the necessity of wholesale Westernization." The three men went in 1928 to teach in Lingnan University (Canton) where they lectured on this subject over a dozen times. In addition, Ch'en made a number of speeches in other schools in the city between 1930 and 1934, thus precipitating another "very lively polemic on civilization," in which Hsü Ti-shan, Hsieh Fu-ya, and Chang Chün-mai, among others, took part (*I-nien-lai kuo-jen tui-yü Hsi-hua t'ai-tu ti pien-hua* [Change of My Countrymen's Attitude toward Westernization during the Past Year, Canton, 1936], p.1).

[195] Ch'en Hsü-ching, *Chung-kuo wen-hua ti ch'u-lu*, pp. 52–53, 106–7.

Actually, civilization does not divide itself into the spiritual and the material. What is called the material aspect of civilization is in reality manifestation of its spiritual aspect; the former is the necessary instrumentality through which the latter expresses itself. The present degree of advancement attained to by Europe in "material civilization" is conditioned by [the degree of advancement of] its "spiritual civilization."[196]

With a view to strengthening his arguments for Westernization but apparently unmindful of involving himself in possible inconsistency, Ch'en asserted that Chinese civilization was not an indivisible unit but contained two separate and widely different segments, "northern" and "southern" civilizations. The former was China's own native product, which originated in the north and spread southward. This was in substance "the Confucian civilization." The latter was the result of China's contact with Western civilization, which contained new tendencies in economic, intellectual, and religious life. This "southern civilization" was China's "new civilization" in contradistinction to the "northern" or "old civilization."[197] Thus, implicitly, as Westernization had already taken root in south China, there was no point in opposing it. In Ch'en's words:

> The Western civilization that has been imported from the West becomes our very own as soon as it comes into our hands. Since it is our own and as it answers our present urgent needs, why should we not devote our efforts to promote and extend it?[198]

Ch'en singled out "individualism" as the "decisive force" of modern Western civilization. He cited the ideas of John Locke, John Stuart Mill, and Henry David Thoreau among other Western thinkers to illustrate what he meant by "individualism." According to him, individualism implied the recognition of the importance of individuality and individual responsiblity, and was for that reason a most potent weapon against traditionalism and cultural stagnation. Herein, Ch'en said, lay the key to "wholesale Westernization" (*ch'üan-p'an hsi-hua*).[199]

Ch'en found in Hu Shih a formidable ally in his campaign for wholesale Westernization, although, as I shall presently show, Hu modified his views in the 1940s away from Ch'en and toward the position taken

[196] Ibid., p. 53.
[197] Ibid., pp. 124–45. Interestingly, Ch'en counted K'ang among those who represented the "intellectual side" of the "southern civilization" (ibid., p. 144).
[198] Ibid., p. 140.
[199] Ibid., pp. 109–23.

by those who recognized the value of Chinese civilization. Hu wrote in 1935:

At present men speak of compromise, of [cultural construction on a] Chinese basis.[200] All this is useless talk. Our efforts can be directed only to the acceptance *in toto* of this new world, this new civilization; there is no other way open [to us]. . . . I for one am in complete agreement with Mr. Ch'en Hsü-ching's wholesale Westernization proposition.[201]

He had arrived at a position quite close to Ch'en's long before 1935. Spirituality, according to Hu, was not the distinguishing mark of the Chinese civilization. In a widely read article dated June 1926,[202] he stated his view in these emphatic terms:

Today the most unfounded and most damaging falsehood is to disparage Western civilization as materialistic and to glorify Eastern civilization as spiritual. This is a very old view but it now shows signs of revival. Formerly, when peoples of the East suffered oppression of the Westerners, they made use of this view as a face-saving device, to console themselves. In recent years the aftermath of the Great War induced in some Westerners a sort of adverse reaction against modern scientific culture. We often hear, therefore, Western scholars praise the "spiritual civilization" of the East. Such talk is merely an expression of transient anomalous psychology, which finds a responsive cord in the magniloquent vanity of Easterners.[203]

Hu then went on to formulate his "basic conceptions." Defining "civilization" as "the total achievement of a given people's efforts exerted in meeting their environment," he asserted, as Ch'en Hsü-ching did later, that the development of a civilization invariably involved two related factors: the material (the forces and resources afforded by the natural environment) and the spiritual (the intelligence, pathos, and aspirations of men). Thus there was no such thing as a purely

[200] Hu was referring to "Declaration for Cultural Construction on a Chinese Basis" (*Chung-kuo pen-wei-ti wen-hua chien-she hsüan-yen*), signed by Sah Meng-wu, Ho Ping-sung, and eight other college professors and printed in *Wen-hua chien-she* (Cultural Construction), 1, no. 4 (Jan. 1935): 3–5; partial translation in de Bary, Chan, and Watson, *Sources of Chinese Tradition*, pp. 854–56.

[201] "Pien-chi hou-chi," *Tu-li p'ing-lun* (The Independent Critic), no. 142; quoted in Ch'en, *I-nien-lai kuo-jen tui-yü Hsi-hua t'ai-tu ti pien-hua*, pp. 20–21.

[202] "Wo-men tui-yü Hsi-yang chin-tai wen-ming ti t'ai-tu," first published in the Japanese monthly journal, *Kaizō*, [Reconstruction] reprinted in *Hsien-tai p'ing-lun*, no. 83 (July 10, 1926) and *Tung-fang tsa-chih*, vol. 23, no. 17 (Sept. 10, 1926). An English version appeared in *Contemporary Review* (July, 1926) and in *Peking Leader Reprints*, no. 24 (1929). The Chinese version is available in *Hu Shih wen-ts'un*, 3rd ser., chüan 1, pp. 1–37. Excerpts translated in de Bary et al., *Sources of Chinese Tradition*, pp. 853–54.

[203] Hu, "Wo-men . . . ti t'ai-tu," *Hu Shih wen-ts'un*, chüan 1, p. 1.

spiritual or a purely materialistic civilization.[204] Western civilization differed from Chinese or Eastern civilization not in being materialistic or nonspiritual, but in being more advanced in the development of both aspects of civilization. Conceiving of "spirituality" in broad utilitarian and pragmatic terms, he contended that modern Western civilization was definitely not materialistic.

> To employ to the fullest extent man's intelligence and wisdom to the search for truth with which to liberate the human mind; to conquer the forces of nature in order to serve man's needs; to change man's material environment; to reform social and political institutions; to work for the greatest happiness of the greatest number of people—a civilization which does these things— . . . is a spiritual civilization, a truly idealistic civilization and is decidedly not a materialistic civilization.[205]

Even science, he argued, "the first distinguishing mark of modern Western civilization," was "spiritual."

> The basic aim of science is the pursuit of truth. Living in the world man is threatened by his physical environment, controlled by habits and customs, and bound by superstitions and preconceptions. Only truth can make him free, give him strength, knowledge, and wisdom, . . . enabling him to attain the dignity that pertains to mankind.[206]

The pursuit of truth, "the greatest innate spiritual need of mankind," was developed fully in the West but suppressed in the East. As a consequence, science flourished in the West while "Eastern sages" perpetuated intellectual laziness, which they justified by the observation, as "life has a limit but knowledge is without limit, to drive the limited in search for the limitless is fatal." In this way Eastern civilization lacked not only science but spirituality. The joy that Newton, Pasteur, or Edison experienced was entirely beyond "the lazy sages of the East."[207]

Frankly, Hu dismissed emotion as an unworthy aspect of life and identified reason, in effect, with "spiritual life." To him, therefore, religious faith or moral sentiments were outside the sphere of spirituality. Modern Western civilization, he said, was definitely moving away from the "old religion" and the "old morality"; for with the advancement of science all religion, all morality that rested on "faith" and "senti-

[204] Ibid., p. 4.
[205] Ibid., pp. 20–21.
[206] Ibid., p. 8.
[207] Ibid. pp. 9–10. The quotation, "life has a limit . . . ," is from the *Chuang-tzu*, Herbert A. Giles translation (Shanghai: Kelly and Walsh, 1926), p. 33.

ment" would be replaced by a "new religion" based on "rationality" and a "new morality" based on "socialization."[208]

In other words, science and socialism were the chief ingredients of the "spiritual civilization" of the modern West. The trend, according to him, was unmistakable. Utilitarianism, which taught the doctrine of "the greatest happiness of the greatest number," came upon the heels of the industrial revolution and contributed to the tendency toward socialization; socialism, which gave rise to the dictatorship of the worker and peasant classes in Soviet Russia, continued to march onward, with impressive achievements. "Such a civilization" he concluded in 1926, "should be able to fulfill the spiritual requirements of man; such a civilization is a spiritual civilization, a truly idealistic civilization; it is absolutely not a materialistic civilization."[209]

"Science," however, was to Hu even more basic than "socialism." This, in his words, was the most significant development in Europe since the sixteenth century:

> The industrial revolution then came about. The method of production was fundamentally changed; the productive power became further and further developed. In two or three centuries, as man's material enjoyments increased, his fellow-feeling and sympathy gradually expanded. . . . Philosophers of the Utilitarian school thereupon set forth the ideal of "the greatest happiness of the greatest number" to serve as the objective of human society.[210]

Moreover, in addition to making it possible for the emergence of humanitarian (or, socialistic) ideals, the advancement of science and technology, which after giving man an unprecedented affluent and comfortable existence, afforded him also opportunities to pursue the higher goals of life—an undertaking denied him before the advent of science. "It is our profound belief," he wrote, "that spiritual civilization must be built on a material basis." Therefore, modern Western civilization in recognizing the importance of this material basis and in furnishing this basis, was superior to Chinese civilization in every respect, in spiritual fulfillment as well as in scientific progress.[211]

[208] Hu, "Wo-men . . . ti t'ai-tu," *Hu Shih wen-ts'un, chüan* 1, pp. 11–18.
[209] Ibid., p. 21.
[210] Ibid., p. 16.
[211] Ibid., pp. 6–8. Hu restated this view in his "The Civilization of the East and West," pp. 34–38. Hu added "the religion of democracy" to socialism as constituents of "the most spiritual phase of the modern civilization of the West" (ibid., pp. 37–38). He probably would have approved of T. S. Ashton's statement, "The in-

Hu took a dim view of China's moral tradition. Admittedly, it contained the ideal of "doing good to the world" but it furnished no workable means of translating such ideal into practical action. As a result, Chinese thinkers turned their attention inward, devoting themselves exclusively to moral cultivation of the individual. The more they did that, the less were they able to keep contact with the external world and to deal with practical problems. Inevitably, such morality ended in dismal failure. "For instance," Hu wrote, "China's eight centuries of Neo-Confucian endeavor remained blind to the inhumanity of footbinding. What has 'enlightenment of mind and cognizance of nature' (*ming hsin chien hsing*) contributed to relieving humanity's sufferings and distress?"[212] He pursued the same line of thought in another connection:

> Let all apologists for the spiritual civilization of the East reflect on this. What spirituality is there in a civilization which tolerates such a terrible form of human slavery as the "rickshaw coolie"? Do we seriously believe that there can be any spiritual life left in those poor human beasts of burden who run and toil and sweat under that peculiar bondage of slavery which knows neither the minimum wage nor any limit of working hours?[213]

Understandably, Hu joined Wu Yü and others in the campaign to destroy "Confucianism."[214]

Hu did not suggest that the Chinese who created such an unspiritual civilization were inherently inhuman. He blamed it all on their failure to develop science and technology, to adopt the modern method of production. "The difference between the Eastern and Western civilizations," he said, "is primarily a difference in the tools used." In the East, civilization was built on human labor as the source of power; in the West, it was built on the basis of the power of machinery.[215] The conclusion was obvious: "China today must first achieve material civilization before she can talk about spiritual civilization."[216]

It hardly requires comment that Hu's endorsement of "machine production," "socialism," and "democracy" reminds one of K'ang's

---

dustrial revolution was also a revolution of ideas" (*The Industrial Revolution, 1760–1830*, p. 22).

[212] Hu, "Wo-men . . . ti t'ai-tu, *Hu Shih wen-ts'un, chüan* 1, p. 15.

[213] Hu, "Civilization of the East and West," pp. 28–29.

[214] "*Wu Yü wen-lu* hsü," *Hu Shih wen-ts'un*, 1st ser., *chüan* 4, pp. 255–59.

[215] "Civilization of the East and West," p. 27.

[216] Lin Yu-t'ang, "Chi-ch'i yü ching-shen," *Hu Shih wen-ts'un*, 3rd ser., *chüan* 1, p. 36.

basic views as set forth in the book of the Great Community of 1902 and the essay on material upbuilding of 1905. K'ang could certainly have approved of Hu's endorsement, and, in a sense, even his denial of "spirituality" to Chinese civilization. Did not K'ang, too, in the 1902 book condemn in equally strong terms and in a much more detailed manner, that "false Confucianism" that had been the ultimate source of human miseries? Did not he, in the 1905 essay, argue also (though in a somewhat less precise way) that without material civilization no prophet could contribute to man's welfare, spiritual and otherwise? There are of course differences between the two men's views. The most important, obviously, is that while Hu perceived nothing really of value in Chinese civilization, K'ang sought to preserve what he deemed to be its valid elements, after having isolated what he believed to be the undesirable ones.

It must be noted, however, that Hu's condemnatory attitude toward Chinese civilization was not consistently maintained. As he gained deeper insight into the matter, he tended to become less severe in his judgment. As early as in 1919 he already showed some interest in the much despised "national heritage," so much so that Wu Chih-hui raised strong objection to his proposal that reassessment of that heritage be included as a task of the "new thought movement."[217] Later, in 1927, Hu denied categorically that the *coup de grâce* had been dealt to that heritage and continued to study aspects of it.[218] He made a statement in 1942 in which he quite explicitly acknowledged its value. According to him, ancient Chinese intellectual tradition contained elements which amounted to being the "philosophical foundations for a democratic China": notably, "the ideal of laissez-faire" in Taoism, "the ideal of universal peace" in the philosophy of Mo-tzu, and "the ideal of a classless society" as well as "the ideal of equitable distribution of wealth in society" in Confucianism. Chinese civilization, after all, was not without "spirituality"; it represented in fact "a way of life" that was worth defending.[219] Still later, in 1959, he implicitly dissociated himself from the anti-Confucian campaign by denying that he had ever taken part in it and claiming that his support of Wu Yü "came from his desire to give all philosophers an equal chance of unbiased evaluation." He merely wished to cut Confucius down to size, not to destroy him. He

---

[217] Chow, *May Fourth Movement*, pp. 319–20.

[218] "Cheng-li kuo-ku yü 'ta-kuei,' " *Hu Shih wen-ts'un*, 3rd ser., *chüan* 2, pp. 209–12. Hu's *An Outline History of Chinese Philosophy*, vol. 1, and many articles on Chinese intellectual history represent some of the results of his reassessment.

[219] Hu Shih, *China, Too, Is Fighting to Defend a Way of Life*, pp. 3–5.

denied also that he shared Ch'en Tu-hsiu's "private opinion"—"that Confucianism and modernism were incompatible." On the contrary, he considered the Confucian principle of *jen*, which pointed to the conceptions of "human rights" and moral integrity, was the heart of "Chinese tradition," presumably not unfit for modern application.[220] And, finally, in 1960, he announced this optimistic view, affirming, in effect, the permanence of Chinese civilization. Despite the "long series of important changes" that had taken place in the many centuries of its existence, its basic nature or essence had remained. The challenge of modern Westernization had made imperative the task of adapting China to the requirements of a new world, but that task was not to be carried out by way of simple Westernization. As a matter of fact, the confrontation of the two civilizations would result in China's cultural "rebirth"—absorbing things from the West without losing her own cultural identity. In Hu's own words:

> The product of this rebirth looks suspiciously occidental. But scratch its surface and you will find that the stuff of which it is made is essentially the Chinese bedrock which much weathering and corrosion only made it stand out more clearly—the humanistic and rationalistic China resurrected by the touch of the scientific and democratic civilization of the new world.[221]

K'ang would have been very happy indeed to nod his consent to this sentiment. This rather dramatic change of Hu's attitude toward Chinese civilization was perhaps partly the result of his reassessment of it, a chore that he began in the 1910s. Over forty years of study and reflection may have persuaded him that there was after all a "bedrock" of Chinese civilization which served appropriately as the basis of cultural reconstruction.

Interestingly, Hu's early training in Western philosophy and later studies in Chinese thought appear to have led him to something like a universalist position. As the former prevented him from committing himself to hidebound Sinocentrism, the latter separated him from naïve Westernization. China must progress with the rest of the world. But while "human progress cannot be measured by a double standard" and "the pace was set by Western achievement," China's own progress must be made on the basis of her own inherent strength, and perhaps also in her own style.[222]

[220] Vincent Y. C. Shih, "A Talk with Hu Shih," pp. 158–59, 160, 161.
[221] "The Chinese Tradition and the Future," pp. 21–22.
[222] Jerome B. Grieder, "Hu Shih: An Appreciation," p. 96.

Hu's changing attitude toward Chinese civilization duplicated, in a way and to some extent, that of K'ang as he revealed it between the concluding decades of the nineteenth century and the first decades of the twentieth. K'ang's initial reaction to "Western learning" was, as he confessed in 1882, "to discard completely" his "old views"; just as years later Hu reacted to Western civilization with a willingness to sound the knell for Chinese tradition. And just as Hu hailed in 1960 the "resurrection" of "the humanistic and rationalistic China" by "the touch of the scientific and democratic civilization of the new world," so did K'ang in 1905 insist upon the abiding value of "Confucianism" (his term for the humanistic and rationalistic China) and sought to enlist the assistance of Western science and democracy to turn them into an effective force in the moral life and social institutions of a modern China. Mature reflection convinced K'ang (as it did Hu) that modernization of China could not be achieved through a process of simple Westernization (and still less could it be done by simply clinging to the "national heritage"), but must be effected through a rationally considered program of synthesis and universalization, aiming at bringing the level of her civilization to that which the West happened to have already attained—without meanwhile losing her cultural identity or surrendering those elements of the "national essence" that were relevant to life in the new world. This program, in K'ang's thinking, could be implemented either by first innovating China's institutional system and intellectual life (as he recommended in 1898) or by first laying for her the necessary material foundation through industrialization (as he urged in 1905). There is no evidence that Hu had seen all the major writings of K'ang dealing with this problem or that he had carefully considered any of them. Had he done so, it is quite conceivable that he might have held a higher opinion of K'ang than he actually did.

One should not, of course, minimize the differences between the views of these two men. While K'ang tended to emphasize the importance of Chinese civilization and to dwell upon the necessity of preserving it, Hu was inclined to think that preservation did not constitute a problem. "The assimilation of the new into the old," to him was almost a natural process which required no particularly strenuous efforts.[223] With an optimism not entirely justified by the course of later events, he announced in the early 1930s that China had "succeeded in bringing about a cultural transformation" and achieved a "new civilization not

---

[223] Shih, "A Talk with Hu Shih," p. 161.

incompatible with the spirit of the new world."[224] With equal optimism he said a little later that cultural synthesis was a natural "process of survival of the fittest," which permitted or required no conscious direction. Moreover, he argued, it was impossible to wipe out "the conservative nature of an indigenous culture." China's adoption of "the scientific and technological world culture and the spiritual civilization behind it" would necessarily bring about a great change in her culture; but "in the future the crystallization of this great change will, of course, be a culture on the 'Chinese basis.' "[225] In other words, while K'ang favored deliberate and planned cultural synthesis, Hu was willing to rely on the process of Darwinian selection in cultural confrontation. Events since the second World War have shown that neither approach has attained any pragmatic success. However, this difference in approach, important as it is, should not be allowed to obscure the fact that in the maturer phases of their thought both K'ang and Hu had come to the essentially identical view that "wholesale Westernization" was not the answer to the problem of China's modernization.

Other important thinkers of the period, with widely different backgrounds and approaches, showed preference for synthesis through universalization to "wholesale Westernization." For instance, Ts'ai Yüan-p'ei, the well-known educator, held the view that "the ultimate objective of existence is to get all elements of the world into a harmonious whole."[226] Liang Ch'i-ch'ao wished to "enrich" Chinese civilization with elements of Western civilization and to "supplement" the latter with the former, "so as to synthesize and transform both to make a new civilization."[227] Liang Sou-ming may have been "vague and dogmatic"[228] in his presentation, but his arguments clearly pointed in the

---

[224] Hu, *Chinese Renaissance*, pp. 1–26, discerned two types of cultural response, change effected by "centralized control" (as in Meiji Japan) and by "diffused penetration" or "diffused assimilation" (as in China). He saw disadvantages of the latent process, but believed that through "evolutionary and gradual" changes—"painfully slow and piecemeal"—it would be possible for China to "achieve a new civilization not incompatible with the spirit of the new world." Hu did not foresee the situation obtaining since 1949.

[225] "P'ing 'Chung-kuo pen-wei wen-hua chien-she hsüan-yen,' " *Hu Shih wen-ts'un*, 4th ser., *chüan* 4, pp. 535–40. Excerpts translated in de Bary et al., *Sources of Chinese Tradition*, pp. 856–57.

[226] From a speech made in 1919, quoted by Robert K. Sakai, "Ts'ai Yüan-p'ei as a Synthesizer of Western and Chinese Thought," pp. 179–85.

[227] Liang, "Ou-yu hsin-ying lu," *Yin-ping-shih ho-chi, chuan-chi*, no. 22, p. 35; partial translation in de Bary et al., *Sources of Chinese Tradition*, p. 847.

[228] Hu Shih, "Tu Liang Sou-ming hsien-sheng ti *Tung-Hsi wen-hua chi ch'i che-*

same general direction. In his view the civilization of China, instead of being less developed than that of the modern West, as Ch'en Hsü-ching alleged, was actually more advanced, in that instead of developing science and technology in order to gratify the human will (as in modern Western civilization), it skipped this first stage of advancement and leaped into the second, devoting its attention to "self-adjustment" of the will. Without the necessary material basis, the "premature civilization" stood helpless in front of modern Western civilization. The remedy was not to throw away this premature civilization but to retrace the path of civilization and adopt the scientific-democratic culture of the West. The ultimate task, Liang added, was not merely to insure the permanence of China's past achievement (in K'ang's phrase, "national essence") but really to bring it into the context of world civilization.[229]

Broadly the same view was expressed years later by Sah Meng-wu and nine other college professors:

> Cultural construction on the Chinese basis is a creative endeavor. . . . Its objective is to enable China and the Chinese . . . not only to keep pace with other countries and peoples, but also to make valuable contributions to a world culture.[230]

Chiang Meng-lin, writing in the 1940s, indicated the hope for a "new civilization" resulting from fusion of "modern science, with special reference to invention and industry," with "China's rich treasures of art and sound morals."[231]

---

hsueh," *Hu Shih wen-ts'un*, 2nd ser., *chüan* 1, pp. 57–85. See Chow, *May Fourth Movement*, pp. 331–32, for evaluation of Hu's criticism.

[229] Liang's views are stated in his *Tung-Hsi wen-hua chi ch'i che-hsüeh*, a series of lectures delivered at the Provincial Education Society, Tsinan, Shantung, August, 1921. See especially pp. 9, 24, 30–42, 53–55, 64–68, 199–200. Summaries of Liang's views are in Chow, *May Fourth Movement*, pp. 329–30 and Harry J. Lamley, "Liang Shu-ming: The Thought and Action of a Reformer," pp. 88–140. Excerpts of Liang's book are translated in de Bary et al., *Sources of Chinese Tradition*, pp. 850–53.

[230] Sa Meng-wu et al., "Chung-kuo pen-wei wen-hua chien-she hsüan-yen," *Wen-hua chien-she*, 1, no. 4 (Jan. 1935): 3–5; partial translation in de Bary et al., *Sources of Chinese Tradition*, pp. 854 ff.

[231] Chiang, *Tides from the West*, p. 272. Chiang's general stand was echoed more recently by a number of writers. E.g., Francis L. K. Hsü, "Cultural Differences between East and West and their Significance for the World Today," *Tsing Hua Journal of Chinese Studies*, n.s., 2, no. 1 (May 1960): 231–34, and Sun Lin-sheng, "Wei-shih-mo yao fa-yang Chung-kuo wen-hua?" *Hsin-wen t'ien-ti*, 3, no. 10 (Dec. 1, 1963): 2. Sun's article was a rejoinder to Richard M. Pfeffer's statement made at a discussion session, August 5, 1963, Taipei, Taiwan, in which Ch'ien Mu, a number of Chinese university professors, and several American graduate students studying in Taiwan

By far the most interesting views were expressed by Fung Yu-lan. In a book published in 1940, he set forth a universalist theory of civilization that curiously paralleled that of K'ang but couched in more philosophical language and expressed in a more systematic fashion. A civilization, Fung said, was definable not by the place of its origin or by the people who evolved it, but by its qualities or characteristics that marked it as of a particular type. Thus "Western civilization" was such not because it was "Western," namely, originated in the Western world and sustained by Western peoples, but because it contained a number of distinctive qualities or elements (such as science, industry, and democracy) that made it the kind of civilization appropriately classified as "modern." The civilization of a given country at a given time was a complex of diverse elements. Some of these determined the type to which it belonged; these were the "essential" ones, while those which were not type determinants were "incidental." A particular combination of incidental elements gave individuality or uniqueness to a civilization, even though (because of the presence of the essential elements) it belonged at the same time to a general type. Now as type-determining elements could be assumed by all civilizations of the same type, it was possible for any country which did not yet possess them to acquire any or all of them. But as the civilization of a country was an individualized entity, it was impossible for another country to adopt it *in toto*, essential and incidental elements all.[232]

It was therefore unmeaning to speak of "wholesale Westernization," or even "Westernization." What China could and should do was to gain possession of the "essential elements" that characterized "modern civilization" and at the same time retain the "incidental elements" that had nothing to do with modernity. In this way, the transformation of her civilization would be "complete" because "to change our civilization in this way is precisely to change it from one type to another."[233] This was, in other words, modernization, not Westernization or de-Sinification.

Most interestingly, Fung credited K'ang with having looked at the problem of civilization from a standpoint similar to his own.

---

took part. Pfeffer took the position that it was well-nigh impossible to adopt Western science and democracy and at the same time to practice "Confucianism" (*Hsin-wen t'ien-ti*, 2, no. 9 (Nov. 1, 1963): 7–8).

[232] Fung Yu-lan, *Hsin shih lun* (*yu ming Chung-kuo tao tzu-yu chih lu*), pp. 8–18.

[233] Ibid., pp. 15–16.

In the eyes of people writing in the early years of the Republic, K'ang Yu-wei was a man who committed himself to preserving the "national essence," and "an old reactionary." In the eyes of people living in late Ch'ing times he was a reformer, a rebel [against tradition]. . . . Judging on the basis of his thought, he was one who identified civilizations by their types. He knew that each type of civilization is a universal, so that more than one country or nation may share it in common. Thus [he thought it possible that the elements which constitute modern civilization] had already been seen by China's ancient sages [and that] when China now transforms her civilization from one type into another [namely from a pre-modern type into a modern type], she would still remain Chinese and could still continue "to follow the Way of her ancient sages."[234]

Fung then went on to say that he disapproved "half of K'ang Yu-wei's views" but concurred with him in the other half.

The points of agreement were soon made clear by Fung. Two types of civilization, Fung said, were known to men of recent times: handicraft civilization and industrial civilization. In the former production was a family affair but in the latter production was "socialized."[235]

The chief characteristic of the postindustrial revolution method of production was the use of machines. Machine production implied large-scale production, . . . the employment of a large number of workers in centralized production. In this way the method of production based on the family was done away with—the system of production based on the family unit was demolished.[236]

[234] Ibid., p. 18.

[235] Ibid., pp. 56–57. Pursuing roughly the same line of reasoning that K'ang followed in the 1905 *Essay*, Fung contrasted agricultural ("country-folk," in his terminology) with industrial ("city-folk") society: the latter enjoyed economic affluence and developed a high degree of knowledge and skill, while the former remained poor and ignorant—constant victim of the latter's "exploitation." "The only way for the country folk of the East to escape the exploitation of the city folk of the West . . . is to achieve the same kind of industrial revolution, the essence of which is to replace handicraft with machine production. . . . England, the first to accomplish such revolution, was the first to acquire the city-folk status in the modern world. Then came Germany and Japan" (ibid., pp. 38–48). Unlike K'ang, however, Fung had no faith in free enterprise but was in favor of socialism (ibid., pp. 49–55). Cf. his *Jen-sheng che-hsüeh*, a book based upon his doctoral dissertation, Columbia University, 1921 (Shanghai, 1926), in which he revealed his early inclination toward socialism. See Robert H. G. Lee, "Fung Yu-lan: A Biographical Profile," pp. 142–43.

[236] Fung, *Hsin shih lun*, pp. 58–59. See also pp. 65–66, 179–82, 186, where Fung stated with approval the Marxist view that "the method of production" determines the form of social organization and human morality. Fung also accepted the Marxist theory of economic classes but regarded "class struggle" merely as propaganda with which the Communists sought to arouse the masses into revolutionary action (ibid., pp. 130, 151–54).

In order to modernize herself, Fung continued, China must effect the same changes that had taken place in the West since the industrial revolution. But this is not saying that China should give up the "non-material" elements that characterized her indigenous culture, or, in the words which he attributed to K'ang, no longer "to follow the Way of ancient sages."

Industrialization eventually would lead to socialization, which in turn would lead to communism when it became world-wide in scope.[237] With the arrival of socialized production and abolition of private property, the importance of the family would be drastically reduced until finally the institution itself became unnecessary. For, Fung explained, in a Communist society all the needs of an individual would be taken care of by society and most of his life would be spent in society.[238] Men and women would have freedom of marriage and women would be emancipated from the duties of the wife and mother. Children would be reared by various nonprofit-making institutions of society. A man's wife would no longer be "a member of the family" but instead would become "a member of society." Like her husband she would have independent skills of her own . . .and would cohabit with him only to fulfill their sexual life.[239] Marriage, in fact, would no longer be permanent, as in a "family-based society."[240]

Fung made it clear, however, all this would come only after the material basis of social changes had been firmly laid. He joined K'ang in warning against wasting efforts in pursuing what the latter called "empty words"—against hastening social changes before the arrival of the appropriate time.

> China's greatest present need is *not any politicalism* but prompt economic development in the direction of socialized production [namely, large-scale machine production]. This is the fundamental [task of modernization].[241]

Fung criticized the leaders of the new culture movement. What they wanted, he said in effect, was not a new culture but really a Westernized culture. The "new literature," for instance, was in reality "Europeanized literature," which was more moribund than the "old literature" that they called "dead."[242] Anti-Confucianism was the product of

[237] Ibid., p. 72.
[238] Ibid., p. 64–65.
[239] Ibid., pp. 98–111.
[240] Ibid., p. 162.
[241] Ibid., p. 184. Emphasis is supplied.
[242] Ibid., pp. 148–51.

naïveté or sheer ignorance. Those who wished to destroy the "old morality" imagined that it was the fabrication of "a few unenlightened men, such as Confucius and Chu Hsi" who, "relying on their prejudices," laid down moral rules and expected men to obey them. These anti-Confucianists failed to understand that the moral values of a country at a given period were conditioned by the mode of production prevailing in that period. Thus, in a society in which the family was the unit of production, as was the case in traditional China, filial piety was of necessity the center and root of all morality. As long as such conditions persisted, no other type of morality could emerge in that society and serve its needs. Only when society was transforming itself into a new type did the family with its appropriate moral values become impediments to progress.[243] That this was a new version of K'ang's idea of social progress in definite stages, into which Fung injected the Marxist interpretation of history, hardly requires comment.

Fung was as emphatic as K'ang in defending the "national essence" while the country was making efforts toward modernization. It was unnecessary, and indeed undesirable, to copy the cultural characteristics of another country, however advanced it might be. Fung put it concretely thus:

> England's is the civilization of socialized production, so is Germany's. . . . England and Germany are therefore identical in this respect. But we cannot say that [in achieving industrialization after England had set the trend] Germany has been Anglicized, because culturally speaking, there still are differences between England and Germany. These differences . . . which make England English and Germany German, are extremely important.

These cultural characteristics, Fung added, which included art and literature, represented not "degree of advancement" but "differences in style."[244] The conclusion from this is obvious:

> If a nation's ways differ in degree of advancement from another nation's ways of the same category, then the nation with less advanced ways should strive to bring her ways up to the more advanced level. Unless this is done, she cannot insure her survival. But if her ways differ only in style [from those of other nations], then each nation should preserve her tradition. Unless this is done, national identity cannot be maintained.[245]

[243] Ibid., pp. 89–91.
[244] Ibid., pp. 135–36.
[245] Ibid., p. 238.

K'ang Yu-wei could not have put the matter in clearer or stronger terms.

He probably would have also approved in principle of Fung's interpretation of the "basis-and-application" (*t'i-yung*) formula.

> If by "Chinese learning as the basis and Western learning for application" is meant that the value system with which to hold society together is China's own, and that what needs to be added is the West's science, technology, and industry, then this phrase does make sense. . . . Since the last years of the Ch'ing to the present day, what China has lacked is this science, technology, and industry that characterize a particular type of civilization. What she possesses is the morality that holds together [Chinese] society [and which therefore constitutes the "basis"].[246]

One gains the impression from the above account that, except for certain details, Fung's ideas of civilization bear a rather striking resemblance to K'ang's views as set forth in the *Ta-t'ung shu* and the essay on material upbuilding. The theory of types of civilization looks suspiciously like the principle of universalization in a different dress; there is even a hint of K'ang's theory of the Three Ages in Fung's conception of social change: handicraft civilization with family as the unit (cf. age of disorder), industrial or socialized civilization (cf. age of emerging peace), and world-wide communism (cf. age of great peace or the Great Community). As Fung expressly said that he approved of half of K'ang's views, there is ample ground to suppose that he had studied both the *Ta-t'ung shu* (published in complete form in 1935) and the essay (sixth printing 1919), and perhaps other published works of K'ang also. The resemblance was presumably no mere coincidence but may be attributed to direct influence of K'ang's thought on the American-educated philosopher.

I have devoted considerable space in the foregoing pages to presenting the views of Ch'en Hsü-ching, Hu Shih, and Fung Yu-lan with a view to showing more precisely the relationship of K'ang's intellectual position to those of some of the most outstanding writers of the period. It turns out that his social thought, his views on civilization, and his solution to the problem of China's modernization were not at all bigoted or unreasonable, shared only by a handful of reactionaries or conservatives, as it was often alleged. On the contrary, despite the loud protests or condemnation raised against them by many of the "new youths," they were knowingly or unknowingly echoed even by writers who were avowedly and unmistakably "progressive" in their intellectual outlook.

[246] Ibid., pp. 228–29.

Arch conservatism, as represented by Ku Hung-ming, found fewer supporters as time went on, although one still encountered an occasional staunch defender of traditional Confucian values. Yen Fu, the "liberal reformer,"[247] who in the 1890s urged Westernization and predicted the impending eclipse of China's heritage,[248] reversed his stand in the 1910s and pinned his hope on "the books of Confucius" and "the beneficient influence of ancient kings."[249] On the other hand, the number of advocates of wholesale Westernization was not on the increase, as Ch'en Hsü-ching claimed in 1936,[250] although people who believed in modernization through cultural synthesis often laid greater emphasis on accepting elements of Western civilization than on preserving the "national essence." Actually, the strident cry "Down with Confucius" was less often heard in the 1930s and 1940s than in the late 1910s or early 1920s.

The Westernizing fervor shown by some writers of the May Fourth period and the emotional commitment to "preserving the national essence" by others appear both to have been naïve reactions to the uncomfortable situation created by the influx of Western culture and the concurrent disintegration of the old order, political, social, moral, and intellectual. Equally concerned about the future of the country, they reacted to the situation in two different directions. The arch conservatives laid the blame on the republican regime and called for a moral and intellectual (if not also a political) restoration. The "new intellectuals," fascinated by what they knew about modern Western civilization, were inclined to trace all evils to "Confucianism." Their " 'wild craze' for Western learning"[251] was as much a symptom of cultural trauma as the fanatical Sinocentrism of their opponents.

Salvation through Westernization was hardly a new idea. Years before, Yung Wing had already expressed the view "that China through western education should be regenerated."[252] Many of the young Chinese studying abroad in the first decade of the present century, too,

[247] Chow Tse-tsung's phrase; see *May Fourth Movement*, p. 64, note t.

[248] See Yen Fu, "Yüan ch'iang," available in *Yen Chi-tao wen-ch'ao*, and *Yen Chi-tao hsien-sheng i-chu.* Cf. *Fa i* (Yen's translation of Montesquieu's *Spirit of Laws*, Shanghai, n.d.), bk. 24, chap. 26, comments. Summary of Yen's political thought in Hsiao Kung-ch'üan, *Chung-kuo cheng-chih ssu-hsiang shih*, pp. 806-8.

[249] "Letters," nos. 39 and 49, quoted in Hsiao, *Chung-kuo cheng-chih ssu-hsiang shih*, p. 808.

[250] Ch'en, *I-nien-lai kuo-jen tui-yü Hsi-hua t'ai-tu ti pien-hua*, pp. 1-3.

[251] John Fryer, *Admission of Chinese Students to American Colleges*, introduction, p. xi.

[252] Yung Wing, *My Life in China and America*, quoted in Tsi C. Wang, *The Youth Movement in China*, p. 50.

were "easily swayed by strange doctrines and revolutionary ideas"[253] that were traceable to the modern West. All this was a natural, and indeed, inevitable development under the circumstances. This, however, does not alter the fact that unconditional Westernization was no better than a simple, all-too-obvious solution to a complex and difficult problem. The Westernizers often seized upon elements of Western civilization without adequate reflection. Some of them made a fetish of "individualism" without taking the trouble to look into "the prequisite of an individualistic system"; others disseminated tenets of the liberal creed without bothering to promote "the basic conditions needed for liberalism." Their "daring and sweeping" ways aroused the enthusiasm of youth,[254] but instead of affording a viable solution to the problem they tended to confuse or complicate it. Their iconoclastic operations worked quite effectively in reducing further the waning influences of the "national essence." The resulting situation was not an entirely happy one. As a recent writer describes it, "the anchor of intellectual life was weighed, but there was no compass to steer it."[255]

The conservative argument, on the other hand, was not more conversant with the practical situation. The vehement opposition to the "new culture" typified by such men as Liu Shih-p'ei, Ku Hung-ming,[256] Yen Fu (in his later years) was perhaps more indicative of emotionalism than calm reflection. These men were not necessarily uninformed about the West. Their anti-Westernization attitude may have also stemmed from their disenchantment with the West. Yen Fu, in particular, had firsthand knowledge of the Western civilization, both in its material and "spiritual" aspects. In recoiling from crass Westernization (from which he was not entirely free in his early days) he appears to have overcorrected himself and ended with something like bigoted Sinocentrism.

The reactions to Western civilization of two Chinese students in America in the early 1920s illustrate in a small way the possibility of a more balanced reaction than either anti-Westernization or anti-Confucianism, even without the wisdom that age sometimes confers.

Discontentment with things at home was one of the greatest forces urging me to go to America. But America I found was not the ideal

---

[253] C. S. Walker, "Army of Chinese Students Abroad," p. 8472.
[254] Y. C. Wang, "Intellectuals and Society in China, 1860–1949," pp. 403–4, 425.
[255] Mu, *Wilting of the Hundred Flowers*, p. 97.
[256] Chow, *May Fourth Movement*, pp. 61–69, summarizes the views of these men.

country which I had envisioned, but far behind us in many things.[257]

I believe that our civilization has to be remade with the help of the western civilization, and that a new civilization may come into being. . . . My change of attitude toward our civilization was perhaps caused by my contact with American friends. Many of them thought that their civilization was the best one and that they had nothing to learn from others. This narrow view I disliked, and became conscious of myself. I wanted to be, not provincial like them, but able to face the fact intelligently.[258]

Here, I believe, were the beginnings of the theory of cultural construction which Hu Shih (in his later years), Fung Yu-lan, and K'ang Yu-wei himself developed, each in his own particular fashion—a theory resting not on a parochial view of civilization but on the willingness "to face the fact intelligently."

A case perhaps may be made that K'ang's views concerning Chinese and Western civilizations, expressed on various occasions during about a half-century's time, constituted a series of varying reactions and attitudes to the historical situation. He began as a scholar of the traditional cast, holding views which presumably were not noticeably different from those of the conservatives of the late nineteenth century and early years of the twentieth. Contact with Western civilization in 1879 persuaded him to devote himself to "extensive inquiry into Western learning" and "to abandon completely" his "old views." For a while he showed perhaps as much "wild craze" for Western learning as some of the "new intellectuals." Almost promiscuously he delved into books on natural sciences and humanities translated from Western-language texts. He was then, potentially, a "wholesale Westernizer." He found fault with the entire intellectual and moral tradition as it then existed; the Confucian texts conveying that tradition he denounced as "false" or "spurious." It may be said that K'ang was a "new intellectual" born a generation's time ahead of Ch'en Tu-hsiu. However, his reinterpretation of Confucianism marked also the beginning of another new phase of his intellectual life: sustained efforts at cultural synthesis by way of universalization. Eventually he arrived at a position that in part foreshadowed that of those who advocated modernization on a "Chinese basis" as well as that of those who subscribed to the newer and more radical ideas of the West. Thus between the 1880s and the 1920s K'ang

---

[257] Statement made at an interview, quoted in Tsi C. Wang, *The Youth Movement in China*, p. 74.

[258] Quoted from a personal letter, in ibid., p. 76.

reflected (in his own unique manner) virtually the entire range of views concerning cultural reconstruction expressed by diverse men writing between the 1910s and 1940s. Whatever may have been the intrinsic worth or practical value of the ideas which he held, there is little doubt that K'ang stood as the most important and most representative thinker of the period of transition from imperial to Communist China. A survey of his ideas amounts practically to a review of the entire range of the major intellectual currents of that period.

To represent transition was, unavoidably, to forfeit the opportunity to say the final word. The "new China" that emerged years after his death bore little resemblance not only to his ideal but to that of those who opposed him. There could have been little comfort to him in knowing that a number of the new intellectuals had somehow come around to his position, or that even before he died, Westernization began to go out of fashion. The self-styled Westernizers who repudiated his universalizing ideas were in turn repudiated by self-styled Marxists who wanted neither Chinese heritage nor Western civilization. Western values, especially individualism and parliamentary democracy, so warmly extolled by Ch'en Tu-hsiu in the 1910s[259] became condemned as manifestations of "bourgeois mentality" detrimental to socialistic construction.[260] Even in the 1920s the decline of the West in Chinese youth circles was already discernible. University professors were taken to task by students for having praised the United States "in the same way old scholars praised the sages Yao, Shun, Yü, T'ang, and the like."[261]

In refuting the plea of Sah Meng-wu and others for "cultural construction on a Chinese basis," Hu Shih optimistically said that "culture itself is conservative" and that violent change "can never completely wipe out the conservative nature of an indigenous culture."[262] Three

[259] See, e.g., Ch'en's article "Tung-Hsi min-tsu ken-pen ssu-hsiang chih ch'a-i," *Hsin ch'ing-nien*, vol. 1, no. 4 (Dec. 1915).

[260] Paul Hollander, "Mores and Morality in Communist China. Privacy: A Bastion Stormed," *Problems of Communism*, 12, no. 6 (Washington, D.C., Nov.–Dec. 1963): 3.

[261] An article written by a student at Nankai University (Tientsin) entitled "The Revolving Education" (Lun-hui chiao-yü), quoted in Y. C. Wang, "Intellectuals and Society in China, 1860–1949," p. 414. "Lun-hui" alludes to the Buddhist doctrine of "transmigration" (or "the wheel of transmigration," *saṁsāra*). See W. E. Soothill and L. Hodous, eds., *A Dictionary of Chinese Buddhist Terms*, p. 445. To the present writer's knowledge, the student was Chou En-lai (now Communist China's premier) who was expelled from the university, partly because of the article.

[262] "P'ing Chung-kuo pen-wei wen-hua chien-she hsüan-yen," *Hu Shih wen-ts'un*, 4th ser., *chüan* 4, pp. 535–40; partial translation in de Bary et al., *Sources of Chinese Tradition*, pp. 856–57.

years after the Communists seized power, he predicted, again optimistically, that "Iron curtain [and bamboo curtain] culture could hardly last for long."[263] This prediction may well prove to be correct. Meanwhile, the Chinese Communists have been relentlessly undermining whatever moral and intellectual values that survived the imperial system and those that were introduced in republican times.[264] Hu Shih's own thought, as is well known, was subjected to the "liquidation" procedure. The question may certainly be raised, how strong will be the "conservative nature" of Chinese culture in face of such determined efforts to undermine it?

It has recently been said of Hu that "the intellectual revolution for which he worked has had an outcome far more harsh and oppressive than he had envisioned."[265] In his early career, in particular, in the May Fourth period, Hu was so deeply absorbed in the task of renovating China by eliminating what he regarded as her moribund culture that even the "experiment" in Soviet Russia made good sense to him. But years later, as I have already suggested above, he took a more lenient view of native culture. Shortly before he died, he reportedly saw no "problem in the assimilation of the new into the old."[266] This, I take it, constituted an implicit admission that after all Chinese tradition was not all "dead" and that wholesale Westernization was not the most rational way to modernization. I suspect that he was disturbed by the "harsh and oppressive" outcome of the intellectual revolution of which he was perhaps the most important leader.

Perhaps it was to K'ang Yu-wei's credit that while he had the courage of visualizing a China and the world of the future drastically different from anything known in the past, he also had the wisdom of foreseeing the risks that inhered in the attempt to realize them and the prudence of counseling against hasty action. This was to him a compelling reason for resisting wholesale Westernization. He was convinced that "sudden and total reversal," however tempting they might seem in face of China's pressing need for modernization, were fraught with perils and that no stable society could be built on "the crumbling ruins of the

[263] "San-pai-nien-lai shih-chieh wen-hua ti ch'ü-shih yü Chung-kuo ying-ch'ü-ti fang-hsiang," *Hu Shih yen-lun chi*, series A, pp. 64–71.

[264] Tooshar Pandit, "Totalitarianism vs. Traditionalism," pp. 10–11. The author overlooks the values and ideas that had gained currency, especially since the New Culture Movement.

[265] Grieder, "Hu Shih: An Appreciation," p. 92.

[266] See note 223, above.

old."[267] He warned, therefore, against dissipating China's "national essence." If, as it was said, K'ang had failed to discover a road that would actually lead to utopia,[268] he at least had uncovered the pitfall of cultural annihilation that awaited the unwary who would choose to take a "great leap" toward the millenium.

This is not suggesting that K'ang was above committing tactical errors. The historical circumstances being such, there was actually no possibility that his views could prevail and take practical effect. But he himself by his own action had rendered it even more difficult for them to gain a fair hearing. Like his opponents and detractors, he inaccurately equated "the Confucian teaching" (which was concerned mainly with morality) with the totality of Chinese civilization, ignoring its non-Confucian components. Unfortunately, "Confucianism" was wedded to the imperial system (without the parental command or knowledge of Confucius) and thus became in that way incompatible, as K'ang's opponents charge, with life in a modern democratic society. K'ang had the perspicacity to realize that this union was a most inauspicious one; he tried to effect a divorce by giving Confucianism a new interpretation, dissociating it from the imperial tradition and bringing it into alignment with modern Western values. But in his desperate attempt to save the "national essence," he sought to wed Confucianism to the abortive "imperial" regime of Yüan Shih-k'ai, giving his opponents a convenient and telling weapon against his cause. Thus, despite the reasonableness of his general stand on civilization, too many of his arguments in support of it proved less than convincing to his critics and remained absolutely futile against the inexorable momentum of cultural disintegration.

---

[267] Sir Rutherford Alcock's remarks, quoted from *Parliamentary Papers, China,* no. 5, "Correspondence Respecting the Revision of the Treaty of Tien-tsin," pp. 137–38, by Mu, *Wilting of the Hundred Flowers,* p. 118.

[268] Mao Tse-tung, "On the People's Democratic Dictatorship" (June 30, 1949), *Selected Works of Mao Tse-tung,* 4: 414: "K'ang Yu-wei wrote *Ta-tung Shu,* or the *Book of Great Harmony,* but he did not and could not find a way to achieve Great Harmony."

POSTSCRIPT: A MODERN
CHINA AND A NEW WORLD

"China's intelligentsia," it has been said, "posed for itself nothing less than the task of defining China's role in the modern world and remodeling her whole intellectual, political, social, and economic fabric to fit that role."[1] Broadly speaking, this was the task that K'ang Yu-wei posed for himself. But he did something more. Convinced that existing institutions, including those of the modern West, fell short of perfection in different ways and to various extents, he undertook to delineate the form and substance of a future world order in which all men would live in total harmony and happiness. In addition to defining China's role in the modern world, he defined a new world in terms of his utopian ideal.

Modern China, as K'ang envisaged it, was to be an independent nation with enough "wealth and power" acquired through modernization to insure for her a fitting place in the family of nations and with a distinctive native culture that would unequivocally justify her nationhood. His position thus differed significantly from that of those Chinese intellectuals who, assuming that unqualified Westernization was the only way to achieve modernization, sought to make China a nation without a national culture. E. R. Hughes's assessment of K'ang's position appears to be essentially correct:

. . . we see that K'ang had not only read the story of other nations and realised that "China was only an eighty-oneth part of the world"; he had

---

[1] Michael Gasster, *Chinese Intellectuals and the Revolution of 1911*, p. 248.

also made this story part of his own experience as a Chinese. He was neither crushed nor dazzled by what he read. On the contrary, his mind was stimulated and invigorated, and the measure of this is found in the easy, natural way in which he turns from Chinese history to Western and vice versa. There is no discounting of foreign history in favour of Chinese, just as there is no sign of indiscriminating admiration of the West.

Hughes goes on to point out that K'ang found two aspects of Western civilization, democratic government and industrialization, particularly valuable. He urged their adoption but at the same time refused to repudiate China's own heritage.[2]

K'ang was not a "nationalist" in the sense that he concerned himself exclusively with the interests of his own country. The influence of Confucian thought and acquaintance with "foreign history" (to use Hughes's phrase) led him first to internationalism and eventually to cosmopolitanism. The "Great Community" was to be the crowning achievement of all mankind, of which the Chinese formed an integral part. The main ingredients of modern civilization, democracy and industry, would continue to expand and to advance; they were to be the dynamic forces that would help to bring a perfect society into being. There would be continuity between the existing modern world and the coming new world.

There would of course be radical changes. Social and political institutions that served man in modern and premodern times would finally become unnecessary. With the elimination of national boundaries all states would no longer exist as separate political entities. Living under a single democratic world government, all men and women would be free and equal citizens of the world. Wealth would be socialized, to be produced and enjoyed by all. Children would be brought up and educated in public institutions; the aged and disabled would be publicly supported. The family and private property, institutions that had existed since antiquity, would vanish. Freed from sufferings inflicted by faulty institutions man would no longer need religion. Deprived of raison d'être, Confucianism, together with Christianity and Islam, would disappear. With humaneness and rationality universally prevailing there would be no more problems—political, social, or moral—to require solution. Life would be a sustained state of unmixed happiness.

It has been suggested that K'ang's utopia was in substance a "Sino-

---

[2] E. R. Hughes, *The Invasion of China by the Western World*, pp. 114–15.

centric universal state."[3] In constructing it K'ang did little more than give the ancient Confucian notion of *t'ien-hsia* ("all-under-heaven") a philosophical twist. In other words, K'ang may be said to have committed himself to something like Sinocentric cultural imperialism. A closer examination of his ideas would show that this is not so. He envisioned, quite explicitly, the withering away not only of the state but the nation and national culture as well. With the amalgamation of all "races" into one homogeneous "mankind," the Chinese along with other nationalities would no longer have distinct existence. A universal language would be spoken by all; mother tongues would fall into desuetude with the fading away of fatherlands. Confucianism, China's "national essence," which K'ang sought to preserve in the modern China that was to evolve, would find no place in the new world. K'ang, in fact, subscribed not to nationalism or imperialism but to cosmopolitanism pure and simple.[4]

This is not saying that K'ang's utopian construct is flawless. One may, for example, criticize him for supposing that science, democracy, and socialism in themselves would surely lead man to perfect society. He did not foresee (and could not have anticipated) the side effects of advanced scientific-technological development—such as air and water pollution—which work to degrade instead of ennobling human existence.[5] Moreover, "triumph of the technological spirit" may tend to lessen the hold of religious or moral values on man.[6] Western democratic societies have been plagued by a variety of problems, material, social, and moral; at any rate, they have not been moving perceptibly in the direction of universal peace and harmony. Socialistic countries face special problems of their own; they are nowhere near the workers' paradise. Their declared willingness to coexist with the democratic societies has not been validated by overt action. The world remains a woefully divided one with no prospect of felicitous union.

One may also criticize K'ang for being unmindful of the fact that social problems are by nature complex and therefore not susceptible to simple solutions, and that solutions to problems often themselves become roots of other problems. His sanguine optimism prevented him from realizing that there are no perfect institutions simply because man

[3] Mary C. Wright, *The Last Stand of Chinese Conservatism*, p. 223.
[4] Cf. Klaus Mehnert, "The Social and Political Role of the Intelligentsia in the New Countries," pp. 125–26.
[5] Cf. Athelstan Spilhaus, "The Next Industrial Revolution," p. 1273.
[6] Cf. Will Herberg, "What Keeps Modern Man from Religion?," pp. 5–11.

who makes them is not infallible.[7] As it is impossible to "eliminate human failing," there will always be faulty institutions; "there will always be pain."[8] And man will continue to try to contrive ways and means to alleviate or remove them.

One cannot deny, however, what K'ang did as reformer and utopian was not without significance; it was an honest attempt to alleviate and remove pain. John Leighton Stuart, an American educator-diplomat serving in China for many years, observed in the early 1950s:

> China could be an enormous asset in a new world order based on reason, righteousness and international good will. . . . The preservation of China's national freedom and her national culture is vitally related to the peace of the Pacific and the progressive welfare of all mankind.[9]

Stuart did not have the 1898 reform in mind when he wrote these words, but they constitute a fitting endorsement of K'ang's efforts at bringing about a modern China. Otto Franke, the noted German Sinologist, had this to say in the opening years of the present century:

> Although world harmony and world peace as taught by Confucianism will remain for numerous generations but a beautiful dream, . . . and the path to the development of the much-yearned-for homogeneous world society appears to be an unfathomable path; yet we should not lose the belief in the development of higher and better goals, because without it our struggle will be purposeless and the history of the world will have no meaning.[10]

It is improbable that when Franke made these remarks, he had seen the manuscript of the *Ta-t'ung shu*. However, had he been acquainted with the "one-world philosophy" set forth in it, he would probably have credited its author with having endeavored, in his own way and to his best ability, to mark a goal for mankind and to give meaning to history.

---

[7] "For all things will never be perfect, until human beings are perfect—which I don't expect them to be for quite a number of years" (Thomas More, *Utopia*, trans. Paul Turner, p. 64).

[8] Günter Grass, *Local Anaesthetic*, pp. 86, 284.

[9] John Leighton Stuart, *Fifty Years in China*, p. 289.

[10] Otto Franke, "Was lehrt uns die ostasiatische Geschichte der letzten fünfzig Jahre?," pp. 70–71; translated in Lonan Wang Grady, "Germany's Role in the Boxer Movement," p. 135, quoted with slight changes.

TABLE OF TRANSLITERATION

Transliterations of personal names not included here will be found
in section B of the bibliography

ai-chih 愛質
ai-li 愛力
ai wu chih chih 愛惡之質
Ajiya Bōeki Shōkai 亞細亞貿易商會

bummei kaika 文明開化

Chan-shih fu 詹事府
Chan T'ien-yu 詹天佑
Chang Kia-ngau (Chang Chia-ao) 張嘉璈
Chang Chü-cheng 張居正
Chang Heng 張衡
Chang Hsüeh-ch'eng 章學誠
Chang Hsün 張勳
Chang Miao-hua 張妙華
Chang Ming-ch'i 張鳴岐
Chang Pai-hsi 張百熙
"Chang san-shih li" 張三世例
Chang Shih-chao 章士釗
Chang Sung-fen 張嵩棻
Chang Tai-nien 張岱年

Chang T'ing-yü 張廷玉
Chang Tsai (Chang Nan-hsüan) 張載 (張南軒)
Chang Yen-ch'iu 張延秋
Chang Yin-huan 張蔭桓
"Ch'ang-hsing hsüeh-chi pa" 長興學記跋
Ch'ang-hsing li 長興里
Ch'ang-hsing shu-chü 長興書局
Ch'ang-yeh pao 昌言報
Chao Heng-t'i 趙恆惕
Chao I 趙翼
Chao P'u 趙普
ch'e-ch'ien fa 掣簽法
Chen Ch'ien-ch'iu 陳千秋
Ch'en Huan-chang 陳序經
Ch'en Shao-po 陳少白
cheng 正, 政
cheng-fu 政府
"Cheng-hsüeh t'ung-i" 政學通議
Cheng K'ang-ch'eng 鄭康成
cheng-lun 政論
cheng-tang i-yüan 政黨議員

601

Cheng-tsai 徵在

Cheng-wen she 政聞社

Ch'eng I 程頤

chi-chin p'ai 急進派

chi-ho yüan-pen 幾何原本

chi-hsieh-shih chih sheng-ming 機械
    式之生命

Chi-tzu 箕子

Ch'i 齊

ch'i (willow) 杞

ch'i (ether) 氣

ch'i ch'iang 騎牆

ch'i-chih 氣質

ch'i hua 氣化

ch'i-shu chih hsüeh 器數之學

ch'i-tien 氣點

ch'i-t'ung 齊同

chia-fa 家法

Chia K'uei 賈逵

chia pu 甲部

chia-shen 甲申

chia-yin 甲寅

chiang-ch'iu   pao-kuo   pao-chung
    pao-chiao chih shih 講求保國保種
    保教之事

Chiang Kuan-yün (Chiang Chih-yu)
    蔣觀雲 (蔣智由)

Chiang Shu-tzu 姜叔子

Ch'iang-hsüeh hui 強學會

chiāo 教

chiao-chu 教主

chiao-hao chih yüeh 交好之約

chiao-huang 教皇

chiao-hui 教會

chiao min chih fa, yang min chih fa,
    an min chih fa, hsin min chih fa
    教民之法養民之法安民之法新民之法

chieh-t'o 解脫

ch'ieh 竊

chien ai 兼愛

Ch'ien-fu shan 千佛山

ch'ien k'un 乾坤

Ch'ien Mu 錢穆

Ch'ien Ting-an 錢定安

chih (govern) 治

chih (intelligence) 智

chih (matter) 質

chih-ch'i 知氣

chih chih chih 智之質

Chih-hsüeh hui 質學會

chih-hui jen-shih 指揮人事

chih-tao 治道

chih-tu chü 制度局

"Chin-kuang meng" 金光夢

Chin-ku hsüeh k'ao 今古學考

Chin-pu tang 進步黨

chin-shih 進士

chin-t'ieh 金鐵

ch'in 親

Ch'in 秦

Ching 經

Ching-chi t'e-k'o 經濟特科

Ching-shih ta-hsüeh-t'ang 京師大學堂

ching-shuang 精爽

Ching-t'u 淨土

Ching-yü chia pien 經語甲編

Ch'ing-chung 輕重

Ch'ing-kuo 清國

Ch'ing-liu tang 清流黨

Chiu-huang wu-ti 九皇五帝

chiu shih 救世

"Chiu-shuo i ching wei shih chih pi"
    舊説以經爲史之弊

"Chiu wang lun" 救亡論

Ch'iu Ch'ang-ch'un 邱長春

Ch'iung-chü 瓊琚

Chōshū 長洲

chou 州

Chou (state) 周

Chou (emperor) 紂

Chou Chi 周姬

Chou-li 周禮

Chou Tun-i 周敦頤

Ch'ou-an hui 籌安會

chu t'ien wu ch'iung 諸天無窮

chu-tsai 主宰

Chu-tzu 楚辭

Chu Tzu-yang (i.e., Chu Hsi) 朱紫陽

Chu Tz'u-ch'i (Chu Chiu-chiang) 朱次琦（朱九江）

ch'u chia 出家

chü 局

chü-jen 舉人

chü luan 據亂

chü-luan shih 據亂世

Ch'ü Hung-chi 瞿鴻機

ch'ü sheng 去聲

chuan-chih 專制

chuan-chih cheng-t'i 專制政體

chuan-men 專門

chuan-shan hsing-shih 專擅行事

chuan-wu chih kuan 專務之官

chüan shou 卷首

ch'üan-mien wei-hsin 全面維新

ch'üan-p'an hsi-hua 全盤西化

ch'üan-shih 權勢

ch'üan shu 權術

ch'üan-ych yin-hang 勸業銀行

Chuang Chou [Chuang-tzu] 莊周 [莊子]

Ch'uang chiao 創教

Ch'uang-hua lun 創化論

ch'uang-tsao shuo 創造説

"Ch'un, Ch'i Ts'ui Chu shih ch'i chün Kuang 春齊崔杼弑其君光

Ch'un-ch'iu 春秋

"Ch'un-ch'iu fen shih-erh shih i-wei san teng" 春秋分十二世以爲三等

Ch'un-ch'iu wei 春秋緯

ch'un shang-yeh hsing 純商業性

chün 均

chün-ch'an chih shuo 均產之説

chün-chu chih jen-cheng 君主之仁政

chün-chu kung-ho 君主共和

chün-chu li-hsien 君主立憲

chün-ch'üan 君權

chün-min kung-chu 君民共主

chung 忠

Chung-hua 中華

Chung-hua hsien-cheng hui 中華憲政會

Chung-kuo chih she-hui chu-i 中國 之社會主義

Chung-kuo hsien-cheng tang 中國憲政黨

Chung-kuo yu-pao 中國郵報

Chung-pei 終北

chung-yang chi-ch'üan 中央集權

erh 二

Erh-wan-chüan shu-lou 二萬卷書樓

fa-chieh 法界

fa jen-shih chih t'ung-shih 發人士之通識

fa-lü chü 法律局

Fa-lü hsüeh-hui 法律學會

Fa pu 法部

fa-shen 法身

fa-ting chin chu-pi 法定金主幣

Fan Chung-yen 范仲淹

Fan Hsü-tung (Fan Hsiu Tung) 范旭東

"Fei hsing" 非相

fen 分

feng-chien 封建

feng-shui 風水

Fu-hsi 伏羲

"Fu kuo" 富國

fu kuo chih fa 富國之法

fukoku kyōhei (fu kuo ch'ing ping) 富國強兵

Fukuzawa Yukichi 福澤諭吉

Fu-lu 附録

Fung Kuo-chang 馮國璋

Godai Tomoatsu 五代友厚

Hai-ch'uang 海幢

Han 漢

"Han-tsu i yu wai-fen wu nei-cheng lun" 漢族宜憂外分母内爭論

Han Yü 韓愈

hanbatsu 藩閥

hang 行

Hirayama Shu 平山周

Ho Chan-li 何旃理

Ho I-i 何易一

"Ho-shih chiu-miu" 何氏糾謬

hou-sheng 後聖

Hou tang 后黨

Hsi-ch'iao shan 西樵山

Hsi-kuo chin-shih hui-pien 西國近世彙編

"Hsi ming" 西銘

"Hsi-tz'u" 繫辭

Hsia 夏

Hsiang 鄉

Hsiang-hsüeh hui 湘學會

Hsiang-kung 襄公

Hsiang-she 鄉社

Hsiao-ching kou-ming chüeh 孝經鈎命決

Hsiao-ching wei 孝經緯

Hsiao-hsien (empress) 孝顯

hsiao-hsin chin-shou 小心謹守

hsiao-k'ang 小康

Hsiao-wen ti 孝文帝

Hsiao Yao-nan 蕭耀南

Hsieh Fu-ya 謝扶雅

hsieh-shih 俠士

hsien 縣

Hsien-cheng hui 憲政會

Hsien-cheng tang 憲政黨

hsien-chih hsien-chüeh 先知先覺

hsien-chu shan wei 賢主禪位

"Hsien-hsüeh" 顯學

hsien ling-shih 縣領事

hsin 信

"Hsin cheng-ts'e tzu hsü" 新政策自序

Hsin chien-she 新建設

hsin hsüeh 心學

hsin-shih shan-ssu 新識深思

hsin-wang chiao-chu 新王教主

hsing (nature) 性

hsing (form, body) 形

hsing-cheng chang-kuan 行政長官

hsing-cheng kuan 行政官

Hsing-chieh hsiang-yu chi (Seikai sō yū ki) 星界想遊記 (by Inoue Enryō 井上圓了)

Hsing Chung hui 興中會

hsing-erh-hsia chih wu-chih hsüeh 形而下之物質學

hsing-erh-shang chih tao-te 形而上之道德

hsing-hai 性海

hsing-ming 性命

hsing-sheng 行省

hsing wei jen chih hou yu li yü hsin 形爲人之後有禮與信

hsü 虛

Hsü Chien-yin 徐建寅

Hsü Chih-ching 徐致靖

Hsü Ch'in 徐勤

hsü-chün kung-ho 虛君共和

Hsü Jun (Hsü Yü-chai) 徐潤 (愚齋)

Hsü Kao-yüan 徐高阮

Hsü Kuang-ch'i 徐光啟

Hsü-lu 叙錄

Hsü Shen 許慎

Hsü Shih-ch'ang 徐世昌

Hsü Shou 徐壽

Hsü Ti-shan 許地山

Hsü T'ung 徐桐

hsü-wu tang 虛無黨

Hsü Ying-k'uei 許應騤

hsüan 玄

Hsüan sheng 玄聖

Hsüan-t'ung 宣統

Hsüan-yeh 玄曄

Hsüan-yüan 軒轅

hsüeh hui 學會

Hsüeh-shih yüan 學士院

hsün cheng 訓政

"Hsün-cheng kang-ling" 訓政綱領

Hsün Ch'ing (Hsün-tzu) 荀卿 (荀子)

hsün-i kuan 訓議官

hsün shun 遜順

Hu-Kuang 湖廣

Hua Heng-fang 華恆芳

Hua-hsü 華胥

Hua-lin 華林

Hua-te-li 華德里

hua wei hsi-jen 化爲西人

Hua-yen 華嚴

Hua-yen ching 華嚴經

Huang Hsing 黃興

"Huang-liang meng" 黃梁夢

Huang Shao-chi 黃紹箕

Hui 回

hun 魂

hun-ch'i 魂氣

hun-chih ("soul substance") 魂質

hun-chih ("soul consciousness") 魂知

hun-p'e 魂魄

hun-yin tzu-yu 婚姻自由

Hung-hsien 洪憲

Hung-lou meng 紅樓夢

Huo-fu shih-li ch'üan-shu 禍福實理全書

i (principle; righteousness) 義

i (town) 邑

i-chen fa-chieh 一眞法界

I-ch'eng yüan-chiao 一來圓教

I-chih 夷之

I-ching 易經

I-ch'uan 伊川

I-ho yüan 頤和園

I-k'uang 奕劻

i-lang 議郎

i-li 義理

"I-lin" 藝林

i min-ch'üan wei kuo 以民權爲國

i shang ti shang 以商敵商

i-shih hui 議事會

i-shih tung-shih 議事董事

I-shu kung-hui 譯書公會

i-ti 夷狄

I-t'ien yüan 一天園

"I-t'ien yüan chi" 一天園記

i-wei 乙未

i wu wei yu 以無爲有

I Yin chih fang T'ai-chia 伊尹之放太甲

I Yin Chou-kung 伊尹周公

i-yu 乙酉

i-yüan 議院 (parliament) 議員 (member of parliament)

Inukai Tsuyoshi 犬養毅

jang i 攘夷

jen 仁

Jen Ch'i-sheng 任啟聖

jen-ch'üan 人權

jen-ch'üan yün-tung 人權運動

jen-ch'ün chin-hua chih li 人羣進化之理

en-ch'ün hui-tang 人羣會黨

jen hsin 人心

"Jen-lui kung-li" 人類公理

"Jen-shen kung-fa" 人身公法

Jen Tsung-ching (Jung Tsung-ching) 榮宗敬

jitsugyōka 實業家

Jiyutō 自由黨

Jōdo shinshū 本願宗

"Ju-lin chuan" 儒林傳

"Ju shih-chieh kuan chung-k'u" 入世界觀衆苦

Jung-ch'ing 榮慶

Jung Hung (Yung Wing) 容閎

Jung-lu 榮禄

kabunakama 株仲間

kai chih 改制

kai ts'ung chi-ch'i pei wen-ming 蓋從機器備文明

k'ai se 開塞

kang-chi i pien 綱紀一變

Kang-chien 綱鑑

Kang-i 剛毅

K'ang Chien-yüan 康建元

K'ang Ch'iung-chü 康瓊琚

K'ang Han-ts'ang 康涵滄

K'ang Hsüeh-hsiu 康學修

K'ang Hui [Wen-yao] 康輝 [文耀]

K'ang I-hsiu [Kuo-hsi] 康懿修 [國熹]

K'ang I-hung 康逸紅

K'ang Kuang-jen [Yu-p'u] 康廣仁 [有溥]

K'ang Kuo-ch'i 康國器

K'ang Kuo-hsi 康國熹

k'ang-lun tang-shih hsiao-mi shih-tsai 抗論當世消弭時災

K'ang Shih-p'eng 康式鵬

K'ang Shih-yao 康世堯

K'ang Ta-chieh 康達節

K'ang Ta-ch'ien 康達遷

K'ang Ta-ch'u 康達初

K'ang Ta-fen 康達棻

K'ang Ta-shou 康達守

K'ang Tao-hsiu 康道修

K'ang T'ung-chieh 康同結

K'ang T'ung-ch'ien 康同籛

K'ang T'ung-wan 康同完

K'ang T'ung-wei 康同薇

K'ang Wei-ch'ing 康惟卿

K'ang Yu-ming 康有銘

K'ang Yu-p'ei 康有霈

K'ang Yüan-yu 康元猷

Kao-teng ta-t'ung hsüeh-hsiao 高等大同學校

Kao-tsu 高祖

Kao-tzu 告子

ken 縣

Keng-sheng 更生

Kido Takayoshi 木戶孝允

Ko Hung 葛洪

ko-jen chi-yeh 箇人企業

"Ko-kuo fen-su chih-tu k'ao" 各國風俗制度考

ko-kuo lü-li 各國律例

ko-ming sheng-jen 革命聖人

Ko Pao-hua 葛寶華

k'ou i 口譯

k'ou-shih 口食

k'ou shuo 口說

ku ho . . . chih ming 孤鶴之鳴

Ku-liang 穀梁

Ku Yen-wu 顧炎武

kuan 觀

Kuan-kung 關公

Kuan Lu 管輅

kuan pan 官辦

kuan-tu shang-pan 官督商辦

Kuan-wen 官文

Kuang-chih shu-chü 廣智書局

Kuang-hsüeh hui 廣學會

kuang-kuai li-lu 光怪離陸

kuang-lu-ssu ch'ing 光祿寺卿

k'uang-che 狂者

kuei-ch'ou 癸丑

kuei-ming kuei-shih 詭名詭實

kuei shen 鬼神

kuei-tzu ya-men 鬼子衙門

K'uei-chün 奎俊

K'un 坤

K'un-kang 崑岡

kung (public, common) 公

kung (industry) 工

kung ch'an 公產

kung cheng-fu 公政府

"Kung-chü shang shu" 公車上書

kung-fa 公法

"Kung-fa hui-t'ung" 公法會通

"Kung-fa shu" 公法書

kung-feng pu 供奉部

kung-fung chih kuan 供奉之官

kung-ho kuo 共和國

kung-ho min-ch'üan 共和民權

kung-i cheng-fu 公議政府

kung-i hui 公議會

kung-i wei ch'üan 公議爲權

kung-i-yüan chih fa 公議院之法

kung kuo 工國

kung-li 公理

"Kung-li shu" 公理書

"Kung-li t'ung" 公理通

Kung-min tzu-chih 公民自治

Kung-sun Hung 公孫弘

kung t'ien-hsia 公天下

Kung-yang 公羊

kung-yeh pen-pu 工業本部

K'ung Chao-yen 孔昭焱

K'ung-chiao 孔教

K'ung-chiao hui 孔教會

K'ung-chiao tsa-chih 孔教雜誌

kuo-chia ch'an-yeh chu-i 國家產業主義

kuo-chia ching-ying 國家經營

kuo-chiao 國教

kuo-ch'üan 國權

Kuo-feng pao 國風報

kuo-hui 國會

kuo hun 國魂

kuo-kuan 國官

Kuo-min hsien-cheng hui 國民憲政會

Kuo-min hsien-cheng tang 國民憲政黨

Kuo-min tang 國民黨

kuo-pao 果報

kuo-shih 國事

kuo ts'ui 國粹

kuo wei kung yu 國為公有

Kuo-wen pao 國聞報

K'uo-p'u-wu-t'ung 闊普武通

Lan shan 藍山

Leng-yen ching 楞嚴經

li (functionary) 吏

li (rites, propriety) 禮

li (a measure of distance) 里

li (principle, reason) 理

Li Fan 李瑶

Li-hsiang k'ao-ch'eng 曆象考成

li-hsüeh 理學

Li Hung-chang 李鴻章

Li Lien-ying 李蓮英

Li Sheng-t'o 李盛鐸

Li Shih-tseng 李石曾

li ts'ai 理財

Li Tuan-fen [Li Pi-yüan] 李端棻 [李苾園]

Li Wen-t'ien 李文田

Li Yüan-hung 黎元洪

Liang-Chiang 兩江

Liang T'ieh-chün 梁鐵君

Lien chou 連州

lien-sheng tzu-chih 聯省自治

Lin Hsü 林旭

ling 靈

ling-hun 靈魂

ling-ming 靈明

Ling shan 靈山

liu-fa shuo 流發說

Liu Hsin 劉歆

Liu Kuang-ti 劉光第

Liu Shih-p'ei 劉師培

liu tao (liu ch'ü) 六道 (六趣)

Liu Tsung-chou 劉宗周

Lo Ch'ang (Lo Chong; Lo Wen-chung, Lo Woon Choon) 羅昌 (羅文仲)

Lo Ying-liu 羅應旒

Lu 魯

Lu Chiu-yüan 陸九淵

Lu Ch'uan-lin 鹿傳霖

Lu Jun-hsiang 陸潤庠

Lu-li 努力

Lu Tso-fu 盧作孚

lun-hui 輪廻

lun kuo chih fu i ti-chia yü wu-chia wei chu 論國之富以地價與屋價為主

Lung-shu 龍樹

Lung Tse-hou 龍澤厚

Lung-wei pi-shu 龍威秘書

Ma-ch'ang 馬廠

Ma Hsiang-po (Ma Liang) 馬相伯 (馬良)

Ma Yung 馬融

Mao shih 毛詩

Matsukata Masayoshi 松方正義

Meirokusha 明六社

Meng[-ku] 蒙古

min-cheng chü 民政局

"Min-cheng p'ien" 民政篇

min-cheng pu 民政部

min-chih 民治

min-chu 民主

min-chu chih kuo 民主之國

min-chu chih t'ai-p'ing 民主之太平

min-ch'üan 民權

min-i-hui 民議會

min-kuan 民官

min-shang 民商

min-sheng chu-i 民生主義

min-tsu chu-i 民族主義

ming (name) 名

ming (fate, mandate) 命

ming (enlightenment) 明
ming hsin chien hsing 明心見性
"Ming-i" 明夷
ming te 明德
Moh Ou-ch'u (Mu Ou-ch'u) 穆藕初
Mo-tzu 墨子
Mou-ch'in tien 懋勤殿
mu-yu 幕友

na-ts'ai, wen-ming, na-chi, na-cheng
　(na-pi), ch'ing-ch'i, ch'in-ying 納采
　問名納吉納徵 (納幣) 請期親迎
Na-t'ung 那桐
Nan-hai 南海
Nan-hsiung 南雄
Nan-hsüeh hui 南學會
"Nan-k'o chi" 南柯記
Nan-k'o meng 南柯夢
nao-ch'i-chin 腦氣筋
"Nan-yang" 南洋
Nara 那拉
Nieh Shih-ch'eng 聶士成
nung hui 農會
nung shang chü 農商局

Ōkubo Toshimichi 大久保利通
Ou Chü-chia 歐榘甲

P'an Tsu-yin 潘祖蔭
pao chiao 保教
pao-ch'üan kuo-t'u kuo-min kuo-
　chiao 保全國土國民國教
pao huang 保皇
Pao-huang hui 保皇會
Pao-kuo hui 保國會
Pao-shang hui 保商會
Pao Shih-ch'en 包世臣
P'ao-hsi 庖羲
p'e 魄
Pei Hua chieh-pao 北華捷報
Pei-ken 倍根
Pi-kan 比干
Pi Yung-nien 畢永年
pien-fa 變法

p'ing 平
po-hsüeh hung-tz'u 博學宏詞
po-shih 博士
po-wu hsüeh 博物學
Po-yu 伯有
pu 不
pu-jen 不忍
pu-jen chih hsin 不忍之心
P'u-i 溥儀

san chung 三重
san kang 三綱
san shih 三世
"San-shih tzu-shu" 三十自述
"San-tai kai-chih chih-wen" 三代改
　制質文
san t'ung 三統
Satsuma 薩摩
seishō 政商
shang 商
shang hsüeh 商學
shang-hsüeh hui 商學會
shang-hsüeh pi-chiao ch'ang 商學比
　較場
shang hui 商會
shang ku 商股
shang pao 商報
shang-pien 上編
shang pu 商部
shang-shu 尚書
Shang-ti 上帝
"Shang t'ung" 尚同
shang-wu chü 商務局
she-hui chih-p'ing chih i 社會至平之義
she-hui chu-i 社會主義
she-hui chün-ch'an i 社會均產義
shen ("gentry") 紳
shen (deity, spirit) 神
shen-chi yüan 審計院
shen-ch'i 神氣
shen-hsien 神仙
shen-hun 神魂
shen i-yüan 紳議員
shen-ming 神明

shen-ming chih i 神明之意

Shen Nung 神農

Shen Pao-chen 沈寶楨

shen-tao 神道

shen-tao she chiao 神道設教

Shen Tseng-chih 沈曾植

shen t'ung 神童

"Sheng-chi t'u" 聖蹟圖

sheng-chiao ta-t'ung 聲教大同

sheng hsien 聖賢

Sheng-hsüeh hui 聖學會

sheng-jen lo-sheng chih tao 聖人樂生
之道

Sheng-jen Wei 聖人為

sheng-ming ts'ai-ch'an ch'üan-li 生命
財產權利

sheng-p'ing 升平

sheng-p'ing shih 升平世

sheng she 聲色

Shibusawa Eiichi 澁澤榮一

shih (scholar) 士

shih (event, affair) 事

shih (age, world) 世

shih (city) 市

shih (circumstance) 勢

shih (substance) 實

shih (history) 史

shih-chieh kung-min 世界公民

shih-chün-tzu 士君子

shih chung 時中

Shih-hsü 世續

Shih hsüan men 十玄門

shih hun-li 士昏禮

shih-jen 士人

shih-lang 侍郎

shih ta-fu 士大夫

Shih-wu pao 時務報

Shih-yen hsüeh-p'ai 實驗學派

Shinran 親鸞

Shou-ch'i 壽者

shou yüeh 守約

Shu-ching 書經

Shu-sun T'ung 叔孫通

shu tsui 贖罪

shu-tu 書牘

shu-yüan 書院

Shun 舜

Shun-t'ien shih-pao 順天時報

Shuo ch'u 説儲

so-chien i tz'u 所見異辭

sonnō jōi 尊皇攘夷

sōshi 壯士

Ssu-i-kuan tsa-chu 四譯館雜著

Ssu-i-kuan ts'ung-pien 四譯館叢編

Ssu-i-kuan wen-chi 四譯館文集

ssu chih 四執

ssu hsieh 四邪

ssu k'u 四苦

ssu li 私利

ssu mi 四迷

ssu shu 四術

ssu-tao 司道

su 俗

Su-hsüeh hui 蘇學會

Su ts'un 蘇村

Su wang 素王

Sun P'i-yang 孫丕揚

Sung Ch'ing 宋慶

Sung Po-lu 宋伯魯

Ta Ch'ing hui-tien 大清會典

Ta Ch'ing lü-li 大清律例

Ta Ch'ing t'ung-li 大清通禮

Ta chu-tsai 大主宰

"Ta ku Tung-ch'iao shu" 答顧東橋書

ta kung-ssu 大公司

Ta-li yüan 大理院

ta-nao, hsiao-nao 大腦, 小腦

ta tao 大道

ta-tao K'ung-chia tien 打倒孔家店

ta-t'ieh kui 打鐵鬼

ta-t'ung 大同

ta-t'ung chih chih 大同之制

ta-t'ung hsüeh 大同學

Ta-t'ung hsüeh-hsiao 大同學校

Ta-t'ung i-shu chü 大同譯書局

Tai Hung-tz'u 戴鴻慈

t'ai-chi 太極

T'ai-hsi hsin-shih lan-yao 泰西新史攬要

T'ai-i 太一

t'ai-p'ing 太平

t'ai-p'ing shih 太平世

T'ai-p'u ssu 太僕寺

T'ai-tsu 太祖

t'ai-yüan 太元

Tan-ju lou 澹如樓

t'an 貪

"T'an-kung shang" 檀弓上

T'an tien 談天

T'ang 唐

T'ang Hsiu 唐修

T'ang-jen shuo-hui 唐人説薈

T'ang Shou-ch'ien 湯壽潛

T'ang T'ai-tsung 唐太宗

T'ang T'ing-shu [Ching-hsing] 唐廷樞 [景星]

T'ang Ts'ai-ch'ang 唐才常

tao (way) 道

tao (circuit, an administrative division) 道

tao hsin 道心

Tao-kuang 道光

tao min sheng ts'ai 導民生財

tao-te 道德

Te-tsung 德宗

"Ti-ch'iu chen-shih" 地球眞史

"Ti-ch'iu hsüeh-an" 地球學案

Ti-ch'iu wan-yin yüan 地球萬音院

ti-fang i-hui 地方議會

ti-fang tzu-chih 地方自治

Ti-pao 邸報

Ti tang 帝黨

Ti-wu-ssu (Deus) 地烏斯

"T'i-jen" 體仁

t'i-p'e 體魄

t'i-yung 體用

T'ieh-liang 鐵良

tien-ch'i 電氣

tien-li 電力

"Tien-shih ts'e" 殿試策

tien-tao 電道

t'ien-fu jen-ch'üan p'ing-teng chih i

天賦人權 平等之義

t'ien-hsia wei kung 天下爲公

t'ien-hsia yu i-chia 天下猶一家

t'ien-li 天理

t'ien-li chih tzu-jan 天理之自然

"T'ien lun" 天論

T'ien-t'ang 天堂

t'ien-tsao chih shih 天造之世

t'ien-yen 天演

T'ien-yen lun 天演論

t'ien yu 天遊

t'ien-yu chih hsüeh 天遊之學

T'ien-yu hua-jen 天遊化人

T'ien-yu t'ang 天遊堂

t'ien yü erh jen li 天欲而人理

ting-wei 丁未

t'ing-nien-ko chih 停年格制

Toba Hung 拓跋宏

Tsai-chen 載振

Tsai-tse 載澤

Ts'ai Chen-fan 蔡鎭藩

Ts'ai O 蔡鍔

Ts'ai-shih-k'ou 菜市口

Tsang 藏

ts'ang fu yü min 藏富於民

ts'ang fu yü shang 藏富於商

ts'ao 曹

Ts'ao K'un 曹錕

Tse Tsan-tai (Hsieh Tsan-t'ai) 謝纘泰

tsei tang 賊黨

Ts'en Ch'un-hsüan 岑春煊

Tseng-tzu 曾子

tsou-i 奏議

ts'u ts'ai 粗材

Ts'ui Liang 崔亮

Ts'ui Shih 崔適

tsun K'ung 尊孔

"Tsun K'ung p'ien" 尊孔篇

Tsun K'ung she 尊孔社

tsung-chiao chia 宗教家

"Tsung-i" 宗儀

tsung-t'ung kung-ho 總統共和

tu-chün 督軍

tu-fu 督撫

tu-hui 都會

Tu-pan cheng-wu ch'u 督辦政務處

Tu-pan min-cheng ta-ch'en 督辦民政大臣

T'u Jen-shou 屠仁守

Tuan Ch'i-jui 段琪瑞

Tuan Yü-ts'ai 段玉裁

Tung-ho tsung-tu 東河總督

T'ung-cheng ssu 通政司

T'ung-chien kang-mu 通鑑綱目

T'ung-jen t'uan-lien chü 同仁團練局

T'ung-meng hui 同盟會

T'ung-wen hsüeh-hsiao 同文學校

Tzu-ch'an 子產

Tzu-cheng yüan 資政院

Tzu-ch'iang hsüeh hui 自強學會

tzu-chu 自主

Tzu-hsia 子夏

Tzu-kung 子貢

tzu-pen chih chuan-chih 資本之專制

Tzu-pu 子部

Tzu-ssu 子思

Tzu-yang shu-yüan 紫陽書院

Tzu-yu 子游

tsu-yu 自由

Tz'u-hsi 慈禧

wai-kuo chih tzu-pen chu-i 外國之資本主義

wai-p'ien 外篇

wan-kuo kung-fa 萬國公法

Wan-kuo tao-te hsüeh-hui 萬國道德學會

"Wan-mu-ts'ao-t'ang k'ou-shuo" 萬木草堂口説

Wan-shen kung-fa 萬身公法

"Wan-shen kung-fa shu-chi" 萬身公法書籍

wan-shih chiao-chu 萬世教主

wan shu-ch'ien pei 萬數千倍

"Wang-chih" 王制

Wang Chüeh-jen 王覺任

Wang Ch'ung 王充

Wang Fu-chih 王夫之

Wang Hsi-ch'i 王錫祺

Wang Hsi-fan 王錫藩

Wang K'ang-nien 汪康年

Wang Mang 王莽

Wang Nien-sun 王念孫

"Wang pa pien" 王覇篇

wang tao 王道

Wang Wen-shao 王文韶

Wei chi 未濟

Wei-hsin hui 維新會

Wei-hsin yüan-nien 維新元年

wei hsüeh 僞學

"Wei jen che t'ien" 爲人者天

Wei Mo-shen (Wei Yüan) 魏默深 (魏源)

wei-shu 緯書

Wei-tzu 微子

wei-yen ta-i 微言大義

wen 文

wen-i 文藝

wen-ming 文明

wen-ming chih kuo 文明之國

Wen-tsung (Hsien-feng) 文宗 (咸豐)

Wen-wang 文王

wen-wu 文物

"Wen-yen" 文言

Wo-yün t'ien 渦雲天

Wu[-wang] 武 [王]

wu 物

wu-chih ("hate disposition") 物質

wu-chih (matter) 物質

wu-chih chih hsüeh 物質之學

Wu-chih yü chi-i 物質與記憶

wu ching erh t'ien che 物競而天擇

Wu-hsü tang-jen 戊戌黨人

wu k'u 五苦

Wu P'ei-fu 吳佩孚

Wu-tao shen 五道神

yang 陽

Yang Hsiung 揚雄

Yang Jui 楊鋭

yang-p'ing sheng 陽平聲

Yang Shen-hsiu 楊深秀

Yang Tu 楊度
Yao Shun 堯舜
Yeh-ho-hwa (Jehova) 耶和華
yeh-se chih kuo 野塞之國
Yeh Shih 葉適
"Yen K'ung ts'ung-shu" 演孔叢書
"Yen K'ung t'u" 演孔圖
yen-li shou-tuan 嚴厲手段
Yen-sheng kung 衍聖公
Yen-tzu 顏子
Yi-yüan (i-yüan) 議員
Yin 殷
yin 因
"Yin-hang" 銀行
yin-hao 銀號
Yin-ho t'ien 銀河天
Yin-kung 隱公
yin-t'an 瀛談
Yin-t'ang hsiang 銀塘鄉
yin tz'u 淫祠
yin yang 陰陽
Yoshida Shōin 吉田松陰

yu-sheng lieh-pai chih li 優勝劣敗之理
Yü 禹
Yü Chin-san 餘晉珊
yü-lu 語録
Yü-yüan lu 愚園路
yüan 圓
"Yüan ch'en" 原臣
yüan-ch'i 元氣
yüan-chih 原質
"Yüan chün" 原君
yüan-lao yüan 元老院
yüan sheng 元聖 (玄聖)
Yüan Shih-k'ai 袁世凱
yüan t'ien 元天
yüan-wai lang 員外郎
yüan-yüan t'ien 元元天
yüeh fa 約法
Yün-chu 雲珠
Yung Chien-ch'iu 雍劍秋

zaibatsu 財閥

BIBLIOGRAPHY

Major collections of shorter works by K'ang Yu-wei are abbreviated in the section of the bibliography listing K'ang's work.

Wen-ch'ao	*K'ang Nan-hai hsien-sheng wen-ch'ao*
Wen-chi	*K'ang Nan-hai wen-chi*
I-kao	*Wan-mu-tsao-t'ang i-kao*
Wu-hsü tsou-kao	*Nan-hai hsien-sheng wu-hsü tsou-kao*
Nien-p'u hsü-pien	*Nan-hai hsien-sheng nien-p'u hsü-pien*

(This sequel to K'ang's *Tzu-pien nien-p'u* was compiled by his daughter, K'ang T'ung-pi. It is given in full in section B, with the other works concerning her father that she compiled or edited.)

Throughout the bibliography the four-volume compilation of Chien Po-tsan et al., *Wu-hsü pien-fa*, is given by author and volume number only.

Manuscripts of K'ang Yu-wei on microfilm are available at the Far Eastern Library, University of Washington.

A. Books and Articles Written or Edited by K'ang Yu-wei 康有爲

Ai-lieh lu 哀列錄. Comp. K'ang Yu-pei 康有霈輯. Kuang-chou, n.d.

"Ch'a Chung-kuo shih tang pien tang-p'ai shuo" 查中國事當辦黨派說. *I-kao*, vol. 1.

[K'ang Tsu-i 康祖詒]. *Ch'ang-hsing hsüeh-chi* 長興學記. Shanghai: Ssu-ch'iu-ch'üeh-chai 思求闕齋, 1892.

"Chi Chu Ting-fu shih-yü wen" 祭朱鼎甫待御文. *Wen-ch'ao*.

"Ch'iang-hsüeh-hui hsü" 強學會序. *Wen-chi, chüan* 8; Chien, vol. 4.

"Chih Chang I-shan shu" 致章一山書. Microfilm, reel 1.

"Chih Chu Shih-hui shu" 致朱師晦書. *I-kao, chüan* 4.

"Chih Kang-t'ien Cheng-shu shu" 致岡田正樹書. *I-kao, chüan* 4.

613

"Chih Li Chung-hao teng shu" 致李忠鎬等書. *I-kao, chüan* 4.

"Chih Li Yüan-hung teng shu" 致黎元洪等書. *I-kao, chüan* 4.

"Chih Lien-san shu" 致蓮冊書. Microfilm, reel 1.

"Chih Ts'ai Sung-p'o shu" 致蔡松坡書. *I-kao, chüan* 4.

"Chih Yüan Shih-k'ai shu" 致袁世凱書. Two letters: 1898, 1916. *I-kao, chüan* 4.

"Chih Yüan Tsung-t'ung shu" 致袁總統書. 1912. *I-kao, chüan* 4.

"Chin-ch'eng *Fa-kuo ko-ming-chi* hsü" 進呈法國革命記序. *Wu-hsü tsou-kao;* Chien, vol. 3.

"Chin-ch'eng *Jih-pen Ming-chih pien-cheng k'ao* hsü" 進呈日本明治變政考序. *Wu-hsü tsou-kao;* Chien, vol. 3.

"Chin-ch'eng *O-lo-ssu Ta-pi-te pien-cheng-chi* hsü" 進呈俄羅斯大彼得變政記序. *Wu-hsü tsou-kao; Nan-hai hsien-sheng ssu shang-shu chi; Pu-jen tsa-chih,* no. 2; Chien, vol. 3.

"Chin-ch'eng *Po-lan fen-mieh-chi* hsü" 進呈波蘭分滅記序. *Wu-hsü tsou-kao;* Chien, vol. 3.

"Chin-ch'eng *T'u-chüeh hsüeh-jo-chi* hsü" 進呈突厥削弱記序. *Wu-hsü tsou-kao;* Chien, vol. 3.

Chin chu-pi chiu-kuo i 金主幣救國議. Shanghai, 1910.

"Ch'in-wang luan-fei pien" 勤王亂匪辨. *I-kao, chüan* 1; microfilm, reel 1.

"Ching hsieh t'ien-en ping [ch'ing] t'ung-ch'ou ch'üan-chü che" 敬謝天恩並[請] 統籌全局摺. Chien, vol. 2.

"Ch'ing chi ch'üan-chü ch'ou chü-k'uan i hsing hsin-cheng chu t'ieh-lu ch'i hai-lu-chün che" 請計全局籌巨疑以行新政策鐵路起海軍摺. Chien, vol. 2.

"Ch'ing ch'ih ko-sheng kai shu-yüan yin-tz'u wei hsüeh-t'ang che" 請飭各省改書院淫祠爲學堂摺. Chien, vol. 2.

"Ch'ing ch'üan nung che" 請勸農摺. *Wu-hsü tsou-kao.*

"Ch'ing Chuang-shih-tun tai-tsou yu-shuo ching-kuo" 請莊士敦代奏游說經過. *K'ang Nan-hai hsien-sheng mo-chi,* vol. 4.

"Ch'ing chün min ho chih Man Han pu fen che" 請君民合治滿漢不分摺. Chien, vol. 2.

"Ch'ing fei pa-ku shih-t'ieh k'ai-fa shih shih kai yung ts'e-lun che" 請廢八股試帖楷法試士改用策論摺. Chien, vol. 2.

"Ch'ing fei ts'ao-yün kai i ts'ao-k'uan chu t'ieh-lu che" 請廢漕運改以漕款築鐵路摺. Chien, vol. 2.

"Ch'ing k'ai chih-tu-chü i hsing hsin-cheng che" 請開制度局議行新政摺. Chien, vol. 2.

"Ch'ing k'ai Ch'ing-chiang-p'u t'ieh-lu che" 請開清江浦鐵路摺. Microfilm, reel 3.

"Ch'ing k'ai hsüeh-hsiao che" 請開學校摺. *Wu-hsü tsou-kao;* Chien, vol. 2.

"Ch'ing k'ai kuo-min ta-hui kung-i li-hsien shu" 請開國民大會公議立憲書. *I-kao, chüan* 4.

"Ch'ing k'ai nung-hsüeh-t'ang ti-chih-chü che" 請開農學地質局摺. Chien, vol. 2.

"Ch'ing kuang-i Jih-pen shu ta-p'ai yu-hsüeh che" 請廣譯日本書大派遊學摺. *Wu-hsü tsou-kao;* Chien, vol. 2.

"Ch'ing kuang k'ai hsüeh-hsiao i yang jen-ts'ai che" 請廣開學校以養人才摺. *Wen-ch'ao*, vol. 5; in Chien, vol. 2, the title is given as "Ch'ing kuang k'ai hsüeh-hsiao che."

"Ch'ing li kung-i chiang ch'uang-hsin che" 請勵工藝奬創新摺. Chien, vol. 2.

"Ch'ing she hsin ching che" 請設新京摺. Chien, vol. 2.

"Ch'ing ting fa-lü che" 請定法律摺. *Wu-hsü tsou-kao*, title only.

"Ch'ing ting-li hsien-fa k'ai kuo-hui che" 請定立憲法開國會摺. Chien, vol. 2.

"Ch'ing tsun K'ung-sheng wei kuo-chiao li chiao-pu chiao-hui i K'ung-tzu chi-nien . . . che" 請尊孔聖爲國教立孝部教會以孔子紀年 . . . 摺. *Wu-hsü tsou-kao; Wen-ch'ao*. Chien, vol. 2.

"Ch'ing tuan-fa i-fu kai-yüan che" 請斷髮易服改元摺. Chien, vol. 2.

"Chiu-wang huan-hsiang chi hsien-miao kao-tsu wen" 久亡還鄉祭先廟告祖文. "Chiu-wang huan-hsiang kao hsien-mu wen" 久亡還鄉告先墓文. *Ai-lieh lu, chüan* 2.

"Chu Chiu-chiang hsien-sheng i-wen hsü" 朱九江先生遺文序. *Pu-jen.*

Chu-t'ien chiang 諸天講. [Shanghai], 1930.

"Ch'üan-fei chih luan wei fu Sheng-chu erh ts'un Chung-kuo shuo" 拳匪之亂爲復聖主而存中國說. Microfilm, reel 2.

Ch'un-ch'iu pi-hsüeh ta-i wei-yen k'ao 春秋筆削大義微言考. N.p., 1913.

"Ch'un-ch'iu pi-hsüeh ta-i wei-yen k'ao fa-fan" 春秋筆削大義微言考發凡. *Wen-ch'ao; Wen-chi.*

Ch'un-ch'iu Tung-shih hsüeh 春秋董氏學. Shanghai, 1898.

"Chün yü kuo pu hsiang-kan . . . lun" 君與國不相干 . . . 論. *Pu-jen*, no. 7, Feb. 1913.

Chung-hua chiu-kuo lun 中華救國論. N.p., n.d. Available in *Pu-jen*, no. 1, pp. 1–58, Feb. 1913; *Pu-jen tsa-chih hui-pien, chüan* 7, pp. 16–18a; *Wen-ch'ao*, 1: 1–22; *Wen-chi, chüan* 1, pp. 1–219.

"Chung-hua min-kuo kuo-hui tai-i-yüan hsüan-chü fa-an" 中華民國國會代議員選擧法案. Microfilm, reel 3.

"Chung-hua min-kuo yüan-lao-yüan hsüan-chü fa-an" 中華民國元老院選擧法案. Microfilm, reel 3.

"Chung-hua ti-kuo Hsien-cheng-hui ko" 中華帝國憲政會歌. *Nan-hai hsien-sheng shih-chi*, Liang Ch'i-ch'ao calligraphy ed.

"Chung-kuo hsüeh-hui pao t'i-tz'u" 中國學會報題詞. *Wen-ch'ao; Wen-chi.*

"Chung-kuo huan-hun lun" 中國還魂論. *Pu-jen; Pu-jen tsa-chih hui-pien.*

"Chung-kuo i ho fang chiu wang lun" 中國以何方救亡論. *Pu-jen*, no. 2, Mar. 1913.

"Chung-kuo pu-hsin ch'u-chiu lun" 中國佈新除舊論. *I-kao, chüan* 1.

"Chung-kuo shan-hou i" 中國善後議. *I-kao, chüan* 1.

"Chung-kuo shan-hou san ts'e" 中國善後三策. In K'ang T'ung-pi, *Nan-hai hsien-sheng tzu-pien pu-i.*

"Chung-kuo tien-wei wu tsai ch'üan fa Ou-Mei erh chin ch'i kuo-ts'ui shuo" 中國顛危在全法歐美而盡棄國粹說. *Pu-jen*, nos. 6, 7; *Pu-jen tsa-chih hui-pien*, no. 2.

"Chung-tzu Lo i-jen mu-chih" 仲姊羅宜人墓誌. *Ai-lieh lu*.

Chung-yung chu 中庸注. Shanghai, ca. 1901.

Fa-kuo ko-ming chi 法國革命記. Written 1898; unpublished?

"Fei sheng lun" 廢省論. *Pu-jen*, nos. 1, 2, 4; *Pu-jen tsa-chih hui-pien*, no. 2.

"Fu Chiao-yü-pu shu" 復教育部書. *Pu-jen*, no. 4.

"Fu Liu Kuan-ch'a Shih-chi shu" 復劉觀察士驥書. *I-kao, chüan* 4.

"Fu Ta-wei hou-chüeh shu" 復大隈侯爵書. *Pu-jen*, nos. 9–10, Dec. 1917 or Jan. 1918.

"Hai-wai Ya Mei Ou Fei Ao wu chou erh-pai pu Chung-hua hsien-cheng hui ch'iao-min kung-shang ch'ing-yüan shu" 海外亞美歐非澳五洲二百埠中華憲政會僑民公上請願書. *Pu-jen*, no. 4, May 1913; *Wen-ch'ao*, vol. 5.

"Han-tsu i yu wai-fen wu nei-cheng lun" 漢族宜憂外分勿內爭論. Microfilm, reel 3.

"Hsi-la yu-chi" 希臘遊記. *Wen-ch'ao*, vol. 11; *Wen-chi, chüan* 6.

"Hsien-cheng-tang chang-ch'eng" 憲政黨章程. Microfilm, reel 3.

Hsien-fa ts'ao-an 憲法草案. Shanghai: Ch'ang-hsing shu-chü 長興書局, n.d.

"Hsien-pi Lao t'ai-fu-jen hsing-chuang" 先妣勞太夫人行狀. *Ai-lieh lu*.

Hsin-hsüeh wei-ching k'ao 新學僞經考. Shanghai, 1891; Peking, 1917; Peiping, 1931; Shanghai, 1936; Peking, 1956.

"Hsin shih-chieh cheng kuo wei kung-yu . . . shuo" 新世界爭國[爲]公有 . . . 說. *Pu-jen*, no. 7.

"Hsin-tang tsei-tang pien" 新黨賊黨辨. *I-kao, chüan* 1.

"Hsü-chuan *Pu-jen tsa-chih* hsü" 續撰不忍雜誌序. *Pu-jen*.

"I K'ung-chiao wei kuo-chiao p'ei t'ien i" 以孔教爲國教配天議. *Pu-jen*, nos. 3, 4, 7, 8; *Wen-ch'ao*.

"I-ta-li yu-chi" 意大義遊記. *Ou-chou shih-i kuo yu-chi, chüan* 1.

"I-yüan cheng-fu wu kan-yü min-su shuo" 議院政府勿干預民俗說. *Pu-jen*, no. 2.

"Jen-tzu chih ko-pu shu" 壬子致各埠書. *I-kao, chüan* 4.

Jih-pen Ming-chih pien-cheng k'ao (*chi*) 日本明治變政考 (記). Manuscript copy (microfilm).

Jih-pen shu-mu chih 日本書目志. Shanghai, 1897(?).

"K'ai-sui hu liu-shih" 開歲忽六十. In K'ang T'ung-pi, *Nan-hai K'ang hsien-sheng tzu-pien nien-p'u pu-i*.

K'ang Kung-pu wu shang-shu kao 康工部五上書稿. N.p., n.d.; *Chih-hsin pao*, no. 45.

K'ang Liang shih-ch'ao 康梁詩鈔. Shanghai, 1914.

K'ang Liang wen-ch'ao 康梁文鈔. Shanghai, 1914.

K'ang Nan-hai hsien-sheng chiang-yen lu 康南海先生講演錄. Hsi-an, 1912(?).

K'ang Nan-hai hsien-sheng mo-chi 康南海先生墨蹟. Comp. Hsieh-an chü-shih 俠安居士. 4 vols. Shanghai, 1934.

K'ang Nan-hai hsien-sheng shih-chi 康南海先生詩集. Comp. K'ang T'ung-wei 康同薇 and K'ang T'ung-pi 康同璧; calligraphy of Ts'ui Ssu-che 崔斯哲. 4 vols. Ch'ang-sa, 1941.

K'ang Nan-hai hsien-sheng shu-tu 康南海先生書牘. Shanghai, 1921.

K'ang Nan-hai hsien-sheng wen-ch'ao (quoted as *Wen-ch'ao*) 康南海先生文鈔. 12 vols. Shanghai, 1914; 3rd printing, 1916.

K'ang Nan-hai hsien-sheng wu-hsü i-pi 康南海先生戊戌遺筆. Shanghai, 1918.

K'ang Nan-hai Liang Jen-kung erh hsien-sheng wen-chi ho-k'e 康南海梁任公二先生文集合刻. Shanghai, 1915.

K'ang Nan-hai Liang Jen-kung wen-chi hui-pien 康南海梁任公文集彙編. Shanghai, 1917.

K'ang Nan-hai wen-chi (quoted as *Wen-chi*) 康南海文集. Shanghai, 1915(?).

"K'ang-shih chia-miao chih pei" 康氏家廟之碑. Manuscript copy in Jung-pang Lo's collection.

"K'ang-shih Chien-yüan i-hou shih-hsi piao" 康氏建元以後世系表. Manuscript copy in Jung-pang Lo's collection.

K'ang tzu nei-wai p'ien 康子內外篇. Manuscript copy, microfilm, reel 2. This work includes: "Ai-wu p'ien" 愛惡篇; "Chao-yü p'ien" 肇域篇; "Chih-yen p'ien" 知言篇; "Chüeh-shih p'ien" 覺識篇; "Ho-p'i p'ien" 闔闢篇; "Hsing-hsüeh p'ien" 性學篇; "Jen-wo p'ien" 人我篇; "Li-ch'i p'ien" 理氣篇; "Li-hsüeh p'ien" 理學篇; "Pu-jen p'ien" 不忍篇; "Shih-je p'ien" 濕熱篇; "Shih-tsu p'ien" 勢祖篇; "Wang-pa p'ien" 王霸篇; "Wei-chi p'ien" 未濟篇.

K'ang Yu-wei shih wen hsüan 康有爲詩文選. Peking, 1958.

"Kao kuo-jen shu" 告國人書. *I-kao, chüan* 4.

"Ko-kuo chin-jih chih mu-ti" 各國今日之目的. Microfilm, reel 2.

Kuan-chih i (also known as *Kuan-chih k'ao*) 官制議 (官制考). Shanghai, 1904; reprinted, 1905, 1906, and 1907; partially printed in *Hsin-min ts'ung-pao*, 1902–3. This work includes: "Chung-kuo chin-jih kuan-chih ta pi i kai lun" 中國今日官制大弊宜改論; "Chung-kuo Han-hou kuan-chih p'ien" 中國漢後官制篇; "Chung-kuo ku kuan-chih p'ien" 中國古官制篇; "Fen-tseng hsing-cheng-pu" 分增行政部; "Hsi chiang tseng li p'ien" 析疆增吏篇; "Hsüan chin-ti-jen wei kuan" 選近地人爲官; "Ko-kuo kuan-chih p'ien" 各國官制篇; "*Kuan-chih i* hsü" 官制議序; "Kuan-chih yüan-li" 官制原理; "Kung-feng sheng chih lun" 供奉省置論; "Kung-min tzu-chih p'ien" 公民自治篇; "Sung kuan-chih tsui shan p'ien" 宋官制最善篇; "Ts'un chiu-kuan lun" 存舊官論.

"Kuei-hsüeh ta-wen" 桂學答問. Peking University, 1929.

Kung-chü shang-shu chi 公車上書記. Peking, 1895.

"*Kung-ho chien-she t'ao-lun-hui tsa-chih* fa-k'an-tz'u" 共和建設討論會發刊詞. Microfilm, reel 1.

Kung-ho cheng-t'i lun 共和政體論. N.p., n.d. Microfilm, reel 2.

Kung-ho p'ing-i 共和平議. Shanghai, 1918. First printed in *Pu-jen*, nos. 9, 10, 1917.

"K'ung-chiao hui hsü" 孔教會序. *Wen-ch'ao*.

K'ung-tzu kai-chih k'ao 孔子改制考. Shanghai, 1897; reprinted, Peking, 1922; Peking and Shanghai, 1958.

Li-ts'ai chiu-kuo lun 理財救國論. Shanghai, ca. 1914; first printed in *Pu-jen*, 1913.

Li-yün chu 禮運注. Shanghai, 1912. Includes: "*Li-yün chu* hsü" 禮運注序. *Wen-ch'ao*.

"*Lien-chou i-chi* hsü" 連州遺集序. *Wen-ch'ao; Wen-chi*.

"*Liu-fen chi* hsü" 留芬集序. *Wen-ch'ao; Wen-chi*.

"Liu-hsing ko" 流星歌. *Chu-t'ien chiang*.

"Lun Chung-kuo pi fen-ko" 論中國必分割. Microfilm, reel 1.

"Lun kung-ho li-hsien" 論共和立憲. *I-kao*.

"Lun Lo-ma li-kuo te-shih" 論羅馬立國得失. *Ou-chou shih-i-kuo yu-chi*.

"Lun sheng fu hsien hsiang i-yüan i chi-k'ai wei pai shih chih pen" 論省府縣鄉議院以亟開爲百事之本. *Wen-ch'ao*, vol. 4.

"Lun tzu-chih" 論自治. *I-kao, chüan* 1.

Lun-yü chu 論語注. Peking, 1917. Includes: "*Lun-yü chu* hsü" 論語注序. *Wen-ch'ao; Wen-chi*.

"Man-ti-chia-lo yu-chi" 滿的加羅遊記. *Ou-chou shih-i kuo yu-chi; Pu-jen*, nos. 9, 10.

Meng-tzu wei 孟子微. Shanghai, 1916; first printed in *Hsin-min ts'ung-pao*, no. 13, 1902. Included are: "*Meng-tzu wei* hsü" 孟子微序. "Meng-tzu wei tsung-lun" 孟子微總論. Available also in *Wen-ch'ao*.

"Ming-kung p'ien" 民功篇. Microfilm, reel 1.

Nan-hai hsien-sheng ch'i shang-shu chi 南海先生七上書記. Shanghai, 1898.

Nan-hai hsien-sheng shih-chi 南海先生詩集. Liang Ch'i-ch'ao's calligraphy. Shanghai, 1908.

Nan-hai hsien-sheng ssu shang-shu chi 南海先生四上書記. Shanghai, 1895.

Nan-hai hsien-sheng wu-hsü tsou-kao (quoted as *Wu-hsü tsou-kao*) 南海先生戊戌奏稿. Comp. Mai Chung-hua 麥仲華編. Yokohama, 1911.

Ni Chung-hua min-kuo hsien-fa ts'ao-an 擬中華民國憲法草案. 2nd printing, Shanghai: Kuang-chih shu-chü, 1916; first printed in *Pu-jen*, 1913.

"Ni ta Chu Yung-sheng hsien-sheng shu" 擬答朱蓉生先生書. Microfilm.

Ou-chou shih-i kuo yu-chi 歐洲十一國遊記. Shanghai, 1905; reprinted, 1906 and 1907.

"Ou-tung A-lien wu kuo yu-chi" 歐東阿連五國遊記. *Pu-jen*, no. 5; *Wen-chi*. Includes: "Pu-chia-li-ya yu-chi" 布加利亞遊記.

"Pa-hsi" 巴西. *Wen-chi, chüan* 6.

"Pa-hsi yu-chi" 巴西遊記. *Wen-ch'ao*.

"Pa-li teng ch'i-ch'iu ko" 巴黎登汽球歌. *K'ang Nan-hai hsien-sheng shih-chi*, Ts'ui Ssu-che calligraphy edition.

"Pa wu-hsü chih Li-t'i-mo-t'ai shu" 跋戊戌致李提摩大書. *K'ang Nan-hai hsien-sheng mo-chi*, vol. 3.

"Pa wu-hsü yü men-jen shu" 跋戊戌與門人書. K'ang Nan-hai hsien-sheng mo-chi, vol. 3.

"Pao kuo hui chang-ch'eng" 保國會章程. Chien, vol. 4.

"Pien yen" 辨言. *Ch'un-ch'iu Tung-shih hsüeh*.

Po-lan fen-mieh chi 波蘭分滅記. 1898; unpublished.

"Pu-chia-li-ya yu-chi" 布加利亞遊記. *Pu-jen*, no. 5.

"Pu-hsing erh yen-chung pu-t'ing che kuo-wang" 不幸而言中不聽則國亡. Shanghai, 1918.

Pu-jen 不忍. A monthly journal; first issue published early in 1913; last (10th) issue late in 1917, all in Shanghai.

Pu-jen tsa-chih hui-pien 不忍雜誌彙編. 2 series; Shanghai, 1914.

"Pu Te-kuo yu-chi" 補德國遊記. *Pu-jen*, nos. 7 and 8; *Wen-ch'ao*, vol. 11; *Wen-chi, chüan* 6.

"Se-erh-wei-ya yu-chi" 塞耳維亞遊記. *Wen-ch'ao*, vol. 11; *Wen-chi, chüan* 6.

"Shang Ch'ing-ti ti-i shu" 上清帝第一書; "Shang Ch'ing-ti ti-erh shu" ("Kung-chü shang-shu") 上清帝第二書 (公車上書); "Shang Ch'ing-ti ti-san shu" 上清帝第三書; "Shang Ch'ing-ti ti-ssu shu" 上清帝第四書; "Shang Ch'ing-ti ti-wu shu" 上清帝第五書; "Shang Ch'ing-ti ti-liu shu" ("Ying-chao t'ung-ch'ou ch'üan-chü che") 上清帝第六書 (應詔統籌全局摺). All in Chien, vol. 2.

"Shang-ti p'ien" 上帝篇. *Chu-t'ien chiang*.

Shih-li kung-fa 實理公法. Manuscript, microfilm. This includes: "Chang-yu men" 長幼門; "Cheng-ch'i ti-ch'iu shu-chi mu-lu kung-lun" 整齊地球書籍目錄公論; "Chiao-shih men" 教事門; "Chih-shih men" 治事門; "Chün-ch'en men" 君臣門; "Li-i men" 禮儀門; "Fu-fu men" 夫婦門; "P'eng-yu men" 朋友門; "Pi-li" 比例; "Shang-ti ch'eng-ming" 上帝稱名; "Shih-ti men" 師弟門.

"*Sung-fen chi* hsü" 誦芬集序. *Wen-ch'ao*, vol. 5; *Wen-chi, chüan* 8.

"Ta chieh-tsai po-i" 大借債駁議. *Wen-chi*.

"Ta Chu Yung-sheng shu" 答朱蓉生書. *I-kao, chüan* 4 *shang*.

Ta-hsüeh chu 大學注. Shanghai (?), 1913.

"Ta P'u chün ta-t'i-hsüeh lun K'ung-hsüeh" 答朴君大提學論孔學. Microfilm.

Ta-t'ung shu 大同書. Edited by Ch'ien An-ting 錢安定. Shanghai, 1935; reprinted, 1936; Peking, 1956; Taipei, 1958; manuscript copy, microfilm.

"T'iao-ch'en shang-wu che" 條陳商務摺. Chien, vol. 2.

"Tien-shih ts'e" 殿試策. *Nan-hai hsien-sheng ssu-shang-shu chi*.

"Ting-ssu Mei-shen-kuan yu-chü shih-chüan" 丁巳美森館幽居詩卷. *K'ang Nan-hai hsien-sheng mo-chi*, vol. 4.

"Ts'ai hsing-sheng i" 裁行省裁議. *Wen-ch'ao*.

"Ts'ai sheng i" 裁省議. Microfilm, reel 3.

"Ts'an-cheng-yüan t'i-i li-kuo ching-shen i shu-hou" 參政院提議立國精神議書後. *Pu-jen*, nos. 9, 10.

"Tsou-ch'ing k'ai kuo-hui che" 奏請開國會摺. Microfilm, reel 3.

"Tsou wei kuo-shih wei-chi . . . ho ch'ing . . . kuei-cheng huang-shang li-ting hsien-fa . . . che" 奏爲國勢危急 . . . 合請 . . . 歸政皇上立定憲法 . . . 摺. *I-kao*, vol. 3.

T'u-chüeh hsüeh-jo chi 突厥削弱記. 1898 (unpublished).

"T'u-chüeh yu-chi" 突厥遊記. *Wen-ch'ao*, vol. 11; *Wen-chi, chüan* 6.

Tzu-pien nien-p'u 自編年譜. Manuscript copy, Jung-pang Lo collection; micro-film, reels 1, 3; mimeographed, Peking, 1958; available also in Chien, vol. 4; Shen Yün-lung, comp. *Chin-tai Chung-kuo shih-liao ts'ung-k'an*, 2nd ser. 沈雲龍, 近代中國史料叢刊, 第二輯. Taipei, 1966.

Wan-mu-ts'ao-t'ang i-kao 萬木草堂遺稿. Comp. K'ang T'ung-pi, 4 vols. Mimeo-graphed, Peking, 1960.

"Wei wang-ying hsieh yen chih Shen I-lao shu" 爲亡媵謝唁致沈乙老書. *I-kao*, vol. 4.

"Wen wu ssu-wan-wan kuo-min te min-ch'üan p'ing-teng tzu-yu hu" 問吾四萬萬國民得民權平等自由乎. *Pu-jen*, no. 6, July, 1913.

Writings, published and unpublished, on microfilm (quoted as microfilm), four reels. University of Washington, Far Eastern Library collection.

Wu-chih chiu-kuo lun 物質救國論. Shanghai, 1919; available also in *Shih-chieh p'ing-lun* 世界評論 (*The World Review*), 10th year, nos. 18 and 19 (Feb. 16 and Mar. 10, 1963), with an introduction by Hsü Kao-yüan 徐高阮.

"Wu-hsü lun-chou-chung chüeh-pi chi wu-wu pa-hou" 戊戌舟中絕筆及戊午跋後. Chien, vol. 1.

Wu-hsü tsou-kao. See *Nan-hai hsien-sheng wu-hsü tsou-kao*.

"Ya-tien yu-chi" 雅典遊記. *Pu-jen*, no. 6.

"Yin-tu yu-chi hsü" 印度遊記序. In K'ang T'ung-pi, *Nien-p'u hsü-pien*.

"Yu yü" 有欲. *Ch'un-ch'iu Tung-shih hsüeh*.

"Yü Chiao-yü-pu tsung-chang Fan Shou-sheng ch'üan kai chin-tu-ching ling shu" 與教育部總長范壽生勸改禁讀經令書. Microfilm, reel 2.

"Yü Hsü t'ai-fu shu" 與徐太傅書. *Pu-jen*, nos. 9, 10, 1917.

"Yü Huang Chung-t'ao pien-hsiu shu" 與黃仲弢編修書. Microfilm, reel 3.

"Yü Shen Tzu-p'ei hsing-pu shu" 與沈子培刑部書. Microfilm, reel 1.

"Yü sheng-nü T'an ta-yin shu" 與甥女譚達印書. *I-kao*, vol. 4.

"Yü tang-jen lun O pai" 與黨人論鄂敗. Microfilm, reel 3.

"Yü wu-ming-che shu" 與無名者書. Microfilm, reel 1.

B. Books and Articles in Chinese and Japanese

Aisin-gioro P'u-yi [Ch'ing Hsüan-t'ung, former Emperor of China] 愛新覺羅溥儀. *Wo-ti ch'ien-pan sheng* 我的前半生. Hong Kong, 1964.

An Wei-chün 安維峻. "Ch'ing hui *Hsin-hsüeh wei-ching k'ao* p'ien" 請毀新學僞經考片. In Su Yü, *I-chiao ts'ung-pien*.

Chang Ch'i-chih et al. 張豈之等. "Kuan-yü K'ang Yu-wei ta-t'ung ssu-hsiang shih-chih-ti shang-chüeh" 關於康有爲大同思想實質的商榷. In Hou Wai-lu, *Wu-hsü pien-fa liu-shih chou-nien chi-yen chi*.

Chang Ch'i-yün 張其昀. *K'ung-tzu hsüeh-shuo yü hsien-tai wen-hua* 孔子學說與現代文化. Taipei, 1958.

Chang Chien 張謇. *Chang Chi-tzu chiu-lu* 張季子九録. 29 vols. Shanghai, 1931. Includes: "Nung-hui i" 農會議; "Shang-hui i" 商會議; "*Shih-yeh lu* 實業録.

———. *Se-weng tzu-ting nien-p'u* 嗇翁自訂年譜. Shanghai (?), 1925.

Chang Chih-tung 張之洞. *Ch'üan-hsüeh p'ien* 勸學篇. Wu-ch'ang, 1898.

———. *Chang Wen-hsiang-kung ch'üan-chi* 張文襄公全集. 120 vols. Peiping, 1928. Includes: "Cha ssu-tao chiang-ch'iu hsin-hsüeh" 札司道講求新學; "Cha t'ung-chü she chü chiang-ch'iu yang-wu" 札同局設局講求洋務; "Chih tsung-shu tien" 致總署電.

Chang Chün-mai [Chang Chia-shen, Carsun Chang] 張君勱 [張嘉森]. "Jen-sheng kuan" 人生觀. In *K'o-hsüeh yü jen-sheng-kuan*, vol. 1.

———. "Jen-sheng-kuan lun-chan chih hui-i" 人生觀論戰之回憶. *Eastern Miscellany, T'ung-fang tsa-chih* 東方雜誌. vol. 31, no. 13, July 1934.

Chang Hsi-t'ang 張西堂. "Liao P'ing *Ku-hsüeh-k'ao* hsü" 廖平古學考序. In Liao, *Ku-hsüeh-k'ao.*

Chang Hsiao-jo 張孝若. *Nan-t'ung Chang Chi-chih hsien-sheng chuan-chi* 南通張季直先生傳記. Shanghai, 1930.

Chang Jo-ku 張若谷. *Ma Hsiang-po hsien-sheng nien-p'u* 馬相伯先生年譜. Shanghai, 1939.

Chang P'eng-yüan 張朋園. *Li-hsien-p'ai yü hsin-hai ko-ming* 立憲派與辛亥革命. Taipei, 1969.

———. *Liang Ch'i-ch'ao yü Ch'ing-chi ko-ming* 梁啟超與清季革命. Taipei, 1964.

Chang Ping-lin 章炳麟. *T'ai-yen wen-lu ch'u-pien* 太炎文錄初編; *T'ai-yen wen pieh-lu* 太炎文別錄. In *Chang-shih ts'ung-shu* 章氏叢書, vols. 16–19. Shanghai, 1924. *Wen-lu* includes: "Hsin-shih shang" 信史上, and "Po chien-li K'ung-chiao i" 駁建立孔教議.

Chang Po-chen 張伯楨. *Nan-hai K'ang hsien-sheng chuan* 南海康先生傳. Peiping, 1932.

Chang T'ing-yü et al. 張廷玉等. *Ming shih* 明史. Shanghai: Chung-hua shu-chü ed., n.d.

Chang Yü-t'ien 張玉田. "Kuan-yü *Ta-t'ung shu* ti hsieh-tso kuo-ch'eng chi ch'i nei-yung fa-chan pien-hua ti t'an-t'ao" 關於「大同書」的寫作過程及其內容發展變化的探討. In *Wen-shih-che* 文史哲, no. 9, 1957.

Chang Yüan-chi 張元濟. "Wu-hsü cheng-pien chih hui-i" 戊戌政變之回憶. In Chien, vol. 4; from *Hsin chien-she* 新建設, vol. 1, no. 3.

Chao Ching 趙靖. "K'ang Yu-wei ti ching-chi ssu-hsiang" 康有為的經濟思想. *Ching-chi yen-chiu* 經濟研究, no. 67, May 1962.

Chao Erh-hsün 趙爾巽. *Ch'ing-shih kao* 清史稿. Mukden ed., 1927, 107: 5a; Hong Kong reprint, 1960, 2: 1377.

Chao Feng-t'ien 趙豐田. "K'ang Chang-su hsien-sheng nien-p'u kao" 康長素先生年譜稿. *Shih-hsüeh nien-pao* 史學年報, vol. 2, no. 1, 1934.

———. *Wan-Ch'ing wu-shih nien ching-chi ssu-hsiang shih* 晚清五十年經濟思想史., Yen-ching Journal of Chinese Studies. Monograph Series no. 18, Peiping, 1939.

Chao Lieh-wen 趙烈文. *Neng-ching-chü jih-chi* 能靜居日記. 6 vols. Taipei, 1964.

Chao Ping-lin 趙炳麟. *Pai-yen wen-ts'un* 栢巖文存. Ch'üan-chou, 1924.

———. *Chao Pai-yen chi* 趙栢巖集. N.p., n.d. Includes *Pai-yen kan-chiu shih-hua* 栢巖感舊詩話.

Chen yin [pseud.] 震瀛. "Chi Ku Hung-ming hsien-sheng" 記辜鴻銘先生, "Pu-chi Ku Hung-ming hsien-sheng" 補記辜鴻銘先生. *Jen-chien-shih* 人間世, nos. 18, 28, Dec. 1934, May 1935.

Ch'en Ch'ang-hua et al. 陳昌華等. "Wo suo chih-tao ti Ku Hung-ming hsien-sheng" 我所知道的辜鴻銘先生. *Jen-chien-shih*, no. 12, Sept. 1934.

Ch'en Chih 陳熾. *Hsü fu-kuo ts'e* 續富國策. In Liang Ch'i-ch'ao, *Hsi-cheng ts'ung-shu. Hsü fu-kuo ts'e* includes: "Chiang-ch'iu nung-hsüeh shuo" 講求農學說 (*chüan* 1); "Ch'üan kung ch'iang kuo shuo" 勸工強國說 (*chüan* 3); "Hua-hsüeh chung-hsüeh shuo" 化學重學說 (essay 4); "I ch'eng-yü hsüeh shuo" 藝成於學說 (*chüan* 3); "Kuang-hsüeh tien-hsüeh shuo" 光學電學說 (essay 5); "Kung-i yang min shuo" 工藝養民說 (*chüan* 3); "Suan-hsüeh t'ien-hsüeh shuo" 算學天學說 (essays 3–5).

————. *Yung shu* 庸書. In Liang Ch'i-ch'ao, *Hsi-cheng ts'ung-shu*. Shanghai, 1896. *Yung shu* includes: "K'ao-kung" 考工 (*chüan* 5); "Ko-chih" 格致 (*chüan* 7); "Li-chin" 釐金 (*chüan* 2); "Nung-cheng" 農政 (*chüan* 2); "Shui-li" 水利 (*chüan* 1); "Tien-hsüeh" 電學 (*chüan* 7); "Ts'an sang" 蠶桑 (*chüan* 2); "Tzu-li" 自立 (*chüan* 8); "Yang min." 養民 (*chüan* 8).

Ch'en Ch'iu 陳虬. *Chih-p'ing t'ung-i* 治平通議. In *Chih-lu ts'ung-shu*, 2nd ser. 蟄廬叢書. Ou-ya-t'ang ed. 甌雅堂, 1893. Included also are *Ching-shih po-i* 經世博議 (*chüan* 4); and *Chiu-shih yao-i* 救時要義 (*chüan* 1).

Ch'en Ch'iu 陳鰲. "Wu-hsü cheng-pien shih fan-pien-fa jen-wu chih cheng-chih ssu-hsiang" 戊戌政變時反變法人物之政治思想. *Yen-ching hsüeh-pao* 燕京學報, no. 25, June 1939.

Ch'en Chou-yeh 陳周業. "Shih-lun K'ang Yu-wei k'ung-hsiang li-lun (*Ta-t'ung shu*) ti chieh-chi chi-ch'u" 試論康有爲空想理論（大同書）的階級基礎 *Chung-hsüeh li-shih chiao-hsüeh* 中學歷史教學, no. 11, 1957.

Ch'en Hsiung 陳熊. "Wu-hsü cheng-pien ch'ien-hou Hu-nan wei-hsin yün-tung ti she-hui chi-ch'u ho ssu-ch'ao ti yen-pien" 戊戌政變前後湖南維新運動的社會基礎和思潮的演變. *Li-shih chiao-hsüeh* 歷史教學, July 1959.

Ch'en Hsü-ching 陳序經. *Chung-kuo wen-hua ti ch'u-lu* 中國文化的出路. Shanghai, 1934.

Ch'en K'uei-lung 陳夔龍. *Meng-chiao-t'ing tsa-chi* 夢蕉亭雜記. In Chien, vol. 1.

Ch'en Kung-lu 陳恭祿. "Chia-wu chan-hou keng-tzu luan-ch'ien Chung-kuo pien-fa yün-tung chih yen-chiu" 甲午戰後庚子亂前中國變法運動之研究. *Wen-che chi-k'an* 文哲季刊 (Wu-Han ta-hsüeh), vol. 3, no. 1, 1933.

————. *Chung-kuo chin-tai shih* 中國近代史. Shanghai, 1935. 6th printing, 1936.

Ch'en Li 陳立. *Kung-yang i-shu* 公羊義疏. In Juan Yüan, *Huang-Ch'ing ching-chieh*.

Ch'en Ling-t'ai 陳冷汰. "Ting-ssu fu-p'i chi" 丁巳復辟記. *Ch'ang-liu* 暢流, vol. 30, no. 10, Jan. 1, 1965.

Ch'en Pao-chen et al. 陳寶琛等, eds. *Te-tsung Ching-huang-ti shih-lu* 德宗景皇帝實錄. In *Ta-Ch'ing li-ch'ao shih-lu* 大清歷朝實錄. Vols. 1071–1180; Tokyo reprint, 1937–38.

————. "Tsou ch'ing li-cheng hsüeh-shu tsao-chiu jen-ts'ai che" 奏請釐正學術造就人才摺. In Yeh Te-hui, *Chüeh-mi yao-lu*.

Ch'en Shou 陳壽. *Wei-chih* 魏志. Shanghai: Chung-hua shu-chü, n.d. Includes: "Kuan Lu chuan" 管輅傳 and "Kuan Lu pieh-chuan" 管輅別傳 (*chüan* 29).

Ch'en T'ien-hua. *See* Ssu-huang.

Ch'en Tu-hsiu 陳獨秀. "Chi-tu-chiao yü Chung-kuo jen" 基督教與中國人. *Hsin ch'ing-nien*, vol. 8, no. 3, Feb. 1, 1920. Subsequent articles by Ch'en Tu-hsiu all appeared in the same journal; volume, number, and year only are given.

————. "Chiang kao ch'ing-nien" 敬告青年. Vol. 1, no. 1, Sept. 1915.

————. "Fa-lan-shi-jen yü chin-shih wen-ming" 法蘭西人與近世文明. Vol. 1, no. 1, Sept. 1915.

————. "Hsien-fa yü K'ung-chiao" 憲法與孔教. Vol. 2, no. 3, Nov. 1916.

————. "Kuan-yü she-hui chu-i ti t'ao-lun" 關於社會主義的討論. Vol. 8, no. 4, Dec. 1910.

————. "K'ung-tzu chih tao yü hsien-tai sheng-huo" 孔子之道與現代生活. Vol. 2, no. 4, Dec. 1916.

————. "Ma-k'e-ssu hsüeh-shuo" 馬克思學說. Vol. 9, no. 6, July 1922.

————. "Pen-chih hsüan-yen" 本誌宣言. Vol. 7, no. 1, Dec. 1919.

————. "Pen-chih tsui-an chih ta-pien-shu" 本誌罪案之答辯書. Vol. 6, no. 1, July 1919.

————. "Po K'ang Yu-wei chih tsung-t'ung tsung-li shu" 駁康有爲致總統總理書. Vol. 2, no. 2, Oct. 1916.

————. "Po K'ang Yu-wei *Kung-ho p'ing-i*" 駁康有爲共和平議. Vol. 4, no. 3, Mar. 1918.

————. "Shih-hsing min-chih ti chi-ch'u" 實行民治的基礎. Vol. 7, no. 1, Dec. 1919.

————. "Tung-Hsi min-tsu ken-pen ssu-hsiang chih ch'a-i" 東西民族根本思想之差異. Vol. 1, no. 4, Dec. 1915.

————. "Wu-jen tsui-hou chih chüeh-wu" 吾人最後之覺悟. Vol. 1, no. 6, Feb. 1916.

————. "Yüan Shih-k'ai fu huo" 袁世凱復活. Vol. 2, no. 4, Dec. 1916.

Cheng Kuan-ying 鄭觀應. *Sheng-shih wei-yen* 盛世危言. 1892. Shanghai: Hua-ying shu-chü 華英書局, 1905. The 1905 edition includes: "Chi-i" 技藝 (essay 26, *chüan* 3); "Chu yin" 鑄銀 (essay 40); "Nung kung" 農工 (essay 28, *chüan* 4); "Shang-chan" 商戰 (essay 25); "Shang-wu" 商務 (essay 24); "T'ieh-lu" 鐵路 (essay 33); "Tien-pao" 電報 (essay 34); "Yin-hang" 銀行 (essay 37–38); "Yu-cheng" 郵政 (essay 35–36).

————. *Sheng-shih wei-yen hou-pien* 盛世危言後編. N.p., 1920. Includes: "Fu k'ao-ch'a shang-wu ta-ch'en Chang Pi-shih shih-lang" 復考察商務大臣張弼士侍郎, *chüan* 8; reprinted in *Yang-wu yün-tung*, vol. 8.

"Cheng-ling i-hsin shuo" 政令一新說. *Wan Kwok Kung Pao*, n.s., vol. 1, no. 5.

Cheng T'an-chou 鄭潭洲. "Shih-chiu shih-chi-mo Hu-nan ti wei-hsin yün-tung" 十九世紀末湖南的維新運動. *Li-shih yen-chiu* 歷史研究, Jan. 1959.

Ch'eng Yen-sheng, comp. 程演生編. *T'ai-p'ing t'ien-kuo shih-liao* 太平天國史料. Peiping, 1926.

Ch'i Ming [pseud.], trans. 起明譯. "O-kuo ko-ming chih che-hsüeh-ti chi-ch'u" 俄國革命之哲學的基礎. Translation of Angelo S. Rapport's article in the July 1917 issue of *The Edinburgh Review; Hsin ch'ing-nien*, vol. 6, nos. 4, 5, April and May 1919.

"Chia-tzu Ch'ing-shih mi-mou fu-p'i wen-cheng" 甲子清室密謀復辟文證. In *Ku-kung ts'ung-kan* 故宮叢刊. Peiping, 1929.

Chiang Meng-lin 蔣夢麟. "Chin-shih wo-kuo hsüeh-shu-chieh-li ti i k'o hui-hsing" 近世我國學術界裏的一顆彗星. *Chung-yang jih-pao* 中央日報 (*Central Daily News*), March 25 and 26, 1963.

―――. "Kai-pien jen-sheng-ti t'ai-tu" 改變人生的態度. *Hsin chiao-yü* 新教育, vol. 1, no. 5, 1918.

―――. "T'an Chung-kuo hsin wen-i yün-tung," 談中國新文藝運動. In *Chung-kuo wen-i fu-hsing yün-tung* 中國文藝復興運動. Taipei, 1960.

Chiang T'ing-fu [Tsiang Tingfu] 蔣廷黻. "Kuo-min-tang yü kuo-min-tang yüan" 國民黨與國民黨員. *Tu-li p'ing-lun* 獨立評論 (*The Independent Critic*), no. 176, Nov. 1935.

Ch'iang-chai [pseud.] 勥齋. "Wan-kuo she-hui-tang ta-hui shih-lüeh" 萬國社會黨大會史畧. *Min pao*, no. 5, June 1906.

Chieh-fang yü kai-tsao 解放與改造. Peking, 1919; renamed *Che-hsüeh* 哲學, 1920.

Chien Po-tsan et al., comp. 翦伯贊等編. *Wu-hsü pien-fa* 戊戌變法. 4 vols. No. 8 of *Chung-kuo chin-tai-shih tzu-liao ts'ung-k'an* 中國近代史資料叢刊, 第八種. Shanghai, 1953.

Ch'ien Hsüan-t'ung 錢玄同. "Ch'ung-yin *Hsin-hsüeh wei-ching k'ao hsü*" 重印新學僞經考序. In K'ang Yu-wei, *Hsin-hsüeh wei-ching k'ao*.

Ch'ien Mu 錢穆. *Chung-kuo chin san-pai nien hsüeh-shu shih* 中國近三百年學術史. Shanghai, 1937.

―――. "K'ung-tzu yü *Ch'un-ch'iu*" 孔子與春秋. *Tung-fang wen-hua* 東方文化 (*Journal of Oriental Studies*), vol. 1, 1954.

Ch'ien Shih-fu 錢實甫. *Ch'ing-chi Chung-kuo chung-yao chih-kuan piao* 清季中國重要職官表. Shanghai, 1959.

Chih-hsin pao 知新報 (*The Reformer China*). Macao, 1897–1900.

Chih-shen [Chu Chih-hsin] 蟄伸 [朱執信]. "Te-i-chih she-hui ko-ming-chia lieh-chuan" 德意志社會革命家列傳. *Min pao*, nos. 2 and 3, Mar. and Apr. 1906.

Chin-liang 金梁. *Chin-shih jen-wu chih* 近世人物志. N.p., 1934.

―――. *Kuang Hsüan hsiao-chi* 光宣小記. N.p., 1933.

Chung-kuo yu-pao 中國郵報. (*China Post*). In Chien, vol. 3.

Ch'ing-i pao 清議報. Yokohama, 1899–1901.

Ch'ing-i pao ch'üan-pien 清議報全編. Yokohama, n.d. (early 1900s).

Ch'ing-shih pien-tsuan wei-yüan-hui 清史編纂委員會. *Ch'ing shih* 清史. 8 vols. Taipei, 1961.

Ch'ing-shih kao 清史稿. *See* K'o Shao-min.

Chu Chieh-ch'in 朱傑勤. *Kung Ting-an yen-chiu* 龔定庵研究. Shanghai, 1940.

Chu Ch'ien-chih 朱謙之. *Chung-kuo ssu-hsiang tui-yü Ou-chou wen-hua chih ying-hsiang* 中國思想對於歐洲文化之影響. Shanghai, 1940.

————. "*Ta-t'ung shu* shih chüan" 大同書十卷. *Tu-shu yüeh-pao* 讀書月報, no. 1, 1957.

Chu Chih-hsin. *See* Chih-shen and Hsüan-chieh.

Chu Ching-nung 朱經農. "Chieh-shu hsün-cheng ti shih-chien wen-t'i" 結束訓政的時間問題. *Tu-li p'ing-lun*, no. 7, July 1932.

Chu Hsi 朱熹. *Chu Wen-kung wen-chi* 朱文公文集. Ssu-pu ts'ung-kan ed. 四部叢刊. Shanghai, n.d. Includes: "Ta Ch'en T'ung-fu shu" 答陳同甫書; *Chu-tzu yü-lei* 朱子語類. Ho Jui-lin ed. 賀瑞麟編. 1876.

Chu I-hsin 朱一新. "Ta K'ang Yu-wei ti-i shu" 答康有爲第一書; "Ta K'ang Yu-wei ti-erh shu" 答康有爲第二書; "Ta K'ang Yu-wei ti-san shu" 答康有爲第三書; "Yü K'ang Yu-wei ti-i shu" 與康有爲第一書; "Yü K'ang Yu-wei ti-erh shu" 與康有爲第二書; "Yü K'ang Yu-wei ti-san shu" 與康有爲第三書; "Yü K'ang Yu-wei ti-ssu shu" 與康有爲第四書. All in Su Yü, *I-chiao ts'ung-pien.*

Chu Shou-p'eng 朱壽鵬: *Tung-hua hsü-lu, Kuang-hsü ch'ao* 東華續錄, 光緒朝. Shanghai, 1909.

Chu Ts'ai 朱采. *Ch'ing-fen-ko chi* 清芬閣集. N.p., 1908.

————. "Hai-fang i" 海防議. In *Yang-wu yün-tung*, vol. 1.

Chuang Ts'un-yü 莊存與. *Ch'un-ch'iu cheng-chieh* 春秋正解. In Juan Yüan, *Huang-Ch'ing ching-chieh.*

Chuang Yü 莊俞. "Chang Chi-chih hsien-sheng chiao-yü t'an" 張季直先生教育談. *Chiao-yü tsa-chih* 教育雜誌, no. 9, Jan. 1917.

Chung-hua shu-chü 中華書局編, comp. *Ch'ing-shih lieh-chuan* 清史列傳. Taipei, 1962.

Chung-kuo li-shih chiao-yen shih 中國歷史教研室編, comp. *Chung-kuo chin-tai ssu-hsiang-chia yen-chiu lun-wen hsüan* 中國近代思想家研究論文選. Peking, 1957.

Chung-kuo k'o-hsüeh-yüan, Che-hsüeh yen-chiu-suo, Chung-kuo che-hsüeh-shih tsu 中國科學院, 哲學研究所, 中國哲學史組編, comp. *Chung-kuo ta-t'ung ssu-hsiang tzu-liao* 中國大同思想資料. Peking, 1959.

Chung-kuo shih-hsüeh hui 中國史學會編, comp. *Yang-wu yün-tung* 洋務運動. 8 vols. Shanghai, 1961 (2nd printing, 1962).

Ch'u Yü-k'un 儲玉坤. *Chung-kuo hsien-fa ta-kang* 中國憲法大綱. Rev. ed., Shanghai, 1948.

Chü-wai p'ang-kuan jen [Robert Hart] 局外旁觀人 (赫德). "Lun t'ung-shang ta-chü" 論通商大局. *Wan Kwok Kung Pao*, n.s., vol. 1, no. 10, Nov. 1889.

Ch'üan Han-sheng 全漢昇. "Chia-wu chan-cheng i-ch'ien Chung-kuo kung-yeh-hua yün-tung" 甲午戰爭以前中國工業化運動. Taipei: Academia Sinica, Institute of History and Philology Bulletin 25, 1954.

————. "Ch'ing-mo Han-yang t'ieh-ch'ang" 清末漢陽鐵廠. In *She-hui k'o-hsüeh lun-ts'ung*, vol. 1, Taipei, April 1950.

————. "Ya-p'ien chan-ch'ien Chiang-su ti mien fang-chih yeh" 鴉片戰前 江蘇的棉紡織業. *Tsing Hua Journal of Chinese Studies*, n.s., vol. 1, no. 3, Sept. 1958.

————. "Sung-tai kuan-li chih ssu-ying shang-yeh" 宋代官吏之私營商業. Taipei: Academia Sinica, Institute of History and Philology Bulletin 7, no. 2, 1936.

Edkins, Joseph 艾約瑟. *Fu-kuo yang-min ts'e* 富國養民策. In Liang Ch'i-ch'ao, *Hsi-cheng ts'ung-shu*.

————. "Jih-pen ko-ku ting-hsin chih ku" 日本革故鼎新之故. *Wan Kwok Kung Pao*, n.s., vol. 1, no. 12, Jan. 1890.

————. "T'ieh-lu i k'uo-ch'ung lun" 鐵路宜擴充論. *Wan Kwok Kung Pao*, n.s., vol. 1, nos. 5–11, June–Dec. 1889.

Fan Wen-lan 范文瀾. *Chung-kuo chin-tai shih, shang-pien, ti-i fen-ts'e* 中國近代史, 上編, 第一分冊. Hong Kong, 1949.

Fang Hao 方豪. *Chung-hsi chiao-t'ung shih* 中西交通史. 5 vols. Taipei, 1954.

Fang Hsiao-ju 方孝孺. *Hsüan-chih-chai chi* 遜志齋集. Ssu-pu ts'ung-k'an ed. Includes: "Min-cheng p'ien" 民政篇; "Tsung-i ti-chiu: T'i-jen" 宗儀第九 體仁.

Fang Hsien-t'ing, ed. 方顯廷. *Chung-kuo ching-chi yen-chiu* 中國經濟研究. 2 vols. Ch'ang-sa, 1939. Includes: "Chung-kuo kung-yeh-hua yü hsiang-ts'un kung-yeh" 中國工業化與鄉村工業; Fang Hsien-t'ing and Ku Yüan-t'ien 方顯廷, 谷源田. "Wo-kuo kang-t'ieh kung-yeh chih niao-k'an" 我國鋼鐵工業之 鳥瞰; Ku Yüan-t'ien 谷源田. "Chung-kuo hsin kung-yeh chih hui-ku yü ch'ien-chan" 中國新工業之囘顧與前瞻.

Fei Hsing-chien 費行簡. *Tz'u-hsi ch'uan-hsin lu* 慈禧傳信錄. Abridged in Chien, vol. 1.

Fu Lan-ya [John Fryer] 傅蘭雅. *K'ao-kung chi-yao* 考工記要; *Kung-ch'eng chih-fu lun* 工程致富論; *Pao fu shu yao* 保富述要; *Tso-chih chu-yen* 佐治芻言. In Liang Ch'i-ch'ao, *Hsi-cheng ts'ung-shu*.

Fung Kuei-fen 馮桂芬. *Chiao-pin-lu k'ang-i* 校邠廬抗議. Kuang-jen-t'ang, ed. 廣仁堂刻. N.d. (author's preface dated 1861: Feng-ch'eng Yü-shih 豐城余 氏 1897). Includes: "Ts'ai hsi-hsüeh" 採西學.

Fung Tzu-yu 馮自由. *Chung-hua min-kuo k'ai-kuo-ch'ien ko-ming shih* 中華民國 開國前革命史. 3 vols. Chungking, 1944.

————. "Lu [Hsiang-kang] *Chung-kuo jih-pao* 'Min-sheng chu-i yü Chung-kuo cheng-chih ko-ming chih ch'ien-t'u' " 錄 [香港] 中國日報民生主義與 中國政治革命之前途. *Min pao*, no. 4, May 1906.

Fung Yu-lan 馮友蘭. *Hsin shih lun* (*Yu Ming Chung-kuo tao tzu-yu chih lu*) 新事論 (又名中國到自由之路). Chungking, 1940; Shanghai, 1946.

————. *Jen-sheng che-hsüeh* 人生哲學. Shanghai, 1926.

————. "K'ang Yu-wei ti ssu-hsiang" 康有為底思想. In Pei-ching ta-hsüeh che-hsüeh hsi, Chung-kuo che-hsüeh-shih chiao-yen shih, ed. 北京大學 哲學系, 中國哲學史教研室編. *Chung-kuo chin-tai ssu-hsiang shih lun-wen chi* 中國 近代思想史論文集. Shanghai, 1958.

Godai Ryūsaku. 五代龍作. *Godai Tomoatsu den* 五代友厚傳. Tokyo, 1933.

Gorai Kinzō 五來欣造. *Ju-chiao tui-yü Te-kuo cheng-chih ssu-hsiang ti ying-hsiang* 儒教對於德國政治思想的影響. Translated by Liu Pai-min and Liu Yen-yung 劉百閔, 劉燕容譯. Shanghai, 1938.

Han-fei-tzu 韓非子. Shanghai: Hung-wen shu-chü 鴻文書局. 1893. Includes: "Hsien-hsüeh" 顯學.

He-te [Robert Hart] 赫德. "Chü-wai p'ang-kuan lun" 局外旁觀論. Wen-ch'ing et al., comp. 文慶等編. *Ch'ou-pan i-wu shih-mo*, T'ung-chih ch'ao 籌辦夷務始末, 同治朝. 40 vols. Peiping, 1929–30.

Ho Ch'i and Hu Li-yüan 何啟胡禮垣. *Hsin-cheng chen-ch'üan* 新政眞詮. Shanghai, 1901. Includes: "Ch'ien tsung-hsü" 前總序; "*Ch'üan-hsüeh p'ien* shu-hou" 勸學篇書後; "Tseng lun shu-hou" 曾論書後.

———. *Hsin-cheng lun-i* 新政論議. Hong Kong, 1895.

Ho Hsiu 何休. *Ch'un-ch'iu Kung-yang chieh-ku* 春秋公羊解詁. In Juan Yüan, ed. 阮元校刻. *Shih-san ching chu-shu* 十三經注疏. Nan-ch'ang, 1916; Taipei reprint, 1959.

Ho Ping-sung 何炳松. "Chung-kuo wen-hua hsi-ch'uan k'ao" 中國文化西傳考. In Pao Tsun-p'eng, *Chung-kuo chin-tai-shih lun-ts'ung*, vol. 2; from *Chung-kuo hsin lun* 中國新論, no. 3, 1935.

Ho Ping-ti 何炳棣. "Chang Yin-huan shih-chi" 張蔭桓事迹. In Pao, *Chung-kuo chin-tai-shih lun ts'ung*; from *Tsing Hua hsüeh-pao* 清華學報, vol. 13, no. 1, 1941.

Hou Hou-p'ei 侯厚培. *Chung-kuo chin-tai ching-chi fa-chan shih* 中國近代經濟發展史. Shanghai, 1929.

Hou O 侯墕. "Liao Chi-p'ing hsien-sheng p'ing-chuan" 廖季平先生評傳. *Ta-kung pao* 大公報 (*L'Impartial*), Wen-hsüeh fu-k'an 文學副刊, Aug. 1, 1932.

Hou Wai-lu 侯外廬. *Chin-tai Chung-kuo ssu-hsiang hsüeh-shuo shih* 近代中國思想學說史. Shanghai, 1947.

———. ed. *Wu-hsü pien-fa liu-shih chou-nien chi-yen chi* 戊戌變法六十週年紀念集. Peking, 1958.

Hsi Wen-fu 嵇文甫. "Yu-li-liao-ti hsüeh-shuo" 游離了的學説. *Hsin shih-hsüeh t'ung-hsün* 新史學通訊, June 1953.

Hsia Ching-kuan 夏敬觀. "K'ang Yu-wei chuan" 康有爲傳. *Kuo-shih-kuan kuan-k'an* 國史館館刊, vol. 1, no. 2, Mar. 1948.

Hsiang Ta et al. 向達等編, comp. *T'ai-p'ing t'ien-kuo* 太平天國. 8 vols. Shanghai, 1952.

Hsiao I-shan 蕭一山編, comp. *T'ai-p'ing t'ien-kuo ts'ung-shu* 太平天國叢書. 1st ser. 10 vols. Shanghai, 1936.

Hsiao Kung-ch'üan 蕭公權. *Chung-kuo cheng-chih ssu-hsiang shih* 中國政治思想史. 2 vols. Shanghai, 1945–46. 2nd printing, 6 vols. Taipei, 1954.

———. "Ti-tiao t'an hsüan-chü: Ti-fang min-i chi-kou ti ch'u-pu chien-t'ao" 低調談選舉: 地方民意機構的初步檢討. *Hsien-cheng yü min-chu* 憲政與民主. Shanghai, 1948.

———. "Woo K'ang. *Les trois théories politiques du Tch'ouen Ts'ieou*" (book review) 吳康. 春秋政治學説 (書評). *Tsing Hua hsüeh-pao*, vol. 8, no. 1, Dec. 1932.

Hsieh Kuo-chen 謝國楨. "Chin-tai shu-yüan hsüeh-hsiao chih-tu pien-ch'ien k'ao" 近代書院學校制度變遷考. In *Chang Chü-sheng hsien-sheng ch'i-shih sheng-jih chi-nien lun-wen chi* 張菊生先生七十生日紀念論文集. Edited by Hu Shih et al. 胡適等編. Shanghai, 1937.

Hsin ch'ing-nien 新青年 (*La Jeunesse*). Shanghai and Peking, 1915–21; Canton, 1921.

Hsin-min ts'ung-pao 新民叢報. Yokohama, 1902–5.

Hsin-min ts'ung-pao hui-pien 新民叢報彙編. Yokohama, 1902–5.

Hsin shih-chi 新世紀 (*The New Century*). Shanghai reprint, 1947.

Hsü Chih-mo 徐志摩. "Tu-yao" 毒藥, *Chih-mo ti shih* 志摩的詩. 1928, 6th printing, Shanghai, 1933.

Hsü Jun 徐潤. *Hsü Yü-chai tzu-hsü nien-p'u* 徐愚齋自叙年譜. Hsiang-shan, 1927. In *Yang-wu yün-tung*, vol. 8.

Hsü Shu-cheng 徐樹錚. *Shih-hsi-hsüan i-kao* 視昔軒遺稿. In *Hsü Shu-cheng hsien-sheng wen-chi nien-p'u ho-k'an* 徐樹錚先生文集年譜合刊. Edited by Hsü Tao-lin [Hsü Dau-lin] 徐道鄰. Taipei, 1962. Includes: "Shang Tuan chih-cheng shu" 上段執政書.

Hsü Su-fu 徐蘇佛. "Chih Jen-kung hsien-sheng shu" 致任公先生書. In Ting Wen-chiang, *Liang Jen-kung hsien-sheng nien-p'u.* . . .

Hsü T'ung-hsin 許同莘. *Chang Wen-hsiang-kung nien-p'u* 張文襄公年譜. Wu-han, 1939; Chungking, 1944; Shanghai, 1946.

Hsüan-chieh [Chu Chih-hsin] 懸解 [朱執信]. "Lun she-hui ko-ming tang yü cheng-chih ko-ming ping-hsing" 論社會革命當與政治革命並行. *Min pao*, no. 5, June 1906.

———. "Ts'ung she-hui chu-i lun t'ieh-tao kuo-yu chi Chung-kuo t'ieh-tao chih kuan-pan ssu-pan" 從社會主義論鐵道國有及中國鐵道之官辦私辦. *Min pao*, no. 4, May 1906.

Hsüeh Fu-ch'eng 薛福成. *Yung-an ch'üan-chi* 庸庵全集. Includes: *Yung-an wen-pien* 庸庵文編; *Hsü-pien* 續編; *Nei-wai-pien* 內外編; *Hai-wai wen-pien* 海外文編; *Ch'ou-yang ch'u-i* 籌洋芻議; *Ch'u-shih Ying Fa I Pi ssu-kuo jih-chi* 出使英法義比四國日記. Shanghai, 1901.

———. *Yung-an ch'üan-chi* also includes the following articles: "Chen pai-kung shuo" 振百工説; "Ch'iang-lin huan-ssu chin ch'en yü-chi shu" 強鄰環視謹陳愚計疏; "Ch'uang-k'ai Chung-kuo t'ieh-lu i" 創開中國鐵路議; "Hsi-yang chu-kuo tao-min sheng-ts'ai shuo" 西洋諸國導民生財説; "Hsi-yang chu-kuo wei min li-ts'ai shuo" 西洋諸國爲民理財説; "Hsüan-chü lun" 選舉論; "K'uang-cheng" 礦政; "Shang-cheng" 商政; "Shang Tseng hou-hsiang shu" 上曾侯相書; "Tai Li po-hsiang i-ch'ing shih-pan t'ieh-lu shu" 代李伯相議請試辦鐵路疏; "Ying chao ch'en yen shu" 籲詔陳言疏; "Yung chi-ch'i chih ts'ai yang min shuo" 用機器殖財養民説.

Hsün-tzu 荀子. Hung-wen shu-chü, 1893. Includes: "Fei hsiang" 非相; "Fu kuo" 富國; "Hsien-hsüeh" 顯學; "T'ien lun" 天論; "Wang-chih" 王制.

Hu Chün-fu 胡君復, comp. *Tang-tai pa-chia wen-ch'ao* 當代八家文鈔. Shanghai, 1925.

Hu Han-min 胡漢民. "*Min pao* chih liu ta chu-i" 民報之六大主義. *Min pao*, no. 3, April 1906.

Hu Pin 胡濱. *Wu-hsü pien-fa* 戊戌變法. Shanghai, 1956.

Hu P'ing-chih and Ch'ien Chün-hsiang 胡聘之, 錢駿祥. "Ch'ing pien-t'ung shu-yüan chang-ch'eng che" 請變通書院章程摺. In Chien, vol. 2.

Hu Shih 胡適. *Hu Shih wen-ts'un*, ch'u-chi, erh-chi, san-chi, ssu-chi 胡適文存, 初集, 二集, 三集, 四集. Taipei, 1953. Articles cited from *Wen-ts'un* below are in ch'u-chi. "Chen-ts'ao wen-t'i" 貞操問題, *Wen-ts'un*, vol. 1; "Cheng-li kuo-ku yü 'ta kuei'—chi Hao-hsü hsien-sheng ti hsin" 整理國故與打鬼—給浩徐先生的信, *Wen-ts'un*, vol. 3; "Chi Ku Hung-ming" 記辜鴻銘, *Wen-hsüeh fu-k'an* 文學副刊, *Ta kung pao* 大公報, no. 164, Aug. 1935; "Chih-hsüeh-ti fang-fa yü ts'ai-liao" 治學的方法與材料, *Wen-ts'un*, vol. 3; "Chung-shen ta-shih" 終身大事, *Hsin ch'ing-nien*, vol. 6, no. 3, Mar. 1919; "Hsin ssu-ch'ao ti i-i" 新思潮的意義, *Hsin ch'ing-nien*, vol. 7, no. 1, Dec. 1919; "Hu Shih ta Lan Chih-hsien shu" 胡適答藍志先書, *Hsin ch'ing-nien*, vol. 6, no. 4, Apr. 1919; "I-pu-sheng chu-i" 易卜生主義, *Hsin ch'ing-nien*, vol. 6, no. 6, June 1918; *Wen-ts'un*, vol. 1; "*K'o-hsüeh yü jen-sheng-kuan* hsü" 科學與人生觀序, *Wen-ts'un*, vol. 2; "Kuei-kuo tsa-kan" 歸國雜感, *Wen-ts'un*, vol. 1; "Mei-kuo ti fu-jen" 美國的婦人, *Wen-ts'un*, vol. 1; "Wo-men tui-yü Hsi-yang chin-tai wen-ming ti t'ai-tu" 我們對於西洋近代文明的態度, *Tung-fang tsa-chih* 東方雜誌, vol. 23, no. 17, Sept. 10, 1926; *Wen-ts'un*, vol. 3; "Ou-yu tao-chung chih shu" 歐遊道中致書, *Wen-ts'un*, vol. 3; "Pai-hua shih" 白話詩, *Hsin ch'ing-nien*, vol. 2, no. 6, Feb. 1917; "Pien-chi hou-chi" 編輯後記, *Tu-li p'ing-lun* 獨立評論, no. 142, 1935; "P'ing Chung-kuo pen-wei wen-hua chien-she hsüan-yen" 評中國本位文化建設宣言, *Wen-ts'un*, vol. 4; "San-pai nien-lai shih-chieh wen-hua ti ch'ü-shih yü Chung-kuo ying-ch'ü-ti fang-hsiang" 三百年來世界文化的趨勢與中國應取的方向, *Yen-lun chi*; "Shih-yen chu-i" 實驗主義, *Hsin ch'ing-nien*, vol. 6, no. 4, Apr. 1919, *Wen-ts'un*, vol. 2; "Tu Liang Sou-ming hsien-sheng ti *Tung-hsi wen-hua chi ch'i che-hsüeh* 讀梁漱溟先生的東西文化及其哲學, *Wen-ts'un*, vol. 2; "*Wu Yü wen-lu* hsü" 吳虞文錄序, *Wen-ts'un*, vol. 1.

———. *Hu Shih yen-lun chi*, chia-chi 胡適言論集, 甲集. Taipei, 1953.

Hu Ssu-ching [T'ui-lu chü-shih] 胡思敬 [退廬居士]. *Wu-hsü li-shuang lu* 戊戌履霜錄. Nan-ch'ang, 1913. In Chien, vol. 1.

Hu Ying-han 胡應漢. *Wu Hsien-tzu hsien-sheng chuan-chi* 伍憲子先生傳記. Kowloon, 1953.

Hua Chih-an [Ernest Faber] 花之安. "Shen li kuo-ts'ai" 愼理國財. *Wan Kwok Kung Pao*, no. 14, Mar. 1890.

———. "Tzu-hsi tsu-tung" 自西徂東. *Wan Kwok Kung Pao*, no. 14, Mar. 1890.

Huang-Ch'ing ching-chieh. *See* Juan Yüan.

Huang-Ch'ing ching-chieh hsü-pien. *See* Wang Hsien-ch'ien.

Huang Chün 黃濬. *Hua-shui-jen-sheng-an chih-i* 花隨人聖菴摭憶. Peking, n.d. (ca. 1943).

Huang Ta-shou 黃大受. *Chung-kuo chin-tai shih* 中國近代史. 3 vols. Taipei, 1955.

Huang Tsun-hsien 黃遵憲. *Jih-pen-kuo chih* 日本國志. Che-chiang shu-chü 浙江書局, 1898. Includes "Kung-i chih" 工藝志, *chüan* 40.

Huang Tsung-hsi 黃宗羲. *Ming-i tai-fang lu* 明夷待訪錄. Hai-shan hsien-kuan ts'ung-shu ed. 海山仙館叢書. Includes "Yüan ch'en" 原臣; "Yüan chün" 原君.

———. *Ming-ju hsüeh-an* 明儒學案. Ssu-ch'ao hsüeh-an ed. 四朝學案. Shanghai, 1936.

———. *Sung Yüan hsüeh-an* 宋元學案. Ssu-ch'ao hsüeh-an ed.

Huang Tzu-t'ung 黃子通. "Hsüeh Fu-ch'eng ti ssu-hsiang" 薛福成的思想. In *Chung-kuo chin-tai-shih lun-wen chi* 中國近代史論文集. Shanghai, 1958.

Ichiko Chūzō 市古宙三. "Hokyō to hempō" 保教と變法. *Kindai Chūgoku no shakai to keizai* 近代中國の社會と經濟. Edited by Niida Noboru 井田仁陛編. Tokyo, 1951.

I-li chu-shu 儀禮注疏. Taipei reprint, 1959.

Itano Chōhachi 板野長八. "Kō Yū-i no daidō shisō" 康有爲の大同思想. *Kindai Chūgoku kenkyū* 近代中國研究. Tokyo, 1948.

Jen Cho-hsüan 任卓宣. "Kuo-fu ti ko-ming ssu-hsiang" 國父的革命思想. *Ko-ming ssu-hsiang* 革命思想, vol. 1, no. 1, July 25, 1955.

Juan Yüan, comp. 阮元輯. *Huang-Ch'ing ching-chieh* 皇清經解. 360 vols. Kuang-chou: Hsüeh-hai-t'ang 廣州學海堂. 1829.

K'ang Kuang-jen 康廣仁. "Chih [Ho] I-i shu" 致 [何] 易一書. In Ting Wen-chiang, *Liang Jen-kung hsien-sheng nien-p'u*. . . .

K'ang Tsan-hsiu 康贊修. "Wen chang-sun Yu-wei sheng" 聞長孫有爲生. In K'ang, *K'ang Nan-hai wen-chi*.

K'ang T'ung-chia 康同家. *K'ang Yu-wei yü wu-hsü pien-fa* 康有爲與戊戌變法. Hong Kong, 1959.

K'ang T'ung-pi, comp. 康同璧編. *Nan-hai K'ang hsien-sheng tzu-pien nien-p'u pu-i* 南海康先生自編年譜補遺. Mimeographed. Peking, 1958.

———, comp. *Nan-hai K'ang hsien-sheng nien-p'u hsü-pien* 南海康先生年譜續編. Mimeographed. Peking, 1960.

———, ed. *Pu K'ang Nan-hai hsien-sheng tzu-pien nien-p'u* 補康南海先生自編年譜. Manuscript copy in collection of Jung-pang Lo. Peking, ca. 1954.

"K'ang Yu-wei lun" 康有爲論. In Chien, vol. 3.

K'ang Yü-chih 康與之. "Tso meng lu" 昨夢錄. In *Shuo Fu* 説郛. Compiled by T'ao Tsung-i 陶宗儀. Shanghai, 1927.

Kao Lao 高勞. "Ti-chih yün-tung shih-mo chi" 帝制運動始末記. *Tung-fang tsa-chih* 東方雜誌 (*Far Eastern Miscellany*), vol. 13, nos. 8, 9, 10, Aug.–Oct. 1916.

Kikuchi Takahara 菊池貴晴. "Kōgakkai to hempō undō—Kōgakkai no setsuritsu ni tsuite" 廣學會と變法運動—廣學の設立について. In *Tōyōshigaku ronshū* 東洋史學論集. Tokyo, 1953.

K'o-hsüeh yü jen-sheng kuan 科學與人生觀. (Comp. Hu Shih?) Shanghai, 1923.

K'o Shao-min 柯劭忞. *Ch'ing-shih kao, lieh-chuan* 清史稿列傳. Peking, 1927.

Ku Chao-hsiung 顧兆熊. "Ma-k'e-ssu hsüeh-shuo" 馬克思學説. *Hsin ch'ing-nien*, vol. 6, no. 5, May 1919.

Ku Chieh-kang 顧頡剛. "Tzu hsü" 自序. *Ku-shih pien* 古史辨, vol. 1. Peking, 1927.

Ku Hung-ming 辜鴻銘. "Hsi-yang i-hui k'ao-lüeh" 西洋議會考畧. In *Chang Wen-hsiang-kung mu-fu chi-wen* 張文襄公幕府紀聞. N.p., 1910 (?).

———. *Tu-I-t'ang wen-chi* 讀易堂文集. Compiled by Ku Neng-i and Ku Wen-ching. 辜能以辜文錦編. Taipei, 1956.

Ku-Wu k'un-hsüeh chü-shih [pseud.] 古吳困學居士. "Kuang-hsüeh-hui ta yu-tsao yü Chung-kuo shuo" 廣學會大有造於中國説, In Chien, vol. 3.

Ku Yüan-t'ien. *See* Fang Hsien-t'ing.

Kuan Lu-yin 關綠茵. "Chan T'ien-yu yü Chung-kuo t'ieh-lu" 詹天佑與中國鐵路. *Ch'ang Liu* 暢流, vol. 35, no. 8, June 1, 1967.

Kuan-tzu 管子. Shanghai: Hung-wen shu-chü, 1893.

Kung Chün 龔駿. *Chung-kuo hsin kung-yeh fa-chan-shih ta-kang* 中國新工業發展史大綱. Shanghai, 1933.

Kung Tzu-chen 龔自珍. *Ting-an ch'üan-chi* 定菴全集. *Wen-chi*, 3 *chüan*; 4 *chüan*; *Wen-chi pu*, 1 *chüan* 文集三卷; 續集四卷; 文集補一卷. Ssu-pu ts'ung-k'an ed. 四部叢刊. Shanghai, n.d. Includes: "Ching-shih yüeh-chi shuo" 京師樂籍説, *Hsü-chi*; "Chuan ssu-teng shih-i" 撰四等十儀, *Hsü-chi*; "I-ping chih-chi chu-i" 乙丙之際著議, *Wen-chi*; "I-ping chih-chi shu-i" 乙丙之際塾議, *Wen-chi*; "Ku-shih kou-ch'en lun" 古史鈎沉論, *Hsü-chi*; "Wu-Ching ta-i chung-shih wen-ta" 五經大義終始問答, *Hsü-chi*.

K'ung Kuang-sen 孔廣森. *Ch'un-ch'iu Kung-yang t'ung-i* 春秋公羊通義. In Juan Yüan, *Huang-Ch'ing ching-chieh*.

Kuo Chan-po 郭湛波. *Chin wu-shih nien Chung-kuo ssu-hsiang shih* 近五十年中國思想史. Peiping, 1935; 2nd printing, 1936.

Kuo Sung-t'ao 郭嵩燾. *Yang-chih-shu-wu wen-chi* 養知書屋文集. In *Yang-chih-shu-wu i-chi*. N.p., 1892. Includes: "Chih Li fu-hsiang shu" 致李傅相書; "Fu Yao Yen-chia" 復姚彥嘉; "Yü yu-jen lun fang-hsiang hsi-fa shu" 與友人論仿行西法書. All are also in *Yang-wu yün-tung*, vol. 1.

Kuo-yü 國語. Cheng-tu: Tsun-ching shu-yüan 成都尊經書院. 1876.

Kuwabara Jitsuzō 桑原隲藏. *Hojukō no jiseki* 蒲壽庚の事蹟. Tokyo, 1935.

Lao Nai-hsüan 勞乃宣. *T'ung-hsiang Lao hsien-sheng i-kao* 桐郷勞先生遺稿. T'ung-hsiang, 1927. Includes: "Chün-chu min-chu p'ing-i" 君主民主平議; "Hsü kung-ho cheng-chieh" 續共和正解; "Jen-shou tzu-ting nien-p'u" 韌叟自訂年譜; "Kung-ho cheng-chieh" 共和正解.

Lao-tzu 老子. Shanghai: Hung-wen shu-chü, 1893.

Li Chi 李季. "She-hui chu-i yü Chung-kuo" 社會主義與中國. *Hsin ch'ing-nien*, vol. 8, no. 6, Apr. 1921.

Li-chi cheng-i 禮記正義. Juan Yüan, ed. *Shih-san ching chu-shü* ed. 十三經注疏, reprinted, Taipei, 1959. Includes: "Chi i" 祭義, 47; "Chiao t'e-sheng" 郊特牲, 25; "Hun i" 昏義, 61; "K'ung-tzu hsien-chü" 孔子閒居, 51; "Li yün" 禮運, 21; "T'an Kung hsia" 檀弓上, 9; "T'an Kung shang" 檀弓下, 6.

Li Chu 黎澍. "Lun she-hui chu-i tsai Chung-kuo ti ch'uan-po" 論社會主義在中國的傳播. *Li-shih yen-chiu* 歷史研究. No. 3, 1954.

Li En-han 李恩涵. *Wan-Ch'ing shou-hui k'uang-ch'üan yün-tung* 晚清收回礦權運動. Taipei, 1963.

Li Jui 李鋭. "Mao Tse-tung t'ung-chih ti ch'u-ch'i ko-ming huo-tung" 毛澤東同志的初期革命活動. *Chung-kuo ch'ing-nien* 中國青年, no. 13, 1953.

Li Kuei 李圭. *Huan-yu ti-ch'iu hsin-lu* 環遊地球新錄. In Wang Hsi-ch'i 王錫祺, comp. *Hsiao-fang-hu-chai yü-ti ts'ung-ch'ao* 小方壺齋輿地叢鈔, 12. Shanghai, c. 1897.

Li Kung-tso 李公佐. "Nan-k'o chi" 南柯記. In Chao-hsi 兆熙, comp., *T'ang-jen shuo-hui* 唐人説薈. N.p., 1864; and in Ma Chün-liang 馬駿良輯, comp. *Lung-wei pi-shu* 龍威秘書. Ta-yu shan-fang 大酉山房, 1794.

Li Kuo-ch'i 李國祁. *Chung-kuo chao-ch'i-ti t'ieh-lu ching-ying* 中國早期的鐵路經營. Taipei: Academia Sinica, Institute of Modern History monograph, 1961.

Li Shou-k'ung 李守孔. "Kuang-hsü wu-hsü ch'ien-hou ko-ming pao-huang liang p'ai chih kuan-hsi" 光緒戊戌前後革命保皇兩黨之關係. *Ta-lu tsa-chih* 大陸雜誌 [*The Continental Magazine*], vol. 25, nos. 1 and 2, July 15 and 31, 1962.

Li Ssu-han 李思涵. "Ch'ing-mo Chin-ling chi-ch'i-chü ti ch'uang-chien yü k'uo-chan" 清末金陵機器局的建設與擴展. *Ta-lu tsa-chih*, vol. 33, no. 12, Dec. 31, 1966.

Li Ta 李達. "Ma-k'e-ssu p'ai she-hui chu-i" 馬克思派社會主義. *Hsin ch'ing-nien*, vol. 9, no. 2, June, 1921.

Li Ta-chao 李大釗. "Wei-wu shih-kuan tsai hsien-tai shih-hsüeh-shang-ti chia-chih" 唯物史觀在現代史學上的價值. *Hsin ch'ing-nien*, vol. 8, no. 4, Dec. 1, 1920.

———. "Wo-ti ma-k'e-ssu chu-i kuan" 我的馬克思主義觀. *Hsin ch'ing-nien*, vol. 6, nos. 5, 6, May and Nov. 1919.

———. "Yu ching-chi-shang chieh-shih Chung-kuo chin-tai ssu-hsiang pien-tung ti yüan-yin" 由經濟上解釋中國近代思想變動的原因. *Hsin ch'ing-nien*, vol. 7, no. 2, Jan. 1, 1920.

Li T'i-mo-t'ai [Timothy Richard] 李提摩太. "Ch'iu ju chiu min shuo" 求儒救民説. In Yü Pao-hsüan, *Huang-ch'ao hsü-ai wen-pien*.

———. "Hsin cheng-ts'e" 新政策. *Wan Kwok Kung Pao*, no. 87, April 1898. Also in Ts'ai Erh-k'ang, ed., *Chung Tung chan chi*; and in Chien, vol. 3.

———. "Shih-shih hsin-lun" 時事新論. Shanghai, 1898.

Li Tse-hou 李澤厚. *K'ang Yu-wei T'an Ssu-t'ung ssu-hsiang yen-chiu* 康有爲譚嗣同思想研究. Shanghai, 1958.

———. "Lun Chung-kuo shih-chiu shih-chi kai-liang-p'ai pien-fa wei-hsin ssu-hsiang ti fa-chan" 論中國十九世紀改良派變法維新思想的發展. *Hsin chien-she* 新建設, no. 5, 1956.

———. "Lun K'ang Yu-wei ti che-hsüeh ssu-hsiang" 論康有爲的哲學思想. *Che-hsüeh yen-chiu* 哲學研究, vol. 1, no. 1, Feb. 1957.

Li Tuan-fen 李端棻. "Ch'ing t'ui-kuang hsüeh-hsiao che" 請推廣學校摺. In Chien, vol. 2.

Li Tz'u-ming 李慈銘. *Yüeh-man-t'ang jih-chi* 越縵堂日記. 51 *ts'e*, Peking, 1922. Includes: *Hsün-hsüeh-chai jih-chi* 荀學齋日記; *T'ao-hua-sheng-chieh-an jih-chi* 桃花聖解庵日記.

Liang Ch'i-ch'ao 梁啟超. *Ch'ing-tai hsüeh-shu kai-lun* 清代學術概論. Shanghai, 1921; 8th printing, 1930.

———. *Ho-chi, chuan-chi* and *Ho-chi, wen-chi*. See *Yin-ping-shih ho-chi*.

———, comp. *Hsi-cheng ts'ung-shu* 西政叢書. Shanghai, 1897. Includes: "*Hsi-cheng ts'ung-shu* hsü" 西政叢書序. Also in *Ho-chi, wen-chi*, 2.

———. *Hsi-hsüeh shu-mu piao* 西學書目表. *Sheng-shih-chi-chai ts'ung-shu* 慎始基齋叢書. N.p., 1897.

———. *Nan-hai K'ang hsien-sheng chuan* 南海康先生傳. Shanghai, 1908. In *Ho-chi, wen-chi*, 6; and in Chien, vol. 4.

———. *Wu-hsü cheng-pien chi* 戊戌政變記. Shanghai and Yokohama, 1899; Hong Kong and New York (16th printing), 1958; Taipei, 1959. Available in *Yin-ping-shih ho-chi, chuan-chi*, 1.

———. *Yin-ping-shih ho-chi* 飲冰室合集. Compiled by Lin Chih-chün 林志鈞. 40. vols. Shanghai, 1936. Includes: "Fu Chang Tung-sun shu lun she-hui chu-i yün-tung" 復張東蓀書論社會主義運動, *Wen-chi*, 36; "Hsin Chung-kuo chien-she wen-t'i" 新中國建設問題, *Wen-chi*, 27; "Hsin min shuo" 新民説, *Chuan-chi*, 4; "Jen-sheng-kuan yü k'o-hsüeh: tui-yü Chang Ting lun-chan ti p'i-p'ing" 人生觀與科學: 對於張丁論戰的批評. *Wen-chi*, 40; "K'ai-ming chuan-chih lun" 開明專制論, *Wen-chi*, 17; "K'o-hsüeh ching-shen yü Tung Hsi wen-hua" 科學精神與東西文化, *Wen-chi*, 39; "Kuan-yü hsüan-hsüeh k'o-hsüeh lun-chan chih 'chan-shih kuo-chi kung-fa'—tsan-shih chü-wai chung-li-jen Liang Ch'i-ch'ao hsüan-yen" 關於玄學科學論戰之 '戰時國際公法' —暫時局外中立人梁啟超宣言, *Wen-chi*, 40; "Lun hsüeh-hui" 論學會, *Wen-chi*, 1; "Ou-yu hsin-ying lu" 歐遊心影錄, *Chuan-chi*, 23; "Pao chiao fei shuo-i tsun-K'ung lun" 保教非所以尊孔論, *Wen-chi*, 9; "P'i fu-p'i lun" 闢復辟論, *Chuan-chi*, 33; "Pien-fa t'ung-i" 變法通議, *Wen-chi*, 1; "Shih-mo shih wen-hua" 什麼是文化, *Wen-chi*, 39; "Tai Tuan Ch'i-jui t'ao Chang Hsün fu-p'i t'ung-tien" 代段祺瑞討張勳復辟通電, *Wen-chi*, 35.

———. "Yü K'ang Yu-wei shu" 與康有爲書. In Chien, vol. 1.

Liang Chia-pin 梁嘉彬. *Kuang-tung shih-san hang k'ao* 廣東十三行考. Shanghai, 1937.

Liang Sou-ming 梁漱溟. "Chiu yüan chüeh i lun" 究源決疑論. *Tung-fang tsa-chih*, vol. 13, May, June, and July, 1916.

―――. *Tung-Hsi wen-hua chi ch'i che-hsüeh* 東西文化及其哲學. Shanghai, 1922; 8th printing, 1930.

Liao P'ing 廖平. "Kai wen ts'ung chih shuo" 改文從質説. In Yü Pao-hsüan, *Huang-ch'ao hsü-ai wen-pien*, vol. 6.

―――. *Ku-hsüeh k'ao* 古學考. Edited and preface by Chang Hsi-t'ang 張西堂 校點並序. Peiping, 1935.

―――. *Liu-i-kuan ts'ung-shu* 六譯館叢書. Ch'eng-tu, 1925. Includes: "Chih mou-jen shu" 致某人書; "Chih-sheng p'ien" 知聖篇; "P'i Liu p'ien" 闢劉篇; "Shih-chieh che-li chin-hua t'ui-hua" 世界哲理進化退化.

Lieh-tzu 列子. Shanghai: Hung-wen shu-chü, 1893. Includes: "Huang-ti" 黃帝; "T'ang wen" 湯問.

Lin K'e-kuang 林克光. "Lun *Ta-t'ung shu*" 論大同書. In *Chung-kuo chin-tai ssu-hsiang-chia yen-chiu lun-wen hsüan* 中國近代思想家研究論文選. Edited by Chung-kuo jen-min ta-hsüeh, Li-shih chiao-yen shih 中國人民大學，歷史教研室編. Peking, 1957.

Lin Yü-t'ang 林語堂. "Chi-ch'i yü ching-sheng" 機器與精神. In *Hu Shih wen-ts'un*, series 3, vol. 1.

―――. "Ku Hung-ming" 辜鴻銘. *Jen-chien-shih* 人間世, no. 12, Sept. 1934.

Ling Shuang [pseud.] 凌霜. "Ma-k'e-ssu hsüeh-shuo p'i-p'ing" 馬克思學説批評. *Hsin ch'ing-nien*, vol. 6, no. 5, May 1919.

Liu Hsü 劉昫. *Chiu T'ang-shu* 舊唐書. Shanghai: Chung-hua shu-chü, n.d.

Liu Feng-lu 劉逢祿. *Kung-yang Ch'un-ch'iu Ho-shih shih-li* 公羊春秋何氏釋例. In Juan Yüan, *Huang-Ch'ing ching-chieh;* see especially "Chang san-shih li" 張三世例.

Liu Kwang-ching 劉廣京. "T'ang T'ing-shu chih mai-pan shih-tai" 唐廷樞之買辦時代. *Tsing Hua Journal of Chinese Studies*, n.s., vol. 2, no. 2, June 1961.

Liu K'un-i 劉坤一. *Liu Chung-ch'eng-kung i-chi* 劉忠誠公遺集. N.p., 1909. Reprinted in *Chin-tai Chung-kuo shih-liao ts'ung-k'an*, compiled by Shen Yün-lung 沈雲龍. Vols. 251–257. Taipei, 1967. Includes: "Fu Fung Hsin-i" 復馮莘坨; "Fu Ou-yang Jun-sheng" 復歐陽潤生. *Shu-tu* 書牘 13 and 12.

Liu Ping-lin 劉秉麟. "Ma-k'e-ssu chuan-lüeh" 馬克思傳畧. *Hsin ch'ing-nien*, vol. 6, no. 5, May 1919.

"Lo Wen-chung hui Ch'ang hsien-sheng hsing-chuan" 羅文仲諱昌先生行狀. Manscript copy in Jung-pang Lo's collection.

Lu Hsün 魯迅. *See also* T'ang Ssu. *Lu Hsün ch'üan-chi* 魯迅全集. Shanghai (?), 1938; 2nd printing, 1946. Includes: "Ch'ing-nien pi-tu shu" 青年必讀書, vol. 3, *Hua-kai chi* 華蓋集; "Hsieh-tsai *Fen* hou-mien" 寫在「墳」後面, vol. 1, *Fen* 墳; "Mo lo shih-li shuo" 摩[訶波羅多]羅[摩衍那]詩力説, vol. 1; "Na-han tzu-hsü" 吶喊自序, vol. 1; "Wen-hua pien-chih lun" 文化偏至論, vol. 1.

―――. "Kuang-jen jih-chi" 狂人日記. *Hsin ch'ing-nien*, vol. 4, no. 5, May 1918.

Lu Nai-hsiang 陸乃翔, Lu Tun-k'uei 陸敦騤. *K'ang Nan-hai hsien-sheng chuan, shang-pien* 康南海先生傳，上編. Shanghai, 1929.

"Lun Chung-kuo pien-cheng ping-wu kuo-chi" 論中國變政並無過激. In Chien, vol. 3.

Ma Chien-chung 馬建忠. *Shih-k'o-chai chi-yen* 適可齋記言. In Liang Ch'i-ch'ao, *Hsi-cheng ts'ung-shu*. Includes: "Chieh chai i k'ai t'ieh-tao shuo" 借債以開鐵道說; "Fu min shuo" 富民說; "Ni-she fan-i shu-yüan i" 擬設翻譯書院議; "Shang Li po-hsiang yen ch'u-yang kung-k'o shu" 上李伯相言出洋功課書; "T'ieh-tao lun" 鐵道論.

Mai Chung-hua 麥仲華, comp. *Huang-ch'ao ching-shih-wen hsin-pien* 皇朝經世文新編. Shanghai, 1898.

―――. *Wu-hsü tsou-kao* 戊戌奏稿. N.p., 1911.

Mai Meng-hua 麥孟華. "Lun Chung-kuo i tsun chün-ch'üan i min-ch'üan" 論中國宜尊君權抑民權. In Chien, vol. 3.

Mao Chien-yü 毛健予. "Wen-t'i chieh-ta" 問題解答. *Hsin shih-hsüeh t'ung-hsün* 新史學通訊, May 1953.

―――. "Tsai wei-hsin pien-fa yün-tung kuo-ch'eng-chung K'ang Yu-wei wei-shih-mo chu *Hsin-hsüeh wei-ching k'ao K'ung-tzu kai-chih k'ao* ho *Ta-t'ung shu*" 在維新變法運動過程中康有為為什麼著新學偽經考和孔子改制考和大同書. *Hsin shih-hsüeh t'ung-hsün*, May 1953.

Mao-tun [Shen Yen-ping] 茅盾. *Tsui-ch'iu* 追求. Part 3 of *Shih* 蝕. Shanghai, 1930.

―――. "Tung-yao" 動搖. *Mao-tun wen-chi* 茅盾文集. Peking, 1958.

Mei-ying [pseud.] 梅影. "Wu-hsü cheng-pien chen-wen" 戊戌政變珍聞. *Jen-wen yüeh-k'an* 人文月刊, vol. 7, no. 10, Dec. 15, 1936.

Meng Ch'i 孟祁. "Chi Ku Hung-ming weng" 記辜鴻銘翁. *Jen-chien-shih*, no. 12, Sept. 1934.

Meng Wen-t'ung 蒙文通. "Ching-ycn Liao Chi-p'ing shih yü chin-tai Chin-wen-hsüeh" 井研廖季平師與近代今文學. *Ta-kung pao* 大公報, "Wen-hsüeh fu-k'an," no. 241 文學副刊, Aug. 15, 1932.

Miao Ch'üan-sun 繆荃孫編, comp. *Hsü pei-chuan chi* 續碑傳集. Chiang-ch'u pien-i shu-chü 江楚編譯書局, 1910.

Min pao 民報, facsimile reprint. Peking: K'o-hsüeh ch'u-pan she 科學出版社, 1957.

Miyazaki Torazō [Miyazaki Tōten] 宮崎寅藏 [宮崎滔天]. *Sanjūsan-nen no yume* 三十三年の夢. Tokyo, 1902; reprinted, Tokyo, 1943.

Mochizuki Shinkō 望月信亨. *Bukkyō daijiten* 佛教大辭典. Tokyo, 1936.

Onogawa Hidemi 小野川秀美. "Kō Yū-i no hempō ron" 康有為の變法論. *Kindai Chūgoku kenkyū*, no. 2 近代中國研究, 二輯, Tokyo, 1958.

―――. *Shimmatsu seiji shisō kenkyū* 清末政治思想研究. Kyoto, 1960.

Ou Chü-chia 歐榘甲. "Lun Chung-kuo pien-fa pi tzu fa-ming ching-hsüeh shih" 論中國變法必自發明經學始. *Chih-hsin pao*, no. 38.

Ou-yang Hsiu 歐陽修. *Hsin T'ang shu* 新唐書. Shanghai: Chung-hua shu-chü, n.d.

Pan Ku 班固. *Han shu* 漢書. Shanghai: Chung-hua shu-chü, n.d.

P'an Shu-fan 潘樹藩. *Chung-hua min-kuo hsien-fa shih* 中華民國憲法史. Shanghai, 1934.

Pao Tsun-p'eng 包遵彭, Li Ting-i 李定一, Wu Hsiang-hsiang 吳相湘, eds. 編. *Chung-kuo chin-tai-shih lun-ts'ung* 中國近代史論叢. 1st ser. 10 vols. Taipei, 1956.

P'eng Tse-i 彭澤益. "Chang Chien ti ssu-hsiang chi ch'i shih-yeh" 張謇的思想及其事業. *Tung-fang tsa-chih*, no. 40, July 1944.

P'i Hsi-jui 皮錫瑞. *Ching-hsüeh t'ung-lun* 經學通論. See especially, "Ch'un-ch'iu t'ung-lun" 春秋通論. Shanghai, 1923.

Sa Meng-wu et al. 薩孟武等. "Chung-kuo pen-wei wen-hua chien-she hsüan-yen" 中國本位文化建設宣言. *Wen-hua chien-she* 文化建設, vol. 1, no. 4, Jan.1935.

Shang Yang 商鞅. *Shang-chün shu* 商君書. Shanghai: Hung-wen shu-chü, n.d.

Shen Chien-shih 沈兼士. "Erh-t'ung kung-yü: ch'e-ti-ti fu-jen wen-t'i chieh-chüeh fa ch'u-fen hsin shih-chieh i-ch'ieh wen-t'i chih so-yüeh" 兒童公育：徹底的婦人問題解決法處分新世界一均問題之鑰鑰. *Hsin ch'ing-nien*, vol. 6, no. 6, Nov. 1919.

Shen Ts'ui-fen 沈粹芬輯, comp. *Kuo-ch'ao wen-hui* 國朝文匯. Shanghai, 1909.

Shen T'ung-sheng 沈桐生, comp. *Kuang-hsü cheng-yao* 光緒政要. Shanghai, 1909.

Shen Yün-ling 沈雲龍. *Hsien-tai cheng-chih jen-wu shu-p'ing*, rev. ed. 現代政治人物述評, 增定本. Taipei, 1967.

——. *K'ang Yu-wei p'ing-chuan* 康有為評傳. Taipei, 1969.

Sheng Hsüan-huai 盛宣懷. "T'iao-ch'en tzu-ch'iang ta-chi shu" 條陳自強大計疏. In Chien, vol. 2.

Shih Min-hsiung 施敏雄. *Ch'ing-tai ssu-chih kung-yeh ti fa-chan* 清代絲織工業的發展. Taipei, 1968.

Shu Hsin-ch'eng 舒新城. *Chin-tai Chung-kuo liu-hsüeh shih* 近代中國留學史. Shanghai, 1927.

Ssu Huang [Ch'en T'ien-hua] 思黃 [陳天華]. "Lun Chung-kuo i kai-ch'uang kung-ho cheng-t'i" 論中國宜改創共和政體. *Min pao*, no. 1, Nov. 1905.

Ssu-k'u ch'üan-shu tsung-mu t'i-yao. See Yung-yung.

Ssu-luan [pseud.] 嗣鸞. "Ku Hung-ming tsai Te-kuo" 辜鴻銘在德國. *Jen-chien-shih* 人間世, no. 12, Sept. 1934.

Ssu-ma Ch'ien 司馬遷. *Shih-chi* 史記. Shanghai: Chung-hua shu-chü, n.d.

Su Chi-tsu 蘇繼祖, comp. *Ch'ing-t'ing wu-hsü ch'ao-pien chi* 清廷戊戌朝變記. Chung-pa 中壩, 1931. In Chien, vol. 1.

Su-ch'ih [Chang Yin-lin] 素癡 [張蔭麟]. "K'ang Yu-wei wu-hsü cheng-pien chih hsin shih-liao" 康有為戊戌政變之新史料. *Ta-kung pao*, "Shih-ti chou-k'an," July 24, 1936.

Su Yü 蘇輿. *Ch'un-ch'iu fan-lu i-cheng* 春秋繁露義證. N.p., n.d.

——, comp. *I-chiao ts'ung-pien* 翼教叢編. Wu-ch'ang, 1898.

Sun Chia-nai 孫家鼐. "Tsou ch'ou-pan ta-hsüeh-t'ang ta-kai ch'ing-hsing che" 奏籌辦大學堂大概情形摺.

——. "I-fu k'ai-pan Ching-shih ta-hsüeh-t'ang che" 議復開辦京師大學堂摺.

——. "Tsou . . . ch'ing yen-chin pei-shu shu" 奏 . . . 請嚴禁悖書疏. All of these three articles are available in Chien, vol. 2.

Sun Lin-sheng 孫麟生. "Wei-shih-mo yao fa-yang Chung-kuo wen-hua?" 爲什麼要發揚中國文化. *Hsin t'ien ti* 新天地, vol. 3, no. 10, Dec. 1, 1963.

Sun Wen [Sun Yat-sen] 孫文 [孫逸仙]. "Chien-kuo fang-lüeh" 建國方畧. *Kuo-fu ch'üan-chi*, vol. 2. Taipei: Cheng-chung wen-k'u ed. 正中文庫, 1954.

―――. *Kuo-fü ch'üan-chi* 國父全集. 6 vols. Chung-yang t'ang-shih shih-liao pien-tsuan wei-yüan-hui 中央黨史史料編纂委員會編輯. Rev. ed., 1957; 2nd ed., Taipei, 1961. Virtually the same material is included in *Sun Chung-shan ch'üan-shu* 孫中山全書. Shanghai: Kuang-i shu-chü, 2nd printing, 1937. *Kuo-fu ch'üan-shu* includes: "Chih-ting Chien-kuo ta-kang hsüan-yen" 制定建國大綱宣言; "Cheng-chien chih piao-shih" 政見之表示; "Chi Lieh-ning wen" 祭列寧文; "Chien-she i hsiu-chih tao-lu wei ti-i yao-cho" 建設以修治道路爲第一要義; "Ch'ien-pi ko-ming" 錢幣革命; "Chung-hua ko-ming shih" 中華革命史; "Chung-kuo chih ti-erh pu" 中國之第二步; "Chung-kuo chih t'ieh-lu chi-hua yü min-sheng chu-i" 中國之鐵路計劃與民生主義; "Chung-kuo kuo-min-tang hsüan-yen" 中國國民黨宣言; "Chung-kuo pi hsien ko-ming erh-hou neng ta kung-ho chu-i" 中國必先革命而後能達共和主義; "Chung-kuo shih-yeh tang ju-ho fa-chan" 中國實業當如何發展; "Hsing-fa shih-yeh wei chiu p'in chih yao-chi" 興發實業爲救貧之藥劑; "Hsiu-chu t'ieh-lu nai Chung-hua min-kuo ts'un-wang chih ta wen-t'i" 修築鐵路乃中華民國存亡之大問題; "Ko-ming ch'eng-kung ko-jen pu-neng yu tzu-yu" 革命成功箇人不能有自由; "Kuo-chi kung-t'ung fa-chan Chung-kuo shih-yeh chi-hua" 國際共同發展中國實業計劃; "Kuo-min cheng-fu chien-kuo ta-kang" 國民政府建國大綱; "Kuo-min-tang cheng-chien hsüan-yen" 國民黨政見宣言; "Lun ch'ou-chu t'ieh-lu shih chih Sung Chiao-jen han" 論籌築鐵路事致宋教仁函; "Po Pao-huang pao" 駁保皇報; "San-min chu-i yü Chung-kuo min-tsu chih ch'ien-t'u" 三民主義與中國民族之前途; "Shih-hsien t'ien-lu cheng-ts'e hsü ch'ü k'ai-fang men-hu chu-i" 實現鐵路政策須取開放門戶主義; "Shih-yeh chi-hua" 實業計劃; "Su hsiu t'ieh-lu i li fu-ch'iang chih chi" 速修鐵路以立富強之基; "Sun Wen hsüeh-shuo" 孫文學說; "Ti-fang tzu-chih k'ai-shih shih-hsing fa" 地方自治開始實行法; "Ti-fang tzu-chih wei chien-kuo chih ch'u-shih" 地方自治爲建國之礎石; "Tsai-fu Li Ts'un-nung lun wai-chai shu" 再復李村農論外債書; "Tzu-chih" 自傳.

―――. "Min pao fa-k'an tz'u" 民報發刊詞. *Min pao*, no. 1, Oct. 1905.

Sun Yü-t'ang 孫毓棠編, comp. *Chung-kuo chin-tai kung-i-shih tzu-liao*, 1st. ser., 2 vols. 中國近代工藝史資料, 第一輯. Shanghai, 1957.

―――, comp. *Chung-kuo ching-chi-shih tzu-liao*, 1st ser. 中國經濟史資料, 第一輯. 2 vols. Peking, 1957.

Sung Yüan Ming Ch'ing ssu-ch'ao hsüeh-an 宋元明清四朝學案. 4 vols. Vols. 1 and 2: Huang Tsung-hsi 黃宗羲, and Ch'üan Tsu-wang 全祖望, *Sung Yüan hsüeh-an* 宋元學案; vol. 3: Huang Tsung-hsi, *Ming-ju hsüeh-an* 明儒學案; vol. 4: Chiang Fan 江藩, *Han-hsüeh shih-ch'eng chi* 漢學師承記, and *Sung-hsüeh yüan-yüan chi* 宋學淵源記; and T'ang Chien 唐鑑, *Ch'ing hsüeh-an hsiao-chih* 清學案小識.

Sung Yün-pin 宋雲彬. *K'ang Yu-wei* 康有爲. Shanghai, 1951.

Ta-Ch'ing li-ch'ao shih-lu, Kuang-hsü 大清歷朝實錄, 光緒.

Tai Chen 戴震. *Meng-tzu tzu-i shu-cheng* 孟子字義疏證. Taipei: Shih-chieh wen-k'u ed. 世界文庫本, 1959.

T'an Ssu-t'ung 譚嗣同. "Chieh-shuo" 界說. *Jen-hsüeh* 仁學. Shanghai, 1917; in *T'an Liu-yang ch'üan-chi* 譚瀏陽全集. 4th printing, Shanghai, 1925.

T'ang Chen 湯震. "Chung hsüeh" 中學. *Wei yen* 危言. Shanghai, 1890.

T'ang Chih-chün 湯志鈞. "Kuan-yü K'ang Yu-wei ti *Ta-t'ung shu*" 關於康有爲的「大同書」. *Wen-shih-che* 文史哲, no. 1, 1957.

———. *Wu-hsü pien-fa chien-shih* 戊戌變法簡史. Peking, 1960.

———. *Wu-hsü pien-fa jen-wu chuan kao* 戊戌變法人物傳稿. 2 vols. Shanghai, 1961.

———. *Wu-hsü pien-fa-shih lun* 戊戌變法史論. Shanghai, 1955.

———. *Wu-hsü pien-fa-shih lun-ts'ung* 戊戌變法史論叢. Wu-han, 1957. Includes: "K'ang Yu-wei ti hsin-cheng chien-i ho Kuang-hsü-ti ti hsin-cheng shang-yü" 康有爲的新政建議和光緒帝的新政上諭; "Wu-hsü pien-fa shih ti hsüeh-hui ho pao-k'an" 戊戌變法時的學會和報刊.

T'ang Ssu [Lu Hsün] 唐俟 [魯迅]. "Wo-chih chieh-lieh kuan" 我之節烈觀. *Hsin ch'ing-nien*, vol. 5, no. 2, Aug. 1918.

———. "Sui-kan lu" 隨感錄. *Hsin ch'ing-nien*, vol. 5, no. 5, Oct. 1918.

T'ao Ch'ien 陶潛. "T'ao-hua-yüan chi" 桃花源記. *Ching-chieh hsien-sheng chi* 靖節先生集. Chiang-su shu-chü 江蘇書局, 1883.

T'ao Mu 陶模. "Fu-ch'en tzu-ch'iang ta-chi shu" 覆陳自強大計疏. In Chien, vol. 2.

Te-tsung shih-lu. See Ch'en Pao-chen.

Ting Wen-chiang 丁文江. "Hsüan-hsüeh yü k'o-hsüeh" 玄學與科學. In *K'o-hsüeh yü jen-sheng-kuan*, vol. 1. Shanghai, 1923.

———, ed. *Liang Jen-kung hsien-sheng nien-p'u ch'ang-pien ch'u-kao* 梁任公先生年譜長編初稿. 3 vols. Taipei: Shih chieh shu-chü, 1958.

T'o-t'o et al. 脫脫等. *Sung shih* 宋史. Shanghai: Chung-hua shu-chü, n.d.

Ts'ai Erh-k'ang 蔡爾康, ed. *Chung Tung chan chi* 中東戰紀, 三編. Shanghai, 1897.

Ts'ai Shang-ssu 蔡尚思. *Chung-kuo ch'uan-t'ung ssu-hsiang tsung p'i-p'an* 中國傳統思想總批判. Shanghai, 1941; 2nd printing, 1950.

Ts'ai Yüan-p'ei 蔡元培. "Lu Hsün hsien-sheng ch'üan-chi hsü" 魯迅先生全集序. In *Lu Hsün ch'üan-chi*, 1st ed.

Tseng Hsieh-kang [Tseng Chi-tse] 曾頡剛 [曾紀澤]. "Hsi-hsüeh lüeh-shu hsü" 西學畧述序. *Wan Kwok Kung Pao*, vol. 1, no. 5, June 1889.

Tseng Kuo-fan 曾國藩. *Tseng Wen-cheng-kung jih-chi* 曾文正公日記. In *Tseng Wen-cheng-kung ch'üan-chi* 曾文正公全集. Shanghai, 1928, reprint of the 1876 Ch'uan-chung shu-chü 傳忠書局 edition. Includes: *Ch'iu-ch'üeh chai jih-chi* 求闕齋日記. Edited by Wang Ting-an.

Tseng Lien 曾廉. "Ying chao shang feng-shih" 應詔上封事. In Chien, vol. 2.

Tso-chuan cheng-i 左傳正義. In Juan Yüan, *Shih-san-ching chu-shu* ed., Taipei reprint, 1959.

Tsuchiya Takao 土屋喬雄. *Nihon no keieisha seishin* 日本の經營者精神. Tokyo, 1959.

Ts'un-t'ung [pseud.] 存統. "Ma-k'e-ssu ti kung-ch'an chu-i" 馬克思底共產主義. *Hsin ch'ing-nien*, vol. 9, no. 4, Aug. 1921.

Tung Chung-shu 董仲舒. *Ch'un-ch'iu fan-lu* 春秋繁露 Pao-ching-t'ang ed. 抱經堂本; 1893; reprinted, Shanghai: Hung-wen shu-chü, 1893. Includes: "Ch'u Chuang-wang" 楚莊王; "San-tai kai chih chih-wen" 三代改制質文; "Shen ch'a ming-hao" 深察名號; "Wei jen che t'ien" 爲人者天.

Wan Kwok Kung Pao 萬國公報. Shanghai, 1868–1904. Microfilm copy made from the original in The Hannold Library, Claremont, California.

Wang Chao 王照. *Fang-chia-yüan tsa-yung chi-shih* 方家國雜詠記事. N.p., 1928. Also in *Shui-tung-chi ch'u-kao* 水東集初稿, Wang-shih chia-k'e 王氏家刻, 1931.

Wang Ch'i-chü 王其榘, comp. "Hsüeh-hui teng tsu-chih" 學會等組織. In Chien, vol. 4.

Wang Ching-wei 汪精衛. "Min-tsu-ti kuo-min" 民族的國民. *Min pao*, no. 2, Nov. 1905.

Wang Ching-yü 汪敬虞編, comp. *Chung-kuo chin-tai kung-yeh-shih tzu-liao*, 2nd ser. 中國近代工業史資料, 第二輯. 1895–1914. 2 vols. Peking, 1957.

Wang Erh-min 王爾敏. *Ch'ing-ping-kung-yeh ti hsing-ch'i* 清季兵工業的興起. Taipei, 1963.

———. "Ch'ing-chi ping-kung-yeh lüeh-lun" 清季兵工業畧論. *Ta-lu tsa-chih* 大陸雜誌, vol. 35, no. 9, Nov. 15, 1967.

Wang Hsien-ch'ien 王先謙編, comp. *Huang-Ch'ing ching-chieh hsü-pien* 皇清經解續編. Chiang-yin: Nan-ch'ing shu-yüan 江陰: 南菁書院, 1888.

Wang Shou-jen 王守仁. *Wang Wen-ch'eng-kung ch'üan-shu* 王文成公全書. 4 vols. Shanghai: Kuo-hsüeh chi-pen ts'ung-shu ed. 國學基本叢書, 1936; Taipei: Cheng-chung shu-chü 正中書局, n.d.; Ssu-pu ts'ung-k'an ed. 四部叢刊, Shanghai: Commercial Press, n.d. Also in *Yang-ming ch'üan-chi* 陽明全集, Ssu-pu pei-yao ed. 四部備要, Shanghai: Chung-hua shu-chü, n.d. Includes: "Ch'uan-hsi lu" 傳習錄; "*Ta-hsüeh* wen" 大學問; "Ta Ku Tung-ch'iao shu" 答顧東橋書.

Wang Shu-huai 王樹槐. *Wai-jen yü wu-hsü pien-fa* 外人與戊戌變法. Taipei: Academia Sinica, Institute of Modern History monograph no. 12, 1965.

Wang T'ao 王韜. *T'ao-yüan wen-lu wai-pien* 韜園文錄外編. Hong Kong, 1883. *Chüan* 1 includes "Yüan jen" 原仁, "Yüan tao" 原道.

Washio Yoshinao 鷲尾義直. *Inukai Mokudō den* 犬養木堂傳. 3 vols. Tokyo, 1938–39.

Wei Shou 魏收. *Wei shu* 魏書. Shanghai: Chung-hua shu-chü, n.d.

Wei Yüan 魏源. *Ch'un-ch'iu fan-lu chu* 春秋繁露注; *Kung-yang ku-wei* 公羊古徵. *Huang-Ch'ing ching-chieh hsü-pien*.

Wei-lien-ch'en [Alexander Williamson] 韋廉臣. "Chih kuo yao wu" 治國要務. *Wan Kwok Kung Pao*, vol. 1, no. 4, May 1889.

Wen-t'i 文悌. "Yen ts'an K'ang Yu-wei che" 嚴參康有爲摺. In Chien, vol. 2.

Weng T'ung-ho 翁同龢. *Weng Wen-kung-kung jih-chi* 翁文恭公日記. 40 vols. Shanghai, 1925.

Wu Chih-hui [Wu Ching-heng] 吳稚暉 [吳敬恆]. *I ko hsin-hsin-yang-ti yü-chou-kuan chi jen-sheng-kuan* 一箇新信仰的字宙觀及人生觀. Nanking: Huang-p'u hsiao ts'ung-shu 黃埔小叢書, 1927.

————. *Wu Chih-hui hsien-sheng wen-ts'ui* 吳稚暉先生文粹. Edited by Yo Ch'in 樂勤編. 4 vols. Shanghai, 1929. Includes: "Chen yang-pa-ku-hua chih li-hsüeh" 箴洋八股化之理學, vol. 3; "Chi-ch'i ch'u-chin ta-t'ung shuo" 機器促進大同説, vol. 2; "Ch'ing-nien yü kung-chü" 青年與工具, vol. 2; "*K'o-hsüeh chou-pao* fa-k'an yü" 科學週報發刊語, vol. 2; "*K'o-hsüeh chou-pao* pien-chi hua" 科學週報編輯話, vol. 2; "K'o-hsüeh yü jen-sheng kuan" 科學與人生觀, vol. 2; "P'ing Chü-p'u chün 'Nan-nü tsa-chiao shuo' " 評鞠普君「男女雜交説」; "T'an wu-cheng-fu chu-i hsien-t'ien" 談無政府主義閑天, vol. 2.

————. *Wu Chih-hui wen-chi* 吳稚暉文集. Shanghai, 1936.

Wu Hsiang-hsiang 吳相湘. *Min-kuo cheng-chih jen-wu* 民國政治人物. Taipei, 1964. Includes: "K'ang Liang yü fu-p'i yün-tung" 康梁與復辟運動.

Wu Hsien-tzu [Wu Chuang] 伍憲子 [伍莊]. *Chung-kuo min-chu hsien-cheng-tang tang-shih* 中國民主憲政黨黨史. San Francisco: *Shih-chieh jih-pao* (*The Chinese World*) 世界日報, ca. 1963.

Wu Tse 吳澤. *K'ang Yu-wei yü Liang Ch'i-ch'ao* 康有爲與梁啓超. Shanghai, 1948.

Wu Yü 吳虞. "Chia-tsu chih-tu wei chuan-chih chu-i chih ken-chü lun" 家族制度爲專制主義之根據論. *Hsin ch'ing-nien*, vol. 2, no. 6, Feb. 1917.

————. *Wu Yü wen-lu* 吳虞文錄. Shanghai, 1921; 4th printing, 1925.

————. *Wu Yü wen hsü-lu* 吳虞文續錄. Chengtu, 1933. Includes: "Tui-yü ssu-K'ung wen-t'i chih wo-chien" 對於祀孔問題之我見.

Yang Fu-li 楊復禮. *K'ang Liang nien-p'u kao-pen* 康梁年譜稿本. 3 vols. Completed in 1928. Mimeographed.

Yang-wu yün-tung. *See* Chung-kuo shih-hsüeh hui.

Yano Jin'ichi 矢野仁一. "Bojutsu no hempō oyobi seihen" 戊戌の變法及び政變. *Shirin* 史林, vol. 8, nos. 1, 2, 3. Kyoto, 1923.

Yeh Te-hui 葉德輝. "Ch'ang-hsing hsüeh-chi po-i" 長興學記駁議. In Su Yü, *I-chiao ts'ung-pien.*

————. *Chüeh-mi yao-lu* 覺迷要錄. Ch'ang-sa (?), 1905.

————. "Ta yu-jen shu" 答友人書; "Yu-hsüan chin-yü p'ing" 輶軒今語評; "Yü Hsü K'o-shih kuan-ch'a shu" 與許恪士觀察書; "Yü Liu Hsien-tuan Huang Yu-wen liang sheng shu" 與劉先端黃郁文兩生書; "Yü Nan-hsüeh hui P'i Lu-men hsiao-lien shu" 與南學會皮鹿門孝廉書; "Yü Shih Tsui-liu shu" 與石醉六書; "Yü Tuan Po-yu mou-ts'ai shu" 與段伯猷茂才書. All in Su Yü, *I-chiao ts'ung-pien.*

Yen Chung-p'ing 嚴中平編, comp. *Chung-kuo chin-tai ching-chi-shih t'ung-chi tzu-liao hsüan-chi* 中國近代經濟史統計資料選輯. Peking, 1955.

————. *Chung-kuo mien-yeh chih fa-chan* 中國棉業之發展. Chungking, 1943.

————. *Chung-kuo mien fang-chih shih-kao* 中國棉紡織史稿. Peking, 1955.

Yen Fu 嚴復, trans. *Heh-hsü-li, T'ien-yen lun* (Huxley, *Evolution and Ethics*) 赫胥黎天演論. Preface dated 1896. Shanghai: Commercial Press, 1930.

———. "Chiu wang chüeh lun" 救亡決論. In Chien, vol. 3.

———. "Yü Hsiung Shun-ju shu" 與熊純如書. In Chien, vol. 2.

———. "Yüan ch'iang" 原強. *Yen Chi-tao wen-ch'ao* 嚴幾道文鈔. Shanghai, 1898; *Yen Chi-tao hsien-sheng i-chu* 嚴幾道先生遺著. Singapore, 1959.

Yen Hsi-shan 閻錫山. "K'ung-tzu shih ko shih-mo chia?" 孔子是什麼家. *Chih Chin cheng-wu ch'üan-shu* 治晉政務全書. 12 vols. Taipei, 1960.

———. *Shih-chieh ta-t'ung* 世界大同. Taipei, 1960.

Yen Hsiu 嚴修. "Tsou-ch'ing she ching-chi chuan-k'o che" 奏請設經濟專科摺. In Chien, vol. 2.

Yung-yung et al. 永瑢等. *Ssu-k'u ch'üan-shu tsung-mu t'i-yao* 四庫全書總目提要. Shanghai: Wan-yu wen-k'u ed. 萬有文庫: 1931.

Yü Pao-hsüan 于寶軒編, comp. *Huang-ch'ao hsü-ai wen-pien* 皇朝蓄艾文編. Shanghai, 1903.

Yüan Ch'ang 袁昶. "I-fu chi-yü shih-chien t'iao-ch'en" 議復寄論事件條陳. In Chien, vol. 2.

Yüan Chen-ying 袁振英. "Ku Hung-ming hsien-sheng ti ssu-hsiang" 辜鴻銘先生的思想. *Jen-chien-shih* 人間世, no. 34, Aug. 1935.

C. Books and Articles in Western Languages

Abbeglan, James C. *The Japanese Factory: Aspects of Its Social Organization.* Glencoe, Ill.: Free Press of Glencoe, 1958.

Aisin-Gioro Pu Yi. *From Emperor to Citizen.* (English version of *Wo-ti ch'ien-pan sheng*). Peking: Foreign Languages Press, 1964.

Alexander, Robert J. *A Primer of Economic Development.* New York: Macmillan Co., 1962.

Allen, George Cyril. *Japan's Economic Expansion.* London and New York: Oxford University Press, 1965.

———. *A Short Economic History of Modern Japan, 1867–1937.* Rev. ed. London and New York: Allen and Unwin, 1962.

———. and Donnithorne, Audrey G. *Western Enterprise in Far Eastern Economic Development: China and Japan.* London: Allen and Unwin; New York: Macmillan Co., 1954.

The Analects of Confucius. Translated by Arthur Waley. London: Allen and Unwin; New York: Macmillan Co., 1938.

Apter, David E. *The Politics of Modernization.* Chicago: University of Chicago Press, 1965.

Aquinas, Saint Thomas. *The Basic Writings.* Edited by A. C. Pegis. New York: Random House, 1945.

Aristotle. *Metaphysics.* Translated by John Warrington. New York: J. M. Dent, Everyman's Library, 1913.

———. *On the Heavens.* Translated by K. C. Guthrie. Cambridge, Mass.: Loeb Classical Library, 1939.

Ashton, T. S. *The Industrial Revolution, 1760–1830.* New York: Oxford University Press, 1948.

de Bary, William, Wing-tsit Chan, and Burton Watson, eds. and trans. *Sources of Chinese Tradition.* New York: Columbia University Press, 1960.

Bashford, James W. *China, an Interpretation.* New York and Cincinnati, 1916. 3rd. ed. New York: Abingdon Press, 1919.

Baudet, Henri. *Paradise on Earth: Some Thoughts on European Images of Non-European Man.* Translated by Elizabeth Wentholt. New Haven and London: Yale University Press, 1965.

Becker, Carl Lotus. *The Heavenly City of the Eighteenth-Century Philosophers.* New Haven: Yale University Press, 1932.

Bellah, Robert N. *Tokugawa Religion: The Values of Pre-Industrial Japan.* Glencoe, Ill.: Free Press, 1957.

Bennett, Arthur. *John Fryer: The Introduction of Western Science and Technology into Nineteenth-Century China.* Harvard East Asian Monograph, no. 24. Cambridge, Mass.: Harvard University Press, 1967.

Beresford, Lord Charles William de la Poer. *The Break-up of China, with an account of its present commerce, currency, waterways, armies, railways, politics, and future prospects.* New York and London: Harper and Bros., 1900.

Bergson, Henri. *Creative Evolution.* Translated by Arthur Mitchell. New York: Henry Holt & Co., The Modern Library, 1911; Random House, 1944.

———. *The Two Sources of Morality and Religion.* Translated by Ashley Audra and Cloudesley Brereton, assisted by W. Horsfall Carter. New York: Doubleday, 1935.

Bernard, Henri. "Notes on the Introduction of the Natural Sciences into the Chinese Empire." *Yenching Journal of Social Studies,* vol. 3, no. 2 (Aug. 1941).

Berneri, Marie Louise. *Journey Through Utopia.* London: Routledge and Paul, 1950.

Berrill, Kenneth, ed. *Economic Development with Special Reference to East Asia.* Proceedings of a Conference held by the International Economic Association. New York: St. Martin's Press, 1964.

Bhagwati, Jagdish. *The Economics of Underdeveloped Countries.* London: World University Library; New York: McGraw-Hill Book Co., 1966.

Biggerstaff, Knight. *The Earliest Modern Government Schools in China.* Ithaca, N.Y.: Cornell University Press, 1961.

———. "The T'ung Wen Kuan." *Chinese Social and Political Science Review* (Peking) vol. 18 (1934).

Bingham, Woodbridge, Hilary Conroy, and Frank W. Iklé. *A History of Asia.* 2 vols. Boston: Allyn and Bacon, 1965.

Blacker, Carmen. *The Japanese Enlightenment: A Study of the Writings of Fukuzawa Yukichi.* Cambridge, Mass.: Harvard University Press, 1964.

Blakney, R. B., trans. *The Way of Life.* New York: New American Library; London: Muller, 1955.

Bland, John O. P. and Edmund Backhouse. *China under the Empress Dowager: Being the History of the Life and Times of Tz'u Hsi.* Philadelphia, 1910. 2nd ed. Peking: N. Vetch, 1939.

Boorman, Howard L., and Richard C. Howard, eds. *Biographical Dictionary of Republican China,* vols. 1, 2. New York: Columbia University Press, 1968.

Borton, Hugh. *Japan's Modern Century.* New York: Ronald Press, 1955.

Bourne, F. D. A. "Possible and Impossible Reforms." *Journal of the North China Branch of the Royal Asiatic Society,* n.s., vol. 33 (1900–1901).

Brière, O., S. J. *Fifty Years of Chinese Philosophy, 1899–1950.* Translated by Laurence G. Thompson. London: Allen and Unwin, 1956.

Broadbridge, Seymour. *Industrial Dualism in Japan. A Problem of Economic Growth and Structural Change.* Chicago: Aldine Publishing Co., 1966.

Brunnert, H. S. and V. V. Hagelstrom. *Present Day Political Organization of China.* Peking, 1911. Reprinted, Hong Kong, n.d.

Bryce, James. *Modern Democracies.* 2 vols. New York: Macmillan Co., 1921.

Cameron, Meribeth Elliot. *The Reform Movement in China, 1898–1912.* Stanford: Stanford University Press, 1931.

Cecil, Gascoyne (assisted by Lady Florence Cecil). *Changing China.* London: J. Nisbet, 1912.

Chan, Wing-tsit, trans. *The Way of Lao-tzu.* Indianapolis: Bobbs-Merrill Co., 1963.

Chang, Carsun. *The Development of Neo-Confucian Thought.* 2 vols. New York: Bookman Associates, 1957, 1962.

————. "Reflections on the Philosophical Controversy in 1923." *The Chung Chi Journal* (Hong Kong), vol. 3, no. 1 (Nov. 1963).

Chang, Chung-li. *The Chinese Gentry: Studies on their Role in Nineteenth-Century China.* Seattle: University of Washington Press, 1955.

————. *The Income of the Chinese Gentry. A Sequel to The Chinese Gentry: Studies on their Role in Nineteenth-Century China.* Seattle: University of Washington Press, 1962.

Chang, John K. "Industrial Development of China, 1912–1949." *Journal of Economic History,* vol. 27, no. 1 (March 1967).

Chang, Kia-ngau. *China's Struggle for Railroad Development.* New York: John Day Co., 1943.

Chang, P'eng. "The Professional Merchants in China, 1842–1911." Ph.D. dissertation, University of Washington, Seattle, 1958.

Ch'en, Ch'i-t'ien [Gideon Chen]. *Modern Industrial Technique in China.* Peiping: Yenching University, 1934–1935.

————. *Tso Tsung-t'ang, Pioneer Promoter of the Modern Dockyard and the Woolen Mill in China.* Peiping: Paragon Press, 1938.

Chen, Chi-yun. "Liang Ch'i-ch'ao's 'Missionary Education': A Case Study of Missionary Influence on the Reformers." Harvard University East Asian Research Center. *Papers on China,* vol. 16 (1962).

Cheng Lin. *The Chinese Railways: An Historical Survey*. Shanghai: China United Press, 1935.

Cheng, Shelley H. "The T'ung-men-hui: Its Organization, Leadership, and Finance, 1905–1912." Ph.D. dissertation, University of Washington, 1962.

Cheng, T'ien-hsi. *China Molded by Confucius. The Chinese Way in Western Light*. London: Stevens and Sons, 1947.

Chiang, Monlin. *Tides from the West: A Chinese Autobiography*. New Haven: Yale University Press, 1947.

Ch'ien, Tuan-sheng. *The Government and Politics of China*. Cambridge, Mass.: Harvard University Press, 1950.

Chinard, Gilbert, ed. *The Correspondence of Jefferson and Du Pont de Nemours*. With an Introduction on Jefferson and the Physiocrats. Baltimore: John Hopkins Press, 1931.

The Chinese Classics. Translated by James Legge. 5 vols. 2nd ed. Hong Kong: Hong Kong University Press, 1960.

Chow, Tse-tsung. *The May Fourth Movement: Intellectual Revolution in Modern China*. Cambridge, Mass.: Harvard University Press, 1960.

Chu, Samuel C. *Reformer in Modern China: Chang Chien, 1853–1926*. New York and London: Columbia University Press, 1965.

Ch'u, Ta-kao, trans. *Tao-te Ching*. London: The Buddhist Society, 1937; reprinted, 1948.

Ch'ü, T'ung-tsu. *Law and Society in Traditional China*. Paris and The Hague: Mouton, 1961.

————. *Local Government in China under the Ch'ing*. Cambridge, Mass.: Harvard University Press, 1962.

Ch'ü Yüan. *Li Sao and other Poems of Ch'ü Yüan*. Translated by Yang Hsien-yi and Gladys Yang. Peking: Foreign Languages Press, 1955.

Cohen, Paul A. *China and Christianity. The Missionary Movement and the Growth of Chinese Antiforeignism, 1860–1870*. Cambridge, Mass.: Harvard University Press, 1963.

The Contemporary Review, vol. 76, July–December, 1899. London: A. Strahan.

Creel, H. G. *Confucius and the Chinese Way*. New York: Harper, 1960. (Published in 1949 by John Day as *Confucius: The Man and the Myth*.)

Dai, Shen-yu. "Mao Tse-tung and Confucianism." Ph.D. dissertation, University of Pennsylvania, 1953. Ann Arbor, Michigan, University Microfilms, 1953.

Davidson, Martha. *A List of Published Translations from Chinese into English, French, and German*. Part I. Literature. Tentative edition. Washington, D.C.: American Council of Learned Societies, 1952.

Davies, Godfrey. *The Early Stuarts, 1603–1660*. Oxford: Clarendon Press, 1937.

Der Ling. *Two Years in the Forbidden City*. New York: Dodd, 1929.

Descartes, René. *The Philosophical Works of Descartes.* Translated by E. S. Haldane and G. R. T. Ross. Cambridge: Cambridge University Press, 1931.

Doig, Peter. *A Concise History of Astronomy.* New York: Philosophical Library, 1951.

Dubs, Homer H. "The Failure of the Chinese to Produce Philosophical Systems." *T'oung Pao,* ser. 2, vol. 26. Leiden: E. J. Brill, 1929.

————, trans. *The Works of Hsüntze.* London: Arthur Probsthain, 1928.

Dunning, W. A. *A History of the Political Theories from Rousseau to Spencer.* New York: Macmillan Co., 1922.

Duyvendak, J. J. L., trans. *The Book of Lord Shang.* London: Arthur Probsthain, 1928; Chicago: University of Chicago Press, 1963.

————, trans. *Tao Te Ching: The Book of the Way and Its Virtue.* London: John Murray, 1954.

Elwes, R. H. M., trans. *The Ethics of Spinoza.* London: M. W. Dunne, 1919.

Engels, Friedrich. *Socialism: Utopian and Scientific.* Translated by Edward Aveling. Chicago: C. H. Kerr, 1905.

England, F. E. *Kant's Conception of God. A Critical Exposition of Its Metaphysical Development.* London: Allen and Unwin, 1929.

Fairbank, John K. *The United States and China.* 1948. Rev. ed. Cambridge, Mass.: Harvard University Press, 1958.

Fang, Hsien-t'ing. *China's Industrialization: A Statistical Survey.* Shanghai: China Institute of Pacific Relations, 1931.

Ferm, Vergilius, ed. *An Encyclopedia of Religion.* New York: Philosophical Library, 1945.

Feuerwerker, Albert. *China's Early Industrialization. Sheng Hsüan-huai (1844–1916) and Mandarin Enterprise.* Cambridge, Mass.: Harvard University Press, 1958.

————. *The Chinese Economy, 1912–1949.* Michigan Papers in Chinese Studies, no. 1. Ann Arbor: University of Michigan Center for Chinese Studies, 1968.

————. "Industrial Enterprise in Twentieth-Century China: The Chee Hsin Cement Co." In *Approaches to Modern Chinese History,* edited by Albert Feuerwerker, Rhoads Murphey, and Mary C. Wright. Berkeley and Los Angeles: University of California Press, 1967.

Forke, Alfred. *Geschichte der neueren chinesischen Philosophie.* Hamburg: De Gruyter and Co., 1938.

Franke, Otto. "Der Ursprung der Reformbewegung in China." *Ostasiatische Neubildungen,* pp. 20–35. Hamburg, 1911.

————. "Was lehrt uns die ostasiatische Geschichte der letzen fünfzig Jahre?" *Ostasiatische Neubildungen,* pp. 70–71. Hamburg, 1911.

Franke, Wolfgang. *Chinas kulturelle Revolution: Die Bewegung vom 4 Mai, 1919.* Munich: R. Oldenbourg, 1957.

————. "Der Kampf der chinesischen Revolution gegen den Konfuzian-ismus," *Gesellschaft für Natur- und Völkerkünde Ostasiens. Nachrichten*, 74. Hamburg, 1953.

————. "Die staatspolitischen Reformsversuche K'ang Yu-weis und seiner Schule." *Mitteilungen des Seminars für Orientalische Sprachen an der Universität Berlin, Ostasiatische Studien* 38. Berlin, 1935.

Fryer, John. *Admission of Chinese Students to American Colleges*. Washington, D.C.: United States Government Printing Office, 1909.

Fukutake, Tadashi. *Asian Rural Society: China, India, Japan*. Seattle: University of Washington Press, 1967.

Fung Yu-lan. *A History of Chinese Philosophy*. Translated by Derk Bodde. 2 vols. Princeton: Princeton University Press, 1953.

Furth, Charlotte. *Ting Wen-chiang: Science and China's New Culture*. Harvard East Asian Series, no. 42. Cambridge, Mass.: Harvard University Press, 1970.

Galbraith, John Kenneth. "Capitalism, Socialism, and the Future of the Industrial State." *The Atlantic*, vol. 219, no. 6 (June 1967).

————. *Economic Development*. Cambridge, Mass.: Harvard University Press, 1964.

————. *Economic Development in Perspective*. Cambridge, Mass.: Harvard University Press, 1962.

Gale, Esson MacDowell. *Salt for the Dragon: A Personal History of China, 1908–1945*. Ann Arbor and East Lansing: Michigan State College Press, 1953.

Gasster, Michael. *Chinese Intellectuals and the Revolution of 1911: The Birth of Chinese Radicalism*. Seattle: University of Washington Press, 1969.

Giles, Lionel, trans. *The Book of Lieh-tzu*. London: John Murray, 1912: reprinted, 1959.

Godwin, William. *Enquiry Concerning Political Justice and Its Influence on Morals and Happiness*. 2 vols. 3rd ed., London: G. G. and J. Robinson, 1798.

Golden, Harry. *Only in America*. New York: Permabooks, 1959.

Goodrich, Joseph King. *The Coming China*. Chicago: A. C. McClurg and Co., 1911.

Gorst, Harold. *China*. New York: E. P. Dutton and Co., 1899.

Grady, Lonan Wang. "Germany's Role in the Boxer Movement." Master's thesis, University of Washington, Seattle, 1964.

Grafer, T. W. "Apologetics." In *Encyclopedia of Religion and Ethics*, edited by James Hastings, vol. 1. 2nd impression, Edinburgh: T. T. Clark, 1930.

Graham, A. C., trans. *The Book of Lieh-tzu*. London: John Murray, 1960.

Grass, Günter. *Local Anaesthetic*. Translated by Ralph Manheim. New York: Harcourt, Brace & World, 1969.

Grieder, Jerome B. "Hu Shih: An Appreciation." *The China Quarterly*, no. 12 (1962).

————. *Hu Shih and the Chinese Renaissance: Liberalism in the Chinese Revolution, 1917–1937*. Cambridge, Mass.: Harvard University Press, 1970.

de Groot, J. J. M. *Religion in China; Universism, a Key to the Study of Taoism and Confucianism.* New York and London: G. P. Putnam's Sons, 1912.

Guillain, Robert. *600 Million Chinese.* Translated by Mervyn Savill. New York: Criterion Press, 1957.

Gundry, R. S. *China Present and Past.* London: Chapman and Hall, 1895.

Gurtov, Melvin. "Recent Developments on Taiwan." *The China Quarterly,* no. 31 (1967).

Hao, Yen-p'ing. "The Abortive Cooperation between Reformers and Revolutionaries (1895–1900)." Harvard University East Asian Research Center. *Papers on China,* vol. 15 (1961).

———. "Cantonese Compradore-Merchants: A Study of Their Functions and Influences, 1842–1884." Ph.D. dissertation, Harvard University, 1966.

Hastie, William, ed. and trans. *Kant's Cosmogony.* Glasgow: J. Maclehose and sons, 1900.

Hastings, James, ed. *Encyclopaedia of Religion and Ethics.* 2nd impression. Edinburgh: T. & T. Clark, 1930.

Hawkes, David, trans. *Ch'u Tz'u: The Songs of the South.* Oxford: Clarendon Press, 1959. Boston: Little, Brown and Co., 1962.

Heilbroner, Robert L. *The Great Ascent: The Struggle for Economic Development in Our Time.* New York: Harper & Row, 1963.

Herberg, Will. "What Keeps Modern Man from Religon?" *The Intercollegiate Review: A Journal of Scholarship and Opinion,* vol. 6, nos. 1–2 (Winter, 1969–70).

Hertzler, Joyce O. *A History of Utopian Thought.* New York: Macmillan Co., 1926.

Hidemi, Onogawa. "K'ang Yu-wei's Idea of Reform." *Studies on Modern China,* no. 2 (Tokyo, 1958), pp. 112–13.

Hinton, Harold C. "The Grain Tribute System of the Ch'ing Dynasty." *Far Eastern Quarterly,* 11, no. 3 (May 1952): 339–54.

Hirschmeier, Johannes, S. V. D. *The Origins of Enterpreneurship in Meiji Japan.* Cambridge, Mass.: Harvard University Press, 1964.

Hirth, Friedrich and W. W. Rockhill. *Chau Ju-kua: His Work on the Chinese and Arab Trade in the Twelfth and Thirteenth Centuries, Entitled Chu-fan-chi.* Translated from the Chinese and annotated: reprinted from the St. Petersburg, 1912, edition with Chinese text. Amsterdam: Oriental Press, 1966.

Ho, Franklin L., and H. D. Fong. "Extent and Effects of Industrialization in China." Presented at the 3rd Biennial Conference of the Institute of Pacific Relations, Kyoto, October 1929. Vol. 9, *Publications and Data Papers.* Tientsin, 1929.

Ho, Ping-ti. "The Salt Merchants of Yang-chou: A Study of Commercial Capitalism in Eighteenth-Century China." *Harvard Journal of Asiatic Studies,* vol. 17, nos. 1 and 2 (June, 1954).

———. "Weng T'ung-ho and the 'One Hundred Days of Reform.' " *Far Eastern Quarterly*, vol. 11, no. 2 (Feb. 1951).

Holt, Robert T., and John E. Turner. *The Political Basis of Economic Development. An Exploration in Comparative Political Analysis.* Princeton: Princeton University Press, 1966.

Honjo, Eijiro. *Economic Theory and History of Japan in the Tokugawa Period* (translation of *Nihon keizai shisō shi*). Tokyo: Maruzen, 1943.

———. *The Social and Economic History of Japan.* Kyoto, 1935. New York: Russell and Russell, 1965.

Houn, Franklin W. *Central Government of China, 1912–1928: An Institutional Study.* 2 vols. Madison: University of Wisconsin Press, 1957.

Howard, Richard C. "K'ang Yu-wei (1858–1927): His Intellectual Background and Early Thought." In *Confucian Personalities*, edited by Arthur F. Wright and Denis Twitchett. Stanford: Stanford University Press, 1962.

Hsiao, Kung-chuan. "The Case for Constitutional Monarchy: K'ang Yu-wei's Plan for the Democratization of China." *Monumenta Serica* 24 (1965): 1–83.

———. "Economic Modernization: K'ang Yu-wei's Ideas in Historical Perspective." *Monumenta Serica* 27 (1968): 1–90.

———. "In and Out of Utopia: K'ang Yu-wei's Social Thought. (1) Path Finding in Two Worlds. (2) Road to Utopia. (3) Detour to Industrial Society." *The Chung Chi Journal*, vol. 7, no. 1 (Nov. 1967); vol. 7, no. 2 (May 1968); vol. 8, no. 1 (Nov. 1968).

———. "K'ang Yu-wei and Confucianism." *Monumenta Serica* 18 (1959): 96–212.

———. "K'ang Yu-wei's Excursion into Science: *Lectures on the Heavens*." In *K'ang Yu-wei: A Biography and a Symposium*, edited by Jung-pang Lo. Tucson: University of Arizona Press, 1967.

———. "Legalism and Autocracy in Traditional China." *Tsing Hua Journal of Chinese Studies*, n.s., 4, no. 2 (Feb. 1964): 108–22.

———. "The Philosophical Thought of K'ang Yu-wei: An Attempt at a New Synthesis." *Monumenta Serica* 21 (1962): 129–93.

———. *Rural China: Imperial Control in the Nineteenth Century.* 1960. Seattle: University of Washington Press, 1967.

———. "Weng T'ung-ho and the Reform Movement of 1898." *Tsing Hua Journal of Chinese Studies*, n.s., 1, no. 2 (April 1957): 111–245.

Hsieh, Pao Chao. *The Government of China, 1644–1911.* Baltimore: John Hopkins Press, 1925.

Hsü, Francis L. K. "Cultural Differences between East and West and Their Significance for the World Today." *Tsing Hua Journal of Chinese Studies*, n.s., vol. 2, no. 1 (May 1960).

Hsü, Immanuel C. Y., trans. Liang Ch'i-ch'ao, *Intellectual Trends in the Ch'ing Period.* Cambridge, Mass.: Harvard University Press, 1959.

————. *The Rise of Modern China*. New York: Oxford University Press, 1970.

Hu Shih. *China, Too, is Fighting to Defend a Way of Life*. San Francisco: Grabhorn Press, 1942.

————. *The Chinese Renaissance*. Haskell Lectures, 1933. Chicago: University of Chicago Press, 1934.

————. "The Chinese Tradition and the Future." Address delivered July 10, 1960, at the Sino-American Conference on Intellectual Cooperation, University of Washington, July 10–15, 1960. Sino-American Conference on Intellectual Cooperation, *Reports and Proceedings*. Seattle: University of Washington Press, 1960.

————. "The Civilizations of the East and the West." In *Whither Mankind: A Panorama of Modern Civilization*, edited by Charles Austin Beard. New York, London, and Toronto: Longmans, 1928.

————. *The Development of the Logical Method in Ancient China*. Shanghai: Oriental Book Co., 1922.

————. "Our Attitude Toward Western Civilization." *Contemporary Review*, no. 83, July 10, 1926; *Peking Leader Reprints*, no. 24. Peking: Peking Leader Press, 1926.

————. "What I Believe," *Living Philosophies, by Twenty-two Representative Modern Thinkers. Forum*, Jan. and Feb., 1930. New York: Simon and Schuster, 1931.

Huang, Joe Chou. "The Political Theories of K'ang Liang School and Their Application to the Reform Movement in China, 1895–1911." Ph.D. dissertation, Southern Illinois University, 1963.

Huang, Philip C. "A Confucian Liberal: Liang Ch'i-ch'ao in Action and Thought." Ph.D. dissertation, University of Washington, 1966.

Hudson, Geoffrey F. *Europe and China: A Survey of Their Relations from the Earliest Times to 1800*. London: E. Arnold & Co., 1931.

Hughes, E. R. *The Invasion of China by the Western World*. New York: Macmillan Co., 1938.

Hummel, Arthur W. *Eminent Chinese of the Ch'ing Period, 1644–1912*. Washington, D.C.: United States Government Printing Office, 1943.

Hummel, William F. "K'ang Yu-wei, Historical Critic and Social Philosopher, 1858–1927." *The Pacific Historical Review*, vol. 4 (1935).

The I-Ching. Translated by James Legge. New York: Dover Publications, 1953.

Ideal Empires and Republics. With an introduction by Charles M. Andrews. New York: Aladdin Book Co., ca. 1901.

Ikei, Masaru. "Japan's Response to the Chinese Revolution of 1911." *The Journal of Asian Studies*, vol. 225, no. 2 (Feb. 1966).

Israel, John. *Student Nationalism in China, 1927–1937*. Stanford: Stanford University Press, 1966.

Jansen, Marius B. *Changing Japanese Attitudes toward Modernization*. Princeton: Princeton University Press, 1965.

————. *The Japanese and Sun Yat-sen.* Cambridge, Mass.: Harvard University Press, 1954.

Japan Information Service. *Japan Report*, vol. 13, no. 16 (New York, Aug. 31, 1967).

Johnston, Bruce F. "Agricultural Production and Economic Development in Japan. *Journal of Political Economy*, vol. 59, no. 6 (Dec. 1951).

Johnston, Reginald F. *Confucianism and Modern China.* The Lewis Fry Memorial Lectures, 1933–1934. New York: D. Appleton-Century Co., 1935.

————. *Twilight in the Forbidden City.* New York: D. Appleton-Century Co., 1935.

Jones, W. T. *A History of Western Philosophy.* New York: Harcourt, 1952.

Kamishima, Jirō. "Modernization of Japan and the Problem of 'Ie' Consciousness." *Acta Asiatica*, Bulletin of the Institute of Eastern Culture (Tokyo), vol. 13 (1967).

K'ang Yu-wei. *Ta T'ung Shu: The One-World Philosophy of K'ang Yu-wei.* Translated by Laurence G. Thompson. London: Allen and Unwin, 1958.

Kant, Immanuel. *Critique of Practical Reason and Other Works on the Theory of Ethics.* Translated by Thomas Kingsmill Abbott. 4th ed., London, 1889. 6th ed., London, New York, and Bombay: Longmans, Green and Co., 1927.

————. *Critique of Pure Reason.* Translated by Norman Kemp-Smith. London: The Macmillan Co., 1929.

————. *Project for a Perpetual Peace.* London, 1796.

Kao, Chung Ju [Bernard]. *Le mouvement intellectuel en Chine et son rôle dans la révolution chinoise (entre 1898 et 1937).* Aix-en-Provence: Saint-Thomas, 1957.

Kao, Hsi-chung [Charles]. "An Analysis of Agricultural Output Increase on Taiwan, 1953–1964." *Journal of Asian Studies*, vol. 26, no. 4 (Aug. 1967).

Kaufmann, M. *Utopias.* London: C. K. Paul, 1879.

Kent, Percy Horace Braund. *Railway Enterprise in China.* London: E. Arnold, 1908.

Klatt, Werner ("W. K."). "Communist China's Agriculture Calamities." *The China Quarterly*, no. 6 (April–June 1961).

Koh, Sung Jae. *Stages of Industrial Development in Asia. A Comparative History of the Cotton Industry in Japan, India, China, and Korea.* Philadelphia: University of Pennsylvania Press, 1966.

Kohn, Harold E. *Thoughts Afield.* Grand Rapids, Michigan, 1959.

Kou Hong Ming [Ku Hung-ming] and Francis Borrey. *Le catéchisme de Confucius. Contribution à l'étude de la sociologie chinoise.* Paris: M. Rivière 1927.

Ku, Chieh-kang. "The Autobiography of a Chinese Historian: Being the Preface to a Symposium on Ancient Chinese History." Translated by Arthur W. Hummel. *Ku-shih pien*, vol. 1. Leiden: E. J. Brill, 1931.

Ku, Hung-ming. *Chinas Verteidigung gegen europäische Ideen*. Jena: E. Diederiches, 1911.

―――. *The Conduct of Life. Or, The Universal Order of Confucius*. Translation of the *Doctrine of the Mean*. London, 1906. Reprinted, London: John Murray, 1920.

―――. *The Discourses and Saying of Confucius*. Shanghai, 1898.

―――. *Papers from a Viceroy's Yamen: A Chinese Plea for the Cause of Good Government and True Civilization in China*. Shanghai: Shanghai Mercury, 1901.

―――. *The Spirit of the Chinese People*. Peking: Peking Daily News, 1915.

―――. *The Story of a Chinese Oxford Movement*. Shanghai: Shanghai Mercury, 1910. 2nd ed., 1912.

Kung-sun Yang. *The Book of Lord Shang*. Translated by J. J. L. Duyvendak. London: Arthur Probsthain, 1928. Chicago: University of Chicago Press, 1963.

Kwok, D. W. Y. *Scientism in Chinese Thought, 1900–1950*. New Haven and London: Yale University Press, 1965.

―――. "Wu Chih-hui and Scientism." *Tsing Hua Journal of Chinese Studies*, n.s., vol. 3, no. 1 (May 1962).

Lach, D. F. *Contributions of China to German Civilization, 1648–1740*. Chicago: University of Chicago Press, 1944.

Lamley, Harry J. "Liang Shu-ming: The Thought and Action of a Reformer." Master's thesis, University of Washington, 1960.

Lang, Olga. *Chinese Family and Society*. New Haven: Yale University Press, 1946.

Latourette, Kenneth Scott. *The Development of China*. 1st ed., 1917; 4th ed., Boston and New York: Houghton Mifflin Co., 1929.

―――. *A History of Modern China*. Melbourne, London and Baltimore: Penguin Books, 1954.

Lee, Robert H. G. "Fung Yu-lan: A Biographical Profile." *The China Quarterly*, no. 14 (April–June 1963).

Leibniz, Gottfried Wilhelm von. *The Monadology and Other Philosophical Writings*. Translated with an introduction and notes by Robert Latta. London, New York, etc., 1898. 2nd impression, London: Clarendon Press, 1925.

Leng, Shao Chuan, and Norman D. Palmer. *Sun Yat-sen and Communism*. New York: Frederick A. Praeger, 1960.

Leroy-Beaulieu, Pierre. *The Awakening of the East*. New York: McClure, Phillips Co., 1900.

Levy, Marion J., Jr. *The Family Revolution in Modern China*. Cambridge, Mass.: Harvard University Press, 1949.

Levy, Marion J., and Shih Kuo-heng. *The Rise of the Modern Chinese Business Class; Two Introductory Essays*. New York: Institute of Pacific Relations, 1949.

Lew, Timothy Tingfang. "The New Culture Movement and Christian Education in China." *China Today Through Chinese Eyes*. 2nd ser. London: Student Christian Movement, 1926.

Lewis, Charlton M. "The Reform Movement in Hunan (1896–1898)." Harvard University East Asian Research Center. *Papers on China*, vol. 15 (1961).

Li, Chien-nung. *The Political History of China, 1840–1928*. Translated by Ssu-yü Teng and Jeremy Ingalls. Princeton: Van Nostrand, 1956.

Liao, W. K., trans. *The Complete Works of Han Fei Tzu*. 2 vols. London: Arthur Probsthain, 1939.

Liang Ch'i-ch'ao. *Intellectual Trends in the Ch'ing Period*. Translated by Immanuel C. Y. Hsü. Cambridge, Mass.: Harvard University Press, 1959.

Lin, Mousheng. *Men and Ideas: An Informal History of Chinese Political Thought*. New York: John Day Co., 1942.

Liu, D. K. *The Growth and Industrialization of Shanghai*. Shanghai: Institute of Pacific Relations, 1936.

Liu, James T. C. *Reform in Sung China; Wang An-shih (1021–1086) and His New Policies*. Cambridge, Mass.: Harvard University Press, 1959.

Liu, Ta-chün and S. T. King. *China's Cotton Industry. A Statistical Study of Ownership, Capital, Output, and Labor Conditions*. Shanghai: Institute of Pacific Relations, 1929.

———. *China's Industrial Development*. Honolulu: Institute of Pacific Relations, 1927.

———. *The Silk Industry of China*. Shanghai: Kelly and Walsh, 1940.

Liu, Wu-chi. *A Short History of Confucian Philosophy*. Baltimore: Penguin Books, 1955.

Living Philosophies. By Twenty-two Representative Modern Thinkers. Forum, 1930. New York: Simon and Schuster, 1937.

Lo, Jung-pang, ed. *K'ang Yu-wei: A Biography and a Symposium*. Tucson: University of Arizona Press, 1967.

Lockwood, William W. *The Economic Development of Japan: Growth and Structural Changes, 1868–1938*. Princeton: Princeton University Press, 1954.

———, ed. *The State and Economic Enterprise in Japan. Essays in the Political Economy of Growth*. Princeton: Princeton University Press, 1965.

Loh, Pichon P. Y. "The Popular Upsurge in China: Nationalism and Westernization, 1919–1927." Ph.D. dissertation, University of Chicago, 1955.

Lund, Renville C. "Imperial University of Peking." Ph.D. dissertation, University of Washington, 1956.

Lung, Cheng-fu. "The Evolution of Chinese Social Thought." Ph.D dissertation, University of Southern California, 1935.

Ma, Te-chih. *Le mouvement réformiste et les événements de la cour de Pékin en 1898*. Ph.D. dissertation, l'Université de Lyon, 1934.

MacNair, Harley Farnsworth. *China*. Berkeley and Los Angeles: University of California Press, 1946.

Mallory, Walter H. *China, Land of Famine*. New York: American Geographical Society, 1926.

Mannheim, Karl. *Ideology and Utopia: An Introduction to the Sociology of Knowledge*. New York: Harcourt, Brace & Co., 1946; Harvest Books ed., n.d.

———. "Utopia." In *Encyclopedia of the Social Sciences*, edited by Edwin R. A. Seligman and Alvin Johnson. New York: Macmillan Co., 1950.

Mao Tse-tung. *On New Democracy*. Peking: Foreign Languages Press, 1954. *Selected Works*, vol. 3. New York: International Publishers, 1955.

———. *On the People's Democratic Dictatorship*. Peking, 1959. *Selected Works*, vol. 3. Peking: Foreign Languages Press, 1961.

Martin, William Alexander Parsons. *A Cycle of Cathay; or China, South and North, with Personal Reminiscences*. Edinburgh, 1896. 3rd ed. New York and Chicago: F. H. Revell, 1900.

Maverick, Lewis A. *China, a Model for Europe*. San Antonio: Paul Anderson Co., 1946.

McCord, William. *The Springtime of Freedom: The Evolution of Developing Societies*. New York: Oxford University Press, 1965.

Mehnert, Klaus. "The Social and Political Role of the Intelligentsia in the New Countries." In *New Nations in a Divided World*, edited by Kurt London. New York and London: Frederick A. Praeger, 1963.

Michael, Franz and George Taylor. *The Far East in the Modern World*. New York: Holt, 1956.

More, Thomas. *Utopia*. Translated by Paul Turner. Baltimore: Penguin Books, 1965.

Morison, Samuel E. *The Oxford History of the American People*. New York: Oxford University Press, 1965.

Morrell, James. "Two Early Chinese Cotton Mills." Harvard University East Asian Research Center. *Papers on China*, vol. 21 (1968).

Morrison, Esther. "The Modernization of the Confucian Bureaucracy." Ph.D. dissertation, Radcliffe College, 1959.

Morse, Hosea Ballou. *The International Relations of the Chinese Empire*. 3 vols. London and New York: Longmans, Green, and Co., 1910–1918.

———. *The Trade and Administration of China*. 3rd ed., rev. London: Longmans, Green, and Co., 1921.

Mountjoy, Alan B. *Industrialization and Underdeveloped Countries*. London, 1966. 2nd ed. Chicago: Aldine Publishing Co., 1967.

Mu, Fu-sheng [pseud.]. *The Wilting of the Hundred Flowers. The Chinese Intelligentsia under Mao*. New York: Heinemann, 1962.

Mumford, Lewis. *The Story of Utopias*. New York: Boni & Liveright, 1922. Compass Book ed., 1962.

Nakayama, Ichiro. *Industrialization of Japan*. Honolulu: East-West Center Press, 1963.

Needham, Joseph. *Science and Civilization in China.* 5 vols. Cambridge: Cambridge University Press, 1954–1965.

Negley, Glenn and Patrick J. Max. *The Quest for Utopia. An Anthology of Imaginary Societies.* New York: Henry Schuman, Inc., 1952. Garden City: Anchor Books ed., 1962.

Neufeld, Maurice F. *Poor Countries and Authoritarian Rule.* Ithaca, N.Y.: Cornell University Press, 1965.

North China Herald (Pei Hua Chieh Pao), Sept. 18, 1886, and Sept. 19, 1898.

Nurkse, Ragnar. *Problems of Capital Formation in Underdeveloped Countries and Patterns of Trade and Development.* New York: Oxford University Press, 1967.

Oda, Makato. "Third-Generation Intellectuals." Translated from Japanese by Ki Chang Lee. *Atlas,* vol. 3, no. 2 (Feb. 1962).

Onslow, Cranley. *Asian Economic Development.* London: G. Allen and Unwin; New York: Frederick A. Praeger, 1965.

van Oort, H. A. "Chinese Culture-Values, Past and Present." *Chinese Culture: A Quarterly Review* (Taipei), vol. 11, no. 1 (March 1970).

Owen, R. G. *Scientism, Man, and Religion.* Philadelphia: Westminster Press, 1952.

Palmer, Norman D. "Makers of Modern China. I. The Reformers: K'ang Yu-wei." *Current History,* vol. 15 (Aug. 1948).

Pandit, Toshar. "Totalitarianism versus Traditionalism." *Problems of Communism,* vol. 12, no. 6 (Nov–Dec. 1963).

Peake, Cyrus H. "Some Aspects of the Introduction of Modern Science into China." *Isis,* no. 22 (1934).

Pelliot, Paul. "La réforme des examens littéraires en Chine." Comité de L'Asie-Française, *Bulletin mensuel.* Paris, April 1903.

Pepper, Suzanne. "Rural Government in Communist China: The Party-State Relationship at the Local Level." Master's thesis, University of Washington, 1963.

Pietrowski, Sylvester A. *Étienne Cabet and the Voyage en Écarie.* Washington, D.C., 1935.

Pipes, Richard, ed. *The Russian Intelligentsia.* New York: Columbia University Press, 1961.

Pokora, T. Review of S. L. Tikhvinsky, *Dvizhenie za reformy v Kitae v kontse XIX veka i Kan Iu-wei. Archiv Orientálni* (Prague), vol. 29, no. 1 (1961).

Pott, F. L. Hawks. *A Short History of Shanghai: Being an Account of the Growth and Development of the International Settlement.* Shanghai: Kelly and Walsh, 1928.

Purcell, Victor. *The Rise of Modern China.* London: Routledge & Kegan Paul, 1962.

Pusey, James R. "K'ang Yu-wei and *Pao-chiao*: Confucian Reform and Reformation." Harvard University East Asian Research Center. *Papers on China,* vol. 20 (Dec. 1966).

Ranis, Gustav. "The Financing of Japanese Economic Development." *Economic History Review*, 2nd ser., vol. 11, no. 3 (April 1959).

Reichwein, Adolf. *China and Europe, Intellectual and Artistic Contacts in the Eighteenth Century*. Translated by J. C. Powell. London: Kegan Paul, French, Trubner & Co., 1925.

Reinsch, Paul S. *An American Diplomat in China*. Garden City, N.Y.: Doubleday, Page and Co., 1922.

————. "Cultural Factors in the Chinese Crisis." *Annals*. The American Academy of Political and Social Science, vol. 16 (1900).

————. *Intellectual and Political Currents in the Far East*. Boston and New York: Houghton Mifflin Co., ca. 1911.

Reischauer, Edwin O. *Japan, Past and Present*. 3rd rev. ed. New York: A. A. Knopf, 1967.

————. "Time Is on Our Side in Asia." *The Reader's Digest*, vol. 90, no. 538 (Feb. 1967).

Renan, Ernest. "Qu'est-ce qu'une nation?" *Discourses et Conférences*, Paris: Colmann-Levy, 1887.

Renouvin, Pierre. *La question d'extrême-orient, 1840–1940*. Paris: Hachette, 1946.

ReQua, Eloise G. and Jane Statham. *The Developing Nations: A Guide to Information Concerning Their Economic, Political, Technical and Social Problems*. Detroit: Gale Research Co., 1965.

Richard, Timothy. *Forty-five Years in China*. London: T. Fisher Unwin, 1916.

Rickett, W. Allyn, trans. "The *Kuan-tzu*: An Annotated Translation of Eight Representative Chapters." Ph.D. dissertation, University of Pennsylvania, 1960.

de Riencourt, Amaury. *The Soul of China*. 1958. Rev. ed., New York: Harper & Row, 1965.

Rosovsky, Henry. *Capital Formation in Japan, 1868–1940*. Glencoe, Ill.: Free Press, 1961.

Ross, Harry. *Utopias Old and New*. London: Nicholson and Watson, 1938.

Rostow, Walt W. *The Process of Economic Growth*. 2nd ed. Oxford: Clarendon Press, 1960.

————. *The Stages of Economic Growth: A Non-Communist Manifesto*. Cambridge, Mass.: Harvard University Press, 1960.

Roy, Andrew T. "Modern Confucian Social Theory: Social Change and Its Concept of Change." Ph.D. dissertation, Princeton University, 1948.

Russell, Bertrand. *The Impact of Science on Society*. Matchette Foundation Lectures, no. 3. New York: Columbia University Press, 1951.

————. *The Problem of China*. New York: The Century Co., 1922.

Russell, Frances Theresa. *Touring Utopia: The Realm of Constructive Humanism*. New York: L. MacVeigh, Dial Press, 1932.

Ruyer, Raymond. *L'utopie et les utopies*. Paris: Presses universitaires de France, 1950.

Sakai, Robert K. "Ts'ai Yüan-p'ei as a Synthesizer of Western and Chinese Thought." Harvard University East Asian Research Center. *Papers on China*, vol. 3 (1949).

Sansom, Sir George Baily. *A History of Japan.* 3 vols. Stanford: Stanford University Press, 1958–63.

———. *The Western World and Japan.* New York: Alfred A. Knopf, 1951.

Scalapino, Robert A., and George T. Yu. *The Chinese Anarchist Movement.* Berkeley: Center for Chinese Studies, University of California, 1961.

Scalapino, Robert A., and Harold Schiffrin. "Early Socialist Currents in the Chinese Revolutionary Movement: Sun Yat-sen versus Liang Ch'i-ch'ao." *The Journal of Asian Studies* 18, no. 3 (May 1959): 321–42.

Schumpeter, Joseph A. *Capitalism, Socialism, and Democracy.* 1942. 3rd ed. New York: Harper, 1950.

———. *The Theory of Economic Development.* (English version of the 1911 German ed.) Cambridge, Mass.: Harvard University Press, 1955.

Schwartz, Benjamin. "Ch'en Tu-hsiu and the Acceptance of the Modern West." *Journal of the History of Ideas* 12 (1951): 61–74.

———. *In Search of Wealth and Power: Yen Fu and the West.* Cambridge, Mass.: Belknap Press, 1964.

———. "The Intelligentsia in Communist China: A Tentative Comparison." In *The Russian Intelligentsia*, edited by Richard Pipes. New York: Columbia University Press, 1961.

De Schweinitz, Karl, Jr. *Industrialization and Democracy: Economic Necessity and Political Possibilities.* New York: Free Press of Glencoe, 1964.

Shapley, Harlow. *Of Stars and Men: Human Response to an Expanding Universe.* Boston: Beacon Press, 1958.

Sheldon, Charles David. *The Rise of the Merchant Class in Tokugawa Japan, 1600–1868: An Introductory Survey.* Locust Valley, N.Y.: J. J. Augustin, 1958.

Shih, Vincent Y. C. "A Talk with Hu Shih." *The China Quarterly*, no. 10 (April–June 1962), pp. 149–65.

Sigmund, Paul, Jr. *The Ideologies of Developing Nations.* New York: Frederick A. Praeger, 1963.

Sinai, I. R. *The Challenge of Modernization. The West's Impact on the Non-Western World.* London: Chatto & Windus, 1964.

Smith, Thomas C. "Japan's Aristocratic Revolution." *Yale Review*, Spring 1961.

———. *Political Change and Industrial Development in Japan: Government Enterprise, 1868–1880.* 1955. Stanford: Stanford University Press, 1966.

So, Kwan-wai. "Western Influence and the Chinese Reform Movement of 1898." Ph.D. dissertation, University of Wisconsin, 1950.

Soothill, William Edward. *Timothy Richard of China: Seer, Statesman, Missionary, and the Most Distinguished Adviser the Chinese Ever Had.* London: Seeley, Service & Co., 1924.

Soothill, William Edward, and Lewis Hodous, ed. *A Dictionary of Chinese Buddhist Terms*. London: Kegan Paul, Trench, Trubner & Co., 1937.

Spence, Jonathan. *To Change China: Western Advisers in China, 1620–1960*. Boston: Little, Brown, and Co., 1969.

Spilhaus, Athelstan. "The Next Industrial Revolution." *Science*, vol. 167 (March 27, 1970).

Spinoza, Baruch. *Improvement of the Understanding, Ethics, and Correspondence*. Translated by R. H. M. Elwes. New York and London: M. Walter Dunne Co., 1901.

Stuart, John Leighton. *Fifty Years in China*. New York: Random House, 1954.

Sun Yat-sen. *San Min Chu I. The Three Principles of the People*. Translated by Frank W. Price; edited by L. T. Chen. Shanghai: Commercial Press, 1927.

Supple, Barry E., ed. *The Economic Development of Japan: Growth and Structural Change, 1868–1938*. Princeton: Princeton University Press, 1954.

————, ed., *The Experience of Economic Growth. Case Studies in Economic History*. New York: Random House, 1963.

Teng, Ssu-yü and John K. Fairbank. *China's Response to the West. A Documentary Survey, 1839–1923*. Cambridge, Mass.: Harvard University Press, 1954.

Thompson, Laurence G., trans. *Ta T'ung Shu: The One-World Philosophy of K'ang Yu-wei*. London: G. Allen and Unwin, 1958.

Tikhvinsky, S. L. *Dvizhenie za reformy v Kitae v kontse XIX veka Kan Iu-wei*. Moscow: Izdatelstvo vastochnoi literatury, 1959.

Tobar, Jérôme, S. J. *Koang-siu et Ts'e-hi, Empéreur de Chine et Impératrice-Douairière: Décrets impériaux 1898. Série d'Orient*, no. 4. Shanghai: Imprimerie de la Presse Orientale, 1900.

Tse, Tsan-Tai. *The Chinese Republic: Secret History of the Revolution*. Hong Kong: South China Morning Post, 1924.

Tseng, Yu-hao. *Modern Chinese Legal and Political Philosophy*. Shanghai: Commercial Press, 1930.

Tsien, Tsuen-hsuin. "Western Impact on China through Translation." *Far Eastern Quarterly*, vol. 13, no. 3 (May 1954).

Tsuchida, Kyoson. *Contemporary Thought of Japan and China*. New York: A. A. Knopf, 1927.

U.S. News and World Report, May 29, 1967.

Walker, C. S. "Army of Chinese Students Abroad." *World's Work*, vol. 13 (Jan. 1907).

Walker, Richard L. *China Under Communism: The First Five Years*. New Haven: Yale University Press, 1955.

Wang, Gungwu. "The Nanhai Trade: A Study of the Early History of Chinese Trade in the South China Sea." *Journal of the Malayan Branch of the Royal Asiatic Society*, vol. 31, no. 2 (June 1958).

Wang, Teh-chao. "The Role of the Chinese Intellectuals in the Revolution of 1911." *Chinese Culture* (Taipei), vol. 7, no. 3 (Sept. 1966).

Wang, Tsi C. *The Youth Movement in China*. New York: New Republic, 1927.

Wang, Y. C. *Chinese Intellectuals and the West, 1872–1949*. Chapel Hill: University of North Carolina Press, 1966.

———. "Intellectuals and Society in China, 1860–1949." *Comparative Studies in Society and History*, vol. 3, no. 4 (July 1961).

Ward, Richard J., ed. *The Challenge of Development: Theory and Practice. A Sourcebook*. Chicago: Aldine Publishing Co., 1967.

Watson, Burton, trans. *Hsün Tzu: Basic Writings*. New York: Columbia University Press, 1963.

Webb, Clement C. J. *Kant's Philosophy of Religion*. Oxford: Clarendon Press, 1926.

Weber, Max. *The Theory of Social and Economic Organization*. Translated by A. M. Henderson and Talcott Parsons. New York: Oxford University Press, 1947.

Wells, H. G. *A Modern Utopia*. London: Chapman and Hall, 1905.

Wen Ching [Lim Boon Keng]. *The Chinese Crisis from Within*. London: Grant Richards, 1901.

Wilhelm, Richard. *Confucius and Confucianism*. Translated by George H. and Annina Periam Danton. New York: Harcourt, Brace & Co., 1931.

———, trans. *The I Ching or Book of Changes*. English translation by Cary F. Baynes. 1950. 2nd ed., New York, 1952. London: Routledge & Kegan Paul, 1965.

Williams, E. T. *China Yesterday and Today*. 1923. Rev. ed. New York: Thomas Y. Crowell Co., 1927.

Wright, Arthur. *Buddhism in Chinese History*. Stanford: Stanford University Press, 1959.

———, ed. *The Confucian Persuasion*. Stanford: Stanford University Press, 1960.

———, ed. *Studies in Chinese Thought*. Chicago: University of Chicago Press, 1953.

Wright, Mary C. *The Last Stand of Chinese Conservatism: The T'ung-chih Restoration, 1862–1874*. Stanford: Stanford University Press, 1957.

Young, George. "Europeanization." In *Encyclopedia of the Social Science*, edited by Edwin R. A. Seligman, vol. 5. New York: Macmillan Co., 1931.

Young, Wing. *My Life in China and America*. New York: H. Holt and Co., 1909.

INDEX

Absolute monarchy: as lowest form of government, 85
Age of Approaching Peace (Minor Peace). *See* Three Ages doctrine
Age of Disorder. *See* Three Ages doctrine
Age of Universal Peace. *See* Three Ages doctrine
Agriculture: reforms proposed for, 305–6
Alcock, Sir John Rutherford, 265n*4*
Allen, Young J., 332
America: as model, 365
Analects, 56, 71, 82–93 *passim*, 114, 117, 422
Anarchist movement: *Ta-t'ung* concept in, 501
"Animal spirit" (*p'e*), 115–16, 150
Animism, 162
Annals, 77, 78, 80
Annam: loss of, 139
Anti-Confucianists, 589
Apocrypha: of Kung-yang school, 83
Approaching Peace doctrine. See *Hsiao-k'ang* (Approaching Peace) doctrine
Aristotle, 181, 186, 525
Arnold, Matthew, 567
Asian Commercial Institute (Ajiya Bōecki Shōkai), 312
Aśoka, 458
Athens, 29
Authoritarianism and economic modernization, 372–76. *See also* K'ang Yu-wei, and reform
Autocracy: outmoding of, 216–17; burden of, 224–25

Backhouse, Sir Edmund T., 23
Bacon, Francis, 383, 384n*24*, 525, 549
Beebe, William, 188n*226*
Bellamy, Edward, 503
Bentham, Jeremy, 159
Beresford, Lord Charles, 360-61n*229*, 400
Bergson, Henri, 142, 183-84n*208*, 185–87, 561–62
Bismarck, Otto von, 475n*236*, 518
Blake, Sir Henry Arthur, 236n*152*
Bland, J. O. P., 23
Board of State Affairs, 275
Book of Changes, 27, 48, 49, 71, 72, 114, 117, 143, 146, 425
Book of Filial Piety, 13, 71–74, 117
Book of History, 71–72
Book of Odes: Mao version, 70; New Text version, 72
Book of Rites, 12, 48, 49, 56, 68, 71, 72, 93, 467
Book Translation Society. *See* I-shu kung hui
Boxer Rebellion, 14, 87, 236n*151*, 237, 239, 515
Brotherly duty: and Confucius, 89
Buddhahood, 171
Buddhism: Mahayāna, 54, 64, 93, 108, 109, 111, 140; and K'ang Yu-wei, 54, 55, 65, 105–6, 108, 109, 110, 111, 118, 138–39, 140, 166; and Confucianism, 65, 110, 125; Ch'an, 108–9, 152; Hua-yen (Avataṁsa), 109, 110, 166; Hīnayāna, 109, 111; and Christianity, 112; Brahmanical, 475n*237*; mentioned, 13, 53, 109, 110, 116, 125, 164, 165–68, 175, 176, 475n*237*, 497

Cabet, Etienne, 501–2, 503, 505, 506
Campanella, Tommaso, 501n*338*, 503 and
    n*347*, 504 and n*353*
Cavour, Camillo, 518
Celestial Peregrination, Academy for, 176,
    178. *See also* K'ang Yu-wei, writings
    discussed
Chamberlain, Houston Stewart, 472
Chan T'ien-yu, 355–56
Chang, Carsun: on moral decay, 392n*58*
Chang Chien, 275, 331n*105*, 353, 362,
    530n*42*
Chang Chih-tung: and K'ang, 23, 102, 237,
    418; and Westernization, 212–13, 507,
    522, 556; and reform, 275, 276–79, 405,
    567; and industry, 302, 360–61n*229*; on
    education, 388–90; mentioned, 14, 122,
    238n*160*, 270n*23*, 293, 319, 333n*105*,
    381n*15*, 412
Chang Chü-cheng, 79
Chang Chün-mai, 550, 551, 561, 564
Chang Heng, 448
Chang Hsüeh-ch'eng, 98n*6*
Chang Hsün, General, 252, 253, 254–56
Chang Miao-hua, 9
Chang Shih-chao, 37n*88*
Chang Tsai, 60, 69, 90, 144, 149
Chang Tung-sun, 184
Chang Yen-ch'iu, 507
Chang Yin-huan, 270n*23*
Chang Yüan-chi, 270n*23*, 272n*31*, 406
Chang-tzu, 498
Chao Heng-t'i, 296
Chao Ping-lin, 530n*42*
Charles I of England, 255
Charles II: restoration of, 255
Ch'en Ch'ien-ch'iu, 55
Ch'en Chih, 328–30, 381n*15*
Ch'en Ch'iu, 327
Ch'en Hsü-ching, 575–77, 585, 590, 591
Ch'en Huang-chang, 131
Ch'en Pao-chen, 102, 118–19, 270n*23*
Ch'en Shao-po, 24
Ch'en Tu-hsiu: as iconoclast, 130, 485; and
    republic, 232–33; and moral decay,
    392n*58*; and New Culture, 482–88; and
    socialism, 489–96; and science vs. meta-
    physics polemic, 549–64; as Westernizer,
    571–75, 594; mentioned, 330, 393, 467,
    528, 582, 593. *See also* "Mr. Democracy";
    "Mr. Science"
Cheng K'ang-ch'eng, 63
Cheng Kuan-ying, 304, 325–27n*81*, 332n*108*,
    354, 355
Ch'eng–Chu tradition, 4, 13, 60–63, 92, 93
Ch'eng I [I-ch'uan], 57, 61, 149
Ch'i (ether or force), 144–45

Ch'i school, 68
Chi-hsüeh hui, 213
Chi-tzu, 87
Chia-fa, 73, 95
Chiang Meng-lin [Chiang Mon-lin], 123,
    537, 556, 585
Ch'iang-hsüeh hui (Society for Study of
    National [Self-] Strengthening; Reform
    Club), 17n*1*, 23, 212–13, 275n*46*, 293,
    404–5
Ch'ien Chün-hsiang, 381n*15*
Ch'ien Hsüan-t'ung, 129
Ch'ien Mu, 23, 49–51, 66, 415, 478
Ch'in, Emperor, 125, 134
Chin-liang, 258n*237*
Chin-pu tang (Progressive Party), 127
China: civilization of, 104, 105, 136, 384–88,
    390, 533–35, 571; Communist, 131–
    32n*138*, 375n*282*, 390, 449, 479, 489–90,
    493, 595; republic of, 260, 352–54, 361,
    372, 390; future of, 565–96
China Constitutional Association. *See* Chung-
    hua hsien-cheng hui; Pao-huang hui
China Merchants Steam Ship Navigation
    Company, 323, 325n*81*, 355
The China Press, 254, 366
Ch'ing government: K'ang supports, 127;
    and reform, 138, 347, 361; and parlia-
    ment, 244–45. *See also* K'ang Yu-wei, and
    reform
Ch'ing, Prince, 238n*160*, 275. *See also*
    I-k'uang
Ch'ing-kuo vs. Chung-hua kuo, 224, 243–44
Ch'ing-liu tang (Chinese Oxford Move-
    ment), 567
Chiu shih (to save the world), 95
Chou dynasty philosophers, 98
Chou, Emperor, 87
Chou Tun-i, 144
Chou-li, 70, 286n*82*
Christianity: influence of, on K'ang, 105–6,
    108; K'ang's view of, 111–12, 113, 165–
    68; and Confucianism, 118, 120; men-
    tioned, 176, 184, 440. *See also* K'ang Yu-
    wei, intellectual influences and develop-
    ment of
Chu Chih-hsin, 491, 492
Chu Hsi [Chu Tzu-yang], 44, 47, 58, 60, 62
    and n*86*, 79, 80, 82, 124, 133, 144, 149,
    157, 309n*28*
Chu Hsi Lu, 61
Chu I-hsin, 74, 75, 102, 129, 149
Chu Ts'ai, 319
Chu-tzu, 58
Chu Tzu-yang. *See* Chu Hsi
Chu Tz'u-ch'i [Chu Chiu-chiang], 4, 6, 60,
    63–65, 67, 138, 160

Ch'ü Hung-chi, 279, 281
Chü-luan shih. See Three Ages doctrine
Chung-hua hsien-cheng hiu (China Constitution Association), 22n*109*, 242, 294
Chung-shan. *See* Sun Yat-sen
Chuang Ts'un-yü, 75
Chün (equality), 90, 91, 94
Ch'un-chiu fan-lu. See Tung Chung-shu
Ch'un-ch'iu wei (apocrypha of the Kung-yang school), 83
Churchill, Winston, 45
City of the Sun, 504
Civilizations, Chinese and Western: evaluation of, 532–95
Classics: K'ang's work on, 78, 94–95. *See also* K'ang Yu-wei, intellectual influences and development; and individual titles
Communication reforms, 313–14
Communism, 495
Comprador-entrepreneurs, 354n*201*
Confucianism: and family, 13; defined, 42–44; revisionists of, 43–44; as state religion, 44, 105–22, 121n*96*, 161, 384–85, 418; defended by K'ang, 55, 56, 122; compared to other teachings, 55, 104, 165–67; imperial, 81, 124–25, 127, 133–34 and nn*142, 143*; as philosophy of reform, 97–105; preservation of, 104, 122; in modern world, 123, 126, 131, 563; as universalistic, 125, 416; eroded by K'ang, 126, 127, 131; as moribund, 390–92; rejection of, 563, 566–73; support by Ku Hung-ming, 566–70
Confucian tradition: K'ang's place in, 122–36
Confucius: doctrines attributed to, 15, 97, 159, 145–46, 163, 582; and K'ang, 27, 69; and supernatural, 28, 162; reinterpretation of, 102–3, 415–16; apotheosis of, 106–7; teaching of equated with Chinese civilization, 571, 576–77, 596. See also *Analects*; K'ang Yu-wei, philosophical influences and development
Conservatism, Chinese, 123
Constitutional monarchy: as transitional form of government, 86, 94, 194, 195, 209, 215, 224n*113*; vs. republicanism, 139; K'ang's crusade for, 252–61; failure of, 372. *See also* K'ang Yu-wei, and reform
"Constitution Protection Movement," 260
Constitutional Party. *See* Hsien-cheng tang
Copernicus, 448, 549
"Cultural cosmopolitanism," 104
Cultural identity: preservation of, 103–4
Cultural nationalism, 104, 543–45

Darwin, Charles, 186

Darwinism, 455, 475
Democracy. See *Min-chu*
Denby, Charles, 212
Der Ling, 404
Descartes, René, 181, 525
De-Sinification: dangers of, 387
Developing countries, 372–73, 496
Dewey, John, 142, 387–88
Dharma (fa-chieh), 109, 110, 166
Divine authority, 114, 115
Doctrine of the Mean, 27, 59, 82, 89, 93
"Dream of the Red Chamber" (*Hung-lou meng*), 33
"The Dream of the Southern Bough" (*Nan-k'o meng*), 35
"The Dream of Yellow Millet" (*Huang-liang meng*), 34
Driesch, Hans, 142

Economic growth, 356–65
Economic nationalism, 318
Edison, Thomas, 575, 578
Edkins, Joseph, 332
Education reform: aftermath of, 388–99
Eight-legged essay, 8, 20, 214n*80*, 268, 270, 526. *See also* K'ang Yu-wei, and reform
Elite leadership: Sun's insistence on, 228–30; current support for, 231
Emperor. *See* Kuang-hsü emperor
Emperor Protection Society. *See* Pao-huang hui
Empress dowager. *See* Tz'u-hsi
England: as model for developing countries, 372, 524, 530
"Enlightened autocracy," concept of, 231
Enlightenment thinkers: and Chinese ethos, 570
Equality. See *Chün*
Ether (*ch'i*), 144–45, 150
Europe: as model for K'ang Yu-wei, 365
Examination system: K'ang Yu-wei's criticism of, 268. *See also* Eight-legged essay; K'ang Yu-wei, and reform

Fa-lü hsüeh hui (study association), 212–13
Family: invalidity of, 81
Fan Wen-lan, 489
Fate (*ming*): and K'ang Yu-wei, 116–17
Filial duty, 429–30, 450–52
Filial piety, 89
First Hague Conference, 479
"Five Emperors," 77
Ford, Henry, 575
Foreign capital, 313, 367–71
Foreign interests, 362
Fourier, Charles, 453–54, 501–2, 504
France: as model for developing countries,

372
Franke, Otto, 600
Frederick the Great: and primary education, 270, 379, 383
Free love, 427–28, 430n85. *See also* K'ang Yu-wei, intellectual influences and development
Freedom (*tzu-yu*), 88
French Revolution, 202–3
Fryer, John, 332, 507–13
Fukuzawa, Yukichi, 341, 342nn147,150
Fung Kuei-fen, 103, 326n82, 412
Fung Kuo-chang, 251n207, 398
Fung Tsu-yu, 491, 492
Fung Yu-lan, 132, 489, 593, 586–90

Galileo, 549, 557
George, Henry, 492
Germany, as model, 524, 529, 530
Godai, Tomoatsu, 340n142
Goethe, 183, 568–69
Golden, Harry, 188n226
Goodrich, Joseph K., 400
Government: proper functions of, 284–85; scope of, 285–86, local, 290–92; centralization vs. federalism, 292–99; in economic reform, 303–4, 358–59n224. *See also* K'ang Yu-wei, and reform
Great Community. See *Ta-t'ung,* doctrine of
Great Learning, 59, 82, 93
Great Unity. See *Ta-t'ung,* doctrine of
Greece, 30

Han Fei, 80
Han learning, 48, 76
Han Yü, 64
Hart, Robert, 264, 400
Harvey, William, 557
Hedonism, 121–22, 158, 159, 179, 309n28, 439–40, 442, 506, 554
Hegel, Georg W. F., 142, 183, 524, 575
Hirayama Shū, 236n152
Ho Chan-li, 10, 163n133
Ho Ch'i, 413n18
Ho Hsiu, 48, 73, 75, 106
Hobbes, Thomas, 549
"Homely Words to Aid Government" (John Fryer): influence on K'ang Yu-wei, 507–13
Hou O, 65–66
Hou tang, 238
House of Calm Contentment (*Tan-ju lou*), 6
Hsi Ming (*The Western Inscription* by Chang Tsai), 60
Hsia dynasty, 98
Hsiang hsüeh hui (study association), 213
Hsiao-ching wei, 117

Hsiao-k'ang (Approaching Peace) doctrine, 48, 49, 50, 56, 57, 79, 80, 127
Hsien-cheng tang (Constitutional Party), 9, 249
Hsin ch'ing-nien (*La Jeunesse*), 130, 483, 484, 485, 487, 488, 492–93, 521, 562, 568, 571
Hsin-min ts'ung-pao, 24
Hsü Chih-ching, 270n23
Hsü Chih-mo, 392
Hsü Ch'in, 250
Hsü Jun [Yu-chai], 354–55
Hsü Kuang-ch'i, 486
Hsü Shou, 355n206
Hsü Shu-cheng, 258n237
Hsü T'ung, 211, 236 and n152
Hsüeh Fu-ch'eng, 304, 321–24, 332n108
Hsüeh-hui (study associations), 104, 199n23, 212–13
Hsün Ch'ing, 58, 179
Hsün-tzu: precepts of, 28, 43, 44, 57, 58, 106, 125, 135; and K'ang Yu-wei, 46, 49, 79, 80, 114; mentioned, 56, 147, 149, 151, 309n28, 423. *See also* K'ang Yu-wei, intellectual influences and development
Hu Han-min, 491
Hu Li-yüan, 413n18
Hu P'ing-chih, 381n15
Hu Shih: and New Culture, 386, 387, 388n42, 482, 484–85; as Westernizer, 393, 395, 397–99, 555, 571, 576–84; and Chinese tradition, 580, 581; mentioned, 55, 392n58, 467, 486–87, 494, 495, 557–58, 561, 575, 590, 592–93
Hua Heng-fang, 355n206
Huang Tsung-hsi, 88n177
Huang Tsun-hsien, 129, 270n23
Hun (spiritual soul), 150
Hun-ch'i (soul ether), 163
Hun-chih (soul substance), 161
Human desires: legitimacy of, 94
Huxley, Thomas H., 51

I-chih, 13
I-ch'uan. *See* Cheng I
I-k'uang (Prince Ch'ing), 275, 279, 281
I-shu kung hui (Book Translation Society), 213
I-ti (barbarian tribes), 85
Icaria, 502, 505
Illiteracy, 350
Imperial system: failure of, 81, 85, 87, 100, 124
"Indian religion," 440
Industrial revolution: as economic reform, 307–8; in Japan, 339–42; as evolutionary process, 373, 374. *See also* K'ang Yu-wei, and reform

Industry: reform in, 306–13

Inoue Enryō, *Narrative of an Imaginary Journey in the Starry Regions (Hsing-chiai hsiang-yu chi)*, 170–71

Institutional reform (*kai chih*), 76, 99

Islam, 120, 165, 167, 184

James, William, 387–88

Japan
—Meiji: monarchical authority in, 208; as model for reform in China, 209, 315, 329, 335–49, 365; commerce policies of, 311–12; feudal system abolished in, 336; agriculture in, 337; industrial revolution in, 338–42, 356–58, 376; Western influence in, 339, 341, 342n*147*, 343, 346; techniques of rule in, 339n*136*, 424n*60*; revolution of ideas in, 341–42; and Confucianism, 344n*160*, 348; leadership in, 356–57; unity in, 360n*226*; schools in, 380; mentioned, 194, 304, 347
—Tokugawa: reformers of, 387; transformation to Meiji, 397; mentioned, 343, 344, 345, 347, 356
—War with, 208, 260. *See also* Sino-Japanese War

Jen, 13, 46, 89, 90, 94, 159, 160

Jōdō Shinshū, 30

Johnston, Reginald F., 258

Judaism, 184

Jung Hung [Yung Wing], 236, 317, 591

Jung-lu, 238n*160*, 240, 241, 242, 275, 276, 405, 515

Kai chih (institutional reform), doctrine of, 76, 99

K'ai-p'ing Coal Mines, 355

Kang-i, 23

K'ang Chien-yüan, 3

K'ang Ch'iung-chü, 15

K'ang Han-ts'ang, 3

K'ang Hsüeh-hsiu, 4

K'ang Hui, 4

K'ang I-hsiu, 5

K'ang I-hung, 15

K'ang Kuang-jen [Yu-p'u], 9, 20–21, 26, 32, 214n*80*, 401

K'ang Kuo-ch'i, 5, 18, 500

K'ang Shih-p'eng, 4

K'ang Shih-yao, 4

K'ang Ta-chieh, 9

K'ang Ta-ch'ien, 4

K'ang Ta-ch'u, 4

K'ang Ta-fen, 9

K'ang Ta-shou, 4

K'ang Tao-hsiu, 4

K'ang Tsan-hsiu, 4

K'ang T'ung-chieh, 12n*55*

K'ang T'ung-ch'ien, 10

K'ang T'ung-pi, 10, 12

K'ang T'ung-wan, 12n*55*

K'ang T'ung-wei, 10, 11

K'ang Tzu-hsiu, 4

K'ang Wei-ch'ing, 3, 4

K'ang Wen-yao, 5

K'ang Yu-ming, 9

K'ang Yu-p'ei, 9

K'ang Yu-p'u. *See* K'ang Kuang-jen

K'ang Yu-wei [Ming-i]
—and Confucianism as a religion: 41–45, 79, 105–22, 127, 384–85, 482
—and contemporaries: regarded as controversial, 17, 36–37n*88*, 195, 196; and overseas Chinese, 35, 243; "Martin Luther of Confucian school," 44, 79; K'ang's attitude toward, 63–69; accused of plagiarism by, 65–66, 68; issue of "religion," 118; Communists, 145, 148; seen as reactionary by, 193, 538–40, 566; Sun Yat-sen, 225–34; recommended by, 270n-23; blamed for moral decay by, 392n*58*; held culpable of reform failure by, 399–401, 403–4; held as too precipitant, 400–403; Hu Shih, 583–84
—intellectual influences and development: philosophical concepts, 6, 13–14, 19, 23, 28, 29, 30–31, 36, 54, 91, 100–101, 130, 139, 140, 142–65, 168–89, 259, 411, 416–19, 427, 489n*291*, 495, 506, 518, 533–34; utopianism, 10, 14–15, 32, 45–46, 49, 82, 85, 86, 91, 100, 111, 143, 153, 167, 179, 194, 198, 410–12, 451–52, 501–6, 595–96, 598–600; Confucian predecessors, 13, 57–63, 69–96, 143, 147–49, 151; Western thought, 14–15, 25, 35, 45, 51, 73, 104, 138–42, 159, 170–171, 177, 179–80n*188*, 181, 183, 184–88, 198, 208, 210–11, 256, 270, 271n*25*, 308, 332, 379, 383, 387–88, 400, 402, 432–34, 453–55, 475, 492, 501–13, 518, 523, 524, 525, 538, 549, 550, 561–62, 568–70, 575; Confucius, 14, 21–22, 27, 41–44, 46–57, 72–78, 93, 122–36, 139–46, 149, 155–60, 165–67, 187, 199, 220, 259, 384, 402, 415, 423, 524, 498, 544–45, 596; religious thought, 30, 35, 118, 120, 141, 160, 161–68, 179–89, 185, 432, 524–25; religious systems, 106, 113, 140, 152, 162–68, 171, 175, 176, 183, 184, 433
—as private individual: early years, 3–13; personal attributes of, 6, 9, 12, 13, 18 and n*4*, 20–26, 31–32, 114, 140–41, 163n*133*, 169, 187, 283nn*71,73*, 309n*28*, 420, 451–52; poetry, 10, 11, 12, 18n*4*, 19, 20, 25, 29; exile and travel, 28, 29–30, 34, 139, 171,

283, 294, 414n*23*, 437, 515; as Sage of Nan-hai, 33, 79, 135–36; and private academy, 176–78, 385, as one of transitional generation, 393, 594; two foci of, 409
—and reform: patterns of, 8, 139, 184, 194, 196, 197–200, 208–10, 212, 214, 268, 270–71, 301–5, 308–9, 310, 311–13, 314–31, 365, 380–88, 404, 434, 533; and emperor, 21, 204, 207, 208, 209, 210, 244–45, 263–73, 379–81, 383, 384, 403; and government, 33, 85, 194–200, 202, 214–15, 224, 243, 249n*199*, 263–73, 283–99, 377–79, 402, 422n*53*, 424, 518, 579; and the West, 142, 201, 434, 524, 525–28, 593: and "people's rule," 153, 198, 251; as antirevolutionist, 193, 196, 202–3, 220–21, 234, 250; as antirepublican, 193, 223, 246–61, 282, 283, 482, 527, 542–44, 546; and constitutional government, 194, 195, 198, 200–207, 209, 216–25, 247–48, 252–61, 519, 527; and Chinese culture, 194, 597–98; democracy, 197–99, 240, 430; and convening parliament, 201, 204, 243–45, 325; and empress dowager, 236, 237, 240–41, 278, 515; industrialization, 306–13, 319–31, 376, 518, 520–21, 522–23; nationalism, 313, 318, 518; transportation and communication, 313–14; and 1898 reform, 399; social precepts, 409–18, 526, 535, 537, 593; socialization, 530
—and restoration of monarchy, 26, 71, 126, 127, 140, 173, 193, 194, 208, 221–22, 234, 252–61, 545
—writings discussed, 48–56, 59, 65, 66, 68, 70, 71, 78, 82, 112–13, 129, 147–48, 221, 224, 250, 257, 283–95, 411, 412, 415, 516; *Ta-t'ung shu* (The Book of the Great Community), 10, 28, 50, 51, 52, 54, 62, 85, 94, 100, 101, 104, 131, 141, 168, 171, 257, 318, 411, 417, 426, 427, 435–513, 436n*105*, 475n*237*, 515, 517, 531, 546, 580–81, 590, 598–99, 600; *K'ung-tzu kai-chih k'ao* (Confucius as Reformer), 23, 49, 55, 66, 67, 71, 94, 97–105 *passim*, 128, 130; *Chu-t'ien chiang* (Lectures on the Heavens), 35, 36, 141, 168–89, 412, 550, 557; *Li-yün chu* (Evolution of Rites Annotated), 49, 51, 52, 56, 79, 80, 81, 84; *K'ang-tzu nei-wai pien* (The Esoteric and Exoteric Essays of Master K'ang), 51, 141, 154, 410, 415, 418–26, 433, 439, 507; *Shih-li kung fa* (Substantial Truths and Universal Laws), 154, 410, 415, 418, 426n*68*, 426–33, 433n*94*, 434, 435, 507
K'ang Yü-chih, 498
Kant, Immanuel, 45, 142, 181–83, 187, 188,

457, 524, 525. *See also* K'ang Yu-wei, intellectual influences and development
Kao-tzu, 148, 151
Kepler, Johannes, 557
Ku Chih-kang, 129–30
Ku Hung-ming: on K'ang Yu-wei, 23; extreme Sinocentrist, 550, 566–70, 591, 592
Ku-liang, 80
Ku-liang Commentary: and Lu school, 68, 73
Ku Yen-wu, 138, 556, 557
Kuan Chung, 423
Kuan Lu, 27
Kuan-wen, 265n*4*
Kuang-shü emperor: and concern with reform, 20, 21, 206–7, 209, 210, 270; memorials to, 26, 217–18, 263–73, 377–78, 381, 383, 384; and empress dowager, 347, 403–5; mentioned, 23, 207, 211, 236n*153*, 252, 365, 404, 519
Kuang-hsüeh hui (Society for the Diffusion of Christian and General Knowledge among the Chinese), 332
K'un-kang (Board of State Affairs), 275
Kung Tzu-chen, 67n*106*, 69, 75, 138
Kung-fa, 85
Kung-yang: influence on K'ang Yu-wei, 33, 106, 108, 139; use of by K'ang Yu-wei, 50, 54, 55; doctrines of, 56, 72–78, 73, 74; and Tung Chung-shu, 59; studies of, 67, 68; scholars of, 69, 99, 125; in Ch'ing times, 75; tradition of, 77, 80, 94, 104; mentioned, 27, 28, 43, 65, 83, 93, 101, 130, 461, 499, 557
Kung-yang Commentary, 68–69, 73, 76. *See also* New Text
Kuo Sung-t'ao, 321
Kuo-ch'üan (rights of the state), 251
Kuo-min hsien-cheng hui (National Constitutional Society: The Constitutional Party; formerly Pao-huang hui), 242, 249
Kuo-min hsien-cheng tang. *See* Pao-huang hui
Kuo-min tang (National People's Party), 127, 249

"Land System of the Heavenly Dynasty": and K'ang, 500
Lao-tzu, 60, 80, 108, 116
Laplace, Pierre Simon de, 179–80n*188*, 186, 187, 550
Latourette, Kenneth Scott, 402
League of Nations, 479
Legalist School, 42, 423
Legge, James, 42
Leibniz, Gottfried von, 186, 570
Lenin, Vladimir, 298

Li Chien-nung, 391–92
Li Fan, 319–20
Li Hung-chang, 213, 238n*160*, 265n*4*, 275, 319, 321, 324, 325n*81*, 359, 366, 383, 516
Li Lien-ying, 240, 241
Li Sheng-t'o, 380n*11*
Li Ta-chao, 493
Li Tuan-fen, 271, 380n*11*
Li Wen-t'ien, 556
Li Yüan-hung, 246, 251, 258n*233*
Li-yün: influence on K'ang, 56, 499–500; in John Fryer's work, 508–9
Liang Ch'i-ch'ao: and Yüan Shih-k'ai, 10, 253, 545n*86*; as reformer, 11, 232, 234, 235, 260, 269n*15*, 270n*23*, 294; view of K'ang, 19, 20, 21, 26, 32–33, 43, 47, 60, 65, 68, 69, 94, 105–6, 108–11, 120, 128–29, 188–89, 207, 435, 456, 478; on Confucianism, 42, 47, 60, 69, 74, 105–6, 120, 128–29; as pupil of K'ang, 50, 55, 537; *Bibliography of Books on Western Learning*, 327; as universalizer, 434–35, 584; and Westernization, 529, 536, 550, 553, 561–62, 564; mentioned, 24, 27, 33, 51, 60, 236n*152*, 237, 238n*162*, 241, 380n*11*, 393, 401, 475n*236*, 516, 521
Liang Sou-ming, 123, 131, 219, 529, 584–85
Liang T'ieh-chün, 24, 238, 239n*162*
Liao P'ing, 63–71, 537
Liberal Party of Japan (Jiyuntō), 312
Lieh-tzu, 498
Lithconia, 503, 504
Liu Feng-lu, 67n*106*, 75
Liu Hsin, 47, 58, 66–67n*106*, 70, 79, 80, 83n*162*
Liu Hsü, 27, 270n*23*
Liu Kuang-ti, 270n*23*
Liu K'un-i, 14, 212–13, 236n*153*, 238n*160*, 275–78, 293, 388–89, 405
Liu Shih-p'ei, 592
Liu Tsung-chou, 4
Lo Chong, 11
Lo Ping-chang, 8
Lo Ying-liu, 320
Locke, John, 576
Lu Chiu-yüan, 44, 50, 60, 61, 62n*86*, 170
Lu Ch'uan-lin, 275
Lu Hsün: as modernizer, 558 and n*137*, 559–62; as Westernizer, 565, 570, 571, 572, 575
Lu–Wang School of Neo-Confucianism, 4, 60, 62, 68, 551. See also *Ku-liang Commentary*; Neo-Confucianism
Luther, Martin, 30

Ma Chien-chung, 304, 324–25n*79*, 332n*108*
Ma Hsiang-po [Ma Liang], 121

Macdonald, Claude M., 399–400
Mai Chung-hua, 11
Mai Meng-hua, 217
Mao Tse-tung: way prepared for, 233–34, 396; and K'ang Yu-wei's ideas, 495; mentioned, 260, 375, 478–79
Mao-tun, 395
Martin, W. A. P., 123, 385
Marxism: climate for, 396
Materialism, 156, 162, 417–18n*35*. See also K'ang Yu-wei, intellectual influences and development
Matsukata Masayoshi, 339
May Fourth movement, 137
May Fourth students, 393–96
Mencius, 32, 43, 44, 57, 58, 61, 73, 86, 88n*177*, 90, 95, 106, 125, 134, 135, 147, 151, 423
Mencius, the, 56, 71, 82, 90n*185*, 93
Meng Wen-t'ung, 68
Mercantilism, 318
Merchant Protection Society, *See* Pao-shang hui
Mill, John Stuart, 576
Min-chu (people's rule), 84, 86, 94, 99, 100, 153, 198, 218–20, 232
Min-ch'üan (people's rights), 199, 203, 217–18, 232, 240, 245, 251, 258
Min pao, 227, 241, 490, 492, 516
Ming-i. *See* K'ang Yu-wei
Minor Peace doctrine. See *Hsiao-k'ang* doctrine
"Mr. Democracy," 233, 528, 551
"Mr. Science," 233, 330, 528, 549, 550, 551, 562, 563, 564, 574
Miyazaki Torazō, 197, 210, 227, 238n*162*
Monarchical republic, 247. *See also* K'ang Yu-wei, and reform
Monck, George, 255n*227*, 256
Monetary reforms, 315–17. *See also* K'ang Yu-wei, and reform
Monotheism, 183
Monte Carlo, 29
Moral tradition: preservation of, 104, 105
Morse, H. B., 400
More, Thomas, 501, 503, 505, 506
Mo-tzu, 13, 92, 93, 440
Muirhead, William, 332
Music: and superior man, 92–93

Nan-hsüeh hui. *See* Hsüeh-hui
National Constitutional Society. *See* Kuo-min hsien-cheng hui
National People's Party. *See* Kuo-min tang
Neo-Confucianism: introduction to, 8; repudiation of, 47, 49, 62, 118, 121, 124, 131, 149; establishment of, 59; mentioned,

551, 573. *See also* K'ang Yu-wei, intellectual influences and development
Neo-Confucians, 44, 60, 62, 64, 74, 95–96, 125, 130, 449
Neo-Platonism, 183
New Culture movement, 384, 386, 390, 398, 522, 563, 564. *See also* Ch'en Tu-hsiu; *Hsin ch'ing-nien*; Hu Shih
Newton, Isaac, 186, 448, 549, 557, 578
Nieh Shih-ch'eng, 213
"Nine Emperors" in *Annals*, 77
New Text: K'ang's work on, 7, 66; doctrines of, 48, 49, 50, 65, 117; authenticity of, 56, 62, 66, 68, 70, 129, 138; deification of Confucius by, 106, 451; mentioned, 43, 130, 415. *See also* K'ang Yu-wei, intellectual influences and development; Kung-yang School

O'Connor, Nicholas, 212
Offices: abolishment of, 272–73. *See also* K'ang Yu-wei, and reform
Old Text classics: K'ang's work on, 7, 66–67; as spurious, 44, 48, 49, 56, 62–63, 68, 70, 83, 101, 131, 415; learning of, 50, 54, 59, 63; accepted, 71; and Confucianism, 128; and imperial authority, 135
"One Hundred Days," 97, 204, 213, 410
Ou Chü-chia, 103
Owen, Robert, 501–2

P'an Tsu-yin, 211
Pantheism, 162, 183
Pao Shih-ch'en, 103
Pao-huang hui (Emperor Protection Society), 20, 126n*118*, 222 and n*109*, 234–46, 519
Pao-kuo hui (Society for National Preservation). See *Hsüeh-hui*
Pao-shang Hui (Merchant Protection Society; precursor to Pao-huang hui), 235
Parliament: convening urged, 201, 204, 243–45, 325
Peking Gazette (*Ti pao*), 8
People's interests: as duty of government, 285
People's rule. See *Min-chu*
Peregrinations of the heavens, 35. *See also* K'ang Yu-wei, intellectual influences and development; writings discussed
Perry, Commodore Matthew, 343
Peter the Great, 208, 523–24
Pi Yung-nien, 236n*152*
Pi-kan, 87
Poland, 203
Political loyalty (*chung*), 87
Political system: and Confucianism, 74,

535; independence of, 104; transformation of, 207–16; decadence of, 357–58; modernization of, 531. *See also* K'ang Yu-wei, and reform
Post-Boxer Reform. *See* Reform, Post-Boxer
Pravraj (*ch'u chia*, "to leave the family"), 15
Presidential republic, 247
Private enterprise, 318, 529–30. *See also* K'ang Yu-wei, and reform; Sun Yat-sen
Pro-emperor party. See *Ti tang*
Pro-empress dowager party. See *Hou tang*
Progressivism, 308
Property: invalidity of, 81
Provincial autonomy, 292–95
Ptolemy, 181
Pu-jen (Compassion, periodical), 172, 411
P'u-i, 259, 389–90

Recruitment of officials, 269. *See also* K'ang Yu-wei, and reform
"Radicalism of impotence," 398n*77*
Red Turbans, 5, 275
Refinement (*wen*), 92, 93
Reform: and K'ang Yu-wei, 74, 81, 101, 118, 124, 293; deterrents to, 347–51 and n*189*; and authoritarianism, 372–76
—1898: failure of, 14, 21, 101, 362, 372, 378; mentioned, 20, 137, 139, 195, 196, 221, 233, 328, 334, 335, 399
—Post-Boxer: 274–82, 292, 388. *See also* K'ang Yu-wei, and reform
Reform Club. *See* Ch'iang-hsüeh hui
Religion: in China, 119; and reform, 118. *See also* K'ang Yu-wei, and Confucianism as a religion; intellectual influences and development of
Republic: as premature, 71, 86, 223, 246, 247
Restoration of dynasty, 71, 126, 253. *See also* K'ang Yu-wei, and restoration of monarchy; P'u-i
Revolution of 1911, 232, 246, 361
Revolutionaries: expatriates as, 516
Reynolds, James, 503, 504, 506
Richard, Timothy: and K'ang, 35, 73, 400; and Reform Club, 212; writings of, 332–34, 567
Roosevelt, Theodore, 188n*226*, 520
Rousseau, Jean Jacques, 524, 575
Rural Reconstruction movement, 219
Russell, Bertrand, 25, 142, 538
Russia, Imperial: as model of reform, 209

Sa[h] Meng-wu, 585, 594
Sage of Nan-hai, 79, 126, 135. *See also* K'ang Yu-wei
Sage of Tung-lu, 135. *See also* Confucius
"Sage's enjoyment in life." See *Sheng-jen lo-*

sheng chih tao
Saint-Simon, Claude Henri de, 492, 505
"Samurai," (H. G. Wells), 505
San Shih. See Three Ages doctrine
San-t'ung (Three Systems doctrine), 78, 82, 99
"To save the world" (*chiu shih*), 95
Schelling, Friedrich, 183
Schools, Western-style, in China, 379n10
Science vs. metaphysics: polemic on, 546–65
Science, Western, 328–29n95
Self-strengthening movement, 195, 302, 402–3n104, 496, 517, 523. See also *Ch'iang-hsüeh hui*
Sexual equality: K'ang Yu-wei's views of, 32
Shang Yang, 423
Shapley, Harlow, 188n225
Shen Chien-shih, 487–88
Shen Tseng-chih, 275
Shen-tsung, Emperor, 273n37
Sheng-hsüeh hui. See *Hsüeh-hui*
Sheng-jen lo-sheng chih tao (Sage's enjoyment in life), 92–93
Sheng-p'ing shih. See Three Ages doctrine
Shibusawa Eiichi, 348n176
Shih chung (the timely mean), 82
Shinran, 30
Shun, Emperor, 85, 90, 99, 527–28
Sino-Japanese War, 211, 302, 363, 486
"Six ways of sentient existence," 177n176
Skeptic movement, 130, 165
"To smash the Confucian shop." See *Ta-tao K'ung-chia tien*
Socialism: K'ang Yu-wei's concept of, 91; and Sun Yat-sen, 366–69, 490; and developing nations, 496; and Hu Shih, 579
Socialization: as premature, 530
Society against Foot-binding, 9
Society for the Diffusion of Christian and General Knowledge among the Chinese (Kuang-hsüeh hui), 332
Society for Religious Freedom, 121
Society for the Study of National [Self-] Strengthening. See Ch'iang hsüeh hui
Soul (*hun*), 115–16
"Soul substance" (*hun-chih*), 161
Soul-ether (*hun-ch'i*), 163
Sovereign-subject relationship, 430
Spinoza, Baruch, 183
Spiritual soul (*hun*), 150
Spring and Autumn Annals, 48, 49, 75–76, 93, 99
Stuart, John Leighton, 600
"Student generation," 393
Study associations. See Hsüeh-hui
Sukarno, 373n274
Sun Chia-nai: and state religion, 102, 119;

and reform, 209, 279, 281, 380, 382n18; and P'u-i, 389
Sun Wen. *See* Sun Yat-sen
Sun Yat-sen [Chung-shan; Sun Wen]: and K'ang, 197, 225–35, 251, 368; "General Principles of Political Reconstruction" (*chien-kuo-ta-kang*), 230; and overseas Chinese, 235; and revolution, 236n152, 237, 241, 244, 310, 366; and *kuo ch'üan*, 251; and republican cause, 260; and centralized authority, 297–99; and economic modernization, 365–72; and socialism, 366–69, 490; and foreign capital, 367–71; and private enterprise, 368–69; and communism, 368n260; and failure of industrialization, 376; and *ta-t'ung* concept, 501; mentioned, 20, 24, 316, 326n82, 491, 492
Sung Ch'ing, 213

Ta-tao K'ung-chia tien (to smash the Confucian shop), 46, 130, 384, 399, 574
Ta-t'ung, doctrine of (Great Unity, Universal Peace), 48, 49, 50, 55, 56, 57, 71, 79, 80, 82, 93, 107, 110, 111, 127, 153, 179, 501
Ta-t'ung shu. See K'ang Yu-wei, writings discussed
Tai Chen, 138, 157, 158n105, 556
T'ai-chi (The Supreme Ultimate), 143
T'ai-p'ing (Taiping) rebellion, 5, 361, 497, 500, 501
T'ai-p'ing shih. See Three Ages doctrine
T'ai-tsung, Emperor, 211
T'an Ssu-t'ung: and K'ang, 15, 27, 145, 537; mentioned, 270n23, 349
T'ang Chen, 275, 537
T'ang Chih-chün, 489
T'ang Shou-ch'ien, 270n23
T'ang T'ing-shu [Ching-hsing; Tong King-sing], 354 and n202
T'ang Ts'ai-ch'ang, 236n152, 237
T'ao Ch'ien, 498
Taoism, 108, 116, 125, 138, 497–98
"Ten Profound Theories" (*Shih hsüan men*), 110
Thompson, Laurence G., 495 and n316
Thoreau, Henry David, 576
Three Ages doctrine (*san-shih*), 54, 56, 57, 75, 77, 79, 80, 82, 84, 99, 107, 220, 402, 461, 490, 590
—Age of Approaching Peace (Minor Peace, *sheng-p'ing shih*), 77, 81, 84, 86, 88, 91, 220
—Age of Disorder (*chü-luan shih*), 77n146, 80, 84, 85, 86, 88, 90, 91, 92, 107, 115, 198, 220, 450, 466, 541
—Age of Universal Peace (*t'ai-p'ing shih*), 60, 77, 81–86, 88, 90, 99, 100, 115, 167
Three Dynasties: principles of, 97

"Three Systems." See *San-t'ung Ti tang*, 238
Tikhvinsky, S. L., 497, 500, 501, 507, 511
"The timely mean." See *Shih chung*
Ting Wen-chiang, 550, 551, 563, 564
Titular monarch: Holy Duke as, 247
Toba Hung [Emperor Hsiao-wen-ti], 224
Tradition, 10, 94, 397
Traditional learning, 10, 555
Traditional moral values, 100
"Transitional generation," 393–94
Translations: of Western and Japanese books, 390
Transportation reforms, 313–14
Treaty of Shimonoseki, 402
Ts'ao K'un, 257, 398
Tse Tan Tai [Hsieh Tsan-t'ai], 236n*152*
Ts'en Ch'un-hsüan, 272n*31*
Tseng Kuo-fan, 8, 265n*4*, 307, 355, 383n*21*, 516, 556
Tseng-tzu, 57, 58, 72, 116
Tso Commentary, 70, 73, 87
Tso Tsung-t'ang, 5, 8, 265n*4*
Ts'ui Liang, 269n*15*
T'u Jen-shou, 302
Tuan Ch'i-jui, 258n*237*
Tung Chung-shu: as Confucian, 44, 55, 59, 60, 106, 125; influence on K'ang Yu-wei, 69, 143–44; mentioned, 13, 27, 28, 73–77, 147, 149, 151
T'ung-chih period, 137
T'ung-meng hui, 222, 241, 516
Tzu-kung, 88
Tzu-ssu, 57, 58
Tzu-yu, 57
Tz'u-hsi (empress dowager): and emperor, 13, 14, 15, 347; and Confucianism, 14, 391; and reform, 206n*46*, 209, 274–82; power of, 208, 238, 403–4; and K'ang Yu-wei, 239, 278, 477; mentioned, 231, 236, and n*153*, 237, 238, 240, 264n*2*, 515

U Thant, 413n*22*
United States: as model for China, 209, 524, 529, 533; as model for developing countries, 372
Unity, and political well-being, 99–100
Universal love. See *Jen*
Universal Peace, Age of. *See* Three Ages doctrine
Universal Peace, doctrine of. See *Ta-t'ung*
Universality of truths, 416–17
Universalizers, 413–14
"Universe of One Reality" (*i-chen fa-chieh*), 110
Utopists, 502–6

Wan Kwok Kung Pao (International News Bulletin), 332, 419
Wang An-shih, 25, 42, 273n*37*, 405, 494
Wang Chao, 24
Wang Ching-wei, 227–28
Wang Fu-chih, 138
Wang Hsi-fan, 270n*23*
Wang Hsien-ch'ien, 412, 556
Wang Mang, 80, 453, 494
Wang Nien-sung, 556
Wang Sho-jen, 44, 50, 60–62, 65, 69, 108
Wang Wen-shao, 213, 275
War lords, 295, 296
Washington, George, 90
Wei Mo-shen, 524
Wei Yüan, 67n*106*, 69, 75
Wei-tzu, 87
Wei-yen ta-i (arcane doctrines and great dogmas), 43
Wells, H. G., 504, 505, 506
Wen ching, 401
Wen, King, 90
Wen-t'i, 47, 102
Weng T'ung-ho, 211
West: impact of on China; 132, 137, 412–18
Western learning: and K'ang Yu-wei, 53–55, 64, 90–92, 93, 95, 111, 122, 140–42; and economic reform, 331–46
Westernization: selective, recommended, 104, 388–90, 542; extremes of, 394–95nn*63,64*, 413–14; vs. universalization, 413
Wheel of transmigration (*lun-hui*), 117, 163, 177
Wilhelm, Richard, 123
Williams, Alexander, 332
Williams, T. E., 42
Wo-jen, 413n*17*
Wu Chih-hui [Wu Ching-heng], 381n*16*, 551–56, 563, 572, 581
Wu, King, 87
Wu P'ei-fu, 296
Wu yü, 130, 485, 580

Yang, C. K., 219
Yang Hsiung, 448
Yang Jui, 270n*23*
Yang Shen-hsiu, 272n*3*
Yao, Emperor, 99, 286, 527–28
Yeh Shih, 58
Yeh Te-hui, 17n*1*, 42, 65, 74, 75
Yellowstone Park, 29–30
Yen Fu, 51, 270n*23*, 393, 400–401, 591, 592
Yen Hsi-shan, 530n*42*
Yen Hsiu, 378
Yen-sheng kung ("the Holy Duke"), 247n*192*

Yen-tzu, 57
Yin, court of, 87
Yin and *yang* principles, 145–46, 150, 155–57
Yoshida Shoin, 349
Yü, Emperor, 92, 98
Yu-chai. *See* Hsü Jun
Yüan (The Prime), 143–44
Yüan Ch'ang, 272n*31*
Yuan Shih-k'ai: as president of republic, 10, 127, 366; and Sun Yat-sen, 366, 370 and
n*265*; and K'ang Yu-wei, 545 and nn*86, 87*, 571, 596; mentioned, 247n*193*, 251, 252n*209*, 253, 260, 275
Yung Chien-ch'iu, 121
Yung Sing-kiu, 236n*152*
Yung Wing. *See* Jung Wing

Zaibatsu, 340, 341, 363
Zoroaster, 146

PUBLICATIONS ON ASIA OF THE INSTITUTE FOR COM-
PARATIVE AND FOREIGN AREA STUDIES
(Formerly Far Eastern and Russian Institute Publications on Asia)

1. Compton, Boyd (trans. and ed.). *Mao's China: Party Reform Documents, 1942–44.* 1952. Reissued 1966. Washington Paperback,
   1966.
2. Chiang, Siang-tseh. *The Nien Rebellion.* 1954.
3. Chang, Chung-li. *The Chinese Gentry: Studies on Their Role in Nineteenth-Century Chinese Society.* Introduction by Franz Michael.
   1955. Reissued 1967. Washington Paperback on Russia and
   Asia-4.
4. *Guide to the Memorials of Seven Leading Officials of Nineteenth-Century
   China.* Summaries and indexes of memorials to Hu Lin-i, Tseng
   Kuo-fan, Tso Tsung-tang, Kuo Sung-tao, Tseng Kuo-ch'uan,
   Li Hung-chang, Chang Chih-tung. 1955.
5. Raeff, Marc. *Siberia and the Reforms of 1822.* 1956.
6. Li Chi. *The Beginnings of Chinese Civilization: Three Lectures Illustrated
   with Finds at Anyang.* 1957. Reissued 1968. Washington Paperback
   on Russia and Asia-6.
7. Carrasco, Pedro. *Land and Polity in Tibet.* 1959.
8. Hsiao, Kung-chuan. *Rural China: Imperial Control in the Nineteenth
   Century.* 1960. Reissued 1967. Washington Paperback on Russia
   and Asia-3.
9. Hsiao, Tso-liang. *Power Relations within the Chinese Communist Movement, 1930–1934.* Vol. I: *A Study of Documents.* 1961. Vol. II:
   The Chinese Documents. 1967.
10. Chang, Chung-li. *The Income of the Chinese Gentry.* Introduction by
    Franz Michael. 1962.
11. Maki, John M. *Court and Constitution in Japan: Selected Supreme Court
    Decisions, 1948–60.* 1964.
12. Poppe, Nicholas, Leon Hurvitz, and Hidehiro Okada. *Catalogue of
    the Manchu-Mongol Section of the Toyo Bunko.* 1964.
13. Spector, Stanley. *Li Hung-chang and the Huai Army: A Study in
    Nineteenth-Century Chinese Regionalism.* Introduction by Franz
    Michael. 1964.
14. Michael, Franz, and Chung-li Chang. *The Taiping Rebellion: History
    and Documents.* Vol. I: *History.* 1966. Vols. II and III: *Documents
    and Comments.* 1971.
15. Shih, Vincent Y. C. *The Taiping Ideology: Its Sources, Interpretations,*

and Influences. 1967.

16. Poppe, Nicholas. *The Twelve Deeds of Buddha: A Mongolian Version of the Lalitavistara; Mongolian Text, Notes, and English Translation.* 1967. Paper.

17. Hsia, Tsi-an. *The Gate of Darkness: Studies on the Leftist Literary Movement in China.* Preface by Franz Michael. Introduction by C. T. Hsia. 1968.

18. Hsiao, Tso-liang. *The Land Revolution in China, 1930–1934: A Study of Documents.* 1969.

19. Gasster, Michael. *Chinese Intellectuals and the Revolution of 1911: The Birth of Modern Chinese Radicalism.* 1969.

20. Thornton, Richard C. *The Comintern and the Chinese Communists, 1928–1931.* 1969.

21. Lin, Julia C. *Modern Chinese Poetry: An Introduction.* 1972.

22. Huang, Philip C. *Liang Ch'i-ch'ao and Modern Chinese Liberalism.* 1972.

23. Gerow, Edwin, and Margery Lang. *Studies in the Language and Culture of South Asia.* 1974.

24. Morrison, Barrie M. *Lalmai, a Cultural Center of Early Bengal.* 1974.

25. Hsiao, Kung-chuan. *A Modern China and a New World: K'ang Yu-wei, Reformer and Utopian, 1858–1927.* 1975.